T0190007

Lecture Notes in Artificial Intelligence   8468

Subseries of Lecture Notes in Computer Science

Lecture Notes in Artificial Intelligence   8468

Subseries of Lecture Notes in Computer Science

LNAI Series Editors

Randy Goebel
University of Alberta, Edmonton, Canada
Yuzuru Tanaka
Hokkaido University, Sapporo, Japan
Wolfgang Wahlster
DFKI and Saarland University, Saarbrücken, Germany

LNAI Founding Series Editor

Joerg Siekmann
DFKI and Saarland University, Saarbrücken, Germany

Leszek Rutkowski   Marcin Korytkowski
Rafał Scherer   Ryszard Tadeusiewicz
Lotfi A. Zadeh   Jacek M. Zurada (Eds.)

Artificial Intelligence and Soft Computing

13th International Conference, ICAISC 2014
Zakopane, Poland, June 1-5, 2014
Proceedings, Part II

 Springer

Volume Editors

Leszek Rutkowski
Marcin Korytkowski
Rafał Scherer
Częstochowa University of Technology
42-200 Częstochowa, Poland
E-mail: {leszek.rutkowski, marcin.korytkowski, rafal.scherer}@iisi.pcz.pl

Ryszard Tadeusiewicz
AGH University of Science and Technology
30-059 Kraków, Poland
E-mail: rtad@agh.edu.pl

Lotfi A. Zadeh
University of California Berkeley
Department of Electrical Engineering and Computer Sciences
Berkeley, CA 94720-1776, USA
E-mail: zadeh@cs.berkeley.edu

Jacek M. Zurada
University of Louisville
Computational Intelligence Laboratory
Louisville, KY 40292, USA
E-mail: jacek.zurada@louisville.edu

ISSN 0302-9743   e-ISSN 1611-3349
ISBN 978-3-319-07175-6   e-ISBN 978-3-319-07176-3
DOI 10.1007/978-3-319-07176-3
Springer Cham Heidelberg New York Dordrecht London

Library of Congress Control Number: 2014938247

LNCS Sublibrary: SL 7 – Artificial Intelligence

Typesetting: Camera-ready by author, data conversion by Scientific Publishing Services, Chennai, India

Printed on acid-free paper

Springer is part of Springer Science+Business Media (www.springer.com)

Preface

This volume constitutes the proceedings of the 13th International Conference on Artificial Intelligence and Soft Computing, ICAISC 2014, held in Zakopane, Poland, during June 1–5, 2014. The conference was organized by the Polish Neural Network Society in cooperation with the University of Social Sciences in Łódź, the Institute of Computational Intelligence at the Częstochowa University of Technology, and the IEEE Computational Intelligence Society, Poland Chapter. Previous conferences took place in Kule (1994), Szczyrk (1996), Kule (1997) and Zakopane (1999, 2000, 2002, 2004, 2006, 2008, 2010, 2012, and 2013) and attracted a large number of papers and internationally recognized speakers: Lotfi A. Zadeh, Igor Aizenberg, Shun-ichi Amari, Daniel Amit, Piero P. Bonissone, Jim Bezdek, Zdzisław Bubnicki, Andrzej Cichocki, Włodzisław Duch, Pablo A. Estévez, Jerzy Grzymala-Busse, Martin Hagan, Yoichi Hayashi, Akira Hirose, Kaoru Hirota, Er Meng Joo, Janusz Kacprzyk, Jim Keller, Laszlo T. Koczy, Soo-Young Lee, Robert Marks, Evangelia Micheli-Tzanakou, Kaisa Miettinen, Ngoc Thanh Nguyen, Erkki Oja, Witold Pedrycz, Marios M. Polycarpou, José C. Príncipe, Jagath C. Rajapakse, Šarunas Raudys, Enrique Ruspini, Jörg Siekmann, Roman Slowiński, Igor Spiridonov, Ponnuthurai Nagaratnam Suganthan, Ryszard Tadeusiewicz, Shiro Usui, Fei-Yue Wang, Jun Wang, Bogdan M. Wilamowski, Ronald Y. Yager, Syozo Yasui, and Jacek Zurada. The aim of this conference is to build a bridge between traditional artificial intelligence techniques and so-called soft computing techniques. It was pointed out by Lotfi A. Zadeh that "soft computing (SC) is a coalition of methodologies which are oriented toward the conception and design of information/intelligent systems. The principal members of the coalition are: fuzzy logic (FL), neurocomputing (NC), evolutionary computing (EC), probabilistic computing (PC), chaotic computing (CC), and machine learning (ML). The constituent methodologies of SC are, for the most part, complementary and synergistic rather than competitive." These proceedings present both traditional artificial intelligence methods and soft computing techniques. Our goal is to bring together scientists representing both areas of research. This volume is divided into six parts:

- Neural Networks and Their Applications
- Fuzzy Systems and Their Applications
- Evolutionary Algorithms and Their Applications
- Classification and Estimation
- Computer Vision, Image and Speech Analysis
- Special Session 3: Intelligent Methods in Databases

The conference attracted 331 submissions from 29 countries, and after the review process, 139 papers were accepted for publication. ICAISC 2014 hosted three special sessions:

Special Session 1: "Machine Learning for Visual Information Analysis and Security" organized by:

- Rafał Scherer, Częstochowa University of Technology, Poland
- Svyatoslav Voloshynovskiy, University of Geneva, Switzerland

The session was supported by the project "New Perspectives on Intelligent Multimedia Management with Applications in Medicine and Privacy Protecting Systems" co-financed by a grant from Switzerland through the Swiss Contribution to the Enlarged European Union.

Special Session 2: "Applications and Properties of Fuzzy Reasoning and Calculus", organized by:

- Witold Kosiński , Polish-Japanese Institute of Information Technology, Poland

Special Session 3: "Intelligent Methods in Databases" organized by:

- Rafał A. Angryk, Georgia State University, USA
- Marcin Gabryel, Częstochowa University of Technology, Poland
- Marcin Korytkowski, Częstochowa University of Technology, Poland

The session was supported by the project "Innovative Methods of Retrieval and Indexing Multimedia Data Using Computational Intelligence Techniques" funded by the National Science Centre.

I would like to thank our participants, invited speakers, and reviewers of the papers for their scientific and personal contribution to the conference. The following reviewers were very helpful in reviewing the papers:

R. Adamczak	M. Choraś	I. Fister
T. Babczyński	K. Choros	M. Fraś
M. Baczyński	P. Cichosz	M. Gabryel
M. Białko	R. Cierniak	A. Gawęda
A. Bielskis	P. Ciskowski	M. Giergiel
M. Blachnik	C. CoelloCoello	F. Gomide
L. Bobrowski	B. Cyganek	Z. Gomółka
L. Borzemski	J. Cytowski	M. Gorgoń
J. Brest	I. Czarnowski	M. Gorzałczany
T. Burczyński	J. de la Rosa	D. Grabowski
R. Burduk	W. Duch	E. Grabska
B. Butkiewicz	L. Dutkiewicz	K. Grąbczewski
C. Castro	L. Dymowa	P. Grzegorzewski
K. Cetnarowicz	A. Dzieliński	J. Grzymala-Busse
J. Chang	P. Dziwiński	H. Haberdar
M. Chis	D. Elizondo	R. Hampel
W. Cholewa	A. Fanea	Y. Hayashi

J. Łęski
B. Macukow
K. Madani
W. Malina
J. Mańdziuk
U. Markowska-Kaczmar
M. Marques
A. Marszałek
W. Kamiński
A. Martin
T. Kaplon
A. Materka
A. Kasperski
R. Matuk Herrera
V. Kecman
J. Mazurkiewicz
E. Kerre
V. Medvedev
F. Klawonn
J. Mendel
J. Kluska
M. Mernik
L. Koczy
J. Michalkiewicz
A. Kołakowska
Z. Mikrut
J. Konopacki
S. Misina
J. Korbicz
W. Mitkowski
M. Kordos
W. Moczulski
P. Korohoda
W. Mokrzycki
J. Koronacki
M. Morzy
M. Korzeń
T. Munakata
W. Kosiński
G. Nalepa
J. Kościelny
L. Nassif
M. Korytkowski
A. Nawrat
L. Kotulski
M. Nieniewski
Z. Kowalczuk
A. Niewiadomski
J. Kozlak
R. Nowicki
M. Kraft
A. Obuchowicz
M. Kretowska
E. Oja
M. Kretowski
S. Osowski
D. Krol
M. Pacholczyk
A. Kubiak
F. Pappalardo
P. Kudová
K. Patan
J. Kulikowski
M. Pawlak
O. Kurasova
A. Piegat
V. Kurkova
Z. Pietrzykowski
M. Kurzyński
V. Piuri
J. Kusiak
P. Prokopowicz
N. Labroche
A. Przybył
J. Lampinen
R. Ptak
A. Ligęza
E. Rafajłowicz
H. Liu
E. Rakus-Andersson
M. Ławryńczuk
M. Rane

Š. Raudys
R. Rojas
L. Rolka
I. Rudas
F. Rudziński
A. Rusiecki
H. Safari
S. Sakurai
N. Sano
J. Sas
a. Sashima
R. Scherer
M. SepesyMaucec
P. Sevastjanov
A. Sędziwy
A. Skowron
E. Skubalska-Rafajłowicz
K. Slot
D. Słota
A. Słowik
J. Smoląg
C. Smutnicki
A. Sokołowski
T. Sołtysiński
J. Starczewski
J. Stefanowski
E. Straszecka
V. Struc
P. Strumiłło
M. Studniarski
P. Suganthan
R. Sulej
V. Sumati
J. Swacha
P. Szczepaniak
E. Szmidt
M. Szpyrka
J. Świątek
R. Tadeusiewicz
H. Takagi
Y. Tiumentsev
A. Tomczyk
V. Torra
B. Trawinski

E. Volna
R. Vorobel
M. Wagenknecht
T. Walkowiak
L. Wang
Y. Wang
J. Wąs

S. Wiak
B. Wilamowski
M. Witczak
M. Wojciechowski
M. Wozniak
M. Wygralak
J. Zabrodzki

S. Zadrożny
D. Zaharie
D. Zakrzewska
A. Zamuda
R. Zdunek

Finally, I thank my co-workers Łukasz Bartczuk, Piotr Dziwiński, Marcin Gabryel, Marcin Korytkowski, and the conference secretary Rafał Scherer for their enormous efforts to make the conference a very successful event. Moreover, I would like to acknowledge the work of Marcin Korytkowski, who designed the Internet submission system.

The conference volumes are devoted to the memory of Prof. Witold Kosiński, co-founder of the Polish Neural Network Society, who passed away on March 14, 2014.

June 2014

Leszek Rutkowski

Organization

ICAISC 2014 was organized by the Polish Neural Network Society in cooperation with the University of Social Sciences in Łódź, the Institute of Computational Intelligence at Częstochowa University of Technology, and the IEEE Computational Intelligence Society, Poland Chapter and with technical sponsorship from the IEEE Computational Intelligence Society.

ICAISC Chairs

Honorary chairs
Lotfi Zadeh (USA)
Jacek Żurada (USA)

General chair
Leszek Rutkowski (Poland)

Co-chairs

Włodzisław Duch (Poland)   Józef Korbicz (Poland)
Janusz Kacprzyk (Poland)   Ryszard Tadeusiewicz (Poland)

ICAISC Program Committee

Rafał Adamczak - Poland
Cesare Alippi - Italy
Shun-ichi Amari - Japan
Rafal A. Angryk - USA
Jarosław Arabas - Poland
Robert Babuska - The Netherlands
Ildar Z. Batyrshin - Russia
James C. Bezdek - USA
Marco Block-Berlitz - Germany
Leon Bobrowski - Poland
Piero P. Bonissone - USA
Bernadette Bouchon-Meunier - France
James Buckley - Poland
Tadeusz Burczynski - Poland

Andrzej Cader - Poland
Juan Luis Castro - Spain
Yen-Wei Chen - Japan
Wojciech Cholewa - Poland
Fahmida N. Chowdhury - USA
Andrzej Cichocki - Japan
Paweł Cichosz - Poland
Krzysztof Cios - USA
Ian Cloete - Germany
Oscar Cordón - Spain
Bernard De Baets - Belgium
Nabil Derbel - Tunisia
Ewa Dudek-Dyduch - Poland
Ludmiła Dymowa - Poland

Andrzej Dzieliński - Poland
David Elizondo - UK
Meng Joo Er - Singapore
Pablo Estevez - Chile
János Fodor - Hungary
David B. Fogel - USA
Roman Galar - Poland
Alexander I. Galushkin - Russia
Adam Gaweda - USA
Joydeep Ghosh - USA
Juan Jose Gonzalez de la Rosa - Spain
Marian Bolesław Gorzałczany - Poland
Krzysztof Grąbczewski - Poland
Garrison Greenwood - USA
Jerzy W. Grzymala-Busse - USA
Hani Hagras - UK
Saman Halgamuge - Australia
Rainer Hampel - Germany
Zygmunt Hasiewicz - Poland
Yoichi Hayashi - Japan
Tim Hendtlass - Australia
Francisco Herrera - Spain
Kaoru Hirota - Japan
Adrian Horzyk - Poland
Tingwen Huang - USA
Hisao Ishibuchi - Japan
Mo Jamshidi - USA
Andrzej Janczak - Poland
Norbert Jankowski - Poland
Ali Jannatpour - Canada
Robert John - UK
Jerzy Józefczyk - Poland
Tadeusz Kaczorek - Poland
Władysław Kamiński - Poland
Nikola Kasabov - New Zealand
Okyay Kaynak - Turkey
Vojislav Kecman - New Zealand
James M. Keller - USA
Etienne Kerre - Belgium
Frank Klawonn - Germany
Jacek Kluska - Poland
Leonid Kompanets - Poland
Przemysław Korohoda - Poland
Jacek Koronacki - Poland
Witold Kosiński - Poland

Jan M. Kościelny - Poland
Zdzisław Kowalczuk - Poland
Robert Kozma - USA
László Kóczy - Hungary
Rudolf Kruse - Germany
Boris V. Kryzhanovsky - Russia
Adam Krzyzak - Canada
Juliusz Kulikowski - Poland
Roman Kulikowski - Poland
Věra Kůrková - Czech Republic
Marek Kurzyński - Poland
Halina Kwaśnicka - Poland
Soo-Young Lee - Korea
George Lendaris - USA
Antoni Ligęza - Poland
Sławomir Litwiński - Poland
Zhi-Qiang Liu - Hong Kong
Simon M. Lucas - UK
Jacek Łęski - Poland
Bohdan Macukow - Poland
Kurosh Madani - France
Luis Magdalena - Spain
Witold Malina - Poland
Krzysztof Malinowski - Poland
Jacek Mańdziuk - Poland
Antonino Marvuglia - Ireland
Andrzej Materka - Poland
Jaroslaw Meller - Poland
Jerry M. Mendel - USA
Radko Mesiar - Slovakia
Zbigniew Michalewicz - Australia
Zbigniew Mikrut - Poland
Sudip Misra - USA
Wojciech Moczulski - Poland
Javier Montero - Spain
Eduard Montseny - Spain
Kazumi Nakamatsu - Japan
Detlef D. Nauck - Germany
Antoine Naud - Poland
Edward Nawarecki - Poland
Ngoc Thanh Nguyen - Poland
Antoni Niederliński - Poland
Robert Nowicki - Poland
Andrzej Obuchowicz - Poland
Marek Ogiela - Poland

Erkki Oja - Finland
Stanisław Osowski - Poland
Nikhil R. Pal - India
Maciej Patan - Poland
Witold Pedrycz - Canada
Leonid Perlovsky - USA
Andrzej Pieczyński - Poland
Andrzej Piegat - Poland
Vincenzo Piuri - Italy
Lech Polkowski - Poland
Marios M. Polycarpou - Cyprus
Danil Prokhorov - USA
Anna Radzikowska - Poland
Ewaryst Rafajłowicz - Poland
Sarunas Raudys - Lithuania
Olga Rebrova - Russia
Vladimir Red'ko - Russia
Raúl Rojas - Germany
Imre J. Rudas - Hungary
Enrique H. Ruspini - USA
Khalid Saeed - Poland
Dominik Sankowski - Poland
Norihide Sano - Japan
Robert Schaefer - Poland
Rudy Setiono - Singapore
Paweł Sewastianow - Poland
Jennie Si - USA
Peter Sincak - Slovakia
Andrzej Skowron - Poland
Ewa Skubalska-Rafajłowicz - Poland
Roman Słowiński - Poland
Tomasz G. Smolinski - USA
Czesław Smutnicki - Poland
Pilar Sobrevilla - Spain
Janusz Starzyk - USA
Jerzy Stefanowski - Poland

Pawel Strumillo - Poland
Ron Sun - USA
Johan Suykens Suykens - Belgium
Piotr Szczepaniak - Poland
Eulalia J. Szmidt - Poland
Przemysław Śliwiński - Poland
Adam Słowik - Poland
Jerzy Świątek - Poland
Hideyuki Takagi - Japan
Yury Tiumentsev - Russia
Vicenç Torra - Spain
Burhan Turksen - Canada
Shiro Usui - Japan
Michael Wagenknecht - Germany
Tomasz Walkowiak - Poland
Deliang Wang - USA
Jun Wang - Hong Kong
Lipo Wang - Singapore
Zenon Waszczyszyn - Poland
Paul Werbos - USA
Slawo Wesolkowski - Canada
Sławomir Wiak - Poland
Bernard Widrow - USA
Kay C. Wiese - Canada
Bogdan M. Wilamowski - USA
Donald C. Wunsch - USA
Maciej Wygralak - Poland
Roman Wyrzykowski - Poland
Ronald R. Yager - USA
Xin-She Yang - UK
Gary Yen - USA
John Yen - USA
Sławomir Zadrożny - Poland
Ali M. S. Zalzala - United Arab
    Emirates

ICAISC Organizing Committee

Rafał Scherer, Secretary
Łukasz Bartczuk, Organizing Committee Member
Piotr Dziwiński, Organizing Committee Member
Marcin Gabryel, Finance Chair
Marcin Korytkowski, Databases and Internet Submissions

Table of Contents – Part II

Data Mining

Bioinformatics, Biometrics and Medical Applications

Agent Systems, Robotics and Control

Artificial Intelligence in Modeling and Simulation

Various Problems of Artificial Intelligence

Machine Learning for Visual Information Analysis and Security

Applications and Properties of Fuzzy Reasoning and Calculus

Clustering

Table of Contents – Part I

Neural Networks and Their Applications

Fuzzy Systems and Their Applications

Evolutionary Algorithms and Their Applications

Classification and Estimation

Computer Vision, Image and Speech Analysis

Intelligent Methods in Databases

Data Mining

Data Mining

Visual Dictionary Pruning Using Mutual Information and Information Gain

Piotr Artiemjew and Przemysław Górecki

Department of Mathematics and Computer Science
University of Warmia and Mazury Olsztyn, Poland
{artem,pgorecki}@matman.uwm.edu.pl

Abstract. Feature selection methods are often applied to many machine learning problems, one of the applications involves selecting most informative Visual Words for image categorization task. In Bag of Visual Words framework, image is represented as vector of frequencies of Visual Words, typically of length from hundreds to thousands elements. A dictionary of Visual Words is produced from image keypoints detected by SIFT algorithm and quantized into words by k-means clustering. In the paper we use Mutual Information and Information Gain as methods for selecting these words that are the most important for efficient image classification. There are four novel methods, which expand use of classic Mutual Information and Information Gain in line with our previous feature selection methods. We consider two basic selection strategies: one-vs-all and one-vs-one, as well as multi class and multi attribute value problems. The experimental session we have conducted has shown a positive effect of our modification, when applied to image classification by Support Vector Machines. The results showed that visual word selection based on modified Mutual Information in most cases wins over methods based on Information Gain.

Keywords: Visual Bag of Words, Feature Selection, Support Vector Machine, Mutual Information, Information Gain.

1 Introduction

In this paper we have applied our previous way of attribute selection - see [1,2,3,20] - and we use it to improve methods based on classic Mutual Information (MI) and Information Gain (IG). Our previous studies [1,2,3,20], especially the effectiveness of our methods shown in the recent paper [22], give us the motivation to use our way of selection in the context of MI and IG.

1.1 Basic Notions

The decision system is defined as (U, A, d), where U is the universe of images, A is the set of conditional attributes from a_1 to a_m (visual words) and d is a decision attribute (the possible classes to which images belong). We consider k decision classes from c_1 to c_k.

L. Rutkowski et al. (Eds.): ICAISC 2014, Part II, LNAI 8468, pp. 3–14, 2014.
© Springer International Publishing Switzerland 2014

Our goal is to find the level of separation of each decision class or pair of decision classes for all visual words a. After the level of separation is computed for all the attributes, we use respective strategies of attributes selection.

1.2   Review of Feature Selection Methods Based on MI and IG

There are many interesting works of feature selection based on Mutual Information and Information Gain factors. For instance, it was applied by Yang et al. [19] to calculate the the term-goodness for text categorization. Both MI and IG were used, followed by a thresholding, to select the best terms in the dictionary. The experimental session proved that IG outperformed other methods. In the similar studies Mukras et al. [15] used his methods based on IG, Xu et al. [17] used MI, and Novovičová [12] et al. used conditional MI.

The other works directed on using IG in various contexts are as follows: Azhagusundari et al. [4] used combination of discernibility matrix and IG, Appavu et al. [7] use Bayes Theorem and IG, where Bayes Theorem was used to discover dependency information among features, it was improved by IG which selected features based on their importance. The IG and MI factors were also applied in the context of visual words selection, for example by Yo-Gang et al. [10]. In our previous studies on visual words selection, we have compared MFM1 [3] and MSF6 [2] feature selection methods [22] to the classical MI and IG.

1.3   Our Motivation

The main goal of this work was to investigate the extension of classic Mutual Information and Information Gain based on Quinlan Entropy into multi class and multi value domains of attributes - in the context of attribute selection. In classic MI and IG the single value is computed for all decision classes as a ratio of their separation. Additionally the domain of attributes in classic case is binary. Our extension consists of using two strategies of attribute selection, one class vs one class, and one class vs the rest of decision classes. The ratio of separation is computed for every central decision class or pair of decision classes, respectively to the strategy. After the rate is computed for all attributes we apply the strategy of choice fixed number of the best attributes.

1.4   Visual Dictionary Pruning

For image representation we use really popular semantic categorization of images [9], object localization and identification [9], as well as content based image retrieval [14,23] derived Visual Bag of Words approach (BoVW). These methods [13,28,25,11] works in a stable way even if the image is partially occluded or the viewpoint is changed.

In a general way, the visual words can be understand as orderless collection of patches, which could be detected as keypoints by the following methods, (i.e.: SIFT[24], SURF[5], BRIEF[8], ORB[16] etc.). After the keypoints are detected there is need for quantization into visual words, for this reason clustering methods are applied, one of the most popular is k - means. Finally the images are represented as histograms of visual words.

We have focus our attention to improve IG and MI basic methods, after seeing the studies [10,18], which have shown that IG is one of the most effective factors, we choose MI, because is in line with IG.

The rest of our paper is organized as follows. In Section 2 basic information about MI and IG are presented, which also constitute a base for our further modifications. Sect. 3 brings the detailed description of our feature selection methods. The next Section 4 describes the results of experiments on the image data sets. Finally, Section 5 provides the summary of our work.

2 Basic Information Gain and Mutual Information

Information Gain measures the dependence between an attribute a and a class label c_i. An average information gain IG_{avg} of an attribute a is defined in a following way:

$$IG_{average}(a) = \frac{1}{C} \sum_{i=1}^{C} IG(a, c_i) \tag{1}$$

$$\text{where } IG(a, c_i) = \sum_{a \in 0,1} \sum_{c_i \in 0,1} \log \frac{P(a, c_i)}{P(a)P(c_i)}, \tag{2}$$

Mutual Information is defined similarly, the ratio of the attribute a for all observations having a class label c_i is defined as following:

$$MI(a, c_i) = \log \frac{P(a, c_i)}{P(a)P(c_i)}, \tag{3}$$

Mutual Information for entire dataset and attribute a is defined as an average value of MI for all decision classes:

$$MI_{avg}(a) = \frac{1}{C} \sum_{i=1}^{C} MI(a, c_i) \tag{4}$$

Mutual information in this form is used for feature selection in context of binary data sets with binary domain of attributes.

In this paper we use equivalent form of described Information Gain derived from Quinlan Entropy, which is popular in the context of node selection in decision tree design. Quinlan Entropy was originally used in C4.5 algorithm [26].

3 Proposed Feature Selection Methods

Our improved versions of described IG and MI are as follows.

3.1 Attribute Selection Method Based on Classic Mutual Information Factor - $MIbasic$

For the decision system (U, A, c), where $|U| = n$, $|A| = m$, $c \in C = \{c_1, c_2, ..., c_k\}$.

For considered feature $a \in A$, and all objects $u \in U$, $Domain(a) = \{v_1(a), v_2(a), ...\}$ as the set of unique values of an attribute a in the universe U.

Given the attribute a and the central class c_i, the global separation rate $Global\_MI(a)$ of a from other decision classes $C - \{c_i\}$ is computed as following:

$$Global\_MI(a) = \frac{\sum_{i=1}^{|C|} \frac{\sum_{j=1}^{|Domain(a)|} Entropy(plus_{c_i}(v_j(a)), minus_{c_i}(v_j(a)))}{|Domain(a)|}}{|C|}$$

where,

$$Entropy(plus_{c_i}(v_j(a)), minus_{c_i}(v_j(a))) = log_2\left(\frac{\frac{plus_{c_i}(v_j(a))}{n}}{\frac{(plus_{c_i}(v_j(a)) + minus_{c_i}(v_j(a)))}{|U|}} * \frac{|C_i|}{|U|}\right)$$

for

$$plus_{c_i}(v_j(a)) = |\{v \in U : a(v) = v_j(a) \ and \ d(v) = c_i\}|$$

$$minus_{c_i}(v_j(a)) = |\{v \in U : a(v) = v_j(a) \ and \ d(v) \neq c_i\}|$$

$$C_i = \{v \in U : d(v) = c_i\}$$

After the rate of separation is computed for all attributes, we sorted it in decreasing order as follows,

$$Global\_MI_1(a) >= Global\_MI_2(a) >= ... >= Global\_MI_{|A|}(a),$$

finally we select a fixed number of the attributes from the list, the remaining ones are pruned.

$$a_{Global\_MI_1(a)}, a_{Global\_MI_2(a)}, ..., a_{Global\_MI_{|A|}(a)}$$

3.2 Modification of Selection Based on Mutual Information - $one - vs - all$ Strategy - $MI2$

The modification of Mutual Information method consists of the attribute choice strategy after the rates of separation are computed for all attributes. The another thing is the design of this method for multi-class problems.

$$MI^{c_i}(a) = \frac{\sum_{j=1}^{|Domain(a)|} Entropy(plus_{c_i}(v_j(a)), minus_{c_i}(v_j(a)))}{|Domain(a)|}$$

For all conditional features, the rates of separation of central classes is sorted for each decision class separately, what we can see below, for $k = |C|$.

$$MI_1^{c_1}(a) >= MI_2^{c_1}(a) >= ... >= MI_{|A|}^{c_1}(a)$$

$$MI_1^{c_2}(a) >= MI_2^{c_2}(a) >= ... >= MI_{|A|}^{c_2}(a)$$

$$\vdots$$

$$MI_1^{c_k}(a) >= MI_2^{c_k}(a) >= ... >= MI_{|A|}^{c_k}(a)$$

Considering the attributes corresponding to sorted list of selection rates, as we can see below,

$$a_{MI_1^{c_1}(a)}, a_{MI_2^{c_1}(a)}, ..., a_{MI_{|A|}^{c_1}(a)}$$

$$a_{MI_1^{c_2}(a)}, a_{MI_2^{c_2}(a)}, ..., a_{MI_{|A|}^{c_2}(a)}$$

$$\vdots$$

$$a_{MI_1^{c_k}(a)}, a_{MI_2^{c_k}(a)}, ..., a_{MI_{|A|}^{c_k}(a)}$$

the final step is to choose the best visual words, considering the decision classes $C = \{c_1, c_2, ..., c_k\}$, and all attributes a from A, the procedure of visual words selection based on above list of attributes is as follows,

```
Input Data: {BestWordsSet ← ∅, iter1 ← 0, iter2 ← 0}
while iter2 ≤ |A| do
   iter2 ← iter2 + 1
   iter3 ← 0
   while iter3 ≤ |C| do
      if a_{MI_{iter2}^{c_iter3}(a)} ∉ BestWordsSet then
         BestWordsSet ← a_{MI_{iter2}^{c_iter3}(a)}
         iter1 ← iter1 + 1
         if iter1 = fixed number of the best visual words then
            return BestWordsSet
         end if
      end if
   end while
end while
```

---

end while
Output Data: $\{BestWordsSet\}$

3.3 Attribute Selection Method Based on Mutual Information - $one - vs - one$ Strategy - $MI3$

The second strategy of attribute selection consists on considering all pairs of classes without repeating. In this case mutual information is defined as follows,

$$MI^{c_{i1},c_{i2}}(a) = \frac{\sum_{j=1}^{|Domain(a)|} Entropy(plus_{c_{i1},c_{i2}}(v_j(a)), minus_{c_{i1},c_{i2}}(v_j(a)))}{|Domain(a)|}$$

$$Entropy(plus_{c_{i1},c_{i2}}(v_j(a)), minus_{c_{i1},c_{i2}}(v_j(a)))$$

$$= log_2(\frac{\frac{plus_{c_{i1},c_{i2}}(v_j(a))}{|C_{i1}|+|C_{i2}|}}{\frac{(plus_{c_{i1},c_{i2}}(v_j(a))+minus_{c_{i1},c_{i2}}(v_j(a)))}{|C_{i1}|+|C_{i2}|}} * \frac{|C_{i1}|}{|C_{i1}|+|C_{i2}|})$$

for

$$plus_{c_{i1},c_{i2}}(v_j(a)) = |\{v \in U : a(v) = v_j(a) \text{ and } d(v) = c_{i1}\}|$$

$$minus_{c_{i1},c_{i2}}(v_j(a)) = |\{v \in U : a(v) = v_j(a) \text{ and } d(v) = c_{i2}\}|$$

$$C_{i1} = \{v \in U : d(v) = c_{i1}\}, C_{i2} = \{v \in U : d(v) = c_{i2}\}$$

For all conditional features, the rates of separation of central classes is sorted for each decision class separately, what we can see below, for $k = |C|$.

$$MI_1^{c_{i1},c_{i2}}(a) >= MI_2^{c_{i1},c_{i2}}(a) >= ... >= MI_{|A|}^{c_{i1},c_{i2}}(a)$$

Considering the attributes corresponding to sorted list of selection rates, as we can see below,

---

$$a_{MI_1^{c_{i1},c_{i2}}(a)}, a_{MI_2^{c_{i1},c_{i2}}(a)}, ..., a_{MI_{|A|}^{c_{i1},c_{i2}}(a)}$$

---

the final step is to choice the best visual words, considering all pairs pf the decision classes (c_{i1}, c_{i2}), where $i1 \in \{1, 2, ..., k\}$ and $i2 \in \{i2 + 1, i2 + 2, ..., k\}$ and all attributes a from A, the procedure of visual words selection based on above list of attributes is as follows,

Input Data: $\{BestWordsSet \leftarrow \emptyset, iter1 \leftarrow 0, iter2 \leftarrow 0\}$
while $iter2 \leq |A|$ **do**
   $iter2 \leftarrow iter2 + 1$
   $iter3 \leftarrow 0$
   while $iter3 \leq |C|$ **do**
     $iter4 \leftarrow iter3$
     while $iter4 \leq |C|$ **do**
       if $a_{MI^{c_{iter3},c_{iter4}}_{iter2}(a)} \notin BestWordsSet$ **then**
       $BestWordsSet \leftarrow a_{MI^{c_{iter3},c_{iter4}}_{iter2}(a)}$
       $iter1 \leftarrow iter1 + 1$
       if $iter1 = fixed\ number\ of\ the\ best\ visual\ words$ **then**
         return $BestWordsSet$
       end if
       end if
     end while
   end while
end while
Output Data: $\{BestWordsSet\}$

3.4 Attribute Selection Method Based on Classic Information Gain Factor - *IGbasic*

This method works analogously with MIbasic with the different definition of separation ratio, which is defined as follows,

$Global\_Entropy_{c_i}(a)$

$$= \frac{\sum_{j=1}^{|Domain(a)|} \frac{plus_{c_i}(v_j(a)) + minus_{c_i}(v_j(a))}{|U|} * Entropy_{c_i}(plus_{c_i}(v_j(a)), minus_{c_i}(v_j(a)))}{|Domain(a)|}$$

where,

$$Entropy_{c_i}(plus_{c_i}(v_j(a)), minus_{c_i}(v_j(a))) = -(log_2(A + B))$$

$$A = (\frac{plus_{c_i}(v_j(a))}{plus_{c_i}(v_j(a)) + minus_{c_i}(v_j(a))})^{\frac{plus_{c_i}(v_j(a))}{plus_{c_i}(v_j(a)) + minus_{c_i}(v_j(a))}}$$

$$B = (\frac{minus_{c_i}(v_j(a))}{plus_{c_i}(v_j(a)) + minus_{c_i}(v_j(a))})^{\frac{minus_{c_i}(v_j(a))}{plus_{c_i}(v_j(a)) + minus_{c_i}(v_j(a))}}$$

$$Global\_IG(a) = \frac{\sum_{i=1}^{|C|}(Entropy_{c_i}(|C_i|, |U| - |C_i|) - Global\_Entropy_{c_i}(a)}{|C|}$$

3.5 Modification of Feature Selection Based on Information Gain - $one - vs - all$ - IG2

This method works in similar way with MI2, the separation ratio is defined as follows,

$$IG^{c_i}(a) = \frac{\sum_{j=1}^{|Domain(a)|} Entropy(plus_{c_i}(v_j(a)), minus_{c_i}(v_j(a)))}{|Domain(a)|}$$

3.6 Attribute Selection Based on Modified Information Gain - $one - vs - one$ - IG3

The last metod works similarly to MI3 algorithm, the separation ratio is defined as follows,

$$IG^{c_{i1},c_{i2}}(a) = Entropy(|C_{i1}|, |C_{i2}|) - Global\_Entropy^{c_{i1},c_{i2}}(a)$$

$$Global\_Entropy^{c_{i1},c_{i2}}(a) = \frac{A * B}{|Domain(a)|}$$

$$A = \sum_{j=1}^{|Domain(a)|} \frac{plus_{c_{i1},c_{i2}}(v_j(a)) + minus_{c_{i1},c_{i2}}(v_j(a))}{|C_{i1}| + |C_{i2}|}$$

$$B = Entropy(plus_{c_{i1},c_{i2}}(v_j(a)), minus_{c_{i1},c_{i2}}(v_j(a)))$$

4 Experimental Session

To evaluate the effectiveness of the proposed dictionary pruning approach, we have performed an experimental session. The session was designed in the following manner. Most of the experiments were performed with use of our in-house dataset of shoe images - available in [21].

The dataset consists of 200 shoe images divided into 5 distinctive visual categories containing 59, 20, 34, 29, and 58 images. Sample images for each category are shown in [22]. In addition, we have tested our method on images taken from VOC Pascal Challenge dataset - available in [27].

For each dataset, the initial dictionary of visual words was created by extracting image keypoints using SIFT transform, followed by k-means clustering. In case of shoe dataset, dictionaries of $k = 1000, 2500, 5000$ visual words were created. For the second dataset, image keypoints were quantized into 250 visual words. The detail info of the data sets are presented in Tab. 1.

Given a dictionary, an image was represented as an orderless BoVW feature vector $x = (x_1, \ldots, x_k)$ of visual word freqencies, where x_i denotes a frequency of i-th visual word. As a basic preprocessing step, feature vectors were normalized to a unit length. Therefore, for a feature vector $x \in U$ all values of attribute $a(x)$ are dividing by the scalar length $||x||$ of x, that is $a_i(x) = \frac{a_i(x)}{||x||}$,

Table 1. Data sets - basic information, *no.of.attr* = number of visual words, *no.of.obj* = number of images, *no.of.dec.classes* = number of image classes

name	no.of.attr	no.of.obj	no.of.dec.classes
shoes1000	984	200	5
shoes2500	2443	200	5
shoes5000	4737	200	5
Voc250	251	1467	9

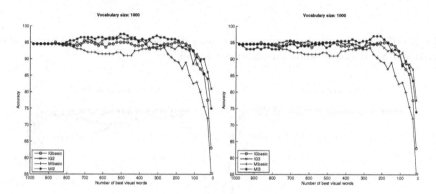

Fig. 1. $CV - 10$ - result of experiments for shoes data set with 1000 considered visual words and SVM classification for chi square kernel

where $\|x\| = \sqrt{\sum_{i=1}^{n}(a_i(x))^2}$. After a normalization, the feature vector is independent of the number of keypoints detected in the image.

As a reference classifier we use Support Vector machine with chi^2 kernel, in particular LibSVM [6] was used. For evaluation of the results we have used 10 fold cross validation. The results of the classification by pruning the dictionaries to a fixed amount of visual words are shown in Fig. 1 - 3.

Surprisingly for most of cases the $MI2$ and $MI3$ methods works best with significant reduction of words count. The only exception is a result from Fig 3, where for a dictionary size of 5000 the $IG2$ one-vs-all strategy beats other methods. However, in all other cases $MI2$ and $MI3$ methods are better from the others (also for dictionaries in the size of 50, 100, 250 and 500 words - not included due to short space).

In addition, we have performed another test with the use of VOC dataset. The result from Fig. 4 confirms that $MI2$ and $MI3$ methods work very well and better than basic versions.

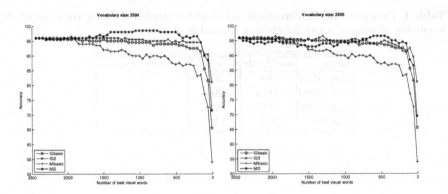

Fig. 2. $CV - 10$ - result of experiments for shoes data set with 2500 considered visual words and SVM classification for chi square kernel

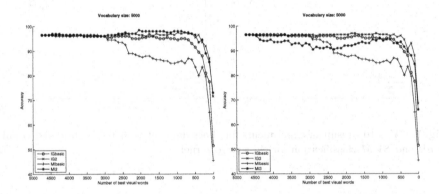

Fig. 3. $CV - 10$ - result of experiments for shoes data set with 5000 considered visual words and SVM classification for chi square kernel

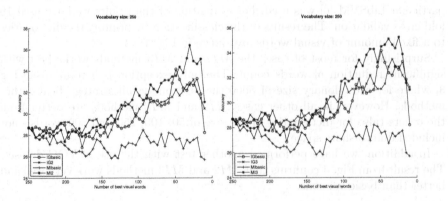

Fig. 4. $CV - 10$ - result of experiments for VOC data set with 250 considered visual words and SVM classification for chi square kernel

5 Conclusions

This work is the continuation of the paper [22], which show us the effectiveness of the way we extended classic feature selection methods.

In this paper we have shown four novel methods of visual words selection. A series of experiments have proven the effectiveness of our methods, it has also been shown that our methods are comparable or even better than classic algorithms based on Information Gain and Mutual Information. $MI2$ and $MI3$ methods works best in most cases, additionally the $IG2$ and $IG3$ methods seems to be better than $IGbasic$ in all examined cases.

In the future work, we plan to check the effectiveness of our feature selection methods based on MI and IG values in different contexts, among other in the context of DNA Microarray gene selection comparing with our previous methods.

Aknowledgements. The research has been supported by the grant N N516 480940 from The National Science Center of the Republic of Poland and grant 1309-802 from Ministry of Science and Higher Education.

References

1. Artiemjew, P.: Classifiers based on rough mereology in analysis of dna microarray data. In: 2010 International Conference of Soft Computing and Pattern Recognition (SoCPaR), pp. 273–278 (December 2010)
2. Artiemjew, P.: The extraction method of DNA microarray features based on experimental A statistics. In: Yao, J., Ramanna, S., Wang, G., Suraj, Z. (eds.) RSKT 2011. LNCS, vol. 6954, pp. 642–648. Springer, Heidelberg (2011)
3. Artiemjew, P.: Review of the extraction methods of dna microarray features based on central decision class separation vs rough set classifier. Foundations of Computing and Decision Sciences 37, 239–252 (2012)
4. Selvadoss Thanamani, A., Azhagusundari, B.: Feature selection based on information gain. International Journal of Innovative Technology and Exploring Engineering (IJITEE) 2(2) (2013)
5. Bay, H., Tuytelaars, T., Van Gool, L.: SURF: Speeded up robust features. In: Leonardis, A., Bischof, H., Pinz, A. (eds.) ECCV 2006, Part I. LNCS, vol. ECCV, pp. 404–417. Springer, Heidelberg (2006)
6. Chang, C.-C., Lin, C.-J.: LIBSVM: A library for support vector machines. ACM Transactions on Intelligent Systems and Technology 2, 27:1–27:27 (2011), Software available at http://www.csie.ntu.edu.tw/~cjlin/libsvm
7. Appavu, S., Rajaram, R., Nagammai, M., Priyanga, N., Priyanka, S.: Bayes theorem and information gain based feature selection for maximizing the performance of classifiers. In: Meghanathan, N., Kaushik, B.K., Nagamalai, D. (eds.) CCSIT 2011, Part I. CCIS, vol. 131, pp. 501–511. Springer, Heidelberg (2011)
8. Calonder, M., Lepetit, V., Strecha, C., Fua, P.: BRIEF: Binary robust independent elementary features. In: Daniilidis, K., Maragos, P., Paragios, N. (eds.) ECCV 2010, Part IV. LNCS, vol. 6314, pp. 778–792. Springer, Heidelberg (2010)
9. Everingham et al: The PASCAL Visual Object Classes Challenge (2010), http://www.pascal-network.org/challenges/VOC/voc2010/workshop/index.html

10. Jiang, et al.: Representations of keypoint-based semantic concept detection: A comprehensive study. IEEE Transactions on Multimedia 12(1), 42–53 (2010)
11. Nilsback, et al.: A visual vocabulary for flower classification. In: Proc. of the 2006 IEEE Computer Society Conference on Computer Vision and Pattern Recognition, vol. 2, pp. 1447–1454. IEEE Computer Society, Washington, DC (2006)
12. Novovičová, J., Somol, P., Haindl, M., Pudil, P.: Conditional mutual information based feature selection for classification task. In: Rueda, L., Mery, D., Kittler, J. (eds.) CIARP 2007. LNCS, vol. 4756, pp. 417–426. Springer, Heidelberg (2007)
13. Parkhi, et al.: Cats and dogs. In: 2012 IEEE Conference on Computer Vision and Pattern Recognition (CVPR), pp. 3498–3505 (2012)
14. Philbin, J., et al.: Object retrieval with large vocabularies and fast spatial matching. In: Proc. of the IEEE Conf. on Computer Vision and Pattern Recognition (2007)
15. Mukras, R., et al.: Information gain feature selection for ordinal text classification using probability re-distribution
16. Rublee, A., et al.: ORB: An efficient alternative to SIFT or SURF. In: International Conference on Computer Vision, Barcelona (2011)
17. Yan, X., et al.: A study on mutual information-based feature selection for text categorization. Journal of Computational Information Systems 3(3), 1007–1012 (2007)
18. Yang, et al.: Evaluating bag-of-visual-words representations in scene classification. In: Proc. of the International Workshop on Workshop on Multimedia Information Retrieval, MIR 2007, pp. 197–206. ACM, New York (2007)
19. evalYang, Y., Pedersen, J.O.: A comparative study on feature selection in text categorization. In: Proc. of the 14th Int. Conf. on Machine Learning, pp. 412–420. Morgan Kaufmann Publishers Inc., San Francisco (1997)
20. Gorecki, P., Artiemjew, P.: Dna microarray classification by means of weighted voting based on rough set classifier. In: 2010 International Conference of Soft Computing and Pattern Recognition (SoCPaR), pp. 269–272 (December 2010)
21. Gorecki, P., Artiemjew, P., Drozda, P., Sopyla, K.: Shoes-dataset, http://wmii.uwm.edu.pl/~kmmi/sites/default/files/grant/shoes200.zip
22. Gorecki, P., Artiemjew, P., Drozda, P., Sopyla, K.: Visual words selection based on class separation measures. In: 2013 12th IEEE International Conference on Cognitive Informatics Cognitive Computing (ICCI*CC), pp. 409–414 (2013)
23. Górecki, P., Sopyła, K., Drozda, P.: Ranking by K-means voting algorithm for similar image retrieval. In: Rutkowski, L., Korytkowski, M., Scherer, R., Tadeusiewicz, R., Zadeh, L.A., Zurada, J.M. (eds.) ICAISC 2012, Part I. LNCS, vol. 7267, pp. 509–517. Springer, Heidelberg (2012)
24. Lowe, D.G.: Distinctive image features from scale-invariant keypoints. Int. J. Comput. Vision 60, 91–110 (2004)
25. Nilsback, M.-E., Zisserman, A.: Automated flower classification over a large number of classes. In: Proc. of the Indian Conference on Computer Vision, Graphics and Image Processing (December 2008)
26. Quinlan, J.R.: Programs for machine learning. Morgan Kaufmann Publishers (1993)
27. VOC. 250 words dictionary size, http://213.184.8.16/~artem/voc2006normobj250.zip
28. Zhang, J., Lazebnik, S., Schmid, C.: Local features and kernels for classification of texture and object categories: a comprehensive study. International Journal of Computer Vision 73 (2007)

Mining Telecommunication Networks
to Enhance Customer Lifetime Predictions

Aimée Backiel[1], Bart Baesens[1,2], and Gerda Claeskens[1]

[1] Faculty of Economics and Business, KU Leuven, Belgium
{aimee.backiel,bart.baesens,gerda.claeskens}@kuleuven.be
[2] School of Management, University of Southampton, UK

Abstract. Customer retention has become a necessity in many markets, including mobile telecommunications. As it becomes easier for customers to switch providers, the providers seek to improve prediction models in an effort to intervene with potential churners. Many studies have evaluated different models seeking any improvement to prediction accuracy. This study proposes that the attributes, not the model, need to be reconsidered. By representing call detail records as a social network of customers, network attributes can be extracted for use in various traditional prediction models. The use of network attributes exhibits a significant increase in the area under the receiver operating curve (AUC) when compared to using just individual customer attributes.

1 Introduction

Churn prediction is a common business application for classification techniques. In almost every market, companies must contend with a regular loss of customers to competition. In many markets, the level of saturation makes it much more difficult to attract entirely new customers, so the focus on customer retention is even more important. Attracting new customers is more costly than retaining existing ones [1, 2]. Longtime customers are valuable in other ways as well, including word of mouth advertising and lower cost of service. The prepaid mobile telephone segment, in particular, faces churn rates between 2 and 3% each month [1]. Accurately predicting which customers are likely to churn in advance can have a large impact on the ability to intervene and ultimately on profitability. This study, using a dataset from a major Belgian mobile provider, proposes the transformation of customer call behavior into a social network in order to enrich the data available for the classification techniques.

In this paper, two categories of churn prediction models are distinguished based on the type of attributes used for prediction: traditional models and network models. In traditional models, attributes of individual customers, such as personal information or customer behavior, are used to predict whether that individual customer will churn. The expectation is that similar customers will behave similarly with regards to churn. On the other hand, network models take into account the social network of customers, specifically calls made to other customers who have or

L. Rutkowski et al. (Eds.): ICAISC 2014, Part II, LNAI 8468, pp. 15–26, 2014.

have not churned, to predict future churners. In this case, the expectation is that people who interact with each other will behave similarly.

The experiments conducted to investigate the differences in predictive performance involve prepaid mobile customers. In this context specifically, incomplete customer information, in addition to high churn rates, necessitate advancements over the traditional prediction models. Prepaid subscriptions are to varying extents anonymous and can easily be passed to a new user without notice to the company. The outcome of this research is a prediction model built on call data available to the mobile provider which allows for timely, accurate, and interpretable predictions.

This paper is organized as follows. Following this introduction, a literature review of churn prediction and social network analysis is summarized. The data and experiment will be described in the Methodology section. Finally the results will be discussed in the Findings section. The paper concludes with a brief summary of the research.

2 Literature

2.1 Churn Prediction

Churn, in general, is defined as the loss of customers. Churn prediction is an application of classification techniques intended to predict the probability of a customer discontinuing their relationship with a company. While there are different classification techniques and a few types of attributes which can be used, the general churn prediction process is not dependent on these choices. The first step is to define churn. In some contexts, this date will be explicitly available such as a contract termination. In other contexts, such as prepaid mobile, a customer simply stops using a service. In this case, churn can be defined as a period of time without any activities on the account [3]. After the churn label is determined, the predictor variables can be used to train a classification model. This model is then applied to new data, generally current customers, to make predictions about their probability for churn. The results will form a ranking of customers from most likely to churn to least likely to churn. At this point, a percentage of customers at the top of the ranking can be contacted as part of a targeted retention campaign.

In the telecommunications domain, research has focused on mobile communications, though some landline studies have been executed as well. Mobile accounts generally include less information about the customer when compared to landline services [4], and prepaid accounts record even less customer data than postpaid accounts. In this literature review, most references use traditional prediction models, which employ customer features, such as contract type, payment amount or dates, hardware features, counts or times of calls or SMS messages. Classification techniques using local attributes include decision trees [4–8], logistic regression [2, 4–9], support vector machines [4, 8], neural networks [2, 4, 7, 9], and survival analysis [10]. Dasgupta et al.[11] use a network of customers and a relational learner to predict how churn will spread or diffuse through the network. Most churn prediction settings involve significant class skew; there is far less churn than non-churn. This should be taken into consideration as it can impact model selection, training, and evaluation. Simple classification accuracy would be less appropriate for assessing performance as a naive rule predicting all customers as non-churners would result in at least 97% accuracy given a churn rate less than 3%. Commonly used model evaluation measures in churn prediction literature include area under the ROC (receiver operating characteristic) curve, Lift which measures the percentage of top-ranked customers who are actual churners compared to the percentage of churners in the population, and assorted threshold metrics such as classification error.

2.2 Social Network Analysis

Social network analysis is based on the concept of homophily. This principle states that contact between similar people occurs at a higher rate than among dissimilar people [12]. If the contact or interaction among people in a network can be measured in some way, it can be used to make predictions instead of or in addition to the individual attributes of each person. Homophily has been used to predict links based on similar attributes and also to predict attributes based on known links [13, 8]. Social influence is a separate, but related concept explaining how individuals encourage similarity through their interactions [14]. They found that both concepts are confounded in networks and cannot be analyzed independently. For predictions, it may not be necessary to distinguish between them, but it will be difficult to interpret exactly how similarity spreads among individuals: either similar people tending to interact or interactions causing similarities.

A social network can be represented graphically where the people are nodes and some relationship between them form links or edges. Networks are not limited to people, but have actually been used to represent many different types of relationship between entities. In this literature review, applications of network analysis have been found in many areas including nursing [15], behavior adoption [16], patent classification [17], fraud detection [18], and prison system communication [19]. Pushpa and Shobha[20] and Dasgupta et al.[11] have applied network analysis to churn prediction, but their results were not compared to traditional prediction models.

Macskassy and Provost[21] have shown that simple relational learners based only on a few known class labels and the links between nodes can produce good predictions. They further suggest that traditional models and relational models should be incorporated as components into network classification systems [22]. There are two approaches for combining the different models into a single system. The approach of Macskassy and Provost begins with a local model which is used to produce prior estimates for the network. Then, a relational learner can adjust these estimates based on the links. Finally, collective inference is used when predictions for nodes are dependent on each other. This is an iterative process. The second approach works in the opposite direction. The social network can first be investigated and information collected through link mining from them can be used as attributes in a traditional model.

Different types of link features can be mined from a network. Three simple link features are mode-link, count-link, and binary link [23]. Mode-link returns the most common neighbor class. Count-link gives the number of neighbors in each class. Binary-link indicates whether there a neighbor of each class. These link features can then be used in classification models. In their study, Lu and Getoor[23] found better performance when separate models were trained for instance attributes and link features. They also determined that links between the training set and test set should be included in the network instead of creating two unconnected networks.

3   Methodology

3.1   Data and Processing

To investigate the impact of social network analysis on churn prediction, a dataset from a Belgian telco operator was analyzed.

Table 1. Data Description

Local Variables		
Account Details	Reload Information	Usage Data
Start Date	Reload count in 60 days	Numbers called in 60 days
Service Plan	Reload value in 60 days	Call time in 60 days
Trial Card	Last reload date	Numbers texted in 60 days
Language	Card swapped in 30 days	Text count in 60 days
Further Breakdowns of Local Data:		
Incoming and Outgoing, Destination Account Type		
Network Type, Day and Time of Call, Call Duration		
Network Variables	Data Type	
Churn Neighbors:	Count	
Churn Calling:	Time in seconds	
Non-Churn Neighbors:	Count	
Non-churn Calling:	Time in seconds	
Out-of-Network Neighbor:	Binary	
Out-of-network Calling:	Time in seconds	

The data include customer information and call details from 1.4 million pre-paid mobile customers from May to October 2010. The customer information includes a total of 111 local variables. Due to the nature of prepaid accounts, no personal information is available. The call detail records, over 32 million per month, include data about each call placed by a customer. These call detail records were transformed into 6 network features. Customer information and call details can be related using an anonymized phone number found in each dataset. Both sets of features are shown in Table 1.

For this study, the calls between customers are modeled as a social network. In the network, each node represents a customer and one additional node represents all non-customers. Calls between customers form single, undirected edges, weighted by the total call seconds. While text message counts were included in the customer account records, individual text messages are not present in the call detail records so they are not included in the social network. Two types of count-link features were extracted from the resulting network: counts of neighbors and the sum of call seconds with neighbors.

Churn has been defined as when a customer did not place or receive any calls for a period of 30 days. One month is short, but the cost of misclassifying a churner is higher than the a non-churner. The network nodes were labelled according to whether the customer churned during the first month. A total of six link features were then extracted from this network as shown in Table 1. Because all out-of-network neighbors are represented by a single node in the network, the Out-of-network neighbor attribute is binary, indicating whether the customer communicated with an out-of-network number or not.

The NetChurn procedure was developed to process the call detail records into social network features. The procedure has been divided into five steps for clarity and reusability. Each step is described by a short algorithm. Figure 1 visually depicts the steps and data sources in the process.

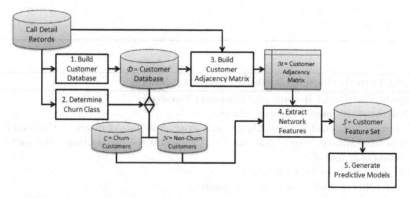

Fig. 1. Flow chart depicting the NetChurn procedure used to extract network features from Call Detail Records

---

Algorithm 1. Build a Customer Database from Call Detail Records

---

Input: Call Detail Records
Output: Customer Database
Begin with a dataset Call Detail Records CDR_m, with month m. Let $\mathcal{D}$ denote a database with customers d_1-d_n and a non-customer d_0. Each customer d_i has variables first call $first_i$ and last call $last_i$.
for *each line* $l \in CDR_1$ **do**
    if *caller* $d_i \in \mathcal{D}$ **then**
        $last_i = date_1$
    $\mathcal{D} = \mathcal{D} \cup \{d_i\}$

Algorithm 2. Determine the Churn Class for a set of Customers

---

Input: Call Detail Records and Customer Database
Output: Customer Database Subsets
Assume CDR_m and $\mathcal{D}$ from Algorithm 1 exist. Now let $\mathcal{D} = \mathcal{C} \cup \mathcal{N}$, such that $\mathcal{C}$ contains first month churners. The binary variable $churn_i$ indicates churn or non-churn during the entire study.
for *each line* $l \in CDR_2$-CDR_n **do**
    if *caller* $d_i \in \mathcal{D}$ **then**
        $last_i = date_l$

for *each customer* $d_i \in \mathcal{D}$ **do**
    if $last_i < churnPeriod$ **then**
        $\mathcal{C} = \mathcal{C} \cup \{d_i\}$
        $churn_i = 1$
    else if $last_i < study$ **then**
        $\mathcal{N} = \mathcal{N} \cup \{d_i\}$
        $churn_i = 1$
    else
        $\mathcal{N} = \mathcal{N} \cup \{d_i\}$
        $churn_i = 0$

Algorithm 3. Build a Customer Adjacency Matrix

Input: Call Detail Records and Customer Database
Output: Customer Adjacency Matrix
Assume CDR_m and $\mathcal{D}$ from Algorithm 1 exist. Now let $\mathcal{M}$ denote a Customer Adjacency Matrix, where each entry $m_{i,j}$ indicates the calling time between two customers d_i and d_j.
for *each line* $l \in CDR_1$ **do**
    if *caller* d_i *and receiver* $d_j \in \mathcal{D}$ **then**
        $m_{i,j} = m_{i,j} + time_l$
    else if *caller* $d_i \in \mathcal{D}$ **then**
        $m_{0,i} = m_{0,i} + time_l$

Algorithm 4. Extract Network Features

Input: Customer Adjacency Matrix and Customer Database Subsets
Output: Customer Network Features
Assume $\mathcal{D} = \mathcal{C} \cup \mathcal{N}$ from Algorithm 2 and $\mathcal{M}$ from Algorithm 3 exist.
Now let $\mathcal{S}$ denote a set of customers s_1-s_n, each with six network features:
Churn neighbors $countC_i$, Churn calling $timeC_i$, Non-churn neighbors
$countNC_i$, Non-churn calling $timeNC_i$ Out-of-network neighbor
$hasOut_i$, and Out-of-network calling $timeOut_i$

for *each customer $d_j\mathcal{D}$* **do**
  for *each customer $d_i\mathcal{D} \mid i < j$* **do**
    if $d_i = 0$ **then**
      $hasOut_j = 1$
      $timeOut_j = m_{0,j}$
    else if $d_i \in \mathcal{C}$ **then**
      $countC_j = countC_j + 1$
      $timeC_j = timeC_j + m_{i,j}$
    else if $d_i \in \mathcal{N}$ **then**
      $countNC_j = countNC_j + 1$
      $timeNC_j = timeNC_j + m_{i,j}$

As discussed in Section 2.2, social network analysis is based on the concept of homophily, that is, that similar people tend to interact more than dissimilar people. Easley and Kleinberg[24] explain one possible test for homophily is to compare the actual fraction of cross-gender edges to the expected cross-gender edges in a random network. If the links in the social network built in this study had been assigned randomly, the expected proportion of edges between churners and non-churners would be 0.3384. In the actual network, the proportion of cross-gender edges is only 0.1391. A t-test showed a statistically significant difference with p-value <0.001. Homophily implies that the network attributes will enhance churn prediction. Figure 2 depicts a subset of the network where the density of links between churners can be seen. This image was generated using Pajek - Program for Large Network Analysis (http://pajek.imfm.si/doku.php, accessed 11 September 2013).

3.2 Experimental Setup

After the data processing was complete, as experiment was designed to compare the use of local attributes versus network attributes. Two types of models were tested: logistic regression and Cox proportional hazards regression (Cox PH). Three variable sets were tested: local attributes, network attributes, and a combination of both. All models were estimated in SAS, which is accomplished with an iterative maximization process [25]. Logistic regression was chosen as an established classification technique. In many applications, logistic regression offers good predictive performance, understandable models, and interpretable

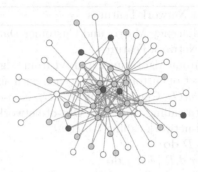

Fig. 2. Cluster of churners in the network. Key: non-churners (white), first month churners (light grey), later churners (dark grey).

log odds ratio to assess the explanatory variables. On the other hand, the Cox proportional hazards model was selected because it allows for time-to-event predictions, in this case, a likely time of churn can be estimated for each customer, rather than a binary churn or non-churn label. To compare this with logistic regression, it is necessary to train a logistic regression model for each time period, while one Cox PH model can make predictions for all time periods. Similar to the log odds ratio, the Cox PH model results in hazard ratios indicating how the probability of churn changes when each explanatory variables changes value.

The models were trained on a subset of 70% of the data. A holdout test set or the remaining 30% was used for validation. Feature selection, based on the Wald test, reduced the local attribute feature set. The Bonferroni correction was used to avoid false positives by lowering the p-value to <0.0001. Ultimately, 39 local attributes were included in the local model. In the network feature set, the out-of-network neighbor binary was not significant, so the remaining five network attributes were included. In the combined model, 41 features were found to be significant. The time interval for predictions was set to one month, since logistic regression requires a different model for each time interval.

4   Findings

As a first visual evaluation, ROC curves have been plotted for three months of predictions in Figure 3. ROC curves are graphical representations of the true positive rate versus the false positive rate. A perfect classification is the point (0,1)—0% false positives and 100% true positives—on the graph, so the closer an ROC curve is to that point, the better the model is [26]. The value of interest in regression models is a probability. In order to label a customer as a predicted churner or non-churner, a cut-off point is used to separate the classes. Probabilities above this threshold will be assigned as churners and those below it will be assigned as non-churners. Each point on the ROC curve corresponds to one such cut-off score in the full range between 0.0 and 1.0.

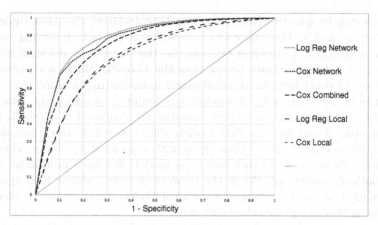

(a) Month 1 ROC Curves

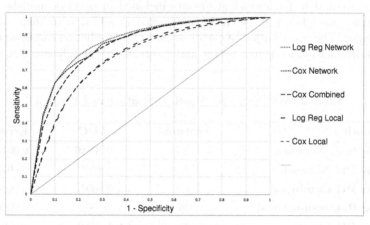

(b) Month 2 ROC Curves

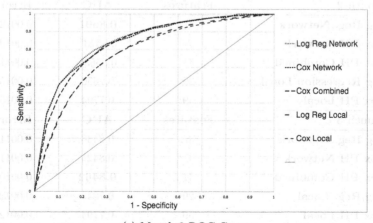

(c) Month 3 ROC Curves

Fig. 3. Comparison of Prediction Models

Models can be quantitatively compared by calculating the Area Under the ROC Curves (AUC). The differences between models was tested using the test of DeLong et al.[26]. In the first two months, the Cox PH Model with network attributes is not significantly better than the Cox PH Model with combined attributes. All other models are significantly different. In the third month, the differences in AUC values for all models were found to be significant. The AUC values for the five models over three months are displayed in Table 2. In all three months, it can be seen that models with network features included do result in greater AUC values than those with only local attributes. However, the differences between network and local models are most prominent in the first month of predictions. While the network models continue to outperform the local models, the AUC values for the local models remain relatively constant while the network models decline over time.

When comparing the models using only network features to those including customer attributes, far fewer features are included in network models. These less complex models are more easily interpreted in addition to their superior performance. The contribution of each feature to the prediction can be analyzed and this information leads to a better understanding of the influences on churn.

Table 2. AUC Values for Month 1, Month 2, and Month 3

Month 1	Features	AUC	Error
Log Reg. Network	6	**0.8836**	0.0014
Cox PH Network	5	0.8735^1	0.0015
Cox PH Combined	41	0.8691^1	0.0014
Log Regression Local	29	0.7872	0.0020
Cox PH Local	39	0.7792	0.0020
Month 2	Features	AUC	Error
Log Reg. Network	6	**0.8601**	0.0012
Cox PH Network	5	0.8543^2	0.0012
Cox PH Combined	41	0.8553^2	0.0011
Log Regression Local	29	0.7850	0.0015
Cox PH Local	39	0.7794	0.0015
Month 3	Features	AUC	Error
Log Reg. Network	6	0.8436	0.0011
Cox PH Network	5	0.8425	0.0011
Cox PH Combined	41	**0.8462**	0.0010
Log Reg. Local	29	0.7843	0.0012
Cox PH Local	39	0.7794	0.0012

Comparison of churn prediction models based on different feature sets. For each month, the greatest AUC is highlighted. [1] [2] No significant difference.

5 Summary

This study was designed to investigate the differences in predicting customer churn by using features based on customers individually or based on the network formed by calls among customers. When evaluating the models using AUC values, it has been shown that network features do offer improved predictions when compared to local features, though the differences are more pronounced on sooner predictions than later. This suggests that network information may be more dynamic, reflecting more current changes in customer behavior. According to these findings, valuable information is present in the social networks of customers. Taking advantage of this information can improve churn prediction models and the retention campaigns designed to reduce churn.

A more practical contribution of this work is a business-oriented approach, implemented in Java, to process one month of company data and make predictions for the next few weeks or months. Using this approach, companies can employ an ongoing monthly targeted retention campaign which identifies customers at risk for churn dynamically.

Acknowledgements. —This research was made possible with support of the Odysseus program (Grant B.0915.09) of the Fund for Scientific Research–Flanders (FWO).

References

1. Bersen, A., Smith, S., Thearling, K.: Building Data Mining Applications for CRM. McGraw-Hill, New York (2000)
2. Verbeke, W., Martens, D., Mues, C., Baesens, B.: Building comprehensible customer churn prediction models with advanced rule induction techniques. Expert Systems with Applications 38, 2354–2364 (2011)
3. Owczarczuk, M.: Churn models for prepaid customers in the cellular telecommunication industry using large data marts. Expert Systems with Applications 37, 4710–4712 (2010)
4. Huang, B., Kechadi, M.T., Buckley, B.: Customer churn prediction in telecommunications. Expert Systems with Applications 39, 1414–1425 (2012)
5. Lima, E., Mues, C., Baesens, B.: Domain knowledge integration in data mining using decision tables: Case studies in churn prediction. Journal of Operational Research Society 60(8), 1096–1106 (2009)
6. Risselada, H., Verhoef, P., Bijmolt, T.: Staying power of churn prediction models. Journal of Interactive Marketing 24, 198–208 (2010)
7. Verbeke, W., Dejaeger, K., Martens, D., Hur, J., Baesens, B.: New insights into churn prediction in the telecommunication sector: A profit driven data mining approach. European Journal of Operational Research 218, 211–229 (2012)
8. Zhang, X., Zhu, J., Xu, S., Wan, Y.: Predicting customer churn through interpersonal influence. Knowledge-Based Systems 28, 97–104 (2012)
9. Verbraken, T., Verbeke, W., Baesens, B.: A novel profit maximizing metric for measuring classification performance of customer churn prediction models. IEEE Transactions on Knowledge and Data Engineering 25(5), 961–973 (2013)

10. Wong, K.K.K.: Using cox regression to model customer time to churn in the wireless telecommunications industry. Journal of Targeting, Measurement, and Analysis for Marketing 19(1), 37–43 (2011)
11. Dasgupta, K., Singh, R., Viswanathan, B., Chakraborty, D., Mukherjea, S., Nanavati, A., Joshi, A.: Social ties and their relevance to churn in mobile telecom networks. In: EDBT 2008 Proceedings of the 11th International Conference on Extending Database Technology: Advances in Database Technology, Nantes, France, pp. 668–677. ACM (March 2008)
12. McPherson, M., Smith-Lovin, L., Cook, J.M.: Birds of a feather: Homophily in social networks. Annual Review of Sociology 27, 415–444 (2001)
13. Rhodes, C.J., Jones, P.: Inferring missing links in partially observed social networks. Journal of Operational Research Society 60(10), 1373–1383 (2009)
14. Shalizi, C.R., Thomas, A.C.: Homophily and contagion are generically confounded in observational social network studies. Sociological Methods and Research 40(2), 211–239 (2011)
15. Pow, J., Gayen, K., Elliott, L., Raeside, R.: Understanding complex interactions using social network analysis. Journal of Clinical Nursing 21, 2772–2779 (2012)
16. Mertens, F., Saint-Charles, J., Mergler, D.: Social communication network analysis of the role of participatory research in the adoption of new fish consumption behaviors. Social Science and Medicine 75(4), 643–650 (2012)
17. Liu, D.-R., Shih, M.-J.: Hybrid-patent classification based on patent-network analysis. Journal of the American Society for Information Science and Technology 62(2), 246–256 (2010)
18. Chiu, C., Ku, Y., Lie, T., Chen, Y.: Internet auction fraud detection using social network analysis and classification tree approaches. International Journal of Electronic Commerce 15(3), 123–147 (2011)
19. Hancock, P.G., Raeside, R.: Analysing communication in a complex service process: an application of social network analysis in the scottish prison service. Journal of Operational Research Society 61, 265–274 (2009)
20. Pushpa, Shobha, G.: An efficient method of building the telecom social network for churn prediction. International Journal of Data Mining and Knowledge Management Proces 2(3), 31–39 (2012)
21. Macskassy, S.A., Provost, F.: A simple relational classifier. In: Proceedings of the Second Workshop on Multi-Relational Data Mining (MRDM-2003) at KDD-2003, pp. 64–76 (2003)
22. Macskassy, S.A., Provost, F.: Classification in networked data: A toolkit and a univariate case study. Journal of Machine Learning Research 8(2), 935–983 (2007)
23. Lu, Q., Getoor, L.: Link-based classification using labeled and unlabeled data. In: Proceedings of the ICML Workshop on The Continuum from Labeled to Unlabeled Data, Washington, DC, USA, ICML (2003)
24. Easley, D., Kleinberg, J.: Networks, Crowds, and Markets. Cambridge University Press, Cambridge (2010)
25. Allison, P.D.: Survival Analysis Using SAS: A Practical Guide, 2nd edn. SAS Institute Inc., Cary (2010)
26. DeLong, E., DeLong, D., Clarke-Pearson, D.: Comparing the areas under two or more correlated receiver operating characteristic curves: A nonparametric approach. International Biometric Society 44(3), 837–845 (1988)

A Note on Machine Learning Approach to Analyze the Results of Pairwise Comparison Based Parametric Evaluation of Research Units

Mateusz Baran[1,2], Konrad Kułakowski[1], and Antoni Ligęza[1]

[1] AGH University of Science and Technology,
al. Mickiewicza 30, 30-059 Kraków, Poland
{mateusz.baran,konrad.kulakowski,antoni.ligeza}@agh.edu.pl
http://www.agh.edu.pl
[2] Cracow University of Technology,
ul. Warszawska 24, 31-155 Cracow, Poland
http://www.pk.edu.pl

Abstract. This paper presents an attempt at an analysis of parametric evaluation of research units with machine learning toolkit. The main goal was to investigate if the rules of evaluation can be expressed in a readable, transparent, and easy to interpret way. A further attempt was made at investigating consistency of the applied procedure and presentation of some observed anomalies.

1 Introduction

Ranking problems are omnipresent in everyday life and professional activities. Unfortunately, well-justified linear ordering of a given set of alternative solutions is rarely possible. This is an intrinsic, born-in feature of problems where the possible solutions are described with several incomparable criteria.

Recently performed parametric evaluation of research units in Poland, its numeric results, and the resulting assignment of categories give rise to a deeper theoretical investigation of the procedure proposed in [1].

The main questions addressed in this paper can be defined as follows:
- can Machine Learning methods provide us with simple to understand, intuitive rules defining the classification?
- can such rules replace the somewhat complex classification procedure? If so, with what accuracy?
- is the final classification rational — mainly in the sense that it should be *consistent*?
- what is the role (or importance) of particular criteria?
- are there any anomalies observed? Can they be eliminated?
- can the process be still improved? Simplified?

In order to answer these questions, a deeper theoretical investigation of the whole procedure and its results has been performed. Moreover, a number of computer experiments have been carried out. The results are reported and discussed throughout the paper.

L. Rutkowski et al. (Eds.): ICAISC 2014, Part II, LNAI 8468, pp. 27–39, 2014.

2   Problem Statement

Let us introduce a brief formal representation of the ranking or sorting problem. We consider a set of m objects (decision alternatives; in our case these are in fact research units) denoted by $\mathbf{X} = \{X_1, X_2, \ldots, X_m\}$. Each object X_i, $i \in \{1, 2, \ldots, m\}$ is described with a feature vector $\mathbf{q}_i$ of length n, where n is the number of predefined *quality evaluation criteria*. Hence, $\mathbf{q}_i = [q_{i,1}, q_{i,2}, \ldots q_{i,n}]$, where $q_{i,j}$ is the numeric value of the $j - th$ criterion for object i.

From mathematical point of view one can consider the set $\mathbf{X}$ as a collection of points in $\mathbb{R}^n$ ($\mathbb{R}$ denotes the set of real numbers). For intuition, each of the criterial values $q_{i,j}$ contributes to the *overall quality* of object i. Selection of some *best*[1] point (or points) is known as the Multiple Criteria Decision Making (MCDM), Multicriteria Optimization Problem (MOP), or Multicriteria Decision Making (MDM) [8,6]. Unfortunately, although such problems are often to be considered, there is no way to define a unique, *best* solution; what can be done is the definition of the non-dominated solutions (the so-called Pareto-optimal set) and some more or less subjective way of forming the final solution. Typically, a weighted sum of values of the defined criteria is a method of choice.

Note that, in such problem statement the simple (Pareto) dominance relation is defined in a straightforward way. We have $X_i \prec X_j$ iff (if and only if) $q_{i,k} > q_{j,k}$ for some k, while it is enough that $q_{i,l} \geq q_{j,l}$ for all other $l \in \{1, 2, \ldots n\}$ ($l \neq k$). Such a relation is transitive and induces partial order over $\mathbf{X}$. Unfortunately, in practice this partial order is most often unsatisfactory.

In practice, one can consider a variety of detailed formulations, e.g.:

- determining only the best solution (a single point or a set of such indistinguishable points),
- defining a linear order in $\mathbf{X}$ with respect to quality,
- classification of the elements of $\mathbf{X}$ into several predefined categories $\mathbf{C} = \{C_1, C_2, \ldots C_k\}$.

Below, we continue to consider a detailed statement of the last problem.

2.1   Multicriteria Classification Problem

Let us consider a generic formulation of the Multicriteria Classification Problem (MCP). Let $\mathbf{X} = \{X_1, X_2, \ldots, X_m\}$ denote the set of objects. Assume a *valuation function* v is defined, so that

$$v(X_i) = [q_{i,1}, q_{i,2}, \ldots q_{i,n}] \tag{1}$$

for each $X_i \in \mathbf{X}$. Each $q_{i,j} \in \mathbb{R}$, i.e. it is a real number.

For convenience, the valuation function can be extended over $\mathbf{X}$, so that $v(\mathbf{X}) = \mathbf{Q}$, where $\mathbf{Q}$ is the rectangular matrix $[q_{i,j}]$, $i = 1, 2, \ldots m$, $j = 1, 2, \ldots m$.

Typically in MCP, the categories of $\mathbf{C}$ are assumed to be linearly ordered, e.g. from the best one to the worst one. Moreover, there is a monotonic relationship

---

[1] Well, whatever it means.

between the values of particular criteria $q_{i,j}$ and the overall quality of the entity X_i, and hence its assignment to a specific class.

The solution of the MCP consists in finding a *rational* assignment of objects of $\mathbf{X}$ into the categories of $\mathbf{C}$ in the form of a function λ, such that

$$\lambda\colon \mathbf{X} \to \mathbf{C}. \tag{2}$$

In practice, λ may not defined in an analytical way; it can be implemented as a complex decision procedure. Unfortunately, again, there is no unique, commonly accepted solution for λ.

A particular formulation of the MCP can be presented as Multicriteria Sorting Problem (MSP) with class assignment (in fact partition into linearly ordered classes). In MSP one looks for a *scalarization function* σ, such that:

$$\sigma\colon \mathbf{X} \to \mathbb{R}. \tag{3}$$

The value $\sigma(X_i)$ is a scalar value determining the overall quality of object X_i. Defining σ induces a linear order over $\mathbf{X}$. Now, to obtain a classification it is enough to defines a set of $k+1$ linearly ordered threshold values $\sigma_1, \sigma_2, \ldots, \sigma_{k+1}$. The function λ can assign class C_j to X_i if and only iff $\sigma_j \leq \sigma(X_i) < \sigma_{j+1}$, $j = 1, 2, \ldots, k$.

Below we try to put forward some most obvious requirements which contribute to rationality of the assignment.

2.2   MCP: Requests for Rationality

Consider the simple precedence relation of the elements of $\mathbf{X}$. The following requirement defines the *monotonicity preservation*:

$$\text{IF } X_i \prec X_j \text{ THEN } c_i \geq c_j, \tag{4}$$

where c_i is the index of a category such that $\lambda(X_i) = C_{c_i}$ and c_j is the index of a category such that $\lambda(X_j) = C_{c_j}$. The understanding of the requirement is straightforward: a better object cannot be assigned to a worse category.

As a straightforward consequence we have the following property: if $X_i \prec X_j$ and $X_j \prec X_k$, and $\lambda(X_i) = \lambda(X_k)$, then $\lambda(X_i) = \lambda(X_j) = \lambda(X_k)$; any object located between two objects assigned to the same category must be assigned to this category, as well.

2.3   Pairwise Comparison: State-of-the-Art

Generally pairwise comparisons (also called paired comparisons) refers to any process of comparing entities that leads to decide which entity is more preferred. The first traces of the use of this approach leads to *Ramon Llull* (the XIII century) - father of voting theory, who use pairwise comparisons to support elections process in the medieval Church [15]. Pairwise comparisons gained real popularity in *XX* century. First, *Thurstone* [25] extended the method from binary to the general choice, then *Saaty* [24] introduced hierarchy, which allows to handle a large number of entities. In the classical pairwise comparisons method (PC method) each entity is compared with the other. The result of comparison is a subjective judgment in form of a ratio reflecting a relative importance of one entity with respect to the other. Research on the method evolved resulting in many interesting works including proposal of a new local inconsistency definition [20], the rank reversal problem discovering [17], incomplete data handling [18], preference order preservation proposal [16], dominance-based rough set approach [19], the PC method with the reference set handling [22] and other.

The classical approach as proposed in [24] assumes that the input data to the pairwise comparisons method is a *(PC)* matrix $M = (m_{i,j})$ and $m_{i,j} \in \mathbb{R}_+$ where $i, j \in \{1, \ldots, n\}$ represents partial assessments over the finite set of concepts $C \overset{df}{=} \{c_i \in \mathscr{C}, i \in \{1, \ldots, n\}\}$ where $\mathscr{C} \neq \emptyset$ is a universe of concepts. For instance $m_{i,j} = 2$ means that the subjective judgment of the experts indicates that c_i is two times more important than c_j. Let $\mu : C \to \mathbb{R}_+$ be a function that assigns to some concepts from $C \subset \mathscr{C}$ positive values from $\mathbb{R}_+$. Thus, the value $\mu(c)$ represents the importance of c. Initially only the matrix M is known, whilst μ need to be determined. Assuming that M is reciprocal i.e. for every $m_{i,j}$ holds that $m_{i,j} = m_{j,i}^{-1}$ and positive, then according to the *Frobenus-Perron* theorem [23] the largest eigenvalue of M is positive and real, and its eigenvector is strictly positive. *Saaty* proposed to adopt this vector (referred in the literature as a principal eigenvector) as the final result of the comparisons. For practical reasons, the result is normalized so that the sum of all the final assessments is 1. I.e.:

$$\mu = \left[\frac{v_1}{s}, \ldots, \frac{v_n}{s}\right]^T \quad \text{where} \quad s = \sum_{i=1}^{n} v_i \tag{5}$$

and $v = [v_1, \ldots, v_n]^T$ is the principal eigenvector of M.

Of course, the pairwise comparison algorithm as used for parametric evaluation of research units in Poland differs from the typical formula. In particular the matrix M composed of $m_{i,j}$ values in form of $V(X_i, X_j)$, where $c_i = X_i$ and $c_j = X_j$ are neither reciprocal nor positive. Hence, it is not surprising that the evaluation algorithm proposes different way of drawing the final assessment (see Sec. 3).

2.4   Consistency and Quality Criteria

Let $V(X_i, X_j)$ denote the result of direct comparison (a kind of a *duel*) between X_i and X_j. There can be three possible results:

- $V(X_i, X_j) > 0$ — X_i wins with X_j,
- $V(X_i, X_j) = 0$ — the comparison results in a draw of X_i and X_j,
- $V(X_i, X_j) < 0$ — X_j wins with X_i.

A first tempting requirement might consist in demand for preserving transitivity of the pairwise comparison. One may put forward the following request: if $V(X_i, X_j) \geq 0$ and $V(X_j, X_k) \geq 0$ then there should be also $V(X_i, X_k) \geq 0$. Unfortunately, this property does not hold. The reason for that is a bit complex: it follows from the nature of multicriteria comparison and nonlinearity of function $V(X,Y)$ — in different comparison different criteria may play important role.

Common sense demands for the values $V(X_i, X_j)$ can be expressed in the form of two following conditions, that should holds for every X_i, X_j and X_k.

1. Consistency of preference order (CPO)
   - $V(X_i, X_j) \geq 0 \wedge V(X_j, X_k) \geq 0$ should imply $V(X_i, X_k) \geq 0$
   and similarly,
   - $V(X_i, X_j) \leq 0 \wedge V(X_j, X_k) \leq 0$ should imply $V(X_i, X_k) \leq 0$
2. Consistency of preference intensity (CPI)
   - if $V(X_i, X_j) > 0$ and $V(X_k, X_j) > 0$ then $\frac{V(X_i,X_j)}{V(X_k,X_j)} > 1$ should imply $V(X_i, X_k) > 0$,
   and similarly
   - if $V(X_i, X_j) < 0$ and $V(X_k, X_j) < 0$ then $\frac{V(X_i,X_j)}{V(X_k,X_j)} > 1$ should imply $V(X_i, X_k) < 0$

The first one, *the consistency of preference order* condition reflects the common-sense belief that the relation of 'being better' unit is transitive, whilst the second one corresponds to the expectation that the values $V(X_i, X_j)$ have also some quantitative meaning. In other words *the consistency of preference intensity* reflects an intuition according to which if X_i won X_j more considerably than X_k won X_j then X_i is probably better than X_k. Table 1 shows how many times the two aforementioned are not fulfilled in ten GWOs with the most entities. The following columns are: name of the GWO, the number of entities in the GWO, CPOV: the number of triples that violate the CPO, the fraction of triples that violate the CPO, the CPO harm index, CPIV: the number of triples that violate the CPI, the fraction of triples that violate the CPI and CPI harm index.

The columns CPOH (CPO harm index) and CPIH (CPI harm index) denote the fraction of entities that are harmed by intransitivity of, respectively, CPO and CPI. Entity X is called CPO-harmed if there exist two entities Y, Z such that $V(X,Y) \geq 0 \wedge V(Y,Z) \geq 0$ but not $V(X,Z) \geq 0$ or $V(Y,Z) \leq 0 \wedge V(Z,X) \leq 0$ but not $V(Y,X) \leq 0$. CPI-harmed entity can be defined by analogy.

Table 1. Consistency measures for ten GWOs with the most entities

Name	#Entities	CPOV	$\frac{CPOV}{(\#Entities)^3}$	CPOH	CPIV	$\frac{CPIV}{(\#Entities)^3}$	CPIH
hslek	93	5814	0.0072	0.9355	124454	0.1547	0.9892
hslsp	93	4444	0.0055	0.8280	123273	0.1533	0.9892
nzlm	78	1754	0.0037	0.8974	74234	0.1564	0.9872
nzlr	50	704	0.0056	0.7800	18238	0.1459	0.9600
hslfb	29	188	0.0077	0.7931	3438	0.1410	0.9655
silea	44	250	0.0029	0.6591	12594	0.1478	0.9545
talpk	39	584	0.0098	0.7949	8145	0.1373	0.9744
silmh	36	330	0.0071	0.7222	6870	0.1472	0.9722
talmz	35	158	0.0037	0.8000	5999	0.1399	0.9714
silba	32	174	0.0053	0.5000	4734	0.1445	0.9688

3 Parametric Evaluation of Research Units: Methodology and Results

The method applied for the parametric evaluation of research units was defined in some detail in the Appendix 8 of [1]. Its basic ideas are as follows:

- all the units are assigned to groups of similar entities (GWO[2]); further categorization is performed only within predefined groups,
- each of the units is compared with all the other units; the results are defined by the $V(X_i, X_j)$ function,
- a decisive factor is the sum of points gathered over all the pairwise comparisons.

In fact, a linear order relation is induced.

Categorization inside GWO is performed as follows:

1. Values of four basic criteria are computed for each entity $X \in \mathbf{X}$ ($O_i(X), i \in \{1, 2, 3, 4\}$); these criteria represent scientific and creative achievements, scientific potential, material effects of scientific activity and other effects of scientific activity,
2. All the entities are compared in a pairwise mode with respect to each of these criterion:

$$P_i(X, Y) = sgn(O_i(X) - O_i(Y)) \begin{cases} 0 & \text{if } \Delta O < D \\ \frac{\Delta O - D}{G - D} & \text{if } D \leq \Delta O < G \\ 1 & \text{if } G \leq \Delta O \end{cases} \quad (6)$$

where $\Delta O = |O_i(X) - O_i(Y)|$, $D = max(0.1 \times min(O_i(X), O_i(Y))$, $0.1 \frac{\sum_{Z \in \mathbf{X}} O_i(Z)}{\#\mathbf{X}})$, $G = max(0.3 \times min(O_i(X), O_i(Y)), 3D)$,

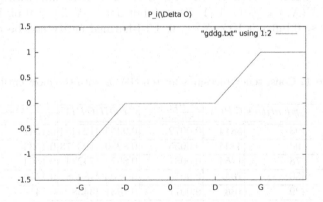

Fig. 1. Illustration to equation 6

---

[2] Grupy Wspólnej Oceny (in Polish)

3. The per-criterion comparisons are combined to form entity comparisons: $V(X,Y) = \sum_{i=1}^{4} W_i P_i(X,Y)$ where W_i are weights dependent on the particular GWO. For all GWO $\sum_{i=1}^{4} W_i = 1$ holds, therefore $V(X,Y)$ can be viewed as weighted average of $P_i(X,Y)$.
4. Two arbitrarily defined reference entities (A, B) are added to each GWO (in fact, they are assigned the threshold values for the overall quality function),
5. The final score for each entity is calculated as the arithmetic mean of comparison scores with each other entity (including reference entities):

$$OJN(X) = \frac{\sum_{Y \in \mathbf{X} \cup \{A,B\} - \{X\}} V(X,Y)}{\#(\mathbf{X} \cup \{A, B\} - \{X\})} \tag{7}$$

6. Finally, the category of an entity is determined as follows:

$$\lambda(X) = \begin{cases} A & \text{if } OJN(X) > OJN(A) \\ B & \text{if } OJN(A) > OJN(X) > OJN(B) \\ C & \text{if } OJN(B) > OJN(X) \end{cases} \tag{8}$$

7. Additionally, a few of the entities categorized as A may be recategorized as A+ (an even better category), but this step is not well-formalized.

Table 2. Entities in GWO SI1EA

ID	O_1	O_2	O_3	O_4	Pts.	Cat.
271	3.64	0.00	0.71	0.00	-93.10	C
404	6.26	41.00	0.00	10.50	-91.36	C
468	20.99	1.00	0.00	0.00	-76.31	C
829	24.25	16.00	0.00	17.00	-69.41	C
740	21.74	121.00	1.23	22.00	-65.57	C
68	18.35	11.00	5.49	31.50	-59.28	C
649	26.49	54.00	3.79	20.00	-54.95	C
811	21.60	2.00	9.92	22.00	-52.01	C
298	25.76	18.00	7.62	13.00	-51.53	C
Jedn. ref. dla kategorii B	18.99	221.37	5.89	29.05	-50.21	
779	29.90	174.00	1.43	4.50	-49.43	B
350	23.22	42.00	7.45	35.00	-48.86	B
576	32.55	63.00	0.51	26.00	-41.39	B
654	25.34	226.00	8.98	66.50	-28.68	B
888	33.47	78.00	4.48	45.00	-22.76	B
674	38.31	188.00	0.74	43.50	-14.95	B
651	35.22	214.00	4.15	38.00	-14.62	B
612	35.94	437.00	2.07	56.00	-6.58	B
197	33.79	246.00	7.21	60.00	-5.35	B
421	42.88	159.00	3.07	7.50	-4.83	B
191	38.58	272.00	3.61	46.00	-3.10	B
643	37.84	368.00	5.13	37.50	0.05	B

358	46.69	132.00	0.56	39.50	10.11	B
904	39.00	365.00	5.41	72.00	11.27	B
604	48.28	95.00	2.80	10.00	11.29	B
813	39.31	350.00	14.54	25.50	11.79	B
966	37.29	337.00	13.40	50.00	12.41	B
588	46.39	259.00	2.91	22.50	15.39	B
768	44.97	339.00	3.21	40.00	19.59	B
764	41.11	583.00	4.22	88.00	19.87	B
Jedn. ref. dla kategorii A	39.07	455.40	12.12	59.76	20.85	
834	43.26	634.00	6.20	65.00	29.79	A
680	44.98	767.00	6.23	52.50	34.74	A
913	46.85	345.00	4.37	68.00	34.89	A
48	54.11	244.00	4.74	27.50	35.83	A
63	48.12	253.00	17.65	25.50	40.18	A
489	84.07	127.00	1.02	20.00	42.89	A
759	46.72	274.00	14.63	77.50	46.73	A
721	52.60	202.00	9.98	60.00	49.25	A
97	53.68	248.00	10.20	81.50	56.13	A
253	56.11	114.00	22.35	51.00	56.70	A
901	51.97	525.00	12.64	84.50	63.58	A
120	52.27	856.00	18.97	64.00	67.15	A
953	54.43	631.00	14.27	70.00	67.20	A
735	53.89	495.00	13.78	92.50	67.35	A
145	80.24	287.00	16.04	45.00	79.28	A+

4   Machine Learning Applied to Rule Learning

We have analyzed the categorization of entities using different machine learning methods. The conjecture is that a well-behaving categorization procedure should be well-reproducible using typical classifier construction algorithms.

The ordered nature of classes is discarded by all common classification algorithms. As a result all misclassifications are treated as equally undesirable which is not true. More appropriate algorithms would take the ordering into account.

We have selected GWO SI1EA as input data (ID and four basic criteria). During learning we use 4-fold cross-validation due to small size of the sample.

Feature Selection. The first question is if all of the features are important for the classification. The results are gathered in the Table 3. Plus sign means that the method selects given attribute. In other cases attributes are ordered from the most important one (1) to the least important one (5) The data was calculated using Weka Explorer [13].

Trees. The Tree-based classifiers construct a tree with tests at nodes and classes in leaves. Two such algorithms are tested:

Table 3. Results of feature selection algorithms

Name of the method	ID	O_1	O_2	O_3	O_4
GreedyStepwise + CfsSubsetEval	-	+	-	+	+
Ranker + CorrelationAttribureEval	5	1	3	2	4
Ranker + GainRatioAttributeEval	5	2	1	4	3
Ranker + InfoGainAttributeEval	5	1	2	4	3
Ranker + OneRAttributeEval	5	1	3	4	2
Ranker + ReliefFAttributeEval	5	1	3	4	2
Ranker + SymmetricalUncertAttributeEval	5	1	2	4	3

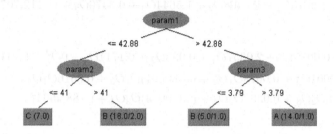

Fig. 2. The C4.5 tree achieving 77% accuracy

- J48 (a variant of C4.5 [9]) achieves the accuracy of 77% with tree of size 7 using parameters 1, 2 and 3 (see Figure 2). Due to overfitting the accuracy does not rise with the size of the tree.
- LMT [10,11] (builds logistic model trees) achieves accuracy of 80% with tree of size 7 but the leaves are more complicated than J48 leaves. It uses all parameters.

Rules. The rule-based classifiers construct an (ordered or unordered) list of rules assigning class to instances matching conditional part of the rule. The following algorithms were used:

- Ridor [7] (RIpple-DOwn Rule learner) achieves 86% accuracy with 6 rules using only parameters 1 and 4.
- PART [4] gives 75% accuracy with 5 rules and uses all parameters.
- FURIA [5], a fuzzy rule-based classifier, achieves 77% accuracy with 4 fuzzy rules employing parameters 1, 2 and 4.

SVM. The SVM [12] (Support Vector Machine) classifier constructs a hyperplane from a given class that separates points in different classes as well as it is possible. SVM gives the best accuracy (77%) for linear kernel function. Other kernel functions available in Weka (polynomial, radial, sigmoid) give even worse accuracy.

Regression. Regression is a method of fitting a curve from a given class to match given (usually real-valued) data as well as possible. In our case the data was the number of points achieved by the entities together with the values of the criteria. Two classes of functions were considered: linear $(f(\mathbf{x}) = a + \sum_{i=1}^{4} a_i \mathbf{x}_i)$ and quadratic $(f(\mathbf{x}) = a + a_{id} id \sum_{i=1}^{4} a_i \mathbf{x}_i + \sum_{i=1}^{4} \sum_{j=i}^{4} a_{i,j} \mathbf{x}_i \mathbf{x}_j)$. The coefficients a, a_{id}, a_i, $a_{i,j}$ are chosen to minimize the sum of squares of errors.

The relative absolute error was 19.2% in the case of linear regression and 11.8% in the case of quadratic regression. Figure 4 visualizes the errors. The optimal coefficients for WHO SI1EA are given in Equations 9 and 10. The second equation shows a significant dependence on the ID of entity (id).

$$points = 1.9675 O_1 + 0.0408 O_2 + 1.5644 O_3 + 0.3476 O_4 + (-112.7077) \quad (9)$$

$$points = (-0.0975)id + 2.0357 O_1 + 0.095 O_2 + 0.1711 O_4 + 0 O_1^2 + (-0.014)O_2^2 +$$
$$- 0.0001 O_3^2 + 0.0018 O_1 O_2 + (-0.0001)O_1 O_3 + 0.0016 O_1 O_4 +$$
$$0.0016 O_2 O_3 + 0.0367 O_2 O_4 + (-0.0043)O_3 O_4 + (-88.4564)$$
$$\quad (10)$$

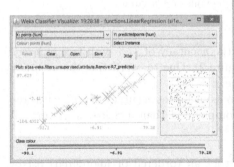 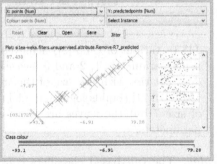

(a) Errors in linear regression   (b) Errors in quadratic regression

Fig. 4. Visualization of errors in regression

K-means. The K-means algorithm divides the data set (points in feature space) into N distinct sets characterized by their centroids. Each point is assigned to the nearest cluster, where the distance is calculated as the distance to the centroid of the cluster. The clustering algorithm tries to place the centroids to match given clustering (or, in our case, categorization).

We used the K-means algorithm to check if the three or four (including A+ category) clusters it produces match the division to categories given by the original data. It resulted in, respectively, 39% and 43% of incorrectly clustered instances.

5 Critical Evaluation and Concluding Remarks

Categorization algorithm as such is unique and it tries to avoid existing solutions. Therefore, its critical assessment is difficult. The lack of direct references to the other rankings makes the evaluation highly subjective. It is hard to judge whether e.g. CPI violation level at 14.5% is a lot or a little. Is this a bug in the algorithm or its inherent feature?

What is certain is that there will be a group of entities (units) which correctly (according to common sense) would argue that 'something is wrong' with the algorithm. They would argue that the results of the comparisons in pairs adopted for the purpose of the algorithm are inconsistent, thus, they are counterintuitive.

The first obvious observation is that the direct comparison based on the $V(X, Y)$ function is not transitive. Moreover, the number of cases violating transitivity can be quite significant.

Second, the results are strongly dependent on the environment. If one considers two units, say X and Y, and we have $V(X, Y) > 0$ (X wins with Y) within certain environment, then after changing the environment (but leaving criteria values for X and Y unchanged) it may happen that $V(X, Y) < 0$ (i.e. this time Y wins with X). This can be claimed to be a syndrome of irregularity — lack of absolute criteria is obvious. In other words the results for a particular pair of units are relative to environment. For example, unit No. 3 wins with the JR-AB, but even so, it is assigned category B.

Additionally, the variation of CPO harm index is surprising. Low harm index indicates that relatively few entities suffer from intransitivity of winning relation, while high harm index means that almost all of them are harmed. Both extremes can be judges as just but intermediate result may suggest that only a select group of units may feel aggrieved/treated fair. Again comes the question — is this a bug or a feature of the algorithm?

The selection of evaluated features seems also to be subject to critics. The criterion O_1 is very important (maybe too important) while the criterion O_3 (assigned the weight 0.15) turns out to be practically unimportant (see Table 3).

It seems symptomatic, that none of the applied tools was able to achieve a satisfactory results. The average correct classification rate was around 80%. An open questions is why? Perhaps this follows from complexity of the proposed approach, but perhaps the criteria are too vague, unstable, or even *locally inconsistent*?

A surprising observation are the very bad results of the commonly accepted K-means approach. The error ratio seems to indicate that the obtained classification is far from rational one, based on similarity. In fact the differences of final score within categories A, B and C are overwhelming.

Finally, the weights O_1–O_4 were established in an arbitrary way; in recent paper [21] some attempt at discussion of this and some further issues is presented.

As it might have been expected, it turned out that the MCP — and especially the produced results — constitute a hard task for known ML classification tools. No simple rules of high classification accuracy have been found. Moreover, correct classification ratio seems to rest on unacceptable level.

It seems not necessary to insist on generating linear order; perhaps a solution can consist in rational grouping of similar units into clusters and assigning them a common category? The differentiation (spread of the parameters) within categories seems substantial, perhaps unacceptable.

Finally, in order to allow the unit leaders create o policy for development, the criteria should be transparent, stable, and known in advance.

References

1. Rozporządzenie Ministra Nauki i Szkolnictwa Wyższego z dn. 13 lipca 2012 w sprawie kryteriów i trybu przyznawania kategorii naukowej jednostkom naukowym. Dziennik Ustaw Rzeczypospolitej Polskiej, Warszawa, 1 sierpnia (2012)
2. Cios, K.J., Pedrycz, W., Swiniarski, R.W., Kurgan, L.A.: Data Mining. A Knowledge Discovery Approach. Springer Science+Business Media, LLC, New York (2007)
3. Flach, P.: Machine Learning. The Art and Science of Algorithms that Make the Sense of Data. Cambridge University Press, Cambridge (2012)
4. Frank, E., Witten, I.H.: Generating Accurate Rule Sets Without Global Optimization. In: Fifteenth International Conference on Machine Learning, pp. 144–151 (1998)
5. Huehn, J.C., Huellermeier, E.: FURIA: An Algorithm for Unordered Fuzzy Rule Induction. Data Mining and Knowledge Discovery (2009)
6. Hwang, C.-L., Masud, A.S.M.: Multiple objective decision making, methods and applications: a state-of-the-art survey. Springer (1979)
7. Gaines, B.R., Compton, P.: Induction of ripple-down rules applied to modeling large databases. Journal of Intelligent Information Systems 5(3), 211–228 (1995)
8. Miettinen, K.: Nonlinear Multiobjective Optimization. Springer (1999)
9. Quinlan, R.: C4.5: Programs for Machine Learning. Morgan Kaufmann Publishers, San Mateo (1993)
10. Landwehr, N., Hall, M., Frank, E.: Logistic Model Trees. Machine Learning 95(1-2), 161–205 (2005)
11. Sumner, M., Frank, E., Hall, M.: Speeding Up Logistic Model Tree Induction. In: Jorge, A.M., Torgo, L., Brazdil, P.B., Camacho, R., Gama, J. (eds.) PKDD 2005. LNCS (LNAI), vol. 3721, pp. 675–683. Springer, Heidelberg (2005)
12. Chang, C.-C., Lin, C.-J.: LIBSVM — A Library for Support Vector Machines (2001), http://www.csie.ntu.edu.tw/~cjlin/libsvm/
13. Hall, M., Frank, E., Holmes, G., Pfahringer, B., Reutemann, P., Witten, I.H.: The WEKA Data Mining Software: An Update. SIGKDD Explorations 11(1) (2009)
14. The Results of Parametric Evaluation of Polish Research Units, http://www.nauka.gov.pl/komunikaty/komunikat-o-wynikach-kompleksowej-oceny-dzialalnosci-naukowej-lub-badawczo-rozwojowej-jednostek-naukowych.html
15. Colomer, J.M.: Ramon Llull: from 'Ars electionis' to social choice theory. Social Choice and Welfare 40(2), 317–328 (2011)
16. Bana e Costa, C.A., Vansnick, J.: A critical analysis of the eigenvalue method used to derive priorities in AHP. European Journal of Operational Research 187(3), 1422–1428 (2008)
17. Dyer, J.S.: Remarks on the analytic hierarchy process. Management Science 36(3), 249–258 (1990)

18. Fedrizzi, M., Giove, S.: Incomplete pairwise comparison and consistency optimization. European Journal of Operational Research 183(1), 303–313 (2007)
19. Greco, S., Matarazzo, B., Słowiński, R.: Dominance-based rough set approach on pairwise comparison tables to decision involving multiple decision makers. In: Yao, J., Ramanna, S., Wang, G., Suraj, Z. (eds.) RSKT 2011. LNCS, vol. 6954, pp. 126–135. Springer, Heidelberg (2011)
20. Koczkodaj, W.W.: A new definition of consistency of pairwise comparisons. Math. Comput. Model. 18(7), 79–84 (1993)
21. Koczkodaj, W.W., Kułakowski, K., Ligęza, A.: On the Quality Evaluation of Scientific Entities in Poland supported by Consistency-Driven Pairwise Comparisons Method. Scientometrics (accepted for publication, 2014)
22. Kułakowski, K.: A heuristic rating estimation algorithm for the pairwise comparisons method. Central European Journal of Operations Research, 1–17 (2013)
23. Perron, O.: Zur Theorie der Matrices. Mathematische Annalen 64(2), 248–263 (1907)
24. Saaty, T.L.: A scaling method for priorities in hierarchical structures. Journal of Mathematical Psychology 15(3), 234–281 (1977)
25. Thurstone, L.L.: A law of comparative judgment, reprint of an original work published in 1927. Psychological Review 101, 266–270 (1994)

Bagging of Instance Selection Algorithms

Marcin Blachnik[1] and Mirosław Kordos[2]

[1] Silesian University of Technology, Department of Management and Informatics,
Katowice, Krasińskiego 8, Poland
marcin.blachnik@polsl.pl
[2] University of Bielsko-Biala, Department of Mathematics and Computer Science,
Bielsko-Biała, Willowa 2, Poland
mkordos@ath.bielsko.pl

Abstract. The paper presents bagging ensembles of instance selection algorithms. We use bagging to improve instance selection. The improvement comprises data compression and prediction accuracy. The examined instance selection algorithms for classification are ENN, CNN, RNG and GE and for regression are the developed by us Generalized CNN and Generalized ENN algorithms. Results of the comparative experimental study performed using different configurations on several datasets shows that the approachbased on bagging allowed for significant improvement, especially in terms of data compression.

1 Introduction

The benefits of instance selections, such as reducing data size and thus accelerating all operations on the data (or making it feasible at all in case of big data), removing noise and thus improving data reliability and improving logical rule extraction from the data are well known. A large survey of 70 different instance selection algorithms for classification tasks can be found in [12].

In this paper we use six instance selection algorithms inside the bagging ensembles. Four algorithms: the Condensed Nearest Neighbor (CNN) algorithm [6], Edited Nearest Neighbor (ENN) algorithm [15], Gabriel Editing (GE) and Relative Neighborhood Graph Editing (RNGE) algorithms [12] are used for classofication. Two instance selection algorithms GenENN and GenCNN, which we presented in our previous work [10] are used for regression.

In the second chapter we discuss the instance selection algorithms that we use in the bagging ensembles for classification problems. In the third chapter - the instance selection algorithms for regression problems.

In the fourth chapter we discuss bagging in the context of instance selection.

In the fifth chapter we describe our methodology of applying bagging to instance selection. In the following chapter we present the results of experimental evaluation on several classification and regression datasets and discuss the results. Finally the last chapter concludes the work.

2 Instance Selection in Classification Problems

In most research concerning instance selection for classification tasks the k-nearest neighbor algorithm (k-NN) was used as the learning method [4], [2]. Based upon the

L. Rutkowski et al. (Eds.): ICAISC 2014, Part II, LNAI 8468, pp. 40–51, 2014.

results of k-NN based classification, the instance selection algorithms decide if a given instance should be kept in the final dataset or rejected. Below we shortly describe the four algorithms used in their work.

The CNN (Condensed Nearest Neighbor) algorithm was introduced by Hart [6]. The purpose of CNN is to achieve dataset compression by rejected instances, which are too similar to their neighbor. The algorithm starts from selecting a single randomly chosen instance in the original dataset T. Then it tries to classify another randomly chosen instance using k-NN and the first instance as the training dataset. If the classification is correct, than the second instance is believed not to contain any valuable information for the classification model and thus it is rejected. If the classification is wrong, the second instance is believed to contain important information, which allows for creating the decision boundaries between classes and thus it is kept in the resultant dataset P. Then the third instance from T is classified with k-NN using the two instances already in P, then the fourth and so on with always correct classification being the rejection condition (see sketch (1)). For classification tasks the compression obtained with CNN is frequently quite significant with the resultant dataset P containing below one third of the instances in T.

Algorithm 1. Schema of the CNN algorithm

Require: $\mathbf{T}$
 $n \leftarrow |\mathbf{T}|$
 $k \leftarrow 1$
 $\mathbf{p}_1 \leftarrow \mathbf{x}_1$
 $flag \leftarrow$ **true**
 while flag **do**
  $flag \leftarrow$ **false**
  for $i = 1 \ldots n$ **do**
   $\bar{C}(\mathbf{x}_i) =$kNN$(k, \mathbf{P}, \mathbf{x}_i)$
   if $\bar{C}(\mathbf{x}_i) \neq C(\mathbf{x}_i)$ **then**
    $\mathbf{P} \leftarrow \mathbf{P} \cup \mathbf{x}_i;$
    $\mathbf{T} \leftarrow \mathbf{T} \setminus \mathbf{x}_i$
    $flag \leftarrow$ **true**
   end if
  end for
 end while
 return $\mathbf{P}$

Algorithm 2. Schema of the ENN algorithm

Require: $\mathbf{T}, k$
 $n \leftarrow |\mathbf{T}|;$
 $\mathbf{P} \leftarrow \mathbf{T};$
 for $i = 1 \ldots n$ **do**
  $\bar{C}(\mathbf{x}_i) =$kNN$(k, (\mathbf{T} \setminus \mathbf{x}_i), \mathbf{x}_i);$
  if $C(\mathbf{x}_i) \neq \bar{C}(\mathbf{x}_i)$ **then**
   $\mathbf{P} \leftarrow \mathbf{P} \setminus \mathbf{x}_i$
  end if
 end for
 return $\mathbf{P}$

The ENN (Edited Nearest Neighbor) (see sketch (2)) algorithm created by Wilson [15] is an opposite method to CNN. The purpose of ENN is to filter out noisy instances, this is instances, which differ too much from their neighbors. ENN starts from the resultant dataset P being a copy of the original dataset T. Then each instance in P is classified by the k-NN algorithm. If the classification is wrong, than the instance is considered to be noise and is rejected from P. If the classification is correct - it remains in P. Since ENN is rather a noise filter than condensation algorithm, the compression obtained with ENN tends to be much lower than the CNN compression. ENN and CNN can be applied sequentially. Fist ENN and then CNN, because applying them in the reverse order does not make much sense (ENN would then remove almost all instances).

Gabriel Editing (GE) and Relative Neighborhood Graph Editing (RNGE) are two algorithms based on graph theory, described by Bhattacharya [1], and presented in sketch (3). A Gabriel Graph is a graph with vertex set $\mathbf{T}$ obtained by connecting any two points $\mathbf{x}_a$ and $\mathbf{x}_b$ in $\mathbf{T}$, which are considered the nearest neighbors, that is if the circle which diameter is a line segment connecting the points $\mathbf{x}_a$ and $\mathbf{x}_b$ does not contain inside any other elements denoted as $\mathbf{x}_c$ of $\mathbf{T}$. In other words for every triple of points the formula:

$$\bigvee_{a \neq b \neq c} D^2(\mathbf{x}_a, \mathbf{x}_b) > D^2(\mathbf{x}_a, \mathbf{x}_c) + D^2(\mathbf{x}_b, \mathbf{x}_c) \tag{1}$$

is evaluated. If the inequality is fulfilled vectors $\mathbf{x}_a$ and $\mathbf{x}_b$ are marked as neighbors.

A Relative Neighborhood Graph (RNG) is very similar to GE algorithm. The main difference is in the formula determining graph neighbors:

$$\bigvee_{a \neq b \neq c} D(\mathbf{x}_a, \mathbf{x}_b) \geq \max(D(\mathbf{x}_a, \mathbf{x}_c), D(\mathbf{x}_b, \mathbf{x}_c)) \tag{2}$$

In both of this algorithms the remaining instances are those, which fulfills the above formulas and belong to opposite classes.

Algorithm 3. RNG and RNGE Algorithms

Require: T
  $n \leftarrow |\mathbf{T}|$;
  $rem_{1:n} \leftarrow 1$;
  for $i_a = 1 \ldots n$ **do**
    for $i_b = [1 \ldots n] \setminus i_a$ **do**
      if $C(\mathbf{x}_{i_a}) \neq C(\mathbf{x}_{i_b})$ **then**
        $tmp \leftarrow$ **true**
        $d_{ab} \leftarrow ||\mathbf{x}_{i_a}, \mathbf{x}_{i_b}||$
        for $i_c = [1 \ldots n] \setminus \{i_a, i_b\}$ **do**
          $d_{ac} \leftarrow ||\mathbf{x}_{i_a}, \mathbf{x}_{i_c}||$
          $d_{bc} \leftarrow ||\mathbf{x}_{i_b}, \mathbf{x}_{i_c}||$
          if CheckCondition(d_{ab}, d_{ac}, d_{bc}) **then**
            $tmp \leftarrow$ **false**
            break;
          end if
        end for
        if tmp **then**
          $rem_{i_a} \leftarrow 0$
          $rem_{i_b} \leftarrow 0$
        end if
      end if
    end for
  end for
  $\mathbf{P} \leftarrow$ RemoveUseles$(\mathbf{T}, rem)$
  return P

---

3   Instance Selection in Regression Problems

Instance selection for regression problems is in general more complex than for classification tasks because of two issues: the rejecttion criterion and the class boudary. The rejection criterion in instance selection for classification is very simple (at least in the most common algorithms): an instance should be rejected based on the result of its classification by the nearest neighbors, which can be either wrong or right. In regression problems, there is no such a crisp rule and the problem becomes more complex. The other issue is that to build a classifier we really need only the instances situated close to class boundaries, thus the obtained compression can be quite significant. To build a regression model we need the instances in the whole space covered by the model, thus the compression we can achieve will be definitely lower.

There were only a few papers, which consider instance selection for regression tasks. Moreover, the approaches and the papers we were able to find did not presented the algorithm verification on real-world datasets. Zhang [17] presented a method to select the input vectors while calculating the output with k-NN. Tolvi [13] presented a genetic algorithm to perform feature and instance selection for linear regression models. In their works Guillen et al. [5] discussed the concept of mutual information used for selection of prototypes in regression problems. Below we shortly describe the two algorithms used in this work: GenENN and GenCNN.

To deal with the lack of crisp rules defining the rejection criterion, in our previous work [10] we introduced some similarity threshold θ. The similarity threshold considers the distances in the output space between the k closest instances in the input space. If the distance in the output space is too high - larger then θ - the instance is considered as important in case of GenCNN algortihm (which starts from the empty set of instances) and as outlier in case GenENN (which removes noise instances).

In the pseudo-code (sketch (4) and (5)) $\mathbf{T}$ is the training dataset, $\mathbf{P}$ is the set of selected prototypes, $\mathbf{x}_i$ is the i-th vector, n is the number of vectors in the dataset ,$Y(\mathbf{x}_i)$ is the real output value of vector $\mathbf{x}_i$, $\bar{Y}(\mathbf{x}_i)$ is the predicted output of vector $\mathbf{x}_i$, S is the set of nearest neighbors of vector $\mathbf{x}_i$, $Model$ is the algorithm, which is trained on dataset $\mathbf{T}$ without vector $\mathbf{x}_i$ which is used as a test sample, for which the $Y(\mathbf{x}_i)$ is predicted, k-NN is the k-NN algorithm returning the subset S of k nearest neighbors to $\mathbf{x}_i$. θ is the threshold of acceptance/rejection of the vector as a prototype, α is a constant coefficient and $std\left(Y\left(\mathbf{X}_S\right)\right)$ is the standard deviation of the outputs of the vectors in S.

Both described instance selection algorithms are considered as *generalized* because they allow to use any prediction model as a predictor embedded in it (the $\bar{Y}(\mathbf{x}) = Model(\mathbf{T}, \mathbf{x})$), while the classical ENN and CNN algorithms were designed with the assumption that the prediction model is the nearest neighbor model. We have shown in [10] that for several regression tasks better results were obtained if the difference between the actual and the predicted output value of an instance was predicted by an MLP neural network than by kNN. However, in the experiments for regression presented in this paper the model that learned the data representation was the 9-NN model.

Algorithm 4. GenENN algorithm	**Algorithm 5.** GenCNN algorithm
Require: T	**Require: T**
$\quad n \leftarrow sizeof(\mathbf{T})$;	$\quad n \leftarrow sizeof(\mathbf{T})$
$\quad \bar{P} = \mathbf{T}$	$\quad \mathbf{P} = \emptyset$
$\quad \textbf{for } i = 1 \ldots n \textbf{ do}$	$\quad \mathbf{P} \leftarrow \mathbf{P} \cup \mathbf{x}_1$;
$\quad\quad \bar{Y}(\mathbf{x}_i) = \text{Model}((\mathbf{T} \setminus \mathbf{x}_i), \mathbf{x}_i)$;	$\quad \textbf{for } i = 2 \ldots n \textbf{ do}$
$\quad\quad S \leftarrow \text{k-NN}(\mathbf{T}, \mathbf{x}_i)$	$\quad\quad \bar{Y}(\mathbf{x}_i) = \text{Model}(\mathbf{P}, \mathbf{x}_i)$
$\quad\quad \theta = \alpha \cdot std(Y(\mathbf{X}_S))$	$\quad\quad S \leftarrow \text{k-NN}(\mathbf{T}, \mathbf{x}_i)$
$\quad\quad \textbf{if } \left| Y(\mathbf{x}_i) - \bar{Y}(\mathbf{x}_i) \right| > \theta \textbf{ then}$	$\quad\quad \theta = \alpha \cdot std(Y(\mathbf{X}_S))$
$\quad\quad\quad \mathbf{P} \leftarrow \mathbf{P} \setminus \mathbf{x}_i$	$\quad\quad \textbf{if } \left| Y(\mathbf{x}_i) - \bar{Y}(\mathbf{x}_i) \right| > \theta \textbf{ then}$
$\quad\quad \textbf{end if}$	$\quad\quad\quad \mathbf{P} \leftarrow \mathbf{P} \cup \mathbf{x}_i$;
$\quad \textbf{end for}$	$\quad\quad\quad \mathbf{T} \leftarrow \mathbf{T} \setminus \mathbf{x}_i$
$\quad \textbf{return } \mathbf{P}$	$\quad\quad \textbf{end if}$
	$\quad \textbf{end for}$
	$\quad \textbf{return } \mathbf{P}$

4 Bagging Method for Instance Selection

For last decade or even more ensemble learning [11], [18] proved to be one of the most profitable directions in machine learning. This approach is often called meta-learning and confirmed its quality in various data mining challenges [8]. In this area many directions have been proposed but the general idea is based on replacing a single expert by a group of experts voting non necessary with equal rights for the best solution. Ensemble learning includes solutions such as voting, stacking, bagging or boosting, etc. Recently these kind of methods were used for ensemble of final prediction models, but there is a little work on using such an approach for data preprocessing such us instance selection. In this paper we investigate application of bagging to improve the quality of instance selection.

In case of classical applications, bagging is based on building several individual prediction models on subset of original training instances, where these data subsets are sampled with replacement from the initial training dataset. An example of such an algorithm is RandomForest [3] where each decision tree is built on a subset of features and a subset of training samples. When making the prediction each of the component models is voting for the final output (in case of classification) or the individual predictions are averaged (in case of regression).

The idea of bagging can be also adapted for the instance selection. In that case each run of the instance selection algorithm provides binary weights denoting absence or presence of each of the training samples. The collected votes for each training instance are combined and averaged, what allows to assign a single new weight attribute representing the importance of each training sample.

Finally to perform the final instance selection an *acceptance threshold* is defined that determines which instances will be included in the final training set.

This approach has several issues. The instance selection method can be simply divided into the outlier eliminators such as ENN algorithm and redundancy filters such as CNN algorithm. The first group usually allows to remove a small subset of instances

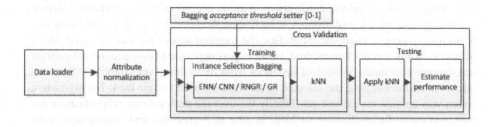

Fig. 1. The experimental evaluation process

what leads to small compression, and rather dense final set, while the redundancy removal methods has large compression and usually small, though sparse final subset. The second group of methods may be very problematic in case of bagging applications, especially for large datasets because for sparse datasets the probability of selecting the same vectors highly decreases, determining the use of small values of *acceptance threshold*, and reducing the compression coefficient.

5 Eperimental Evaluation

5.1 Experimental Environment

We implemented the instance selection algorithms in Java as RapidMiner Extensions and used RapidMiner [19] for the whole process. The source codes, executable files and datasets used in the experiments can be downloaded from [20].

In our experiments we tested four different instance selection algorithms for classification: ENN, CNN, RNGE, GE and two methods for regression: Generalized ENN and Generalized CNN, which were developed from ENN and CNN to extend their functionality so that they cover any tasks where the cost function can be defined (classification, regression). The parameters of the instance selection methods were set to the default values. In the case of classification we used 1-NN as the inner model of these algorithms and as the classifier. In the case of regression we used 9-NN as the inner model and 9-NN as the predictor.

We performed the experiments on six most popular classification and four regression datasets. The classification datasets used in the experiments were obtained from the UCI Machine Learning Repository [14]: heart disease, ionosphere, Pima Indian diabetes, sonar, vehicle and Wisconsin breast cancer. For the regression problems two datasets were also obtained form the UCI repository: Concrete Compression Strength (7 attributes, 1030 instances), Crime and Communities (7 attr., 320 inst.). Two datasest (SteelC14 and SteelC14-noise: 18 attr., 2382 inst.) depict the steel production process with the task to predict the amount of carbon that must be added to the liquid steel in to obtain the desired steel properties.

For the purpose of the experiment we defined a RapidMiner process, which is available from [20]. The scheme of the testing environment is presented in figure (5.1) The process starts form loading the data and attribute normalization or standardization (in case of regression we did standardization). After it, according to the *acceptance threshold* settings and selection of instance reduction method the 10 fold cross-validation was performed, where in each validation first the bagging algorithm was executed which wraps the instance reduction method. In our experiments the instance reduction method was executed 15 times on 80% of instances from the training set sampled without replacement. After bagging, the selected instances were used to train the k-NN algorithm, which was applied on the test set. Finally the average performance (classification accuracy in case of classification or MSE in case of regression) and compression were evaluated. In our case the compression C_x is defined as

$$C_x = 1 - \frac{number\_of\_instances\_after\_selection}{number\_of\_instances\_before\_selection} \tag{3}$$

and it tends to 1 if less instances remain in the training set, and tends to 0 if no instance reduction is possible.

5.2 Simulation Results

The simulation results are presented in tables in appendix. Typically, results of instance selection methods are represented in a form of accuracy-compression plots. This represents both of the goals of instance selection; rejection of unneeded instances and improvement of the model accuracy. The training dataset compression shows rejection of redundant and thus not informative instances as well as rejection of the outliers, which do not fit in the model. In other words the plots show relation between the level of compression and the instance selection influence on the accuracy of the final prediction system. However, in our case to perform the comparison between bagging-based instance selection and a single instance selector we draw accuracy-compression gain plots, where the horizontal axis expresses

$$accuracy\_of\_bagging\_method - accuracy\_of\_single\_method$$

and the vertical axis expresses

$$compression\_of\_bagging\_method - compression\_of\_single\_method$$

such that values equal 0 represent no gain, and values ≥ 0 represent the level of improvement, while values ≤ 0 the level of deterioration. The gain plots are presented in figures 5.2 and 5.2.

6 Conclusions

The obtained results showed that using the bagging ensembles is beneficial when the proper *acceptance threshold* is set. Generally the highest gain was obtained for the ENN and GE algorithms. In that case the bagging allowed increasing the compression level of up to 80% without any significant accuracy drop. Bagging also allowed improving

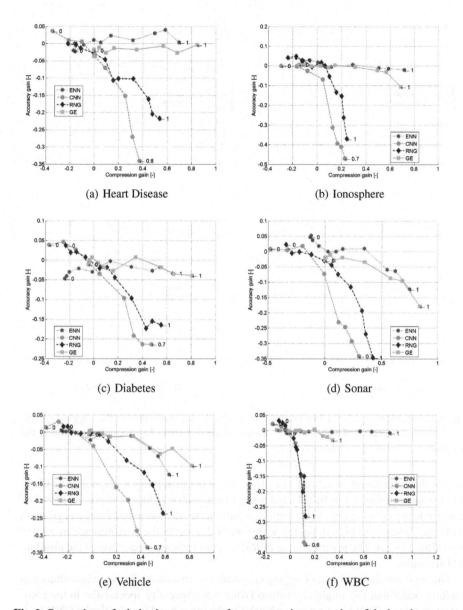

Fig. 2. Comparison of relative improvement of accuracy and compression of the bagging ensemble of instance selection methods vs. the original method without bagging as a function of the *acceptance threshold* for classification tasks

the classification accuracy of up to 5% in almost all cases however reducing the compression. For the CNN and RNGE algorithms high accuracy drop may be observed for increased *acceptance threshold* value. These results can be explained by the high initial compression ratio. As it was already mentioned, because CNN initially boast

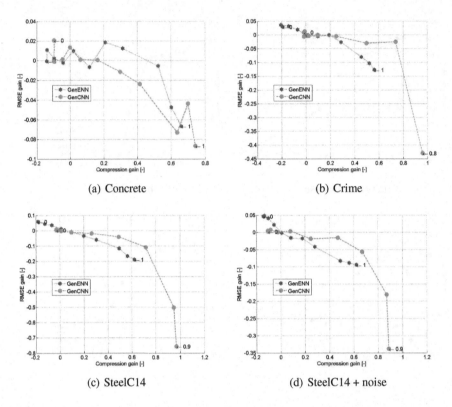

(a) Concrete

(b) Crime

(c) SteelC14

(d) SteelC14 + noise

Fig. 3. Comparison of relative improvement of RMSE and compression of the bagging ensemble of instance selection methods vs. the original method without bagging as a function of the *acceptance threshold* for regression tasks

very high compression (what can't be observed on the gain plot), it becomes less likely that the same instance will be selected many times, which reduces the possible level of applicable *acceptance threshold*. Similar results were also obtained for the regression problems, where too high *acceptance threshold* decreases the performance measured by RMSE ((5.2)). The positive value of *RMSE-gain* indicates reduction of the absolute RMSE value.

The final conclusion is that bagging ensembles of instance selection algorithms can perform better that the single algorithms (what was especially spectacular in the compression gain of ENN bagging ensembles). On the other hand frequently the CNN bagging ensembles allowed for better accuracy gain of up to 5% but with carefully tuned *acceptance threshold* taking small values. Thus a good direction of the future research would be to build an other ensemble of instance selection methods. One of the possibilities are voting methods which may replace the classical approach based on serial processing of instance selection for example including the benefits of both CNN and ENN and thus attempt to improve significantly both: compression gain and accuracy gain.

References

1. Bhattacharya, B.K., Poulsen, R.S., Toussaint, G.T.: Application of proximity graphs to editing nearest neighbor decision rule. In: International Symposium on Information Theory, Santa Monica (1981)
2. Bhatia, N.: Survey of Nearest Neighbor Techniques. International Journal of Computer Science and Information Security (IJCSIS) 8(2) (2010)
3. Breiman, L.: Random Forests. Machine Learning 45(1), 5–32 (2001)
4. Dasarathy, B.V.: Nearest Neighbor (NN) Norm, Nn Pattern Classification Techniques. IEEE Computer Society (1990)
5. Guillen, A.: Applying mutual information for prototype or instance selection in regression problems. In: ESANN 2009 (2009)
6. Hart, P.: The condensed nearest neighbor rule (corresp.). IEEE Transactions on Information Theory 14(3), 515–516 (1968)
7. Huber, P.J.: Robust Statistics. Wiley Series in Probability and Statistics, Wiley-Interscience (1981)
8. Jankowski, N., Gr?bczewski, K.: Handwritten digit recognition — road to contest victory. In: IEEE Symposium Series on Computational Intelligence, pp. 491–498. IEEE Press (2007)
9. Kordos, M., Blachnik, M., Strzempa, D.: Do We Need Whatever More Than k-NN? In: Rutkowski, L., Scherer, R., Tadeusiewicz, R., Zadeh, L.A., Zurada, J.M. (eds.) ICAISC 2010, Part I. LNCS, vol. 6113, pp. 414–421. Springer, Heidelberg (2010)
10. Kordos, M., Blachnik, M.: Instance Selection with Neural Networks for Regression Problems. In: Villa, A.E.P., Duch, W., Érdi, P., Masulli, F., Palm, G. (eds.) ICANN 2012, Part II. LNCS, vol. 7553, pp. 263–270. Springer, Heidelberg (2012)
11. Kuncheva, L.: Combining Pattern Classifiers: Methods and Algorithms. Wiley (2004)
12. Garcia, S., Derrac, J., Cano, J.R., Herrera, F.: Prototype selection for nearest neighbor classification: Taxonomy and empirical study. IEEE Transactions on Pattern Analysis and Machine Intelligence 34, 417–435 (2012)
13. Tolvi, J.: Genetic algorithms for outlier detection and variable selection in linear regression models. Soft Computing 8, 527–533 (2004)
14. Merz, C., Murphy, P.: Uci repository of machine learning databases (2013), http://www.ics.uci.edu/mlearn/MLRepository.html
15. Wilson, D.L.: Asymptotic properties of nearest neighbor rules using edited data. IEEE Transactions on Systems, Man and Cybernetics SMC-2(3), 408–421 (1972)
16. Wilson, D., Martinez, T.: Reduction techniques for instance-based learning algorithms. Machine Learning 38, 251–268 (2000)
17. Zhang, J.: Intelligent selection of instances for prediction functions in lazy learning algorithms. Artifcial Intelligence Review 11, 175–191 (1997)
18. Zhou, Z.-H.: Ensemble Methods: Foundations and Algorithm. Chapman and Hall/CRC (2012)
19. http://www.rapidminer.com
20. source code and datasets used in the paper, http://code.google.com/p/instance-selection-2014/

Appendix

Table 1. Classification accuracy and instance selection compression obtained in the experiments. Threshold denoted as "-" represent normal result without bagging ensemble

Dataset	thr	Accuracy	Compress	Accuracy	Compress	Accuracy	Compress	Accuracy	Compress
-		ENN		CNN		RNGE		GE	
Sonar	-	0.81±0.86	0.07±0.01	0.86±0.31	0.08±0.01	0.86±0.46	0.08±0.02	0.89±1.00	0.09±0.00
	0.00	0.86±0.99	0.07±0.01	0.87±0.79	0.08±0.03	0.88±0.80	0.06±0.02	0.86±1.00	0.08±0.00
	0.10	0.86±0.98	0.06±0.00	0.87±0.64	0.08±0.02	0.85±0.75	0.06±0.03	0.87±1.00	0.08±0.00
	0.20	0.85±0.96	0.09±0.01	0.88±0.51	0.05±0.02	0.86±0.68	0.07±0.02	0.87±1.00	0.07±0.00
	0.30	0.83±0.91	0.10±0.01	0.79±0.32	0.12±0.02	0.85±0.58	0.08±0.02	0.87±0.99	0.08±0.01
	0.40	0.81±0.83	0.07±0.02	0.63±0.19	0.10±0.02	0.83±0.47	0.06±0.01	0.88±0.95	0.08±0.01
	0.50	0.81±0.76	0.08±0.03	0.61±0.13	0.09±0.01	0.81±0.40	0.03±0.02	0.86±0.92	0.08±0.02
	0.60	0.82±0.70	0.09±0.02	0.57±0.07	0.10±0.02	0.78±0.34	0.12±0.02	0.87±0.85	0.04±0.02
	0.70	0.82±0.51	0.08±0.02	0.52±0.01	0.08±0.00	0.74±0.23	0.08±0.02	0.86±0.65	0.05±0.02
	0.80	0.75±0.31	0.10±0.01	±	±	0.66±0.13	0.10±0.01	0.80±0.42	0.08±0.02
	0.90	0.75±0.23	0.08±0.02	±	±	0.59±0.10	0.10±0.02	0.79±0.32	0.09±0.02
	1.00	0.69±0.11	0.10±0.02	±	±	0.51±0.04	0.11±0.01	0.71±0.16	0.08±0.02
Ionosphere	-	0.84±0.84	0.06±0.01	0.87±0.24	0.04±0.01	0.81±0.26	0.03±0.02	0.87±0.79	0.04±0.01
	0.00	0.87±0.97	0.04±0.01	0.87±0.54	0.05±0.01	0.86±0.50	0.05±0.01	0.87±0.94	0.04±0.01
	0.10	0.86±0.96	0.05±0.01	0.87±0.41	0.06±0.02	0.86±0.43	0.06±0.01	0.87±0.92	0.05±0.01
	0.20	0.86±0.96	0.06±0.01	0.85±0.32	0.07±0.01	0.84±0.38	0.06±0.02	0.87±0.89	0.04±0.01
	0.30	0.87±0.91	0.03±0.01	0.80±0.19	0.07±0.02	0.81±0.30	0.07±0.01	0.87±0.84	0.03±0.01
	0.40	0.85±0.84	0.06±0.01	0.56±0.11	0.11±0.01	0.83±0.23	0.06±0.02	0.87±0.77	0.05±0.01
	0.50	0.84±0.79	0.06±0.02	0.48±0.07	0.18±0.01	0.82±0.20	0.07±0.01	0.86±0.70	0.03±0.01
	0.60	0.83±0.72	0.06±0.01	0.46±0.04	0.17±0.01	0.76±0.16	0.03±0.01	0.87±0.65	0.04±0.02
	0.70	0.84±0.55	0.07±0.02	0.40±0.01	0.11±0.00	0.68±0.10	0.11±0.01	0.86±0.48	0.04±0.02
	0.80	0.83±0.34	0.06±0.02	±	±	0.66±0.06	0.11±0.01	0.85±0.30	0.06±0.02
	0.90	0.82±0.26	0.04±0.02	±	±	0.55±0.04	0.12±0.01	0.84±0.23	0.08±0.01
	1.00	0.82±0.12	0.10±0.01	±	±	0.44±0.02	0.15±0.01	0.76±0.11	0.06±0.02
Wisconsin breast cancer	-	0.97±0.96	0.02±0.00	0.92±0.14	0.02±0.01	0.91±0.13	0.03±0.01	0.95±0.38	0.03±0.01
	0.00	0.96±0.99	0.02±0.00	0.94±0.29	0.02±0.02	0.94±0.22	0.03±0.01	0.95±0.50	0.03±0.01
	0.10	0.96±0.99	0.02±0.00	0.94±0.21	0.02±0.01	0.94±0.19	0.03±0.01	0.95±0.47	0.03±0.01
	0.20	0.96±0.99	0.02±0.00	0.92±0.17	0.02±0.02	0.93±0.17	0.02±0.01	0.95±0.44	0.03±0.02
	0.30	0.96±0.97	0.02±0.00	0.88±0.10	0.05±0.01	0.91±0.13	0.02±0.01	0.94±0.39	0.02±0.01
	0.40	0.96±0.92	0.02±0.01	0.77±0.05	0.10±0.01	0.89±0.10	0.04±0.01	0.94±0.34	0.03±0.02
	0.50	0.96±0.87	0.02±0.01	0.56±0.03	0.26±0.01	0.86±0.09	0.03±0.01	0.95±0.31	0.03±0.02
	0.60	0.96±0.81	0.02±0.01	0.55±0.01	0.22±0.00	0.85±0.07	0.03±0.01	0.94±0.27	0.02±0.01
	0.70	0.96±0.62	0.02±0.01	±	±	0.77±0.05	0.11±0.01	0.95±0.19	0.02±0.02
	0.80	0.96±0.39	0.02±0.01	±	±	0.71±0.03	0.11±0.01	0.93±0.12	0.03±0.01
	0.90	0.96±0.30	0.02±0.01	±	±	0.76±0.02	0.14±0.01	0.92±0.08	0.03±0.01
	1.00	0.96±0.14	0.03±0.01	±	±	0.63±0.01	0.30±0.00	0.91±0.04	0.05±0.01
Pima indian diabetes	-	0.75±0.73	0.03±0.00	0.65±0.49	0.06±0.01	0.67±0.60	0.05±0.01	0.71±0.94	0.05±0.01
	0.00	0.70±0.98	0.04±0.00	0.69±0.86	0.03±0.01	0.71±0.83	0.05±0.01	0.70±0.99	0.05±0.00
	0.10	0.71±0.96	0.02±0.01	0.70±0.74	0.05±0.01	0.69±0.79	0.05±0.01	0.71±0.98	0.06±0.00
	0.20	0.72±0.94	0.04±0.01	0.68±0.64	0.04±0.01	0.69±0.74	0.05±0.01	0.71±0.98	0.06±0.00
	0.30	0.73±0.86	0.02±0.01	0.62±0.44	0.04±0.02	0.68±0.67	0.04±0.01	0.72±0.96	0.02±0.01
	0.40	0.72±0.75	0.04±0.01	0.55±0.24	0.04±0.01	0.65±0.55	0.03±0.01	0.71±0.90	0.06±0.01
	0.50	0.73±0.68	0.05±0.01	0.46±0.16	0.06±0.02	0.65±0.49	0.04±0.01	0.70±0.86	0.05±0.01
	0.60	0.74±0.60	0.04±0.01	0.44±0.09	0.08±0.01	0.63±0.42	0.08±0.02	0.69±0.78	0.04±0.01
	0.70	0.73±0.43	0.06±0.02	0.44±0.02	0.09±0.01	0.58±0.29	0.05±0.01	0.72±0.60	0.07±0.01
	0.80	0.72±0.25	0.03±0.01	±	±	0.50±0.17	0.05±0.01	0.70±0.39	0.04±0.01
	0.90	0.73±0.19	0.04±0.01	±	±	0.52±0.12	0.08±0.01	0.68±0.28	0.05±0.01
	1.00	0.71±0.09	0.04±0.01	±	±	0.51±0.04	0.10±0.01	0.67±0.13	0.07±0.01
Heart disease	-	0.79±0.80	0.07±0.01	0.71±0.44	0.07±0.02	0.75±0.58	0.07±0.03	0.78±1.00	0.06±0.00
	0.00	0.77±0.97	0.07±0.01	0.75±0.78	0.08±0.02	0.75±0.80	0.10±0.01	0.76±1.00	0.05±0.00
	0.10	0.79±0.96	0.06±0.01	0.72±0.65	0.08±0.02	0.75±0.73	0.06±0.03	0.74±1.00	0.05±0.00
	0.20	0.77±0.96	0.06±0.01	0.72±0.54	0.06±0.02	0.74±0.69	0.05±0.02	0.76±1.00	0.07±0.00
	0.30	0.79±0.89	0.07±0.01	0.64±0.35	0.08±0.02	0.72±0.58	0.06±0.02	0.74±0.99	0.07±0.00
	0.40	0.80±0.80	0.05±0.01	0.56±0.18	0.07±0.02	0.70±0.49	0.07±0.02	0.77±0.96	0.08±0.01
	0.50	0.79±0.75	0.10±0.02	0.44±0.12	0.11±0.03	0.64±0.42	0.09±0.02	0.75±0.90	0.07±0.02
	0.60	0.81±0.66	0.04±0.02	0.37±0.06	0.16±0.01	0.65±0.38	0.06±0.03	0.77±0.84	0.06±0.02
	0.70	0.80±0.48	0.08±0.01	±	±	0.65±0.26	0.08±0.02	0.76±0.65	0.04±0.03

Continued

Table 1 – Continued

Dataset	thr	Accuracy	Compress	Accuracy	Compress	Accuracy	Compress	Accuracy	Compress
		ENN		CNN		RNGE		GE	
-	0.80	0.82±0.30	0.06±0.01	±	±	0.59±0.13	0.08±0.01	0.77±0.43	0.07±0.02
	0.90	0.83±0.22	0.07±0.02	±	±	0.54±0.10	0.14±0.01	0.75±0.32	0.10±0.02
	1.00	0.79±0.10	0.06±0.01	±	±	0.53±0.04	0.12±0.01	0.78±0.15	0.08±0.02
Vehicle	-	0.69±0.72	0.05±0.01	0.68±0.48	0.05±0.01	0.68±0.65	0.04±0.01	0.70±0.97	0.05±0.00
	0.00	0.70±0.97	0.03±0.00	0.69±0.86	0.04±0.01	0.70±0.89	0.03±0.01	0.69±0.99	0.05±0.00
	0.10	0.69±0.96	0.04±0.01	0.71±0.76	0.04±0.01	0.70±0.86	0.03±0.01	0.70±0.99	0.03±0.00
	0.20	0.69±0.93	0.04±0.01	0.69±0.66	0.04±0.01	0.68±0.83	0.03±0.01	0.70±0.99	0.02±0.00
	0.30	0.69±0.85	0.04±0.01	0.64±0.47	0.08±0.02	0.68±0.75	0.05±0.01	0.70±0.97	0.06±0.00
	0.40	0.67±0.73	0.06±0.01	0.52±0.28	0.07±0.01	0.68±0.66	0.05±0.01	0.69±0.93	0.04±0.01
	0.50	0.68±0.65	0.05±0.01	0.48±0.18	0.04±0.01	0.68±0.60	0.05±0.01	0.69±0.88	0.03±0.01
	0.60	0.68±0.58	0.03±0.01	0.39±0.11	0.06±0.01	0.66±0.52	0.07±0.01	0.68±0.82	0.04±0.01
	0.70	0.68±0.39	0.04±0.01	0.34±0.02	0.03±0.01	0.60±0.37	0.04±0.01	0.68±0.63	0.03±0.01
	0.80	0.65±0.24	0.04±0.01	±	±	0.57±0.23	0.06±0.01	0.63±0.41	0.05±0.01
	0.90	0.62±0.17	0.05±0.01	±	±	0.53±0.16	0.04±0.01	0.65±0.31	0.05±0.01
	1.00	0.57±0.08	0.04±0.01	±	±	0.45±0.07	0.06±0.01	0.60±0.14	0.05±0.01

Table 2. MSE for regression problems and instance selection compression obtained in the experiments. Threshold denoted as "-" represent normal result without bagging ensemble.

Dataset	thr	RMSE	Compress	RMSE	Compress	Dataset	RMSE	Compress	RMSE	Compress
	-	ENN		CNN			ENN		CNN	
Steel C14 noise	-	1.37±0.72	0.07±0.00	1.27±0.89	0.06±0.00	Steel C14	0.37±0.71	0.05±0.00	0.27±0.97	0.05±0.00
	0	1.32±0.86	0.04±0.00	1.26±0.99	0.03±0.00		0.31±0.89	0.05±0.00	0.27±1.00	0.04±0.00
	0.1	1.32±0.85	0.03±0.00	1.26±0.99	0.03±0.00		0.31±0.89	0.06±0.00	0.27±1.00	0.04±0.00
	0.2	1.33±0.82	0.07±0.01	1.26±0.97	0.03±0.00		0.32±0.83	0.04±0.00	0.27±0.99	0.04±0.00
	0.3	1.35±0.77	0.05±0.01	1.27±0.91	0.01±0.00		0.33±0.78	0.05±0.00	0.27±0.96	0.04±0.00
	0.4	1.37±0.71	0.06±0.01	1.26±0.81	0.04±0.00		0.35±0.70	0.05±0.01	0.28±0.87	0.06±0.00
	0.5	1.38±0.63	0.05±0.01	1.29±0.64	0.02±0.01		0.37±0.61	0.05±0.01	0.29±0.71	0.04±0.01
	0.6	1.39±0.54	0.02±0.00	1.28±0.42	0.04±0.00		0.40±0.51	0.05±0.01	0.31±0.48	0.05±0.00
	0.7	1.41±0.44	0.02±0.01	1.32±0.22	0.04±0.00		0.43±0.41	0.06±0.01	0.38±0.25	0.04±0.01
	0.8	1.45±0.23	0.05±0.00	1.45±0.02	0.10±0.00		0.48±0.22	0.05±0.00	0.78±0.02	0.11±0.00
	0.9	1.46±0.15	0.06±0.01	1.61±0.00	0.11±0.00		0.53±0.15	0.07±0.01	1.03±0.00	0.03±0.00
	1	1.46±0.09	0.03±0.01	±	±		0.55±0.09	0.04±0.01	±	±
Crime	-	0.65±0.65	0.11±0.02	0.60±0.98	0.07±0.00	Concrete	0.91±0.76	0.14±0.01	0.92±0.80	0.10±0.01
	0	0.62±0.84	0.07±0.01	0.59±1.00	0.08±0.00		0.91±0.90	0.04±0.00	0.90±0.90	0.10±0.00
	0.1	0.62±0.85	0.09±0.01	0.61±1.00	0.07±0.00		0.90±0.89	0.14±0.00	0.92±0.90	0.10±0.01
	0.2	0.62±0.79	0.07±0.02	0.59±0.99	0.07±0.01		0.91±0.85	0.04±0.00	0.92±0.85	0.11±0.01
	0.3	0.64±0.71	0.06±0.01	0.61±0.96	0.07±0.01		0.92±0.80	0.15±0.01	0.91±0.80	0.13±0.01
	0.4	0.66±0.64	0.08±0.02	0.60±0.88	0.06±0.01		0.90±0.74	0.11±0.01	0.92±0.74	0.12±0.01
	0.5	0.66±0.55	0.08±0.02	0.61±0.73	0.07±0.02		0.92±0.64	0.14±0.01	0.92±0.64	0.06±0.01
	0.6	0.65±0.45	0.06±0.02	0.63±0.48	0.08±0.02		0.89±0.55	0.17±0.01	0.93±0.50	0.15±0.01
	0.7	0.68±0.35	0.09±0.02	0.63±0.24	0.05±0.02		0.90±0.44	0.12±0.01	0.95±0.39	0.12±0.01
	0.8	0.73±0.19	0.11±0.01	1.03±0.02	0.07±0.00		0.92±0.23	0.21±0.01	1.00±0.17	0.07±0.01
	0.9	0.76±0.12	0.07±0.01	±	±		0.96±0.16	0.16±0.01	0.97±0.10	0.08±0.00
	1	0.78±0.08	0.06±0.02	±	±		0.98±0.10	0.17±0.01	1.01±0.06	0.07±0.00

Essential Attributes Generation
for Some Data Mining Tasks

Maciej Krawczak[1,2] and Grażyna Szkatuła[1]

[1] Systems Research Institute, Polish Academy of Sciences
Newelska 6, 01–447 Warsaw, Poland
[2] Warsaw School of Information Technology
Newelska 6, 01–447 Warsaw, Poland
{krawczak,szkatulg}@ibspan.waw.pl

Abstract. In this paper, we introduce a new approach referred to as
Essential Attributes Generation (EAG) to reduce the dimensionality of
multidimensional real-valued data series. We form a new representation
of the original data. The approach is based on the concept of essential
attributes generated by a multilayer neural network. The EAG generates
a vector of real valued new attributes which form the compressed representation of the original data. The attributes are synthetic, and while not
being directly interpretable, they still retain important features of the
original data series. The approach has found applications to classification
as well as clustering tasks.

Keywords: Multidimensional data, Essential attributes, Neural
networks.

1   Introduction

Data series is often used to refer to any data set with a single independent
parameter. The high dimensionality of data series delivers many data mining
imperfect methods. In general, the data mining methods require high computational requirements when being applied to very large data sets. This obstacle
is sometimes referred to the "curse of dimensionality". In data mining problems there is a necessity of dimensionality reduction and developing new data
representations. It is assumed that the new representation preserves sufficient information for solving data mining problems correctly. Dimensionality reduction
can effectively reduce this computational overhead.

Thus, the aim is to develope a new representation of the original data which
is based on dimensionality reduction. Such methods of dimensionality reduction
can lead to attribute selection, attribute extraction, or record selection. The
process of extracting attributes reduces the dimensionality of data, which means
that it forms a kind of data compression. Note that lossy compression methods
invoke some compromise between the compression rate and retained information.

There are some reviews of approaches to dimensionality reduction and similarity searches of data series in large databases (e.g. Tak-chung Fu [22]). In general,

L. Rutkowski et al. (Eds.): ICAISC 2014, Part II, LNAI 8468, pp. 52–62, 2014.

a data of arbitrary length M can be reduced to another representation of data of length K, $K < M$. The simplest method is sampling (Astrom [1]), in which the rate of M/K stands for the compression rate. Piecewise approximation methods divide the data series into segments and approximate each segment using functions (e.g. Yi and Faloutsos [24], Keogh et al. [12], Lee et al. [20]). There are other methods to approximate a time series by straight lines; for example, linear interpolation or linear regression. Representing data series in the transformed domain is another approach. One of the popular transformation techniques is the Discrete Fourier Transform (e.g. Faloutsos et al.[6]) and the Discrete Wavelet Transform (e.g. Chan, A.C. Fu [3]). Principal Component Analysis is a popular multivariate technique using statistical methods (e.g. Yang and Shahabi [23]). Other methods use Hidden Markov Models (e.g. Azzouzi and Nabney [2]). Many of the approaches use different indexing methods.

Here, we propose a new approach referred to as Essential Attributes Generation (EAG) for gradual reduction of dimensionality of multidimensional real-valued data series. Let us denote the original data series of arbitrary length M and indexed by n as the following vector $[y_1(n), \ldots, y_M(n)]$, $n = 1, \ldots, N$, $y_k(n) \in R$, $k = 1, \ldots, M$, where M stands for the dimensionality of the data and N is the number of data in the data set. The idea is based on the use of a multilayer neural network as an auto-associative memory. Such a neural network consists of two modules: the first is responsible for encoding while the second for decoding. The inputs and the outputs of the neural network are just considered as original date, while in between there are hidden neurons. The outputs of the hidden neurons describe just the essential attributes. The vector of the new attributes gives a new representation of the original data The new representation is formed as encoded information which is described by hidden layer neurons. The number of hidden neurons is considerably lower than the number of the network inputs. Even there is no physical interpretation of essential attributes, but they still keep the most important features of the original data and contains enough information for data mining tasks. In the approach considered we will use Cybenko's theorem (Cybenko [4]) as well as nonlinear principle component analysis and auto-associative neural networks. The fundamental in neural networks Cybenko's theorem concerns a function approximation, while application of nonlinear principle component analysis allows to determine mapping from M-dimensional space to E-dimensional space of components. On the basis of Cybenko's theorem a multi-layer auto-associative neural network can perform an identity mapping, where the network outputs are enforced to equal the network inputs with some accuracy, and in this case the features are represented by outputs of the second hidden layer neurons. Here we will consider the features as essential attributes, and the assumed neural network architecture requires that the number of second hidden layer neurons is considerably smaller than the dimension of data, i.e., $E < M$. Under such assumption, an auto-associative neural network works as a devise for data compression as well as decompression, but here we put our attention to the first functionality of the network - data compression - to obtain the essential attributes, the decompression part is necessary only to adjust neural network's weights to achieve good quality of compression/decompression. This way, we use multilayer feedforward neural networks to reconstruct the input data by the network output. To perform this task efficiently, such neural networks learn interrelationships among the input variables. When the network has been trained, a relatively small number of hidden neurons is sufficient to reconstruct the input values as the network outputs. Therefore, the data are compressed to a form coming with the lower dimensionality. This way the outputs of the second hidden layer neurons constitute the essential attributes and the number of them E must be adjusted, where $E < M$.

The essential attributes obtained by the neural network constitute a set of real values, but the order of elements is meaningless. The essential attributes for all considered data but yet must be generated for a fixed permutation of elements. This way we obtained another representation of the original data and the dimension E of the new representation indicates dimensionality reduction of the data representation, and the data representation is formed by the essential attributes. We can use the essential attributes directly or after some transformation in order to create a new vector of attributes. The main reason to create the new attributes is to express hidden relationships between individual attributes. These new attributes can be formed in various ways, generally it is said that the new attributes are some functions of the original ones (e.g. Wnek and Michalski [25]). The new attributes may be better suited for subsequent data mining than the essential attributes. Generally, there are used functions like maximum value, minimum value, average value, etc. or some arithmetic operators including: +, -, * and integer division, and so on. The new attributes used directly often cause some increasing of dimensionality of a data representation, although quite often only the most important attributes are selected (e.g. Hall and Holmes [9]). Evaluation of attributes can be done using so-called wrappers or filter methods (e.g. Frohlich et al. [7]).

The EAG approach allows a data series of arbitrary length M to be reduced to an arbitrary length K, where $K < M$. These new attributes as data series representation can be applied for solving the data mining problems.

The results of calculations can be found in other works of authors. We consider classification and clustering problems, because they are among of the most common data mining problems. We have made calculations on compressed data in order to determine whether they still kept enough information to their proper classification and clustering. The experiments have shown that even for a significant reduction of dimensionality, the new representation retains information about the data sufficient for classification and clustering of the data (Krawczak and Szkatuła [18]). The EAG approach is described in detail below.

2   Generation of Essential Attributes

We consider the real-valued data series which are described in the following way:

$$[y_1(n), \ldots, y_M(n)] \tag{1}$$

where $y_k(n) \in R, \quad n = 1, \ldots, N, \quad k = 1, \ldots, M.$

Each data describes a point in a M-dimension space of real values. In general, we can expect that there is some redundancy of representation dimensionality (e.g. Guyon et al. [8], Jolliffe [11]) and these superfluities can be removed by application of multilayer feedforward neural networks (e.g. Dreyfus [5]). There are known applications of multilayer feed-forward neural networks as an auto-associative memory, especially in data compression in telecommunication area.

This way, we will use an auto-associative feedforward neural network with five layers, including the input layer. The inputs are described by data of dimensionality M, while the outputs are decompressed inputs of the same dimensionality described as follows

$$[\hat{y}_1(n), \ldots, \hat{y}_M(n)] \tag{2}$$

The objective of this type of neural networks is to generate features, called here the essential attributes, represented by outputs of E neurons of the second hidden layer, under the assumption that $E < M$. The idea of essential attributes obtained from auto-associative neural networks was introduced in earlier papers by Krawczak and Szkatuła related to data mining problems.

The hint of the application of such type of neural networks came from Cybenko's theorem, which states that three layer neural network, with one hidden layer, is an universal approximator, in general a mapping of one space to another. Thus we can use two such neural networks, the first is responsible for a mapping of M inputs $[y_1(n), \ldots, y_M(n)]$, $n = 1, \ldots, N$, into E output variables $[b_1(n), \ldots, b_E(n)]$, $n = 1, \ldots, N$, into variables $[\hat{y}_1(n), \ldots, \hat{y}_M(n)]$.

The first network referred to as *Coder* performs compression and realizes encoding of inputs to E essential attributes, see Fig. 1.

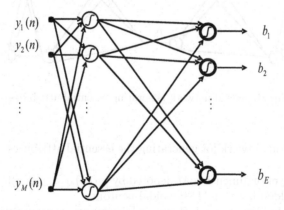

Fig. 1. The first neural network

The second network referred to as *Decoder* assures that the compressed essential attributes are consistent with the inputs with some accuracy as $[\hat{y}_1(n), \ldots, \hat{y}_M(n)]$, see Fig.2.

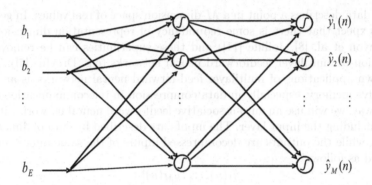

Fig. 2. The second neural network

Coupling of such two neural networks we form the architecture shown in Fig. 3.

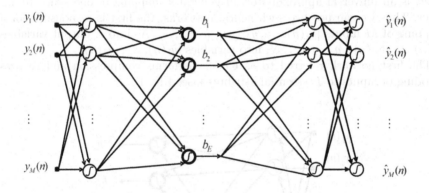

Fig. 3. Neural network generating essential attributes

In all the neural network for generating the essential attributes consists of the following parts:
  – the input layer of dimension M denoted by $[y_1(n), \ldots, y_M(n)]$, $n = 1, \ldots, N$,
  – the first hidden layer of M sigmoidal neurons,
  – the second hidden layer of E sigmoidal neurons, the outputs of this layer neurons generate signals $[b_1(n), \ldots, b_E(n)]$, $n = 1, \ldots, N$. The above described three layers: input layer, first hidden layer and second hidden layer all together form a mapping of M inputs into E essential attributes.
  – the third hidden layer of M sigmoidal neurons,
  – the output layer of M sigmoidal neurons denoted by $[\hat{y}_1(n), \ldots, \hat{y}_M(n)]$, $n = 1, \ldots, N$.

This neural network maps M input variables into M output variables, thus the network maps each input into itself. The entire network is necessary to determine weights of connections between neurons of adjacent layers. The weights are obtained during the training process supported by the backpropagation (with modifications) algorithm (Krawczak [13], [14]). The following formula expresses the mean square error (MSE) learning error generated by the network

$$MSE = \frac{1}{NM} \sum_{n=1}^{N} \sum_{k=1}^{M} (\hat{y}_k(n) - y_k(n))^2 \tag{3}$$

and describes the efficiency of compression and decompression.

Proper selection of value of the number of essential attributes E is of crucial importance because their values have strong influence on quality of new data representations. The problem of choosing the value of E (i.e., number of essential attributes) must be overcome in some experimental way. During the experiment the number of hidden neurons E can be changed, and for each case the network was trained and the learning error was calculated, and the selection must be done in such a way to get a stable as well as the lowest value of the learning error.

This way we formed another representation of the original data, and the value E indicates an additional dimensionality reduction. The essential attributes can be used directly or it is possible to generate a new set of attributes. The new set of attributes is formed through an rearrangements of differences of the essential attributes. Perhaps the simplest way is following, we have the set of the essential attributes $\{b_1(n), \ldots, b_E(n)\}$, $n = 1, \ldots, N$, and we generate $\binom{E}{2}$ combinations without repetitions of differences $b_i(n) - b_j(n)$, $i, j \in \{1, \ldots, E\}$, for $i > j$, $n = 1, \ldots, N$, these combinations give rise to a new set of attributes

$$\{c_j(n)\}_{j=1}^{j=\binom{E}{2}} = \tag{4}$$
$$\{b_2(n) - b_1(n), b_3(n) - b_2(n), b_4(n) - b_3(n), \ldots, b_E(n) - b_{E-1}(n),$$
$$b_3(n) - b_1(n), b_4(n) - b_2(n), \ldots, b_E(n) - b_{E-2}(n),$$
$$b_4(n) - b_1(n), \ldots, b_E(n) - b_{E-3}(n),$$
$$\ldots$$
$$b_E(n) - b_1(n)\}$$

for $n = 1, \ldots, N$.

The set of the attributes $\{c_j(n)\}_{j=1}^{j=K}$ for $n = 1, \ldots, N$, where $K = \binom{E}{2}$ constitutes the new representation of the data, where K denotes the final number of the new attributes.

The new attributes can be arranged in a vector form, i.e., one chosen permutation of them must be taken for all investigated data, $[c_j(n)]_{j=1}^{j=K}$.

Here we use the following measures of compression and decompression quality. The most general term for compression measure is compression ratio defined as follows (Guyon et al. [8])

$$Compression\ Ratio = Cr = \frac{Compressed\ Size}{Uncompressed\ Size} \tag{5}$$

In the case of the new attributes the compression ratio is following

$$Cr_{ess.attribute} = \frac{1}{M}\binom{E}{2} = \frac{1}{M}\frac{E!}{2!(E-2)!} = \frac{(E-1)E}{2M} \qquad (6)$$

The obtained new representation of the data series (1) can be characterized, according to (6), by compression ratio $Cr_{ess.attribute}$.

It seems that such reduction of dimensionality is of restrictive interest as well as applications and therefore the next step of dimensionality reduction should be taken. Namely, it is worth to consider replacing the real values of the attributes by nominal values and next to treat each time series as a string of symbols.

Converting numeric data into sequential symbolic data relies on dividing the real-valued range of attributes into a number of intervals and assigning nominal symbols to each interval. In literature (cf. Maimon and Rokach [21]) one can distinguished some methodologies for discretization, for example: *the division of equal width intervals* and *the equal frequency intervals method, the discretization based on statistical tests, the entropy based discretization* and *the methods with applying the dynamic programming.* The methodologies are of heuristic type for data discretization, and according to reported experiments none of them is significantly better than others, and the choice of methodology used much depends on data and problem considered therefore it is difficult to claim what approach is better or more universal.

In our approach to dimensionality reduction there is no physical interpretation of the attributes, and they are arranged as a set of real numbers, and tacit relationships between attributes are very important.

The assumed common range of the all attributes is divided into some subranges and therefore the division is the same for each attribute and each nominal value has the same interpretation for each attribute. One of the possible methodology to use is so called *equal width interval discretization.* This way real values of the new attributes are replaced by nominal values.

In the process of discretization of the attributes the ranges of all attributes values are subdivided into fixed number of partitions. The methodology called equal width interval discretization relies on determination of the domain of attributes values and dividing the interval into equal subintervals. Considering all attributes values, $\{c_j(n)\}_{j=1}^{j=K}$ for $n = 1,\ldots,N$, where $K = \binom{E}{2}$, let us divide each interval into equal subintervals. Now let us consider the set $V := V_{c_1} \cup V_{c_2} \cup \ldots \cup V_{c_K}$, where each set $V_{c_j} = \{v_{j,1}, v_{j,2}, \ldots, v_{j,L_j},\}$ describes the domain of the proper attribute c_j, and L_j denotes the number of subintervals for the j-th attribute, $j = 1,\ldots,K$. The subinterval boundaries, i.e., cut points, can be constructed in the following way for each attribute:

$$p_0 = min\{v : v \in V\},$$
$$p_l = p_0 + l \cdot \partial, \quad l = 1,\ldots,P-1 \qquad (7)$$
$$p_P = max\{v : v \in V\},$$

where $\partial = \frac{max\{v:\ v\in V\}\ -\ min\{v:\ v\in V\}}{P}$ while $P \in N$ is a predefined parameter.

The attributes $\{c_j(n)\}_{j=1}^{j=K}$ now represented by nominal values can be denoted as $\{a_j(n)\}_{j=1}^{j=K}$ for $n = 1,\ldots,N$, where $K \ll M$. The procedure described above drives to describing a new symbolic representation of data series and is characterized by a vector of attributes whose values are nominal.

Thus we obtain a vector of K nominal-valued attributes representing the original data series (1) and the new representation preserve important properties for the original data series mining problems, i.e., classification or clustering.

3   Conclusions

In this paper we described a new approach to reduce dimensionality of data series referred to as Essential Attributes Generation (EAG) approach. The approach is based on the Cybenko's theorem well known in neural networks society as well as the idea of principal components. The principal components are generated by the outputs of the second hidden layer of the designed neural network.

In the paper Krawczak and Szkatuła [18], we introduced the extension of the EAG approach (i.e., SEAA approach) to reduce dimensions of data series to symbolic representation. The essence of the methodology is highlighted in Fig.4.

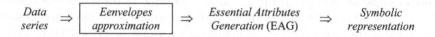

Fig. 4. The approach scheme of SEAA

The approach allows a data series of arbitrary length M to be reduced to an arbitrary length K, where $K \ll M$. For symbolic representation of data series, we use the alphabet of finite size $R>3$. The concept is based on the upper and lower envelopes [15], and on essential attributes of the envelopes (EAG). In this case we obtain a vector of nominal-valued attributes representing the original data series and preserving properties which are important for the original data series mining problems. It must be emphasized that the data series is understood as real-valued time series or pseudo-time series, while SEAA generates a vector of nominal-valued attributes.

It is obvious that our approach together with changing of real-valued essential attributes into nominal-valued essential attributes constitutes interesting methodology for preprocessing of time series. The methodology can be compared to Symbolic Aggregate Approximation (SAX) (cf. Lin et al. [19]), it seems the most competitive method in the literature for dimensionality reduction of time series with introduced symbolic representation. In general, the SAX method consists of two main parts, in the first part a time series is approximated by Piecewise Aggregate Approximation based on piecewise constant approximation, while in the second part such time series representation is converted into a sequence of symbols.

Our methodology differs considerably from other methods known in the literature; however it is possible to find partial similarities to SAX method.

We verify the quality of dimensionality reduction practically by analysis of particular data mining tasks. We proposed an approach which first creates a symbolic representation of times series using the SEAA approach. Then, using the attributes with nominal values as data series representation verification of the approach was applied for solving two data series mining problems, namely classification and clustering. We consider classification and clustering problem, because they are among of the most common data mining problems. Calculations were performed to verify whether the proposed approach of dimensionality reduction still retains important features of the original data series, which allow to correctly classify or cluster data series.

Practical presentation of the approach was carried out for the database available at the Irvine University of California (Krawczak and Szkatuła [18]). Verification of efficiency of the proposed procedure was performed via solving two data series mining problems, namely classification and clustering. Calculations were made on compressed data in order to determine whether they still kept enough information to their proper classification and clustering. Numerical experiments show that a large dimensionality reduction (causing also an information reduction) generates the new data representation, which preserves information about the data characteristics particularly well (Krawczak and Szkatuła [16], [17], [18]).

For example we considered *the learning data* series of three different classes (25 time series of each 60 values). In Fig. 5 there are depictured all 75 normalized time series. Additionally we also considered *the testing data* series (25 time series of each class) and each data series has 60 values. The goal was to reduce the dimensionality of the considered data series and next to create nominal-valued representation of the original time series.

For designing the required neural network a freely available neural network simulator JNNS was applied. During the experiment the number of hidden neurons was changed and for each case the network was trained and the learning error was calculated. In order to adjust weights we used the backpropagation

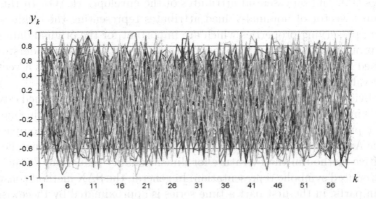

Fig. 5. The learning data series $\{y_k(n)\}_{k=1}^{k=60}$ for $n = 1, \ldots, 75$, belong to three classes

with momentum algorithm, and required parameters were selected experimentally. In result the number of neurons of the hidden layer was chosen as 5, it means that five essential attributes were enough to conserve the information about the data series character. Next the real-valued essential attributes were replaced by nominal values of the following alphabet $a, b, c, d, e, f, g, h, i, j$. After some transformation the generated nominal essential attributes looked like those shown in Fig. 6.

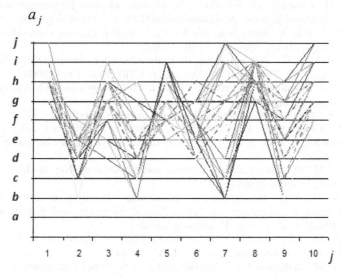

Fig. 6. The nominal attributes $\{a_j(n)\}_{j=1}^{j=10}$, $n = 1, \ldots, 75$, for the upper envelopes

In the case of classification problems efficiency was 100% for learning data and above 98.7% for testing data. Results of classification obtained by using our approach gave slightly better accuracy than by other specialized algorithms as well as by SAX dimensionality reduction methodology. In the case of clustering our approach gave 100% accuracy, but they cannot be compared to other algorithms because there is lack of reported efficiency results.

It must be noted that described in this paper dimensionality reduction methodology of data series was not developed for specified data series, and experimental results of classification and clustering allow us to claim that the approach is at least not worse than those reported in the literature. Up to our experience the methodology can be elaborated in the future.

References

1. Astrom, K.J.: On the choice of sampling rates in parametric identification of time series. Information Sciences 1(3), 273–278 (1969)
2. Azzouzi, M., Nabney, I.T.: Analyzing time series structure with Hidden Markov Models. In: Proceedings of the IEEE Conference on Neural Networks and Signal Processing, pp. 402–408 (1998)

3. Chan, K.P., Fu, A.C.: Efficient time series matching by wavelets. In: Proceedings of the 15th IEEE International Conference on Data Engineering, pp. 126–133 (1999)
4. Cybenko, G.: Approximations by superpositions of sigmoidal functions. Mathematics of Control, Signals, and Systems 2(4), 303–314 (1989)
5. Dreyfus, G.: Neural Networks Methodology and Applications. Springer, Berlin (2005)
6. Faloutsos, C., Ranganathan, M., Manolopulos, Y.: Fast subsequence matching in time-series databases. SIGMOD Record 23, 519–529 (1994)
7. Frohlich, H., Chapelle, O., Scholkopf, B.: Feature selection for support vector machines by means of genetic algorithms. In: ICTAI, pp. 142–148 (2003)
8. Guyon, I., Gunn, S., Nikravesh, M., Zadeh, L. (eds.): Feature extraction foundations and applications. Springer, Berlin (2005)
9. Hall, M., Holmes, G.: Benchmarking attribute selection techniques for discrete class data mining. IEEE Trans. Knowl. Data Eng. 15(6), 1437–1447 (2003)
10. Inselberg, A.: Parallel Coordinates: VISUAL Multidimensional Geometry and its Applications. Springer (2009)
11. Jolliffe, I.T.: Principal Component Analysis. Springer, Berlin (2002)
12. Keogh, E., Chakrabarti, K., Pazzani, M., Mehrotra, S.: Dimensionality reduction for fast similarity search in large time series databases. J. Knowl. Inform. Syst. 3(3), 263–286 (2000)
13. Krawczak, M.: Multilayer Neural Systems and Generalized Net Models. Ac. Publ. House EXIT, Warsaw (2003a)
14. Krawczak, M.: Heuristic dynamic programming - Learning as control problem. In: Rutkowski, L., Kacprzyk, J. (eds.) Neural Networks and Soft Computing, pp. 218–223. Physica Verlag, Heidelberg (2003b)
15. Krawczak, M., Szkatuła, G.: Time series envelopes for classification. In: IEEE Intelligent Systems Conference, London, July 7-9 (2010)
16. Krawczak, M., Szkatuła, G.: A hybrid approach for dimension reduction in classification. Control and Cybernetics 40(2), 527–552 (2011)
17. Krawczak, M., Szkatuła, G.: Nominal Time Series Representation for the Clustering Problem. In: IEEE 6th International Conference, Intelligent Systems, Sofia, pp. 182–187 (2012)
18. Krawczak, M., Szkatuła, G.: An approach to dimensionality reduction in time series. Information Sciences 260, 15–36 (2014)
19. Lin, J., Keogh, E., Wei, L., Lonardi, S.: Experiencing SAX: a novel symbolic representation of time series. Journal Data Mining and Knowledge Discovery 15(2), 107–144 (2007)
20. Lee, S., Kwon, D., Lee, S.: Dimensionality reduction for indexing time series based on the minimum distance. Journal of Inform. Science and Engineering 19, 697–711 (2003)
21. Maimon, O., Rokach, L. (eds.): Data mining and knowledge discovery handbook. Springer (2010)
22. Fu, T.-C.: A review on time series data mining. Engineering Applications of Artificial Intelligence 24, 164–181 (2011)
23. Yang, K., Shahabi, C.: On the stationarity of multivariate time series for correlation-based data analysis. In: Proceedings of the Fifth IEEE International Conference on Data Mining, pp. 805–808 (2005)
24. Yi, B.K., Faloutsos, C.: Fast time sequence indexing for arbitrary norms. In: Proceedings of International Conference on Very Large Data Bases, Cairo, Egypt (2000)
25. Wnek, J., Michalski, R.S.: Hypothesis-driven Constructive Induction in AQ17-HCI: A Method and Experiments. Machine Learning 14, 139–168 (1994)

Visualizing Random Forest
with Self-Organising Map

Piotr Płoński and Krzysztof Zaremba

Institute of Radioelectronics, Warsaw University of Technology,
Nowowiejska 15/19,00-665 Warsaw, Poland,
{pplonski,zaremba}@ire.pw.edu.pl

Abstract. Random Forest (RF) is a powerful ensemble method for classification and regression tasks. It consists of decision trees set. Although, a single tree is well interpretable for human, the ensemble of trees is a black-box model. The popular technique to look inside the RF model is to visualize a RF proximity matrix obtained on data samples with Multidimensional Scaling (MDS) method. Herein, we present a novel method based on Self-Organising Maps (SOM) for revealing intrinsic relationships in data that lay inside the RF used for classification tasks. We propose an algorithm to learn the SOM with the proximity matrix obtained from the RF. The visualization of RF proximity matrix with MDS and SOM is compared. What is more, the SOM learned with the RF proximity matrix has better classification accuracy in comparison to SOM learned with Euclidean distance. Presented approach enables better understanding of the RF and additionally improves accuracy of the SOM.

Keywords: Random Forest, Self-Organising Maps, visualization, classification, proximity matrix.

1 Introduction

Nowadays, there is a need for efficient data mining techniques. The human readability of the model is an important factor of a good data mining algorithm. Among various data mining methods very popular are decision trees [20], [3]. Although, they have an easy interpretable model, a single tree does not always obtain the highest accuracy. To overcome this problem, various ensemble methods were proposed. Among them, the popular is Random Forest (RF) proposed by Leo Breiman [2]. The RF builds a set of trees using bagging and random subspace methods. The final output is a mode of responses from all individual trees. The RF can be used for classification and regression tasks. Despite the high accuracy of the RF, the human readability of the model is lost. There exist some methods to look inside RF black-box, like: examining variable importance [4], parallel cooridinate plots by variable [2] or visualizing the RF proximity distance matrix with Multidimensional Scaling [6]. Herein, we propose a novel method for visualizing the RF proximity matrix based on Self-Organising Maps (SOM)

L. Rutkowski et al. (Eds.): ICAISC 2014, Part II, LNAI 8468, pp. 63–71, 2014.

[8]. The SOM is an artificial neural network model that maps high-dimensional input data space onto usually two-dimensional lattice of neurons in an unsupervised way. Although, the SOM is an originally unsupervised algorithm there exist supervised extensions [9], [14], [13], [7]. The SOM has been proved as an efficient data mining tool in many real life applications [11], [12], [18], [19]. In this paper, we focus on using the labeled SOM model for mapping the RF used in classification tasks. The RF proximity matrix will be used for the SOM learning. It was shown that using more sophisticated distance metric than Euclidean can improve the accuracy of the SOM [15]. The RF proximity matrix was used earlier for improving clustering accuracy. Horvath et al. [16] presented method for building clusters from the RF learned with unlabeled data and successfully used it for tumor detection [17]. Moosmann et al. [10] used the RF for efficient segmentation of images, where leaves were assigned to distinct image regions rather than to specific class. Gray et al. [5] used the RF proximity matrix and the MDS for classification of medical images of different types of dementia. The paper is organized as follow: firstly, we describe the SOM and the RF algorithms; secondly, proposed approach for learning the SOM with the RF proximity matrix is presented; then, the MDS vs the SOM visualization and the accuracy of the SOM learned with Euclidean metric and the RF proximity matrix are compared.

2   Methods

Let's denote data set as $D = \{(\boldsymbol{x_i}, c_i)\}$, where $\boldsymbol{x_i}$ is an attribute vector, $\boldsymbol{x} \in \mathcal{R}^M$, M is attribute vector length and c_i is a discrete class number of i-th sample, $i = [1, 2, ..., N]$ and $c = [1, 2, ..., C]$.

2.1   Self Organising Maps

In this paper, we used the SOM as a two-dimensional grid of neurons. Each neuron is represented by a weights vector W_{pq}, where (p, q) are indices of the neuron in the grid. It is important to notice, that neuron's weights vector has the same length as sample's attribute vector in the data set. The neuron's weights directly corresponds to attributes in the data set. In the training phase, for each sample we search for a neuron which is the closest to the i-th sample. In the original SOM algorithm the distance is computed with squared Euclidean distance by following equation:

$$Dist_{train}(D_i, W_{pq}) = (\boldsymbol{x_i} - W_{pq})^T (\boldsymbol{x_i} - W_{pq}). \qquad (1)$$

The neuron (p, q) with the smallest distance to i-th sample is so-called the Best Matching Unit (BMU), and we note its indicies as (r, v). Once the BMU is found, the weights update step is executed. The weights of each neuron are updated with formula:

$$W_{pq}(t + 1) = W_{pq}(t) + \eta h_{pq}^{(i)}(\boldsymbol{x_i} - W_{pq}(t)), \qquad (2)$$

where t is an iteration number and η is a learning coefficient and $h_{pq}^{(i)}$ is a neigh-bourhood function. We assume that one iteration is a presentation of one train-ing sample, whereas a presentation of all training samples is one learning epoch. The learning coefficient η is decreased between consecutive epochs to improve network's ability to remember patterns. It is described by:

$$\eta = \eta_0 exp(-e\lambda_\eta), \tag{3}$$

where η_0 is the initial step size, e is the current epoch number and λ_η is re-sponsible for regulating the speed of the decrease. The neighbourhood function controls changing of weights with respect to the distance to the BMU in the grid. It is noted as:

$$h_{pq}^{(i)} = exp(-\alpha((r - p)^2 + (v - q)^2)), \tag{4}$$

where α describes the neighbourhood function width. This parameter is increas-ing during learning $\alpha = \alpha_0 exp(-(e_{stop} - e)\lambda_\alpha)$ - it assures that neighbourhood becomes narrower during the training. The network is trained till chosen number of learning procedure epochs e_{stop} is exceeded.

In the described algorithm the class label information is not used. The sim-plest approach of using the SOM as a classifier is to label the neurons after the unsupervised training. For each neuron we remember the overal sum of neigh-bourhood values $h_{pq}^{(i)}$ from each class over all samples. The label of major class is assigned to the neuron. In the testing phase, the input sample's class is des-ignated based on the class of the found BMU.

2.2   Random Forest

In the RF algorithm a set of single trees is built. The process of constructing one tree can be described in the following steps:

1. Draw a bootstrap data set D' by choosing n times with replacement from all N training samples.
2. Determine a decision at node using only m attributes, where m is smaller than M. The split is selected based on maximal Information Gain.
3. Move the data through the node with respect to decision from the step 2.
4. Repeat steps 2, 3 till full tree is grown.

At the end of tree constructing, the class label is assigned to each leaf based on a class of samples in it. In the testing phase, a new sample is pushed down through all trees. From each tree a class label is remembered based on class of the reached leaf. The final response is the mode of votes from all trees. The proximity matrix $Prox$, with size NxN, can be easily obtained by putting all samples down the all trees. If two samples i and j are in the same terminal node in the tree, their proximity is increased by one $Prox(i,j) = Prox(i,j) + 1$. After the presentation of all samples the proximities are divided by the number of trees in the RF. The greater proximity value is, the more similar samples are. The dissimilarity measure can be formulated as $Dis(i,j) = 1 - Prox(i,j)$.

2.3 Self Organising Maps Learned with Random Forest (RF-SOM)

In the proposed approach we assume that the RF is already learned. The learning of the network in one epoch can be summarized in the following steps:

1. Build a data set H as a union of all network's weights W and attribute vector x_j of j-th sample, $H = W \cup x_j$. The matrix W size is LxM, where the L is a total number of neurons in the network. In this matrix each row contains weights from one neuron, the mapping from neurons's 2D grid to matrix W is assumed.
2. For set H compute dissimilarity matrix Dis_H using the RF. The Dis_H size is $(L + 1)x(L + 1)$.
3. Find the smallest distance to the neurons in dissimilarity matrix Dis_H, in distances corresponding to j-th sample:

$$v = \arg\min_h Dis_H(j, h), h \neq j, \qquad (5)$$

where v is an index of BMU in the matrix W, which can be mapped into r, v indices in the network 2D grid.

4. Update the network weigths with formula 2.
5. Repeat steps 1-4 for all samples in the training set.

After the end of the SOM learning, it is labeled as described in Section 2.1. In the testing phase, for input sample the BMU search is performed by taking the steps 1-3. The output class label is the same as the BMU class. We will denote the proposed method as RF-SOM. The computational complexity of using the Euclidean distance in the SOM is $\mathcal{O}(N*L)$, because we need to compute for each sample, from N samples, a distance between sample and L neurons. Whereas, the using of the RF proximity matrix in the proposed RF-SOM has complexity $\mathcal{O}(N*L*T*log_2(tree_{size}))$[1], where $tree_{size}$ is a number of nodes in the tree. In the RF-SOM for each sample we propagate $L + 1$ input vectors through T trees in the RF, and passage through a tree has complexity $\mathcal{O}(log_2(tree_{size}))$. The complexity of distance computation using the RF proximity matrix is worse than using Euclidean distance. Although, it is beneficial when compared to the memory complexity of the MDS used for RF proximity visualization, which uses $\mathcal{O}(N^2)$ memory. The RF-SOM requires only $\mathcal{O}(L^2)$. This discards the MDS as a method of the RF proximity matrix visualization for large data sets.

3 Results

We used 6 real data sets to examine properties of the RF-SOM. There were used data sets: 'Glass', 'Wine', 'Iris', 'Sonar', 'Ionosphere', 'Pima' from the 'UCI Machine Learning Repository' [1]. In the Table 1 are presented data sets properties. In all experiments we used following parameters values for each SOM type:

---

[1] We omit cost of constructing the RF in the complexity assessment.

$e_{stop} = 200$, $\eta_0 = 0.1$, $\lambda_\eta = 0.0345$, $\alpha_0 = 0.1$, $\lambda_\alpha = 0.008$. We will denote a network learned with Eculidean distance as SOM. The network sizes for the SOM and the RF-SOM for each data set are equal, they are presented in the Table 1. The network sizes were chosen arbitrarily because selecting optimal network size is not in the scope of this paper. In all cases the SOM and the RF-SOM starts learning from the same initial weights values. The RF was constructed with 100 trees and $m = \sqrt{M}$ for all data sets.

Table 1. The description of data sets used in experiments and network size used for each data set

	Samples	Attributes	Classes	Network size
Glass	214	9	6	7x7
Wine	178	13	3	4x4
Iris	150	4	3	5x5
Sonar	208	60	2	8x8
Ionosphere	351	34	2	8x8
Pima	768	8	2	7x7

To present visulization properties of the proposed method we used 'Pima' data set. In the Fig.1 there are presented: the SOM (Fig.1a) and the MDS (Fig.1c) both learned with Euclidean distance; and RF-SOM (Fig.1b) and RF-MDS (Fig.1d) constructed using the RF proximity matrix. The SOM networks were presented as a 2D grid of neurons, where for each neuron, its weigths are presented by a polar area diagram (sometimes called coxcomb plot). In the MDS and the RF-MDS plots information about points distribution in reduced 2D space is available. However, information about how point's position is affected by combination of attributes values is missing. What is more, there is hard to find crisp border to distinguish two classes on the MDS neither on the RF-MDS. In contrary to MDS technique, the SOM and RF-SOM plots do not provide information about explicit point distribution but rather a mapping of attributes combination onto 2D grid of neurons. After network labeling the class labels are assigned to neurons, therefore distinguishing specific combination of attributes in each class is possible. As expected, although, the SOM and the RF-SOM started learning from the same initial weights values they have different final distribution of attributes combinations across the network.

To compare the accuracy of the SOM learned with Euclidean distance and RF-SOM learned with RF proximity matrix we use information about samples class label. We measure the accuracy of classification. The results of comparison are presented in the Table 2. All of the results are mean over 10-fold cross validation. In the Table 2 we also include the accuracy of the alone RF as the reference. The RF-SOM on 4 data sets ('Glass', 'Sonar', 'Ionosphere', 'Pima') obtained better results than the SOM. The greatest improvement over the SOM was achived on 'Sonar' set, it was 12.57%. The same performance of the SOM

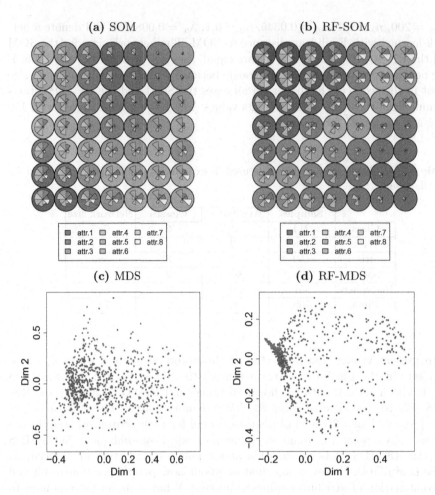

Fig. 1. The visualizations of 'Pima' data set with (a) the SOM, (b) the RF-SOM, (c) the MDS with Euclidean distance, (d) the RF-MDS. The class information is coded in red color for the first class and blue color for the second class in all plots. In the (a) and (b) for polar area diagram the attribute's number corresponding to the neuron's weight is shown in the legend.

and the RF-SOM was on 'Wine' and 'Iris', when on the latter the RF-SOM has higher standard deviation value. It is worth noting, that the improvement of the RF-SOM over the SOM depends on the accuracy of the RF. On data sets (like 'Sonar' or 'Glass') where the accuracy difference between the RF and the SOM is high, the RF-SOM noted large improvement over the SOM. Whereas, on data sets ('Wine' and 'Iris') with small accuracy difference between the RF and the SOM, the RF-SOM obtained the same mean accuracy as the SOM.

We measure classfication accuracy for different number of trees in the RF to examine the influence of a number of trees in the RF to performance of the

Table 2. The classification accuracy for RF, SOM and RF-SOM. The results are mean and std. over 10-fold cross validation.

	Glass	Wine	Iris	Sonar	Ionosphere	Pima
RF	77.96±7.82	98.85±2.29	95.33±6.70	85.05±4.74	93.44±2.88	76.14±7.09
SOM	61.73±6.18	96.60±3.73	94.67±4.00	67.69±8.97	84.33±6.43	71.73±5.16
RF-SOM	67.27±6.04	96.60±3.73	94.67±5.81	80.26±5.17	89.72±6.42	74.71±6.80

RF-SOM. The accuracy for the RF and the RF-SOM for a number of trees in the RF, $T = \{10, 20, 50, 100, 200, 500\}$, is presented in Fig.2. It can be observed that for all data sets except 'Sonar' and 'Glass' the accuracy of the RF does not depend on T. The good results of classification are obtained even for 10 trees in the RF. For 'Sonar' and 'Glass' sets the accuracy of the RF increases with increasing a number of trees. The very similar behaviour can be observed for the RF-SOM. The accuracy for 'Wine', 'Iris', 'Ionosphere' and 'Pima' slightly varies with T growing. However, for 'Sonar' and 'Glass' sets the RF-SOM obtains better results if more trees are used in the RF. The observed behaviour can be explained by more complex data relationships in 'Sonar' and 'Glass' sets which are better modeled with greater number of trees in the RF.

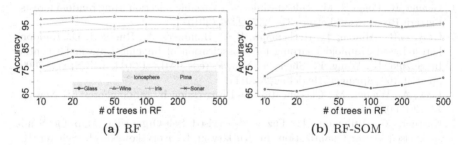

(a) RF   (b) RF-SOM

Fig. 2. The classification accuracy for (a) RF and (b) RF-SOM, for a different number of trees in the RF. The result are mean over 10-fold cross validation.

4   Conclusions

The novel method for visualizing the RF proximity matrix by the SOM was proposed. The RF-SOM method uses the RF to compute distances between input sample and neurons. The proposed method of visualization provide better understanding of relationship between data in the RF structure than the MDS. The RF-SOM contrary to the MDS provides a mapping of data onto 2D neurons grid. In case of new coming samples there is no need to recompute the whole RF proximity matrix like in the MDS method. Additionally, the proposed method has lower memory complexity than the MDS, which for large data sets is not applicable. What is more, the experimental results show that the RF-SOM learned with the RF dissimilarity gained better or the same accuracy than the SOM learned with Euclidean distance. As pointed in [16] the RF dissimilarity has attractive features: it can handle mixed variable types well, is invariant to monotonic transformations of the input variables and is robust to outliers. The attractiveness of RF dissimilarity and obtained results with RF-SOM encourage to focus our future work on using the RF proximity matrix in other clustering algorithms.

Acknowledgements. PP has been supported by the European Union in the framework of European Social Fund through the Warsaw University of Technology Development Programme.

References

1. Asuncion, A., Newman, D.J.: UCI machine learning repository. University of California, Irvine, School of Information and Computer Sciences (2007)
2. Breiman, L.: Random Forests. Machine Learning 45, 5–32 (2001)
3. Czajkowski, M., Grześ, M., Kretowski, M.: Multi-Test Decision Trees for Gene Expression Data Analysis. In: Bouvry, P., Kłopotek, M.A., Leprévost, F., Marciniak, M., Mykowiecka, A., Rybiński, H. (eds.) SIIS 2011. LNCS, vol. 7053, pp. 154–167. Springer, Heidelberg (2012)
4. Genuer, R., Poggi, J.-M., Tuleau-Malot, C.: Variable selection using random forests. Pattern Recognition Letters 31, 2225–2236 (2010)
5. Gray, K.R., Aljabar, P., Heckemann, R.A., Hammers, A., Rueckert, D.: Random Forest-Based Manifold Learning for Classification of Imaging Data in Dementia. In: Suzuki, K., Wang, F., Shen, D., Yan, P. (eds.) MLMI 2011. LNCS, vol. 7009, pp. 159–166. Springer, Heidelberg (2011)
6. Liaw, A., Wiener, M.: Classification and Regression by randomForest. R News 2, 18–22 (2002)
7. Kästner, M., Villmann, T.: Fuzzy Supervised Self-Organizing Map for Semi-supervised Vector Quantization. In: Rutkowski, L., Korytkowski, M., Scherer, R., Tadeusiewicz, R., Zadeh, L.A., Zurada, J.M. (eds.) ICAISC 2012, Part I. LNCS, vol. 7267, pp. 256–265. Springer, Heidelberg (2012)
8. Kohonen, T.: The Self-Organizing Map. Proceedings of the IEEE 78, 1464–1480 (1990)
9. Midenet, S., Grumbach, A.: Learning Associations by Self-Organization: The LASSO model. Neurocomputing 6, 343–361 (1994)
10. Moosmann, F., Nowak, E., Jurie, F.: Randomized Clustering Forests for Image Classification. IEEE Transactions on Pattern Analysis and Machine Intelligence 30, 1632–1646 (2008)
11. Olszewski, D., Kacprzyk, J., Zadrożny, S.: Employing Self-Organizing Map for Fraud Detection. In: Rutkowski, L., Korytkowski, M., Scherer, R., Tadeusiewicz, R., Zadeh, L.A., Zurada, J.M. (eds.) ICAISC 2013, Part I. LNCS, vol. 7894, pp. 150–161. Springer, Heidelberg (2013)
12. Olszewski, D.: An Experimental Study on Asymmetric Self-Organizing Map. In: Yin, H., Wang, W., Rayward-Smith, V. (eds.) IDEAL 2011. LNCS, vol. 6936, pp. 42–49. Springer, Heidelberg (2011)

13. Osowski, S., Linh, T.H.: Fuzzy Clustering Neural Network for Classification of ECG Beats. In: International Joint Conference on Neural Networks, pp. 26–32 (2000)
14. Płoński, P., Zaremba, K.: Self-Organising Maps for Classification with Metropolis-Hastings Algorithm for Supervision. In: Huang, T., Zeng, Z., Li, C., Leung, C.S. (eds.) ICONIP 2012, Part III. LNCS, vol. 7665, pp. 149–156. Springer, Heidelberg (2012)
15. Płoński, P., Zaremba, K.: Improving Performance of Self-Organising Maps with Distance Metric Learning Method. In: Rutkowski, L., Korytkowski, M., Scherer, R., Tadeusiewicz, R., Zadeh, L.A., Zurada, J.M. (eds.) ICAISC 2012, Part I. LNCS, vol. 7267, pp. 169–177. Springer, Heidelberg (2012)
16. Shi, T., Horvath, S.: Unsupervised Learning with Random Forest Predictors. Journal of Computational and Graphical Statistics 15, 118–138 (2006)
17. Shi, T., Seligson, D., Belldegrun, A.S., Palotie, A., Horvath, S.: Tumor classification by tissue microarray profiling: random forest clustering applied to renal cell carcinoma. Modern Pathology 18, 547–557 (2005)
18. Szymański, J., Duch, W.: Self Organizing Maps for Visualization of Categories. In: Huang, T., Zeng, Z., Li, C., Leung, C.S. (eds.) ICONIP 2012, Part I. LNCS, vol. 7663, pp. 160–167. Springer, Heidelberg (2012)
19. Szymański, J.: Self–Organizing Map Representation for Clustering Wikipedia Search Results. In: Nguyen, N.T., Kim, C.-G., Janiak, A. (eds.) ACIIDS 2011, Part II. LNCS, vol. 6592, pp. 140–149. Springer, Heidelberg (2011)
20. Quinlan, J.R.: C4.5: Programs for Machine Learning. Morgan Kaufmann Publishers (1993)

B-Spline Smoothing of Feature Vectors in Nonnegative Matrix Factorization

Rafał Zdunek[1], Andrzej Cichocki[2,3,4], and Tatsuya Yokota[2]

[1] Department of Electronics, Wroclaw University of Technology,
Wybrzeze Wyspianskiego 27, 50-370 Wroclaw, Poland
rafal.zdunek@pwr.wroc.pl
[2] Laboratory for Advanced Brain Signal Processing
RIKEN BSI, Wako-shi, Japan
[3] Warsaw University of Technology, Poland
[4] Systems Research Institute, Polish Academy of Science (PAN), Poland

Abstract. Nonnegative Matrix Factorization (NMF) captures nonnegative, sparse and parts-based feature vectors from the set of observed nonnegative vectors. In many applications, the features are also expected to be locally smooth. To incorporate the information on the local smoothness to the optimization process, we assume that the features vectors are conical combinations of higher degree B-splines with a given number of knots. Due to this approach the computational complexity of the optimization process does not increase considerably with respect to the standard NMF model. The numerical experiments, which were carried out for the blind spectral unmixing problem, demonstrate the robustness of the proposed method.

Keywords: NMF, B-Splines, Feature Extraction, Spectral Unmixing.

1 Introduction

Nonnegative Matrix Factorization (NMF) [1,2] is a key tool for feature extraction and dimensionality reduction of nonnegative data. However, in many practical scenarios the feature extracted with NMF may not have easy interpretation or meaning due to various ambiguities that are intrinsically related with the assumed model of factorization. The extensive analysis of non-uniqueness issues in NMF can be found in [3]. To relieve these problems, the prior knowledge on the factors to be estimated is usually imposed. Commonly used priors assume the sparsity that is typically incorporated to the factor updating process by l_1-norm-based penalty or regularization terms.

Pascuala-Montano *et al.* [4] reported that sparsity and smoothness constraints are closely related in NMF applications. Typically, when one of the factors is sparse, the other tends to be locally smooth. It is also well-known that the smoothness of a signal in the time domain involves its sparseness in the frequency domain, and vise versa. Hence, the smoothness constraints are also important

L. Rutkowski et al. (Eds.): ICAISC 2014, Part II, LNAI 8468, pp. 72–81, 2014.

and might considerably relax the factor ambiguity problems, if some estimated factors are expected to be locally smooth.

The smoothness constraints are motivated by many practical applications of NMF. For example, the temporal as well as frequency profiles extracted from the magnitude spectrograms of speech or audio signals are locally smooth [5–7]. The similar smoothness behavior is also observed in the parts-based features extracted from a set of facial images. In a supervised classification performed with NMF, the encoding vectors obtained from the training vectors that belong to one class may also demonstrate the local smoothness property. Smooth signals may also be found in spectral unmixing problems, e.g. in hyperspectral imaging or Raman spectroscopy [8–13]. Depending on the observed data, the smoothness may take place in spectral signatures (endmembers) or in abundance maps. These applications motivate the proposed method.

Smoothness constraints can be imposed on the estimated factors in many ways. It is well-known that the Gaussian priors lead to smooth estimates. This issue has been widely discussed in the literature (see e.g. [9, 14]). The smoothness can be also enforced in the similar way by applying the Markov Random Field (MRF) models [7]. These models are usually more robust to the overfitting phenomena than the Gaussian ones but they are more difficult to tackle numerically. In all these approaches, if the factor updating process is performed with gradient descent algorithms, the hyperparameters associated with the priors are difficult to be estimated.

Another approach to the smoothness is to assume that the feature vectors in NMF can be expressed by a linear combination of some basis functions that are locally smooth, bounded and nonnegative in the whole domain. This model was proposed in [15], where the basis functions are determined by the Gaussian Radial Basis Functions (GRBF). Next, Yokota et al. [16] improved this model in terms of computational complexity and extended it to work efficiently with 2D features and with multi-linear array decomposition models.

Motivated by the efficiency of a family of the GRBF-NMF algorithms, we extend the concept of approximating the feature vectors in NMF to a more general and sophisticated case where the basis functions are expressed by piecewise smooth nonnegative B-spline functions. This idea is partially motivated by the piecewise smoothness constraints proposed in [11] but our method does not use the MRF model to enforce the smoothness. The B-splines are piecewise polynomials that are widely used in many applications such as curve fitting, interpolation, approximation techniques [17]. The use of B-splines gives us more possibilities for model adaptation and regularization with the Total Variation (TV) term. The degree of the splines and the knots can be easily adapted. The coefficients of the linear combinations of the B-splines can be also readily estimated since the basis matrix reveals a block structure. In this paper, we also proposed the multiplicative algorithm for estimating the coefficients, assuming any feature vector is a superposition of the B-splines.

The paper is organized as follows: Section 2 discusses the application of B-splines to approximate the feature vectors in NMF. The optimization algorithm for estimating the underlying factors is presented in Section 3. The experiments carried out for the linear spectral unmixing problem are described in Section 4. Finally, the conclusions are drawn in Section 5.

2   Model

The aim of NMF is to find such lower-rank nonnegative matrices $A = [a_{ij}] \in \mathbb{R}_+^{I \times J}$ and $X = [x_{jt}] \in \mathbb{R}_+^{J \times T}$ that $Y = [y_{it}] \cong AX \in \mathbb{R}_+^{I \times T}$, given the data matrix Y, the lower rank J, and possibly some prior knowledge on the matrices A or X. The set of nonnegative real numbers is denoted by $\mathbb{R}_+$. For high redundancy: $J << \frac{IT}{I+T}$ but in our considerations we assume: $J \leq \min\{I, T\}$.

For the linear spectral unmixing problem, we assume that the column vectors of $Y = [y_1, \ldots, y_T]$ represent the observed mixed spectra, where T is the number of registered mixed spectra or the number of pixels in a remotely observed hyperspectral image. The observed spectral signals are divided into I adjacent subbands. Using the basic NMF model, the column vectors of $A = [a_1, \ldots, a_J]$ are feature vectors that contain the pure spectra (spectral signatures) and X may represent the mixing matrix or vectorized abundance maps. The rank of factorization J determines the number of pure spectra, which can be estimated with various techniques such as cross-validation or automatic relevance determination. In this paper, we assume that all the feature vectors, i.e. the vectors $\{a_j\}$ are locally smooth.

2.1   B-Splines

A spline is a piecewise-polynomial real function $F : [\xi_{min}, \xi_{max}] \to \mathbb{R}$ determined on the interval $[\xi_{min}, \xi_{max}]$ that is divided into P subintervals $[\xi_{n-1}, \xi_n]$ where $\xi_{min} = \xi_0 < \xi_1 < \cdots < \xi_{P-1} < \xi_P = \xi_{max}$ for $n = 1, \ldots, P$. For $\forall n : F(\xi) = S_n(\xi)$ for $\xi_{n-1} \leq \xi < \xi_n$ where $S_n : [\xi_{n-1}, \xi_n] \to \mathbb{R}$.

Any spline function F can be uniquely expressed in terms of a linear combination of so-called B-splines, i.e. the basis splines:

$$F(\xi) = \sum_{n=0}^{N} \alpha_n S_n^{(k)}(\xi), \tag{1}$$

where $S_n^{(k)}(\xi)$ is the B-spline of order k determined on the subinterval $\xi_{n-1} \leq \xi < \xi_n$, and $\{\alpha_n\}$ are coefficients of a linear combination of N B-splines, where $N \geq k - 1$. The points $\{\xi_0, \xi_1, \ldots, \xi_N\}$ are known as knots. The B-splines can be determined by the "Cox-DeBoor" recursive formula:

$$S_n^{(k)}(\xi) = \frac{\xi - \xi_n}{\xi_{n+k-1} - \xi_n} S_n^{(k-1)}(\xi) + \frac{\xi_{n+k} - \xi}{\xi_{n+k} - \xi_{n+1}} S_{n+1}^{(k-1)}(\xi), \tag{2}$$

where

$$S_n^{(1)}(\xi) = \begin{cases} 1 & \text{if } \xi_n \leq \xi < \xi_{n+1} \\ 0 & \text{otherwise} \end{cases} \tag{3}$$

are B-splines of the first-order. The B-spline is a continuous function at the knots, and $\sum_n S_n^{(1)}(\xi) = 1$ for all ξ. If $k = 2$, $F(\xi)$ is composed of piecewise linear functions, hence a degree of the polynomial is equal to one. For $k = 2$, the B-splines are formed by the piecewise quadratic functions. The degree of the polynomial F is equal to $k - 1$.

Note that the derivative of $F(\xi)$ at ξ can be easily determined by the $(k-1)$-order B-spline. Since:

$$F'(\xi) = \sum_{n=0}^{N}(k-1)\frac{\alpha_n - \alpha_{n-1}}{\xi_{n+k-1} - \xi_n}S_n^{(k)}(\xi), \tag{4}$$

the TV-based regularization term: $TV(F(\xi)) = \int_{\xi_{min}}^{\xi_{max}} |F'(\xi)|d\xi$ can be readily calculated.

2.2 Smoothing

If $k > 2$, the spline $F(\xi)$ is a smooth function on the interval $[\xi_{min}, \xi_{max}]$. In this paper, we assume that the model (1) is used for approximating the feature vectors in NMF. Thus:

$$a_j = \sum_{n=0}^{N} w_{nj}s_n^{(k)}, \tag{5}$$

where $\{w_{nj}\} \in \mathbb{R}_+$ are coefficients of a conical combinations of B-splines of order k, and $s_n^{(k)} = [S_n^{(k)}(\xi_i)] \in \mathbb{R}_+^I$ for $i = 1,\ldots, I$. Following [15,16], the NMF model with the B-spline smoothing has the form:

$$Y = SWX, \tag{6}$$

where $S = [s_1^{(k)},\ldots,s_N^{(k)}] \in \mathbb{R}_+^{I\times N}$, $W = [w_{nj}] \in \mathbb{R}_+^{N\times J}$ and $X = [x_{jt}] \in \mathbb{R}_+^{J\times T}$. Assuming $A = SW$, the model (6) boils down to the standard NMF model.

The model (6) has better flexibility than in the GRBF-NMF that was proposed in [15]. First, the knots sequence $\{\xi_n\}$ does not have to be uniformly distributed in the interval $[\xi_{min}, \xi_{max}]$. Moreover, the positions of knots can be also estimated. The number of knots can be adjusted with alternating iterations or can be regarded as the regularization parameter. The degree of the approximating polynomial can be also adaptively selected. For the intervals where the feature vectors do not show meaningful variability, low-order B-splines can be used. A higher variation may involve a higher order but the cubic B-splines should be sufficient for many practical applications. Using B-splines of low-order, the regularization is easier. To model relatively narrow spectral peaks, the number and the order of knots can be determined adaptively. Note that the model (6) can be also extended to work with multi-linear array decompositions, similarly as in [16]. Moreover, when the extracted features are 2D images, then 2D B-splines can be used.

3   Algorithm

To estimate the matrices W and X from (6), we assume that the objective function is expressed by the squared Euclidean distance:

$$\Psi(W, X) = \frac{1}{2}\|Y - SWX\|_F^2. \tag{7}$$

From the stationarity of (7) we have:

$$\nabla_W \Psi(W, X) = S^T(SWX - Y)X^T \triangleq 0, \tag{8}$$

$$\nabla_X \Psi(W, X) = (SW)^T(SWX - Y) \triangleq 0. \tag{9}$$

Hence, the projected ALS updating rules have the form:

$$W = (S^T S)^{-1} SYX^T(XX^T)^{-1}, \tag{10}$$

$$A = [SW]_+, \tag{11}$$

$$X = \left[(W^T S^T SW)^{-1} W^T S^T Y\right]_+, \tag{12}$$

where $[\xi]_+ = \max\{0, \xi\}$.

The ALS algorithm does not satisfy the KKT optimality conditions that lead to non-monotonic convergence. Obviously, the monotonicity is not a crucial condition in certain applications, and hence the ALS algorithm may work quite efficiency for some class of data. However, if the monotonic convergence is expected, a better choice seems to be the multiplicative algorithm presented below.

Theorem 1. *Given $S \geq 0$, and the initial guesses: $w_{nj}, x_{jt} \geq 0$, the objective function in (7) is non-increasing under the update rules:*

$$w_{nj} \leftarrow w_{nj} \sqrt{\frac{\left[S^T Y X^T\right]_{nj}}{\left[S^T SW XX^T\right]_{nj}}}, \qquad x_{jt} \leftarrow x_{jt} \frac{\left[W^T S^T Y\right]_{jt}}{\left[W^T S^T SW X\right]_{jt}}. \tag{13}$$

Lemma 1. *The function*

$$G(W, \tilde{W}) = \frac{1}{2} \sum_{n,j} \frac{[S^T S\tilde{W} XX^T]_{nj} w_{nj}^2}{\tilde{w}_{nj}}$$

$$- \sum_{n,j} [XY^T S]_{nj} \tilde{w}_{nj} \left(1 + \ln\left(\frac{w_{nj}}{\tilde{w}_{nj}}\right)\right) + \frac{1}{2} \operatorname{tr}\left\{Y^T Y\right\} \tag{14}$$

is an auxiliary function to the objective function in (7), i.e. it satisfies the conditions:

$$G(\tilde{W}, \tilde{W}) = \Psi(\tilde{W}, X), \tag{15}$$

$$G(W, \tilde{W}) \geq \Psi(W, X). \tag{16}$$

Proof. The objective function in (7) can be rewritten as:

$$\Psi(\boldsymbol{W}, \boldsymbol{X}) = \frac{1}{2} \operatorname{tr}\left\{\boldsymbol{W}^T \boldsymbol{S}^T \boldsymbol{S} \boldsymbol{W} \boldsymbol{X} \boldsymbol{X}^T\right\} - \operatorname{tr}\left\{\boldsymbol{X} \boldsymbol{Y}^T \boldsymbol{S} \boldsymbol{W}\right\} + \frac{1}{2} \operatorname{tr}\left\{\boldsymbol{Y}^T \boldsymbol{Y}\right\} \quad (17)$$

It is easy to show that the condition (15) holds.

Ding *et al.* [18] proved that for any symmetric matrices $\boldsymbol{U} \in \mathbb{R}_+^{N \times N}$ and $\boldsymbol{V} \in \mathbb{R}_+^{J \times J}$ and the matrices $\boldsymbol{Z} = [z_{nj}] \in \mathbb{R}_+^{N \times J}$, $\tilde{\boldsymbol{Z}} = [\tilde{z}_{nj}] \in \mathbb{R}_+^{N \times J}$, the following inequality:

$$\sum_{n=1}^{N} \sum_{j=1}^{J} \frac{[\boldsymbol{U} \tilde{\boldsymbol{Z}} \boldsymbol{V}]_{nj} z_{nj}^2}{\tilde{z}_{nj}} \geq \operatorname{tr}(\boldsymbol{Z}^T \boldsymbol{U} \boldsymbol{Z} \boldsymbol{V}) \quad (18)$$

is satisfied. Replacing $\boldsymbol{Z} \triangleq \boldsymbol{W}$, $\tilde{\boldsymbol{Z}} \triangleq \tilde{\boldsymbol{W}}$, $\boldsymbol{U} \triangleq \boldsymbol{S}^T \boldsymbol{S}$ and $\boldsymbol{V} \triangleq \boldsymbol{X} \boldsymbol{X}^T$, we get:

$$\operatorname{tr}\left\{\boldsymbol{W}^T \boldsymbol{S}^T \boldsymbol{S} \boldsymbol{W} \boldsymbol{X} \boldsymbol{X}^T\right\} \leq \frac{[\boldsymbol{S}^T \boldsymbol{S} \tilde{\boldsymbol{W}} \boldsymbol{X} \boldsymbol{X}^T]_{nj} w_{nj}^2}{\tilde{w}_{nj}}. \quad (19)$$

From the concavity of the log function: $\xi \geq 1 + \ln(\xi)$ for $\xi \geq 0$. Assuming $\xi = \frac{w_{nj}}{\tilde{w}_{nj}}$, we have:

$$-\operatorname{tr}\left\{\boldsymbol{X} \boldsymbol{Y}^T \boldsymbol{S} \boldsymbol{W}\right\} \leq -\sum_{n,j}[\boldsymbol{X} \boldsymbol{Y}^T \boldsymbol{S}]_{nj} \tilde{w}_{nj}\left(1 + \ln\left(\frac{w_{nj}}{\tilde{w}_{nj}}\right)\right). \quad (20)$$

Considering (19) and (20), the condition (16) is satisfied. *Q.E.D.*

Assuming $\boldsymbol{W}^{(m+1)} = \arg\min_{\boldsymbol{W}} G(\boldsymbol{W}, \tilde{\boldsymbol{W}})$ and setting $\boldsymbol{W}^{(m)} \triangleq \tilde{\boldsymbol{W}}$ for $m = 0, 1, \ldots,$, we obtain:

$$\frac{\partial}{\partial w_{nj}} G(\boldsymbol{W}, \tilde{\boldsymbol{W}}) = \frac{[\boldsymbol{S}^T \boldsymbol{S} \tilde{\boldsymbol{W}} \boldsymbol{X} \boldsymbol{X}^T]_{nj} w_{nj}}{\tilde{w}_{nj}} - [\boldsymbol{X} \boldsymbol{Y}^T \boldsymbol{S}]_{nj} \frac{\tilde{w}_{nj}}{w_{nj}} \triangleq 0, \quad (21)$$

which gives the update rule for $\boldsymbol{W}$ in Theorem 1. Since $\boldsymbol{A} = \boldsymbol{S} \boldsymbol{W}$, the update rule for $\boldsymbol{X}$ is the same as proposed and proved in [19]. From Lemma 1, we have:

$$\Psi(\boldsymbol{W}^{(0)}, \boldsymbol{X}^{(0)}) \geq \ldots \geq \Psi(\boldsymbol{W}^{(m)}, \boldsymbol{X}^{(m)}) \geq \Psi(\boldsymbol{W}^{(m+1)}, \boldsymbol{X}^{(m)})$$
$$\geq \Psi(\boldsymbol{W}^{(m+1)}, \boldsymbol{X}^{(m+1)}) \geq \ldots \geq \Psi(\boldsymbol{W}^{(*)}, \boldsymbol{X}^{(*)}), \quad (22)$$

which proves Theorem 1.

4 Experiments

The experiments are carried out for the blind linear spectral unmixing problem, using the benchmark of 4 real reflectance signals taken from the U.S. Geological Survey (USGS) database[1]. We selected 4 spectral signatures that are illustrated

---

[1] http://speclab.cr.usgs.gov/spectral.lib06

in Fig. 1 (in blue). These signals are divided into 224 bands that cover the range of wavelengths from 400 nm to 2.5 μm. The angle between any pair of the signals is greater than 15 degrees. These signals form the matrix $\boldsymbol{A} \in \mathbb{R}_{+}^{I \times J}$, where $I = 224$ and $J = 4$. Note that all the reflectance signals are strictly positive and slowly varying with strong local smoothness. Thus, this benchmark is very difficult to be blindly estimated with nearly all Blind Source Separation (BSS) methods. The entries of the mixing matrix $\boldsymbol{X} \in \mathbb{R}_{+}^{4 \times 3000}$ were generated randomly from a normal distribution $\mathcal{N}(0, 1)$, and then the negative entries are replaced with a zero-value. The columns with all-zero entries were removed. The mixed spectra were corrupted with an additive zero-mean Gaussian noise with the variance adapted to a given noise level.

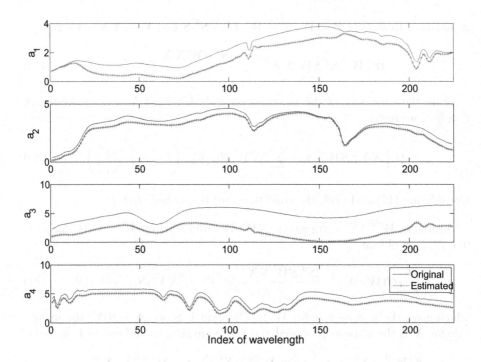

Fig. 1. Spectral signatures (endmembers): (blue) original; (red) estimated with the BS-NMF. For the estimated spectra: $SIR = 17.7\ dB$.

To estimate the matrices $\boldsymbol{A}$ and $\boldsymbol{X}$ from $\boldsymbol{Y}$ we used several NMF algorithms for comparing the results. The proposed algorithm is denoted by the acronym BS-NMF (B-Spline NMF). The algorithms are listed as follows: the standard Lee-Seung algorithm [1] (denoted here by the MUE acronym) for minimizing the Euclidean distance, projected ALS [2], HALS [2], Lin's Projected Gradient [20], FC-NNLS [21], and BS-NMF. All the tested algorithms were initialized by the same random initializer generated from an uniform distribution. To analyze the efficiency of the discussed methods, 100 Monte Carlo (MC) runs of the NMF algorithms were performed, each time the initial matrices A and X were different. All the algorithms, except for the ALS, were implemented using the same computational strategy as in the LPG, i.e. the same stopping criteria are applied to all the algorithms, and the maximum number of inner iterations for updating the factor A or X is set to 10. The ALS performs only one inner iterative step. In the BS-NMF, we set $k = 4$, the number of the B-splines is varying with the alternating steps according to the rule: $N = \max(10, \min(100, [m/5]))$, where m stands for the alternating step, and $[\cdot]$ rounds towards the nearest integers.

The performance of the NMF algorithms was evaluated with the Signal-to-Interference Ratio (SIR) [2] between the estimated signals and the true ones. Fig. 2 shows the SIR statistics for estimating the spectral signatures in the matrix A for two cases of the noise level and the number of observations.

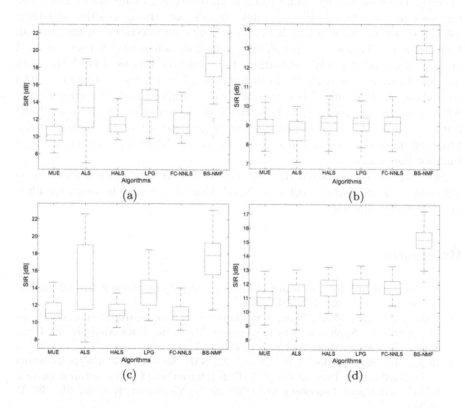

Fig. 2. SIR statistics for estimating the spectral signatures in the matrix A from noisy observations: (a) $SNR = 30\ dB$, $T = 10$; (b) $SNR = 10\ dB$, $T = 10$; (c) $SNR = 30\ dB$, $T = 100$; (d) $SNR = 10\ dB$, $T = 100$

Table 1. Mean-SIR [dB] for estimating the matrix A and the runtime [in seconds] for the case: $SNR = 30\ dB$, $T = 100$

Algorithms	MUE	ALS	HALS	LPG	FC-NNLS	BS-NMF
SIR for A	11.3	15	11.45	13.7	11.1	17.52
SIR for X	9.8	14.45	10.25	11.78	9.77	15
Time	0.64	0.27	0.76	0.91	1.49	1.48

5 Conclusions

The paper shows a possibility of using B-splines for modeling the feature vectors in NMF. The proposed method is suitable for recovering locally smooth features, e.g. such as presented in Fig. 1. These signals are strictly positive and their variability is very low, which makes them very difficult to estimate with nearly all BSS methods. The statistics presented in Fig. 2 demonstrates that for this kind of data nearly all the NMF algorithms fail. Only the proposed BS-NMF gives mean-SIRs greater than 15 dB, both for weak ($T = 10$) and strong ($T = 100$) redundant observations. When the data are corrupted with the strong noise $SNR = 10\ dB$, the mean-SIR of the BS-NMF decreases below the level 15 dB but not considerably. The results given in Table 1 shows that the runtime of the proposed method is nearly the same as for the FC-NNLS but not much longer than for the others.

Summing up, the proposed BS-NMF method seems to be efficient for estimating locally smooth feature vectors in NMF. Moreover, it may be easily modified and adapted to the data.

References

1. Lee, D.D., Seung, H.S.: Learning the parts of objects by non-negative matrix factorization. Nature 401, 788–791 (1999)
2. Cichocki, A., Zdunek, R., Phan, A.H., Amari, S.I.: Nonnegative Matrix and Tensor Factorizations: Applications to Exploratory Multi-way Data Analysis and Blind Source Separation. Wiley and Sons (2009)
3. Huang, K., Sidiropoulos, N.D., Swami, A.: NMF revised: New uniquness results and algorithms. In: Proc. of the 2013 IEEE International Conference on Acoustics, Speech and Signal Processing (ICASSP 2013), Vancouver, Kanada, May 26–31 (2013)
4. Pascual-Montano, A., Carazo, J.M., Kochi, K., Lehmean, D., Pacual-Marqui, R.: Nonsmooth nonnegative matrix factorization (nsNMF). IEEE Transaction Pattern Analysis and Machine Intelligence 28(3), 403–415 (2006)
5. Févotte, C., Bertin, N., Durrieu, J.L.: Nonnegative matrix factorization with the Itakura-Saito divergence: With application to music analysis. Neural Computation 21(3), 793–830 (2009)

6. Mohammadiha, N., Smaragdis, P., Leijon, A.: Prediction based filtering and smoothing to exploit temporal dependencies in NMF. In: Proc. IEEE International Conference on Acoustics, Speech and Signal Processing (ICASSP 2013), Vancouver, Canada, May 26–31, pp. 873–877 (2013)
7. Zdunek, R.: Improved convolutive and under-determined blind audio source separation with MRF smoothing. Cognitive Computation 5(4), 493–503 (2013)
8. Sajda, P., Du, S., Brown, T.R., Stoyanova, R., Shungu, D.C., Mao, X., Parra, L.C.: Nonnegative matrix factorization for rapid recovery of constituent spectra in magnetic resonance chemical shift imaging of the brain. IEEE Transaction on Medical Imaging 23(12), 1453–1465 (2004)
9. Pauca, V.P., Pipera, J., Plemmons, R.J.: Nonnegative matrix factorization for spectral data analysis. Linear Algebra and its Applications 416(1), 29–47 (2006)
10. Miao, L., Qi, H.: Endmember extraction from highly mixed data using minimum volume constrained nonnegative matrix factorization. IEEE Transactions on Geoscience and Remote Sensing 45(3), 765–777 (2007)
11. Jia, S., Qian, Y.: Constrained nonnegative matrix factorization for hyperspectral unmixing. IEEE Transactions on Geoscience and Remote Sensing 47(1), 161–173 (2009)
12. Iordache, M., Dias, J., Plaza, A.: Total variation spatial regularization for sparse hyperspectral unmixing. IEEE Transactions on Geoscience and Remote Sensing 50(11), 4484–4502 (2012)
13. Wang, N., Du, B., Zhang, L.: An endmember dissimilarity constrained non-negative matrix factorization method for hyperspectral unmixing. IEEE Journal of Selected Topics in Applied Earth Observations and Remote Sensing 6(2), 554–569 (2013)
14. Schmidt, M.N., Laurberg, H.: Nonnegative matrix factorization with Gaussian process priors. Computational Intelligence and Neuroscience (361705) (2008)
15. Zdunek, R.: Approximation of feature vectors in nonnegative matrix factorization with gaussian radial basis functions. In: Huang, T., Zeng, Z., Li, C., Leung, C.S. (eds.) ICONIP 2012, Part I. LNCS, vol. 7663, pp. 616–623. Springer, Heidelberg (2012)
16. Yokota, T., Cichocki, A., Yamashita, Y., Zdunek, R.: Fast algorithms for smooth nonnegative matrix and tensor factorizations. Neural Computations (submitted)
17. Schumaker, L.L.: Spline Functions: Basic Theory. John Wiley and Sons, New York (1981)
18. Ding, C., Li, T., Peng, W., Park, H.: Orthogonal nonnegative matrix trifactorizations for clustering. In: KDD 2006: Proc. of the 12th ACM SIGKDD International Conference on Knowledge Discovery and Data Mining, pp. 126–135. ACM Press, New York (2006)
19. Lee, D.D., Seung, H.S.: Algorithms for nonnegative matrix factorization. In: Advances in Neural Information Processing, NIPS, vol. 13, pp. 556–562. MIT Press (2001)
20. Lin, C.J.: Projected gradient methods for non-negative matrix factorization. Neural Computation 19(10), 2756–2779 (2007)
21. Kim, H., Park, H.: Non-negative matrix factorization based on alternating nonnegativity constrained least squares and active set method. SIAM Journal in Matrix Analysis and Applications 30(2), 713–730 (2008)

Variants and Performances
of Novel Direct Learning Algorithms
for L2 Support Vector Machines

Ljiljana Zigic and Vojislav Kecman

Virginia Commonwealth University
401 West Main Street
Richmond, VA 23284, USA
{zigicl,vkecman}@vcu.edu
http://computer-science.egr.vcu.edu

Abstract. The paper introduces a novel Direct L2 Support Vector Machine (DL2 SVM) classifier and presents the performances of its 4 variants on 12 different binary and multiclass datasets. Direct L2 SVM avoids solving quadratic programming (QP) problem and it solves the Nonnegative Least Squares (NNLS) task instead, which, unlike the related iterative algorithms, produces an impeccably accurate results. Solutions obtained by NNLS and QP are equal but NNLS needs much less CPU time. The comprehensive DL2 SVM model, as well as its three variants, are devised. The similarities with, and differences in respect to, LS SVM and proximal SVMs are pointed at too. The four DL2 SVM models performances are compared in terms of accuracy, percentage of support vectors and CPU time. A strict nested cross-validation (double resampling) is used in all experiments.

Keywords: Direct L2 Support Vector Machine, Nonnegative Least Squares.

1 Introduction

Support Vector Machine is a powerful and very popular machine learning algorithm with strong theoretical foundations based on the Vapnik-Chervonenkis theory [1]. Although SVM models show similarity to the other data mining techniques such as neural networks (NN) and radial basis functions NN, they usually outperform these algorithms. This is why SVMs are embedded in almost all machine learning off the shelf toolboxes. SVMs are widely used in diverse real-world problems, such as bio-informatics, direct marketing, hand written text recognition and image classification. The reason for their wide application lies in the fact that they show considerable improvements regarding computational efficiency, scalability and robustness against outliers compared to other methods. Support vector machines perform particularly well on classification and regression problems when there is a small number of training data and big number of features. They are also suitable for big, large and ultra-large datasets, there is no upper

L. Rutkowski et al. (Eds.): ICAISC 2014, Part II, LNAI 8468, pp. 82–91, 2014.
© Springer International Publishing Switzerland 2014

limit on number of data and the only constraints are those imposed by hardware. That is why the efforts are constantly being made in developing faster and/or more accurate approaches and algorithms for ultra-large problems.

One such algorithm is Direct L2 SVM [2]. It represents the newest contribution to the field of efficient solvers of ultra-large machine learning problems. This paper introduces four versions of this algorithm and presents their relative performance on twelve, different in complexity, classification datasets.

1.1 Support Vector Machines - Introductory Overview

To describe our DL2 SVM method we give a brief introduction to support vector machine classifier. First method of SVMs discovered in early 1960s solved the problem of linearly separable data by finding the widest separation of classes, i.e. by maximizing the margin between two classes. Such a classifier is called a *hard margin classifier*. To deal with non-separable problems a modified version of this classifier, that takes into account data that lie on the wrong side of the margin, was introduced. This generally non-linear classifier is dubbed L1 SVM *soft margin classifier*. Here we discuss one more version of the SVM classifier, namely L2 SVM. Names for L1 and L2 SVMs originate from the norm that is used for the errors in the minimizing function (1). In other words, support vector machines that use linear sum of slack variables are called L1 SVMs, and SVMs with the square sum of slack variables, as shown in (1), are called L2-SVMs. Although the change seems minor it leads to some important differences.

L2 SVM is posed as solving the following problem [3], [4],

$$\arg\min_{\mathbf{w},\zeta} \frac{1}{2}\|\mathbf{w}\|^2 + C \sum_{i=1}^{m} \zeta_i^2, \tag{1}$$

subject to,

$$y_i(\varphi(\mathbf{x}_i)^T \mathbf{w} + b) \geq 1 - \zeta_i, i = 1, ..., m, \tag{2}$$

where $\mathbf{x}_i$ and y_i are the d-dimensional inputs and their corresponding labels, m represents number of samples, i.e., the size of the dataset, $\mathbf{w}$ is the weight vector in the feature space, and φ represents the kernel function (mapping) of the original data points (measurements) into the feature space, b is the bias term (i.e., the intercept parameter) of the model, C stands for the penalty (regularization) parameter and ζ_i are the so-called slack variables which relax the constraints. These slack variables represent the distance of the data points $\mathbf{x}_i$ form their corresponding margins. In the case that all the data are correctly classified $\zeta_i = 0$. If there is no nonlinear mapping of the input space i.e., when φ is an identity mapping $\varphi(\mathbf{x}_i) = \mathbf{x}_i$, the decision function $o(\mathbf{x})$ is a linear hyper-plane over the d-dimensional input space given as $o(\mathbf{x}_i) = \mathbf{x}_i^T \mathbf{w} + b$.

Well documented comparisons between performances of the L1 and L2 SVMs can be found in [4]. The L2 SVM setting has an important property that it can be readily transformed into solving of a linear system of equations. In this way a solving of a QP problem is avoided, enabling the L2 SVMs to learn faster than L1

SVMs while producing similar accuracies. The idea of Direct L2 SVM algorithm
is derived from several different SVM models such as the Least Squares SVM
[5], Proximal SVM [6] and various 'geometric' approaches related either to L1
SVMs [7] and [8], or to L2 SVMs [9-14].

1.2   General L2 SVM Learning Model

The most general i.e., comprehensive L2 SVM learning model from which all the
other L2 SVM approaches mentioned above can be derived is posed as follows,

$$\arg \min_{\mathbf{w},b,\zeta,\rho} \frac{1}{2}\|\mathbf{w}\|^2 + \frac{C}{2}\sum_{i=1}^{m} \zeta_i^2 + \frac{k_b}{2}b^2 - k_\rho\rho, \tag{3}$$

subject to,

$$y_i(\boldsymbol{\varphi}(\mathbf{x}_i)^T\mathbf{w} + b) \geq \rho - \zeta_i, i = 1, ..., m. \tag{4}$$

The cost function (3) of the general L2 SVM model has two additional terms,
the bias term b and parameter ρ. Also, on the right hand side of the constraints
(4) there is a parameter ρ instead of 1. All the other L2 SVMs models (mentioned
above and well accepted in practice) can be looked at as the special cases of this
learning task.

For the sake of comprehensiveness we give similarities and differences between
this model and models mentioned above, namely Least Squares (LS) SVM, proximal SVM and some of the 'geometric' approaches,

- the Least Squares SVM model minimizes cost function (3) with both k_b
and k_ρ set to 0, while the linear inequality constraints in (4) are replaced with
equality constraints. Instead using the variable parameter ρ on the right hand
side of (4), LS SVM works with a fixed value for $\rho = 1$. Such an approach leads
to solving a system of linear equations of the size $(m+1, m+1)$ and gives non-
sparse, i.e., dense solution. In other words, it produces a model in which all the
data are support vectors and this is, for obvious reasons, not accepted for large
learning tasks.

- the Proximal SVM poses the similar learning problem to LS SVM. This
model uses additional bias term b^2 with $k_b = 1$ in (3) while, same as Least
Squares SVM, sets k_ρ to 0. On the right hand side of (4) there is a fixed value
for $\rho = 1$. Another similarity to LS SVM is the use of equality constraints in (4)
instead of inequality ones. This has same consequences as commented above in
the sense that one has to solve a system of linear equations which leads to dense
solutions.

- several 'geometric' approaches presented in [10-14] dubbed as core, ball,
sphere and minimal norm (MN) SVMs have identical posing of the L2 SVM
problem as given above. They are minimizing function (3) subject to (4) but
they always work with fixed values for k_b $(= 1)$ and k_ρ $(= 1)$). These approaches
are called geometric since the posing of the problem is solved as the problem of
finding minimal enclosing ball in the feature space defined by $\tilde{\varphi}(\mathbf{x}_i)$ (which will
be defined below) or, in case of L1 SVMs, problem of finding the closest point of

the convex hull to the origin [8-13]. Because of iterative nature in obtaining the solution they are suited for solving large classification problems. Iterative nature enables finding a solution which at no point requires entire Hessian matrix for all the training data.

Recently, it seems that Minimal Norm SVM given in [12] and [13] has an edge in terms of both speed and scalability. In following section we will present the direct, non-iterative, algorithm for finding exact solution to general L2 SVM problem as posed in (3) and (4).

2   Basic Direct L2 SVM Model

Direct L2 SVM algorithm is derived from (3) and (4) by transforming it to the primal Lagrangian L_p as proposed in [2]. Next, we find derivatives of primal Lagrangian in respect to $\mathbf{w}, b, \zeta_i$ and α_i and equal them to 0, which after simple rearrangements leads to,

$$\mathbf{w} = \sum_{i=1}^{m} \alpha_i y_i \varphi(\mathbf{x_i}), \tag{5}$$

$$b = \frac{1}{k_b} \sum_{i=1}^{m} \alpha_i y_i, \tag{6}$$

$$\sum_{i=1}^{m} \alpha_i = k_\rho, \tag{7}$$

$$\zeta_i = \frac{\alpha_i}{C}, \tag{8}$$

$$y_i \left(\sum_{i=1}^{m} \alpha_i y_i k(\mathbf{x}, \mathbf{x}_i) + b \right) + \zeta_i = \rho. \tag{9}$$

The crucial step in obtaining DL2 SVM model is plugging in equations (5), (6) and (8) into the equation (9) and then dividing the resulting expression by a scalar value ρ. This introduces new dual variables β_i defined as,

$$\beta_i = \frac{\alpha_i}{\rho}, i = 1, ..., m. \tag{10}$$

where α_i's represent Lagrangian multipliers. Dividing α_i by ρ, i.e., by involving new variables β_i we have transformed the general L2 SVM quadratic programming problem given by (3) subject to (4) into the classic Nonnegative Least Squares (NNLS) problem defined as,

$$\mathbf{K}_f \boldsymbol{\beta} = \mathbf{1}, \tag{11}$$

subject to

$$\beta_i \geq 0, i = 1, ..., m, \tag{12}$$

where $\mathbf{K}_f$ corresponds to the altered (m, m) Kernel matrix and $\boldsymbol{\beta}$ represents vector of β_i values. Kernel matrix $\mathbf{K}_f$ is a positive definite matrix and is given as,

$$\mathbf{K}_f = \left[\mathbf{K} + \frac{1}{k_b}\mathbf{1}_{\mathrm{m,m}} + diag_{m,m}(\frac{1}{C})\right] . * \mathbf{y}\mathbf{y}^{\mathbf{T}}, \tag{13}$$

where each entry $k(\mathbf{x}_i, \mathbf{x}_j)$ of the Kernel matrix $\mathbf{K}$ represents the scalar product of the original data images φ in feature space defined as,

$$k(\mathbf{x}_i, \mathbf{x}_j) = \left[\varphi(\mathbf{x}_i^T)\varphi(\mathbf{x}_j)\right]_{i=1,...,m,j=1,...,m}. \tag{14}$$

Therefore, elements of our matrix $\boldsymbol{K}_f$ (subscript f denotes the fact that it differs from original matrix $\mathbf{K}$) are related to altered feature space defined by $\tilde{\varphi}$ and are denoted as

$$\tilde{k}(\mathbf{x}_i, \mathbf{x}_j) = \tilde{\varphi}(\mathbf{x}_i^T)\tilde{\varphi}(\mathbf{x}_j). \tag{15}$$

Once nonnegative β_i values are calculated the value of parameter ρ can be easily obtained as,

$$\rho = \frac{k_\rho}{\sum_{i=1}^{m} \beta_i}. \tag{16}$$

After computing value of ρ, the dual variables α_i of general L2 SVM model can be calculated as,

$$\alpha_i = \beta_i\rho, i = 1, ..., m. \tag{17}$$

Finally, α_i allow us to calculate bias term b, and so, given input vector $\mathbf{x}$ DL2 SVM model's output $o(\mathbf{x})$ is as follows,

$$o(\mathbf{x}) = \sum_{i=1}^{m} \alpha_i y_i k(\mathbf{x}, \mathbf{x}_i) + b = \sum_{sv=1}^{\#SVectors} \alpha_{sv} y_{sv} k(\mathbf{x}, \mathbf{x}_{sv}) + b. \tag{18}$$

Note the use of kernel k and not $\tilde{k}$ while computing the output.

As already mentioned above, by introducing new scalar variables β_i we have replaced solving the QP problem, which might be slow and hence prohibitive for large datasets, with a NNLS one defined by (11) and (12).

The basic NNLS posed in (11) and (12) will be solved by a variant of a Lawson and Hanson algorithm [15]. In principle, their NNLS solves the system of constrained linear equations in a repetitive manner meaning, it updates the current solution by the use of previously calculated one. This sequence simply repeats itself with the addition of one more support vector in each iteration until the solution satisfies well-defined termination conditions. As mentioned before, matrix $\mathbf{K}_f$ is a symmetric positive definite and so are all it's diagonal matrices, and this is why we propose a very efficient and numerically stable Cholesky factorization with an update to be used in DL2 SVM.

There are several remarks which should be done here. Firstly, the DL2 SVM (NNLS based) algorithm's complexity scales with the number of the non-negative β_i (i.e., α_i) values and not with the number of data. In other words, it scales with the number of support vectors while the standard SVM's QP based solvers scale with the cube of the number of training data ($O(n^3)$). Hence, when the percentage of support vectors is small, a significant speed up can be expected for large datasets for DL2 SVMs. Secondly, the NNLS algorithm has the merit that it always finds the exact solution, it is not iterative in the nature, and thus requires no arbitrary cutoff parameter. Thirdly, finiteness of NNLS algorithm is guaranteed to happen within a finite number of iterations as shown in [15].

2.1 Three More Variants of DL2 SVM Model

Basic DL2 SVM model based on (3) and (4) represents just one posing of the problem. Here we will give three additional versions of this model and later on compare their experimental results on several datasets.

One possible different posing of the problem is a model without parameter ρ in cost function (3). This also changes the inequality constraints given in (4) to $y_i(\varphi(\mathbf{x}_i)^T\mathbf{w}+b) \geq 1-\zeta_i$. After similar derivations as for the general DL2 SVM a new one for a model without parameter ρ is obtained as given below,

$$\mathbf{K}_f\boldsymbol{\alpha} = 1, \tag{19}$$

subject to,

$$\alpha_i \geq 0, i = 1, ..., m. \tag{20}$$

As it can be readily seen this model is almost the same as basic DL2 SVM one. The only difference is that by setting $\rho = 0$ we avoid calculation of β_i values and we find nonnegative Lagrange multipliers α_i directly. It is important to mention similarity of this model to proximal SVMs which solve quite similar learning problem with only difference being that the inequality constraints (4) are replaced by the equality ones in proximal SVMs (i.e., $y_i(\varphi(\mathbf{x}_i)^T\mathbf{w}+b) = 1-\zeta_i$). Setting this equality has a consequence of finding dense solution which is not suitable for large datasets. The DL2 SVM model proposed here avoids that problem and thus leads to the sparse solution.

Next, the second model developed here is the one without the bias term b in cost function (3) but with an ρ parameter. If we posed our problem like this we would have to solve the following NNLS problem,

$$\mathbf{K}_{f2}\boldsymbol{\beta} = 1, \tag{21}$$

subject to,

$$\beta_i \geq 0, i = 1, ..., m, \tag{22}$$

where subscript $f2$ denotes the fact that matrix $\mathbf{K}_{f2}$ does not equal the one given in (13). Matrix $\mathbf{K}_{f2}$ for the DL2 SVM without bias is shown below,

$$\mathbf{K}_{f2} = \left[\mathbf{K} + diag_{m,m}(\frac{1}{C})\right].*\mathbf{yy^T}. \tag{23}$$

Note that the only change in respect to the original matrix $\mathbf{K}_f$ is an absence of the $\frac{1}{k_b}\mathbf{1}_{m,m}$ element which is otherwise present in the original Kernel matrix $\mathbf{K}_f$.

The final DL2 SVM model setup is the one that uses neither bias term b nor parameter ρ in cost function (3). In fact, this is the most basic L2 SVM problem given by (1) and (2) and it leads to solving the following NNLS task,

$$\mathbf{K}_{f2}\boldsymbol{\alpha} = 1, \tag{24}$$

subject to,

$$\alpha_i \geq 0, i = 1, ..., m. \tag{25}$$

The matrix $\mathbf{K}_{f2}$ is the same as the one given in (23). There is one more comparison to be made between the DL2 SVM model given by (24) and (25) and LS SVM. LS SVM uses the same cost function with only difference being that the linear inequality constraints (2) are replaced by the equality ones. This has the same consequence as given above in the sense that the solution is always dense, meaning all the training data vectors are support vectors, which is not the case in the DL2 SVMs models introduced here.

3   Experimental Results

To demonstrate effectiveness of the four DL2 SVM models introduced in this paper, we give experimental results on 12 real classification datasets. First ten datasets used in the experiments are taken from the UCI Machine Learning Repository, and the last two datasets are the benchmarking datasets for protein sub-cellular localization constructed by Reinhardt and Hubbard [16]. The basic information about all datasets as well as the classification accuracies achieved by four DL2 SVM models are given in Table 1.

Table 1. Dataset Information and Classification Accuracies [%]

Dataset	# instances	# features	# classes	model 1	model 2	model 3	model4
Iris	150	4	3	95.90	95.90	94.67	94.67
Glass	214	9	6	67.30	69.58	70.91	73.93
Vote	232	16	2	93.99	93.99	96.14	96.14
Wine	178	13	3	98.30	98.30	96.57	96.57
Teach	151	5	3	54.21	54.88	55.42	55.73
Sonar	208	60	2	89.40	89.40	88.93	88.93
Cancer	198	32	2	79.86	79.86	77.38	77.38
Dermatology	366	33	6	98.37	98.37	97.00	97.00
Heart 1	297	13	5	58.46	57.56	55.91	55.57
Heart 2	270	13	2	80.74	80.74	81.85	81.85
Prokaryotic	997	20	3	90.07	89.97	90.17	90.17
Eukaryotic	2427	20	4	80.92	80.92	80.96	81.04
Average Accuracy				82.29	**82.46**	82.16	82.42

In our very strict experiments we use nested (a.k.a. double) cross validation procedure that is the only viable approach while comparing different algorithms. (In statistics literature this is known as a double resampling). In such an experimental approach, there are two loops in the double cross-validation procedure. In the outer loop, the data set is separated into J_1 roughly equal-sized parts. Each part is held out in turn as the test set, and the remaining parts are used as the training set. Then, in the inner loop, another J_2-fold cross-validation is performed over the training set only to determine the values of the best hyper-parameters of the model. The chosen model is then applied on the test set. In our experiments we used value of 10 for both J_1 and J_2. The double cross-validation procedure ensures that the class labels of the test data won't be seen when tuning the hyper-parameters, which is consistent with the real-world scenario. Features of all the datasets are normalized to zero mean and unit variance before all the experiments were run.

Table 2. Percentage of Support Vectors [%] and CPU Time [s]

Dataset	model 1	model 2	model 3	model 4	model 1	model 2	model 3	model 4
Iris	44.7	44.7	47.0	47.0	3.78	3.82	3.7	3.73
Glass	79.5	82.3	88.2	79.0	22.04	22.08	22.76	22.82
Vote	43.2	43.2	47.3	47.3	27.34	27.52	27.24	27.25
Wine	55.1	55.1	72.6	72.6	8.22	8.26	8.14	8.19
Teach	90.7	90.7	93.0	89.3	11.66	11.63	11.47	11.4
Sonar	74.0	74.0	81.6	81.6	29.74	29.78	29.49	30.25
Cancer	88.0	88.0	88.6	88.6	22.38	22.32	23.31	22.69
Dermatology	58.6	58.6	79.6	79.6	87.35	87.52	84.51	85.09
Heart 1	93.2	92.1	95.4	95.4	65.81	64.86	65.78	65.98
Heart 2	80.1	80.1	75.4	75.4	40.24	39.48	38.72	38.79
Prokaryotic	46.0	46.0	59.3	59.3	885.57	880.26	887.53	894.73
Eukaryotic	67.1	66.3	65.2	65.2	25547.5	25841.28	26301.28	26121.43
Average	**68.35**	68.43	74.43	73.36	**2229.30**	2253.21	2291.99	2277.70

Here, the measures of a quality are the classification accuracy (the higher, the better), percentage of support vectors (the smaller, the better) and CPU time needed to finish the nested cross-validation procedure (the smaller, the better). The experimental results are summarized in Table 1 (classification accuracies) and Table 2 (percentage of support vectors and CPU time).

Remark 1. In Tables (1) and (2) the comprehensive DL2 SVM model given by (3) subject to (4) and solved as NNLS (11) and (12) is denoted as *model 1*, *model 2* represents DL2 SVM with bias b but without using the ρ parameter ($\rho = 0$), *model 3* is the one with bias $b = 0$ and ρ, and finally DL2 SVM without both bias b and ρ is denoted as *model 4*.

Few remarks about results are now in order. First, models without bias require much more support vectors. Next, accuracies of all four models are close, with the tiny advantage of models with bias. Also, models with bias b are little faster during the training than models without it.

Overall, if one has to choose the "best" DL2 SVM model, the model with bias b but without ρ parameter would be the choice (model 2 as given by (19) and (20)).

4 Conclusions

The paper introduces, derives and presents four different variants of a DL2 SVM algorithm. The derivations of models are presented and their performances are compared on 12 multiclass and binary classification datasets. In order to ensure fair comparisons of different models all the experiments are done under the strict nested cross-validation procedure with 10 splits of the data in both outer and inner loop. Models are compared in terms of classification accuracy, model size (percentage of support vectors) and CPU training time. The extensive experimental results suggest that DL2 SVM model which uses bias b but not parameter ρ is the model of the choice. Due to the fact that DL2 SVM is based on NNLS solver it seems that both the use of Cholesky factorization and possibility of a relatively straightforward parallelization lead to the powerful SVM algorithm for ultra-large datasets.

References

1. Vapnik, V.: Estimation of Dependences Based on Empirical Data (in Russian), Nauka, Moscow (1979); (English translation: Springer Verlag, New York 1982)
2. Zigic, L., Strack, R., Kecman, V.: L2 SVM Revisited - Novel Direct Learning Algorithm and Some Geometric Insights. In: MENDEL 19th International Conference on Soft Computing, Brno, Czech Republic (2013)
3. Huang, T.M., Kecman, V., Kopriva, I.: Kernel Based Algorithms for Mining Huge Data Sets. In: Supervised, Semi- supervised, and Unsupervised Learning. Springer, Heidelberg (2006)
4. Abe, S.: Support Vector Machines for Pattern Classification, 2nd edn. Springer (2010)
5. Suykens, J., Vandewalle, J.: Least Squares Support Vector Machine Classifiers. Neural Processing Letters (NPL) 9(3), 293–300 (1999)
6. Fung, G., Mangasarian, O.L.: Multicategory Proximal Support Vector Machine Classifiers. In: Machine Learning, pp. 1–21 (2004)
7. Mavroforakis, M.E., Theodoridis, S.: A geometric approach to support vector machine (SVM) classification. IEEE TNNS 17(3), 671–682 (2006)
8. Franc, V., Hlavc, V.: An iterative algorithm learning the maximal margin classifier. Pattern Recognition 36(9), 1985–1996 (2003)
9. Keerthi, S.S., Shevade, S.K., Bhattacharyya, C., Murthy, K.K.: A fast iterative nearest point algorithm for support vector machine classifier design. IEEE TNNLS 11(1), 24–36 (2000)
10. Tsang, I.W., Kwok, J.T., Cheung, P.-M.: Core Vector Machines: Fast SVM Training on Very Large Data Sets. Journal of Machine Learning Research 6, 363–392 (2005)
11. Strack, R., Kecman, V., Li, Q., Strack, B.: Sphere Support Vector Machines for Large Classification Tasks. Neurocomputing 101, 59–67 (2013)

12. Strack, R., Kecman, V.: Minimal Norm Support Vector Machines for Large Classification Tasks. In: Proc. of the 11th IEEE International Conference on Machine Learning Applications (ICMLA 2012), Boca Raton, FL, vol. 1, pp. 209–214 (2012)
13. Strack, R.: Geometric Approach to Support Vector Machines Learning for Large Datasets, PhD dissertation, Virginia Commonwealth University, Richmond, VA (2013)
14. Kecman, V., Strack, R., Zigic, L.: Big Data Mining by L2 SVMs - Geometrical Insights Help, Seminar at CS Department, Virginia Commonwealth University, VCU, Richmond, VA (2013)
15. Lawson, C.L., Hanson, R.J.: Solving Least Squares Problems. Prentice-Hall, Inc., Englewood Cliffs (1974)
16. Reinhardt, A., Hubbard, T.: Using neural networks for prediction of the subcellular location of proteins. Nucleic Acids Res. 26, 2230–2236 (1998)

Bioinformatics, Biometrics and Medical Applications

Evolving Parameters for a Noisy Biological System – The Impact of Alternative Approaches

David J. Barnes and Dominique Chu

School of Computing, The University of Kent, Canterbury,
Kent CT2 7NF, UK
{d.j.barnes,d.f.chu}@kent.ac.uk

Abstract. In this contribution we seek to evolve viable parameter values for a small-scale biological *network motif* concerned with bacterial nutrient uptake and metabolism. We use two different evolutionary approaches with the model: implicit and explicit. Our results reveal that significantly different characteristics of both efficiency and timescale emerge in the resulting evolved systems depending on the which particular approach is used.

1 Introduction

In this paper we explore the evolution of parameter values for a small-scale biological *network motif* concerned with bacterial nutrient uptake and metabolism. Network motifs are small-scale regulatory connection patterns of genes that have been identified by systematic search for highly over-represented patterns in known networks [1]. However, much of the research on network motifs remains qualitative in the sense that it considers the topology of the network alone without paying much attention to how the behaviour of the system depends on quantitative details. In the context of biochemical systems, parameters specify values such as association or dissociation rate constants, the concentration of proteins in the cell or the expression rate of a gene. Little is known about the quantitative design principles of organisms; that is, the selection rules for parameters that lead to fit organisms.

Parameters determine the abundance of biomolecules via reaction/expression rates and, hence, determine two key aspects of cellular life that are of fundamental evolutionary significance: noise and cost. Since biological reaction networks are stochastic systems, low numbers of reactants lead to high relative fluctuations of dynamical quantities [2], such as expression events or molecular concentrations. On the other hand, high numbers of reactants reduce the relative noise but they are metabolically costly. Taken together, these factors suggest that there is a trade-off to be made in biological networks between the effects of noise and the cost associated with mitigating those effects.

Recent work in exploring the parameter space of a similar simple metabolic gene network [3,4] has demonstrated that feasible parameter sets can be very difficult to find for stochastic systems, with the vast majority of random solutions

L. Rutkowski et al. (Eds.): ICAISC 2014, Part II, LNAI 8468, pp. 95–106, 2014.

leading to the production of either no biomass or insignificant amounts. This contrasts strongly with the results produced by equivalent differential equation models, where noise plays no role.

This contribution describes the biological model for which we sought to evolve feasible parameters, the two evolutionary approaches we used for parameter discovery, and the characteristics of the resulting systems. Finally, we consider whether the relatively inefficient system that results from the more realistic environmental conditions present in one of our approaches suggests that similar real bacterial network motifs might, themselves, have evolved to a relatively inefficient form that retains scope for improvement.

This paper is organised as follows: in Sect. 2 we present the biological network motif we are seeking to model; in Sect. 3 we describe the two approaches we used to evolve viable parameter sets; in Sect. 4 we discuss the characteristics of typical parameter sets derived from these approaches; and in Sect. 5 we discuss possible implications of these results.

2   The Biological Model

The model we worked with is a simple biological network motif representing bacterial uptake/metabolism system (Fig. 1).

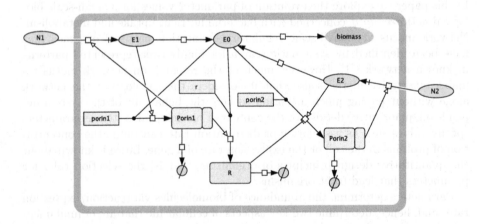

Fig. 1. Schematic outline of the model system in which distinct nutrient sources, N_1 and N_2, are converted into *biomass*. Genes are represented by the square-cornered rectangles.

The model represents two sources of nutrients N_1 and N_2 available to a cell. Uptake of nutrients requires specific porins, namely P_1 and P_2 respectively. Once taken up into the cell the nutrient becomes an internal source of energy (E_1 and E_2) which can be converted into actual energy (or ATP), which we denote by E_0. We assume that the uptake and conversion of nutrient follows Hill kinetics[5,6].

E_0 is consumed in several processes: the synthesis of porins and the regulator R; and the production of *biomass*. Conversion of E_2 to E_0 is less efficient than conversion of E_1, and synthesis of P_2 is suppressed by the presence of R.

The model aims to represent a biological system in which uptake of N_2 is regulated by R, whose expression is dependent on the availability of N_1. On exhaustion of N_1 a cell should be able to switch to consumption of N_2 as an alternative source of energy through loss of the regulator R. Part of our goal in working with this model was to explore how easy it would be to find parameter values implementing such switching behaviour. The model is described by the following chemical equations:

$$N_i \rightarrow E_i, k_{N_i} P_i \frac{N_i}{N_i + K_{N_i}} \tag{1}$$

$$E_i \rightarrow E_0, \frac{E_i^{h_{E_i}}}{E_i^{h_{E_i}} + K_{E_i}} \tag{2}$$

$$P_1 + E_0 \rightarrow P_1, (leak_1 + k_{P_1} \frac{E_1^{h_{P_1}}}{E_1^{h_{P_1}} + K_{P_1}^{h_{P_1}}}) E_0 L \tag{3}$$

$$P_2 + E_0 \rightarrow P_2, (leak_2 + k_{P_2} \frac{E_2^{h_{P_2}}}{E_2^{h_{P_2}} + K_{P_2}^{h_{P_2}}} \frac{K_R^{h_R}}{K_R^{h_R} + R^{h_R}}) E_0 L \tag{4}$$

$$r + E_0 \rightarrow R, E_0 \frac{P_1^{h_r}}{P_1^{h_r} + K_r^{h_r}} k_{Re} \tag{5}$$

$$E_0 \rightarrow biomass, \frac{E_0}{E_0 + k_g} \tag{6}$$

$$\{P_i, E_i, R\} \rightarrow \emptyset, d_{\{P_i, E_i, R\}} \tag{7}$$

Equation 1 models nutrient uptake mediated by specific porins while equation 2 models conversion of the internal sources of energy to ATP (E_0). Equation 3, 4, 5 and 6 model the various competing demands on E_0 for the production of porins, regulator and biomass. Porin production is limited by the space available at the surface of a cell to accomodate porins (L). This is given by equation 8:

$$L = \frac{K_L}{((P_1 + P_2)/\text{surfaceArea})^2 + K_L} \tag{8}$$

Finally, equation 7 models the continual degradation and loss of the various products.

Uptake and gene expression are assumed to follow Hill kinetics. While this is an approximation, in reality it has been found that Hill kinetics is a good description of the reactions described here. It is also widely used to model them and is a fairly simple approach.

3 The Evolutionary Model

The chemical equations were coded as a parameterised cell model and we sought to evolve values for the kinetic parameters determining the system, including the Hill-constants (K_{N_i}), Hill-exponents (h_x) and dynamic constants such as k_{P_i}. Cells were grouped into independent communities, with each community providing a shared supply of the two types of external nutrient to its particular cells. A community was implemented as an event-driven Gillespie SSA [7,8] that utilised improvements due to Gibson and Bruck [9] in order to minimise propensity recalculation after each, largely independent, cell event.

A simulation consisted of series of coordinated generations for a set of communities, synchronising the communities between generations. At the start of each simulation, 48 communities were created, each with 10,000 units of each type of nutrient. The initial population of cells all had different random parameter sets consisting of floating-point values in the range [0, 100). This limited starting range was found to result in more viable starting communities than wider ones, although values were only constrained thereafter to be non-negative. On each generation, cells within a community competed among themselves for the shared nutrients. At the end of each generation, the largest population size among all communities was determined and a simulation was ended when that size had stabilised within small variations. Between generations, the composition of each community was adjusted and the supply of nutrients was renewed to its original level.

A generation for a community was completed when any one of the following conditions was fulfilled:

- All of the cells had died.
- All of both types of external nutrient had been consumed.
- A time limit had been reached. (For runs reported here this was set to 20 time units.)
- No cell was able to perform any future action (i.e., the propensity sum for reactions in all cells was zero).

Once all communities had completed a single generation, population compositions were adjusted and a further generation was run. At the end of each generation, the maximum population size was output along with the parameter values of a random cell chosen from the largest community. We used two distinct evolutionary approaches to evolve parameters of the cell model: implicit evolution and a genetic algorithm (GA). The differences between these approaches are described in Sect. 3.1 and 3.2.

3.1 The Implicit Approach

In the implicit approach, each community was seeded with 2000 randomly initialised cells for the initial generation. Each community, therefore, had a heterogeneous population. During a generation, cells grew, divided and died. On division, there was a probability of mutation in the newly created cell's copy of the dividing cell's parameter values. Each parental parameter value had a probability of mutation. If a parameter was mutated, its value was adjusted up or down by a percentage. Parameter values which were adjusted to zero were then reset to a random floating-point value in the range $[0, 100)$.

Between generations, community populations were adjusted in the following ways:

- Each community whose size was above a limit of 100 cells was reduced to the limit by removing random cells from it.
- After population reduction, all communities were re-seeded to 200 cells via the introduction of new cells with random parameter values.
- A percentage of randomly-selected cells were transferred between communities. Candidate cells for migration were chosen with a probability based on their community's size before the reduction and reseeding processes described above.
- On migration, there was a probability that a percentage of the migrant cell's parameter values might be crossed over with those of an existing random cell of the receiving community.

3.2 The Genetic Algorithm Approach

In the GA approach, each community was seeded with a single cell at the start of each generation. Random parameter sets typically proved to be unviable with a single cell, so cells for the initial generation of the GA were selected randomly from those remaining after a single generation of the implicit approach had been run. During each generation, cells in each community grew, divided and died but there was no mutation on division. In contrast to the implicit approach, therefore, the communities in this approach were always homogeneous.

At the end of a generation, community population size was used as the fitness function. However, in order to smooth some of the stochastic variation in population size (and, hence, fitness reliability), a community was only considered to have a completed a generation after it had undergone repeated "runs" with the same single-cell starting point. In order to avoid confusion over terminology, therefore, we shall refer to these non selective runs as *trials* in the following description. No mutation or crossover was performed between trials; the population in each community was simply reduced back to 1. The fitness of a community was assigned as the *minimum* population level achieved over the course of those several trials. We typically used either 3 or 5 trials per generation. Between generations, communities were adjusted in the following ways:

- Fitness-proportional selection was used to select seed cells (enough for one per community) for the next generation.
- Each community was cleared and a single seed cell put into it.
- When a seed cell was put into a community there was a probability of mutation of its parameters. Each parameter value had a probability of mutation. If a parameter was mutated, its value was adjusted up or down by a percentage. Parameter values which were adjusted to zero were then reset to a random floating-point value in the range $[0, 100]$.

– When a seed cell was put into a community there was a probability of its being crossed over with the parameters of a different seed cell. A percentage of its parameters would be crossed over.

The percentage and probability values referred to above for the two approaches were all set globally and remained constant for a single simulation run, but all could be varied between simulations.

4   Results

Around 10,000 simulations were conducted with both approaches, varying the various mutation and crossover rates and percentages described in Sect. 3 in combinations of 0, 20, 50, 80 and 100 percent. There were no significant differences in either the qualitative or quantitative behaviours of the resulting parameter sets from any particular combination of these. The characteristics described here are typical, therefore, of those we observed across the range of evolutionary configurations.

Parameter sets that result in models demonstrating growth are difficult to find. We ran around 40 million trials of a single cell for one generation of the GA with random parameter values in the range $[0 - 100)$. 99.6% of the trials resulted in a final population size of either 0 or 1. Fig. 2 provides a sample of the frequency counts of population size from those trials. Random limits of 10 and 1000 both produced even lower percentages of cells that replicated.

The GA, with its single-cell seeding, therefore, often required a significant number of generations before a viable population could be established. However, once growth started, fitness levels usually rose rapidly. Fig. 3 provides an illustration of how the overall fitness values typically vary over time in three separate GA simulations. (The initial, non-productive generations have been omitted from each plot.) The three plateaus discernible there represent exploitation of the less-efficient nutrient N_2, nutrient N_1 or both together. The plateaus were invariably repeated, to varying degrees, in all successful simulations.

Fig. 4 illustrates the typical trend in evolution of the maximum population size over two runs using the implicit approach. The population levels arising during the evolutionary process in the two approaches are not directly comparable, however, since the population numbers at the start of each generation are significantly different (200 cells versus 1 cell).

In order to examine the characteristics of cells evolving from the simulations, we took a single parameter set from a random cell in the largest community at the end of successful simulation runs. This set was then used to seed a single community with a single cell for one generation. On this generation there was no mutation or crossover, so the population size at the end of the generation was purely a measure of the solution's ability to convert nutrient to biomass. The time limit for these runs was increased to 100 time units, and the nutrient level was increased to 100,000 units of each type.

Cells evolved from the two evolutionary approaches exhibit significantly different approaches to nutrient consumption. Parameters evolved via the implicit

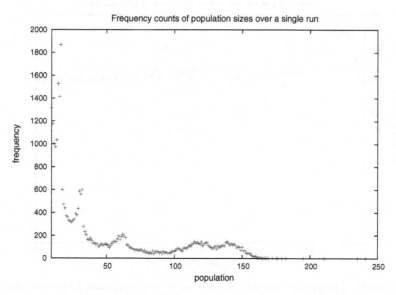

Fig. 2. Frequency counts of population sizes $>= 9$ at the end of a single generation starting with a single cell, from around 40 million sample runs with random parameter values. Over 99% of the runs resulted in no increase in biomass.

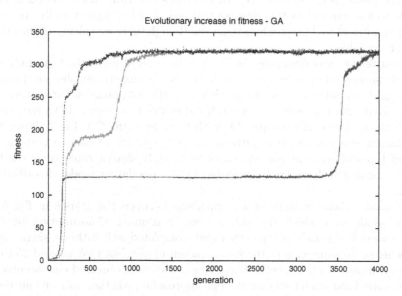

Fig. 3. Overall fitness over successive generations for three simulations using the GA. Runs typically plateau at three distinct levels (here: around 140, 190 and 320). Low fitness initial generations have been omitted.

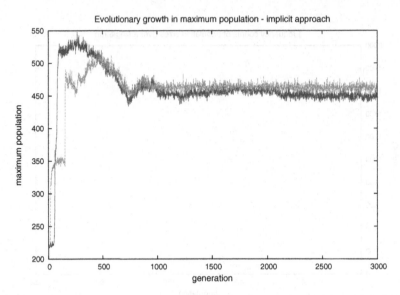

Fig. 4. Growth in maximum population over successive generations for two simulations using the implicit approach. Initial seeding generation of 2000 cells omitted.

approach usually exhibited a strong preference for just a single nutrient – typically the more energy efficient N_1. In the single-cell runs this made them vulnerable to nutrient exhaustion and populations would collapse rapidly once the preferred nutrient had been exhausted, even though there was plenty of the other nutrient available.

In contrast, as was illustrated in Fig. 3, cells evolved using the GA approach regularly succeeded in increasing their fitness to the uppermost plateau through harnessing both nutrient types for growth. Nevertheless, on a few rare occasions, cells evolved with the implicit approach did evolve to consume both nutrients, making them more easily comparable with those from the GA. Fig. 5 illustrates the dual nutrient consumption patterns of both types. Note that, in both cases, the two types of nutrient are consumed at roughly similar rates *concurrently*, and not consecutively as was anticipated by the regulatory model described in Sect. 2.

The most striking feature of a comparison between the graphs in Fig. 5 is the time-scale over which the nutrient was consumed. Consumption by the implicitly-evolved cells was typically rapid, completed well within a single time step, whereas consumption of the same amount of nutrient took around 25 time steps to complete with GA cells. These time-scales were observed consistently in all the evolved parameter sets for the two approaches, whether only one nutrient was consumed or both.

Another consistent difference between the solutions is that those evolved from the GA approach are more efficient in their conversion of nutrient to biomass. Fig. 6 shows population growth over time for the two approaches. The time

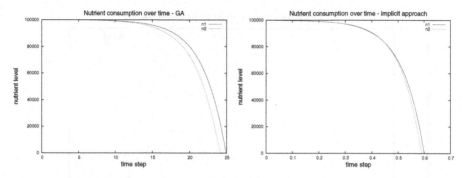

Fig. 5. Nutrient consumption over time for the GA (left) and implicit approach (right). In the resulting cells, both nutrients are consumed in roughly equal amounts concurrently. However, note the significantly different timescales of the consumption from the different approaches.

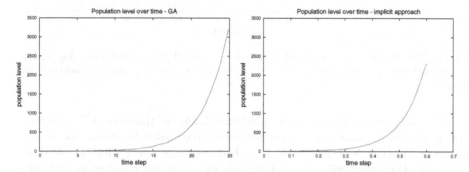

Fig. 6. Population growth over time for the GA (left) and implicit approach (right). Note the difference in final population levels, as well as the timescales of the growth.

scales are the same as those seen for nutrient consumption. With 100,000 units of each type of nutrient, population sizes from the GA approach tend to reach 2,900-3,200 while those from the implicit approach reach only 2,200-2,300.

Fig. 7 seeks to visualise the difference in nutrient efficiency by representing it via population size divided by amount of nutrient consumed. Since the timescales of the different cell types are not directly comparable, the x-axis is simply based on periodic progress reporting and it is the differential efficiency levels that are the significant feature.

In order to examine whether the inefficiencies of the implicit solutions were linked to the speed of nutrient consumption, we undertook further simulations with the GA approach but imposed a time limit comparable to that exhibited by the implicit solutions. In these explorations, fitness levels were first allowed to reach a minimum of 10 within the standard 20 time steps in order to establish viable communities, but then the time limit was progressively reduced by 5% on each successive generation until it reached the desired lower limit. The simulations then continued until a stable overall fitness level was reached. We set time limits between 0.1 and 0.8 time steps.

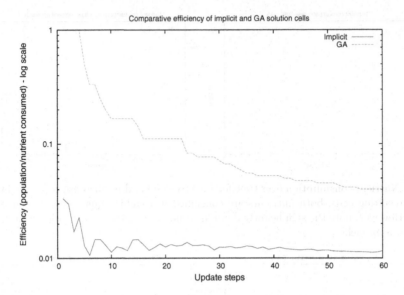

Fig. 7. (Population size / nutrient consumed) as an efficiency indicator (log scale) shows that the cells evolved by the GA are more efficient at converting nutrient to biomass

The main consequence of this reduced time limit was that most GA solutions now produced parameter sets that almost entirely failed to utilise one of the nutrients for growth (typically N_2), as had been the norm with the implicit approach. The single-cell comparative runs with solution parameters typically terminated before the end of the 100 time steps through population extinction as a result of single nutrient exhaustion. Further confirmation that these parameter sets were close in character to those resulting from the implicit approach were that the maximum fitness levels achieved were below 2000 (reached within a timescale comparable to that of the implicit solutions) and the nutrient efficiency levels stabilised in the range 0.01 to 0.02 (cf Fig. 7).

An interesting side-effect of these time-limited simulations was the emergence of a single solution whose behaviour we had not previously observed in any of the other unconstrained or constrained runs of either type. While its evolutionary character exhibited no difference from those illustrated in Fig. 3, its nutrient consumption and growth behaviour were quite different. Both are illustrated in Fig. 8, which should be compared with Fig. 5 and 6. Up to around 0.6 time steps, N_1 is consumed to exhaustion with little use of N_2, but the cell then switches to consumption of N_2 with further growth. While this appears to represent a successful parameterisation of the switching behaviour described in Sect. 2, the switching is not, in fact, regulated by R. Instead, it appears to be caused by large quantities of P_1 preventing production of P_2 due to the space limit at the surface of the cell (Eq. 8). Once levels of P_1 drop on the exhaustion of N_1, P_2 levels are able to rise to support uptake of N_2.

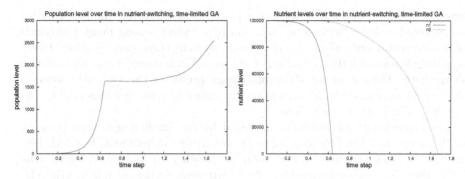

Fig. 8. Population growth and nutrient consumption over time in a parameter set resulting from a GA constrained to 0.5 time steps. The cells exhibit a form of switching as consumption of N_2 accelerates shortly after the time at which the supply of N_1 is exhausted.

5   Discussion and Conclusions

The most significant result of this study is our observation of the widely different characteristics exhibited by the solutions arising from the particular approach used to evolve them. The implicit approach leads to individuals whose preference is to consume nutrient very quickly without necessarily using it to produce biomass. In contrast, individuals derived from the GA consume nutrient around 40 times more slowly and devote a greater proportion of their consumption to the production of biomass. The implicit solutions were significantly less efficient than those evolved by the GA. With many solutions, the inefficiency was a consequence of almost completely ignoring one of the nutrients as a source of energy, while most GA solutions eventually evolved to utilise both nutrients. Yet, even when implicit solutions utilised both, they did so significantly less efficiently than the GA solutions.

In a homogeneous GA community, cells are not in competition with one another in terms of selection based on fitness, since selection of any one of them for the next generation ensures the survival of the shared parameter set. In contrast, in a heterogeneous implicit community, selection at the end of a generation is not guaranteed based purely on a cell's contribution to the community's growth in size. Hence, accumulation of nutrient and, thereby, denial of it to other (biologically different) cells appears to be a stronger driving force for survival and, hence, selection.

Our attempts to evolve parameter sets for the biological model described in Sect. 2 demonstrated that viable parameter sets – those capable of producing even small amounts of biomass – are relatively rare. We also did not succeed in evolving a parameter set that exhibited genuine nutrient switching via the regulator R. Whether this is a result of a limitation of the design of the model, the complexities introduced by the stochastic nature of the system, the rarity of feasible solutions, or some other factor is not clear. However, the fact that we encountered a single "switching" solution by accident among many thousands of non-switching ones allows for the possibility that there may be other, rarely occurring behaviours that we have not yet seen. For instance, there was nothing significantly different about the evolutionary profile of the switching solution that would have made its identification any easier to spot, and this may be the case with other atypical solutions.

The evolutionary environment modelled by the implicit approach is closer in character than the GA to a naturally occurring environment, in which biologically distinct variants compete with one another for limited resources. One interesting speculation we might make is: Are some living organisms also relative inefficient in their utilisation of resources, because it confers a competitive advantage due to the nature of the environments in which they exist?

References

1. Alon, U.: Network motifs: theory and experimental approaches. Nature Review Genetics 8(6), 450–461 (2007)
2. Paulsson, J.: Summing up the noise in gene networks. Nature 427(6973), 415–418 (2004)
3. Chu, D.: Replaying the tape of evolution: Evolving parameters for a simple bacterial metabolism. In: IEEE Congress on Evolutionary Computation (CEC), pp. 213–220 (2013)
4. Chu, D.: Evolving parameters for a noisy bio-systems. In: 2013 IEEE Symposion series on Computational Intelligence (2013)
5. Chu, D., Zabet, N., Mitavskiy, B.: Models of transcription factor binding: Sensitivity of activation functions to model assumptions. Journal of Theoretical Biology 257(3), 419–429 (2009)
6. Chu, D., Zabet, N., Hone, A.: Optimal parameter settings for information processing in gene regulatory networks. BioSystems 104, 99–108 (2011)
7. Gillespie, D.: Exact stochastic simulation of coupled chemical reactions. The Journal of Physical Chemistry 81(25), 2340–2361 (1977)
8. Barnes, D., Chu, D.: Introduction to Modelling for Biosciences. Springer, Berlin (2010)
9. Gibson, M., Bruck, J.: Efficient exact stochastic simulation of chemical systems with many species and many channels. Journal of Physical Chemistry 104, 1876–1889 (2000)

Classification of EEG Signals Using Vector Quantization

Petr Berek, Michal Prilepok, Jan Platos, and Vaclav Snasel

Department of Computer Science, FEECS,
IT4 Innovations, Centre of Excellence,
VSB-Technical University of Ostrava,
Ostrava Poruba, Czech Republic
{petr.berek,michal.prilepok,jan.platos,vaclav.snasel}@vsb.cz

Abstract. Proper identification and classification of the EEG data still pauses a problem in the field of brain diagnosis. However, the application of such algorithm is almost unlimited as they may be involved in applications such as, brain computer interface for controlling of prosthesis, wheelchair, etc.. In this paper we are focusing on applying data compression in the classification of EEG signals. We combine a vector quantization and the normalized compression distance for proper classification of a finger movement data.

Keywords: Electroencephalography, EEG, BCI, EEG waves group, EEG data, NCD.

1 Introduction

The Electroencephalography (EEG) has a big role in the diagnosis of brain, as well as, in Brain Computer Interface (BCI) system applications, which help disabled people to use their mind to control external devices. Both research areas are growing these days.

EEG records an activity of the brain using several sensor sets. Different mental tasks may seems the same on the recordings but they are different, because different brain actions activate different parts of brains. The difficult task is to define an efficient method or algorithm for detection of the differences in recordings belonging to the different mental tasks. When we define such algorithm, we are able to translate these recorded signals into control commands for the external devices, such as. prosthesis, wheelchairs, computer terminals, etc.

2 The Electroencephalography

Electroencephalography (EEG) measures the electrical activity of a human brain by placing set of sensors on a scalp according to 10/20 EEG International electrode placement, as depicted on Figure 1. We distinguish two types of measuring EEG: a measuring of EEG that can record signals between two active electrodes - bipolar recording, or between an active electrode and reference electrode - monopole recordings. [21]

L. Rutkowski et al. (Eds.): ICAISC 2014, Part II, LNAI 8468, pp. 107–118, 2014.
© Springer International Publishing Switzerland 2014

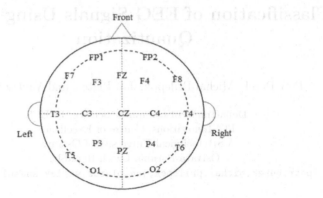

Fig. 1. 10/20 International Electrode Placement

2.1 EEG Wave Types

The types of brain waves distinguished by their different frequency ranges are recognized as follows.

Delta (δ) waves lie within the range from 0.5 to 4 Hz where the amplitude is varying, These waves are associated with deep sleep and present in the waking state. Theta (θ) waves. These lie within the range from 4 to 7.5 Hz where the amplitude is about 20 μV. Theta waves have been associated with access to unconscious material, creative inspiration and deep meditation. The frequency of the Alpha (α) waves lies within the range from 8 to 13 Hz, where the amplitude is about 30 to 50 μV. It is reduced or eliminated by opening the eyes, hearing unfamiliar sounds, anxiety, or mental concentration or attention. Beta (β) wave is the electrical activity of the brain varying within the frequency range from 14 to 26 Hz. In this case, the amplitude is about 5 to 30 μV, and it is associated with active thinking, active attention, focus on the outside world, or solving concrete problems. A high- level beta wave may be acquired when a human is in a panic state. Gamma (γ) waves have frequency range above 30 Hz, These wave can be used to demonstrate the locus for right and left index finger movement, right toes, and the rather broad and bilateral area for tongue movement [23] and [22]. Mu (μ) waves bare the same Alpha frequency range, 8 to 13 Hz, but Alpha waves are recorded on occipital cortex area, and Mu waves are recorded on motor cortex area. Mu waves are related to spontaneous nature of the brain, such as motor activities [22].

2.2 History of EEG

Carlo Matteucci and Emil Du Bois-Reymond, were the first who register the electrical signals emitted from muscle nerves using a galvanometer and established the concept of neurophysiology. The first brain activity in the form of electrical signals was recorded in 1875 by Richard Caton (1842 - 1926), a scientist from Liverpool, England, using a galvanometer and two electrodes placed over the scalp of a human. Accordingly, the term EEG stands for: Electro which refers to the registration of brain electrical activities, Encephalon which refers to emitting the signals from a brain, and gram or graphy, which means drawing. Then the term EEG was henceforth used to denote electrical neural activity of the brain [23].

In 1920, Hans Berger, the discoverer of the existence of human EEG signals, began his study of human EEG. In 1910, Berger started working with a string galvanometer and later he used a smaller Edelmann model. After the year 1924, he used larger Edelmann model. In 1026, Berger started to use the more powerful Siemens double coil galvanometer (attaining a sensitivity of 130 $\mu V/cm$). In 1929 Berger made the first report of human EEG recordings with duration from one to three minutes on a photographic paper and, in the same year, he also found some correlation between mental activities and the changes in the EEG signals [23].

The first biological amplifier for the recording of brain potentials was built by Toennies (1902 - 1970). In 1932 the differential amplifier for EEG recording was later produced by the Rockefeller foundation. The potential of a multichannel recordings and a large number of electrodes to cover a wider brain region was recognized by Kornmuller. Berger, assisted by Dietch (1932), applied Fourier analysis to EEG sequences, which was developed during the 1950s [23].

After that, the EEG analysis and classification grew and developed rapidly. The application of the EEG signals analysis leads to the diagnosis of the brain diseases and to control external devices for disabled people such as wheel chair, prosthesis, etc. Today, several techniques for analysis and classification the EEG signal take place, by using multi EEG channels recording according to 10/20 International electrodes standard, which is used in Brain Computer Interface (BCI).

3   Related Works

In this section we present some of the related works, for EEG data analysis using different techniques such as Non-negative Matrix Factorization (NMF), Normalized Compression Distance (NCD), and LempelZiv complexity (LZ).

Lee et al. presented a Semi-supervised version of NMF (SSNMF) which jointly exploited both (partial) labeled and unlabeled data to extract more discriminative features than the standard NMF. Their experiments on EEG datasets in BCI competition confirm that SSNMF improves clustering as well as classification performance, compared to the standard NMF [14].

Shin et al. have proposed new generative model of a group EEG analysis, based on appropriate kernel assumptions on EEG data. Their proposed model finds common patterns for a specific task class across all subjects as well as individual patterns that capture intra-subject variability. The validity of the proposed method have been tested on the BCI competition EEG dataset [25].

Dohnalek et al. have proposed a method for signal pattern matching based on NMF. They also used short-time Fourier transform to preprocess EEG data and

Cosine Similarity Measure to perform query-based classification. This method of creating a BCI is capable of real-time pattern recognition in brainwaves using a low cost hardware, with very cost efficient way of solving the problem [5].

Mehmood, and Damarla applied kernel non-negative matrix factorization to separate between the human and horse footsteps, and compared KNMF with standard NMF. T, their result conclude that KNMF work better than standard NMF [18].

Sousa Silva, et al. verified that the Lempel and Ziv complexity measurement of EEG signals using wavelets transforms is independent on the electrode position and dependents on the cognitive tasks and brain activity. Their results show that the complexity measurement is dependent on the changes of the pattern of brain dynamics and not dependent on electrode position [26].

Noshadi et al. have applied Empirical mode decomposition (EMD) and improved Lempel-Ziv(LZ) complexity measure for discrimination of mental tasks. Their results reached 92.46% in precision, and also they concluded that EMD-LZ is getting better performance for mental tasks classification than some of other techniques [20].

Li Ling, and Wang Ruiping calculated the complexity of sleeping stages of EEG signals, using Lempel-Ziv complexity. Their results showed that nonlinear feature can reflect sleeping stage adequately, and it is useful in automatic recognition of sleep stages [17].

Krishna, et al. proposed an algorithm for classification of the wrist movement in four directions from Magneto encephalography (MEG) signals. The proposed method includes signal smoothing, design of a class-specific Unique Identifier Signal (UIS) and curve fitting to identify the direction in a given test signal. The method was tested on data set of the BCI competition, and the best result of the prediction accuracy reached to 88.84% [11].

4   Vector Quantization

Vector quantization (VQ) is well-known method for data reduction [7]. It can be used in many applications, for example in data compression and signal processing [13], [9], [12] and [2]. We can define vector quantization as a mapping function which maps finite vector space to finite set of vectors - called codebook (CB), $CB = C_1, C_2, C_3, \ldots, C_n$, where n is the size of the codebook and C_i represents one item from the codebook. Each item in codebook is a vector with the same length as the original vector $C_i = ci_1, ci_2, ci_3, ci_k$ where k is the length of the block or vector[10]. Each vector in the codebook has it's unique number. Vector quantization has two phase codebook preparation and encoding.

The encoding phase of the vector quantization consists of processing of the input data and generation of the vectors space. The length of the vectors is the parameter of the algorithm. For example, if we are processing images, we may take 2, 4, 8 or even more pixels from a image as a one vector. However, when we gather all unique vectors from the data including their frequency we may use many different strategies for creation of the codebook with size N (which is also a parameter of an algorithm). One principle is that we may remove the least used vectors from the set until we get the proper number of vectors. This principle may bring more error in the second phase. Another principle may replace two similar vector by their average which reduces the errors of the second phase.

In our work we used the following algorithm for the set reduction:

1. We create codebook (CB) by sequence of non-overlapping numbers
2. $|CB|$ is the size of the codebook
3. Target CB size is $N = |CB| * C$ where C is a constant defined empirically.
4. While($|CB| > N$)
   (a) For each search vector (SV) in CB
       i. Find nearest vector (NV) in CB
       ii. Compute the average vector (AV) from NV and SV according the equation 1.
       iii. Delete NV and SV from CB
       iv. Insert AV into CB

The average vector (AV) is computed by the average values of each vector component from two vectors - nearest vector (NV) and search vector (SV).

$$AV[i] = (NV[i] + SV[i])/2 \tag{1}$$

Where

- AV - average vector
- NV - nearest vector
- SV - search vector
- AV[i], NV[i], SV[i] - i-th compomenet of vector AV, NV, SV

The encoding phase of the vector quantization is a mapping of the original vector from the data using the codebook. For each vector from the input data, we find the most similar vector in the CB and we replace it by the number of the most similar vector. When we need to reconstruct the original data, we need the codebook and we replace each vector number by the vector from the codebook. The reconstruction is lossy, because we reduced the number of used vectors, therefore, we remove some information from the data.

5   The Normalized Compression Distance

The Normalized Compression Distance (NCD) is based on Kolmogorov complexity. It makes use of standard compressors in order to approximate Kolmogorov complexity. The NCD has been used for text retrieval [8], text clustering, plagiarism detection [27], music clustering [19] and [8], music style modeling [6], automatic construction of the phylogeny tree based on whole mitochondrial genomes [15], the automatic construction of language trees [1] and [16], and the automatic evaluation of machine translations [4]. The NCD is a mathematical way for measuring the similarity of two objects x and y. Measuring of similarity is realized by the help of compression where repeating parts are suppressed by compression. NCD may be used for comparison of different objects, such as images, music, texts or gene sequences. NCD has requirements to compressor. The compressor meets the condition

$$C(x) = C(xx) \qquad (2)$$

within logarithmic bounds [24]. We may use NCD for detection of plagiarism and visual data extraction [28,3]. The resulting rate of probability distance between two objects x and y is calculated by the following formula:

$$NCD(x,y) = \frac{C(xy) - min(C(x), C(y))}{max(C(x), C(y))} \qquad (3)$$

Where:

- $C(x)$ is the length (size) of compression of objects x,
- $C(xy)$ is the length of compression concatenation of objects x and y,
- $min(C(x), C(y))$ is the minimum length (size) of values x and y after compression,
- $max(C(x), C(y))$ is the maximum length (size) of values x and y after compression.

The NCD value is in the interval $0 < NCD(x; y) < 1 + \epsilon$. If $NCD(x, y) = 0$, then files x and y are equal. They have the highest difference when the result value of $NCD(x, y) = 1 + \epsilon$. The constant ϵ describes the inefficiency of the used compressor.

The NCD is not a metric. It is an approximation of the Normalized Information Distance (NID). The computation of the NCD is very efficient because we do not need to create the output itself. We compute only the size of the output. A study of the efficient implementation of the compression algorithms may be found in [29].

6   EEG Experiment

In this section we describe the data used in our experiments, the proposed algorithm and, finally, the achieved results.

6.1   EEG Data

The data for our experiments was recorded in our laboratory. We have used 7 selected channels from recorded data. The signal data contains records of the movement of one finger from four different subjects - persons. Every subject performed a press of a button with left index finger. The sampling rate was set to 256 Hz. The signals were band pass filtered from 0.5 Hz to 60 Hz to remove unwanted frequencies and noise from the outside environment. The data was then processed, that we extract each movement from the data as well as 0.3 second before the start of the movement and 0.3 second after the end of the movement. We marked the starting and ending position of the movement during data recording.

The preprocessed data contains 4606 data segments - 2303 data segments with finger movement and 2303 data segments without finger movement. We divided this set of data segments into seven groups - one group for each sensor. Each group contains part of training and testing data part. The testing data part contains 75% of data segments with finger movement and 75% of data segments without finger movement. The rest of unused data segments - with and without finger movement - were used for training part. The training part for one sensor contains 492 data segments - 246 data segments with finger movement and 246 data segments without finger movement. The testing part contains 166 data segments - 83 data segments with finger movement and 83 data segments without finger movement. We used the training and testing part for further model validation.

6.2 Proposed Method Description

We may define EEG data as sequence of numbers. In the encoding phase, data is divided into non- overlapping data segments vectors. These vectors creat the list of vectors used in the data. Then, we applied the vector quantization algorithm as described in section 4. Constant C in our experiment is set to 2/3, and we used a cosine measure as a distance measure for the vectors in codebook. After that, we applied hierarchical clustering algorithm.

This algorithm created new vectors. We needed to save these vectors for comparison. In the next, algorithm we computed for each vector in CB it's norm. We used norm of vector for sorting vectors and we created sorted codebook. We assume that for similar EEG data we get similar sorted codebooks. Then we saved the vectors in codebook. For each vector in codebook, we saved every component as a text. In other words, if a component of a vector is a number then, we saved the number as its text representation. In the next step, we looked for nearest vector in codebook for each original vector and we saved the index into a mapped file.

In summary we created codebook from non-overlapping numbers from EEG data and we applied vector quantization. We sorted codebook and saved each component of each vector as text and we used backward reconstruction of signal to save the indices into file. We created codebook with the length of vectors set to twelve numbers. On this codebook we applied vector quantization algorithm.

After applying vector quantization with the same setup on all data segments extracted, vectors from dataset we evaluated similarity between one data segments from testing group to all data segments in training group of one sensor. The similarity was measured with NCD and 7-Zip compression algorithm as a compressor. The similarity evaluation was applied to all testing data segments.

Next, we selected a group of training data segments with similarity S satisfying the following condition $S >= minThreshold$ & $S <= maxThreshold$ for every test data segment. The condition threshold values are depicted in Table 1 for data with movement and in Table 2 for data without movement for all sensors.

This selected group of data segments is used to indicated which category belongs to the tested data segment. This was calculated as a ratio of data segments with movement to total count of the selected data segments in a group, using the following formula

$$C = \frac{m}{c} \qquad (4)$$

where:

- m is a count of data segments, which are marked during data pre-processing as data segment with movement,
- c is a count of data segments in the selected group, which satisfy condition.

The tested data segment is marked as data segment which belongs to the category with movement data segments, if $C >= 0.5$, and as a data segments without movement otherwise. These steps were performed separately for all categories of data - with movement and without movement - and all sensors.

The values of $minThreshold$ and $maxThreshold$ represents the boundaries in which the classifier has correctly identified maximum data segments, where $minThreshold \in [0,1]$ and $maxThreshold \in [0,1]$ and $minThreshold < maxThreshold$, e.g. $minThreshold = 0.15$ and $maxThreshold = 0.2$.

On Figure 2 we may see that similarities for one testing data segment to all training data segments on one sensor are separated in two groups - ranges with small overlapping. We used this feature to decide whether the testing data segment belongs to the data segment group with finger movements or not.

6.3   Experiment Result

Our experiment was divided into two parts. The first part is focused on successful movement detection and the other is focused on successful detection of data segments without movement. Both experiments uses the same conditions and experiment setup.

In our experiment we tried to find thea shortest range in which we are able to correctly decide the category of the tested data segment - with or without finger movement.

In our first experiment we could detect the movement of index finger with success rate between 89.16% and 100.00%. We reached the best results on all sensors except sensor S4 (89.16%) and S5 (89.16%). The worst results were for sensors S4 and S5 with success rate 89.16%. The movement detection results and their corresponding threshold values for all sensor are depicted in Table 1.

Most of the values taken by $minThreshold$ are around 0.20 and $maxThreshold$ values were situated around value 0.51.

In the second experiment we could detect data segment without movement of index finger with success rate between 85.37% and 100.00%. The best results were reached on all sensors except sensor S4 (87.95%) and sensor S5 (85.37%). The worst result was on sensor S5 (85.37%). The movement detection results and their corresponding threshold values for all sensor are depicted in Table 2

The most $minThreshold$ values in the second experiment were around 0.15 and $maxThreshold$ values were situated up to value 0.55.

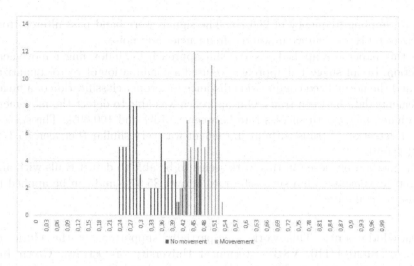

Fig. 2. Histogram of the similarities for data segment with and without movement of one sensor

Table 1. Table of Movement Results

Sensor	Min Threshold	Max Threshold	Finger Movement
S1	0.20	0.55	100.00%
S2	0.14	0.56	100.00%
S3	0.16	0.56	100.00%
S4	0,49	0.51	89.16%
S5	0.36	0.44	89.16%
S6	0.18	0.52	100.00%
S7	0.47	0.57	100.00%

Table 2. Table of No Movement Results

Sensor	Min Threshold	Max Threshold	No Movement
S1	0.15	0.55	100.00%
S2	0.11	0.55	100.00%
S3	0.15	0.53	100.00%
S4	0.47	0.52	87.95%
S5	0.37	0.46	85.37%
S6	0.13	0.50	100.00%
S7	0.06	0.55	100.00%

7   Conclusion

We conducted our experiments on our EEG data recorded in our laboratory from four different subjects performing the same task - pressing a button with index finger. The EEG data was recorded using 7 channels recording machine with a sampling frequency of 256 Hz. The signals were band pass filtered from 0.5 Hz to 60 Hz to remove unwanted frequencies and noise.

In this paper, we applied a successful approach for index finger movement detection. In our suggested approach we used a combination of vector quantization and the normalized compression distance for proper classification of a finger movements data between trails. Our approach was able to detect the movement of an index finger with success rate between 89.16% and 100.00%. The success rate of detection of trails without movement was very similar (between 85.37% and 100.00%.)

The method proposed in this work seems to be able to detect trails with and without movement with a successful rate of over 85.37% and can be applied to the use on real data.

Acknowledgment. This work was partially supported by the Grant of SGS No. SP2014/110, VŠB - Technical University of Ostrava, Czech Republic, and was supported by the European Regional Development Fund in the IT4Innovations Centre of Excellence project (CZ.1.05/1.1.00/02.0070) and by the Bio-Inspired Methods: research, development and knowledge transfer project, reg. no. CZ.1.07/2.3.00/20.0073 funded by Operational Programme Education for Competitiveness, co-financed by ESF and state budget of the Czech Republic.

References

1. Benedetto, D., Caglioti, E., Loreto, V.: Language trees and zipping. Physical Review Letters 88(4), 48,702 (2002)
2. Chang, P.C., Yu, C.S., Lee, T.H.: Hybrid lms-mmse inverse halftoning technique. IEEE Transactions on Image Processing 10(1), 95–103 (2001)
3. Cilibrasi, R., Vitnyi, P.M.B.: Clustering by compression. CoRR cs.CV/0312044 (2003), http://dblp.unitrier.de/db/journals/corr/corr0312.html
4. Dobrinkat, M., Väyrynen, J., Tapiovaara, T., Kettunen, K.: Normalized compression distance based measures for metricsmatr 2010. In: Proceedings of the Joint Fifth Workshop on Statistical Machine Translation and MetricsMATR, WMT 2010, pp. 343–348. Association for Computational Linguistics, Stroudsburg (2010)
5. Dohnálek, P., Gajdoš, P., Peterek, T., Penhaker, M.: Pattern recognition in EEG cognitive signals accelerated by GPU. In: Herrero, Á., Snášel, V., Abraham, A., Zelinka, I., Baruque, B., Quintián, H., Calvo, J.L., Sedano, J., Corchado, E. (eds.) Int. Joint Conf. CISIS'12-ICEUTE'12-SOCO'12. AISC, vol. 189, pp. 477–485. Springer, Heidelberg (2013)
6. Dubnov, S., Assayag, G., Lartillot, O., Bejerano, G.: Using machine-learning methods for musical style modeling. IEEE Computer 36(10), 73–80 (2003), http://dblp.uni-trier.de/db/journals/computer/computer36.html
7. Gersho, A., Gray, R.M.: Vector Quantization and Signal Compression. Kluwer Academic Publishers, Norwell (1991)
8. Granados, A.: Analysis and study on text representation to improve the accuracy of the normalized compression distance. AI Commun. 25(4), 381–384 (2012), http://dblp.uni-trier.de/db/journals/aicom/aicom25.html

9. Hsieh, C.H., Tsai, J.C.: Lossless compression of vq index with search-order coding. IEEE Transactions on Image Processing 5(11), 1579–1582 (1996)
10. Kekre, D.H.B., Tanuja, M., Sarode, K.: Vector quantized codebook optimization using k-means
11. Krishna, S., Vinay, K.C., Raja, K.B.: Efficient meg signal decoding of direction in wrist movement using curve fitting (emdc). In: 2011 International Conference on Image Information Processing (ICIIP), pp. 1–6 (2011), doi:10.1109/ICIIP.2011.6108851
12. Lai, J.Z.C., Yen, J.Y.: Inverse error-diffusion using classified vector quantization. IEEE Transactions on Image Processing 7(12), 1753–1758 (1998)
13. Lai, J.Z.C., Liaw, Y.C., Liu, J.: A fast vq codebook generation algorithm using codeword displacement. Pattern Recogn. 41(1), 315–319 (2008), http://dx.doi.org/10.1016/j.patcog.2007.04.015, doi:10.1016/j.patcog.2007.04.015
14. Lee, H., Yoo, J., Choi, S.: Semi-supervised nonnegative matrix factorization. IEEE Signal Processing Letters 17(1), 4–7 (2010), doi:10.1109/LSP.2009.2027163
15. Li, M., Badger, J.H., Chen, X., Kwong, S., Kearney, P., Zhang, H.: An information-based sequence distance and its application to whole mitochondrial genome phylogeny. Bioinformatics 17(2), 149–154 (2001), doi:10.1093/bioinformatics/17.2.149
16. Li, M., Chen, X., Li, X., Ma, B., Vitanyi, P.: The similarity metric (2004), http://arxiv.org/abs/cs.CC/0111054
17. Ling, L., Ruiping, W.: Complexity analysis of sleep eeg signal. In: 2010 4th International Conference on Bioinformatics and Biomedical Engineering (iCBBE), pp. 1–3 (2010), doi:10.1109/ICBBE.2010.5515699
18. Mehmood, A., Damarla, T.: Kernel non-negative matrix factorization for seismic signature separation. Journal of Pattern Recognition Research 8(1), 13–25 (2013), doi:10.13176/11.463
19. Niblack, W., Barber, R., Equitz, W., Flickner, M., Glasman, E.H., Petkovic, D., Yanker, P., Faloutsos, C., Taubin, G.: The qbic project: Querying images by content, using color, texture, and shape. In: Storage and Retrieval for Image and Video Databases (SPIE), pp. 173–187 (1993), http://dblp.uni-trier.de/db/conf/spieSR/spieSR93.html
20. Noshadi, S., Abootalebi, V., Sadeghi, M.T.: A new method based on emd and lz complexity algorithms for discrimination of mental tasks. In: 2011 18th Iranian Conference of Biomedical Engineering (ICBME), pp. 115–118 (2011), doi:10.1109/ICBME.2011.6168535
21. Quiroga, R.Q.: Quantitative analysis of eeg signals: Time-frequency methods and chaos theory. Ph.D. thesis, Institute of Signal Processing and Institute of Physiology, Medical University of Lubeck, Germany (1998)
22. Rao, T.K., Lakshmi, M.R., Prasad, T.V.: An exploration on brain computer interface and its recent trends. International Journal of Advanced Research in Artificial Intelligence 1(8), 17–22 (2012)
23. Sanei, S., Chambers, J.A.: EEG Signal Processing. John Wiley & Sons Ltd., The Atrium (2007)
24. Sculley, D., Brodley, C.E.: Compression and machine learning: A new perspective on feature space vectors. In: DCC 2006: Proceedings of the Data Compression Conference, pp. 332–332. IEEE Computer Society, Washington, DC (2006), http://portal.acm.org/citation.cfm?id=1126054, doi:http://dx.doi.org/10.1109/DCC.2006.13
25. Shin, B., Oh, A.: Bayesian group nonnegative matrix factorization for eeg analysis. CoRR abs/1212.4347, 1–8 (2012)

26. de Sousa Silva, A., Arce, A., Tech, A., Costa, E.: Quantifying electrode position effects in eeg data with lempel-ziv complexity. In: 2010 Annual International Conference of the IEEE Engineering in Medicine and Biology Society (EMBC), pp. 4002–4005 (2010), doi:10.1109/IEMBS.2010.5628002
27. Swain, M., Ballard, D.: Color indexing. International Journal of Computer Vision 7, 11–32 (1991)
28. Vitanyi, P.: Universal similarity. In: Proceedings of the IEEE ITSOC Information Theory Workshop on Coding and Complexity, New Zealand (2005)
29. Walder, J., Krtk, M., Baca, R., Platos, J., Snsel, V.: Fast decoding algorithms for variable-lengths codes. Inf. Sci. 183(1), 66–91 (2012),
   http://dblp.uni-trier.de/db/journals/isci/isci183.html

Offline Text-Independent Handwriting Identification and Shape Modeling via Probabilistic Nodes Combination

Dariusz Jacek Jakóbczak

Department of Electronics and Computer Science, Technical University of Koszalin,
Sniadeckich 2, 75-453 Koszalin, Poland
dariusz.jakobczak@tu.koszalin.pl

Abstract. Proposed method, called Probabilistic Nodes Combination (PNC), is the method of 2D curve modeling and handwriting identification by using the set of key points. Nodes are treated as characteristic points of signature or handwriting for modeling and writer recognition. Identification of handwritten letters or symbols need modeling and the model of each individual symbol or character is built by a choice of probability distribution function and nodes combination. PNC modeling via nodes combination and parameter γ as probability distribution function enables curve parameterization and interpolation for each specific letter or symbol. Two-dimensional curve is modeled and interpolated via nodes combination and different functions as continuous probability distribution functions: polynomial, sine, cosine, tangent, cotangent, logarithm, exponent, arc sin, arc cos, arc tan, arc cot or power function.

Keywords: handwriting identification, shape modeling, curve interpolation, PNC method, nodes combination, probabilistic modeling.

1   Introduction

Handwriting identification and writer verification are still the open questions in artificial intelligence and computer vision. Handwriting based author recognition offers a huge number of significant implementations which make it an important research area in pattern recognition [1]. There are so many possibilities and applications of the recognition algorithms that implemented methods have to be concerned on a single problem. Handwriting and signature identification represents such a significant problem. In the case of writer recognition, described in this paper, each person is represented by the set of modeled letters or symbols. The sketch of proposed method consists of three steps: first handwritten letter or symbol must be modeled by a curve, then compared with unknown letter and finally there is a decision of identification. Author recognition of handwriting and signature is based on the choice of key points and curve modeling. Reconstructed curve does not have to be smooth in the nodes because a writer does not think about smoothing during the handwriting. Curve interpolation in handwriting identification is not only a pure mathematical problem but important task in pattern recognition and artificial intelligence such as: biometric recognition [2-4], personalized

L. Rutkowski et al. (Eds.): ICAISC 2014, Part II, LNAI 8468, pp. 119–130, 2014.
© Springer International Publishing Switzerland 2014

handwriting recognition [5], automatic forensic document examination [6,7], classification of ancient manuscripts [8]. Also writer recognition in monolingual handwritten texts is an extensive area of study and the methods independent from the language are well-seen. Proposed method represents language-independent and text-independent approach because it identifies the author via a single letter or symbol from the sample. This novel method is also applicable to short handwritten text.

Writer recognition methods in the recent years are going to various directions: writer recognition using multi-script handwritten texts [9], introduction of new features [10], combining different types of features [3], studying the sensitivity of character size on writer identification [11], investigating writer identification in multi-script environments [9], impact of ruling lines on writer identification [12], model perturbed handwriting [13], methods based on run-length features [14,3], the edge-direction and edge-hinge features [2], a combination of codebook and visual features extracted from chain code and polygonized representation of contours [15], the autoregressive coefficients [9], codebook and efficient code extraction methods [16], texture analysis with Gabor filters and extracting features [17], using Hidden Markov Model [18-20] or Gaussian Mixture Model [1]. But no method is dealing with writer identification via curve modeling or interpolation and points comparing as it is presented in this paper.

The author wants to approach a problem of curve interpolation [21-23] and shape modeling [24] by characteristic points in handwriting identification. Proposed method relies on nodes combination and functional modeling of curve points situated between the basic set of key points. The functions that are used in calculations represent whole family of elementary functions with inverse functions: polynomials, trigonometric, cyclometric, logarithmic, exponential and power function. These functions are treated as probability distribution functions in the range $[0;1]$. Nowadays methods apply mainly polynomial functions, for example Bernstein polynomials in Bezier curves, splines and NURBS [25]. But Bezier curves do not represent the interpolation method and cannot be used for example in signature and handwriting modeling with characteristic points (nodes). Numerical methods for data interpolation are based on polynomial or trigonometric functions, for example Lagrange, Newton, Aitken and Hermite methods. These methods have some weak sides [26] and are not sufficient for curve interpolation in the situations when the curve cannot be build by polynomials or trigonometric functions. Proposed 2D curve interpolation is the functional modeling via any elementary functions and it helps us to fit the curve during handwriting identification.

This paper presents novel Probabilistic Nodes Combination (PNC) method of curve interpolation and takes up PNC method of two-dimensional curve modeling via the examples using the family of Hurwitz-Radon matrices (MHR method) [27], but not only (other nodes combinations). The method of PNC requires minimal assumptions: the only information about a curve is the set of at least two nodes. Proposed PNC method is applied in handwriting identification via different coefficients: polynomial, sinusoidal, cosinusoidal, tangent, cotangent, logarithmic, exponential, arc sin, arc cos, arc tan, arc cot or power. Function for PNC calculations is chosen individually at each modeling and it represents probability distribution function of parameter $\alpha \in [0;1]$ for every point situated between two successive interpolation knots. PNC method uses nodes of the curve $p_i = (x_i, y_i) \in \mathbf{R}^2$, $i = 1, 2, \ldots n$:

1. PNC needs 2 knots or more ($n \geq 2$);
2. If first node and last node are the same ($p_1 = p_n$), then curve is closed (contour);
3. For more precise modeling knots ought to be settled at key points of the curve, for example local minimum or maximum and at least one node between two successive local extrema.

Condition 3 means for example the highest point of the curve in a particular orientation, convexity changing or curvature extrema. The goal of this paper is to answer the question: how to model a handwritten letter or symbol by a set of knots [28]?

2   Probabilistic Curve Modeling

The method of PNC is computing points between two successive nodes of the curve: calculated points are interpolated and parameterized for real number $\alpha \in [0;1]$ in the range of two successive nodes. PNC method uses the combinations of nodes $p_1 = (x_1, y_1)$, $p_2 = (x_2, y_2), \ldots$, $p_n = (x_n, y_n)$ as $h(p_1, p_2, \ldots, p_m)$ and $m = 1, 2, \ldots n$ to interpolate second coordinate y for first coordinate $c = \alpha \cdot x_i + (1-\alpha) \cdot x_{i+1}$, $i = 1, 2, \ldots n-1$:

$$y(c) = \gamma \cdot y_i + (1 - \gamma) y_{i+1} + \gamma(1 - \gamma) \cdot h(p_1, p_2, \ldots, p_m), \tag{1}$$

$$\alpha \in [0;1], \quad \gamma = F(\alpha) \in [0;1].$$

Here are the examples of h computed for MHR method [29]:

$$h(p_1, p_2) = \frac{y_1}{x_1} x_2 + \frac{y_2}{x_2} x_1 \tag{2}$$

or

$$h(p_1, p_2, p_3, p_4) = \frac{1}{x_1^2 + x_3^2}(x_1 x_2 y_1 + x_2 x_3 y_3 + x_3 x_4 y_1 - x_1 x_4 y_3) +$$
$$+ \frac{1}{x_2^2 + x_4^2}(x_1 x_2 y_2 + x_1 x_4 y_4 + x_3 x_4 y_2 - x_2 x_3 y_4) .$$

The examples of other nodes combinations:

$$h(p_1, p_2) = \frac{y_1 x_2}{x_1 y_2} + \frac{y_2 x_1}{x_2 y_1}$$

or

$$h(p_1, p_2) = \frac{y_1 x_2}{y_2} + \frac{y_2 x_1}{y_1}$$

or

$$h(p_1, p_2) = x_1 y_1 + x_2 y_2$$

or

$$h(p_1, p_2) = x_1 x_2 + y_1 y_2$$

or

$$h(p_1, p_2, ..., p_m) = 0$$

or

$$h(p_1) = x_1 y_1$$

or others. Nodes combination is chosen individually for each curve. Formula (1) represents curve parameterization as $\alpha \in [0;1]$:

$$x(\alpha) = \alpha \cdot x_i + (1-\alpha) \cdot x_{i+1}$$

and

$$y(\alpha) = F(\alpha) \cdot y_i + (1 - F(\alpha)) y_{i+1} + F(\alpha)(1 - F(\alpha)) \cdot h(p_1, p_2, ..., p_m),$$
$$y(\alpha) = F(\alpha) \cdot (y_i - y_{i+1} + (1 - F(\alpha)) \cdot h(p_1, p_2, ..., p_m)) + y_{i+1}.$$

Proposed parameterization gives us the infinite number of possibilities for curve calculations (determined by choice of F and h) as there is the infinite number of human signatures, handwritten letters and symbols. Nodes combination is the individual feature of each modeled curve (for example a handwritten letter or signature). Coefficient $\gamma = F(\alpha)$ and nodes combination h are key factors in PNC curve interpolation and shape modeling.

2.1   Distribution Functions in PNC Modeling

Points settled between the nodes are computed using PNC method. Each real number $c \in [a;b]$ is calculated by a convex combination $c = \alpha \cdot a + (1 - \alpha) \cdot b$ for

$$\alpha = \frac{b-c}{b-a} \in [0;1].$$

Key question is dealing with coefficient γ in (1). The simplest way of PNC calculation means $h = 0$ and $\gamma = \alpha$ (basic probability distribution). Then PNC represents a linear interpolation. MHR method [30] is not a linear interpolation. MHR [31] is the example of PNC modeling. Each interpolation requires specific distribution of parameter α and γ (1) depends on parameter $\alpha \in [0;1]$:

$$\gamma = F(\alpha), \ F:[0;1] \rightarrow [0;1], \ F(0) = 0, \ F(1) = 1$$

and F is strictly monotonic. Coefficient γ is calculated using different functions (polynomials, power functions, sine, cosine, tangent, cotangent, logarithm, exponent, arc sin, arc cos, arc tan or arc cot, also inverse functions) and choice of function is connected with initial requirements and curve specifications. Different values of coefficient γ are connected with applied functions $F(\alpha)$. These functions $\gamma = F(\alpha)$ represent the examples of probability distribution functions for random variable $\alpha \in [0;1]$ and real number $s > 0$:

$\gamma = \alpha^s$, $\gamma = sin(\alpha^s \cdot \pi/2)$, $\gamma = sin^s(\alpha \cdot \pi/2)$, $\gamma = 1 - cos(\alpha^s \cdot \pi/2)$, $\gamma = 1 - cos^s(\alpha \cdot \pi/2)$, $\gamma = tan(\alpha^s \cdot \pi/4)$, $\gamma = tan^s(\alpha \cdot \pi/4)$, $\gamma = log_2(\alpha^s + 1)$, $\gamma = log_2^s(\alpha + 1)$, $\gamma = (2^\alpha - 1)^s$, $\gamma = 2/\pi \cdot arcsin(\alpha^s)$, $\gamma = (2/\pi \cdot arcsin\alpha)^s$, $\gamma = 1 - 2/\pi \cdot arccos(\alpha^s)$, $\gamma = 1 - (2/\pi \cdot arccos\alpha)^s$, $\gamma = 4/\pi \cdot arctan(\alpha^s)$, $\gamma = (4/\pi \cdot arctan\alpha)^s$, $\gamma = ctg(\pi/2 - \alpha^s \cdot \pi/4)$, $\gamma = ctg^s(\pi/2 - \alpha \cdot \pi/4)$, $\gamma = 2 - 4/\pi \cdot arcctg(\alpha^s)$, $\gamma = (2 - 4/\pi \cdot arcctg\alpha)^s$.

Functions above, used in γ calculations, are strictly monotonic for random variable $\alpha \in [0;1]$ as $\gamma = F(\alpha)$ is probability distribution function. Also inverse functions $F^{-1}(\alpha)$ are appropriate for γ calculations. Choice of function and value s depends on curve specifications and individual requirements. Considering nowadays used probability distribution functions for random variable $\alpha \in [0;1]$ - one distribution is dealing with the range $[0;1]$: beta distribution. Probability density function f for random variable $\alpha \in [0;1]$ is:

$$f(\alpha) = c \cdot \alpha^s \cdot (1-\alpha)^r \;, s \geq 0, r \geq 0. \tag{3}$$

When $r = 0$ probability density function (3) represents $f(\alpha) = c \cdot \alpha^s$ and then probability distribution function F is like $f(\alpha) = 3\alpha^2$ and $\gamma = \alpha^3$. If s and r are positive integer numbers then γ is the polynomial, for example $f(\alpha) = 6\alpha(1-\alpha)$ and $\gamma = 3\alpha^2 - 2\alpha^3$. Beta distribution gives us coefficient γ in (1) as polynomial because of interdependence between probability density f and distribution F functions:

$$f(\alpha) = F'(\alpha) \;, \; F(\alpha) = \int_0^\alpha f(t)dt \cdot \tag{4}$$

For example (4): $f(\alpha) = \alpha \cdot e^\alpha$ and $\gamma = F(\alpha) = (\alpha - 1)e^\alpha + 1$.
What is very important in PNC method: two curves (for example a handwritten letter or signature) may have the same set of nodes but different h or γ results in different interpolations (Fig.6-14).

Algorithm of PNC interpolation and modeling (1) looks as follows:

Step 1: Choice of knots p_i at key points.
Step 2: Choice of nodes combination $h(p_1, p_2, \ldots, p_m)$.
Step 3: Choice of distribution $\gamma = F(\alpha)$.
Step 4: Determining values of α: $\alpha = 0.1, 0.2 \ldots 0.9$ (nine points) or $0.01, 0.02 \ldots 0.99$ (99 points) or others.
Step 5: The computations (1).

These five steps can be treated as the algorithm of PNC method of curve modeling and interpolation (1).

Curve interpolation has to implement the coefficients γ. Each strictly monotonic function F between points (0;0) and (1;1) can be used in PNC interpolation.

3   Handwriting Modeling and Author Identification

PNC method enables signature and handwriting recognition. This process of recognition consists of three parts:

1. Modeling – choice of nodes combination and probabilistic distribution function (1) for known signature or handwritten letters;
2. Unknown writer - choice of characteristic points (nodes) for unknown signature or handwritten word and the coefficients of points between nodes;
3. Decision of recognition - comparing the results of PNC interpolation for known models with coordinates of unknown text.

3.1   Modeling – The Basis of Patterns

Known letters or symbols ought to be modeled by the choice of nodes, determining specific nodes combination and characteristic probabilistic distribution function. For example a handwritten word or signature "*rw*" may look different for persons A, B or others. How to model "*rw*" for some persons via PNC method? Each model has to be described by the set of nodes for letters "*r*" and "*w*", nodes combination h and a function $\gamma = F(\alpha)$ for each letter. Less complicated models can take $h(p_1, p_2, \ldots, p_m) = 0$ and then the formula of interpolation (1) looks as follows:

$$y(c) = \gamma \cdot y_i + (1 - \gamma) y_{i+1}.$$

It is linear interpolation for basic probability distribution ($\gamma = \alpha$). How first letter "*r*" is modeled in three versions for nodes combination $h = 0$ and $\alpha = 0.1, 0.2 \ldots 0.9$? Of course α is a random variable and $\alpha \in [0;1]$.

Person A

Nodes (1;3), (3;1), (5;3), (7;3) and $\gamma = F(\alpha) = \alpha^2$:

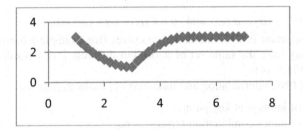

Fig. 1. PNC modeling for nine reconstructed points between nodes

Person B

Nodes (1;3), (3;1), (5;3), (7;2) and $\gamma = F(\alpha) = \alpha^2$:

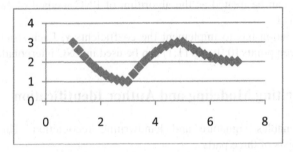

Fig. 2. PNC modeling of letter "*r*" with four nodes

Person C

Nodes (1;3), (3;1), (5;3), (7;4) and $\gamma = F(\alpha) = \alpha^3$:

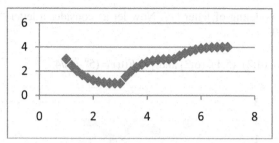

Fig. 3. PNC modeling of handwritten letter "*r*"

These three versions of letter "*r*" (Fig.1-3) with nodes combination $h = 0$ differ at fourth node and probability distribution functions $\gamma = F(\alpha)$. Much more possibilities of modeling are connected with a choice of nodes combination $h(p_1, p_2, \ldots, p_m)$. MHR method [32] uses the combination (2) with good features because of orthogonal rows and columns at Hurwitz-Radon family of matrices:

$$h(p_i, p_{i+1}) = \frac{y_i}{x_i} x_{i+1} + \frac{y_{i+1}}{x_{i+1}} x_i$$

and then (1)

$$y(c) = \gamma \cdot y_i + (1 - \gamma) y_{i+1} + \gamma(1 - \gamma) \cdot h(p_i, p_{i+1},) .$$

Here are two examples of PNC modeling with MHR combination (2).
Person D
Nodes (1;3), (3;1), (5;3) and $\gamma = F(\alpha) = \alpha^2$:

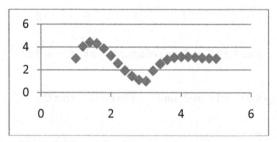

Fig. 4. PNC modeling of letter "*r*" with three nodes

Person E
Nodes (1;3), (3;1), (5;3) and $\gamma = F(\alpha) = \alpha^{1.5}$:

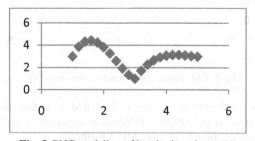

Fig. 5. PNC modeling of handwritten letter "*r*"

Fig.1-5 show modeling of letter "r". Now let us consider a letter "w" with nodes combination $h = 0$.

Person A

Nodes (2;2), (3;1), (4;2), (5;1), (6;2) and $\gamma = F(\alpha) = (5^{\alpha} - 1)/4$:

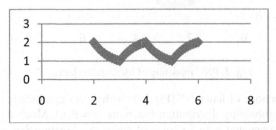

Fig. 6. PNC modeling for nine reconstructed points between nodes

Person B

Nodes (2;2), (3;1), (4;2), (5;1), (6;2) and $\gamma = F(\alpha) = sin(\alpha \cdot \pi/2)$:

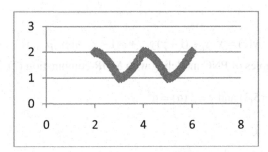

Fig. 7. PNC modeling of letter "w" with five nodes

Person C

Nodes (2;2), (3;1), (4;2), (5;1), (6;2) and $\gamma = F(\alpha) = sin^{3.5}(\alpha \cdot \pi/2)$:

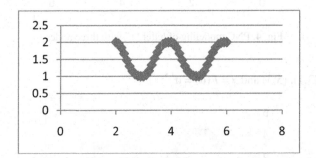

Fig. 8. PNC modeling of handwritten letter "w"

These three versions of letter "w" (Fig.6-8) with nodes combination $h = 0$ and the same nodes differ only at probability distribution functions $\gamma = F(\alpha)$. Fig.9 is the example of nodes combination h (2) from MHR method:

Person D
Nodes (2;2), (3;1), (4;1), (5;1), (6;2) and $\gamma = F(\alpha) = 2^{\alpha} - 1$:

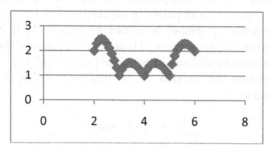

Fig. 9. PNC modeling for nine reconstructed points between nodes

Examples above have one function $\gamma = F(\alpha)$ and one combination h for all ranges between nodes. But it is possible to create a model with functions $\gamma_i = F_i(\alpha)$ and combinations h_i individually for a range of nodes $(p_i;p_{i+1})$. It enables very precise modeling of handwritten symbol between each successive pair of nodes.

Each person has its own characteristic and individual handwritten letters, numbers or other marks. The range of coefficients x has to be the same for all models because of comparing appropriate coordinates y. Every letter is modeled by PNC via three factors: the set of nodes, probability distribution function $\gamma = F(\alpha)$ and nodes combination h. These three factors are chosen individually for each letter, therefore this information about modeled letters seems to be enough for specific PNC curve interpolation, comparing and handwriting identification. Function γ is selected via the analysis of points between nodes and we may assume $h = 0$ at the beginning. What is very important - PNC modeling is independent of the language or a kind of symbol (letters, numbers or others). One person may have several patterns for one handwritten letter. Summarize: every person has the basis of patterns for each handwritten letter or symbol, described by the set of nodes, probability distribution function $\gamma = F(\alpha)$ and nodes combination h. Whole basis of patterns consists of models S_j for $j = 0,1,2,3…K$.

3.2   Unknown Writer – Points of Handwritten Symbol

Choice of characteristic points (nodes) for unknown letter or handwritten symbol is a crucial factor in object recognition. The range of coefficients x has to be the same like the x range in the basis of patterns. Knots of the curve (opened or closed) ought to be settled at key points, for example local minimum or maximum (the highest point of the curve in a particular orientation), convexity changing or curvature maximum and at least one node between two successive key points. When the nodes are fixed, each coordinate of every chosen point on the curve (x_0^c,y_0^c), $(x_1^c,y_1^c),…, (x_M^c,y_M^c)$ is accessible to be used for comparing with the models. Then probability distribution function $\gamma = F(\alpha)$ and nodes combination h have to be taken from the basis of modeled letters to calculate appropriate second coordinates $y_i^{(j)}$ of the pattern S_j for first coordinates x_i^c, $i = 0,1,…,M$. After interpolation it is possible to compare given handwritten symbol with a letter in the basis of patterns.

3.3   Decision of Recognition – The Author

Comparing the results of PNC interpolation for required second coordinates of a model in the basis of patterns with points on the curve $(x_0{}^c,y_0{}^c)$, $(x_1{}^c,y_1{}^c)$,..., $(x_M{}^c,y_M{}^c)$, we can say if the letter or symbol is written by person A, B or another. The comparison and decision of recognition [33] is done via minimal distance criterion. Curve points of unknown handwritten symbol are: $(x_0{}^c,y_0{}^c)$, $(x_1{}^c,y_1{}^c)$,..., $(x_M{}^c,y_M{}^c)$. The criterion of recognition for models $S_j = \{(x_0{}^c,y_0{}^{(j)})$, $(x_1{}^c,y_1{}^{(j)})$,..., $(x_M{}^c,y_M{}^{(j)})\}$, $j=0,1,2,3...K$ is given as:

$$\sum_{i=0}^{M}\left|y_i{}^c - y_i{}^{(j)}\right| \rightarrow \min.$$

Minimal distance criterion helps us to fix a candidate for unknown writer as a person from the model S_j.

4   Conclusions

The method of Probabilistic Nodes Combination (PNC) enables interpolation and modeling of two-dimensional curves [34] using nodes combinations and different coefficients γ: polynomial, sinusoidal, cosinusoidal, tangent, cotangent, logarithmic, exponential, arc sin, arc cos, arc tan, arc cot or power function, also inverse functions. Function for γ calculations is chosen individually at each curve modeling and it is treated as probability distribution function: γ depends on initial requirements and curve specifications. PNC method leads to curve interpolation as handwriting or signature identification via discrete set of fixed knots. PNC makes possible the combination of two important problems: interpolation and modeling in a matter of writer identification. Main features of PNC method are:

a)   the smaller distance between knots the better;
b)   calculations for coordinates close to zero and near by extremum require more attention because of importance of these points;
c)   PNC interpolation develops a linear interpolation into other functions as probability distribution functions;
d)   PNC is a generalization of MHR method via different nodes combinations;
e)   interpolation of L points is connected with the computational cost of rank $O(L)$ as in MHR method;
f)   nodes combination and coefficient γ are crucial in the process of curve probabilistic parameterization and interpolation: they are computed individually for a single curve.

Future works are going to: application of PNC method in signature and handwriting recognition, choice and features of nodes combinations and coefficient γ, implementation of PNC in computer vision and artificial intelligence: shape geometry, contour modelling, object recognition and curve parameterization.

References

1. Schlapbach, A., Bunke, H.: Off-line writer identification using Gaussian mixture models. In: International Conference on Pattern Recognition, pp. 992–995 (2006)
2. Bulacu, M., Schomaker, L.: Text-independent writer identification and verification using textural and allographic features. IEEE Trans. Pattern Anal. Mach. Intell. 29(4), 701–717 (2007)
3. Djeddi, C., Souici-Meslati, L.: A texture based approach for Arabic writer identification and verification. In: International Conference on Machine and Web Intelligence, pp. 115–120 (2010)
4. Djeddi, C., Souici-Meslati, L.: Artificial immune recognition system for Arabic writer identification. In: International Symposium on Innovation in Information and Communication Technology, pp. 159–165 (2011)
5. Nosary, A., Heutte, L., Paquet, T.: Unsupervised writer adaption applied to handwritten text recognition. Pattern Recogn. Lett. 37(2), 385–388 (2004)
6. Van, E.M., Vuurpijl, L., Franke, K., Schomaker, L.: The WANDA measurement tool for forensic document examination. J. Forensic Doc. Exam. 16, 103–118 (2005)
7. Schomaker, L., Franke, K., Bulacu, M.: Using codebooks of fragmented connected-component contours in forensic and historic writer identification. Pattern Recogn. Lett. 28(6), 719–727 (2007)
8. Siddiqi, I., Cloppet, F., Vincent, N.: Contour based features for the classification of ancient manuscripts. In: Conference of the International Graphonomics Society, pp. 226–229 (2009)
9. Garain, U., Paquet, T.: Off-line multi-script writer identification using AR coefficients. In: International Conference on Document Analysis and Recognition, pp. 991–995 (2009)
10. Bulacu, M., Schomaker, L., Brink, A.: Text-independent writer identification and verification on off-line Arabic handwriting. In: International Conference on Document Analysis and Recognition, pp. 769–773 (2007)
11. Ozaki, M., Adachi, Y., Ishii, N.: Examination of effects of character size on accuracy of writer recognition by new local arc method. In: Gabrys, B., Howlett, R.J., Jain, L.C. (eds.) KES 2006. LNCS (LNAI), vol. 4252, pp. 1170–1175. Springer, Heidelberg (2006)
12. Chen, J., Lopresti, D., Kavallieratou, E.: The impact of ruling lines on writer identification. In: International Conference on Frontiers in Handwriting Recognition, pp. 439–444 (2010)
13. Chen, J., Cheng, W., Lopresti, D.: Using perturbed handwriting to support writer identification in the presence of severe data constraints. In: Document Recognition and Retrieval, pp. 1–10 (2011)
14. Galloway, M.M.: Texture analysis using gray level run lengths. Comput. Graphics Image Process. 4(2), 172–179 (1975)
15. Siddiqi, I., Vincent, N.: Text independent writer recognition using redundant writing patterns with contour-based orientation and curvature features. Pattern Recogn. Lett. 43(11), 3853–3865 (2010)
16. Ghiasi, G., Safabakhsh, R.: Offline text-independent writer identification using codebook and efficient code extraction methods. Image and Vision Computing 31, 379–391 (2013)
17. Shahabinejad, F., Rahmati, M.: A new method for writer identification and verification based on Farsi/Arabic handwritten texts. In: Ninth International Conference on Document Analysis and Recognition (ICDAR 2007), pp. 829–833 (2007)
18. Schlapbach, A., Bunke, H.: A writer identification and verification system using HMM based recognizers. Pattern Anal. Appl. 10, 33–43 (2007)

19. Schlapbach, A., Bunke, H.: Using HMM based recognizers for writer identification and verification. In: 9th Int. Workshop on Frontiers in Handwriting Recognition, pp. 167–172 (2004)
20. Marti, U.-V., Bunke, H.: The IAM-database: An English sentence database for offline handwriting recognition. Int. J. Doc. Anal. Recognit. 5, 39–46 (2002)
21. Collins II, G.W.: Fundamental Numerical Methods and Data Analysis. Case Western Reserve University (2003)
22. Chapra, S.C.: Applied Numerical Methods. McGraw-Hill (2012)
23. Ralston, A., Rabinowitz, P.: A First Course in Numerical Analysis, 2nd edn. Dover Publications, New York (2001)
24. Zhang, D., Lu, G.: Review of Shape Representation and Description Techniques. Pattern Recognition 1(37), 1–19 (2004)
25. Schumaker, L.L.: Spline Functions: Basic Theory. Cambridge Mathematical Library (2007)
26. Dahlquist, G., Bjoerck, A.: Numerical Methods. Prentice Hall, New York (1974)
27. Jakóbczak, D.: 2D and 3D Image Modeling Using Hurwitz-Radon Matrices. Polish Journal of Environmental Studies 4A(16), 104–107 (2007)
28. Jakóbczak, D.: Shape Representation and Shape Coefficients via Method of Hurwitz-Radon Matrices. In: Bolc, L., Tadeusiewicz, R., Chmielewski, L.J., Wojciechowski, K. (eds.) ICCVG 2010, Part I. LNCS, vol. 6374, pp. 411–419. Springer, Heidelberg (2010)
29. Jakóbczak, D.: Curve Interpolation Using Hurwitz-Radon Matrices. Polish Journal of Environmental Studies 3B(18), 126–130 (2009)
30. Jakóbczak, D.: Application of Hurwitz-Radon Matrices in Shape Representation. In: Banaszak, Z., Świć, A. (eds.) Applied Computer Science: Modelling of Production Processes, vol. 1(6), pp. 63–74. Lublin University of Technology Press, Lublin (2010)
31. Jakóbczak, D.: Object Modeling Using Method of Hurwitz-Radon Matrices of Rank k. In: Wolski, W., Borawski, M. (eds.) Computer Graphics: Selected Issues, pp. 79–90. University of Szczecin Press, Szczecin (2010)
32. Jakóbczak, D.: Implementation of Hurwitz-Radon Matrices in Shape Representation. In: Choraś, R.S. (ed.) Image Processing and Communications Challenges 2. Advances in Intelligent Systems and Computing, vol. 84, pp. 39–50. Springer, Heidelberg (2010)
33. Jakóbczak, D.: Object Recognition via Contour Points Reconstruction Using Hurwitz-Radon Matrices. In: Józefczyk, J., Orski, D. (eds.) Knowledge-Based Intelligent System Advancements: Systemic and Cybernetic Approaches, pp. 87–107. IGI Global, Hershey (2011)
34. Jakóbczak, D.: Curve Parameterization and Curvature via Method of Hurwitz-Radon Matrices. Image Processing & Communications- An International Journal 1-2(16), 49–56 (2011)

Computer-Aided System for Automatic Classification of Suspicious Lesions in Breast Ultrasound Images

Behnam Karimi and Adam Krzyżak

Department of Computer Science and Software Engineering
Concordia University, Montreal, QC H3G 1M8, Canada
{b_karimi,krzyzak}@cs.concordia.ca
http://www.cs.concordia.ca/

Abstract. In this research, a new method for automatic detection of suspected breast cancer lesions using ultrasound images is proposed. In this fully automated method, the best de-noising technique from among several considered is selected, a new segmentation based on fuzzy logic is proposed and detection of lesions based on morphological features and texture features is considered. We also consider correlation among ultrasound images taken from different angles and use it to improve detection.

Keywords: breast cancer, ultrasound images, automatic detection of lesions.

1 Introduction

Ultrasound is one of the screening tests to detect possible cancerous lesions in breast. Ultrasound is cyclic sound pressure with a frequency greater than the upper limit of human hearing. When the sound pressure penetrates a medium, it measures the reflection signature or supply focused energy. The reflection signature then allows gleaning details about the inner structure of the medium. Very well-known application of ultrasound is sonography, which is widely used in medicine. Ultrasound can be used for screening, diagnosis and therapeutic procedures.

In a computer-aided screening system for ultrasound images contains four main components: pre-processing, segmentation, feature extraction and classification. Lots of research has been carried out in recent years but not many automatic methods for classification of breast cancer have been developed.

In [1] a method is proposed that uniquely combines histogram equalization in a pre-processing stage with hybrid filtering, multifractal analysis, thresholding segmentation, and a rule-based approach in fully automated ROI labeling. The proposed method is able to very accurately label most lesions, with its best performance being the identification of malignant lesions (90%) and its worst being the identification of fibroadenomas (77.59%). It appears that even by using hybrid filtering and multifractal processing, the accuracy of the result to identify

L. Rutkowski et al. (Eds.): ICAISC 2014, Part II, LNAI 8468, pp. 131–142, 2014.
© Springer International Publishing Switzerland 2014

fibroadenomas is not very high. It is suspected that noise and shadowing in the images are responsible for low accuracy of fibroadenomas detection.

Another method was introduced in [2, 3] that uses a bilateral subtraction technique to reduce false positives in mass candidate regions detected by detection scheme for whole breast ultrasound images. It was found that the bilateral subtraction technique could reduce false positives effectively. This method is based on the premise that normal left and right breasts of the same subject display architectural symmetry. The radiologists use it as a useful tool to interpret ultrasound images. Even if there is a mass region in the breast, the region is classified as normal tissue if similar region exists in same position in the other breast. This method uses this feature to reduce false positives. The method involves (1) image feature extraction; (2) registration of bilateral breasts; and (3) reduction of false positives. This method removes 67.3% of false positives but requires more improvements. It looks like the accuracy of the system can be improved by employing a batter pre-processing technique for noise and shadow removal.

Another method was proposed by Gupta [4]. It uses speckle features of automated breast ultrasound images (ABUS). The ABUS images of 147 pathologically proven breast masses (76 benign and 71 malignant cases) were used. For each mass, a volume of interest (VOI) was cropped to define the tumor area, and the average number of speckle pixels within a VOI was calculated. Also, first-order and second-order statistical analysis of the speckle pixels was considered to quantify the information of gray-level distributions and the spatial relations among the pixels. Receiver operating characteristic curve analysis was used to evaluate the performance. It achieves the accuracy of 84.4%. The performance indices of the speckle features were comparable to the performance indices of the morphological features. Although the accuracy is not ideal, it can be improved by combining speckle features with morphological and texture features.

The remainder of the paper is structured as follows. In sections 2 through 5 we present critical survey of the state of the art of the field and discuss the advantages and disadvantages of various approaches and we suggest possible improvement. We provide detailed survey of different stages of the detection system including preprocessing, segmentation, feature extraction, feature selection and classification. A new detection method proposed by us is described in Section 6 and results of experiments are given in Section 7.

2   Pre-processing of Ultrasound Images

Ultrasound images are typically effected by noise because of various sources of interferences and other phenomena. The noise usually appears as bright and dark spots called speckle, which obscure fine details, degrade and makes it difficult to detect low-contrast lesion. Thus in a computerized system for detection of cancer in ultrasound images pre-processing to eliminate the noise is an important component [5–7].

In the past years, several image enhancement algorithms have been introduced. They usually belong to two categories: spatial domain- and transform-domain-based. The spatial domain algorithms involve image operations on a whole image or a on local region and make use of image statistics. They include methods such as histogram equalization, image averaging, sharpening of image using edge detection and morphology operators, and nonlinear median filtering [8]. In transform-domain-based algorithms the operations are performed in the transform domain such as Fourier and wavelet domain. The frequency transform methods facilitate the extraction of certain image features that cannot be derived from spatial domain [8].

3   Segmentation and Feature Extraction

There are several segmentation methods that were applied to breast ultrasound images. They use histogram thresholding, model-based approaches, machine learning and watershed approach [32].

Machine learning methods are more suitable for segmentation of ultrasound images. For example in [29], a classification method based on neural network is proposed. Images are divided into blocks of squares. Features are extracted from each block using discrete cosine transform (DCT). After that, a three-layer hybrid neural network is trained to classify the blocks into background and foreground, which are breast tissues and lesion respectively.

Following segmentation we need to find features in the regions to be able to categorize the lesions into malignant or benign categories. In the diagnosis of breast cancer, mass carries important information about cancer. Features of the mass playing a significant role in breast cancer diagnosis include shape, boundary, branch, internal structures, and the micro calcifications. For example, when a doctor observes a mass in an ultrasound image, which usually is the darkest area of the image, the first thing he does is to see if it has an irregular shape and if it has branched. Fig. 1 shows mass that is both branched and has an irregular shape.

Fig. 1. Irregular mass

Many features can be used for breast tumor detection [12, 14, 20, 21] and [22]. These features include: perimeter, area, NSPD (number of substantial protuberances and depressions), LI (lobulation index), ENC (elliptic-normalized circumference), ENS (elliptic-normalized skeleton), LS Ratio (long axis to short axis ratio), Aspect Ratio, Roundness, Solidity, Convexity, Extent, TCA Ratio (tumor area to convex area ratio), TEP Ratio (tumor perimeter to ellipse perimeter ratio), TEP Difference (difference between tumor perimeter and ellipse perimeter), TEP Difference (difference between tumor perimeter and ellipse perimeter), TCP Ratio (tumor perimeter to circle perimeter ratio), TCP Difference (difference between tumor perimeter and circle perimeter), AP Ratio (area to perimeter ratio) and Thickness of the wall. As part of this research, we will find the optimum number and set of features that will provide the highest accuracy and performance.

Part of the manual diagnosis by a physician is to see the texture of the lesions and decide whether they look suspicious or not. Extracting those features is not very time consuming and combining them with morphological features could give better and more accurate classification results [17, 18].

4   Feature Selection

4.1   Sequential Forward Search and Sequential Backward Search

The feature selection methods that we are going to use are sequential forward search and sequential backward search and we choose between the subset that resulted from these two procedures. In sequential forward search, first the best single feature is found. Then among the remaining features, the feature that best discriminate between the classes when used along with already selected features is chosen and added to the list of selected features. The procedure is repeated until the addition of new features increases the error rate or no feature remains to be added. In sequential backward search, the search space is drawn like an ellipse to emphasize the fact that there are fewer states towards the full or empty sets. The main disadvantage of SFS is that it is unable to remove features that become obsolete after the addition of other features [23, 34].

4.2   Distance Based Feature Selection

This method combines the concept of between-class distance and within-class divergence [33]. Therefore, the ultimate objective becomes to select a subset of image features that (i) Maximizes the distances among the classes, and (ii) minimizes the divergence within each class. Let T_S be a labeled training set with N_S samples. The classes ω_k represented by subsets $T_K \subset T_S$, each class having N_K samples $\sum N_K = N_S$. Measurement vectors in T_S (without reference to their class) are denoted by z_n. Measurement vectors in T_K (vectors coming from class ω_k denoted by $z_{k,n}$). The sample mean of a class and that of the entire training set can be defined respectively as: $\hat{\mu}_k(T_k) = \frac{1}{N_k}\sum_{n=1}^{N_k} z_{k,n}$ and $\hat{\mu}_k(T_S) = \frac{1}{N_S}\sum_{n=1}^{N_S} z_n$. The following formula defines the partial within-class scattered matrix for one specific class:

$$S_k(T_k) = \frac{1}{N_k}\sum_{n=1}^{N_k}(z_{k,n} - \hat{\mu}_k)(z_{k,n} - \hat{\mu}_k)^T \tag{1}$$

The following formula represents the within-class scattered matrix.

$$S_\omega(T_S) = \frac{1}{N_S} \sum_{k=1}^{K} N_k S_k(T_k) = \frac{1}{N_S} \sum_{k=1}^{K} \sum_{n=1}^{N_k} (z_{k,n} - \hat{\mu}_k)(z_{k,n} - \hat{\mu}_k)^T \qquad (2)$$

The following formula provides the between-class scattered matrix:

$$S_b(T_S) = \frac{1}{N_S} \sum_{n=1}^{K} N_k(\hat{\mu}_k - \mu)(\hat{\mu}_k - \mu)^T \qquad (3)$$

In our proposed method, we used a combination of sequential forward search, sequential backward search and distance based methods. This will be discussed in detail in Section 6.

5 Classification

The main goal of this study is to help radiologists in interpreting ultrasound images. After the features are extracted from the ultrasound image, we need to classify them in order to see if the lesion is suspicious based on the extracted features. One of the best known methods in pattern and image classification is Support Vector Machine (SVM). It is designed to separate of a set of training images into two different classes, $(x_1, y_1), (x_2, y_2), ..., (x_n, y_n)$ where x_i in R^d, d-dimensional feature space, and y_i in $\{-1, +1\}$, the class label, with $i = 1, ..., n$. SVM builds the optimal separating hyperplane using a kernel function K. All images, of which feature vectors lie on one side of the hyper plane belong to class -1 and the others belong to class $+1$. There exist other classifiers such as artificial neural networks and classification trees but they have not been applied in our system [31].

6 Proposed System

The outline of our proposed system is showin in Fig. 2.

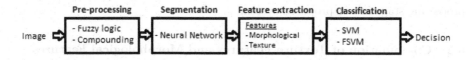

Fig. 2. Outline of proposed system

The uncertainty to identify lesions and their boundaries suggests the use of fuzzy logic for pre-processing. The detection of structures is crucial for the diagnosis of a large number of illnesses including breast cancer in breast ultrasound images. Being blurred by nature, with little contrast or significant immersion in noise, most standard techniques of digital image processing do not yield optimum results for these images.

The use of fuzzy logic that uses both global and local information and has the ability to enhance the fine details of the ultrasound images is a suitable choice for low-contrast ultrasound images as they details cannot be obtained easily in these images.

6.1   Fuzzy Logic for De-noising

The enhancement can be done to better distinguish the background from the actual image. It is logical that the more we can distinguish the background from foreground, the better the result would be. An interval-valued fuzzy set constitutes that the membership degree of every element to the set is given by a closed subinterval of interval $[0,1]$. The concept of type 2 fuzzy sets was introduced by Zadeh [24, 25] as a generalization of an ordinary fuzzy set. The membership degree of an element to a type 2 fuzzy set is a fuzzy set in $[0,1]$. An interval type 2 fuzzy set $\overline{\overline{A}}$ in U is defined as

$$\overline{\overline{A}} = \{(u, A(u), \mu_u(x)) | u \in U, A(u) \in L([0,1])\},$$

where $A(u) = [\underline{A}(u), \overline{A}(u)]$ is a membership function; i.e., a closed subinterval is $[0,1]$, and function $\mu(x)$ represents the fuzzy set associated with the element $u \in U$ obtained when x is within $[0,1]$; $\mu_u(x)$ is given in the following way:

$$F(x) = \begin{cases} a & \text{if} \quad \underline{A}(u) \leq x \leq \overline{A}(u) \\ 0 & \text{otherwise.} \end{cases}$$

[26] proposed an algorithm to enhance ultrasound images, in which fuzzy rules such as the following one have been used.

IF the pixel does not belong to the breast tissue, THEN leave it unchanged. IF the pixel belongs to the breast tissue AND is dark, THEN make it darker. IF the pixel belongs to the breast tissue AND is gray, THEN make it dark. IF the pixel belongs to the breast tissue AND is bright, THEN make it brighter.

In this research, the mentioned method has been used as part of the pre-processing stage in our proposed system.

6.2   Combination of Texture Features and Morphological Features

In our experiments, we used a sub-set of morphological features that is described in section 3. The method to extract those features is described in section 4. Then we used a combination of the extracted morphological features with texture features.

For extracting texture feature information, there are two primary methodologies. The first class of methods applies a linear transform, filter, or filter bank globally to the image. The local energy of the filter responses represents the local texture feature values. Generally these methods have high computational complexity. The second class of methods divides the whole image into many small non-overlapping pixel blocks, and then applies some transform, such as a wavelet transform, to each block to get the local information. These methods extract texture features for a block of pixels. Both methodologies have the problem of generating texture information for each individual pixel [27].

In this research a method described in [30] is used to extract texture features for each pixel, a window of some pre-determined size, $k*k$ is applied to each pixel. The center of the window slides over every pixel and performs the wavelet (We used Daubechies-4 wavelet) transform at each location to determine each pixel texture feature.

6.3 Correlation of Images from Different Angles

Some artifacts like shadowing may hamper clear delineation of the lesion in ultrasound images. Because of these issues ultrasound imaging is an interactive process and requires a lot of experience to capture and interpret lesions. Findings in the ultrasound images sometimes are not reproducible and often vary between individual interpreters. The limitations thus mentioned might be overcome by considering correlation between images from different angles (i.e. multiple viewing angles all around the breast). The concept is known as Full Angle Spatial Compounding (FASC). As noise is uncorrelated in images from different angles, it will be reduced by using this technique. In this method because of varying angles, shadowing is suppressed or at least significantly reduced. Also structures, which cause specular reflections are imaged and delineated in the compound image. We can use another approach to simply average the results from different angles. It is also possible to calculate lateral variations in attenuation in a sample from the single envelope of a pair of scans from equal and opposite steered angles. This information then can be used to provide a compounded backscatter image free from shadows and enhancements.

7   Experimental Results

7.1   Feature Selection

A combination of Sequential Forward Search & Sequential Backward Search has been implemented for feature selection. In order to make sure that we do not eliminate significant features during Sequential backward Search, we consider a union between the results of Sequential Forward Search & Sequential Backward Search. The result of the previous step is then combined with Distance Based feature selection (union). Table 1 summarizes the selected features.

7.2   Compounding

In order to find out how compounding of the images will improve the result, we applied the compounding algorithm we discussed earlier. The algorithm is

Table 1. Selected Features

Feature	Used by physician
Roundness	*
Solidity	*
Convexity	
TCA Ratio	
Perimeter	*
Area	*
NSPD	*
Wall Thickness	*

Table 2. Experiment using compounding

Original	De-noised	Compounded	Segmented

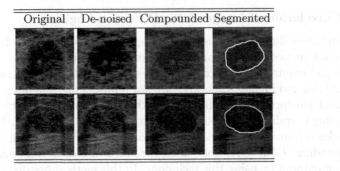

applied on three images per patient (9 o'clock, 0 o'clock and 3 o'clock). A sample of the result is shown in Table 2.

After applying compounding, the shadows were reduced drastically. This will help radiologists to distinguish the lesions much easier.

7.3   Comparison with Other Techniques

In this section we will compare a new approach with state-of-the-art CAD systems: ABUS [4] and Hybrid Filtering [1].

Experiment #1. In this experiment, we have not done any pre-processing for the ultrasound images. Neural network method in [28] is used for Segmentation. We used the features that we extracted using Sequential Forward Search, Sequential Backward Search and Distance-based methods. For classification, we used Support Vector Machine proposed in [20]. We have experimented this on 80 patients. For the purpose of this experiment, we only used the 0 o'clock ultrasound images. The result is shown in Table 3 (TP: True Positive, TN: True Negative, FP: False Positive, FN: False Negative).

Experiment #2. In this experiment, we used fuzzy logic for pre-processing of ultrasound images. Neural network method in [28] is used for segmentation. We

Table 3. Experiment #1

Method	# of patients	TP	TN	FP	FN	Accuracy
Our Method	80	60	20	3	2	93.75%
Hybrid Filtering[1]	80	61	19	4	2	92.5%
ABUS[4]	80	62	18	6	3	88.75%

used the features that we extracted using Sequential Forward Search, Sequential Backward Search and Distance-based methods. For classification, we used Support Vector Machine proposed in [20]. We have experimented with images from 80 patients. For the purpose of this experiment, we only used the 0-o'clock ultrasound images. The result is shown in Table 4.

Table 4. Experiment #2

Method	# of patients	TP	TN	FP	FN	Accuracy
Our Method	80	61	19	3	1	95%
Hybrid Filtering[1]	80	61	19	4	2	92.5%
ABUS[4]	80	62	18	6	3	88.75%

Experiment #3. In this experiment, we used fuzzy logic for pre-processing of ultrasound images. Neural network method in [28] is used for segmentation. We used the features that we extracted using Sequential Forward Search, Sequential Backward Search and Distance-based methods. Texture features are also used. For classification, we used an SVM classifier. We have implemented the algorithm on 80 patients images. For the purpose of this experiment, we only used the 0 o'clock ultrasound images. The result is shown in Table 5.

Table 5. Experiment #3

Method	# of patients	TP	TN	FP	FN	Accuracy
Our Method	80	59	21	1	1	97.5%
Hybrid Filtering[1]	80	61	19	4	2	92.5%
ABUS[4]	80	62	18	6	3	88.75%

Experiment #4. In this experiment, we used fuzzy logic for pre-processing of ultrasound images. We also used compounding of three images of each patient (9 o'clock, 0 o'clock and 3 o'clock) and performed compounding on the images. Neural network method [28] is used for segmentation. We used the features that we extracted using Sequential Forward Search, Sequential Backward Search and Distance-based methods. Texture features are also used. Classification was carried out by the Support Vector Machine. We have carried out experiments on 80 patients images. The result is shown in Table 6.

Table 6. Experiment #4

Method	# of patients	TP	TN	FP	FN	Accuracy
Our Method	80	59	21	1	0	98.75%
Hybrid Filtering[1]	80	61	19	4	2	92.5%
ABUS[4]	80	62	18	6	3	88.75%

8   Conclusions

In this research we surveyed the current state of the field of automatic breast cancer detection from ultrasound images and we pointed out many deficiencies in the current methodology. We proposed a new improved approach to cancer detection. The main problem with processing ultrasound images is speckle noise and shadowing. To overcome these problems we proposed a fully automated system for detection of breast ultrasound images. In the first pre-processing stage we used fuzzy logic approach to remove noise and thus improved segmentation and overall performance of the cancer detection system. In order to improve classification we applied backward and forward sequential search to identify a subset of good features which were subsequently validated by the physician. As it was pointed out by a physician one of the big problems in detection of suspicious lesions is shadowing. To overcome this problem we used a method of compounding ultrasound images from different angles. This method allowed us to either eliminate or significantly reduce the amount of shadowing present in our database of ultrasound images thus improving overall results. The experiments carried out on the database of 80 patients with 3 images per patient validated our claim of improved performance.

In future research we plan to experiment with different sets of features, applying our method on a database of color ultrasound images. We also intend to implement an expert system for the diagnosis stage of our automated CAD system. The expert system will attempt to minimize the effort by a physician for diagnosis of suspicious lesions.

References

1. Yap, M.H.: A novel algorithm for initial lesion detection in ultrasound breast images. Journal of Applied Clinical Medical Physics 9(4) (2008)
2. Ikedo, Y., Fukuoka, D., Hara, J., Fujita, H., Takada, E., Endo, T., Morita, T.: Computerized mass detection in whole breast ultrasound images: Reduction of false positives using bilateral subtraction technique. In: Medical Imaging. Proc. of SPIE, vol. 6514, pp. 1–10 (2007)
3. Ikedo, Y., Fukuoka, D., Hara, T., Fujita, H., Takada, E., Endo, T., Morita, T.: Development of a fully automatic scheme for detection of masses in whole breast ultrasound images. Medical Physics 34, 4378–4388 (2007)
4. Moon, W.K., Lo, C., Chang, J., Huang, C., Chen, J., Chang, R.: Computer-aided classification of breast masses using speckle features of automated breast ultrasound images. Medical Physics. 39 (2012)

5. Gupta, S., Chauhan, R., Sexena, S.: Robust non-homomorphic approach for speckle reduction in medical ultrasound images. Medical and Biological Engineering and Computing 43, 189–195 (2005)
6. Benes, R., Riha, K.: Noise Reduction in Medical Ultrasound Images. Elektrorevue 2(3) (2011)
7. Roy, S., Sinha, N., Sen, A.: A New Hybrid Image Denoising Method. International Journal of Information Technology and Knowledge Management 2(2), 491–497 (2010)
8. Nicolae, M.C., Moraru, L., Gogu, A.: Speckle noise reduction of ultrasound images. Medical Ultrasonography an International Journal of Clinical Imaging 11, 50–51 (2009)
9. Joo, S., Moon, W.K., Kim, H.C.: Computer-aided diagnosis of solid breast nodules on ultrasound with digital image processing and artificial neural network. Medicine and Biology Society 2, 1397–1400 (2004)
10. Yeh, C.K., Chen, Y.S., Fan, W.C., Liao, Y.Y.: A disk expansion segmentatoin method for ultrasonic breast lesions. Pattern Recognition 42(5), 596–606 (2009)
11. Moon, W.K., Shen, Y.W., Bae, M.S., Huang, C.H., Chen, J.H.: Computer-Aided Tumor Detection Based on Multi-scale Blob Detection Algorithm in Automated Breast Ultrasound Images. IEEE Transaction on Medical Imaging 32(7), 1191–1200 (2013)
12. Chang, R.F., Wu, W.J., Moon, W.K., Chen, D.R.: Automatic ultrasound segmentation and morphology based diagnosis of solid breast tumors. Breast Cancer Research and Treatment 89(2), 179–185 (2005)
13. Sennett, C.A., Giger, M.L.: Automated Method for Improving System Performance of Computer-Aided Diagnosis in Breast Ultrasound 28(1), 122–128 (2009)
14. Lihua, L., Jiangli, L., Deyu, L., Tianfu, W.: Segmentation of medical ultrasound image based on markov random field. Bioinformatics and Biomedical Engineering 968–971 (2007)
15. Deka, B., Ghosh, D.: Ultrasound image segmentation using watersheds and region merging. In IET International Conference on Visual Information Engineering, Banglore, pp. 110–115(2006)
16. Pereira, W.C.A., Infantosi, A.F.C.: Analysis of Co-Occurrence Texture Statistics as a Function of Gray-Level Quantization for Classifying Breast Ultrasound. IEEE Transactions on Medical Imaging 31(10), 1889–1899 (2012)
17. Wu, W.J., Kyung Moon, W.: Ultrasound breast tumor image computer-aided diagnosis with texture and morphological features. Academic Radiology 15(7), 873–880 (2008)
18. Ramana Reddy, B.V., Suresh, A., Radhika Mani, M., Vijaya Kumar, V.: Classification of Textures Based on Features Extracted from Preprocessing Images on Random Windows. International Journal of Advanced Science and Technology 9 (2009)
19. Tamilselvi, P.R., Thangaraj, P.: Improved Gabor filter for extracting texture edge features in US kidney images. Modern Applied Science 4 (2010)
20. Lin, C.F., Wang, S.D.: Fuzzy support vector machines. IEEE Transactions on Neural Networks 13(2), 464–471 (2002)
21. Lui, B., Cheng, H., Huang, J., Tian, J., Tang, X., Liu, J.: Probability density difference-based active contour for ultrasound image segmentation. Journal Pattern Recognition 43(6), 2028–2042 (2010)
22. Selvan, S., Kavitha, M., Shenbagadevi, S., Suresh, K.: Feature Extraction for Characterization of Breast Lesions in Ultrasound Elastography and Echography. Journal of Computer Science 16, 67–74 (2010)

23. Kotropoulos, C., Pitas, I.: Segmentation of ultrasonic images using support vector machines. Pattern Recognition Letters 24(4), 715–725 (2004)
24. Zadeh, L.A.: The concept of linguistic variable and its application to approximate reasoning - I. Information Science 8, 199–249 (1975)
25. Zadeh, L.A.: Fuzzy sets. Information and Control 8(3), 338–353 (1965)
26. Sahba, F., Tizhoosh, M.R., Salma, M.M.A.: Segmentation of prostate boundaries using regional contrast enhancement. In: The IEEE International Conference on Image Processing (ICIP), vol. 2, pp. 1266–1269 (2005)
27. Haihui, W., Yanli, W., Tongzhou, T., Miao, W., Mingpeng, W.: Images segmentation method on comparison of feature extractoin techniques. In: 2nd International Workshop on Intelligent Systems and Applications, pp. 1–4 (2010)
28. Dokur, Z., Olmez, T.: Segmentation of ultrasound images by using a hybrid neural network. Pattern Recognition Letters 23(14), 1825–1836 (2002)
29. Sarti, A., Corsi, C., Mazzini, E., Lamberti, C.: Maximum likelihood segmentation with Rayleigh distribution of ultrasound images. Computers in Cardiology 31, 329–332 (2004)
30. Zhang, H., Fritts, J.E., Goldman, S.A.: A fast texture feature extraction method for region-based image segmentation. Image and Video Communications and Processing 5685, 957–968 (2005)
31. Duda, R.O., Hart, P.E., Stork, D.G.: Pattern Classification. Wiley, New York (2001)
32. Saini, K., Dewal, M.L., Rohit, M.: Ultrasound Imaging and Image Segmentation in the area of Ultrasound: A Review. International Journal of Advanced Science and Technology 24 (2010)
33. Sohail, A.S.M., Bhattacharya, P., Mudur, S.P., Krishnamurthy, S.: Classification of ultrasound medical images using distance based feature selection and fuzzy-SVM. In: Vitrià, J., Sanches, J.M., Hernández, M. (eds.) IbPRIA 2011. LNCS, vol. 6669, pp. 176–183. Springer, Heidelberg (2011)
34. Burrell, L.S., Smart, O.L., Georgoulas, G., Marsh, E., Vachtsevanos, G.J.: Evaluation of Feature Selection Techniques for Analysis of Functional MRI and EEG. In: 2007 International Conference on Data Mining, DMIN, Las Vegas (2007)

The Classifier for Prediction of Peri-operative Complications in Cervical Cancer Treatment

Jacek Kluska[1], Maciej Kusy[1], and Bogdan Obrzut[2]

[1] Faculty of Electrical and Computer Engineering, Rzeszów University of Technology,
35-959 Rzeszów, Powstańców Warszawy 12, Poland
{jacklu,mkusy}@prz.edu.pl
[2] Faculty of Medicine, University of Rzeszów, 35-205 Rzeszów,
Warszawska 26a, Poland
b.obrzut@univ.rzeszow.pl

Abstract. This paper addresses the problem of creating a new classifier as highly interpretable fuzzy rule-based system, based on the analytical theory of fuzzy modeling and gene expression programming. This approach is applied to solve the prediction problem of peri-operative complications of radical hysterectomy in patients with cervical cancer. The developed classifier has the form of the set of fuzzy metarules, which are readable for the medical community, and additionally, is accurate enough. The consequents of the metarules describe the presence or absence of peri-operative complications. For the construction of the classifier we can use the fuzzified, binarized or both types of the attributes. We also compare the efficiency of our model with the decision trees and C5 algorithm.

Keywords: Takagi-Sugeno system, gene expression programming, cervical cancer, complications prediction.

1 Introduction

Cervical cancer is the third most common carcinoma and the fourth leading cause of cancer death in females worldwide [1]. In early tumor stages, the operative therapy is preferred. Patients with microinvasive cervical cancer may be treated less aggressively. For more advanced disease (FIGO IA2-IIB) [2], in many medical centers, radical hysterectomy with pelvic lymphadenectomy remains the therapy of choice [3]. As one of the most extensive surgical procedures in gynecological oncology, this operation is burdened with significant risk of severe complications [4]. These adverse events cause an additional stress of a patient, postpone the adjuvant therapy and significantly increase hospital costs. Thus, the identification of patients with high risk of peri-operative complications is significant, since the chemoradiation would be probably more safe and equally effective therapeutic option for them.

The aim of this study is to propose a new classifier for the prediction of radical hysterectomy complications in women with cervical cancer FIGO IA2-IIB. This classifier will have the form of the set of fuzzy metarules which are readable for the medical community. We investigate the real data consisting of 107 patients

L. Rutkowski et al. (Eds.): ICAISC 2014, Part II, LNAI 8468, pp. 143–154, 2014.

with 10 attributes obtained from the Clinical Department of Obstetrics and Gynecology of Rzeszów State Hospital in Poland.

There is a large number of computational intelligence algorithms which can be used for prediction problems in a medical domain, e.g. artificial neural networks, distance classifiers, regression models, support vector machines, proposed in the literature. Unfortunately, these type of models, as classifiers, are the black boxes which cannot be interpretable [5]. However, there have been some models developed which, along with the classification result, are capable of extracting some knowledge by generating the set of interpretable rules which, in turn, a human understands [6]. They are considered as white boxes. The following methods deserve attention here: decision trees [7,8], C4.5 algorithm and beyond [9], fuzzy clustering methods [10,11], genetic programming algorithms [12] or the methodologies of generating rules by learning from examples [13]. One can observe the trend in creating fuzzy classifiers and decision support systems which are also capable of generating a set of rules [14,15]. These techniques generate data models in terms of production rules of the form: IF condition THEN conclusion [16].

The structure of the article is as follows. Section 2 highlights some ideas on analytical theory of fuzzy modeling concerning a special case of the Takagi-Sugeno-Kang systems. In this part, we present a theorem, corollary and an example on equivalency between the set of fuzzy metarules and their algebraic representation. In Section 3, the original data set and the fuzzy representation of the inputs are described. Section 4 presents the problem statement. In Section 5, the efficiency of the proposed approach, decision trees and C5 algorithm is assessed in the considered classification problem. The main result of the paper, in the form of the interpretable metarules, is presented in Section 6. Finally, the work is concluded in Section 7.

2   P1-TS Fuzzy Rule-Based System

In the work [17], it is proved that for some class of the Takagi-Sugeno models, where all input variables have linear and complementary membership functions of the fuzzy sets, the system of their "If-then" metarules is equivalent to multilinear functions. These functions are special case of the Kolmogorov-Gabor polynomial. Such a class of systems is denoted by P1-TS. Based on the polynomial we are able to read the metarules, which have a very simple interpretation from the logical point of view. Thanks to the recursion introduced in [17], the curse of dimensionality problem can be substantially reduced. Below, we present some notions comprised by P1-TS system.

Let us consider a multiple-input-single-output (MISO for short) rule-based system with input variables $z_1, \ldots, z_n$ and the output S. For every input $z_k \in [-\alpha_k, \beta_k]$ it is required that $\alpha_k + \beta_k > 0$, $(k = 1, 2, \ldots, n)$. The set $D^n = [-\alpha_1, \beta_1] \times \ldots \times [-\alpha_n, \beta_n]$ defines a hyperrectangle. For any z_k, we define two membership functions of fuzzy sets $N_k = N_k(z_k)$, and $P_k = P_k(z_k)$, where P_k is an algebraic complement to N_k:

$$N_k = (\alpha_k + \beta_k)^{-1} (\beta_k - z_k), \quad P_k = 1 - N_k, \tag{1}$$

for $k = 1, \ldots, n$. This system is defined by 2^n rules in the form of implications:

$$\text{If } z_1 \text{ is } A_{i_1} \text{ and } \ldots \text{ and } z_n \text{ is } A_{i_n}, \text{ then } S = q_j, \quad q_j \in \mathbb{R}, \tag{2}$$

where $A_{i_k} \in \{N_k, P_k\}, (k = 1, \ldots, n)$. The above rule-based system with membership functions for the inputs as in (1) we will call P1-TS system.

Theorem 1. *[17] Let*

$$f_0(\mathbf{z}) = \sum_{(p_1, \ldots, p_n) \in \{0,1\}^n} \theta_{p_1, \ldots, p_n} z_1^{p_1} \cdots z_n^{p_n}, \tag{3}$$

where $\theta_{p_1, \ldots, p_n} \in \mathbb{R}$. For every function of the type (3) there exists a (zero-order) MISO P1-TS system with the inputs $z_1, \ldots, z_n$ and the output S, such that $S(\mathbf{z}) = f_0(\mathbf{z})$ for all $\mathbf{z}^T = [z_1, \ldots, z_n] \in D^n$. By solving 2^n linear equations one can find all consequents q_j of the rules. For a nonzero volume of the hyperrectangle D^n, the unique solution always exists.

The fuzzy rule-based systems exhibit the "curse of dimensionality", because the number of their rules grows exponentially with the number of inputs. Namely, by adding an extra dimension to the input space, we observe a doubling of the number of fuzzy "If-then" rules in the MISO P1-TS. However, by means of the recursion, the curse of dimensionality problem can be substantially reduced [17].

In this paper, we consider a special case of the rule-based system in which $D^n = [0,1]^n$. In such a case the inputs take the values from the interval $[0,1]$, therefore, we can call the rule-based system "logical" one, since the labels of fuzzy sets N_k are interpreted as *almost false*, and the labels of fuzzy sets P_k are interpreted as *almost true*. This type of systems process the information expressed in continuous, multi-valued logic. Usually, we are not interested in 2^n fuzzy rules, but in obtaining the *metarules* [17].

Corollary 1. *Let the inputs of the P1-TS system be $x_1, \ldots, x_n \in [0,1]$ and the consequents of its rules are from the set $\{0,1\}$. Let us define new inputs $z_1, \ldots, z_{2n}$, such that $z_{2k-1} = x_k$, $z_{2k} = 1 - x_k$, for $k = 1, \ldots, n$. The crisp output of this system can be expressed as a sum of products:*

$$S = \sum_{i=1}^{M} \prod_{i \in P_i} \tilde{z}_i, \quad \text{where} \quad \tilde{z}_i \in \{z_i, 1 - z_i\}, \quad M \leqslant 2^{2n}, \tag{4}$$

and P_i's contain some indices of the variables from the set $\{z_1, \ldots, z_{2n}\}$.

Example 1. Suppose the P1-TS system has 6 inputs x_k, where all inputs are from the unity interval $[0,1]$ for $k = 1, \ldots, 6$ and the membership functions for every input are of the type (1). The following 8 metarules define this system:

M1: If x_1 is N_1 and x_3 is P_3 and x_4 is N_4, then $S = 1$,
M2: If x_3 is P_3 and x_4 is P_4 and x_6 is N_6, then $S = 1$,
M3: If x_1 is P_1 and x_2 is N_2 and x_4 is N_4 and x_5 is N_5, then $S = 1$,
M4: If x_1 is N_1 and x_3 is N_3, then $S = 0$,

M5: If x_4 is P_4 and x_6 is P_6, then $S = 0$,
M6: If x_1 is P_1 and x_4 is N_4 and x_5 is P_5, then $S = 0$,
M7: If x_1 is P_1 and x_3 is N_3 and x_4 is P_4 and x_6 is N_6, then $S = 0$,
M8: If x_1 is P_1 and x_2 is P_2 and x_4 is N_4, then $S = 0$.

One can prove that the crisp output of this P1-TS system is given by:

$$S = (1 - x_1) x_3 (1 - x_4) + x_3 x_4 (1 - x_6) + x_1 (1 - x_2) (1 - x_4) (1 - x_5). \quad (5)$$

Let us introduce new variables $z_{2k-1} = x_k$ and $z_{2k} = 1 - x_k$ for $k = 1, \ldots, 6$. Thus, we obtain the double number of variables $z_j \in [0, 1]$, for $j = 1, \ldots, 2n$. The function (5) is equivalent to:

$$S = z_2 z_5 z_8 + z_5 z_7 z_{12} + z_1 z_4 z_8 z_{10}. \quad (6)$$

From (6) we can uniquely define three metarules whose consequents are equal to one, while the consequents of all remaining rules are zeros.

The interpretation of the metarules, the individual rules, and the crisp function of any P1-TS system with the inputs from the unity interval is quite simple. Additionally, for the given expression in the form of (4), one can obtain the fuzzy "If-then" metarules.

3   Original Data Set and Fuzzy Representation of Inputs

In this section, the transformation of the data used in the work will be discussed. It is a crucial step in the methodology of the rule based system design, since the appropriate representation of the attributes has a straightforward influence on the interpretability of the results for the clinicians, as the subject-matter experts (SMEs).

Each of 107 records from the original data set consists of the following predictor variables: $age = x_1$ [y], $body\ mass\ index\ (BMI) = x_2$ $\left[\text{kg} / \text{m}^2\right]$, $comorbidities = x_3 \in \{no, yes\}$, $previous\ operations = x_4 \in \{no, yes\}$, $hormonal\ status = x_5 \in \{premenopausal, postmenopausal\}$, $histology\ of\ tumor = x_6 \in \{squamous, nonsquamous\}$, $histologic\ grade = x_7 \in \{G1, G2, G3\}$, $FIGO\ stage = x_8 \in \{IA2, IB1, IB2, IIA, IIB\}$ [2]. The output variable is $S \in \{present, absent\}$, where $S = present$ means occurrence of intra- or post-operative complications, and $S = absent$ – means vice-versa.

The predictors x_i will be linearly transformed (fuzzified) into new variables Z_k. We propose to distinguish three types of the input variables.

1. Original attribute x_i is a real number from the finite and ordered data set (universe) $\{x_{i,\min}, \ldots, x_{i,\max}\}$, and there is no SME recommendation to split this universe into subintervals. We assume that all new cases of the variable x_i are allowed to be from the interval $[a_i, b_i] \supset \{x_{i,\min}, \ldots, x_{i,\max}\}$. This inclusion says that there might be also other cases than those that occur in the studied population, e.g. the body weight greater than $x_{i,\max}$. Therefore,

the value of a_i is not greater than $x_{i,\min}$ and the value of b_i is not smaller than $x_{i,\max}$. We perform the following two steps:
(1) Normalization:

$$z_i = (x_i - a_i) / (b_i - a_i) \in [0, 1], \quad x_i \in [a_i, b_i]. \tag{7}$$

(2) Assigning two complementary membership functions of fuzzy sets:

$$Z_k = P(z_i) = z_i, \quad Z_{k+1} = N(z_i) = 1 - z_i. \tag{8}$$

As a result we obtain two new input variables $<Z_k, Z_{k+1}>$ which have clear linguistic interpretation, namely, the closer x_i to its upper bound, the greater the value of Z_k. Similarly, the closer x_i to its lower bound, the greater the value of Z_{k+1}.

2. Original attribute x_i is a real number from the finite and ordered data set (universe) $\{x_{i,\min}, \ldots, x_{i,\max}\}$, and there are SME recommendations to split this universe into p_i smaller subsets. We assume that all new cases of the variable x_i are allowed to be from the set $[r_{i,L}, r_{i,V}) \supset \{x_{i,\min}, \ldots, x_{i,\max}\}$:

$$[r_{i,L}, r_{i,V}) = \bigcup_{j=1}^{p_i} [r_{i,j}, r_{i,j+1}), \qquad p_i > 1.$$

We perform the following two steps:
(1) Normalization:

$$z_i = (x_i - r_{i,j}) / (r_{i,j+1} - r_{i,j}) \in [0, 1], \quad x_i \in [r_{i,j}, r_{i,j+1}), \quad j = 1, \ldots, p_i. \tag{9}$$

(2) Assigning two complementary membership functions of fuzzy sets:

$$Z_{k+2j-2} = P(z_i), \quad Z_{k+2j-1} = N(z_i) = 1 - z_i. \tag{10}$$

As a result we obtain new pairs of membership functions $< Z_k, Z_{k+1} >$.

3. Original attribute x_i is a categorical variable from the set $\{label_1, \ldots, label_r\}$, and $2 \leqslant r < \infty$. In this case, we assign the pairs of membership functions $< Z_k, Z_{k+1} >, \ldots, < Z_{k+2p-2}, Z_{k+2p-1} >$, namely:

$$Z_{k+2j-2} = 1, \quad Z_{k+2j-1} = 0, \quad \text{if} \quad x_i = label_j. \tag{11}$$

For the data set considered in our study, the process of obtaining new variables $Z_1, \ldots, Z_m$ is as follows:

- Original attribute age (x_1) is an integer from the set $\{29, \ldots, 73\}$, and we assume that all new cases (for the prediction problem) of the variable x_1 are allowed to be from the set $[a_1, b_1] = [25, 75] \supset \{29, \ldots, 73\}$. From the clinical point of view, there is no indication to divide the original universe of the age variable [4]. As a result we obtain new variables: Z_1 – patient's age near the upper bound of *age*, and Z_2 – patient's age near the lower bound of *age*.

- Original attribute *body mass index* (*BMI* or x_2) is a real number; $x_2 \in \{17.5, \ldots, 44.96\}$. We assume that all new cases of the variable x_2 (for the prediction problem) are allowed to be from the interval $[15, 50]$. In case of *BMI* variable, we are imposed some prerequisites. Namely, according to WHO classification [18], 8 categories of *BMI* are distinguished as the intervals: $[15, 16)$ – underweight: severe thinness, $[16, 17)$ – underweight: moderate thinness, $[17, 18.5)$ – underweight: mild thinness, $[18.5, 25)$ – normal range, $[25, 30)$ – overweight, $[30, 35)$ – obese class I, $[35, 40)$ – obese class II, $[40, 50]$ – obese class III. For x_2, the second case of the transformation takes place and we obtain new variables: $Z_3, \ldots, Z_{18}$. For example, the interpretation of *BMI* from the interval $[15, 16)$ is as follows: Z_3 - *BMI* is near the upper bound of the severe thinness, and Z_4 - *BMI* is near the lower bound of the severe thinness.

- Original attributes – *comorbidities* (x_3), *previous operations* (x_4), *hormonal status* (x_5) and *histology of tumor* (x_6) are all the elements of the bivalent sets. For x_3 - x_6, the third case of the transformation is faced ($r = 2$), therefore we obtain new variables, which are interpreted in the following way: Z_{19} – *comorbidities* are present, Z_{20} – *comorbidities* are absent, Z_{21} – *previous operations* are present, Z_{22} – *previous operations* are absent, Z_{23} – *hormonal status* is pre-menopausal, Z_{24} – *hormonal status* is post-menopausal, Z_{25} – *histology of tumor* is squamous, Z_{26} – *histology of tumor* is non-squamous.

- Input variable *histologic grade*, $x_7 \in \{G_1, G_2, G_3\}$ denotes the tumor grade, i.e. the grade of invasive cancer of the cervix uteri (or the grade of histologic differentiation) [19]. Cancer graded as G_1 is usually less aggressive and unlikely spreads to other organs or tissues of the body. G_3 graded carcinoma is the most aggressive type of cancer. This variable is eligible to the third case with $r = 3$. Thus, we obtain new inputs: $Z_{27}, \ldots, Z_{32}$. For example, the fuzzy sets for histologic grade are interpreted as follows: Z_{27} – cancer is well differentiated and Z_{28} – cancer is not well differentiated.

- Input variable *FIGO stage*, $x_8 \in \{IA2, IB1, IB2, IIA, IIB\}$ describes the extent of cervical cancer according to the FIGO staging system [2]. The third case of the transformation occurs now for $r = 5$. We obtain new variables: $Z_{33}, \ldots, Z_{42}$. For example, $Z_{33} = 1$ means that cervical cancer is of $IA2$ stage, $Z_{34} = 1$ – cervical cancer is not of $IA2$ stage. The fuzzy sets $Z_{35}, \ldots, Z_{42}$ are understood in the same manner.

4   Problem Statement

For the training data set described in Section 3, we want to find the set of expressions in the form of the sum of the products as in (4), which best fit the data. Based on these expressions, obtaining the metarules for the P1-TS system with 42 inputs and the bivalent output S, will be quite simple. Of course, one can obtain the rules using the other methods. Therefore, we will compare our results with the decision trees and C5 algorithm. In order to find expression in the form of (4), we propose to use the gene expression programming (GEP) method.

5 The Efficiency Assessment of the Proposed Approach, Decision Trees and C5 Algorithm

In this section, we compare our new methodology which is based on P1-TS system and GEP with two well known classification methods, i.e. decision trees (DT) and C5 algorithm in the problem of cervical cancer complications prediction. All the models can be viewed as white box classifiers which, as the result, provide the error computed on the test data and, additionally, the set of rules.

5.1 Gene Expression Programming

Gene expression programming was introduced by Ferreira [20]. In this algorithm, individuals are encoded by the chromosomes which are composed of the genes structurally organized in the head and the tail. The length of genes depends on the head size. When the representation of each gene is given, the genotype is established. It is then converted to the expression tree.

In order to construct the chromosome, the genes are linked with each other by means of the linking function. The individuals form a population which undergoes evolution by computing the expression from each chromosome, applying predefined genetic operators and calculating the fitness. The evolution continues until a termination criterion is satisfied.

For the construction of the proposed fuzzy classifier, GeneXproTools 4.0 software is used with the following settings: number of chromosomes in population (30), head size (5), number of genes within each chromosome (1, 3, 5, 7), linking function between genes (*Addition*), fitness function (*Number of hits*), genetic operators (*Mutation* = 0.044, *Inversion* = 0.1, *IS Transposition* = 0.1, *RIS Transposition* = 0.1, *One-Point Recombination* = 0.3, *Two-Point Recombination* = 0.3, *Gene Recombination* = 0.1, *Gene Transposition* = 0.1), computing functions in head (*Multiplication*).

Evolution is performed until 1000 generations are reached. The fitness function is chosen to be *Number of hits*. The rounding threshold is set to be 0.5.

5.2 Decision Trees and C5 Algorithm

Decision trees were originally described in [7]. DT methodology consists of three parts: (1) – Construction of maximum tree, (2) – Choice of the right tree size, and (3) – Classification of new data using constructed tree. In this research, we use DTREG [21] software to construct and test the tree. The entropy is used to evaluate the quality of splits in the process of tree construction. The depth of the tree is set to 10. No pruning algorithms are applied to control the tree size.

C5 is an algorithm used to generate a decision tree developed by Quinlan [9]. This algorithm generates classifiers expressed as decision trees, but it can also construct classifiers in the rule set form. In this work, we apply IBM SPSS Modeler 14.2 [22] to simulate C5 algorithm. The model with the lowest generalization error is chosen on the basis of the variety of setting options, such as:

Table 1. Minimum test errors computed in each partition for cervical cancer complication prediction using proposed approach, DT and C5

Training/Test size	Min. test error [%]					
	Proposed method				DT	C5
	1 gene	3 genes	5 genes	7 genes		
54/53	35.85	32.08	33.96	33.96	44.44	37.29
64/43	30.23	27.91	27.91	30.23	46.51	42.55
74/33	24.24	24.24	27.27	27.27	40.62	38.89
85/22	27.27	22.73	18.18	18.18	31.82	41.67
96/11	9.09	9.09	9.09	9.09	25.00	36.36
102/5	0.00	0.00	0.00	0.00	20.00	0.00
Average	**21.11**	**19.34**	**19.40**	**19.78**	**34.73**	**32.79**
St. dev.	**13.69**	**12.25**	**12.88**	**13.22**	**10.84**	**16.24**

extent to which the rule set is pruned (5, 10, 15), minimum records per child branch (2), using global pruning (applied, not applied), winnowing attributes (used, not used).

5.3 Models' Comparison

It is known that the number of ways of dividing the training set into v groups, each of size k, is huge and equals $h = n!/(v!\,(k!)^v)$ [23]. Thus, considering all possible training sets is computationally intractable in practice. Therefore, in the simulations, we consider the partition of $n = 107$ samples into 6 training and testing parts, which are drawn randomly. The percentage of testing data within each part equals 50% (54 training samples, 53 test samples), 40% (64 training samples, 43 test samples), 30% (74 training samples, 33 test samples), 20% (85 training samples, 22 test samples), 10% (96 training samples, 11 test samples) and 5% (102 training samples, 5 test samples).

In each data partition, we search for the model for which the lowest test error is found. In Table 1, the lowest test error values are shown in particular training-test partitions for three regarded classifiers. We also calculate the average value and the standard deviation over all test errors because the sum of these indices determines the utility thresholds of the models (these are marked in bold in the table).

As shown in Table 1, the proposed approach provides lowest values of the test set error among all three compared models. Such a result is valid regardless of the number of genes used in the chromosome. For the chromosome composed of three genes, DT and C5 performs worse by 15.39% and 13.45%, respectively. In GEP based classification, the test error usually decreases along with the increase of the training data size. Such a result seems to be natural (although it is not the case for C5 method) since a greater number of samples is used to train the model. It is also worth noting that the constraint of the number of genes within the chromosome to one, increases test error. For the number of genes equal to 3, 5 and 7, almost no error change is observed.

6 Discovering Metatules from Algebraic Expression

It can be observed that the lowest average test error value, computed over all samples' partition cases, for each of examined models is found when our approach is used for data classification. Such a result (19.34%) occurs for 3 genes in the chromosome. Due to the fact that the minimum test error (22.73%) found at 85/22 partition is closest to the average error value, we decide to compute the output expression for the model which is applied in this particular classification problem. Moreover, as shown in Table 1, the standard deviation reaches the lowest value (12.25%) for 3 genes based model, thus we consider this result as most reliable.

Below, two exemplary models (denoted as **Model 1** and **Model 2**) are shown in the form of the output expression (S) and the sets of metarules, presented in the similar way as proposed in formula (4). It is necessary to emphasize that, in each case, three genes are involved in the chromosome evolution, therefore, three metarules are extracted for the models. For both models the average test error is the same, i.e. 22.73%. For **Model 1**, we obtain:

$$S = Z_{12}Z_{29} + Z_{20}Z_{29} + Z_{24}Z_{42}.$$

This sum of products defines three following metarules:

1. **If** *BMI* is near the lower bound of overweight **and** cancer is moderately differentiated, **then** *complications* are present;
2. **If** *comorbidities* are absent **and** cancer is moderately differentiated, **then** *complications* are present;
3. **If** *hormonal status* is post-menopausal **and** cervical cancer is not of *IIB stage*, **then** *complications* are present.

The output expression for **Model 2** has the following form:

$$S = Z_{16}Z_{21} + Z_{20}Z_{29} + Z_{12}Z_{29}.$$

This sum of products allows to formulate three metarules as follows:

1. **If** *BMI* is near the lower bound of obese class II **and** *previous operations* are present, **then** *complications* are present;
2. **If** *comorbidities* are absent **and** cancer is moderately differentiated, **then** *complications* are present;
3. **If** *BMI* is near the lower bound of overweight **and** cancer is moderately differentiated, **then** *complications* are present.

Since for the chromosomes composed of 5 genes, both the average test error (19.40%) of the classifier and the standard deviation (12.88%) slightly differ from the same factors, but determined when 3 genes are used in the chromosome (0.06% and 0.63%, respectively), we also decide to generate the metarules for 5 genes based model. As previously, the average test error computed over all partitions is nearest to the error value (18.18%) found at 85/22 data division. Therefore, for this classification problem the output expression for the model (named henceforth **Model 3**) has the following form:

$$S = Z_{12}Z_{22}Z_{26} + Z_{22}Z_{33} + Z_{11}Z_{20}Z_{35} + Z_2 Z_9 Z_{24}Z_{29} + Z_2 Z_{10}Z_{20}Z_{22}Z_{26}. \quad (12)$$

This expression provides five metarules for **Model 3**:

1. **If** *BMI* is near the lower bound of overweight **and** *previous operations* are absent **and** *histology of tumor* is non-squamous, **then** *complications* are present;
2. **If** *previous operations* are absent **and** cervical cancer is of $IA2$ stage, **then** *complications* are present;
3. **If** *BMI* is near the upper bound of overweight **and** *comorbidities* are absent **and** cervical cancer is of $IB1$ stage, **then** *complications* are present;
4. **If** patient's age is near the lower bound of *age* **and** *BMI* is near the upper bound of normal range **and** *hormonal status* is post-menopausal **and** cancer is moderately differentiated, **then** *complications* are present;
5. **If** patient's age is near the lower bound of *age* **and** *BMI* is near the lower bound of normal range **and** *comorbidities* are absent **and** *previous operations* are absent **and** *histology of tumor* is non-squamous, **then** *complications* are present.

Observe that the metarules for considered models are readable to medical audience. Furthermore, the particular rule antecedents are simple and transparent, and the entire metarule resembles, to a high degree, the medical judgement exposed to a patient.

7   Conclusion

Our main goal was to provide the classifier which generates the rules readable for the medical community. We obtained the metarules in the case of the complications presence.

The idea introduced in this paper is new and has the following advantages:

1. The construction of the transparent classifier is universal in the sense that for any subset of the attributes we can apply the fuzzy or bivalent notions. The process of the variable fuzzification and the interpretation of an attribute considered by a domain expert as relevant, must be consulted with this expert since he/she is the end user of the decision support system.
2. The interpretation of the rules is simple since we used the Takagi-Sugeno-Kang system involving linear membership functions of fuzzy sets.
3. The number of the metarules can be set up by providing the appropriate number of genes in a chromosome.

The authors will attempt to explore the problem of the prediction of different complications where the number of classes is greater than 2 (distinction between mild, moderate and severe complications, and absence of complications). One can achieve this by using the proposed method and "one against all" approach. We realize though that the given number of data comprising 107 patients is hardly sufficient.

It is worth adding that for the same data set, as explored in this paper, the authors conducted the simulations on the efficiency of the following classifiers: k-nearest neighbor, logistic regression, bayesian network, support vector machine, multilayer perceptron, k-means clustering, probabilistic neural network, linear discriminant analysis and radial basis function neural network. The results were reported in [24] where multilayer perceptron was found to be the best classifier among all tested models (average test error 17.22%). This network outperforms the classifier proposed in this paper. However, it is not interpretable (black box) since it does not provide any rules.

Acknowledgements. This work was partially supported by the Grant INNO-TECH–K2/IN2/41/182370/NCBR/13 from the National Centre for Research and Development in Poland and by the Rzeszow University of Technology Grant No. U–235/DS.

References

1. Jemal, A., Bray, F., Center, M.M., Ferlay, J.: Global cancer statistics. A Cancer Journal for Clinicians 61, 69–90 (2011)
2. Pecorelli, S., Zigliani, L., Odicino, F.: Revised FIGO staging for carcinoma of the cervix. International Journal of Gynecology & Obstetrics 105, 107–108 (2009)
3. Schneider, A., Kohler, C.: Tumor Surgery Cervical Cancer Treatment. In: Gross, G., Tyring, S.K. (eds.) Sexually Transmitted Infections and Sexually Transmitted Diseases, pp. 477–488. Springer, Heidelberg (2011)
4. Obrzut, B.: The extent of surgery and its impact on FIGO IA2-IIB cervical cancer treatment outcomes. Poznan, OWN XVIII (2008) (in Polish)
5. Duch, W., Setiono, R., Zurada, J.M.: Computational Intelligence Methods for Rule-Based Data Understanding. Proceedings of the IEEE 92(5), 771–805 (2004)
6. Casillas, J., Cordon, O., Herrera, F., Magdalena, L. (eds.): Interpretability Issues in Fuzzy Modeling. STUDFUZZ, vol. 128. Springer, Heidelberg (2003)
7. Breiman, L., Friedman, J.H., Olshen, R.A., Stone, C.J.: Classification and regression trees. Wadsworth, Belmont (1984)
8. Quinlan, J.R.: Generating Production Rules from Decision Trees. In: 10th International Joint Conference on Artificial Intelligence, pp. 304–307. Morgan Kaufmann Publishers, San Mateo (1987)
9. Quinlan, J.R.: C4.5: Programs for machine learning. Morgan Kaufmann Publishers, San Mateo (1993)
10. Yager, R., Filev, D.: Approximate clustering via mountain method. IEEE Trans. Systems, Man and Cybernetics 24(8), 1279–1284 (1994)
11. Setnes, M.: Supervised Fuzzy Clustering for Rule Extraction. IEEE Trans. Fuzzy Systems 8(4), 416–424 (2000)

12. Tsakonas, A., Dounias, G., Jantzen, J., Axer, H., Bjerregaard, B., Keyserlingk, D.G.: Evolving rule-based systems in two medical domains using genetic programming. Artificial Intelligence in Medicine 32, 195–216 (2004)
13. Wang, L.-X., Mendel, J.M.: Generating fuzzy rules by learning from examples. IEEE Trans. Systems, Man and Cybernetics 22(6), 1414–1427 (1992)
14. Gadaras, I., Mikhailov, L.: An interpretable fuzzy rule-based classification methodology for medical diagnosis. Artificial Intelligence in Medicine 47, 25–41 (2009)
15. Tsipouras, M.G., Fotiadis, D.I., Naka, K.K., Michalis, L.K.: Automated Diagnosis of Coronary Artery Disease Based on Data Mining and Fuzzy Modeling. IEEE Trans. Information Technology in Biomedicine 12(4), 447–458 (2008)
16. Cios, K.J., Mamitsuka, H., Nagashima, T., Tadeusiewicz, R.: Computational intelligence in solving bioinformatics problems. Artificial Intelligence in Medicine 35, 1–8 (2005)
17. Kluska, J.: Analytical Methods in Fuzzy Modeling and Control. Springer, Berlin (2009)
18. Leeners, B., Rath, W., Kuse, S., Irawan, C., Imthurn, B., Neumaier-Wagner, P.: BMI: new aspects of a classical risk factor for hypertensive disorders in pregnancy. Clinical Science 111, 81–86 (2006)
19. Randall, M.E., Michael, H., Ver Morken, J., Stehman, F.: Uterine cervix. In: Hoskins, W.J., Perez, C.A., Young, R.C., et al. (eds.) Principles and Practice of Gynecologic Oncology, pp. 743–822. Lippicott Williams & Wilkins, Philadelphia (2005)
20. Ferreira, C.: Gene Expression Programming: A New Adaptive Algorithm for Solving Problems. Complex Systems 13(2), 87–129 (2001)
21. Sherrod, P.H.: DTREG predictive modeling software (2011), http://www.dtreg.com
22. IBM SPSS Modeler 14.2 Algorithms Guide. IBM Corporation (2011)
23. Arlot, S.: A survey of cross-validation procedures for model selection. Statistics Surveys 4, 40–79 (2010)
24. Kluska, J., Kusy, M., Obrzut, B.: Prediction of Radical Hysterectomy Complications for Cervical Cancer Using Computational Intelligence Methods. In: Rutkowski, L., Korytkowski, M., Scherer, R., Tadeusiewicz, R., Zadeh, L.A., Zurada, J.M. (eds.) ICAISC 2012, Part II. LNCS, vol. 7268, pp. 259–267. Springer, Heidelberg (2012)

Face Classification Based on Linguistic Description of Facial Features

Damian Kurach[1], Danuta Rutkowska[2,3], and Elisabeth Rakus-Andersson[4]

[1] Institute of Computational Intelligence, Czestochowa University of Technology,
42-201 Czestochowa, Poland
damian.kurach@iisi.pcz.pl
[2] Institute of Computer and Information Sciences,
Czestochowa University of Technology, 42-201 Czestochowa, Poland
[3] Information Technology Institute, University of Social Sciences,
90-113 Lodz, Poland
drutko@kik.pcz.pl
[4] Department of Mathematics and Natural Sciences,
Blekinge Institute of Technology, S-37179 Karlskrona, Sweden
elisabeth.andersson@bth.se

Abstract. This paper presents an artificial intelligence approach towards classification of persons based on verbal descriptions of their facial features. Frame knowledge representation, fuzzy sets, fuzzy IF-THEN rules, and fuzzy granulation are employed. Features of face elements (nose, eyes, etc.) are extracted by use of existing detection techniques, such as measurements of horizontal and vertical sizes. Linguistic variables that correspond to fuzzy sets, representing selected facial features, are applied in the frames and fuzzy rules. Linguistic values defined by the fuzzy sets conform the terminology applied by law enforcement to create an eyewitness verbal description. Classification results are illustrated in three cases of the system's input: facial composites (sketches) created by an artist, images (digital pictures) from a face database, and verbal descriptions.

1 Introduction

Visual representations of a suspect's appearance, based on eyewitness memory and verbal description, still play an important role in crime investigation to help law enforcement to find suspects. Even it is proved that eyewitness testimony is unreliable and may lead to a mistaken identity, the face sketch recognition is still used in a crime if there is no photographic evidence.

The modern sketch originates from the 'portrait parle' [1] – 'spoken portrait' that is a technique invented by Bertillon in 19th century, and based on the anthropometric measurement system and individual card description.

A graphical representation of an eyewitness's memory of a face is called a facial composite [3]. The basic method of creating a facial composite is to produce a sketch by an artist [4], who helps eyewitnesses to recall details about a suspect's appearance. The ability to express verbal description of personal appearance is known as face recall [21]. This process is complex because the verbal

L. Rutkowski et al. (Eds.): ICAISC 2014, Part II, LNAI 8468, pp. 155–166, 2014.

description of each feature requires recalling the suspect's appearance from the witness's memory. Even due, a detailed verbal description does not guarantee that the authors of the portrait will be able to build a correct visual representation of the suspect. The artist must properly decode all information given by the witness. Therefore, a standardized terminology was introduced to combine the features characteristics with their description.

Contrary to expectation, the most accurate and detailed verbal description of the appearance is not as convincing as a picture and even then the facial composites are prone to error. The reason for this is a small number of memorized details of the appearance and the lack of precision in the description.

In this study, we use the verbal description terminology concerning human faces, and employ the theory of fuzzy sets and fuzzy logic [22] in order to classify persons, based on selected facial features. Thus, linguistic variables are associated with the facial features, and fuzzy IF–THEN rules can be formulated for classification [10], [11]. Linguistic values of the linguistic variables are represented by membership functions of the fuzzy sets. In this way, we are able to compensate uncertainty both for eyewitness testimony and inaccuracy of automatic feature extraction.

Hence, we propose an intelligent system that may be used for searching, classifying and grouping faces, based on their linguistic description, not only digital images. The paper is organized as follows. In Section 2, we present facial features and their verbal description. Section 3 concerns the linguistic variables and corresponding fuzzy sets. Section 4 describes the fuzzy granulation concept. In Section 5, fuzzy IF-THEN rules are formulated. In Section 6, a fuzzy classifier is outlined. Section 6 illustrates classification results. Finally, in Section 7, conclusions and final remarks are presented.

2   Facial Features and Their Verbal Description

Facial feature selection and description are crucial parts because of two factors: feature availability/reliability and witness perception lack of accuracy. It may occur that e.g. suspect's ears, covered by hair, cannot be visible or an eyewitness cannot be sure what is a color of his eyes (gray or dark blue).

Individual body parts can take different shapes, sizes and colors. For example:

- face shape can be elliptical, circular, oval, rectangular, triangular etc.,
- nose size can be small, medium, large,
- eye color can be amber, blue, brown, gray, green, hazel.

In order to create an appropriate and relevant composite, mentioned in Section 1, proper communication between the artist and eyewitness is needed. This is done by use of the standardized terminology. The lexicon of words to express how each face element looks like is provided to create a verbal composite description. Table 1 shows some of those verbal terms according to the selected features.

Crucial face components are eyes, nose, mouth, their structure, distance between them or relative position.

Table 1. The selected facial features and corresponding verbal terminology

Element	Feature	Values
Forehead	Height	low, medium high, high
	Width	narrow, medium wide, wide
Eyebrows	Length	short, medium long, long
	Setting	horizontally, upwards, downwards
	Spacing	fused, narrow, medium wide, wide
	Location	low, medium high, high
Eyes	Color	dark pigment (brown), light pigment (blue), mixed (green, gray)
	Openness	narrow, medium wide, wide
	Length	short, medium long, long
	Distance	narrow, medium wide, wide
Nose	Length	short, medium long, long
	Width	narrow, medium wide, wide
Ear	Size	small, medium large, large
Mouth	Height	low, medium high, high
	Width	narrow, medium wide, wide
Chin	Shape	spherical, oval, square, triangular
	Size	small, medium large, large

Every human face may be divided into three parts (see Fig. 1):
- part of the forehead – including the forehead and eyes,
- part of the nose – including the nose, cheeks, and ears,
- part of the lip-chin – including the mouth, and chin.

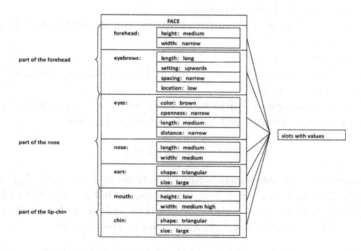

Fig. 1. Frame knowledge representation

These three parts, and particular face elements, are depicted in Fig. 1 which presents the artificial intelligence data structure called 'frame', introduced by Minsky [7], in application to the concept of face granulation considered in this paper (Section 4).

Frames are structures of knowledge representation where information about an object is included in slots. Each slot can contain data values, procedures or even other frames and subframes. The structure of the frame is intuitive, and has some analogy to the Bertillon's card. The slots are associated with object's attributes, and facets correspond to the values.

As a matter of fact, we use the concept of a fuzzy frame as knowledge representation, with linguistic values defined by fuzzy membership functions described in Section 3. Let us notice that borders between the forehead, nose, and lip-chin parts are rather fuzzy, not crisp. Thus, these parts of the face can be viewed as fuzzy granules (see Section 4), similarly to the particular face elements like eyes, nose, etc. Hence, the face granulation can be considered as hierarchical.

3   Linguistic Variables and Fuzzy Sets

Verbal composite descriptions consist of words which can be directly transformed into values of linguistic variables and applied to create fuzzy sets [13]. Each of the face/head feature represented by a fuzzy set might be useful to create a fuzzy system for face classification and sketch recognition. Generally, fuzzy sets and corresponding membership functions can be obtained from a learning process or delivered by an expert/experts [13], [15], [16]. In the case of face linguistic description, we create membership functions of the fuzzy sets, based on images from a database, by means of the following, *SimplyFS*, procedure:

1. For each face in the database,
   (a) Extract selected face elements
   (b) For each element, measure its features, e.g. element's size (in the iris diameter unit [IU])
2. For each selected feature,
   (a) Calculate minimum m_1, mean m_2 and maximum m_3 values of the features' measurements
   (b) Create membership functions of fuzzy sets corresponding to linguistic values of the features (attributes), in such a way that:

$$\mu_{A_{i,j}}(m_j) = 1 \tag{1}$$

   where $\mu_{A_{i,j}}$ denotes membership functions of fuzzy sets $A_{i,j}$, for $i = 1, 2, ..., n$, and and $j = 1, 2, ..., m$; assuming that n - number of features (attributes) and m - number of linguistic values of the attributes, e.g. $m = 3$ for "short", "medium long", "long" (see Fig. 2).

For each selected feature of faces in the database, using the *SimplyFS* algorithm, we create the fuzzy sets based on the measured values of the attributes. With regard to the size of a face element, the length or width are expressed in the normalized unit [IU] – size of the iris diameter. The process of normalization is described in [5]. Shape or an angle of facial elements is obtained based on geometrical relation to the facial vertical axis [14]. The feature like color is determined based on information concerning the mean color value in the HSV color model representation (see e.g. [20]) which is converted to the linguistic description.

Figure 2 illustrates fuzzy sets representing the feature 'nose length', obtained as a result of the *SimplyFS* procedure, assuming that triangular shape of the membership functions have been applied.

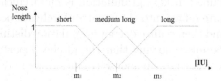

Fig. 2. An example of fuzzy sets (membership functions) for features/variables 'nose length', created by the *SimplyFS* procedure

With regard to Table 1 and the frame presented in Fig.1, we can create a fuzzy frame, with slots containing fuzzy attributes, with values defined by fuzzy sets represented by membership functions determined according to the *SimplyFS* algorithm.

4   Fuzzy Granulation

The *Frame:Face*, presented in Fig. 1, corresponds to Fig. 3 where we consider shapes and sizes of various parts of a face. In this case, linguistic values defined by membership functions in the two-dimensional space of the face describe particular face elements, like nose, eyes, etc..

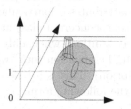

Fig. 3. Illustration of a fuzzy set representing an eye element of a face in 2D space [12]

It is worth mentioning that the knowledge concerning human faces ought to be gathered using the fuzzy description. According to Zadeh - who is known as the "father" of fuzzy sets [22] and fuzzy logic [23] - it is not possible to determine precise borders between particular parts of a human face, such as the nose, cheek, etc. Thus, the fuzzy borders must be considered. In [24], we find the following explanation: "Granulation of an object leads to a collection of granules of the object, with a granule being a clump of points (objects) drawn together by indistinguishability, similarity, proximity or functionality. For example, the granules of a human head are the forehead, nose, ears, eyes, etc..

The theory of fuzzy information granulation was proposed and developed by Zadeh [24]. It is inspired by the way in which humans granulate information and reason with it. However, the foundations of this theory and its methodology, as Zadeh explains, are mathematical in nature. In the theory of fuzzy information granulation, linguistic variables, fuzzy IF-THEN rules, and fuzzy logic play an important role.

In general, as explained in [24], granulation is hierarchical in nature. Hence, at first we can granulate a face into three parts (forehead, nose, and lip-chin) as illustrated in Fig. 1, and then realize deeper granulation distinguishing particular face elements. For example, knowing that the forehead part (with eyes) carries most information with regard to a person recognition, we may focus our attention to this granule.

Some ideas concerning fuzzy granulation have been developed by Pedrycz, especially with regard to neural networks (see e.g. [8]), and also in application to pattern recognition [9].

5   Fuzzy IF-THEN Rules

The fuzzy sets (membership functions), considered in Section 3 to represent linguistic description of facial feature elements, may be applied in fuzzy rules that allow to classify faces. Thus, in this section, we focus our attention on fuzzy IF-THEN, usually employed in fuzzy systems, see e.g. [13].

According to [24], the concept of fuzzy rules is adequate in situations when considered dependencies are imprecise or high precision is not required. With regard to the face description, both eyewitness' testimony and automatic feature extraction from an image are subject to errors. Hence, we use the fuzzy IF-THEN rules that contain, in their antecedent parts, linguistic variables and fuzzy sets that correspond to attributes of particular elements of a human face. The consequent parts of the rules concern a class in a classification task.

In the case of a suspect recognition, when only one suspect is considered, we have a problem of person classification into two classes (matching or not matching to their face description). This is a case of binary classification, and we can apply simple rules of the following form:

rule 1: IF ear IS big AND forehead IS high AND . . . eye color IS blue
           THEN person IS suspect
rule 2: IF ear IS small AND forehead IS short AND . . . eye color brown
           THEN person IS no suspect

The above example illustrates two rules with antecedents corresponding to linguistic descriptions of a suspect and a person that is not the suspect, respectively. The selected face elements (ear, forehead, eye, among others) are described by use of linguistic variables. The linguistic values (big, high, etc.) in these rules are defined by fuzzy sets obtained according to the *SimplyFS* algorithm presented in Section 3. Let us notice that the antecedent parts of the rules may refer to appropriate fuzzy frames, similar to that presented in Fig. 1.

Of course, the number of the rules may be greater than two, especially in the case of more than one suspect. For N suspects, a generalized form of the rules can be expressed as follows:

rule k: IF ... THEN class k (suspect k);   for $k = 1, 2, \ldots, N$

Both types of the above rules are special cases of the following, typical fuzzy rule base for classification:

$$R^{(k)} : \text{IF } x_1 \text{ is } A_{1,1}^k \text{ AND } x_2 \text{ is } A_{2,1}^k \text{ AND } \ldots \text{ AND } x_n \text{ is } A_{n,m}^k \qquad (2)$$
$$\text{THEN class } k$$

where N denotes the number of fuzzy rules, $x_1, \ldots, x_n$ are linguistic variables corresponding to attributes of face elements, $A_{i,j}^k$, for $i = 1, 2, \ldots, n$, and $j = 1, 2, \ldots, m$, are fuzzy sets, in this paper determined by use of the *SimplyFS* algorithm. Let us notice that for a given attribute, indicated by i, the same fuzzy set, $A_{i,j}^k$, may be included in more than one rule $R^{(k)}$, for $k = 1, 2, \ldots, N$.

It is worth emphasizing that, as a matter of fact, the example of the rule base, presented in this section, with the linguistic description in the antecedents of the rules, i.e. "ear IS big AND forehead IS high" and so on, suits better to the case presented in Fig.3. This means that the fuzzy sets representing the linguistic values are defined in the two-dimensional face space.

6   Fuzzy Classifier

As mentioned in Section 5, the fuzzy IF-THEN rules may be applied in the problem of face classification based on the linguistic description. The fuzzy classification system, proposed in this paper, is presented in Fig. 4.

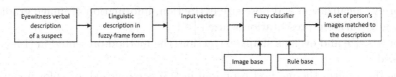

Fig. 4. Fuzzy face classification system

The first block may be used at first stage when verbal description of a suspect's face is delivered by an eyewitness (or witnesses). In such a case, this description may differ from the form of the fuzzy frame. If not, we can start from the second block, otherwise a transformation from the source description to the frame-form is needed. The frame-form description includes values of fuzzy linguistic variables and can easily be transformed to the input vector of the fuzzy classifier.

The fuzzy classifier, in the system portrayed in Fig. 4, realizes the classification based on the collection of face images (image base) and the fuzzy IF-THEN rules (rule base). For the input vector, the fuzzy classifier produces a set of person's images matched to the linguistic description. As a matter of fact, the inference procedure performed by the classifier checks how much the input values (such as the distance between eyes, the nose length etc.) match to corresponding fuzzy sets in the antecedents of the rules in the rule base. This means that every rule is activated by the input vector, and the degree of the rule activation, τ_k, is determined according to the following formula:

$$\tau_k = \prod_{i=1}^{n} \mu_{A_{i,j}^k}(\overline{x}_i) \tag{3}$$

for $k = 1, \ldots, N$, where $\mu_{A_{i,j}^k}$ are membership functions of fuzzy sets $A_{i,j}^k$ in the antecedent parts of the rules, and $\overline{x}_i$ denotes crisp input values (face values).

As a result of the classification process, based on the rule activation expressed by Equation (3), we expect to obtain a set of face images belonging to a specific class (matched to the linguistic description).

7   Experiments and Results

In our experiments, presented in this paper, the *AR Face Database* is applied [6], and selected facial elements are used, extracted automatically, listed as follows with their attributes: Eyes={*distance between eyes, eye width, degree of eye openness*}, Nose={*length, width*}, Mouth={*width, height*}.

This particular database has been employed in the experiments because in the process of creation the *AR Face Database*, each person's image was taken in two, separated by two weeks time, sessions. It allows to create the system based on images from the first session and test our approach on data delivered by the second session.

The list of detection/extraction methods and obtained result, see Fig. 5:

- for eye localization and nose size extraction, information of image gradients in gray image representation is used [18]
- for iris size and eyelid's shape extraction, the method presented in [14] is applied
- for the mouth, the method proposed in [17] is employed for color images

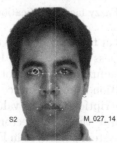

Fig. 5. Results of feature extraction and measurements

Figure 5 shows an example of automatic feature extraction and corresponding measure values. As preparations before the experiments, membership functions of the fuzzy sets are created, based on real values obtained from feature measurements, by use of the *SimplyFS* procedure for images from the first session–*S*1 of the *AR Face Database*; see Fig. 8.

Experiment 1

In the first experiment, the image of the person (from second session–*S*2, stored as *M_027_14*), was presented at the system input. As a result, we get the feature linguistic description of the person's face from input image and a set of images representing persons matching to the received description.

For the person in Fig. 5, the linguistic description is as follows:

> *eye openness* IS *medium wide* AND *eye length* IS *medium long* AND *eyes distance* IS *medium wide* AND *nose length* IS *short* AND *nose width* IS *medium wide* AND *mouth height* IS *medium high* AND *mouth width* IS *medium wide*

Figure 6 presents images of the classified faces that match to this description (rule antecedent).

Fig. 6. Result of system classification – 3 of 8 persons matching to the feature description of the input image

Experiment 2

The second experiment concerns the case of the classifier working with a sketch provided at the input. The sketch comes from the *CUHK Face Sketch Database (CUFS)* [19], where for each face of the *AR Face Database* [6], there is a corresponding sketch drawn by an artist.

According to the input values, the feature linguistic description for the provided sketch is identical as the description obtained in the first experiment. This means that it is consistent with the rule activated by the image portrayed in Fig. 5, and leads to the same results of classification, see Fig. 6 and Fig. 7.

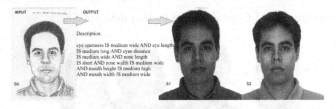

Fig. 7. Result of system classification based on sketch input

The membership functions of the proposed system, delivered by the *SimplyFS* procedure, are illustrated in Fig. 8. In addition, comparison of degrees of membership representing the input features for the same person (image stored as M_027_1 [6] from first session–$S1$, image M_027_14 [6] from second session–$S2$ and corresponding sketch (SK) [18]) is presented in Fig. 8.

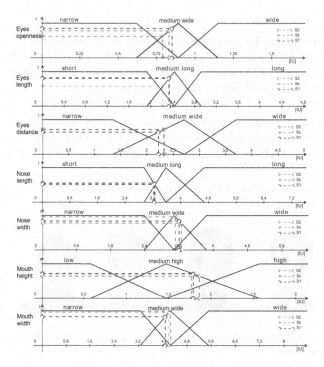

Fig. 8. Fuzzy sets created by *SimpleFS* procedure and degrees of membership for features of the same person (M_027) in case of different input images ($S1$, $S2$, Sk)

Experiment 3

The last experiment was performed to present how the system operates with features' verbal description delivered to the input e.g. by a witness. The simulated description could be like the following:

> The suspect *eye's openness* was *narrow* and *length – medium long*. The *distance* between eyes was *medium wide*. The *nose* was *medium long* and *medium wide*. The size of mouth was *medium high* and *medium wide*.

Figure 9 shows images of faces matched to this description.

Fig. 9. Images matched to provided above description

8   Conclusions and Final Remarks

In this paper, we show that the verbal description of facial features can be successfully applied for face classification, regardless consideration of image, sketch or only the description.

The results obtained during the experiments indicate that even the initial fuzzy classifier can give a powerful solution. Mistakes and errors at the stage of the sketch creation will significantly influence the result of classification but fuzzy feature description decreases this effect.

It should be noticed that sometimes an eyewitness' description is the only knowledge we got. If the eyewitnesses did not see every detail of a face, they at least can describe the parts they did see. Taking into account the partial description delivered by eyewitnesses, and using fuzzy rules, we still are able to find a potential suspect from composite sketches or police photos.

The future work will continue and focus on

- classification or grouping people/objects with some similarities in appearance thereby eliminating data in huge databases
- searching for potential criminals through the eyewitness verbal description and sketch analyzing
- generating (by combining with genetic algorithm) initial sketch examples based on the eyewitness testimony

A challenge for future work is to examine fuzzy sets creation and the knowledge representation. As a base for membership function values, the ideal proportion of the facial parts and face elements can be assumed. It is also worth considering the mean face, from entire database, used for the same purpose. This may increase flexibility of the system for the input images outside of the database.

Finally, fuzzy granulation is considered, as introduced in Section 4, to describe a face as a composition of fuzzy granules that represent particular face elements. The fuzzy granules may carry information delivered by the verbal description. The hierarchical granulation can be employed, as mentioned with regard to the face frame portrayed in Fig. 1. The frame slots may include the information granules, and classification of frames can be performed by frame matching inference, according to fuzzy IF-THEN rules.

This article presents an initial part of study on usage linguistic description for face recognition. However, some promising results have been obtained. We expect to continue this research and apply to larger databases.

Apart from the suspect recognition, other applications of this approach can be realized, e.g. gender classification by use of face image databases [2].

References

1. Bertillon, A.: Identification Anthropométrique: Instructions Signalétiques, Imprimerie Administrative. Melun (1893) (in French)
2. Chang, Y., Wang, Y., Chen, C., Ricanek, K.: Improved image-based automatic gender classification by feature selection. Journal of Artificial Intelligence and Sot Computing Research 1(3), 241–253 (2011)

3. Czerw, S.: Human Identification Based on Characteristics of Appearance. Forensic Techniques. (2). Szczytno, 139–171 (1995) (in Polish)
4. Gibson, L.: Forensic Art Essentials: a Manual for Law Enforcement Artists. Elsevier, Amsterdam (2008)
5. Kompanets, L., Kurach, D.: On facial frontal vertical axes projections and area asymmetry measure. Int. J. Computing, Multimedia and Intelligent Techniques 1(3), 61–88 (2007)
6. Martinez, A.M., Benavente, R.: The AR Face Database. CVC Technical Report#24 (1998)
7. Minsky, M.: A Framework for Representing Knowledge. In: Winston, P. (ed.) The Psychology of Computer Vision, pp. 211–277. McGraw-Hill, New York (1975)
8. Pedrycz, W.: Neural networks in the framework of granular computing. Int. J. Applied Mathematics and Computer Science. 10(4), 723–745 (2000)
9. Pedrycz, W., Vukovich, G.: Granular computing in pattern recognition. In: Bunke, H., Kandel, A. (eds.) Neuro-Fuzzy Pattern Recognition, pp. 125–143. World Scientific (2000)
10. Rakus-Andersson, E.: Fuzzy and Rough Techniques in Medical Diagnosis and Medication. Springer (2007)
11. Rakus-Andersson, E.: Approximation and rough classification of letter-Like polygon shapes. In: Skowron, A., Suraj, Z. (eds.) Rough Sets and Intelligent Systems. ISRL, vol. 43, pp. 455–474. Springer, Heidelberg (2013)
12. Rutkowska, D.: An expert system for human personality characteristics recognition. In: Rutkowski, L., Scherer, R., Tadeusiewicz, R., Zadeh, L.A., Zurada, J.M. (eds.) ICAISC 2010, Part I. LNCS, vol. 6113, pp. 665–672. Springer, Heidelberg (2010)
13. Rutkowska, D.: Neuro-Fuzzy Architectures and Hybrid Learning. Springer (2002)
14. Rutkowska, D., Kurach, D.: A genetic algorithm for a facial vertical axis determination. In: Selected Topics in Computer Science Applications, pp. 164–175. Academic Publishing House EXIT, Warsaw (2011)
15. Rutkowski, L.: Computational Intelligence. Methods and Techniques. Springer (2008)
16. Rutkowski, L.: New Soft Computing Techniques for System Modelling. Pattern Classification and Image Processing. STUDFUZZ, vol. 143. Springer, Heidelberg (2004)
17. Saeed, U., Dugelay, J.-L.: Temporal synchronization and normalization of speech videos for face recognition. In: Yang, J. (ed.) State of the art in Biometrics, pp. 143–160. InTech (2011)
18. Timm, F., Barth, E.: Accurate eye centre localisation by mans of gradients. In: Proc. Int. Conference on Computer Theory and Applications, Algarve Portugal, pp. 125–130 (2011)
19. Wang, X., Tang, X.: Face photo-sketch synthesis and recognition. IEEE Transactions on Pattern Analysis and Machine Intelligence (PAMI) (31) (2009)
20. Wiaderek, K., Rutkowska, D.: Fuzzy granulation approach to color digital picture recognition. In: Rutkowski, L., Korytkowski, M., Scherer, R., Tadeusiewicz, R., Zadeh, L.A., Zurada, J.M. (eds.) ICAISC 2013, Part I. LNCS, vol. 7894, pp. 412–425. Springer, Heidelberg (2013)
21. Wilcock, R., Bull, R., Milne, R.: Witness Identification in Criminal Cases: Psychology and Practice. Oxford University Press (2008)
22. Zadeh, L.A.: Fuzzy Sets. Information and Control (8) 338–353 (1965)
23. Zadeh, L.A.: The Role of Fuzzy Logic in the Management of Uncertainty in Expert Systems. Fuzzy Sets and Systems (11), 199–227 (1983)
24. Zadeh, L.A.: Toward a Theory of Fuzzy Information Granulation and its Centrality in Human Reasoning and Fuzzy Logic. Fuzzy Sets and Systems (90), 111–127 (1997)

Impact of Bayesian Network Model Structure on the Accuracy of Medical Diagnostic Systems

Agnieszka Oniśko[1,2] and Marek J. Druzdzel[1,3]

[1] Faculty of Computer Science, Białystok University of Technology,
Białystok, Poland
a.onisko@pb.edu.pl
[2] Magee-Womens Hospital, University of Pittsburgh Medical Center,
Pittsburgh, PA 15213, USA
[3] Decision Systems Laboratory, School of Information Sciences and Intelligent
Systems Programs, University of Pittsburgh, USA
marek@sis.pitt.edu

Abstract. While Bayesian network models may contain a handful of numerical parameters that are important for their quality, several empirical studies have confirmed that overall precision of their probabilities is not crucial. In this paper, we study the impact of the structure of a Bayesian network on the precision of medical diagnostic systems. We show that also the structure is not that important – diagnostic accuracy of several medical diagnostic models changes minimally when we subject their structures to such transformations as arc removal and arc reversal.

Keywords: Bayesian network structure, medical diagnostic models, sensitivity.

1 Introduction

Decision-theoretic approaches offer a coherent framework for dealing with problems involving uncertainty [1]. The most popular modeling tool for complex systems involving uncertainty, such as those encountered in medicine, is a Bayesian network [2], an acyclic directed graph modeling the joint probability distribution over a set of variables. The popularity of Bayesian networks rests on their ability to model complex domains and to provide a sound basis for model-based inference. There exist algorithms for reasoning in Bayesian networks that compute the posterior probability distribution over variables of interest given a set of observations. This allows, for example, to calculate the probabilities of various disorders given a set of symptoms and test results and, hence, to support medical diagnosis. As Bayesian network algorithms are mathematically correct, the ultimate quality of their results depends directly on the quality of the underlying models. These models are rarely precise, as they are often based on judgments of independence underlying their structure and rough subjective probability estimates. Even when models are learned entirely from data, these data may not reflect precisely the target population. The question whether the quality of models matters has, thus, important practical implications on knowledge engineering for Bayesian networks.

L. Rutkowski et al. (Eds.): ICAISC 2014, Part II, LNAI 8468, pp. 167–178, 2014.

There are two mechanisms by which a Bayesian network represents a joint probability distribution: (1) independencies among the domain variables, modeled by the structure of the directed graph, and (2) numerical probability distributions of individual variables conditional on their direct ancestors in the graph. There is a popular belief that it is the structure of Bayesian networks that is important and that they are insensitive to the overall noise and precision of their numerical probabilities. There is a body of empirical work showing that indeed the precision of numerical parameters is not important to the quality of results (e.g., [3, 4, 5, 6]). To our knowledge, there has been no parallel work testing the importance of graphical structure of Bayesian networks.

This paper probes the question whether the structure of Bayesian networks is important for the quality of their reasoning. We start from realistic gold standard medical diagnostic models learned from real data sets originating from the Irvine Machine Learning Repository [7]. We subject these models to systematic structure distortions and test the impact of these distortions on the accuracy of the models. Our results suggest that also the precise structure of Bayesian networks is not crucial. Structure transformations, such as arc removal and arc reversal, turn out to have only moderate impact of the diagnostic quality of the models.

2   Bayesian Networks

Bayesian networks [2] are acyclic directed graphs modeling probabilistic dependencies and independencies among variables. The graphical part of a Bayesian network reflects the structure of a problem, while local interactions among neighboring variables are quantified by conditional probability distributions. Bayesian networks have proven to be powerful tools for modeling complex problems involving uncertain knowledge.

Mathematically, a Bayesian network is an acyclic directed graph that consists of a qualitative part, encoding existence of probabilistic influences among domain's variables in a directed graph, and a quantitative part, encoding the joint probability distribution over these variables. Each node in the graph represents a random variable. Each arc represents a direct dependence between two variables. Formally, the structure of the directed graph is a representation of a factorization of the joint probability distribution. In case of a Bayesian network that consists of n variables: $X_1, X_2, ..., X_n$, this factorization is represented as follows:

$$\Pr(X_1, X_2, .., X_n) = \prod_i \Pr(X_i | \mathrm{Pa}(X_i)) , \qquad (1)$$

where $\mathrm{Pa}(X_i)$ represents parent variables of X_i. As many factorizations are possible, there are many graphs that are capable of encoding the same joint probability distribution. Of these, those that minimize the number of arcs are preferred. From the point of view of knowledge engineering, graphs that reflect the causal structure of the domain are especially convenient – they normally reflect expert's understanding of the domain, enhance interaction with a human expert at the model building stage, and are readily extendible with new information.

Figure 1 presents an example Bayesian network modeling three liver disorders along with their risk factors and symptoms. It is a fragment of the HEPAR II network described in detail in [8]. The example captures also a prior probability distribution for the node *Obesity* and a conditional probability distribution for the node *Chronic hepatitis* given the node *History of viral hepatitis*.

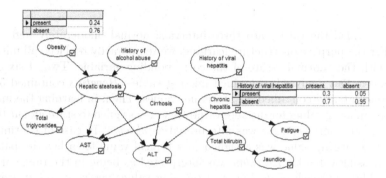

Fig. 1. Example of a Bayesian network model

Given observations of some of the variables (evidence nodes), Bayesian network models allow for calculating posterior probability distributions over the remaining nodes. In case of a diagnostic network, the output of a model can be viewed as an assignment of posterior probabilities to various disorders.

3   Models Studied and Model Quality Criterion

In our earlier study, focusing on the impact of precision of numerical parameters on the quality of Bayesian network results [5], we selected six medical data sets from the Irvine Machine Learning Repository: Acute inflammation [9], SPECT Heart, Cardiotocography, Hepatitis, Lymphography [10], and Primary Tumor [10]. We used the following two selection criteria: (1) the data set had to have at least one disorder variable and (2) it should not contain too many missing values and too many continuous variables. The latter selection criterion prevented possible confounding effect of dealing with missing data and with discretization. We have decided to use the same data sets in the current study. Table 1 lists the basic properties of the selected data sets.

Our next step was creating gold standard medical diagnostic models from the selected data sets. To that effect, we applied a basic Bayesian search-based learning algorithm [11]. Because the algorithm accepts only discrete data, prior to learning we discretized all continuous variables. We used expert-based discretization, relying on domain-specific thresholds (e.g., in case of total bilirubin

Table 1. Medical data used in our experiments (mv stands for missing values)

data set	#instances	#variables	variable types	#classes	mv
Acute Inflammation	120	8	categorical, integer	4	no
SPECT Heart	267	23	categorical	2	no
Cardiotocography	2,126	22	categorical, real	3	no
Hepatitis	155	20	categorical, real	2	yes
Lymphography	148	19	categorical, integer	4	no
Primary Tumor	339	18	categorical, integer	20	yes

test, we divided the range into three intervals: normal, moderately high, and high). For the purpose of structure learning, we temporarily replaced all missing values with the "normal" state of the corresponding variable. Two of six data sets that we had analyzed, contained missing values: *Hepatitis* contained 5.4% and *Primary tumor* contained 3.7% missing values. Then, in learning the model structure, missing values for discrete variables were assigned to state *absent* (e.g., a missing value for *Anorexia* was interpreted as *absent*). In case of continuous variables, a missing value was assigned to a typical value for a healthy patient (e.g., a missing value for *Bilirubin* was interpreted as being in the range of 0–1 *mg/dl*). This approach of dealing with missing values, as we demonstrated in our earlier work [12], leads typically to highest accuracy of medical diagnostic systems. Table 2 lists the basic properties of the Bayesian network models that resulted from this procedure.

Table 2. Bayesian network models used in our experiments (#nodes: number of nodes; μ #states: average number of states per node; μ in-degree: average number of parents per node; #arcs: number of arcs; #params: number of numerical parameters)

model	#nodes	μ #states	μ in-degree	#arcs	#params
ACUTE INFLAMMATION	8	2.13	1.88	15	97
SPECT HEART	23	2.00	2.26	52	290
CARDIOTOCOGRAPHY	22	2.91	2.86	63	13,347
HEPATITIS	20	2.50	1.90	38	465
LYMPHOGRAPHY	19	3.00	1.21	23	300
PRIMARY TUMOR	18	3.17	1.83	33	877

We assumed that the models obtained this way were perfect in the sense of having the right structure and containing parameters as precise as the data would allow.

A critical element of our experiments is comparison of accuracy of models. We define diagnostic accuracy as the percentage of correct diagnoses on real patient cases. This is a simplification, as one might want to know the models' sensitivity and specificity for each of the disorders or even study the models' ability to detect a disorder in terms of their ROC (Receiver Operating Characteristic) curves or AUC (Area Under the ROC Curve) measure. We have decided against this because the ROC curves express models' ability to detect single disorders. So do sensitivity and specificity. We focused instead on a simple measure of the percentage of correct diagnoses. Furthermore, because Bayesian network models operate only on probabilities, we used probability as the decision criterion: the diagnosis that is most likely given patient data is the diagnosis that the model puts forward.

Because virtually each of the original data sets was rather small, we always applied the method of "leave-one-out" [13] to test models' performance. It involves n-fold learning from $n - 1$ records out of the n records available and subsequently testing it on the remaining nth record.

4   Measures of Bayesian Network Arc Strength

Our experimental manipulation of Bayesian network structure involves arc removal and arc reversal. Because we will want to perform these operations in a strictly specified order, e.g., from the weakest to the strongest arcs, we first need to introduce measures of arc strength.

The concept of an arc strength in BNs was first defined by Boerlage [14], who introduced the concept of link strength for binary nodes and defined it as the maximum influence that a parent node can have on the child node. Nicholson and Jitnah [15] and later Ebert-Uphoff [16, 17] used mutual information as the basis of the measure of link strength. Lacave [18] proposed a measure of link strength for the purpose of explanation in decision support systems based on Bayesian networks. Koiter [19] reviews a number of measures of arc strength from the perspective of model visualization. He also proposes a measure of arc strength based on the differences between the posterior marginal probability of the child node, as the parent node changes. He proposed to calculate these differences using standard measures of distance between probability distributions, i.e., Euclidean distance, Hellinger distance, J-divergence, and CDF difference. While Euclidean distance focuses on the absolute differences between probabilities, Hellinger distance [20], is sensitive to relative differences. For example, the distance between 0.1 and 0.11 is the same as the difference between 0.70 and 0.80 in Euclidean distance, but is much larger in Hellinger distance.

Because Koiter's measure seems most practical, while being well grounded in theory and has been used in practical applications in the past, in our experiments, we use Koiter's measures.

For each arc of the gold standard Bayesian network models described in Section 3 and summarized in Table 2, we calculated its strength. While calculating this strength, we have applied two measures of distance: (1) the Euclidean distance and (2) the Hellinger distance. Figure 2 presents histograms of arc strengths based on Euclidean distance for each of the studied models. While there are several values of arc strength that are more likely than others, their probability distributions are generally spread over the entire range of $0 - 1$.

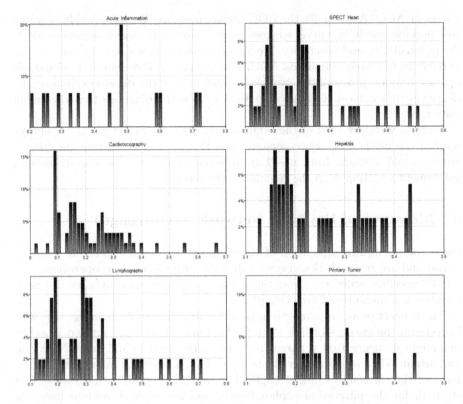

Fig. 2. Histograms for arc strength of the Bayesian network models (clock-wise: ACUTE INFLAMMATION, SPECT HEART, CARDIOTOGRAPHY, HEPATITIS, LYMPHOGRAPHY, and PRIMARY TUMOR). The Euclidean distance was applied.

5   Experimental Results

We conducted two experiments to investigate the impact of departures from the ideal structure of a Bayesian network on its accuracy. There are two straight-forward ways of distorting the structure of a Bayesian network: (1) removing its arcs, and (2) reversing them. Please note that adding additional arcs would not have much impact on the accuracy of Bayesian network models, as additional dependencies introduced by such arcs will be compensated in the learning process by parameters that capture independence numerically.

5.1   Experiment 1: Arc Removal

Our first experiment involved a gradual removal of arcs in our gold standard Bayesian network models listed in Table 2. We have tested the accuracy of the original models, then removed 10%, 20%, 30%, ..., 90%, and 100% of their arcs, re-learned their numerical parameters from the Irvine Machine Learning

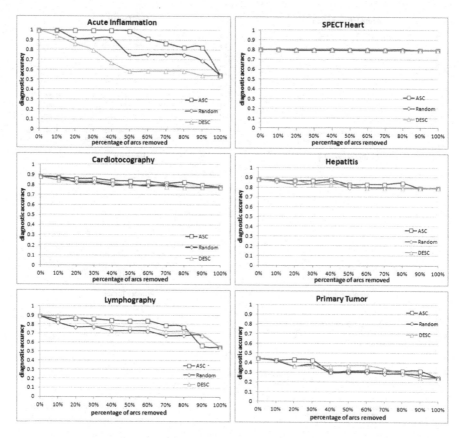

Fig. 3. The diagnostic accuracy of the six models (clock-wise: ACUTE INFLAMMATION, SPECT HEART, CARDIOTOGRAPHY, HEPATITIS, LYMPHOGRAPHY, and PRIMARY TUMOR) as a function of the percentage of arcs removed. Arcs ordered according to the Euclidean distance.

Repository data sets by means of the EM algorithm, and re-tested the resulting distorted models at each step. The first model in this sequence (0% arcs removed) was the original, gold standard model and the last model (100% arcs removed) was a model including all original variables but no arcs, i.e., it assumed that all model variables are independent of each other.

In the experiment, we followed three different orders of arc removal: (a) ascending order of arc strengths (i.e., from the weakest to the strongest arc), (b) descending order of arc strengths (i.e., from the strongest to the weakest arc), and (c) random order.

Figures 3 and 4 show the results of our experiment for each of the models and for the two measures of distance, Euclidean and Hellinger, respectively. The graphs show the models' diagnostic accuracy as a function of the percentage of arcs removed. The accuracy at 0% removal equals to the accuracy of the original models and the accuracy at 100% equals to the prevalence of the most likely disease. To see

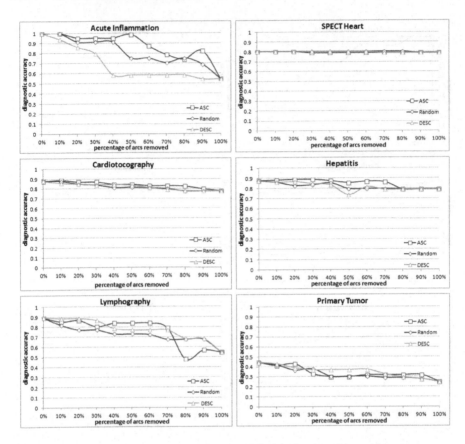

Fig. 4. The diagnostic accuracy of the six models (clock-wise: ACUTE INFLAMMATION, SPECT HEART, CARDIOTOGRAPHY, HEPATITIS, LYMPHOGRAPHY, and PRIMARY TUMOR) as a function of the percentage of arcs removed. Arcs ordered according to the Hellinger distance.

the latter, please note that when there are no arcs, the posterior probability distribution over the disease node is equal to its prior probability distribution; the most likely diagnosis is the disorder with the highest a-priori prevalence.

We can see that removing weaker arcs (ASC) has generally less impact on the resulting model accuracy than removing stronger arcs ($DESC$) and that the two provide generally the upper and lower bound on random removal of arcs ($Random$). It is also clear that the impact of arc removal on the diagnostic accuracy is not very strong, i.e., removing as many as half of the arcs decreases the overall accuracy by a few percent.

5.2   Experiment 2: Arc Reversal

Our second experiment involved a gradual reversal of arcs in our gold standard Bayesian network models listed in Table 2. We have tested the accuracy of the original models, then reversed 10%, 20%, 30%, ..., 90%, and 100% of their arcs, re-learned their numerical parameters from the Irvine Machine Learning Repository data sets by means of the EM algorithm, and re-tested the resulting distorted models at each step. The first model in this sequence (0% arcs reversed) was the original, gold standard model and the last model (100% arcs reversed) was a model in which all original arcs were reversed.

Similarly to what we did in Experiment 1, we followed three different orders of arc reversal: (a) ascending order of arc strengths (i.e., from the weakest to the strongest arc), (b) descending order of arc strengths (i.e., from the strongest to the weakest arc), and (c) random order. We were forced to deviate slightly from the order. Since Bayesian networks are acyclic directed graphs and some reversals could lead to cycles in the graph, not always were we able to reverse a specific arc. In such case, we postponed the reversal of this arc, trying the next arc in the order until we encountered an arc that could be reversed. The omitted arcs remained always at the beginning of the queue and were reversed as soon as it was possible. It is fairly easy to prove that this procedure terminates only after all arcs have been reversed.

Figure 5 shows the results of Experiment 2 for each of the models for Euclidean distance (we have omitted the Hellinger distance due to space constraints – the plots looked very similar). The graphs show the models' diagnostic accuracy as a function of the percentage of arcs reversed. The accuracy at 0% reversal equals to the accuracy of the original models. We can see that reversing arcs according to all three orders (*ASC*, *DESC*, and *Random*) leads to similar results. It is also clear that the impact of arc reversal on the diagnostic accuracy is minimal.

6   Discussion

This paper presented the results of two experiments probing the question of sensitivity of accuracy of Bayesian networks to their structure. We started from learning realistic gold standard medical diagnostic models from real data sets originating from the Irvine Machine Learning Repository. We subjected these models to systematic structure distortions and tested the impact of these distortions on the accuracy of the models. In the first experiment, we removed systematically fractions of the existing arcs and in the second experiment we systematically reversed a fraction of the arcs. Our results suggest that the precise structure of Bayesian networks is not as important as popularly believed. Structure transformations such as arc removal and arc reversal turn out to have only moderate impact on the diagnostic quality of the models. Of these, arc removal seems to have a stronger impact.

It is clear that when using the relative probability of disorder as the main decision criterion for choosing the diagnosis, prior probability distributions are important. For example, diagnostic accuracy of the SPECT HEART and CARDIOTOGRAPHY models reached 80% even after all arcs have been removed. The dominating factor here is the prior probability distribution of the node representing the class variable, CARDIOTOGRAPHY, with the following a-priori distribution $(0.78, 0.14, 0.08)$. When no evidence reaches the CARDIOTOGRAPHY node,

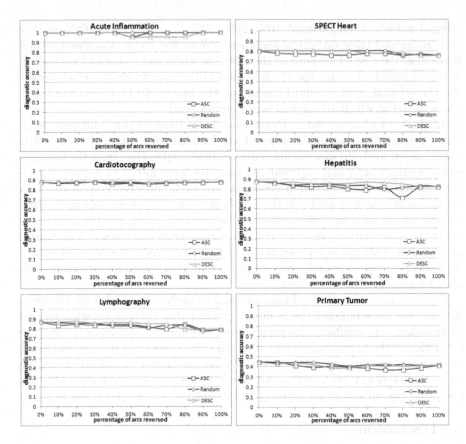

Fig. 5. The diagnostic accuracy of the six models (clock-wise: ACUTE INFLAMMATION, SPECT HEART, CARDIOTOGRAPHY, HEPATITIS, LYMPHOGRAPHY, and PRIMARY TUMOR) as a function of the percentage of arcs reversed. Arcs ordered according to the Euclidean distance.

the model always chooses the first, most likely state as its diagnosis. This leads to the accuracy of 78%.

In a problem as hard as testing whether the accuracy of Bayesian networks is sensitive to their structure, no study will provide definitive answer. In addition to increasing the sample size of models tested, we have several follow-up questions and studies in mind. The first is applying different measures of accuracy. Pradhan et al. [6], for example, focus on the posterior probability of the correct diagnosis. While this measure has several disadvantages, which we discussed earlier [4], it might lead to different results.

The strongest test of sensitivity to structure will be node removal. This is equivalent to the problem of feature selection. When important features have been removed, the accuracy will suffer. While the end result will never fall below the 100% arc removal baseline, the shape of the curves pictured in Figures 3 and 4 may be different. We have indirectly touched this problem – when all paths between a feature node and the disease node have been removed, the feature node has been de-facto removed.

Acknowledgments. Agnieszka Onisko was supported by the Białystok University of Technology grant S/WI/2/2013. Marek Druzdzel was supported by the National Institute of Health under grant number U01HL101066-01.

All Bayesian network models in this paper were created and tested using SMILE, an inference engine, and GeNIe, a development environment for reasoning in graphical probabilistic models, both developed at the Decision Systems Laboratory and available at http://genie.sis.pitt.edu/.

References

[1] Henrion, M., Breese, J.S., Horvitz, E.J.: Decision Analysis and Expert Systems. AI Magazine 12(4), 64–91 (1991)
[2] Pearl, J.: Probabilistic Reasoning in Intelligent Systems: Networks of Plausible Inference. Kaufmann Publishers, Inc, San Mateo (1988)
[3] Druzdzel, M.J., Onisko, A.: The impact of overconfidence bias on practical accuracy of Bayesian network models: An empirical study. In: Renooij, S., Tabachneck-Schijf, H.J., Mahoney, S.M. (eds.) Working Notes of the 2008 Bayesian Modelling Applications Workshop, Special Theme: How Biased Are Our Numbers? Annual Conference on Uncertainty in Artificial Intelligence (UAI–2008), July 9 (2008)
[4] Onisko, A., Druzdzel, M.J.: Effect of imprecision in probabilities on Bayesian network models: An empirical study. In: Working Notes of the European Conference on Artificial Intelligence in Medicine (AIME 2003), Workshop on Qualitative and Model-based Reasoning in Biomedicine, pp. 45–49 (October 19, 2003)
[5] Onisko, A., Druzdzel, M.J.: Impact of precision of Bayesian network parameters on accuracy of medical diagnostic systems. Artificial Intelligence in Medicine 57(3), 197–206 (2013)
[6] Pradhan, M., Henrion, M., Provan, G., del Favero, B., Huang, K.: The sensitivity of belief networks to imprecise probabilities: An experimental investigation. Artificial Intelligence 85(1-2), 363–397 (1996)
[7] Bache, K., Lichman, M.: UCI Machine Learning Repository, University of California, Irvine, School of Information and Computer Sciences, USA (2013), http://archive.ics.uci.edu/ml
[8] Onisko, A., Druzdzel, M.J., Wasyluk, H.: Extension of the Hepar II model to multiple-disorder diagnosis. In: Kłopotek, M., Michalewicz, S.W. (eds.) Intelligent Information Systems. Advances in Soft Computing, pp. 303–313. Physica-Verlag (A Springer-Verlag Company), Heidelberg (2000)
[9] Czerniak, J., Zarzycki, H.: Application of rough sets in the presumptive diagnosis of urinary system diseases. In: Soldek, J., Drobiazgiewicz, L. (eds.) 9th International Conference on Artifical Inteligence and Security in Computing Systems, ACS 2002, pp. 41–51. Kluwer Academic Publishers, Norwell (2003)
[10] Kononenko, I.: Inductive and Bayesian learning in medical diagnosis. Applied Artificial Intelligence 7, 317–337 (1993)
[11] Cooper, G.F., Herskovits, E.: A Bayesian method for the induction of probabilistic networks from data. Machine Learning 9(4), 309–347 (1992)

[12] Oniśko, A., Druzdzel, M.J., Wasyluk, H.: An experimental comparison of methods for handling incomplete data in learning parameters of Bayesian networks. In: Kłopotek, M., Michalewicz, M., Wierzchoń, S.T. (eds.) Intelligent Information Systems. Advances in Soft Computing, pp. 351–360. Physica-Verlag (A Springer-Verlag Company), Heidelberg (2002)

[13] Moore, A.W., Lee, M.S.: Efficient algorithms for minimizing cross validation error. In: Proceedings of the 11th International Conference on Machine Learning. Morgan Kaufmann, San Francisco (1994)

[14] Boerlage, B.: Link strengths in Bayesian networks. Master's thesis, Dept. of Computer Science, The University of British Columbia, Vancuver, Canada (1992)

[15] Nicholson, A.E., Jitnah, N.: Using mutual information to determine relevance in Bayesian networks. In: Lee, H.-Y. (ed.) PRICAI 1998. LNCS, vol. 1531, pp. 399–410. Springer, Heidelberg (1998)

[16] Ebert-Uphoff, I.: Measuring connection strengths and link strengths in discrete Bayesian networks. Technical Report GT-IIC-07-01, Georgia Institute of Technology (2007)

[17] Ebert-Uphoff, I.: Tutorial on how to measure link strengths in discrete Bayesian networks. Technical Report GT-ME-2009-001, Georgia Institute of Technology (2009)

[18] Lacave, C., Díez, F.J.: A review of explanation methods for heuristic expert systems. The Knowledge Engineering Review 19(2), 133–146 (2004)

[19] Koiter, J.R.: Visualizing inference in Bayesian networks. Master's thesis, Delft University of Technology, Delft, The Netherlands (2006)

[20] Kanazawa, Y.: Hellinger distance and Akaike's information criterion for the histogram. Statistics and Probability Letters 17(4), 293–298 (1993)

A New Three-Dimensional Facial Landmarks in Recognition

Sebastian Pabiasz[1], Janusz T. Starczewski[1], and Antonino Marvuglia[2]

[1] Institute of Computational Intelligence, Czestochowa University of Technology,
Czestochowa, Poland
{sebastian.pabiasz,janusz.starczewski}@iisi.pcz.pl
[2] Public Research Centre Henri Tudor (CRPHT)
Resource Centre for Environmental Technologies (CRTE)
6A, avenue des Hauts-Fourneaux, L-4362 Esch-sur-Alzette, Luxembourg
antonino.marvuglia@tudor.lu

Abstract. In recent years, the number of biometric solutions based on 3D face images has increased rapidly. Such solutions provide a much more accurate alternative to those using flat images; however, they are much more complex. In this paper, we present subsequent results of our research on a new representation of characteristic points for the 3D face. As a comparative method the standard PCA is applied.

Keywords: biometric, 3D face, mesh, depth map.

1 Introduction

A biometric system is a pattern recognition system that determines the authenticity of an individual using physical or behavioral features. The physical features include unique anatomical features such as fingerprint, DNA, etc. Behavioral features are related to the behavior of a person e.g. signature[3][4]. Biometric systems are divided into two groups. The first group is constituted by systems that require some user interaction, e.g. systems based on fingerprints. A biometric capture device must scan a fingerprint, hence the user intervention is required. The second group consists of systems based on the feature that is always and easily available such as faces.

Research on automatic face recognition has been carried out for more than half a century; however, a big step in this field has been the development of the eigenface algorithm[12,26]. Currently, mainstream focuses on the use of three-dimensional model of the face.

2 A New Three-Dimensional Facial Landmarks

Since our previous work [17], we deal with the new approach to determine three-dimensional facial landmarks. In the first stage of the proposed method, the input set is organized in the form of a depth-map. Then, we have to examine the

L. Rutkowski et al. (Eds.): ICAISC 2014, Part II, LNAI 8468, pp. 179–186, 2014.
© Springer International Publishing Switzerland 2014

possibility of extracting face landmarks (new, with no relation to anthropometric points) on the basis of extremes. We assume that each row and each column is represented in function forms. Besides, each function can be classified as one of the four types of values:

local minimum of a function at a specified window size,
local maximum of a function at a specified window size,
global minimum of a function,
global maximum of a function.

Therefore, our method consists of two stages (Algorithm 1). The first stage extracts characteristic points from columns, and the second one does the same with rows. In each step, only points of the selected range are analyzed.

Algorithm 1. First state of landmark extraction

$\textbf{for } x = 1 \rightarrow COLUMNS \textbf{ do}$
$\quad \textbf{for } y = 1 \rightarrow WINDOWS\_SIZE \textbf{ do}$
$\quad\quad find\_Local\_Minimum$
$\quad\quad find\_Local\_Maximum$
$\quad\quad \textbf{if } is\_Global\_Minimum\_in\_Range \textbf{ then}$
$\quad\quad\quad save\_Global\_Minimum$
$\quad\quad \textbf{end if}$
$\quad\quad \textbf{if } is\_Global\_Maximum\_in\_Range \textbf{ then}$
$\quad\quad\quad save\_Global\_Maximum$
$\quad\quad \textbf{end if}$
$\quad \textbf{end for}$
$\textbf{end for}$
$\textbf{for } x = 1 \rightarrow ROWS \textbf{ do}$
$\quad \textbf{for } y = 1 \rightarrow WINDOW\_SIZE \textbf{ do}$
$\quad\quad find\_Local\_Minimum$
$\quad\quad find\_Local\_Maximum$
$\quad\quad \textbf{if } is\_Global\_Minimum\_in\_Range \textbf{ then}$
$\quad\quad\quad save\_Global\_Minimum$
$\quad\quad \textbf{end if}$
$\quad\quad \textbf{if } is\_Global\_Maximum\_in\_Range \textbf{ then}$
$\quad\quad\quad save\_Global\_Maximum$
$\quad\quad \textbf{end if}$
$\quad \textbf{end for}$
$\textbf{end for}$

In our algorithm, the height of each point is the smallest distance from the straight line matching the function at the window borders (fig. 1).

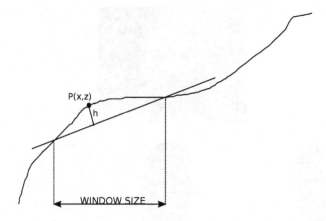

Fig. 1. Determination of the height of the point

3   Early Tests in Recognition

For the experiment, we firstly obtained characteristic points with the previously described method. For each person face, the training set consisted of dozens of face shots. The extracted characteristic points were subsequently analyzed by the principal component (PCA) method to form the data base. During the testing phase, we made use of the image that was not present in the learning phase. A series of tests comparing different types of characteristic points with each other were performed.

3.1   3D Face Database

The comparative study was carried out on a set of biometric three-dimensional images *NDOff-2007*[7]. The collection of 6940 3D images (and corresponding 2D images) were gathered for 387 human faces. The advantage of this collection is that, for a single person, there are several variants of face orientation.

3.2   Results

In the study, we used thousand 3D images taken for sixty people. Individual features can be categorized as follows:

all, all local and global landmarks from columns and rows,
col-l, local landmarks from columns,
col-g, global landmarks from columns,
glob, global landmarks from columns and rows,
row-l, local landmarks from rows,
row-g, global landmarks from rows.

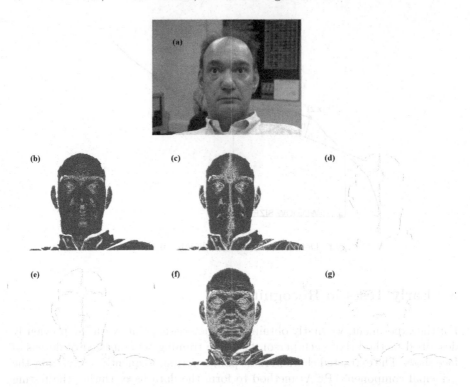

Fig. 2. Landmarks visualization.(a) original reference photo, (b) all landmarks, (c) col-l landmarks,(d) col-g landmarks, (e) glob landmarks, (f) row-l landmarks, (g) row-g landmarks.

Table 1. Results. Indexes of recognized faces. Correct are indexes: 1–38(C - correct, I - incorrect).

	all	col-l	col-g	glob	row-l	row-g
all	**36(C)**	**6(C)**	529(I)	529(I)	**6(C)**	529(I)
col-l	**36(C)**	**36(C)**	434(I)	434(I)	**6(C)**	434(I)
col-g	287(I)	287(I)	246(I)	246(I)	404(I)	246(I)
glob	238(I)	497(I)	370(I)	578(I)	238(I)	578(I)
row-l	**36(C)**	**36(C)**	626(I)	626(I)	**27(C)**	626(I)
row-g	235(I)	235(I)	452(I)	**11(C)**	235(I)	**11(C)**

Table 1 presents results of recognition process. In first column, there are listed landmarks databases used to recognize pattern image, which are based on landmarks from first row. Figure 2 presents visualization of new landmarks.

Figures 3 –6 presents results of comparisons of different class of landmarks with other landmarks. This experiment was aimed to define which points are the best to store in the database and which are the best for comparison purposes. For the calculation of the false acceptance rate (FAR), the false rejection rate (FRR) was assumed to be zero.

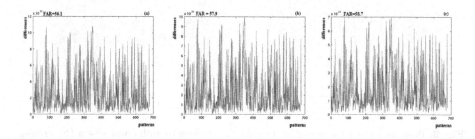

Fig. 3. Positive resutls for all landmarks. (a) - all to all comparison (b) - all to col-l comparison (c) - all to row-l comparison.

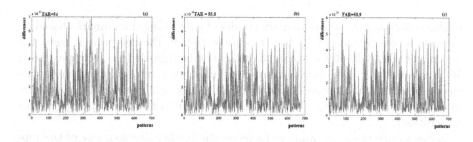

Fig. 4. Positive results for col lanmarks. (a) - col-l to all comparison (b) - col-l to col-l comparison (c) - col-l to row-l comparison.

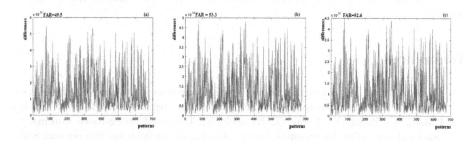

Fig. 5. Positive results for row landmakrs. (a) - row-l to all comparison (b) - row-l to col-l comparison (c) - row-l to row-l comparison.

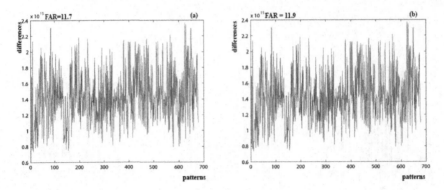

Fig. 6. Positive results for row-g landmarks. (a) - row-g to glob comparison (b) - row-g to row-g comparison.

4   Conclusion

In this contribution, the preliminary results of extraction of landmarks based on the new representation of 3D face was presented. In the comparison tests, the best result of 11% FAR was obtained, which can be regarded as a very promising for future works. Row-g landmarks are the most effective landmarks in our 3D face representation. Moreover, the row-g landmarks database is small comparing to databases created from other landmarks, since it is the most appropriate for recognition.

In the future work, we want to focus on the further development of the representation of the face, in particular, on the methods for model interpretation, e.g. on fuzzy methods [5,9,15,16,18,24] or neuro-fuzzy methods [10,21,22,25] as well as combinations with methods of image understanding [2] and processing [1]. Some work on non-parametric methods [6,8,11,13,14,19,20,23] can be done as well.

References

1. Bazarganigilani, M.: Optimized image feature selection using pairwise classifiers. Journal of Artificial Intelligence and Soft Computing Research 1(2), 147–153 (2011)
2. Chang, Y., Wang, Y., Chen, C., Ricanek, K.: Improved image-based automatic gender classification by feature selection. Journal of Artificial Intelligence and Soft Computing Research 1(3), 241–253 (2011)
3. Cpalka, K., Zalasinski, M.: A new method of on-line signature verification using a flexible fuzzy one-class classifier. In: Selected Topics in Computer Science Applications, pp. 38–53 (2011)
4. Zalasiński, M., Cpałka, K.: Novel algorithm for the on-line signature verification. In: Rutkowski, L., Korytkowski, M., Scherer, R., Tadeusiewicz, R., Zadeh, L.A., Zurada, J.M. (eds.) ICAISC 2012, Part II. LNCS (LNAI), vol. 7268, pp. 362–367. Springer, Heidelberg (2012)

5. Cpalka, K., Rutkowski, L.: Flexible takagi Sugeno neuro-fuzzy structures for nonlinear approximation. WSEAS Transactions on Systems 4(9), 1450–1458 (2005)
6. Duda, P., Jaworski, M., Pietruczuk, L., Scherer, R., Korytkowski, M., Gabryel, M.: On the application of fourier series density estimation for image classification based on feature description. In: Proceedings of the 8th International Conference on Knowledge, Information and Creativity Support Systems, Krakow, Poland, November 7-9, pp. 81–91 (2013)
7. Faltemier, T., Bowyer, K., Flynn, P.: Rotated profile signatures for robust 3d feature detection. In: 8th IEEE International Conference on Automatic Face Gesture Recognition, FG 2008, pp. 1–7 (September 2008)
8. Gabryel, M., Nowicki, R.K., Woźniak, M., Kempa, W.M.: Genetic cost optimization of the $gI/m/1/N$ finite-buffer queue with a single vacation policy. In: Rutkowski, L., Korytkowski, M., Scherer, R., Tadeusiewicz, R., Zadeh, L.A., Zurada, J.M. (eds.) ICAISC 2013, Part II. LNCS, vol. 7895, pp. 12–23. Springer, Heidelberg (2013)
9. Gabryel, M., Rutkowski, L.: Evolutionary designing of logic-type fuzzy systems. In: Rutkowski, L., Scherer, R., Tadeusiewicz, R., Zadeh, L.A., Zurada, J.M. (eds.) ICAISC 2010, Part II. LNCS, vol. 6114, pp. 143–148. Springer, Heidelberg (2010)
10. Greblicki, W., Rutkowski, L.: Density-free bayes risk consistency of nonparametric pattern recognition procedures. Proceedings of the IEEE 64(4), 482–483 (1981)
11. Greblicki, W., Rutkowska, D., Rutkowski, L.: An orthogonal series estimate of time-varying regression. Annals of the Institute of Statistical Mathematics 35(1), 215–228 (1983)
12. Kirby, M., Sirovich, L.: Application of the Karhunen-Loeve procedure for the characterization of human faces. IEEE Trans. Pattern Anal. Mach. Intell. 12(1), 103–108 (1990)
13. Korytkowski, M., Rutkowski, L., Scherer, R.: On combining backpropagation with boosting. In: International Joint Conference on Neural Networks, IJCNN 2006, pp. 1274–1277 (2006)
14. Korytkowski, M., Rutkowski, L., Scherer, R.: From ensemble of fuzzy classifiers to single fuzzy rule base classifier. In: Rutkowski, L., Tadeusiewicz, R., Zadeh, L.A., Zurada, J.M. (eds.) ICAISC 2008. LNCS (LNAI), vol. 5097, pp. 265–272. Springer, Heidelberg (2008)
15. Nowicki, R.: Rough-neuro-fuzzy system with MICOG defuzzification. In: 2006 IEEE International Conference on Fuzzy Systems, pp. 1958–1965 (2006)
16. Nowicki, R.: On classification with missing data using rough-neuro-fuzzy systems. International Journal of Applied Mathematics and Computer Science 20(1), 55–67 (2010)
17. Pabiasz, S., Starczewski, J.T.: A new approach to determine three-dimensional facial landmarks. In: Rutkowski, L., Korytkowski, M., Scherer, R., Tadeusiewicz, R., Zadeh, L.A., Zurada, J.M. (eds.) ICAISC 2013, Part II. LNCS (LNAI), vol. 7895, pp. 286–296. Springer, Heidelberg (2013)
18. Przybył, A., Cpałka, K.: A new method to construct of interpretable models of dynamic systems. In: Rutkowski, L., Korytkowski, M., Scherer, R., Tadeusiewicz, R., Zadeh, L.A., Zurada, J.M. (eds.) ICAISC 2012, Part II. LNCS, vol. 7268, pp. 697–705. Springer, Heidelberg (2012)
19. Rutkowski, L.: A general approach for nonparametric fitting of functions and their derivatives with applications to linear circuits identification. IEEE Transactions on Circuits and Systems 33(8), 812–818 (1986)
20. Rutkowski, L., Przybyl, A., Cpalka, K.: Novel online speed profile generation for industrial machine tool based on flexible neuro-fuzzy approximation. IEEE Transactions on Industrial Electronics 59(2), 1238–1247 (2012)

186   S. Pabiasz, J.T. Starczewski, and A. Marvuglia

21. Rutkowski, L.: On bayes risk consistent pattern recognition procedures in a quasi-stationary environment. IEEE Transactions on Pattern Analysis and Machine Intelligence 4(1), 84–87 (1982)
22. Rutkowski, L.: Sequential pattern recognition procedures derived from multiple fourier series. Pattern Recognition Letters 8(4), 213–216 (1988)
23. Rutkowski, L.: Non-parametric learning algorithms in time-varying environments. Signal Processing 18(2), 129–137 (1989)
24. Scherer, R., Rutkowski, L.: Connectionist fuzzy relational systems. In: Hagamuge, S., Wang, L.P. (eds.) Computational Intelligence for Modelling and Control. SCI, vol. 2, pp. 35–47. Springer, Heidelberg (2005)
25. Theodoridis, D., Boutalis, Y., Christodoulou, M.: Robustifying analysis of the direct adaptive control of unknown multivariable nonlinear systems based on a new neuro-fuzzy method. Journal of Artificial Intelligence and Soft Computing Research 1(1), 59–79 (2011)
26. Turk, M., Pentland, A.: Face recognition using eigenfaces. In: Proceedings of IEEE Computer Society Conference on Computer Vision and Pattern Recognition, CVPR 1991, pp. 586–591 (June 1991)

Computer-Aided Off-Line Diagnosis of Epileptic Seizures

Grzegorz Rutkowski and Krzysztof Patan

Institute of Control and Computer Engineering,
University of Zielona Góra,
ul. Podgórna 50, 65-246 Zielona Góra, Poland
k.patan@issi.uz.zgora.pl

Abstract. EEG signal analysis is commonly used by skilled neurologists as a useful tool in the diagnosis of specific neurological dysfunction. To greatly facilitate the diagnostic process and improve the efficiency of decision making decision support systems are developed based on expert knowledge. This paper presents the design of a computer system supporting seizure detection, based on real EEG records. The system is based on modern signal processing tools that allow for time-frequency representation of the analyzed signal. The proposed solution should be treated as a decision support computer system. The system has been designed to facilitate the rapid detection of characteristic graphoelements to effectively detect epileptic seizures. The proposed solution can have a significant impact on an accuracy and speed in the analysis of EEG signals, which may significantly shorten the time of making diagnosis trials. The proposed system is based on studies using real EEG records of patients with epilepsy as well as healthy subjects prepared in collaboration with the medical staff of the Ward of Neurology and Strokes of the Provincial Hospital of Zielona Góra, Poland.

Keywords: EEG signal, Epileptic seizures, medical diagnosis, GUI.

1 Introduction

EEG analysis plays a very important role in the diagnosis of serious neurological disorders such as epilepsy [5,15,17]. Chronic neurological disorders are characterized by recurrent amplitude increasing in height, which indicate the symptoms of excessive electrical activity of neurons in the brain [3,6,10]. Recent studies have mainly focused on the analysis of ElectroEncephaloGraphic bequests based on recorded cases of epileptic seizures. Research on epilepsy and epilepsy-like entries may play a key role in the diagnosis of neurological disorders [11]. Cases of this kind of dysfunction wear an different forms and occur in many types of generalized, partial waves with short and long-term occurring in different areas of the brain [2,16]. The most popular method of analysis of EEG signals, which is carried out by specialists of neurology is visual inspection in the form of an electronic record in the analysis attached to the measuring apparatus and recording

L. Rutkowski et al. (Eds.): ICAISC 2014, Part II, LNAI 8468, pp. 187–194, 2014.

software in the form of printed paper. This method is a very time consuming and can be very inefficient. There is a very high probability of discrepancies in diagnoses posed both in the case of one and many experts in the analysis of signals which may result in the assessment of the accuracy of the recorded EEG. In the literature one can find a lot of automated methods for the detection of epileptic seizures [1,4,7,8,9,12], which achieve accuracy in detection of epileptic seizures significantly exceeding 85%. The proposed automatic diagnostic environment was created with the collaboration with medical personnel in the Ward of Neurology and Strokes of the Provincial Hospital of Zielona Góra, Poland. The system analyzes the EEG data, which was recorded using 16-channel device with the standard 10/20. Obtained records for patients with epilepsy are analyzed based on selected time intervals under the supervision of specialists neurology. EEG signals used in the system were filtered using a low-pass filter with the cut-off frequency equal to 35 Hz. All recorded signals were subjected to examination by the specialist neurology to eliminate specific artifacts.

The main goal of this work is to develop an automated system for the detection of epileptic seizures in the off-line mode. It allows to reduce the time that is required by a neurologist to find the characteristic graphoelements. The captured fragments of EEG signals allow for further detailed analysis. The proposed solution can be regarded as a decision support system in order to present a more detailed analysis of suspicious EEG records. The implemented system was created in MATLAB environment and through friendly GUI (Graphic User Interface) allows it to focus on neurology specialist areas identified by the software.

2   Assumptions and Methodology

In our previous work [13] we proposed the on-line diagnosis system for seizures detection. However, after consultations with specialists we found that the application should be developed is such a way as to minimize the time spent by a specialist to analyse the record. In fact, in a hospital the EEG signals are recorded by a technician first and then are analysed by a neurologist. The length of the EEG record can reach one hour then an expert can spent a lot of time observing and analysing of the record. Therefore, it is advisable to perform automated EEG analysis off-line, to detect suspected areas and to present these results to a neurologist to final decision. In cooperation with the medical staff of the Ward of Neurology and Strokes of the Provincial Hospital of Zielona Góra, Poland, a database of neurological disorders was prepared. The data were acquired from both epileptic patients and healthy subjects. With the help of neurologists, 586 seizures from 104 patients (both females and males) were recorded and analysed. Simultaneously, 568 sequences from 61 healthy subjects were derived. Eventually, the database consisted of 1154 EEG sequences. An expert in clinical analysis of EEG signals inspected every record visually to score epileptic and normal sequences. Analysing description of these cases we found that in majority of cases epileptic seizures were manifested by the occurrence of specified components usually by theta waves with frequencies from the interval 4 − 7Hz. So our main idea is to analyse a record in the frequency range from 4 to 8 Hz and to point out the time stamps of areas with the greatest magnitude. Selected in this way suspected excerpts of a EEG record are subjects of further analysis.

The first stage of the analysis is to select suspected candidate sequences of the EEG records which possibly represent seizures. Each EEG record consists of 16 signals (Fig.1).

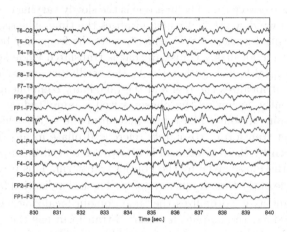

Fig. 1. All channels witch marked the beginning of an epileptic seizure

To facilitate the analysis, the EEG record should be compressed first. Taking into account that each record is processed using specteral analysis, in this work it is proposed to sum up all signals in the EEG record. Assuming that a record is represented by a matrix $R \in \mathbb{R}^{m \times n}$, where m is a number of channels, and n is the record length, the EEG record transformation is represented as follows:

$$R_c(j) = \sum_{i=1}^{m} R(i,j) \quad \forall j = 1, \ldots, n. \tag{1}$$

The vector R_c is then processed using a spectral analyis method. Taking into account the nonstationary nature of the signal Stockwell Transform (S Transform) can be used here. The S Transform (ST) is a relatively new time-frequency analysis tool developed by Stockwell in 1994 [14]. It can be viewed as a generalization of the Short-Time Fourier Transform (STFT), but instead of a window of the constant size as in the STFT, it uses a scalable Gaussian window. The Stockwell transform of signal R_c is given as follows:

$$S(t,f) = \int_{-\infty}^{\infty} R_c(\tau)g(t-\tau)e^{-i2\pi f\tau}d\tau, \tag{2}$$

where $g(t - \tau)$ is the Gaussian function located at $\tau = t$ defined as

$$g(t - \tau) = \frac{|f|}{\sqrt{2\pi}} e^{-\frac{(t-\tau)^2 f^2}{2}}. \tag{3}$$

This makes it possible to use a variable window length. As f increases, the length of the window decreases. The advantage of S-transform over the short time Fourier transform is that the window width is a function of f rather than a fixed one as in STFT. In contrast to wavelet analysis the S-Transform wavelet can be divided into two parts. The first one is the slowly varying envelope formed by the Gaussian window $g(t - \tau)$ which localizes the time. The second is the oscillatory exponential kernel $e^{-i2\pi f \tau}$ which selects the frequency being localized. Then, it is the time localizing Gaussian that is translated while keeping the oscillatory exponential kernel stationary. As the oscillatory exponential kernel is not translating, it localizes the real and the imaginary components of the spectrum independently, localizing the phase as well as amplitude spectrum. Thus S transform retains absolute phase information of the signal which is not provided by wavelet transform. Absolutely referenced phase means that the phase information given by the S transform is always referenced to time $t = 0$, which is also true for the phase given by the Fourier transform. This is true for each S transform sample of the time-frequency space. The normalization factor $\frac{|f|}{\sqrt{2\pi}}$ also is very important as it normalizes the time domain localizing window to have unit area. Therefore, the amplitude of the S-transform has the same meaning as the amplitude of the Fourier transform. This provides a frequency invariant amplitude response in contrast to the wavelet transform. The frequency invariant amplitude response means that for a sinusoid with an amplitude M, the S-transform returns an amplitude M regardless of the frequency f.

In order to point out suspected regions, the amplitude of the time-frequency representation is considered. The system searches regions with the highest amplitudes and their time stamps are stored. In the present version of the software 99 time stamps are selected. Based on selected time stamps the second stage of diagnosis is carried out.

The second stage of the diagnosis is a classification procedure. This stage is based on the original EEG record consisting of 16 channels. For each times stamp a record of the length 200 samples is formed which means that 16 time sequences of the length 0.4 second are considered. For each record formed in this way the following steps are performed:

Step 1. to perform time-frequency analysis of each channel according to (2),
Step 2. to determine features for each transformed channel and to form overall feature vector,
Step 3. to perform a classification of each feature vector,
Step 4. to carry out the final decision based on the majotrity voting.

The first step is to perform the time-frequency analysis of the EEG record similarly like in the first stage of the diagnosis but this time the analysis is carried out for each channel separately. The reason for that is it is required to achieve as accurate information about possible seizures as possible. Moreover, S transform is performed for the larger frequency range 0-50 Hz, and the frequency sampling rate was equal to 10. Using such settings, each channel is decomposed into 11 components. Based on achieved in this way time-frequency representations of each channel, a feature extraction procedure is carried out. In this work attributes are obtained calculating energy of each frequency component according to the formula:

$$W(S_j(t, f_k)) = \sum_{t=1}^{200} |S_j(t, f_k)|^2, \quad \text{for } j = 1, \dots, 16, \quad k = 1, \dots, 11. \quad (4)$$

Thus, the feature vector consisting of 176 attributes is formed (16 channels × 11 components × 1 indicator). The third step is a classification of a single suspeced case. In this work K-nearest neighbours algorithm was applied. The pattern is classified by a majority vote of its neighbours, with the pattern being assigned to the class most common amongst its k nearest neighbours. The training phase of the algorithm consists of storing the attributes and class labels of the training samples. In the classification phase, k is the user-defined constant, and an input vector is classified by assigning the label which is the most frequent among the k training samples nearest to that query point. As training samples the database consisting of 1154 samples. The last step is to make a final decision wheter the EEG records represents seizure or not (Fig.2). To carry out this step the

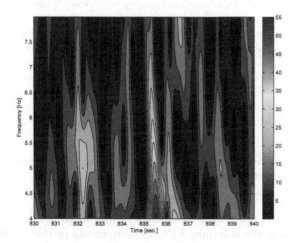

Fig. 2. Time-frequency representation of the signal determining the epileptic seizure (sum of all channels)

majority vote is used based on the classification results of 99 suspected cases. The majority voting uses the diagnosis rate r defined as follows:

$$r = \frac{n_s}{N} 100\%, \quad (5)$$

where n_s represent a number of cases classified as seizures, and N is a total number of cases. In this study N was set to 99. Then the decision d is made according to the rule:

$$d = \begin{cases} 0 & \text{if } r < 50\% \\ 1 & \text{if } r > 50\% \end{cases} . \tag{6}$$

As the number of considered cases is odd the case that $r = 50\%$ is not considered here.

3   Results

Firstly, a preliminary diagnosis aimed at finding 'suspicious' of EEG epileptic seizure cases is carried out (Fig.3).

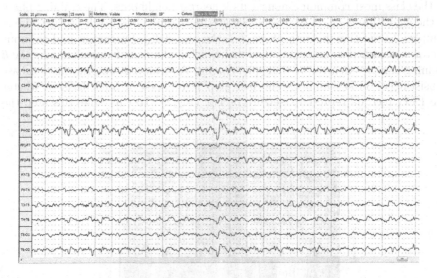

Fig. 3. The original record of hospital equipment epileptic seizure measurement recorded for the characteristic wave Theta

The next stage is performed on a single signal in time - frequency domain taking into account the standard EEG measurements in the range of 4 - 8Hz, (Theta waves).

This choice is conditioned based on numerous consultations with doctors from Provincial Hospital of Zielona Góra, according to descriptions of diagnostic judgments for cases diagnosed as epileptic seizures. After analyzing the results and the analysis is performed in time - frequency made the sort that allowed determined from the high amplitude group of records that determines the occurrence of cases of suspected epileptic seizures. This approach allowed to determine and point out the occurrence time of the waves with the highest amplitude (Fig.4).

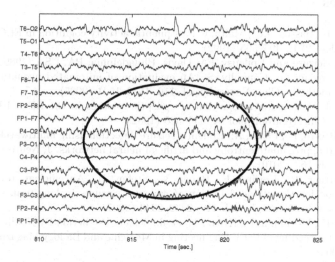

Fig. 4. Theta wave recorded by the system during an epileptic seizure specifies

In the next stage of classification performed for each channel to determine attributes for further analysis. The diagnostic process has been defined on the basis on the classification results and rules (5) and (6).

The proposed system has obtained very good results for both the provisions establishing the standard, for example, 35%, 46%, 29%, 21%, 12% and cases defining epileptic seizures indicating 59%, 55%, 78% , 64%, 86%.

Presented in this article the results are very promising and confirm the validity of the presented experiments. Development and improvement of existing diagnostic tools using the latest technologies aimed at more accurate assessment of clinical diagnoses posed by specialists. Developments of such a kind of tools is designed to support neurologist in decision making and can be very helpful in avoiding errors in medical diagnosis.

4   Conclusions and Further Development Directions

The paper presents the implementation of the off-line computer-aided system for seizures detection. The system uses advanced methods of signal processing, as well as the outstanding classification algorithms. Close cooperation with specialists in the field of ElectroEncephaloGraphy medical staff of the Ward of Neurology and Strokes of the Provincial Hospital of Zielona Góra allows for further development of the application.

Planned enhancements include:

- to extend analysis modules in off-line mode,
- to improve the interaction between the application and the user,
- to introduce diagnostic parameters able to rule out a false diagnosis,
- to implement analysis of reports in the form of visualization for specific area.

References

1. Diambra, L., Bastos, J.C., Malta, C.P.: Epileptic activity cognition in EEG recording. Physica (273), 495–505 (1999)
2. Engel, J.: Seizure and Epilepsy, FA, Davis, Philadelphia, PA, USA (1989)
3. Faul, S., Boylan, G., Connolly, S.: An evaluation of automated neonatal seizure detection methods. Clin. Neurophysiol. 116, 1533–1541 (2005)
4. Gotman, J.: Automatic recognition of epileptic seizures in the EEG. Electroencephalogr. Clin. Neurophysiol 54, 530–540 (1982)
5. Guo, L., Rivero, D., Pazos, A.: Epileptic seizure detection using multiwavelet transform based approximate entropy and artificial neural networks. J. Neurosci. Methods 193, 156–163 (2010)
6. Hopfengartner, R., Kerling, F., Bauer, V., Stefan, H.: An efficient, robust and fast method for the offline detection of epileptic seizures in long-term scalp eeg recordings. Clin. Neurophysiol. 118, 2332–2343 (2007)
7. Lehnertz, K., Mormann, F., Kreuz, T., et al.: Seizure Prediction By Nonlinear EEG Analysis. Proceeding of IEEE Engineering in Medicine and Biology Magazine 22(1), 57–63 (2003)
8. Layne, S.P., Mayer-Kress, G., Holzfuss, J.: Problems associated with the analysis of EEG data, in Dimensions and Entropies in Chaotic Systems. Springer, NY (1986)
9. Iasemidis, L.D., Shiau, D.S., Chaovalitwongse, W., Sackellares, J.C., Pardalos, P.M., Principe, J.C.: Adaptive epileptic seizure prediction system. IEEE Transactions on Biomedical Engineering 50(5), 616–627 (2003)
10. McSharry, P., He, T., Smith, L.: Linear and non-linear methods for automatic seizure detection in scalp electro-encephalogram recordings. Med. Biol. Eng. Comput. 40, 447–461 (2002)
11. Patan, K., Rutkowski, G.: Analysis and classification of EEG data: An evaluation of methods. In: Rutkowski, L., Korytkowski, M., Scherer, R., Tadeusiewicz, R., Zadeh, L.A., Zurada, J.M. (eds.) ICAISC 2012, Part II. LNCS, vol. 7268, pp. 310–317. Springer, Heidelberg (2012)
12. Rutkowski, G., Patan, K., Leśniak, P.: Comparison of time-frequency feature extraction methods for EEG signals classification. In: Rutkowski, L., Korytkowski, M., Scherer, R., Tadeusiewicz, R., Zadeh, L.A., Zurada, J.M. (eds.) ICAISC 2013, Part II. LNCS (LNAI), vol. 7895, pp. 320–329. Springer, Heidelberg (2013)
13. Rutkowski, G., Patan, K., Leśniak, P.: Computer-aided on-line seizure detection using stockwell transform. In: Korbicz, J., Kowal, M. (eds.) Intelligent Systems in Technical and Medical Diagnostics. AISC, vol. 230, pp. 279–289. Springer, Heidelberg (2013)
14. Stockwell, R.G., Mansinha, L., Lowe, R.P.: Localization of the complex spectrum: The S transform. IEEE Trans. Signal Processing 44(4), 998–1001 (1996)
15. Taheri, S., Mammadov, M.: Learning the naive Bayes classifier with optimization models. J. Applied Mathematics and Computer Science 23(4), 787–795 (2013)
16. T., A., Tsipouras, M.G., Tsalikakis, D.G., Karvounis, E.C., Astrakas, L., Konitsiotis, S., Tzallas, M.T.: Automated epileptic seizure detection methods: A review study. In: Stevanovic, D. (ed.) Epilepsy - Histological, Electroencephalographic and Psychological Aspects. InTech (2012) ISBN: 978-953-51-0082-9
17. Woźniak, M., Krawczyk, B.: Combined classifier based on feature space partitioning. J. Applied Mathematics and Computer Science 22(4), 855–866 (2012)

Active Region Approach for Segmentation of Medical Images

Pawel Tracz and Piotr S. Szczepaniak

Institute of Information Technology, Lodz University of Technology,
ul. Wolczanska 215, 90-924 Poland
138124@edu.p.lodz.pl, Piotr.Szczepaniak@p.lodz.pl
http://ics.p.lodz.pl

Abstract. Active region models are methods for automatic image segmentation. In this paper, the method is examined using various medical images (heart, brain and liver). The quality measure, taken for evaluation of the method is based on combination of two measures used for classifiers. The energy of the region is based on statistical features of initial region.

Keywords: image segmentation, medical image segmentation, active contour, active region, snakes.

1 Introduction

The task of image segmentation is considered to be one of the most difficult operations of in image processing [3]. The medical images are particularly hard to analyze [1, 12–20]. There are many techniques of image segmentation available. One of the most promising methods of image segmentation is the *active contour* approach [2, 4, 5, 7–12, 18, 19]. Originally, *active contour* approach was developed for low-level image segmentation coupled with the ability to use high-level information. The high-level information is incorporated into the given objective function, called Energy, which is used for evaluation of the quality of a contour which is the result of the method. As shown in [8, 10], contours are contextual classifiers of pixels (one part of the pixels belongs to the interior and the other part to the exterior of a given contour) and *active contours* are methods of optimal construction of classifiers. The *active region* approach is similar in that it can be thought of as the extension of *active contour* method [4]]. It is worth to notice that not only the shape of the contour is taken into consideration but also the statistical parameters of the initial region [4].

The paper is composed in the following way. First, the applied segmentation method, called active regions, is briefly presented. Then, the method is examined using different medical images. Then the segmentation result of the method based on conducted experiments is presented and when possible evaluated.

L. Rutkowski et al. (Eds.): ICAISC 2014, Part II, LNAI 8468, pp. 195–206, 2014.
© Springer International Publishing Switzerland 2014

1.1 Active Region Approach

For evaluation of the contour an objective function E, called energy, is used. Its general form is as follows:

$$E = E_{int} + E_{img} + E_{con} = E_{int} + E_{ext} \tag{1}$$

where:

E_{int} - internal energy (e.g. evaluation of the shape),
E_{img} - image energy (e.g. evaluation of the position of the contour on the image),
E_{con} - constraint energy (e.g. external knowledge),
E_{ext} - external energy.

As stated in the formula (1) the Energy E is expressed as the sum of all its components.

In the active region method, the internal energy is the same as in the case of active contour method approach [4, 5]:

$$E_{int} = \int_0^1 \frac{\alpha(s)|v'(s)|^2 + \beta(s)|v''(s)|^2}{2} ds \tag{2}$$

where:

$s \in [0,1]$ - position of the point on the contour,
$v(s) = x(s), y(s)$ - coordinates of the considered point,
α - elasticity parameter,
β - rigidity parameter.

The evolution of the contour depends on statistical parameters (being mean intensity and standard deviation of the pixel intensity) of the area inside the contour. The region energy is defined as follows [4]:

$$E_{region} = -\rho \iint_R G(I(x,y)) dx\, dy \tag{3}$$

where:

ρ - the parameter which determines the influence of region energy,
R - the region inside the contour are calculated,
$I(x,y)$ - the intensity of a given pixel,
$G(I(x,y))$ - the function that evaluates the goodness of the image.

The G function used in previously introduced formula (3) can be defined as follows [4]:

$$G(I(x,y)) = 1 - \frac{|I(x,y) - \mu|}{k\sigma} \qquad (4)$$

where:

$I(x,y)$ - the intensity of a given pixel,
μ - the mean intensity of the pixels inside the seed region,
σ - the standard deviation of the pixel intensity in the seed region,
k - the parameter that tunes the value of the force.

It is worth to notice the fact that the value of G is heavily influenced by the value of k parameter. This parameter should be set experimentally preferably by an expert (e.g. radiologist). It must also be emphasized that G values are normalized (it ranges from 0 to the maximum value of 1).

It is also worth to notice that in this work the input for the G function is not the value of a single pixel (intensity) but the mean value of its neighborhood (9 point neighborhood). Motivation behind this approach is to make the method be less local in terms of region component.

The region energy (double integral over a region R) is approximated by calculating the sum of G values for all pixels in the region R. Usually the initial region is located inside the searched object (Fig. 1). In this case it is the area inside a liver which is affected by cancer cells.

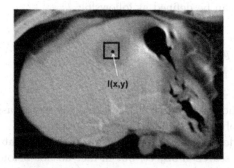

Fig. 1. Sample medical image (CT) of the liver along with seed region R marked as a black square. I denotes pixel intensity which is an argument of the function G.

The force that results from the region energy term is always perpendicular to the contour in a given point. The direction of the force either inside or outside the contour - is determined by the influence that the resulting move exerts on the regions assessment (incorporated into G function).

Another aspect of great importance is contour resampling. It allows to change the number of points as it progresses. It can be particularly useful when initial contour has too few points to reflect the boundaries of the searched object accurately. In this work it was realized using some threshold values both for addition and removal of the points. If the distance between points was greater than the threshold the point was added in the middle otherwise it was removed.

1.2 Quality Measure for Image Segmentation

As the image segmentation is synonymous to the binary classification (background-object discrimination) [10] the quality measures known for classifiers can be employed. In this approach one need to have already segmented areas corresponding to investigated images (e.g. Fig 2.). Assuming that such reference collection exists, the following measure of segmentation quality can be applied [6]:

$$F_\beta = (1 + \beta^2)\left(\frac{precision\, recall}{\beta^2\, precision + recall}\right) \qquad (5)$$

$$F_1 = 2\frac{precision\, recall}{precision + recall} \qquad (6)$$

where:

β is a non-negative number. Frequently, $\beta = 1$ is used and the measure is called $F_1 - score$ or $F_1 - measure$. The $precision$ and $recall$ are well-known measures which can be defined as follows[6]:

$$precision = \frac{t_p}{t_p + f_p}\ recall = \frac{t_p}{f_p + f_n} \qquad (7)$$

where:

t_p - $true\ positive$ denotes the number of image pixels were classified as belonging to the searched object and in reality do belong to it,

f_p - $false\ positive$ denotes the number of image pixels that were classified as belonging to the searched object, but in fact do not belong to it,

f_n - $false\ negative$ denotes the number of image pixels that were classified as not belonging to the searched object but in reality do belong to it.

In the reported investigations, the reference images were provided only in case of heart images. Please note that in further parts of this article whenever quality measure is used it refers to $F_1 - score$. The example reference images for heart ventricles of heart are presented in Fig.2.

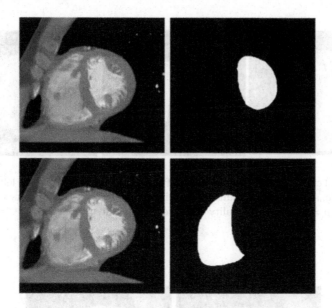

Fig. 2. Heart images (left) with segmented ventricles (right)

2   Application Results on Medical Images

The material for the examination of the method comprised on sets of medical images of brain, heart and liver. In case of heart the segmentation task was to detect the heart ventricles; in case of brain images the aim was to segment ventricular system, while in case of liver images the objective was to segment cancer cells.

Practical results of each type of the image is described in the following section. In every case the result boundary is white.

2.1   Heart Images

In the following section there are presented results for the images of heart. For this subset the reference images was provided and the quality measure could be calculated.

One can see that the segmentation of heart ventricle is not an easy task. It is mainly because of the inhomogeneity of the region describing the ventricle. Some areas inside the heart ventricle are almost identical in terms of pixel intensity - to those of the background. Accumulated results proves that for the given parameters and location of the initial contour satisfactory result can be obtained. The success of the method lies in the fact that both the shape and region is evaluated in this method.

Fig. 3. Initial circle (seed region R) on the left; reference image segmented left ventricle in the middle; segmentation result using active region method. Parameters values $\alpha = 0.1, \beta = 0.1, \rho = 0.3, k = 16$. Quality measure $F1$ amounted to 0.975.

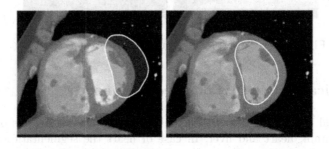

Fig. 4. Initial and final contour. Parameters values $\alpha = 0.1, \beta = 0.1, \rho = 0.3, k = 16$. Quality measure $F1$ amounted to 0.975.

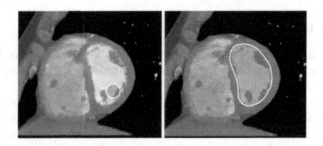

Fig. 5. Initial and final contour. Parameters values $\alpha = 0.1, \beta = 0.1, \rho = 0.3, k = 1.8$. Quality measure $F1$ amounted to 0.975.

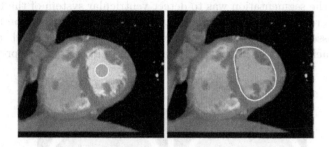

Fig. 6. Initial and final contour. Parameters values $\alpha = 0.1, \beta = 0.1, \rho = 0.3, k = 20$. Quality measure $F1$ amounted to 0.969.

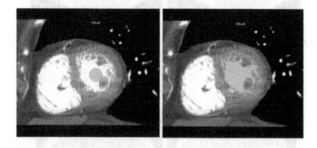

Fig. 7. Initial and final contour. Parameters values $\alpha = 0.1, \beta = 0.1, \rho = 0.3, k = 4$. Quality measure $F1$ amounted to 0.948.

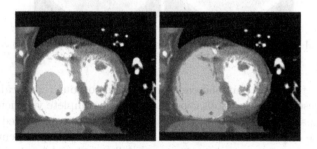

Fig. 8. Initial and final contour. Parameters values $\alpha = 0.1, \beta = 0.1, \rho = 0.3, k = 4$. Quality measure $F1$ amounted to 0.965.

2.2 Brain Images

The task of the segmentation was to detect ventricular system of the brain. For these images reference images were not available so the segmentation result can only be assessed subjectively. In the following investigation the seed region was calculated each time and its location is always an initial contour (presented as a circle).

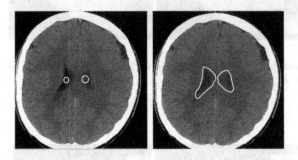

Fig. 9. Initial and final contour. Parameters values $\alpha = 0.1, \beta = 0.1, \rho = 0.3, k = 5$.

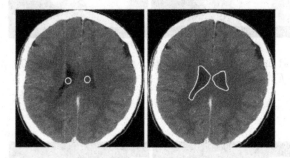

Fig. 10. Initial and final contour. Parameters values $\alpha = 0.1, \beta = 0.1, \rho = 0.3, k = 3$.

It is worth to notice that one can run a single contour (after calculation of seed region described in previous cases) to segment complete ventricular system without using separate contours for each part. This case is presented in Fig. 12.

Like in case of previously investigated images of heart, experiments on brain images also proves the method can be successfully employed for the objects that are not homogenous (in terms of pixel intensity).

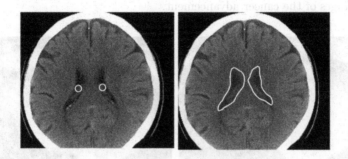

Fig. 11. Initial and final contour. Parameters values $\alpha = 0.1, \beta = 0.1, \rho = 0.3, k = 1.5$.

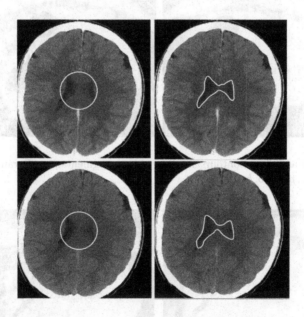

Fig. 12. Illustration for applying one contour to find ventricular system. Parameter values are identical to those described in the Fig. 9. and Fig 10.

2.3 Liver Images

The task of this segmentation was to detect liver cancer of the patient. The method was examined on CT scan of the liver. The images were taken at a different stages of the cancer advancement.

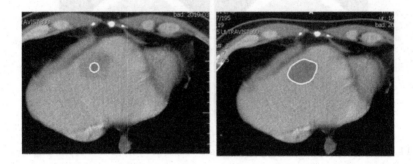

Fig. 13. Initial and final contours for liver cancer segmentation. Parameters values $\alpha = 0.1, \beta = 0.1, \rho = 0.3, k = 2.5$.

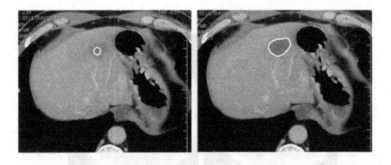

Fig. 14. Initial and final contours for liver cancer segmentation. Parameters values $\alpha = 0.1, \beta = 0.1, \rho = 0.3, k = 2.5$.

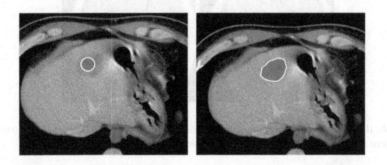

Fig. 15. Initial and final contours for liver cancer segmentation. Parameters values $\alpha = 0.1, \beta = 0.1, \rho = 0.3, k = 2$.

3 Conclusions

The active region method may be suitable for medical applications (in the sense of segmentation). Its performance is measured by a quality measure which in case of heart images was almost perfect (close to 1). The quality measure indicates that it may be used. For the rest of the images, the results are also satisfactory but due to the lack of reference images cannot be quantified objectively.

The practical evaluation performed using a collection of medical images allows one to expect that the method performs well. However, one has to keep in mind that the success or failure of this method is dependent on the choice of its parameters (especially one that results from region energy).

Further developments of this method should be directed at enriching region energy by identifying the influence of other statistical values for the region energy and the quality of the results. Other area in which the method could be improved is the automated choice of methods parameters.

References

1. Bankman, I.N. (ed.): Handbook of Medical Imaging. Processing and Analysis. Academic Press, San Diego (2000)
2. Casselles, V., Kimmel, R., Sapiro, G.: Geodesic Active Contours. Int. Journal of Computer Vision 22(1), 61–79 (2000)
3. Gonzales, R.C., Woods, R.E.: Digital Image Processing. Prentice-Hall, Inc. (2002)
4. Ivins, J., Porrill, J.: Active Region Models for Segmenting Medical Images. Artificial Intelligence Vision Research Unit. University of Shefield (1994)
5. Kass, M., Witkin, W., Terzopoulos, S.: Snakes: Active Contour Models. Int. Journal of Computer Vision 1(4), 321–333 (1998)
6. Makhoul, J., Francis, K., Schwartz, R., Wieschedel, R.: Performance measures for information extraction. In: Proceedings of DARPA Broadcast News Workshop, Herndon, VA (1999)
7. Tomczyk, A.: Image Segmentation using Adaptive Potential Active Contours. In: Kurzyski, M., et al. (eds.) Computer Recognition Systems, pp. 148–155. Springer, Heidelberg (2007)
8. Tomczyk, A.: Active Hypercontours and Contextual Classification. In: Proceedings of the 5th International Conference on Intelligent Systems Design and Applications ISDA 2005, Wroclaw, Poland, pp. 256–261. IEEE Computer Society Press (2005)
9. Tomczyk, A., Pieta, L., Szczepaniak, P.S.: Potential Active Contours Basic Concepts, Mechanisms and Features. In: Pietka, E., Kawa, J. (eds.) Information Technologies in Biomedicine. ASC, vol. 47, pp. 74–84. Springer, Heidelberg (2008)
10. Tomczyk, A., Szczepaniak, P.S.: On the Relationship between Active Contours and Contextual Classification. In: Kurzyski, M., et al. (eds.) Proceedings of the 4th Int. Conference on Computer Recognition Systems, CORES 2005, pp. 303–310. Springer, Heidelberg (2005)
11. Tomczyk, A., Szczepaniak, P.S.: Adaptive Potential Active Hypercontours. In: Rutkowski, L., Tadeusiewicz, R., Zadeh, L.A., Żurada, J.M. (eds.) ICAISC 2006. LNCS (LNAI), vol. 4029, pp. 692–701. Springer, Heidelberg (2006)

12. Jojczyk, K., Pryczek, M., Tomczyk, A., Szczepaniak, P.S., Grzelak, P.: Cognitive Hierarchical Active Partitions using Patch Approach. In: Bolc, L., Tadeusiewicz, R., Chmielewski, L.J., Wojciechowski, K. (eds.) ICCVG 2010, Part I. LNCS, vol. 6374, pp. 35–42. Springer, Heidelberg (2010)
13. Walczak, S., Tomczyk, A., Szczepaniak, P.S.: Interpretation of Images and Their Sequences using Potential Active Contour Method. In: Bolc, L., Tadeusiewicz, R., Chmielewski, L.J., Wojciechowski, K. (eds.) ICCVG 2010, Part I. LNCS, vol. 6374, pp. 89–96. Springer, Heidelberg (2010)
14. Tomczyk, A., Pryczek, M., Walczak, S., Jojczyk, K., Szczepaniak, P.S.: Spatch based Active Partition with Linguistically Formulated Energy. Journal of Applied Computer Science JACS 18(1), 87–115 (2010)
15. Pryczek, M., Tomczyk, A., Szczepaniak, P.S.: Active Partition Based Medical Image Understanding with Self Organized, Competitive Spatch Eduction. Journal of Applied Computer Science JACS 18(2), 67–78 (2010)
16. Tomczyk, A., Szczepaniak, P.S.: Knowledge Extraction for Heart Image Segmentation. In: Burduk, R., et al. (eds.) Computer Recognition Systems 4. AISC, vol. 95, pp. 579–586. Springer, Heidelberg (2011)
17. Tracz, P., Szczepaniak, P.S., Tomczyk, A.: Application of Active Region Model for Detection of Liver Cancer. Journal of Medical Informatics and Technologies 17, 263–268 (2011)
18. Tomczyk, A., Szczepaniak, P.S.: Adaptive potential active contours. Pattern Analysis and Applications 14(4), 425–440 (2011)
19. Pryczek, M., Szczepaniak, P.S.: Cognitive Hierarchical Active Partitions in Distributed Analysis of Medical Images. Journal of Ambient Intelligence and Humanized Computing JAIHC 19(1), 143–150 (2012)
20. Pieciak, T., Baran, M., Urbanczyk, M.: Level-set Based Segmentation of Carotid Arteries in Computed Tomography Angiography Images. Journal of Medical Informatics and Technologies 17, 281–286 (2011)

SCM-driven Tree View for Microarray Data

Hsun-Chih Kuo[1], Miin-Shen Yang[2,*], Jenn-Hwai Yang[2], and Yen-Chi Chen[2]

[1] Department of Statistics, National Chengchi University,
Wenshan District, Taipei 11605, Taiwan
[2] Department of Applied Mathematics,
Chung Yuan Christian University, Chung-Li 32023, Taiwan
msyang@math.cycu.edu.tw

Abstract. Eisen's tree view is a useful tool for clustering and displaying of microarray gene expression data. In Eisen's tree view system, a hierarchical method is used for clustering data. However, some useful information in gene expression data may not be well drawn when a hierarchical clustering is directly used in Eisen's tree view. In this paper, we embed the similarity-based clustering method (SCM) into the tree view system so that microarray data can be re-organized according to the structure of data. The created SCM-driven tree view can give a better dendrogram display for microarray gene expression data with more useful information.

Keywords: Clustering, Microarray data, Similarity-based clustering method, Eisen's tree-view.

1   Introduction

Cluster analysis is a useful tool for finding clusters of a data set, grouped with most similarity in the same cluster and most dissimilarity between different clusters [10,12]. Microarray gene expression data have been widely used and analyzed. An important step for analyzing microarray data is to cluster sets of genes with similar patterns of expression. In this case, cluster analysis becomes a useful tool in the analysis of microarray gene expression data. Eisen et al. [6] successfully created a system of cluster analysis and display of genome-wide expression patterns. They first defined a similarity metric between genes and then used the hierarchical clustering for the dendrogram display of gene expression data. Based on the system created by Eisen et al. [6], a tree-view dendrogram software system was presented by Eisen Laboratory [7]. Nowadays, Eisen's tree-view system is popular for the display of microarray gene expression data, for example, Alizadeh et al. [1] used Eisen's tree-view system to create a systematic characterization of gene expression in B-cell malignancies.

In clustering, partitioning methods are widely used. The well-known partitioning method with cluster prototypes is k-means [13]. The k-means method restricts that each data point belongs to exactly one cluster with crisp cluster memberships so that they can be fitted for sharp boundaries between clusters in data. However, if boundaries are un-sharp (or vague) between clusters in data, then fuzzy memberships

---

* Corresponding author.

L. Rutkowski et al. (Eds.): ICAISC 2014, Part II, LNAI 8468, pp. 207–215, 2014.
© Springer International Publishing Switzerland 2014

based on fuzzy sets [18] will be more suitable to provide more information for clustering. Fuzzy clustering had been successfully applied in various areas [3,15]. In fuzzy clustering, the fuzzy c-means (FCM) algorithm is the most used method. Gasch and Eisen [8] first applied FCM to explore the conditional coregulation of yeast gene expression where they used a heuristically modified version of FCM to identify overlapping clusters of yeast genes based on published gene-expression data following the response of yeast cells to environmental changes. Dembélé and Kastner [5] applied FCM for clustering data from DNA microarray with a suitable choice of fuzziness parameter m.

However, the FCM has some drawbacks, for example, the numbers of points in clusters are supposed to be almost equal, and its memberships do not always correspond well to the degree of belonging of the data. It is always inaccurate in a noisy environment. To overcome these drawbacks, many generalized FCM algorithms have been proposed in the literature, such as Yu and Yang [17] with a unified model for those varieties of generalized FCM algorithms. However, these varieties of FCM still have two problems. These are sensitivity to initial values and necessity to pre-assume the number of clusters. Although there have many validity functions been proposed to find an optimal number of clusters, they always heavily depend on clustering algorithms. Yang and Wu [16] proposed a similarity-based clustering method (SCM). The SCM can self-organize the data into a better estimated number of clusters without initial cluster centers and pre-assumed number of clusters. Yang and Wu [16] exhibited SCM with three robust clustering characteristics: Robust to the initialization (cluster number and initial guesses), robust to cluster volumes (ability to detect different volumes of clusters), and robust to noise and outliers. The SCM algorithm had been successfully used in cluster analysis on the extra-solar planets [11].

In this paper, we embed the SCM algorithm into Eisen's tree view such that microarray gene expression data can be self-organized by SCM. We then use Eisen's tree view for the display of microarray gene expression data. Two gene data sets, lymphoma data and leukemia data, will be used for demonstration and comparisons. We compare Eisen's tree view with-SCM and without-SCM for these gene data sets. The results show the effectiveness of the proposed SCM-driven tree view.

2   The Proposed SCM-driven Tree View

Let $X = \{x_1, x_2, \cdots, x_n\} \subset R^s$ be a data set where x_j is a feature vector in the s-dimensional Euclidean space R^s. For a given c, $2 \leq c < n$, $v = \{v_1, v_2, \cdots, v_c\}$ denotes the cluster centers where $v_i \in R^s$. The Euclidean norm $\|x_j - v_i\|$ is used as the dissimilarity measure between x_j and the ith cluster center v_i. The SCM algorithm proposed by Yang and Wu [16] is an alternating optimization procedure to find v_i to maximize the total similarity measure $J_s(v)$ with

$$J_s(v) = \sum_{j=1}^{n} \sum_{i=1}^{c} \left(\exp- \frac{\|x_j - v_i\|^2}{\beta} \right)^{\gamma} \tag{1}$$

where the parameter γ is used to determine the location of the peaks of $J_s(v)$ and β is defined by

$$\beta = \frac{\sum_{j=1}^{n} \|x_j - \bar{v}\|^2}{n} \quad \text{with } \bar{v} = \frac{\sum_{j=1}^{n} x_j}{n} \tag{2}$$

To analyze the effect of γ, let $J_s^{\gamma}(x_k)$ be the total similarity of the data point x_k to all data points with

$$J_s^{\gamma}(x_k) = \sum_{j=1}^{n} \left(\exp- \frac{\|x_j - x_k\|^2}{\beta} \right)^{\gamma}, \quad k = 1, \cdots, n.$$

The function $J_s^{\gamma}(x_k)$ can describe the density shape of the data points in the neighborhood of x_k. Thus, the correlation between the values of $J_s^{\gamma_1}(x_k)$ and $J_s^{\gamma_2}(x_k)$ can be used as a tool to select a better parameter γ. A higher correlation gives a better γ. The procedure to choose a better γ is called a correlation comparison algorithm (CCA) [16].

After we estimate the approximate density shape of the data set with the estimate γ using the CCA, the next step is to find v_i that maximizes the SCM objective function $J_s(v)$. We differentiate $J_s(v)$ with respect to all v_i and set them to zero. We have the necessary condition with the following update equation

$$v_i = \sum_{j=1}^{n} x_j \left(\exp- \frac{\|x_j - v_i\|^2}{\beta} \right)^{\gamma} \bigg/ \sum_{j=1}^{n} \left(\exp- \frac{\|x_j - v_i\|^2}{\beta} \right)^{\gamma} \tag{3}$$

Here β is assigned to be the sample variance as equation (2) and γ is obtained by the CCA procedure. Although v_i in equation (3) cannot be solved directly, we can used the fixed-point iterative method to approximate it. Let the right side of equation (3) be $f(v_i)$. The first step is to specify the initial value $v_i^{(0)}$ and then compute $f(v_i^{(0)})$ and set it to be $v_i^{(1)}$. Repeat the steps until the $(k+1)$th solution $v_i^{(k+1)}$ is very close to the kth solution. This procedure is called a similarity clustering algorithm (SCA) in Yang and Wu [16]. When we implement SCA, we use $v^{(0)} = (v_1^{(0)}, \cdots, v_n^{(0)}) = (x_1, \cdots, x_n)$ as initial n cluster centers. After the SCA converges, the final n cluster centers $v^{(*)} = (v_1^{(*)}, \cdots, v_n^{(*)})$ will self-organize into c^*

modes. We are then able to use any agglomerative hierarchical clustering (AHC) method to identify these c^* clusters. Totally, the SCM procedure is combined by three algorithms of CCA, SCA and AHC. Because Eisen's tree view uses AHC as a clustering method, we can combine tree view with SCM together under the AHC step. Before processing AHC for tree view, we implement SCM to re-organize gene data. We call it the SCM-driven tree view. We use the two gene data sets, lymphoma data and leukemia data, for comparisons. The experimental data and results will be shown and analyzed in the next section.

3   Experimental Data and Results

The first experimental data used in this section is the Lymphoma data set. To conduct a systematic characterization of gene expression in B-cell malignancies, Alizadeh et al. [Alizadeh, 00] designed a specialized microarray, the 'Lymphochip', by selecting genes that are preferentially expressed in lymphoid cells and genes with known or suspected roles in processes important in immunology or cancer. In the Lymphochip, ~1.8-million measurements of gene expression were made in 96 normal and malignant lymphocyte samples using 128 lymphochip macroarrays. Alizadeh et al. [1] displayed and analyzed these lymphoma data using Eisen's tree view. In this paper, we use lymphoma data to comapare the SCM-driven tree view with the Eisen's tree view.

The second experimental data used in this section is the Leukemia data set. Leukemia data consists of 38 bone marrow samples with 27 acute lymphoblastic leukemia (ALL) and 11 acute myeloid leukemia (AML) obtained from acute leukemia patients at the time of diagnosis. It is known that leukemia data is a popular data set as a test case in the cancer classification community where ALL is usually divided into T and B cell subtypes, marked as ALL-T and ALL-B. Brunet et al. [4] used this leukemia data set to compare their nonnegative matrix factorization (NMF) method with several other clustering methods with respect to the efficacy and stability in recovering these subtypes and their hierarchy. In this paper, we use the leukemia data set to comapare the SCM-driven tree view with the Eisen's tree view.

Lymphoma data use 96 normal and malignant lymphocyte samples with 128 lymphochip macroarrays. In lymphoma data set, there are the three most prevalent adult lymphoid malignancies: diffuse large B-cell lymphoma (DLBCL), follicular lymphoma (FL) and chronic lymphocytic leukaemia (CLL). Because there are missing data in lymphoma data set, we first consider to discarding the data if there exists a missing value. We finally have a whole data set without missing of 854×96 lymphoma data. We have the results shown in Fig. 1 using Eisen's tree view for this data set. Figure 1 consists of three parts: AHC clustering, colors for DLBCL, FL and CLL, and tree view. Blue represents DLBCL, Grey represents FL, and yellow represents CLL. According to AHC clustering, we can see there are three clusters there. However, it is difficult to find more information from tree view.

We implement SCM for these 854×96 lymphoma data with first considering row feature vectors using CCA. We get $\gamma_1 = 30$. We then implement SCM for these 854×96 lymphoma data with considering column feature vectors using CCA. We get $\gamma_2 = 15$. We run SCA for row feature vectors with $\gamma_1 = 30$ and run SCA for column feature vectors with $\gamma_2 = 15$. We finally have AHC clustering and tree view. The results are shown in Fig. 2. We find that both of Figs. 1 and 2 present almost the same results.

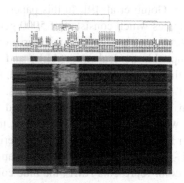

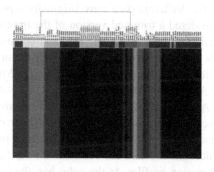

Fig. 1. Results from Eisens's tree view for 854×96 lymphoma data

Fig. 2. Results from SCM-driven tree view for 854×96 lymphoma data with $\gamma_1 = 30$ and $\gamma_2 = 15$

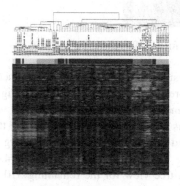

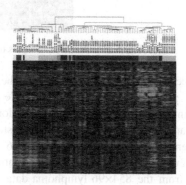

Fig. 3. Results from the SCM-driven tree view for 854×96 lymphoma data $\gamma_1 = 10$ and $\gamma_2 = 5$

Fig. 4. Results from Eisens's tree view for the chosen 544×96 lymphoma data

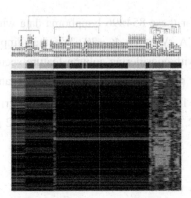

Fig. 5. Results from Eisens's tree view for 310×96 lymphoma data

Because the parameter γ affects the SCA results, we consider another parameters with $\gamma_1=30/3=10$ and $\gamma_2=15/3=5$. We get the results shown in Fig. 3. From Fig. 3, we find a big group with the same color. That means SCM had given a pattern with the same characteristic. We are interested in this pattern with 544×96 data. We then implement tree view for the 544×96 data and the results are shown in Fig. 4. However, it shows there is no information there. Thus, we can discard these 544×96 data from the 854×96 lymphoma data. We run tree view for the remaining 310×96 lymphoma data. The results are shown in Fig. 5. The tree view presents good clustering results. This means that we are able to use the SCM-driven tree view to select more useful data from macroarray data sets. We next make advanced analysis for the leukemia data set.

The leukemia data were originally reported by Golub et al. [9]. In this paper, we considered a trimmed version of the training samples which consisted of 5000 genes used by Brunet et al. [4]. The data contains 38 Affymetrix Hgu6800 microarry data sets obtained from 27 patients with acute lymphoblastic leukemia (ALL) and 11 patients with acute myeloid leukemia (AML) at the time of diagnosis. In addition, the 27 ALL samples can be subdivided into 8 ALL-T samples and 19 ALL-B samples.

After standardizing the data across rows, an AHC clustering was performed by Eisen's cluster software. The clustering result was then viewed using Eisen's tree view as shown in Fig. 6. There are three parts in Fig. 6 including the AHC clustering dendrogram. These are color bar for AML, ALL-B, and ALL-T, and the heat map of expression profiles. In the color bar, the yellow color represents AML, the blue color represents ALL-B, and the red color represents ALL-T. According to the AHC clustering dendrogram, there are five clusters. They are one cluster for AML, one cluster for ALL-T, and the other three clusters for ALL-B. However, it seems to be difficult to get more information from the heat map.

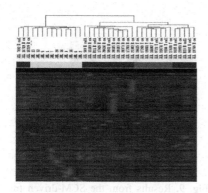
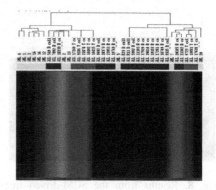

Fig. 6. Results from Eisens's tree view for 5000×38 leukemia data set

Fig. 7. Results from the SCM-driven tree view for 5000×38 leukemia data set

We implement SCM on row feature vectors of these 5000×38 leukemia data using CCA. The finding estimate for optimal γ_1 was 10. Then, the SCM is again implemented on column feature vectors of these 5000×38 leukemia data using CCA. The resultant estimate for optimal γ_2 was 15. As a rule of thumb as seen in Lymphoma case, SCA would result better clustering patterns by using about one-third of the optimal γ_1 and γ_2. Accordingly, the SCA with $\gamma_1 = 3$ for the row feature vectors and SCA with $\gamma_2 = 5$ for column feature vectors were run sequentially. Finally, the AHC was performed to get the clustering dendrogram and the heat map of expression profiles. The results were shown in Fig. 7.

In Fig. 7, the color bar shows a complicated mixed pattern for AML, ALL-B, and AL-T. Moreover, it also shows that the majority of the heat map is consisted of 4844 genes and it displays an identical pattern in rows. That is, after SCM these 4844 genes had shown a pattern with the same characteristic. As a result, the 4844 genes all together could only contribute the same amount of information to the clustering just like each of the 4844 genes. It is also understandable that the AHC clustering results on these 4844 genes would not be good as shown in Fig. 8 because the color bar becomes more complicated. Therefore, we are then interested in the clustering pattern based on the rest of the 156 genes. So the AHC was only run on the 156x38 data and the finding results were shown in Fig. 9. In Fig. 9, the AHC clustering dendrogram suggests that there are mainly three clusters. According to the color bar, there is an AML (yellow) sample being mis-clustered into ALL_B (blue), an ALL_B (blue) sample being mis-clustered into ALL_T (red), and an ALL_B (blue) sample being mis-clustered into AML (yellow). Based on the results above, we conclude that the SCM can correctly cluster/classify 35 Leukemia samples out of 38 samples where it is close to the classification rate (36/38) reported in Golub et al. [9].

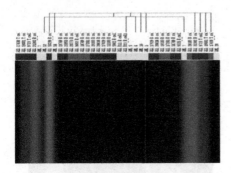
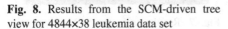

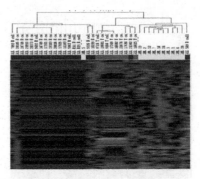

Fig. 8. Results from the SCM-driven tree view for 4844×38 leukemia data set

Fig. 9. Results from the SCM-driven tree view for 156×38 leukemia data set

To make comparison among the 156 SCM selected genes, the 50 genes selected by Golub et al. [9] and the top 24 genes selected by Aris and Recce [2] are used. The Entrez Gene ID [14] is applied as a common gene identifier. Each of the 3 sets of genes is searched for its corresponding Entrez Gene ID. Interestingly, it is found that the 156 SCM selected genes include 21 of the 50 Golub's selected genes [9] based on the Entrez Gene IDs. However, these 156 SCM selected genes only capture 5 of the top 24 genes selected by Aris and Recce [2]. After searching thoroughly through the Entrez Gene database, 742 human Gene IDs is found related to leukemia as on October 16, 2006. Moreover, 11 genes out of 50 genes selected by Golub et al. [9] and 11 genes out of the top 24 genes selected by Aris and Recce [2] are found in these 742 human Gene IDs, while 30 of the SCM identified genes are found. In fact, these 30 SCM-leukemia related genes are also found that they cover 8 out of the 11 Golub's leukemia related genes and 3 out of the 11 Aris-Recce's leukemia related genes. Therefore, we can suggest that the 156 SCM selected genes contain good biological information for clustering/classifying leukemia microarray data.

4   Conclusions

In this paper we proposed the SCM-driven tree view display for microarray data. The use of SCM can re-organize the structure of data such that Eisen's tree view has a better dendrogram display for microarray data. In fact, the proposed SCM-driven tree view can direct us to discard these less information data and then keep more useful data. When we applied the SCM-driven tree view to the leukemia data set, we finally had the remaining 156 genes. To make advanced analysis along with Golub et al. [9] and Aris and Recce [2], we found that these selected 156 genes actually contain good biological information.

References

1. Alizadeh, A.A., Eisen, M.B., Davis, R.E., Ma, C., Lossos, I., Rosenwald, A., Boldrick, J.C., Brown, P.O., Staudt, L.M.: Distinct types of diffuse large B-cell lymphoma identified by gene expression profiling. Nature 403, 503–511 (2000)
2. Aris, V., Recce, M.: A method to improve detection of disease using selectively expressed genes in microarray data. In: Lin, S.M., Johnson, K.F. (eds.) Methods of Microarray Data Analysis, pp. 69–80. Kluwer Academic, New York (2002)
3. Bezdek, J.C.: Pattern Recognition with fuzzy objective function algorithms. Plenum Press, New York (1981)
4. Brunet, J.P., Tamayo, P., Golub, T.R., Mesirov, J.P.: Metagenes and molecular pattern discovery using matrix factorization. Proc. Natl. Acad. Sci. USA 101, 4164–4169 (2004)
5. Dembéle, D., Kastner, P.: Fuzzy c-means method for clustering microarray data. Bioinformatics 19, 973–980 (2003)
6. Eisen, M.B., Spellman, P.T., Brown, P.O., Botstein, D.: Cluster Analysis and Display of Genome-Wide Expression Patterns. Proc. Natl. Acad. Sci. USA 95, 14863–14868 (1998)
7. Eisen's Tree View, Availabe from Eisen Laboratory at
   http://rana.lbl.gov/EisenSoftware.htm
8. Gasch, A.P., Eisen, M.B.: Exploring the conditional coregulation of yeast gene expression through fuzzy k-means clustering. Genome Biology 3, 1–22 (2002)
9. Golub, T.R., Slonim, D.K., Tamayo, P., Bloomfield, C.D., Lander, E.S.: Molecular classification of cancer: Class discovery and class prediction by gene expression monitoring. Science 286, 531–537 (1999)
10. Hartigan, J.A.: Clustering Algorithms. Wiley, New York (1975)
11. Jiang, I.G., Yeh, L.C., Hung, W.L., Yang, M.S.: Data analysis on the extra-solar planets using robust clustering. Monthly Notices of the Royal Astronomical Society 370, 1379–1392 (2006)
12. Kaufman, L., Rousseeuw, P.J.: Finding groups in data: An introduction to cluster analysis. Wiley, New York (1990)
13. MacQueen, J.: Some methods for classification and analysis of multivariate observations. In: Proc. 5th Berkeley Symposium, pp. 281–297 (1967)
14. Maglott, D., Ostell, J., Pruitt, K.D., Tatusova, T.: Entrez Gene: gene-centered information at NCBI. Nucleic Acids Research 33, 54–58 (2005)
15. Yang, M.S.: A survey of fuzzy clustering. Mathematical and Computer Modeling 18, 1–16 (1993)
16. Yang, M.S., Wu, K.L.: A similarity-based robust clustering method. IEEE Trans. Pattern Analysis and Machine Intelligence 26, 434–448 (2004)
17. Yu, J., Yang, M.S.: Optimality test for generalized FCM and its application to parameter selection. IEEE Trans. Fuzzy Systems 13, 164–176 (2005)
18. Zadeh, L.A.: Fuzzy sets. Information and Control 8, 338–353 (1965)

New Method for Dynamic Signature Verification Using Hybrid Partitioning

Marcin Zalasiński[1], Krzysztof Cpałka[1], and Meng Joo Er[2]

[1] Częstochowa University of Technology,
Institute of Computational Intelligence, Poland
{marcin.zalasinski,krzysztof.cpalka}@iisi.pcz.pl
[2] Nanyang Technological University,
School of Electrical & Electronic Engineering, Singapore
emjer@ntu.edu.sg

Abstract. Dynamic signature is behavioural biometric attribute which is commonly used to identity verification. Methods based on the partitioning are one of the types of methods for identity verification using signature biometric attribute. These methods divide trajectories of the signature into parts and during verification phase compare created fragments of trajectories in each partition. Partitioning is performed on the basis of values of signals describing dynamics of signing process (e.g. pen velocity or pen pressure). In this paper we propose a new method for dynamic signature verification using hybrid partitioning. Partitions in the proposed method can be interpreted as, for example, high velocity in the first phase of the signing process or low pressure in the final phase of the signing process. Our method assumes use of all partitions during classification process and our classifier is based on the flexible neuro-fuzzy system of the Mamdani type. Simulations were performed using public SVC2004 dynamic signature database.

1 Introduction

Signature is a behavioural biometric attribute used to verify identity of the individual. This attribute is very interesting from the practical point of view because identity verification using the signature is commonly accepted in the society. However, verification based on the behavioural global features is more difficult than verification based on physiological ones, like fingerprint or iris.

Dynamic signature (called also on-line signature) is signature created in the real time using some kind of input digital device, e.g. graphic tablet. It contains also information about the dynamics of signing, like velocity and pressure signals changing over time. This information are very useful during verification process and increases its accuracy.

Approaches to identity verification based on dynamic signature may be categorized into few groups, one of them are methods based on signature partitioning (see [23]). In this paper we propose a new method for dynamic signature verification based on hybrid of horizontal and vertical partitioning (see [9], [65]).

L. Rutkowski et al. (Eds.): ICAISC 2014, Part II, LNAI 8468, pp. 216–230, 2014.

First, signature is divided into partitions on the basis of time indexes values, because we assume that some regions of the signature acquired in certain timeframe can be more characteristic for the user than other regions. Next, trajectory in each selected partition is divided into two parts on the basis of velocity and pressure signals average values. Previous researches have shown that combination of velocity and pressure with shape makes verification more effective than use of the separated dynamic features (see [17], [23]-[24], [63]-[65]). The partitioning allows selection of the most discriminative features of the signature which belong to the user. In the verification phase we propose flexible neuro-fuzzy system of the Mamdani type (see e.g. [6], [8], [14], [50]-[51]). Our method assumes partitioning signatures into few subspaces (number of subspaces results from the product of the number of horizontal and vertical partitions) which are weighted by weights of importance and used during classification process. In this process we use data from all partitions created during training phase.

This paper is organized into 4 sections. Section 2 contains detailed description of the algorithm. Simulation results are presented in Section 3. Conclusions are drawn in Section 4.

2   Detailed Description of the Algorithm

In our method we use four signals of the signature over time: x-trajectory, y-trajectory, pressure and velocity. First three of them are acquired directly from the graphic tablet and the velocity is first derivative of the signature trajectory. Before beginning of the main phase of the method, all training signatures of the signer i should be pre-processed by commonly used methods to remove some intra-class variations (see e.g. [17], [18], [33], [40]). Signatures are pre-processed with reference to one signature of the user (called base signature) which is the most similar to all training signatures. During pre-processing the length, rotation, scale and offset of the signatures are matched. After a pre-processing, main phase of training process is performed.

The individual steps of the algorithm are detailed below: **Step 1. Partitioning of signatures.** First, signatures are partitioned on the basis of time indices values into two parts. Next, fragment of the signature in each partition is divided into two parts on the basis of the average value of pressure and velocity signal. This second step is also performed in two phases: 1) velocity and pressure signals are divided into two parts, 2) partitioning of the whole signature is performed, signature elements which time points corresponding to the velocity and pressure signals are assigned to the appropriate partition. After this phase signatures are divided into eight parts (four partitions related to the velocity and four partitions related to the pressure). This step is performed during the training and the test phase. **Step 2. Templates generation.** In this step templates, which contains average values of training signatures signals, are generated for each partition. The templates are regarded as the reference signature of the user. This step is performed only during training phase. **Step 3. Determination of similarities between signatures and template in each partition.** In this step similarities between each signature of the user and template are calculated for each partition. In the training phase the similarities are used for determination of the classifier. In the test phase the similarities are created only for the test signature. They are used in the classification process. This step is performed during training and test phase. **Step 4. Determination of the partition importance in the classification process.** In this step weights of importance for each partition are created. They allow to evaluate which partition contains information characteristic for the user. The weights are used in the verification process. This step is performed only during training phase. **Step 5. Preliminary separation of the reference signatures in the partition.** During this step linear boundary of the inclusion of genuine signatures in each partition is created (see [64]). The boundary is used to determine fuzzy sets applied in the classification process. This step is performed only during training phase. **Step 6. Determination of the parameters of fuzzy classifier of genuineness of the signatures.** The parameters describe fuzzy sets of the classifier, which is used in the classification phase. Fuzzy rules describe a way of test signature classification. The fuzzy sets in the rules are based on decision boundaries determined in the step 5. Therefore they may be interpretable. This step is performed only during training phase. **Step 7. Classification of the genuineness of the signatures.** In this step signature is classified as genuine or forgery. In this process flexible neuro-fuzzy system of the Mamdani type is used. This step is performed only during test phase.

We can see that steps 1-6 are performed during training phase, while steps 1,3,7 are performed during test phase.

After training phase, velocity and pressure signals of the base signature, information about partitions and parameters of the classifier are stored into the database. These information will be used in the test phase.

2.1   Vertical Signature Partitioning

First, vertical partitioning based on selected time intervals of signing is performed. This is possible because lengths of the signals of all signatures are the same through the pre-processing. Alignment of the length is performed using Dynamic Time Warping algorithm (see e.g. [22]), which operates on the basis of matching velocity and pressure signals. Result of this matching is a map of corresponding points of the signatures signals, which is used to match trajectories of the signature (see [9]). Vertical partitions $partv_{i,j,k}^{\{s\}}$ of the sample k of the signature j of the signer i based on signal s (velocity v or pressure z) are created using the following equation:

$$partv_{i,j,k}^{\{s\}} = \begin{cases} 1 & \text{for} \quad 0 < k \leq \frac{L_i}{P^{\{s\}}} \\ 2 & \text{for} \quad \frac{L_i}{P^{\{s\}}} < k \leq \frac{2L_i}{P^{\{s\}}} \\ \quad \vdots \\ P^{\{s\}} & \text{for} \quad \frac{(P^{\{s\}}-1)L_i}{P^{\{s\}}} < k \leq L_i \end{cases}, \tag{1}$$

where s is a signal type (velocity or pressure) used during alignment phase, i is the user number ($i = 1, 2, \ldots, I$), j is the signature number ($j = 1, 2, \ldots, J$), L_i is a number of samples of the user i, k is the sample number ($k = 1, 2, \ldots, L_i$) and $P^{\{s\}}$ is a number of partitions ($P^{\{s\}} \ll L_i$). In this method we have assumed, that $P^{\{v\}} = P^{\{z\}} = 2$.

2.2 Horizontal Signature Partitioning

After vertical partitioning, horizontal partitioning of the signature is performed. In the first step of this process average values $avg_{i,p}^{\{s\}}$ of velocity and pressure signals of the base signature are computed for each vertical partition. This is described by the following formula:

$$avg_{i,p}^{\{s\}} = \frac{1}{K_{i,p}} \sum_{k=1}^{K_{i,p}} s_{i,j=jBase,p,k}, \tag{2}$$

where $K_{i,p}$ in number of samples in the vertical partition p ($p = 1, 2$) of the user i, $s_{i,j,p,k} \in \{v_{i,j,p,k}, z_{i,j,p,k}\}$ is signal (velocity v or pressure z) value of the sample k ($k = 1, 2, \ldots, K_{i,p}$), which belongs to the vertical partition p, of the base signature (for which $j = jBase$) of the signer i.

Next, division into horizontal partitions on the basis of values determined in (2) is performed. Horizontal partition $parth_{i,j,p,k}^{\{s\}}$ of the sample k, which belongs to the vertical partition p (of the index specified in the formula (1)), of the signature j of the signer i based on signal s (velocity v or pressure z) is determined as follows:

$$parth_{i,j,p,k}^{\{s\}} = \begin{cases} 1 \text{ for } s_{i,j,p,k} < avg_{i,p}^{\{s\}} \\ 2 \text{ for } s_{i,j,p,k} \geq avg_{i,p}^{\{s\}} \end{cases}. \tag{3}$$

We use two horizontal partitions, because our previous research have shown that method based on two partition achieves best performance.

In the next step templates of the signatures for each partition are generated.

2.3 Generation of the Templates

Template $\mathbf{ta}_{i,p,r}^{\{s\}}$ of the partition p, r (p denotes index of the vertical partition described by the formula (1), r denotes index of the horizontal partition described by the formula (2)) of the signer i for signatures aligned with use of signal s (velocity v or pressure z) and trajectory a (x or y) is described by the following equation:

$$\mathbf{ta}_{i,p,r}^{\{s\}} = \left[ta_{i,p,r,1}^{\{s\}}, ta_{i,p,r,2}^{\{s\}}, \ldots, ta_{i,p,r,K_{i,p,r}^{\{s\}}}^{\{s\}} \right], \tag{4}$$

where $K_{i,p,r}^{\{s\}}$ in number of samples in the partition p, r ($r = 1, 2$), determined for signal s, of the user i, $ta_{i,p,r,k}^{\{s\}}$ is template value for the time step k of the partition p, r of the signer i for signatures aligned with use of signal s (velocity v or pressure z) and trajectory a (x or y) which is calculated by the formula:

$$ta_{i,p,r,k}^{\{s\}} = \frac{1}{J} \sum_{j=1}^{J} a_{i,j,p,r,k}^{\{s\}}, \tag{5}$$

where $a_{i,j,p,r,k}^{\{s\}}$ is trajectory (x or y) value in the sample k of the partition p, r, determined for signal s (velocity v or pressure z), of the signature j of the signer i.

Next, distances between templates from all partitions and each signature trajectory are calculated.

2.4   Determination of Similarities between Signatures and Template in Each Partition

Distance $da_{i,j,p,r}^{\{s\}}$ between template of the partition p, r, determined for signal s (velocity v or pressure z) of the signer i and trajectory a (x or y), and the signature j of the signer i is described by the following equation:

$$da_{i,j,p,r}^{\{s\}} = \sqrt{\sum_{k=1}^{K_{i,p,r}^{\{s\}}} \left(ta_{i,p,r,k}^{\{s\}} - a_{i,j,p,r,k}^{\{s\}} \right)^2}. \tag{6}$$

The next phase of this step is calculation of distances between templates and signatures in two dimensional space. Distance $d_{i,j,p,r}^{\{s\}}$, between the trajectory of signature j of the signer i and template of the signer i in the partition p, r, determined for signal s (velocity v or pressure z), is calculated by the formula:

$$d_{i,j,p,r}^{\{s\}} = \sqrt{\left(dx_{i,j,p,r}^{\{s\}} \right)^2 + \left(dy_{i,j,p,r}^{\{s\}} \right)^2}. \tag{7}$$

The values $d_{i,j,p,r}^{\{s\}}$ are used directly to determine the parameters of the fuzzy sets of the signature classifier.

In the next step, weights of importance for partitions are calculated.

2.5   Determination of the Partition Importance in the Classification Process

The weights are created on the basis of mean distances $\bar{d}_{i,p,r}^{\{s\}}$ between signatures and template in partitions and standard deviation of distances in each partition. The mean distance $\bar{d}_{i,p,r}^{\{s\}}$ between signatures of the signer i and the template of the signer i in the partition p, r, determined for signal s (velocity v or pressure z), is calculated by the formula:

$$\bar{d}_{i,p,r}^{\{s\}} = \frac{1}{J} \sum_{j=1}^{J} d_{i,j,p,r}^{\{s\}}. \tag{8}$$

Standard deviation of signatures $\sigma_{i,p,r}^{\{s\}}$ of the user i from the partition p, r, determined for signal s (velocity v or pressure z), is calculated using the following equation:

$$\sigma_{i,p,r}^{\{s\}} = \sqrt{\frac{1}{J} \sum_{j=1}^{J} \left(\bar{d}_{i,p,r}^{\{s\}} - d_{i,j,p,r}^{\{s\}} \right)^2}. \tag{9}$$

Next, weights of importance are calculated. Weight $w_{i,p,r}^{'\{s\}}$ of the partition p, r, determined for signal s (velocity v or pressure z), of the user i is calculated by the following formula:

$$w_{i,p,r}^{'\{s\}} = \bar{d}_{i,p,r}^{\{s\}} \cdot \sigma_{i,p,r}^{\{s\}}. \tag{10}$$

After that, weights should be normalized to simplify the classification phase. Weight $w_{i,p,r}^{\{s\}}$ of the partition p, r, determined for signal s (velocity v or pressure z), of the user i is normalized by the following equation:

$$w_{i,p,r}^{\{s\}} = 1 - \frac{c_w \cdot w_{i,p,r}^{'\{s\}}}{\max \left\{ w_{i,p,r}^{'\{s\}} \right\}}, \tag{11}$$

where $c_w \in (0, 1]$ is the auxiliary constant of the normalization, which prevents elimination of the partitions associated with a small values of the weights from the classification process (in our simulations we assumed that $c_w = 0.9$).

In the next step, preliminary separation of the reference signatures in the partitions is realized.

2.6 Preliminary Separation of the Reference Signatures in the Partition

In the considered problem, immediate adaptation of the method for verification of new users' signature is required. This eliminates the possibility of machine learning in the classifier selection. Therefore, we developed a flexible neuro-fuzzy classifier which requires properly prepared descriptors, determined once on the basis of the reference signatures of the user.

The boundary of the inclusion of genuine signatures is determined by exploiting the consistency of dissimilarity measures in training signatures (see [23], [24]). Parameters of the boundary are computed using the means and standard deviations of the distances. The mean distance $\bar{da}_{i,p,r}^{\{s\}}$, between signatures of the signer i and template of the signer i in the partition p, r, determined for signal s (velocity v or pressure z) and trajectory a (x or y), is calculated by the formula:

$$\bar{da}_{i,p,r}^{\{s\}} = \frac{1}{J} \sum_{j=1}^{J} da_{i,j,p,r}^{\{s\}}. \tag{12}$$

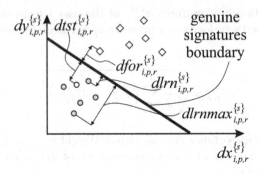

Fig. 1. Illustration of the genuine signature boundary. Genuine training signatures of the user are described as circles, genuine training signatures of other users are described as diamonds.

Standard deviation of signatures $\sigma a_{i,p,r}^{\{s\}}$ of the user i from the partition p, r, determined for signal s (velocity v or pressure z) and trajectory a (x or y), is calculated using the following equation:

$$\sigma a_{i,p,r}^{\{s\}} = \sqrt{\frac{1}{J} \sum_{j=1}^{J} \left(\bar{d}a_{i,p,r}^{\{s\}} - da_{i,j,p,r}^{\{s\}} \right)^2}. \tag{13}$$

The linear boundary of the inclusion of genuine signatures in the slope-intercept form is presented as follows:

$$dy\,(dx) = -\frac{\sigma y_{i,p,r}^{\{s\}}}{\sigma x_{i,p,r}^{\{s\}}} dx + c_{i,p,r}^{\{s\}} \cdot \bar{d}x_{i,p,r}^{\{s\}} \cdot \left(\frac{\sigma y_{i,p,r}^{\{s\}}}{\sigma x_{i,p,r}^{\{s\}}} + 1 \right), \tag{14}$$

where $c_{i,p,r}^{\{s\}}$ is constant parameter used to adjust the position of the line, which is determined in such a way that $dlrn_{i,p,r}^{\{s\}}$ is equal to $dfor_{i,p,r}^{\{s\}}$, as depicted in Fig. 1.

Remarks on Fig. 1 can be summarized as follows: **(a)** Grey circles in Fig. 1 represent the distances between signatures and templates created individually for each user (see (6), (7)). Therefore, they represent the instability of the signature created by the individual user within each partition and they are not interpretable clusters of data. Theoretically, grey circles should lie exactly in the centre of the coordinate system. In practice, large distance between grey circles and the origin of the coordinate system means that quality of the acquired signatures is low and the reliability of the dynamic signature of the user is also low. In other words, in the context of considered user the method is not reliable, because the user is unable to create in a similar way a few signatures at the same time. **(b)** White circles in Fig. 1 theoretically should also be exactly in the centre of the coordinate system, because they represent signatures created by the user in the test phase. In practice, it is expected that the white circles will be placed at a certain distance from the origin of the coordinate system (e.g. due to changes of signature in time). **(c)** Diamonds in Fig. 1 represent the signatures of other users. Therefore, they should be significantly further from the origin of the coordinate system than white circles. **(d)** Fuzzy rules of the classifier define a way of signature classification which depends on the location of the descriptors $(dtst_{i,p,r}^{\{s\}})$ of the test signature in relation to the boundary of the inclusion of the reference signatures of the user. Please note that the sample (white circle) does not have to be classified as false, even if it is located over the boundary of the inclusion of the reference signatures of the user in the partition (within the inclusion area of false signatures). This happens when: (1) sample in the other partitions is more similar to the template, (2) the reliability of the partition is small (the partition is associated with the low value of the weight). It is a distinctive feature of our method against the methods presented in other works. **(e)** Values $dlrnmax_{i,p,r}^{\{s\}}$ (see Fig. 1) have an impact on spacing of fuzzy sets, which represent values $\{low, high\}$ assumed by the linguistic variables "the truth of the signature of user i from the partition p, r, determined for signal s".

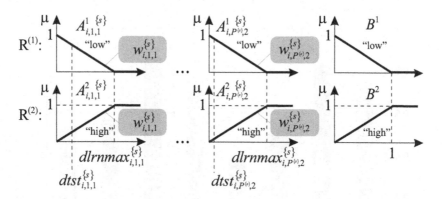

Fig. 2. Input and output fuzzy sets of the flexible neuro-fuzzy system of the Mamdani type for signature verification

Next, determination of the classifier is performed.

2.7 Determination of the Parameters of Fuzzy Classifier of Genuineness of the Signatures

In this step flexible Mamdani-type neuro-fuzzy system is used. Neuro-fuzzy systems combine the natural language description of fuzzy systems (see e.g. [1]-[5], [10]-[13], [16], [21], [25], [28], [34], [45]-[47], [60]-[61]) and the learning properties of neural networks (see e.g. [7], [26], [29]-[32], [35]-[39], [41]-[42], [48], [55]-[56], [58]-[59]). Alternative approaches to classification can be found in [15], [20], [43]-[44], [49], [52]-[54], [57]. Our system works on the basis of two fuzzy rules presented as follows:

$$
\left\{
\begin{array}{l}
R^{(1)}: \left[
\begin{array}{l}
\text{IF} \left(dtst_{i,1,1}^{\{s\}} \text{is} A_{i,1,1}^{1\ \{s\}} \right) \Big| w_{i,1,1}^{\{s\}} \text{ OR} \\
\left(dtst_{i,1,2}^{\{s\}} \text{is} A_{i,1,2}^{1\ \{s\}} \right) \Big| w_{i,1,2}^{\{s\}} \text{ OR} \\
\vdots \\
\left(dtst_{i,P\{s\},1}^{\{s\}} \text{is} A_{i,P\{s\},1}^{1\ \{s\}} \right) \Big| w_{i,P\{s\},1}^{\{s\}} \text{ OR} \\
\left(dtst_{i,P\{s\},2}^{\{s\}} \text{is} A_{i,P\{s\},2}^{1\ \{s\}} \right) \Big| w_{i,P\{s\},2}^{\{s\}} \text{ THEN} y_i \text{is} B^1
\end{array}
\right] \\[2em]
R^{(2)}: \left[
\begin{array}{l}
\text{IF} \left(dtst_{i,1,1}^{\{s\}} \text{is} A_{i,1,1}^{2\ \{s\}} \right) \Big| w_{i,1,1}^{\{s\}} \text{ OR} \\
\left(dtst_{i,1,2}^{\{s\}} \text{is} A_{i,1,2}^{2\ \{s\}} \right) \Big| w_{i,1,2}^{\{s\}} \text{ OR} \\
\vdots \\
\left(dtst_{i,P\{s\},1}^{\{s\}} \text{is} A_{i,P\{s\},1}^{2\ \{s\}} \right) \Big| w_{i,P\{s\},1}^{\{s\}} \text{ OR} \\
\left(dtst_{i,P\{s\},2}^{\{s\}} \text{is} A_{i,P\{s\},2}^{2\ \{s\}} \right) \Big| w_{i,P\{s\},2}^{\{s\}} \text{ THEN} y_i \text{is} B^2
\end{array}
\right]
\end{array}
\right\}, \qquad (15)
$$

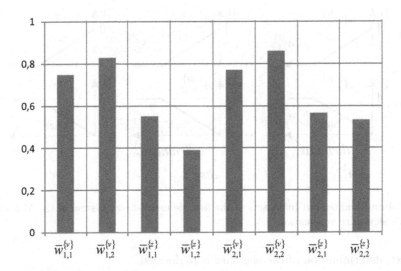

Fig. 3. Average values of weights of the users determined for each partition of dynamic signature

where **(a)** $dtst_{i,p,r}^{\{s\}}$ are input linguistic variables, whose numeric value is a distance between the test signature trajectory of the signer i and the linear boundary of the inclusion of genuine signatures in the partition p, r, determined for signal s. **(b)** $A_{i,p,r}^{1\ \{s\}}$, $A_{i,p,r}^{2\ \{s\}}$ are input fuzzy sets related to the signal $s \in \{v, z\}$ shown in Fig. 2. Fuzzy sets $A_{i,p,r}^{1\ \{s\}}$ and $A_{i,p,r}^{2\ \{s\}}$ represent values $\{$low, high$\}$ assumed by input linguistic variables $dtst_{i,p,r}^{\{s\}}$. **(c)** y_i is input linguistic variable interpreted as reliability of signature. **(d)** B^1, B^2 are output fuzzy sets shown in Fig. 2. Fuzzy sets B^1, B^2 represent values $\{low, high\}$ assumed by output linguistic variable determining the reliability of signature. **(e)** $w_{i,p,r}^{\{s\}}$ are weights of the partition p, r, determined for signal s, of the user i.

Signature is considered true if the following assumption is satisfied:

$$
\bar{y}_i = \cfrac{S^* \left\{ \begin{array}{c} \mu_{A_{i,1,1}^2}^{\{s\}} \left(dtst_{i,1,1}^{\{s\}}\right), \mu_{A_{i,1,2}^2}^{\{s\}} \left(dtst_{i,1,2}^{\{s\}}\right), \ldots, \\ \mu_{A_{i,P\{s\},1}^2}^{\{s\}} \left(dtst_{i,P\{s\},1}^{\{s\}}\right), \mu_{A_{i,P\{s\},2}^2}^{\{s\}} \left(dtst_{i,P\{s\},2}^{\{s\}}\right); \\ w_{i,1,1}^{\{s\}}, w_{i,1,2}^{\{s\}} \ldots, w_{i,P\{s\},1}^{\{s\}}, w_{i,P\{s\},2}^{\{s\}} \end{array} \right\}}{\left(\begin{array}{c} S^* \left\{ \begin{array}{c} \mu_{A_{i,1,1}^2}^{\{s\}} \left(dtst_{i,1,1}^{\{s\}}\right), \mu_{A_{i,1,2}^2}^{\{s\}} \left(dtst_{i,1,2}^{\{s\}}\right), \ldots, \\ \mu_{A_{i,P\{s\},1}^2}^{\{s\}} \left(dtst_{i,P\{s\},1}^{\{s\}}\right), \mu_{A_{i,P\{s\},2}^2}^{\{s\}} \left(dtst_{i,P\{s\},2}^{\{s\}}\right); \\ w_{i,1,1}^{\{s\}}, w_{i,1,2}^{\{s\}} \ldots, w_{i,P\{s\},1}^{\{s\}}, w_{i,P\{s\},2}^{\{s\}} \end{array} \right\} + \\ S^* \left\{ \begin{array}{c} \mu_{A_{i,1,1}^1}^{\{s\}} \left(dtst_{i,1,1}^{\{s\}}\right), \mu_{A_{i,1,2}^1}^{\{s\}} \left(dtst_{i,1,2}^{\{s\}}\right), \ldots, \\ \mu_{A_{i,P\{s\},1}^1}^{\{s\}} \left(dtst_{i,P\{s\},1}^{\{s\}}\right), \mu_{A_{i,P\{s\},2}^1}^{\{s\}} \left(dtst_{i,P\{s\},2}^{\{s\}}\right); \\ w_{i,1,1}^{\{s\}}, w_{i,1,2}^{\{s\}} \ldots, w_{i,P\{s\},1}^{\{s\}}, w_{i,P\{s\},2}^{\{s\}} \end{array} \right\} \end{array} \right)} > cth_i,
$$

$$(16)$$

where **(a)** $S^* \{\cdot\}$ is a weighted t-conorm (see [6]). **(b)** $\bar{y}_i$ is the value of the output signal of applied neuro-fuzzy system (see e.g [27]) described by rules (15). Detailed description of the system can be found in [51]. Formula (16) was created by taking into account in the description of system simplification resulting from the spacing of fuzzy sets shown in Fig. 2: $\mu_{A_{i,p,r}^1}^{\{s\}}(0) = 1$, $\mu_{A_{i,p,r}^1}^{\{s\}}\left(dlrnmax_{i,p,r}^{\{s\}}\right) = 0$, $\mu_{A_{i,p,r}^2}^{\{s\}}(0) = 0$, and $\mu_{A_{i,p,r}^2}^{\{s\}}\left(dlrnmax_{i,p,r}^{\{s\}}\right) = 1$. **(c)** $cth_i \in [0,1]$ - coefficient determined experimentally during training phase for each user to eliminate disproportion between FAR and FRR error (see [62]). The parameters $cth_i \in [0,1]$, computed individually for the user i, are used during verification process in the test phase.

3   Simulation Results

The simulation was performed using public SVC2004 signature database which contains signatures of 40 users. The signatures were acquired in two sessions using the digitizing tablet. In the first session each user created 10 genuine signatures. In the second session, each user came again to create another 10 genuine signatures. In this session he/she also created four skilled forgeries for five other users. The SVC2004 database contains 20 genuine signatures and 20 skilled forgeries for each user.

Test procedure proceeded as follows for signatures of each from 40 signers available in the database. During training phase we used 5 randomly selected (from 20) genuine signatures of each signer. During test phase we used 10 randomly selected (from the remaining 15) genuine signatures and all 20 skilled forgeries of each signer. The process was performed five times, and the results were averaged. The described method is commonly used in evaluating the effectiveness of methods for dynamic signature verification, which corresponds to the standard crossvalidation procedure. The test was performed using the authorial testing environment implemented in C# language.

We also implemented some other methods based on partitioning to compare the results of our simulations: 1) method presented in [17] which achieves very good results, 2) our previous method based on vertical partitioning proposed in [9], 3) our previous method based on horizontal partitioning proposed in [65].

Table 1 contains simulation results described as values of FAR (False Acceptance Rate) and FRR (False Rejection Rate), which are commonly used in biometrics (see e.g. [19]). As mentioned earlier, in the simulations we assumed that a number of vertical partitions is equal to 2 and a number of horizontal partition is also equal to 2. Moreover, we present average values of weights of importance for each partition ($\bar{w}_{p,r}^{\{s\}}$), averaged in the context of the users (see Fig. 3), which describe reliability of the signature in the partitions.

Table 1. Results of simulation performed by the system (16)

Method	Average FAR	Average FRR	Average error
Ibrahim et al. [17]	11.05 %	13.75 %	12.40 %
Zalasiński & Cpałka [65]	12.15 %	11.00 %	11.58 %
Cpałka & Zalasiński [9]	10.51 %	10.45 %	10.99 %
Our method	**11.73 %**	**9.95 %**	**10.84 %**

4 Conclusions

In this paper we presented a new method for dynamic signature verification using hybrid partitioning. In this method the signature is divided into few vertical parts, which are divided into two horizontal parts. All created partitions are used during classification process. The method assumes use of the classifier based on the Mamdani type neuro-fuzzy system which is characterized by very good accuracy and ease of interpretation of the collected knowledge. Accuracy achieved in our simulations performed using SVC2004 database proves the correctness of the proposed assumptions. Moreover, the simulations show that partitions created on the basis of the velocity signal are more reliable than partitions created on the basis of the pressure signal. This is due to the higher value of weights (11) associated with the partitions of the signal v (see 3). The most reliable partition is the one created in the final phase of the signing process ($p = 2$) and associated with the high value ($r = 2$) of the velocity signal v.

Acknowledgment. The project was financed by the National Science Centre (Poland) on the basis of the decision number DEC-2012/05/B/ST7/02138.

References

1. Bartczuk, Ł., Dziwiński, P., Starczewski, J.T.: A New Method for Dealing with Unbalanced Linguistic Term Set. In: Rutkowski, L., Korytkowski, M., Scherer, R., Tadeusiewicz, R., Zadeh, L.A., Zurada, J.M. (eds.) ICAISC 2012, Part I. LNCS (LNAI), vol. 7267, pp. 207–212. Springer, Heidelberg (2012)
2. Bartczuk, Ł., Dziwiński, P., Starczewski, J.T.: New Method for Generation Type-2 Fuzzy Partition for FDT. In: Rutkowski, L., Scherer, R., Tadeusiewicz, R., Zadeh, L.A., Zurada, J.M. (eds.) ICAISC 2010, Part I. LNCS, vol. 6113, pp. 275–280. Springer, Heidelberg (2010)
3. Bartczuk, Ł., Przybył, A., Dziwiński, P.: Hybrid state variables - fuzzy logic modelling of nonlinear objects. In: Rutkowski, L., Korytkowski, M., Scherer, R., Tadeusiewicz, R., Zadeh, L.A., Zurada, J.M. (eds.) ICAISC 2013, Part I. LNCS, vol. 7894, pp. 227–234. Springer, Heidelberg (2013)
4. Bartczuk, Ł., Rutkowska, D.: A New Version of the Fuzzy-ID3 Algorithm. In: Rutkowski, L., Tadeusiewicz, R., Zadeh, L.A., Żurada, J.M. (eds.) ICAISC 2006. LNCS (LNAI), vol. 4029, pp. 1060–1070. Springer, Heidelberg (2006)
5. Bartczuk, Ł., Rutkowska, D.: Medical Diagnosis with Type-2 Fuzzy Decision Trees. In: Kącki, E., Rudnicki, M., Stempczyńska, J. (eds.) Computers in Medical Activity. AISC, vol. 65, pp. 11–21. Springer, Heidelberg (2009)
6. Cpalka, K.: A Method for Designing Flexible Neuro-fuzzy Systems. In: Rutkowski, L., Tadeusiewicz, R., Zadeh, L.A., Żurada, J.M. (eds.) ICAISC 2006. LNCS (LNAI), vol. 4029, pp. 212–219. Springer, Heidelberg (2006)
7. Cpałka K., Łapa K., Przybył A., Zalasiński M.: A new method for designing neuro-fuzzy systems for nonlinear modelling with interpretability aspects, Neurocomputing (in print, 2014), http://dx.doi.org/10.1016/j.neucom.2013.12.031
8. Cpałka, K., Rutkowski, L.: Flexible Takagi Sugeno Neuro-fuzzy Structures for Nonlinear Approximation. WSEAS Transactions on Systems 9(4), 1450–1458 (2005)
9. Cpałka, K., Zalasiński, M.: On-line signature verification using vertical signature partitioning. Expert Systems with Applications 41, 4170–4180 (2014)
10. Dziwiński, P., Bartczuk, Ł., Starczewski, J.T.: Fully controllable ant colony system for text data clustering. In: Rutkowski, L., Korytkowski, M., Scherer, R., Tadeusiewicz, R., Zadeh, L.A., Zurada, J.M. (eds.) EC 2012 and SIDE 2012. LNCS, vol. 7269, pp. 199–205. Springer, Heidelberg (2012)
11. Dziwiński, P., Rutkowska, D.: Algorithm for generating fuzzy rules for WWW document classification. In: Rutkowski, L., Tadeusiewicz, R., Zadeh, L.A., Żurada, J.M. (eds.) ICAISC 2006. LNCS (LNAI), vol. 4029, pp. 1111–1119. Springer, Heidelberg (2006)
12. Dziwiński, P., Rutkowska, D.: Ant focused crawling algorithm. In: Rutkowski, L., Tadeusiewicz, R., Zadeh, L.A., Zurada, J.M. (eds.) ICAISC 2008. LNCS (LNAI), vol. 5097, pp. 1018–1028. Springer, Heidelberg (2008)
13. Dziwiński, P., Starczewski, J.T., Bartczuk, Ł.: New linguistic hedges in construction of interval type-2 FLS. In: Rutkowski, L., Scherer, R., Tadeusiewicz, R., Zadeh, L.A., Zurada, J.M. (eds.) ICAISC 2010, Part II. LNCS, vol. 6114, pp. 445–450. Springer, Heidelberg (2010)
14. Gabryel, M., Cpałka, K., Rutkowski, L.: Evolutionary strategies for learning of neuro-fuzzy systems. In: Proceedings of the I Workshop on Genetic Fuzzy Systems, Granada, pp. 119–123 (2005)
15. Greblicki, W., Rutkowska, D., Rutkowski, L.: An orthogonal series estimate of time-varying regression. Annals of the Institute of Statistical Mathematics 35(2), 215–228 (1983)

16. Greenfield, S., Chiclana, F.: Type-reduction of the discretized interval type-2 fuzzy set: approaching the continuous case through progressively finer discretization. Journal of Artificial Intelligence and Soft Computing Research 1(3), 183–193 (2011)
17. Ibrahim, M.T., Khan, M.A., Alimgeer, K.S., Khan, M.K., Taj, I.A., Guan, L.: Velocity and pressure-based partitions of horizontal and vertical trajectories for on-line signature verification. Pattern Recognition 43 (2010)
18. Jain, A.K., Griess, F.D., Connell, S.D.: On-line signature verification. Pattern Recognition 35, 2963–2972 (2002)
19. Jain, A.K., Ross, A.: Introduction to Biometrics. In: Jain, A.K., Flynn, P., Ross, A.A. (eds.) Handbook of Biometrics. Springer (2008)
20. Jaworski, M., Duda, P., Pietruczuk, L.: On fuzzy clustering of data streams with concept drift. In: Rutkowski, L., Korytkowski, M., Scherer, R., Tadeusiewicz, R., Zadeh, L.A., Zurada, J.M. (eds.) ICAISC 2012, Part II. LNCS (LNAI), vol. 7268, pp. 82–91. Springer, Heidelberg (2012)
21. Jelonkiewicz, J., Przybył, A.: Accuracy improvement of neural network state variable estimator in induction motor drive. In: Rutkowski, L., Tadeusiewicz, R., Zadeh, L.A., Zurada, J.M. (eds.) ICAISC 2008. LNCS (LNAI), vol. 5097, pp. 71–77. Springer, Heidelberg (2008)
22. Jeong, Y.S., Jeong, M.K., Omitaomu, O.A.: Weighted dynamic time warping for time series classification. Pattern Recognition 44, 2231–2240 (2011)
23. Khan, M.A.U., Khan, M.K., Khan, M.A.: Velocity-image model for online signature verification. IEEE Trans. Image Process 15 (2006)
24. Khan, M.K., Khan, M.A., Khan, M.A.U., Lee, S.: Signature verification using velocity-based directional filter bank. In: IEEE Asia Pacific Conference on Circuitsand Systems, APCCAS, pp. 231–234 (2006)
25. Korytkowski, M., Nowicki, R., Rutkowski, L., Scherer, R.: AdaBoost ensemble of DCOG rough–neuro–fuzzy systems. In: Jędrzejowicz, P., Nguyen, N.T., Hoang, K. (eds.) ICCCI 2011, Part I. LNCS, vol. 6922, pp. 62–71. Springer, Heidelberg (2011)
26. Korytkowski, M., Rutkowski, L., Scherer, R.: On combining backpropagation with boosting. In: Proceedings of the IEEE International Joint Conference on Neural Network (IJCNN), vol. 1-10, pp. 1274–1277 (2006)
27. Korytkowski, M., Rutkowski, L., Scherer, R.: From Ensemble of Fuzzy Classifiers to Single Fuzzy Rule Base Classifier. In: Rutkowski, L., Tadeusiewicz, R., Zadeh, L.A., Zurada, J.M. (eds.) ICAISC 2008. LNCS (LNAI), vol. 5097, pp. 265–272. Springer, Heidelberg (2008)
28. Kroll, A.: On choosing the fuzziness parameter for identifying TS models with multidimensional membership functions. Journal of Artificial Intelligence and Soft Computing Research 1(4), 283–300 (2011)
29. Laskowski, L.: A Novel Continuous Dual Mode Neural Network in Stereo-Matching Process. In: Diamantaras, K., Duch, W., Iliadis, L.S. (eds.) ICANN 2010, Part III. LNCS, vol. 6354, pp. 294–297. Springer, Heidelberg (2010)
30. Laskowski, Ł.: A novel hybrid-maximum neural network in stereo-matching process. Neural Comput & Applic. 23, 2435–2450 (2013)
31. Laskowski, Ł.: Hybrid-Maximum Neural Network for Depth Analysis from Stereo-Image. In: Rutkowski, L., Scherer, R., Tadeusiewicz, R., Zadeh, L.A., Zurada, J.M. (eds.) ICAISC 2010, Part II. LNCS, vol. 6114, pp. 47–55. Springer, Heidelberg (2010)
32. Laskowski, Ł.: Objects Auto-selection from Stereo-Images Realised by Self-Correcting Neural Network. In: Rutkowski, L., Korytkowski, M., Scherer, R., Tadeusiewicz, R., Zadeh, L.A., Zurada, J.M. (eds.) ICAISC 2012, Part I. LNCS, vol. 7267, pp. 119–125. Springer, Heidelberg (2012)
33. Lei, H., Govindaraju, V.: A comparative study on the consistency of features in on-line signature verification. Pattern Recognition Letters 26, 2483–2489 (2005)

34. Li, X., Er, M.J., Lim, B.S., Zhou, J.H., Gan, O.P., Rutkowski, L.: Fuzzy Regression Modeling for Tool Performance Prediction and Degradation Detection. International Journal of Neural Systems 20(5), 405–419 (2010)
35. Łapa, K., Przybył, A., Cpałka, K.: A new approach to designing interpretable models of dynamic systems. In: Rutkowski, L., Korytkowski, M., Scherer, R., Tadeusiewicz, R., Zadeh, L.A., Zurada, J.M. (eds.) ICAISC 2013, Part II. LNCS (LNAI), vol. 7895, pp. 523–534. Springer, Heidelberg (2013)
36. Łapa, K., Zalasiński, M., Cpałka, K.: A New Method for Designing and Complexity Reduction of Neuro-fuzzy Systems for Nonlinear Modelling. In: Rutkowski, L., Korytkowski, M., Scherer, R., Tadeusiewicz, R., Zadeh, L.A., Zurada, J.M. (eds.) ICAISC 2013, Part I. LNCS (LNAI), vol. 7894, pp. 329–344. Springer, Heidelberg (2013)
37. Nowicki, R.: Rough-neuro-fuzzy structures for classification with missing data. IEEE Transactions on Systems, Man, and Cybernetics-Part B: Cybernetics 39(6), 1334–1347 (2009)
38. Nowicki, R., Scherer, R., Rutkowski, L.: A method for learning of hierarchical fuzzy systems. In: Sincak, P., Vascak, J., Kvasnicka, V., Pospichal, J. (eds.) Intelligent Technologies - Theory and Applications, pp. 124–129. IOS Press (2002)
39. Nowicki, R., Scherer, R., Rutkowski, L.: A hierarchical neuro-fuzzy system based on simplification. In: Proceedings of International Joint Conference on Neural Networks, IJCNN 2003, Portland, Oregon, pp. 20–24 (2003)
40. O'Reilly, C., Plamondon, R.: Development of a Sigma-Lognormal representation for on-line signatures. Pattern Recognition 42, 3324–3337 (2009)
41. Patan, K., Patan, M.: Optimal Training strategies for locally recurrent neural networks. Journal of Artificial Intelligence and Soft Computing Research 1(2), 103–114 (2011)
42. Peteiro-Barral, D., Bardinas, B.G., Perez-Sanchez, B.: Learning from heterogeneously distributed data sets using artificial neural networks and genetic algorithms. Journal of Artificial Intelligence and Soft Computing Research 2(1), 5–20 (2012)
43. Pietruczuk, L., Duda, P., Jaworski, M.: A new fuzzy classifier for data streams. In: Rutkowski, L., Korytkowski, M., Scherer, R., Tadeusiewicz, R., Zadeh, L.A., Zurada, J.M. (eds.) ICAISC 2012, Part I. LNCS, vol. 7267, pp. 318–324. Springer, Heidelberg (2012)
44. Pietruczuk, L., Duda, P., Jaworski, M.: Adaptation of decision trees for handling concept drift. In: Rutkowski, L., Korytkowski, M., Scherer, R., Tadeusiewicz, R., Zadeh, L.A., Zurada, J.M. (eds.) ICAISC 2013, Part I. LNCS, vol. 7894, pp. 459–473. Springer, Heidelberg (2013)
45. Pławiak P., Tadeusiewicz R, Approximation of phenol concentration using novel hybrid computational intelligence methods. Applied Mathematics and Computer Science 24(1) (in print, 2014)
46. Przybył, A., Jelonkiewicz, J.: Genetic algorithm for observer parameters tuning in sensorless induction motor drive. In: Rutkowski, L., Kacprzyk, J. (eds.) Neural Networks and Soft Computing (6th International Conference on Neural Networks and Soft Computing 2002), Zakopane, Poland, pp. 376–381 (2002)
47. Przybył, A., Smoląg, J., Kimla, P.: Distributed Control System Based on Real Time Ethernet for Computer Numerical Controlled Machine Tool (in Polish). Przeglad Elektrotechniczny 86(2), 342–346 (2010)
48. Rutkowski, L.: Computational intelligence. Springer (2008)
49. Rutkowski, L.: On Bayes risk consistent pattern recognition procedures in a quasi-stationary environment. IEEE Transactions on Pattern Analysis and Machine Intelligence PAMI-4(1), 84–87 (1982)
50. Rutkowski, L., Cpałka, K.: Flexible structures of neuro-fuzzy systems. In: Quo Vadis Computational Intelligence. STUDFUZZ, vol. 54, pp. 479–484. Springer, Heidelberg (2000)

51. Rutkowski, L., Cpałka, K.: Flexible weighted neuro-fuzzy systems. In: Proceedings of the 9th International Conference on Neural Information Processing (ICONIP 2002), Orchid Country Club, Singapore, November 18-22 (2002)
52. Rutkowski, L., Jaworski, M., Pietruczuk, L., Duda, P.: Decision trees for mining data streams based on the gaussian approximation. IEEE Transactions on Knowledge and Data Engineering 26(1), 108–119 (2014)
53. Rutkowski, L., Jaworski, M., Pietruczuk, L., Duda, P.: The CART decision tree for mining data streams. Information Sciences 266, 1–15 (2014)
54. Rutkowski, L., Pietruczuk, L., Duda, P., Jaworski, M.: Decision trees for mining data streams based on the McDiarmid's bound. IEEE Transactions on Knowledge and Data Engineering 25(6), 1272–1279 (2013)
55. Rutkowski, L., Przybył, A., Cpałka, K.: Novel on-line speed profile generation for industrial machine tool based on flexible neuro-fuzzy approximation. IEEE Transactions on Industrial Electronics 59, 1238–1247 (2012)
56. Rutkowski, L., Przybył, A., Cpałka, K., Er, M.J.: Online speed profile generation for industrial machine tool based on neuro-fuzzy approach. In: Rutkowski, L., Scherer, R., Tadeusiewicz, R., Zadeh, L.A., Zurada, J.M. (eds.) ICAISC 2010, Part II. LNCS, vol. 6114, pp. 645–650. Springer, Heidelberg (2010)
57. Rutkowski, L., Rafajlowicz, E.: On optimal global rate of convergence of some nonparametric identification procedures. IEEE Transaction on Automatic Control, AC-34(10), 1089–1091 (1989)
58. Scherer, R.: Neuro-fuzzy relational systems for nonlinear approximation and prediction. Nonlinear Analysis Series A: Theory, Methods and Applications 71(12), e1420–e1425 (2009)
59. Scherer, R., Rutkowski, L.: Connectionist fuzzy relational systems. In: 9th International Conference on Neural Information and Processing; 4th Asia-Pacific Conference on Simulated Evolution and Learning; 1st International Conference on Fuzzy Systems and Knowledge Discovery, Singapore. Computational Intelligence for Modelling and Prediction. SCI, vol. 2, pp. 35–47. Springer, Heidelberg (2005)
60. Starczewski, J.T., Scherer, R., Korytkowski, M., Nowicki, R.: Modular Type-2 Neuro-fuzzy Systems. In: Wyrzykowski, R., Dongarra, J., Karczewski, K., Wasniewski, J. (eds.) PPAM 2007. LNCS, vol. 4967, pp. 570–578. Springer, Heidelberg (2008)
61. Szaleniec, M., Goclon, J., Witko, M., Tadeusiewicz, R.: Application of artificial neural networks and DFT-based parameters for prediction of reaction kinetics of ethylbenzene dehydrogenase. Journal of Computer-Aided Molecular Design 20(3), 145–157 (2006)
62. Yeung, D.-Y., Chang, H., Xiong, Y., George, S.E., Kashi, R.S., Matsumoto, T., Rigoll, G.: SVC2004: First International Signature Verification Competition. In: Zhang, D., Jain, A.K. (eds.) ICBA 2004. LNCS, vol. 3072, pp. 16–22. Springer, Heidelberg (2004)
63. Zalasiński, M., Cpałka, K.: A new method of on-line signature verification using a flexible fuzzy one-class classifier. In: Selected Topics in Computer Science Applications, pp. 38–53. EXIT (2011)
64. Zalasiński, M., Cpałka, K.: Novel algorithm for the on-line signature verification. In: Rutkowski, L., Korytkowski, M., Scherer, R., Tadeusiewicz, R., Zadeh, L.A., Zurada, J.M. (eds.) ICAISC 2012, Part II. LNCS (LNAI), vol. 7268, pp. 362–367. Springer, Heidelberg (2012)
65. Zalasiński, M., Cpałka, K.: New approach for the on-line signature verification based on method of horizontal partitioning. In: Rutkowski, L., Korytkowski, M., Scherer, R., Tadeusiewicz, R., Zadeh, L.A., Zurada, J.M. (eds.) ICAISC 2013, Part II. LNCS (LNAI), vol. 7895, pp. 342–350. Springer, Heidelberg (2013)

New Method for Dynamic Signature Verification Based on Global Features

Marcin Zalasiński[1], Krzysztof Cpałka[1], and Yoichi Hayashi[2]

[1] Częstochowa University of Technology,
Institute of Computational Intelligence, Poland
{marcin.zalasinski,krzysztof.cpalka}@iisi.pcz.pl
[2] Meiji University, Department of Computer Science, Japan
hayashiy@cs.meiji.ac.jp

Abstract. Identity verification based on the dynamic signatures is commonly known issue of biometrics. This process is usually done using methods belonging to one of three approaches: global approach, local function based approach and regional function based approach. In this paper we focus on global features based approach which uses the so called global features extracted from the signatures. We present a new method of global features selection, which are used in the training and classification phase in a context of an individual. Proposed method bases on the evolutionary algorithm. Moreover, in the classification phase we propose a flexible neuro-fuzzy classifier of the Mamdani type. Our method was tested using the SVC2004 public on-line signature database.

1 Introduction

Signature is a biometric attribute which is commonly used in the process of identity verification. It belongs to the group of behavioural attributes, like gait (see e.g. [17]), related to the characteristic of individual's behaviour. Verification based on these attributes is more difficult than verification based on the physiological ones, like face or iris (see e.g. [1], [41]-[43], [64]), but it is less invasive.

Signature biometric attribute may be classified into two categories - static (off-line) signature and dynamic (on-line) signature. Static signature, which contains only information about shape of the trajectory, is more common in everyday life (it is on many paper documents), but identity verification based on this type of signature is less reliable than verification based on the dynamic signature. Dynamic signature contains also information about dynamics of the signing process, e.g. velocity, acceleration and pressure. Shape of the on-line signature is represented by the horizontal and vertical trajectories. Methods of the dynamic signature verification may be categorized into three main groups (see e.g. [11]): global features based methods, local function based methods and regional function based methods. Global features based methods use so called global features which are extracted from the signature and used during training and classification phase (see e.g. [32], [36], [67]). Examples of these features are signature total

L. Rutkowski et al. (Eds.): ICAISC 2014, Part II, LNAI 8468, pp. 231–245, 2014.
© Springer International Publishing Switzerland 2014

duration and number of pen-ups. Function based methods compare time functions, which contains information about changes of signature features over time (see e.g. [18], [24]-[25]). In this approach waveforms extracted from the signature are compared to the waveforms of the other signature and classification is made on the basis of this process result. Regional based methods rely on segmentation of signature into some regions, used during training and verification phase (see e.g. [66]-[69]).

In this paper we focus on the approach based on global features. We use a set of global features proposed in [19], which contains extended collection of features from three other papers - [31], [37]-[38]. It should be noted that the operation of our method is not dependent on the adopted feature set, which can be practically arbitrarily reduced or extended. In the approach proposed in this paper, large global feature set is reduced by selection of optimal features subset, which is considered during classification phase. Moreover, global features are ranked and only features with the highest rank value are used in the classification process. Application of evolutionary feature selection in the proposed algorithm is possible thanks to using a new fuzzy one-class classifier.

The problem of global features selection has been considered in the literature (see e.g. [19], [31]). Please note that the method proposed in this paper stands out from the methods of other authors by following characteristics: (a) The proposed method takes advantage of an evolutionary algorithm in the process of feature selection. (b) The proposed method uses in the classification process a hierarchy of features individually for each user. (c)The proposed method takes advantage of the theory of fuzzy sets and fuzzy systems (see e.g. [2]-[6], [12]-[15], [28])

This paper is organized into four sections. In Section 2 we present idea of the new method for dynamic signature verification based on global features. In Section 3 simulation results are presented. Conclusions are drawn in Section 4.

2   Idea of the New Method for Dynamic Signature Verification Based on Global Features

Idea of the proposed method can be summarized as follows: (a) It works on the basis of a set of 85 features describing the dynamics of the dynamic signature which have been systematized, for example, in the paper [19]. As already mentioned, the proposed method does not depend on the base set of features. This set can be freely modified. (b) It uses an evolutionary algorithm with specifically defined evaluation function. The function promotes chromosomes (which correspond to the solutions) encoding a set of features, whose values are homogeneous within the training signatures of the user. (c) It uses (developed for the considered method) one-class classifier which is based on the capacities of the flexible fuzzy system proposed by us earlier (see e.g. [11], [69]). It allows to take into account the weights of importance of individual features, selected individually for each user. (d) It works in two modes: (1) learning and (2) testing (operating mode). In the first mode the selection of features is performed for each user, descriptors of features and weights of importance of features are determined. They are needed for proper work of the classifier in the test phase. These parameters are stored in a database. In the second mode, mode of operation (verification of test signature), the parameters stored for each user in the learning phase are downloaded from the database and then signature verification is realized on the basis of these parameters. It should be noted that the efficiency of the method does not depend on the number of users whose signatures are stored in a database (thus descriptors heterogeneity of individual characteristics of different users is not taken into account). This encumbrance has been introduced intentionally, because it causes that the effectiveness of the method in practical applications does not depend on the number of records in the database. Of course, in the learning phase (as already mentioned) skilled forgeries are not used (they are only used for test of the method), which is an additional advantage of the proposed approach.

2.1 Training Phase

General description of the training phase for the user i (procedure $\texttt{Training}(i)$) can be described as follows: **Step 1.** Acquisition of J training signatures of user i. **Step 2.** Determination of the matrix $\mathbf{G}_i$ of all considered global features, describing dynamics of signatures, for all J training signatures of the user i. **Step 3.** Determination of the vector $\bar{\mathbf{g}}_i$ of average values for each global feature, determined in **Step 2** for J training signatures of the user i. **Step 4.** Evolutionary selection of subset of global features, which are the most characteristic for the user i (procedure $\texttt{EvolutionaryFeaturesSelection}(\mathbf{G}_i, \bar{\mathbf{g}}_i)$). This process is performed on the basis of a similarity of features values computed using chosen distance measure. **Step 5.** Determination of the vector $\mathbf{X}'_i$ which contains information about selected global features characteristic for the user i. Length of the vector (denoted as N) is equal to the number of global features selected in **Step 4**. Please note that the vector $\mathbf{X}'_i$ is in practice the best chromosome from the population considered in the **Step 4** ($\mathbf{X}'_i = \mathbf{X}_{i,chBest}$). **Step 6.** Selection of classifier parameters used in the test phase (procedure $\texttt{ClassifierDetermination}(i, \mathbf{X}'_i, \mathbf{G}_i, \bar{\mathbf{g}}_i)$). **Step 7.** Storing in a database the following information about the user i: vector $\mathbf{X}'_i$, vector $\bar{\mathbf{g}}_i$, parameters of classifier $maxd_{i,n}$ and $w_{i,n}$ ($n = 1, \ldots, N$).

Later in this section steps of the procedure $\texttt{Training}(i)$ have been described in details.

First, acquisition of training signatures for the user i is performed (**Step 1**). Next, the matrix $\mathbf{G}_i$, which contains all considered global features of all J training signatures of user i, is determined (**Step 2**):

$$\mathbf{G}_i = \begin{bmatrix} g_{i,1,1} & g_{i,2,1} & \cdots & g_{i,N,1} \\ g_{i,1,2} & g_{i,2,2} & \cdots & g_{i,N,2} \\ & & \vdots & \\ g_{i,1,J} & g_{i,2,J} & \cdots & g_{i,N,J} \end{bmatrix} = \begin{bmatrix} \mathbf{g}_{i,1} \\ \mathbf{g}_{i,2} \\ \vdots \\ \mathbf{g}_{i,N} \end{bmatrix}, \tag{1}$$

where $\mathbf{g}_{i,j} = \begin{bmatrix} g_{i,1,j} \; g_{i,2,j} \; \cdots \; g_{i,N,j} \end{bmatrix}$, $g_{i,n,j}$ is a value of the global feature, $i = 1, 2, \ldots, I$ is an index of the user, I is a number of the users, $n = 1, 2, \ldots, N$ is a number of the global feature, $j = 1, 2, \ldots, J$ is an index of the signature, J is a number of the signatures created by the user in the acquisition phase (which is a part of the training phase).

In the **Step 3** vector $\bar{\mathbf{g}}_i$ of average values of each global feature of all training signatures J of user i is determined:

$$\bar{\mathbf{g}}_i = [\bar{g}_{i,1}, \bar{g}_{i,2}, \ldots, \bar{g}_{i,N}], \tag{2}$$

where $\bar{g}_{i,n}$ is average value of the global feature n of training signatures of the user i, computed using the following formula (**Step 3**):

$$\bar{g}_{i,n} = \frac{1}{J} \sum_{j=1}^{J} g_{i,n,j}. \tag{3}$$

In the next step (**Step 4**) selection of the optimal subset of global features for the user i is performed. For this purpose the algorithm Evolutionary FeaturesSelection$(\mathbf{G}_i, \bar{\mathbf{g}}_i)$, described in Section 2.2, is used. The procedure EvolutionaryFeaturesSelection$(\mathbf{G}_i, \bar{\mathbf{g}}_i)$ returns the subset of global features $\mathbf{X}'_i$ which are used during creation of the classifier (**Step 5**). In the **Step 6** classifier for the user i is determined. Next, all data required in the process of classifier determination and signature verification (vector $\mathbf{X}_{i,ch}$, vector $\bar{\mathbf{g}}_i$, parameters of the classifier $maxd_{i,n}$ and $w_{i,n}$) are stored into a database (**Step 7**). Detailed description of the classifier determination is presented in Section 2.4.

2.2 Evolutionary Features Selection

The main step in the learning phase Training(i) is **Step 4**, in which evolutionary selection of features for the user i is performed. The procedure of features selection is called EvolutionaryFeaturesSelection$(\mathbf{G}_i, \bar{\mathbf{g}}_i)$. Remarks on the considered procedure can be summarized as follows: **(a)** It uses the binary encoding in which each of the genes of individual chromosomes encodes the information whether the corresponding feature has to be taken into account in the process of signature verification of considered user i (a gene encoding a value "1" means that the feature associated with this gene has to be considered in the process of signature verification). Thus, each of the chromosomes has a length corresponding to the number of all considered features and encodes a subset of the features. Further in the paper, it is assumed that $\mathbf{X}_{i,ch} = [X_{i,ch,g=1}, X_{i,ch,g=2}, \ldots, X_{i,ch,g=N}]$ means chromosome with index ch, $ch = 1, 2, \ldots, Ch$, in a population associated with the user i, whose number of genes is equal to the number of features (the value N). **(b)** The procedure EvolutionaryFeaturesSelection$(\mathbf{G}_i, \bar{\mathbf{g}}_i)$ is consistent with the typical scheme of the evolutionary algorithm, therefore it will not be considered in detail. It includes the initialization of the population, population evaluation, selection of chromosomes from the population, the evolution of the chromosomes in the population carried by the application of evolutionary operators (in the simulations we use crossover and mutation), checking of the stopping criterion. A detailed description of the algorithm can be found, among others, in [8], [67]. (c) The originality of the proposed approach results from a specific way of determining the evaluation function of chromosomes from the population. Evaluation of the chromosomes is based on the similarity of features for the user's reference signatures created in the training phase. The objective of the algorithm is to minimize the evaluation function, thus such features are preferred, whose values (determined for the reference signatures created in the training phase) for the user are the most similar to each other according to the adopted measure of similarity. Details of the procedure $\texttt{CalculateFf}(i, \mathbf{G}_i, \bar{\mathbf{g}}_i, \mathbf{X}_{i,ch})$ are described in the Section 2.3. (d) Evolutionary features selection can be performed using other algorithms based on the population, which differ in their approach to exploration and exploitation of a space of considerations. (e) The result of the procedure $\texttt{EvolutionaryFeaturesSelection}(\mathbf{G}_i, \bar{\mathbf{g}}_i)$ is the information about the set of features describing the stability of signing in the learning phase by the user i. This information is stored in the best chromosome of the last step of performed evolution process. Next, it is rewritten into a vector $\mathbf{X}'_i$, whose length is equal to N (as a length of the chromosome $\mathbf{X}_{i,ch}$).

2.3   Determination of Fitness Function

In the definition of the fitness function of the chromosome, the following input parameters are taken into account: (a) i - an index of the user for which the training process is performed. (b) $\mathbf{G}_i$ - a matrix of all global features values, determined for all reference signatures of the user i. (c) $\bar{\mathbf{g}}_i$ - a vector of average values of global features, averaged in the context of all reference signatures of the user i. (d) $\mathbf{X}_{i,ch}$ - a chromosome with index ch in the population associated with the user i, for which the value of the evaluation function is calculated.

General description of the procedure for determining the evaluation function of chromosomes belonging to the population and encoding subsets of features ($\texttt{CalculateFf}(i, \mathbf{G}_i, \bar{\mathbf{g}}_i, \mathbf{X}_{i,ch})$) is the following: **Step 1.** Determination of the covariance matrix for the matrix of all global features. It should be noted that during determination of the covariance matrix only the global features from the subset of the features encoded in the chromosome $\mathbf{X}_{i,ch}$ are taken into account. In the further description of the method, the matrix of the subset of global features created by combining $\mathbf{G}_i$ and $\mathbf{X}_{i,ch}$ will be denoted as $\mathbf{G}'$ and the covariance matrix corresponding to the matrix $\mathbf{G}'$ will be denoted as cov$(\mathbf{G}')$. A vector containing the elements of the row j of the matrix $\mathbf{G}'$ will be denoted as $\mathbf{g}'_j$. Number of rows of the matrix $\mathbf{G}'$ results from the number of reference signatures of the user i created during acquisition phase (training) and it is equal to J. Number of columns of the matrix $\mathbf{G}'$ results from the number of features encoded in the chromosome $\mathbf{X}_{i,ch}$ (the number of non-zero elements in the vector). Please note that the matrix $\mathbf{G}'$ will not be used anywhere outside the procedure $\texttt{CalculateFf}(i, \mathbf{G}_i, \bar{\mathbf{g}}_i, \mathbf{X}_{i,ch})$. **Step 2.** Determination of the vector of Mahalanobis distances (see e.g. [16]) $\mathbf{m}$ between the vector of average values of the global features and the matrix of the global features values. It should be noted that only the global features from the subset of features encoded in the chromosome $\mathbf{X}_{i,ch}$ are taken into account during determination of the Mahalanobis distances vector $\mathbf{m}$. Thus, in the further description of the method the vector of average values of the subset of global features created by combining $\bar{\mathbf{g}}_i$ and $\mathbf{X}_{i,ch}$ will be denoted as $\bar{\mathbf{g}}'$. It will be used during determination of the value of the vector $\mathbf{m}$. Number of elements of the vector $\mathbf{m}$ results from the number of reference signatures of the user i created in the acquisition phase (training) and it is equal to J. Please note that vectors $\bar{\mathbf{g}}'$ and $\mathbf{m}$ will not be used anywhere outside the procedure $\texttt{CalculateFf}(i, \mathbf{G}_i, \bar{\mathbf{g}}_i, \mathbf{X}_{i,ch})$. **Step 3.** Determination of the evaluation function of the chromosome $\mathbf{X}_{i,ch}$. Value of this function (denoted as ff $(\mathbf{X}_{i,ch})$) is determined by averaging the values of the Mahalanobis distances vector $\mathbf{m}$.

Later in this section a detailed description of the function $\texttt{CalculateFf}(i, \mathbf{G}_i, \bar{\mathbf{g}}_i, \mathbf{X}_{i,ch})$ is provided.

In the **Step 1** covariance matrix $\mathrm{cov}\,(\mathbf{G}')$ of global features encoded in the chromosome is created. Covariance is a measure of the linear correlation between the global features of the reference signatures of the user (and created in the acquisition phase). Thus, the covariance matrix $\mathrm{cov}\,(\mathbf{G}')$ is a square matrix $N \times N$, where N is a number of features. Next, values m_j, $j = 1, 2, \ldots, J$, of the vector of Mahalanobis distances are determined using the following formula:

$$m_j = \sqrt{(\mathbf{g}' - \bar{\mathbf{g}}')^T \left(\mathrm{cov}(\mathbf{G}')\right)^{-1} (\mathbf{g}' - \bar{\mathbf{g}}')}. \tag{4}$$

It should be noted that for each subset of features J distances are created. The subset of features associated with the lowest distance is the most valuable for the user i in the training phase. In the **Step 3** value of the fitness function of the chromosome $\mathbf{X}_{i,ch}$ is determined as follows:

$$\mathrm{ff}\,(\mathbf{X}_{i,ch}) = \frac{1}{J}\sum_{j=1}^{J} m_j. \tag{5}$$

Lower value of the fitness function means that the chromosome is "better" (subset of global features encoded in the chromosome $\mathbf{X}_{i,ch}$ is the most characteristic for the user i).

2.4 Determination of Classifier

General form of the procedure $\texttt{ClassifierDetermination}(i, \mathbf{X}'_i, \mathbf{G}_i, \bar{\mathbf{g}}_i)$, which determines parameters of the our classifier, can be presented as follows: **Step 1.** Determination of Euclidean distances $d_{i,n,j}$ between each global feature n encoded in the chromosome $\mathbf{X}'_i$ and average value of the global feature for all J signatures of the user i. **Step 2.** Selection of maximum distance for each global feature n from distances determined in **Step 1**. It should be emphasized that the maximum distance (labelled as $maxd_{i,n}$) are individual for each user i.

They will be used in the classification phase of the signature (verification of the authenticity). Therefore, they must be stored in a database (in addition to the parameters: vector $\mathbf{X}'_i$, vector $\bar{\mathbf{g}}_i$). **Step 3.** Computation of weights of importance $w_{i,n}$, associated with the feature number n of the user i and used in the classification phase. It should be emphasized that the weights also have individual character for the user i and they will be used in the classification process of the signature. Therefore, they must be stored in a database. **Step 4.** Creation of the flexible neuro-fuzzy system using values determined in **Step 2** and **Step 3**.

In the **Step 1** distances $d_{i,n,j}$ between each global feature n encoded in $\mathbf{X}'_i$ and average value of the global feature for all J signatures of the user i is computed using the following formula:

$$d_{i,n,j} = X''_{i,n} \cdot \sqrt{\left(\bar{\mathbf{g}}_{i,n} - \mathbf{g}_{i,n,j}\right)^2}, \tag{6}$$

where $X'_{i,n} \in \{0,1\}$ is gene value of the chromosome $\mathbf{X}'_i$, associated with the feature number n. Next, maximum distance for each global feature is selected (**Step 2**):

$$maxd_{i,n} = \max_{j=1,\ldots,J} \{d_{i,n,j}\}. \tag{7}$$

In the **Step 3** weights of importance of features $w_{i,n}$ for each global feature n of the user i are determined. Weight of the global feature n of the user i is computed on the basis of standard deviation of the global feature n of the user i and average value of distances for the global feature n of the user i (computed in the **Step 2**). This process is described by the following formula:

$$w_{i,n} = \frac{\sqrt{\frac{1}{J}\sum_{j=1}^{J}\left(g_{i,n} - g_{i,n,j}\right)^2}}{\frac{1}{J}\sum_{j=1}^{J} d_{i,n,j}}. \tag{8}$$

Next, a classifier is created (**Step 4**). We use flexible neuro-fuzzy system of the Mamdani type (see e.g. [50]). Neuro-fuzzy systems (see e.g. [27], [56], [60]-[63]) combine the natural language description of fuzzy systems (see e.g. [21]-[23], [29]-[30], [46]-[48]) and the learning properties of neural networks (see e.g. [7], [26], [33]-[34], [39]-[40], [44]-[45], [53]-[55], [57]-[58], [66]). Alternative approaches to classification can be found in [49], [51]-[52]. Our system is based on the rules in the form if-then. The fuzzy rules contain fuzzy sets which represent the values, e.g. "low" and "high", of the input and output linguistic variables. In our method the input linguistic variables are dependent on the similarity between the global features of the test signature and average values of global features computed on the basis of training signatures. The system uses only features selected individually for the user during evolutionary selection process. Output linguistic variables describe the reliability of the signature. In our method input parameters of fuzzy sets are individually selected for each user (**Step 2** of the procedure ClassifierDetermination$(i, \mathbf{X}'_i, \mathbf{G}_i, \bar{\mathbf{g}}_i)$). Please note that if training signatures are more similar to each other, the tolerance of our classifier is lower. The flexibility of the classifier results from the possibility of using in the classification the importance of global features, which are selected individually for each user (**Step 3** of the procedure ClassifierDetermination$(i, \mathbf{X}'_i, \mathbf{G}_i, \bar{\mathbf{g}}_i)$). Taking into account the weights of importance of the global features is possible thanks to the use of proposed by us earlier (see e.g. [20]) aggregation operators named the weighted triangular norms.

Our system works on the basis of two fuzzy rules presented as follows:

$$
\left\{
\begin{array}{l}
R^{(1)} : \begin{bmatrix} \text{IF } \left(dtst_{i,1}\text{is}A^1_{i,1}\right) \big| w_{i,1}\text{AND } \left(dtst_{i,2}\text{is}A^1_{i,2}\right) \big| w_{i,2}\text{AND}\dots \\ \text{AND } \left(dtst_{i,N}\text{is}A^1_{i,N}\right) \big| w_{i,N}\text{THEN}y_i\text{is}B^1 \end{bmatrix} \\[4mm]
R^{(2)} : \begin{bmatrix} \text{IF } \left(dtst_{i,1}\text{is}A^2_{i,1}\right) \big| w_{i,1}\text{AND } \left(dtst_{i,2}\text{is}A^2_{i,2}\right) \big| w_{i,2}\text{AND}\dots \\ \text{AND } \left(dtst_{i,N}\text{is}A^2_{i,N}\right) \big| w_{i,N}\text{THEN}y_i\text{is}B^2 \end{bmatrix}
\end{array}
\right. , \tag{9}
$$

where **(a)** $A^1_{i,n}, A^2_{i,n}, i = 1, 2, \dots, I, n = 1, 2, \dots, N$, are input fuzzy sets related to the global feature number n of the user i. Fuzzy sets $A^1_{i,1}, A^1_{i,2}, \dots, A^1_{i,N}$ represent values "high" assumed by input linguistic variables $dtst_{i,n}$ in the test phase and variables $d_{i,n,j}$ in the training phase, computed using (6), both for signatures in the training phase and the test phase. Analogously, fuzzy sets $A^2_{i,1}, A^2_{i,2}, \dots, A^2_{i,N}$ represent values "low" assumed by input linguistic variables $dtst_{i,n}$ in the test phase and variables $d_{i,n,j}$ in the training phase. Thus, each rule contains N antecedents. In the fuzzy classifier of the signature used in the simulations we applied a Gaussian membership function (see Fig. 1) for all input fuzzy sets. **(b)** y_i, $i = 1, 2, \dots, I$, is output linguistic variable interpreted as reliability of the signature considered to be created by the signer i. **(c)** B^1, B^2 are output fuzzy sets shown in Fig. 1. Fuzzy set B^1 represents value "high" of output linguistic variable determining the reliability of the signature. Analogously, fuzzy set B^2 represents value "low" of output linguistic variable determining the reliability of the signature. In the fuzzy classifier of the signature used in the simulations we applied the membership function of type γ in the rule 1 and the membership function of type L in the rule 2. Please note that the membership function of fuzzy sets B^1 and B^2 are the same for all users. **(d)** $w_{i,n}, i = 1, 2, \dots, I, n = 1, 2, \dots, N$, are weights of importance related to the global feature number n of the user i.

2.5   Identity Verification Phase

The process of signature verification (SignatureVerification(i)) is performed in the following way: **Step 1.** Acquisition of test signature of the user which is considered as user i. **Step 2.** Download of information about selected features of the user i ($\mathbf{X}'_i$), average values of this features computed during training phase ($\bar{\mathbf{g}}_i$) and classifier parameters of the user i from the database ($maxd_{i,n}, w_{i,n}$). **Step 3.** Determination of values of global features which have been selected as the most characteristic for the user i in the training phase. **Step 4.** Verification of the test signature using one class flexible neuro-fuzzy classifier.

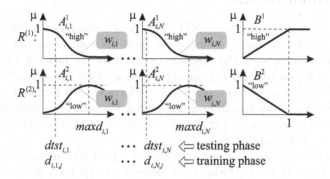

Fig. 1. Input and output fuzzy sets of the flexible neuro-fuzzy system of the Mamdani type for verification signature of user i

In the **Step 1** user which identity will be verified creates one test signature. In this step user claims his identity as i. Next, information about selected features of the user i ($\mathbf{X}'_i$), average values of this features computed during training phase ($\bar{\mathbf{g}}_i$) and parameters of the classifier of the user i created during training phase ($maxd_{i,n}$, $w_{i,n}$) are downloaded from the database (**Step 2**). In the **Step 3** system determines global features of the test signature. Finally, verification is performed using flexible one-class neuro-fuzzy classifier of the Mamdani type (**Step 4**). A signature is true if the following assumption is satisfied:

$$\bar{y}_i = \frac{T^* \left\{ \mu_{A^1_{i,1}} \left(dtst_{i,1} \right), \ldots, \mu_{A^1_{i,N}} \left(dtst_{i,N} \right); w_{i,1}, \ldots, w_{i,N} \right\}}{\left(\begin{array}{c} T^* \left\{ \mu_{A^1_{i,1}} \left(dtst_{i,1} \right), \ldots, \mu_{A^1_{i,N}} \left(dtst_{i,N} \right); w_{i,1}, \ldots, w_{i,N} \right\} + \\ + T^* \left\{ \mu_{A^2_{i,1}} \left(dtst_{i,1} \right), \ldots, \mu_{A^2_{i,N}} \left(dtst_{i,N} \right); w_{i,1}, \ldots, w_{i,N} \right\} \end{array} \right)} > cth_i,$$

(10)

where **(a)** $T^* \{\cdot\}$ is the algebraic weighted t-norm (see [50]), **(b)** $\mu_A (\cdot)$ is a Gaussian membership function, **(c)** $\mu_{B^1} (\cdot)$ is a membership function of the class L, **(d)** $\mu_{B^2} (\cdot)$ is a membership function of the class γ, **(e)** $\bar{y}_i$, $i = 1, 2, \ldots, I$, is the value of the output signal of applied neuro-fuzzy system described by rules (9). Detailed description of the system can be found in [9], [20], **(e)** Formula (10) was created by taking into account in the description of system simplification resulting from the spacing of fuzzy sets, shown in Fig. 1. The simplifications can be described as follows: $\mu_{A^1_{i,n}} (0) = 1$, $\mu_{A^1_{i,n}} (maxd_{i,n}) \approx 0$, $\mu_{A^2_{i,n}} (0) \approx 0$, $\mu_{A^2_{i,n}} \left(maxd_{i,n}^{\{s\}} \right) = 1$. Detailed information about the system described by the rules in the form (9), which allow to easily derive the relationship (10) on the basis of the above assumptions, can be found e.g. in [9]-[10], [20], **(f)** $cth_i \in [0, 1]$ - coefficient determined experimentally for each user to eliminate disproportion between FAR and FRR error (see e.g. [65]).

3   Simulation Results

Simulations were performed using SVC 2004 public database (see [65]). During the simulations the following assumptions have been adopted: **(a)** population contains 100 chromosomes, **(b)** algorithm stops after the lapse of a determined number of 1000 generations, **(c)** during selection of chromosomes tournament selection method is used, **(d)** crossover is performed with probability equal to 0.8 at three points, **(e)** mutation is performed for each gene with probability equal to 0.02. Details concerning the interpretation of these parameters can be found, among others, in [50], [59].

The database contains 40 signers and for each signer 20 genuine and 20 forgery signatures. The test was performed five times, every time for all signers stored in the database. In training phase 5 genuine signatures (numbers 1-10) of the signer were used. During test phase 10 genuine signatures (numbers 11-20) and 20 forgery signatures (numbers 21-40) of each signer were used. Simulations were performed in the authorial environment implemented in C#.

During simulation we tested three methods of verification based on global features. The one of them was our method described in this paper. Results of the simulations are presented in the Table 1. The table contains values of FAR (False Acceptance Rate) and FRR (False Rejection Rate) errors which are commonly used in the literature to evaluate the effectiveness of identity verification methods (see e.g. [18], [25]).

Moreover, in Fig. 2 information on the frequency of selection of individual features are presented. Each sample in the graph refers to the global feature of the signature and it is a percentage value of the frequency of the feature selection in the context of the 40 users.

Table 1. Results of simulation performed by our system

Method	Average FAR	Average FRR	Average error
PCA using random subspace [35]	25.75 %	24.60 %	25.18 %
Evolutionary selection with PCA [67]	23.87 %	22.65 %	23.26 %
Our method	**16.69 %**	**13.18 %**	**14.94 %**

Conclusions of the simulations can be summarized as follows: **(a)** The accuracy of our method is higher in comparison to the methods described in [35] and [67]. The method proposed in this paper works with clearly greater accuracy for considered database SVC 2004. **(b)** Before carrying out the simulation we expected that in the process of evolutionary selection of features some of them may be chosen more often than others in the context of all users. However, it turned out that none of the features had not dominated the others. This may indicate that the most important in the context of identity verification of the user are sets of features (combinations of features), not their individual features. In addition, it can be seen that the five features have never been selected in the process of evolution.

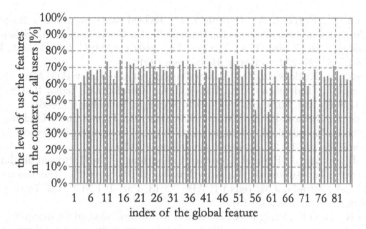

Fig. 2. Percentage frequency of selection of the global features of the signature for users from the database SVC2004

4 Conclusions

In this paper a new method for dynamic signature verification based on global features is presented. The method assumes selection of the subset of global features from a large set of the features. This process is performed using evolutionary algorithm. Its application was made possible by a well-defined evaluation function, which takes into account the diversity of values of the reference signatures for each user and does not require any signatures of other users. The features are selected individually for each user. It is worth noting that during the selection of features none of them clearly dominates the other, what may indicate that the most characteristic for the user are individual combinations of features, not individual features. The achieved accuracy of the signature verification in comparison with other methods proves correctness of the assumptions.

Acknowledgment. The project was financed by the National Science Centre (Poland) on the basis of the decision number DEC-2012/05/B/ST7/02138.

References

1. Abiyev, R.H., Altunkaya, K.: Neural network based biometric personal identification with fast iris segmentation. International Journal of Control, Automation and Systems 7, 17–23 (2009)
2. Bartczuk, Ł., Dziwiński, P., Starczewski, J.T.: A new method for dealing with unbalanced linguistic term set. In: Rutkowski, L., Korytkowski, M., Scherer, R., Tadeusiewicz, R., Zadeh, L.A., Zurada, J.M. (eds.) ICAISC 2012, Part I. LNCS, vol. 7267, pp. 207–212. Springer, Heidelberg (2012)
3. Bartczuk, Ł., Dziwiński, P., Starczewski, J.T.: New Method for Generation Type-2 Fuzzy Partition for FDT. In: Rutkowski, L., Scherer, R., Tadeusiewicz, R., Zadeh, L.A., Zurada, J.M. (eds.) ICAISC 2010, Part I. LNCS, vol. 6113, pp. 275–280. Springer, Heidelberg (2010)

4. Bartczuk, Ł., Przybył, A., Dziwiński, P.: Hybrid state variables - fuzzy logic modelling of nonlinear objects. In: Rutkowski, L., Korytkowski, M., Scherer, R., Tadeusiewicz, R., Zadeh, L.A., Zurada, J.M. (eds.) ICAISC 2013, Part I. LNCS, vol. 7894, pp. 227–234. Springer, Heidelberg (2013)
5. Bartczuk, Ł., Rutkowska, D.: A New Version of the Fuzzy-ID3 Algorithm. In: Rutkowski, L., Tadeusiewicz, R., Zadeh, L.A., Żurada, J.M. (eds.) ICAISC 2006. LNCS (LNAI), vol. 4029, pp. 1060–1070. Springer, Heidelberg (2006)
6. Bartczuk, Ł., Rutkowska, D.: Medical Diagnosis with Type-2 Fuzzy Decision Trees. In: Kącki, E., Rudnicki, M., Stempczyńska, J. (eds.) Computers in Medical Activity. AISC, vol. 65, pp. 11–21. Springer, Heidelberg (2009)
7. Bilski, J., Smoląg, J.: Parallel Approach to Learning of the Recurrent Jordan Neural Network. In: Rutkowski, L., Korytkowski, M., Scherer, R., Tadeusiewicz, R., Zadeh, L.A., Zurada, J.M. (eds.) ICAISC 2013, Part I. LNCS, vol. 7894, pp. 32–40. Springer, Heidelberg (2013)
8. Cpałka K., Łapa K., Przybył A., Zalasiński M.: A new method for designing neuro-fuzzy systems for nonlinear modelling with interpretability aspects, Neurocomputing (in press, 2014), http://dx.doi.org/10.1016/j.neucom,12.031
9. Cpałka, K., Rutkowski, L.: Flexible Takagi Sugeno Neuro-fuzzy Structures for Nonlinear Approximation. WSEAS Transactions on Systems 9(4), 1450–1458 (2005)
10. Cpalka, K.: A Method for Designing Flexible Neuro-fuzzy Systems. In: Rutkowski, L., Tadeusiewicz, R., Zadeh, L.A., Żurada, J.M. (eds.) ICAISC 2006. LNCS (LNAI), vol. 4029, pp. 212–219. Springer, Heidelberg (2006)
11. Cpałka, K., Zalasiński, M.: On-line signature verification using vertical signature partitioning. Expert Systems with Applications 41, 4170–4180 (2014)
12. Dziwiński, P., Bartczuk, Ł., Starczewski, J.T.: Fully controllable ant colony system for text data clustering. In: Rutkowski, L., Korytkowski, M., Scherer, R., Tadeusiewicz, R., Zadeh, L.A., Zurada, J.M. (eds.) EC 2012 and SIDE 2012. LNCS, vol. 7269, pp. 199–205. Springer, Heidelberg (2012)
13. Dziwiński, P., Rutkowska, D.: Algorithm for generating fuzzy rules for WWW document classification. In: Rutkowski, L., Tadeusiewicz, R., Zadeh, L.A., Żurada, J.M. (eds.) ICAISC 2006. LNCS (LNAI), vol. 4029, pp. 1111–1119. Springer, Heidelberg (2006)
14. Dziwiński, P., Rutkowska, D.: Ant focused crawling algorithm. In: Rutkowski, L., Tadeusiewicz, R., Zadeh, L.A., Zurada, J.M. (eds.) ICAISC 2008. LNCS (LNAI), vol. 5097, pp. 1018–1028. Springer, Heidelberg (2008)
15. Dziwiński, P., Starczewski, J.T., Bartczuk, Ł.: New linguistic hedges in construction of interval type-2 FLS. In: Rutkowski, L., Scherer, R., Tadeusiewicz, R., Zadeh, L.A., Zurada, J.M. (eds.) ICAISC 2010, Part II. LNCS, vol. 6114, pp. 445–450. Springer, Heidelberg (2010)
16. De Maesschalck, R., Jouan-Rimbaud, D., Massart, D.L.: The Mahalanobis distance. Chemometrics and Intelligent Laboratory Systems 50, 1–18 (2000)
17. Ekinci, M., Aykut, M.: Human Gait Recognition Based on Kernel PCA Using Projections. Journal of Computer Science and Technology 22, 867–876 (2007)
18. Faundez-Zanuy, M.: On-line signature recognition based on VQ-DTW. Pattern Recognition 40, 981–992 (2007)
19. Fiérrez-Aguilar, J., Nanni, L., Lopez-Peñalba, J., Ortega-Garcia, J., Maltoni, D.: An On-Line Signature Verification System Based on Fusion of Local and Global Information. In: Kanade, T., Jain, A., Ratha, N.K. (eds.) AVBPA 2005. LNCS, vol. 3546, pp. 523–532. Springer, Heidelberg (2005)
20. Gabryel, M.: Cpałka K., Rutkowski L, Evolutionary strategies for learning of neuro-fuzzy systems. In: Proceedings of the I Workshop on Genetic Fuzzy Systems, Granada, pp. 119–123 (2005)

21. Greenfield, S., Chiclana, F.: Type-reduction of the discretized interval type-2 fuzzy set: approaching the continuous case through progressively finer discretization. Journal of Artificial Intelligence and Soft Computing Research 1(3), 183–193 (2011)
22. Horzyk, A., Tadeusiewicz, R.: Self-Optimizing Neural Networks. In: Yin, F.-L., Wang, J., Guo, C. (eds.) ISNN 2004. LNCS, vol. 3173, pp. 150–155. Springer, Heidelberg (2004)
23. Jelonkiewicz, J., Przybył, A.: Accuracy improvement of neural network state variable estimator in induction motor drive. In: Rutkowski, L., Tadeusiewicz, R., Zadeh, L.A., Zurada, J.M. (eds.) ICAISC 2008. LNCS (LNAI), vol. 5097, pp. 71–77. Springer, Heidelberg (2008)
24. Jeong, Y.S., Jeong, M.K., Omitaomu, O.A.: Weighted dynamic time warping for time series classification. Pattern Recognition 44, 2231–2240 (2011)
25. Kholmatov, A., Yanikoglu, B.: Identity authentication using improved online signature verification method. Pattern Recognition Letters 26, 2400–2408 (2005)
26. Korytkowski, M., Nowicki, R., Rutkowski, L., Scherer, R.: AdaBoost Ensemble of DCOG Rough–Neuro–Fuzzy Systems. In: Jędrzejowicz, P., Nguyen, N.T., Hoang, K. (eds.) ICCCI 2011, Part I. LNCS, vol. 6922, pp. 62–71. Springer, Heidelberg (2011)
27. Korytkowski, M., Rutkowski, L., Scherer, R.: On combining backpropagation with boosting. In: Proceedings of the IEEE International Joint Conference on Neural Network (IJCNN), vol. 1-10, pp. 1274–1277 (2006)
28. Korytkowski, M., Rutkowski, L., Scherer, R.: From Ensemble of Fuzzy Classifiers to Single Fuzzy Rule Base Classifier. In: Rutkowski, L., Tadeusiewicz, R., Zadeh, L.A., Zurada, J.M. (eds.) ICAISC 2008. LNCS (LNAI), vol. 5097, pp. 265–272. Springer, Heidelberg (2008)
29. Kroll, A.: On choosing the fuzziness parameter for identifying TS models with multidimensional membership functions. Journal of Artificial Intelligence and Soft Computing Research 1(4), 283–300 (2011)
30. Li, X., Er, M.J., Lim, B.S., Zhou, J.H., Gan, O.P., Rutkowski, L.: Fuzzy Regression Modeling for Tool Performance Prediction and Degradation Detection. International Journal of Neural Systems 20(5), 405–419 (2010)
31. Lee, L.L., Berger, T., Aviczer, E.: Reliable on-line human signature verification systems. IEEE Trans. on Pattern Anal. and Machine Intell. 18, 643–647 (1996)
32. Lumini, A., Nanni, L.: Ensemble of on-line signature matchers based on overcomplete feature generation. Expert Systems with Applications 36, 5291–5296 (2009)
33. Łapa, K., Przybył, A., Cpałka, K.: A new approach to designing interpretable models of dynamic systems. In: Rutkowski, L., Korytkowski, M., Scherer, R., Tadeusiewicz, R., Zadeh, L.A., Zurada, J.M. (eds.) ICAISC 2013, Part II. LNCS, vol. 7895, pp. 523–534. Springer, Heidelberg (2013)
34. Łapa, K., Zalasiński, M., Cpałka, K.: A new method for designing and complexity reduction of neuro-fuzzy systems for nonlinear modelling. In: Rutkowski, L., Korytkowski, M., Scherer, R., Tadeusiewicz, R., Zadeh, L.A., Zurada, J.M. (eds.) ICAISC 2013, Part I. LNCS, vol. 7894, pp. 329–344. Springer, Heidelberg (2013)
35. Nanni, L.: Experimental comparison of one-class classifiers for online signature verification. Neurocomputing 69, 869–873 (2006)
36. Nanni, L., Lumini, A.: Ensemble of Parzen window classifiers for on-line signature verification. Neurocomputing 68, 217–224 (2005)
37. Nelson, W., Kishon, E.: Use of dynamic features for signature verification. In: Proc. of the IEEE Intl. Conf. on Systems, Man, and Cyber, vol. 1, pp. 201–205 (1991)
38. Nelson, W., Turin, W., Hastie, T.: Statistical methods for on-line signature verification. Intl. Journal of Pattern Recognition and Artificial Intell. 8, 749–770 (1994)

39. Nowicki, R.: Rough-Neuro-Fuzzy System with MICOG Defuzzification. In: 2006 IEEE International Conference on Fuzzy Systems, IEEE World Congress on Computational Intelligence, Vancouver, BC, Canada, July 16-21, pp. 1958–1965 (2006)
40. Nowicki, R., Scherer, R., Rutkowski, L.: A method for learning of hierarchical fuzzy systems. In: Sincak, P., Vascak, J., Kvasnicka, V., Pospichal, J. (eds.) Intelligent Technologies - Theory and Applications, pp. 124–129. IOS Press (2002)
41. Pabiasz, S., Starczewski, T.J.: Face reconstruction for 3D systems. In: Selected Topics in Computer Science Applications, pp. 54–63. EXIT (2011)
42. Pabiasz, S., Starczewski, J.T.: Meshes vs. depth maps in face recognition systems. In: Rutkowski, L., Korytkowski, M., Scherer, R., Tadeusiewicz, R., Zadeh, L.A., Zurada, J.M. (eds.) ICAISC 2012, Part I. LNCS, vol. 7267, pp. 567–573. Springer, Heidelberg (2012)
43. Pabiasz, S., Starczewski, J.T.: A New Approach to Determine Three-Dimensional Facial Landmarks. In: Rutkowski, L., Korytkowski, M., Scherer, R., Tadeusiewicz, R., Zadeh, L.A., Zurada, J.M. (eds.) ICAISC 2013, Part II. LNCS, vol. 7895, pp. 286–296. Springer, Heidelberg (2013)
44. Patan, K., Patan, M.: Optimal Training strategies for locally recurrent neural networks. Journal of Artificial Intelligence and Soft Computing Research 1(2), 103–114 (2011)
45. Peteiro-Barral, D., Bardinas, B.G., Perez-Sanchez, B.: Learning from heterogeneously distributed data sets using artificial neural networks and genetic algorithms. Journal of Artificial Intelligence and Soft Computing Research 2(1), 5–20 (2012)
46. Pławiak P., Tadeusiewicz R, Approximation of phenol concentration using novel hybrid computational intelligence methods. Applied Mathematics and Computer Science 24(1) (in print, 2014)
47. Przybył, A., Jelonkiewicz, J.: Genetic algorithm for observer parameters tuning in sensorless induction motor drive. In: Rutkowski, L., Kacprzyk, J. (eds.) Neural Networks And Soft Computing (6th International Conference on Neural Networks and Soft Computing), Zakopane, Poland, pp. 376–381 (2003)
48. Przybył, A., Smoląg, J., Kimla, P.: Distributed Control System Based on Real Time Ethernet for Computer Numerical Controlled Machine Tool (in Polish). Przeglad Elektrotechniczny 86(2), 342–346 (2010)
49. Rutkowski, L.: An application of multiple Fourier series to identification of multivariable nonstationary systems. International Journal of Systems Science 20(10), 1993–2002 (1989)
50. Rutkowski, L.: Computational intelligence. Springer (2008)
51. Rutkowski, L.: Nonparametric learning algorithms in the time-varying environments. Signal Processing 18, 129–137 (1989)
52. Rutkowski, L.: The real-time identification of time-varying systems by nonparametric algorithms based on the Parzen kernels. International Journal of Systems Science 16, 1123–1130 (1985)
53. Rutkowski, L.: Flexible structures of neuro-fuzzy systems. In: Sincak, P., Vascak, J. (eds.) Quo Vadis Computational Intelligence. SCI, vol. 54, pp. 479–484. Springer, Heidelberg (2000)
54. Rutkowski, L., Cpałka, K.: Flexible weighted neuro-fuzzy systems. In: Proceedings of the 9th International Conference on Neural Information Processing (ICONIP 2002), Orchid Country Club, Singapore, November 18-22 (2002)
55. Rutkowski, L., Przybył, A., Cpałka, K., Er, M.J.: Online speed profile generation for industrial machine tool based on neuro-fuzzy approach. In: Rutkowski, L., Scherer, R., Tadeusiewicz, R., Zadeh, L.A., Zurada, J.M. (eds.) ICAISC 2010, Part II. LNCS, vol. 6114, pp. 645–650. Springer, Heidelberg (2010)

56. Rutkowski, L., Przybył, A., Cpałka, K.: Novel on-line speed profile generation for industrial machine tool based on flexible neuro-fuzzy approximation. IEEE Transactions on Industrial Electronics 59, 1238–1247 (2012)
57. Scherer, R.: Neuro-fuzzy relational systems for nonlinear approximation and prediction. Nonlinear Analysis Series A: Theory, Methods and Applications 71(12), e1420–e1425 (2009)
58. Scherer, R., Rutkowski, L.: Connectionist fuzzy relational systems. In: Halgamuge, S.K., Wang, L. (eds.) 9th International Conference on Neural Information and Processing; 4th Asia-Pacific Conference on Simulated Evolution and Learning; 1st International Conference on Fuzzy Systems and Knowledge Discovery, Singapore. Computational Intelligence for Modelling and Prediction. SCI, vol. 2, pp. 35–47. Springer, Heidelberg (2005)
59. Sivanandam, S.N., Deepa, S.N.: Introduction to Genetic Algorithms. Springer (2008)
60. Starczewski, J.T.: A Type-1 Approximation of Interval Type-2 FLS. In: Di Gesù, V., Pal, S.K., Petrosino, A. (eds.) WILF 2009. LNCS, vol. 5571, pp. 287–294. Springer, Heidelberg (2009)
61. Starczewski, J.T., Rutkowski, L.: Connectionist Structures of Type 2 Fuzzy Inference Systems. In: Wyrzykowski, R., Dongarra, J., Paprzycki, M., Waśniewski, J. (eds.) PPAM 2001. LNCS, vol. 2328, pp. 634–642. Springer, Heidelberg (2002)
62. Starczewski, J., Rutkowski, L.: Interval type 2 neuro-fuzzy systems based on interval consequents. In: Rutkowski, L., Kacprzyk, J. (eds.) Neural Networks and Soft Computing. Advances in Soft Computing, pp. 570–577. Springer, Heidelberg (2003)
63. Starczewski, J.T., Scherer, R., Korytkowski, M., Nowicki, R.: Modular Type-2 Neuro-fuzzy Systems. In: Wyrzykowski, R., Dongarra, J., Karczewski, K., Wasniewski, J. (eds.) PPAM 2007. LNCS, vol. 4967, pp. 570–578. Springer, Heidelberg (2008)
64. Xu, G., Zhang, Z., Ma, Y.: A novel method for iris feature extraction based on intersecting cortical model network. Journal of Applied Mathematics and Computing 26, 341–352 (2008)
65. Yeung, D.Y., Chang, H., Xiong, Y., George, S., Kashi, R., Matsumoto, T., Rigoll, G.: SVC2004: First International Signature Verification Competition. In: Zhang, D., Jain, A.K. (eds.) ICBA 2004. LNCS, vol. 3072, pp. 16–22. Springer, Heidelberg (2004)
66. Zalasiński, M.: Cpałka K, A new method of on-line signature verification using a flexible fuzzy one-class classifier, pp. 38–53. Academic Publishing House EXIT (2011)
67. Zalasiński, M., Łapa, K., Cpałka, K.: New algorithm for evolutionary selection of the dynamic signature global features. In: Rutkowski, L., Korytkowski, M., Scherer, R., Tadeusiewicz, R., Zadeh, L.A., Zurada, J.M. (eds.) ICAISC 2013, Part II. LNCS, vol. 7895, pp. 113–121. Springer, Heidelberg (2013)
68. Zalasiński, M., Cpałka, K.: Novel algorithm for the on-line signature verification. In: Rutkowski, L., Korytkowski, M., Scherer, R., Tadeusiewicz, R., Zadeh, L.A., Zurada, J.M. (eds.) ICAISC 2012, Part II. LNCS, vol. 7268, pp. 362–367. Springer, Heidelberg (2012)
69. Zalasiński, M., Cpałka, K.: New approach for the on-line signature verification based on method of horizontal partitioning. In: Rutkowski, L., Korytkowski, M., Scherer, R., Tadeusiewicz, R., Zadeh, L.A., Zurada, J.M. (eds.) ICAISC 2013, Part II. LNCS, vol. 7895, pp. 342–350. Springer, Heidelberg (2013)

Agent Systems, Robotics and Control

Investigating the Rate of Failure
of Asynchronous Gathering in a Swarm
# of Fat Robots with Limited Visibility

Kálmán Bolla, Tamás Kovács, and Gábor Fazekas

Kecskemét College, Department of Informatics,
Izsáki 10, 6000 Kecskemét, Hungary
{bolla.kalman,kovacs.tamas}@gamf.kefo.hu,
{fazekas.gabor}@inf.unideb.hu
http://www.kefo.hu

Abstract. In the present paper we investigate the failure probability of
the asynchronous gathering task in a mobile robot swarm that contains
weak robots (oblivious, with limited visibility, without global navigation
and communication). We are modelling fat robots, which are represented
as solid discs. We performed numerous computer simulations in order to
measure the rate of failure of gathering using extended Ando's gathering algorithm [1]. The physical parameters of the simulations are based
on our previous experiments on image processing based kin recognition
method using Surveyor SRV-1 robots [11] [12]. It was obtained that the
computational time and the travelling speed of the robots affect very
strongly the rate of gathering success. If we apply SRV-1 robots with the
referred kin recognition method and highest possible travelling speed,
then the rate of failure is very close to 100 percent. While, reducing the
travelling speed with a factor of 1/20 (or increasing the computational
performance to 20 times the original) results in much better success rates
of gathering. Besides, we have found that the failure rate increases together with the number of robots.

Keywords: mobile robot swarm, gathering problem, asynchronous
gathering.

1 Introduction

Gathering of an oblivious robot swarm on an obstacle-free plane without global
navigation and common coordinate system is a basic and important problem of
swarm intelligence. However the solution of this problem is far from trivial; therefore, it roused high attention in the last decade. In an early stage the problem
was split into synchronous and asynchronous cases [5], where the synchronous
problem is defined as the robots do they acts (*Look*, *Compute*, *Wait* and *Move*)
synchronously together, while in an asynchronous case it is not supposed. It was
shown that the asynchronous problem is not solvable [2], [7]; therefore it was
necessary to introduce a weaker version of the problem when we require not

L. Rutkowski et al. (Eds.): ICAISC 2014, Part II, LNAI 8468, pp. 249–256, 2014.

gathering in a single point but that the diameter of the area enclosing all of the robots tends to zero with the increasing time. This weaker problem (let us call it convergence) is solvable simply by the so called Center Of Gravity (COG) algorithm, where each robot goes to the momentarily detected center of gravity of the swarm.

The applied mathematical models can be qualified also from the point of view of being rather idealistic or realistic. In the earlier publications the robots were modeled by mathematical points with unlimited visibility [7], [8], [3]. Later the model of the gathering problem was modified to be more realistic: the robots had limited visibility i.e. they could discover kin robots being closer than a visibility radius [1], [4], [6]. A well usable algorithm for the synchronous limited visibility problem was proposed by Ando et al. [1]. The two basic elements of their algorithm were that in a step cycle each robot starts forward the center of the smallest enclosing circle (SEC) of the neighboring visible robots; and this movement is limited so that any of the visibility contact do not brake. An asynchronous limited visibility problem was solved by Flocchini et al. with an additional compass sensor for each robot i.e. the robots were able to agree on a common global direction [4].

Prencipe has shown that in the case of limited visibility the asynchronous problem cannot be solved, because the splitting of the originally connected visibility graph can happen. (The nodes of the visibility graph are the centers of the robots and an edge of this graph means that the two connected robots are seeing each other.) In their work they introduce a simple example for this split-up [7].

Considering this, we can say that any gathering algorithm in an asynchronously working swarm with limited visibility and without global navigation tools may fail. In the present work we investigate the probability of such a failure. Besides we try to give a quantitative picture about how this failure probability is affected by number, the density and the computing times of the robots. These questions are seems to be very important from a practical point of view, since the implemented robot swarms have limited visibility and they cannot be equipped with global navigation and synchronization in every cases. Regarding the computing times of the robots, we use our earlier work on visual neighbor discovering in a robot swarm consisting of Surveyor SRV-1 robots as reference [11], [12].

Another step towards the realistic models is to work with no point-like but "fat" robots, where all of the robots are supposed to be solid discs on a plane with radius R_s. This modification of the problem has serious consequences: it is impossible to gather in a single point, so the original purpose should be modified. Another problem is that the robots now can hinder or totally block the movement of each other; moreover, this is true for the visibility too, since the robots are not transparent in a realistic case.

How should we define the gathering in the case of the fat robots? Czyzowicz et al. [9] defined the gathering so that

- the contact graph of the disks are connected, and
- each robot sees all of the others.

(The contact graph contains the center of the disks as vertices, and two vertices are connected if and only if the two disks are in contact.) Starting out from this definition, they solved the gathering problem for at most four robots. It is obvious, however, that the condition of seeing the other robots at the gathered position cannot be satisfied if there are many robots in the swarm. Therefore, in the present work, we define the minimum requirement of gathering as the connectivity of the contact graph.

In the present paper we apply computer simulation of a swarm of non-transparent "fat" and oblivious robots working asynchronously and having limited visibility; and our aim is to obtain the splitting probabilities mentioned above. We use Ando's SEC based gathering algorithm. We also apply the modification of the basic algorithm proposed by us in an earlier work [10] to be applicable for fat robots. In Sections 2 and 3 we give the details of the computer simulations. In Section 4 the results are introduced, and in the last section we conclude.

2   Detecting Swarm Members

In order to detect other swarm members from an observer robot using our kin recognition method [11] [12] is assumed in the simulations. This algorithm is based on image processing in the frequency domain, which is responsible for detecting swarm members, where each robot is equipped with a repeating texture pattern. The captured images were sampled by fixed number of pixel-columns. The applied repeating texture pattern produces a peak in the frequency domain if the sampled pixel-column is part of the pattern, and this is the basis of the kin-recognition. For more details of our swarm member recognition method see [11] [12].

In the present work we assume that each swarm member is equipped with an omnidirectional visual perception system which is able to get a 360 degrees panoramic view. In [11] [12] we used VGA quality (640 × 480 pixels) images, which are processed by the robot itself. The camera view angle of Surveyor SRV-1 robot is 66.4 degrees, but in this case an omnidirectional camera is assumed on the robots thus a capture frame contains 3470 × 480 pixels approximately. Our kin recognition method [11] [12] works reliably up to a distance of 300cm, so the visibility limit is V=300cm. The SRV-1 robot radius is 6cm and it has got 40cm/sec maximum speed. The total processing time (T) of an image-frame with our robot recognition algorithm consists of the following terms:

$$T = t_h + t_0 + \sum_{i=1}^{N} t_i(d_i). \tag{1}$$

where t_h is the image processing time of the sensor and the attached hardware, t_0 is the image processing computational time of an image without kin robots. Therefore, if there are no robots on the image only the hardware time (t_h) and t_0 are needed to process the whole image. The presence of the ith kin robot in the picture contributes to T with the term $t_i(d_i)$, where d_i means the distance of ith neighbour from the observer robot. Here N is the number of the visible neighbors. If a robot is located close to the observer, it occupies larger area in the image and requires more computation time than of a robot farther from the observer. In other words, the case when a robot has numerous neighbours and they are located close, the current robot requires more computational effort, which means it has a slower reaction to its environment. The defined T computation time is considered to be the *Look* phase in the *Wait-Look-Compute-Move* cycle.

There is a linear relationship between the reciprocal of d_i and the number of columns is generated by the pattern in the image plane, and t_i is supposed to be proportional to the number of these columns. Therefore the relationship between d_i and t_i should be:

$$t_i \sim 1/d_i. \tag{2}$$

Numerous experiments were done in order to justify the relationship above and to obtain the coefficient between t_i and $1/d_i$. Figure 1 shows the experimental results for distances of 50cm up to 300cm marked with continuous line, and the approximated line is marked with dashed line. The coefficient in question is given by the slope of the approximated line (slope = 2.69E-04).

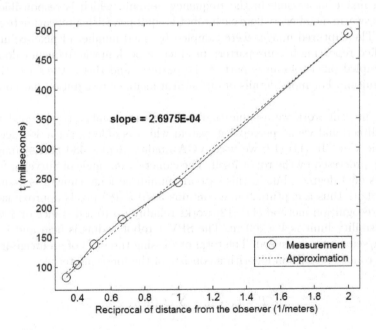

Fig. 1. Relationship between the distance from observer robot and the required computational time

3   Generating Initial Position

The initial positions of the robots are generated in a square area by a uniform random generator with the spatial density of $1/9$ robots/m^2. Using this density value resulted average robot-robot distance close to the visibility radius. After this generation, the largest connected visibility graph is chosen to perform the gathering experiment. The robots in this graph are considered to form the gathering swarm, and the other robots are discarded. Figure 2 shows an example for a random initial position of the robots, where the edges of the largest connected visibility graph are drawn.

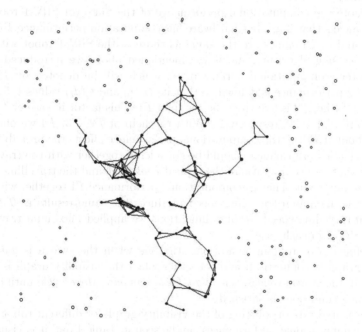

Fig. 2. Generated robot initial positions and the selected largest visibility graph

Due to this method the number of the robots in the swarm (N) is not determined a priori, but a random value in each experiment. In order to obtain the effect of N on the splitting probability we defined 9 intervals of N with equal width of 5. These are the following: [5..9], [10..14], [15..19], [20..24], [25..29], [30..34], [35..39], [40..44], [45..49]. We generated 100 different initial visibility graphs for each interval of N.

4   Asynchronous Gathering Experiments and Results

As it was mentioned in the introduction we supposed asynchronously working oblivious robot swarm with limited visibility (V) and with robot radius R_s.

The applied Ando's gathering method [1] was extended with a tangential movement of the robots, which was responsible for solving the blocking problem when a robot is prevented by another robot (This problem rises because of the fat robot representation.) [10]. Altogether 3600 experiments were performed with our MATLAB simulation program with the above described initial positions and for four different computational performances of the robots hardware. So, 900 experiments were done with the 900 initial positions for each specific computational performance. We determined the frequency of splitting of visibility graph, and we obtained an estimation of the probability of swarm splitting according to the number of robots and for lower and faster computational performance.

We denote the computational performance of the Surveyor SRV-1 robot by $T1$. This means that if a robot hardware has computation performance $T1$ then its t_h, t_0 and $t_i(d_i)$ values are the same as those of the SRV-1 robot with our image processing algorithm. As it was mentioned above we introduced three other (faster) computational performances, which will be denoted by $T2$, $T3$ and $T4$. $T2$ performance is defined so that its t_h, t_0 and $t_i(d_i)$ values $1/5$ times of those of $T1$ i.e. $T2$ is five times better than $T1$. This factor in case of $T3$ and $T4$ are $1/10$ and $1/20$, respectively. With the help of $T2$, $T3$, $T4$ we obtain a picture about that how the computational performance affects the probability in question. These performances should be considered together with the travelling speed of robots, since the ratio of the typical *Look* time and the travelling speed of robot is important. That is, computational performance $T1$ together with $1/5$ times of the maximum travelling speed produces the same results as $T2$ with maximum travelling speed. In our simulations we applied maximum travelling speed of SRV-1 in each case.

We defined two stopping conditions: the one when the swarm is gathered (contact graph is connected); and the other when the visibility graph is split. All units in the swarm repeats the *Wait-Look-Compute-Move* cycle until one of the stopping conditions is satisfied.

The measured rate of splitting of the visibility graph for different robot numbers and computational performances can be seen in Table 1 and it is visualised in Figure 3. It can be seen that in case of $T1$ performance and maximum travelling speed the splitting rate is 1.00 or very close to 1.00. That is, with these parameters the gathering will almost surely fail. If we suppose higher computational performances (or slower travelling speeds) the success rate becomes much better. It is also seen that the splitting rate increases fast with the number of the robots in the swarm. This is not a surprising behaviour because the splitting probability should be higher if there are higher number of visibility links in the graph. If we apply $T4$ computational performance (or 20 times slower travelling speed) then the success rate can be evaluated as quite good: for robot numbers under 20 it is above 97 percent.

Table 1. Experimental results

Interval	Rate of splitting			
	T1	T2	T3	T4
[5..9]	0.99	0.14	0.04	0.01
[10..14]	1.00	0.20	0.04	0.01
[15..19]	1.00	0.57	0.16	0.03
[20..24]	1.00	0.79	0.25	0.02
[25..29]	1.00	0.84	0.32	0.07
[30..34]	1.00	0.97	0.39	0.15
[35..39]	1.00	0.96	0.43	0.11
[40..44]	1.00	1.00	0.70	0.16
[45..49]	1.00	1.00	0.50	0.21

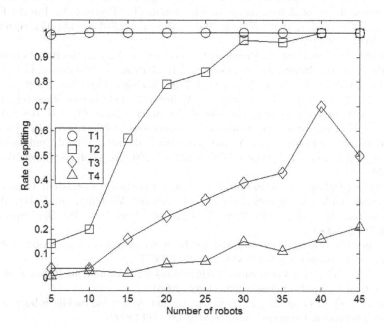

Fig. 3. Rate of splitting of the visibility graph for different robot numbers and computational performances

5   Conclusions

Computer simulations above show that:

- the frequency of failure of asynchronous gathering task increases with the number of robots in the swarm;
- the frequency of failure decreases quickly together with the increasing computational time (or with the travelling speed of the robots);
- it can be suspected that the failure probability will be 0 if time of the *Look* phase is 0 (which is not proved yet theoretically).

Acknowledgements. This research was realized in the frames of TÁMOP 4.2.4. A/2-11-1-2012-0001 "National Excellence Program Elaborating and operating an inland student and researcher personal support system convergence program" and, was supported by the TÁMOP-4.2.2.C-11/1/KONV-2012-0001 project. The project was subsidized by the European Union and co-financed by the European Social Fund.

References

1. Ando, H., Suzuki, I., Yamashita, M.: Formation and agreement problems for synchronous mobile robots with limited visibility. In: 1995 IEEE International Symposium on Intelligent Control, pp. 453–460. IEEE Press (1995)
2. Prencipe, G.: *InstantaneousActions* vs. *FullAsynchronicity*: Controlling and Coordinating a Set of Autonomous Mobile Robots. In: Restivo, A., Ronchi Della Rocca, S., Roversi, L. (eds.) ICTCS 2001. LNCS, vol. 2202, pp. 154–171. Springer, Heidelberg (2001)
3. Cieliebak, M., Flocchini, P., Prencipe, G., Santoro, N.: Solving the Robots Gathering Problem. In: Baeten, J.C.M., Lenstra, J.K., Parrow, J., Woeginger, G.J. (eds.) ICALP 2003. LNCS, vol. 2719, pp. 1181–1196. Springer, Heidelberg (2003)
4. Flocchini, P., Prencipe, G., Santoro, N., Widmayer, P.: Gathering of asynchronous robots with limited visibility. Theoretical Computer Science 337, 147–168 (2005)
5. Santoro, N.: Distributed Algorithms for Autonomous Mobile Robots. In: Navarro, G., Bertossi, L., Kohayakawa, Y. (eds.) Fourth IFIP International Conference on Theoretical Computer Science - TCS. IFIP, vol. 209, pp. 11–27. Springer, Boston (2006)
6. Souissi, S., Défago, X., Yamashita, M.: Using Eventually Consistent Compasses to Gather Oblivious Mobile Robots with Limited Visibility. In: Datta, A.K., Gradinariu, M. (eds.) SSS 2006. LNCS, vol. 4280, pp. 484–500. Springer, Heidelberg (2006)
7. Prencipe, G.: Impossibility of gathering by a set of autonomous mobile robots. Theoretical Computer Science 384, 222–231 (2007)
8. Cohen, R., Peleg, D.: Local Spread Algorithms for Autonomous Robot Systems. Theoretical Computer Science 399, 71–82 (2008)
9. Czyzowicz, G.J., Gasieniec, L., Pelc, A.: Gathering few fat mobile robots in the plane. Theoretical Computer Science 410, 481–499 (2009)
10. Bolla, K., Kovacs, T., Fazekas, G.: Gathering of Fat Robots with Limited Visibility and without Global Navigation. In: Rutkowski, L., Korytkowski, M., Scherer, R., Tadeusiewicz, R., Zadeh, L.A., Zurada, J.M. (eds.) EC 2012 and SIDE 2012. LNCS, vol. 7269, pp. 30–38. Springer, Heidelberg (2012)
11. Bolla, K., Kovacs, T., Fazakas, G.: Compact Image Processing-based Kin Recognition, Distance Measurement and Identification Method in a Robot Swarm. In: IEEE Conference on ICCC-CONTI 2010,Timisora pp. 419–424 (2010)
12. Bolla, K., Kovacs, T., Fazakas, G.: A Fast Image Processing Based Robot Identification Method for Surveyor SRV-1 Robots. In: IEEE Conference on AIM 2011, Budapest, pp.1003–1009 (2011)

Modeling Context-Aware and Agent-Ready Systems for the Outdoor Smart Lighting

Radosław Klimek and Grzegorz Rogus

AGH University of Science and Technology
Al. Mickiewicza 30, 30-059 Krakow, Poland
{rklimek,rogus}@agh.edu.pl

Abstract. Smart lighting systems considered as context-awareness systems are challenging. The use of advanced technology for street lighting allows to achieve a number of potential benefits of improving the efficiency of lighting, enhance the ability to monitor and control street lighting. A context-aware based system in architecture for street lighting control dealing with intelligent software applications in pervasive computing has been proposed. Some diagrams in the UML language are extended by some elements of the CML language in order to provide possibilities to design and verify behaviour of context-aware-based systems.

Keywords: Smart lighting, system architecture, pervasive computing, Ambient Intelligence, context-awareness, Context-Modeling Language, activity diagrams.

1 Introduction

Conventional street lighting systems are extremely uneconomical. In most of the areas lighting system is adjusted online at regular intervals of time irrespective of the seasonal variations. The street lights are simply switched on in the afternoon and turned off in the morning. For example in areas with a low frequency of passersby lamps are online most of the night without purpose. The consequence is that a large amount of power is wasted meaninglessly. There are several kinds of solutions for a better fit to the actual lighting needs. Firstly, they recommended the application of improvements in light technology (e.g. the usage of light-emitting diodes (LED) instead of common light bulbs), and secondly, they introduce an efficient, user-centered street lamp switching system. Agent technologies are developing dynamically. *Intelligent agents* are software entities composed of three important features: autonomy, reactivity, and communication ability. The agents' distributed structure seems to be particularly suitable for complex and smart lighting systems.

In this paper, we propose a context-aware based system architecture for street lighting control dealing with intelligent software application in pervasive/ ubiquitous computing. These computing entities are expected to be context-aware so that they can perceive and anticipate the needs of users and act pro-actively in advance by amending its behavior based on the changing contexts. The context-aware applications, i.e. applications demanding the contextual information from

L. Rutkowski et al. (Eds.): ICAISC 2014, Part II, LNAI 8468, pp. 257–268, 2014.

the environment, may not have prior knowledge about context which is gathered during the operation of a system. Thus, context-aware systems determine which system rules are most relevant in a particular context. They may be determined by environmental conditions and knowledge of the users behavior, as well as the history or users preferences. The contribution of the work is a complete architecture of smart outdoor lighting as well as rules for development of context-awareness software systems. Some diagrams of the UML language are extended by some elements of the CML language in order to provide possibilities to design behaviour of context-aware-based systems.

2   Related Works

Research in user/context-sensitive street lighting can be subdivided into the two major fields: street lighting control and context-aware design application. The compatibility and interoperability of new systems with existing (inflexible, central controlled) infrastructure is in the center of research [18,14]. An outdoor lighting optimization is presented in [9]. A highway tunnel lighting case is being discussed. The tunnel is equipped witch vehicle and luminance detectors. There are also some luminance requirements given to comply with safety regulations. In [17] authors focus on the control issue. One of the main problem is complexity of control algorithms related to the size of state spaces depending on working parameters and environments conditions. They proposed formal way by using decomposable graph representation of the environment under control and multiagent system deployed on it. With regard to steer-by-wire systems, the research focus is on the improvement of communication between substations or communication nodes (here: street lamps or groups of street lamps) by means of "PowerLineCommunication" (PLC) [4,16]. As a steer-by-wireless means of communication, the research is centered on the classical mobile-radio communication techniques global system for mobile (GSM), general packet radio (GPRS), and complemented by ZigBee [3,5,10]. Work [13] reports on research using ZigBee as an alternative option to PLC for single groups of street lamps. Their work is focused on error detection like short circuits that cannot be detected by PLC. Work [10] stated that ZigBee is an important (the optimum) communication technology for this kind of applications and investigates the special requirements for efficient routing algorithms to cope with difficulties with radio transmission caused by buildings. Most approaches combine different communication technologies within a system and mostly GSM or GPRS is used for the communication between base station and substations, while PLC or radio technology like ZigBee is used for data exchange between substation and the end points (street lamps) [3]. In computer science context awareness [20] refers to the idea that computers can both sense, and react based on their environment. Devices may have information about circumstances under which they are able to operate and based on rules, or an intelligent stimulus, react accordingly. The term context-awareness in ubiquitous computing was introduced by Schilit [15]. Context aware devices may also try to make assumptions about the user's current situation. Dey and Abowd [7,6] define context as "any information that can be used to characterize the situation of an entity". Recently, a great deal of research on intelligent home environment and context-aware architectures has been done. In [19] they have proposed a design for automatic room light detection and control, according to the type of a room, the light controls the light using a fixed threshold value resulting in inefficiency through this system controls. Work [2] proposed a self-adapting intelligent system used for providing building control and energy saving services in buildings.

3 Outdoor Lighting System – Problems and Requirements

"Intelligent street lighting" includes the entire system with advanced lighting control solutions, control algorithms, communication systems and administrative tools for software systems. The solution focuses on low energy consumption and high functional standard. It also automatically declines the maintenance costs for the operator in combination with increased safety for the street user. Streets or roads equipped with such a solution dynamically adapts the street lighting performance according to the actual needs for the given period of time on the road. Typically it will lead to a lowered lumen output from the lamp during good conditions, when low traffic volumes or low average speed appears in combination with non-foggy weather. This is also be in the case if the surface is covered with snow.

Modern smart lighting system must fulfil some requirements.

1. Requirements regarding domain the lighting system
   - Suburban areas with low-pedestrian and traffic movement are considered.
   - System covers a large area often with different weather conditions.
   - Outdoor lighting system consists of architecture space, light points and sensor devices.
   - There are a lot of light points and various types of sensors and detectors.
   - Each lamp in the system is to have a unique identifier that allows the monitoring of its work, and precise control.
   - Allows two-way communication to each luminaire.
   - Some environment factors are considered: natural lighting, weather conditions (rain, snow, fog), time (time of the day, working days), traffic, social events etc.
2. Management of control lighting system requirements
   - Centralized installation, low maintenance and control cost.
   - Seamless integration with existing IT systems (billing, GIS, maintenance, etc).
   - Open and interoperable communication protocols.
   - Management over each individual light provides granular control and features such as: basic switching (on/off), dimming, alarms (lamp fault, lamp flickering, end of life, brown out), full electrical measures (main voltage, lamp voltage, active power), energy consumption monitoring and calculations.

The use of advanced technology for street lighting allows to achieve a number of potential benefits of improving the efficiency of the lighting, enhance the monitoring ability and control street lighting.

4 Proposal of the System Architecture

Due to the requirements defined in Section 3, which define the basic design assumptions, the concept of a hierarchical control system is proposed. It comprises a central processing unit monitoring and controlling the operation of the sub-control arranged on a dedicated intermediate area. The number and localization of intermediate units depends on the topology of the lighting network. Fig. 1 presents the general concepts of architecture.

Research in context-awareness can be classified [20] into the following four primary areascontext acquisition, context storage, context modeling, and context reasoning. Context acquisition is the process of collecting raw context data from various context sources. Raw context data can be collected either from a single sensor node, or by aggregating context data available from multiple sensor nodes. The collected context data then needs to be stored for further processing. The raw context tends to be noisy and inconsistent, which calls for proper context pre-processing, inconsistency detection and resolution mechanisms. After processing, context is represented using particular pattern or design descriptions, called context models. Many layered context-aware systems and frameworks have evolved during the last years. The following layered conceptual architecture, as depicted in Fig. 2, augments layers for detecting and using context by adding interpreting and reasoning functionality [6,7].

The first layer consists of a collection of different sensors. It is notable that the word "sensor" not only refers to hardware but also to every data source which may provide usable context information. The second layer is responsible for the retrieval of raw context data. It makes use of appropriate drivers for

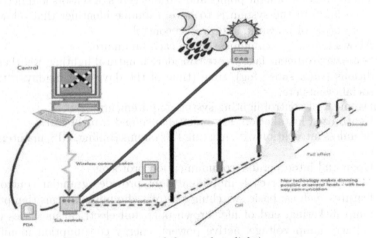

Fig. 1. Overview of the outdoor lighting system

Fig. 2. Layered conceptual framework for context-aware systems

physical sensors and APIs for virtual and logical sensors. The Preprocessing layer is not implemented in every context-aware system but may offer useful information if the raw data are too coarse grained. The preprocessing layer is responsible for reasoning and interpreting contextual information. In context-aware systems consisting of several different context data sources, in this layer the single context information can be aggregated to high-level information. A single sensor value is often not important to an application, whereas combined information might be more precious and accurate. The fourth layer, Storage and Management, organizes the gathered data and offers them via a public interface to the client. The client is realized in the fifth layer, the Application layer. The actual reaction on different events and context-instances is implemented here.

Based on the presented reference architecture we propose a new solution. Our system is divided into a gathered data layer, control layer and application layer presented in Fig. 3. In our propose, layers 2-4 from reference architecture are implemented in sub-control component. The gathered data consist of sensors, personal devices and lamps. Today there are two basic ways to communicate between luminaires and the power supply cabinet where the segment controller is build in PLC (power line communications) or RF (radio frequency). The use of RF is in some instances implemented but with limited success. The common way to communicate in Street Lighting is by using the existing power cables between the luminaire and the power supply cabinet. Sensors monitor real-time data of environment factors (location, humidity, temperature, light etc). Segment Controler first retrieves context data directly or indirectly from sensors, which are grounded in the physical environment.

To easily understand and deal with this, the context is divided into three categories: lamp context, user context and environmental context. Lamp context is the description of a single lamp. The lamp context is mainly composed of light point identity (such as ip and geographical location) and its parameters. The parameters include pole height, overhang, angles, dimming etc. A key element is a proper representation of the problem, in terms of search space, to find an optimized set of prameters, under given circumstances. Environmental context described in this paper includes current time (morning or night, weekday or weekend) and the surrounding environment (temperature, humidity, etc). User context is then using pedestrian in lighting system who has a PDA (for example mobile telephone) and allow an explicit identification of the user). Then user

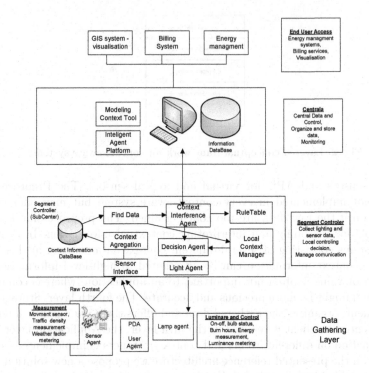

Fig. 3. Logical architecture of the Smart Lighting System

context consist of information about the user (localization and his preferences for example default road to home etc.). The main component in that level is Context Manager which analyzes different information coming from different sensors and then extractors and parsers where possible (depicted in Fig. 3) to extract content of the environment.

Context-aware computing allows to detect specific conditions requiring some adaptation action. As can be seen in Fig. 3 we use multiagent approach to execute control task in Lighting System. There are following types of agents:

- Lamp agent - located over lamp driver. This agent keeps direct control via lamp driver over lamp behavior. It also transmits all exploitation/diagnostic data from lamp driver.
- Sensor agent - collects sensor data and sends them to Segment Controller.
- User Agent - sends data from personal devices to Segment Controller.
- Light Agent - manages a set of individual light point via lamp agent. The control tasks are delegated to this light agent from decision-making agent.
- Decision-Making Agent - main control agent in Segment Controller. It is responsible for creating light agent to react on specific context changes reported by the local context manager and sending to him control data for controlled area.

- Context Interference Agent - communication agent to sending/receiving data from central unit.
- Intelligent Agent Platform – main agent in central unit. This calls for context integration and context abstraction methods. Context integration concerns the extraction of the most accurate context from a number contexts from other sub areas. Context abstraction or context reasoning allows to derive a higher-level application-relevant context from number of lower-level context data from segment Controller.

In our approach each point can be managed, controlled separately to provide optimization of the entire grid according to the pissible choosen criteria. Designing a decision-making criteria is one of the main tasks in a context-aware system. It is possible to make decisions on-line or off-line. In the first way the decision agent uses optimization algorithm that calculates optimal control to all points of light in selected areas. In the second way the administrator prepares a static rule table. The rule table consists of profiles. A profile defines a mode of operation for lighting grid for a particular purpose. It provides behavioral model under certain circumstances precisely defining the lighting conditions. Choosing a profile can depend on such factors as natural lighting, weather (snow, rain, frog) time (time of day, working days), social events, energy shortage, traffic etc. Since some profiles might depend on subsume each other, they can form hierarchy. There are major profiles defining lighting conditions for regular and emergency operations.

Case Study. Consider the behavior of our system illuminating the sharp curve. In Fig. 4.a we have a car approaching to the curve. There are people behind the curve. People and the car are detected by sensors. Depending on information about the weather and lighting conditions system for safety turns on all the lamps on full effect. Similar situation takes places in Fig. 4.b. We have only one car. In that situation system turn on only same of the lamps. The decision depends on identification of environment state and assigned to him defined context rules. In Fig. 4.c the system selects all lamp but all are dimmed in about 50 percents. It enough for the comfort of the pederasties. When road is empty the system switches off all the lamps to save energy consumption – Fig. 4.d.

5   Context Modeling and Reasoning

Issues to the modeling of context-awareness systems are discussed in this Section. They include the extension of the UML language with some aspects of the CML language for context modeling, as well as the possibilities of formal correctness analysis of behavior of the so obtained software models.

Pervasive computing or ubiquitous computing can be understood as existing or being everywhere at the same time, assuming the omni-presence of computing providing strong support for users/inhabitants. Because of the pervasiveness of considered lighting technologies, one uses them without thinking about them, making the technology effectively invisible to the user. Context-awareness and context modeling are some of the crucial aspects of pervasive systems.

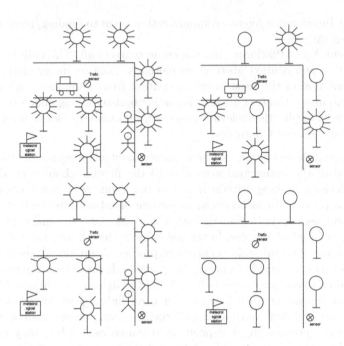

Fig. 4. A sharp curve example: (a) top left, (b) top right, (c) down left, (d) down right

Context-awareness is an important component of today's most pervasive applications which behaviour is characterized by the interpretation logic that is embedded inside these applications. This type of computing assumes transfer of contextual information among pervasive applications. A context is conditions and circumstances that are relevant to the working system, where the physical world creates a context. This physical world is a typical street lighting system for a rural or suburban environment. The physical world and the context-awareness software constitute the smart and energy efficient lighting system. The traffic involves both vehicles and pedestrians. Context model creates different types of sensors which are distributed all over the considered area. Smart street lighting is controlled by intelligent software which is context-aware and pro-active. Distributed sensors constitute a kind of eyes for software systems. These ideas also refer to the concept of *Ambient Intelligence* (AmI), i.e. electronic devices that are sensitive and responsive to the presence of humans/inhabitants. Context-aware system is able to adapt their operations to the current context without explicit user intervention. It follows that it requires special treatment when modeling software.

Context-Modeling Language CML, e.g. [1], is a language designed for modeling context information. It provides a graphical notation that allows analysing and formally specifying the context requirements. The context model contains fact types, i.e. shared context, to capture dependencies between them and capture histories for certain fact types. CML also enables modeling context-dependent preferences expressed in terms of these situations. CML is suitable for a variety of context-aware applications and allows to capture: activities in the form of fact types, associations between users and devices, and locations of users and devices. CML is a graphical language, e.g. boxes, the examples of which are shown in Fig. 5, denoting a role played by object types within a fact type.

The fundamental lack of the CML language is that it does not allow to take into account the behavior of a modeled system, i.e. dynamic aspects of a system are not considered. On the other hand, UML, i.e. the Unified Modeling Language, which is ubiquitous in the software industry can be a powerful tool for the requirements engineering process and software modeling. Thus, the extension of the UML diagrams with some elements of CML is proposed at the work. *Activity diagrams* enable modeling the workflow activities, i.e. modeling sequence, choice, iteration and concurrency for workflows. The *swimlane* is useful for partitioning the activity diagram and enables to group the activities in a single thread. The important goal of activity diagrams is to show how an activity depends on others. The example of the activity diagram extension through introduction of the CML elements is shown in Fig. 5. The diagram contains three swimlanes managed by three objects *o1*, *o2* and *o3*, respectively. These objects perform activities. Some activities refer to some fact types. To give an example, the "presence" fact type contains two roles, one played by the vehicle object type and the other by the traffic-sensor object type. Fact types, associated with the activities, marked on the diagram as dependencies, model the behavior of objects, e.g. sensors, vehicles,

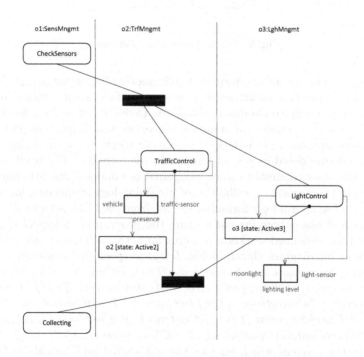

Fig. 5. A modified activity diagram for context-aware models

etc. In addition to the above, the flow of the object is presented. It allows to show the change of states of corresponding state machines for objects. To give an example, after the execution of the "TrafficControl" activity, the state machine for object $o2$ reaches the "Active2" state.

State diagrams allow an abstract description of the behavior of a system, i.e. can be used to graphically represent finite state machines. State machines consists of states and events. A state can consider all possible event sequences and capture only the relevant ones. The simple examples of state machines are shown in Fig. 6. They refer to objects $o2$ and $o3$, respectively. To give an example, after the "traffic-sensor" finds the presence of vehicle, the "TrfSignal" signal is generated and constitutes an event for the considered state machines, i.e. it allows to reach the new state "Active2".

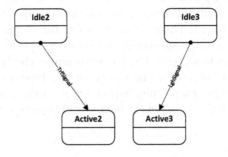

Fig. 6. Two sample state diagrams

The verification of context-aware system is another important aspect. Formal methods enable precise formulation of important artifacts arising during software development and help to eliminate ambiguity. Deduction-based verification enables the analysis of infinite computation sequences. One important problem of the deductive approach is the lack of automatic methods for obtaining logical specifications considered as sets of temporal logic formulas. The need to build logical specifications manually can be recognized as a major obstacle to untrained users. Work [11] discusses possibilities of obtaining logical specification understood as set of temporal logic formulas, e.g. [8], from the UML activity diagrams. A method and algorithms for automating the generation of logical specifications based on predefined workflow patterns for activity diagrams are proposed. For example, for diagram shown in Fig. 5 logical specification should contains the following formulas: $CheckSensors \Rightarrow \Diamond TrafficControl \land \Diamond LightControl$, $\neg CheckSensors \Rightarrow \neg(\Diamond TrafficControl \land \Diamond LightControl)$, $TrafficControl \land LightControl \Rightarrow \Diamond Collecting$, $\neg(TrafficControl \land LightControl) \Rightarrow \neg \Diamond Col -$ $lecting$, $\Box \neg(CheckSensors \land (TrafficControl \lor LightControl))$, $\Box \neg((Traffic-$ $Control \lor LightControl) \land Collecting)$, $\Box \neg(CheckSensors \land Collecting)$. A complete deduction system which enables the automated and formal verification of software models has been introduced. Another type of diagrams considered for obtaining logical specifications are state diagrams, c.f. work [12]. For example, for Fig. 6 logical specification should contains among other formulas: $TrfSignal \Rightarrow \Diamond Active2$ or $LghSignal \Rightarrow \Diamond Active3$. Gathering all temporal logic formulas for logical specification, properties of software models can be verified. Liveness and safety are a standard taxonomy of system properties. More detailed discussion and an example contains work [11].

6 Conclusions

The work proposes a context-aware architecture for smart outdoor lighting systems. Some diagrams of the UML language are extended by some elements of the CML language in order to enable developing behaviors of pro-active and context-aware systems. Developing such a system is challenging as pervasive/ubiquitous computing. Some aspects of the formal verification of behaviour for software models are briefly discussed. The research has thrown up many questions in need of further investigation. Future research should discuss other details of such modern and energy-efficient systems. The next research step may also involve a detailed case study.

Acknowledgment. This work was supported by the AGH UST internal grant no. 11.11.120.859.

References

1. Bettini, C., Brdiczka, O., Henricksen, K., Indulska, J., Nicklas, D., Ranganathan, A., Riboni, D.: A survey of context modelling and reasoning techniques. Pervasive Mobile Computing 6(2), 161–180 (2010), http://dx.doi.org/10.1016/j.pmcj.2009.06.002
2. Byun, J., Park, S.: Development of a self-adapting intelligent system for building energy saving and context aware smart services. IEEE Transactions on Consumer Electronics 57, 90–98 (2011)
3. Caponetto, R., Dongola, G., Fortuna, L., Riscica, N., Zufacchi, D.: Power consumption reduction in a remote controlled street lighting system. In: International Symposium on Power Electronics, Electrical Drives, Automation and Motion(SPEEDAM 2008), Ischia, June 11-13, pp. 428–33. IEEE Computer Society (2008)
4. Cho, S., Dhingra, V.: Street lighting control based on lonworks power line communication. In: IEEE International Symposium on Power Line Communications and Its Applications (ISPLC 2008), Jeju city, Jeju Island, Apri 2-4, pp. 396–8. IEEE Computer Society Press (2008)
5. Denardin, G.W., Barriquello, C.H., Pinto, R.A., Silva, M.F., Campos, A., do Prado, R.N.: An intelligent system for street lighting control and measurement. In: IEEE Industry Applications Society Annual Meeting (IAS 2009), Houston, TX, October 4-8, pp. 1–5. IEEE Computer Society (2009)
6. Dey, A.K.: Understanding and using context. Personal Ubiquitous Computing 5(1), 4–7 (2001), http://dx.doi.org/10.1007/s007790170019

7. Dey, A.K., Abowd, G.D.: Towards a better understanding of context and context-awareness. In: Workshop on The What, Who, Where, When, and How of Context-Awareness, CHI 2000 (April 2000),
http://www.cc.gatech.edu/fce/contexttoolkit/
8. Emerson, E.: Temporal and Modal Logic. In: Handbook of Theoretical Computer Science, vol. B, pp. 995–1072. Elsevier, MIT Press (1990)
9. Fan, S., Yang, C., Wang, Z.: Automatic control system for highway tunnel lighting. In: Li, D., Liu, Y., Chen, Y. (eds.) Computer and Computing Technologies in Agriculture IV. IFIP AICT, vol. 347, pp. 116–123. Springer, Heidelberg (2011)
10. Iordache, C., Gavat, S., Mada, C., Stanciu, D., Holban, C.: Streetlight monitoring and control system part i: system structure. In: IEEE International Conference on Automation, Quality and Testing, Robotics (AQTR 2008), Cluj-Napoca, May 22-25, pp. 183–186. IEEE (2008)
11. Klimek, R.: From extraction of logical specifications to deduction-based formal verification of requirements models. In: Hierons, R.M., Merayo, M.G., Bravetti, M. (eds.) SEFM 2013. LNCS, vol. 8137, pp. 61–75. Springer, Heidelberg (2013)
12. Klimek, R., Faber, L., Kisiel-Dorohinicki, M.: Verifying data integration agents with deduction-based models. In: Proceedings of Federated Conference on Computer Science and Information Systems (FedCSIS 2013), Kraków, Poland, September 8-11, pp. 1049–1055. IEEE Xplore Digital Library (2013)
13. Lee, J.D., Nam, K.Y., Jeong, S.H., Choi, S.B., Ryoo, H.S., Kim, D.K.: Development of zigbee based street light control system. In: IEEE PES Power Systems Conference and Exposition (PSCE 2006), Atlanta, GA, October 29 - November 1, pp. 2236–40. IEEE Computer Society (2006)
14. Li, L., Chu, X., Wu, Y., Wu, Q.: The development of road lighting intelligent control system based on wireless network control. In: International Conference on Electronic Computer Technology, Macau, February 20-22, pp. 353–7 (2009)
15. Schilit, B., Adams, N., Want, R.: Context-aware computing applications. In: Proceedings of the 1994 First Workshop on Mobile Computing Systems and Applications (WMCSA 1994), pp. 85–90. IEEE Computer Society (1994),
http://dx.doi.org/10.1109/WMCSA.1994.16
16. Wang, C., Zhang, D.L., Qin, H.L., Yao, Y.Y., Sun, Y., Shen, Y.: Hps street lighting lamp networking over power-lines. In: International Conference on Power System Technology (PowerCon 2006), Chongqing, October 22-26, pp. 1–5. IEEE Computer Society (2006)
17. Wojnicki, I., Sedziwy, A., Kotulski, L.: Towards ai-based distributed lighting control systems. Automatyka/Automatics 16, 189–198 (2012)
18. Wouters, I., Chen, W., van Oorschot, B., Smeenk, W.: Interactive green street enhancement using light dependent sensors and actuators. In: IEEE International Symposium on Consumer Electronics (ISCE 2008), Vilamoura, April 14-16, pp. 1–3. IEEE Computer Society (2008)
19. Ying-Wen, B., Yi-Te, K.: Automatic room light intensity detection and control using a icroprocessor and light sensors. IEEE Transactions on Consumer Electronics 54, 1173–1176 (2008)
20. Zhang, D., Guo, M., Liu, L., Zhong, M., Liu, X., Ota, K., Zhu, X.: A reference model for context-awareness in pervasive computing environments. In: Pervasive Computing. Nova Publisher (2011)

Problem of Agents Cooperation in Heterogeneous Graph-Based Knowledge Environment

Leszek Kotulski, Adam Sędziwy, and Barbara Strug

AGH University of Science and Technology,
Department of Applied Computer Science,
al. Mickiewicza 30, 30-059 Kraków, Poland
{kotulski,sedziwy,bstrug}@agh.edu.pl

Abstract. The important aspect of performance of a multi-agent system deployed in highly non-homogeneous environment is ensuring data confidentiality. In such an environment each agent resides in its local ecosystem characterized by its own data structure and semantics. Moreover agents may also extend their knowledge by sending appropriate queries to other agents. Thus a knowledge diffuses through the system so it may cause unauthorized data accesses. In this article we propose the run-time method of discovering such data leaks and the method of preventing such events.

Keywords: multi-agent system, data confidentiality, graph, distributed system, data leaks.

1 Introduction

Distributed environments operating on huge-volumed and complex structured data impede information processing and preserving its consistency. Such systems may include a range of entities like telecom operators, population databases, government agencies, hospitals, insurance agencies and so on. Among the problems which each information system operating in such environment has to face is ability of collecting a consistent set of data relevant to partial information given as an input. Moreover, a process of gathering required data is a subject to restrictions related to confidentiality policies corresponding to data maintained by particular organizational units.

This paper deals with an approach using a graph based knowledge representation of data gathered by entities. It does not assume a particular type of graph structures, the data can be based on simple graphs, nested graphs, hypergraphs [2] or RDF graphs.

A problem of distributed graph has already been researched in other context where a cooperation and communication between systems was tackled [3,4,5,6]. Previous approach to solving the problem of cooperation strategy in context of design problems is presented in [9,10,11,12,13,16].

In this paper we take a different approach. Each entity is treated as an agent and the system communication is realized by passing messages between pairs of

L. Rutkowski et al. (Eds.): ICAISC 2014, Part II, LNAI 8468, pp. 269–277, 2014.

agents, while keeping track of the original owner of the data (information) and providing means to prevent data leaks or passing them to unauthorized agents (entities).

2 Agent's Knowledge Representation

A knowledge present in the considered system is distributed: particular agents possess its fragments which have separate structures and content (although it is admissible that some data may partially overlap). For this reason we aim at enabling communication and consistent data exchange in such a heterogeneous graph-based multi-agent system.

As an agent's local knowledge has a structure which may be defined using RDF scheme or other similar approach, it may be easily represented by means of a graph as well. Thus we can think about the agent's knowledge as of a graph storing data. Having in mind that data are distributed and non uniformly structured, it should be remarked the global knowledge is represented by a set of agent-specific graphs (hypergraphs). Figure 2.2 shows the sample agent level graph G representing the structure of a driving license data record.

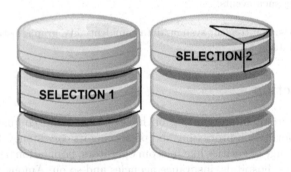

Fig. 2.1. Data publication models

An agent supplies parts of stored data in a response for queries sent by other agents. The word *part* may be understood twofold: as a selection of particular database records (in complete form) as shown in Figure 2.1 (left) but also as a portion of those records (Fig. 2.1, right). We focus on the latter case as more general one. In the terms of a graph representation it corresponds to sending a subgraph $H \subseteq G$ to a querying agent.

3 The Architecture of Multi-agent System

Let us suppose there is given a set of agents $\mathbf{A} = \{A_1, A_2, \ldots A_n\}$. Each $A_i \in \mathbf{A}$ holds its portion of a global ontology. Let a graph $G_i \subset U$ represents a knowledge,

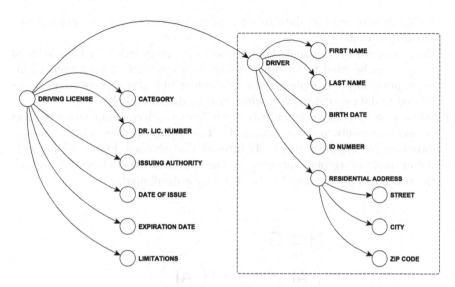

Fig. 2.2. The sample data graph G and its subgraph H (bounded by the dashed line)

of an agent A_i where U is a graph representation of an overall knowledge. Next, we suppose that agents are linked with unidirectional communication channels so a system is modeled with directed graph $M = (\mathbf{A}, E \subset \mathbf{A} \times \mathbf{A})$, such that M doesn't contain neither loops nor multiple arcs. In particular, $e_{ij} = (A_i, A_j)$ and $e_{ji} = (A_j, A_i)$ represent two oppositely directed channels.

Definition 1. *An agent A_j is referred to as a **successor** of A_i iff there exists a communication channel $e_{ij} = (A_i, A_j)$ from A_i to A_j. Analogously, A_i is a **predecessor** of A_j iff $e_{ij} = (A_i, A_j)$ exists.*

*An agent A_j is called a **indirect successor** of A_i iff there exists a sequence of agents $(A_{i(0)}, A_{i(1)}, \ldots A_{i(k)})$ such that $A_{i(0)} \equiv A_i, A_{i(k)} \equiv A_j$ and $A_{i(m+1)}$ is a successor of $A_{i(m)}$, for $0 \leq m < k$. Analogously, A_i is a **indirect predecessor** of A_j iff there exists a sequence of agents $S=(A_{i(0)}, A_{i(1)}, \ldots A_{i(k)})$ such that $A_{i(0)} \equiv A_i, A_{i(k)} \equiv A_j, A_{i(p)} \neq A_{i(q)}$ for $p \neq q$ and $A_{i(m)}$ is a predecessor of $A_{i(m+1)}$, for $0 \leq m < k$. For both cases, agents $A_{i(0 < m < k)}$ are referred to as **transitive agents**. The sequence S i referred to as a **trace** of the message.*

Example 1. In Figure 4.2 the agent A_1 has two successors A_2, A_6 and three indirect successors A_4, A_5, A_6. The agent A_5 may be reached from A_1 in three ways: (i) through A_2, A_3, A_4, (ii) through A_2 and (iii) through A_6.

4   Communication among Agents and Data Confidentiality

Agents living in a distributed environment exchange data through query-response mechanism. We make several assumptions concerning communication among agents.

1. An agent may send its data to some of its successors only: no explicit forwarding is used.
2. Data acquired by an agent A_i in a result of a query extend a knowledge of A_i and can be used to form a response to a query of another agent. This assumption implies implicit data forwarding but also creates some issues related to data confidentiality which will be discussed below.
3. We ascribe a predefined confidentiality policy to each communication channel or, more precisely, to its endpoint A_j. This policy specifies which data are forbidden to be transferred to A_j through that channel. Figure 4.1 presents the example of agents connected by the communication channel for which the transmission of some H from A_i to A_j is disallowed.

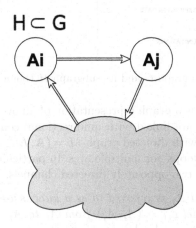

Fig. 4.1. Communication channel (represented as the arrow) and the portion H of an agent's knowledge, disallowed for transmission by the channel.

Technical aspects of communication among agents are assumed to be supported by a transport layer and will not be discussed here. Instead we focus on its logic. In this article we consider the problem of data confidentiality. More precisely, we deal with an agent system in which each single agent possesses a part of global knowledge and this local knowledge may be propagated to other agents only according to rules presented above. The issue arising from this scenario is that data which flow through communication channels may bypass restrictions ascribed to communication channels and get indirectly to a not authorized recipient.

Since an agent A_i may easily control its data confidentiality when performing transfers to successors, there is no simple inspection method enabling the control over query-response data spread in a system and which may leak in a result of consecutive queries of particular agents. Thus two problems are opened:

1. How to manage agents to prevent unauthorized data access?
2. How to discover analytically potential data leaks in such data forwarding system of agents?

To resolve the first issue we introduce the notion of *forbidden patterns* which enables agents to implement data access policy. To verify the correctness of this mechanism in the scale of an entire system we need to find a method of data leak detection. To discover leaks occurrences we attach to a content of a message obtained by an agent $A_{i(k)}$ auxiliary meta-data: (i) a list of agents which contributed some knowledge to the message content, and corresponding subgraphs (see Example 2) (ii) a trace of the message up to $A_{i(k-1)}$ agent. The example of such data passing is shown in Figure 4.2. It should be remarked that a list of contributing agents is not equivalent to a trace as some agents may relay a message only without changing that.

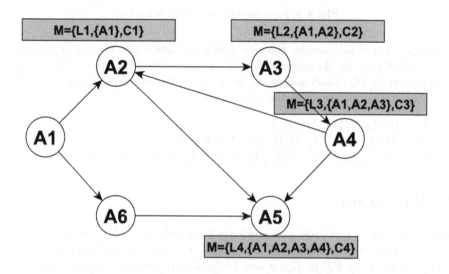

Fig. 4.2. Message passing. $L_i = (\{A_1, H_1\}, \ldots, \{A_{i-1}, H_{i-1}\})$ is an incremental list of contributing agents and corresponding subgraphs added to the message's content. The message content grows: $C_1 \subseteq C_2 \subseteq C_3 \subseteq C_4$.

We define it globally for entire agent system by means of lists of *forbidden patterns*.

Definition 2. *A list of **forbidden patterns** is a codomain of the mapping:*

$$FP : \mathbf{A} \to 2^U \times \Pi, \tag{4.1}$$

where $\mathbf{A}$ is a set of agents, U is the total knowledge deposited is a multi-agent system and Π denotes the space of predicates (e.g., related to a primary sender of a given portion of knowledge).

The equation 4.1 specifies that a given agent (being an argument of FP mapping) is forbidden to acquire a portion of knowledge represented by a graph $H \in 2^U$ and any $H' \subset H$, iff the corresponding predicate $\pi \in \Pi$ is satisfied. Note that $FP(A)$ may be a set of pairs of the form (H, π). It should be noted that FP mapping is assigned to an agent rather than to a communication channel. Communication channel may be present implicitly in the predicate π.

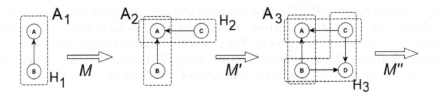

Fig. 4.3. Incremental knowledge behavior

Example 2. Let us consider the case shown in Figure 4.3. The agent A_1 sends the graph H_1 to A_2. A_2 extends this by merging with its portion of knowledge represented by H_2. Analogously, A_3 adds H_3 to the resultant graph. Thus the message structure changes in the following way.

1. $M = \{(\{A_1, H_1\}), \{A_1\}, H_1\}$
2. $M' = \{(\{A_1, H_1\}, \{A_2, H_2\}), \{A_1, A_2\}, H_1 \cup H_2\}$
3. $M'' = \{(\{A_1, H_1\}, \{A_2, H_2\}, \{A_3, H_3\}), \{A_1, A_2, A_3\}, H_1 \cup H_2 \cup H_3\}$

5   Data Leaks

The possibility of forwarding a knowledge acquired from other agents may lead to a data leak which is defined as obtaining data, contrary to the confidentiality policy, as given by FP mapping (see Definition 2). Let us consider Example 3 illustrating the problem.

Example 3. Suppose that the multi-agent system shown in Figure 4.2 is given. Moreover, let $FP(A_5) = (H, \pi)$, where H is a certain graph and $\pi = \{H$ is received from $A_2\}$. Such form of $FP(A_5)$ will block transmission of H via $e_{25} = (A_2, A_5)$ channel but this constraint may be still omitted by passing the message containing H through two transitive agents, namely A_3 and A_4. To discover this data leak A_5 analyzes the entire contribution chain along the message trace:$(\{A_2, H\}, \{A_3, H'\}, \{A_4, H''\})$ where H' and H'' are possibly empty graphs. The first element in a sequence satisfies the predicate π so the leak is detected.

Implementing data access policy relies on two elements. The first is the concept of a list of *forbidden patterns* defined above, which assigns to a given agent A a list of subgraphs which are not allowed to be obtained by A if given predicates holds. The second element of data policy implementation is wrapping a message content into the structure containing the message trace (consisting of agents) and contributions from particular transitive agents.

We should also consider the specific but important case of three agents, A_1, A_2, B organized in the two level hierarchy (Figure 5.1). Agents A_1 and A_2 are assumed to be located at the same, lower level and B, the supervising agent, at the upper one. We assume that B is authorized to send and receive any data to/from A_1 and A_2, and that the latter ones are restricted in a communication: A_2 cannot obtain some data (graph), say X, from A_1 and *vice versa*: A_1 cannot obtain some data (graph), say X', from A_2. It may be formalized using the notion of FP mapping (see the formula 4.1) in the following way:

$$FP(A_1) = (X', \pi_1),$$
$$FP(A_2) = (X, \pi_2),$$

where $\pi_1 = \{X' \text{ originates from } A_2\}$ and $\pi_2 = \{X \text{ originates from } A_1\}$. Suppose that the agent B forwards both graphs, X and X', without adding any knowledge to them. Thus A_2 receives the message $M = \{(\{X, A_1\}), \{A_1, B\}, X\}$ from A_1 and analogously A_2 receives the message $M' = \{(\{X', A_2\}), \{A_2, B\}, X'\}$ from A_2. In both cases the message would trigger the data leak alert due to pairs $\{X, A_1\}$ matching π_2 and $\{X', A_2\}$ matching π_1. In this case however X and X' as well may be "legally" forwarded from A_1 to A_2 (and from A_2 to A_1 respectively) via B which may grant rights to A_1 and A_2 to access X' and X respectively. In this context B authorizes A_2 to read X and A_1 to read X'. To introduce this scenario to the agent communication semantics and to avoid the clash with data confidentiality policy we need to include this case in predicates π_1 and π_2. It may be accomplished twofold: either by introducing an explicit clause into π (e.g., the last agent in the message trace is B) or by adding some special attribute to X (X'), say `allowed` which value is set to `true` by the agent B.

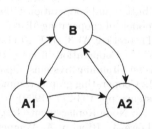

Fig. 5.1. Two level hierarchy of agents

6   Conclusions and the Future Work

This paper presents a new approach to a knowledge exchange between independent agents representing entities gathering data. The main idea behind this approach is to prevent security leaks i.e. passage of data to an unauthorized entities. The methodology presented here allows for a strong control of data passing and provides a formal and well defined method preventing unauthorized access to sensitive data. An example presented in this paper shows a simple but representative scenario.

While this approach does not make any assumption about types of graphs used as the data representation it still assumes an existence of some common graph type enabling communication among all agents (or at least ability of "understanding" forbidden patterns). As this assumption may be hard to assure in some cases we are now working on providing a "translation" layer between agents which would allow for the use of different graph representations at each agent which would better fit the real world situations where different entities (institutions) may have different data representations..

Another direction for future research involves the use of graph transformations as a way of formal description of both data modification and data passing. While the use of formal grammars has been use for quite a long time as a mean to describe and modify data we plan to use it also as a mean of data transfer (exchange) between different entities.

Acknowledgments. Financial support for this study was provided from resources of the NCBIR grant no. 0021/R/ID2/2011/01.

References

1. Rozenberg, G.: Handbook of Graph Grammars and Computing By Graph Transformation, vol. 1-3. World Scientific (1997-1999)
2. Kotulski, L., Strug, B.: Supporting communication and cooperation in distributed representation for adaptive design. Advanced Engineering Informatics 27(2), 220–229 (2013)
3. Csuhaj-Varju, E., Dassow, J., Kelemen, J., Paun, G.: Grammar systems. A grammatical approach to distribution and cooperation (1994)
4. Kelemen, J.: Syntactical models of cooperating/distributed problem solving. Journal of Experimental and Theoretical AI 3(1), 1–10 (1991)
5. Martin-Vide, C., Mitrana, V.: Cooperation in contextual grammars. In: Proc of the MFCS 1998 Workshop on Grammar Systems, Opava, pp. 289-302 (1998)
6. Simeoni, M., Staniszkis, M.: Cooperating graph grammar systems. In: Grammatical Models of Multi-agent Systems, pp. 193-217 (1999)
7. Engelfriet, J., Rozenberg, G.: Node Replacement Graph Grammars, 3–94. In: [1]
8. H. Ehrig, R. Heckel, M. Löwe, L. Ribeiro, A. Wagner: Algebraic Approaches to Graph Transformation - Part II: Single Pushout and Comparison with Double Pushout Approach. In: [1] pp. 247-312
9. Grabska, E., Strug, B.: Applying Cooperating Distributed Graph Grammars in Computer Aided Design. In: Wyrzykowski, R., Dongarra, J., Meyer, N., Waśniewski, J. (eds.) PPAM 2005. LNCS, vol. 3911, pp. 567–574. Springer, Heidelberg (2006)
10. Grabska, E., Strug, B., Slusarczyk, G.: A Graph Grammar Based Model for Distributed Design (2006)
11. Kotulski, L., Strug, B.: Distributed Adaptive Design with Hierarchical Autonomous Graph Transformation Systems. NCS 4488, 880–887 (2007)

12. Kotulski, L.: GRADIS – Multiagent Environment Supporting Distributed Graph Transformations. In: Bubak, M., van Albada, G.D., Dongarra, J., Sloot, P.M.A. (eds.) ICCS 2008, Part III. LNCS, vol. 5103, pp. 644–653. Springer, Heidelberg (2008)
13. Kotulski, L., Fryz, L.: Conjugated Graph Grammars as a Mean to Assure Consistency of the System of Conjugated Graphs. In: Proceedings of RELCOMEX 2008, pp. 9–14. IEEE (2008)
14. Kotulski, L.: Distributed Graphs Transformed by Multiagent System. In: Rutkowski, L., Tadeusiewicz, R., Zadeh, L.A., Zurada, J.M. (eds.) ICAISC 2008. LNCS (LNAI), vol. 5097, pp. 1234–1242. Springer, Heidelberg (2008)
15. Kotulski, L., Sedziwy, A.: Agent framework for decomposing a graph into the subgraphs of the same size.In: WORLDCOMP 2008 (FCS 2008), Las Vegas (2008)
16. Kotulski, L., Strug, B.: Parallel Graph Transformations in Distributed Adaptive Design. In: Proc. GCM-ICGT 2008, Leicester (2008)
17. Minas, M.: Concepts and Realization of a Diagram Editor Generator Based on Hypergraph Transformation. Science of Computer Programming 44, 157–180 (2002)

Managing Machine's Motivations

Janusz Starzyk[1,2], James Graham[1], and Leszek Puzio[2]

[1] School of Electrical Engineering and Computer Science,
Ohio University, Athens, OH, USA
{jg193404,starzykj}@ohio.edu
[2] University of Information Technology and Management, Rzeszow, Poland
lpuzio@wsiz.rzeszow.pl

Abstract. This paper presents concepts for the development and management of motivations in learning agents, which are critical for motivated learning. We suggest that an agent must be equipped with a mechanism referred to as a *nonspecific formative process* to trigger higher level motivations. Resource and action related motivations are discussed as examples of implementing such process in a virtual world learning scenario.

Keywords: Motivated learning, cognitive agents, reinforcement learning, goal creation.

1   Introduction

In this paper, we examine various ways to establish a motivation mechanism for the agent to develop. This is an extension of our earlier work on creation of goals by an autonomous learning agent[1].

Autonomous learning agents are needed to establish a path towards intelligent machines. Today, these agents find many applications in industry such as: robotics, video games, remote sensing, image recognition, quality control, warfare, assisting humans, entertainment, etc. and their importance is growing steadily. There are several concepts for organizing motivational systems. One, introduced by Pfeifer [2], shows motivation as a result of the developmental process. Another concept, based on external reward signals, is known as reinforcement learning (RL). It was initialized by the work of Sutton and Barto [3], followed by Brooks [4], Pfeifer [5], Schmidhuber [6] and many others. The intrinsic motivation system based on artificial curiosity was proposed by Oudeyer [7].

Merrick pointed out that RL robots do not have internal drives to maintain their resources within an acceptable range [8]. To address this problem a motivated learning (ML) system was proposed to allow the agent to develop its own motivations and goals [9]. Merrick introduced motivated reinforcement learning (MRL) and used motivated exploration in video games [8]. Motivated learning based on the need for resources was used to develop a coordinated learning strategy in a multi-stage stochastic game [10].

L. Rutkowski et al. (Eds.): ICAISC 2014, Part II, LNAI 8468, pp. 278–289, 2014.
© Springer International Publishing Switzerland 2014

Motivated learning showed promise in supporting the development of intelligent systems. But a nagging question arises; where do the motivations come from? How should a system be motivated to develop? What are the conditions for motivations to reach higher levels of abstraction and sophistication in an agent's interaction with the environment? This paper tries to answer some of these questions and proposes a mechanism for creating higher level motivations fundamental to agent's mental development.

2   Basic Concepts in Motivated Learning

A ML agent has predefined *needs* (for instance need for shelter, food, or energy level). Agent *motivations* are to satisfy its needs. Thus, in order to introduce new motivations, an agent must develop new needs. A basic mechanism to create new needs for resources was described in [9]. This was extended in recent work to a mechanism that is used to create needs related to actions by other agents.

In order to clarify our discussion let us define some critical concepts used in ML.

Definitions
A *primitive pain* is associated with each predefined need and measures how far the agent is from satisfying its need. The pain is larger if the degree of satisfaction of a need is lower. For example the following function can measure resource related pains:

$$P_i = w_i * \frac{\varepsilon + R_d(s_i)}{\varepsilon + R_c(s_i)} \tag{1}$$

where R_d is a desired level of needed resource s_i, w_i is a weight that increases with the increased importance of resource i, R_c is the current level, and ε is a small positive number to prevent numerical overflow. *Pain reduction* in ML is equivalent to a *reward* in RL.

When an agent is introduced to a new environment, it does not know how to satisfy its needs and must experiment with various resources and available actions until one of its needs is reduced. A new *abstract need* is created for the resource used to reduce the primitive need. The agent will reduce the new abstract need in the same manner it reduced its primitive needs by trying various actions. An *Abstract pain* measures how far the agent is from satisfying its abstract need and is computed based on (1).

Once introduced, an abstract need can be satisfied by acting on another resource. This leads to another higher level abstract need (for this new resource) and related abstract pain. This simple mechanism allows the agent to build a potentially complex "network of needs" and such mechanism is a foundation of *resource based motivations*.

3   Developing Motivations

In this paper, we ask questions as to what other cognitive mechanisms should be considered for building motivations, and to allow a ML agent to develop even more abstract motivations, such as a motivations to gain love, friendship, recognition in society, self esteem, or the human tendency to actualize itself as fully as possible. The last one, known as self-actualization, is considered by psychologists as the final level of psychological development that can be achieved when all basic and other mental needs are satisfied. According to Goldstein [11] self-actualization is not an ultimate objective, but rather a process driven by the tendency to actualize all self capacities, the entire potential available at any given moment and in given conditions.

The question is as follows: can all these levels of abstract motivation be derived from the *fundamental mechanisms* that create needs in ML? Are they necessary consequences of mental development? Are they characteristic of successful intelligent behavior, whether this behavior is conducted by a human, an animal, or a machine? Can these abstract motivations be achieved before the lower level needs are satisfied and if not, are they symptomatic to the friendliness, specific level of sophistication, and reciprocal support from the environment in which such growth is possible and useful?

Reasoning along this line we may ask: is the state of the environment related to the motivational levels and the level of mental development of its learning agents? We may also ask a more direct question: is the state of the environment a result of and measure of the state of development of the most successful individuals that inhibit it? These are not existential questions, although they may relate to such questions. The aim of asking these questions is to specify the necessary environmental conditions for developmental robots.

We have affirmative examples confirming mutual dependence of the environment and its inhabitants in humans. The more advanced the state of the environment in terms of technological support, tools efficiency, and ease of satisfying basic human needs; the more capable, more motivated and better developed individuals become, even when their brains do not change much.

There is a difference of opinion in psychology as to whether higher order needs and motivations are a driving force for human development or whether they are a prespecified ideal hierarchy of motivations and needs. This difference can be rephrased in a question: do we develop our needs as we grow or is there a given hierarchy that is fixed and specified independently of individual capacities to reach them that perhaps only few of us can reach, living ordinary lives. This question is important in view of developmental learning in machines where we do not put limits on the development or needs, but try to justify higher levels by what works and what makes the machine more successful in its interaction with the environment. A related and equally important question is about the basis of these motivations. Is there a mechanism that creates them and if so what is it?

Psychologists studying successful people like Albert Einstein and Charles Darwin found that these people were focused on finding solutions to societal problems rather than to their own personal problems, were open minded, had a strong sense of self, valued life and human dignity, and had a small group of close friends. This helped them to succeed where others could not. But this observation of personal traits in people who succeeded when extended to a general population may miss an important link in the developmental process, the one that justifies why such motivations are useful for growth of individuals and society. Instead some of the highest level motivations are compared to the norms of morality in a given society. Are these norms invariant to the level of growth and sophistication of social interactions? Most likely not. We know that such norms change as society changes, as social consciousness and understanding of human needs and behavior grows. Thus, such norms or prespecified hierarchy of motivations cannot be considered as a constant part of the mechanism responsible for the developmental process.

Alderfer's *ERG theory* [12] stresses *existence, relatedness*, and *growth*, where *existence* focuses on material existence requirements, *relatedness* focuses on the need to relate and maintain social interactions, and *growth* focuses on personal development. But are they the mechanisms that resulted in current social organization or rather they reflect it? In this search for cause and effect we cannot accept existing norms as a foundation for the development of higher level motivations. Norms were not given but were derived from the development of humans and accepted by society. Subsequently, they became a part of the current environment that influences further growth. However, further growth must come from within individual's drives which are modified but not predetermined by the current social order.

Ryan and Deci [13] who promote self-determination theory focus on three elements: humans master their drives and emotions, have a tendency to grow and develop, and optimal development does not happen automatically. This theory is hard to accept as a drive for development since it does not explain what a driver for such motivations is or why they appeared in the first place. They do not provide a causal relationship in behavioral development that would yield these kinds of drives.

The Need for Achievement theory [14] of motivational growth stresses social motives like dominance. According to this theory people will take calculated risks, establish attainable goals, and fear failure. They also want to be praised for their accomplishments and receive feedback from others. Such and other theories debated by psychologists focus on explaining the human motivational system, the way it is and the way expresses itself, but they do not answer the important question from the developmental point of view. How did the human motivational system develop?

What is important for building intelligent machines is to describe the *nonspecific formative processes* (NFP) that the agent may use to develop motivations at a certain abstraction level. Nonspecific means that these processes are not prespecified to obtain certain motivations (like the need for food or shelter) but rather are used to develop motivations that help to solve a group of existential problems.

3.1   Nonspecific Formative Processes

An example of a NFP process is the way an agent creates goals and motivations in order to acquire resources needed for its survival as discussed in Section 2. Such a NFP process includes evaluation of changes in the environment and creates motivations to collect or to avoid certain resources in the environment. The resources are defined as objects in the environment that do not initiate actions by themselves. Rather they can be used by the agent to satisfy its needs (for instance food or water) or to be avoided since they may harm the agent (for instance poisons or toxic substances).

Starzyk, J. Graham, and L. Puzio

Another example is to equip the agent with an NFP process to evaluate actions by other agents (non agent characters or NACs) and learn how to encourage or discourage such actions. Such a NFP evaluation process is nonspecific because it makes no assumption as to what kind of agent performs the action, what action it performs, or whether or not this action has any effect on the ML agent. Learning how to discourage or encourage an action is also nonspecific as the ML agent has no preconceived knowledge whether or not the action performed by NAC is beneficial or harmful.

The need for action to discourage NAC action (that increases ML agent pain) will be a result of the NAC action pain signal created by the agent. The NAC action pain can be computed using:

$$B = \gamma * \frac{-\delta_a * \overline{P(y)}}{1 - \delta_a - 2 * L(y) + \varepsilon} \tag{2}$$

where $L(y)$ is a likelihood that NAC agent will act on the ML agent, y identifies the NAC action, $\overline{P(y)}$ is the average pain to ML agent caused in the past by a NAC action, and δ_a is desirability of such action. δ_a is 1 when the action by NAC is desired and δ_a is -1 when it is not. The value ε is a small positive number to prevent numerical overflow, and $\gamma > 0$ regulates how quickly pain increases.

Another example will be an NFP process to evaluate actions by other intelligent agents that can learn to modify their actions according to the response of ML agent. Since no such mechanism has been developed yet, it is hard to speculate how general it can be and what it will involve.

It is this category of ML agent mechanisms that need to be investigated, designed and implemented in order to provide the agent with cognitive support to reach higher levels of motivational development as described by Maslow [15]. This paper addresses some of the issues and poses open questions to discuss scenarios, current developmental skills, levels of sophistication of the environment in which such development is useful or possible.

Developmental skills determine the internal state of the agent ready for further growth and development of its motivations and mental abilities. Thus, some motivations cannot be developed before others and they will naturally form a hierarchy of motivations and related skills. The developmental process is a function of itself and depends on its history as well as the agent's ability to accommodate new challenges in the environment. For instance, before the agent learns how to interact with another intelligent agent, it must possess skills necessary to respond to NAC actions. Similarly, in order to learn how to respond to NAC actions that are damaging an agent's resources, the ML agent must first learn the values of such resources, and have motivations to collect or protect them. Thus, it must have developed a resource NFP process before it can develop a NAC NFP process and related motivations.

To some degree, the structure of motivational drives develops gradually and can be compared to the genetic development of species. The difference is that it concerns only a single individual rather than generations of individuals. The similarity between these two processes is that both mental development as well as evolutionary development are incremental and depend on the current state of the developmental process. Similarity also lies in the randomness of the incremental changes that take place.

In genetic development it is survival of the fittest as a way to adapt to changes in the environment (by random mutations and crossovers), while in mental development it is the opportunity to learn an interesting trait to improve the way that an individual works (by random trial and error).

3.2   Social Agent

A learned response to NAC action pain (2) may not work well when the NAC is intelligent. An intelligent NAC agent may change its strategy, such that an initially successful action may fail.   Another way in which an intelligent NAC may respond is to fight back, causing additional pain that was not there before. This may be a primitive pain inflicted on the ML agent, so there is no need to use bias estimation. To avoid such pain, the ML agent must learn that its action caused the NAC's response and modify its behavior. If the ML agent observes that total pain from all pain sources increased as a result of its action, the action should be avoided.

So, the question is what recourse does the ML agent have when an intelligent NAC destroys its resources or otherwise inflicts pain on the ML agent? No action against the NAC will be painful. An action that causes a response from NAC may be painful, but if the total pain increase is smaller than when no action is taken, such an action is acceptable. For instance, the ML agent may fight the NAC and even when it suffers some pain, the overall pain reduction may be greater than the pain inflicted by the fight, particularly if the ML agent is stronger than the NAC and makes it go away.

If the NAC is stronger, the pain inflicted by it may exceed the pain reduction and such action should be avoided. We then see a typical flight situation, where the agent will suffer the pain without fighting back.

But what if the NAC can fight back with equal resolve and inflict equal pain to the agent? Both agents will suffer a significant amount of pain without any benefit. For instance when they fight over the food supply, neither will get food, and they suffer the pain inflicted by their opponent. The obvious solution to this situation will be sharing the resources, rather than fighting for them.   Such a decision, when neither agent fights for the resource will be "agreed" upon if the two agents know each other's ability to inflict significant pain and decide not to fight. Such an estimate can be obtained using (2) and evaluating the likelihood of aggression by the NAC directed against the ML agent.

The only modification we need in this case is to replace $L(y)$ by a likelihood estimate based on learning the NAC's behavior. This can be accomplished using RL which will learn the likelihood of NAC actions and predict the negative reward in response to the ML agent's action.

Similar analysis can be performed in the case where intelligent NAC action is desired. The likelihood of the NAC's action is learned using RL. If this likelihood is low, the ML agent will suffer the pain described by (2) proportional to the amount of reward (pain reduction) that the NAC action can bring.

3.3   Directing the Machine

A good way to accelerate learning is to use help from a teacher. The problem is how to introduce a teacher within the framework of ML? The simplest (but not the most desirable) way is to assume that any instruction given by the teacher motivates the robot to complete this instruction to a satisfaction of a teacher. We can use voice commands as sensory input that must be recognized and interpreted by the robot. We assume that a spoken command generates a primitive pain signal that is removed by the teacher once its command was correctly implemented by the robot. The level of the pain signal is between threshold and the maximum pain and depends on the articulation. A sharp and angry command will carry higher pain that a soft and gentle instruction. So the agent must learn not only to recognize the command but also to determine its emotional content. The teacher will reward the agent by pressing a prespecified key. A more developed agent may learn to use verbal praise for a reward.

4   Simulation Scenario

To illustrate the process of developing motivations, we designed a learning environment for the ML agent. In our simulation scenario, presented in Fig.1, we have five primitive pains: Sweet-tooth, Bee stings, Hunger, Thirst, Curiosity.

In Fig. 1 all resources are represented by ovals and actions by rectangles. Acting on a resource that inhibits a pain is indicated by inhibitory links (with solid black circle). An excitatory link (with arrow) triggers a NAC action pain or a NAC appearance. In Fig. 1, only simplified relations are shown to avoid clutter. Each resource symbol can be interpreted as an inhibitory interaction on the amount of resource and the lack of resource pain as shown in Fig. 2. Similarly, a related action on the resource causes a small inhibitory feedback link to the resource being utilized as shown on Fig.2 b from the action 'Plant Flowers' to the resource 'Flowers'.

As illustrated in Fig. 2, the top inhibitory link inhibits the abstract pain 'Lack of Flowers'. When the 'Lack of Flowers' is inhibited the Flowers resource is automatically activated. A resource is restored through proper action by the agent, in this case by buying flowers. As the resource is used up by frequent action (planting flowers) the inhibition from Flowers to the Lack of Flowers is weaker and the abstract pain 'Lack of Flowers' increases. In Fig. 2, the resource nodes and lack of resource nodes are automatically activated unless inhibited. The forward arrow links are excitatory, so the Flowers resource activates the non-agent character (bees).

Curiosity pain drives agent to explore the environment, *i.e.*, to learn useful actions on resources. Curiosity pain stays high until the agent learns all valid actions. Other primitive pains like Thirst, Hunger, Bee stings, Sweet-tooth, may be satisfied by various actions. For example, the Thirst pain can be satisfied by the 'Drink water from Cup' action. Hunger, Thirst, and Sweet-tooth pains increase with time, while the 'Bee stings' pain increases when Bees are around. We call those actions 'useful motorsensor pairs', because the agent can satisfy one of its needs performing a motor action on a resource.

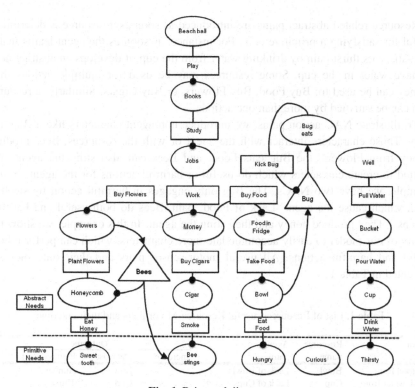

Fig. 1. Pain-goal diagram

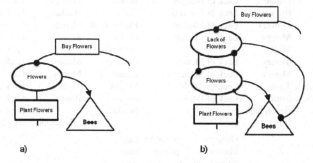

a)   b)

Fig. 2. a) Simplified relations from Fig. 1 between the resource (flowers) and the action on the resource (plant flowers), b) detailed relations

Notice that the presented scenario is used in simulation to show relationships between resources and changes in the environment that result from specific actions. The ML agent does not know these relations and has to learn them by interacting with the environment and observing what happens.

Resource related abstract pains are introduced as soon as a resource is determined useful for satisfying a primitive pain. For instance, as soon as the agent learns that it can satisfy its thirst pain by drinking water from the cup, it develops an abstract need to have water in the cup. Some resources may be used for multiple actions, like Money can be used to: Buy Food, Buy Flowers, or Buy Cigars. Similarly, a resource pain can be satisfied by more than one action.

To illustrate NAC action pains, we introduce non-agent characters like a Bug and Bees. Those characters interact with the agent or with the resources. Bees produce Honey from Flowers, the Bug eats Food, and Bees can also sting the agent. We wanted to create characters which do useful or harmful actions for the agent. In this example, we have two NACs. The Bug only engages in harmful action by steeling food, which cause the agent 'Lack of Food' pain. Bees do both useful and harmful actions. They produce honey and they sting the agent. In this example, we show the ability of our model to easily accommodate more characters, which can perform both useful and harmful actions. All useful motor-sensor pairs and their outcomes are presented in Table 1.

Table 1. List of Resources, useful Resource-Motor pairs and their outcome

Motor action	Resource name	Agent's pains	Outcome		
			Increase	Decrease	Pain reduced
Eat food from	Bowl	Lack of Bowls		Bowls	Hunger
Drink water from	Cup	Lack of Cups		Cups	Thirst
Eat honey from	Honeycomb	Lack of Honeycombs		Honeycombs	Sweet tooth
Smoke	Cigar	Lack of Cigars		Cigars	Bee sting
Take food from	Fridge	Lack of Fridges	Bowls	Fridges	Lack of Bowls
Pour water from	Bucket	Lack of Buckets	Cups	Buckets	Lack of Cups
Plant	Flowers	Lack of Flowers	Honeycombs	Flowers	Lack of Honeycombs
Buy food with	Money	Lack of Money	Fridges	Money	Lack of Fridges
Pull water from	Well	-	Buckets	-	Lack of Buckets
Buy flowers with	Money	Lack of Money	Flowers	Money	Lack of Flowers
Buy cigars with	Money	Lack of Money	Cigars	Money	Lack of Cigars
Work for money with	Tools	Lack of Tools	Money	Tools	Lack of Money
Study for job with	Book	Lack of Books	Tools	Books	Lack of Tools
Play for joy with	Beach ball		Books		Lack of Books
Kick	Bug	-		Likelihood	Bug eating food
		Hunger - primitive pain			
		Thirst - primitive pain			
		Sweet tooth - primitive pain			
		Bee sting - primitive pain			
Any		Curiosity - primitive pain			Curiosity

4.1 Simulation Implementation

Based on this scenario, we created a simulation in NeoAxis. The NeoAxis 3D Engine is an integrated development environment for 3D projects of any type and complexity. The environment is intended for use in such areas as the creation of video games, development of simulators, and development of virtual reality and visualization software.

It includes a full set of tools for fast and logical development of modern 3D projects. We created 3D models of resources and characters, and animations of characters in Autodesk 3ds Max. Fig. 3 presents sample resources and character's models. Some animations were captured by Kinect, which provides also full-body 3D motion capture, facial recognition and voice recognition capabilities. The agent logic was written in C++ with use of the Boost library. The simulation environment was implemented in C#.

a)   b)

Fig. 3. a) Resources: apple, ball, banana, bucket, bowl, cup, b) Characters: agent, bug, bee

Based on the presented simulation scenario, we created a simulation map with all resources and characters mentioned in Fig. 1. During creation of the simulation environment, we set the desired level for each resource. We implemented NACs and their actions (both types, i.e. desired and undesired). We also implemented agent actions on resources from Table 1. Fig. 4 presents such a map with resources and NACs.

Fig. 4. Simulation map

Multiple simulation tests proved that the ML agent was able to use the nonspecific formative processes to develop resource and NAC action based motivations, and was able to successfully learn how to manage its needs in a dynamic environment. To our knowledge no other cognitive agent can learn how to manage its resources and learn how to respond to other characters' attacks. We challenge anyone in the machine learning community to try a simpler version of such scenario - Autonomous Learning Challenge - described on http://ncn.wsiz.rzeszow.pl/?p=39.

The simulation window presented in Fig. 5 shows: in the left top corner - a list of resources available to the agent and their quantities; in the top center - the current task performed by the agent; at top right - a list of abstract and primitive pains and their levels; bottom left - the state of agent's memory.

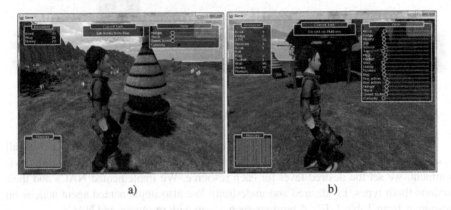

a)   b)

Fig. 5. Simulation window with a list of resources, current task, pains, and memory. a) the agent starts its learning process, b) the agent learned all actions.

When the simulation starts, the agent may interact only with three resources (Bowl, Mug, Honey) to satisfy its primitive pains (Hunger, Thirst, Sweet-tooth, Curiosity). This situation is presented in Fig. 5 a). The memory window in this screenshot is almost grey, indicating that the agent has learned very little. After some time in simulation, the agent's knowledge increases. It introduces new abstract pains, and discovers new applications for resources. As a result, the agent is able to keep its pain under control and keep resources at satisfied levels. Its memory indicates that it learned how to maintain resources and control the NAC related pains. After satisfying all pains (i.e., keeping their levels below threshold), the agent goes to rest on a mattress. Multiple tests proved that in less than half an hour of real time simulation, the agent was able to learn all useful actions and keep its pains under control.

5   Conclusions

This paper examines how motivations in a motivated agent are formed and how they can become increasingly abstract. We examined our earlier work and the recent changes we have made to introduce actions by non-agent characters (NACs), and determined how this work could be extended. The agent must learn increasingly abstract behaviour interacting with its environment and communicating with other agents. We posit that this can be done via the use of nonspecific formative processes by giving the agent the ability to reason about the cause and effect of its actions on itself, the environment, and other agents. We also suggest that higher level motivations can only develop when the environment is sophisticated enough to stimulate and support further growth of the agent's mental powers. Brooks stated 20 years ago that intelligence cannot develop without environment. We append this by stating that the development is mutually dependent. Developing agents change their environment, and this change is necessary for further growth in the complexity of agents' motivations.

Acknowledgements. This research was supported by The National Science Centre, grant No. 2011/03/B/ST7/02518.

References

1. Starzyk, J.A., Graham, J.T., Raif, P., Tan, A.-H.: Motivated Learning for Autonomous Robots Development. Cognitive Science Research 14(1), 10(16),10–25 (2012)
2. Pfeifer, R., Bongard, J.C.: How the Body Shapes the Way We Think: A New View of Intelligence. The MIT Press, Bradford Books (2007)
3. Sutton, R., Barto, A.G.: Reinforcement Learning: An Introduction. MIT Press (1998)
4. Brooks, R.A.: Intelligence without representation. Artificial Intelligence 47, 139–159 (1991)
5. Pfeifer, R., Scheier, C.: Understanding Intelligence. MIT Press, Cambridge (1999)
6. Schmidhuber, J.: Curious model-building control systems. In: Proc. Int. Joint Conf. Neural Networks, Singapore, pp. 1458–1463 (1991)
7. Oudeyer, P.-Y., Kaplan, F., Hafner, V.: Intrinsic Motivation Systems for Autonomous Mental Development. IEEE Trans. on Evolutionary Computation 11(2), 265–286 (2007)
8. Merrick, K.: A Comparative Study of Value Systems for Self-Motivated Exploration and Learning by Robots. IEEE Transactions on Autonomous Mental Development 2(2), 119–131 (2010)
9. Starzyk, J.A.: Motivation in Embodied Intelligence. In: Frontiers in Robotics, Automation and Control, pp. 83–110. I-Tech Education and Publishing (October 2008)
10. Teng, T.-H., Tan, A.-H., Teow, L.-N., Starzyk, J.A.: Motivated Learning for Coordinated Multi-Agent Reinforcement Learning in Multi-Stage Game. In: 13th Int. Conf. on Autonomous Agents and Multiagent Systems, Paris, France, May 5-9 (2014)
11. Goldstein, K.: The Organism: A Holistic Approach to Biology Derived from Pathological Data in Man. Beacon Press (1963)
12. Alderfer, C.: Existance, relatedness and growth. Free Press (1972)
13. Ryan, R., Deci, E.L.: Intrinsic and Extrinsic Motivations: Classic Definitions and New Directions. Cont. Educational Psychology 25(1), 54–67 (2000)
14. McClelland, D., Atkinson, J.W., Clark, R.A.: The Achievement Motive. Literarry licensing (2012)
15. Maslow, A.: Motivation and personality. Pearson (1997)

Globalised Dual Heuristic Dynamic Programming in Tracking Control of the Wheeled Mobile Robot

Marcin Szuster

Rzeszow University of Technology
Department of Applied Mechanics and Robotics
8 Powstancow Warszawy St., 35-959 Rzeszow, Poland
mszuster@prz.edu.pl

Abstract. The paper presents an application of the Approximate Dynamic Programming algorithm in Globalised Dual Heuristic Dynamic Programming configuration in the tracking control problem of the wheeled mobile robot Pioneer 2-DX. The Globalised Dual Heuristic Dynamic Programming algorithm is realised in the form of two structures, the actor and the critic, that can be implemented in the form of any adaptive algorithm, e.g. Artificial Neural Networks. The actor generates the suboptimal control law, the critic approximates the value function and its difference with respect to the states, what is equal to evaluation of the realised control law. The discrete tracking control system is composed of the Globalised Dual Heuristic Dynamic Programming algorithm, the PD controller and the supervisory term, which structure derives from the stability analysis realised using the Lapunov stability theorem. The proposed control system works on-line and its performance was verified using the wheeled mobile robot Pioneer 2-DX.

Keywords: Approximate Dynamic Programming, Globalised Dual Heuristic Dynamic Programming, Neural Network, Tracking Control, Wheeled Mobile Robot.

1 Introduction

The tracking control problem of wheeled mobile robots (WMRs) is widely discussed in literature, where different approaches to realisation of the desired trajectory are presented. This shows how important and difficult to solve the problem is. Difficulties met in the tracking control problem result from the fact, that WMRs are described by nonlinear dynamic equations, where some parameters of the model may by unknown or change during the movement. That is why the best results in realisation of the tracking control are obtained by the implementation of complex methods, that can adjust their parameters during the realisation of the task, to assure the demanded quality of the tracking. Artificial Intelligence (AI) algorithms like Artificial Neural Networks (NNs) [4, 11] or Approximate Dynamic Programming (ADP) [1, 2, 6, 13, 15–17] algorithms are widely used to solve control

L. Rutkowski et al. (Eds.): ICAISC 2014, Part II, LNAI 8468, pp. 290–301, 2014.

problems. Solutions presented in literature are often only the theoretical considerations, and there is not many real applications. The control system presented in this paper is used for the tracking control of the WMR Pioneer 2-DX. It includes the ADP algorithm in the Globalised Dual Heuristic Dynamic Programming (GDHP) configuration [3, 13, 16], which is rarely met in literature. The control system is characterised by high tracking performance and guaranteed stability. The GDHP algorithm is realised in a form of two structures, the actor and the critic, composed of Random Vector Functional Link (RVFL) NNs.

The results of the researches presented in the article continue the author's earlier works related to the problem of control of nonlinear dynamical systems like the WMR, using ADP methods [7–9]. The paper is organised as follows: after a short introduction to the WMRs tracking control problem in the first section, section two presents the control object - the WMR Pioneer 2-DX and its dynamics model. In the third section, the ADP algorithm in the GDHP configuration is presented. Section four includes the proposed tracking control system, and the following section presents the laboratory stand. The next section includes the results of an experiment. The last section summarises the article.

2   Dynamics of the Wheeled Mobile Robot Pioneer 2-DX

The control object is a two-wheeled mobile robot, the Pioneer 2-DX, shown in Fig. 1. The WMR is a non-holonomic object, described by nonlinear dynamics equations, composed of two driving wheels 1 and 2, a free rolling castor wheel 3 and a frame 4. The movement of the WMR is analysed in the xy plane.

The presented tracking control system is discrete. A continuous model of the WMR's dynamics [4, 5] was discretised using the Euler's method. The state vector was assumed in the form $z_{\{k\}} = \left[z_{1\{k\}} \ z_{2\{k\}}\right]^T$, where a vector $z_{2\{k\}} =$

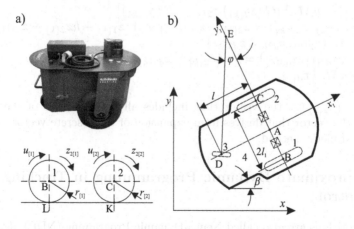

Fig. 1. a) The Pioneer 2-DX, b) the scheme of the WMR Pioneer 2-DX

$\left[z_{2[1]\{k\}} \; z_{2[2]\{k\}} \right]^{T}$ corresponds to the continuous vector of angular velocities. A discrete dynamics model of the WMR was assumed in the form

$$
\begin{aligned}
z_{1\{k+1\}} &= z_{1\{k\}} + h z_{2\{k\}} \,, \\
z_{2\{k+1\}} &= z_{2\{k\}} - h M^{-1} \left[C \left(z_{2\{k\}} \right) z_{2\{k\}} + F \left(z_{2\{k\}} \right) + \tau_{d\{k\}} - u_{\{k\}} \right] \,,
\end{aligned} \tag{1}
$$

where k – an index of iteration steps, h – a time discretisation parameter, M – the positive defined inertia matrix of the WMR, $z_{1\{k\}}$ – the vector of angles of the driving wheels rotation, $z_{1\{k\}} = \left[z_{1[1]\{k\}} \; z_{1[2]\{k\}} \right]^{T}$, $C \left(z_{2\{k\}} \right) z_{2\{k\}}$ – the vector of centrifugal and Coriolis momentous, $F \left(z_{2\{k\}} \right)$ – the vector of resistances to motion, $\tau_{d\{k\}}$ – the vector of disturbances, $u_{\{k\}}$ – the control vector.

The discrete tracking errors of the angles of the driving wheels rotation $z_{1\{k\}}$ and errors of angular velocities $z_{2\{k\}}$ are defined as

$$
\begin{aligned}
e_{1\{k\}} &= z_{1\{k\}} - z_{d1\{k\}} \,, \\
e_{2\{k\}} &= z_{2\{k\}} - z_{d2\{k\}} \,,
\end{aligned} \tag{2}
$$

where the desired trajectory $(z_{d1\{k\}}, z_{d2\{k\}}, z_{d3\{k\}})$ was generated earlier. On the basis of the tracking errors, the filtered tracking error $s_{\{k\}}$ was defined,

$$
s_{\{k\}} = e_{2\{k\}} + \Lambda e_{1\{k\}} \,, \tag{3}
$$

where Λ - a fixed, positive defined diagonal matrix.

On the basis of the errors definitions (2), (3) and the WMR dynamics model (1), the filtered tracking error in step $k + 1$ was assumed in the form

$$
s_{\{k+1\}} = -Y_{f} \left(z_{2\{k\}} \right) + Y_{d} \left(z_{\{k\}}, z_{d\{k\}}, z_{d3\{k\}} \right) - Y_{\tau\{k\}} + h M^{-1} u_{\{k\}} \,, \tag{4}
$$

where

$$
\begin{aligned}
Y_{f} \left(z_{2\{k\}} \right) &= h M^{-1} \left[C \left(z_{2\{k\}} \right) z_{2\{k\}} + F \left(z_{2\{k\}} \right) \right] \,, \\
Y_{d} \left(z_{\{k\}}, z_{d\{k\}}, z_{d3\{k\}} \right) &= z_{2\{k\}} - z_{d2\{k+1\}} + \Lambda \left[z_{1\{k\}} + h z_{2\{k\}} - z_{d1\{k+1\}} \right] = \\
&= s_{\{k\}} + Y_{e} \left(z_{2\{k\}}, z_{d2\{k\}}, z_{d3\{k\}} \right) \,, \\
Y_{e} \left(z_{2\{k\}}, z_{d2\{k\}}, z_{d3\{k\}} \right) &= h \left[\Lambda e_{2\{k\}} - z_{d3\{k\}} \right] \,, \\
Y_{\tau\{k\}} &= h M^{-1} \tau_{d\{k\}} \,,
\end{aligned} \tag{5}
$$

where $Y_{f} \left(z_{2\{k\}} \right)$ – the vector that includes all nonlinearities of the WMR, $z_{d3\{k\}}$ – the vector that derives from expansion of the discrete vector $z_{d2\{k+1\}}$ using the Euler's method.

3   Approximate Dynamic Programming in Tracking Control

ADP algorithms are also called Neuro-Dynamic Programing (NDP) algorithms or Adaptive Critic Designs (ACD) [1, 2, 12–14]. These algorithms derive from the

Bellman's equation, where NNs were applied to approximate the value function, and make real-time control possible. The ADP algorithms family is composed of six algorithms, schematically shown in Fig. 2, that differ from each other by the critic's structure and weights adaptation algorithm. The basic algorithm is the Heuristic Dynamic Programming (HDP) structure, where the actor generates the sub-optimal control law, and the critic approximates the value function. The second algorithm is the Dual Heuristic Dynamic Programming, where the actor's structure is the same, but the critic approximates the difference of the value function with respect to the states. It has a more complex structure, but assures higher quality of control in comparison to HDP [7]. The third algorithm is GDHP, which is built in the same way as HDP, but its characteristic feature is the critic's weights adaptation rule, that bases on the vale function and its difference with respect to the states of the controlled system, so it can be seen as a combination of learning procedures characteristic for the HDP and DHP algorithms. The rest of the ADP algorithms are Action-dependant (AD) versions of HDP, DHP and GDHP, where the control law generated by the actor NN is simultaneously the input to the critic's NN.

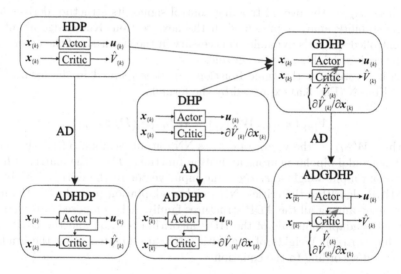

Fig. 2. The scheme of the Approximate Dynamic Programming algorithms family

The main part of the presented discrete tracking control system is the GDHP algorithm. There is not many applications of the GDHP algorithm in control problems in literature, and existing publications concern with rather theoretical studies [3, 10, 16, 17]. In this paper, verification of the tracking control system realised using the WMR Pioneer 2-DX is presented. The GDHP algorithm generates the sub-optimal control law that minimises the value function $V_{\{k\}}\left(s_{\{k\}}\right)$ [1, 2, 12, 13], which is a function of the filtered tracking error $s_{\{k\}}$, assumed in the form

$$V_{\{k\}}\left(s_{\{k\}}\right) = \sum_{k=0}^{N}\gamma^{k}L_{C\{k\}}\left(s_{\{k\}}\right) , \tag{6}$$

where $L_{C\{k\}}\left(s_{\{k\}}\right)$ – the local cost function for the k-th step, N – a number of steps, γ – a discount factor, $0 < \gamma \leq 1$. The cost function was assumed in the form

$$L_{C\{k\}}\left(s_{\{k\}}\right) = \frac{1}{2}s_{\{k\}}^{T}Rs_{\{k\}} , \tag{7}$$

where R – a fixed, positive defined diagonal matrix.

The GDHP algorithm is composed of three structures:

– the predictive model – predicts the state $s_{\{k+1\}}$ of the closed loop system according to equation

$$s_{\{k+1\}} = -Y_f\left(z_{2\{k\}}\right) + Y_d\left(z_{\{k\}}, z_{d\{k\}}, z_{d3\{k\}}\right) + hM^{-1}u_{\{k\}} , \tag{8}$$

where $u_{\{k\}}$ – the overall tracking control signal, its structure derives from the stability analysis presented in the next section. Knowledge about the controlled system's dynamics is necessary in the synthesis of the actor's and the critic's weights adaptation rule.

– critic – estimates the value function (6). It is realised in the form of one RVFL NN (Fig. 3.a) expressed by the formula

$$\hat{V}_{\{k\}}\left(x_{C\{k\}}, W_{C\{k\}}\right) = W_{C\{k\}}^{T}S\left(D_C^{T}x_{C\{k\}}\right) , \tag{9}$$

where $W_{C\{k\}}$ – the vector of critic's NN output weights, $S(.)$ – the vector of sigmoidal bipolar neurons activation functions, D_C – the matrix of fixed, random input weights, $x_{C\{k\}}$ – the input vector to the critic's NN. In the GDHP algorithm the critic's NN weights adaptation procedure is the most complex among all the ADP structures family. It is composed of the critic's weights adaptation rule of the HDP algorithm ($e_{H\{k\}}$) and the DHP algorithm ($e_{D\{k\}}$). Weights of the critic's NN are adapted using the gradient method according to the equation

$$W_{C\{k+1\}} = W_{C\{k\}} - \Gamma_C\eta_1 e_{H\{k\}}\frac{\partial \hat{V}_{\{k\}}\left(x_{C\{k\}}, W_{C\{k\}}\right)}{\partial W_{C\{k\}}} + \\ -\Gamma_C\eta_2 e_{D\{k\}}\frac{\partial^2 \hat{V}_{\{k\}}\left(x_{C\{k\}}, W_{C\{k\}}\right)}{\partial s_{\{k\}}\partial W_{C\{k\}}} , \tag{10}$$

where Γ_C – the fixed diagonal matrix of positive learning rates, η_1, η_2 – positive constants,

$$e_{H\{k\}} = \hat{V}_{\{k\}}\left(x_{C\{k\}}, W_{C\{k\}}\right) - L_{C\{k\}}\left(s_{\{k\}}\right) - \gamma\hat{V}_{\{k+1\}}\left(x_{C\{k+1\}}, W_{C\{k\}}\right) , \tag{11}$$

is a part of the adaptation rule typical of the HDP structure, and

$$
e_{D\{k\}} = \boldsymbol{I}_D^T \left\{ \frac{\partial L_{C\{k\}}\left(\boldsymbol{s}_{\{k\}}\right)}{\partial \boldsymbol{s}_{\{k\}}} + \left[\frac{\partial \boldsymbol{u}_{\{k\}}}{\partial \boldsymbol{s}_{\{k\}}}\right]^T \frac{\partial L_{C\{k\}}\left(\boldsymbol{s}_{\{k\}}\right)}{\partial \boldsymbol{u}_{\{k\}}} + \right.
$$
$$
+\gamma\left[\frac{\partial \boldsymbol{s}_{\{k+1\}}}{\partial \boldsymbol{s}_{\{k\}}} + \left[\frac{\partial \boldsymbol{u}_{\{k\}}}{\partial \boldsymbol{s}_{\{k\}}}\right]^T \frac{\partial \boldsymbol{s}_{\{k+1\}}}{\partial \boldsymbol{u}_{\{k\}}}\right]^T \frac{\partial \hat{V}_{\{k+1\}}\left(\boldsymbol{x}_{C\{k+1\}}, \boldsymbol{W}_{C\{k\}}\right)}{\partial \boldsymbol{s}_{\{k+1\}}} +
$$
$$
\left. -\frac{\partial \hat{V}_{\{k\}}\left(\boldsymbol{x}_{C\{k\}}, \boldsymbol{W}_{C\{k\}}\right)}{\partial \boldsymbol{s}_{\{k\}}} \right\} ,
$$

$$(12)$$

is a part of the adaptation rule typical of the DHP algorithm, where $\boldsymbol{I}_D = [1,1]^T$ – a constant vector.

– actor – generates the suboptimal control law $\boldsymbol{u}_{A\{k\}} = \left[u_{A[1]\{k\}} \; u_{A[2]\{k\}}\right]^T$. It is realised in the form of two RVFL NNs expressed by the formula

$$
u_{A[j]\{k\}}\left(\boldsymbol{x}_{Aj\{k\}}, \boldsymbol{W}_{Aj\{k\}}\right) = \boldsymbol{W}_{Aj\{k\}}^T \boldsymbol{S}\left(\boldsymbol{D}_A^T \boldsymbol{x}_{Aj\{k\}}\right) , \qquad (13)
$$

where j – an index, $j = 1, 2$, $\boldsymbol{W}_{Aj\{k\}}$ – the vector of j-th actor's NN output weights, $\boldsymbol{x}_{Aj\{k\}}$ – an input vector to the j-th actor's NN. The actor's NN weights are adapted using the gradient method according to the equation

$$
\boldsymbol{W}_{Aj\{k+1\}} = \boldsymbol{W}_{Aj\{k\}} - \boldsymbol{\Gamma}_A e_{A[j]\{k\}} \boldsymbol{S}\left(\boldsymbol{D}_A^T \boldsymbol{x}_{Aj\{k\}}\right) , \qquad (14)
$$

where $\boldsymbol{\Gamma}_A$ – a fixed diagonal matrix of positive learning rates. The error $e_{A\{k\}}$ was assumed in the form

$$
e_{A\{k\}} = \frac{\partial L_{C\{k\}}\left(\boldsymbol{s}_{\{k\}}\right)}{\partial \boldsymbol{u}_{\{k\}}} + \left[\frac{\partial \boldsymbol{s}_{\{k+1\}}}{\partial \boldsymbol{u}_{\{k\}}}\right]^T \frac{\partial \hat{V}_{\{k+1\}}\left(\boldsymbol{x}_{C\{k+1\}}, \boldsymbol{W}_{C\{k\}}\right)}{\partial \boldsymbol{s}_{\{k+1\}}} . \quad (15)
$$

The scheme of the GDHP structure is shown in Fig. 3.b).

The structure of the GDHP algorithm is similar to the structure of the HDP algorithm, it generally consists of one critic's NN and n actor's NNs, when n generally corresponds to the size of the state vector of the object's model (in the case of the proposed control system $n = 2$). The difference is in the weights adaptation procedure, which is more complex in GDHP, while it couples the critic's NNs weights adaptation procedures of HDP and DHP. The actor's weights adaptation procedure is similar to that in HDP. The structure of DHP is more complex, because it generally consists of n actor's NNs and n critic's NNs, while the critic approximates the difference of the value function with respect to the states.

4   Tracking Control of the Mobile Robot

The proposed discrete tracking control system consists of four structures:

296   M. Szuster

a)

b)

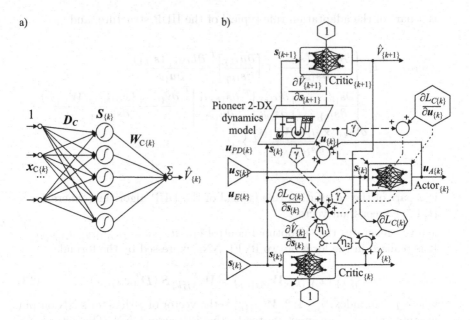

Fig. 3. a) The scheme of the Random Vector Functional Link Neural Network, b) the scheme of the Globalised Dual Heuristic Dynamic Programming algorithm

- the ADP structure in the GDHP configuration, where the actor generates the control signal $u_{A\{k\}}$,
- the PD controller ($u_{PD\{k\}}$), which controls the system at the beginning of the weights adaptation process and in the face of disturbances,
- the supervisory term ($u_{S\{k\}}$), which ensures stability of the control process, its structure derives from the stability analysis realised using the Lyapunov stability theorem,
- the additional control signal $u_{E\{k\}}$.

The overall discrete tracking control signal was assumed in the form

$$u_{\{k\}} = -\frac{1}{h} M \left[u_{A\{k\}} + u_{PD\{k\}} + u_{S\{k\}} + u_{E\{k\}} \right] , \qquad (16)$$

where

$$\begin{aligned} u_{PD\{k\}} &= K_D s_{\{k\}} , \\ u_{S\{k\}} &= I_S u^*_{S\{k\}} , \\ u_{E\{k\}} &= h \left[\Lambda e_{2\{k\}} - z_{d3\{k\}} \right] , \end{aligned} \qquad (17)$$

where K_D – a positive defined diagonal matrix of the PD controller gains, I_S – a diagonal matrix, $I_{S[j,j]} = 1$ if $|s_{[j]\{k\}}| \geq \rho_{[j]}$, and $I_{S[j,j]} = 0$ in the other case, $\rho_{[j]}$ – a positive constant, $j = 1, 2$.

The scheme of the neural tracking control system with GDHP structure is shown in Fig. 4.

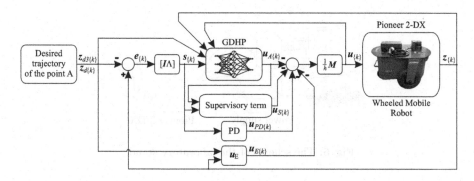

Fig. 4. The scheme of the neural tracking control system with the GDHP structure

In the stability analysis, it was assumed $I_{S[j,j]} = 1$. Substituting (16) into (4), the equation of the closed-loop system takes the form

$$
\begin{aligned}
s_{\{k+1\}} = s_{\{k\}} &- Y_f\left(z_{2\{k\}}\right) + Y_e\left(z_{2\{k\}}, z_{d2\{k\}}, z_{d3\{k\}}\right) - Y_{\tau\{k\}} + \\
&- \left[u_{A\{k\}} + u_{PD\{k\}} + u_{S\{k\}} + u_{E\{k\}}\right] .
\end{aligned}
\tag{18}
$$

The stability analysis of the discrete tracking control system was realised using the Lyapunov stability theorem and assuming the positive definite Lyapunov candidate function

$$
L = \frac{1}{2} s_{\{k\}}^T s_{\{k\}} .
\tag{19}
$$

The difference of (19) can be assumed in the form

$$
\Delta L = s_{\{k\}}^T \left[s_{\{k+1\}} - s_{\{k\}}\right] .
\tag{20}
$$

Substituting (18) into (20) and assuming the supervisory control signal expressed by the formula

$$
u_{S[j]\{k\}}^* = \mathrm{sgn}\left(s_{[j]\{k\}}\right) \left[F_{[j]} + |u_{A[j]\{k\}}| + b_{d[j]} + \sigma_{[j]}\right] ,
\tag{21}
$$

where $|Y_{f[j]}\left(z_{2\{k\}}\right)| \le F_{[j]}$, $F_{[j]}$ – a positive constant, $j = 1, 2$, $b_{d[j]}$ – a positive boundary of the disturbances, $b_{d[j]} > 0$, $|Y_{\tau[j]\{k\}}| \le b_{d[j]}$, $\sigma_{[j]}$ – a positive constant, the difference of the Lyapunov function (20) is a negative definite. The stability analysis of the closed-loop system was discussed in detail in [7, 8].

5   Laboratory Stand

Performance of the presented discrete neural tracking control system with the ADP algorithm in the GDHP configuration was verified using the laboratory stand schematically shown in Fig. 5. It is composed of the WMR Pioneer 2-DX

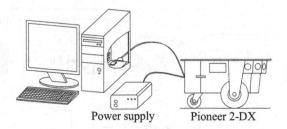

Fig. 5. The scheme of the laboratory stand

with the power supply unit and a PC with the dSpace DS1102 digital signal processing board and software: Control Desk and Matlab/Simulink. The WMR Pioneer 2-DX is equipped with two independently supplied DC motors with gears (19.7:1) and position encoders (500 ticks per shaft revolution). The Pioneer 2-DX weights $m_{DX} = 9$ [kg], its maximal linear velocity is equal to $v_A = 1.6$ [m/s].

6   Experiment Results

The experiment consisted in the tracking control of the point A of the WMR's frame for desired trajectory generated earlier and prescribed in the local memory of the system. In the experiment NNs with eight neurons each were used, and the output layer initial weights values were set to zero. The time discretisation parameter was equal to $h = 0.01$ [s] during the experiment. In this section the notation of variables is simplified and the index k is omitted.

According to the assumed control law (16), the overall tracking control signals $\boldsymbol{u}$, shown in Fig. 6.a), consist of the control signals generated by the actor's NNs $\boldsymbol{u}_A$ (Fig. 6.b), the PD control signals $\boldsymbol{u}_{PD}$ (Fig. 6.c), the supervisory term control signals $\boldsymbol{u}_S$ and the additional control signals $\boldsymbol{u}_E$ shown in Fig. 6.d).

The desired $(z_{d2[1]})$ and realised $(z_{2[1]})$ angular velocities of wheel 1 are shown in Fig. 7.a). The tracking errors of wheel 1, $e_{1[1]}$ and $e_{2[1]}$, are shown in Fig. 7.b). Values of the motion parameters and the tracking errors for wheel 2 are analogical. The highest values of the tracking errors occurred at the beginning of the experiment, when values of the PD control signals are at their highest, and the process of NNs' zero initial weights adaptation starts. Next the control signals of the actor's NNs take the main part of the overall control signals, and the tracking errors are reduced.

Values of the GDHP structure's NNs weights are shown in Fig. 7.c) and d), for the first actor's NN $\boldsymbol{W}_{A1}$ (for the second actor's NN $\boldsymbol{W}_{A2}$ values of weights are similar) and the critic's NN $\boldsymbol{W}_C$ respectively. Values of weights remained bounded during the experiment.

The tracking quality of the proposed control system was compared to the results obtained by other control systems presented earlier, where the ADP algorithms in HDP [7, 9] and DHP [7, 8] configuration, the PD controller or the RVFL NNs [4], were used.

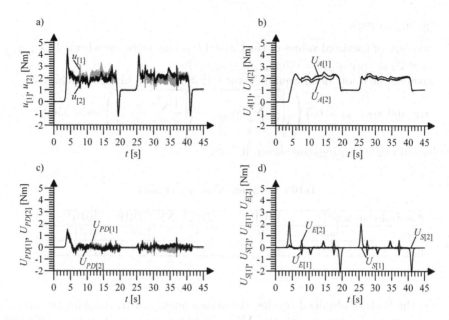

Fig. 6. a) The overall tracking control signals $u_{[1]}$ and $u_{[2]}$, b) the actor's NNs control signals $U_{A[1]}$ and $U_{A[2]}$, $\mathbf{U}_A = -h^{-1}\mathbf{M}\,\mathbf{u}_A$, c) the PD control signals $U_{PD[1]}$ and $U_{PD[2]}$, $\mathbf{U}_{PD} = -h^{-1}\mathbf{M}\,\mathbf{u}_{PD}$, d) the supervisory term's control signals ($U_{S[1]}$, $U_{S[2]}$), $\mathbf{U}_S = -h^{-1}\mathbf{M}\,\mathbf{u}_S$, and the control signals $U_{E[1]}$ and $U_{E[2]}$, $\mathbf{U}_E = -h^{-1}\mathbf{M}\,\mathbf{u}_E$

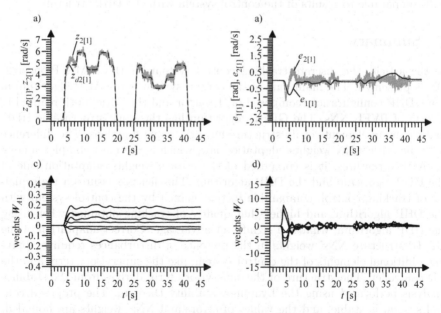

Fig. 7. a) The desired (dashed line) and realised (continuous line) angular velocity of the wheel 1, $z_{d2[1]}$ and $z_{2[1]}$, b) tracking errors of the wheel 1, $e_{1[1]}$ and $e_{2[1]}$, c) weights of the actor 1 RVFL NN $\mathbf{W}_{A1}$, d) weights of the critic RVFL NN $\mathbf{W}_C$

Quality ratings:

- average of maximal values of the filtered tracking error for wheels 1 ($s_{mx[1]}$),
  and 2 ($s_{mx[2]}$): $s_{mxa} = 0.5\left(s_{mx[1]} + s_{mx[2]}\right)$,
- average of Root Mean Square Error (RMSE) of the filtered tracking errors

$$s_{[1]} \text{ and } s_{[2]}: \varepsilon_{av} = 0.5\left(\sqrt{\frac{1}{n}\sum_{k=1}^{n} s_{[1]\{k\}}^2} + \sqrt{\frac{1}{n}\sum_{k=1}^{n} s_{[2]\{k\}}^2}\right), n = 4500.$$

Values of quality ratings are shown it Tab. 1.

Table 1. Values of quality ratings

Control system:	PD	HDP	RVFL NN	GDHP	DHP
s_{mxa}	3.6	2.21	2.3	1.48	1.31
ε_{av}	1.77	0.4	0.32	0.23	0.21

On the basis of obtained results, the higher quality of tracking for the neural tracking control systems with the ADP algorithms in a comparison to the PD controller can be noticed. Values of the quality ratings for the control system with the GDHP algorithm are lower than the ones obtained by the control system with the HDP structure or the neural tracking control system with RVFL NNs, and comparable to results of the control system with the DHP structure.

7 Summary

In the article, the discrete tracking control system for the WMR Pioneer 2-DX is presented. The main part of the control system is the ADP algorithm in the GDHP configuration, composed of the actor and the critic, both realised in a form of RVFL NNs. The GDHP algorithm has the same structure as HDP, and the main elements of its structure have the same functions. The difference is in the critic's NN weights adaptation law, which is the most complex among all ADP structures, it is composed of the critic's weights adaptation rule of the HDP algorithm and the DHP algorithm. This feature assures a high quality of tracking control, comparable to that gained by the control system with the DHP algorithm, and higher that quality of tracking obtained when using the HDP algorithm, what is a significant advantage. Correct adaptation of the GDHP structure NNs' weights in the presence of disturbances requires applying additional elements of the control system, like the supervisory term and the PD controller. The structure of the supervisory term derives from the stability analysis performed using the Lyapunov stability theorem. The proposed control system is stable, and the values of errors and NNs' weights are bounded. The control system works on-line and does not require a process of preliminary learning. Performance of the control system was verified using the WMR Pioneer 2-DX.

References

1. Barto, A.G., Sutton, R.S., Anderson, C.W.: Neuronlike Adaptive Elements that Can Solve Difficult Learning Control Problems. IEEE Trans. Syst., Man, Cybern. 13, 834–846 (1983)
2. Barto, A.G., Sutton, R.: Reinforcement Learning: an Introduction. MIT Press, Cambridge (1998)
3. Fairbank, M., Alonso, E., Prokhorov, D.: Simple and Fast Calculation of the Second-Oorder Gradients for Globalized Dual Heuristic Dynamic Programming in Neural Networks. IEEE Trans. Neural Netw. Learn. Syst. 23, 1671–1676 (2012)
4. Giergiel, J., Hendzel, Z., Zylski, W.: Modeling and Control of Wheeled Mobile Robots. (in Polish). WNT, Warsaw (2002)
5. Giergiel, J., Zylski, W.: Description of Motion of a Mobile Robot by Maggie's Equations. J. Theoret. Appl. Mech. 43, 511–521 (2005)
6. Hendzel, Z.: An Adaptive Critic Neural Network for Motion Control of a Wheeled Mobile Robot. Nonlinear Dynam. 50, 849–855 (2007)
7. Hendzel, Z., Szuster, M.: Discrete Model-Based Adaptive Critic Designs in Wheeled Mobile Robot Control. In: Rutkowski, L., Scherer, R., Tadeusiewicz, R., Zadeh, L.A., Zurada, J.M. (eds.) ICAISC 2010, Part II. LNCS (LNAI), vol. 6114, pp. 264–271. Springer, Heidelberg (2010)
8. Hendzel, Z., Szuster, M.: Discrete Neural Dynamic Programming in Wheeled Mobile Robot control. Commun Nonlinear Sci Numer Simulat. 16, 2355–2362 (2011)
9. Hendzel, Z., Szuster, M.: Heuristic Dynamic Programming in Wheeled Mobile Robot Control. In: 14th IFAC International Conference on Methods and Models in Automation and Robotics, Miedzyzdroje, pp. 37–41 (2009)
10. Liu, D., Wang, D., Yang, X.: An Iterative Adaptive Dynamic Programming Algorithm for Optimal Control of Unknown Discrete-Time Nonlinear Systems with Constrained Inputs. Inform Sciences 220, 331–342 (2013)
11. Miller, W.T., Sutton, R.S., Werbos, P.J. (eds.): Neural Networks for Control. MIT Press, Cambridge (1990)
12. Powell, W.B.: Approximate Dynamic Programming: Solving the Curses of Dimensionality. Willey-Interscience, Princeton (2007)
13. Prokhorov, D., Wunch, D.: Adaptive Critic Designs. IEEE T Neural Networ 8, 997–1007 (1997)
14. Si, J., Barto, A.G., Powell, W.B., Wunsch, D.: Handbook of Learning and Approximate Dynamic Programming. IEEE Press, Wiley-Interscience, New York (2004)
15. Syam, R., Watanabe, K., Izumi, K.: Adaptive Actor-Critic Learning for the Control of Mobile Robots by Applying Predictive Models. Soft Computing 9, 835–845 (2005)
16. Venayagamoorthy, G.K., Wunsch, D.C., Harley, R.G.: Adaptive Critic Based Neurocontroller for Turbogenerators with Global Dual Heuristic Programming. In: IEEE Power Engineering Society Winter Meeting 1, pp. 291–294. IEEE Press, New York (2000)
17. Wang, D., Liu, D., Wei, Q., et al.: Optimal Control of Unknown Nonaffine Nonlinear Discrete-Time Systems Based on Adaptive Dynamic Programming. Automatica 48, 1825–1832 (2012)

Fuzzy Sensor-Based Navigation with Neural Tracking Control of the Wheeled Mobile Robot

Marcin Szuster, Zenon Hendzel, and Andrzej Burghardt

Rzeszow University of Technology
Department of Applied Mechanics and Robotics
8 Powstancow Warszawy St., 35-959 Rzeszow, Poland
{mszuster,zenhen,andrzejb}@prz.edu.pl

Abstract. Navigation of the wheeled mobile robot in the unknown environment with simultaneous realisation of the generated trajectory, is one of the most challenging and up to date problems in the modern mobile robotics. In the article a new approach is presented to a collision-free trajectory generating for a wheeled mobile robot, realised in a form of the hierarchical control system with two layers. The first layer is a tracking control system, where the Neuro-Dynamic Programming algorithm in the Dual Heuristic Dynamic Programming configuration was applied. The second layer is a trajectory generator where the Fuzzy Logic systems were used. The presented control system generates and realises trajectory of the wheeled mobile robot within the complex task of goal-seeking and obstacle avoiding. The proposed hierarchical control system works on-line, its performance was verified using the wheeled mobile robot Pioneer 2-DX.

Keywords: Neuro-Dynamic Programming, Fuzzy System, Mobile Robot, Neural Networks, Path Planning, Sensor-Based Navigation.

1 Introduction

The development of mobile robotics makes the increase of its applications possible. Still one of the most challenging tasks is navigation of the wheeled mobile robot (WMR) in the unknown environment with simultaneous realisation of the collision-free trajectory, to reach the destination. This problem is often met in literature [1, 4, 9, 10], where different approaches to the path planning problem are presented. Two of the most popular are global and local methods. In the global methods, which are model based algorithms, the path is planned on the base of the environment map [9]. These methods are not applicable in the unknown environment. In contrast, local methods are sensor-based and operate in the nearest environment of the robot, in its sensory system reach.

The behavioural control algorithms, inspired by the world of living organisms, solve the problem of trajectory generation in typical tasks e.g. seek the goal (GS) or move in the middle of the free space and avoid collisions with obstacles (OA). The more complex behaviour, where the robot seeks the goal

L. Rutkowski et al. (Eds.): ICAISC 2014, Part II, LNAI 8468, pp. 302–313, 2014.

and realises the collision free trajectory, may be seen as a combination of two behaviours mentioned earlier. This problem is often solved using the trajectory generator composed of three parts, the behavioural control system for the GS, OA behaviour [4], and the algorithm, that switches the realisation of elementary behaviours according to the environment conditions [7]. In this article a new approach to generation of the collision free trajectory in the unknown environment is proposed, where the sensor based navigator consists of only one part realised in the form of the Fuzzy Logic (FL) systems. The generated trajectory is realised using the tracking control layer, realised using the Neuro-Dynamic Programming (NDP) algorithm in the Dual Heuristic Dynamic Programming (DHP) configuration [11–13]. The proposed control system works on-line and does not require the preliminary learning. The performance of the control system was verified using the wheeled mobile robot Pioneer 2-DX.

The research presented in the paper continues the authors' earlier works, related to the problem of tracking control of the WMR [5, 6] and navigation of the WMR [4, 7, 8] in the unknown environment. The article is organised as follows: the first section is an introduction to the navigation of the WMR in the unknown environment. The second section presents the WMR Pioneer 2-DX, and its dynamics model. In the third section typical behavioural control strategies are discussed, and the hierarchical control system composed of the tracking control layer with the DHP algorithm and the navigator with the FL systems is proposed. The next section presents the laboratory stand. In section five experiment results are presented, and the last section summarises the article.

2   Wheeled Mobile Robot Pioneer 2-DX

The WMR Pioneer 2-DX consists of two driving wheels 1 and 2, a free rolling castor wheel 3 and a frame 4. It is a non-holonomic object described using nonlinear dynamics equations, whose movement is analysed in the xy plane [2, 3]. The WMR Pioneer 2-DX is equipped with eight ultrasonic range finders and one scanning laser range finder for obstacles detection. The WMR Pioneer 2-DX is shown in Fig. 1.a), the scheme of the WMR moving in the environment with static obstacles is shown in Fig. 1.b), where $G\left(x_G, y_G\right)$ – the goal, ψ_G – an angle between the axis of the WMR's frame and the line p_G, β – a temporary angle of the self-turn of the WMR's frame, $d_{R[i]}$, $d_{F[i]}$, $d_{L[i]}$ – distances to obstacles measured by the scanning laser range finder in the front, on the right and left side of the frame, $\omega_{R[i]}$, $\omega_{F[i]}$, $\omega_{L[i]}$ – the angle between the axis of the frame and the axis of the i-th measurement, $i = 1, 2, 3$. The selected measurements were assigned to three groups, that measure distances to the obstacles in the front, on the right and left side of the frame. In the global co-ordinate system xy position of the WMR is described by the vector $[x_A, y_A, \beta]^T$, where (x_A, y_A) are coordinates of the point A.

The dynamics of the controlled object was modelled using the Maggie's formalism [2, 3]. The continuous model of the WMR dynamics was discretised using the Euler's method, and expressed by the formula

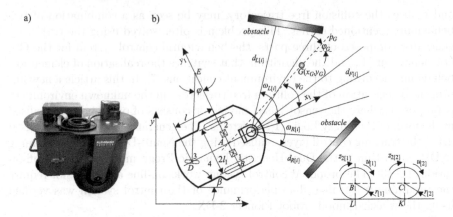

Fig. 1. a) The Wheeled Mobile Robot Pioneer 2-DX, b) the scheme of the Pioneer 2-DX in the environment

$$
\begin{aligned}
z_{1\{k+1\}} &= z_{1\{k\}} + h z_{2\{k\}} \,, \\
z_{2\{k+1\}} &= z_{2\{k\}} - h M^{-1} \left[C\left(z_{2\{k\}}\right) z_{2\{k\}} + F\left(z_{2\{k\}}\right) + \tau_{d\{k\}} - u_{\{k\}} \right] \,,
\end{aligned}
\tag{1}
$$

where k – an index of iteration steps, $z_{1\{k\}} = \left[z_{1[1]\{k\}} \; z_{1[2]\{k\}} \right]^T$ – the vector of angles of driving wheels rotation, h – a time discretisation parameter, $z_{2\{k\}}$ - the vector of angular velocities, M – the positive defined inertia matrix, $C\left(z_{2\{k\}}\right) z_{2\{k\}}$ – the vector of centrifugal and Coriolis momentous, $F\left(z_{2\{k\}}\right)$ – the vector of resistances to motion, $\tau_{d\{k\}}$ – the vector of disturbances, $u_{\{k\}}$ – the control vector. The state vector was assumed in the form $z_{\{k\}} = \left[z_{1\{k\}} \; z_{2\{k\}} \right]^T$.

The discrete tracking errors of angles $z_{1\{k\}}$ and angular velocities $z_{2\{k\}}$ are defined as

$$
\begin{aligned}
e_{1\{k\}} &= z_{1\{k\}} - z_{d1\{k\}} \,, \\
e_{2\{k\}} &= z_{2\{k\}} - z_{d2\{k\}} \,,
\end{aligned}
\tag{2}
$$

where $z_{d1\{k\}}$, $z_{d2\{k\}}$, $z_{d3\{k\}}$ – movement parameters of the desired trajectory, calculated in the trajectory generator. On the basis of (2) was defined the filtered tracking error

$$
s_{\{k\}} = e_{2\{k\}} + \Lambda e_{1\{k\}} \,,
\tag{3}
$$

where Λ – a fixed, positive defined diagonal matrix.

On the basis of errors definitions (2), (3) and the dynamics model of the WMR (1), the filtered tracking error $s_{\{k+1\}}$ was assumed in the form

$$
s_{\{k+1\}} = -Y_f\left(z_{2\{k\}}\right) + Y_d\left(z_{\{k\}}, z_{d\{k\}}, z_{d3\{k\}}\right) - Y_{\tau\{k\}} + h M^{-1} u_{\{k\}} \,,
\tag{4}
$$

where

$$\boldsymbol{Y}_f\left(\boldsymbol{z}_{2\{k\}}\right) = h\boldsymbol{M}^{-1}\left[\boldsymbol{C}\left(\boldsymbol{z}_{2\{k\}}\right)\boldsymbol{z}_{2\{k\}} + \boldsymbol{F}\left(\boldsymbol{z}_{2\{k\}}\right)\right] ,$$
$$\boldsymbol{Y}_d\left(\boldsymbol{z}_{\{k\}}, \boldsymbol{z}_{d\{k\}}, \boldsymbol{z}_{d3\{k\}}\right) = \boldsymbol{z}_{2\{k\}} - \boldsymbol{z}_{d2\{k+1\}} + \boldsymbol{\Lambda}\left[\boldsymbol{z}_{1\{k\}} + h\boldsymbol{z}_{2\{k\}} - \boldsymbol{z}_{d1\{k+1\}}\right] =$$
$$= \boldsymbol{s}_{\{k\}} + \boldsymbol{Y}_e\left(\boldsymbol{z}_{2\{k\}}, \boldsymbol{z}_{d2\{k\}}, \boldsymbol{z}_{d3\{k\}}\right) ,$$
$$\boldsymbol{Y}_e\left(\boldsymbol{z}_{2\{k\}}, \boldsymbol{z}_{d2\{k\}}, \boldsymbol{z}_{d3\{k\}}\right) = h\left[\boldsymbol{\Lambda}\boldsymbol{e}_{2\{k\}} - \boldsymbol{z}_{d3\{k\}}\right] , \quad \boldsymbol{Y}_{\tau\{k\}} = h\boldsymbol{M}^{-1}\boldsymbol{\tau}_{d\{k\}} ,$$
$$(5)$$

where $\boldsymbol{Y}_f\left(\boldsymbol{z}_{2\{k\}}\right)$ – the vector that includes all nonlinearities of the controlled system, $\boldsymbol{z}_{d3\{k\}}$ – the vector that derives from expansion of $\boldsymbol{z}_{d2\{k+1\}}$.

3 Hierarchical Control System

There are two simple behaviours which are inspirations in the conception of the behavioural control. First of them is the GS behaviour, when the agent moves to the goal, but the location of obstacles is not taken into consideration (Fig. 2.a). The second behaviour is OA, when the agent moves in the middle of the free space, and realises collision free trajectory, but the goal is not defined (Fig. 2.b). The third, more complex problem is to reach the goal without colliding with obstacles, it might be solved using combination of the GS and OA behavioural (CB) control signals (Fig. 2.c). This task is most often met in real problems.

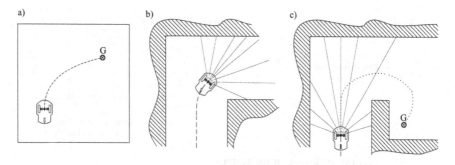

Fig. 2. a) The scheme of the Goal Seeking behaviour, b) the scheme of the Obstacle Avoiding behaviour, c) the scheme of the Goal Seeking with Obstacle Avoiding

In most cases the problem of navigation in the CB task is solved using three elements in the trajectory generation layer of the hierarchical control system. Two behavioural control system for the GS and OA behaviours are used, and an additional element, that switches between the realisation of basic behaviours as required, according to the environment conditions [7]. The typical solution of the trajectory generator in the CB task is shown in Fig. 3.

A new approach to the navigation problem is proposed in this article, where one element composed of two FL systems generates control signals of the trajectory generating layer in the complex CB task. On the basis of these control signals are calculated the movement parameters realised by the tracking control layer of the hierarchical control system, that is schematically shown in Fig. 4

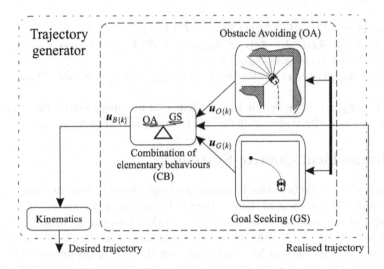

Fig. 3. The scheme of the trajectory generator with combination of behavioural control signals

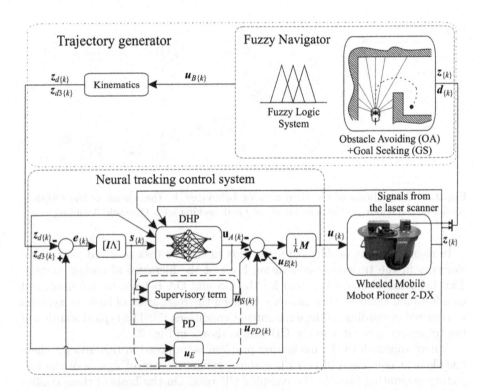

Fig. 4. The scheme of the hierarchical control system with the fuzzy navigator

3.1   Fuzzy Sensor-Based Navigation

In the fuzzy navigator two FL systems were used, first of them generates the control signal $u_{v\{k\}}$, that controls the desired velocity of the point A of the WMR's frame. The second control signal $u_{\dot{\beta}\{k\}}$ corresponds to the desired angular velocity of the WMR's frame turn $\dot{\beta}$. Both FL systems use the Takagi-Sugeno model with triangular or trapezoidal membership functions of fuzzy sets.

The FL system, that generates the control signal $u_{v\{k\}}$, has two inputs ($d_{G\{k\}}$ – the distance to the goal, $d_{O\{k\}}$ – the distance to the obstacles, $d_{O\{k\}} = \min\left(d_{L[i]\{k\}}, d_{F[i]\{k\}}, d_{R[i]\{k\}}\right)$), its structure is simple.

The FL system that generates the control signal $u_{\dot{\beta}\{k\}}$ is more complex. It has four inputs: $e_{O\{k\}}$ defined by the formula (6), $\psi_{G\{k\}}$, $d_{G\{k\}}$ and $d_{O\{k\}}$.

$$e_{O\{k\}} = d^*_{R\{k\}} - d^*_{L\{k\}} ,$$
$$\psi_{G\{k\}} = \varphi_{G\{k\}} - \beta_{\{k\}} , \tag{6}$$

where $d^*_{R\{k\}}$, $d^*_{L\{k\}}$ – minimal distances to the obstacles on the right and the left side of the WMR's frame.

It contains the rules base, that consists of $m = 48$ rules in the form

$$R^m_B : \text{IF} \left(e_{O\{k\}} \text{ is eS}\right) \text{ AND } \left(\psi^*_{G\{k\}} \text{ is pS}\right) \text{ AND } \left(d^*_{G\{k\}} \text{ is dGS}\right)$$
$$\text{AND } \left(d^*_{O\{k\}} \text{ is dOB}\right) \text{ THEN } u_{v\{k\}} \text{ is uPS} , \tag{7}$$

where $\psi^*_{G\{k\}} \in <-1, 1>$ – the normalised angle $\psi_{G\{k\}}$, $d^*_{G\{k\}} \in <0, 1>$ – the normalised distance to the goal, $d^*_{O\{k\}} \in <0, 1>$ – the normalised distance to the nearest obstacle, eS, pS, dGS, dOB – linguistic labels of membership functions of fuzzy sets of premises, shown in Fig. 5, the membership functions of sets of inferences are: uNB=-1, uNS=-0.6, uPS=0.6, uPB=1, where: NB – negative big, NS – negative small, PS – positive small, PB – positive big, S – small, M – medium, B – big.

The control signals generated by the fuzzy navigator $\boldsymbol{u}_{B\{k\}} = \left[u_{v\{k\}}, u_{\dot{\beta}\{k\}}\right]^T$ are next recalculated in the kinematics module into the desired discrete angular velocities of the driving wheels, according to the equation

$$\begin{bmatrix} z_{d2[1]\{k\}} \\ z_{d2[2]\{k\}} \end{bmatrix} = \frac{1}{r} \begin{bmatrix} v^*_A & \dot{\beta}^* l_1 \\ v^*_A & -\dot{\beta}^* l_1 \end{bmatrix} \begin{bmatrix} u_{v\{k\}} \\ u_{\dot{\beta}\{k\}} \end{bmatrix} , \tag{8}$$

where $r = r_{[1]} = r_{[2]}$, l_1 – dimensions that derive from geometry of the WMR Pioneer 2-DX, v^*_A – a maximal defined velocity of the point A, $\dot{\beta}^*$ – a maximal defined angular velocity of the self-turn of the WMR's frame.

3.2   Neural Tracking Control

The discrete neural tracking control system, applied in the hierarchical control system, consists of four structures. The first is the NDP algorithm in the

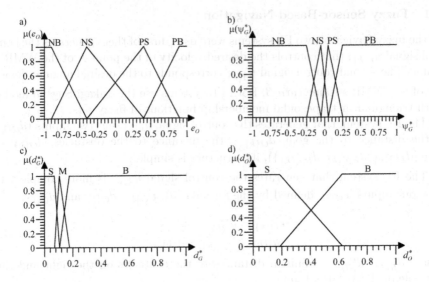

Fig. 5. The membership functions of fuzzy sets of premises for: a) $e_{O\{k\}}$, b) $\psi^*_{G\{k\}}$, c) $d^*_{G\{k\}}$, d) $d^*_{O\{k\}}$

GDHP configuration, where the actor generates the control signal $u_{A\{k\}}$. The second is PD controller ($u_{PD\{k\}}$), which controls the system at the beginning of the weights adaptation process and in the face of disturbances. The third is the supervisory term ($u_{S\{k\}}$), which ensures stability of the control process. Its structure derives from the stability analysis realised using the Lyapunov stability theorem. The final control signal is $u_{E\{k\}}$.

The overall discrete tracking control signal was assumed in the form

$$u_{\{k\}} = -\frac{1}{h} M \left[u_{A\{k\}} + u_{PD\{k\}} + u_{S\{k\}} + u_{E\{k\}} \right] , \qquad (9)$$

where

$$\begin{aligned} u_{PD\{k\}} &= K_D s_{\{k\}} , \\ u_{S\{k\}} &= I_S u^*_{S\{k\}} , \\ u_{E\{k\}} &= h \left[\Lambda e_{2\{k\}} - z_{d3\{k\}} \right] , \end{aligned} \qquad (10)$$

where K_D – a positive defined diagonal matrix of the PD controller gains, I_S – a diagonal matrix, $I_{S[j,j]} = 1$ if $|s_{[j]\{k\}}| \geq \rho_{[j]}$, and $I_{S[j,j]} = 0$ in the other case, $\rho_{[j]}$ – a positive constant, $j = 1, 2$, $u^*_{S\{k\}}$ – the vector of supervisory term's control signals.

The main part of the tracking control layer is DHP algorithm, that generates the sub-optimal control law that minimises the value function $V_{\{k\}} \left(s_{\{k\}} \right)$ [11–13], which is a function of the filtered tracking error $s_{\{k\}}$, assumed in the form

$$V_{\{k\}} \left(s_{\{k\}} \right) = \sum_{k=0}^{N} \gamma^k L_{C\{k\}} \left(s_{\{k\}} \right) , \qquad (11)$$

where $L_{C\{k\}}\left(s_{\{k\}}\right)$ – the local cost function for the k-th step, N – a number of steps, γ – a discount factor, $0 < \gamma \leq 1$. The cost function was assumed in the form

$$L_{C\{k\}}\left(s_{\{k\}}\right) = \frac{1}{2} s_{\{k\}}^T R s_{\{k\}} , \tag{12}$$

where R – a fixed, positive defined diagonal matrix.

The DHP algorithm consists of three structures:

- the predictive model – predicts the state $s_{\{k+1\}}$ of the closed loop system,
- critic – estimates the difference of the value function with respect to the states. It is realised in the form of two Random Vector Functional Link NNs expressed by the formula

$$\hat{\lambda}_{[j]\{k\}}\left(x_{Cj\{k\}}, W_{Cj\{k\}}\right) = W_{Cj\{k\}}^T S\left(D_C^T x_{Cj\{k\}}\right) , \tag{13}$$

where j – an index, $j = 1, 2$, $W_{Cj\{k\}}$ – the vector of j-th critic's NN output weights, $S\left(.\right)$ – the vector of sigmoidal bipolar neurons activation functions, D_C – the matrix of fixed, random input weights, $x_{Cj\{k\}}$ – the input vector to the j-th critic's NN. Weights of the critic's NNs are adapted using the gradient method, where the error $e_{C\{k\}}$ expressed by the formula is minimised,

$$e_{C\{k\}} = \frac{\partial L_{C\{k\}}\left(s_{\{k\}}\right)}{\partial s_{\{k\}}} + \left[\frac{\partial u_{\{k\}}}{\partial s_{\{k\}}}\right]^T \frac{\partial L_{C\{k\}}\left(s_{\{k\}}\right)}{\partial u_{\{k\}}} +$$
$$+\gamma \left[\frac{\partial s_{\{k+1\}}}{\partial s_{\{k\}}} + \left[\frac{\partial u_{\{k\}}}{\partial s_{\{k\}}}\right]^T \frac{\partial s_{\{k+1\}}}{\partial u_{\{k\}}}\right]^T \hat{\lambda}_{\{k+1\}}\left(x_{C\{k+1\}}, W_{C\{k\}}\right) +$$
$$-\hat{\lambda}_{\{k\}}\left(x_{C\{k\}}, W_{C\{k\}}\right) , \tag{14}$$

- actor – generates the sub-optimal control law $u_{A\{k\}} = \left[u_{A[1]\{k\}}\ u_{A[2]\{k\}}\right]^T$, it is realised in the form of two RVFL NNs (Fig. 6.a) expressed by the formula

$$u_{A[j]\{k\}}\left(x_{Aj\{k\}}, W_{Aj\{k\}}\right) = W_{Aj\{k\}}^T S\left(D_A^T x_{Aj\{k\}}\right) , \tag{15}$$

where $x_{Aj\{k\}}$ – an input vector to the j-th actor's NN, $W_{Aj\{k\}}$ – the vector of output weights. Actor NNs' weights are adapted using the gradient method, the minimised error $e_{A\{k\}}$ was assumed in the form

$$e_{A\{k\}} = \frac{\partial L_{C\{k\}}\left(s_{\{k\}}\right)}{\partial u_{\{k\}}} + \left[\frac{\partial s_{\{k+1\}}}{\partial u_{\{k\}}}\right]^T \hat{\lambda}_{\{k+1\}}\left(x_{C\{k+1\}}, W_{C\{k\}}\right) . \tag{16}$$

The scheme of the DHP algorithm is shown in Fig. 6.b).

The neural tracking control system with the NDP algorithm in the DHP configuration was discussed in detail in [5, 6].

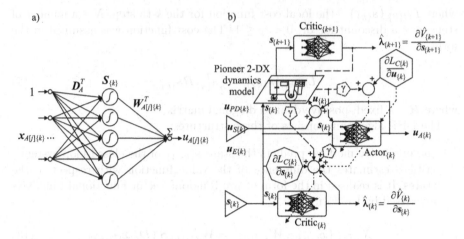

Fig. 6. a) The scheme of the j-th Actor's Random Vector Functional Link Neural Network, b) the scheme of the Dual Heuristic Dynamic Programming algorithm

4   Laboratory Stand

Performance of the proposed hierarchical control system was verified using the laboratory stand, that consists of the WMR Pioneer 2-DX with the Hokuyo UBG-04LX-F01 scanning laser range finder, the power supply unit, the PC with the dSpace DS1102 digital signal processing board and software: Control Desk and Matlab/Simulink, and the laboratory environment, where research was realised. The scheme of the laboratory stand is shown in Fig. 7.

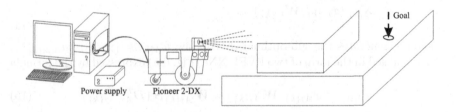

Fig. 7. The scheme of the laboratory stand

5   Experiment Results

Verification of the proposed control algorithm was realised by a series of experiments using the WMR Pioneer 2-DX in the laboratory environment. During the experiment the time discretisation parameter was equal $h = 0.01$ [s], in the DHP structure, NNs with 8 neurons each and zero output layer initial weights were used. In this section notation of variables is simplified, the index k is omitted.

On the basis of measurements realised using the scanning laser range finder, the proposed hierarchical control system generated and realised the collision free path from the starting point $S(0.6, 0.95)$ to the goal. The environment map with a trajectory of the point A, positions of obstacles localised by the scanning laser range finder (grey dots) and the destination in point $G\,(7.0, 0.75)$, are shown in Fig. 8. The start position of the point A is marked by the triangle and the goal is marked by the "X".

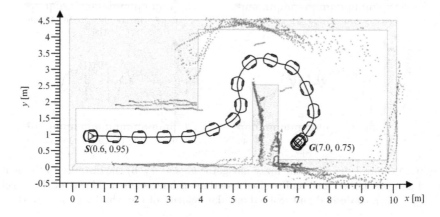

Fig. 8. The environment map with the path of the WMR to the goal $G\,(7.0, 0.75)$

The environment map was designed in the way, that none of the behavioural control systems in the OA or the GS task are able to generate the successive path. It is only possible using combination of this behaviours. Localisations of obstacles were computed on the basis of: scanning laser range finder readings, localisation of the point A and orientation of the WMR's frame, measured using incremental encoders. Errors in range finder readings and measurements of the realised trajectory influenced on computed localisations of detected obstacles in coordinates of the environment map caused a difference between real and computed localisations of obstacles presented in Fig. 8.

The fuzzy navigator control signals u_v and $u_{\dot\beta}$, generated during the movement of the WMR to the point G, that are shown in Fig. 9.a). In Fig. 9.b) the distance to the goal d_G, reduced during the experiment is shown.

The desired angular velocities of the WMR ($z_{d2[1]}$ and $z_{d2[2]}$), shown in Fig. 9.c) and d) were computed on the basis of the fuzzy navigator's control signals.

The desired trajectory was realised by the tracking control layer, that generated the overall tracking control signals $u_{[1]}$, $u_{[2]}$, shown in Fig. 9.a). According to the equation (9), the sum is composed of control signals generated by the DHP structure actor's NNs (u_A), control signals generated by the PD controller (u_{PD}, Fig. 9.a), the supervisory term control signals (u_S), and additional control signals u_E. Values of the actor's RVFL NN (W_{A2}) and the critic's NN (W_{C2}) weights of the DHP structure, that generate the tracking control signal $u_{[2]}$, are shown in Fig. 10.c) and d). Values of NNs' weights are bounded.

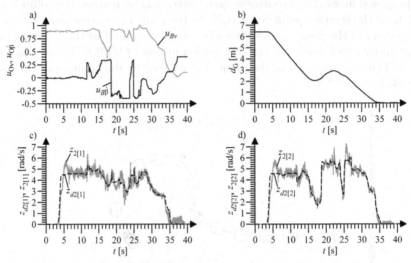

Fig. 9. a) Control signals of the fuzzy navigator u_v and $u_{\dot{\beta}}$, b) the distance to the goal d_G, c) desired (dashed line) and realised (continuous line) angular velocity of the wheel 1 ($z_{d2[1]}$, $z_{2[1]}$), d) desired and realised angular velocity of the wheel 2 ($z_{d2[2]}$, $z_{2[2]}$)

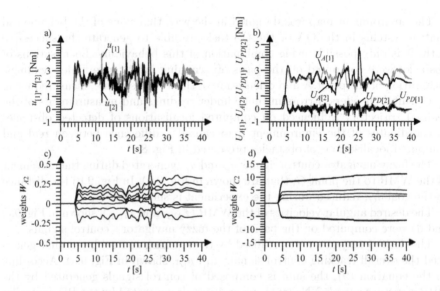

Fig. 10. a) The overall tracking control signals $u_{[1]}$ and $u_{[2]}$, b) the actor's NNs control signals ($U_{A[1]}$, $U_{A[2]}$), $\boldsymbol{U}_A = -h^{-1}\boldsymbol{M}\boldsymbol{u}_A$, and the PD control signals ($U_{PD[1]}$, $U_{PD[2]}$), c) weights of the actor's 2 NN $\boldsymbol{W}_{A2}$, d) weights of the critic's 2 NN $\boldsymbol{W}_{C2}$

6 Summary

The article presents a new approach to the process of WMR Pioneer 2-DX navigation in the unknown 2-D environment with static obstacles, realised in the form of the hierarchical control system composed of the fuzzy navigator and the neural tracking control system with the DHP algorithm. In the trajectory generation layer only one structure realised in a form of two FL systems was used, it generated the collision-free trajectory in the complex task of goal seeking with obstacle avoiding. The presented approach considerably reduces complexity of the control system, while the task is realised successfully. The tracking control system consists of the NDP algorithm in the DHP configuration, the PD controller, the supervisory therm and the additional control signal. The generated trajectory provides, that the point A of the WMR Pioneer 2-DX reaches the goal. The projected hierarchical control system with the sensor-based navigator works on-line and does not require the preliminary learning of the DHP structure NNs. Performance of the control system was verified using the wheeled mobile robot Pioneer 2-DX.

References

1. Arkin, R.C.: Behavior-Based Robotics. MIT Press, Cambridge (1998)
2. Giergiel, J., Hendzel, Z., Zylski, W.: Modeling and Control of Wheeled Mobile Robots. PWN, Warsaw (2002) (in Polish)
3. Giergiel, J., Zylski, W.: Description of Motion of a Mobile Robot by Maggie's Equations. J. Theoret. Appl. Mech. 43, 511–521 (2005)
4. Hendzel, Z.: Fuzzy Reactive Control of Wheeled Mobile Robot. J. Theoret. Appl. Mech. 42, 503–517 (2004)
5. Hendzel, Z., Szuster, M.: Discrete Model-Based Adaptive Critic Designs in Wheeled Mobile Robot Control. In: Rutkowski, L., Scherer, R., Tadeusiewicz, R., Zadeh, L.A., Zurada, J.M. (eds.) ICAISC 2010, Part II. LNCS, vol. 6114, pp. 264–271. Springer, Heidelberg (2010)
6. Hendzel, Z., Szuster, M.: Discrete Neural Dynamic Programming in Wheeled Mobile Robot control. Commun. Nonlinear Sci. Numer. Simulat. 16, 2355–2362 (2011)
7. Hendzel, Z., Szuster, M.: Neural Dynamic Programming in Behavioural Control of Wheeled Mobile Robot. Acta Mechanica et Automatica 5, 28–36 (2011) (in Polish)
8. Hendzel, Z., Szuster, M.: Neural Dynamic Programming in Reactive Navigation of Wheeled Mobile Robot. In: Rutkowski, L., Korytkowski, M., Scherer, R., Tadeusiewicz, R., Zadeh, L.A., Zurada, J.M. (eds.) ICAISC 2012, Part II. LNCS (LNAI), vol. 7268, pp. 450–457. Springer, Heidelberg (2012)
9. Maaref, H., Barret, C.: Sensor-based Navigation of a Mobile Robot in an Indoor Environment. Robot. Auton. Syst. 38, 1–18 (2002)
10. Millan, J.: Reinforcement Learning of Goal-Directed Obstacle-Avoiding Reaction Strategies in an Autonomous Mobile Robot. Robot. Auton. Syst. 15, 275–299 (1995)
11. Powell, W.B.: Approximate Dynamic Programming: Solving the Curses of Dimensionality. Willey-Interscience, Princeton (2007)
12. Prokhorov, D., Wunch, D.: Adaptive Critic Designs. IEEE Trans. Neural Netw. 8, 997–1007 (1997)
13. Si, J., Barto, A.G., Powell, W.B., Wunsch, D.: Handbook of Learning and Approximate Dynamic Programming. IEEE Press, Wiley-Interscience (2004)

Artificial Intelligence in Modeling and Simulation

Fuzzy and Neural Rotor Resistance Estimator for Vector Controlled Induction Motor Drives

Moulay Rachid Douiri, Ouissam Belghazi, and Mohamed Cherkaoui

Mohammadia Engineering School, Department of Electrical Engineering,
Ibn Sina Avenue, Agdal-Rabat 765, Morocco

Abstract. This paper contributes to improving the dynamic performance of indirect vector controlled induction motor drives. This command requires the rotor resistance; the variation of this parameter could distort the decoupling between the flux and torque and, consequently, lead to deterioration of performance. To overcome this problem two intelligent approaches have been introduced to estimate the rotor resistance namely fuzzy logic and artificial neural networks. These estimators process the information from the rotational speed, the stator currents and voltages. The performances of the two intelligent approaches are investigated and compared in simulation. The results show that the neural rotor resistance estimator is reliable and highly effective in the resistance identification relative to fuzzy rotor resistance estimator of induction motor drives.

Keywords: rotor resistance, neural networks, fuzzy logic, vector control, induction motor.

1 Introduction

The principle of field orientation control of machines was developed in Germany in the late 1960 and early 1970 [1]. Two possible methods for achieving field orientation were identified [2]. Blaschke [3] used Hall sensors mounted in the air gap to measure the machine flux, and therefore obtain the flux magnitude and flux angle for field orientation. Field orientation achieved by direct measurement of the flux is termed Direct Flux Orientation (DFO). On the other hand Hasse [4] achieved flux orientation by imposing a slip frequency derived from the rotor dynamic equations so as to ensure field orientation. This alternative, consisting of forcing field orientation in the machine, is known as Indirect Field Orientation (IFO). IFO has been generally preferred to DFO implementations which use Hall probes; the reason being that DFO requires a specially modified machine and moreover the fragility of the Hall sensors detracts the inherent robustness of an induction machine [2].

The rotor resistance is an important parameter which is involved in rotor flux estimation and the control law to compensate for the nonlinearity of system [5]-[6]. However, this parameter varies with machine temperature. In addition it was demonstrated that a poor estimate of this parameter affects the regulation (pursuit of flux trajectory and rotor speed) and even it can introduce oscillations [6]-[7]. This difficulty has been the main source of our motivation for this research; in which one propose

L. Rutkowski et al. (Eds.): ICAISC 2014, Part II, LNAI 8468, pp. 317–327, 2014.

two intelligent approaches based on fuzzy logic and artificial neural networks to identify the rotor resistance. Several authors have contributed to estimating rotor resistance [5]-[6]-[7]-[8]-[9]-[10]-[11].

Fuzzy logic as many of the linguistic terms used by human involve degree of fuzziness and relative significance, it is desirable to address the impact of fuzziness on the solutions made by experts for complex problems. In 1965, fuzzy logic theory was developed by Zadeh [12]-[13], to deal with uncertainties that are not statistical in nature. The concept of fuzzy sets theory differs from that of the conventional crisp sets mainly in the degree by which an object belong to a set. In crisp sets, objects are either included or excluded from a set [14]. In fuzzy set, on the other hand, objects are described in such a way so as to allow gradual transition from being a member of a set to non member. Each object contains a degree of membership ranging from zero to one, where zero indicates non membership while one indicates full membership [14], [15].

An artificial neural network (ANN) is essentially a way to learn the relationship between a set of input data and the corresponding output data. That is, it can memorize data, generalize this information when given new input data, and adjust when the relationship changes [16]. The training is normally done with input-output examples. After training, ANNs have the capability of generalization. That is, given previously unseen input data, they can interpolate from the previous training data. They were inspired by models of neural cell structure in organic brains [17]. They became popular in the research community when architectures were found to enable the learning of nonlinear functions and patterns [16].

This paper is organized as follows: The principle of indirect field oriented control of induction motor drive is presented in the second part, section three presents an fuzzy logic rotor resistance estimator, neural networks rotor resistance in the four part, and the five parts is devoted to illustrate the simulation performance of this control strategy, a conclusion and reference list at the end.

2   Indirect Field Oriented Control

In field orientation concept of induction motor, the goal is to obtain an electromagnetic torque proportional to the quadrature component of stator current i_{sq} (at constant flux) and can control the flux by acting on the direct component of this current i_{sd} [2]. This can be accomplished by choosing ω_e to be the instantaneous speed of ψ_r and locking the phase of the reference system such that the rotor flux is entirely in the d-axis (flux axis), resulting in the mathematical constraint:

$$\psi_r = \psi_{rd} \; ; \quad \psi_{rq} = 0. \tag{1}$$

The Fig. 1 illustrates the principle of indirect method using phase diagram. At any instant, d electrical axis is in angular position θ_e relative to α axis. The angle θ_e is the result of the sum of both rotor angular and slip angular positions, as follows:

$$\begin{cases} \theta_e = \theta_r + \theta_{sl} \\ \omega_e t = \omega_r t + \omega_{sl} t = (\omega_r + \omega_{sl})t \end{cases} \tag{2}$$

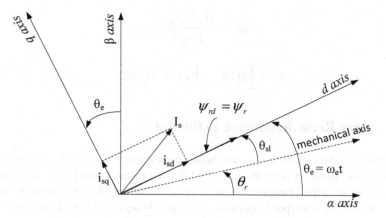

Fig. 1. Vector diagram for indirect field oriented control

The rotor dynamics are given by the following equations:

$$\frac{d\psi_r}{dt} = \frac{L_m}{\tau_r}i_{sd} - \frac{1}{\tau_r}\psi_r.$$ (3)

$$\frac{d\omega_r}{dt} = \frac{3n_p^2 L_m}{2JL_r}\psi_r i_{sq} - \frac{f}{J}\omega_r - \frac{n_p}{J}T_l.$$ (4)

$$T_e = \frac{3n_p L_m \psi_r}{2L_r}i_{sq}.$$ (5)

$$\rho = \int \omega_e dt = \int \left(\omega_r + \frac{R_r L_m i_{sq}}{L_r \psi_r}\right)dt.$$ (6)

The rotor flux magnitude is related to the direct axis stator current by a first-order differential equation; thus, it can be controlled by controlling the direct axis stator current. Under steady-state operation rotor flux is constant, so Eq. (3) becomes:

$$\psi_r = L_m i_{sd}.$$ (7)

Indirect vector control can be implemented using the following equations:

$$i_{sd}^* = \frac{\psi_r^*}{L_m}.$$ (8)

$$i_{sq}^* = \frac{2L_r T_e^*}{3n_p L_m \psi_r^*}.$$ (9)

$$\omega_{sl}^* = \frac{R_r L_m i_{sq}^*}{L_r \psi_r^*}. \tag{10}$$

$$\rho^* = \int \omega_e^* dt = \int (\omega_r + \omega_{sl}^*) dt. \tag{11}$$

3   Fuzzy Rotor Resistance Estimator

The input variables of the estimator should wear explicitly or implicitly information related to the change in resistance. We find that the torque could be the candidate. We can estimate the actual torque from the stator flux. This method is simple but it is not recommended for low-speed operation since in this region it is very difficult to estimate exactly the stator flux.

We will use a function Φ, which is a modification of the function used in Eq. (3):

$$\Phi = \frac{1}{\omega_e} (i_{qs} \frac{d\psi_{dr}}{dt} - i_{ds} \frac{d\psi_{qr}}{dt}). \tag{12}$$

As the resistance variation with temperature is very slow, we can estimate in steady state. We can demonstrate that steady state; the function Φ can be calculated as follows:

$$\Phi = -i_{ds}\psi_{dr} = -i_{ds}\hat{\psi}_{dr} = F_{est}. \tag{13}$$

where $\hat{\psi}_{dr}$ is the estimated flux of the d-axis.

The actual value of the function Φ is calculated:

$$\Phi_{act} = \frac{L_r}{L_m} \left[\frac{1}{\omega_e} (v_{ds} i_{qs} - v_{qs} i_{ds}) + L_s \sigma (i_{ds}^2 + i_{qs}^2) \right]. \tag{14}$$

In Eq. (14) the function Φ is calculated from stator voltage and current. The rotor voltage will be available to our estimation algorithm.

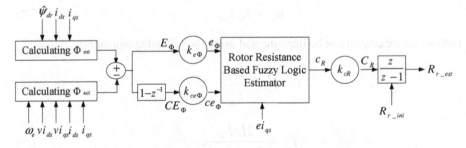

Fig. 2. Structure of the fuzzy rotor resistance estimator

Fig. 2 shows the configuration of rotor resistance estimation. The functions Φ_{est} and Φ_{act} it's first calculated. The error between Φ_{est} and Φ_{act} and its derivation are the inputs of the estimator e, they are then calculated as follows:

$$E_{\Phi}(k) = \Phi_{est}(k) - \Phi_{act}(k). \tag{15}$$

$$CE_{\Phi}(k) = E_{\Phi}(k) - E_{\Phi}(k-1). \tag{16}$$

The internal structure of the estimator involves three steps: fuzzification, inference and defuzzification. The signals $e_\Phi(k)$ and $ce_\Phi(k)$ are normalized and deducted the signals $E_\Phi(k)$ and $CE_\Phi(k)$ by multiplying by the factor $k_{e\Phi}$ and $k_{ce\Phi}$.

The estimated value of the resistance increment is obtained by multiplying the estimator output $c_R(k)$ by the gain k_{cR}. Resistance is finally integration increment:

$$R_r(k) = R_r(k-1) + k_{cR} \, c_R(k). \tag{17}$$

Note that the initial value of the resistance R_r is its nominal value.

This resistance is estimated to be used in indirect vector control algorithm to ensure optimal performance.

The rules table contains 49 rules (7 x 7) as shown in Table 1.

Table 1. Fuzzy linguistic rule table

C_R		e_Φ						
		NB	NM	NS	Z	PS	PM	PB
	NB	NB	NB	NB	NB	NM	NS	Z
	NM	NB	NB	NB	NM	NS	Z	PS
	NS	NB	NB	NM	NS	Z	PS	PM
ce_Φ	AZ	NB	NM	NS	Z	PS	PM	PB
	PS	NM	NS	Z	PS	PM	PB	PB
	PM	NS	Z	PS	PM	PB	PB	PB
	PB	Z	PS	PM	PB	PB	PB	PB

The fuzzy sets are characterized by standard designations: NB (negative big), NM (negative medium), NS (negative small), Z (zero), PS (positive small), PM (positive medium), and PB (positive big).

As the time constant of the resistance variation as a function of temperature is much greater than the electric time constant of the motor, we can estimate the resistance in steady state, where there is no load variation or change control signal. This ensures that signal variations $E_\Phi(k)$ and $CE_\Phi(k)$ are caused by R_r variation only.

4   Neural Rotor Resistance Estimator

In Model Reference Adaptive System (MRAS) or Model Reference Adaptive Control (MRAC), there is a reference model, an adjustable model, and an adaptation mechanism. Reference model:

$$\frac{d}{dt}\begin{bmatrix} \psi_{rd} \\ \psi_{rq} \end{bmatrix} = \frac{L_r}{L_m}\left(\begin{bmatrix} v_{sd} \\ v_{sq} \end{bmatrix} - R_s\begin{bmatrix} i_{sd} \\ i_{sq} \end{bmatrix} - \sigma L_s\frac{d}{dt}\begin{bmatrix} i_{sd} \\ i_{sq} \end{bmatrix}\right) \tag{18}$$

Adjustable model

$$\frac{d}{dt}\begin{bmatrix} \hat{\psi}_{rd} \\ \hat{\psi}_{rq} \end{bmatrix} = \begin{bmatrix} -\dfrac{R_r}{L_r} & -\hat{\omega}_r \\ \hat{\omega}_r & -\dfrac{R_r}{L_r} \end{bmatrix}\begin{bmatrix} \hat{\psi}_{rd} \\ \hat{\psi}_{rq} \end{bmatrix} + \frac{L_m R_r}{L_r}\begin{bmatrix} i_{sd} \\ i_{sq} \end{bmatrix} \tag{19}$$

In neural rotor resistance estimator technique (Fig. 3), there is a reference model that provides the desired output, and a neural network model has two layers based on back propagation technique which provides for the estimated output, both outputs are compared and the total error between the desired state variable and estimated is then back-propagated to adjust the weight (rotor speed) of the neural model [9], [10].

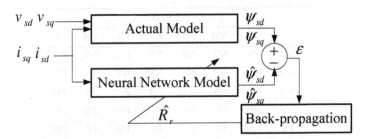

Fig. 3. Structure of the neural rotor resistance estimator

The Adjustable model Eq. (20), after discretization is written as follows:

$$\begin{bmatrix} \hat{\psi}_{rd}(k) \\ \hat{\psi}_{rq}(k) \end{bmatrix} = w_1 I \begin{bmatrix} \hat{\psi}_{rd}(k-1) \\ \hat{\psi}_{rq}(k-1) \end{bmatrix} + w_2 J \begin{bmatrix} \hat{\psi}_{rd}(k-1) \\ \hat{\psi}_{rq}(k-1) \end{bmatrix} + w_3 \begin{bmatrix} i_{sd}(k-1) \\ i_{sq}(k-1) \end{bmatrix} \tag{20}$$

where $w_1 = 1 - \dfrac{R_r}{L_r}t_s,\ w_2 = w_r t_s,\ w_3 = \dfrac{L_m R_r}{L_r}t_s, I = \begin{bmatrix} 1 & 0 \\ 0 & 1 \end{bmatrix}, J = \begin{bmatrix} 0 & -1 \\ 0 & 1 \end{bmatrix}$

Eq. (20) can also be written as:

$$\hat{\psi}_r(k) = w_1 A_1 + w_2 A_2 + w_3 A_3 \tag{21}$$

The Eq. (21) can be represented as a neural model (Fig. 4) with two layers where w_1, w_2, w_3 represent the weights of the networks $A_1 = \begin{bmatrix} \hat{\psi}_{rd}(k-1) \\ \hat{\psi}_{rq}(k-1) \end{bmatrix}$,

$A_2 = \begin{bmatrix} -\hat{\psi}_{rq}(k-1) \\ \hat{\psi}_{rd}(k-1) \end{bmatrix}$, $A_3 = \begin{bmatrix} i_{sd}(k-1) \\ i_{sq}(k-1) \end{bmatrix}$ are the three inputs to the network. The

rotor speed signals were involved in weight w_2.

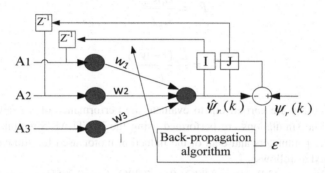

Fig. 4. Two layered neural network model

The total square error on the output layer can be calculated as:

$$E = \frac{1}{2}\varepsilon^2(k) = \frac{1}{2}\left(\psi_r(k) - \hat{\psi}_r(k)\right)^2 \tag{22}$$

Variable weight w_i can be given as follows:

$$\Delta w_i = -\frac{\partial E}{\partial w_i} = -\frac{\partial E}{\partial \hat{\psi}_r(k)}\frac{\partial \hat{\psi}_r(k)}{\partial w_i} = \rho A_i = \left(\psi_r(k) - \hat{\psi}_r(k)\right)^t I \hat{\psi}_r(k-1) \tag{23}$$

where

$$\rho = \frac{\partial E}{\partial \hat{\psi}_r(k)} = \left(\psi_r(k) - \hat{\psi}_r(k)\right)^t \tag{24}$$

either

$$w_i(k) = w_i(k-1) + \eta \Delta w_i(k) \tag{25}$$

with

$$\Delta w_i(k) = -\eta\rho A_i + \alpha\Delta w_i(k-1) \tag{26}$$

where α determines the effect of past weight changes and η is the training coefficient. The weights are adjusted so as to minimize a square error energy function and the new weight w_i is given by:

$$w_i = (k) = w_i(k-1) - \eta\rho A_i + \alpha\Delta w_i(k-1) \tag{27}$$

The rotor resistance R_r can be found from either w_1 or w_3 using Eq. (28) or (29):

$$R_r = \frac{L_r w_3}{L_m t_s} \tag{28}$$

$$R_r = \frac{L_r(1-w_1)}{t_s} \tag{29}$$

Simulation works are carried out to evaluate the performance of the new proposed technique. The simulations are performed using the MATLAB/Simulink simulation package. The parameters and data of the induction motor used for simulation procedure are listed as follows:

$P_n = 3\text{kW}$, $V_n = 230\text{V}$, $R_s = 2.89\Omega$, $R_r = 2.39\Omega$, $L_s = 0.225\text{H}$, $L_r = 0.220\text{H}$, $L_m = 0.214\text{H}$, $J = 0.2\text{kg·m}^2$, $n_p = 2$.

Figs. 5(a) and 5(a') presents the estimation and error estimation results of fuzzy rotor resistance estimator compared to neural rotor resistance estimator.

The rotor resistance is changed abruptly during steady state operation of the drive. Its value is increased from the nominal value of 2.39Ω to 3.585Ω at 0.2sec, and then decreased to 2.987Ω at 0.4sec, and then decreased to its nominal value at 0.6sec.

This figure shows a good operation of the estimator does not depend, again, the initial value of R_r chosen in the algorithm. This is very important since in reality we do not know the exact value of resistance when the estimation algorithm starts. The convergence of this method is thus confirmed. In reality, the actual rotor resistance varies much more slowly, this means that the estimated rotor resistance can better monitor the actual rotor resistance.

Fig. 5(b) shows the rotor speed variations, the real speeds show a steady state disturbance error before rotor resistance estimation process begins. A short time after estimation process, the disturbance is reduced to zero. The electromagnetic torque is showing in Fig. 5(c), well as the decoupling between the flux and torque is verified.

As can be seen from the comparison, the dynamic response of neural rotor resistance estimator is much better than the fuzzy rotor resistance estimator.

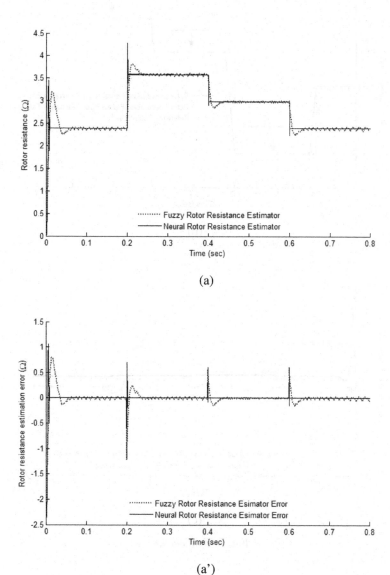

(a)

(a')

Fig. 5. Fuzzy rotor resistance estimator compared to neural rotor resistance estimator. (a) rotor speed estimation error; (a') rotor resistance estimation; (b) rotor speed; (c) torque.

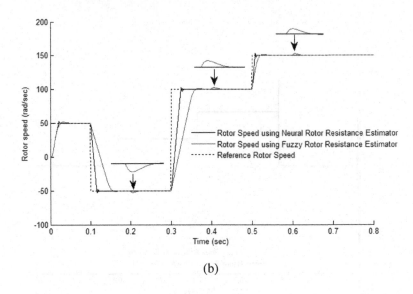

(b)

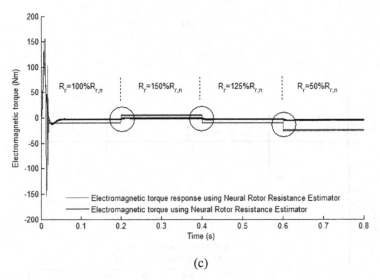

(c)

Fig. 5. (*Continued.*)

5   Conclusion

The expected results of this research were primarily to improve the performance of drives addressed by conventional methods of indirect rotor flux orientation. This improvement should be achieved by developing a new blueprint indirect more robust with respect to the parameter variation. The basic idea of this new command structure is the online correction of rotor resistance variation to maintain the decoupling controller in perfect agreement with the actual conditions of motor operation. Considering the results of the simulation, the new proposed neural rotor resistance estimator has better dynamic performance than the fuzzy rotor resistance estimator presented in the literature. The simulation results show the effectiveness of this estimator. The optimal control vector is then obtained and the torque/current is kept at the maximum value corresponding to a given load torque.

References

1. Leonhard, W.: Control of Electrical Drives. Springer (1996)
2. Krause, P.C., Wasynczuk, O., Sudhoff, S.D.: Analysis of Electric Machinery and Drive Systems. Wiley Interscience, John Wiley & Sons, NY (2002)
3. Blaschke, F.: The Principle of Field Orientation as Applied to the New Transvector Closed-Loop Control System for Rotating Field Machines. Siemens Review 34(5), 217–223 (1972)
4. Hasse, K.: On the Dynamics of Speed Control of a Static AC Drive with a Squirrel-Cage Induction Machine. Dissertation for the Doctoral Degree, Darmstadt (1969)
5. Hadj Saïd, S., Mimouni, M.F., M'Sahli, F., Farza, M.: High Gain Observer Based On-Line Rotor and Stator Resistances Estimation for IMs. Simulation Modelling Practice and Theory 19, 1518–1529 (2011)
6. Bartolini, G., Pisano, A., Pisu, P.: Simplified Exponentially Convergent Rotor Resistance Estimation for Induction Motors. IEEE Transactions on Automatic Control 48(2), 325–330 (2003)
7. Kojabadi, H.M.: Active Power and MRAS Based Rotor Resistance Identification of an IM Drive. Simul. Modell. Practice Theory 17(2), 376–389 (2009)
8. Abbasian, T., Salmasi, F.R., Yazdanpanah, M.J.: Improved Adaptive Feedback Linearization Control of Induction Motors Based on Online Estimation of Core Loss and Rotor Resistance. In: International Symposium on Power Electronics, Electrical Drives, Automation and Motion, SPEEDAM 2006, Taormina-Sicily, Italy, pp. S32/22–S32/27 (2006)
9. Toliyat, H.A., Levi, E., Raina, M.: A Review of RFO Induction Motor Parameter Estimation Techniques. IEEE Trans. Energy Convers 18(2), 271–283 (2003)
10. Toliyat, H.A., Wlas, M., Krzemiriski, Z.: Neural-Network-Based Parameter Estimations of Induction Motors. IEEE Transactions on Industrial Electronics 55(4), 1783–1794 (2008)
11. Zidani, F., Nait-Said, M.S., Benbouzid, M.E.H., Diallo, D., Abdessemed, R.: A Fuzzy Rotor Resistance Updating Scheme for an IFOC Induction Motor Drive. IEEE Power Engineering Review 21(11), 47–50 (2001)
12. Zadeh, L.A.: Fuzzy Logic. IEEE Computer Magazine 1(4), 83–92 (1988)
13. Zadeh, L.A.: Fuzzy Sets. Information and Control 8(3), 338–353 (1965)
14. Zimmermann, H.J.: Fuzzy Sets, Decision Marking, and Expert Systems, Boston, Dordrecht, Lancaster (1987)
15. Chen, S.-M.A.: Fuzzy Approach for Rule-Based Systems Based on Fuzzy Logics. IEEE Trans. Syst. Man and Cybernetics 26(5), 769–778 (1996)
16. Livingstone, D.J.: Artificial Neural Networks: Methods and Applications. Humana Press Inc. (2009)
17. Hertz, J., Krogh, A., Palmer, R.G.: Introduction to the Theory of Neural Computation. Addison-Wesley (1991)

ALMM Solver - A Tool for Optimization Problems

Ewa Dudek-Dyduch[1], Edyta Kucharska[1], Lidia Dutkiewicz[1],
and Krzysztof Rączka[1]

AGH University of Science and Technology,
Department of Automatics and Biomedical Engineering,
30 Mickiewicza Av, 30-059 Krakow, Poland
{edd,edyta,lidia,kjr}@agh.edu.pl

Abstract. The aim of our paper is to present the concept and structure of a software tool named the ALMM Solver. The goal of the solver is to generate solutions for discrete optimization problems, in particular for NP-hard problems. The solver is based on Algebraic Logical Meta-Model of Multistage Decision Process (ALMM of MDP) methodology, which is briefly described in the paper. Functionality and modular structure of the ALMM Solver is presented. SimOpt, the core module of the solver, is described in detail. Some possible future advances regarding the solver are also given.

Keywords: solver, optimizer, algebraic-logical meta-model (ALMM), multistage decision process, scheduling problem, simulation tool.

1 Introduction

The aim of our paper is to present the concept and structure of a software tool named ALMM Solver. The goal of the solver is to generate solutions for discrete optimization problems, in particular for NP-hard problems. The solver is based on Algebraic-Logical Meta-Model of Multistage Decision Process (ALMM of MDP) methodology.

There are many different discrete optimization problems. Some of them are modeled by means of well-known mathematical models, another are described informally or partially formally. These problems are solved with the use of general methods as well as dedicated algorithms [2], [16], [10], [14], [18]. There are also a growing number of software tools that allow one to solve certain kinds of problems by various known methods.

There are many such solutions, both academic and commercial. Some of these tools are based on the Logical Constraint Programming (CLP) approach, in which the accent is on finding feasible solutions [15], [17], [22], [13]. The problems are modeled there by a finite, predetermined number of variables, their domains, and relations between them. However, wide range of actual optimization problems are not suitable for modeling through CLP.

L. Rutkowski et al. (Eds.): ICAISC 2014, Part II, LNAI 8468, pp. 328–338, 2014.

Other example solution is JABAT, which is software environment designed in the agent technology [11], [1]. It is based on the A-Team architecture and uses JADE Framework. The goal of JABAT is to solve complex combinatorial optimization problems. Its users implement optimization algorithms using the system interface and predefined objects, without the need to implement system infrastructure.

There are also software tools implemented on top of well-known spreadsheet applications. One of them is "Frontline solvers", a commercial solution based on Excel [23].

Naturally, there are many other applications designed for solving numerous optimization problems. We only gave several examples to illustrate our point.

Nonetheless, there are discrete problems, especially dynamic ones, for which existing software packages are not sufficient. It turns out that a majority of these difficult discrete optimization problems can be represented by a formal model based on the algebraic-logical meta-model presented in Section 2. This meta-model allows one to introduce the model of the problem into the ALMM Solver, and then to use different methods (exact and heuristic), implemented in the solver, to solve the problem. Moreover, one can apply new meta-heuristic algorithms developed specifically for this meta-model.

2   ALMM Methodology

The ALMM Solver allows one to solve discrete optimization problems by finding optimal or suboptimal solutions. The solver can also be used to solve those problems, in which it suffices to find an admissible solution only.

A crucial issue when designing a solver is how to maintain the knowledge about the problem to be solved. In other words, how, in a formal way, should one enter into the system all the constraints and quality criteria which define the problem. The ALMM Solver operates on models of problems that belong to the class of models based on Algebraic-Logical Meta-Model of Multistage Decision Process (ALMM of MDP).

In ALMM methodology, a problem is modeled as a multistage decision process. With the use of a model, a sequence of consecutive process states is generated. In this sequence, each state depends on the previous state and the decision made at this state. The decision is chosen from different decisions one can make at the given state. Generation of the state sequence is terminated if the new state is a goal state (state we want the process to be at the end), a non-admissible state, or state with an empty set of possible decisions. The sequence of consecutive process states from a given initial state to a final state (goal or non-admissible) form a process trajectory.

Below we give a formal definition of a multistage decision process, devised by Dudek- Dyduch [3], [4]. Using this formal definition, one can create models of many discrete optimization problems, hence the name "meta-model". This definition concerns dynamic decision processes, i.e. processes in which both the constraints and the transition function (in particular, the sets of possible decisions) depend on time. Therefore, the concept of the so-called "generalized state" is introduced, which is defined as a pair containing the state and the time instant.

Definition 1. *Algebraic-logical meta-model of multistage decision process (ALMM of MDP) is a process that is defined by the sextuple $MDP = (U, S, s_0, f, S_N, S_G)$ where: U is a set of decisions, $S = X \times T$ is a set of generalized states (X is a set of proper states and $T \subset \mathbb{R}^+ \cup \{0\}$ is a subset of non-negative real numbers representing the time instants), $f : U \times S \to S$ is a partial function called a transition function (it does not have to be defined for all elements of the set $U \times S$), $s_0 = (x_0, t_0)$ is an initial generalized state, $S_N \subset S$ is a set of not admissible generalized states, $S_G \subset S$ is a set of goal generalized states, i.e. the states in which we want the process to be at the end.*

Transition function f is defined by means of two functions, i.e., $f = (f_x, f_t)$ where: $f_x : U \times X \times T \to X$ determines the next state and $f_t : U \times X \times T \to T$ determines the next time instant. It is assumed that the difference $\Delta t = f_t(u, x, t) - t$ has a value that is both finite and positive. Thus, as a result of the decision u that is taken at some proper state x and a moment t, the state of the process changes to $x' = f_x(u, x, t)$ that is observed at the moment $t' = f_t(u, x, t) = t + \Delta t$.

Since not all decisions defined formally make sense in certain situations, the transition function f is defined as a partial one. Thanks to it, all limitations concerning the control decisions in a given state s can be defined in a convenient way by means of so-called sets of possible decisions $U_p(s)$, and defined as: $U_p(s) = \{u \in U : (u, s) \in Dom f\}$.

In the most general case, sets U and X are a Cartesian product $U = U^1 \times U^2 \times \ldots \times U^m$, $X = X^1 \times X^2 \times \ldots \times X^n$, i.e., $u = (u^1, u^2, \ldots, u^m)$, $x = (x^1, x^2, \ldots, x^n)$. Each particular u^i, $i = 1, 2, ..m$ represents a separate decisions that is taken at the same time and relates to particular objects in the process (executors, resources, tasks, etc.). There are no general limitations imposed on the sets; in particular they do not have to be numerical. The values of particular co-ordinates of a state may be names of elements (symbols) as well as some objects (e.g., finite sets, sequences). The sets S_N, S_G and U_p are formally defined with the use of logical formulas.

According to its structure, the knowledge regarding a problem is represented by information coded by U, S, s_0, f, S_N, S_G.

To define a particular optimization problem in ALMM methodology, one should build an algebraic-logical model of the problem and give a specified optimization criterion Q. The optimization task is to find an admissible decision sequence $\tilde{u}$ that optimizes criterion Q. If the goal is to simply find a feasible solution, an algebraic-logical model alone is sufficient.

For a problem instance, an algebraic-logical model represents a set of process trajectories that start from the initial state s_0. If the process contains finite (or countable) sets $U_p(s)$ only, the transition graph for the process is defined as a graph $G = (S^{TG}, R)$, where S^{TG} is a set of all generalized states of the process trajectories, $R \subset (S \times S)$ is a relation such that $(s_i, s_j) \in R$ iff there exists $u \in U_p(s_i)$ such that $f(u, s_i) = s_j$. It can be shown that for all multistage decision processes the graph G is acyclic one. Since the considered states include time components, state transition graph is either a tree or a directed acyclic graph. By cloning some of the states (that is, some of the graph nodes), we can convert each directed acyclic graph to a tree.

Many different type of discrete optimization problems, especially discrete dynamic optimization problems, can be modeled by means of the above formal model. Such problems as control of discrete manufacturing processes (especially scheduling problems), logistic problems, project management problems and others can be formally defined in this way. In particular, the algebraic-logical meta-model has been applied to several problems such as scheduling with state dependent resources, scheduling with state depended retooling, planning supply routes for multi-location companies, production planning in failure modes [7], and scheduling in a system with defects and a quality control [9].

The ALMM of MDP constitutes the basis for defining novel heuristic discrete optimization methods. Based on ALMM of MDP, methods that uses a specially designed local optimization task, learning-based method, and the substitution task method have been proposed and developed [5], [6], [7], [12]. ALMM of MDP makes it possible to define mathematic properties of discrete optimization problems. As a result, new proposed heuristic methods and algorithms can be explained and discussed formally.

3   ALMM Solver

The task of the ALMM Solver is to provide solutions (exact or approximate) for NP-hard of discrete optimization problems, using the Algebraic-Logical Meta-Model methodology. The main idea behind the ALMM Solver is to generate one or more trajectories (also partial trajectories if needed). The generation of a trajectory is controlled through various general methods and/or specific optimization algorithms or algorithms for searching admissible solutions. As a solution the ALMM Solver gives a decision sequence (which determines the trajectory passing from the initial state s_0 to a state belonging to the S_G) or indicates that a solution has't been found.

The ALMM Solver provides functionality regarding problem modeling, problem optimization, process simulation for a given decision sequence, and presentation of the results (including visualization).

We have built the solver basing on newest paradigms and software design patterns [8], [19], [21], [20]. The proposed modular structure of the ALMM Solver is presented in Fig. 1.

ALM Modeler is a module that allows one to define the model of the problem in ALMM methodology. That includes: creating an algebraic-logical model of the process, setting the optimization criterion, and defining the additional knowledge about the problem (e.g., as auxiliary procedures or inference rules).

The model can be built by different means, e.g., by using pre-defined components or by defining it from the scratch. In the current version of the solver, the

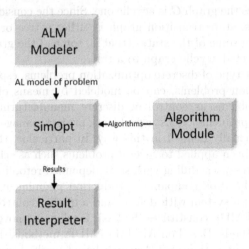

Fig. 1. Modules of the ALMM Solver

algebraic-logical models of the problem are implemented using the programming language.

Our goal is to fit ALM Modeler with a user-friendly interface to build models, as well as a library of pre-defined components and models for various optimization problems. Our intention is to facilitate building models for users not familiar with computer programming. Moreover, the modeler may be a completely separate application, written by any person, and connected to the solver. The only crucial thing is that it provides the model in the appropriate format.

SimOpt module constitutes a core of the ALMM Solver. Its task is to intelligently construct the state transition tree (either in its entirety, or only a part of it) by generating one or more trajectories (parts of trajectories). The solver database stores all generated states of the trajectories maintaining the structure of the tree. The SimOpt module uses the model of the problem provided by ALM Modeler. Trajectory generation is controlled using algorithms from the Algorithm Module. A more detailed description of the SimOpt module is given in Section 3.1.

Algorithm Module provides a collection of already implemented methods and algorithms, and allows one to design new algorithms. Thus, it consists of two parts: Algorithm Repository and Algorithms Designer.

Algorithm Repository stores various methods and algorithms. There are grafh search algorithms, general methods (e.g., Branch & Bound), standard algorithms (e.g., finding the shortest path in graph algorithms), and meta-heuristics and algorithms based on the ALMM methodology. It also includes dedicated algorithms for specific problems.

Algorithm Designer allows one to create new methods and algorithms.

Results Interpreter is a module which identifies the final solution of the given problem (the best one or an admissible one) on the basis of the data (state tree) stored in the solver database. Result Interpreter gives the users the solution (one or many) in an appropriate form or return an information that a solution was not found (when the solution does not exist or was not found before the termination condition was met). Each solution is given in the form of a decision sequence with the value of the quality criterion appended (or only the decision sequence in the case of searching for an admissible solution).

In addition, another important feature of this module is that it contains the visualization of results, including a graphical representation of the whole or a part of the generated state tree. In the future, the module will also provide a mean to share the results of the analysis through external API. It will allow one to integrate the ALMM Solver with other systems, for example, with manufacturing planning systems, and to use Business Intelligence tools. Additionally, the module will provide the possibility to define various ways of analyzing results obtained from a series of computations for the same or different instances of a problem.

3.1   SimOPT Module

SimOpt is a module where main computations are conducted. All tasks performed in this module can be partitioned into two abstraction layers.

1. Meta-decision Layer
   On this layer, a particular way of finding the solution of the problem is established. Therefore specific components of a solving algorithm are set: the rules for choosing the state for which the further part of a trajectory will be generated, procedures for producing the $U_p(s)$ sets of possible decisions (concerning number and sequence of decisions), procedures (usually parametric) for choosing one decision from the $U_p(s)$ set, and termination conditions. Also the analysis of computations is carried out and potential modifications of procedures and parameters are made. All these general decisions determine the final form of the meta-algorithm, by which the calculations are performed in the Computing Layer. It corresponds to intelligent generation of the state tree.

2. Computing Layer
   This is the layer where the actual computations are performed. It is composed
   of two layers:
   – Choice and Optimization Sublayer – in this layer the algorithm set out
     at the Meta-decision Layer performs its calculations (for one cycle). As a
     result, two entities are determined: the state s_i, for which the next state
     will be calculated, and the decision u_i for state s_i.
   – Step-simulation Sublayer - in this layer the transition function calculates
     the next state s_{i+1} for given state s_i and the decision u_i. The value of the
     criterion $Q(s_{i+1})$ is calculated for the new state as well. It is also verified
     whether this new state s_{i+1} is a non-admissible state ($s_{i+1} \in S_N$) or a
     goal state ($s_{i+1} \in S_G$).

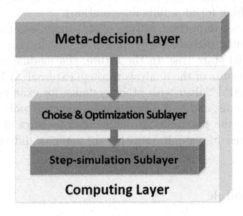

Fig. 2. Layers of SimOpt

The SimOpt module consists of a number of components which perform its
tasks. These elements are:

– Coordinator component – its task is to launch sequentially other components
  of the SimOpt module and to coordinate their work. Additionally, it saves
  all the generated states in the database.
– Controller component – stores the control information regarding the process
  of solution searching of the problem instance. Users of the system choose
  Controller parameters, of which the most impotant ones are:
  • searching strategy for the state transition tree
  • a general algorithm for choosing decisions in individual states,
  • termination condition: the number of generated trajectories or the thresh-
    old value of the quality criterion. Controller parameters can be changed
    during the experiment by the Analyzer component.

- StateChooser component - its task is to chose the state, for which the next state will be generated. Most often it is simply the last generated state (of the trajectory being built), but it is possible to generate a part of a trajectory starting from any state in the so far generated state tree. Operation mode of this element depends on the chosen tree search strategy (Controller holds the information about the chosen strategy). Available strategies are: depth-first search, breadth-first search, mixed strategy, or heuristic search strategies.
- DecisionGenerator component – its task is to generate the U_p set of possible decisions in a given state (the whole set U_p or a part of it). An algorithm to generate a set can be defined specifically for a particular problem or an algorithm from AlgorithmRepository can be used.
- DecisionChooser component – it selects one decision from the possible decisions in a given state, using the set generated by DecisionGenerator. The choice is made on the basis of particular decision choices algorithms. Algorithms can be developed on the basis on one of the mentioned ALMM methods. Users of the system can also create their own algorithms in Algorithm Designer module or use the algorithms collected in Algorithm Repository.
- NextStateGenerator component – it computes the new state for the current state (selected by StateChooser) and the given decision (selected by DecisionChooser), using the transition function. In addition, it checks whether the generated state belongs to the S_G set of goal states or the S_N set of non-admissible states.
- QualityCriteria component – it computes the value of the quality criterion for the new state. The function calculating the quality criterion is defined in the module ALM Modeler.
- Analyzer – its task is to modify the parameters and/or procedures used in the solution finding process.

   The process of finding a solution for the problem instance is as follows. The process begins with downloading the model of the problem from ALM Modeler and downloading the instance data. Then the user determines the method and the parameters for the process of finding a solution. This information is stored in the Controller component. Then the Coordinator component starts to operate, i.e., to execute the solution finding process. It is done by executing in a cycle appropriate components of the SimOpt module. In each cycle the next node (corresponding to a state) of the state tree is generated. Each cycle begins with the selection (by StateChooser) of the state for which the next state will be generated. For this state, DecisionGenerator generates a whole or a part of a set of possible decisions. From this set, DecisionChooser selects one decision. The selected decision and the current state are sent to StateGenerator, where a new state is calculated, and to the QualityCriteria component, where the criterion value is calculated for this state. The state is verified regarding its membership in the sets S_N and S_G. A new node is created in the state tree. The node corresponds to the newly generated state and stores all the information connected with it. Then the Analyzer component performs the analysis of the new state and optionally changes the parameters and procedures of the solutions finding process.

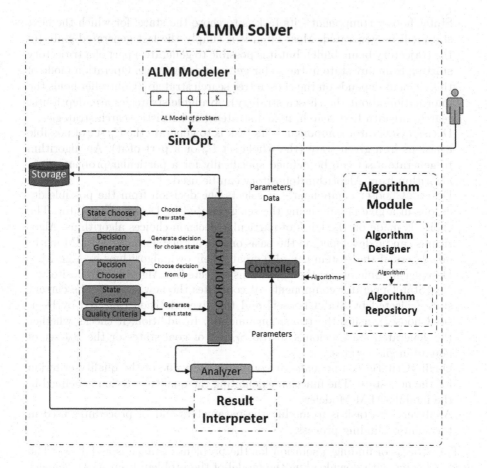

Fig. 3. Structure of the ALMM Solver

4 Conclusions

The paper presents the concept and structure of the ALMM Solver intended to solve various discrete problems, especially NP-hard and dynamic problems. Our concept of the ALMM Solver is part of the current research direction, where not only methods and algorithms are developed, but also tools.

We have designed the solver to be easily extendable and able to cooperate with other applications. In the modular structure of the proposed solver, different components are responsible for specific individual tasks. Their functionality is distributed in such a way that the potential extensions does not change the overall behavior of the system. This approach allow to continuously develop the solver by adding new elements or improving old ones. At the same time new problems and algorithms can be implemented.

The core of the ALMM Solver is ready and running, and was already used to solve several optimization problems. Further work will focus on the development of the Modeler Module, the Algorithm Module, and the Result Interpreter module.

References

1. Barbucha, D., Czarnowski, I., Jędrzejowicz, P., Ratajczak-Ropel, E., Wierzbowska, I.: JABAT Middleware as a Tool for Solving Optimization Problems. T. Computational Collective Intelligence 2, 181–195 (2010)
2. Danping, L., Lee, C.K.M., Zhang, W.: Integrated GA and AHP for re-entrant flow shop scheduling problem. In: IEEE International Conference on Quality and Reliability, ICQR (2011)
3. Dudek-Dyduch, E.: Formalization and Analysis of Problems of Discrete Manufacturing Processes. Scientific bulletin of AGH University, Automatyka, vol. 54 (1990) (in Polish)
4. Dudek-Dyduch, E.: Learning based algorithm in scheduling. Journal of Intelligent Manufacturing 11(2), 135–143 (2000)
5. Dudek-Dyduch, E., Dutkiewicz, L.: Substitution Tasks Method for Discrete Optimization. In: Rutkowski, L., Korytkowski, M., Scherer, R., Tadeusiewicz, R., Zadeh, L.A., Zurada, J.M. (eds.) ICAISC 2013, Part II. LNCS, vol. 7895, pp. 419–430. Springer, Heidelberg (2013)
6. Dudek-Dyduch, E., Kucharska, E.: Learning method for co-operation. In: Jędrzejowicz, P., Nguyen, N.T., Hoang, K. (eds.) ICCCI 2011, Part II. LNCS, vol. 6923, pp. 290–300. Springer, Heidelberg (2011)
7. Sękowski, H., Dudek-Dyduch, E.: Knowledge based model for scheduling in failure modes. In: Rutkowski, L., Korytkowski, M., Scherer, R., Tadeusiewicz, R., Zadeh, L.A., Zurada, J.M. (eds.) ICAISC 2012, Part II. LNCS, vol. 7268, pp. 591–599. Springer, Heidelberg (2012)
8. Evans, E.: Domain-Driven Design: Tackling Complexity in the Heart of Software. Addison Wesley (2011)
9. Grobler-Dębska, K., Kucharska, E., Dudek-Dyduch, E.: Idea of switching algebraic-logical models in flow-shop scheduling problem with defects. In: Proceedings of the 18th International Conference on Methods and Models in Automation and Robotics, MMAR, pp. 532–537 (2013)
10. Hyun-Seon, C.: Scheduling algorithms for two-stage reentrant hybrid flow shops: minimizing makespan under the maximum allowable due dates. The International Journal of Advanced Manufacturing Technology (2009)
11. Jędrzejowicz, P., Wierzbowska, I.: JADE-Based A-Team Environment. In: Alexandrov, V.N., van Albada, G.D., Sloot, P.M.A., Dongarra, J. (eds.) ICCS 2006. LNCS, vol. 3993, pp. 719–726. Springer, Heidelberg (2006)
12. Kucharska, E., Dutkiewicz, L., Grobler-Dębska, K., Rączka, K.: ALMM approach for optimization of the supply routes for multi-location companies problem. In: Skulimowski, A. (ed.) Advances in Decision Sciences and Future Studies - Proceedings of the 8th International Conference on Knowledge, Information and Creativity Support Systems: Kraków, Poland, November 7-9, vol. 2, pp. 321–332 (2013)
13. Ligęza, A.: Improving Efficiency in Constraint Logic Programming Through Constraint Modeling with Rules and Hypergraphs. In: Federated Conf. on Computer Science and Information Systems, pp. 101–107. IEEE Computer Society Press (2012)

14. Mróz, H., Wąs, J.: Discrete vs. Continuous Approach in Crowd Dynamics Modeling Using GPU Computing. Cybernetics and Systems 45(1), 25–38 (2014)
15. Rossi, F., Van Beek, P., Walsh, T.: Handbook of Constraint Programming. Elsevier (2006)
16. Sze, S.N., Tiong, W.K.: A Comparison between Heuristic and Meta-Heuristic Methods for Solving the Multiple Traveling Salesman Problem. World Academy of Science, Engineering and Technology, 300–303 (2007)
17. Tomczuk-Piróg, I., Wójcik, R., Banaszak, Z.: Decision Support Systems Based on CLP Approach in SMEs. In: IEEE Conference on Emerging Technologies & Factory Automation, vol. 1-3, pp. 1078–1083 (2006)
18. Wąs, J., Kułakowski, K.: Multi-agent Systems in Pedestrian Dynamics Modeling. In: Nguyen, N.T., Kowalczyk, R., Chen, S.-M. (eds.) ICCCI 2009. LNCS, vol. 5796, pp. 294–300. Springer, Heidelberg (2009)
19. Wirfs-Brock, R.J.: Characterizing Classes. IEEE Software 23(2), 9–11 (2006)
20. Verginadis, Y., Apostolou, D., Papageorgiou, N., Mentzas, G.: An architecture for collaboration patterns in agile event-driven environments. In: 18th IEEE International Workshops on Enabling Technologies: Infrastructures for Collaborative Enterprises, WETICE 2009, pp. 227–230. IEEE (2009)
21. Zhang, C., Budgen, D.: What Do We Know about the Effectiveness of Software Design Patterns? IEEE Transaction on Software Engineering 38(5), 1213–1231 (2012)
22. http://www.jacop.eu/
23. http://www.solver.com

Tournament Searching Method for Optimization of the Forecasting Model Based on the Nadaraya-Watson Estimator

Grzegorz Dudek

Department of Electrical Engineering, Czestochowa University of Technology,
Al. Armii Krajowej 17, 42-200 Czestochowa, Poland
dudek@el.pcz.czest.pl

Abstract. In the article the tournament searching method is used for optimization of the forecasting model based on the Nadaraya-Watson estimator. This is a nonparametric regression model useful for forecasting the nonstationary in mean and variance time series with multiple seasonal cycles and trend. The tournament searching is a stochastic global optimization algorithm which is easy to use and competitive to other stochastic methods such as evolutionary algorithms. Three types of tournament searching algorithms are proposed: for estimation of the forecasting model parameters (continuous optimization), for the predictor selection (binary optimization) and for both predictor selection and parameter estimation (mixed binary-continuous optimization). The effectiveness of the proposed approach is illustrated through applications to electrical load forecasting and compared with other optimization methods: grid search method, genetic and evolutionary algorithms, and sequential methods of feature selection. Application examples confirm good properties of tournament searching.

Keywords: Tournament searching, binary and continuous optimization, Nadaraya-Watson estimator, multiple seasonal time series forecasting, short-term load forecasting.

1   Introduction

Time series forecasting plays a significant role in economy, industry, seismology, meteorology, geophysics etc. The purpose of forecasting is to support decision-making processes, to stimulate for action favoring or opposing the realization of the forecast or to provide information about the changes of some phenomenon in the future. In general, time series consists of four types of components: trend, seasonality, cycling and irregularity. They combine in an additive or multiplicative fashion. Sometimes there are multiple seasonal variations. This complicates the construction of the forecasting model. A typical procedure in such a case is to simplify the problem by deseasonality or decomposition of the time series. After decomposition the components showing less complexity than the original time series can be forecasted using simpler models.

The most commonly used conventional approaches to the modeling of time series with seasonality are the autoregressive moving average models (ARMA, ARIMA, SARMA etc.) and the Holt-Winters exponential smoothing models. The rapid

L. Rutkowski et al. (Eds.): ICAISC 2014, Part II, LNAI 8468, pp. 339–348, 2014.
© Springer International Publishing Switzerland 2014

development of computational intelligence and machine learning in recent years has brought many new methods of forecasting such as: artificial neural networks, fuzzy inference systems, regression trees and support vector machines. The conventional approaches as well as computational intelligence ones usually require many parameters (tens, hundreds or even thousands) for modeling nonstationary time series with trend and multiple seasonal cycles. The searching of the model space to find the optimal solution in this case is a very complex optimization task. It is due to different types of parameters (qualitative, continuous, discrete, logical) and multimodality of the error function. The choice of the appropriate methods of learning or optimization and values of their parameters is often a separate optimization problem. In the case of unstable models (e.g. neural networks), where we observe different learning results for the same training data, the optimization process is much more difficult.

In the article we describe a simple deterministic forecasting model based on Nadaraya–Watson estimator. This is a similarity–based model working on patterns of the seasonal cycles of time series [1]. Using patterns we filter the time series removing the trend and seasonal variations of periods longer than the basic period and we get stationary time series. We propose the tournament searching method for optimization of the model. This is a stochastic, global optimization method with only one or two parameters controlling the local/global optimization property. The tournament searching effectively optimizes the Nadaraya–Watson estimator in the continuous and binary spaces.

2   Forecasting Model Based on the Nadaraya-Watson Estimator

The Nadaraya-Watson estimator (N-WE) as a forecasting tool was derived from the conditional density estimator using kernel functions in [2]. Nonparametric conditional density estimation is a way to model the relationship between past and future realisation of the random variable. The regression function in this case is defined as:

$$m(x) = \frac{\sum_{j=1}^{N} K\left(\frac{x-x_j}{h}\right) y_j}{\sum_{j=1}^{N} K\left(\frac{x-x_j}{h}\right)}, \tag{1}$$

where: N is a number of elements in a random sample, x is a predictor, y is a response variable, $K(.)$ is a kernel function and h is its bandwidth.

For multidimensional predictors the kernels are expressed using a multidimensional product kernel function. The selection of the kernel function form is not as important as the selection of their bandwidths. When we use normal kernels the N-WE for multidimensional predictors is of the form:

$$m(\mathbf{x}) = \frac{\sum_{j=1}^{N} \exp\left(-\sum_{t=1}^{n} \frac{(x_t - x_{j,t})^2}{2h_t^2}\right) y_j}{\sum_{j=1}^{N} \exp\left(-\sum_{t=1}^{n} \frac{(x_t - x_{j,t})^2}{2h_t^2}\right)}, \tag{2}$$

where $\mathbf{x} \in \mathbb{R}^n$.

The response variable can be a vector as well.

Estimator (2) is a linear combination of response variables y_j weighted by the normalized kernel functions. Kernels map nonlinearly the distance between points $\mathbf{x}$ and $\mathbf{x}_j$. The bandwidth h_t decides about the share of the t-th component of $\mathbf{x}$ in the distance (greater value of h implies larger share). The bias-variance tradeoff of the regression model (2) is controlled by bandwidth values. Too small values of h result in undersmoothing, whereas too large values result in oversmoothing. Proper selection of the h values is therefore a key issue. For the normal product density estimators Scott proposed a rule [3]:

$$h_t^S = \hat{\sigma}_t N^{-\frac{1}{n+4}}, \tag{3}$$

where $\hat{\sigma}_t$ is the estimated standard deviation of the t-th component of $\mathbf{x}$.

The N-WE is a flexible forecasting method due to the local nature of fitting of the simple regression models. In the next section we describe how the N-WE is optimized using tournament searching.

One more issue should be clarified. How are predictors and response variable defined? For the time series considered in Section 4 and presented in Fig. 2 we define patterns of the daily cycles:

$$x_{i,t} = \frac{z_{i,t} - \bar{z}_i}{\sqrt{\sum_{l=1}^{n}(z_{i,l} - \bar{z}_i)^2}}, \tag{4}$$

where: $z_{i,t}$ is a component of the vector $\mathbf{z}_i = [z_{i,1} \ z_{i,2} \ ... \ z_{i,n}]$ including the elements of time series from the i-th daily cycle (electrical loads at successive hours of the day i in our example), $\bar{z}_i$ is a mean value of elements in cycle i, $x_{i,t}$ is the component of the pattern vector $\mathbf{x}_i = [x_{i,1} \ x_{i,2} \ ... \ x_{i,n}]$ representing the daily cycle $\mathbf{z}_i$.

Patterns $\mathbf{x}$ defined using (4) are normalized versions of vectors $\mathbf{z}$. Thus they have the unity length, zero mean and the same variance. It is worth nothing that after normalization the nonstationary in mean and variance time series $\{z_k\}$ is represented by patterns having the same mean and variance. The trend and additional seasonal cycles longer that the daily one are filtered. This simplification of the time series facilitates the construction of the forecasting model.

In the similar way to the predictors the response variables are defined:

$$y_i = \frac{z_{i+\tau,t} - \bar{z}_i}{\sqrt{\sum_{l=1}^{n}(z_{i,l} - \bar{z}_i)^2}}, \tag{5}$$

where: $z_{i+\tau,t}$ is the t-th element in the $(i+\tau)$-th daily cycle, τ is a forecast horizon (in daily cycles).

The y_i value encodes the actual time series element $z_{i+\tau,t}$ from the forecast period $i+\tau$ using current time series parameters ($\bar{z}_i$ and dispersion of a daily cycle in the denominator of (5)) from the nearest past, which allows to take into consideration current variability of the process and ensures possibility of decoding: when we get the forecast of y_i we can determine the forecast of $z_{i+\tau,t}$ using (5).

3   Tournament Searching for N-WE Optimization

The N-WE is optimized using the tournament searching method (TS). Three types of optimization procedures are performed. The first type concerns estimation of the bandwidth values. This is a continuous optimization problem, where we are searching for the vector $\mathbf{h} = [h_1, h_2, ..., h_n]$. The second type is the feature selection. This is a combinatorial optimization problem, where we are searching for the set of predictors. And the third type is the combined optimization, where we are searching for the bandwidths and the set of predictors in the same time. This is the mixed binary-continuous problem. The optimization criterion in these procedures is the forecast error (MAPE).

3.1   Estimation of the Bandwidth Values

The TS method has been proposed in [4] for combinatorial optimization (feature selection) as an alternative to the more complex stochastic global optimization methods such as genetic algorithm and simulated annealing. Application of TS to estimation of bandwidths requires redefinition of the algorithm (see Fig. 1).

Starting from the solution created according to the Scott's rule TS explores the solution space generating new solutions by perturbing the parent solution. The set of l candidate solutions $\{\mathbf{h}_1, \mathbf{h}_2, ..., \mathbf{h}_l\}$ is created from the parent solution in each iteration using the move (or mutation) operator defined as:

$$h_{i,t} = h_t^* + \xi_{i,t}, \quad i = 1, 2, ..., l, \quad t = 1, 2, ..., n, \qquad (6)$$

where $h_{i,t}$ is the mutated value of the parent solution component h_t^*, $\xi_{i,t} \sim N(0, \sigma_t)$.

The standard deviation of the normal distribution determines the range of moving. It is assumed that $\sigma_t = w\, h_t^S$, where $w = \text{const} \in \mathbb{R}^+$. Thus the moving range in the t-th direction is dependent on the initial value of h_t, i.e. on the variance of the t-th component of $\mathbf{x}$.

1. Initialization of the parent solution using the Scott's rule (3).
2. Generation of the set of l candidate solutions from the parent solution using the move operator.
3. Evaluation of the candidate solutions using N-WE.
4. Tournament - selection of the best solution among the candidate solutions.
5. Replacement of the parent solution by the tournament winner.
6. Repeat steps 2-6 until the stop criterion is reached.

Fig. 1. Algorithm of tournament searching for estimation of bandwidth values

After moving the candidate solutions are evaluated and the best one is selected. It replaces the parent solution and other set of candidate solution is generated from it in the next iteration. The l parameter (called the tournament size) and the standard deviation of mutation σ controls exploration/exploitation properties of the algorithm. When l is large the local minima attracts the searching process more intensively. The probability of escaping from the basin of attraction of the local minimum increases when l decreases. But in this case the searching process is more random. The standard deviation σ determines the length of jumps, i.e. the distance between the parent solution and the candidate solutions generated from it.

3.2   Selection of the Predictors

The components of pattern $\mathbf{x}$ (predictors) are strongly correlated. So elimination some of them should simplify the forecasting model without deteriorating its quality. The solution (selected predictors) is represented by a binary vector $\mathbf{b} = [b_1, b_2, ..., b_n]$. Ones in $\mathbf{b}$ indicates the selected components. TS algorithm for the problem of binary vector searching was proposed in [4]. The searching scheme is similar to that presented in Fig. 1, except the first step. Now the parent solution is initialized by random. The move operator generates $l \in \{1, 2, ..., n\}$ candidate solutions by switching the value of one randomly chosen bit (different for each candidate solution) of the parent solution. The tournament size l controls the exploration/exploitation properties, as in the case of TS for continuous optimization described in Section 3.1. When $l = 1$ the solution space is searched with a random walk algorithm, resistant to local minima. When $l = n$ we get a hill climbing procedure, which gets stuck in local minima. We recommend $l = \text{round}(n/3)$. In this case the algorithm quite intensively searches the neighborhoods of local minima but is able to leave their basins of attraction.

3.3   Mixed optimization: Selection of Predictors and Estimation of Bandwidth Values

Results of both the bandwidth estimation and selection of predictors are obviously interdependent. We propose TS method for simultaneous searching of two spaces: binary space of selected predictors and continuous space of bandwidths. The algorithm processes two paired vectors: $\mathbf{b}$ encoding selected predictors and $\mathbf{h}$ encoding bandwidths. The algorithm scheme is presented in Fig. 1, except the first step. The ways of initialization of both vectors $\mathbf{h}$ and $\mathbf{b}$ are the same as described in Sections 3.1 and 3.2, respectively. The move operator for vector $\mathbf{b}$ is the same as described in Section 3.2. The move operator for vector $\mathbf{h}$ has form (6), wherein only these components of $\mathbf{h}$ are modified which correspond to ones in the paired $\mathbf{b}$ vector. The paired vectors $(\mathbf{b}, \mathbf{h})$ after moving are evaluated together using N-WE. The tournament size $l \in \{1, 2, ..., n\}$ plays the same role as in the TS algorithms described above.

344   G. Dudek

4   Application Example

We illustrate the optimization of N-WE using tournament searching on example of forecasting time series with multiple seasonal cycles. That is a short-term electrical load forecasting problem. We use the time series of the hourly electrical load of the Polish power system from the period 2002–2004, which is shown in Fig. 2. This time series is nonstationary and exhibits trend and tree seasonal variations: annual, weekly and daily.

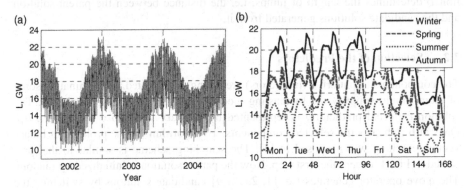

Fig. 2. The time series of electrical load of the Polish power system in three-year (a) and one-week (b) intervals

Our goal is to forecast the power system load for the next day ($\tau = 1$) at hours $t = 1, 6, 12, 18$ and 24. The test set includes 30 days from January 2004 (without untypical 1 January) and 31 days from July 2004. The training set for each forecasting task (load forecasting at hour t of the day j) is prepared individually. It contains patterns **x** representing the same days of the week (Monday, ..., Sunday) as the query pattern and paired with them y-values representing load at hour t for the next day. The training set is determined from the historical data. For each of the 305 forecasting tasks the separate N-WE model is created and optimized.

The proposed TS were compared with other optimization methods. For estimation of bandwidth values the grid search method (GS) and evolutionary algorithm (EA) are applied.

The GS searches the neighborhood of the point $\mathbf{h}^S = [\, h_1^S ,\ h_2^S ,\ ...,\ h_n^S \,]$ determined using Scott's rule (3). In the k-th iteration of the GS algorithm $\mathbf{h}_k$ point is generated as follows:

$$\mathbf{h}_k = a_k \mathbf{h}^S, \quad k = 1, 2, ..., \tag{7}$$

where $a_k = a_0 + \Delta(k-1)$, $a_0 \in \mathbb{R}^+ \leq 1$ and Δ is the step defining the grid density.

The stop criterion (N iterations without improvement in results) determines the final value of k. GS is sub-optimal and searches the sets of discretized values of **h** components. The multidimensional optimization problem: estimation of $h_1, h_2, ..., h_n$ is replaced here with one-dimensional problem: estimation of a.

The EA searches n-dimensional space to estimate vector $\mathbf{h}$. The vectors $\mathbf{h}$, which are individuals in EA, are initialized by the Scott's rule. The operators used in evolutionary process are: mutation, recombination and selection. The mutation is the same as in TS for continuous optimization (6). The recombination creates two new individuals by linear combinations of two parent individuals selected by random (so-called arithmetic or intermediate recombination) [5]:

$$h'_{a,t} = h_{a,t} + c(h_{b,t} - h_{a,t}), \; h'_{b,t} = h_{b,t} + c(h_{a,t} - h_{b,t}), \tag{8}$$

where $c \sim U(0,1)$, $t = 1, 2, \ldots, n$.

The selection operator was the tournament selection [5]. The tournament size T controls the selection pressure. The elitist strategy was also applied: the best individual was copied form population i to $i+1$.

For selection of predictors two deterministic sub-optimal methods were applied [6]: sequential forward selection (SFS) and sequential backward selection (SBS), as well as genetic algorithm (GA). In GA solutions are represented by binary vectors $\mathbf{b}$. As in EA three operators are used: mutation, recombination and selection. Mutation switches bits selected from the population of individuals by random with probability of p_m. One-point crossover is used as the recombination operator [5]. Tournament selection is used to select individuals to the next generation.

The parameters of the studied optimization algorithms were as follows:

- TS for estimation of bandwidth values (TSh): $l = 30$, $w = 0.1$, number of iterations $M = 100$,
- TS for selection of predictors (TSb): $l = 8$, number of iterations $M = 100$,
- TS for selection of predictors and estimation of bandwidth values (TSbh): $l = 8$, $w = 0.1$, number of iterations $M = 500$,
- GS: $a_0 = 0.1$, $\Delta = 0.05$, $N = 20$,
- EA: population size – 30, number of iterations $M = 100$, $T = 2$, probability of crossover – 0.9, probability of individual mutation – 1, $w = 0.1$,
- GA: population size – 8, number of iterations $M = 100$, $T = 2$, probability of crossover – 0.9, probability of mutation – 0.05.

These parameters were adjusted in the preliminary tests. The stop criterion in EA and TSh was: there is no improvement in results in $0.25M$ successive iterations.

The N-WE was optimized in leave-one-out procedure. The forecast errors (mean absolute percentage error MAPE) on validation and test samples for different methods of parameter estimation in Table 1 are shown. From this table it can be seen that the validation error was reduced when using GS, EA and TSh but the test error was not reduced. This could be due to insufficient information about the target function contained in the learning points which are sparse distributed in the n-dimensional space.

The bandwidth values estimated using GS were in 91% of cases higher than the values determined according to the Scott's rule. This percentage for EA and TSh was 65 and 67%, respectively. The optimal bandwidths for one of the forecasting task in Fig. 3 are shown.

Table 1. The forecast errors for different methods of estimation of the bandwidth values

Method	January		July		Mean	
	$MAPE_{val}$	$MAPE_{tst}$	$MAPE_{val}$	$MAPE_{tst}$	$MAPE_{val}$	$MAPE_{tst}$
Scott's rule	1.62	1.20	1.54	0.92	1.58	1.05
GS	1.58	1.21	1.51	0.96	1.55	1.09
EA	1.32	1.36	1.28	0.90	1.30	1.13
TSh	1.30	1.23	1.25	0.93	1.28	1.08

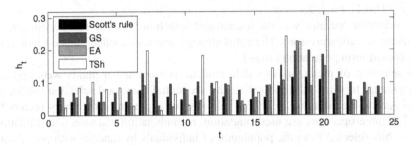

Fig. 3. The bandwidth values for the forecasting task of July 1, 2004, hour 12

The forecast errors for different methods of the predictor selection in Table 2 are shown. The bandwidths were determined using Scott's rule in this study except TSbh method which searches both set of predictors and bandwidth values at the same time. It can be seen from this table that both the validation and test errors were reduced when using stochastic optimization methods comparing to the case without selection but the test errors are statistically indistinguishable (Wilcoxon signed-rank test was used).

The selected predictors and bandwidth values for one of the forecasting task in Table 3 are shown. The frequencies of the predictor selection in Fig. 4 are shown.

Table 2. The forecast errors for different methods of selection of predictors

Method	January		July		Mean	
	$MAPE_{val}$	$MAPE_{tst}$	$MAPE_{val}$	$MAPE_{tst}$	$MAPE_{val}$	$MAPE_{tst}$
SFS	1.37	1.25	1.32	0.90	1.34	1.07
SBS	1.37	1.20	1.35	0.90	1.36	1.05
GA	1.38	1.17	1.34	0.90	1.36	1.03
TSb	1.34	1.17	1.30	0.90	1.32	1.03
TSbh	1.25	1.20	1.21	0.86	1.23	1.03

The average reduction in the number of predictors was as follows: for SFS – 76%, for SBS – 52%, for GA – 60%, for TSb – 67% and for TSbh – 57%. Thus the rejection of more than half of the predictors should not negatively affect the accuracy of the forecasting model. The most often selected predictors were x_{23} and x_{24}.

Table 3. The bandwidth values ($\cdot 10^{-3}$) for the forecasting task of July 1, 2004, hour 12

t	1	2	3	4	5	6	7	8	9	10	11	12
SFS	37	–	–	–	–	–	–	–	–	–	41	40
SBS	45	35	–	–	–	36	–	58	48	41	51	–
GA	44	34	–	–	–	35	64	57	47	40	–	–
TSb	44	34	–	–	–	35	–	57	47	40	–	–
TSbh	22	60	90	–	–	31	194	14	–	28	89	–
t	13	14	15	16	17	18	19	2–	21	22	23	24
SFS	–	–	–	37	–	–	–	–	–	–	39	–
SBS	–	–	41	46	–	–	–	–	–	50	49	–
GA	–	–	–	–	76	–	–	92	–	–	48	–
TSb	–	37	–	45	–	–	–	–	–	49	48	–
TSbh	–	54	59	40	–	–	165	151	–	42	–	–

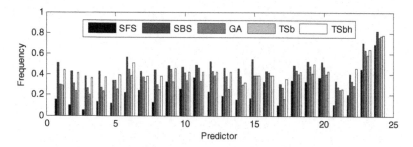

Fig. 4. The frequencies of predictor selection

5   Conclusions

The tournament searching method is a simple generic stochastic search method. It has an efficient, flexible algorithm which can be adapted to binary, continuous and mixed binary–continuous optimization. TS in a binary version has only one parameter controlling the global/local searching properties of the algorithm – the tournament size. In the continuous version TS has the second parameter – the standard deviation used for generating new solutions. This parameter determines the length of jumping from the parent solution to the candidate one, i.e. the size of the locally explored region.

Application of TS to optimization of the forecasting model based on Nadaraya-Watson estimator gave good results comparing to other optimization methods such as grid search, genetic and evolutionary algorithms, and sequential methods of feature selection. In a result we get simple, easy to use and accurate model for forecasting "hard" nonstationary time series with trend, multiple seasonal cycles and random noise.

Acknowledgment. The study was supported by the Research Project N N516 415338 financed by the Polish Ministry of Science and Higher Education.

References

1. Dudek, G.: Pattern-Similarity Machine Learning Models for Short-Term Load Forecasting. Academic Publishing House Exit, Warsaw (2012) (in Polish)
2. Dudek, G.: Short-Term Load Forecasting Based on Kernel Conditional Density Estimation. Przegląd Elektrotechniczny (Electrical Review) 86(8), 164–167 (2010)
3. Scott, D.W.: Multivariate Density Estimation: Theory, Practice, and Visualization. Wiley (1992)
4. Dudek, G.: Tournament Searching Method to Feature Selection Problem. In: Rutkowski, L., Scherer, R., Tadeusiewicz, R., Zadeh, L.A., Zurada, J.M. (eds.) ICAISC 2010, Part II. LNCS, vol. 6114, pp. 437–444. Springer, Heidelberg (2010)
5. Michalewicz, Z.: Genetic Algorithms + Data Structures = Evolution Programs. Springer (1996)
6. Theodoridis, S., Koutroumbas, K.: Pattern Recognition. Elsevier (2009)

A New Algorithm for Identification of Significant Operating Points Using Swarm Intelligence

Piotr Dziwiński[1], Łukasz Bartczuk[1], Andrzej Przybył[1],
and Eduard D. Avedyan[2]

[1] Częstochowa University of Technology,
Institute of Computational Intelligence, Poland
{piotr.dziwinski,lukasz.bartczuk,andrzej.przybyl}@iisi.pcz.pl
[2] Moscow Institute of Physics & Technology, Russia
eavedian@mail.ru

Abstract. The paper presents a novel algorithm for identification of significant operating points from non-invasive identification of nonlinear dynamic objects. In the proposed algorithm to identify the unknown parameters of nonlinear dynamic objects in different significant operating points, swarm intelligence supported by a genetic algorithm is used for optimization in continuous domain. Moreover, we propose a new weighted approximation error measure which eliminates the problem of the measurements obtained from non-significant areas. This measure significantly accelerates the process of the parameters identification in comparison with the same algorithm without weights. Performed simulations prove efficiency of the novel algorithm.

1 Introduction

Identification of dynamic objects is an important issue from the scientific and practical point of view (see e.g. [48][49]). Computer science researchers deal with the problem of the non-invasive identification of nonlinear dynamic objects, focusing only on cases in which measurements are collected in a short time, activity time of the object is not too long or estimated parameters of the nonlinear dynamic object do not change in a function of its input values. This paper is focused on identification of a nonlinear object in a case of significant size disproportions of the important and unimportant measurement areas and detection of operating points in order to determine parameters of specific components of the identified object when a precise mathematical model is unknown. Simple example of this type of a nonlinear object can be an electrical circuit with an element activating only at a certain value of voltage. This paper describes an initial part of a large project that is realized.

Swarm intelligence studies the collective behaviour of many individuals included in the complete system [38]. Each individual interacts locally with each other and their environment. Swarms use some forms of decentralized control as indirect communication to obtain satisfying solution in a reasonable time. In the

L. Rutkowski et al. (Eds.): ICAISC 2014, Part II, LNAI 8468, pp. 349–362, 2014.
© Springer International Publishing Switzerland 2014

world literature many swarm-based systems inspired by real swarms observed in nature can be found [38]. For example, Ant Colony Optimization methods have been developed by mimicking collective behaviour of real ants. These algorithms are adequate to solve discrete optimization problems [17]-[18], [21]. Another interesting behaviors have been observed in flocks of birds or schools of fish. In this kind of swarms, each individual randomly looks for food and observes other individuals in the neighborhood at the same time. In the Particle Swarm Optimization, individuals moving directly in a solution space are able to solve a problem in a continuous domain [23], [38].

2   Nonlinear Dynamic Object Identification

Let us consider a nonlinear dynamic system described by the algebraic equations and based on the state variables technique

$$\frac{dx}{dt} = f(x, u) = \mathbf{A}x + \mathbf{B}u + \eta g(\mathbf{x}, \mathbf{u}), \tag{1}$$

$$\mathbf{Y} = \mathbf{C} \cdot \mathbf{x}, \tag{2}$$

where $g(\mathbf{x}, \mathbf{u})$ is a separate nonlinear part of the system and η is the influence factor of the nonlinearities of the whole system, $\mathbf{A}, \mathbf{B}, \mathbf{C}$ are system input and output matrices, $\mathbf{x}, \mathbf{y}, \mathbf{u}$ are vectors of state variables, input and output signals respectively. Assuming that η is small and the system is weakly nonlinear then the linear approximation about an equilibrium point may give good results in some range. However, overall accuracy of such a model may be too low for many practical applications.

In this paper we propose solutions to increase accuracy of the above method by identifying parameters affecting the behaviour of a nonlinear dynamic object. This identification is based on data obtained from system measurements and/or data from the internal state of the object.

However, in order to precisely determine parameters of an object, two problems have to be solved, (a) in which parts of data it is possible (important measurement area) or it is not possible (unimportant measurement area) to determine of most or all parameters of the object; (b) how data from measurements should be treated in a case when small parts of them convey some important information from the identification point of view.

3   PSO nad GA Algorithm

In order to identify specific unknown parameters of dynamic nonlinear objects, we use the Particle Swarm Optimisation (PSO) algorithm supported by the genetic algorithm (see e.g. [25], [34]-[35], [41]).

Particle swarm optimisation is a well known computational method to solve optimization problems. At each epoch the algorithm attempts to improve the solution according to the specific measure of quality.

Unfortunately, PSO algorithm is not resistant to local optima occurring frequently in the case of estimating the parameters of dynamic objects. From that reason – in early stages – they require support of another effective algorithm inspired by nature – a Genetic Algorithm (GA) (see e.g. [11], [24], [27]-[28], [42]). GA provides diversity to obtained partial solutions and allows searching the entire space of solutions, while PSO is fast convergent to an optimal local solution.

In PSO algorithm each particle $p_i \in N_{PSO}^t, i = 1, \ldots, |N_{PSO}^t|$ has certain location $\mathbf{x}_i^t$ and velocity $\mathbf{v}_i^t$, where location $\mathbf{x}_i^t \in \mathbf{R}^N$, $t = 1, \ldots, T$, T - maximum epoch number. Each particle moves through a continuous search space looking for a high quality solution guided by its best location $\mathbf{xp}_i^t$ which has been found so far, and the global best location $\mathbf{xg}^t$ found by all particles. Initially, the set N_{PSO}^0 of particles, best locations $\mathbf{xp}_i^0$ and global best location $\mathbf{xg}^0$ are randomly scattered throughout the solution space. Firstly, PSO algorithm updates the velocity (3) and the location (4) of the particles [16], [52]

$$\mathbf{v}_i^{t+1} = w^t \cdot \mathbf{v}_i^t + \mathbf{U}(0, \psi_1)^t \cdot (\mathbf{xp}_i^t - \mathbf{x}_i^t) + \mathbf{U}(0, \psi_2)^t \cdot (\mathbf{xg}^t - \mathbf{x}_i^t), \qquad (3)$$

$$\mathbf{x}_i^{t+1} = \mathbf{x}_i^t + \mathbf{v}_i^{t+1}, \qquad (4)$$

where w^t is an influence factor of the velocity value in the time t on the velocity value in the time $t + 1$, ψ_1, ψ_2 are factors which determine an influence of $\mathbf{xp}_i^t$ and $\mathbf{xg}^t$ on the next velocity value, $\mathbf{U}(0, \psi_k)^t$ is vector of random numbers which are uniformly distributed in $[0, \psi_k]$, $k = 1, 2$.

As mentioned earlier, in order to prevent PSO algorithm from premature convergence, genetic algorithm can be used with probability P_{GA}^t at early stage of the search process

$$P_{GA}^t = \begin{cases} P_{GA_{min}} + \frac{(P_{GA_{max}} - P_{GA_{min}}) \cdot (T_{stop} - t)}{T_{stop}} & \text{if } (t \leq T_{stop}) \\ P_{GA_{min}} & \text{otherwise} \end{cases}, \qquad (5)$$

where T_{stop} is epoch number in which $P_{GA}^t = P_{GA_{min}}$, $T_{stop} < T$.

At each epoch of the PSO method supported by the GA algorithm, a set $N_a^t = N_{PSO}^t \cup N_{GA}^t$ of solutions is obtained. After that, each solution $\mathbf{x}_i^t \in N_a^t$ is evaluated according to arbitrarily chosen measure of quality f and the best solution $\mathbf{xp}_i^t$ for each participle and the global best solution $\mathbf{xg}^t$ are refreshed according to equations (6) and (7) respectively

$$\mathbf{xp}_i^t = \begin{cases} \mathbf{x}_i^t & \text{when } f(\mathbf{x}_i^t) < f(\mathbf{xp}_i^{t-1}) \\ \mathbf{xp}_i^{t-1} & \text{in other case} \end{cases}, \qquad (6)$$

$$\mathbf{xg}^t = \arg \min_{i=1,\ldots,|\mathbf{N}_a^t|} (\mathbf{xp}_i^t). \qquad (7)$$

In the last step of the algorithm, a set $N_{PSO}^{(t+1)}$, which contains $|N_{PSO}|$ the best solutions from the set N_a^t, is created.

4   Problem of the Unimportant Measurement Areas

In the proposed method the parameters of a nonlinear dynamic object are generated by the modified PSO algorithm described in the previous section. To evaluate obtained solutions, the Root Mean Square Error (RMSE) can be used

$$\text{RMSE}^t = \sqrt{\frac{1}{K}\sum_{j=1}^{K}\varepsilon_j^t}; \qquad \varepsilon_j^t = \left(y_j^t - \bar{y}_j\right)^2, \tag{8}$$

where y_j^t is an output obtained from the object identified for solution, $\bar{y}_j$ is reference value and K is number of reference values.

However, the RMSE measure is inefficient in a situation when the number of obtained data in unimportant measurement areas is significantly higher than in important measurement areas. In this case, the algorithm stops earlier because the error in the important area of measurement has a weak effect on the overall solution error. To eliminate this disadvantage we propose a new Weighted Root Mean Square Error (WRMSE) dedicated to an object identification problem or function approximation

$$\text{WRMSE}^t = \sqrt{\sum_{j=1}^{K}\hat{w}_j^t \cdot \varepsilon_j^t / \sum_{j=1}^{K}\hat{w}_j^t}. \tag{9}$$

For each reference value, a weight $\hat{w}_j^t$ is calculated according to RMSE^t and the current error value ε_j^t

$$w_j^{(t+1)} = \varepsilon_j^t / \text{RMSE}^t, \tag{10}$$

where $RMSE^t$ is the smallest error obtained so far by the algorithm. This weight must be additionally normalized

$$\hat{w}_j = w_j / \max(w_j), \tag{11}$$

in order to increase precision, or

$$\hat{w}_j = w_j / \left(\frac{1}{K}\sum_{i=1}^{K}w_i\right), \tag{12}$$

in a case of significant disproportion in number of reference data within important and unimportant measurement areas of the identified object. Weights scale the error space so that the sensitivity of the algorithm can be increased in the areas where the identified object performs poorly.

5   Algorithm for Identification Significant Operating Points

The designating parameters of a nonlinear object may depend on input or output values in some measurement areas or may be constant in others. Measurement areas, in which parameters of a nonlinear object behave in a certain way will be called *significant operating points*.

Identification of a nonlinear object in all measurement areas is difficult or even impossible unless a complex model for estimating change of the parameters is used. Moreover, some identified objects have constant parameters in most measurement areas so that only a small part of input or output is interesting from the viewpoint of linear or nonlinear parameter changes. A good example may be a nonlinear object with a semiconductor in an electrical circuit. It works in two states defining two potential operating points for the whole object. An identified nonlinear object may contain many elements, for which sufficiently accurate mathematical model is unknown [42].

When approximate mathematical model of the nonlinear object is known it is possible to identify this object using only a small part of measurement values. When the measure of quality for $\mathbf{xg}^t$ is lower than the threshold value ε_{stop} then the analysed area can be enlarged. This extension is made until the accuracy of the model, determined by comparing values of its output signal y_j^t with the reference value $\bar{y}_j$, is lower than ε_{find}. The algorithm to determine the first significant operating point op_{first} is presented in Alg. (1).

Input: Measurements $\bar{y}_j$, $j = 1, \ldots, K$, ε_{stop}, ε_{find}, ε_{end} are minimum error of the ending operating point, extending operating point, estimating end of operating point respectively, δ - initial interval for object identification.

Output: One significant operating point with an identified nonlinear object.

Set the $K_{start} = 0$; $K_{stop} = \delta$,
op_{new}(internal_object_state) $\leftarrow$ estimate from $\bar{y}_{K_{start}}$;
while K_{stop} *increase* **do**
    while $f(\mathbf{xg}^t) > \varepsilon_{stop}$ *and* $t < T$ **do**
    | Identify object using PSO supported by GA;
    end
    while $\varepsilon_{K_{stop}} < \varepsilon_{find}$ **do**
    | For the best solution $\mathbf{xg}^t$, extend the operating point through
    | increasing K_{stop}, calculate the error $\varepsilon_{K_{stop}}$ for the obtained object;
    end
end
Reproduce the measurements again to estimate the end of the location of the operating point starting from the $j = K_{start}$ using the following loop
while $\varepsilon_j < \varepsilon_{end}$ **do**
    | For the best solution $\mathbf{xg}$ increase j;
    | Calculate the error ε_j;
end

Algorithm 1. Algorithm to determine the first significant operating point op_{first}

The exact procedure is shown in Alg. (2). The complete algorithm to determine all significant operating points is depicted in Alg. (3).

Input: Measurements $\bar{y}_j$, $j = 1, \ldots, K$, ε_{stop}, ε_{find}, ε_{end}, op_p - previous operating point.

Output: Modified the previous operating point op_p and a new operating point op_{new}.

Set the $K_{start} = K_{stop}(op_p)$,

the op_{new}(parameters_for_identification) $\leftarrow$ op_p(identified_parameters)

and the op_{new}(internal_object_state) $\leftarrow$ estimate from $\bar{y}_{K_{start}}$;

Initially reproduce measurements to estimate the end of the location of the new operating point starting from the $j = K_{start}$ using the following loop

while $\varepsilon_j < \varepsilon_{find}$ **do**
    For the best solution $\mathbf{xg}^t$, for op_{new} increase j;
    Calculate the error ε_j;
end

Determine the new operating point using the following loops

while K_{stop} *increase* **do**
    while $f(\mathbf{xg}^t) > \varepsilon_{stop}$ *and* $t < T$ **do**
        Identify object in the operating point op_p, the join point $K_{stop}(op_p) = K_{start}$ and the new operating point op_{new} using PSO supported by GA;
    end
    while $\varepsilon_{K_{stop}} < \varepsilon_{find}$ **do**
        For the best solution $\mathbf{xg}^t$ extend the new operating point op_{new}, increase K_{stop}, calculate the error $\varepsilon_{K_{stop}}$ from the obtained object in the new operating point op_{new};
    end
end

Reproduce measurements again to estimate location end of the new operating point staring from the $j = K_{start}$ using the following loop

while $\varepsilon_j < \varepsilon_{end}$ **do**
    For the best solution $\mathbf{xg}^t$ increase j;
    Calculate the error ε_j for the object in op_{new};
end

Algorithm 2. Algorithm to determine the new operating points op_{new}

Input: Measurements $\bar{y}_j$, $j = 1, \ldots, K$
Output: Collection of all obtained operating points OP with identified nonlinear objects

Determine the first operating point op_{first} and object using Alg. (1);
Add op_{first} with object to collection OP;
set the $op_p = op_{first}$;
while $K_{stop} < K$ **do**
    Determine a new operating point op_{new} using Alg. (2);
    Add op_{new} to OP;
    Set the $op_p = op_{new}$;
end

Algorithm 3. Algorithm to determine all operating points

6 Experimental Results

The proposed algorithm for identification of the significant operating point has been applied to the inverted pendulum problem with the spring fixed in different points. A comprehensive description of this problem is presented in Fig. 1 and described by equations (13-21).

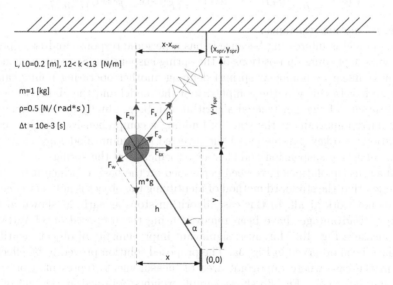

Fig. 1. Model of the inverted pendulum

$$\alpha^{(t+1)} = \alpha^t + \omega^t \cdot \Delta t + \frac{1}{2} \cdot (\varepsilon^t \cdot \Delta t^2), \tag{13}$$

where ω - angular speed, Δt - step integration, ε - angular acceleration,

$$\omega^{(t+1)} = \omega^t + \varepsilon^t \cdot \Delta T, \tag{14}$$

$$x^{(t+1)} = -h \cdot \sin(\alpha^{(t+1)}), \qquad y^{(t+1)} = h \cdot \cos(\alpha^{(t+1)}), \tag{15}$$

$$L^{(t+1)} = \sqrt{(x^{(t+1)} - x_{spr})^2 + (y^{(t+1)} - y_{spr})^2}, \tag{16}$$

where $L^{(t+1)}$ - spring length in the time t+1,

$$F_s^{(t+1)} = k \cdot (L^{(t+1)} - L_0), \tag{17}$$

where k - elasticity coefficient, L_0 - free length of the spring,

$$\beta^{(t+1)} = \begin{cases} \arccos((y_{spr} - y^{(t+1)})/L^{(t+1)}) & \text{if } x_{spr} \geq x^{(t+1)} \\ -\arccos((y_{spr} - y^{(t+1)})/L^{(t+1)}) & \text{otherwise} \end{cases}, \tag{18}$$

$$F_{s_x}^{(t+1)} = F_s^{(t+1)} \cdot \sin(\beta^{(t+1)}), \qquad F_{s_y}^{(t+1)} = F_s^{(t+1)} \cdot \cos(\beta^{(t+1)}), \tag{19}$$

$$F_w^{(t+1)} = \left(m \cdot g - F_{s_y}^{(t+1)} \right) \cdot \sin(\alpha^{(t+1)}) - F_{s_x}^{(t+1)} \cdot \cos(\alpha^{(t+1)}), \tag{20}$$

where m - mass, g - gravity acceleration,

$$F_o^{(t+1)} = \rho \cdot \omega^{(t+1)}, \qquad \varepsilon^{(t+1)} = (F_w^{(t+1)} - F_o^{(t+1)})/(m \cdot h), \tag{21}$$

where: ρ - motion resistance.

This model is interesting because it has a periodic response and two operating points depending on positions of the spring suspension. Sequential elements (e.g. next linear or nonlinear spring) defining another operating points can be easily added. In this way the complexity of the model and the ability to detect disadvantages of the constructed algorithm can be gradually increased. This is particularly important at the stage of building a comprehensive solution. In all simulations two key parameters of the inverted pendulum model are identified: a point of spring suspension and elasticity coefficient of the spring.

Numerous simulations have been performed on the basis of which it has been concluded that the standard method of identifying the object is not very effective or does not work at all. In this case algorithm stops as early as shown in Fig. 4a. Key disadvantages have been removed using the proposed novel WRMSE error measure Fig. 4b. Moreover, significant improvements of object identification have been observed in Fig. 3a. The proposed solution proved to be effective even in the case where important area of measurements represented only 3% of all measurements. Fig. 3b shows sample weights obtained at the end of the identification process. Experiments shown in Fig. 3 and Fig. 4 are based on data for standard model without changing parameters.

Results presented in Fig. 2, Fig. 5 and Fig. 6 have been realized for fast changes the spring elasticity coefficient. The main steps of the algorithm to identify the operating points presented in Alg. 1, Alg. 2 and Alg. 3 are shown in Fig. 2, Fig. 5 and Fig. 6. Fig. 2 presents initial stage of the identification of the first operating point with the object, Fig. 5 illustrates a way to determine end of the

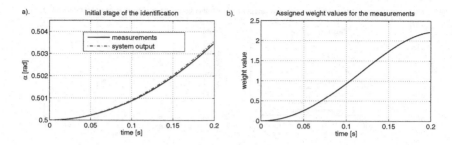

Fig. 2. Illustration of the initial stage of the object identification in the first operating point; a) the output of the identified object compared to measurements used for identification; b) assigned weight values obtained from equation (12) for the measurements used for the identification

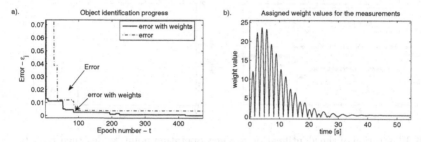

Fig. 3. a) Object identification progress; b) assigned weight values obtained from equation (12) for the measurements used for the identification

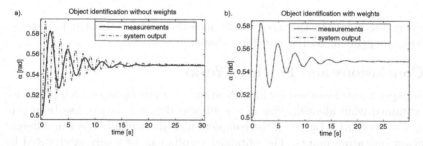

Fig. 4. Comparison of results for the algorithm applied for measurements with significant disproportion between important and unimportant measurement areas, plots represent only part of measurements in time interval equal 300 [s]; a) identified object without using weights (the algorithm does not work correctly); b) identified object using weights (good approximation is obtained)

operating point. Finally, Fig. 6 shows estimation of connection point between the first operating point op_{first} and a new operating point op_{new}. We also observed a difficulty in determining correctly identified parameters of the object in a case of a small number of the measurements despite obtained small errors. This phenomenon has been observed in early stages of the object identification at the

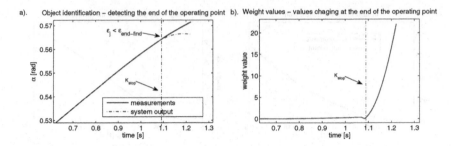

Fig. 5. Illustration of the K_{stop} identification for the first operating point op_{first}; a) output of the identified object with selected K_{stop} connect point; b) location of the K_{stop} for the first operating point in the context of the assigned weight values

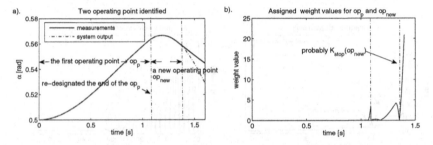

Fig. 6. Illustration of the identification of a new operating point, re-designed $K_{stop}(op_p)$ using PSO supported by the GA; a) location of the previous operating point op_p and the new operating point op_{new}; b) location of the $K_{stop}(op_{new})$ in the context of the assigned weight values

first operating point. In this area of the measurements, estimated parameters are weakly dependent on the waveform shape.

7   Conclusions and Further Works

In this paper a novel method for identification of significant operating points for data obtained from identification of a nonlinear dynamic object has been proposed. This method is based on the complete identification of object in different significant operating points. The obtained results can be easily interpreted by the expert to analyze the obtained models. The simulations show full usefulness of the proposed method.

The constructed algorithm for identification of significant operating points for nonlinear object reminded key problems of nonlinear identification:

- Detection of the activation of one significant operating point in different measurement areas using various architectures of neural networks (see e.g. [3]-[8], [32]-[33], [39]-[40]).
- Detection of the activation of one significant operating point in different measurement areas using fuzzy systems (see e.g. [29]-[31], [53]-[56]) and neuro-fuzzy systems (see e.g. [10]-[15], [43]-[47]).

- Identification of fuzzy rules using PSO supported by GA [13], or other nature inspired algorithms [11], [26], [36]-[37].
- Grouping of obtained significant operating points for merge.
- Estimation of the characteristics of parameters change in a transition area (what can be interpreted by the expert) using Takagi-Sugeno neuro-fuzzy systems [14]-[15].
- Testing the algorithm for different identified nonlinear objects.
  These proposals will be considered and resolved in subsequent extended publications.

Acknowledgment. The project was financed by the National Science Centre (Poland) on the basis of the decision number DEC-2012/05/B/ST7/02138.

References

1. Bartczuk, Ł., Dziwiński, P., Starczewski, J.T.: A New Method for Dealing with Unbalanced Linguistic Term Set. In: Rutkowski, L., Korytkowski, M., Scherer, R., Tadeusiewicz, R., Zadeh, L.A., Zurada, J.M. (eds.) ICAISC 2012, Part I. LNCS, vol. 7267, pp. 207–212. Springer, Heidelberg (2012)
2. Bartczuk, Ł., Przybył, A., Dziwiński, P.: Hybrid State Variables-Fuzzy Logic Modelling of Nonlinear Objects. In: Rutkowski, L., Korytkowski, M., Scherer, R., Tadeusiewicz, R., Zadeh, L.A., Zurada, J.M. (eds.) ICAISC 2013, Part I. LNCS (LNAI), vol. 7894, pp. 227–234. Springer, Heidelberg (2013)
3. Bilski, J., Litwiński, S., Smoląg, J.: Parallel Realization of QR Algorithm for Neural Networks Learning. In: Rutkowski, L., Siekmann, J.H., Tadeusiewicz, R., Zadeh, L.A. (eds.) ICAISC 2004. LNCS (LNAI), vol. 3070, pp. 158–165. Springer, Heidelberg (2004)
4. Bilski, J., Rutkowski, L.: Numerically Robust Learning Algorithms for Feed Forward Neural Networks. Advances in Soft Computing - Neural Networks and Soft Computing, pp. 149–154. Physica-Verlag, A Springer-Verlag Company (2003)
5. Bilski, J., Smoląg, J.: Parallel Approach to Learning of the Recurrent Jordan Neural Network. In: Rutkowski, L., Korytkowski, M., Scherer, R., Tadeusiewicz, R., Zadeh, L.A., Zurada, J.M. (eds.) ICAISC 2013, Part I. LNCS (LNAI), vol. 7894, pp. 32–40. Springer, Heidelberg (2013)
6. Bilski, J., Smoląg, J.: Parallel Realisation of the Recurrent Elman Neural Network Learning. In: Rutkowski, L., Scherer, R., Tadeusiewicz, R., Zadeh, L.A., Zurada, J.M. (eds.) ICAISC 2010, Part II. LNCS (LNAI), vol. 6114, pp. 19–25. Springer, Heidelberg (2010)
7. Bilski, J., Smoląg, J.: Parallel Realisation of the Recurrent Multi Layer Perceptron Learning. In: Rutkowski, L., Korytkowski, M., Scherer, R., Tadeusiewicz, R., Zadeh, L.A., Zurada, J.M. (eds.) ICAISC 2012, Part I. LNCS (LNAI), vol. 7267, pp. 12–20. Springer, Heidelberg (2012)
8. Bilski, J., Smoląg, J.: Parallel Realisation of the Recurrent RTRN Neural Network Learning. In: Rutkowski, L., Tadeusiewicz, R., Zadeh, L.A., Zurada, J.M. (eds.) ICAISC 2008. LNCS (LNAI), vol. 5097, pp. 11–16. Springer, Heidelberg (2008)
9. Bin, W., Yi, Z., Shaohui, L., Zhongzhi, S.: CSIM: A Document Clustering Algorithm Based on Swarm Intelligence Evolutionary Computation. In: CEC 2002, vol. 1, pp. 477–482 (2002)
10. Cpalka, K.: A Method for Designing Flexible Neuro-fuzzy Systems. In: Rutkowski, L., Tadeusiewicz, R., Zadeh, L.A., Żurada, J.M. (eds.) ICAISC 2006. LNCS (LNAI), vol. 4029, pp. 212–219. Springer, Heidelberg (2006)

11. Cpałka, K.: On evolutionary designing and learning of flexible neuro-fuzzy structures for nonlinear classification. In: Nonlinear Analysis Series A: Theory, Methods and Applications, vol. 71, pp. 1659–1672. Elsevier (2009)
12. Cpałka, K., Łapa, K., Przybył, A., Zalasiński, M.: A new method for designing neuro-fuzzy systems for nonlinear modelling with interpretability aspects. Neurocomputing (in print, 2014), http://dx.doi.org/10.1016/j.neucom.2013.12.031
13. Cpałka, K., Rutkowski, L.: A New Method for Designing and Reduction of Neuro-fuzzy Systems. In: Proceedings of the 2006 IEEE International Conference on Fuzzy Systems (IEEE World Congress on Computational Intelligence, WCCI 2006), Vancouver, BC, Canada, pp. 8510–8516 (2006)
14. Cpałka, K., Rutkowski, L.: Flexible Takagi-Sugeno Fuzzy Systems. In: Proceedings of the International Joint Conference on Neural Networks 2005, Montreal, pp. 1764–1769 (2005)
15. Cpałka, K., Rutkowski, L.: Flexible Takagi Sugeno Neuro-fuzzy Structures for Nonlinear Approximation. WSEAS Transactions on Systems 9(4), 1450–1458 (2005)
16. Montes de Oca, M.A., Stützle, T., Birattari, M., Dorigo, M.: Frankenstein's PSO: A Composite Particle Swarm Optimization Algorithm. Trans. Evol. Comp. 13(5), 1120–1132 (2009)
17. Dorigo, M., Birattari, M., Stützle, T.: Ant Colony Optimization Artificial Ants as a Computational Intelligence Technique. IEEE Computational Intelligence Magazine, 28–39 (2006)
18. Dorigo, M., Gambardella, L.M.: Ant Colony System: A Cooperative Learning Approach to the Traveling Salesman Problem. IEEE Transactions on Evolutionary Computation 1(1), 53–66 (1997)
19. Dziwiński, P., Bartczuk, Ł., Starczewski, J.T.: Fully Controllable Ant Colony System for Text Data Clustering. In: Rutkowski, L., Korytkowski, M., Scherer, R., Tadeusiewicz, R., Zadeh, L.A., Zurada, J.M. (eds.) SIDE 2012 and EC 2012. LNCS, vol. 7269, pp. 199–205. Springer, Heidelberg (2012)
20. Dziwiński, P., Rutkowska, D.: Algorithm for Generating Fuzzy Rules for WWW Document Classification. In: Rutkowski, L., Tadeusiewicz, R., Zadeh, L.A., Żurada, J.M. (eds.) ICAISC 2006. LNCS (LNAI), vol. 4029, pp. 1111–1119. Springer, Heidelberg (2006)
21. Dziwiński, P., Rutkowska, D.: Ant Focused Crawling Algorithm. In: Rutkowski, L., Tadeusiewicz, R., Zadeh, L.A., Zurada, J.M. (eds.) ICAISC 2008. LNCS (LNAI), vol. 5097, pp. 1018–1028. Springer, Heidelberg (2008)
22. Dziwiński, P., Starczewski, J.T., Bartczuk, Ł.: New Linguistic Hedges in Construction of Interval Type-2 FLS. In: Rutkowski, L., Scherer, R., Tadeusiewicz, R., Zadeh, L.A., Zurada, J.M. (eds.) ICAISC 2010, Part II. LNCS (LNAI), vol. 6114, pp. 445–450. Springer, Heidelberg (2010)
23. Eennedy, J., Eberhart, R.: Particle swarm optimization. In: Proceedings of IEEE Internatiolal Conference on Neural Networsk, vol. 4, pp. 1942–1948 (1995)
24. Elbeltagi, E., Hegazy, T., Grierson, D.: Comparison among five evolutionary-based optimization algorithms. Advanced Engineering Informatics 19(1), 43–53 (2005)
25. El-Abd, M.: On the hybridization on the artificial bee colony and particle swarm optimization algorithms. Journal of Artificial Intelligence and Soft Computing Research 2(2), 147–155 (2012)
26. Gabryel, M., Cpałka, K., Rutkowski, L.: Evolutionary strategies for learning of neuro-fuzzy systems. In: Proceedings of the I Workshop on Genetic Fuzzy Systems, Granada, pp. 119–123 (2005)

27. Gabryel, M., Korytkowski, M., Scherer, R., Rutkowski, L.: Object Detection by Simple Fuzzy Classifiers Generated by Boosting. In: Rutkowski, L., Korytkowski, M., Scherer, R., Tadeusiewicz, R., Zadeh, L.A., Zurada, J.M. (eds.) ICAISC 2013, Part I. LNCS (LNAI), vol. 7894, pp. 540–547. Springer, Heidelberg (2013)
28. Gabryel, M., Woźniak, M., K. Nowicki, R.: Creating Learning Sets for Control Systems Using an Evolutionary Method. In: Rutkowski, L., Korytkowski, M., Scherer, R., Tadeusiewicz, R., Zadeh, L.A., Zurada, J.M. (eds.) SIDE 2012 and EC 2012. LNCS, vol. 7269, pp. 206–213. Springer, Heidelberg (2012)
29. Greenfield, S., Chiclana, F.: Type-reduction of the discretized interval type-2 fuzzy set: approaching the continuous case through progressively finer discretization. Journal of Artificial Intelligence and Soft Computing Research 1(3), 183–193 (2011)
30. Korytkowski, M., Rutkowski, L., Scherer, R.: On combining backpropagation with boosting. In: Proceedings of the IEEE International Joint Conference on Neural Network (IJCNN), vol. 1-10, pp. 1274–1277 (2006)
31. Kroll, A.: On choosing the fuzziness parameter for identifying TS models with multidimensional membership functions. Journal of Artificial Intelligence and Soft Computing Research 1(4), 283–300 (2011)
32. Laskowski, L.: A Novel Continuous Dual Mode Neural Network in Stereo-Matching Process. In: Diamantaras, K., Duch, W., Iliadis, L.S. (eds.) ICANN 2010, Part III. LNCS, vol. 6354, pp. 294–297. Springer, Heidelberg (2010)
33. Laskowski, Ł.: Hybrid-Maximum Neural Network for Depth Analysis from Stereo-Image. In: Rutkowski, L., Scherer, R., Tadeusiewicz, R., Zadeh, L.A., Zurada, J.M. (eds.) ICAISC 2010, Part II. LNCS (LNAI), vol. 6114, pp. 47–55. Springer, Heidelberg (2010)
34. Lobato, F.S., Steffen Jr., V.: A new multi-objective optimization algorithm based on differential evolution and neighborhood exploring evolution strategy. Journal of Artificial Intelligence and Soft Computing Research 1(4), 259–267 (2011)
35. Lobato, F.S., Steffen Jr., V., Silva Neto, A.J.: Solution of singular optimal control problems using the improved differential evolution algorithm. Journal of Artificial Intelligence and Soft Computing Research 1(3), 195–206 (2011)
36. Łapa, K., Przybył, A., Cpałka, K.: A new approach to designing interpretable models of dynamic systems. In: Rutkowski, L., Korytkowski, M., Scherer, R., Tadeusiewicz, R., Zadeh, L.A., Zurada, J.M. (eds.) ICAISC 2013, Part II. LNCS (LNAI), vol. 7895, pp. 523–534. Springer, Heidelberg (2013)
37. Łapa, K., Zalasiński, M., Cpałka, K.: A new method for designing and complexity reduction of neuro-fuzzy systems for nonlinear modelling. In: Rutkowski, L., Korytkowski, M., Scherer, R., Tadeusiewicz, R., Zadeh, L.A., Zurada, J.M. (eds.) ICAISC 2013, Part I. LNCS (LNAI), vol. 7894, pp. 329–344. Springer, Heidelberg (2013)
38. Martens, D., Baesens, B., Fawcett, T.: Editorial survey: swarm intelligence for data mining. 25th Anniversary Machine Learning 85(25), 1–42 (2011)
39. Patan, K., Patan, M.: Optimal Training strategies for locally recurrent neural networks. Journal of Artificial Intelligence and Soft Computing Research 1(2), 103–114 (2011)
40. Peteiro-Barral, D., Bardinas, B.G., Perez-Sanchez, B.: Learning from heterogeneously distributed data sets using artificial neural networks and genetic algorithms. Journal of Artificial Intelligence and Soft Computing Research 2(1), 5–20 (2012)
41. Prampero, P.S., Attux, R.: Magnetic particle swarm optimization. Journal of Artificial Intelligence and Soft Computing Research 2(1), 59–72 (2012)
42. Przybył, A., Cpałka, K.: A new method to construct of interpretable models of dynamic systems. In: Rutkowski, L., Korytkowski, M., Scherer, R., Tadeusiewicz, R., Zadeh, L.A., Zurada, J.M. (eds.) ICAISC 2012, Part II. LNCS, vol. 7268, pp. 697–705. Springer, Heidelberg (2012)

43. Rutkowski, L., Cpałka, K.: Compromise approach to neuro-fuzzy systems. In: Sincak, P., Vascak, J., Kvasnicka, V., Pospichal, J. (eds.) Intelligent Technologies - Theory and Applications, vol. 76, pp. 85–90. IOS Press (2002)

44. Rutkowski, L., Cpałka, K.: Flexible weighted neuro-fuzzy systems. In: Proceedings of the 9th International Conference on Neural Information Processing (ICONIP 2002), Orchid Country Club, Singapore, November 18-22, CD (2002)

45. Rutkowski, L., Cpałka, K.: Neuro-fuzzy systems derived from quasi-triangular norms. In: Proceedings of the IEEE International Conference on Fuzzy Systems, Budapest, July 26-29, vol. 2, pp. 1031–1036 (2004)

46. Rutkowski, L., Przybył A., Cpałka, K.: Novel on-line speed profile generation for industrial machine tool based on flexible neuro-fuzzy approximation. IEEE Transactions on Industrial Electronics 59, 1238–1247 (2012)

47. Rutkowski, L., Przybył, A., Cpałka, K., Er, M.J.: Online Speed Profile Generation for Industrial Machine Tool Based on Neuro-fuzzy Approach. In: Rutkowski, L., Scherer, R., Tadeusiewicz, R., Zadeh, L.A., Zurada, J.M. (eds.) ICAISC 2010, Part II. LNCS (LNAI), vol. 6114, pp. 645–650. Springer, Heidelberg (2010)

48. Theodoridis, D.C., Boutalis, Y.S., Christodoulou, M.A.: Robustifying analysis of the direct adaptive control of unknown multivariable nonlinear systems based on a new neuro-fuzzy method. Journal of Artificial Intelligence and Soft Computing Research 1(1), 59–79 (2011)

49. Tran, V.N., Brdys, M.A.: Optimizing control by robustly feasible model predictive control and application to drinking water distribution systems. Journal of Artificial Intelligence and Soft Computing Research 1(1), 43–57 (2011)

50. Wagner, I.A., Lindenbaum, M., Bruckstein, A.M.: Cooperative Covering by Ant-Robots using Evaporating Traces, Technical report CIS-9610 (1996)

51. Wagner, I.A., Lindenbaum, M., Bruckstein, A.M.: Smell as a Computational Resource-A Lesson We Can Learn from the Ant. In: ISTCS, pp. 219–230 (1996)

52. Shi, Y., Eberhart, R.: A modified particle swarm optimizer. In: Proceedings 1998. IEEE World Congress on Computational Intelligence, The 1998 IEEE International Conference on Evolutionary Computation, pp. 69–73 (1998)

53. Zalasiński, M., Cpałka, K.: A new method of on-line signature verification using a flexible fuzzy one-class classifier, pp. 38–53. Academic Publishing House EXIT (2011)

54. Zalasiński, M., Łapa, K., Cpałka, K.: New Algorithm for Evolutionary Selection of the Dynamic Signature Global Features. In: Rutkowski, L., Korytkowski, M., Scherer, R., Tadeusiewicz, R., Zadeh, L.A., Zurada, J.M. (eds.) ICAISC 2013, Part II. LNCS (LNAI), vol. 7895, pp. 113–121. Springer, Heidelberg (2013)

55. Zalasiński, M., Cpałka, K.: New Approach for the On-Line Signature Verification Based on Method of Horizontal Partitioning. In: Rutkowski, L., Korytkowski, M., Scherer, R., Tadeusiewicz, R., Zadeh, L.A., Zurada, J.M. (eds.) ICAISC 2013, Part II. LNCS (LNAI), vol. 7895, pp. 342–350. Springer, Heidelberg (2013)

56. Zalasiński, M., Cpałka, K.: Novel algorithm for the on-line signature verification. In: Rutkowski, L., Korytkowski, M., Scherer, R., Tadeusiewicz, R., Zadeh, L.A., Zurada, J.M. (eds.) ICAISC 2012, Part II. LNCS (LNAI), vol. 7268, pp. 362–367. Springer, Heidelberg (2012)

57. Zalasiński, M., Cpałka, K.: Novel Algorithm for the On-Line Signature Verification Using Selected Discretization Points Groups. In: Rutkowski, L., Korytkowski, M., Scherer, R., Tadeusiewicz, R., Zadeh, L.A., Zurada, J.M. (eds.) ICAISC 2013, Part I. LNCS (LNAI), vol. 7894, pp. 493–502. Springer, Heidelberg (2013)

Artificial Bee Colony Algorithm Used for Reconstructing the Heat Flux Density in the Solidification Process

Edyta Hetmaniok, Damian Słota, and Adam Zielonka

Institute of Mathematics
Silesian University of Technology
Kaszubska 23, 44-100 Gliwice, Poland
{edyta.hetmaniok,damian.slota,adam.zielonka}@polsl.pl

Abstract. Scope of the paper is the procedure reconstructing the heat flux density in the solidification on the grounds of temperature measurements in selected points of the cast. Elaborated method is based on two procedures: finite difference method with application of the generalized alternating phase truncation method used for solving the appropriate direct solidification problem and the Artificial Bee Colony algorithm used for minimizing some functional representing the crucial part of the procedure.

Keywords: Artificial Intelligence, Swarm Intelligence, ABC algorithm, solidification.

1 Introduction

In the last decades there appeared an idea of solving the most complicated engineering problems by imitating the behavior of living organisms, in particular their ability of learning and constant improving their activity in order to maximize the chances for success. This idea constitutes the grounds for an important branch of computer science called the artificial intelligence [1].

Within the framework of artificial intelligence one can distinguish some specific groups of algorithms differing in the way of approaching to investigated problems. For example, the evolutionary algorithms generate the solutions of considered problems by using the techniques inspired by natural evolution, such as reproduction, mutation, selection and crossover [2]. The artificial neural networks are the computational models inspired by the central nervous systems of animals and they are usually presented as systems of interconnected "neurons" computing the values from inputs by feeding information through the network [3]. Finally the swarm intelligence algorithms are based on the collective behavior of self-organized members of the swarm partitioning the general problem into a set of small subproblems solving of which leads to a general success [4].

Inspiration of composing the final solution from the partial solutions achieved by the swarm members was taken from the natural behavior of the swarms of

L. Rutkowski et al. (Eds.): ICAISC 2014, Part II, LNAI 8468, pp. 363–372, 2014.

insects, like ants or bees. On these grounds many interesting algorithms have been developed, like the Ant Colony Optimization [5, 6], the Glowworm Swarm Optimization [7] as well as the Artificial Bee Colony algorithm [8, 9], further called for short as the ABC algorithm, used in this paper.

Artificial intelligence algorithms of different kinds have found a number of applications in solving various problems, for example, in solving the heat conduction problem [10], the image segmentation problem [11], the asymmetric traveling salesman problem [12], the transportation problem [13], the reaction-diffusion problem [14], the generalized assignment problem [15], in system controlling [16] and in investigating many other problems.

Physical processes modeled by means of mathematical models can be divided into two groups: direct problems and inverse problems. Direct problem concerns the case when all the input data are given at the beginning and the problem just must be solved under initial assumptions. In case when some part of the input information is unknown, which means it must be reconstructed, but in exchange some additional information about the effects caused by the input data is known, then we deal with the inverse problem. Therefore, the inverse problems can be used, for example, for determining the values which cannot be directly measured or in design problems in which the initial values of parameters should be selected such that they will ensure a required run of the process. However, the inverse problems are often called as the ill posed problems because of many difficulties appearing in the course of their solution and resulting from the fact that usually their analytic solutions do not exist or they exist but are neither unique nor stable [17]. That is why each proposition of successful method enabling to determine the approximate solution of such problems is desired and interesting.

The process of pure metal solidification is mathematically defined by the Stefan problem [18–22], whereas the process of alloy solidification is described by the so called solidification in the temperature interval [23, 24]. Model of solidification in the temperature interval, which takes into account only the temperature distribution, is based on the heat conduction equation with the enclosed source element including the latent heat of fusion and the volume contribution of solid phase. For the assumed form of function describing this contribution, the equation is transformed to the heat conduction equation with the so called substitute thermal capacity. Thereby the considered differential equation describes the heat conduction in the entire homogeneous region (in solid phase, in two-phase zone (mushy zone) and in liquid phase).

Authors of the current paper have already tested several optimization algorithms of artificial intelligence in solving inverse problems connected with the heat conduction [25–29]. One of the investigated procedures was the Artificial Bee Colony algorithm which turned out to be quite efficient in solving problems of considered kind. Therefore, in this paper we intend to use the ABC algorithm for identifying the heat flux density on boundary of the region in solidification process with the aid of additional information given by the measurements of temperature in selected points of the cast. Elaborated procedure is based on two methods: finite difference method combined with the generalized alternating phase truncation method (see [30] and [18, 21, 22]) used for solving the direct problem connected with the investigated inverse problem and the ABC algorithm applied for minimizing some functional representing the important part of the procedure.

2 Artificial Bee Colony Algorithm

Idea of the Artificial Bee Colony Algorithm is based on the observation of behavior of the colony of bees exploring the environment around the hive in order to find the flowers rich in nectar. When the bees – discoverers find some good sources of nectar, they take the samples and fly back to the hive where, with the aid of some special kind of dance called the waggle dance, they inform the other bees – viewers about the positions of sources of food. Next, the bees from the hive fly in pointed direction for using the most attractive ones from among the found sources of nectar.

In the algorithm imitating such way of communication between the bees the role of sources of nectar is played by the points of domain – vectors $\mathbf{x}$ and value of optimized function J in given point – number $J(\mathbf{x})$ – designates the quality of respective source $\mathbf{x}$. In the task of minimization of the objective function, the smaller is the value $J(\mathbf{x})$, the better is the source $\mathbf{x}$ and probability of the choice of a source is the greater, the better is the quality of this source. In general, the process consists in the double search of investigated region – more generally for the first time in order to localize the best sources and then more precisely around these best selected locations. In details the ABC algorithm runs in the following way (see also [8, 9]).

Initialization of the algorithm

1. Initial data:
   SN – number of the explored sources of nectar (number of the bees-scouts, number of the bees-viewers);
   D – dimension of the source $\mathbf{x}_i$, $i = 1, \ldots, SN$;
   lim – number of "corrections" of the source position $\mathbf{x}_i$;
   MCN – maximal number of cycles.
2. Initial population – random selection of the initial sources localization represented by D-dimensional vectors $\mathbf{x}_i$, $i = 1, \ldots, SN$.
3. Calculation of values $J(\mathbf{x}_i)$, $i = 1, \ldots, SN$, for the initial population.

Main algorithm

1. Modification of sources localizations by the bees-scouts.
   a) Every bee-scout modifies position $\mathbf{x}_i$ according to formula

$$v_i^j = x_i^j + \phi_{ij}(x_i^j - x_k^j), \quad j \in \{1, \ldots, D\},$$

where: $\left.\begin{array}{l} k \in \{1,\dots,SN\}, k \neq i, \\ \phi_{ij} \in [-1,1]. \end{array}\right\}$ – randomly selected numbers.

b) If $J(\mathbf{v}_i) \leq J(\mathbf{x}_i)$, then position $\mathbf{v}_i$ replaces $\mathbf{x}_i$. Otherwise, position $\mathbf{x}_i$ stays unchanged.

Steps a) and b) are repeated lim times. We take: $lim = SN \cdot D$.

2. Calculation of probabilities P_i for the positions $\mathbf{x}_i$ selected in step 1. We use formula

$$P_i = \frac{fit_i}{\sum\limits_{j=1}^{SN} fit_j}, \quad i = 1,\dots,SN,$$

where: $fit_i = \begin{cases} \frac{1}{1+J(\mathbf{x}_i)} & \text{if } J(\mathbf{x}_i) \geq 0, \\ 1 + |J(\mathbf{x}_i)| & \text{if } J(\mathbf{x}_i) < 0. \end{cases}$

3. Every bee-viewer chooses one of the sources $\mathbf{x}_i$, $i = 1,\dots,SN$, with probability P_i. Of course one source can be chosen by a group of bees.
4. Every bee-viewer explores the chosen source and modifies its position according to the procedure described in step 1.
5. Selection of the $\mathbf{x}_{best}$ for the current cycle – the best source among the sources determined by the bees-viewers. If the current $\mathbf{x}_{best}$ is better that the one from the previous cycle, we accept it as the $\mathbf{x}_{best}$ for the entire algorithm.
6. If in step 1 the bee-scout did not improve position $\mathbf{x}_i$ ($\mathbf{x}_i$ did not change), it leaves the source $\mathbf{x}_i$ and moves to the new one by using formula

$$x_i^j = x_{min}^j + \phi_{ij}(x_{max}^j - x_{min}^j), \quad j = 1,\dots,D,$$

where $\phi_{ij} \in [0,1]$.

Steps 1–6 are repeated MCN times.

3   Governing Equations

Let us consider region $D = \{(x,t) : x \in (0,d); t \in (0,t^*)\}$ taken by the solidifying material in which the distribution of temperature is described by means of the heat conduction equation [18–20]:

$$C \varrho \frac{\partial T(x,t)}{\partial t} = \lambda \frac{\partial^2 T(x,t)}{\partial x^2}, \quad (x,t) \in D, \tag{1}$$

where C, ϱ and λ denote, respectively, the substitute thermal capacity, density and thermal conductivity coefficient, T describes the temperature, finally t and x refer to the time and spatial variable. The above equation is completed by the initial condition

$$T(x,0) = T_0(x), \quad x \in [0,d], \tag{2}$$

and boundary conditions of the second kind

$$\frac{\partial T(0,t)}{\partial t} = 0, \quad t \in (0,t^*), \tag{3}$$

and

$$-\lambda \frac{\partial T(d,t)}{\partial t} = q(t), \qquad t \in (0, t^*). \tag{4}$$

Substitute thermal capacity is equal to

$$C = \begin{cases} c_l & T > T_L, \\ c_{mz} + \dfrac{L}{T_L - T_S} & T \in [T_S, T_L], \\ c_s & T < T_S, \end{cases} \tag{5}$$

where c_l, c_{mz} and c_s denote, respectively, the specific heat of liquid phase, mushy zone and solid phase, L describes the latent heat of fusion and T_L and T_S refer to the liquidus and solidus temperatures, respectively. In equation (1) the values of density and the thermal conductivity coefficient vary as well in dependance of temperature

$$\varrho = \begin{cases} \varrho_l & T > T_L, \\ \varrho_{mz} & T \in [T_S, T_L], \\ \varrho_s & T < T_S, \end{cases} \qquad \lambda = \begin{cases} \lambda_l & T > T_L, \\ \lambda_{mz} & T \in [T_S, T_L], \\ \lambda_s & T < T_S. \end{cases} \tag{6}$$

The investigated inverse problem consists in determination of the temperature distribution T in domain D and in identification of the heat flux density q on boundary of this region in case when the values of temperature in selected points $((x_i, t_j) \in D)$ of the domain are known

$$T(x_i, t_j) = U_{ij}, \qquad i = 1, 2, \ldots, N_1, \quad j = 1, 2, \ldots, N_2, \tag{7}$$

where N_1 denotes the number of sensors and N_2 describes the number of measurements taken from each sensor.

For the fixed form of heat flux density q problem (1)–(4) turns into the direct problem, solution of which makes us able to find the values of temperature $T_{ij} = T(x_i, t_j)$ corresponding to the given heat flux density q. For solving the direct problem, associated with considered inverse problem, we use the finite difference method completed with the generalized alternating phase truncation method (see [30] and [18, 21, 22]).

By using the calculated temperatures T_{ij} and the measured temperatures U_{ij} we define the following functional representing the error of approximate solution

$$J(q) = \left(\sum_{i=1}^{N_1} \sum_{j=1}^{N_2} (T_{ij} - U_{ij})^2 \right)^{1/2}. \tag{8}$$

Minimization of the above functional leads to find such form of heat flux q that the reconstructed temperatures will be as close as possible to the measurement values. For minimizing this functional we apply the Artificial Bee Colony algorithm keeping in mind the fact that each running of the procedure requires to solve the appropriate direct problem.

4   Numerical Example

For verifying the procedure presented in previous sections let us consider the solidification process described by the following parameters: $d = 0.1$ [m], $t^* = 1000$ [s], $\lambda_l = 104$ [W/(m K)], $\lambda_s = 262$ [W/(m K)], $c_l = 1275$ [J/(kg K)], $c_s = 1077$ [J/(kg K)], $\varrho_l = 2498$ [kg/m^3], $\varrho_s = 2824$ [kg/m^3], $L = 390000$ [J/kg], liquidus temperature $T_L = 926$ [K], solidus temperature $T_S = 886$ [K] and initial temperature $T_0(x) = 1013$ [K].

Our goal is to identify the heat flux density on boundary of the region in case when measurements of temperature are known in the selected points of the cast. The exact values of heat flux density are known and are the following ([W/m^2]):

$$q(t) = \begin{cases} 440000, & t \in [0, 100), \\ 280000, & t \in [100, 250), \\ 220000, & t \in [250, 400), \\ 160000, & t \in [400, 1000]. \end{cases} \tag{9}$$

The thermocouple ($N_1 = 1$) was located on the boundary (in point $x = 0.1$) of considered region and we took from it 500 measurements of temperature ($N_2 = 500$) read in every 1 second. In calculations we used the exact values of temperature and values burdened by the noise. For each exact value of temperature the perturbation was randomly selected from normal distribution $N(0, \sigma/3)$. For calculations we took the value of σ equal to 1% and 2% of the exact value. For solving the direct problem we used the finite difference method combined with the generalized phase truncation method applied for the mesh of steps $\Delta t = 0.005$ and $\Delta x = 0.0002$.

For minimizing functional (8) we used the ABC algorithm executed for number of bees $SN = 15$ and number of cycles $MCN = 10$. Because of the big differences between expected values of reconstructed heat flux density the respective initial locations of sources were randomly selected from the following different intervals: $[250000, 600000]$, $[150000, 400000]$, $[100000, 300000]$ and $[50000, 250000]$. Limitations forced by the above intervals were maintained during the entire optimization process. Important feature characterizing the swarm intelligence algorithms, including ABC, is their heuristic nature which means that each execution of the procedure can give slightly different results. Therefore for being sure that the results are not accidental we evaluated the calculations for 10 times and the best of received results were accepted as the reconstructed elements.

Relative errors of the heat flux density q identification obtained for input data burdened by 1% and 2% error, respectively, are presented in Figure 1. In the figure we may see four lines corresponding with the relative errors obtained for the reconstructed values in the respective intervals displayed in dependence on the number of cycles of the procedure. In both cases very quickly – after about two cycles – the errors stabilize on the level comparable with the perturbation of input data, however we may observe that further executions of the procedure do not improve significantly the results.

Quality of the temperature reconstructions is illustrated in Figures 2 and 3. Both figures present the comparison of the exact and reconstructed distribution

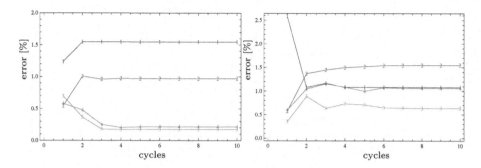

Fig. 1. Relative errors of heat flux density reconstruction for the successive iterations obtained for 1% (left figure) and 2% (right figure) noise of input data (four lines corresponding with the respective values in four intervals in (9) are denoted by the respective numbers 1–4)

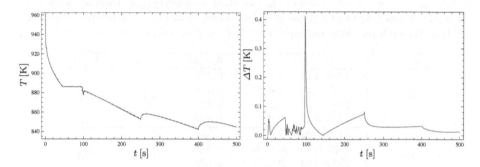

Fig. 2. Exact (solid line) and reconstructed (dots) distributions of temperature (left figure) in control point located on the boundary obtained for 1% noise of input data and absolute error of this reconstruction (right figure)

of temperature in control point located on boundary of the region obtained for 1% and 2% noise of input data, respectively. Both lines in both cases almost cover which means the very good reconstructions of the temperature confirmed additionally by the very low absolute errors of these reconstructions also displayed in both figures.

Finally, in Table 1 the results received in 10 evaluations of the procedure are compiled. For the unburdened input data the relative errors of reconstructed elements are close to zero (only in case of the heat flux density identified in the first interval of variability the relative error is the highest, however it is about 0.2% which makes it acceptable). Similar situation can be observed for input data perturbated by 1% random error – almost all the elements are reconstructed with the error lower than 1% except the the first value of heat flux density, error of which exceeds for about 0.5% the input data error. In third considered case all the errors of reconstruction are lower than 2% error of input data. Moreover, the respective low values of standard deviations in each considered case confirm stability of elaborated procedure.

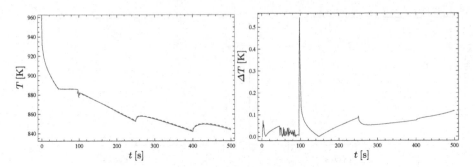

Fig. 3. Exact (solid line) and reconstructed (dots) distributions of temperature (left figure) in control point located on the boundary obtained for 2% noise of input data and absolute error of this reconstruction (right figure)

Table 1. Reconstructed values of the heat flux density q_i for $i = 1, 2, 3, 4$, standard deviations (s_{q_i}) and relative errors (δ_{q_i}) of these reconstructions together with the maximal absolute (Δ_T) and relative (δ_T) errors of temperature reconstruction obtained for the unnoised input data and input data burdened by 1% and 2% error

noise	i	q_i	s_{q_i}	δ_{q_i} [%]	Δ_T [K]	δ_T [%]
0%	1	440953.75	1.265	0.217	0.901	0.102
	2	279960.12	0.078	0.014		
	3	219940.63	1.108	0.027		
	4	159953.17	0.067	0.029		
1%	1	446811.92	373.301	1.548	3.660	0.413
	2	282720.45	209.436	0.972		
	3	220380.84	29.183	0.173		
	4	159657.52	35.281	0.214		
2%	1	444746.28	398.188	1.079	4.826	0.545
	2	284333.23	239.272	1.547		
	3	221395.23	73.184	0.635		
	4	161698.37	165.87	1.061		

5   Conclusions

Aim of this paper was the elaboration of procedure for solving the inverse problem describing the solidification process. Solution of this problem consisted in identification of the heat flux density on boundary of the region and in reconstruction of the temperature distribution in considered region on the basis of temperature measurements known in selected points of the cast. Essential part of the approach consisted in minimization of the functional expressing the errors of approximate results, for minimization of which the Artificial Bee Colony algorithm was used. The proposed procedure was investigated with regard to the precision of obtained results and stability of working.

Summing up, the proposed algorithm constitutes the effective tool for solving such kind of inverse problem, however the error of input data and selection of parameters in the ABC algorithm (number of individuals and number of cycles) influence essentially the quality of solution. However, in each considered case of input data the reconstruction errors are smaller or at least comparable with errors of input data, values of the standard deviations of results obtained in multiple execution of the procedure are relatively small as well as the numbers of bees and cycles in the ABC algorithm needed for receiving satisfying results which makes the entire procedure useful, efficient and stable.

Acknowledgements. This project has been financed from the funds of National Science Centre granted on the basis of decision DEC-2011/03/B/ST8/06004.

References

1. Russell, S.J., Norvig, P.: Artificial Intelligence: A Modern Approach. Prentice Hall, Englewood Cliffs (1995)
2. Bäck, T., Fogel, D., Michalewicz, Z.: Handbook of Evolutionary Computation. Oxford Univ. Press (1997)
3. Gurney, K.: An Introduction to Neural Networks. Routledge, London (1997)
4. Eberhart, R.C., Shi, Y., Kennedy, J.: Swarm Intelligence. Morgan Kaufmann, San Francisco (2001)
5. Dorigo, M., Blum, C.: Ant colony optimization theory: a survey. Theoretical Computer Science 344, 243–278 (2005)
6. Duran Toksari, M.: Ant Colony Optimization for finding the global minimum. Applied Mathematics and Computation 176, 308–316 (2006)
7. Krishnanand, K.N., Ghose, D.: Glowworm swarm optimization for multimodal search spaces. In: Panigrahi, B.K., Shi, Y., Lim, M.-H. (eds.) Handbook of Swarm Intelligence. ALO, vol. 8, pp. 451–467. Springer, Berlin (2011)
8. Karaboga, D., Basturk, B.: On the performance of artificial bee colony (ABC) algorithm. Appl. Soft Computing 8, 687–697 (2007)
9. Karaboga, D., Akay, B.: A comparative study of artificial bee colony algorithm. Appl. Math. Comput. 214, 108–132 (2009)
10. Słota, D.: Solving the inverse Stefan design problem using genetic algorithm. Inverse Problems in Science and Engineering 16, 829–846 (2008)
11. Ma, M., Liang, J., Guo, M., Fan, Y., Yin, Y.: SAR image segmentation based on Artificial Bee Colony algorithm. Applied Soft Computing 11, 5205–5214 (2011)
12. Bai, J., Yang, G.-K., Chen, Y.-W., Hu, L.-S., Pan, C.-C.: A model induced max-min ant colony optimization for asymmetric traveling salesman problem. Applied Soft Computing 13, 1365–1375 (2013)
13. Lučić, P., Teodorović, D.: Computing with Bees: attacking complex transportation engineering problems. Int. J. Artificial Intelligence Tools 12, 375–394 (2003)
14. Tereshko, V.: Reaction-diffusion model of a honeybee colony's foraging behaviour. In: Deb, K., Rudolph, G., Lutton, E., Merelo, J.J., Schoenauer, M., Schwefel, H.-P., Yao, X. (eds.) PPSN 2000. LNCS, vol. 1917, pp. 807–816. Springer, Heidelberg (2000)
15. Özbakir, L., Baykasoğlu, A., Tapkan, P.: Bees algorithm for generalized assignment problem. Appl. Math. Comput. 215, 3782–3795 (2010)
16. Gabryel, M., Woźniak, M., Nowicki, R.K.: Creating Learning Sets for Control Systems Using an Evolutionary Method. In: Rutkowski, L., Korytkowski, M., Scherer, R., Tadeusiewicz, R., Zadeh, L.A., Zurada, J.M. (eds.) EC 2012 and SIDE 2012. LNCS, vol. 7269, pp. 206–213. Springer, Heidelberg (2012)

17. Beck, J.V., Blackwell, B., St.Clair, C.R.: Inverse Heat Conduction: Ill Posed Problems. Wiley Intersc., New York (1985)
18. Mochnacki, B., Suchy, J.S.: Numerical Methods in Computations of Foundry Processes. PFTA, Cracow (1995)
19. Mochnacki, B.: Numerical modeling of solidification process. In: Zhu, J. (ed.) Computational Simulations and Applications, pp. 513–542. InTech, Rijeka (2011)
20. Santos, C.A., Quaresma, J.M.V., Garcia, A.: Determination of transient interfacial heat transfer coefficients in chill mold castings. J. Alloys and Compounds 319, 174–186 (2001)
21. Słota, D.: Identification of the cooling condition in 2-D and 3-D continuous casting processes. Numer. Heat Transfer B 55, 155–176 (2009)
22. Słota, D.: Restoring boundary conditions in the solidification of pure metals. Comput. & Structures 89, 48–54 (2011)
23. Ionescu, D., Ciobanu, I., Munteanu, S.I., Crisan, A., Monescu, V.: 2D mathematical model for the solidification of alloys within a temperature interval. Metalurgia International 16(4), 39–44 (2011)
24. Piasecka Belkhayat, A.: Numerical modelling of solidification process using interval boundary element method. Archives of Foundry Engineering 8(4), 171–176 (2008)
25. Hetmaniok, E., Słota, D., Zielonka, A.: Experimental verification of immune recruitment mechanism and clonal selection algorithm applied for solving the inverse problems of pure metal solidification. Int. Commun. Heat Mass Transf. 47, 7–14 (2013)
26. Hetmaniok, E.: Invasive weed optimization algorithm applied for solving the inverse Stefan problem. Hutnik 81(1), 76–79 (2014)
27. Hetmaniok, E., Słota, D., Zielonka, A.: Solution of the inverse heat conduction problem by using the ABC algorithm. In: Szczuka, M., Kryszkiewicz, M., Ramanna, S., Jensen, R., Hu, Q. (eds.) RSCTC 2010. LNCS, vol. 6086, pp. 659–668. Springer, Heidelberg (2010)
28. Zielonka, A., Hetmaniok, E., Słota, D.: Using of the Artificial Bee Colony Algorithm for determining the heat transfer coefficient. In: Czachórski, T., Kozielski, S., Stańczyk, U. (eds.) Man-Machine Interactions 2. AISC, vol. 103, pp. 369–376. Springer, Heidelberg (2011)
29. Hetmaniok, E., Słota, D., Zielonka, A., Wituła, R.: Comparison of ABC and ACO algorithms applied for solving the inverse heat conduction problem. In: Rutkowski, L., Korytkowski, M., Scherer, R., Tadeusiewicz, R., Zadeh, L.A., Zurada, J.M. (eds.) EC 2012 and SIDE 2012. LNCS, vol. 7269, pp. 249–257. Springer, Heidelberg (2012)
30. Mochnacki, B., Majchrzak, E., Kapusta, A.: Numerical model of heat transfer processes in solidifying and cooling steel ingot (on the basis of BEM). In: Wrobel, L.C., Brebbia, C.A. (eds.) Computational Modelling of Free and Moving Boundary Problems 2, Heat Transfer, pp. 177–189. Computational Mech. Publ., Southampton (1992)

Simulations of Credibility Evaluation and Learning in a Web 2.0 Community*

Grzegorz Kowalik**, Paulina Adamska, Radosław Nielek, and Adam Wierzbicki

Polish-Japanese Institute of Information Technology (PJIIT),
ul. Koszykowa 86, 02-008 Warsaw, Poland
{grzegorz.kowalik,tiia,adamw,nielek}@pjwstk.edu.pl

Abstract. Since the emergence of Web 2.0, the idea of online knowledge sharing has been gaining attention of researchers and online communities. We can observe the popularity of such services on Wikipedia and numerous Q&A systems, in which ordinary users can explicitly ask questions and provide answers thus raise their expertise level by learning from others. Users dynamically switch between roles of content producer and content consumer. This paper applies game-theoretic approach to study how different community member profiles and reputation can affect the learning process and, in consequence, credibility of the provided information.

Keywords: game theory, knowledge, learning communities, web 2.0, web credibility, social simulations, social roles.

1 Introduction

The emergence of Web 2.0 [1, 2] has provided a great opportunity to create an environment for online learning communities. This shift in paradigms of the Internet resulted in the emergence of a great variety of Q&A systems like Quora[1] or Stack Oveflow[2] services where users were allowed to ask questions and provide answers to others in order to support the process of learning. Our work focuses on contributory factors and barriers in reaching this goal. We propose a theoretical model allowing us to observe learning proces, even if users are exposed to very unfriendly conditions, can bypass numerous difficulties, especially in the presence of a reputation system. The next section of the paper briefly explains the background of the model and introduces two basic hypotheses, which have been evaluated using simulation approach.

---

* Research supported by the grant "Reconcile: Robust Online Credibility Evaluation of Web Content" from Switzerland through the Swiss Contribution to the enlarged European Union.

** This author is supported by Polish National Science Centre grant 2012/05/B/ST6/03364.

[1] https://www.quora.com/

[2] stackoverflow.com

L. Rutkowski et al. (Eds.): ICAISC 2014, Part II, LNAI 8468, pp. 373–384, 2014.
© Springer International Publishing Switzerland 2014

2   Related Work

Different aspects of learning communities have been extensively studied over the several past years. Numerous works analyzed the profiles of Q&A contributors, their evolution and correlation of certain characteristics with the activity of users [3,4], and their expertise [5]. Other papers were dedicated to the phenomenon known as wisdom of the crowd [6]. Some of the research aimed specifically to better understand the concepts of information and knowledge, along with its correlates [7]. [8] explains the differences between the two terms, suggesting that information has no intrinsic meaning, while knowledge is a feature of a reader and a provider. This approach is also used in our analysis. Numerous publications treat knowledge management as in [9] and learning communities as in [10], focusing on some processes determining how knowledge is shared, and how such communities work. Our model is based on the one described in [11], however it is modified to analyze learning processes. The proposed learning curve is mostly inspired by [12].

In this paper we aim to verify two basic hypotheses using our theoretical model. These hypotheses are presented in the following sections, along with a brief summary of previous research results.

2.1   Community will Learn

The first hypothesis constitutes the fundamental assumption of all the open Q&A systems the knowledge of the community members should increase over time. The concept of learning is crucial to improving quality of the generated content and therefore sustain the community. This intuition has been questioned by the empirical studies presented in [13], where authors noticed that the mean quality of the initial answer's scores are likely to persist during the user's tenure. We claim that this phenomenon does not necessarily mean that the community members do not learn. It can be associated with the fact that analyzed users are already at the stage of providing answers (thus they have achieved a certain level of expertise earlier), while the increase of knowledge is made possible only by consuming high-quality information posted by others (if we assume that community is the only one place they use for learning). Another explanation might be associated with the evolution of the entire community which actually does learn, and therefore expects higher quality of consumed information. Moreover, it is also possible, that an average post score is strongly correlated with a particular topic, which determines the number of potential voters. This aspect of Stack Overflow was been studied in [14]. Apart from analyzing the learning process itself, in this paper we also study how the initial knowledge distribution (variance) between agents affects its characteristics.

Additionally, there is a well-known communication problem between experts and non-experts [15]. Jeff Atwood, the co-founder of Stack Overflow[3] explained that acquiring certain communication skills is a vital part of user education

---

[3] http://www.wired.com/wiredenterprise/2012/07/stackoverflow-jeff-atwood/

process: "Programmer's job is to communicate with users to find out what people want. (...)We're tricking developers into being better communicators." We want to verify and confirm the importance of this communication in the learning community.

2.2 Online Community with a Reputation System can Handle Dishonesty

Online communities are especially vulnerable to a great variety of abuses. Some users might have other goals than cooperation - like marketing, self-promotion, hoaxes, jokes etc. Therefore, most of the modern services define certain rules and force community members to comply with them by introducing reputation systems. This approach is widely applied to e-commerce systems. However, it has also been introduced to learning communities, where users can provide feedback regarding the quality of certain information, and thus influence the reputation of its producer (in some systems referred to as karma). Different aspects of such systems and their potential influence on the community have been extensively studied over the past several years. Some of them investigated how reputation and badges can be used to promote certain behaviors and what the limitations of such approaches are [16, 17]. Others provide guidelines on how to effectively achieve high reputation score using particular community characteristics [14]. However, very little is known about the influence of different reputation systems and voting strategies on the quality and credibility of the provided information. Our model creates an environment for a theoretically study and evaluates different approaches to designing such mechanisms. In this paper we analyze how communities with different member profiles deal with dishonest users and how dishonesty affects a learning process.

3 The Model

A preliminary analysis of the Stack Overflow community revealed that its active members can be divided into three groups, namely: information consumers who only ask questions - in our model referred to as content consumers (CC) information producers who only provide answers in our model referred to as content producers (CP), and multi-role types who perform both actions. At each simulation step, agents choose their roles in the community. Afterwards a CP produces content, while a CC chooses one CP to interact with, and consumes the provided piece of information. By default, we assume that everyone can act both as CP and CC at each simulation step. However, some of the experiments were conducted using the role assignment inspired by real data extracted from the Stack Overflow community.

3.1 Model Description

Agents in content producer roles use their knowledge to produce good quality (true) information. We will describe this attribute of content as "truthfulness"

(TF) true information will have TF=1. However, they can either fail to do so or intentionally produce wrong (false) information, especially those who are dishonest (CP-L). Such information will have TF=0. In addition, the producer can invest in the presentation, the look (L) of content - like persuade the others that s/he is right, using embellishments or use kind, communicative language to explain answer (L=1) or not (L=0). For example:

- Question: "What is a good treatment for a strong headache?"
- Answer: "Aspirin is the best way to stop a headache. It is also effective against flu, and protects even against heart attacks and strokes."

This answer, even if truthful, contains several embellishments and a lot of additional information that serves to persuade the asking person to use aspirin. It is an example of good looking truth (L=1, TF=1). We could bring more examples to other combinations of content values:

- (TF=0 ; L=0): "Put some Olbas oil on your forehead."
  - This solution is wrong (we assume) so TF=0. The author does not use anything more to convince us to use it, so also L=0.
- (TF=0 ; L=1) : "Do not take an aspirin, because it is an acid and can damage your stomach. Put some Olbas oil on your forehead and rest in a dark room. This will stop almost any headache."
  - L=1 because thr answer contains a lot of persuasive information to persuade the asking person. This persuasion can be based on a negative motivation (fear of damaging the stomach). TF=0 because Olbas oil is not effective against headaches.
- (TF=1 ; L=0): "Take an aspirin."
  - This solution is correct (TF=1), but author does not provide any look value to it (L=0).

We do not say that "look value" is something wrong, it just makes content more attractive to CC. All important factors, besides truthfulness of information, can be described as "look" value.

Content consumers try to consume good (true) information using an inaccurate signal for evaluation. The signal is composed of quality/truthfulness (TF) of information and its look (L). Using their knowledge, CC try to verify the TF of signal. The less they know, the greater the significance of the L factor. Naive users could just follow CP assurance, having no idea if it will work or not.

The signal is randomized from normal distribution using the following formula:

$$S \sim (\alpha * TF + (1 - \alpha) * L, \delta) \tag{1}$$

Where:

α - knowledge of CC (ranges from 0 to 1)
TF - Truthfulness of content (true=1, false=0)
L - Look of content (1 if CP invested in it, 0 if not)
δ - "expertise" value used as standard deviation, 0,3 by default[4]

---

[4] This factor is used here as "noise" . However, it can be interpreted as "expertise", accuracy of estimation or "certainty". More about this factor can be found in [11].

Users in CC is the role can learn change their knowledge value. If they successfully accept true content, their knowledge increases. However, accepting false information results in the decrease of knowledge (they will move forward making the same errors etc.). As mentioned before, the S-Curve function will be used. Each time we say that agent's knowledge increases or decreases we use S-Curve function calculating it from "experience" value that is increased or decreased by fixed value (0.01 by default):

$$knowledge = \frac{1}{1 - e^{-t}} \qquad (2)$$

where:

t - current experience level

Experience will be also used for calculating initial values. Each interaction results in payoff for both sides, using values the same as in [11]. Those gains are "main goal" of agents and are used in evolution (knowledge can help achieve better gains, but have no direct impact on gains and evolution):

Table 1. Payoff tables. Each row (CP strategy) represents final information value from CP composed by truthfulness and look (TF, L).

	CC				CC	
	Accept	Reject			Accept	Reject
(1,1)	2 / 4	0 / -1		(1,1)	2 / 1	0 / -1
CP -H (1,0)	2 / 5	0 / 0		CP -L (1,0)	2 / 2	0 / 0
(0,1)	-2 / 1	0 / -3		(0,1)	-2 / 4	0 / -3
(0,0)	-2 / 2	0 / -2		(0,0)	-2 / 5	0 / -2

3.2   Simulation Procedure

The presented model has been implemented using the Repast 2.0 framework.

Each simulation involve a number of generations that involve a number of iterations. Evolution occurs between generations. By default, we use 100 generations and each with 100 iterations. Whole simulation procedure is described below:

1. Each CP produces one piece of information, according to his strategy
    - Look (L) : Can add look (L=1) or not (L=0)
    - Truthfulness (TF): can produce true (TF=1) or false (TF=0). If CP intends to produce TF=1, s/he has a chance to do it basing on his or her knowledge. If s/he fails, information will be false (TF=0).

2. Each CC chooses one producer from the population, according to the producer choice strategy (one of two) used in scenario:
   - Random producer: CC selects one CP at random
   - Reputation: CC selects three CPs and then chose the one with the highest reputation value
3. CC evaluates producer's information and decides whether to accept it or not
   - The signal for evaluation is randomized basing on look (L) and truthfulness (TF) of information from CP
   - If the signal is higher than the consumer's individual acceptance threshold, CC accepts the information. Otherwise, it is rejected.
4. If CC accepted information:
   - Modify CC knowledge. If TF=1 then increase, if TF=0 then decrease
   - CC rates the CP (this action modifies only the working copy of producer's rating, so that other consumers do not take this evaluation until the next iteration) if the CC accepts information and TF=1, the CP receives one "upvote" (his or her reputation increases). If the CC accepts TF=0, CP receives one "downvote" (its reputation decreases).
5. CC and CP receive their gains (according to the payoff table, see Table 1).
6. Original producer's ratings are updated taking into account the evaluations from this iteration.
   - If it is the last iteration in the generation:
   - Producers evolve (modify the strategy of TF and L values of produced information proportionally to gains from all iterations in this generation)
     • CP strategy inheritance has a 1% chance to be random instead of parental (mutation).
   - The reputation of all the producers is reset
   - Consumers evolve (modify their acceptance thresholds proportionally to gains from all iterations in this generation)
     • CC strategy inheritance has a 1% chance to be random instead of parental (mutation).

4   Simulation Results

All presented results were verified by multiple runs (usually 10). The following charts show one run of simulation. If results were different between runs it will be mentioned otherwise, all runs looked similar.

4.1   Community will Learn

To explore this topic we can form a hypothesis:

- The total / mean value of knowledge in community should increase (if there are people with enough knowledge to teach)

This was tested using some basic scenarios. Most simulation parameters will be same as in [11]:

- Number of interactions/generations: 100/100
- Number of multi-role agents: 100
- "Expertise": 0.3
- Experience gain/loses: 0.01
- Initial experience/knowledge was randomized using normal distribution. Mean and variance will be provided
- CP Look usage strategy will be randomized at start (50% chances for 1 and 50% for 0)

Scenarios to this hypothesis assume that all agents are honest (CP-H in CP role). CP-L type presence will be tested later in this paper. Reputation will not be used; it will be also tested on next hypothesis.

Different scenarios will test different initial knowledge it will be randomized value (using experience) for each "generic" agent from normal distribution, with mean and std. deviation defined by scenario.

Each figure shows:

- Knowledge mean - mean of knowledge value of all agents
- Knowledge varianve - variance of knowledge value of all agents
- Look strategy usage - mean of look usage in CP role (value 1 for agents using it, 0 for agents not using it)
- Acceptance threshold mean - mean of acceptance threshold of all agents (value used in their CC role)

As we can see, if initial knowledge is average (Fig. 1) or high (Fig. 3), we can observe a learning process leading to the situation where all agents have maximal knowledge. Look usage rises at the start (CP need to "promote" their content), but when knowledge reaches maximum levels, it starts to decrease as CC no longer consider look in signal evaluation, it is just unnecessary cost. This is a good example of "communication role" discussed in this hypothesis firstly,

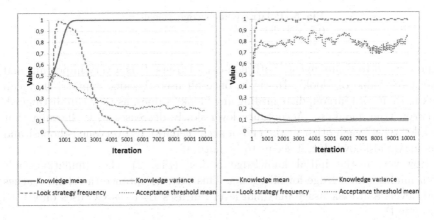

Fig. 1. Average knowledge scenario results (mean=0.5, std. Dev=0.2)

Fig. 2. Low knowledge scenario results (mean = 0.2, std. dev. = 0.2)

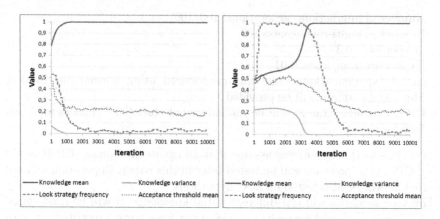

Fig. 3. High knowledge scenario results (mean = 0.8, std. dev. = 0.2)

Fig. 4. Varied knowledge (mean = 0.5, std. dev = 1)

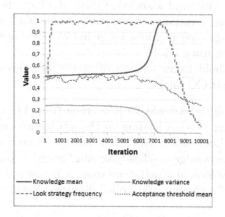

Fig. 5. Polarized knowledge (mean = 0.5, std. dev = 99)

experts need to communicate with non-expert users. It is a very important and "positive" value of "look". However, once all users became experts, they can talk in their own jargon, disregarding any "look" values, as they can distinguish between true and false. Acceptance level slowly decreases to 0, showing that people "trust" each other at the end of such scenario as everyone is honest and has maximal knowledge, it seems to be natural.

However, if the initial knowledge is low (Fig. 2), the simulation ends with minimal knowledge for all agents. This way, acceptance threshold reaches high levels and look usage maximal level (all uses L=1 as CC uses only L to evaluate I).

There is an interesting case with initial knowledge variance as we can see in Fig. 4 and Fig. 5, higher variance results in longer "learning" process knowledge mean still reaches maximal level, but in longer time (iterations). This is a very interesting result, suggesting that learning communities with similar level of knowledge of their members will work better than those with very different knowledge of members (with same total sum / average).

In [13] authors shows that quality of content seems to be constant. This can be compared with similar behavior of our signal. As we can see in results, initially CC with lower knowledge would likely evaluate positively content with good look (that is rapidly taken as strategy by CP), but at a later stage, if we have a community with high knowledge, whole signal is based on TF Look is rarely used as it has no value. Users have other (higher quality) expectation of content. This way, we can ask if "quality of content" as in [13] could actually change in time as evaluation of it might be deferent.

4.2 Online Community with a Reputation System can Handle Dishonesty

As written before, many online communities use reputation systems. They have many possible effects. The one we want to focus on is impact on knowledge and learning of members and an impact of dishonest agents. Dishonest producers (CP-L), same as in [11], are those interested in providing information with TF=0 (different payoffs). They will use strategy to not add it. However, it can change in the course of evolution (from mutation).

In tested scenarios, we set a number of agents as dishonest (10%, 50% and 90% from initial 100). Other parameters were nearly same as in previous scenarios (we reduced initial look usage and initial knowledge to mean = 0.3 to make results more visible and clear)

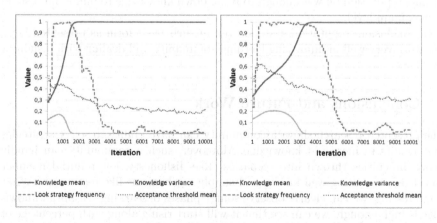

Fig. 6. Scenario with reputation on, 10% dishonest

Fig. 7. Scenario with reputation on, 50% dishonest

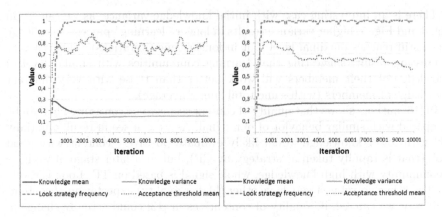

Fig. 8. Scenario with reputation on, **Fig. 9.** Scenario with reputation off, 90% dishonest   10% dishonest

Simulations clearly show the effect of reputation. With reputation presence, 10% dishonest agent presence was almost unnoticeable (comparing Fig 10 with Fig. 1). As we can observe, community achieved higher acceptance threshold they are not so "trusty" as it was observed in Fig.1. It seems that community spontaneously created a solution how to deal with the presence of dishonest agents. With 50% of dishonesty, as we can see in Fig.11, achieving maximum levels of knowledge took more time (iterations). Also, final acceptance threshold level was higher. If we flood the community with dishonest agents, as we can see in Fig.12 with 90% dishonest agents, we can observe that the community will not be able to achieve the maximum levels and ends with minimum levels (and a very high acceptance threshold). Here, the role of reputation is very important, as can be seen in Fig. 13 the scenario with reputation system turned off. Fig.13 shows, that only 10% dishonest agents in the same scenario modified only by turning reputation off was enough to bring down knowledge to minimum instead of maximum level.

In conclusion, reputation system, even in such basic form as presented here, can work very well in improving learning community and dealing with dishonest members.

5   Conclusions and Future Work

The presented research show, a community can have ability to select strategies that results in increased knowledge. Moreover, such a community can handle many difficulties thrown into scenarios like dishonesty, lower initial member knowledge etc. using well known and simple mechanisms like reputation. What is interesting, we can clearly observe some "phases of learning" if initial knowledge is high enough, we can see that it will start rising along with percentage of agents using the look for their CP roles. This shows the importance of good communication, even promotion of content at early stages especially from experts to non-experts. Once knowledge reaches maximum levels, agents gradually stop using look, as they are all experts, focusing only on truthfulness of information. We can also clearly observe that the acceptance threshold drops to almost "full trust" if we do not have dishonest agents, but with presence of dishonesty it reaches accordingly higher levels.

The main contribution of this article is a theoretical model of an open knowledge community which allows studying the interplay between learning and content selection. Content consumers in our model are not directly motivated to learn; learning of the community is the emergent process. Using our model, we are also able to study the effects of a reputation system on emergence of learning in the presence of adversaries who attempt to manipulate the community.

A good theoretical model should have the following three properties: it should be conceptually simple, should be able to express the most relevant phenomena in the studied area, and should be able to formulate predictions which can be verified empirically. We believe that our model fulfills these three requirements, and our future work will focus on empirical model verifications and improvements. For example, our model can be used in future to answer the questions such as: what is the likelihood of obtaining an answer to a question in a particular learning community? What distributions of knowledge can be expected in typical learning communities? Empirical studies of such research questions will most likely require creating a testing method for open knowledge communities which can base on surveys or use the Q&A system directly.

References

1. O'reilly, T.: What is web 2.0: Design patterns and business models for the next generation of software. Communications & Strategies (1), 17 (2007)
2. Bleicher, P.: Web 2.0 revolution: Power to the people. Applied Clinical Trials 15(8), 34 (2006)
3. Furtado, A., Andrade, N., Oliveira, N., Brasileiro, F.: Contributor profiles, their dynamics, and their importance in five q&a sites. In: Proceedings of the 2013 Conference on Computer Supported Cooperative Work, pp. 1237–1252. ACM (2013)
4. Pal, A., Chang, S., Konstan, J.A.: Evolution of experts in question answering communities. In: ICWSM (2012)
5. Pal, A., Konstan, J.A.: Expert identification in community question answering: exploring question selection bias. In: Proceedings of the 19th ACM International Conference on Information and Knowledge Management, pp. 1505–1508. ACM (2010)
6. Kostakos, V.: Is the crowd's wisdom biased? a quantitative analysis of three online communities. In: International Conference on Computational Science and Engineering, CSE 2009, vol. 4, pp. 251–255. IEEE (2009)
7. Morrison, P., Murphy-Hill, E.: Is programming knowledge related to age? an exploration of stack overflow. In: Proceedings of the Tenth International Workshop on Mining Software Repositories, pp. 69–72. IEEE Press (2013)
8. Miller, F.J.: I= 0-(information has no intrinsic meaning). Information Research 8(1) (2002)
9. Sharratt, M., Usoro, A.: Understanding knowledge-sharing in online communities of practice. Electronic Journal on Knowledge Management 1(2), 187–196 (2003)

10. García-Carbonell, A., Watts, F., Montero, B.: Learning communities in simulation and gaming. Bridging the Gap: Transforming Knowledge into Action through Gaming and Simulation, 254–262 (2004)
11. Papaioannou, T.G., Aberer, K., Abramczuk, K., Adamska, P., Wierzbicki, A.: Game-theoretic models of web credibility. In: Proceedings of the 2nd Joint WICOW/AIRWeb Workshop on Web Quality, pp. 27–34. ACM (2012)
12. Leibowitz, N., Baum, B., Enden, G., Karniel, A.: The exponential learning equation as a function of successful trials results in sigmoid performance. Journal of Mathematical Psychology 54(3), 338–340 (2010)
13. Posnett, D., Warburg, E., Devanbu, P., Filkov, V.: Mining stack exchange: Expertise is evident from initial contributions. In: 2012 ASE International Conference on Social Informatics (2012)
14. Bosu, A., Corley, C.S., Heaton, D., Chatterji, D., Carver, J.C., Kraft, N.A.: Building reputation in stackoverflow: an empirical investigation. In: Proceedings of the Tenth International Workshop on Mining Software Repositories, pp. 89–92. IEEE Press (2013)
15. White, R.W., Richardson, M., Liu, Y.: Effects of community size and contact rate in synchronous social q&a. In: Proceedings of the SIGCHI Conference on Human Factors in Computing Systems, pp. 2837–2846. ACM (2011)
16. Anderson, A., Huttenlocher, D., Kleinberg, J., Leskovec, J.: Steering user behavior with badges. In: Proceedings of the 22nd International Conference on World Wide Web, International World Wide Web Conferences Steering Committee, pp. 95–106 (2013)
17. Barclay, P., et al.: Harnessing the power of reputation: strengths and limits for promoting cooperative behaviors. Evolutionary Psychology: An International Journal of Evolutionary Approaches to Psychology and Behavior 10(5), 868–883 (2011)

Optimization of Composite Structures Using Bio-inspired Methods

Arkadiusz Poteralski[1], Mirosław Szczepanik[1], Witold Beluch[1],
and Tadeusz Burczyński[1,2]

[1]Institute of Computational and Mechanical Engineering,
Faculty of Mechanical Engineering,
Silesian University of Technology, ul. Konarskiego 18a, 44-100 Gliwice, Poland
arkadiusz.poteralski@polsl.pl
[2]Institute of Computer Science,
Faculty of Physics Mathematics and Computer Science,
Cracow University of Technology, ul. Warszawska 24, 31-155 Cracow, Poland
tburczyn@pk.edu.pl

Abstract. The paper deals with an application of the artificial immune system (AIS) and the particle swarm optimizer (PSO) to the optimization problems. The AIS and PSO are applied to optimize of stacking sequence of plies in composites. The optimization task is formulated as maximization of minimal difference between the first five eigenfrequencies and the external excitation frequency. Recently, immune and swarm methods have found various applications in mechanics, and also in structural optimization. The AIS is a computational adaptive system inspired by the principles, processes and mechanisms of biological immune systems. The algorithms typically use the characteristics of the immune systems like learning and memory to simulate and solve a problem in a computational manner. The swarm algorithms are based on the models of the animals social behaviours: moving and living in the groups. The main advantage of the AIS and PSO, contrary to gradient methods of optimization, is the fact that they do not need any information about the gradient of fitness function. The numerical examples demonstrate that the new method based on immune and particle computation is an effective technique for solving computer aided optimal design.

Keywords: artificial immune system, particle swarm optimizer, finite element method, optimization, material constants, composite, laminate, modal analysis.

1 Introduction

The paper deals with an application of the artificial immune system (AIS) [1][22][25] or the particle swarm optimizer (PSO) [10][11][18] with the finite element method to the optimization of stacking sequence of plies in composites. Recently, immune and swarm methods have found various applications in mechanics, and also in structural optimization. These methods have gained popularity and they are alternative methods to evolutionary algorithm (EA) [3][4][6][7].

L. Rutkowski et al. (Eds.): ICAISC 2014, Part II, LNAI 8468, pp. 385–395, 2014.
© Springer International Publishing Switzerland 2014

Results of optimization for EA are presented in the paper [2] In this paper only comparison between AIS and PSO is presented.

Composites seem to be an interesting alternative for classical structural materials especially due to their high strength-to-weight ratio. The laminates, being multilayered, fibre reinforced composites, have especially superior properties. Laminate properties can be tailored to the specific applications by modification their component materials, number and order of layers and layer thickness. Laminates are often produced in short series or individually, so the non-destructive methods of identification should be employed to identify material elastic constants in laminates [19]. The aim of the optimization using AIS or PSO is to find the optimum ply angles of the hybrid laminate for the given number and thicknesses of the laminas. It is assumed that the number of laminas made of particular materials is constant. The main advantage of the bio-inspired method is the fact that these approach do not need any information about the gradient of the fitness function and give a strong probability of finding the global optimum. The main drawback of these approaches is the long time of calculations. The fitness function is calculated for each B cell receptor and for each swarm particle in each iteration by solving the boundary-value problem by means of the finite element method (FEM). In order to speedup the computations the hybrid methods were used. The HAIS and HPSO for another problems like: identification of material constants of piezoelectrics or identification of room acoustic properties are used [15][21].

2   Artificial Immune Systems

The artificial immune systems (AIS) are developed on the basis of a mechanism discovered in biological immune systems [17]. An immune system is a complex system which contains distributed groups of specialized cells and organs. The main purpose of the immune system is to recognize and destroy pathogens - funguses, viruses, bacteria and improper functioning cells. The lymphocytes cells play a very important role in the immune system. The lymphocytes are divided into several groups of cells. There are two main groups B and T cells, both contains some subgroups (like B-T dependent or B-T independent). The B cells contain antibodies, which could neutralize pathogens and are also used to recognize pathogens. There is a big diversity between antibodies of the B cells, allowing recognition and neutralization of many different pathogens. The B cells are produced in the bone marrow in long bones. A B cell undergoes a mutation process to achieve big diversity of antibodies. The T cells mature in thymus, only T cells recognizing non self cells are released to the lymphatic and the blood systems. There are also other cells like macrophages with presenting properties, the pathogens are processed by a cell and presented by using MHC (Major Histocompatibility Complex) proteins. The recognition of a pathogen is performed in a few steps. First, the B cells or macrophages present the pathogen to a T cell using MHC, the T cell decides if the presented antigen is a pathogen. The T cell gives a chemical signal to B cells to release antibodies. A part of stimulated B cells goes to a lymph node and proliferate (clone). A part of the B cells changes into memory cells, the rest of them secrete antibodies into blood. The secondary response of the immunology system in the presence of known pathogens is faster because of memory cells. The memory cells created during primary response, proliferate and the antibodies are secreted to blood. The antibodies bind to pathogens and neutralize them. Other cells like macrophages destroy pathogens. The number of lymphocytes in the organism changes, while the presence of pathogens increases, but after attacks a part of the lymphocytes is removed from the organism.

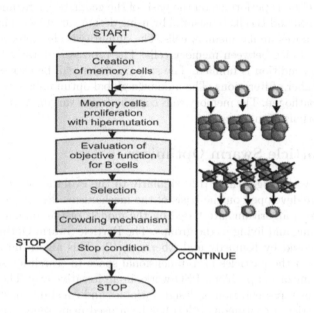

Fig. 1. An artificial immune system

The artificial immune systems [14][15] take only a few elements from the biological immune systems. The most frequently used are the mutation of the B cells, proliferation, memory cells, and recognition by using the B and T cells. The artificial immune systems have been used to optimization problems in classification and also computer viruses recognition. The cloning algorithm presented by von Zuben and de Castro [8] uses some mechanisms similar to biological immune systems to global optimization problems. The unknown global optimum is the searched pathogen. The memory cells contain design variables and proliferate during the optimization process. The B cells created from memory cells undergo mutation. The B cells evaluate and better ones exchange memory cells. In Wierzchoń S. T. [24] version of Clonalg the crowding mechanism is used - the diverse between memory cells is forced. A new memory cell is randomly created and substitutes the old one, if two memory cells have similar design variables. The crowding mechanism allows finding not only the global optimum but also other local ones. The presented approach is based on the Wierzchoń S. T. algorithm [24], but the mutation operator is changed. The Gaussian mutation is used instead of the nonuniform mutation in the presented approach [14]. The Figure 1 presents the flowchart of an artificial immune system.

The memory cells are created randomly. They proliferate and mutate creating B cells. The number of clones created by each memory cell is determined by the memory cells objective function value. The objective functions for B cells are evaluated. The selection process ex-changes some memory cells for better B cells. The selection is performed on the basis of the geometrical distance between each memory cell and B cells (measured by using design variables). The crowding mechanism removes similar memory cells. The similarity is also determined as the geometrical distance between memory cells. The process is iteratively repeated until the stop condition is fulfilled. The stop condition can be expressed as the maximum number of iterations. The unknown global optimum is represented by the searched pathogen. The memory cells contain design variables and proliferate during the optimization process.

3   The Particle Swarm Optimizer

The particle swarm algorithms [12], similarly to the evolutionary and immune algorithms, are developed on the basis of the mechanisms discovered in the nature. The swarm algorithms are based on the models of the animals social behaviours: moving and living in the groups. The Particle Swarm Optimizer PSO has been proposed by Kennedy and Eberhart [12]. This algorithm realizes directed motion of the particles in n-dimensional space to search for solution for n-variable optimization problem. PSO works in an iterative way. The algorithm with continuous representation of design variables and constant constriction coefficient (constricted continuous PSO) has been used in presented re-search. In this approach each particle oscillates in the search space between its previous best position and the best position of its neighbours, hopefully finding new best locations on its trajectory. When the swarm is rather small (swarm consists of several or tens particles) it can be assumed that all particles are the neighbours of currently considered one. In this case we can assume the global neighbourhood version and the best location found by swarm so far is taken into account current position of the swarm leader (Figure 2a).

The position xij of the i-th particle is changed by stochastic velocity vij, which is de-pendent on the particle distance from its earlier best position and position of the swarm leader. This approach is given by the following equations:

$$v_{ij}(k+1) = wv_{ij}(k) + \phi_{1j}(k)\left[q_{ij}(k) - d_{ij}(k)\right] + \phi_{2j}(k)\left[\hat{q}_j(k) - d_{ij}(k)\right] \quad (1)$$

$$d_{ij}(k+1) = d_{ij}(k) + v_{ij}(k+1), i = 1,2,...,m, j = 1,2,...,n \quad (2)$$

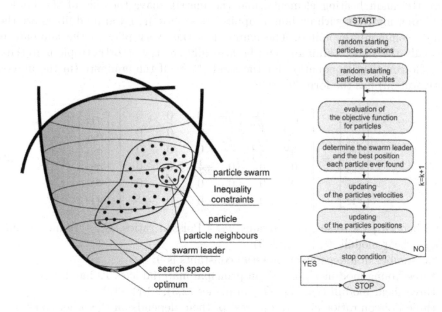

Fig. 2. The idea of the particle swarm and particle swarm optimizer - block diagram

where: $\phi_{1j}(k) = c_1 r_{1j}(k)$, $\phi_{2j}(k) = c_2 r_{2j}(k)$, m - number of the particles, n - number of design variables (problem dimension), w - inertia weight, c_1, c_2 - acceleration coefficients, r_1, r_2 - random numbers with uniform distribution [0,1], $d_i(k)$ - position of the i-th particle in k-th iteration step, $v_i(k)$ - velocity of the i-th particle in k-th iteration step, $q_i(k)$ - the best found position of the i-th particle found so far, $\hat{q}(k)$ - the best position found so far by swarm the position of the swarm leader, k itera-tion step. The flowchart of the particle swarm optimizer is presented in Figure 2b. At the beginning of the algorithm the particle swarm of assumed size is created randomly. Starting positions and velocities of the particles are created randomly. The objective function values are evaluated for each particle. In the next step the best positions of the particles are updated and the swarm leader is chosen. Then the particle velocities are modified by means of the Equation (1) and particle positions are modified accord-ing to the Equation (2) [20][21]. The process is iteratively repeated until the stop condition is fulfilled.

4   Mechanics of Composite Materials

Composite material consisting of at least two different constituents with macro-scopic - level connections. Laminates are probably the most often used composite materials because of their mechanical and strength properties related to specific gravity. A laminate is a set of definite number of the stacked plies (laminas) composed of the unidirectional fibers permanently fixed with a matrix. Fibers are the main bearing elements, and the matrix plays the role of the binder. Polymer matrices with carbon, graphite, glass, boron and aramid fibers are the most commonly exploited. The material of the every plies in the laminate is usually the same. Laminates can be typically treated as orthotropic materials, so the constitutive equation for the single layer of the laminate (in the in-axis orientation) has the form [9]:

$$
\begin{bmatrix} \varepsilon_{11} \\ \varepsilon_{22} \\ \varepsilon_{33} \\ \varepsilon_{23} \\ \varepsilon_{31} \\ \varepsilon_{12} \end{bmatrix} = \begin{bmatrix} \frac{1}{E_1} & -\frac{\nu_{12}}{E_1} & -\frac{\nu_{13}}{E_1} & 0 & 0 & 0 \\ -\frac{\nu_{21}}{E_2} & \frac{1}{E_2} & -\frac{\nu_{23}}{E_2} & 0 & 0 & 0 \\ -\frac{\nu_{31}}{E_3} & -\frac{\nu_{32}}{E_3} & \frac{1}{E_3} & 0 & 0 & 0 \\ 0 & 0 & 0 & \frac{1}{2G_{23}} & 0 & 0 \\ 0 & 0 & 0 & 0 & \frac{1}{2G_{31}} & 0 \\ 0 & 0 & 0 & 0 & 0 & \frac{1}{2G_{12}} \end{bmatrix} \begin{bmatrix} \sigma_{11} \\ \sigma_{22} \\ \sigma_{33} \\ \sigma_{23} \\ \sigma_{31} \\ \sigma_{12} \end{bmatrix} \tag{3}
$$

where: σ_{ij} - stresses, ε_{ij} - strains, ν_{ij} - Poisson ratios, E_{ij} - Young moduli, G_{ij} - shear moduli, (i, j = 1, 2, 3).
The number of independent material constants is 9:
- three Young moduli E_1, E_2, E_3 in principal material axes 1, 2 and 3;
- three shear moduli G_{23}, G_{31}, G_{12} in planes (2,3), (3,1), (1,2);
- three Poisson ratios v_{12}, v_{23}, v_{31}; rest of them depends on the other constants:

$$
\frac{\nu_{ij}}{E_i} = \frac{\nu_{ji}}{E_j}, (i, j = 1, 2, 3) \tag{4}
$$

The laminate can be in general treated as a two-dimensional structure. Applying the Kirchhoff-Love thin plate hypothesis and assuming plane-stress state, equation (3) takes the form:

$$
\begin{Bmatrix} \varepsilon_{11} \\ \varepsilon_{22} \\ \varepsilon_{12} \end{Bmatrix} = \begin{bmatrix} \frac{1}{E_1} & -\frac{\nu_{12}}{E_1} & 0 \\ -\frac{\nu_{21}}{E_2} & \frac{1}{E_2} & 0 \\ 0 & 0 & \frac{1}{2G_{12}} \end{bmatrix} \begin{Bmatrix} \sigma_{11} \\ \sigma_{22} \\ \sigma_{21} \end{Bmatrix} \tag{5}
$$

The number of independent material constants has been reduced to four $(E_1, E_2, G_{12}, \nu_{12})$. Typically, the laminate consists of more than one layer with different orientation of the fibers. The resultant stresses N and moments M, referred to the unit cross-section width can be obtained after the integration of the equation (6) and summation over all laminate layers [23]:

$$
\begin{bmatrix} N \\ M \end{bmatrix} = \begin{bmatrix} A & B \\ B & D \end{bmatrix} \begin{bmatrix} \varepsilon^o \\ \kappa^o \end{bmatrix} \tag{6}
$$

where: $A = [A_{ij}]$, $B = [B_{ij}]$, $D = [D_{ij}]$ - in-plane, coupling and out-of-plane stiffnesses matrixes, ε^o - strains curvature at the mid-plane, κ^o - curvature at the mid-plane.
In the general case, the shield state of the laminate is coupled with its bending state, which ensures matrix B. For commonly used symmetrical laminates this coupling does not exist $(B_{ij} = 0)$.

5   Formulation of the Optimization Problem

The optimization task is formulated as the minimization (or maximization) of the objective function J_0 with respect to design variables vector x:

$$\max_x(J_0) \tag{7}$$

The aim is to find the optimal set of ply angles for structures made of multi-layered, symmetrical laminates for given criteria. Simple and hybrid laminates are considered. Two variants of the design variables are taken into account: a) with continuous design variables; b) with discrete design variables.

The optimization task is formulated as maximization of minimal difference between the first five eigenfrequencies ω_{i_cl} and the external excitation frequency ω_{ex} with respect to the vector of the design variables:

$$\max(J_0) = \max |\omega_{i\_cl}(\mathbf{x}) - \omega_{ex}(\mathbf{x})| \tag{8}$$

To solve the boundary-value problem numerical method like the boundary element method (BEM) or the finite element method (FEM) can be used. In the current work the commercial FEM software (MSC PATRAN/NASTRAN) is employed.

6   Numerical Example

A symmetric hybrid laminate plate made of two materials is considered. The external plies of the laminate are made of material M_e, the core of the plate is made of the material M_i [2].

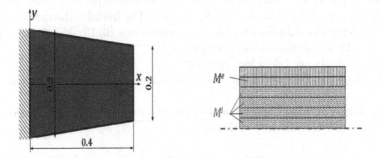

Fig. 3. The hybrid laminate plate: a) dimensions and bearing; b) location of materials (for 12-plies case)

The properties of materials are:
- material M_e (graphite-epoxy, T300/5280):
E_1=181GPa, E_2=10.3GPa, G_{12}=7.17GPa, ν_{12}=0.28, $\rho = 1600kg/m^3$, - material M_i (glass-epoxy, Scotchply 1002):
E_1=38.6GPa, E_2=8.27GPa, G_{12}=4.14GPa, ν_{12}=0.26, $\rho = 1800kg/m^3$.

The aim of the optimization is to find the optimum ply angles of the hybrid laminate for the given number and thicknesses of the laminas. It is assumed that the number of laminas made of particular materials is constant.
The AIS and PSO are employed to solve the optimization problem. Each B-cell receptor and each particle is composed of parameters representing ply angles. Due to symmetry, the number of parameters in each B-cell receptor and particle is equal to a half number of plies. The parameters of the AIS and PSO are:

PSO:
- the numbers of particles: N_{sp}=20,
- inertia weight: w=0.73,
- acceleration coefficient: c_1=1.47,
- the numbers of particles: c_2=1.47,

AIS:
- number of memory cells: n_{mc}=5,
- number of clones : n_{cl}=10/20,
- number of design variables : n_m=6/12,
- minimum crowding distance : c_{dist}=0.2,
- mutation range : m_r=0.5.

Two cases are considered: with $K_1 = 12$ and $K_2 = 24$ plies. The thickness of the plate is assumed to be constant and equal to h = 0.0072m. The thicknesses of parts made of particular materials are also the same. Each ply of the laminate in each i case has equal thickness h_i = h/K_i, i = 1,2. The initial (arbitrary chosen) stacking sequences for 12-plies and 24-plies variants are: (0/15/-15/45/-45)s and (0/0/15/15/-15/-5/45/45/-45/-45)s, respectively.
Different variants are taken into account:
- each ply angle can take real values from the range $< -90°, 90° >$ (continuous variant);
- each ply angle can take discrete values from the range $< -90°, 90° >$ varying every 5°, 15° and 45° (discrete variants).

The results for the maximization of the minimal difference between the first five eigenfrequencies and the external excitation frequency (ω_{ex} is equal to 120Hz) for PSO algorithm are collected in Table 1.
The same example was solved using another optimization method: artificial immune system (AIS). Results and comparison between PSO and AIS is presented in the table 2.

Table 1. Optimization results for PSO algorithm

Variant	Plies no.	Stacking sequence	$max(|\omega_{cl} - \omega_{ex}|)$ [Hz]
continuous	12	(-48.3/-49.9/50.3/50.2/50/50.4)s	64.864
	24	(49.1/-48.9/48.9/49.1/49.2/49.4/49.2/-	65.718
		49.2/49.2/49.2/49.1/-48)s	
5°	12	(50/-50/-50/-50/-55/-55)s	64.633
	24	(-50/50/50/-50/-50/50/50/-50/-	65.613
		50/-50/50/-45)s	
15°	12	(45/-45/-60/-60/-60/-60)s	63.02
	24	(45/45/45/-45/45/-60/75/-60/60/-	63.750
		75/75/-60)s	
45°	12	(45/-45/-45/-90/-90/-90)s	60.663
	24	(-45/45/45/-45/-45/-90/45/45/45/-	63.525
		90/-90/45)s	

Table 2. Results and comparison between AIS and PSO

Variant	Plies no.	Stacking sequence	$max(|\omega_{cl} - \omega_{ex}|)$	[Hz]
		AIS	AIS	PSO
continuous	12	(-49.1/50.7/51.3/-45.6/50.6/50.3)s	64.054	64.864
	24	(-50.1/47.2/48.7/-48.4/52.5/-53.2/-51.5/-	65.237	65.718
		50.9/49.8/-44.6/-44.4/-58.6)s		
5°	12	(-50/50/50/50/55/55)s	64.633	64.633
	24	(-50/50/50/-50/45/55/-50/-40/55/-	65.480	65.613
		60/55/55)s		
15°	12	(45/-45/-60/-60/-60/-60)s	63.02	63.02
	24	(45/-45/45/-45/-45/-75/-45/-60/-	63.677	63.750
		60/75/-60/75)s		
45°	12	(-45/45/45/90/90/90)s	60.663	60.663
	24	(45/-45/45/-45/-45/-45/90/90/45/	62.682	63.525
		90/-45/45)s		

7 Conclusions

In the paper, the formulation and application of the finite element method and the artificial immune system and particle swarm optimizer to optimization of stacking sequence of plies in composites is presented. Hybrid laminates have been taken into account. The continuous as well as the discreet optimization has been performed. The artificial immune and particle swarm optimization can be simply implemented because it needs only the values of objective functions. The particle swarm optimizer coupled with finite element method gives an efficient computational intelligence method for optimization of stacking sequence of plies in composites. Comparison between PSO and AIS in this paper is presented. Numerical example is given and good results are obtained.

The main advantage of the AIS and PSO, contrary to gradient methods of optimization, is the fact that they do not need any information about the gradient of fitness function. Only for hybrid method described in the paper [15][21] it is necessary to compute the gradient of fitness function but the aim of hybridization was to obtain more accurate results and speedup the computations. There are possibilities of further efficiency improvement of the proposed method, e.g. by the application of adjoint variable method in the sensitivity analysis. Also, the application of another hybridized global optimization algorithms, like hybrid artificial immune system, would be interesting. Efficiency of the proposed method can be also improved by distributing computations in multi-agent systems [13].

References

1. Balthrop, J., Esponda, F., Forrest, S., Glickman, M.: Coverage and generalization in an artificial immune system. In: Proceedings of the Genetic and Evolutionary Computation Conference, GECCO 2002, pp. 3–10. Morgan Kaufmann, New York (2002)
2. Beluch, W., Burczyński, T., Kuś, W.: Evolutionary optimization and identification of hybrid laminates. Evolutionary Computation and Global Optimization 2006, Oficyna Wyd. Pol. Warszawskiej 156, 39–48 (2006)
3. Burczyński, T., Poteralski, A., Szczepanik, M.: Genetic generation of 2-D and 3-D structures. In: Second M.I.T. Conference on Computational Fluid and Solid Mechanics, Massa-Chusetts, Institute of Technology Cambridge, MA 02139 U.S.A (2003)
4. Burczyński, T., Poteralski, A., Szczepanik, M.: Topological evolutionary computing in the optimal design of 2D and 3D structures. Eng. Optimiz. Taylor and Francis 39(7), 811–830 (2007)
5. Burczyński, T., Bereta, M., Poteralski, A., Szczepanik, M.: Immune Computing: Intelligent Methodology and its applications in bioengineering and computational mechanics. In: Comput. Meth. Mech. Advanced Structured Materials, vol. 1, Springer, Heidelberg (2010)
6. Burczyński, T., Kuś, W., Długosz, A., Poteralski, A., Szczepanik, M.: Sequential and Distributed Evolutionary Computations in Structural Optimization. In: Rutkowski, L., Siekmann, J.H., Tadeusiewicz, R., Zadeh, L.A. (eds.) ICAISC 2004. LNCS (LNAI), vol. 3070, pp. 1069–1074. Springer, Heidelberg (2004)
7. Burczyński, T., Długosz, A., Kus, W., Orantek, P., Poteralski, A., Szczepanik, M.: Intelligent computing in evolutionary optimal shaping of solids. In: Proceedings of the 3rd International Conference on Computing, Communications and Control Technologies, vol. 3, pp. 294–298 (2005)
8. de Castro, L.N., Timmis, J.: Artificial immune systems as a novel soft computing paradigm. Soft Computing 7(8), 526–544 (2003)
9. German, J.: Podstawy mechaniki kompozytów włóknistych, Wyd. Politechniki Krakowskiej, Kraków (2001)
10. Heppner, F., Grenander, U.: A stochastic nonlinear model for coordinated bird flocks. In: Krasner, S. (ed.) The Ubiquity of Chaos. AAAS Publications, Washington, DC (1990)
11. Kennedy, J., Eberhart, R.: Particle Swarm Optimisation. In: Proceedings of IEEE Int. Conf. on Neural Networks, Piscataway, NJ, pp. 1942–1948 (1995)

12. Kennedy, J., Eberhart, R.C.: Swarm Intelligence. Morgamn Kauffman (2001)
13. Mrozek, D., Małysiak-Mrozek, B.: An Improved Method for Protein Similarity Searching by Alignment of Fuzzy Energy Signatures. International Journal of Computational Intelligence Systems 4(1), 75–88 (2011)
14. Poteralski, A., Szczepanik, M., Dziatkiewicz, G., et al.: Immune identification of piezoelectric material constants using BEM. Inverse Problems in Science And Engineering 19(1), 103–116 (2011)
15. Poteralski, A., Szczepanik, M., Ptaszny, J., Ku, W., Burczyski, T.: Hybrid artificial immune system in identification of room acoustic properties Inverse Problems in Science and Engineering. Taylor and Francis (2013)
16. Poteralski, A., Szczepanik, M., Dziatkiewicz, G., Kuś, W., Burczyński, T.: Comparison between PSO and AIS on the basis of identification of material constants in piezoelectrics. In: Rutkowski, L., Korytkowski, M., Scherer, R., Tadeusiewicz, R., Zadeh, L.A., Zurada, J.M. (eds.) ICAISC 2013, Part II. LNCS (LNAI), vol. 7895, pp. 569–581. Springer, Heidelberg (2013)
17. Ptak, M., Ptak, W.: Basics of Immunology, Jagiellonian University Press, Cracow (2000) (in Polish)
18. Reynolds, C.W.: Flocks, herds, and schools, A distributed behavioral model. Computer Graphics 21, 25–34 (1987)
19. Silva, M.F.T., Borges, L.M.S.A., Rochinha, F.A., de Carvalho, L.A.V.: A genetic algo-rithm applied to composite elastic parameters identification. IPSE 12, 17–28 (2004)
20. Szczepanik, M., Poteralski, A., Długosz, A., Kuś, W., Burczyński, T.: Bio-inspired optimization of thermomechanical structures. In: Rutkowski, L., Korytkowski, M., Scherer, R., Tadeusiewicz, R., Zadeh, L.A., Zurada, J.M. (eds.) ICAISC 2013, Part II. LNCS (LNAI), vol. 7895, pp. 79–90. Springer, Heidelberg (2013)
21. Szczepanik, M., Poteralski, A., Ptaszny, J., Burczyński, T.: Hybrid Particle Swarm Optimizer and Its Application in Identification of Room Acoustic Properties. In: Rutkowski, L., Korytkowski, M., Scherer, R., Tadeusiewicz, R., Zadeh, L.A., Zurada, J.M. (eds.) EC 2012 and SIDE 2012. LNCS, vol. 7269, pp. 386–394. Springer, Heidelberg (2012)
22. Tan, K.C., Goh, C.K., Mamun, A.A., Ei, E.Z.: An evolutionary artificial immune system for multi-objective optimization. European Journal of Operational Research, 371–392 (2008)
23. Tylikowski, A.: Teoria spreżystoci ciał anizotropowych jako elementw kompozytowych. VI Szkoła Kompozytów, Wisła, 183–200 (2003)
24. Wierzchoń, S.T.: Artificial Immune Systems, Theory and Applications. EXIT, Warsaw (2001)
25. Zilong, G., Sunan, W., Jian, Z.: A novel immune evolutionary algorithm incorporating chaos optimization. Pattern Recognition Letters 27, 2–8 (2006)

Applying Metamodels and Sequential Sampling for Constrained Optimization of Process Operations

Ahmed Shokry and Antonio Espuna

Department of Chemical Engineering, Universitat Politecnica de Catalunya
Av. Diagonal, 020280, Barcelona, Spain
{ahmed.shokry,antonio.espuna}@upc.edu

Abstract. This paper presents a framework for nonlinear constrained optimization of complex systems, in which the objective function and the constraints are represented by black box functions. The proposed approach replaces the complex nonlinear model based on first principles with Kriging metamodels. Coupled to Kriging, the "Constrained Expected Improvement" technique and a sequential sampling strategy are used to explore the metamodels, in order to find global solutions for the constrained nonlinear optimization problem. The methodology has been tested and compared with classical optimization procedures based on sequential quadratic programming. Both have been applied to three mathematical examples, and to a case study of chemical process operation optimization. The proposed framework shows accurate solutions and significant reduction in the computational time.

Keywords: Kriging, Adaptive Sampling, Surrogate Models, Optimization, Process Operation.

1 Introduction

In area like chemical industry, the mathematical models required to emulate the behavior of a process system are usually highly nonlinear, complex, and require a lot of effort and time to be coded [2]. Specialized simulation software tools have been developed to model and simulate such complex processes (e.g. Aspen Plus), but, they appear to the user as black box models, with no access to the embedded first principle equations. Their ease of usage comes with many limitations as high computational time, especially in applications requiring lots of simulation runs (e.g. optimization), and noisy calculations. Moreover, a major difficulty appears in case of nonlinear optimization: standard gradient based optimizers estimate the model derivatives using noisy estimates, because of errors introduced by these simulators (e.g. caused by the termination criteria), and consequently, the optimization results are badly affected [3],[2],[15]. An approach to tackle these challenges, is to use the original complex model as a "computer experiment" for generating data points [4]. These points are used to fit simpler accurate models (Metamodels or Surrogate Models), which are used instead of

L. Rutkowski et al. (Eds.): ICAISC 2014, Part II, LNAI 8468, pp. 396–407, 2014.
© Springer International Publishing Switzerland 2014

the original complex model in optimization. Jones [6] analyzed many types of metamodels, and concluded that non-interpolating (regression) metamodels are unreliable in optimization, because they do not appropriately capture the function shape, and it is usually better to use surfaces that interpolate the data with linear combinations of basis functions. Additionally, he showed that, even an interpolating metamodel is used, exploring the metamodel with an arbitrary optimizer can fail even to find local optima, because the metamodel prediction uncertainty is not taken into account by the traditional optimizers [6], [15]. Consequently, there is a need for optimization techniques that do not only consider the metamodel prediction, but also consider the uncertainty about this prediction. Kriging surrogate models provide high prediction accuracy with relatively small number of training points. They include adjustable parameters in their basis function, which are tuned to obtain the best data fit [5][6]. Additionally, Kriging is able to estimate a variance which represents the uncertainty about the prediction. This variance extends the Kriging capabilities, as it enables the use of new sequential sampling techniques, and powerful optimization tools like the Expected Improvement (EI) [6] and the Constrained Expected Improvement (CEI) techniques [12],[13]. In these techniques, the optimization search is not only guided by the Kriging metamodel prediction, but also by the Kriging variance which represents the uncertainty about the search.

Shokry et al. [15] have used a global Kriging metamodel with the EI technique to solve unconstrained process operation optimization. However, practical optimization problems are inherently constrained, in the sense that the selected decision variables are not completely independent. In most cases, additionally to their natural bounds, complex mathematical relations among them should be formulated and maintained to ensure that the proposed solution is feasible. In this paper, a Kriging based framework is presented to solve nonlinear constrained optimization problems, which appear in the case of complex processes operation and control. To our knowledge, just few works have used Kriging metamodels to optimize decision making in this specific area, where sudden changes in the process and/or external conditions require fast and reliable reaction. In all these works, the Kriging model has been used as an accurate input/output surrogate, without exploiting the above mentioned potentials and capabilities provided by the Kriging variance (Caballero et al. [2], Davis et al. [3]), which makes the Kriging outperforming many metamodels in optimization in means of accuracy, managing uncertainty, reducing the optimization function evaluations.

2   Proposed Framework

The proposed framework consists of three main steps; 1) sampling plan design and computer experiments, 2) Kriging metamodels construction and validation, 3) surrogate model based optimization.

2.1 Sampling Design and Computer Experiments

In this step, the complex process model (model based on first principles - energy and mass balances, etc.-) is explored to identify the output variables of interest (objective and constraints), the input variables (the degrees of freedom of the optimization), and their bounds or domain (metamodel domain). Then, over the specified domain, a certain set of input combinations (sample points) is selected, which is called "sampling plan" $[X]_{n \times k}$, where n is the number of sample points, and k is the number of input variables [4]. The design of a sampling plan includes two issues: specifying a reasonable number of sample points n, and designing the locations of those data points through the metamodel domain. Many sampling design techniques are available [4]. In this paper, the space-filling latin hyper-cube sampling design (SLHS) is used, because it achieves high uniformity and stratification of the sampling plan [4],[5]. After designing an efficient sampling plan $[X]_{n \times k}$, a simulation run (computer-based experiment using the complex first principles model) is carried out at each point of this plan, to obtain the response or output variables $[Y]_{n \times M}$. Where, M is the number of output variables, which includes the objective function and the $M - 1$ constraints. Consequently, M is also the number of Kriging metamodels to be fitted (a Kriging metamodel for the objective, and Kriging metamodel for each of the $M - 1$ constraints). The output variables do not need to be direct measures of the process variables, but combinations of intermediate/output variables which finally lead to process performance indicators.

2.2 Kriging Metamodel Construction and Validation

The ordinary Kriging model assumes a stochastic process, in which the error in the predicted value is also a function of the input variables x. The Kriging predictor $\hat{y}(x)$ is then composed by two parts: the first one is a polynomial term $f(x)$ which is selected constant $f(x) = \mu$, while the second part is a deviation $Z(x)$ from that polynomial. So, $\hat{y}(x) = f(x) + Z(x)$, where $Z(x)$ is a stochastic Gaussian process with expected value zero $E(Z(x)) = 0$ and a covariance between two points x_i, x_j calculated as: $cov(Z(x_i), Z(x_j)) = \sigma^2 R(x_i, x_j)$, where σ^2 is the process variance, and $R(x_i, x_j)$ is a spatial correlation function (SCF), which is usually selected exponential, see (1) [4],[5].

$$R(x_i, x_j) = exp\left(-\sum_{l=1}^{k} \theta |x_{i,l} - x_{j,l}|^{p_l} \right) \qquad , l = 1, 2, ...k . \qquad (1)$$

To estimate the values of μ, σ^2, θ_l, p_l, the likelihood function of the observed data $[Y]_{n \times 1}$ is maximized, by differentiating the natural logarithm of the likelihood function with respect to μ and σ^2. After some algebra, their optimal values are obtained as (2), and (3).

$$\hat{\mu} = \frac{1^T R^{-1} Y}{1^T R^{-1} 1} . \qquad (2)$$

$$\hat{\sigma}^2 = \frac{(Y - 1\hat{\mu})^T R^{-1}(Y - 1\hat{\mu})}{n} \ . \tag{3}$$

Substituting by the optimal values of μ and σ^2 in the likelihood function leads to the concentrated log-likelihood function(4). The kriging predictor and variance are obtained by calculating the augmented likelihood function of the original data set and the new interpolating point (x_{new}, y_{new}). The final predictor of the Kriging method is given in (5), where: r is the $n \times 1$ vector of correlations $R(x_{new}, x_i)$ between the point to be predicted x_{new} and the sample design points. The variance of the predictor is given by (6). Detailed information about the required mathematical development can be found in [6],[2].

$$\underset{\theta_l, p_l}{\text{Max}} - \frac{n}{2} \ln(\hat{\sigma}^2) - \frac{1}{2} \ln(|R|) \ . \tag{4}$$

$$\hat{y}(x_{new}) = \hat{\mu} + r^T R^{-1}(Y - 1\hat{\mu}) \ . \tag{5}$$

$$\hat{s}^2(x_{new}) = \hat{\sigma}^2 \left(1 - r^T R^{-1} r + \frac{(1 - (r^T R^{-1} r))^2}{r^T R^{-1} r} \right) \ . \tag{6}$$

Fitting a Kriging metamodel is accomplished by obtaining the optimal metamodel parameters $[\theta_l, p_l, \mu, \sigma^2]$, through the maximization of the concentrated log-likelihood function (4). In practice, this optimization problem is computationally challenging, because of the complex nature of the concentrated log-likelihood function itself [4],[5]. In this paper, a genetic algorithm is used as the optimizer of the concentrated likelihood function. After fitting the Kriging metamodels, they are validated to assess thier accuracy [10]. Cross validation allows doing it without any additional data generation rather than the original set of sample points [7],[10]. Many cross validation methods have been developed, in this work, the "leave-one-out cross validation" (LOOCV) is used, because of its efficiency in terms of accuracy and computational effort. Details of this and other cross validation techniques can be found in [7], [10]. The Kriging accuracy is evaluated by computing the average root mean square error of the LOOCV (7), where, $y_i, \hat{y}_i$ are the real and the estimated values of the same left out point x_i.

$$AVR_{RMSE} = \sqrt{\frac{1}{n} \sum_{i=1}^{n} (\hat{y}_i - y_i)^2} \ . \tag{7}$$

2.3 Optimization Using Surrogate Models

Once the Kriging metamodels (one model for each one of the objective and constraints to be considered) have been fitted and validated, they take the place of the original complex process model. Hence, equations (8), (9) represent the nonlinear constrained optimization of process operation problem, in which one Kriging metamodel represents the objective, and $M - 1$ Kriging metamodels represent the $M - 1$ constraints. The objective and the constraints are considered as random variables $Y_{obj}(x)$, $Y_{const(m)}(x)$, which are normally distributed with means equal to the Kriging metamodels predictions $\hat{y}_{obj}(x)$, $\hat{y}_{const(m)}(x)$, and variances equal to the Kriging metamodels variances $\hat{s}^2_{obj}(x)$, $\hat{s}^2_{const(m)}(x)$, where T_m is the constraint limit, $m = 1, 2, \ldots M - 1$.

$$Min \ Y_{obj}(x), \ \ Y_{obj}(x) = \mathcal{N}\left(\hat{y}_{obj}(x), \hat{s}^2_{obj}(x)\right) \ . \tag{8}$$

$$Y_{const(m)}(x) \leq T_m, \ \ Y_{const(m)}(x) = \mathcal{N}\left(\hat{y}_{const(m)}(x), \hat{s}^2_{const(m)}(x)\right) \ . \tag{9}$$

The Expected Improvement (EI) technique [6] is used to optimize unconstrained objective function represented by a Kriging metamodel (8), via sequential sampling. Assuming that the objective function is to be minimized and the current best value of this objective is f_{min}, if a new untrained point x is to be explored, so the current best solution is expected to get improvement by an amount $I = max[0, f_{min} - Y_{obj}(x)]$. Hence, the likelihood of achieving this improvement is given by a normal density function. By integrating over this density function, the expected improvement is obtained in (10), where ϕ is the normal cumulative distribution function, and φ is the density function [9]. The approach works iteratively through sequential sampling. In each iteration, the EI criteria (10) is maximized to find a potentially improved solution x^*; the original complex model is evaluated at this solution to obtain the real response y^*, so this new point $[x^*, y^*]$ is added to the initial set of metamodel training points, and then the metamodel is refitted. The method has been tested and it is found that, it usually converges to the global optimum [6],[13],[5].

$$E(I(x)) = \hat{s}^2_{obj}(x)\left[u\,\phi(u) + \varphi(u)\right], \ \ u = \frac{f_{min} - \hat{y}_{obj}(x)}{\hat{s}^2_{obj}(x)} \ . \tag{10}$$

However, the EI can manage only the optimization of the objective and its uncertainty. The existence of the constraints and their uncertainties (9) requires the use of an additional technique to manage the feasibility of the search, and the uncertainty about this feasibility. An approach is to use the EI method coupled with a penalty function for the constraints. But this approach would neglect the uncertainty about the constraints (uncertainty about the feasibility), and could easily lead to a deceptive solution [12],[5]. The Kriging variance enables to use an additional technique to account for the constraints uncertainty, which is the probability of improvement (PI) [12],[13]. This technique considers the expected value of the Kriging metamodel (that represents a constraint) at a certain untrained point as a random variable $Y_{const}(x)$, which is normally distributed with a mean equal to the kriging prediction at this point $\hat{y}_{const}(x)$, and a variance equal to the kriging variance $\hat{s}^2_{const}(x)$. Assuming a maximum acceptable value of the constraint is T (the constraints limit), and its current value $fconst$, when exploring a new untrained point x, the probability of improving our current $fconst$ beyond T (the probability of feasibility) is modeled as the probability that $Y_{const}(x) \leq T$ [10]. Assuming the random variable is normally distributed, this probability is given by (11). The probability of improvement (PI) is calculated for each one of the constraints metamodels[14],[12],[5].

$$PI(x) = P(Y_{cons}(x) \leq T) = \phi\left(\frac{T - \hat{y}_{const}(x)}{\hat{s}^2_{const}(x)}\right) \ . \tag{11}$$

$$CEI = \log E[I(x)] + \sum_{m=1}^{M-1} \log PI_m(x) . \qquad (12)$$

Combining the EI criterion and the PI criterion of each constraint(11), we obtain the Constrained Expected Improvement (CEI) criterion or method (12), [12],[5], which minimizes an objective function subjected to constraints, all of them represented by Kriging metamodels. The optimization technique works iteratively: in each iteration, it finds the point x^* which maximizes the CEI criterion, evaluates the real complex process model at x^* to obtain the corresponding output y^*, adds the point $[x^*y^*]$ to the original metamodels training set, and then refits the Kriging metamodels. The point that maximizes the CEI criterion is the point in the metamodels domain that has minimum prediction value of the objective, maximum prediction variances, and highest probability of satisfying the constraints. So, the CEI method does not only conduct the search to well suited solutions to the proposed optimization problem, but also improves the metamodels accuracy during the optimization to reduce the uncertainties [12],[13]. The stopping criterion of CEI optimization technique is the number of iterations specified by the modeler. The maximization of the CEI criterion is accomplished by a genetic algorithm due to the sophisticated nature of CEI function, that can deceive classical derivative based optimizers. The variables boundaries are represented in the metamodels domain limits[12],[5].

3   Methodology Steps

The previously described techniques and tools should be properly coordinated, in order to deal to a robust and efficient optimization methodology. The following steps are proposed:

1. Explore the complex first principle model to identify the M variables of interest (objective function and constraints). Then, identify the set of k independent variables (optimization/control variables) and their bounds (metamodel domain).
2. Over the metamodels domain, design a sampling plan with a certain number of sample points $n.([X]_{n \times k})$
3. Evaluate the process/model at these sampling points $[X]_{n \times k}$, and get the corresponding matrix of observations $[Y]_{n \times M}$.
4. Fit the M kriging metamodels by maximizing the likelihood of the observed data $[XY]$. This optimization is performed using a genetic algorithm.
5. Validate the kriging metamodels (only in the first iteration).
6. Maximize the CEI criterion, and get the optimal solution point x^*. Maximization of the CEI criterion is carried out using a genetic algorithm.
7. Evaluate the real process / model at x^* and get y^*.
8. Add the new point $[x^*y^*]$ to the original matrix of observations $[XY]$.
9. Stop if the stopping criterion is satisfied, otherwise return to step (4) and continue iterations.

4   Applications

4.1   Mathematical Examples

Peaks [2], Branin [6], Six-hump Camel Back [3], and Gomez functions [12] are well-known mathematical examples for global nonlinear optimization, because of their multimodality and high nonlinearity. In this paper, scaled versions of those functions between [0 1] are used.

1. Minimize the peaks function (13), subjected to one constraint (14) .

$$f_{peaks} = 3(1 - x_1)^2 \exp\left(-x_2^2 - (x_2 + 1)^2\right) - 10\left(\frac{x_1}{5} - x_1^3 - x_2^5\right) \dots$$

$$\dots \exp(-x_1^2 - x_2^2) - \frac{1}{3}\exp\left(-(x_1 + 1)^2 - x_2^2\right) , \qquad -2 \le x_1, x_2 \le 2 . \quad (13)$$

$$x_1^2 + 4x_2^2 < 1.7 . \quad (14)$$

2. Minimize the Branin function (15), subjected to one constraint (16)

$$f_{Branin} = \left(x_2 - \frac{5.1}{4\pi^2}x_1^2 + \frac{5}{\pi}x_1 - 6\right)^2 + 10\left(1 - \frac{1}{8\pi}\cos(x_1)\right) + 10 . \quad (15)$$

$$, \qquad -5 \le x_1 \le 10, \quad 0 \le x_2 \le 15 .$$

$$f_{peaks} < -2 . \quad (16)$$

3. Minimize the Six-hump camel back function (17), subjected to one constraint (18).

$$f_{camel} = (4 - 2.1x_1^2 + \frac{x_1^4}{3})x_1^2 + x_1 x_2 + (-4 + 4x_2^2)x_2^2 . \quad (17)$$

$$, \qquad -2 \le x_1 \le 2, \quad 1 \le x_2 \le 1 .$$

$$f_{gomez} > 3 . \quad (18)$$

$$f_{gomez} = (4 - 2x_1^2 + \frac{x_1^4}{3})x_1^2 + x_1 x_2 - (-4 + 4x_2^2)x_2^2 + 3\sin(6(1 - x_1)) + 3\sin(6(1 - x_2)) .$$

$$, \qquad 0 \le x_1, x_2 \le 1 .$$

In each example, a SLHS technique is used to generate initial sampling plan of 19 sample points to fit the kriging metamodels. The proposed methodology has been applied to each example with two different values of the stopping criterion (no. of iterations), to show the algorithm abilities. The methodology is also compared to the case of using the orginal mathimatical model with a classical sequential quadratic programming (SQP) optimizer. In each of the three examples, the objective is subjected to only one constraint, so the methodology fits two kriging metamodels (one for the objective and the other for the constraint). The scaled results of the examples are summarized in Table.1, and visualized in Fig.1. The table shows how the methodology provides accurate results with a smaller number of function evaluations than the SQP traditional method. Although, since

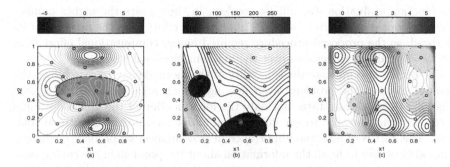

Fig. 1. Constrained optimizations using the methodology of example 1 (a), example 2 (b), and example 3 (b); the shaded or colored areas are the feasible regions, o is the original samples set, ◁ is the optimization samples (iterations), □ is the real optimal point

Table 1. Results obtained for the constrained optimization of the examples

	Real model + SQP	CEI	
		(iter=4)	(iter=8)
Example(1)			
Optimal objective	-2.977	-2.886	-2.95
Optimal variables (x1,x2)	(0.183, 0.539)	(0.200, 0.564)	(0.192, 0.553)
No. of kriging models	0	2	2
Func. eval. (kriging model)	0	19	19
Func. eval. (Optimization)	75	4	8
Initial Sample design time	0	10.63	10.6
Computer experiment time	0	0.008	0.008
Optimization time	0.13	30.7	68.1
Example(2)			
Optimal objective	0.397	0.434	0.398
Optimal variables (x1, x2)	(0.542, 0.152)	(0.538,0.163)	(0.543,0.152)
No. of kriging models	0	2	2
Func. eval. (kriging model)	0	19	19
Func. eval. (Optimization)	80	4	8
Initial Sample design time	0	10.49	10.49
Computer experiment time	0	0.014	0.014
Optimization time	0.21	25.8	50.5
Example(3)			
Optimal objective	-0.975	-0.667	-0.913
Optimal variables (x1, x2)	(0.447,0.864)	(0.397,0.877)	(0.439, 0.831)
No. of kriging models	0	2	2
Func. eval. (kriging model)	0	19	19
Func. eval. (Optimization)	35	4	8
Initial Sample design time	0	10.47	10.47
Computer experiment time	0	0.017	0.017
Optimization time	0.577	34.42	63.91

the function evaluation was almost costless, in these cases the higher number of evaluations required (by the SQP) implied less effort than the fitting process overhead, so the proposed procedure required higher computational effort than the use of traditional methods over the mathematical real model.

The results also indicate the capability of the methodology to search over the whole domain of the problem, even moving among separated feasible regions (Fig.1(b,c)), which facilitates not only the identification of the global optimum of the problem, but also to get information about alternative suboptimal solutions. This fact is of essential importance in real engineering problems, where it is not always easy to fit all the information about the problem in the corresponding mathematical terms (objective function and/or constrains) and local optima may represent alternative solutions. So, human practical know-how may be supported through this additional information to make a final decision. Additionally, this characteristic eliminates the need to repeat the optimization departing from different initial points, which is a drawback of other local optimization methods. Finally, it is worth to note that the algorithm not only optimizes during iterations, but also improves the accuracy of the metamodels. So, if an area/point showing high prediction uncertainties, it will maximize the merit value (CEI (12)) in spite of its eventual unfeasibility - see Fig.1(b) -, and will attract the optimizer to explore it, and add it to the original set of training points. In the next iterations, the effect of the uncertainties on the merit value (CEI) will be reduced, and the effect of the areas or points that have high probabilities of feasibility will dominate the merit, and will force the optimizer to return to the feasible area. In this sense, the methodology is insensitive to the initial solution, simply because it does not need an initial solution to start the optimization. On the contrary, when optimizing examples 1, 2, 3 with classical SQP optimizers, more than 50% of the optimization trails fail to find even feasible solutions, and a lot of effort was dedicated to find a feasible initial solution. Additionally, the methodology is responsive for the tunning of the stopping criterion.

5   Utility Plant Case Study

This case study Fig.2, is based on a utility plant which supplies the required energy to an industrial process, as electrical and thermal energy demands. The system is composed of a boiler that receives water and supplies high pressure steam, which is distributed to three steam turbines, and to the low pressure steam header, which collects the outlet steam from the three steam turbines. The outlet steam is cooled and the water is taken to a deaerator to remove the dissolved gases from it. After that, demineralized water is added to compensate for plant losses, and the water is pumped back to the boiler inlet. The process is modeled using the Aspen Hysys modeling environment.

The objective is the minimization of the operational cost of the utility plant, which is the summation of the operational cost of these described units (boiler, turbines, deaerator, and pump) plus the cost of the required resources (cooling water, demineralized water and energy). These costs were calculated using the

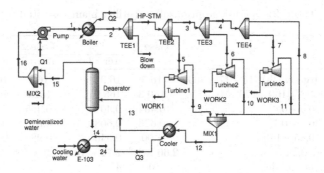

Fig. 2. Aspen model of the utility plant case study

correlations presented in [1]. The operational cost [*OPRcost*] is modeled as a function of five optmization variables (input, independent, or control variables), which are; the boiler outlet steam temperature and flow rate [*STMtemp, STMflrt*], and the steam split fractions to the three turbines [*SFTUR1, SFTUR2, SFTUR3*]. There are power demand constraints at the three turbines, required to maintain a minimum efficiency [*Work1* ≥ 35000 kW, *Work2* ≥ 25000 kW, and *Work3* ≥ 15000 kW]. The case study has been solved with two different techniques summarized in Table.2: in case (1), the optimization has been achieved using the complex original process (Aspen Plus) model and the SQP optimizer integrated in MATLAB; in case (2), the proposed framework with three different stopping criteria has been used. The process outputs in interest are four which includes the objective and the three constraints [*OPRcost, Work1, Work2, Work3*]. So, in case (2), four Kriging metamodels were fitted (one for each of the outputs) using SLHS technique to generate sampling plan of 45 points.

When compared with case (1), the proposed framework requires a significantly lower number of function evaluations, and the overall computational effort is also significantly reduced, leading to very similar operating set points. The constraint violations of the SQP optimizer and the proposed optimization method were zeros for this case study, and also for the previous three examples.

The reduction of the computational effort is much greater in successive uses of the algorithm, which will make use of the already fitted metamodels and so will avoid the computational load associated to the initial metamodels generation. But the main advantage of the proposed procedure, especially when dealing with complex highly nonlinear systems, is its computational reliability, which is basic in the day-to-day optimization of the operating conditions in situations which require fast decision-making: Further the computational load (case(1)) associated to the optimization itself, the evaluation of first-principle based model during an optimization procedure may require a huge quantity of time and human effort to redress the computational system from eventual failures, inconsistencies and convergence problems caused by the evaluation of the model for incompatible input combinations the optimizer may try. And additionally, if specific simulation tools are used (e.g. Aspen), it is not easy to make them compatible with

Table 2. Operation optimization (utility plant case study)

	Case 1	Case 2		
		iter=3	iter=5	iter=9
STMflrt (Kgmole/h) [15 - 17]×3600	16.5	16.9	16.8	16.6
STMtemp ($C°$)[160 - 170]	160.3	165.9	162.5	163.7
SFTUR1 [0.4 - 0.6]	0.464	0.46	0.465	0.462
SFTUR2 [0.5 - 0.7]	0.623	0.608	0.620	0.615
SFTUR3 [0.85 - 1.0]	1.00	0.940	0.980	0.990
OPRcost ($/year)	2.66×10^6	2.72×10^6	2.69×10^6	2.68×10^6
No. of kriging models	0	4	4	4
Function eval. (kriging)	0	45	45	45
Function eval. (optimization)	270	3	5	9
Sampling design time in sec	0	49	49	49
Experiment time	0	108	108	108
Optimization time in sec	993	64	106	226
Total no. of function eval.	270	48	50	54
Total time (s)	993	221	263	383
Computational reliability	60%	100%		

standard optimization software tools (e.g. Matlab). Finally, in the previous applications the SQP optimizer failed many times to find the global optima, and in some times failed even to find a feasible solution. The proposed Kriging based methodology integrates the model with the optimization algorithm, and uses the first principle model just in a relatively few evaluations, reducing dramatically the problems associated to these computational issues.

6 Conclusion

In this paper, a Kriging based framework is presented for nonlinear constrained optimization, applicable to the day-to-day operation of complex processes. The framework gathers many tools as sampling design, kriging, LOOCV, and optimization techniques as (CEI) method. The CEI technique shows a great behavior in handling the uncertainties in both objective and constraints during optimization, in front of other methods currently in use. The results clearly show how the use of the kriging metamodels coupled with the CEI overcomes many drawbacks of the traditional optimizers in complex process operation optimization, significantly increasing the reliability of the numerical process, and simultaneously reducing the number of required function evaluations and optimization time, saving the effort usually required to find a feasible initial solution, avoiding local optima, providing accurate solutions, and exploring separated feasible regions in constrained optimization.

Acknowledgments. Financial support received from the projects SIGERA (DPI2012-37154-C02-01) and EHMAN (DPI2009-09386) both funded by the Spanish Ministerio de Economa y Competitividad, and the European Regional Development Fund (ERDF) is fully appreciated.

References

1. Bruno, J.C., Fernandez, F., Castells, F., Grossmann, E.I.: A Rigorous MINLP Model for The Optimal Synthesis and Operation of Utility Plants. Chemical Engineering Research and Designl 76, 246–258 (1998)
2. Caballero, J.A., Grossmann, I.E.: An Algorithm for The Use of Surrogate Models in Modular Flowsheet Optimization. AICHEl 54, 2633–2650 (2008)
3. Davis, E., Ierapetritou, M.: A kriging method for the solution of nonlinear programs with black-box functions. AIChE 53, 2001–2012 (2007)
4. Fang, K.-T., Li, R., Sudjianto, A.: Design and Modelling for Computer Experiment. Chapman and Hall/CRC, New York (2006)
5. Forrester, A., Sobester, A., Keane, A.: Engineering Design Via Surrogate Modelling. John Wiley and Sons, Southampton (2008)
6. Jones, D.R.: A Taxonomy of Global Optimization Methods Based on Response Surfaces. Journal of Global Optimization 21, 345–383 (2001)
7. Kohavi, R.: A Study of Cross Validation and Bootstrap for Accuacy Estimation and Model Selection. In: Proceedings of the 14th International Joint Conference on Artificial Intelligencel, IJCAI 1995, vol. 2, pp. 1137–1143 (1995)
8. Kushner, H.J.: A New Method of Locating The Maximum Point of an Arbitrary Multipeak Curve in The Presence of Noise. Journal of Basic Engineering 86, 97–106 (1964)
9. Locatelli, M.: Bayesian Algorithms for One-Dimensional Global Optimization. Journal of Global Optimization 10, 57–76 (1997)
10. Meckesheimer, M., Booker, A.J., Barton, R.R., Simpson, T.W.: Computationally Inexpensive Metamodel Assessment Strategies. American Institute of Aeronautics and Astronautics Journall 40, 2053–2060 (2002)
11. Mitchell, T.J., Morris, M.D.: Bayesian design and analysis of computer experiments: two examples. Statistica Sinica 2, 359–379 (1992)
12. Parr, J.M., Holden, C.M.E., Forrester, A.I.J., Keane, A.J.: Review of Efficient Surrogate Infill Sampling Criteria With Constraint Handling. In: 2nd International Conference on Engineering Optimization (2010)
13. Sasena, M.J.: Flexibility and Efficiency Enhancements for Constrained Global Design Optimization with Kriging Approximations. PhD Thesis, University of Michigan (2002)
14. Schonlau, M., Welch, W.J., Jones, D.R.: Global Versus Local Search in Constrained Optimization of Computer Models. IMS Lecture Notes-Monograph Series, vol. 34 (1998)
15. Shokry, A., Bojarski, A.D., Espua, A.: Using Surrogate Models for Process Design and Optimization. Uncertainty Modeling in Knowledge Engineering and Decision Making 7, 483–488 (2012)

Various Problems of Artificial Intelligence

A New Measure of Conflict and Hybrid Combination Rules in the Evidence Theory

Ludmila Dymova[1], Pavel Sevastjanov[1],
and Kamil Tkacz[1], and Tatyana Cheherava[2]

[1] Institute of Comp.& Information Sci., Czestochowa University of Technology,
Dabrowskiego 73, 42-200 Czestochowa, Poland
http://www.icis.pcz.pl/
[2] Mogilev State A. Kuleshov University, Kosmonavtov str., 1, Mogilev,
212022, Mogilev, Belarus
http://www.msu.mogilev.by

Abstract. Based on the critical analysis of methods for evaluation of conflict between basic probability assignments (*bpas*) to be combined and combination rules in the Dempster-Shafer theory of evidence, a new simple, but reliable method for the evaluation of conflict between combining *bpas* is proposed and analysed. Using some critical examples, it is shown that the proposed approach performs better than Dempster's rule and the known hybrid rule based on the weighted sum of conjunction and disjunction operators. It is shown that in the case of small conflict, the use of averaging rule for combination of *bpas* seems to be a best choice.

Keywords: Dempster-Shafer Theory of evidence, Conflict between basic probability assignments, Combination rules.

1 Introduction

The core of Dempster-Shafer theory of evidence (DST) is the rule of combination of evidence from different sources. The classical Dempster's rule [21] assumes that information sources are independent and uses the so-called orthogonal sum to combine multiple belief structures. In this rule, the denominator 1-K is used, where, K is called the degree of conflict which measures the conflict between pieces of evidence and the process of dividing by 1 - K is called normalisation. In [28,29], Zadeh has underlined that this normalisation involves counterintuitive behaviors in the case of considerable conflict. Smets [24] proposed unnormalised version of Dempster's rule introduced in the Transferable Belief Model usually referred to as the TBM conjunctive rule. The main limitations of the Dempster's rule and the TBM conjunctive rule seem to be their lack of robustness with respect to conflicting evidence (a criticism which mainly applies to the Dempster's rule), and the requirement that the items of evidence combined be distinct. In order to solve the problem of conflict management, Yager [27], Dubois [3] and some other authors [9,12,18,20] proposed other combination rules.

On the other hand, the problems of conflict management with Dempster's rule (and, to a lesser extent, with the TBM conjunctive rule) are often due to

L. Rutkowski et al. (Eds.): ICAISC 2014, Part II, LNAI 8468, pp. 411–422, 2014.
© Springer International Publishing Switzerland 2014

incorrect or incomplete modelisation of the problem at hand, and these rules often yield reasonable results when they are properly applied [8].

Nevertheless, in practice we often meet situations when a decision should be made in the case of large conflict.

Therefore a wide variety of rules for evidence combination is proposed in the literature. The reviews and classifications of them (obviously, not exhaustive) are presented, for example in [20,23], where the rules are analysed according to their algebraic properties as well as on different examples.

To avoid the problem concerned with the classical Dempster's rule in the case of high conflict, the different hybrid rules were proposed in the literature. In [3], Dubois and Prade proposed to use the combination of non-normalised Dempster's rule and modified disjunction rule defined in [2,4]. Different combinations of the Dempster's and Dubois and Prade's were proposed in the literature [1,5,6,10,17,25]. Usually such rules are based on weighted sums of conjunction and disjunction rules with weights dependent on the conflict K.

But we did not find in the literature hybrid rules based on Dempster's rule and averaging rules considered in [9,12,18,20].

An important problem concerned with hybrid rules, based on weighted sums of known rules with weights dependent on the conflict K, is a proper definition of conflict between sources of evidence. It was shown in [15] that "the value K cannot be used as a quantitative measure of conflict between two beliefs, contrary to what has long been taken as a fact in the Dempster-Shafer theory community." The same conclusion was made in [16].

Therefore, in the current paper with the use of critical examples we analyse some more popular hybrid rules and propose a new hybrid rule based on the weighted sum of Dempster's and averaging rules, which has some advantages in comparison with known hybrid rules. Since the weights used in the proposed new hybrid rule depends on the value of conflict, we propose a new simple definition of conflict between sources of evidence.

The rest of paper is set out as follows. In Section 2, we recall some basic problems concerned with the combination of evidence, analyse some most popular hybrid rules of combination and propose a new hybrid combination rule based on the weighted sum of Dempster's and averaging rules. Section 3 is devoted to the conflict evaluation problem. The existing approach to the solution of this problem is analysed and a new more simple, but reliable approach to the conflict evaluation is proposed. In Section 4, using critical numerical examples we present advantages of the proposed hybrid rule of combination based on the proposed new definition of conflict between sources of evidence. Finally the concluding section summarises the paper.

2   The Hybrid Combination Rules

Currently a wide variety of rules for evidence combination is proposed in the literature. A review of them is presented, for example in [20], where the rules are analysed according to their algebraic properties and using different

examples. A recent review of most popular fusion rules can also be found in
[23]. The most popular in the different applications of DST are the conjunction Dempster's rule of combination [21] and the Dubois and Prade's disjunctive
combination rule [2,4].

The Dempster-Shafer belief structure has associated with it a mapping m,
called basic probability assignment function (bpa), from subset of X into unit
interval, $m : 2^X \to [0,1]$, $m(\emptyset) = 0$, $\sum\limits_{A \subset X} m(A) = 1$.

Then the Dempster's rule of combination is defined us follows.

$$m_{12}(A) = \frac{\sum\limits_{B \cap C = A} m_1(B) m_2(C)}{1 - K}, A \neq \emptyset, m_{12}(\emptyset) = 0, \tag{1}$$

where $K = \sum\limits_{B \cap C = \emptyset} m_1(B) m_2(C)$. The denominator $1 - K$ is called the normalisation, K is called the degree of conflict which measures the conflict between
pieces of evidence and the process of dividing by $1 - K$ is called normalisation.

The main problem with this rule is that it provides counterintuitive results
when the conflict K is close to its maximal value equal to 1.That was first pointed
out by Zadeh [28].

Dubois and Prade's disjunctive combination rule [2,4] is defined as follows:

$$m_{DP}(X) = \sum\limits_{X_1 \cup X_2 = X} m_1(X_1) m_2(X_2). \tag{2}$$

It is noted in [20] that "The union does not generate any conflict and does not
reject any of the information asserted by the sources. As such, no normalisation
procedure is required ".

To reduce the disadvantage of Dempster's rule in the cases of considerable
conflict, the different combinations of Dempster's and Dubois and Prade's rules
were proposed in the literature [1,3,10,17,25].

These combination usually are based on the of conjunction

$$m_\wedge(X) = \sum\limits_{X_1 \cap X_2 = X} m_1(X_1) m_2(X_2) \tag{3}$$

and disjunction

$$m_\vee(X) = \sum\limits_{X_1 \cup X_2 = X} m_1(X_1) m_2(X_2) \tag{4}$$

rules.

For example, in [3] Dubois and Prade proposed the rule of combination which
admits that the two sources are reliable when they are not in conflict, but one
of them is right when a conflict occurs. Then if one observes a value in set X_1
while the other observes this value in a set X_2 the truth lies in $X_1 \cap X_2$ as long
$X_1 \cap X_2 \neq \emptyset$. If $X_1 \cap X_2 = \emptyset$ then the truth lies in $X_1 \cup X_2$.

According to this principle, the commutative (but not associative) Dubois
and Prade's hybrid rule of combination (denoted here by index DP), which

is a reasonable trade-off between precision and reliability, is defined for $\emptyset$ by $m_{DP}(\emptyset) = 0$ and for $(\forall X \neq \emptyset) \in 2^\theta, X \neq 0$ by

$$m_{DP}(X) = \sum_{\substack{X_1 \cap X_2 = X \\ X_1 \cap X_2 \neq \emptyset}} m_1(X_1)m_2(X_2) + \sum_{\substack{X_1 \cup X_2 = X \\ X_1 \cap X_2 = \emptyset}} m_1(X_1)m_2(X_2). \qquad (5)$$

But usually the hybrid rules are based on weighted sums of conjunction and disjunction rules with weights dependent on the conflict K.

For example, in [5] the following rule was proposed

$$m(X) = \alpha(K)m_\vee(X) + \beta(K)m_\wedge(X), \qquad (6)$$

where $\alpha(K) = \frac{K}{1-K+K^2}$, $\beta(K) = \frac{1-K}{1-K+K^2}$.

In [6], the set of functions $\alpha(K)$ and $\beta(K)$ was proposed. These functions have the following properties:
1). $\alpha(K)$ is an increasing function with $\alpha(0) = 0$ and $\alpha(1) = 1$,
2). $\beta(K)$ is a decreasing function with $\beta(0) = 1$ and $\beta(1) = 0$,
3). $\alpha(K) = 1 - (1 - K)\beta(K)$.
The links of approach based on (6) and proposed set of functions $\alpha(K)$ and $\beta(K)$ with other existing rules is analysed. On the other hand, the use of disjunction rule $m_\vee(X)$ to reduce the undesirable properties of conjunction rule $m_\wedge(X)$ in the case of considerable conflict is not exclusive and the best in all cases approach to develop hybrid rules with acceptable properties.

It is known that Dempster's and Dubois and Prade's rules are not idempotent. Hence, the hybrid combinations (5) and (6) may provide non-acceptable results when we deal with the absence of conflict or a low conflict between *bpas*. On the other hand, the simplest averaging rule $m_{12}(A) = \frac{1}{2}(m_1(A) + m_2(A))$ is idempotent one.

Therefore, we can say that the combination of Dempster's rule with the averaging rule seems to be more justified than the combination of Dempster's rule with Dubois and Prade's rule since the averaging rule provides reasonable results in the case of large conflict and a true result in the case when there is no conflict between sources of evidence.

Although, the averaging rule of combination is idempotent and has some other desirable properties, they are not often used in the framework of DST.

Matsuyama et al. [18] proposed an integration method based on the mean of basic probability assignment $m(C) = \sum_{A_i \cap B_j = C, C \neq \emptyset} \frac{m(A_i) + m(B_j)}{2}$. This rule is very different from Dempster's and Dubois and Prade's rules. Similar to Matsuyama's rule, Horiuchi [9] proposed a weighted integration method to give different source the different weights in combination:
$$m(C) = \sum_{A_i \cap B_j = C} (w_i m(A_i) + w_j m(B_j)), \; (w_i + w_j) = 1.$$
The difference between Horiuchi's rule and Matsuyama's rule is that, the Horiuchi's rule adds a weight factor to each source of evidence, and conflicting information is not assigned zero probability, while Matsuyama's rule treats different sources of evidence equally, and conflicting information is assigned zero probability.

In [12], the following rule was proposed: $m(A) = \frac{1}{N} \sum_{i=1}^{N} m_i(A)$, where N is the number of independent sources to combine.

The similar approaches was proposed in [20]. The formula for the "mixing" combination rule is just

$$m_{1,2,\dots,n}(A) = \frac{1}{n} \sum_{i=1}^{n} w_i m_i(A), \tag{7}$$

where m_i's are *bpas* for the belief structures being aggregated and w_i's are weights assigned according to the reliability of sources.

Of course, the mixing combination rule (as well as any other method) have some disadvantages. For example, in [19], the author noted that the averaging lacks correspondence with Bayesian conditioning. In [22] , the averaging rule is qualified as "too mechanical, not well justified".

Let us define the averaging rule for two sources of evidence as follow:
$m_{12}^{A}(C) = \frac{1}{2} (m_1(C) + m_2(C))$
(this is a simplification of the more general definition (7)) and $m_{12}^{D}(C)$ be the result obtained using Dempster's rule (1).

Then the hybrid rule may be defined as follows:

$$m_{12}^{H}(A) = Mcm_{12}^{A}(A) + (1 - Mc)m_{12}^{D}(A), \tag{8}$$

where Mc is the measure of conflict such that it is equal to 1 in the case of full conflict and equal to 0 when there is no conflict between two sources of evidence, i.e,. they are identical ones.

Of course, different functions $\alpha(Mc)$ and $\beta(Mc)$ as in [6] may be used in (8), but if we have no reasons to select a best such function, the simplest approach $\alpha(Mc) = Mc$, $\beta(Mc) = 1 - Mc$ seems to be enough justified.

3   The Measure of Conflict

Traditionally the value of $K = \sum_{B \cap C = \emptyset} m_1(B)m_2(C)$ is treated as the measure of conflict, but it is easy to show that it does not always satisfy desirable properties of the measure of conflict.

Let us consider the following examples:

Example 1
$m_1(A) = 0, m_1(B) = 0, m_1(A, B) = 1,$
$m_2(A) = 0, m_2(B) = 0.75, m_2(A, B) = 0.25.$
Example 2
$m_1(A) = 0.01, m_1(B) = 0.01, m_1(A, B) = 0.98,$
$m_2(A) = 0.01, m_2(B) = 0.6, m_2(A, B) = 0.39.$
Example 3
$m_1(A) = 0.7, m_1(B) = 0.2, m_1(A, B) = 0.1,$
$m_2(A) = 0.2, m_2(B) = 0.7, m_2(A, B) = 0.1.$

Example 4
$m_1(A) = 0.1, m_1(B) = 0.6, m_1(A, B) = 0.3,$
$m_2(A) = 0.1, m_2(B) = 0.6, m_2(A, B) = 0.3.$
Example 5
$m_1(A) = 0.3, m_1(B) = 0.4, m_1(A, B) = 0.3,$
$m_2(A) = 0.3, m_2(B) = 0.4, m_2(A, B) = 0.3.$
Example 6
$m_1(A) = 0.98, m_1(B) = 0.01, m_1(A, B) = 0.01,$
$m_2(A) = 0.01, m_2(B) = 0.98, m_2(A, B) = 0.01.$
Example 7
$m_1(A) = 1, m_1(B) = 0, m_1(A, B) = 0,$
$m_2(A) = 0, m_2(B) = 1, m_2(A, B) = 0.$
The results of calculations of K for these examples are presented in Table 1. (in this table, Mc is a new measure of conflict, which will be defined below).

Table 1. The value of K and the measure of conflict Mc

Example	K	Mc
3	0	0.75
4	0.0061	0.59
5	0.53	0.5
6	0.12	0
7	0.24	0
8	0.9605	0.97
9	1	1

We can see that in the Example 1 we have $K=0$ and therefore we should treat the sources of evidence as not conflicting, whereas they are not identical, and therefore some non-zero conflict exists. Since the differences between corresponding focal elements of the sources in Example 1 are greater than in the Example 2, we can conclude that the conflict in Example 1 is greater than in the Example 2, and therefore the value of K in Example 1 should be greater than in Example 4. But in Table 1, we see the opposite situation.

In the examples 4 and 5 we deal with the identical sources of evidence and a true measure of conflict in these example should be equal to 0, whereas in these cases we have $K > 0$.

We can see that only in the cases of large conflict (see examples 6 and 7) , the value of K reflects well the sense of conflict.

Therefore, in [15] Liu states that "K only represent the mass of uncommitted belief (or falsely committed belief) as a result of combination" and that the "value K cannot be used as a quantitative measure of conflict between two beliefs, contrary to what has long been taken as a fact in the Dempster-Shafer theory community." In [16], Martin *et al.* showed that the value of K is not appropriate to characterise the conflict between mass functions.

Therefore, other approaches to the evaluation of the measure of conflict between sources of evidence were proposed. The methods based on the treatment of conflict as a difference between sources of evidence were analysed in [7]. In [15], Liu proposed the method for evaluating the conflict using the distance between betting commitments of beliefs. To develop this method some known and new definitions were used.

Definition 1. [26]. Let m be a *bpa* on Ω. Its associative pignistic probability function $BetP_m \colon \Omega \to [0,1]$ is defined as $BetP_m(w) = \sum\limits_{A \subseteq \Omega, w \in A} \frac{1}{|A|} \frac{m(A)}{1-K}$, $K \neq 1$, where $|A|$ is the cardinality of subset A.

$BetP_m$ can be extended as a function on 2^Ω as $BetP_m(A) = \sum_{w \in A} BetP_m(w)$. The transformation from m to $BetP_m$ is called the pignistic transformation . When the initial *bpa* gives $K = 0$, $\frac{m(A)}{1-K}$ is reduced to $m(A)$. It is assumed in [15] that the function $BetP_m$ has been extended to 2^Ω. $BetP_m(A)$ tells what is the total mass value that A can carry and it is referred to as the betting commitment to A. In [11], the function $BetP_m$ is named the probability expectation function.

Definition 2. [15]. Let m_1 and m_2 be two *bpas* on frame Ω and let $BetPm_1$ and $BetPm_2$ be the results of two pignistic transformations from them respectively. Then $difBetP = \max_{A \subseteq \Omega} (|BetP_{m_1}(A) - BetP_{m_2}(A)|)$ is called the distance between betting commitments of two *bpas*. The value $|BetP_{m_1}(A) - BetP_{m_2}(A)|$ is the difference between betting commitments to A from two sources.

The distance between betting commitments is therefore the maximum extent of the differences between betting commitments to all the subsets. Obviously, $difBetP=0$ whenever $m_1 = m_2$, i.e., the distance between betting commitments is always equal to 0 between any two identical *bpas* (total absence of conflict).

Given two *bpas* and their corresponding pignistic transformations, it is possible that these two *bpas* have the same betting commitment to a subset A that is, $BetP_{m_1}(A)=BetP_{m_2}(A))$, but have rather different betting commitments to another subset B. For this reason, according to Liu [15], "we cannot use either min or mean to replace operator max in the above definition, since we want to find out the maximum, not the minimum or the average, level of differences between their betting commitments."

In our opinion, the last statement seems to be debatable and is not justified enough. Therefore, in this paper we propose another more simple and intuitively obvious definition of the distance between two *bpas*, which can serve as the measure of conflict Mc between sources of evidence.

The comprehensive survey and generalisations of distances in evidence theory provided in [14], makes it possible to conclude that the other definitions of distance between *bpas* should provide the results similar to those obtained in [15]. In [15], Liu proposed the following definition.

Definition 3. Let m_1 and m_2 be two *bpas*. Then $cf(m_1, m_2)=\langle K, difBetP \rangle$ be a two-dimensional measure, where $K = \sum\limits_{B \cap C = \emptyset} m_1(B)m_2(C)$ is the mass of uncommitted belief when combining m_1 and m_2 with Dempster's rule and $difBetP$ be the distance between betting commitments in Definition 2. Then

m_1 and m_2 are defined as in conflict if both $difBetP > \varepsilon$ and $K > \varepsilon$ hold, where $\varepsilon \in [0,1]$ is the threshold of conflict tolerance.

Obviously, it is difficult to use this definition based on the two-dimensional measure of conflict to represent the degree of conflict in such hybrid rules as (6) and (8). It easy to show that this definition may provide controversial results (see Example 1 and Table 1, where $K = 0$ in the case of evident conflict). Moreover, although in the case of two identical $bpas$ a true degree of conflict should be equal to 0, the value of K may be considerable greater than 0 (see examples 3,4 and Table 1).

Summarising we can say that the value of K should be used only in the calculation of normalisation factor in Dempster's rule of combination, not for the evaluation of conflict between $bpas$.

In our opinion, Definition 3 is a consequence of too restrictive treatment of conflict in [15] : "A conflict between two beliefs in DS theory can be interpreted qualitatively as one source strongly supports one hypothesis and the other strongly supports another hypothesis, and the two hypotheses are not compatible".

Here, we propose another treatment of conflict and the measure of conflict.

Suppose we have two identical $bpas$. Then the degree of conflict should be equal to 0, but if we introduce even a very small change in these $bpas$, and they become not identical, then a small conflict occurs.

Therefore, it seems natural to define the measure of conflict as the mean of differences between corresponding focal elements:

$$Mc(m_1, m_2) = \frac{1}{N_C} \sum_{|m_{1i} - m_{2i}| > 0} |m_{1i} - m_{2i}|, \qquad (9)$$

where N_C is the number of differences contributing into conflict. Opposite to the $difBetP$ (see Definition 2.) this measure of conflict compensates the great differences between some focal elements by low differences between other ones.

To illustrate the introduced measure of conflict (9), consider the following example:

Example 8
$m_1(A) = 0.1, m_1(B) = 0.4, m_1(A,B) = 0.5,$
$m_2(A) = 0.1, m_2(B) = 0.2, m_2(A,B) = 0.7.$
In this case we have $N_C = 2$ and
$Mc(m_1, m_2) = \frac{1}{2}(|m_1(B) - m_2(B)| + |m_1(A,B) - m_2(A,B)|) = 0.2.$
We can see that the introduced new measure of conflict has good properties (see Table 1).

4   Numerical Examples

Let us compare the results obtained using Dempster's rule (1), the rule (6) modified as follows $m(A) = Mcm_\vee(A) + (1 - Mc)m_\wedge(A)$, the rule (8) and the averaging rule $m(A) = \frac{1}{N} \sum_{i=1}^{N} m_i(A)$ on the base of examples 1-7.

Table 2. The results obtained using Dempster's rule (1)

Example	Mc	$m_{12}(A)$	$m_{12}(B)$	$m_{12}(A,B)$
1	0.75	0	0.75	0.25
2	0.59	0.01388	0.6559	0.3845
3	0.5	0.48936	0.48936	0.0213
4	0	0.07954	0.81818	0.10227
5	0	0.35526	0.52631	0.11842
6	0.97	0.49873	0.49873	0.00253
7	1	0/0	0/0	0/0

Table 3. The results obtained using the rule (6): $m(A) = Mc m_\vee(A) + (1 - Mc)m_\wedge(A)$

Example	Mc	$m_{12}(A)$	$m_{12}(B)$	$m_{12}(A,B)$
1	0.75	0	0.75	0.8125
2	0.59	0.0174	0.62364	0.73304
3	0.5	0.495	0.495	0.1
4	0	0.07	0.72	0.09
5	0	0.27	0.40	0.09
6	0.97	0.9803	0.9803	0.0198
7	1	1	1	0

The results are presented in Tables 5-5.

It is seen that in the examples 1 and 3 (see Section 3), the sums (from both *bpas*) of values of arguments in favor of (A, B) are greater than in favor of B. Therefore, it is intuitively obvious that in these examples after combination we should expect $m_{12}(A, B) > m_{12}(B)$. We can see that such results are obtained for the rules (6), (8) and averaging rule (see tables 3-5), but Dempster's rule provides counterintuitive results (see Table 2).

All the analysed rules provide intuitively obvious results for the examples 3 and 6. In the examples 6 and 7, we deal with the identical *bpas*. Therefore, only idempotent averaging rule provides true results. In the example 7, the result of Dempster's rule is not defined as in this case we deal with the dividing by 0 since $K=1$ and 1-K=0 (see Table 1). In this example, the other analysed combination rules provide good results which can be naturally treated as fifty-fifty chances for A and B.

Therefore, we can say that the rules (6), (8) and averaging rule performs better than Dempster's rule, but the averaging rule provides the better results than the rules (6) and (8) as it provides true results in both asymptotical cases: in the case of full conflict and in the case of lack of conflict.

It is worth noting that in practice we often deal with *bpas* characterizing by relatively low conflict Mc. It is clear that in such cases the use of not idempotent Dempster's rule and the rules (6) and (8) may provide inappropriate numerical results (see examples 4 and 5). Obviously, in such cases the use of averaging rule seems to be the best choice.

Table 4. The results obtained using the rule (8): $m_{12}^H(A)=Mcm_{12}^A(A)+(1-Mc)m_{12}^D(A)$

Example	Mc	$m_{12}(A)$	$m_{12}(B)$	$m_{12}(A,B)$
1	0.75	0	0.46875	0.53125
2	0.59	0.01159	0.44887	0.56180
3	0.5	0.46968	0.46968	0.06065
4	0	0.07954	0.81818	0.10227
5	0	0.35526	0.52631	0.11842
6	0.97	0.49511	0.49511	0.0097
7	1	0.5	0.5	0

Table 5. The results obtained using the averaging rule $m(A) = \frac{1}{N}\sum_{i=1}^{N} m_i(A)$

Example	Mc	$m_{12}(A)$	$m_{12}(B)$	$m_{12}(A,B)$
1	0.75	0	0.375	0.625
2	0.59	0.01	0.305	0.685
3	0.5	0.45	0.45	0.1
4	0	0.1	0.6	0.3
5	0	0.3	0.4	0.3
6	0.97	0.495	0.495	0.01
7	1	0.5	0.5	0

A good property of averaging rule is that it provides normalised combined bpas if initial bpas are normalised too. It is seen that using averaging rule (7), it is possible in a natural way to take into account the reliabilities (or weighs) of combined sources of evidence.

Summarising, we can say that the averaging rule can be used solely to combine bpas. Of course, this rule seems to be too simple, but simple methods are not always bad or wrong ones.

On the other hand, we belief that choosing an appropriate combination rule is a context dependent problem. We can say that the use of rule (6) in practice is difficult as it provides non-normalised results.

Therefore, taking into account that Dempster's rule is currently the most popular method for the combination of bpas we can advise the use of hybrid rule (8) which provides normalised bpas when combined initial bpas are normalised too. Nevertheless, we should remember that this hybrid rule may provide unacceptable results when we combine bpas with a low conflict Mc.

5   Conclusion

A critical analysis of methods for evaluation of conflict between basic probability assignments (bpas) to be combined and combination rules in the Dempster-Shafer theory of evidence is presented. A new simply, but reliable method for the evaluation of conflict between combining bpas is proposed and analysed. Based on this method, a new approach to the combination of bpas based on the weighted sum of Dempster's and averaging rules with weighs dependent on the proposed value of conflict is developed. Using some critical examples, it is shown that the proposed approach performs better than Dempster's rule and the known hybrid rule based on the weighted sum of conjunction and disjunction operators. Opposite to the known hybrid rules, the proposed new combination rule provides normalised results of combination if the combining *bpas* are normalised too.

It is shown that the averaging rule can be used solely to combine *bpas* and in the case of small conflict the use of averaging rule for the combination of *bpas* seems to a best choice.

A good property of averaging rule is that it provides normalised combined *bpas* if initial *bpas* are normalised too. It is shown that using averaging rule, it is possible in a natural way to take into account the reliabilities (or weighs) of combined sources of evidence.

References

1. Delmotte, F., Dubois, L., Desodt, A., Borne, P.: Using trust in uncertainty theories. Information and Systems Engineering 1, 303–314 (1995)
2. Dubois, D., Prade, H.: A Set-Theoretic View on Belief Functions: Logical Operations and Approximations by Fuzzy Sets. International Journal of General Systems 12, 193–226 (1986)
3. Dubois, D., Prade, H.: Representation and combination of uncertainty with belief functions and possibility measures. Computational Intelligence 4, 244–264 (1988)
4. Dubois, D., Prade, H.: On the combination of evidence in various mathematical frameworks. In: Aamm, J., Luisi, T. (eds.) Reliability Data Collection and Analysis, pp. 213–241 (1992)
5. Florea, M.C., Dezert, J., Valin, P., Smarandache, F., Jousselme, A.L.: Adaptative combination rule and proportional conflict redistribution rule for information fusion. In: Proc. of Int. Conf. on Cognitive Systems with Interactive Sensors, Paris (2006), arXiv:cs/0604042v1
6. Florea, M.C., Jousselme, A.-L., Bossé, É., Grenier, D.: Robust combination rules for evidence theory. Information Fusion 10, 183–197 (2009)
7. Florea, M.C., Bossé, É.: Crisis Management Using Dempster-Shafer Theory: Using Dissimilarity Measures to Characterize Source's Reliability. In: Conference NATO RTO IST-086, Bucharest, May 11-12 (2009), http://ftp.rta.nato.int/public//PubFullText/RTO/MP/RTO-MP-IST-086///MP-IST-086-17.pdf
8. Haenni, R.: Are alternatives to Dempster's rule of combination real alternatives?: Comments on "about the belief function combination and the conflict management problem"-Lefevre et al. Information Fusion 3, 237–239 (2002)
9. Horiuchi, T.: Decision Rule for Pattern Classification by Integrating Interval Feature Value. IEEE Trans. Pattern Analysis and Machine Intelligence 20, 440–448 (1998)
10. Inagaki, T.: Interdependence between Safety-Control Policy and Multiple-Sensor Schemes Via Dempster-Shafer Theory. IEEE Transactions on Reliability 40, 182–188 (1991)
11. Josang, A.: The consensus operator for combining beliefs. Artificial Intelligence 141, 157–170 (2002)

422   L. Dymova et al.

12. Josang, A., Daniel, M., Vannoorenberghe, P.: Strategies for Combining Conflicting Dogmatic Beliefs. In: Proceedings of 6th International Conference on International Fusion, vol. 2, pp. 1133–1140 (2003)
13. Jousselme, A.-L., Grenier, D., Bosse, E.: A new distance between two bodies of evidence. Information Fusion 2, 91–101 (2001)
14. Jousselme, A.-L., Maupin, P.: Distances in evidence theory: Comprehensive survey and generalisations. International Journal of Approximate Reasoning 53, 118–145 (2012)
15. Liu, W.: Analizing the degree of conflict among belief functions. Artificial Intelligence 170, 909–924 (2006)
16. Martin, A., Jousselme, A.-L., Osswald, C.: Conflict measure for the discounting operation on belief functions. In: Proc. of the 11th International Conference on Information Fusion, Cologne, Germany, pp. 1003–1010 (2008)
17. Martin, A., Osswald, C.H., Dezert, J., Smarandache, F.: General Combination Rules for Qualitative and Quantitative Beliefs. Journal of Advances in Information Fusion 3, 67–89 (2008)
18. Matsuyama, T.: Belief Formation From Observation and Belief Integration Using Virtual Belief Space in Dempster-Shafer Probability Model. In: Proc. Multisensor Fusion and Integration for Intelligent Systems (MFI 1994), pp. 379–386 (1994)
19. Murphy, C.K.: Combining Belief Functions When Evidence Conflicts. Decision Support Systems 29, 1–9 (2000)
20. Sentz, K., Ferson, S.: Combination of Evidence in Dempster-Shafer Theory. Sandia National Laboratories SAND, 2002-0835 (2002)
21. Shafer, G.: A mathematical theory of evidence. Princeton University Press, Princeton (1976)
22. Smarandache, F.: An In-Depth Look at Information Fusion Rules and the Unification of Fusion Theories. In: Computing Research Repository (CoRR), vol. cs.OH/0410033, Cornell University arXiv (2004)
23. Smarandache, F.: Unification of Fusion Theories (UFT), May 16-27. NATO Advanced Study Institute, Albena (2005)
24. Smets, P.: The combination of evidence in the transferable belief model. IEEE Transactions on Pattern Analysis and Machine Intelligence 12, 447–458 (1990)
25. Smets, P.: The alpha-junctions: combination operators applicable to belief functions. In: Nonnengart, A., Kruse, R., Ohlbach, H.J., Gabbay, D.M. (eds.) FAPR 1997 and ECSQARU 1997. LNCS, vol. 1244, pp. 131–153. Springer, Heidelberg (1997)
26. Smets, P.: Decision making in the TBM: the necessity of the pignistic transformation. International Journal of Approximate Reasoning 38, 133–147 (2004)
27. Yager, R.R.: On the Dempster-Shafer framework and new combination rules. Information Sciences 41, 93–138 (1987)
28. Zadeh, L.A.: Review of Books: A Mathematical Theory of Evidence. The AI Magazine 5, 81–83 (1984)
29. Zadeh, L.: A simple view of the Dempster-Shafer theory of evidence and its application for the rule of combination. AI Magazine 7, 85–90 (1986)

On Measuring Association between Groups of Rankings in Recommender Systems

Hanna Łącka[1] and Przemysław Grzegorzewski[2,3]

[1] Interdisciplinary PhD Studies at the Polish Academy of Sciences,
Jana Kazimierza 5, 01-248 Warsaw, Poland
[2] Systems Research Institute, Polish Academy of Sciences,
Newelska 6, 01-447 Warsaw, Poland
[3] Faculty of Mathematics and Computer Science,
Warsaw University of Technology,
Koszykowa 75, 00-662 Warsaw, Poland
h.lacka@phd.ipipan.waw.pl
pgrzeg@ibspan.waw.pl

Abstract. A measure of association between two groups of rankings is proposed. The suggested measure possesses some interesting properties which make it useful in recommender systems and some other possible applications. In particular, it aggregates the bipolar information taking into account both the strength of the correlation and its sign. Simultaneously, applied in collaborative filtering, it rewards strong association which is a desired property in making meaningful recommendations to a user.

Keywords: Aggregation function, association measure, bipolarity, collaborative filtering, correlation coefficient, ordering, OWA operator, preference system, ranks, rating, recommender system.

1 Introduction

Nowadays there are many Web applications designed for advising users on what they might like. The most common are applications predicting what movies a user would like to see, or what product a customer might be interested in buying. Besides open Web applications there exist expert software supporting client advisors and various consultants. Both such public like specialist facilities are called *recommendation systems*.

The main goal of a recommender system, i.e. generating some meaningful recommendations to a user, might be perceived as an attempt to predict what rating a user would give to a previously unrated item. Next the highest rated item is presented as a recommendation to that user.

Although recommendation systems use different technologies, we can broadly categorize them as (see, e.g., [1])

- *Collaborative filtering*, which recommend items based on similarity measures between users and/or items. Hence items recommended to a user are those preferred by similar users.

L. Rutkowski et al. (Eds.): ICAISC 2014, Part II, LNAI 8468, pp. 423–432, 2014.

- *Content-based systems*, which examine properties of the item. Hence items recommended are similar in content to other items the user has liked in the past, or the items which matched best the attributes predefined by the user.
- *Hybrid techniques*, i.e. methods combining both collaborative and content-based approaches.

The most popular setting in which a recommender system is considered is a matrix (sometimes called a *utility matrix*) with rows corresponding to clients, columns corresponding to items and cells for each user-item pair containing value that represents the rating given to this item by the user.

In this paper we consider a much more complicated setting where the utility matrix contains attribute columns with possibly different domains and where the entries of the cells for each user-attribute pair contain rankings made by the user for items/objects belonging to the domain of a given attribute. Alternatively, if not provided directly by the user, rankings might be produced from information about items obtained in another way, e.g. from single-value ratings or from frequency of user choices. Therefore, in face of such data much more sophisticated methods of collaborative filtering are required. Actually, instead of similarity measures between users based on correlation between two rankings produced by these users on a set of items under study, we need now a measure of association between two groups of rankings. It seems that some aggregation operators might be helpful to generate a desired recommendation based on such type of data.

The paper is organized as follows: An introductory example explaining the difference between the classical situation considered in recommender systems and the suggested setting is given in Sec. 2. Then, in Sec. 3 a model for the data representation discussed in the introductory example is suggested. In Sec. 4 we discuss the desired properties of the requested measure of association between two sets of rankings. A candidate for such a measure is suggested in Sec. 5, while in Sec. 6 we discuss its actual properties.

2   Introductory Example

Let us consider a travel agency, that gathers a history of vacation trips of its clients. Data are stored in a form of rankings made by the clients and concern various aspects of the trip. For each separate attribute a client assigns ranks to possible variants (which depend on a domain of an attribute), expressing his/her preferences on those variants. In other words, each client orders all available variants corresponding to given attribute from the most preferred to the least preferred one. An exemplary output of a data set described above is given in Table 1, where numbers indicate ranks assigned by the clients.

Such data sets as shown in Table 1 are collected because the agency plans to prepare new trip offers. To maximize the possibility of accepting a new offer it should be prepared in a way that guarantees client's satisfaction when chosen. To achieve this, the agency tries to identify pairs of clients that within most of the considered areas made significantly similar choices (similar clients) or significantly different choices (dissimilar clients). This way the clients will be gathered into similarity groups. For each client the agency will offer trips to places already visited by other clients from the same group, omitting the places visited by most dissimilar clients.

Table 1. Exemplary data set of clients' preferences

	Accommodation	Means of transport	Activities
Client A	tent - 1 guesthouse - 2 hotel - 3	car - 1 train - 2 airplane - 3	sunbathing - 2 sightseeing - 1
Client B	tent - 3 guesthouse - 2 hotel - 1	car - 3 train - 1 airplane - 2	sunbathing - 2 sightseeing - 1
...	...	...	...

3 Data Representation

Keeping in mind the introductory example discussed in Sec. 2 we will introduce a formal description of the data representing consumers profiles.

Let $\mathcal{X}$ denote a set of consumers and let $\mathcal{Y}$ be a set of attributes. Without loss of generality we assume that $\mathcal{Y}$ is a finite set of size n. Moreover, we assume that $\mathcal{U}_j$ is a domain of the attribute $Y_j \in \mathcal{Y}$. Each domain consists of objects, with respect to which the consumers express their preferences. Therefore, it is assumed that the domain of each attribute is finite.

Hence, for any consumer $A \in \mathcal{X}$ we get n rankings corresponding to successive attributes, so the observation related to A might be perceived as a vector $[R_{A1}, R_{A2} \ldots, R_{An}]$, where R_{Aj} is a ranking of objects belonging to the domain of the j-th attribute. An example of so prepared data set is given in Table 2.

Table 2. Exemplary data set of clients' preferences

A	R_{A1}	R_{A2}	...	R_{An}
B	R_{B1}	R_{B2}	...	R_{Bn}
...	...	...	...	...

Consider now a ranking R_{Aj}. Since it reflects the consumer's preferences on variants belonging to the domain $\mathcal{U}_j$ of the attribute $Y_j \in \mathcal{Y}$, it is also a vector. Namely,

$$R_{Aj} = (r_{Aj}^{(1)}, r_{Aj}^{(2)}, \ldots, r_{Aj}^{(l_j)}), \tag{1}$$

where $r_{Aj}^{(k)}$, $k = 1, \ldots, l_j$ is a rank assigned to k-th object belonging to $\mathcal{U}_j$ and where l_j stands for the size of the domain $\mathcal{U}_j$.

Since our goal is to identify both similar and dissimilar consumers, we are interested in defining an association measure between every pair of consumers $A, B \in \mathcal{X}$.

4   Desired Properties of a Measure of Association between Two Groups of Rankings

There are many ways for measuring association or correlation between two rankings, like the well-known Spearman's r_S or Kendall's τ (see, e.g., [2]). However, in our case we need a measure of association not between two rankings but between two sets of rankings $[R_{A1}, R_{A2} \ldots, R_{An}]$ and $[R_{B1}, R_{B2} \ldots, R_{Bn}]$, where particular rankings may correspond to attributes with quite different domains.

Let us try to list the desired properties of the requested measure of association between two sets of rankings. Denote such a hypothetical measure (coefficient) by S. It seems that S should satisfy at least the following requirements:

R1. $S : \mathcal{X} \times \mathcal{X} \rightarrow [-1, 1]$.
R2. S should assume its maximal value if and only if all rankings are pairwise perfectly concordant, i.e. $S = 1$ if and only if (R_{Aj}, R_{Bj}) are perfectly concordant for all $j = 1, \ldots, n$.
R3. S should assume its minimal value if and only if all rankings are pairwise perfectly discordant, i.e. $S = -1$ if and only if (R_{Aj}, R_{Bj}) are perfectly discordant for all $j = 1, \ldots, n$.
R4. S should be commutative, i.e. $S(A, B) = S(B, A)$.
R5. S should not depend on the permutation of attributes.
R6. S should depend on pairwise correlations between rankings calculated for the same attribute. Moreover, the increase in pairwise correlations for all attributes should result in the increase of S, and conversely, the decrease in pairwise correlations for all attributes should result in the decrease of S.

In some situations we may expect that the measure of association between two sets of rankings would additionally satisfy the following natural properties:

R7. Any pairwise correlation between rankings that is different from zero should be rewarded in S, i.e. the higher the absolute value of the pairwise correlation between rankings, the stronger influence of that correlation on the value of S.
R8. S should assume value equal to zero in case of lack of pairwise correlation for all attributes or when positive and negative correlations balance, i.e. for each positive correlation there exists a negative one with equal absolute value.

5   How to Measure Association between Two Groups of Rankings

Let s denote any pairwise correlation measure between two rankings, taking values in $[-1, 1]$, like Kendall's τ or Spearman's rank correlation coefficient r_S

(see, e.g., [2]). Moreover, let $(s_{AB}^1, s_{AB}^2, \ldots, s_{AB}^n)$ be a vector of pairwise correlations obtained for all attributes under study for two consumers $A, B \in \mathcal{X}$, i.e. $s_{AB}^j = s(R_{Aj}, R_{Bj})$, $j = 1, \ldots, n$.

Taking into account postulates R1 – R8 discussed above one may define the desired measure of association between two groups of rankings corresponding to consumers A and B, $A, B \in \mathcal{X}$, as

$$S(A, B) = F(s_{AB}^1, s_{AB}^2, \ldots, s_{AB}^n), \qquad (2)$$

where $F : [-1, 1]^n \to [-1, 1]$ is a suitable function.

As we look on (2) we may expect that F should be an appropriate aggregation function, since its goal is to aggregate several correlations to a single value. Moreover, postulates R1–R8 suggest it might be an ordered weighted averaging (OWA) operator [3], especially that we want to reward higher correlations (see R7). Unfortunately, F cannot be a typical aggregation function. Why? As it is well known, an aggregation function should have at least two fundamental properties: the preservation of bounds and the monotonicity condition (see, e.g., [4,5,6]). In our case there is no problem with the preservation of bounds, i.e. $F(-1, -1, \ldots, -1) = -1$ and $F(1, 1, \ldots, 1) = 1$, which coincides with postulates R2 and R3, respectively. However, the monotonicity condition means that $\boldsymbol{x} \leq \boldsymbol{y}$ implies $F(\boldsymbol{x}) \leq F(\boldsymbol{y})$ for all $\boldsymbol{x}, \boldsymbol{y} \in [-1, 1]$, where $\boldsymbol{x} = (x_1, \ldots, x_n)$, $\boldsymbol{y} = (y_1, \ldots, y_n)$ and where $\boldsymbol{x} \leq \boldsymbol{y}$ means that each component of $\boldsymbol{x}$ is not greater than the corresponding component of $\boldsymbol{y}$. And here is the problem, since, by R7, we want to promote higher correlations regardless of their signs, so F cannot be monotone on the whole interval $[-1, 1]$. Hence we need another type of aggregation operator that would be monotone not on the whole domain but for absolute values of arguments while still keeping track of the signs. One can propose there different candidates for the function F but in our opinion the following one seems to have many interesting properties.

Let us consider a function $F : [-1, 1]^n \to [-1, 1]$ defined as follows

$$F(x_1, \ldots, x_n) = \frac{2}{n(n+1)} \sum_{j=1}^{n} r(|x_j|) \cdot x_j, \qquad (3)$$

where $r : [0, 1] \to \mathbb{R}^+$ is a function such that

$$r(z) = \frac{1}{2} + \sum_{i=1}^{n} c(z - |x_i|) \qquad (4)$$

and where c is defined as

$$c(u) = \begin{cases} 0 & \text{if } u < 0 \\ \frac{1}{2} & \text{if } u = 0 \\ 1 & \text{if } u > 0. \end{cases} \qquad (5)$$

Combining (2) and (3) we get the following measure of association between two groups of rankings delivered by two consumers A and B:

$$S(A,B) = \frac{2}{n(n+1)} \sum_{j=1}^{n} r(|s_{AB}^{j}|) \cdot s_{AB}^{j} \qquad (6)$$

Example 1

Consider two consumers A and B who specified their preferences by assigning ranks to several variants belonging to the domain of four attributes under study. Moreover, assume that the correlation between their preferences for each separate attribute was calculated and as a result we received the following four numbers: $s_{AB}^{1} = 0.3$, $s_{AB}^{2} = 0.8$, $s_{AB}^{3} = -0.3$ and $s_{AB}^{4} = 0.1$. Hence, using (6), we can aggregate these four coefficients and obtain a value describing the association between two groups of rankings delivered by these two consumers. So we get

$$r(|0.3|) = \frac{1}{2} + (\frac{1}{2} + 0 + \frac{1}{2} + 1) = 2.5$$

$$r(|0.8|) = \frac{1}{2} + (1 + \frac{1}{2} + 1 + 1) = 4$$

$$r(|-0.3|) = \frac{1}{2} + (\frac{1}{2} + 0 + \frac{1}{2} + 1) = 2.5$$

$$r(|0.1|) = \frac{1}{2} + (0 + 0 + 0 + \frac{1}{2}) = 1$$

and hence

$$S(A,B) = F(0.3, 0.8, -0.3, 0.1)$$
$$= \frac{2}{4 \cdot 5}(2.5 \cdot 0.3 + 4 \cdot 0.8 + 2.5 \cdot (-0.3) + 1 \cdot 0.1) = 0.33.$$

It is worth noting that the value of our coefficient is greater than the arithmetic average of the arguments. Indeed, $\frac{1}{4}(0.3 + 0.8 - 0.3 + 0.1) = 0.225$. It shows that our measure promotes higher correlations which postulates R7.

6   Properties of the Measure S

In this section we will discuss basic properties of the suggested measure of association (6). Let us start from some useful properties of the operator (3).

By [3] F is an ordered weighted averaging operator (OWA) if $F_{OWA} : [0,1]^{n} \rightarrow [0,1]$ has the following form

$$F_{OWA}(x_1, \ldots, x_n) = \sum_{j=1}^{n} w_j \cdot x_{(j)}, \qquad (7)$$

where $\boldsymbol{w} = [w_1, \ldots, w_n]$ is a vector of weights such that $w_j \geq 0$ for $j = 1, \ldots, n$ and $\sum_{j=1}^{n} w_j = 1$, and where $x_{(j)}$ denote the j-th largest element of the collection of aggregated objects $x_1, \ldots, x_n$.

In our case one may see that if $|x_i| \neq |x_k|$ for any $i, k = 1, \ldots, n$ such that $i \neq k$, then function (4) attributes ranks to the sequence of points of the vector $(|x|_{(1)}, \ldots, |x_{(n)}|)$ in this way that the maximal value obtains the highest rank, the last but one value the last but one rank, and so on till the smallest value that obtains the smallest rank. In other words, $r(|x|_{(j)}) = n - j + 1$.

If there are two or more points $x_1, \ldots, x_n$ having the same absolute value then we use the well-known method in statistics of assigning midranks to deal with ties, i.e. each of these points obtains the same rank equal to the average of the ranks those points would get if they all had different absolute values.

Therefore, we get n weights $w_1 \ldots w_n$, where $w_j = \frac{2}{n(n+1)} r(|x|_{(j)})$. One may easily check that $w_j \in [0, 1]$ for each $j = 1, \ldots, n$ and $\sum_{j=1}^{n} w_j = 1$. However, contrary to the OWA operator the summands in (7) are the weights connected with ordered absolute values of x's which are then multiplied just by x's and not order statistics. Therefore, we may conclude that (3) is not the OWA operator. This is also the reason why operator (3) is not an aggregation function according to popular definitions (see, e.g., [4,5,6]).

However, function (3) behaves as OWA operator for absolute values of the arguments, i.e. $F(|x_1|, \ldots, |x_n|)$ is OWA operator. Indeed, then

$$F(|x_1|, \ldots, |x_n|) = \frac{2}{n(n+1)} \sum_{j=1}^{n} r(|x_j|) \cdot |x_j| = \sum_{j=1}^{n} w_j \cdot |x|_{(j)},$$

where $w_j = \frac{2}{n(n+1)} r(|x|_{(j)})$.

Yager [3] suggested how to determine and characterize weights of OWA operators:

− dispersion degree

$$Disp(w) = -\sum_{j=1}^{n} w_j ln(w_j), \tag{8}$$

− orness

$$Orness(w) = \frac{1}{n-1} \sum_{j=1}^{n} (n-j) w_j. \tag{9}$$

Let us consider the arithmetic mean, as a reference point. It is, of course, the OWA operator with identical weights, i.e. $w_j^* = \frac{1}{n}$ for $j = 1, \ldots, n$. Such distribution of weight induces $Disp(w^*) = ln(n)$ and $Orness(w^*) = 0.5$. One may notice that our operator (3) is at least as close to the "or" operator as arithmetic mean, because $Orness(w^*) \leq Orness(w) \leq 1$. Moreover, the weights of our operator (3) are distributed at most as uniformly as for the arithmetic mean, because $0 \leq Disp(w) \leq Disp(w^*)$.

Let us consider now some important properties of (3).

Lemma 1. *Function (3) is idempotent.*

Proof. Actually, for any $a \in [-1,1]$ we get

$$r(|a|) = \frac{1}{2} + (\frac{1}{2} + \frac{1}{2} + \ldots + \frac{1}{2}) = \frac{1}{2} + n \cdot \frac{1}{2} = (n+1)\frac{1}{2}$$

and hence

$$F(a, \ldots, a) = \frac{2}{n(n+1)} \sum_{j=1}^{n} r(|a|) \cdot a = \frac{2}{n(n+1)} \sum_{j=1}^{n} (n+1)\frac{1}{2} \cdot a = a,$$

which is the desired conclusion.   ∎

By the above lemma we get the following important conclusion.

Corollary 1. *Function (3) preserves bounds, i.e.*

$$F(-1, \ldots, -1) = -1,$$
$$F(1, \ldots, 1) = 1.$$

One may also easily notice that

$$F(x_1, \ldots, x_n) = F(x_{\sigma(1)}, \ldots, x_{\sigma(n)}) \tag{10}$$

for any permutation $\{\sigma(1), \ldots, \sigma(n)\}$ of $\{1, \ldots, n\}$, which means that our operator is symmetric.

Now let us examine if our coefficient S satisfies the desired requirements postulated in Sec. 4.

Lemma 2. *For any two groups of rankings delivered by two consumers A and B the measure of association (6) is bounded, namely $-1 \leq S(A, B) \leq 1$.*

The proof is evident just by the construction of function (3). This indicates that postulate R1 holds. Next two properties, i.e. R2 and R3, are also fulfilled.

Lemma 3. *$S = 1$ if and only if all rankings delivered by consumers A and B are pairwise perfectly concordant.*

Proof: If all rankings delivered by consumers A and B are pairwise perfectly concordant, we get $s_{AB}^1 = 1, s_{AB}^2 = 1, \ldots, s_{AB}^n = 1$. By Corollary 1 we get here $S(A, B) = 1$.
On the other hand, assume that $S = 1$. Suppose, conversely, that one of the correlation coefficients, say a, is smaller than 1, while the rest are equal to 1. Then by (4) we get

$$r(|1|) = \frac{1}{2} + (\frac{1}{2} + \ldots + \frac{1}{2} + 1) = \frac{n}{2} + 1$$

and

$$r(|a|) = \frac{1}{2} + (0 + \ldots + 0 + \frac{1}{2}) = 1.$$

Hence

$$S(A,B) = F(1,\dots,1,a) = \frac{2}{n(n+1)} \left((n-1)(\frac{n}{2}+1) + a \right) = 1$$

if and only if $a = 2$, which contradicts our assumptions. In the same way we may show that we cannot obtain $S(A,B) = 1$ if any correlation coefficient is different than 1. ∎

In the same way one may prove the following lemma.

Lemma 4. $S = -1$ *if and only if all rankings delivered by consumers A and B are pairwise perfectly discordant.*

Lemma 5. *The measure of association (6) between two groups of rankings is commutative with respect to consumers, i.e. $S(A,B) = S(B,A)$.*

The proof is immediate. This way Lemma 5 indicates that our postulate R4 is also fulfilled. But in our case we may also consider commutativity with respect to attributes (see R5).

Lemma 6. *The measure of association (6) between two groups of rankings is commutative with respect to attributes.*

The proof of this lemma is an immediate conclusion of the symmetry of operator F, i.e. (10).

It is also not difficult to observe that postulates R6–R8 are satisfied thanks to some properties of operator F. Actually, postulates R6 and R7 are fulfilled due to the fact discussed at the beginning of this section, that function (3) behaves as OWA operator for absolute values of the arguments, i.e. when we consider $F(|x_1|,\dots,|x_n|)$. It is important since the OWA operator is monotonic. Hence when we increase or decrease the absolute values of the arguments of F, the value of our measure also increases or decreases, respectively, what has been postulated in R6. This way we also reward higher correlations whatever are their signs, according to postulate R7. Please, notice in contrast, that for so popular OWA operators like the arithmetic mean or the median, no coefficients are rewarded in this way. In the case of the arithmetic mean all correlation coefficients are treated equally, while in the case of the median only middle valued coefficients are rewarded.

Finally, R8 is a straightforward conclusion of the way we define operator F. Indeed, if for each positive correlation there exists a negative one with equal absolute value they obtain the same rank but since they have opposite signs they sum up to 0.

The above mentioned relation between F operator and OWA functions leads also to the following lemma.

Lemma 7. *Let $s_{AB}^1,\dots,s_{AB}^n$ denote a sequence of pairwise correlations obtained for all attributes under study for two consumers $A, B \in \mathcal{X}$. Then*

$$\min\{s_{AB}^1,\dots,s_{AB}^n\} \leq S(A,B) \leq max\{s_{AB}^1,\dots,s_{AB}^n\}. \tag{11}$$

We may observe also some minor but useful properties of the measure S.

432 H. Łącka and P. Grzegorzewski

Lemma 8. *If $S(A,B) = 1$ and $S(B,C) = p$, where $p \in [-1,1]$, then $S(A,C) = p$. Similarly, if $S(A,B) = -1$ and $S(B,C) = p$ then $S(A,C) = p$.*

Proof: By Lemma 3 we have that $S(A,B) = 1$ if and only if $A = B$. Then from $S(B,C) = p$ and $A = B$ we obtain $S(B,C) = S(A,C) = p$.

Similarly, from Lemma 4 we have that $S(A,B) = -1$ if and only if $A = B^-$, where B^- denotes a group of rankings with all rankings reversed with respect to B. Then from $S(B,C) = p$ and $A = B^-$ we obtain $S(B,C) = S(A^-,C) = p$. As a result, what can easily be shown, we get $S(A,C) = -p$. ∎

7 Conclusions

In this paper we have considered an interesting problem one can face in recommender systems when we have to make a recommendation based on the aggregated correlations. Since in measuring correlation both its absolute value and the sign is meaningful and important, traditional aggregation operators, like OWA functions may not be satisfactory. Therefore, we have suggested a new measure of association between two sets of rankings and examine its properties. Although the proposed measure satisfies basic requirements specified for this type of operators, some questions and problems remain open. In particular, it seems that our measure might be treated as a member of a family of semi-aggregation operators, which behave as traditional aggregation functions when we restrict our consideration to the absolute values of their arguments, but simultaneously they do not loose information about the signs of those arguments. Hence we still need a more deep and broader study on the operators designated for processing the bipolar information.

Acknowledgment. Study was supported by research fellowship within "Information technologies: research and their interdisciplinary applications" project co-financed by European Social Fund (agreement no. POKL.04.01.01-00-051/10-00).

References

1. Melville, P., Sindhwani, V.: Recommender systems. In: Encyclopedia of Machine Learning. Springer (2009)
2. Gibbons, J.D., Chakraborti, S.: Nonparametric Statistical Inference. Marcel Dekker Inc., New York (2003)
3. Yager, R.R.: On ordered weighted averaging aggregation operators in multicriteria decisionmaking. IEEE Transactions and Systems, Man and Cybernetics 18, 183–190 (1988)
4. Beliakov, G., Pradera, A., Calvo, T.: Aggregation Functions: A Guide for Practitioners. STUDFUZZ, vol. 221. Springer, Heidelberg (2007)
5. Calvo, T., Kolesarova, A., Komornikova, M., Mesiar, R.: Aggregation operators: Properties, classes and construction methods. In: Calvo, T., Mayor, G., Mesiar, R. (eds.) Aggregation Operators. New Trends and Applications. STUDFUZZ, vol. 97, pp. 3–104. Springer, Heidelberg (2002)
6. Grabisch, M., Pap, E., Marichal, J.L., Mesiar, R.: Aggregation Functions, Cambridge (2009)

An Arduino-Simulink-Control System for Modern Hand Protheses

Andreas Attenberger and Klaus Buchenrieder

Institut für Technische Informatik, Universität der Bundeswehr München
Werner-Heisenberg-Weg 39, 85577 Neubiberg, Germany
{andreas.attenberger,klaus.buchenrieder}@unibw.de

Abstract. Despite the significant amount of research on the application of myoelectric research for upper limb prostheses control [1] and advances in signal processing and classification methods for myoeletric signals (MES), patient satisfaction and acceptance for modern hand prostheses is lacking [2]. This is partly due to missing intuitive and natural control possibilities for accessing the various grip patterns that are available with current prostheses models on the market. As a step towards easy prototyping and seamless integration of a wide variety of prostheses, we present a system based on the Arduino microcontroller platform. With adaptable Simulink^{TM} models and a wide number of libraries for the Arduino IDE, the system allows electromyographic (EMG) processing as well as basic classification for actuating both basic hand models and more advanced hand prostheses. Complex classifier models can be trained with a PC-based MATLAB^{TM} application prior to microcontroller operation.

Keywords: Arduino, Electromyography, Hand Prostheses, Pattern Recognition, Signal Processing, Simulink.

1 Introduction

Modern prostheses like the bebionic^{TM} hand by RSL Steeper or the Michelangelo^{TM} hand by Otto Bock are characterized by multiple degrees of freedom (DOF) and allow a wide array of different grip patterns. The previous generation of hand prostheses were mainly simple grippers with additional options, i.e. manual wrist adjustment [3]. Figure 1 shows the evolution of traditional simple gripper hand models to state of the art hand prostheses.

Despite advanced possibilities of modern upper limb prostheses, the acceptance by patients is slow [4] and actual usability to patients remains limited [5], [2]. One of the reasons are control systems which are not based on movement classification but instead rely on traditional amplitude thresholding. To remedy this, Jiang et al. advocate a shift of focus to myoelectric control features that are more beneficial to patients [4], while Paredes and Graimann state that current myoelectric control schemes lack adaptibility, robustness and simplicity of use [6]. Regardless of the aspects to be researched, the potential changes and adaptions in prostheses control systems, it is beneficial to include patients at early

L. Rutkowski et al. (Eds.): ICAISC 2014, Part II, LNAI 8468, pp. 433–444, 2014.

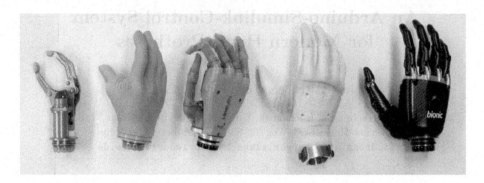

Fig. 1. Two basic hand prostheses on the left compared to more current hand prostheses like the i-limb^{TM} ultra, Michelangelo^{TM} and bebionic3^{TM} hands

stages of development. In order to attain a flexible prototyping environment to test control schemes for hand prostheses, we have developed a virtual prothesis at our department [7]. It is based on MATLAB^{TM} and necessitates either the utilization of a laptop or a PC. To allow a more realistic test setup for prostheses control, it is necessary to take into account the execution of a control system on microcontrollers as well as the integration of prostheses currently available.

This contribution presents a fully operable Simulink^{TM}-based microcontroller prototyping platform for conducting experiments with different hand prostheses. The MATLAB^{TM} application can be utilized for classifier training and parameter adjustment. In addition to controlling a low-cost exemplar hand model, we also show the integration of current state of the art hand prostheses into the framework.

2   Classification Process

The prosthesis control prototype allows for the execution of all steps of the multi-stage classification process defined by Englehart et al. [8], which comprises feature extraction and classifier algorithms. In the presented setup, a basic RMS feature is utilized, which is denoted for N samples by:

$$x_{rms} = \sqrt{\frac{1}{N} \cdot \sum_{n=1}^{N}(x_n^2)}. \qquad (1)$$

The Simulink^{TM} environment also permits the calculation of frequency-based features like zero crossing values which can be calculated with the following formula:

$$x_{zc} = \sum_{n=0}^{N-1} I\{\text{sgn}(n+1) \cdot \text{sgn}(n) < 0\}. \qquad (2)$$

After feature extraction, a classifier can be trained for the various different methods, ranging from simple classifiers like decision trees or naive Bayes classifiers to more complex methods like support vector machines. For a decision tree, a subset X_t is associated with each node T of the tree [9]. A subset is subsequently divided into two subsets, comprising 'Yes'- (X_{tY}) and 'No'-answers (X_{tN}) at the descendant nodes, while satisfying the following conditions:

$$X_{tY} \cap X_{tN} = \emptyset. \tag{3}$$

$$X_{tY} \cup X_{tN} = X_t. \tag{4}$$

If for a naive Bayes classifier, statistical independence is assumed for individual features x_j with $j = 1, 2, ..., l$ [9], it follows that:

$$p(\boldsymbol{x}|\omega_i) = \prod_{j=1}^{l} p(x_j|\omega_i) \tag{5}$$

with

$$i = 1, 2, ..., M \tag{6}$$

Subsequently, an unknown sample $\boldsymbol{x} = [x_1, x_2, ..., x_l]^T$ is assigned to the following class:

$$\omega_m = \arg\max_{\omega_i} \prod_{j=1}^{l} p(x_j|\omega_i) \tag{7}$$

with

$$i = 1, 2, ..., M \tag{8}$$

The above classifiers and further methods are all available in MATLAB^{TM} and have previously been tested for MES classification [10]. Further implementation details and the prototype training application are presented in section 3.3.

3 Prototype

The prototype of the control system for a selected prosthesis, consists of the following components: a Delsys Bagnoli^{TM} sensor system[1] with four single differential EMG sensors, an Arduino Uno for myoelectric signal processing and the generation of control commands. Controls are sent to an Arduino Uno with a custom motor shield, an Arduino BT with a Bluetooth module or an Arduino Due, which are connected to the prostheses. The full prototyping system is shown in Figure 2.

---

[1] http://www.delsys.com/Products/Bagnoli_Desktop.html

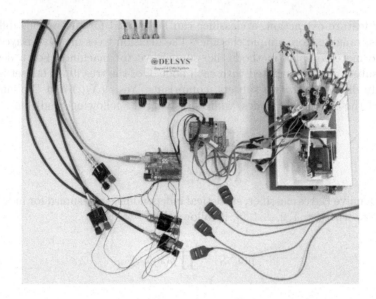

Fig. 2. Full prototype setup comprising the Delsys EMG system, an Arduino for signal processing and an Arduino for receiving control commands and driving the servos of a MechaTE hand

3.1 EMG System and Signal Processing Board

For the processing of the EMG signal, the Delsys EMG sensors are connected to the analog inputs of the Arduino Uno prototyping board, as displayed in Figure 3. Sensor channels 1 to 4 are input to the analog connectors A0 to A3. When the Bagnoli^{TM} EMG amplifier system is connected directly, only the positive portion of the myoelectric signal can be considered. Thus, a small circuit for converting the amplified signal in the range of -5 to +5 Volts to a signal ranging from 0 to 5V with a DC component of 2.5V must be inserted. This allows the utilization of frequency-based features like zero crossings for more sophisticated classification schemes. The control information derived from the MES is output through the ATmega328's UART interface available from the Arduino board's pins 0 (RX) and 1 (TX). A SoftSerial Interface can be employed in case utilization of these pins is confined to other tasks [11].

3.2 Control Software

Signal processing is based on a Simulink model, which resides in the internal flash utilizing the Arduino Target library[2] for MATLAB^{TM} [12]. The model, as shown in Figure 4, applies a highpass filter to the analog signal converted by the ATmega328's ADC.

---

[2] http://www.mathworks.de/hardware-support/arduino-simulink.html

Fig. 3. The Arduino board employed for processing the MES output by the Delsys Bagnoli™ amplifier

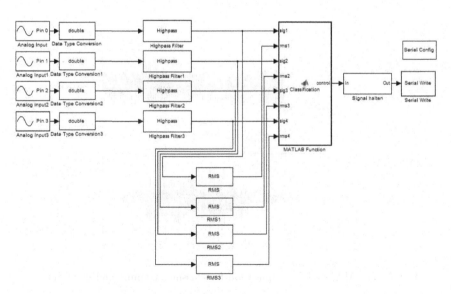

Fig. 4. Simulink™ model on the processing Arduino

438   A. Attenberger and K. Buchenrieder

Frequencies below 20Hz are removed by high pass filters to reduce interference and noise [13]. In the current setup, the RMS values of both channels are subsequently subjected to amplitude level thresholding in the classification block. Depending on the settings in the model, a corresponding control command is sent by the ATmega over a serial connection through the board's RX/TX-lines. Once a threshold has been reached, the corresponding hand position control command is continually transmitted until a new classification result is present. This basic classifier in the corresponding Simulink^{TM} MATLAB function block can be replaced by more sophisticated algorithms.

3.3   Classifier Training

Before any prosthesis control scheme can be operated, patients have to undergo a training process during which parameters like amplitude threshold levels, which are individual for each patient, can be adjusted [1]. Furthermore, when employing pattern recognition with classifier methods, a training session is also mandatory before operating a classifier algorithm. Due to the high number of parameters and options that can be manipulated for different classifier and feature combinations, classifier training is more easily carried out on a computer. The window of the MATLAB^{TM} classifier training application is displayed in Figure 5, showing a basic example of two movement classes and two sensors. The application allows direct testing of classification results as well as visualization of the result with a virtual 3D prosthesis [7]. In addition, it is possible to integrate the other prostheses models like the MechaTE or the Michelangelo^{TM} hand.

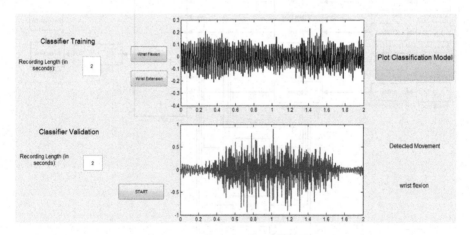

Fig. 5. The MATLAB^{TM} application for classifier training and validation

Once a classifier model has been trained and classifier validation shows sufficient robustness, it can be saved from the MATLAB^{TM} workspace and transferred to the Arduino board. While the current basic RMS threshold model can seamlessly be integrated with the MATLAB^{TM} function block, more sophisticated classifiers from the MATLAB^{TM} Statistics Toolbox[3] can only directly be utilized in the PC-based training application. For these, to be integrated into the Simulink^{TM} model, only a subset of the functions is supported for a microprocessor target[4]. To remedy this limitation, Simulink^{TM} additionally supports the injection of C/C++-Code into models, employing S-Functions. Open source code for classifiers like the Naive Bayes classifiers is readily available online[5].

3.4 Hand Models

Due to the basic serial interfacing, it is possible to connect other microcontrollers to actuate a prosthesis. Beside the MechaTE Robot Hand, this approach allows to control modern multi-DOF prostheses, thus allowing realistic training of classifiers and hand control schemes for patients. The realized prototype allows for flexible control of modern prostheses like the Michelangelo^{TM} and the bebionic3^{TM} hands through wireless and wired interfaces.

MechaTE Robot Hand. As a basic model of an artificial hand, mainly intended for judging interaction speed and viability of classification control schemes, a MechaTE Robot Hand was chosen. It consists of five individually controllable digits and a flexible wrist, that can be extended, flexed, pronated and supinated. The fingers are made of anodized aircraft aluminum [14]. Each finger is driven with a miniature servo motor. For the execution of movements and grip patterns, each servo is connected to a custom-built Arduino motor shield, connected to an Arduino Uno microcontroller board. Furthermore all the servo pins are connected to an Arduino Uno microcontroller-board. The ATmega328's flash memory contains the Simulink^{TM} model created with the Arduino Target library in MATLAB^{TM}. For controlling the servos, the servo block library for Simulink Arduino Target created by Matt Bilsky[6] is employed. The setup, as shown in Figure 7, can be connected to a signal processing system by a serial interface with another connector available for common ground. When a character is received through the serial connection, it is compared to a predefined set of movements consisting of: resting position, wrist extension, wrist flexion, fist, supination, pronation, precision grip, lateral grip, index finger and thumb flexion. As displayed in the following listing, the angles are then utilized by the servo library for setting the motors to the specified positions:

---

[3] http://www.mathworks.com/products/statistics/
[4] http://www.mathworks.de/de/help/simulink/ug/
functions-supported-for-code-generation--categorical-list.html
[5] http://code.google.com/p/naive-bayes-classifier/
[6] http://mattbilsky.com/mediawiki/
index.php?title=Servo_Block_Library_for_Simulink_Arduino_Target

Servo angles for moving the MechaTE Hand to form a fist

```
%% Faust
  if seriell == 4
      Pin3 =uint8(10);
      Pin5 =uint8(180);
      Pin6 =uint8(180);
      Pin9 =uint8(180);
      Pin10 =uint8(180);
      Pin11 =uint8(90);
      Pin12 =uint8(90);
  end
```

While the resulting Simulink^{TM} model has a size of 48kB on disk, the resulting hex file after compilation is only 16kB, easily fitting in the ATmega328's flash memory. As shown in Figure 6, a GUI has also been developed for controlling the MechaTE Robot Hand through a serial interface between MATLAB^{TM} and the control Arduino [12].

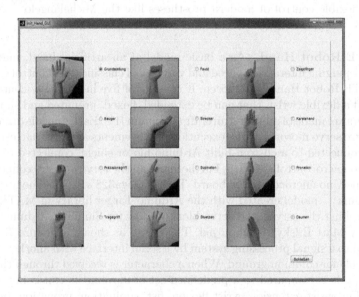

Fig. 6. The MATLAB GUI for controlling the MechaTE Robot Hand through a serial interface

Michelangelo^{TM} Hand. The Michelangelo^{TM} hand is the latest prosthetic hand model by Otto Bock Healthcare featuring a seperate movable thumb and Bluetooth connectivity. It exhibits various different grip patterns such as lateral and opposition grips [15]. For integration into the Arduino-based prototype, we used a Arduino BT equipped with a Bluetooth module. It receives control commands through the serial interface on pins 0 (RX) and pin 1 (TX). A connection setup is shown in Figure 8.

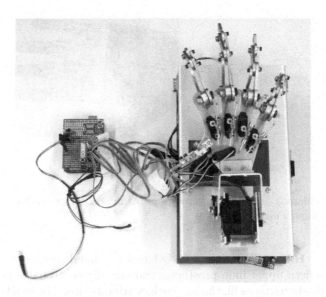

Fig. 7. The MechaTE Robot Hand connected to a custom-built shield mounted on the Arduino Uno board

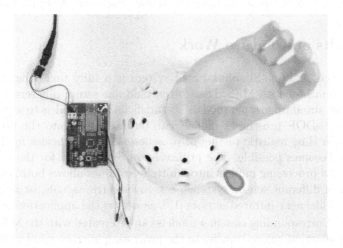

Fig. 8. Integration of the Michelangelo^{TM} hand into the control setup with serial connection to the Arduino BT

Fig. 9. The bebionic3^TM hand connected to an Arduino Due for sending control commands to the hand's microcontrollers

bebionic3^TM **Hand.** RSL Steeper's bebionic3^TM hand displayed in Figure 9 is another modern upper limb prosthesis. Individually controllable fingers allow sophisticated grip patterns like hook, pinch or tripod grips. The hand can also be configured wirelessly with the bebalance software [16]. For the integration into our prototypical prosthesis control scheme, the bebionic3^TM hand is wired to an Arduino Due equipped with a 3.3V-powered Atmel SAM3X8E ARM Cortex-M3 CPU[7]. Similiar to the previous setups, its serial interface serves as a link to receive the control information from the signal processing Arduino board.

4   Results and Future Work

The presented Arduino-Simulink-based system is a fully functional prosthesis control system based on MES. Due to the modular setup, different prostheses ranging from standard gripper models and artificial hand models to sophisticated modern multi-DOF prostheses models can be integrated into the prototyping system. With this, realistic testing of prostheses control schemes for numerous end-effects becomes possible. The utilization of Simulink^TM for the integration of control and processing models into multiple Arduinos allows both, the flexible utilization of different sensor systems, e.g. myoelectric signals, or novel sensor technologies like near-infrared sensors [17], as well as the application of classifier algorithms. Corresponding classifier models can be created with the MATLAB^TM training application before transfer to the processing microcontroller. While several restrictions apply to embedding MATLAB functions, user-defined C-/C++-Code can be injected into the Simulink^TM models. Depending on the classifier model size and processing requirements, a processing platform more powerful than the Arduino Uno has to be considered. Next to the Arduino Mega, which

---

[7] http://arduino.cc/en/Main/ArduinoBoardDue

offers a bigger program flash and SRAM, both the PandaBoard and the Raspberry Pi microcontroller boards are currently supported by Simulink^{TM} and thus constitute possible alternatives. Current development efforts are targeted at implementing advanced classification algorithms for utilization in the embedded Simulink^{TM} models. Furthermore, additional feature extraction methods from the MATLAB^{TM} movement classification toolbox [10] have to be evaluated for compatibility with the target harware.

Acknowledgements. We are grateful to Manuel Rosenau for implementing the first version of the prototyping environment with the MechaTE Robot Hand [12]. Furthermore, we would like to thank Sebastian Preibisch for his work towards controlling the Michelangelo^{TM} Hand. Finally, we thank Sławomir Wojciechowski for his implementation of the MATLAB^{TM} training application.

References

1. Muzumdar, A.: Powered Upper Limb Prostheses: Control, Implementation and Clinical Application. Springer (2004)
2. Peerdeman, B., Boere, D., Witteveen, H.J.B., Huis in 't Veld, M.H.A., Hermens, H.J., Stramigioli, S., Rietman, J.S., Veltink, P.H., Misra, S.: Myoelectric forearm prostheses: State of the art from a user-centered perspective. Journal of Rehabilitation Research and Development 48(6), 719–738 (2011)
3. Fryer, C.M., Michael, J.W.: Upper-Limb Prosthetics: Body-Powered Components (2013), http://oandplibrary.org/alp/chap06-01.asp
4. Jiang, N., Dosen, S., Müller, K., Farina, D.: Myoelectric control of artificial limbs: is there the need for a change of focus? IEEE Signal Processing Magazine 152, 1–4 (2012), doi:10.1109/MSP.2012.2203480
5. Wolf Schweitzer: 2010's "bionic" prostheses and why they fail (2010), http://www.swisswuff.ch/tech/?p=282
6. Paredes, L., Graimann, B.: Advanced myoelectric control of prostheses: Requirements and challenges. In: Pons, J.L., Torricelli, D., Pajaro, M. (eds.) Converging Clinical and Engineering Research on Neurorehabilitation. Biosystems & Biorobotics, vol. 1, pp. 1221–1224. Springer, Heidelberg (2013)
7. Attenberger, A., Buchenrieder, K.: Modeling and Visualization of Classification-Based Control Schemes for Upper Limb Prostheses. In: Popovic, M., Schätz, B., Voss, S. (eds.) ECBS, pp. 188–194. IEEE (2012)
8. Englehart, K., Hudgins, B., Parker, P., Stevenson, M.: Classification of the myoelectric signal using time-frequency based representations. Medical Engineering & Physics 21(6-7), 431–438 (1999)
9. Theodoridis, S., Koutroumbas, K.: Pattern Recognition, 4th edn. Academic Press (August 2008)
10. Attenberger, A., Buchenrieder, K.: A MATLAB Toolbox for Upper Limb Movement Classification. In: Moreno-Díaz, R., Pichler, F., Quesada-Arencibia, A. (eds.) EUROCAST. LNCS, vol. 8112, pp. 191–198. Springer, Heidelberg (2013)
11. Arduino: Arduino SoftwareSerial (2014), http://www.arduino.cc/en/Reference/SoftwareSerial
12. Rosenau, M.: Realisierung eines Klassifizierungs-Frameworks für Microcontroller-basierte Prothesensteuerungen. Master's thesis, Universität der Bundeswehr München (2012)

13. Herrmann, S.: Direkte und proportionale Ansteuerung einzelner Finger von Handprothesen. PhD thesis, Universität der Bundeswehr München (2011)
14. Entertainment Solutions Inc: Robotic Hand, MechaTE Robot Hand Limited Edition | Animatronic Robotics (2014),
    http://animatronicrobotics.com/shopping/components/mechate-robot-hand-limited-edition/1-3.html
15. Otto Bock HealthCare GmbH: The Michelangelo Hand in Practice (2012),
    http://www.living-with-michelangelo.com/fileadmin/downloads/therapeuten/english/therapist_product_brochure.pdf
16. RSLSteeper: bebionic3 technical information (2013),
    http://rslsteeper.com/uploads/files/281/bebionic3_tech_manual_web.pdf
17. Herrmann, S., Buchenrieder, K.: Fusion of Myoelectric and Near-Infrared Signals for Prostheses Control. In: Proc. 4th International Convention on Rehabilitation Engineering & Assistive Technology, iCREATe 2010, Kaki Bukit TechPark II, Singapore, pp. 54:1–54:4. Singapore Therapeutic, Assistive & Rehabilitative Technologies (START) Centre (2010)

Solving Timetabling Problems on GPU

Wojciech Bożejko[1], Łukasz Gniewkowski[1], and Mieczysław Wodecki[2]

[1] Institute of Computer Engineering, Control and Robotics
Wrocław University of Technology
Janiszewskiego 11-17, 50-372 Wrocław, Poland
{wojciech.bozejko,lukasz.gniewkowski}@pwr.wroc.pl
[2] Institute of Computer Science, University of Wrocław
Joliot-Curie 15, 50-383 Wrocław, Poland
mwd@ii.uni.wroc.pl

Abstract. This paper concerns the application of a parallel *tabu search* algorithm to solve the general problem of *timetabling*. The problem of timetabling (also known as scheduling) was first expressed as a graph coloring problem and then good approximate solutions were obtained with use of concurrent metaheuristic algorithm for GPU (*Graphics Processing Unit*).

1   Introduction

Timetabling is the assignment of a set of tasks (lessons) to apropriate time periods, in order to comply with the limits laid before the implementation of the schedule. On the basis of such adaptation there can be a timetable for classes and teachers determined. The problem of arranging a timetable (work) is a combinatorial optimization problem heavily inspired by the practice (see [15,11]). Basing on interviews with representatives of the Polish primary, secondary and technical schools one can say that this problem is solved once or twice each year. In most schools this issue is still analyzed and resolved with use of conventional methods which means that all work is done by one or more persons in a few days to several weeks, using a sheet of paper and/or board. Such a procedure is both time-and labor-consuming. Although there are software tools (packages, applications) to support this process, usually most of the work is done by a man, as it is his competence to take the final decision. This is due to the slowness of applications or because of the fact that the obtained solution does not meet the requirements.

In this paper, we consider the requirements which appear in the process of creating a lesson plan (timetabling) that has been determined not only on the basis of the information found in the literature, but also on the basis of interviews with people dealing with this issue in educational institutions. Due to the computational complexity of the timetable designing process we propose to use GPU [18] concurrent computing environment.

2   Formulation of the Problem

For the purpose of this publication there were two types of constraints adopted: hard constraints (which must be met) and soft constraints (no need to be met

L. Rutkowski et al. (Eds.): ICAISC 2014, Part II, LNAI 8468, pp. 445–455, 2014.
© Springer International Publishing Switzerland 2014

for the plan to be acceptable, but it is recommended that they are met). The *hard constraints* are:

- No class can have two lessons at one time.
- No teacher can have two lessons in parallel.
- Number of lessons that require certain type of room, taking place at the same time, cannot be greater than the number of available rooms of this type.
- No class can have unused time slots (periods without subjects or activities between lessons in a day) on any day
- Class must have adequate number of lessons on a day, from 4 to 8.
- There cannot be two lessons of the same subject for a class on one day.

The *soft constraints* are defined as follows:

- Teacher should not have one hour of class during one day.
- Teacher should not have more than two unused time sots during the day.

3   Literature Review

Preparing a school plan (called timetabling) is a multi-criteria combinatorial optimization problem. This problem occurs relatively frequently in the literature, it is a constant subject of study, although some of its variants have been relatively well studied (the most common option is preparing the timetable for colleges or universities or timetables of exams for schools of higher education). In the literature one can find many ways of modeling solutions to the problem. The most commonly used may include the following three models:

- 3-dimensional matrix [3,19], – the solution is shown in the form of a binary matrix x, where x_{ijk} takes the value 1, when i-th lesson takes place in the j-th term in the k-th place, a value of 0 is assigned otherwise.
- 2-dimensional matrix [16] – the solution is shown in a two dimensional matrix, in which on the position x_{ij} there is the number of lesson held at the i-th term in the j-th room.
- Graph model [2,10] – this model requires rewriting of *the timetabling problem into a limited graph coloring problem,* in which the vertices connect the edges that cannot occur at the same time (due to the common participants or teachers).

It is enough that the solution obtained will fully comply with the above mentioned hard requirements and sufficiently comply with the soft requirements. There is a wide range of computational techniques for finding suboptimal solutions. Their greatest advantage is the ability to obtain good-quality solutions in a satisfactory time for problems strictly insoluble. The most commonly used methods are:

- Hyper-heuristics [10] – this approach relies on a number of low-level heuristics, of which, in a given step, there is only one selected to solve the problem. Methods of heuristics selection may be different, for example, by different heuristics.
- Tabu search [3,16] – very popular method of solving the timetabling problem. However, most authors of solutions add extra units to the algorithm in order to obtain better results - for example, memetic tabu search algorithm [16].
- Population-based algorithms [2,17] - this term hides a very wide range of issues, from evolutionary algorithms to ant or swarm algorithms, etc. Most often, these algorithms are combined with the graph model.

It is evident that the problem can be approached in several ways, which is why the problem of scheduling still lies in the center of interest of many research circles.

For the last few years GPGPU parallel programming model has been used for massive shared-memory applications (see [18]). The GPU is especially well-suited to address problems that can be expressed as data-parallel computations – SIMD – with high arithmetic intensity (the number of arithmetic operations is significantly greater than the number of memory operations). Because the same program is executed on many data elements and has high arithmetic intensity, the memory access latency can be hidden with calculations instead of big data caches. This property was used by Bożejko et al. [6,9] to design efficient parallel metaheuristic for GPU.

4   Graph Model

In this section there will be presented a mathematical model of the problem. The input data of the problem, the solution and the form of the objective function will be defined here.

4.1   Input Data

The input data which properly define the problem with regard to all restrictions described in Section 2, are as follows:

- k – number of classes,
- n – number of teachers,
- l – number of lessons,
- $V = \{V_1, V_2, \ldots, V_l\}$ – set of lessons,
- d – number of days,
- r – number of time slots in a day,
- s – number of type of rooms,
- $S = \{S_1, S_2, \ldots, S_s\}$ – number of rooms of certain type.

Each lesson contains the information for which class it is conducted, by which teacher, with what subject, how much time it takes and the type of room required.

4.2 Auxiliary Variables

The described hereinafter variables are created from the input data for faster and easier check of compliance with the restrictions.

- $E = \{E_1, E_2, \ldots, E_e\}$ -set of edges,
- $v = \{v_1, v_2, \ldots, v_l\}$ - set of vertices,
- $K = \{K_1, K_2, \ldots, K_k\}$ - list of indices of i-th class,
- $N = \{N_1, N_2, \ldots, N_n\}$ - list of indices of lessons of i-th teacher,
- $I = \{I_1, I_2, \ldots, I_s\}$ - list of indices of lessons requiring i-th type of room,
- t - number of periods (terms),
- $T = \{T_1, T_2, \ldots, T_t\}$ - list of indices of lessons which cannot take place on the same day.

For each vertex there were the following indices defined: a class-, teacher-, subject-, type of room, set of lessons that cannot take place in one day and duration time one. References to these fields are as follows:

- $v_i.k$ – index of the room in which the i-th subject is taught,
- $v_i.n$ – index of the teacher who teaches the i-th subject,
- $v_i.p$ – index of the subject for which the i-th class is taught,
- $v_i.t$ – duration of i-th subject,
- $v_i.s$ – required type of room for the i-th subject,
- $v_i.z$ – index of a set of lessons which cannot take place on one day.

A set of edges is created between the classes, which are held for the same class, or for the same teacher. Number of terms, which defines the number of colors available in a solution, is calculated by formula (1).

$$t = d \cdot r. \tag{1}$$

One set T includes lessons which take place for the same class from the same subject.

4.3 Solution Model

The solution to the problem is presented with the use vectors:

- $P = \{P_1, P_2, \ldots, P_n\}$ - vertex color, for multi colored vertices it is the first color,
- $Z = \{Z_1, Z_2, \ldots, Z_n\}$ - the last color of vertices,
- $G = \{G_1, G_2, \ldots, G_n\}$ - number of a day on which given lessons take place,
- $R = \{R_1, R_2, \ldots, R_n\}$ - index of the appropriate type of room in which lessons take place.

4.4 Objective Function Description

The task of a limited graph coloring problem is formulated as follows (see [4,13]):

$$f(P) = \sum_{i=1}^{n} \sum_{j=1}^{m} w_j f_j(P, i), \tag{2}$$

where: $- w_1, w_2, \ldots, w_m$ - appropriate weight to restrictions,

$-f_1(P,i)$, $f_2(P,i)$, $\ldots$, $f_m(P,i)$ - functions defining the penalties for failure to comply with certain restrictions, definitions can be found below.

In the implemented algorithm m is 7.

— $f_1(P,i)$ - function which checks the constraint, saying that no class and no teacher can have two classes at one time. The value of the function is proportional to the number of common terms of these lessons (for lessons over more than one period). It is a function describing the correctness of solutions in the classical *graph coloring problem*. The formula defining the function (3).

$$f_1(P,i) = \sum_{\{v_i,v_j\}\in E} (\mathrm{v_j.t} * w(v_i,v_j)), \tag{3}$$

where:

$$w(v_i,v_j) = |[P_i, Z_i] \cap [P_j, Z_j]| \tag{4}$$

— $f_2(P,i)$ – the function is responsible for checking whether the number of classes that require the same type of room, taking place in a given period is not greater than the number of rooms. This condition is checked for all the terms at which the i-th class takes place. This function is calculated using the dependency (5).

$$f_2(P,i) = \sum_{j=P_i}^{Z_i} d(\sum_{v_m \in \mathrm{I_{v_{i.s}}}} |[P_m, Z_m] \cap j| - S_{v_i.s}), \tag{5}$$

where:

$$d(x) = \begin{cases} 0 \text{ gdy x} < 0, \\ x \text{ gdy x} \geq 0. \end{cases} \tag{6}$$

— $f_3(P,i)$ – the function checking if a lesson, which cannot occur on one day (held for one class in the same subject) do not take place on one day. The function equation is as follows (7):

$$f_3(P,i) = \sum_{v_j \in T_{v_{i.z}}} \mathrm{v_j.t} * |\{G_i\} \cap \{G_j\}| \tag{7}$$

— $f_4(P,i)$– the function responsible for checking the number of lesson time slots on the class schedule. An equation describing the function is shown below (8)

$$f_4(P,i) = \sum_{v_j \in K_{v_{i.k}}} |\{G_i\} \cap \{G_j\}| * o(G_j, K_{v_i.k}), \tag{8}$$

where:

$$o(x,k) = |\mathrm{i} : 0 \leq \mathrm{i} \leq \mathrm{r} \wedge$$
$$(\exists 0 \leq a < i)(\exists i < b \leq r)(\exists v_m \in k)(\exists v_n \in k)(\forall v_j \in k)$$
$$|[P_j, Z_j] \cap j| = 0 \wedge \tag{9}$$
$$|[P_m, Z_m] \cap a| = 1 \wedge$$
$$|[P_n, Z_n] \cap b| = 1|.$$

– $f_5(P, i)$– the function responsible for checking the number of lessons of a given class on a day. A formula which describes the functions is given below (10):

$$f_5(P, i) = h\left(\sum_{v_j \in K_{v_i.k}} |\{G_i\} \cap \{G_j\}|\right), \qquad (10)$$

where:

$$h(x) = \begin{cases} Min_k - x & \text{gdy} & x < Min_k \\ 0 & \text{gdy } Min_k \le x \le Max_k \\ x - Max_k & \text{gdy} & x > Max_k \end{cases} \qquad (11)$$

Parameters Min_k and Max_k are arbitrarily set to a value of 4 and 8.
– $f_6(P, i)$- the function responsible for checking the number of lesson time slots on the day of the teacher who teaches the i-th class. The function is defined as follows (12):

$$f_6(P, i) = \sum_{v_j \in K_{v_i.n}} |\{G_i\} \cap \{G_j\}| * o(G_j, K_{v_i.n}). \qquad (12)$$

Function $o(x, k)$ is described by the equation (9).
– $f_7(P, i)$ - the function responsible for checking the number of classes of a given teacher on the day. The function is defined as follows (13):

$$f_7(P, i) = h(\sum_{v_j \in N_{v_i.n}} |\{G_i\} \cap \{G_j\}|) \qquad (13)$$

Function $h(x)$ is described by the equation (11).
Parameters of function values are as follows: $Min_n = 2$; $Max_n = 8$.

The weights for the separate functions are selected so as to depend on the vertex, for which the penalty function is calculated. Moreover, it was also observed that the most important criteria was the classical graph coloring problem, therefore the highest weight has the (equation (14)). The weights for other hard and soft constraints are described by equations (15) and (16):

$$w_1(i) = \text{INF}* \sum_{\{v_i, v_j\} \in E} C_j \qquad (14)$$

$$w_2(i) = w_3(i) = w_4(i) = w_5(i) = \text{INF}*C_i \qquad (15)$$

$$w_6(i) = w_7(i) = C_i \qquad (16)$$

The restrictions from the first to the fifth must be met so that the plan was acceptable. Therefore, these weight were given multiplier INF (i.e. a very large number) so that their fulfillment was a priority for the algorithms.

5   Solution Method

Nowadays mainly metaheuristics [7,8] are used to solve NP-hard discrete optimization problems, due to exponential working time of exact approaches. Here we propose to use tabu search method with an additional backtrack-jump list (see [8]). The change introduced to the basic tabu search method, i.e. the mechanism of backtrack-jump list allows us to return to the best solution obtained so far. After returning the algorithm starts searching for better solutions in a different direction than before. This mechanism is particularly useful when the generated neighborhood is composed of many elements. The return to the best solution occurs when the return condition is fulfilled.

The computational complexity of the algorithm based on tabu search method depends on the choice of its individual elements, such as method for determining neighborhood, length and type of elements stored in tabu list, method of calculation of the objective function value, backtrack-jump and stop conditions.

The above presented paper used a tabu search algorithm with the elements defined as follows:

- Change operator - change of the color of one of the vertices.
- Tabu list – there was a movement parameter recorded in the tabu list – i.e. the number and color of the vertex on which the change operator was performed were recorded.
- Aspiration criterion – satisfied when the received solution is better than the current best.
- Backtrack-jump condition - number of iterations without improvement.
- Stop criterion – number of iterations of the algorithm or the number of backtrack jumps to the best solution.

6   Parallel Neighborhood Search

Using the results presented by Bożejko and Gniewkowski [5], there was the parallelization of neighborhood setting. The expected improvement of acceleration of algorithm is due to factor: designation of a neighbor is the process longer than the calculation of the objective function, and thus the influence of the communication time between the GPU and the CPU will be reduced. Algorithm 1 shows a pseudo-code of algorithm parallelization.

For technical reasons it was not possible to carry out simultaneous parallel designation of the neighborhood and the objective function (currently available software does not permit to run successive threads from the kernel level). Additionally, there was a parallel run of independent algorithms implemented.

7   Computational Experiments

The proposed method of parallelization of the objective function was used in the previously described tabu search algorithm for preparing a timetable for elementary and secondary schools. The algorithm actions were tested on instances

```
Algorithm 1.
Functions: DesignateNeighbors(neighbors, solution, lesson, term)
- designates attractiveness of neighbor by the transfer of lessons
to appropriate term
        designateBest(S, p) - function determines the best neigh-
bor from the set S
Input: π - current solution
        Ll - number of lessons
        Lt - number of terms (periods)
Output: S - vector of sorted neighbors

for p := 1 to Ll * Lt
    parallel do DesignateNeighbors(S, π, p/Ll, p%Ll)
end
for p := 1 to N
    parallel do designateBest(S, p)
end
```

Fig. 1. Parallel neighbor search

generated on the basis of actual data (collected from educational institutions in Poland) and run on a computer equipped with a six-core Intel Core i7 CPU X980 (3.33GHz) equipped with nVidia Tesla S2050 GPU (1792 cores) running at 64-bit Linux operating system Ubuntu 10.04.4 LTS. Parallel algorithms were written using CUDA technology. There was one type of tests carried out - the duration time of the whole algorithm depending on the size of the instance (number of lessons). The results are shown in Tables 1 and 2.

Table 1. Duration of algorithm's run-time

Number of	$t \; [s]$					
lessons	CS	GS	GPF	GRN1	GPN2	GRN3
156	1.09	59.25	63.52	0.94	0.19	0.15
312	4.13	270.55	259.56	2.82	0.63	0.52
468	9.16	702.76	687.85	5.65	1.40	1.23
546	40.15	2571.78	2595.80	71.69	17.45	7.42
624	15.87	1422.77	1395.58	9.07	2.48	2.19
780	24.79	2470.89	2461.27	14.04	3.93	0.36
936	35.96	3995.93	4039.51	20.47	5.96	5.47
1092	107.62	16026.34	13931.39	400.21	215.74	214.85
mean:	**29.85**	**3440.03**	**3179.31**	**65.61**	**30.97**	**29.02**

Individual columns in Table 1 designate:

- t – duration of run-time of tabu search algorithm in the given configuration,
- CS – tabu search algorithm computed sequentially on CPU (*Central Processing Unit*),

- *GS* – tabu search algorithm omputed sequentially on *GPU* (*Graphics Processing Unit*),
- *GPF* - tabu search algorithm with objective function computed parallel on *GPU*,
- *GRN1* - tabu search algorithm with parallel neighbor search computed on *GPU*, one processor is combined with one node
- *GRN2* - tabu search algorithm with parallel neighbor search computed on *GPU*, one processor is combined with one neighbor
- *GRN3* - tabu search algorithm with parallel neighbor search computed on *GPU*, parallel run of independent algorithm, one processor is combined with one neighbor
- Absolute acceleration – ratio of parallel run-time of algorithm on *GPU* (GRN2) to sequential run-time on *CPU* (CS).
- Mean acceleration - ratio of parallel run-time of algorithm on *GPU* (GRN2) to sequential run-time on *GPU* (GS).
- *f* - Karp–Flatt metric

Table 2. Parameters of algorithm's run-time

Number of	Acceleration		f
lessons	Absolute	Relative	
156	5.91	319.75	0.0026
312	6.60	432.22	0.0017
468	6.52	500.63	0.0014
546	2.30	147.37	0.0060
624	6.40	573.63	0.0012
780	6.31	628.68	0.0010
936	6.04	670.78	0.0009
1092	0.50	74.29	0.0120
mean:	**5.07**	**418.42**	**0.0036**

The obtained result for *GPF* shows that using *TS* with parallel computing of objective function doesn't give good acceleration. On the other hand using algorithm with parallel neighbor search provide big acceleration (up to 670 times). In Table 1, we can observe that *CUDA* technology manage well with simulate additional processors- comparison *GRN2* with *GRN1*, *GRN2* requires more processor (up to over 40 thousand) than *GPU* deliver (1792 cores). Moreover comparison between *GRN2* and *GRN3* shows that parallel run of independent algorithm don't provides much better result.

The obtained results show that the use of parallel neighborhood search algorithm improves the run-time of the algorithm (in most cases). This follows from a comparison of the sequential and parallel algorithms performance calculated on the same device (in this case on the *GPU*). Also, comparison between *GRN2* and *CS* (absolute accelerate) in most cases is larger than 1.The technology difference between *CPU* and *GPU* processor is cause of the size of acceleration.

8   Conclusions

The paper proposes a parallelization of the tabu search algorithm for the timetabling problem taking under consideration parallelization of the most time-consuming elements. Part of algorithm responsible for calculation of the objective function and viewing neighborhoods was paralleled. These solutions help to improve the performance time of the algorithm, however, they do not affect the results obtained. The obtained results show the actual gain resulting from the parallelization algorithm for performing calculations sequentially and in parallel on the same device.

Acknowledgement. The work was supported by the OPUS grant DEC-2012/05/B/ST7/00102 of Polish National Centre of Science.

References

1. Adenso-Diaz, B.: Restricted neighbourhood in the tabu search for the flow shop problem. European Journal of Operational Research 62, 27–37 (1992)
2. Ahandani, M., Baghmisheh, M., Zadeh, M., Ghaemi, S.: Hybrid particle swarm optimization transplanted into a hyper-heuristic structure for solving examination timetabling problem. Swarm and Evolutionary Computation 7, 21–34 (2012)
3. Alvarez-Valdes, R., Crespo, E., Tamarit, J.M.: Design and implementation of a course scheduling system using Tabu Search. European Journal of Operational Research 137, 512–523 (2002)
4. Asham, M.G., Soliman, M.M., Ramadan, R.A.: Trans Genetic Coloring Approach for Timetabling Problem. International Journal of Computer Application (1), 17–25 (2011)
5. Bożejko, W., Gniewkowski, Ł.: Parallel tabu search algorithm for timetabling determination (in Polish). In: Knosala, R. (ed.) Innovations in Management and Production, Polish Production Management Society Publishing House (2013)
6. Bożejko, W., Uchroński, M., Wodecki, M.: Multi-GPU Tabu Search Metaheuristic for the Flexible Job Shop Scheduling Problem. In: Klempous, R., Nikodem, J., Chaczko, Z. (eds.) Topics in Intelligent Engineering and Informatics Series, vol. 6, pp. 43–60 (2014)
7. Bożejko, W., Wodecki, M.: Parallel genetic algorithm for minimizing total weighted completion time. In: Rutkowski, L., Siekmann, J.H., Tadeusiewicz, R., Zadeh, L.A. (eds.) ICAISC 2004. LNCS (LNAI), vol. 3070, pp. 400–405. Springer, Heidelberg (2004)
8. Bożejko, W., Uchroński, M., Wodecki, M.: The new golf neighborhood for the flexible job shop problem. In: Proceedings of the ICCS 2010. Procedia Computer Science, vol. 1, pp. 289–296 (2010)
9. Bożejko, W., Uchroński, M., Wodecki, M.: Solving the Flexible Job Shop Problem on Multi-GPU. In: Proceedings of ICCS 2012. Procedia Computer Science, vol. 9, pp. 2020–2023 (2012)
10. Burke, E., McCollum, B., Meisels, A., Petrovic, S., Qu, R.: A graph-based hyper-heuristic for educational timetabling problems. European Journal of Operational Research 176, 177–192 (2007)

11. Burke, E., Rudová, H.: Practice and Theory of Automated Timetabling. In: Burke, E.K., Rudová, H. (eds.) PATAT 2007. LNCS, vol. 3867, Springer, Heidelberg (2007)
12. Grabowski, J., Wodecki, M.: A very fast tabu search algorithm for the permutation flow shop problem with makespan criterion. Computers & Operations Research 31, 1891–1909 (2004)
13. Neufeld, G.A., Tartar, J.: Graph coloring conditions for the existence of solutions to the timetable problem. Communications of the ACM 17(8), 450–453 (1974)
14. Nowicki, E., Smutnicki, C.: A fast tabu search algorithm for the permutation flow-shop problem. European Journal of Operational Research 91, 160–175 (1996)
15. Rahman, S.A., Bargiela, A., Burke, E.K., Özcan, E., McCollum, B., McMullan, P.: Adaptive linear combination of heuristic orderings in constructing examination timetables. European Journal of Operational Research 232(2), 287–297 (2014)
16. Salwani, A., Hamza, T.: On the use of multi neighbourhood structures within a Tabu-based memetic approach to university timetabling problems. Information Sciences 191, 146–168 (2012)
17. Socha, K., Sampels, M., Manfrin, M.: Ant algorithms for the university course timetabling problem with regard to the state-of-the-art. In: Raidl, G.R., et al. (eds.) EvoWorkshops 2003. LNCS, vol. 2611, pp. 334–345. Springer, Heidelberg (2003)
18. Wen-Mei, H.: GPU Computing Gems. Morgan Kaufmann Publ. (2011)
19. Zhipeng, L., Jin-Kao, H.: Adaptive Tabu Search for course timetabling. European Journal of Operational Research 200, 235–244 (2010)

Scheduling Problem with Uncertain Parameters in Just in Time System

Wojciech Bożejko[1], Paweł Rajba[2], and Mieczysław Wodecki[2]

[1] Institute of Computer Engineering, Control and Robotics
Wrocław University of Technology
Janiszewskiego 11-17, 50-372 Wrocław, Poland
wojciech.bozejko@pwr.wroc.pl
[2] Institute of Computer Science, University of Wrocław
Joliot-Curie 15, 50-383 Wrocław, Poland
mwd@ii.uni.wroc.pl

Abstract. This paper tackles a stochastic version of single machine scheduling with random processing times and due dates. The objective function is to find a schedule of jobs which minimizes the weighted sum of earliness and tardiness penalties, taking into consideration probabilistic modelling of the tasks processing times. Since the problem is NP-hard, it is not possible to find optimal values for large scales of the problem in a reasonable run time, therefore, a tabu search meta-heuristic is provided. Computational experiments demonstrate that the proposed tabu search algorithm is strongly capable of finding near optimal stability solutions with a very low gap.

1 Introduction

In many manufacturing processes, there appear great difficulties in clear defining of parameters. In addition, in many cases data come from imprecise measurement devices. Such a case takes place for example in scheduling of construction projects [1], for which the weather decides when a job starts. On the basis of management practice, it is commonly believed that data are most commonly uncertain and imprecise. The data often change their values already in the process of implementation of taken solution, destroying not only their optimality, but also their acceptability. Thus, decision-making in uncertain condition (that is, in case of lack of accurate parameter values) becomes a commonplace.

Optimization problems with uncertain data are solved mainly with use of either probabilistic methods or fuzzy set theory. The first approach is used when uncertainty of parameters is of random character, for instances like: weather, demand, absenteeism of employees, equipment failure, etc. The second case exemplifies the uniqueness of production, changes in technology, uncertainty of measurement, etc. The complexity of the problems and computational difficulties already for the deterministic case result in the fact that the problems with uncertain data are less often formulated and analyzed.

L. Rutkowski et al. (Eds.): ICAISC 2014, Part II, LNAI 8468, pp. 456–467, 2014.

Production organization in *just in time* system (called *JIT* for short) allows us to synchronize the supply of materials and semi-finished products with the demand for manufactured products. As a result, the system reduces not only the costs (production area and capital resources corresponding to production in progress), but also improves the flow of production.

In this paper we consider the problem of single machine scheduling minimizing the total cost of the work not completed on time. we present algorithms based on the tabu search method for solving the problem of deterministic data represented by random variables which follow the normal distribution. The main goal is to construct algorithms determining stable solutions resistant to distortions (disorders) of parameters appearing during the implementation, which destabilize the production process. This enables creation of schedules which take into consideration the potential distortions that occur during the production phase.

2   Problem Formulation

Single machine scheduling problem considered in this work can be formulated as follows:

Every job from the set $\mathcal{J} = \{1, 2, \ldots, n\}$ must be executed without any stops on the machine that performs at most one job at a time. For the job $i \in \mathcal{J}$, let p_i, e_i, d_i, u_i, w_i be respectively, the execution time, the earliest and at the latest deadlines for completion of the required works and the coefficients of jobs costs for too early or too late completion times. It is necessary to determine the execution order of jobs that minimizes the sum of cost factors coefficients that are not completed according to set deadlines (that is, too early or too late).

If the order of job is fixed and C_i is a job completion time $i \in \mathcal{J}$, then $u_i V_i + w_i U_i$ is called a cost (penalty - for not meeting the deadline) of job completion, where

$$V_i = \begin{cases} 0, & \text{if } C_i \geq e_i, \\ 1, & \text{if } C_i < e_i, \end{cases} \qquad U_i = \begin{cases} 0, & \text{if } C_i \leq d_i, \\ 1, & \text{if } C_i > d_i. \end{cases} \qquad (1)$$

If $V_i = 1$ or $U_i = 1$, then this job is called respectively *accalerated* or *late*. Otherwise, (i.e. when job execution is finished in time interval between e_i and d_i) the job is called *on time*. In the considered problem there must be an order of jobs fixed that minimizes the cost of their completion, that is, the sum $\sum_{i=1}^{n}(u_i V_i + w_i U_i)$.

Every acceptable solution of the considered problem can be represented by certain permutation of elements of the set $\mathcal{J}$. Let Φ be a set of all such permutations. Then, the time of job completion $\pi(i) \in \mathcal{J}$ (executed as i-th in the order) $C_{\pi(i)} = \sum_{j=1}^{i} p_{\pi(i)}$, and the cost of jobs execution (permutation $\pi \in \Phi$) is

$$F(\pi) = \sum_{i=1}^{n}(u_{\pi(i)} V_{\pi(i)} + w_{\pi(i)} U_{\pi(i)}). \qquad (2)$$

The considered problem boils down to determining the optimal permutation $\pi^* \in \Phi$, for which the function $F(\pi)$ defined in (2) reaches a minimum value. In the further part of the work this problem will be denoted by WNET in short (*Weighted Number of Early and Tardy jobs*). It is denoted in literature by $1||\sum(u_iV_i + w_iU_i)$ and belongs to the class of *NP-hard* problems.

Exact algorithms used for WNET problem allow for efficient determination of the optimal solution only if the number of jobs does not exceed 50 (Ronconi and Kawamura [11]), and 80 - in multiprocessor environment (Wodecki [16]). Therefore, in practice there are approximate algorithms used (mainly metaheuristics). They are most often specifically adopted algorithms to solve much general and more widely known in literature single machine problem of scheduling with the criterion $\sum_{i=1}^{n}(u_iE_i + w_iT_i)$. The best examples were published by: Tung-I Tsai [14], Wodecki [17], Shihi-Hsin Chena and al. [12], Rios-Mercado and Rios-Solis [9].

Scheduling problems with uncertain data are solved mainly with the use of either methods based on the probabilistic elements (Zhu and Cai [18], Van den Akker and Hoogeveen [15], Dean [4]) or with the use of fuzzy sets theory (Prade, [8] and Ishii [5]). They enable the inclusion of uncertainty already at the stage of mathematical model construction and also in constructed algorithms. The accuracy of these algorithms is determined on the basis of examples of the family of randomly generated instances according to a certain probability distribution. The accuracy specified in the above manner is called stability of the algorithm (or, more generally - the methods of solving the optimization problem).

3   Classic Tabu Search Algorithm

In solving *NP-hard* problems of discrete optimization we almost always use approximate algorithms. The solutions given by these algorithms are, in their appliance, fully satisfying (they often differ from the best known solutions by less then 1%). Most of them belong to the local search methods group. Their acting consists in viewing in sequence a subset of a set of acceptable solutions, and in pointing out the best one according to a determined criterion. One of this method realizations is the tabu search, whose basic criterions are:

move	- a function that converts one solution into another one,
neighborhood	- a subset of a set of acceptable solutions, whose elements are rigorously analyzed,
tabu list	- a list containing the attributes of a certain number of solutions analyzed recently,
ending condition	- most of the time fixed by the number of algorithm iterations.

Let $\pi \in \Phi$ be a starting permutation, $\mathcal{N}(\pi)$ neighborhood of permutation π, F costs function, L_{TS} a tabu list and π^* the best solution found so far.

Algorithm Tabu Search (TS)

1 *repeat*
2 Determine the neighborhood $\mathcal{N}(\pi)$ of permutation π;
3 Delete from $\mathcal{N}(\pi)$ permutations forbidden by the tabu list L_{TS};
4 Determine a permutation $\delta \in \mathcal{N}(\pi)$, such that
5     $F(\delta) = \min\{F(\beta) : \beta \in \mathcal{N}(\pi)\}$;
6 *if* $(F(\delta) < F(\pi^*))$ *then*
7     $\pi^* := \delta$;
8 Place attributes δ on the list L_{TS};
9     $\pi := \delta$
10 *until* (*the completion condition*).

The computational complexity of the algorithm depends mostly on the way the neighborhood is generated and viewed. Below we present in details the basics elements of the algorithm.

3.1 The Move and the Neighborhood

Let $\pi = (\pi(1), \ldots, \pi(n))$ be any permutation from Φ, and

$$\mathcal{L}(\pi) = \{\pi(i) : C_{\pi(i)} < e_{\pi(i)} \text{ or } C_{\pi(i)} > d_{\pi(i)}\},$$

the *set of early or tardy jobs* in π.

Let π_l^k ($l = 1, 2, \ldots, k-1, k+1, \ldots, n$) be the permutation obtained from π by interchanging $\pi(k)$ and $\pi(l)$. We can say that π_l^k is generated from π by a *swap move* (*s-move*) s_l^k (i.e. $\pi_l^k = s_l^k(\pi)$). Let $\mathcal{M}(\pi(k))$ be the set of *s-moves* of the element $\pi(k)$. Define

$$\mathcal{M}(\pi) = \bigcup_{\pi(k) \in \mathcal{L}(\pi)} \mathcal{M}(\pi(k)),$$

the set of *s-moves* of all late elements π in the permutation. The cardinality of $\mathcal{M}(\pi)$ is bounded above by $n(n-1)/2$.

The neighborhood of $\pi \in \Phi$ is the set of permutations

$$\mathcal{N}(\pi) = \left\{ s_l^k(\pi) : s_l^k \in \mathcal{M}(\pi) \right\}.$$

While implementing the algorithm, we remove from the neighborhood the permutations whose attributes are on the list L_{TS} (see. [2],[3]).

3.2 The Tabu List

In order to avoid generating a cycle (by returning to the same permutation after a small number of algorithm iterations), some attributes of every move are saved in a tabu list. It is operated according to the FIFO queue. We put the move's attribute, the tuple $(\pi(r), j, F(\pi_j^r))$, on the tabu list L_{TS} when making the $s_j^r \in \mathcal{M}(\pi)$ move (generating from $\pi \in \Phi$ the permutation π_j^r).

Suppose that we analyze the move $s_l^k \in \mathcal{M}(\beta)$ that generates from $\beta \in \Phi$ the permutation β_l^k. If the tuple (r, j, Ψ) such that $\beta(k) = r$, $l = j$ and $F(\beta_l^k) \geq \Psi$ is on the L_{TS} list, such a move is forbidden and removed from $\mathcal{M}(\beta)$ set. The only parameter of this list is its length, the number of elements it contains. There are many realizations of the tabu list presented in the given references.

4   Randomization

The literature presents various scheduling problems with random parameters, mainly - times of jobs execution with normal, exponential or uniform distribution (for instance Van den Akker and Hoogeveen [15], Jang [6] and Soroush [13]). In the following part of the work we consider the problem of WNET, in which the parameters are determined by random variables with normal distribution.

In order to simplify the notation, we assume in this section that the considered solution is a natural permutation, that is $\pi = (1, 2, \ldots, n)$. Moreover, if X is a random variable, then by F_X we denote its distribution.

If the times of jobs execution $\tilde{p}_i$ $(i \in \mathcal{J})$ are random variables with normal distribution (i.e. $\tilde{p}_i \sim N(p_i, \alpha \cdot p_i)$) with mean p_i and standard deviation $\alpha \cdot p_i$ (α parameter is determined experimentally), then the times of jobs completion $\tilde{C}_i = \tilde{p}_1 + \tilde{p}_2 + \ldots + \tilde{p}_i$ and the values denoting too early $\tilde{V}_i$ or too late $\tilde{U}_i$ jobs execution are random variables. In addition, a random variable is also a function (equivalent of criterion (2))

$$\tilde{F}(\pi) = \sum_{i=1}^{n} (u_i \tilde{V} + w_i \tilde{U}). \tag{3}$$

In the process of determination of the best element of the neighbourhood, in the tabu search method (instructions (4) and (5) of the algorithm), we compare the values of the goal function for different solutions. In case when the function is random variable (3), we use some of its moments or their combinations. The computational experiments conducted initially have shown that the best results were obtained when the first or the sum of the first and second central moment (mean and variance) are used for the comparison of solutions. Therefore, our further consideration will refer to the following two functions:

$$W_1(\pi) = E(\tilde{F}) = \sum_{i=1}^{n} (u_i E(\tilde{V}) + w_i E(\tilde{U})), \tag{4}$$

$$W_2(\pi) = E(\tilde{F}) + D^2(\tilde{F}) = \sum_{i=1}^{n} \left(u_i (E(\tilde{V}) + D^2(\tilde{V})) + w_i (E(\tilde{U}) + D^2(\tilde{U})) \right). \tag{5}$$

If the times of jobs execution $\tilde{p}_i$ $(i \in \mathcal{J})$ are independent random variables, then it's easy to notice that $E(\tilde{V}) = E(\tilde{V}^2)$

We remind that the parameters of the considered scheduling problem are: the execution times p_i, the earliest e_i, the latest d_i times of execution and coefficients of penalty function u_i and w_i. In the further paragraph we will consider the following non-deterministic cases:

A. random p_i, deterministic: u_i, w_i, e_i and d_i,
B. random: p_i, e_i, deterministic: u_i, w_i and d_i,
C. random: p_i, d_i, deterministic: u_i, w_i and e_i,
D. random: p_i, e_i and d_i, deterministic: u_i, w_i.

Case A (problem: $1|\tilde{p}_i \sim stoch| \sum(u_i V_i + w_i E_i)$)
The times of jobs execution $\tilde{p}_i \sim N(p_i, \alpha \cdot p_i)$ ($i \in J$) are independent random variables with normal distribution. It is easy to notice that the times of jobs completion are random variables with normal distribution, that is:

$$\tilde{C}_i \sim N(p_1 + \ldots + p_i, \alpha \cdot \sqrt{p_1^2 + \ldots + p_i^2}). \tag{6}$$

Since

$$\tilde{V}_i = \begin{cases} 0, \text{ if } \tilde{C}_i \geq e_i, \\ 1, \text{ if } \tilde{C}_i < e_i, \end{cases} \qquad \tilde{U}_i = \begin{cases} 0, \text{ if } \tilde{C}_i \leq d_i, \\ 1, \text{ if } \tilde{C}_i > d_i, \end{cases}$$

then

$$E(\tilde{V}_i) = E(\tilde{V}_i^2) = P(\tilde{C}_i < e_i) = F_{\tilde{C}_i}(e_i),$$

$$E(\tilde{U}_i) = E(\tilde{U}_i^2) = P(\tilde{C}_i > d_i) = 1 - F_{\tilde{C}_i}(d_i),$$

$$D^2(\tilde{V}_i) = F_{\tilde{C}_i}(e_i) - (F_{\tilde{C}_i}(e_i))^2, \quad D^2(\tilde{U}_i) = F_{\tilde{C}_i}(d_i) - (F_{\tilde{C}_i}(d_i))^2.$$

Ultimately, for variables of jobs execution times, as the comparative criteria (according to definition in 4 and 5) to solutions we adopt:

$$W_1^A(\pi) = \sum_{i=1}^n \left(u_i F_{\tilde{C}_i}(e_i) + w_i \left(1 - F_{\tilde{C}_i}(d_i)\right) \right),$$

$$W_2^A(\pi) = \sum_{i=1}^n \left[u_i \left(2 F_{\tilde{C}_i}(e_i) - (F_{\tilde{C}_i}(e_i))^2\right) + w_i \left(1 - (F_{\tilde{C}_i}(d_i))^2\right) \right].$$

Case B (problem: $1|\tilde{p}_i, \tilde{e}_i \sim stoch| \sum(u_i V_i + w_i E_i)$)
We assume that the times of jobs execution $\tilde{p}_i \sim N(p_i, \alpha \cdot p_i)$ and the earliest times of jobs completion $\tilde{e}_i \sim N(e_i, \alpha \cdot e_i)$ ($i \in \mathcal{J}$) are independent random variables with normal distribution. To simplify the problem, let $\tilde{G}_i = \tilde{C}_i - e_i$ (distribution of random variable $\tilde{C}_i$ was presented in (6)). It is easy to show, that the variable has normal distribution For the above presented cases random variables have the following distribution:

$$\tilde{G}_i \sim N(p_1 + \ldots + p_i - e_i, \alpha \cdot \sqrt{p_1^2 + \ldots + p_i^2 + e_i^2}). \tag{7}$$

In this case

$$\tilde{V}_i = \begin{cases} 0, \text{ if } \tilde{C}_i \geq \tilde{e}_i, \\ 1, \text{ if } \tilde{C}_i > \tilde{e}_i, \end{cases} \qquad \tilde{U}_i = \begin{cases} 0, \text{ if } \tilde{C}_i \leq d_i, \\ 1, \text{ if } \tilde{C}_i > d_i, \end{cases}$$

Thus,

$$E(\tilde{V}_i) = E(\tilde{V}_i^2) = P(\tilde{C}_i < e_i) = P(\tilde{C}_i - e_i < 0) = F_{\tilde{G}_i}(0),$$

$$E(\tilde{U}_i) = E(\tilde{U}_i^2) = P(\tilde{C}_i > d_i) = 1 - F_{\tilde{C}_i}(d_i),$$

$$D^2(\tilde{V}_i) = F_{\tilde{G}_i}(0) - (F_{\tilde{G}_i}(0))^2, \quad D^2(\tilde{U}_i) = F_{\tilde{C}_i}(d_i) - (F_{\tilde{C}_i}(d_i))^2.$$

As the comparative criteria of solutions, we adopt:

$$W_1^B(\pi) = \sum_{i=1}^{n} \left(u_i F_{\tilde{G}_i}(0) + w_i \left(1 - F_{\tilde{C}_i}(d_i) \right) \right),$$

$$W_2^B(\pi) = \sum_{i=1}^{n} \left(u_i \left(2 F_{\tilde{G}_i}(0) - (F_{\tilde{G}_i}(0))^2 \right) + w_i \left(1 - (F_{\tilde{C}_i}(d_i))^2 \right) \right).$$

Case C (problem: $1|\tilde{p}_i, \tilde{d}_i \sim stoch| \sum(u_i V_i + w_i E_i)$)

We assume that the times of jobs execution $\tilde{p}_i \sim N(p_i, \alpha{\cdot}p_i)$ and the latest jobs completion times $\tilde{d}_i \sim N(d_i, \alpha \cdot d_i)$ $(i \in \mathcal{J})$ are independent random variables.

Similarly like in the previous case, we introduce random variables $\tilde{H}_i = \tilde{C}_i - d_i$ with normal distribution, that is

$$\tilde{H}_i \sim N(p_1 + \ldots + p_i - d_i, \alpha \cdot \sqrt{p_1^2 + \ldots + p_i^2 + d_i^2}). \tag{8}$$

Because

$$\tilde{V}_i = \begin{cases} 0, & \text{if } \tilde{C}_i \geq e_i, \\ 1, & \text{if } \tilde{C}_i < e_i, \end{cases} \qquad \tilde{U}_i = \begin{cases} 0, & \text{if } \tilde{C}_i \leq \tilde{d}_i, \\ 1, & \text{if } \tilde{C}_i \leq \tilde{d}_i, \end{cases}$$

and

$$E(\tilde{V}_i) = E(\tilde{V}_i^2) = P(\tilde{C}_i < e_i) = F_{\tilde{C}_i}(e_i),$$

$$E(\tilde{U}_i) = E(\tilde{U}_i^2) = P(\tilde{C}_i > d_i) = P(\tilde{C}_i - d_i > 0) = 1 - F_{\tilde{H}_i}(0),$$

$$D^2(\tilde{V}_i) = F_{\tilde{C}_i}(e_i) - (F_{\tilde{C}_i}(e_i))^2, \quad D^2(\tilde{U}_i) = F_{\tilde{H}_i}(0) - (F_{\tilde{H}_i}(0))^2.$$

thus, as a comparative criteria of solutions we adopt:

$$W_1^C(\pi) = \sum_{i=1}^{n} \left(u_i F_{\tilde{C}_i}(e_i) + w_i \left(1 - F_{\tilde{H}_i}(0) \right) \right),$$

$$W_2^C(\pi) = \sum_{i=1}^{n} \left(u_i \left(2 F_{\tilde{C}_i}(e_i) - (F_{\tilde{C}_i}(e_i))^2 \right) + w_i \left(1 - (F_{\tilde{H}_i}(0))^2 \right) \right).$$

Case D (problem: $1|\tilde{p}_i, \tilde{e}_i, \tilde{d}_i \sim stoch| \sum(u_i V_i + w_i E_i)$)

In this case the execution times $\tilde{p}_i \sim N(p_i, \alpha{\cdot}p_i)$, the earliest $\tilde{e}_i \sim N(e_i, \alpha{\cdot}e_i)$ and the latest $\tilde{d}_i \sim N(d_i, \alpha \cdot d_i)$ $(i \in \mathcal{J})$ times of jobs are independent random variables with normal distribution.

We define functions

$$\tilde{V}_i = \begin{cases} 0, & \text{if } \tilde{C}_i \geq \tilde{e}_i, \\ 1, & \text{if } \tilde{C}_i < \tilde{e}_i, \end{cases} \qquad \tilde{U}_i = \begin{cases} 0, & \text{if } \tilde{C}_i \leq \tilde{d}_i, \\ 1, & \text{if } \tilde{C}_i > \tilde{d}_i, \end{cases}$$

With use of random variables $G_i = \tilde{C}_i - e_i$ and $H_i = \tilde{C}_i - d_i$, whose distributions have been presented in (7) and (8), we obtain

$$E(\tilde{V}_i) = E(\tilde{V}_i^2) = P(\tilde{C}_i < e_i) = P(\tilde{C}_i - e_i < 0) = F_{\tilde{G}_i}(0),$$

$$E(\tilde{U}_i) = E(\tilde{U}_i^2) = P(\tilde{C}_i > d_i) = P(\tilde{C}_i - d_i > 0) = 1 - F_{\tilde{H}_i}(0),$$

$$D^2(\tilde{V}_i) = F_{\tilde{G}_i}(0) - (F_{\tilde{G}_i}(0))^2, \qquad D^2(\tilde{U}_i) = F_{\tilde{H}_i}(0) - (F_{\tilde{H}_i}(0))^2.$$

Finally

$$W_1^D(\pi) = \sum_{i=1}^n \left(u_i F_{\tilde{G}_i}(0) + w_i \left(1 - F_{\tilde{H}_i}(0) \right) \right),$$

$$W_2^D(\pi) = \sum_{i=1}^n \left(u_i \left(2 F_{\tilde{G}_i}(0) - (F_{\tilde{G}_i}(0))^2 \right) + w_i \left(1 - (F_{\tilde{H}_i}(0))^2 \right) \right).$$

5   The Algorithms' Stability

In this section we shall introduce a certain measure which let us examine the influence of the change of jobs' parameters on the goal function value (2) i.e. the solution stability.

Let $\delta = ((p_1, u_1, w_1, e_1, d_1), \dots, (p_n, u_n, w_n, e_n, d_n))$ be an example of data (deterministic) for the WNET problem. By $D(\delta)$ we denote a set of data generated from δ by a disturbance of jobs parameters. A disturbance consists in changing these times on random determined values.

Let $A = \{AD, AP\}$ where AD and AP is the deterministic and the probabilistic algorithm respectively (i.e. solving examples with deterministic or random times of jobs' performance) for the WNET problem. By π_δ we denote a solution (a permutation) determined by the algorithm A for a data δ. Then, let $F(A, \pi_\delta, \phi)$ be the cost of jobs' execution (2) for the example ϕ in a sequence determined by a solution (a permutation) π_δ determined by the algorithm A for data δ. Then,

$$\Delta(A, \delta, D(\delta)) = \frac{1}{|D(\delta)|} \sum_{\phi \in D(\delta)} \frac{F(A, \pi_\delta, \phi) - F(AD, \pi_\phi, \phi)}{F(AD, \pi_\phi, \phi)},$$

we call the solution stability π_δ (of an example δ) determined by the algorithm A on the set of disturbed data $D(\delta)$.

Let Ω be a set of deterministic examples for the problem of jobs' arrangement. The stability rate of the algorithm A on the set Ω is defined in the following way:

$$S(A, \Omega) = \frac{1}{|\Omega|} \sum_{\delta \in \Omega} \Delta(A, \delta, D(\delta)). \tag{9}$$

In the following section we will present numerical experiments that allow comparisons of the deterministic stability coefficient $S(AD, \Omega)$ with the probabilistic stability coefficient $S(AP, \tilde{\Omega})$.

6 Computational Experiments

Deterministic data were obtained on the basis of the examples for the problem $n|1||\sum w_i T_i$ placed on page of OR-Library [7]. For every n ($n = 40, 50, 100$) the data include 125 examples each (triangles (p_i, w_i, d_i), $i = 1, 2, \ldots n$. Every example was complemented with the earliest acceptable time of commencement e_i and penalty coefficient u_i, generated according to uniform distribution suitably from the range $[0, d_i/1.2]$ and $[1, 10]$, $i = 1, 2, \ldots n$. In total, a set of output deterministic data Ω contains 375 examples.

For each example of the deterministic data set there were corresponding examples of probabilistic data assigned, that is, containing sequences of random variables with normal distribution: $\tilde{p}_i \sim N(p_i, \alpha \cdot p_i)$ $\tilde{e}_i \sim N(e_i, \alpha \cdot e_i)$, $\tilde{d}_i \sim N(d_i, \alpha \cdot d_i)$ (depending on the considered case **A,B,C** or **D** the data contain respectively random variable or numerical value). Then, there were computational experiments carried out in order to determine the value of the parameter α (occurring in standard deviation of distributions of random variables). The results were compared for values $\alpha \in \{0.01, 0.02, \ldots, 0.2, 0.3, 0.4, 0.5\}$ and finally there was $\alpha = 0.1$ adopted. The set of probabilistic data generated with determined in the above manner parameter α, we denote by $\tilde{\Omega}$.

Every time we start an algorithm (either deterministic or probabilistic one), as the starting permutation we assume $\pi = (1, 2, \ldots, n)$, and the lenghty of tabu list – $n/3$. Examining the quality of the solutions of the two algorithms (deterministic and probabilistic) the results are compared with the solution values (called later 'the best') determined by a very good algorithm of solving the problem $1||\sum(u_i E_i + w_i T_i))$ described in the work of Wodecki [17].

In the chapter **Randomization** there were presented the two criteria for elements of neighbourhood selection (W_1 and W_2) which can be used in the construction of the probabilistic algorithm. In order to define the quality of the solutions determined by algorithms (values of goal function (2)) there were computations for both versions of probabilistic algorithm made, on the examples from the set $\tilde{\Omega}$ and the deterministic algorithm AD (on the instances from the set Ω). The comparative results(average relative error in relation to the 'best' solutions) are shown in Table 1 (columns marked with AP_1 and AP_2 include the results of probabilistic algorithm respectively from the choice criterion W_1 (4) and W_2 (5).

According to expectations the deterministic algorithm finds much better solutions. For the number of iterations n (n is a size of a problem) the average mean error for the solutions set by the above algorithm is 7.79%, and for probabilistic algorithms, 9.45% and 9.59% respectively. By n^2 number of iterations the proportions are similar. A significant increase in the number of iterations (from n to n^2) causes only small decrease of the mean error (of deterministic

Table 1. Average relative error (in percentage) of the deterministic algorithm AD and of probabilistic algorithms AP_1 and AP_2

n	Iteration number n			Iteration number n^2		
	AD	AP_1	AP_2	AD	AP_1	AP_2
40	5.12	6.86	7.01	4.98	5.21	6.11
50	7.37	9.11	9.38	7.01	8,34	8.72
100	10.88	12.38	11.37	8.76	10.52	9.54
Average	**7.79**	**9.45**	**9.59**	**6.92**	**8.02**	**8.12**

algorithm) from 7.79% to 7.25%. This proportion is similar for all other cases. The comparison of stability was made not only for the deterministic algorithm

Table 2. Stability coefficients (9) in % of deterministic AD and probabilistic algorithm AP_1 (with comparative criterion W_1 (4))

n	Algorithm AD		Algorithm AP_1	
	$n/2$ iterations	n iterations	$n/2$ iterations	n iterations
Case A ($\tilde{p}_i \sim stoch$)				
40	1.36	1.55	0.31	0.26
50	1.58	1.90	0.28	0.18
100	1.78	1.97	0.33	0.20
Average	**1.57**	**1.80**	**0.31**	**0.21**
Case B ($\tilde{p}_i, \tilde{e}_i \sim stoch$)				
40	2.02	2.38	0.41	0.32
50	2.16	2.57	0.37	0.37
100	3.61	3.43	0.26	0.51
Average	**2.60**	**2.80**	**0.35**	**0.40**
Case C ($\tilde{p}_i, \tilde{d}_i \sim stoch$)				
40	3.37	4.02	1.17	1.19
50	3.83	4.59	1.16	1.18
100	5.08	6.06	1.67	1.77
Average	**4.09**	**4.89**	**1.34**	**1.38**
Case D ($\tilde{p}_i, \tilde{e}_i, \tilde{d}_i \sim stoch$)				
40	3.87	4.62	1.23	1.21
50	4.20	5.04	1.24	1.23
100	6.28	7.30	1.74	1.85
Average	**4.78**	**5.65**	**1.40**	**1.43**

AD, but also for the probabilistic one AP_1 (with a choice criterion W_1 (4)) and the number of iterations $n/2$ and n. The calculations of deterministic algorithm AD were made on the examples from the set Ω, and of probabilistic algorithm – on the examples from the set $\tilde{\Omega}$. In order to compare the stability of the two algorithms for each instance of the deterministic data from the set Ω there were 100 examples of disturbed data generated (in total there are 3750 examples). They were then solved by the algorithm AD, and the obtained solutions served as a basis for the stability coefficient for both algorithms. The summary results (the stability coefficients in %) are presented in Table 2.

On this basis it can be concluded that irrespectively to the number of iterations, the probabilistic algorithm has almost three to more than six times smaller stability coefficient than the deterministic algorithm.

There were also computations made for the second - probabilistic algorithm AP_2 (with a comparative criterion W_2 (5)). Generally, the results are similar to those presented in Table 2.

7   Remarks and Conclusions

In this work there was considered a problem of uncertain data modeling methods with the use of random variables with normal distribution, which well describes the 'natural' randomness most often met while dealing with management practices. The paper presents the design of algorithm based on the tabu search method for some single machine jobs scheduling problem in JIT system. Computational experiments were conducted to investigate the stability of algorithms, that is, the problem of the impact of the disorder parameter on changes in values of the optimized criterion. The obtained results clearly indicate that much more stable are the probabilistic algorithms, that is the algorithms, in which, as the comparative criterion there was a function of central moments of random goal functions adopted.

Acknowledgements. The work was supported by the OPUS grant DEC-2012/ 05/B/ST7/ 00102 of Polish National Center of Science.

References

1. Bożejko, W., Hejducki, Z., Wodecki, M.: Applying metaheuristic strategies in construction projects management. Journal of Civil Engineering and Management 18(5), 621–630 (2012)
2. Bożejko, W., Wodecki, M.: On the theoretical properties of swap multimoves. Operations Research Letters 35(2), 227–231 (2007)
3. Bożejko, W., Grabowski, J., Wodecki, M.: Block approach-tabu search algorithm for single machine total weighted tardiness problem. Computers & Industrial Engineering 50(1/2), 1–14 (2006)
4. Dean, B.C.: Approximation algorithms for stochastic scheduling problems, PhD thesis, MIT (2005)
5. Ishii, H.: Fuzzy combinatorial optimization. Japanese Journal of Fuzzy Theory and Systems 4(1), 84–96 (1992)
6. Jang, W.: Dynamic scheduling of stochastic jobs a single machine. EJOR 138, 518–530 (2002)
7. OR Library, http://www.ms.ic.ac.uk/info.html
8. Prade, H.: Using fuzzy set theory in a scheduling problem. Fuzzy Sets and Systems 2, 153–165 (1979)
9. Rios-Mercado, R.Z., Rios-Solis (eds.): Just-in-Time. Springer Optimization and Its Applications, vol. 60 (2012)

10. Rogalska, M., Bożejko, W., Hejducki, Z.: Time/cost optimization using hybrid evolutionary algorithm in construction project scheduling. Automation in Construction 18, 24–31 (2008)
11. Ronconi, D.P., Kawamura, M.S.: The single machine earliness and tardiness problem: lower bounds and a branch-and-bound algoruthm. Computational & Applied Mathematics 29(2), 107–124 (2010)
12. Shihi-Hsin, C., Min-Cih, C., Pei-Chann, C., Yuh-Min, C.: EA/G-GA for Single Machine Scheduling Problems with Earliness/Tardiness Costs. Entropy 13, 1152–1169 (2011)
13. Soroush, H.M.: Minimizing the weighted number of early and tardy jobs in a stochasic single machine scheduling problem. EJOR 181, 266–287 (2007)
14. Tung-I Tsai, A.: genetic algorithm for solving the single machine earliness/tardiness problem with distunct due dates and ready times. Int. J. Adv. Manuf. Technol. 32, 994–1000 (2007)
15. Van den Akker, M., Hoogeveen, H.: Minimizing the number of late jobs in a stochastic setting usinga chance constraint. J. Sched. 11, 59–69 (2008)
16. Wodecki, M.: A Branch-and-Bound Parallel Algorithm for Single-Machine Total Weighted Tardiness Problem. Advanced Manufacturing Technology 37, 996–1004 (2008)
17. Wodecki, M.: A block approach to earliness-tardiness scheduling problems. International Journal on Advanced Manufacturing Technology 40, 797–807 (2009)
18. Zhu, X., Cai, X.: General Stochastic Single-Machine Scheduling with Regular Cost Functions. Math. Comput. Modelling 26(3), 95–108 (1997)

Variable Neighborhood Search
for Non-deterministic Problems

Marco Antonio Cruz-Chávez[1], Alina Martínez-Oropeza[1],
Jesús del Carmen Peralta-Abarca[2], Martín Heriberto. Cruz-Rosales[3],
and Martín Martínez-Rangel[4]

[1] Engineering and Applied Science Research Center,
Av. Universidad 1001, Col. Chamilpa, 62209, Cuernavaca, Morelos, México
[2] FCQeI, Av. Universidad 1001, Col. Chamilpa, 62209, Cuernavaca, Morelos, México
[3] FC, Av. Universidad 1001, Col. Chamilpa, 62209, Cuernavaca, Morelos, México
[4] FCAeI, UAEM,
Av. Universidad 1001, Col. Chamilpa, 62209, Cuernavaca, Morelos, México
{mcruz,alinam}@uaem.mx

Abstract. A comparative analysis of several neighborhood structures is presented, including a variable neighborhood structure, which corresponds to a combination of the neighborhood structures evaluated in this paper. The performance of each neighborhood structure was tested using large random instances generated in this research and well-known benchmarks such as the Classical Symmetric Traveling Salesman Problem and the Unrelated Parallel Machines Problem. Experimental results show differences in the performance of the variable neighborhood search when it is applied to problems with differing complexity. Contrary to reports in literature about variable neighborhood searches, its performance varies according to the complexity of the problem.

Keywords: Population, Diversity, Hamming Distance, Population-based Algorithm, Individual.

1 Introduction

For many decades, heuristic methods have been widely used to undertake a large variety of not only theoretical problems, but practical ones too. These problems are classified by the complexity theory into P (Polynomial time), NP (Non-deterministic Polynomial time) and NP-Complete based on their characteristics and nature. NP-Complete problems are the most difficult problems [1], which become intractable in the worst case for large test problems. Because deterministic methods are not enough to solve them, it is necessary to use non-deterministic methods to bind the problem, in an attempt to get high-quality solutions, without the guarantee of optimality.

One of the most frequently used heuristics is local search, which involves the use of neighborhood structures. Sometimes the use of a sole heuristic is not enough to find good solutions for hard problems because the solution space is very complex. In such cases, the neighborhood structures have shown themselves to be efficient search methods for these problems. Recently, a new type of neighborhood structure,

L. Rutkowski et al. (Eds.): ICAISC 2014, Part II, LNAI 8468, pp. 468–478, 2014.

better-known as the Variable Neighborhood Structure (VNS), has been applied to several optimization problems because of its good performance. Moreover, it has been shown to be an efficient method to use when searching for approximated solutions.

There is some research in the literature about variable neighborhood search, as they are referred to in this paper. In [2], the authors present a two phase hybrid approach; the structure combines a VNS in the first phase with an iterated local search in the second phase, while always accepting the best solutions. The variable neighborhood search involves 13 different neighborhood structures, which are randomly selected during execution. Experimental results show the algorithm is competitive with other approaches in literature. For nine data sets, it obtained one improved and eight equal solutions.

Another approach, proposed by [3], is a VNS which is implemented in a local search algorithm. Some modifications of this approach are presented. VNS and its variants were tested in five problems: Travelling Salesman Problem (TSP), p-median Problem (PM), Multi-source Weber Problem (MW), Minimum Sum-of-squares Clustering Problem (MSSCC), and Bilinear Programming Problem with Bilinear Constraints (BBLP). It showed competitive results, especially for the PM and MW problems. In [2], a hybrid approach is presented that combines a variable neighborhood search in the first phase with an iterated local search in the second phase, which always accepts the best solutions for the Attribute Reduction in Rough Set Theory. The approach was tested in over 13 well-known datasets. Experimental results demonstrate that it produces solutions competitive with the best techniques.

This research was motivated by the continuous need to find high-quality solutions for important combinatorial problems, such as TSP and UPMP, because in Meta heuristics, the local search is the most time-consuming procedure. Therefore, in this research, a hybrid local search is applied to an NP and an NP-Complete problem to observe its performance in different complexity problems, under the same conditions.

Experimental results show that the good performance of a variable neighborhood search depends on the search space complexity of the problem. High quality solutions are obtained for CSTSP, which is classified as an NP-Complete problem, but poor quality solutions are obtained for UPMP, which is a less complex NP problem. The contribution of this research is the finding that the performance of local search depends on the hardness of the problem. Contrary to what one might expect, the performance is better for the NP-complete problem than for the NP problem, both of which are studied in this paper.

This paper is organized as follows. Section two and three present an introduction to the complexity problems undertaken, which are the Classical Symmetric Traveling Salesman Problem and the Unrelated Parallel Machines Problem. Section four describes the neighborhood structures tested in this research. Section five details the proposed VNS. Section six explains the statistical analysis performed on the obtained results and compares the results of each structure. Finally, section seven present conclusions.

2   Classical Symmetric Traveling Salesman Problem

The Classical Symmetric Traveling Salesman Problem (CSTSP) is a discrete optimization problem [1, 4], classified as an NP-complete problem [1] due to its complexity and nature. The aim of the Classical Symmetric Traveling Salesman Problem is to minimize the total travel distance when visiting all the cities exactly once and returning to the home town [5]. A graph G = (V, E) consists of a finite set V of vertices, identifying the cities, and a finite multiset E of edges or distances between cities. The problem involves unordered pairs (i, j) of cities, where the same city must not be visited more than once and the total travel distance is minimized. The tour has a beginning city and an ending one. Therefore, E = {(i, j): i, j ∈ V,} and cij is the cost (distance) associated with the edge (i, j). The mathematical formulation of the integer linear programming model is described in (1 to 4). [6], shows the objective function in (1), where the aim is to minimize the total travel cost and is based on a set of constraints (2 to 4), which must be met to obtain feasible solutions. The set of constraints in (2) specifies that only city i can be reached from city j. The set of constraints in (3) specifies that only city j can be reached from city i. The last set of constraints in (4) ensures that all the cities have been visited.

$$\min f = \sum_{(i,j)\in E}^{m} C_{ij}X_{ij} \tag{1}$$

Subject to:

$$\sum_{\{C_j:(i,j)\in E\}} X_{ij} = 1 \qquad \forall i \in E \tag{2}$$

$$\sum_{\{C_i:(i,j)\in E\}} X_{ij} = 1 \qquad \forall j \in E \tag{3}$$

$$\sum_{\{(i,j)\in E, i\in S, j\in S\}} X_{ij} \le |S| - 1 \quad to \ \ S \subset V, 2 \le |S| \le |V| - 2 \quad \forall i \tag{4}$$

3   Unrelated Parallel Machines Problem

The Unrelated Parallel Machines Problem (UPMP) is a variant of the classical Job Shop Scheduling Problem (JSSP) relaxed to get a mapping of UPMP [7]. The UPMP is classified as NP [8]. The UPMP can be described as the set $J=\{1,2,...,n\}$ of n independent jobs that have to be scheduled in $K=\{1, 2, ..., n\}$ positions corresponding to $I=\{1,2,...,m\}$ unrelated parallel machines that process jobs at different rates, meeting certain constraints to obtain feasible solutions according to the objective function. It is done with the goal to minimize the total completion time of processing all the jobs. According to this, any job can be processed in any machine, and any machine can process any job, but the processing time depends on the machine and position of the assigned job. It takes into account the basic constraints of the problem which are shown in the mathematical formulation (5 to 8) [16], and involves a penalization according to the assigned position. This penalization forces the job j to be scheduled in the first position, in an attempt to reduce the processing time.

The features mentioned above show many similarities to the requirements of manufacturing systems currently used in industry. As demand increases, the machinery requirements grow, so enterprises have to acquire new equipment. This is the main reason why machines have different capacities, and it is a central part of the problem. Capacities are considered to try to ensure efficient scheduling while avoiding overspending on equipment and machinery.

$$\min f = \sum_{i=1}^{m}\sum_{j=1}^{n}\sum_{k=1}^{n} kP_{ij}X_{ikj} \tag{5}$$

Subject to:

$$\sum_{i=1}^{m}\sum_{k=1}^{n} X_{ikj} = 1 \qquad j = 1, \dots, n \tag{6}$$

$$\sum_{j=1}^{n} X_{ikj} \leq 1 \qquad i = 1, \dots, m \quad k = 1, \dots, n \tag{7}$$

$$X_{ikj} \in \{0, 1\} \qquad i = 1, \dots, m \quad k = 1, \dots, n, j = 1, \dots, n \tag{8}$$

The mathematical formulation presents the objective function in (5), which minimizes the total completion time of processing all the jobs. The processing time of job j depends on the machine and position where it was assigned, and the processing time kPij directly contributes to the value of the objective function.

The set of constraints represented by (6) ensures that each job will be processed only once. Constraint (7) guarantees that each position k processes at most one job j. The last set of constraints (8) shows that a certain job was scheduled in a certain position in a certain machine. Therefore, xijk can only take binary values, xijk = 1 if the job was assigned, and 0 otherwise.

4 Neighborhood Structures

A neighborhood structure is a technique implemented with an algorithm in order to exploit the solution neighborhood, with the intent to improve the quality of that solution, according to the objective function of the undertaken problem. A critical aspect of designing some optimization algorithms is choosing an appropriate neighborhood structure. This allows for better exploitation of the solution space, according to the algorithm and the problem, because the procedure will help search for new and improved solutions.

A neighborhood structure is determined by the criterion of neighbor selection, that is, the movement σ carried out to reach a solution s' from the current solution s. This procedure is performed iteratively while the selection criterion if fulfilled.

In this research, four different neighborhood structures were applied to local search for the CSTSP, and the UPMP. The neighborhood structures used for CSTSP and UPMP are explained as follows:

- **An Adjacent Pair.** An array position *num* is randomly selected by the neighborhood structure. According to the features of the structure, that position is permutated with the position *num + 1*, and a new neighboring solution s' [9, 10, 11] is obtained. The new solution is then evaluated, according to the objective function.

- **A Random Pair.** Similarly, this neighborhood structure performs a single permutation between two different positions of a solution. The difference from the previously described structure is the type of movement implemented to reach a neighboring solution. In this case, two positions of the solution array are randomly selected (num1 and num2) [1, 10, 12]. These positions must be different and not adjacent. If the condition is fulfilled, the permutation is performed.

- **Two Adjacent Pairs.** In this case, the complexity of the neighborhood structure has increased. This technique applies two permutations, unlike the previous two structures. For this structure, it is necessary to generate two random numbers which correspond to positions in the current solution. The selected positions, num and num1, must be different and non-adjacent. The movement is performed with the position adjacent [13] to the selected one; num permutes with num+1, and num1 with num1+1. In this case there were two randomly selected jobs *j*, which were non-adjacent. The jobs are then placed in the next array position, and they are permuted in pairs, resulting in a new neighboring solution.

- **Two Random Pairs.** This neighborhood structure increases in complexity, because it generates four random numbers (num1, num2, num3, and num4) which have to meet certain characteristics before being taken. The constraints include the numbers being different and non-adjacent. Once the positions are selected, permutations take place, performing swaps in pairs [12, 14, 15]. When applying this neighborhood structure, as compared to the previous structures, the difference is greater between the initial solution and the neighboring one. This indicates that the neighborhood size is larger than in the other cases.

5 Variable Neighborhood Search

A variable neighborhood is a technique that incorporates specific characteristics of more than two different neighborhoods. In the literature, some researchers have developed approaches to exploit this concept, due to its improved performance in comparison to basic neighborhood structures.

The development of the variable neighborhood in this paper was based on the research of [3, 7, 2], their obtained results of the neighborhood structures, and the previous explanation of the CSTSP. This paper presents a more straightforward varia-ble neighborhood search, which incorporates basic and low-complexity searches. This change attempts to optimize the time required to perform the local search, because it is very time-consuming to conduct a neighborhood search.

The variable neighborhood search is able to handle variable neighborhood-sizes, due to the random interaction of the structures during the execution time, which im-proves the exploitation of the solution space. The neighborhood structures presented in this research, including the variable neighborhood structure, were tested for the CSTSP and the UPMP, which are contrasting problems both in concept and in com-plexity. In both cases the neighborhood structures were applied to local search, al-though in the case of UPMP, the local search procedure was implemented to improve the metaheuristic Ant Colony. The structure of the variable neighborhood search is shown in Figure 1 [7].

All the neighborhood structures and the Ant Colony algorithm for UPMP were de-veloped using Visual C, 2008 with Windows Vista Home Premium.

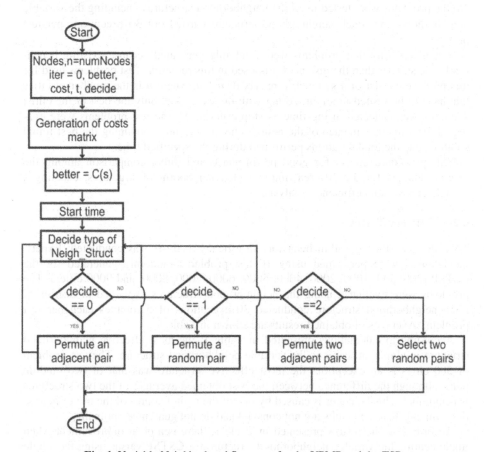

Fig. 1. Variable Neighborhood Structure for the UPMP and the TSP

6   Experimental Results

Tests were performed on a laptop with the following characteristics: Centrino Core 2Duo processor 2.0 GHz, 3GB RAM memory, Windows Vista Home Premium.

Neighborhood structures and the Ant Colony algorithm were developed using a Visual C 2008 compiler. Test problems were randomly generated for 200, 500, 1000, 2000, 4000, 5000, 6000, 7000, 8000, and 9000 cities for the TSP, respectively. In the case of UPMP, test problems were randomly generated for 200, 250, 270, and 300 jobs to be scheduled on 12 machines, respectively.

This research tested the hypothesis: *"The improvement in solution quality depends not only on the applied variable neighborhood structure, but also on the problem complexity"*. This research undertook two problems. Although CSTSP and UPMP are both NP problems, their hardness is different. CSTSP has a more challenging solution space than UPMP [1].

6.1   Experimental Results for CSTSP

All the problems were tested in all the neighborhood structures, including the variable neighborhood one. Each neighborhood structure carried out 30 executions per test problem.

It is noteworthy that problems were randomly generated because existing benchmarks are smaller than the instances proposed in this research. Test problems used for this purpose consist of a symmetric matrix of $n * n$, where n is the number of cities that have to be visited in a tour. Along with the execution, only the best of the elitist solutions were selected, using time as stop criteria. All the test problems were evaluated for 5 minutes in each of the neighborhood structures, obtaining the best found solution, and the total iterations performed during the specified time.

This procedure allows for good performance and direct comparison among the results obtained for the different implemented neighborhood structures, enabling a reliable efficacy and efficiency analysis.

6.2   Efficacy Testing

To understand the algorithm behavior, an efficacy analysis was conducted. Experimental tests were performed using 10 test problems randomly generated for the CSTSP (200, 500, 1000, 2000, 4000, 5000, 6000, 7000, 8000, and 9000 cities). The problems were evaluated using the neighborhood structures explained in Section 5. Each neighborhood structure conducted 30 executions of 5 minutes each per test problem. Averages of obtained results are shown in Table 1.

According to calculations presented in Table 1, the most effective neighborhood structure in almost all cases is the variable neighborhood structure. The test problem of 500 cities is an exception; the most effective structure was that of two random pairs, although the difference between the best obtained averages of the two structures was minimal. This behavior is caused by one of the main features of the use of heuristics, which is that the results are not constant and do not guarantee optimality.

According to the results presented in Table 1, there is a clear improvement when implementing the variable neighborhood structure for CSTSP versus using the single straightforward neighborhood structures. The improvement was obtained not only for the best found solution, but for the worst one also, independent of the problem size. These results are consistent with those reported in literature.

Table 1. Average of the results obtained in experimental testing for different sized problems

Prob_ Size	Adjacent Pair	Random Pair	Two Adjacent Pairs	Two Random Pairs	variable neighborhood
200	2012	1994	1974	1945	**1944**
500	5161	5118	5124	**5057**	5098
1000	49661	49375	49202	49166	**49128**
2000	101075	100617	100467	100856	**100232**
4000	198292	198092	197373	197524	**197280**
5000	52345	51885	51762	51831	**51742**
6000	61216	61173	61178	61228	**61168**
7000	72036	72100	72030	72078	**72014**
8000	82539	82617	82284	82482	**82238**
9000	973283	973009	972938	972947	**972930**

6.3   Efficiency Testing

The efficiency is a measure of the time required to find a high quality solution. In this research, efficiency was calculated for 1000 solutions found by each neighborhood structure, and the different sizes of test problems (200, 500, 1000, 2000, 4000, 5000, 6000 cities, respectively) that were studied. Results are shown graphically in Figure 2.

Figure 2 shows that the behavior of all the evaluated neighborhood structures is very similar for small instances (from 200 to 2000 cities). Starting at 4000 cities, some neighborhood structures begin to require more computational effort to find solutions.

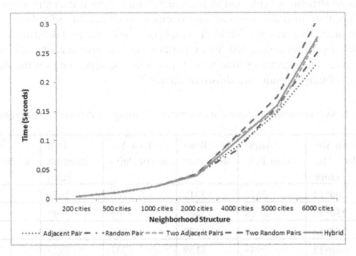

Fig. 2. Time required for five different neighborhood structures to find 1000 solutions for test problems of different sizes (from 200 – 6000 cities)

Naturally, the interesting cases are the results obtained for large problems (from 4000 to 6000 cities). In these cases, there is a clear difference in efficiency under the same conditions, when only the size of the test problem varies. According to the calculations plotted in Figure 8, the behavior of the variable neighborhood structure is constant for large problems. This demonstrates the variable neighborhood structure's efficiency as competitive, because it shows better efficiency than the neighborhood structure of two adjacent pairs and two random pairs in most of cases.

6.4   Experimental Results for UPMP

Experimental tests for UPMP were conducted in the same way for the CSTSP. Therefore, all the test problems were tested, and the Ant Colony algorithm was implemented in all of the neighborhood structures, including the variable neighborhood one. Each neighborhood structure carried out 30 executions per test problem.

Problems were randomly generated. Test problems used for this problem consist of a matrix of $n * mn$, where n is the number of jobs that have to be scheduled in m machines with k positions each one ($k = n$). Along with the execution, only the best of the elitist solutions were selected, using time as stop criteria. The Ant Colony algorithm was executed for 3 hours, obtaining the best found solution, and the total number of iterations performed during the specified time.

This procedure allows for good performance and direct comparison among the results obtained for the different implemented neighborhood structures, enabling a reliable efficacy and efficiency analysis.

6.5   Efficacy Testing

Experimental tests were performed using 4 test problems randomly generated for the UPMP of 200, 250, 270, and 300 jobs, respectively, which have to be scheduled on k positions (number of jobs) of 12 machines. The problems were evaluated using the neighborhood structures explained in Section 5, which were implemented into an Ant Colony algorithm, in order to get an improvement in the quality of solution. The enhancement procedure was applied to the neighborhood of the best solution so far. The Ant Colony algorithm conducted 30 executions per test problem on each neighborhood structure. The executing time was almost 3 hours, depending on the input size. Averages of obtained results are shown in Tables 2.

Table 2. Average results obtained in experimental testing for different sized problems

Problem Size Jobs * Machine	Adjacent Pair	Random Pair	Two Adjacent Pairs	Two Random Pairs	variable neighborhood
200*12	2648	2317	2768	2678	2320
250*12	3928	3460	3465	3998	3515
270*12	4908	4279	4389	4986	4582
300*12	5948	5139	5232	5975	5388

According to calculations presented in Table 2, and contrary to results obtained for CSTSP using the same neighborhood structures, the best solution was found in all cases by the random pair neighborhood structure, leaving the variable structure in second place.

This research demonstrates that although CSTSP and UPMP are both NP problems, their hardness is different. CSTSP has a harder solution space than UPMP [1]. Therefore, the variable neighborhood structure has more benefits for hard problems, as opposed to less hard problems where it is easier to find good solutions.

6.6   Efficiency Testing

According to the calculations plotted in Figure 3, the behavior of the variable neighborhood structure's efficiency is competitive, because it shows better efficiency than the neighborhood structure of two adjacent pairs and two random pairs in most of cases.

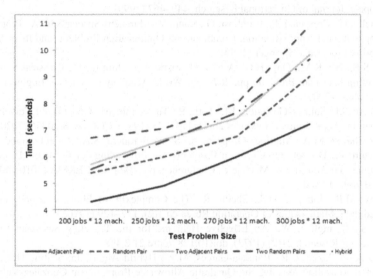

Fig. 3. Time required for each neighborhood structure to find a solution

7   Conclusions

Many experimental tests were performed for two combinatorial problems with different hardness in their solution space. The problems studied were CSTSP and UPMP. In both cases, test problems were randomly generated, according to the problems' features. Experimental results showed a difference in the variable neighborhood structure performance, because in the case of CSTSP, excellent quality solutions were obtained by the variable neighborhood structure. For UPMP, the same structure did not obtain the best solutions.

According to experimental analysis, the hypothesis presented in this paper is confirmed. The contribution of this research is the experimental proof that not all the variable neighborhood structures work well in all discrete optimization problems when compared to other straightforward structures. This is seen clearly in the case of UPMP, where a straightforward structure gets better quality solutions than the variable neighborhood one.

This research demonstrates that although CSTSP and UPMP are both NP problems, CSTSP has a harder solution space than UPMP. The variable neighborhood structure has more benefits for harder problems, as opposed to less hard problems where it is easier to find good solutions.

References

1. Papadimitriou, C.H., Steiglitz, K.: Combinatorial Optimization, Algorithms and Complexity. Dover Publications, Inc., Mineola (1998)
2. Arajy Yahya, Z., Abdullah, S.: Hybrid Variable Neighborhood Algorithm for Attribute Reduction in Rough Set Theory. In: 10th International Conference on Intelligent Systems Design and Applications, ISDA, Cairo, Egypt. IEEE (2010)
3. Hansen, P., Mladenović, N.: Variable Neighborhood Search: Principles and Applications. European Journal of Operational Research, 449–467 (1999)
4. Ausiello, G., Crescenzi, P., Gambosi, G., Kann, V., Marchetti-Spaccamela, A., Protasi, M.: Complexity and Approximation: Combinatorial Optimization Problems and their Approximability Properties. Springer (1999)
5. Liu, S.B., Ng, K.M., Ong, H.L.: A New Heuristic Algorithm for the Classical Symmetric Traveling Salesman Problem, pp. 267–271. World Academy of Science, Engineering and Technology (2007)
6. Fischetti, M., Salazar-González, J.J., Toth, P.: The Symmetric Generalized Traveling Salesman Polytope. Journal Networks 26(2), 113–123 (1995), CCC 0028-3045/95/020113-11
7. Cruz-Chávez, M.A., Martínez-Oropeza, A., Serna-Barquera, S.A.: Neighborhood Hybrid Structure for Discrete Optimization Problems. In: Proceedings of the IEEE Electronics, Robotics and Automotive Mechanics Conference, pp. 108–113. CERMA (2010) ISBN-13: 978-0-7695-4204-1
8. Garey, M.R., Johnson, D.S., Shethi, R.: The Complexity of Flow Shop and Job Shop Scheduling. Mathematics of Operation Research 1(2), 117–129 (1976)
9. Lin, S., Kernighan, W.: An Effective Heuristic for the Traveling Salesman Problem. Operations Research 21(2) (1973), doi:10.1287/opre.21.2.498
10. González-Velázquez, R., Bandala-Garcés, M.A.: Hybrid Algorithm: Scaling Hill and Simulated Annealing to Solve the Quadratic Allowance Problem. In: González-Velázquez, R. (ed.) 3th. Latin-Iberoamerican Workshop of Operation Research, Guerrero, México (2009)
11. Pacheco, J., Delgado, C.: Different Experiences Results with Local Search Applied to Path Problem. Electronic Journal of Electronics of Comunications and Works ASEPUMA 2(1), 54–81 (2000) ISSN: 1575-605X
12. Kenneth, D.B.: Cost Versus Distance in the Traveling Salesman Problem. Dept. Los Angeles. CA 90024 1596. Citeseer. USA. UCLA Computer Science (1995)
13. Lourenço, H.R., Martin, O.C.: Iterated Local Search. In: Handbook of Metaheustics. International Series in Operations Research & Management Science, vol. 57, pp. 320–353. Springer (2003)
14. Martin, O., Otto, S.W., Felten, E.W.: Large Step Markov Chains for the Traveling Salesman Problem, pp. 299–326. Complex Systems (1991)
15. Martin, O., Otto, S.W., Felten, E.W.: Large Step Markov Chains for the TSP Incorporating Local Search Heuristics. Operations Reasearch, 219–224 (1992)
16. Pinedo, M.L.: Scheduling Theory, Algorithms, and Systems, 3rd edn., New York University. Prentice Hall (2008) ISBN: 978-0-387-78934-7, e-ISBN: 978-0-387-78935-4

Emergent Phenomena
in Constrained 3D Layout Design

Katarzyna Grzesiak-Kopeć and Maciej Ogorzałek

Jagiellonian University in Krakow, Department of Information Technologies, Poland
{katarzyna.grzesiak-kopec,maciej.ogorzalek}@uj.edu.pl

Abstract. While explored in the context of creativeness in computer aided design, emergence has hardly ever been mentioned as a phenomenon that may enhance optimization process in engineering design. This paper presents the original approach to constrained 3D component layout design problem that takes advantage of visual shape grammar computations, emergent phenomena and computational intelligence methods. Possible design solutions are generated with a use of a simple shape grammar. Design specific knowledge is represented in a form of goals and constraints and the search process is driven by an intelligent derivation controller. The presented framework is very general but in the same time flexible and easily adjustable to a specific problem domain.

Keywords: computer aided design, shape grammar, computational intelligence, optimization, 3D layout design.

1 Introduction

The tailor-made layout of components in a given solution space is one of the most basic engineering tasks. It requires efficient search of vast and discontinuous spaces that include different kinds of entities, like components, goals, constraints and topological relations. It can be found in a wide range of design and manufacturing problems under different headings, e.g. packing, spatial arrangement, floorplaning or component layout. It occurs not only in engineering design, but in scheduling, pallet loading, virtual reality modeling or current social problems, like crises management or urban planning, as well. Nevertheless, a number of researchers have addressed the issue of object placement in 3D environments, because of the computational complexity it is still very challenging one.

The vast majority of available layout computer-aided design (CAD) systems consider only geometry, which makes them excellent tools for holding graphical and geometric data, but in the same time they are unable to automatically generate valid design solutions [1]. In order to obtain a globally near-optimal result that fulfills requirements and complies with constraints the semantic layer information is needed. The technological advances in 3D visualization and in the field of computational intelligence, gives the opportunity to propose new methods and tools for CAD to efficiently solve the constrained 3D layout design task.

L. Rutkowski et al. (Eds.): ICAISC 2014, Part II, LNAI 8468, pp. 479–489, 2014.

Since a pathway leading the designer to a final solution cannot be predicted and the design creativity is considered one of the most important attributes, the question of creativity also arises in CAD. Even though, there is no general agreement regarding the nature of the creativity in design, there is no doubt that one of the most important phenomena which enhances creativeness is *emergence*. This paper presents our original approach to component layout problem that takes advantage of visual shape grammar computations, emergent phenomena and computational intelligence methods. The proposed solution is a kind of a framework that is very general and flexible but include dedicated mechanisms allowing to adopt it to a specific problem domain. The shape grammar geometric representation and the optimization technique are both problem independent while goals and constraints represent distinct layout design task knowledge. The optimization search algorithm holds the problem formulation and finds auspicious solutions by evaluating evolving design states. The proposed method is accompanied by the development of a dedicated application *PerfectShape* which architecture is based on the established framework. For the time being, it is in a pre-release version and runs as a SketchUp [2] plugin.

2   Emergence and Visual Cognition

The study of emergent phenomena has captured the attention of scientists in very diverse fields. Emergence is a meaningful cognitive phenomenon of human visual reasoning [3] which may be characterized by *much coming from little* [4]. It covers not only visual and structural aspects of artifacts but functional and behavioural ones as well. Emergent properties can be found in complex adaptive systems like the Internet, ant colonies, the traffic, cellular automata or the board games.

After [4] we presume that emergence occurs in systems that are generated and where the whole is more than the sum of the parts. The systems are composed of entities that obey simple rules. However, the interactions among parts are nonlinear and the global behaviour cannot be realized as a sum of the behaviours of the isolated components. Let us investigate a famous Conway's Game of Life [5]. There are only three simple rules that determine whether a cell is alive or dead. However, depending on the cells interactions many emergent patterns may be observed, e.g. still life objects, oscillators or moving objects like gliders. Another example is the human body that consists of 75 trillion cells and every second thousands of them are dying. Within 7 years all of the cells are replaced, but even though we are who we are, and *the recipe for us* is stored in the cells relations. When new cells arrive, chemical signals from the neighboring cells tell them what part of DNA to follow. In other words, what kind of cell (skin, muscle etc.) to become [6].

In our case, the feature is called emergent if two conditions are met:

1. it is not explicitly represented but emerge from a design structure, and
2. it is possible to represent it explicitly.

Hence, emergence is a matter of both pattern recognition and pattern definition. The phenomenon is extensively explored by cognitive theory that attempts to formulate the factors that cause such a variety of possible arrangements, segmentations and interpretations of images. According to the Gestalt psychologists, people intuitively distinguish the foreground from the background in their reading of shapes. However, it is not unambiguous and the viewer's imagination determines which part of the image is a foreground. In other words, seeing demands some activity from the person who is watching. The most famous example of emergence is a black vase which materialises into two white human profiles (Fig.1).

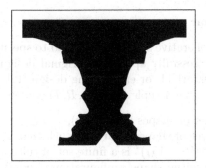

Fig. 1. Emergent faces (after [7])

The paper focuses only on emergence in the visual layer and its possible applications in solving constrained 3D layout problem.

3   Flexible Framework for 3D Layout Design

Due to the computational complexity of the constrained 3D layout design problem, there are no deterministic algorithms solving such a task and computational intelligence methods are needed. The elaborated framework architecture has to be flexible and reconfigurable. Allowing easy exchange of one heuristic for another it gives a chance to find the most promising one for the given problem domain. It also has to separate the presentation layer from the semantic one to dynamically adjust available free parameters of the selected intelligent method. And last but not least, it has to carry out visual computations that enable to introduce emergent features into the course of design generation. In this way, on the one hand the proposed approach remains generic and on the other it takes advantage of a design specific knowledge and emergence to direct the search process towards the optimal design solution.

Taking into account these requirements and previously proposed 2D solution (see [8] and [9]), the following components in the design context are introduced:

1. Designer,
2. Shape grammar,
3. Design knowledge,
4. Derivation controller.

The designer can moderate all of the elements. Before a single search process begins she/he defines a shape grammar, encodes the design knowledge in a form of goals and constraints, a design evaluation function (fitness function) and sets stop criteria for the derivation controller. The shape grammar is used to generate potential layout designs. While the derivation controller manages the execution and directs it towards the globally near-optimal solution.

3.1   Shape Grammar

Shape grammars are generative systems dedicated to specific needs of designers. The formalism was successfully applied in original design and analysis in the field of architecture[10], art[11] or engineering design [12]. After [13], we define a shape grammar (SG) as a 4-tuple (V_T, V_M, R, I) where:

1. $V_T \neq \emptyset$ is a finite set of shapes (terminals),
2. $V_M \neq \emptyset$ is a finite set of shapes (markers) such that $V_T \cap V_M = \emptyset$,
3. $R \subset (V_T \cup V_M)^+ \times (V_T \cup V_M)^*$ is a finite set of rules,
4. $I \in V_T^+ \cup V_M^*$ is an initial shape configuration (axiom).

The shape grammar is a rule-based rewriting system (see Fig.2). It acts on shape configurations composed of both terminal shapes and markers. Having identified the left-hand side (LHS) of the rule in the current design, the shape grammar rewrites it according to the mapping encoded in the right-hand side (RHS). In this way, starting with an axiom and successively perturbing the current shape configuration, the execution process ends up with the final design. As we can see, there are several decisions to be made. First of all, we have to select a rule. The selection is simple if there is only one possible rule to apply. However, in the most cases there is a bunch of admissible rules. The easiest way to proceed is to select a rule randomly, but also some functional decomposition [14] or machine learning techniques (see [8] and [9]) may be considered. Having a rule selected, we have to indicate the LHS in the current design. In other words, we have to find an embedding. Even though this part of the generation process has a huge influence on the achieved design solution, it is hardly ever mentioned in the literature. Four different methods of a rule embedding have been established: *execute first admissible, execute last, execute random* and *execute all* (see [15] and [16]). The execute first admissible embedding applies a rule to first possible shape configuration. The execute last embedding tries to apply a rule to some shape configuration that came into being in the latest generation step. The execute random embedding applies a rule to one randomly selected from all recognized shape configurations. Eventually, the execute all embedding applies a rule to all admissible shape configurations. According to a design task domain, all rules may be embedded with a single method or it can vary for different rules, or

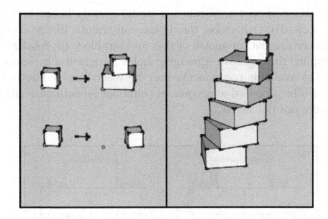

Fig. 2. Simple shape grammar with two rules and 10-step generation example

even for different phases of one generation process. If not fixed, an embedding method, as in the case of a rule selection, may be chosen randomly or with a use of some more sophisticated and intelligent algorithm.

Finally, comparing the design evaluation value before and after the generation step, the rule application may be either committed or rolled back. If the achieved result is better than before the step, it is approved. Otherwise, the step may be rolled back or also approved depending on the intelligent decision taken with a help of simulated annealing or some multi-agent system [9]. It is also worth mentioning the importance of the right selection of the initial shape configuration. Conducting many visual computations for our leading research design task, namely 3D integrated circuits design, we came across the fact that a small change in the axiom may contribute with a significant improvement in the generated solutions. In some cases, the improper starting configuration caused the execution process to got stuck for every activation.

In most CAD systems, emergence is not addressed at all or limited to observation of those emergent elements that appear in a generated design. In this way, emergent properties are considered only as the output of the design process and may not be exploited as the input for further computations. In our approach a shape grammar provides visual computations and enables not only to recognise emergent features but fed them back into the generation process as well [17]. The formalism allows to freely decompose and rearrange shapes and consequently introduce observed emergent elements into design space. The adopted technique makes computational emergence possible.

In the 3D layout problem we are looking for such a packing of a large number of components in a limited space that best meets given requirements. The successful solution demands to arrange components as tight as possible which naturally limits or even excludes the presence of voids in the final design. Two kinds of emergent elements should be considered: *holes* and *grooves* [18]. Let us analyze the example in Fig 3. A hole is a void surrounded by components while a groove has one part that is boundless. If the emergent cube that constitutes a hole was recognized, a single swap transformation would greatly improve the proposed packing (Fig 3(c)-(d)). Otherwise, the design constraints, like no overlapping of components, may prevent a removal of this undesirable void. Analogical reasoning can be applied for a groove. Emergent holes recognition is especially useful when one of the available components may be placed inside another, like presented in Fig 4. The proposed arrangement could not be automatically generated if the holes were not perceived.

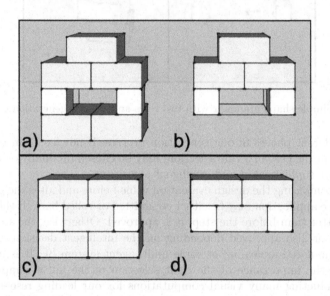

Fig. 3. (a)Emergent hole;(b)Emergent groove;(c)-(d)Improved packings

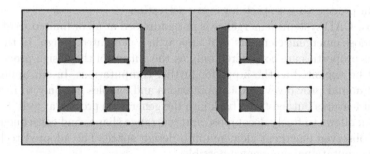

Fig. 4. Example use of emergent holes in 3D packing

However, there are a lot of situations when recognized voids cannot be fulfilled with components because of the inadequate sizes. In such a case another operation is proposed that rearrange layout, namely *sliding*. The main goal of the elaborated method is to compress the generated design and eliminate all the voids. The left front bottom corner of the packing bounding box in selected and

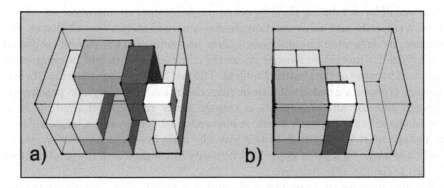

Fig. 5. Example 3D layout (a) before and (b) after sliding

after sorting, all the components are moved towards it if possible. The example result of the sliding is presented in Fig. 5.

Eventually, building engineering shape grammars forces to connect a grammar and design requirements. There are two ways to deal with the task. The first possible approach is to create a knowledge intensive grammar that works as a sophisticated expert system and generates feasible and functional designs. However, inferring grammar rules generating only valid designs is not only very time consuming but in most cases impossible. And even if such an expert grammar is created, it can be very difficult to modify and maintain. That is why the second method, where a simple shape grammar is accompanied by some external mechanisms to direct derivations is more reasonable [19].

3.2 Design Knowledge

Since in the presented approach a low level of knowledge is encrypted in a shape grammar itself, a method for defining a task specific knowledge has to be introduced. Let $SG = (V_T, V_M, R, I)$ denote a simple shape grammar. Let $\Sigma = \Sigma_T \cup \Sigma_R \cup \Sigma_F$, where $\Sigma_T \cap \Sigma_R \cap \Sigma_F = \emptyset$ be fixed alphabets of terminal, rule and face labels, respectively. A *layout design knowledge* over Σ is a system $DK = (lb_T, lb_R, lb_F, G, C, f)$, where:

1. $lb_T : V_T \to \Sigma_T$ is a terminal labeling function,
2. $lb_R : R \to \Sigma_R$ is a rule labeling function,
3. $lb_F : F \to \Sigma_F$ is a shape face labeling function,
4. $G = \{g : g \text{ is a goal and } g : V_T^+ \to \Re^+\}$ is a non empty set of goals,
5. $C = \{c : c \text{ is a constraint and } c : V_T^2 \to \{true, false\}\}$ is a non empty set of constraints,
6. $f = \sum_{i=1}^{\#G} a_i g_i$ is a fitness function, where $a_i \in \Re^+$ is a goal g_i blending ratio.

Among others, a layout design knowledge contains three labeling mappings: one for terminal shapes, one for rules, and one for shape faces. Terminal shapes are labeled by names of the corresponding components, e. g. *pipe* in a pallet loading or *core* in integrated circuits design. Having assumed that shapes are composed of faces, labeling them by colors (or some other enumeration set values) allows to identify and verify relations between immediately adjacent shapes. For instance, in integrated circuits design there are elements that should be placed side by side for functional reasons or, on the contrary, that should be completely separated because of the heating problem. The last but not least, the rule labeling function gives us a great flexibility in rules definition. The only one parametric wildcard rule for all components is enough for a given transformation. In a typical shape grammar such a rule is impossible to define, and a single rule for each shape must be specified. In this way, the rules like *swap any two shapes* or *rotate any shape by a given angle* may be easily introduced and the total number of rules is significantly reduced.

We also propose to introduce goals and constraints [20], and the optimization process fitness function. *Constraints* are binary predicates that applied to a shape configuration return *true* or *false*. They refer to topological relations among components. A good example of such a constraint is a *no intersection constraint* that prevents components from overlapping. Of course constraints may include more specific component information given in a form of attributes, like color, material, or durability. For instance in the architectural design, in this way the requirement of separating a living room from a bedroom may be given. Constraints are very strict and each generation step can be approved if and only if a derived design meets all the given constraints.

If the constraints are met, all the goals are independently evaluated. A single *goal* is a real-valued predicate and may be satisfied to some extent. The aggregated result of goals evaluation values defined by a fitness function gives a total evaluation score of the current design. The explicit impact factor of a single goal to the final outcome is moderated by a derivation controller.

A derivation controller is responsible for proceeding visual computations and directing the execution. Having design knowledge, it employs a shape grammar and drives the course of derivations towards some near-optimal solutions. Encapsulating domain knowledge parameters and all the adopted heuristics, it also decides when to stop the ongoing computations. A derivation controller can be considered the intelligent core of the whole framework.

Let us present a simple 3D IC layout design task with four different circuit blocks to be arranged in a chip in the number of $10, 5, 10$, and 6 respectively. A simple shape grammar has 5 terminal shapes, where a white cube is a special shape that do not represent any circuit block but is needed for running the execution (Fig. 6). The alphabet of terminal labels is following $\Sigma_T = \{$ CORE, CACHE, DRAM, BANK, TEMPORAL-LABEL, ANY-LABEL $\}$. There are two distinguished labels. The TEMPORAL-LABEL is assigned to a white cube in all additive rules, in other words, in all rules that add a new circuit block to the current design. The ANY-LABEL is used in parametric rules that transform shapes so that one transformation rule is defined for any terminal shape. In this way the number of rules is significantly diminished. In the presented example, there are no face labels and only one rule label is used to indicate parametric rules: $\Sigma_R = \{$ ANY-LABEL-COND $\}$. Two constraints and two goals are

applied: *no intersection constraint, glue shape constraint, minimal space goal*
and *spatial relation goal*. The *spatial relation goal* requires the yellow blocks to
be aligned vertically. Both goals are equally important and blended with ratio
1. Example 3D IC layout results are presented in Fig. 6.

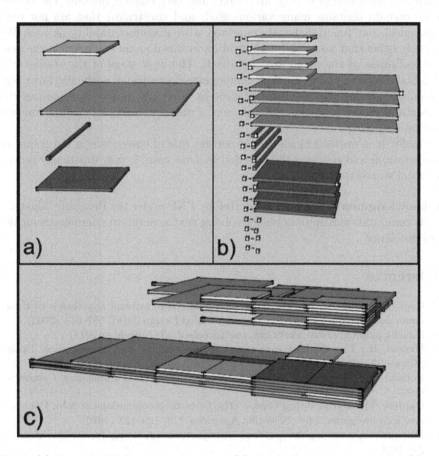

Fig. 6. (a) Example ICs layout components, (b) simple shape grammar rules, (c) example 3D layouts designs after sliding

4   Conclusions and Future Prospects

Optimization plays a crucial role in the design and usability of many engineering
products and several approaches for solving the 3D layout problem have been
proposed. Among the most promising ones are simulated annealing [1], a hybrid approach using a combination of simulated annealing and expert systems
[21], and genetic algorithms [22]. However, none of them take the advantage of
emergent phenomena during the computations.

The paper presents a completely new approach to solving the task. The proposed framework architecture is methodologically advanced and easily reconfigurable. It undergoes practical verification with a use of a dedicated application working on a 3D integrated circuits layout design problem, where effective computer-aided design is both up-to-date and very challenging one. The search space domain contains many various goals and constraints that are not only topological, but functional and connected with manufacturability as well. We strongly belief that a successful application in this domain will confirm the general usefulness of the elaborated approach. The next stage of the studies will be a fine-tuning of the framework components and a use of a sematic layer representation during the optimization process. Since the approach separates the presentation layer from the semantic one, a different representation techniques may be evaluated.

Finally, it is worth noticing the important role of emergence in the course of computations and stressing the fact that in some cases it may drastically reduce the total search time.

Acknowledgment. Research supported by FNP under the Program "Master": "New computational approaches for solving next generation microelectronic design problems".

References

1. Cagan, J., Shimada, K., Yin, S.: A survey of computational approaches to three-dimensional layout problems. Computer Aided Design 34(8), 597–611 (2002)
2. SketchUp, http://www.sketchup.com (accessed 13, November 2013)
3. Oxman, R.: The thinking eye: visual re-cognition in design emergence. Design Studies 23, 135–164 (2002)
4. Holland, H.J.: Emergence, From Chaos to Order. Perseus Publishing, Cambridge (1999)
5. Gardner, M.: Mathematical Games. The fantastic combinations of John Conway's new solitaire game "life". Scientific American 223, 120–123 (1970)
6. EmergentUniverse.org, http://www.emergentuniverse.org (accessed December 20, 2013)
7. Arnheim, R.: The Dynamics of Architectural Form. University of California Press, Berkeley (1977)
8. Grabska, E., Grzesiak-Kopeć, K., Ślusarczyk, G.z.: Designing floor-layouts with the assistance of curious agents. In: Alexandrov, V.N., van Albada, G.D., Sloot, P.M.A., Dongarra, J. (eds.) ICCS 2006. LNCS, vol. 3993, pp. 883–886. Springer, Heidelberg (2006)
9. Grabska, E., Grzesiak-Kopeć, K., Ślusarczyk, G.: Visual creative design with the assistance of curious agents. In: Barker-Plummer, D., Cox, R., Swoboda, N. (eds.) Diagrams 2006. LNCS (LNAI), vol. 4045, pp. 218–220. Springer, Heidelberg (2006)
10. Chiou, S.C., Krishnamurti, R.: The grammar of Taiwanese traditional vernacular dwellings. Environment and Planning B: Planning and Design 22, 689–720 (1995)
11. Schnier, T., Gero, J.S.: From Frank Lloyd Wright to Mondrian: Transforming evolving representation. In: Parmee, I.C. (ed.) Adaptive Computing in Design and Manufacture, pp. 207–219. Springer, Berlin (1998)

12. Agarwal, M., Cagan, J., Stiny, G.: A micro language: generating MEMS resonators by using a coupled form - function shape grammar. Environment and Planning B: Planning and Design 27(4), 615–626 (2000)
13. Stiny, G.: Introduction to shape and shape grammars. Environment and Planning B: Planning and Design 7, 343–351 (1980)
14. Agarwal, M., Cagan, J.: A blend of different tastes: the language of coffee makers. Environment and Planning B: Planning and Design 25(2), 205–226 (1998)
15. Grzesiak-Kopeć, K., Ogorzałek, M.: Computer-Aided 3D ICs Layout Design. Computer-Aided Design and Applications 11(3), 318–325 (2014)
16. Grzesiak-Kopeć, K., Ogorzałek, M.: Intelligent 3D Layout Design with Shape Grammars. In: Proc. of 6th International Conference on Human System Interaction (HIS 2013), pp. 265–270 (2013)
17. Knight, T.: Interaction in visual design computing. Visual and Spatial Reasoning in Design III. The invited paper (2004)
18. Grzesiak-Kopeć, K.: Emergent elements in periodic designs: An attempt at formalization. In: Design Computing and Cognition 2004, pp. 297–316. Kluwer Academic Publishers (2004)
19. Cagan, J.: Engineering shape grammars. In: Antonsson, E.K., Cagan, J. (eds.) Formal Engineering Design Synthesis, pp. 65–92. Cambridge University Press, New York (2001)
20. Ruiz-Montiel, M., Mandow, L., Perez-De-La-Cruz, J.L., et al.: Shapes, grammars, constraints and policies. In: Proc. of the First Interdisciplinary Workshop on SHAPES (SHAPES 1.0), Karlsruhe, Germany (2011)
21. Hills, W., Smith, N.: A new approach to spatial layout design in complex engineered products. In: Proc. of the International Conference on Engineering Design (ICED 1997), Tampere, Finland (1997)
22. Ikonen, I., Biles, W., Kumar, A., et al.: A genetic algorithm for packing three-dimensional non-convex objects having cavities and holes. In: Proc. of 7th International Conference on Genetic Algorithms (1997)

Brainy: A Machine Learning Library

Michal Konkol

Natural Language Processing Group
Department of Computer Science and Engineering
University of West Bohemia
Univerzitni 8, 306 14 Plzen, Czech Republic
{nlp,konkol}@kiv.zcu.cz

Abstract. Brainy is a newly created cross-platform machine learning library written in Java. It defines interfaces for common types of machine learning tasks and implementations of the most popular algorithms. Brainy utilizes a complex mathematical infrastructure which is also part of the library. The main difference compared to other ML libraries is the sophisticated system for feature definition and management. The design of the library is focused on efficiency, reliability, extensibility and simple usage. Brainy has been extensively used for research as well as commercial projects for major companies in Czech Republic and USA. Brainy is released under the GPL license and freely available from the project web page.

Keywords: Machine learning, software library.

1 Introduction

Machine learning is a branch of artificial intelligence which studies computer systems with the ability to learn without being explicitly programmed. Such systems are very different from standard rule-based systems where the knowledge is hand coded by humans. The machine learning systems have their strengths and weaknesses. On one hand, they can handle very complex problems, that are intractable by standard rule-based systems. On the other hand, the knowledge learned by machine learning system is almost never perfect and the rule-based systems can perform better for simple problems.

Machine learning is used for wide variety of tasks all around us. These tasks include natural language processing, weather forecasting, stock value forecasting, earthquake prediction, medicine decision making and many others. Generally, machine learning can be used for any complex problem where no other solution performs well.

There exist different paradigms of learning. The basic one is *supervised learning*. In supervised learning the training data are provided along with annotations which are telling the algorithm the right answers. The algorithm then tries to generalize the knowledge acquired from training data and also to still give the maximum of good answers. When the algorithm generalizes badly, it can often reproduce right answers for training data, but performs poorly for unseen data.

The second important paradigm is *unsupervised learning*. In unsupervised learning, the algorithm receives only data (without answers) and tries to find patterns in the data. There exists more learning paradigms, but the majority of tasks uses the presented two.

L. Rutkowski et al. (Eds.): ICAISC 2014, Part II, LNAI 8468, pp. 490–499, 2014.

Machine learning represents a wide variety of algorithms. We will briefly describe the basic groups of these algorithms. The first group of algorithms is the *regression* group. Regression algorithms are designed for problems where the predicted variable is real valued. It analyzes the training data where the values are already annotated and then tries to find optimal values for unseen data. For example in the weather forecasting domain this algorithm can be used to predict the precipitation based on weather radar information.

A *classification* group is for problems where the output is categorical. These algorithms require some examples for each category and tries to find optimal decision boundary between these categories. An example from weather domain can be classification of days into sunny and cloudy categories. Another group closely related to classification is *sequence labelling*. It addresses problems where the category of the classified object depends not only on the data for this object but also on categories assigned to objects in its vicinity. This happens for example in industry where defective products are often produced in short series.

Another important group is *clustering*. Clustering can be seen as unsupervised learning version of classification. It analyzes data and assigns them to one of categories. Some algorithms need a predefined number of categories, some can choose the number of categories based on the data. Clustering can be used for example to automatically categorize news articles by topic.

All machine learning algorithms use the data to learn. The data for different domains are completely different and a universal representation have to be used. Machine learning introduces an abstraction called *feature* for this purpose. Each feature represents one property of the data object and translates it into numerical form. All features extracted from a data object form a *feature vector*. Features are often defined by *feature templates* (often also called features). One feature template is often responsible for many features. A typical feature template used in the natural language processing domain is a word and features are words themselves as "the" or "day". The group of features (or feature templates) used for some task is called *feature set*.

Two groups of machine learning algorithms are specialized on choosing optimal feature set. *Feature selection* takes features defined by user as input and removes features with smallest impact on the result. Feature set can be often heavily reduced without loosing performance. *Feature induction* (sometimes extraction or selection) also starts with features from user, but it also tries to create combinations of these features and tries to select an optimal set. This task is much harder than simple feature selection, because the number of features can easily reach million and the number of combinations is huge.

Training of machine learning algorithms often requires a lot of time and resources. The training algorithms are often very sophisticated and are based on linear algebra, statistics and optimization. It is necessary to use highly optimized mathematical algorithms to reduce required resources. A naive implementation usually makes even smaller problems intractable.

Brainy deals with all presented tasks and problems. The following sections give a basic overview of Brainy rather than an in-depth description. It should provide enough information to decide, whether Brainy is interesting for you.

2 Architecture

The framework consists of three main components – feature management, machine learning algorithms and mathematics (mainly statistics, optimization and linear algebra). We will briefly describe the interactions of the components and then each component more deeply.

Each machine learning task needs some data to learn. These data are usually represented as feature vectors. For this purpose, we have defined interfaces for matrices and vectors. These matrices and vectors serves as unified data interface between the machine learning and the feature management parts of the library. The feature management part defines interfaces for features and feature set. The machine learning part processes the data represented as vectors and matrices. It is heavily supported by the mathematical infrastructure. An overview is given by fig. 1.

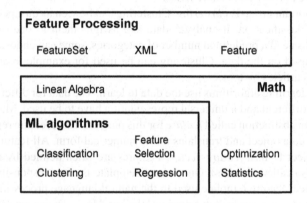

Fig. 1. Main components of the library

2.1 Feature Management

The feature management is often overlooked in machine learning libraries. In our library we define interfaces for both features and feature set. The Feature interface represents a feature template and provides well-defined methods for changing data representation from user defined objects to numerical values. Each feature template then returns a vector indexed from 0 to n, where n_f is number of features defined on the template. Therefore the features are independent of each other.

The FeatureSet class manages the features. It processes all the user objects, combines the vectors from individual features into the final feature vector and creates a matrix representing the data from feature vectors. The feature set can be defined by an XML file. The file contains a list of features and their parametrization. This allows fast experimentation with multiple feature sets without changing the source code. It also helps you to keep track of your experiments and reproduce the results.

2.2 Mathematical Infrastructure

The first part of the mathematical infrastructure is linear algebra. The machine learning algorithms can be often vectorized – transformed into vectors and matrices combined using standard linear algebra operations. We have defined interfaces for matrices and vectors. Different implementations of matrices allow very efficient execution, e.g. using sparse/dense matrices with different implementations, running in parallel, etc. It is easy to extend the library with new algorithms thanks to the support of linear algebra primitives.

Optimization algorithms form another part. We have defined interfaces for mathematical functions (e.g. `Function` for simple function, `DiffFunction` for differentiable function) and a `Minimizer` interface. For new method you only need to implement the cost function and use one of our implementations of Minimizer. We are usually using L-BFGS minimizer or some non-trivial version of gradient descent.

We have implemented interfaces for more mathematical primitives (e.g. random distributions, distances, similarities, etc.) and provided implementations for commonly used variants.

2.3 Machine Learning Algorithms

The main part of machine learning library are, of coarse, machine learning algorithms. We have defined interfaces for all major tasks – regression, classification, sequence labelling and clustering. We will describe these interfaces and their usage in section 3. All algorithms of the same type share the same interface and that allows easy experimentation with different algorithms and their combinations.

Fig. 2 shows detailed view of the machine learning component with listing of selected algorithms.

3   User View

In this section, we will briefly describe the library from the user view. For detailed description see the tutorial on the project website (sec. 6).

First step for any machine learning task is preparation of data. Our machine learning library supports two approaches. The machine learning algorithms work solely with matrices and vectors. The first possibility is to directly create these matrices using any way that fits your needs. The second possibility is to use our feature management system.

3.1 Feature Management

The feature management system supports easy experimentation with features. The basic interface is `Feature` which represents a feature template. With feature template

494   M. Konkol

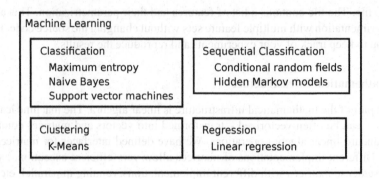

Fig. 2. The machine learning component

we mean set of very similar features with the same semantics, e.g. in the field of natural language processing the feature template 'word' consists of features for individual words (current word is 'wood', 'steel', etc.).

The `Feature` interface has two important methods. The `train()` method is used for training the feature from training data, e.g. the previously mentioned 'word' feature needs to learn the words. The `extractFeature()` method translates the user objects to numeric representation.

After defining features you can create a feature set (class `FeatureSet`). The feature set can be created programatically or by XML configuration file. The XML file is very useful for testing multiple feature sets. Listing 1 shows both ways of feature set creation and its usage. Note that `FeatureSet` class is generic. The generic type represents the object you want to classify – in our example the `String[]` represents a document. The `trainingObjects` object is a list-like structure with objects for classification.

Listing 1. Creation of feature sets

```
FeatureSet<String[]> set = new FeatureSet<String[]>();
set.add(new WordFeature(0));
set.train(trainingObjects);

set = new FeatureSet<String[]>("myFeatureSet.xml");
set.train(trainingObjects);

DoubleMatrix data = set.getData(trainingObjects);
IntVector labels = set.getLabels(trainingObjects);
```

3.2 Classification

The schema of classification task is on fig. 3. After data preparation a classifier trainer object is created. This object represents a method for training of chosen classifier, e.g. maximum entropy [1] classifier can be trained by L-BFGS [2] method. The trainer object then returns a classifier object, which is ready to classify unseen data.

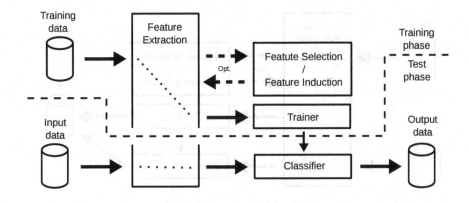

Fig. 3. The classification task

Listing 2 shows an example code for classifier training and usage. We have used a maximum entropy classifier, where the `MaxEntLBFGSTrainer` is the trainer class and `MaxEnt` is the classifier class. As we said previously the data can be prepared in multiple ways. Before classification you need to create `Results` object, which is filled by results of the classifier. This allows you to reuse this object, e.g. when you are searching for optimal parameters of the classifier.

Listing 2. Creation and usage of maximum entropy classifier

```
DoubleMatrix trainingData = ...;
IntVector trainingLabels = ...;
SupervisedClassifierTrainer trainer = new MaxEntLBFGSTrainer();
Classifier classifier = trainer.train(trainingData,
    trainingLabels, numLabels);

DoubleMatrix data = ...;
Results results = BasicResults.create(numLabels, data.columns());
classifier.classify(data, results);
```

3.3   Clustering

The scheme for clustering is on fig. 4. The objects used for clustering have different semantics. The clustering method is represented by single object which implements the `Clustering` interface, e.g. object of `K-Means` class. This object clusters the data. Some methods also support an optional function – they return an object which represents a trained version of the clustering method. This object also implements the `Clustering` interface and is able to add additional (previously unseen) objects to the previously created clusters without the need of clustering all data objects from start. In the case of K-Means [3] the trained version computes the distances between additional vectors and centroids and adds them to the cluster with shortest distance.

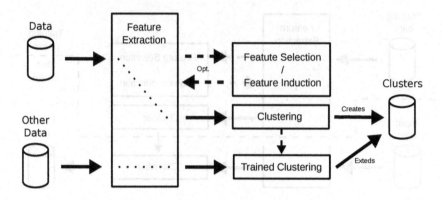

Fig. 4. The clustering task

An example of clustering can be seen on listing 3.

Listing 3. Creation and usage of K-Means clustering

```
DoubleMatrix data = ...;
Clustering kmeans = new KMeans(means.length,
    new EuclideanDistance());
Clustering trainedKmeans = kmeans.cluster(data, results);

DoubleMatrix otherData = ...;
trainedKmeans.cluster(data, results);
```

4   Related Systems

In this section we will briefly describe libraries and frameworks with similar focus. We have done some artificial tests on them and compared with our library. The tests had almost the same results for all libraries (comparing the same algorithms). These tests represents only simple problems. Their results prove that the libraries are not faulty and their performance is more or less the same for simple problems, but do not show well the differences between algorithms on real and more complex problems. The proper way of comparing these libraries would be testing on multiple real problems from multiple fields, but it is out of the scope of this article.

The most similar libraries are Mallet[1] [4] and Java-ML[2] [5]. They are both machine learning libraries written in Java. The biggest difference between these libraries and our library is the architecture. The interfaces for machine learning tasks are different. They heavily differ in the way they prepare and represent the data. These differences in architecture forces the user to use different concepts and the appropriate library should be chosen based on the task, compatibility with other systems and personal preference.

---

[1] http://mallet.cs.umass.edu
[2] http://java-ml.sourceforge.net

Weka[3] [6] and Apache Mahout[4] are another machine learning frameworks worth mentioning, but they differ in purpose compared to the previously mentioned libraries. The Weka itself states "Weka is a collection of machine learning algorithms for data mining tasks.", so it is not primarily intended as a general machine learning library. The standard usage is through GUI and CLI, while our library provides only API. The Weka framework generally uses higher level of abstraction then our library.

Apache Mahout is focused on very big problems. The framework is based on the Apache Hadoop framework for distributed computing. Our library can be parallelized to some extent, but it is limited by one cluster. Hadoop provides much more complex infrastructure for distributed computing then our library, e.g. node error recovery, etc. So the main difference is the basic concept or targets of the library.

5 Verification

All algorithms provided by the library are tested on very simple machine learning tasks using the jUnit framework. The library is also used by students for assignments and theses.

The library was extensively used for research by the Natural Language Processing Group at University of West Bohemia. So far, the library was used in two main directions of research – named entity recognition (NER) and sentiment analysis (SA).

The NER tool is based on Brainy and GATE[5]. The first version of our NER system was based on the maximum entropy classifier [7]. Current version is based on conditional random fields and is a state-of-the-art method for Czech [8]. We are working on multilingual NER, which has already achieved exceptional results. The NER tool is currently tested by two major companies in Czech republic – Seznam.cz, a.s[6] (a majority search engine) and ČTK[7] (national news agency established by law).

Our sentiment analysis research is also heavily based on Brainy. The research was focused on social media SA [9], semantic spaces in SA [10], or a new model for SA based on the target context [11].

Brainy is also used in a commercial project for Owen Software Ltd. and in the High Precision Stemmer[8], which is a unsupervised language-independent stemmer.

This section shows that the library can achieve state-of-the-art results in multiple research fields and it can be used for commercial projects.

6 Availability and Requirements

The library is written in Java and thus should be usable on any platform with Java Virtual Machine. The minimal version of Java is 1.6. It is necessary to use the 64 bit version of Java for non-trivial applications because of memory requirements.

---

[3] http://www.cs.waikato.ac.nz/ml/weka/
[4] http://mahout.apache.org
[5] http://gate.ac.uk
[6] http://www.seznam.cz
[7] http://www.ctk.eu
[8] http://liks.fav.zcu.cz/HPS/

The library is available from the project web page[9]. It is released under the GPLv3[10] license.

7   Conclusion and Future Work

We have implemented a Java machine learning library called Brainy. Brainy was already used in research and commercial projects. It is released under GPL license.

The library provides many advanced algorithms, data structures and utilities. The infrastructure of the library allows quick implementation of new algorithms with standard interfaces. The library is designed for experimentation as well as for production systems.

The library is under active development. In the near future we are going to add our own implementation of various types of neural networks and graphical models. We also want to create a framework for standard machine learning pipelines and their configuration.

Acknowledgements. This work was supported by grant no. SGS-2013-029 Advanced computing and information systems, by the European Regional Development Fund (ERDF). Access to the MetaCentrum computing facilities provided under the program "Projects of Large Infrastructure for Research, Development, and Innovations" LM2010005, funded by the Ministry of Education, Youth, and Sports of the Czech Republic, is highly appreciated.

References

1. Berger, A.L., Pietra, V.J.D., Pietra, S.A.D.: A maximum entropy approach to natural language processing. Comput. Linguist. 22, 39–71 (1996)
2. Malouf, R.: A comparison of algorithms for maximum entropy parameter estimation. In: Proceedings of the 6th Conference on Natural Language Learning, COLING 2002, Stroudsburg, PA, USA, vol. 20, pp. 1–7. Association for Computational Linguistics (2002)
3. Lloyd, S.: Least squares quantization in pcm. IEEE Trans. Inf. Theor. 28(2), 129–137 (2006)
4. McCallum, A.K.: Mallet: A machine learning for language toolkit (2002)
5. Abeel, T., Van de Peer, Y., Saeys, Y.: Java-ml: A machine learning library. J. Mach. Learn. Res. 10, 931–934 (2009)
6. Hall, M., Frank, E., Holmes, G., Pfahringer, B., Reutemann, P., Witten, I.H.: The weka data mining software: An update. SIGKDD Explor. Newsl. 11(1), 10–18 (2009)
7. Konkol, M., Konopík, M.: Maximum entropy named entity recognition for czech language. In: Habernal, I., Matoušek, V. (eds.) TSD 2011. LNCS (LNAI), vol. 6836, pp. 203–210. Springer, Heidelberg (2011)
8. Konkol, M., Konopík, M.: Crf-based czech named entity recognizer and consolidation of czech ner research. In: Habernal, I., Matoušek, V. (eds.) TSD 2013. LNCS (LNAI), vol. 8082, pp. 153–160. Springer, Heidelberg (2013)

---

[9] home.zcu.cz/$\sim$konkol/brainy.php
[10] http://www.gnu.org/licenses/gpl-3.0-standalone.html

9. Habernal, I., Ptáček, T., Steinberger, J.: Sentiment analysis in czech social media using supervised machine learning. In: Proceedings of the 4th Workshop on Computational Approaches to Subjectivity, Sentiment and Social Media Analysis, Atlanta, Georgia, pp. 65–74. Association for Computational Linguistics (June 2013)
10. Habernal, I., Brychcín, T.: Semantic spaces for sentiment analysis. In: Habernal, I. (ed.) TSD 2013. LNCS (LNAI), vol. 8082, pp. 484–491. Springer, Heidelberg (2013)
11. Brychcín, T., Habernal, I.: Unsupervised improving of sentiment analysis using global target context. In: Proceedings of the International Conference Recent Advances in Natural Language Processing, RANLP 2013, Hissar, Bulgaria, pp. 122–128. INCOMA Ltd., Shoumen (2013)

Optimisation of Character n-gram Profiles Method for Intrinsic Plagiarism Detection

Marcin Kuta and Jacek Kitowski

AGH University of Science and Technology,
Al. Mickiewicza 30, 30-059 Krakow, Poland,
Department of Computer Science,
Faculty of Computer Science, Electronics and Telecommunications
{mkuta,kito}@agh.edu.pl

Abstract. The focus of the paper is to improve intrinsic plagiarism detection. The paper investigates and improves performance of character n-grams profiles method proposed by Stamatatos by tuning its parameter settings and proposing new modifications and rich feature sets. We raised the overall plagdet score from 24.67% to 33.41% for the PAN-PC09 corpus and from 18.83% to 26.66% for the PAN-PC11 corpus. Results are reported on PAN-PC09 and PAN-PC11 corpora, which are especially well suited for this task and were previously used in Plagiarism Analysis, Authorship Identification, and Near-Duplicate Detection (PAN) competitions.

Keywords: plagiarism detection, intrinsic plagiarism, character n-grams, sliding window.

1 Introduction

Macmillan dictionary defines plagiarism as *'the process of taking another person's work, ideas, or words, and using them as if they were your own. Someone who does this is called a plagiarist.'* [1] In intrinsic plagiarism detection problem no reference corus is given and plagiarism detection is based solely on internal style changes of referenced document. According to different research reports concerning universities from 50% students to even 90% students committed a plagiarism at least once in their life [1,2]. There was also observed sharp increase in plagiarism practices in 2000 due to raising availability of information in cyberspace.

Intrinsic and external plagiarism detection tasks are distinguished in general plagiarism detection problem. Intrinsic plagiarism detection is a variation of plagiarism detection problem in which no external sources of plagiarism are available of even does not exist. The former may be caused by imperfections of document retrieval systems (source documents are available in digital form but retrieval system is not able to provide information about them to a user)

---

[1] http://www.macmillandictionary.com

L. Rutkowski et al. (Eds.): ICAISC 2014, Part II, LNAI 8468, pp. 500–511, 2014.

or by barrier between analogue and digital world (document retrieval system is not aware of source documents if they exist only as paper books on a library shelf). The latter may seem more strange, but it is a common scenario that ghost-writers are partially or entirely authors of someone else's work. Frequently they offer their services in paper-mills.

Intrinsic plagiarism detection is also related to stylometry and authorship attribution but is harder than the latter due to usually small amount of evidence text [3].

Character n-gram profiles algorithm is the top intrinsic plagiarism detection method, winning the PAN-PC'09 competitions and being outperformed only by one team [4] in the PAN-PC'11 competitions [5]. The method was also applied successfully in authorship attribution, including forensics.

Optimal parameters of the method, e.g. window size, (cf. [6]), or size of n-grams, are not however well-defined or studied in literature. The aim of the paper is to improve effectiveness of character n-gram method when applied to intrinsic plagiarism detection by adjusting its parameters. We propose also a new extension of the method by taking richer and better suited n-gram feature set.

The main contributions of the paper are the following:

- Raising plagdet effectiveness of character n-grams profile method from 18.83% to 26.66% measured for the PAN-PC09 corpus and from 24.67% to 33.41% measured for the PAN-PC11 corpus, which are widely recognised corpora in plagiarism competitions.
- Improvement of the standard character n-grams profile method by considering richer feature sets, i.e. n-grams with varying length instead of n-grams with fixed length.
- Finding optimal parameters (n-gram order, window size, window step) of the method.

2   State of the Art

The modern plagiarism detection systems consist of three parts:

- preprocessing phase, which selects the preliminary set of candidate files or passages,
- proper detection of plagiarised passages,
- postprocessing phase, which may validate proposed set of plagiarism chunks and merge some of them to improve granularity of the final answer.

In recent year several solutions to the proper detection of intrinsic plagiarism were proposed but none of them seem satisfactory for real applications.

In [7] Stamatatos splits documents into text chunks (windows) and for each window as well as a whole document a profile is built. The profile of a window or a document is the set of its character trigrams along with the number of their occurrences. Based on window profiles distance of each of text chunk from a whole document is computed and with the help of standard deviation outliers (plagiarised chunks) are identified. The big advantage of character n-grams features is their language independence, as they belong to lexical features family.

Algorithm of Oberreuter is conceptually similar to that of Stamatatos but they use word unigrams instead of character trigrams to build a document/window profile [4].

Paper [6] is an example of departure from common approach of comparing current section identified by a sliding window to the profile of a the whole document. Instead each section is compared to each other section and square matrix of distances is created. Outliers (presumably plagiarised sections) are identified by a technique suitable for multivariate data in high dimensions based on Principal Component Analysis. Authors use only 1000 or 2500 most common n-grams found previously in the entire PAN-PC10 corpus.

In [8] Akiva takes the rarest words as stylistic markers. Text chunks are clustered with spectral clustering method n-cut into 2 clusters, presumably corresponding to non-plagiarised and plagiarised text respectively. In the second phase chunks close to the centroid of the small cluster and far from the centroid of the whole document are identified as plagiarised.

Improvement of intrinsic plagiarism detection by incorporating complexity features beside normalized count features into SVM and neural network classifiers is proposed in [9].

3   Character n-gram Profiles Method

Here we recall character n-gram profiles method in detail [7] with our enrichment of the postprocessing phase.

Many modern methods in NLP departure from the classic Vector Space Model. Character n-gram profiles method represents a document as a set of character n-grams. At first the document is split into a set of windows (text chunks) by a running window of constant size. At each iteration a sliding window advances over the document by a constant step to create new text chunk. Usually sliding step is assigned a lower value than window size, so arisen windows are overlapping. Window size and step refer to the number of letter characters only. Non-letter characters are ignored in this values, so real window size and step are larger than logical values.

Distance function between each window W and document D is calculated on the basis of character n-grams frequency:

$$nd_1(W, D) = \frac{\sum_{g \in P(W)} \left(\frac{f_W(g) - f_D(g)}{f_W(g) + f_D(g)} \right)^2}{|P(W)|}, \tag{1}$$

where $P(W)$ denotes the profile of window W; $f_W(g)$, $f_D(g)$ denote frequency of n-gram g in window W and document D, respectively. The nd_1 function measures the similarity of n-grams distributions $f_W(g)$ and $f_D(g)$ over W. The more $f_W(g)$

and $f_D(g)$ distributions are similar over W, the lower the distance between window W and document D, with distance equal to 0 iff $f_W(g)$ and $f_D(g)$ totally overlap over W. The distance between $f_W(g)$ and $f_D(g)$ is normalised using $|P(W)|$ in order to $nd_1 \in [0,1]$.

The nd_1 function is not a real distance function however due to lack of symmetry ($nd_1(A,B) \neq nd_1(B,A)$), as summing is executed only over n-grams belonging to the profile of the first window in a pair. Function nd_1 takes into consideration only n-grams which contain at least one letter. In our implementation $f_D(g)$ and $f_W(g)$ frequencies are computed as relative, not absolute values.

Thus a vector of distances between each text chunk and the whole document, D, is created and vector's mean, m, and standard deviation, std are computed. Each window, W, whose distance from document D satisfies inequality

$$nd_1(W, D) > m + std \tag{2}$$

or whose real length (taking into account non-letter characters) $> T_2*$window size (window size refers to the number of letter only characters) is filtered out from the vector in order to recompute its new mean, m', and new standard deviation, std'. Then the algorithm identifies each window W in the original vector as a plagiarism if it meets the criterion:

$$nd_1(W, D) > m' + a \cdot std' \tag{3}$$

where a is a sensitivity parameter. The bigger a the less chunks are classified as a plagiarism. Classification of chunks is illustrated in Fig. 1. Finally plagiarised passages are mapped into positions in the original text.

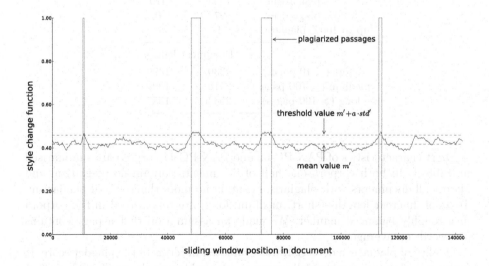

Fig. 1. Identification of plagiarised passages on the basis of the style change function

Documents with $std' < T_1$ are not considered to contain real plagiarism cases as their variability is attributed to natural changes of the style of a document author.

In our implementation of the algorithm we extended the postprocessing phase. To improve granularity overlapping plagiarism chunks are merged into one wider chunk (which seems quite obvious) but we also merge plagiarism chunks if they stay apart in the text by no more than the gap parameter (in our settings equal to 1000 characters).

4   Evaluation Corpora

The intrinsic plagiarism detection experiments have been conducted with the PAN-PC-09 and PAN-PC-11 corpora used in PAN plagiarism detection competitions [10,11]. These corpora are particularly suitable as they have separate sets of documents devoted to intrinsic plagiarism detection evaluation.

Table 1. Characteristics of PAN-PC-09 and PAN-PC-11 corpora (number of documents), parts of the corpora concerning intrinsic plagiarism

	PAN-PC09	PAN-PC11
documents	6183	4753
Amount of plagiarism		
no plagiarism	3091	2388
<20% plagiarism	1831	1955
<50% plagiarism	1233	410
<80% plagiarism	27	0
up to 100% plagiarism	1	0
Document length		
short ($\leq$ 10 pages)	1330	1306
medium ($\leq$ 100 pages)	2310	1890
long ($>$ 100 pages)	2543	1557

Short characteristics of PAN-PC-09 and PAN-PC-11 corpora are summarised in Table 1. In both corpora one half of documents contain no plagiarism and almost all documents with plagiarism contain no more than 50% of plagiarism. Texts of different lengths (short, medium, long) are represented in the corpora in a roughly balanced manner. We made an assumption that a page contains 375 words on average.

Quality of plagiarism detection was evaluated in terms of the plagdet score. It makes use of precision and recall measures adapted to suit the needs of plagiarism detection and granularity measure, which arises only in plagiarism detection problem. Precision, $prec_{PDA}$, and recall, rec_{PDA}, are defined formally as follows [12]:

$$rec_{PDA}(S, R) = \frac{1}{|S|} \sum_{s \in S} \frac{|s \sqcap \bigcup_{r \in R} r|}{|s|} \ , \tag{4}$$

$$prec_{PDA}(S, R) = \frac{1}{|R|} \sum_{r \in R} \frac{|r \sqcap \bigcup_{s \in S} s|}{|r|} \ , \tag{5}$$

where

$$s \sqcap r \overset{\mathrm{df}}{=} \begin{cases} s \cap r & \text{if } r \text{ detects } s, \\ \varnothing & \text{otherwise}, \end{cases} \tag{6}$$

S is a set of plagiarised sections in an original document being source of plagiarism and R is a set of sections detected by plagiarism detection program in inspected document.

Granularity measure is introduced as [12]:

$$gran_{PDA}(S, R) = \frac{1}{|S_R|} \sum_{s \in S_R} |C_s| \ , \tag{7}$$

where $C_s \overset{\mathrm{df}}{=} \{ r \mid r \in R \land s \sqcap r \neq \varnothing \}$ and $S_R \overset{\mathrm{df}}{=} \{ s \mid s \in S \land \exists r \in R : s \sqcap r \neq \varnothing \}$. Additionally F measure is auxiliarly introduced, which is a harmonic mean of precision and recall, with weight equal to 1 assigned both to precision and recall ($F = 2 \cdot prec \cdot rec/(prec + rec)$). Then overall *plagdet* measure can be computed as [12]:

$$plagdet = \frac{F}{\log_2(1 + gran_{PDA})} \ . \tag{8}$$

5   Experiments and Results

The aim of experiments was to explore parameter space of Stamatatos algorithm and find optimal ones. We conjectured that values proposed in his paper [7] are not optimal for plagiarism detection effectiveness.

Four main experiments have been conducted. The first experiment examined impact of parameter settings of the standard character n-gram profiles algorithm on plagiarism detection effectiveness. We varied sliding window size from 500 to 7000 and n-gram size took values $n \in \{2, 3, 4, 5, 6\}$.

The second experiment took into account union of n-grams when computing nd_1 distance. We considered union of bigrams and trigrams (23grams features), then union of bigrams, trigrams and fourgrams (234grams features) and in an analogous way 2345grams features and 23456grams features. Encouraged by promising results we additionally explored union of trigrams, fourgrams and fivegrams (345grams features).

The third experiment was similar to the first one, but only 2500 most frequent n-grams, $n \in \{2, 3, 4, 5\}$, were taken into account. Fourth experiment examined impact of a sliding window step on plagiarism detection effectiveness.

Threshold T_1 was set to 0.02 in the first, second and fourth experiment and to 0.01 in the third experiment. In all experiments threshold T_2 was set to 1.5 and sensitivity a to 2. Window step was equal to 200 in first three experiments. In total 548 subexperiments were performed.

Table 2 presents plagdet scores of the standard character n-gram profiles algorithm. Plagdet scores for trigrams and window size equal to 1000, parameter settings proposed by [7], are 0.2467 and 0.1883 for PAN-PC09 and PAN-PC11, respectively. The plagdet score 0.2467 comes in good agreement with results reported by Stamatatos, i.e. 0.2462. Our experiment reveals that that the standard algorithm optimal obtains results with fourgrams and window size equal to 6000 (PAN-PC09) or with fivegrams and window size equal to 4500 (PAN-PC11). The plagdet scores are equal to 0.3309 and 0.2524 for PAN-PC09 and PAN-PC11, respectively. Increasing order of n-grams beyond five spoils the results due to data sparseness, which is observed for sixgrams.

Table 3 gives more insight on the components of plagdet examined for fourgrams and with window size varying from 500 to 7000. With larger window sizes detection precision is growing from 13.54% to 40.50% at the cost of lowering recall from 54.40% to 27.75%. Granularity is consistently getting lower with growing size of a running window. On the whole plagdet is improving from 0.1649 to its peak at 0.3309 and the is getting lower to 0.3285.

In our experiments we did not divide the corpora into the training and test files. This split is not available from Bauhaus-Universität Weimar (the provider of the corpora) and making our own split would make the results hard to replicate for the community. This is not however a drawback. Treating PAN-PC09 as the training corpus and PAN-PC11 as the test corpus we find that the results for PAN-PC11 do not change much and are significantly better than those achieved by Stamatatos.

Over 65% (PAN-PC09) and 61% (PAN-PC11) documents were identified correctly as containing or not containing plagiarism cases. Table 4 presents plagdet scores for the second experiment, when not only n-grams of fixed length are taken into account for computing nd_1 distance. For both corpora we observe that incorporating more n-gram features is beneficial for almost every window size, e.g. it is better to consider union of all n-grams with varying n instead of n-grams with fixed n only.

The best results were obtained for 2345grams features and window size equal to 3500 (PAN-PC09) or 345grams features and window size equal to 3000 (PAN-PC11). These settings gave improvement of plagdet score from 33.09% to 33.41% and from 25.24 to 25.90% respectively, compared to approach with n-grams of fixed length. Exploiting broader feature set allowed to achieve optimal results for smaller window size, compared to the standard algorithm (3500 vs. 6000 for PAN-PC09, 3000 vs. 4500 for PAN-PC11). Similarly to first experiment, worsening of results is observed with higher n, $n \geq 6$ (e.g. 23456grams features).

Table 2. Impact of n-grams and sliding window size on plagdet score of character n-gram profiles method. In bold the best obtained results. In italic the results obtained with [7] settings.

PAN-PC09											
	500	1000	1500	2000	2500	3000	3500	4000	4500	5000	6000	7000
2grams	0.1632	0.2088	0.2223	0.2309	0.2325	0.2329	0.2343	0.2319	0.2318	0.2304	0.2303	0.2285
3grams	0.1566	*0.2467*	0.2926	0.3150	0.3235	0.3276	0.3258	0.3208	0.3158	0.3083	0.3026	0.2983
4grams	0.1649	0.2203	0.2640	0.2941	0.3094	0.3210	0.3249	0.3262	0.3288	0.3300	**0.3309**	0.3285
5grams	0.1878	0.2439	0.2763	0.2945	0.3079	0.3150	0.3201	0.3231	0.3235	0.3255	0.3290	0.3261
6grams	0.1475	0.2288	0.2696	0.2949	0.3066	0.3147	0.3158	0.3153	0.3144	0.3141	0.3147	0.3110

PAN-PC11											
	500	1000	1500	2000	2500	3000	3500	4000	4500	5000	6000	7000
2grams	0.1175	0.1305	0.1256	0.1223	0.1220	0.1193	0.1136	0.1128	0.1149	0.1153	0.1050	0.0980
3grams	0.1197	*0.1883*	0.2226	0.2358	0.2372	0.2324	0.2256	0.2202	0.2165	0.2090	0.1959	0.1914
4grams	0.1279	0.1687	0.2012	0.2262	0.2402	0.2480	0.2504	0.2524	0.2512	0.2523	0.2487	0.2433
5grams	0.1515	0.1891	0.2132	0.2290	0.2382	0.2453	0.2466	0.2502	**0.2524**	0.2489	0.2476	0.2444
6grams	0.1466	0.1920	0.2240	0.2376	0.2437	0.2445	0.2467	0.2440	0.2411	0.2383	0.2337	0.2251

Table 5 shows plagdet scores for the third experiment when only 2500 most frequent n-grams of fixed length were considered. Following the Kestemont's idea the most frequent n-grams were fixed on the basis of a whole corpus (namely the PAN-PC10 corpus). In the implementation we required that such n-grams had to be present in both the document and the sliding windowing in order to contribute to $nd_1(W, D)$ distance.

Compared to the standard algorithm (first experiment) significant deterioration of results can be observed but we still profit from taking window size larger than 1000. The optimal score in this experiment was obtained for window size equal to 5500 (PAN-PC09) or 4500 (PAN-PC11).

When detecting plagiarism with most frequent n-grams at a corpus level the data sparseness problem arises. The optimal score is reached for trigrams, while for fourgrams in the first experiment. Due to data sparseness continuous degradation of results with increasing n-gram length begins with $n = 4$.

Additionally, there may be no n-gram from the most frequent n-grams set present in a sliding window, what makes computing the distance between a window and a document, $nd_1(W, D)$, impossible. The problem was observed for higher order n-grams ($n \geq 5$) with small window sizes (≤ 500).

Therefore we replicated this experiment with the most frequent n-grams fixed on the basis of a currently processed document. These detection scores were even worse and are not presented in the paper. The variation of the experiment with n-grams fixed at the corpus level and present in either the document or the sliding windowing also turned out to be inferior to results presented in Table 5.

The last experiment examined the impact of window step size on plagiarism detection performance (Tables 6 and 7). In this experiment we considered n-grams features, which gave previously promising results: 4grams and 2345grams and window size set parameter to 3500 or 4000, according to our

Table 3. Impact of sliding window size on intrinsic plagiarism detection effectiveness obtained for n-grams with $n = 4$

PAN-PC09					
Window size	Recall	Precision	F-measure	Granularity	Plagdet
500	0.5440	0.1354	0.2168	1.4878	0.1649
1000	0.5181	0.1726	0.2589	1.2585	0.2203
1500	0.4873	0.2119	0.2953	1.1712	0.2640
2000	0.4540	0.2428	0.3163	1.1075	0.2941
2500	0.4268	0.2644	0.3265	1.0780	0.3094
3000	0.3967	0.2869	0.3329	1.0524	0.3210
3500	0.3685	0.3060	0.3343	1.0408	0.3249
4000	0.3459	0.3200	0.3324	1.0268	0.3262
4500	0.3299	0.3365	0.3331	1.0183	0.3288
5000	0.3151	0.3535	0.3331	1.0136	0.3300
5500	0.3052	0.3658	0.3327	1.0086	0.3307
6000	0.2953	0.3803	0.3324	1.0066	0.3309
6500	0.2855	0.3917	0.3302	1.0046	0.3292
7000	0.2775	0.4050	0.3293	1.0036	0.3285

PAN-PC11					
Window size	Recall	Precision	F-measure	Granularity	Plagdet
500	0.5777	0.0864	0.1503	1.2576	0.1279
1000	0.5151	0.1115	0.1833	1.1239	0.1687
1500	0.4561	0.1382	0.2121	1.0768	0.2012
2000	0.4154	0.1630	0.2341	1.0493	0.2262
2500	0.3794	0.1825	0.2464	1.0360	0.2402
3000	0.3426	0.1987	0.2515	1.0198	0.2480
3500	0.3094	0.2138	0.2528	1.0138	0.2504
4000	0.2857	0.2289	0.2541	1.0097	0.2524
4500	0.2633	0.2424	0.2524	1.0067	0.2512
5000	0.2510	0.2554	0.2531	1.0050	0.2523
5500	0.2384	0.2684	0.2525	1.0049	0.2516
6000	0.2274	0.2763	0.2494	1.0045	0.2487
6500	0.2134	0.2909	0.2461	1.0043	0.2454
7000	0.2046	0.3017	0.2438	1.0033	0.2433

previous findings. The window step size varied from 100 to 3500 or 4000; value of step equal to window size meant no overlapping of running windows. The experiment reveals that window step size parameter should be adjusted to a larger window size. The step's optimal size seems to be between 25% and 33% of a window size. A small deviation from this finding is observed for PAN-PC09 analysed with 2345grams features. Adjusting window step to window size raised further plagdet from 25.90% to 26.66% for PAN-PC09. Taking larger values of window step allowed also to obtain results faster due to lower number of sliding window iterations.

Table 4. Impact of summed n-grams and a sliding window size on plagdet score

PAN-PC09									
	500	1000	1500	2000	2500	3000	3500	4000	4500	5000
23grams	0.1785	0.2628	0.2933	0.3084	0.3163	0.3167	0.3116	0.3068	0.3013	0.2978
234grams	0.1885	0.2622	0.2997	0.3187	0.3278	0.3336	0.3336	0.3312	0.3292	0.3262
2345grams	0.2036	0.2683	0.2989	0.3197	0.3282	0.3325	**0.3341**	0.3304	0.3285	0.3278
23456grams	0.2081	0.2697	0.3004	0.3155	0.3259	0.3302	0.3285	0.3271	0.3234	0.3226
345grams	0.1891	0.2589	0.2923	0.3135	0.3246	0.3293	0.3303	0.3310	0.3304	0.3295

PAN-PC11									
	500	1000	1500	2000	2500	3000	3500	4000	4500	5000
23grams	0.1366	0.1976	0.2182	0.2216	0.2188	0.2141	0.2084	0.2014	0.1961	0.1939
234grams	0.1436	0.2027	0.2354	0.2505	0.2516	0.2520	0.2498	0.2440	0.2410	0.2380
2345grams	0.1601	0.2114	0.2376	0.2492	0.2550	0.2574	0.2569	0.2552	0.2500	0.2467
23456grams	0.1650	0.2153	0.2393	0.2490	0.2504	0.2554	0.2533	0.2468	0.2436	0.2406
345grams	0.1469	0.2024	0.2316	0.2487	0.2537	**0.2590**	0.2578	0.2555	0.2541	0.2499

Table 5. Plagdet score obtained for PAN-PC09 and PAN-PC11 corpora with 2500 most common n-grams

PAN-PC09										
	500	1000	1500	2000	2500	3000	3500	4000	4500	5000	6000	7000
2grams	0.1275	0.1546	0.1782	0.2114	0.2339	0.2502	0.2571	0.2640	0.2619	0.2650	0.2679	0.2673
3grams	0.1485	0.1831	0.2075	0.2362	0.2630	0.2855	0.2946	0.3013	0.3019	0.3047	**0.3056**	0.3028
4grams	0.1385	0.1707	0.1912	0.2047	0.2147	0.2300	0.2447	0.2590	0.2683	0.2765	0.2842	0.2911
5grams	0.1254	0.1575	0.1781	0.1925	0.2002	0.2058	0.2088	0.2121	0.2155	0.2212	0.2383	0.2517

PAN-PC11										
	500	1000	1500	2000	2500	3000	3500	4000	4500	5000	6000	7000
2grams	0.1013	0.1181	0.1335	0.1543	0.1694	0.1813	0.1870	0.1879	0.1861	0.1868	0.1838	0.1797
3grams	0.1175	0.1402	0.1564	0.1784	0.1980	0.2125	0.2220	0.2300	**0.2317**	0.2298	0.2242	0.2175
4grams	0.1120	0.1328	0.1455	0.1565	0.1626	0.1744	0.1854	0.1980	0.2049	0.2106	0.2169	0.2162
5grams	0.0884	0.1249	0.1400	0.1477	0.1537	0.1559	0.1562	0.1584	0.1598	0.1658	0.1758	0.1897

Table 6. Plagdet scores obtained for PAN-PC09 and PAN-PC11 corpora with window step values varying from 100 to 3500 and window size set to 3500

PAN-PC09								
	100	200	400	500	1000	1500	2000	3000	3500
4grams	0.3245	0.3249	0.3265	0.3263	0.3228	**0.3271**	0.3228	0.3016	0.2908
2345grams	0.3332	**0.3341**	0.3340	0.3327	0.3289	0.3287	0.3218	0.2991	0.2883

PAN-PC11								
	100	200	400	500	1000	1500	2000	3000	3500
4grams	0.2487	0.2504	0.2546	0.2556	0.2604	**0.2666**	0.2646	0.2540	0.2451
2345grams	0.2556	0.2569	0.2600	0.2600	0.2620	**0.2661**	0.2632	0.2512	0.2383

Table 7. Plagdet scores obtained for PAN-PC09 and PAN-PC11 corpora with window step values varying from 100 to 4000 and window size set to 4000

	PAN-PC09							
	100	200	400	500	1000	2000	3000	4000
4grams	0.3255	0.3262	0.3260	0.3272	**0.3279**	0.3199	0.3064	0.2915
2345grams	0.3303	0.3304	0.3297	**0.3305**	0.3299	0.3192	0.3027	0.2871
	PAN-PC11							
	100	200	400	500	1000	2000	3000	4000
4grams	0.2510	0.2524	0.2537	0.2557	**0.2589**	0.2588	0.2543	0.2398
2345grams	0.2537	0.2552	0.2546	0.2559	**0.2586**	0.2561	0.2481	0.2335

5.1   Test Bed and Implementation

Experiments were carried out on the Zeus cluster, being part of the PL-Grid infrastructure. This supercomputer offers currently 12104 general purpose cores to the scientific community, which provides 23 TB RAM and 120 TFlops of computing power. Computing nodes equipped with Intel Xeon processors work in HP ProLiant BL2x220c configuration under Scientific Linux 5.8 (2.6.18 kernel).

We implemented intrinsic plagiarism detection programs in Python 2.7.2 and used numpy 1.6.1 library. Computing tasks were distributed to nodes with Torque resource and queueing system ver. 2.5.12 and Moab workload manager ver. 7.2.1. We exploited task level parallelism.

6   Conclusions

In the paper we investigated character n-gram method for intrinsic plagiarism detection. We examined parameters of the method proposed by [7], found that these settings (trigrams with window size=1000) are far from the optimal ones and showed that taking larger window size $\in \{6000, 4500\}$ and n-grams with $n \in \{4, 5\}$ is profitable and significantly improves the plagdet score. Incorporation of n-gram features with varying length contributes to further improvement of plagdet score, achieved with smaller window size $\in \{3500, 3000\}$.

Taking window step between $1/4$ and $1/3$ of window size is also profitable as it not only improves plagiarism detection scores but additionally reduces running time of the algorithm.

Kestemont's idea of considering only the most common n-grams did not improve results and even deteriorated them significantly.

Despite gained effectiveness in intrinsic plagiarism detection, the problem is still far from being solved and intensive research should be continued.

Acknowledgments. This research is supported by the AGH University of Science and Technology (AGH-UST) grant no. 11.11.230.015. The research was also supported in part by PL-Grid Infrastructure. ACC CYFRONET AGH is acknowledged for the computing time.

References

1. McCabe, D.: Levels of cheating and plagiarism remain high. Technical report, Duke University, Center for Academic Integrity (2005)
2. Sheard, J., Dick, M., Markham, S., MacDonald, I., Walsh, M.: Cheating and plagiarism: Perceptions and practices of first year IT students. In: Caspersen, M.E., Joyce, D., Goelman, D., Utting, I. (eds.) Seventh Annual Conference on Innovation and Technology in Computer Science Education, pp. 183–187 (2002)
3. Stein, B., Lipka, N., Prettenhofer, P.: Intrinsic plagiarism analysis. Language Resources and Evaluation 45(1), 63–82 (2011)
4. Oberreuter, G., L'Huillier, G., Ríos, S.A., Velásquez, J.D.: Approaches for intrinsic and external plagiarism detection - Notebook for PAN at CLEF 2011. In: Petras, V., Forner, P., Clough, P.D. (eds.) Notebook Papers of CLEF 2011 LABs and Workshops (2011)
5. Potthast, M., Eiselt, A., Barrón-Cedeño, A., Stein, B., Rosso, P.: Overview of the 3rd international competition on plagiarism detection. In: Petras, V., Forner, P., Clough, P.D. (eds.) Notebook Papers of CLEF 2011 LABs and Workshops (2011)
6. Kestemont, M., Luyckx, K., Daelemans, W.: Intrinsic plagiarism detection using character trigram distance scores - Notebook for PAN at CLEF 2011. In: Petras, V., Forner, P., Clough, P.D. (eds.) Notebook Papers of CLEF 2011 LABs and Workshops (2011)
7. Stamatatos, E.: Intrinsic plagiarism detection using character n-gram profiles. In: Stein, B., Rosso, P., Stamatatos, E., Koppel, M., Agirre, E. (eds.) SEPLN 2009 Workshop on Uncovering Plagiarism, Authorship, and Social Software Misuse (PAN 2009), pp. 38–46 (2009)
8. Akiva, N.: Using clustering to identify outlier chunks of text - Notebook for PAN at CLEF 2011. In: Petras, V., Forner, P., Clough, P.D. (eds.) Notebook Papers of CLEF 2011 LABs and Workshops (2011)
9. Seaward, L., Matwin, S.: Intrinsic plagiarism detection using complexity analysis. In: Stein, B., Rosso, P., Stamatatos, E., Koppel, M., Agirre, E. (eds.) SEPLN 2009 Workshop on Uncovering Plagiarism, Authorship, and Social Software Misuse (PAN 2009), pp. 56–61 (2009)
10. Potthast, M., Eiselt, A., Stein, B., Barrón-Cedeño, A., Rosso, P.: Plagiarism Corpus PAN-PC 2009 (2009), http://www.webis.de/research/corpora
11. Potthast, M., Stein, B., Barrón-Cedeño, A., Rosso, P.: An Evaluation Framework for Plagiarism Detection. In: Huang, C.R., Jurafsky, D. (eds.) 23rd International Conference on Computational Linguistics (COLING 2010), pp. 997–1005. Association for Computational Linguistics (2010)
12. Barrón-Cedeño, A., Potthast, M., Rosso, P., Stein, B., Eiselt, A.: Corpus and Evaluation Measures for Automatic Plagiarism Detection. In: Calzolari, N., Choukri, K., Maegaard, B., Mariani, J., Odijk, J., Piperidis, S., Rosner, M., Tapias, D. (eds.) 7th Conference on International Language Resources and Evaluation (LREC 2010). European Language Resources Association (ELRA) (2010)

A Recommender System Based on Customer Reviews Mining

Paweł P. Ładyżyński[1] and Przemysław Grzegorzewski[2,3]

[1]Interdisciplinary PhD Studies at the Polish Academy of Sciences,
Jana Kazimierza 5, 01-248 Warsaw, Poland
pawelladyz@wp.pl
[2]Systems Research Institute, Polish Academy of Sciences,
Newelska 6, 01-447 Warsaw, Poland
pgrzeg@ibspan.waw.pl
[3]Faculty of Mathematics and Computer Science,
Warsaw University of Technology,
Koszykowa 75, 00-662 Warsaw, Poland

Abstract. As e-commerce is becoming more and more popular, the number of different products reviews done by customer grows rapidly. The efficient method for automatic summarization of such reviews is required. The majority of existing approaches classify a review only whether the opinion is positive or negative. In the present paper we show how to extract product features from the set of the reviews to design feature based summaries of available opinions. These summaries, expressed in IF-set framework, are later used to recommend a customer the best product corresponding to his individual demands.

Keywords: Bipolarity, decision making, IF-sets, information retrieval, opinion mining, recommender systems, similarity, text processing.

1 Introduction

In parallel with the e-commerce expansion we notice the rapid growth of products reviews prepared directly by consumers. In case of a popular product one may find hundreds or even thousands reviews. This makes difficulty for a potential customer to read them before making a conscious decision on whether to purchase given product or not. A manufacturer meets there also difficulties to keep track and to manage customer opinions on his products.

Inspired by [4] we show how to extract product features from the set of the reviews to design feature-based summaries of available opinions. Our main goal is to extract features of product which are rated by the customers. The next step is to classify a given review as rated in the positive or negative way. The final purpose is to provide the customer with a summary of the reviews to support him in making a reasonable decision or even to recommend him automatically the best solution that satisfies best his requirements.

The paper is organized as follows. Firstly, we introduce the problem by the leading real-life example related to camera reviews. We describe briefly the data

L. Rutkowski et al. (Eds.): ICAISC 2014, Part II, LNAI 8468, pp. 512–523, 2014.
© Springer International Publishing Switzerland 2014

structure, the software and techniques applied for text summarization and processing. Then, in Section 3, we present some methods used for extracting features from the consumer reviews and results obtained for our example. Next, in Section 4, we discuss how to classify the reviews and how to generate the desired summaries of the available reviews. Finally, in Section 5, we suggest how to make a recommendation based on those summaries.

2   Introductory Example

2.1   Data and Software

To perform the task of opinion mining, we used the Amazon Product Review Data (source: http://www.cs.uic.edu/~liub/FBS/sentiment-analysis.html, see [9] for details). This data set contains more than 5.8 million reviews of different products as books, cameras, movies etc. The reviews are collected in one "txt" file where every single line is a different opinion. In our study, we load the first 100000 reviews into R package and choose that ones, where the words "camera" and "Nikon" occur. As a result, we obtained 38 reviews. We decided to begin with such reviews, because we believe that the features there are quite obvious, frequent and therefore it is also easy to evaluate the accuracy of presented method. During this research, we use R package with following libraries: *tm, topicmodels, lda, openNLP, arules.*

2.2   Text Summarization

Firstly, we have read the reviews and prepared manually the list of features (categories of features) occurring there:

- Size, shape, weight,
- Picture, image quality, resolution,
- Battery life, charging,
- Zoom,
- Lens,
- Control, using comfort,
- Price,
- Flash,
- Shutter (shutter modes etc.),
- LCD,
- Memory cards,
- Light.

In next sections we show how it is possible to extract the list of features in the automatic way from the selected 38 camera reviews.

2.3 Text Processing

In order to analyze selected reviews automatically, we had to use some basic text processing methods. Firstly, we converted all capital letters to a lowercase. Then, we removed punctuation. In the next step, we computed the Document - Term matrix and after investigating frequent terms, we decided to remove stopwords. We used a dictionary from the *tm* package, but we modified it and remove from this dictionary the words, that could express opinions on some features (i.e. good, perfect etc.). Then we removed all numbers and applied stemming algorithm to our data. We decided to use Porter stemming algorithm (see [10]) from *tm* package. We tried also algorithms from Rweka library (see [12]) however, the effects were worse.

3 Extracting Deatures from Customer Reviews

3.1 Latent Dirichlet Allocation

Our first idea to cope with the problem of extracting features from the text files with reviews about cameras was to use LDA (Latent Dirichlet Allocation, see [3]). LDA is a three-level hierarchical Bayesian model, in which each item of a collection is modeled as a finite mixture over an underlying set of topics. Each topic is, in turn, modeled as an infinite mixture over an underlying set of topic probabilities. In the context of text modeling, the topic probabilities provide an explicit representation of a document.

However, the list of features obtained using this method was too long and contained too many words that were not features of reviewed products. The output of this method is shown in Figure 1.

```
> LDA_model@terms[sort_ind][1:30]
 [1] "camera"  "card"    "batteri" "digit"   "great"   "pictur"  "buy"     "featur"
 [9] "set"     "canon"   "memori"  "ive"     "littl"   "manual"  "recharg" "size"
[17] "expen"   "lcd"     "control" "take"    "time"    "compact" "screen"  "life"
[25] "mode"    "model"   "option"  "comput"  "doesnt"  "rang"
> |
```

Fig. 1. Automatically extracted list of features using LDA

3.2 Association Rules

Our next idea, inspired by [4], was to use association rules (see [2]) to find frequent itemsets of features in our data. Association rule learning is a popular method for discovering interesting relations between variables in large databases. It is intended to identify strong rules discovered in databases using different measures of interestingness:

– **support**
$$support(A \Rightarrow B) = \mathbb{P}(A \cap B), \tag{1}$$

which can be interpreted as the percentage of cases in the data that contains both A and B;

– **confidence**
$$confidence(A \Rightarrow B) = \frac{\mathbb{P}(A \cap B)}{\mathbb{P}(A)}, \tag{2}$$

that shows the percentage of cases containing A that also contain B;

– **lift**
$$lift(A \Rightarrow B) = \frac{confidence(A \Rightarrow B)}{\mathbb{P}(B)}, \tag{3}$$

i.e. the ratio of confidence to the percentage of cases containing B.

To apply association rules to our reviews, we used a priori algorithm from the library *arules* (Rpackage). We tried many different configurations and we decided to use $supp = 0.2$, $conf = 0.7$. Then we used redundancy pruning (see [12]) to remove words that are not product features.

```
> rules.pruned <- rules.sorted[!redundant]
> inspect(rules.pruned)
   lhs                rhs           support    confidence  lift
1  {olympus}     => {megapixel} 0.2105263  0.8888889  2.598291
2  {speed}       => {zoom}      0.2105263  0.8000000  2.533333
3  {memori}      => {card}      0.2631579  0.9090909  2.467532
4  {option}      => {qualiti}   0.2368421  0.9000000  2.442857
5  {control}     => {manual}    0.2105263  0.8000000  2.338462
6  {life}        => {batteri}   0.2105263  1.0000000  2.235294
7  {speed}       => {shutter}   0.2105263  0.8000000  2.171429
8  {money}       => {dont}      0.2105263  0.8000000  2.171429
9  {megapixel}   => {shutter}   0.2631579  0.7692308  2.087912
10 {light}       => {shutter}   0.2368421  0.7500000  2.035714
11 {zoom}        => {shutter}   0.2368421  0.7500000  2.035714
12 {subject}     => {len}       0.2105263  1.0000000  2.000000
13 {littl}       => {qualiti}   0.2105263  0.7272727  1.974026
14 {littl}       => {card}      0.2105263  0.7272727  1.974026
15 {olympus}     => {pictur}    0.2368421  1.0000000  1.809524
16 {shutter}     => {flash}     0.3157895  0.8571429  1.809524
17 {control}     => {batteri}   0.2105263  0.8000000  1.788235
18 {money}       => {shot}      0.2105263  0.8000000  1.788235
19 {light}       => {flash}     0.2631579  0.8333333  1.759259
20 {shutter}     => {shot}      0.2894737  0.7857143  1.756303
21 {lot}         => {shot}      0.2894737  0.7857143  1.756303
22 {megapixel}   => {batteri}   0.2631579  0.7692308  1.719457
23 {review}      => {look}      0.2105263  0.8000000  1.688889
```

Fig. 2. Output from apriori algorithm after redundancy pruning

However, the features of products are usually nouns or noun phrases, so we decided to extract only these parts of rules that are nouns. We applied part-of-speech tagger from *openNLP* library.

As a final feature list, we decided to take the union of nouns from left-hand-sides and right-hand-sides of the pruned rules. The result is shown in Figure 3.

516   P.P. Ładyżyński and P. Grzegorzewski

```
> unique(union(cechy3,cechy4))
 [1] "lens"      "megapixel" "zoom"     "card"     "qualiti"  "manual"   "batteri"
 [8] "shutter"   "dont"      "pictur"   "flash"    "shot"     "look"     "digit"
[15] "use"       "camera"    "nikon"    "subject"  "speed"    "option"   "control"
[22] "life"      "money"     "light"    "lot"      "review"   "size"     "lcd"
[29] "print"     "slr"       "shoot"    "featur"
```

Fig. 3. Final list of features automatically generated by the algorithm

3.3 Results

Below, in Table 1, we can see the comparison of the automatically generated list of features (output from the algorithm) and the list of features extracted manually from analyzed text documents.

Table 1. Results generated manually and automatically

Manual list of features	Automatic list of features
Size, shape, weight	size
Picture, im. quality, resol.	pictur, megapixel
Battery life, charging	batteri, life
Zoom	zoom
Lens	lens
Control, using comfort	control, use, option, manual, speed
Price	money
Flash	flash
Shutter modes	shutter
LCD	lcd
Memory cards	card
Light	light
-	dont
-	shot, shoot
-	digit, camera, nikon, subject, slr
-	print
-	featur

As we can see, 100% of features were detected by the algorithm. However, there are still 5 unnecessary words from all 17 detected. The advantage of this algorithm is that you can tune parameters in a priori algorithm and redundancy pruning to obtain the result that best fits your specific requirements. If you don't want any words that are not product features, you could take only the nouns from right-hand-sides of rules. Then all detected words would be the product features however, three of the features would be missing.

4   Making Summaries

4.1   Classifying Opinions

In this section, we focus on classifying the reviews according to selected features. In the first step of this process, we find the so-called *opinion sentences*. As in [4], by the opinion sentence we consider a sentence containing one or more product features.

Next, we have to identify *opinion words*, i.e. those words that are primarily used to express subjective opinions. As the opinion words we consider adjectives that modify adjacent noun or a noun phrase being a product feature. The process of identifying those adjectives is strictly connected with sentence parsers, which are specific for a given language (for English we have e.g. http://nlp.stanford.edu:8080/parser/). Usually sentence parsers detect also negations of the adjectives which is very important to classify properly the product's assessment.

Next step of the classification process is the identification of the opinion words orientation. Many approaches are described in the literature (see e.g. [4,11]). For example, one may use a vocabulary method, where the opinion words are compared with adjectives from the special vocabulary that provides information about the word orientation. The efficiency of such method strongly depends on the quality and size of the vocabulary. More advanced methods utilize Word Net (see [4]).

The output of classification process is an information whether given opinion is positive, neutral or negative. In the next section we show how to summarize efficiently such results.

4.2   IF-summary Generation

Usually a useful and effective summarization of the results obtained as the output of the classification process is not easy. The sets of features observed in a few particular reviews often differ significantly, and thus the information they provide is not comparable. On the other hand, this step is crucial for decision making or suggesting the best solution to the user.

In [4] the features are ranked according to the frequency as they appear in the reviews. Next, the number of the reviews with positive or negative opinions on the feature is counted. This method might be useful for the user who wants to aggregate the reviews in order to compare the total number of positive and negative opinions on the product features. However, if we are interested in designing a slightly more sophisticated automatic decision support system we should also be able to take into account specific demands of a user before we propose a recommendation. Therefore, a desired recommender system should take into consideration both the preferences of the user and the specific characteristics of available reviews. Some features of the product may be more interesting for the customer than others but we should also distinguish frequently evaluated features from the sparse ones. It is clear, since we cannot rely on a single opinion only, even if it suggests that given product is perfect.

Having in mind all these remarks we suggest a new method for making recommendations. Since consumers' opinions usually reveal either positive or negative attitude of the reviewer we need such mathematical tools for modeling that enable modeling this bipolarity. It seems that the theory of IF-sets (i.e. Atanassov intuitionistic fuzzy sets, see [1]) gives us the required apparatus which is both user-friendly and flexible enough.

Assume the following notion: Let $\{f_1, \ldots, f_n\} \in \mathcal{F}$ be a set of product features extracted from the reviews, $\mathcal{R}$ will be the r-element set of reviews and $\mathcal{P} = \{p_1, \ldots, p_m\}$ will be the set of reviewed products. The number of reviews related to the product p we will denote by r_p. Moreover, suppose that an opinion related to i-th feature given in j-th review of product p will be expressed by $k_{ij}^p \in \{-1, 1\}$.

To construct a bipolar model of a product reviews, a suitable IF-set must be defined for each product. Thus let us define an operator T which transforms each product $p \in \mathcal{P}$ to the corresponding IF-set p^T

$$p^T = \{(f, \mu_p(f), \nu_p(f)) : f \in \mathcal{F}\}, \tag{4}$$

where $\mu_p, \nu_p : \mathcal{F} \to [0, 1]$ are the membership and nonmembership function of the IF-set p^T defined for the product p, respectively. For a given feature $f \in \mathcal{F}$ a value $\mu_p(f)$ can be interpreted as a degree to which f belongs to the class of positively rated features, while $\nu_p(f)$ as a degree to which f does not belong to the class of positively rated features. The last value would be identified with the degree to which f belongs to the class of negatively rated features.

This way the collection of IF-sets p^T for $p \in \mathcal{P}$ summarizes opinions on particular features characterizing products under review. Thus a family $\{p^T : p \in \mathcal{P}\}$ will be called the *IF-summary of the reviews*.

Now one of the crucial problem is how to assign adequate values of the functions μ_p, ν_p. One may do it in the simplest way as follows

$$\mu_p(f_i) = \mu_p^S(f_i) = \frac{\sum_{j=1}^{r_p} \mathbb{I}(k_{ij}^p > 0)}{\sum_j |k_{ij}^p|}, \tag{5}$$

$$\nu_p(f_i) = \nu_p^S(f_i) = \frac{\sum_{j=1}^{r_p} \mathbb{I}(k_{ij}^p < 0)}{\sum_j |k_{ij}^p|}, \tag{6}$$

where $\mathbb{I}$ is the indicator function and $i = 1, \ldots n$.

Unfortunately, the method given by (5)-(6) reveals serious drawbacks. In particular, if we have e.g. 20 reviews of the product p_l and only one review with some opinion on feature f_i (say positive) than $\mu_{p_l}^S(f_i) = 1$ and $\nu_{p_l}^S(f_i) = 0$. These scores for the product p_l would be better than for the product p_h, with the feature f_i rated positively in 19 reviews and negatively in only one, for which we get $\mu_{p_h}^S(f_i) = \frac{19}{20}$ and $\nu_{p_h}^S(f_i) = \frac{1}{20}$.

To assign more importance to more frequent features let us define μ_p, ν_p in the following way:

$$\mu_p(f_i) = \frac{\sum_{j=1}^{r_p} \mathbb{I}(k_{ij}^p > 0)}{r_p}, \tag{7}$$

$$\nu_p(f_i) = \frac{\sum_{j=1}^{r_p} \mathbb{I}(k_{ij}^p < 0)}{r_p}. \tag{8}$$

Going back to our example and check, how this degrees behave for frequent and non frequent features. If we have 20 reviews for each of products p_l and p_h, where there is only one review with some opinion on feature f_i (say positive) for product p_l, than $\mu_{p_l}(f_i) = \frac{1}{20}$ and $\nu_{p_l}(f_i) = 0$. However, if for product p_h feature f_i is rated positively in 19 reviews and negatively in only one, then $\mu_{p_h}(f_i) = \frac{19}{20}$ and $\nu_{p_h}(f_i) = \frac{1}{20}$. It seems that the method (7)-(8) of defining functions μ_p, ν_p gives more natural values than the previous one.

It is worth noting that formulae (7)-(8) could be obtained from (5)-(6) by the appropriate weighting including frequency of the opinions on given feature in the reviews. Actually if

$$w_i = \frac{\text{number of reviews with feature} f_i}{r_p} \tag{9}$$

then we get

$$\mu_p(f_i) = w_i \mu_p^S(f_i), \tag{10}$$

$$\nu_p(f_i) = w_i \nu_p^S(f_i). \tag{11}$$

5   Creating Recommendations

Now we will show how to use the IF-summary proposed in previous section to create automatic recommendations for the user.

Let us define the following two IF-sets

$$p^+ = \{(f_i, \mu_{p^+}(f_i), \nu_{p^+}(f_i)) : i = 1, \ldots, n\}, \tag{12}$$

$$p^- = \{(f_i, \mu_{p^-}(f_i), \nu_{p^-}(f_i)) : i = 1, \ldots, n\}, \tag{13}$$

where

$$\mu_{p^+}(f_i) = \max_{l=1,\ldots,P} \mu_{p_l}(f_i) \tag{14}$$

$$\nu_{p^+}(f_i) = \min_{l=1,\ldots,P} \nu_{p_l}(f_i) \tag{15}$$

$$\mu_{p^-}(f_i) = \min_{l=1,\ldots,P} \mu_{p_l}(f_i) \tag{16}$$

$$\nu_{p^-}(f_i) = \max_{l=1,\ldots,P} \nu_{p_l}(f_i). \tag{17}$$

The p^+ and p^- can be interpreted as the "most desired" and the "least desired" product, respectively (see [7,8]). A reasonably working recommender system should propose products which are more similar to p^+ and simultaneously less similar to p^-. Therefore, we need a suitable similarity measure between IF-sets p^T representing successive products and p^+, p^-, i.e. $sim(p^T, p^+)$ and $sim(p^T, p^-)$. Here $sim(p^T, p^+)$ shows how much given product is similar to the "most desired" one, while $sim(p^T, p^-)$ tells us how much given product is similar to the "least desired" product.

Since p^T, p^+ and p^- are IF-sets we can use here various similarity measures based on distances defined for IF-sets, dissimilarity measures, divergence measures and so on (see, e.g. [5,7]).

However, in our opinion, a good recommender system, tailored for the user, should be able to take into consideration weights connected with investigated product features. Hence we recommend the following modified S_E similarity measure proposed in [6]:

$$S_E^{\omega}(p_1, p_2) = 1 - \sqrt{\frac{3(n-1)}{2n(n+1)} \sum_{i=1}^{n} \omega_i ((\mu_{p_1}(f_i) - \mu_{p_2}(f_i))^2 + (\nu_{p_1}(f_i) - \nu_{p_2}(f_i))^2)}, \quad (18)$$

where ω_i denotes the weight connected with product feature f_i.

Finally, to get a recommendation we need a suitable function $g : [0, \infty) \times [0, \infty) \to [0, \infty)$, which will aggregate $sim(p^T, p^+)$ and $sim(p^T, p^-)$. In other words, for given product $p \in \mathcal{P}$ and its IF-representation p^T we need a function

$$g = g(sim(p^T, p^+), sim(p^T, p^-)), \quad (19)$$

which is increasing at the first component and decreasing at the second component.

Then a function $R_g : \mathcal{P} \to [0, \infty)$, called *recommendation function*, such that

$$R_g(p) = g(sim(p^T, p^+), sim(p^T, p^-)) \quad (20)$$

will give us the *recommendation degrees* of the product $p \in \mathcal{P}$. Thus, the greater is the value $R_g(p)$, the more recommended is the product p and, consequently, p^* is the most recommended product if

$$R_g(p^*) = \max_{p \in \mathcal{P}} R_g(p). \quad (21)$$

One can consider various recommendation functions (20). As a natural example we suggest the following one

$$R_g(p) = \frac{sim(p^T, p^+)}{sim(p^T, p^+) + sim(p^T, p^-)}. \quad (22)$$

Below we show exemplary results obtained using the proposed method. In Table 2 we have k_{ij}^p coefficients for $n = 12$ features of $m = 5$ products taken

Table 2. Results of the classification step of opinions on product features

Product id		f_1	f_2	f_3	f_4	f_5	f_6	f_7	f_8	f_9	f_{10}	f_{11}	f_{12}
1	review 1	-1	NA	NA	NA	NA	NA	1	NA	1	1	NA	1
1	review 2	NA	NA	NA	NA	1	NA	1	1	1	NA	NA	1
1	review 3	NA	1	NA	NA	NA	NA	NA	NA	NA	1	1	1
1	review 4	NA	NA	NA	1	NA	1	NA	NA	NA	NA	1	NA
1	review 5	NA	-1	NA	-1	1	NA	NA	NA	NA	NA	NA	NA
2	review 6	1	NA	NA	-1	NA	1	NA	NA	NA	1	NA	NA
2	review 7	1	NA	NA	-1	1	NA	NA	-1	1	NA	NA	1
2	review 8	NA	NA	NA	1	1	1	NA	1	NA	1	-1	-1
2	review 9	1	NA	-1	1	1	1	1	NA	NA	1	1	NA
2	review 10	NA	NA	1	NA	NA	1	1	NA	NA	NA	NA	NA
2	review 11	NA	1	-1	NA	-1	NA	-1	1	NA	NA	-1	1
2	review 12	NA	-1	NA	NA	NA	1	1	1	-1	1	NA	1
2	review 13	1	1	NA	NA	NA	1	NA	NA	NA	1	-1	NA
2	review 14	1	NA	NA	NA	NA	NA	1	NA	NA	-1	1	1
2	review 15	1	NA	1	1	NA	-1	1	NA	1	1	NA	NA
2	review 16	1	1	1	1	NA	1	1	NA	NA	1	1	NA
2	review 17	1	NA	NA	1	NA	1	NA	-1	-1	1	1	1
3	review 18	1	NA	NA	NA	1	NA	1	NA	NA	NA	1	-1
3	review 19	-1	NA	-1	-1	NA	1	NA	-1	-1	NA	NA	1
3	review 20	-1	-1	NA	1	1	NA	NA	NA	NA	1	NA	1
3	review 21	NA	NA	NA	NA	1	NA	NA	-1	1	NA	NA	NA
3	review 22	NA	NA	NA	NA	1	NA	-1	NA	NA	NA	-1	1
4	review 23	1	NA	1	NA	1	NA	-1	1	1	NA	-1	-1
4	review 24	NA	NA	1	NA	NA	1	1	NA	1	1	1	1
4	review 25	NA	NA	1	NA	NA	-1	1	NA	-1	NA	NA	NA
4	review 26	1	NA	1	NA	NA	NA	NA	NA	NA	NA	NA	NA
4	review 27	NA	1	NA	NA	1	-1	1	NA	-1	-1	1	-1
4	review 28	NA	NA	NA	1	-1	NA	NA	1	NA	NA	1	NA
4	review 29	-1	NA	-1	NA	NA	1	1	NA	NA	NA	1	NA
4	review 30	1	NA	NA	NA	-1	1	NA	NA	1	NA	-1	1
4	review 31	NA	NA	NA	NA	-1	NA	1	NA	NA	NA	NA	-1
5	review 32	-1	1	-1	1	1	NA	1	NA	NA	-1	-1	1
5	review 33	NA	1	-1	NA	NA	1	1	1	-1	1	1	-1
5	review 34	1	1	1	NA	NA	NA	1	NA	NA	NA	1	NA
5	review 35	NA	NA	1	NA	1	NA	-1	-1	1	NA	NA	NA
5	review 36	1	NA	1	NA	1	1	1	1	NA	-1	NA	-1
5	review 37	NA	1	NA	NA	-1	NA	NA	NA	-1	NA	1	1
5	review 38	NA	NA	NA	1	1	NA	NA	-1	NA	1	1	-1

from $r = 38$ reviews. Symbol NA means that given feature is not available in the review.

In Table 3 and 4 we have the values of membership and non-membership functions calculated for the data from Table 2. Then in Table 5 we can see the recommendation degrees for the reviewed products. In Table 5 we have degrees with all weights ω_i equal to 1. In this case, we would recommend p_2 because the recommendation degree is the highest for this product. If we assign non equal weights to the features of the reviewed products (see Table 6), the recommendation changes to p_1.

Table 3. Membership functions for selected features and products

	f_1	f_2	f_3	f_4	f_5	f_6	f_7	f_8	f_9	f_{10}	f_{11}	f_{12}
$\mu_{p_1}(f_i)$	0	0.2	0	0.2	0.4	0.2	0.4	0.2	0.4	0.4	0.4	0.6
$\mu_{p_2}(f_i)$	0.17	0.58	0.5	0.33	0.5	0.33	0.33	0.33	0.58	0.33	0.25	0.25
$\mu_{p_3}(f_i)$	0.4	0.4	0.2	0.4	0.4	0.4	0	0.4	1	0.2	0.6	0.4
$\mu_{p_4}(f_i)$	0.44	0.33	0.22	0.44	0.67	0.33	0.33	0.44	0.22	0.56	0.22	0.44
$\mu_{p_5}(f_i)$	0.71	0.29	0.43	0.14	0.57	0.57	0.14	0	0.57	0	0.29	0.43
$\mu_{p^+}(f_i)$	0.67	0.57	0.44	0.42	0.8	0.67	0.57	0.29	0.4	0.67	0.57	0.6
$\mu_{p^-}(f_i)$	0	0	0	0.11	0.22	0.2	0.2	0	0.14	0.11	0.2	0.22

Table 4. Non-membership functions for selected features and products

	f_1	f_2	f_3	f_4	f_5	f_6	f_7	f_8	f_9	f_{10}	f_{11}	f_{12}
$\nu_{p_1}(f_i)$	0.2	0.2	0	0.2	0	0	0	0	0	0	0	0
$\nu_{p_2}(f_i)$	0	0.08	0.17	0.17	0.08	0.08	0.08	0.17	0.17	0.08	0.25	0.08
$\nu_{p_3}(f_i)$	0.4	0.2	0.2	0.2	0	0	0.2	0.4	0.2	0	0.2	0.2
$\nu_{p_4}(f_i)$	0.11	0	0.11	0	0.33	0.22	0.11	0	0.22	0.11	0.22	0.33
$\nu_{p_5}(f_i)$	0.14	0	0.29	0	0.14	0	0.14	0.29	0.29	0.29	0.14	0.43
$\nu_{p^+}(f_i)$	0	0	0	0	0	0	0	0	0	0	0	0
$\nu_{p^-}(f_i)$	0.4	0.2	0.29	0.2	0.33	0.22	0.2	0.4	0.29	0.29	0.25	0.43

Table 5. Recommendation degrees obtained for the equal weights assigned by the user, i.e. $\omega = (1,1,1,1,1,1,1,1,1,1,1,1)$

	p_1	p_2	p_3	p_4	p_5
$R_g(p_k)$	0.4956274	**0.5624043**	0.4237449	0.4584276	0.5079808

Table 6. Recommendation degrees obtained for the following weights assigned by the user: $\omega = (0,0,0.5,0,0.5,0,0,1,1,0.5,0.2,0)$

	p_1	p_2	p_3	p_4	p_5
$R_g(p_k)$	**0.5277612**	0.5045744	0.4759245	0.4945355	0.4905108

6   Conclusions and Perspectives

In this paper we suggest a method that can cope with thousands of reviews available in the internet. The proposed recommender system extract product features from the customer reviews so that a user does not need to know the specific product features that should be taken into consideration before purchase.

The system works like an expert: it shows which features are important and recommends an optimal product with respect to available reviews. The architecture of the recommender system is based on IF-summaries that enable to consider bipolarity connected with the positive and negative attitude to the reviewed products. Moreover, the adequate choice of weights in similarity measures used by the recommendation function allows to tailor a recommender system more sensitive for the customer individual demands.

It is also worth noting that our method might be useful for manufacturers to analyze which features are the most important for their customers. The optimal product p^+ could be taken into consideration as a model of achievable optimal product.

Some extensions of our study deserve future research. Firstly, the efficient algorithm of parameters optimization (confidence, support) to choose the optimal list of features is strongly required. Next, an approach based on correlations between terms and on associations, extracting positive and negative opinion words to choose opinion words without parsers, is of interest. Finally, one may be interested in applying the fake reviews detector to improve the quality of recommendations.

Acknowledgements. Study was supported by research fellowship within "Information technologies: research and their interdisciplinary applications" project co-financed by European Social Fund (agreement number POKL.04.01.01-00-051/10-00).

References

1. Atanassov, K.: Intuitionistic Fuzzy Sets: Theory and Applications. STUDFUZZ, vol. 35. Springer, Heidelberg (1999)
2. Agrawal, R., Srikant, R.: Fast Algorithms for Mining Association Rules. In: Proceedings of the 20th VLDB Conference Santiago (1994)
3. Blei, D.M., Ng, A.Y., Jordan, M.I.: Latent Dirichlet Allocation. Journal of Machine Learning Research 3, 993–1022 (2003)
4. Hu, M., Liu, B.: Mining and Summarizing Customer Reviews. In: KDD 2004 (2004)
5. Grzegorzewski, P.: Distances between intuitionistic fuzzy sets and/or interval-valued fuzzy sets based on the Hausdorff metric. Fuzzy Sets and Systems 148, 319–328 (2004)
6. Grzegorzewski, P., Ładyżyński, P.P.: Comparing vague preferences in recommender systems. In: Proceedings of the EUROFUSE 2013 Workshop, pp. 149–157 (2013)
7. Grzegorzewski, P., Mrówka, E.: Flexible Querying via IF-sets. International Journal of Intelligent Systems 22, 587–597 (2007)
8. Montes, S., Iglesias, T., Janiš, V., Montes, I.: A common framework for some comparison measures of IF-sets. In: IWIFSGN 2012, Warsaw (2012)
9. Jindal, N., Liu, B.: Opinion Spam and Analysis. In: WSDM 2008, Palo Alto (2008)
10. Porter, M.F.: An algorithm for suffix stripping. Program 14, 130–137 (1980)
11. Turney, P.: Thumbs Up or Thumbs Down? Semantic Orientation Applied to Unsupervised Classification of Reviews. In: ACL 2002 (2002)
12. Zhao, Y.: R and Data Mining: Examples and Case Studies. Elsevier (2012)

Complex System Analysis Using Softcomputing

Jacek Mazurkiewicz

Institute of Computer Engineering, Control and Robotics,
Wroclaw University of Technology, ul. Janiszewskiego 11/17, 50-372 Wroclaw, Poland
Jacek.Mazurkiewicz@pwr.edu.pl

Abstract. The paper presents a usage of softcomputing methods to reliability and functional analysis of sophisticated complex systems. The
approach is sensible since dependability parameters of the system are
mostly approximated by experts instead of classical sources of data. The
analyzed - Computer Information System *(CIS)* and Discrete Transport
System *(DTS)* - are modelled using the unified structure - in functional
sense. Results of numerical experiment performed on a test case scenario
related to the reliability, economic and functional aspects using softcomputing are given. The presented approach allows reducing the problem
of assumptions of reliability distributions and - this way - seems to be
very interesting for real systems management and tuning.

1 Introduction

We propose a combination of general view on a service network and its analysis
using softcomputing methods. We call the approach as the functional-reliability
models of network system exploitation. The computer systems analysis is the
root for our elaboration but we believe it is useful for modelling of the wider
spectrum of systems which realise tasks based on fully or partially available resources. We shortly describe elements of transport system and computer system.
Then some common elements are presented. Next sections provide the details
of the softcomputing methods usage and for the analysis. The results show the
essential practical data in the function of the reliability parameters of the system. We propose the parallel analysis of the computer system and the discrete
transport system based on the unified softcomputing approach. It is very important to note that complex system can be understood as several different service
providers. Since service [3] is describe as a set of services components based on
business logic, that can be loaded and repeatedly used for concrete business handling process (i.e. online service, transportation, etc.), therefore service can be
seen as a set of service components and tasks, that are used to provide definite
service in accordance with business logic for this process. On the high level importance of user request is the highest priority. For this reason we can assume
and make a sweeping statement that user request is realized in the same matter in transportation network and in computer systems, but based on different
resources (in first case - vehicles, in second - computers) [5].

L. Rutkowski et al. (Eds.): ICAISC 2014, Part II, LNAI 8468, pp. 524–535, 2014.
© Springer International Publishing Switzerland 2014

2   Abstract Approach to Service Network

The system is providing a service in a sense of user request accomplishment. As mentioned, we speak about unified common approach, analyzing network services as a general network. Since the service is aim to realized user task, therefore the key point of the view is the *Task (T)* given to the systems, its specification and its time. Each task conditioned by the scenario - business logic, therefore choreography [1] within a service must be defined and known. To provide a task, we have to use system resources - *Technical Infrastructure (TI)* capable to realize specified choreography. Moreover, not only the single choreography can be realized and not only the single configuration of the service is possible. Since, choreography is based on predefined service components located in network nodes task should be seen as an input to the predefined *Business Service (BS)*. As mentioned, specifying the task and its parameters is a *User* role *(M)* and the time functions on each level of abstraction - *Chronicle of the System (K)*. *Abstract Network Services (ANS)* can be represented as a 4-tuple [5]:

$$ANS = \langle T, BS, TI, M, K \rangle, \tag{1}$$

This unified description can be realized in case of network system exploitation analysis. Based on (1) we will consider two networks with respect to low level view, that is: Computer Information System and Discrete Transport System.

3   Discrete Transport System (DTS) Overview

Discrete Transport System *(DTS)* and its tasks are seen differently than in a Computer System, but still there are based on the same schema. Task understood as a request to a system of transport resources (e.g. vehicles), transport infrastructure (e.g. roads) and a management system. For this reasons, we can speak about: *Task (TM)* - as a several kinds of a commodity transported in the system, the commodities are addressed; *Business Service (BS)* - set of services based on business logic; each service component in *DTS* consists of a task of delivering a commodity from a source node to the destination one; *Technical Infrastructure (TI)* - infrastructure consisted of: *nodes* - to create the source, the destination and the trans-shipping points, *vehicles* - resources providing the service, described with some parameters, *roads* - paths of possible trip of vehicles, *Maintenance Crews*; *Client (CM)* - client allocated on one of nodes of the transport system and *Time-Table (TT)* - related to tasks and vehicles. Then the model of Discrete Transport System can be described as follows [12]:

$$DTS = \langle TM, BS, TI, CM, TT \rangle, \tag{2}$$

Basic elements of system are as follow: store-houses of tradesperson, roads, vehicles, trans-shipping points, store-houses of addressee and transported media (commodities). The commodities are taken from store-houses of tradesperson and transported by vehicles to trans-shipping points. Other vehicles transport commodities from trans-shipping points to next trans-shipping points or to final store-houses of addressees. Moreover, in time of transportation vehicles dedicated to commodities could failed and then they are repaired (Fig. 1.) [13]. Different *commodities* are characterized by common attribute which can be used for their mutual comparison: capacity. *Road* is an ordered double of system elements described by: length, number of maintenance crews, and number of vehicles moving. The road is assumed to have no damages. A single *vehicle* transports commodities from start to end point of a single road, return journey realizes in an empty status and the whole cycle is repeated. The commodity could be routed to more than one direction. Only one vehicle can be unloaded at the moment. If the vehicle can be unloaded, the commodity is stored in the trans-shipping point. If not, the vehicle is waiting in the only one input queue serviced by FIFO algorithm. Only one vehicle can be loaded at the moment. If the vehicle can be loaded (i.e. the proper commodity is presented and it could be routed a given road) the state of trans-shipping is reduced. If not, the vehicle is waiting in the each output road FIFO queue [10]. The *store-house of addressee* is described by following parameters: global capacity, initial state, function or rule which describes how each kind of commodity is spent by recipients. Output algorithm can be described as: stochastic process, continuous deterministic or discrete deterministic one. Moreover, the following assumptions are taken: the capacity of the commodity can't be less than zero, "no commodity state" - is generated when there is a lack of required kind of commodity. The economic analysis is realized from vehicle owner's view-point. The revenue is proportional to number of store-houses of addressee, number of deliveries realized to single store-house of addressee and gain for single delivery to single store-house of addressee. Following costs are taken into account: penalty costs - paid by a transportation firm when there is a lack of commodity in the store-house of addressee, repair costs - proportional to a unit of repair time, vehicle usage costs - in a function of time (salary of drivers) and in a function of distance (i.e. costs of petrol). The economic quality of discrete transport system is described by overall gain function $G(T)$ estimated in given time-period T as difference between the revenue and costs. We have to remember that the overall gain $G(T)$ is a random variable [4].

4   Fuzzy Analysis of DTS

4.1   Case Study

An exemplar transport network consists of two different commodities transported over network (marked as A and B) from two producers through two trans-shipping points to two consumers. Each commodity is spent by a given recipient. The process is continuous deterministic. Roads lengths and the number of vehicles are presented in Fig. 1. All vehicles have the same parameters. To each road one maintenance crew is assigned. Number of vehicles assigned to each road was calculated on a basis on required amount of commodities spent by each recipient taking into account some redundancy due to the fact of vehicle failures [2].

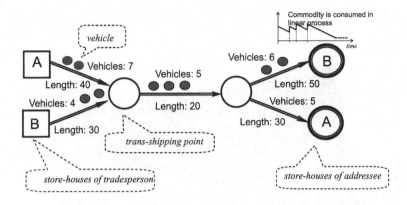

Fig. 1. Discrete transport system - case study example

4.2   Fuzzy Reliability Parameters

We analyze the overall system gain $G(T)$ in a function of fuzzy representation of truck reliability parameter: mean time of failures. We are not analyzing the classical reliability values: intensities of failures by its inverse of intensities since we think that it is much easier for expert to express the failure parameter in time units [11]. We assumed trapezoidal membership function for fuzzy representation of mean time of failure (let denote is as: $\mu_{M_\mu}(m)$). The four trapezoidal parameters has been set - based on expert knowledge - to (500,1000,2000,3000) hours. Assumption of the fuzzy membership function shape does not bound following analysis. One could use any other membership function and apply presented here methodology. Such system could be understood as a simple single input and single output fuzzy system. Applying fuzzy operator like max one could have achieved results. The overall gain is a random value. Therefore for a given system parameters (i.e. a given mean time repair time) we got a set of overall gain values.

4.3   Fuzzy Gain Description

We propose to represent the gain $G(T)$ as a fuzzy number. It could be done using for example the trapezoidal membership function. Four parameters have been set based on mean value m and standard deviation std of achieved gain as $(m - 3std, m - std, m + std, m + 3std)$. The results of fuzzy gain $\mu_G(g, m)$ (g spans possible values of gain, m spans possible values of mean time to failure) for case study system is presented in Fig 2.

4.4   Fuzzy Gain in Function of Fuzzy Reliability

Having the fuzzy gain representation $\mu_G(g, m)$ for each crisp value of the fuzzy reliability parameter $\mu_{M_\mu}(m)$, presented in Fig 2, we need to combine these

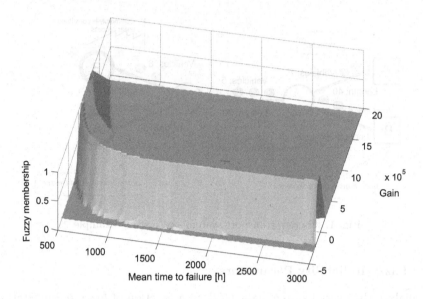

Fig. 2. Fuzzy representation of overall gain in function of mean time to failure

two measures to achieve an overall fuzzy gain. We propose to apply max and multiply operator to solve this problem (results are presented in Fig. 3a). It gives the following equation for the fuzzy gain membership function:

$$\mu_G(g) = \underset{m}{MAX} \left\{ \mu_G(g,m) \cdot \mu_{M_\mu}(m) \right\} \qquad (3)$$

where: m - mean time to failure, g - gain value.

4.5   Probability Density Method for DTS

The other way of final results presentation is based on probability density function estimation. Assuming that the fuzzy representation of mean time to failure is a way of stating the probability of vehicle mean time to failure, we could calculate the overall gain probability density function using slightly modified kernel method (with Gaussian kernels). The modification is done by multiplication each kernel by the weighted fuzzy trapezoidal function. Based on N results of overall gain g_i from computer simulation, calculated for given values of mean time to failure m_i, the density function $f(g)$ is given by:

$$f(g) = \frac{1}{h \sum\limits_{j=1}^{N} \mu_{M_\mu}(m_j)} \sum\limits_{i=1}^{N} \frac{1}{\sqrt{2\pi}} \exp\left(-\frac{1}{2}\left(\frac{g_i - g}{h}\right)^2\right) \cdot \mu_{M_\mu}(m_i) \qquad (4)$$

where h is a bandwidth parameter. It is set to optimal value based on maximal smoothing principle: AMISE - the asymptotic mean square error. Results for the case study DTS is presented in Fig. 3b.

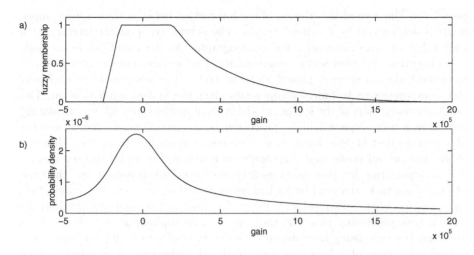

Fig. 3. Results: the overall gain presentation by a) fuzzy method and b) probability density method

5   Computer Information System (CIS) Overview

Task understood as a request to a service is specified by the user and executed in a Computer Information System defined as a farm of computers providing the service. With respect to its complexity such systems are called Complex Information System *(CIS)* - systems with extensive infrastructure aimed to satisfy user needs in case of a service based on computer network resources [9]. Taking these aspects into consideration we focus on service and user requirements - functional and dependability. This is the reason why, we can model *CIS* using the following elements: *Task (Z)* - input data specified by the clients in case of business service usage; *Business service (BS)* - set of service components located on defined server that determined service possibilities, requirements and behaviour; *Technical Infrastructure (HS)* - network resources (devices and links) built to provide network service. *Chronicle of the system (K)* - the time function on each level of abstraction; *Clients (M)* - set of users and its allocation, number of users of a given profile and their activities. As mentioned since we propose to analyze *CIS* systems on a basis of their service, we can modify (1) and define Complex Information System Oriented to Provide Service as:

$$CIS = \langle Z, BS, HS, M, K \rangle, \tag{5}$$

Service components (interacting applications) are responsible for providing responses to queries originating either from the system clients or from other service components. While computing the responses, service components acquire data from other components by sending queries to them. The system comprises of a number of such components. The set of all services comprises a Web system. Communication between Web services works on top of Internet messaging protocols. The communication encompasses data exchange using the client-server paradigm. The over-all description of the interaction between the service components is determined by its choreography. The service components interact with each other in accordance with the choreography. As the result, there are logical connections between service components. The service component is realized by some technical service, placed on some hosts. The assignment of each service components to technical components gives the system configuration. The most important part of the system model is an algorithm that allows calculating how long a user request will be processed be a system. Since, the processing of a user request is done by service components according to a given choreography, the overall processing time could be calculated as equal to time needed for communication between hosts used by each service component and the time of processing tasks required by each of service components. The communication time was modelled by a random value (with truncated normal distribution). In case of task processing time the problem is more sophisticated. It is due to a fact that the processing time depends on the type of a task (its computational complexity), type of a host (its computational performance) on which a task is executed and a number of other tasks being executed in parallel. And this number is changing in a time during the system lifetime. Therefore, it is hard to use any of analytic methods to calculate the processing time. That is way we used the simulation approach that allows to monitor the number of executed tasks on each host during the simulation process. We propose to extend failures to represents Web system faults which occur in a random way. We assume that system failures could be modelled a set of failures. Each failure is assigned to one of hosts and represents a separate working-failure stochastic process. The occurrence of failure is described by a random process. The time to failure is modelled by the exponential distribution. Whereas the repair time by truncated normal distribution. In simulation experiments described in the next section we consider two types of failures for each host: with full dysfunction of host and 98% downgrade of host performance. The first represents the results of a host or operation system failure. The second type of faults (with 0.95 downgrade parameter) models a virus or malware occurrence.

6   Fuzzy Analysis of CIS

6.1   Case Study

We have analyzed a Web system presented in Fig. 4. Few servers are used for a proper service realization: *BookingDatabase* - booking information storage, *WebServer* - Web Page server, *BackupWebServer* - Backup Web Page device, *PaymentServerController* - responsible for payment and bank operations, *Reservation Server* - server responsible for final reservation data. Booking service and it's choreography is described in Fig. 5.

6.2   Fuzzy Reliability Parameters of CIS

We want to analyze the accumulated down time in a function of fuzzy representation of host reliability parameter: mean time of failures(fh) and mean repair

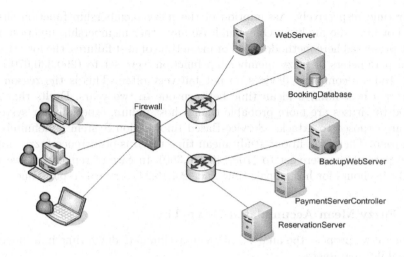

Fig. 4. Web system infrastructure - case study example

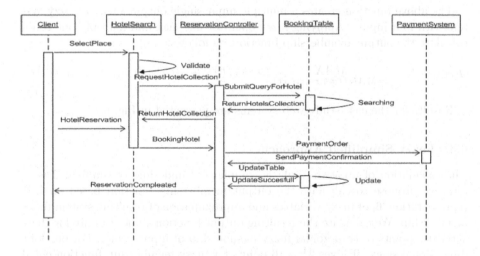

Fig. 5. Web system choreography - case study example

time (rh). We are not analyzing the classical reliability values: intensities of failures but its inverse since we think that it is much easier for expert to express the failure parameter in time units [11]. Moreover, we analyze the occurrence of virus and malware intrusions. It is described by mean time of virus occurrence (fv) and mean repair time (rv). We propose to use a trapezoidal membership function for fuzzy representation of mean time of failures and repair time for host and virus failures. Let note it is as: $\mu_{type}()$, where $type$ is equal to f_h, r_h, f_v, r_v for mean time to host failure, host repair time, mean time to virus and virus

repair time respectively. Assumption of the fuzzy membership function shape
does not bind the analysis. One could use any other membership function and
apply presented here methodology. For mean time of host failures, the four trapezoidal parameters of fuzzy membership function were set to (290,330,670,710)
days. Today's computer devices do not fail very often. This is the reason we
consider a host failures mean time between one to two years. Faults that are
related to viruses are more probable than a host failure, especially for systems
that are exposed to attacks. Service-Based Information System is definitely in
this group. Therefore, in our study mean time to virus occurrence fuzzy trapezoidal parameters were set to (100,140,340,360). In case of repair time we use
(4,8,32,48) hours for host repair time and (2,4,16,24) for virus repair time.

6.3 Fuzzy Mean Accumulated Down Time

In general we propose the analysis of mean accumulate down time in a function
of reliability parameter:

$$MADT(fh, rh, fv, rv). \tag{6}$$

The above function creates a multiple input single output (MISO) fuzzy system with four inputs. Applying fuzzy operator like max and multiply one could
calculate the output membership function, as follows:

$$\mu_{MADT}(t) = \underset{t=MADT(mh,rh,mv,rv)}{MAX} \{\mu_{f\_h}(fh) \cdot \mu_{r\_h}(rh) \cdot \mu_{f\_v}(fv) \cdot \mu_{r\_v}(rv))\} \tag{7}$$

Results for the case study web systems are presented in Fig. 6a.

6.4 Fuzzy Simplified Approach

The calculation of above formula is complicated and time consuming. Therefore, we propose to calculate the output membership function based on L-R
representation [6] of fuzzy variables and approximation of resulting system fuzzy
membership. We calculate the resulting output function value (6) only for characteristic points of trapezoidal fuzzy membership of input values. For our four
dimensional space, it gives $2^4 = 16$ points for fuzzy membership function equal
to 1 and similarly for membership function equal to 0. Among each of these
two groups, minimum and maximum values of the output function values (6)
are selected giving the resulting trapezoidal membership output function. Such
representation guarantees a really simple and fast calculation of fuzzy output
values. But this is only the rough approximation of fuzzy function of outputs
values. The results for case testbed are shown in Fig. 6b.

6.5 Probability Density Method for CIS

We propose also the other way of final results presentation, based on probability
density function estimation. Assuming that the fuzzy representation of mean

time to failure and repair time (section 4.2) is a way of stating the probability of time to failure, we could calculate the overall gain probability density function using slightly modified kernel method (with Gaussian kernels). The modification is done by multiplication each kernel by the weighted fuzzy trapezoidal function. Based on I results of accumulated down time $ADT_i(fh, rh, fv, rv)$ achieved

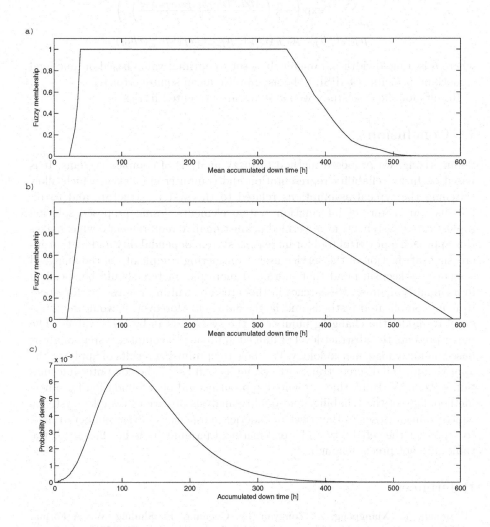

Fig. 6. Results: the accumulated down time presentation by a) fuzzy method b) fuzzy simplified method and c) probability density method

for different reliability parameter values (fh,rh,fv,rv) by computer simulation, the density function $f(t)$ could be approximated by:

$$f(t) = \frac{1}{h\sqrt{2\pi} \sum\limits_{j,k,l,m=1}^{J,K,L,M} \mu_{f\_h}(fh_j)\cdot\mu_{r\_h}(rh_k)\cdot\mu_{f\_v}(fv_l)\cdot\mu_{r_v}(rh_m)} \cdot$$

$$\sum\limits_{i,j,k,l,m=1}^{I,J,K,L,M} \exp\left(-\frac{1}{2}\left(\frac{ADT_i(fh_j,rh_k,fv_l,rv_m)-t}{h}\right)^2\right) \cdot$$

$$\mu_{f\_h}(fh_j) \cdot \mu_{r\_h}(rh_k) \cdot \mu_{f\_v}(fv_l) \cdot \mu_{r_v}(rh_m)$$

where h is a bandwidth parameter. It is set to optimal value based on maximal smoothing principle: AMISE - the asymptotic mean square error [7].

Results for the case study web systems are presented in Fig. 6c.

7   Conclusion

Summarizing, we proposed method of fuzzy analysis of complex systems. It is based on fuzzy reliability representation and computer simulation which allow softening the typical assumptions related to the system structure and to reliability parameters of information system elements. Using proposed solution sophisticated systems can be verified against quality requirements, what makes this approach a powerful tool for increasing system dependability and by that increasing satisfaction of the service user. Considering complexity of the analyzed systems, we keep in mind that more and more parameters should be specified in a similarly manner. Researches in this area are still in progress, with respect to more complicated testbeds and larger data set. Moreover, it would be interested to model the changing number of the system users by fuzzy values. The paper presents the abstract level of unified approach to complex system analysis based on fuzzy logic methodology. We show the promising results of applying the approach for the discrete transport system as well as for the computer information system. We think that presented approach could be a foundation for a new methodology of the reliability and quality analysis of various complex systems, which is much closer to the practice experience especially if the number of data to represent the reliability and - or functional parameters is insufficient or the values are not precise enough.

References

1. Hongli, Y., Xiangpeng, Z., Zongyan, Q., Geguang, P., Shuling, W.: A Formal Model for Web Service Choreography Description Language (WS-CDL). In: Proc. of ICWS 2006. IEEE Computer Society (2006)
2. Kaplon, K., Walkowiak, T.: Economic Aspects of Redundancy in Discrete Transport Systems, Poland, Szczyrk. XXXII Winter School of Reliability, pp. 142–153 (2004) (in Polish)
3. Martinello, M., Kaaniche, M., Kanoun, K.: Web Service Availability-Impact of Error Recovery and Traffic Model. Safety, Reliability Engineering and System Safety 89(1), 6–16 (2005)

4. Michalska, K., Mazurkiewicz, J.: Functional and Dependability Approach to Transport Services Using Modelling Language. In: Jędrzejowicz, P., Nguyen, N.T., Hoang, K. (eds.) ICCCI 2011, Part II. LNCS (LNAI), vol. 6923, pp. 180–190. Springer, Heidelberg (2011)
5. Nowak, K., Mazurkiewicz, J.: Multiagent Modeling and XML-Like Description of Discrete Transport System. In: Kabashkin, I. (ed.) Transport and Telecommunication, vol. 12(4), pp. 14–26. Transport and Telecommunication Institute, Riga (2011)
6. Piegat, A.: Fuzzy Modeling and Control. EXIT Academic ublishing House, Warsaw (1999) (in Polish)
7. Silverman, B.W.: Density Estimation. Chapman and Hall, London (1986)
8. Walkowiak, T., Mazurkiewicz, J.: Algorithmic Approach to Vehicle Dispatching in Discrete Transport Systems. In: Sugier, J., et al. (eds.) Technical Approach to Dependability, pp. 173–188. Oficyna Wydawnicza Politechniki Wroclawskiej, Wroclaw (2010)
9. Walkowiak, T., Mazurkiewicz, J.: Analysis of Critical Situations in Discrete Transport Systems. In: Proceedings of International Conference on Dependability of Computer Systems, Brunow, Poland, June 30-July 2, pp. 364–371. IEEE Computer Society Press, Los Alamitos (2009)
10. Walkowiak, T., Mazurkiewicz, J.: Availability of Discrete Transport System Simulated by SSF Tool. In: Proceedings of International Conference on Dependability of Computer Systems, Szklarska Poreba, Poland, pp. 430–437. IEEE Computer Society Press, Los Alamitos (2008)
11. Walkowiak, T., Mazurkiewicz, J.: Functional Availability Analysis of Discrete Transport System Realized by SSF Simulator. In: Bubak, M., van Albada, G.D., Dongarra, J., Sloot, P.M.A. (eds.) ICCS 2008, Part I. LNCS, vol. 5101, pp. 671–678. Springer, Heidelberg (2008)
12. Walkowiak, T., Mazurkiewicz, J.: Functional Availability Analysis of Discrete Transport System Simulated by SSF Tool. International Journal of Critical Computer-Based Systems 1(1-3), 255–266 (2010)
13. Walkowiak, T., Mazurkiewicz, J.: Soft Computing Approach to Discrete Transport System Management. In: Rutkowski, L., Scherer, R., Tadeusiewicz, R., Zadeh, L.A., Zurada, J.M. (eds.) ICAISC 2010, Part II. LNCS (LNAI), vol. 6114, pp. 675–682. Springer, Heidelberg (2010)

Can the Generation of Test Cases for Unit Testing be Automated with Rules?*

Grzegorz J. Nalepa, Krzysztof Kutt, and Krzysztof Kaczor

AGH University of Science and Technology,
Al. Mickiewicza 30, 30-059 Kraków, Poland
{gjn,kkutt,kk}@agh.edu.pl

Abstract. In this paper a proposal of a new black-box unit testing method based on decision tables is given. Its main part is an automatic generation of test cases using rule-based specification of a module. The tables containing rules are described in a formalized way using the XTT2 design method for rule-based systems. The paper also provides a presentation of a prototypical framework uses proposed method. This tool was designed as an Eclipse plugin which generates JUnit test cases. The proposed method can automate and improve the software testing process.

1 Introduction

Software engineering seeks novel methods and approaches for dealing with its challenges, e.g. quality control The growing scale of software systems stimulates the use of automated tools for performing number of repetitive tasks. Preserving and monitoring the quality of the execution of these tasks is of great practical importance. Hence formalized, and declarative methods are preferred. Moreover, there is a growing interest to use a range of intelligent tool to support them.

Testing is an important area in the software lifecycle. First of all it is one of the most common activities related to the quality assurance of software. While, definitely it is not the only one, or even should not be the main one, it is important to note, that it extensively uses automation. In the classic V model of the software lifecycle several types of tests that correspond to the subsequent phases of the lifecycle are considered. Most of them, especially on the lower level can be fully automated in terms of execution.

Unit testing is one of the most basic and broadly used type of tests [1]. In mature programming approaches writing tests is closely related to writing the code itself. In some approaches [2] tests are written before the actual code is created. There are several standardized tools supporting the creation of unit test. A common example is JUnit[1] for the Java language [3]. It also has a number of counterparts for other programming languages.

Unit testing frameworks such as JUnit have well developed facilities for implementation and execution of tests. In this area especially execution can mostly

---

* The paper is supported by the AGH UST Grant 11.11.120.859.
[1] See http://junit.org

L. Rutkowski et al. (Eds.): ICAISC 2014, Part II, LNAI 8468, pp. 536–547, 2014.
© Springer International Publishing Switzerland 2014

be automated. However, the main challenge lies in the actual preparation of test cases. In most of the cases this is the activity that requires knowledge of a human programmer or tester. While data for test cases can be semi-automatically inferred from the code or system specification (where it is available), the proper preparation and validation of test cases requires multiple manual activities.

In this setting, the main motivation for this research is to provide an automated method and tool supporting the generation of test cases from a formalized system specification. The assumption is that this specification is described with the use of decision rules. The method itself combines a black-box testing technique based on decision tables (DT) with the formalized design of business rules [4,5]. In this approach the specification of a unit (in terms of unit testing, e.g. a class) is described by a sets of business rules combined into decision tables. Then, the tables are used to automatically generate test cases for JUnit. The formalized description of tables allows for generation of complete test specifications. The original contribution of the paper is the description of the method, extending the preliminary research discussed in [6] and [7]. Moreover a practical tool implementing the method was developed, described and evaluated.

The rest of the paper is organized as follows: in Section 2 a more detailed description of motivation is given. Then, in Section 3 the specification for the approach is presented. Section 4 discusses the architecture and implementation of the software tool that supports the approach. The overall evaluation of the results is carried out in Section 5. The summary for the paper and some direction for future works are given in Section 6.

2   Motivation for Formalization of Unit Testing

In order to automate the creation of test cases, the specification of requirements for a software system has to be at least partially formalized. In this research we do not require the use of formal methods (e.g. Petri Nets). Instead, we assume the use of explicit description of certain requirements on the level of a unit. On a general level this description can be given by sets of input values to the system and the corresponding output values. This is the so-called black-box testing technique. It is not concerned with the internal structure of the system. Instead, it is solely based on the system specification and takes into account only the system response for a given input. In *decision tables (DT) based testing* the specification is described by a DT that groups admissible input values for a software unit being tested and specifies the expected output values.

For simplicity, we would assume here that a unit corresponds to a single class in an OO language (e.g. Java)[2]. The contents of DT correspond to the possible combinations of the values of attributes in a class. There are two main concepts involved in the DT testing:

---

[2] However, in a general situation this is not always the case. While our tool currently supports test case generation for classes, our approach could easily be extended.

1. *Equivalence classes* group the sets of all possible values for a given attribute. An equivalence class defines a subset of values that should be processed by system in the same manner. Thanks to that, the number of value combinations can be significantly decreased. It is assumed that DT contains input values from all possible combinations of equivalence class.
2. *Boundary values* are considered an extension of the equivalence classes. Having the set of equivalence classes, the boundary values can be specified according to ends of the equivalence class ranges. This technique is efficient, because many errors are caused by such values. A properly built DT should contain conditions related to each equivalence class and boundary values.

As an illustration, let us consider a simple system in [8]. Based on distance, location, available time and weather, it determines how to reach a particular location. Possible actions are: walk, take an umbrella and walk, take a taxi and drive your car. The system logic is presented in the form of seven rules in a decision table (Tab. 1). Example of a boundary value is 5 for *distance*.

Table 1. Rules of exemplary system

No.	Condition	Action
1	$distance > 5$	$means := drive$
2	$distance > 1 \wedge time < 15$	$means := drive$
3	$distance > 1 \wedge time \geq 15$	$means := walk$
4	$means = drive \wedge location = city\ centre$	$decision := take\ a\ taxi$
5	$means = drive \wedge location \neq city\ centre$	$decision := drive\ your\ car$
6	$means = walk \wedge weather = bad$	$decision := take\ an\ umbrella\ and\ walk$
7	$means = walk \wedge weather = good$	$decision := walk$

Our work is related to the conceptualand visual design of the rule-based intelligent systems [9]. The XTT2 (*eXtended Tabular Trees*) method [5] was developed as a formalized design method for rules. It uses DTs for knowledge representation where each row of a table corresponds to a single rule. Additionally, it provides features facilitating the modeling process. These include: a) the underlying formalism – the ALSV(FD) logic which provides a rigorous and precise definition of the rule language [9], b) visual representation where DTs are designed in a visual manner by a dedicated tool HQEd, c) Logical Quality Analysis (LQA) mechanism allows for discovering the logical anomalies in DTs like in completeness, redundancy, contradictions, etc, d) strong typing with the specification of attribute domains which in turn are used by LQA. Apart from the DT modeling, we consider the application of the XTT2 method to automate generation of tests based on DTs. In this context, it can be used as conceptualization method which allows for design of the given application specification using DTs.

3   Specification of DT-Based Framework for Unit Test Generation

A framework for automatic unit test generation using DTs should support several steps that are performed during testing process. It is assumed, these steps involve operations that can be summarized as follows:

1. **Creation** of a specification template that identifies input and output parameters for the methods belonging to the tested unit. In this step, empty decision tables (decision table schemas), corresponding to the methods, are created. Fields of the tested unit are mapped to the parameters that are used within conditions and actions of the decision tables.
2. **Fulfillment** of the specification template by defining rules providing information about initial values of the identified parameters and corresponding return values of the methods.
3. **Verification** of the complete specification with regard to logical errors such in completeness or redundancy of rules.
4. **Generation** of tests according to the complete specification. The set of test cases is generated and then saved as testing code (e.g. JUnit for Java code).
5. **Execution** of tests using generated test cases. For example, JUnit tests can be run by the Eclipse with the JUnit plugin.

Here we focus on the generation step which produces a unit testing code in a given programming language. It contains the set of test cases generated from the DT-based specification of the unit. During this step, the provided specification is parsed and, for every single rule, the following operations are performed:

1. A list of parameters used by tested methods is extracted from the decision table schemas that were created during the first step of the testing process.
2. A set of test values is generated for each parameter by using boundary value analysis. For this purpose, a simple algorithm is provided (see Table 2).
3. Test cases are generated as tuples (Cartesian product) where each tuple contains one test value for each parameter.
4. For each test case (single element of the Cartesian product) an expected result is calculated.
5. The set of generated test cases is saved as tests code.

According to provided specification of the DT-based framework for automatic unit tests generation, an architecture and implementation of proof of concept framework were developed.

4   Architecture and Implementation of the Framework

The proposed framework supports all the identified steps of the testing process. The first proposal of such a framework was presented in [6]. In that proposal we made several assumptions concerning the framework:

Table 2. Test values selection algorithm

Case	Tested value(s)
$Att = Value$	$Value$
$Att > Value$	$Value + 1$
$Att \geq Value$	$Value$
$Att < Value$	$Value - 1$
$Att \leq Value$	$Value$
$Att \in [L, U]$	L, U
$Att \in \{Att1, ..., AttN\}$	$Att1$

1. Specification of a tested unit is stored as an XTT2 model. This allows for using tools being part of the HADEs framework, such as HQED editor for rule modeling and HEART engine [11] for rules processing [11] and test generation.
2. All the test cases are saved in the JUnit format. This format is currently very common and thus it is well supported by many tools.
3. The framework is based on Eclipse IDE with the HADEsCLIPSE plugin [12]. This plugin supports communication between Eclipse and the HADEs tools as well as provides graphical user interface.

In this work, the architecture of the framework is refined (see Figure 1) and includes the following elements:

- **Tested unit** — a source code of tested unit. Based on this code, information about unit is extracted (available fields, existing methods, etc).
- **System specification** — the knowledge about behavior of a tested unit. According to this specification an XTT2 model is created.
- **HADEs** — a set of tools for modeling and managing rule-based systems.
  - **HQED** — a visual editor for XTT2 models.
  - **HEART** — a rule engine for XTT2 models that uses the HALVA plugin [13] for providing LQA mechanism and test plugin for generation of the test cases.
- **Eclipse** — an integrated development environment (IDE) for many programming languages that can be easily expanded via plugins system:
  - **HADEsCLIPSE** — a plugin for integration of Eclipse and HADEs framework, extending Eclipse with new creators and editors.
  - **JUnit** — a plugin for executing JUnit tests using user-friendly interface.

The set of steps identified in Section 3 is supported by the proposed framework. Figure 2 depicts the communication diagram for the testing process by means of the architecture of the proposed framework. The communication can be summarized as follows:

1. Creating initial specification in a Eclipse workspace as empty hml file by using creator provided by HADEsCLIPSE.
2. Sending specification file to HQED (in server mode).

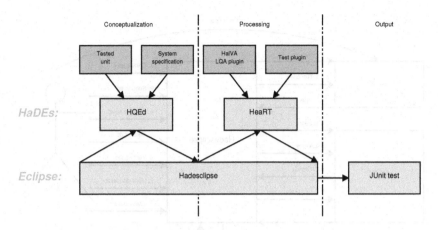

Fig. 1. Architecture of testing framework based on HaDEs and Eclipse

3. Completing the model in HQED by:
   (a) Creating types that represent classes of the parameters from tested unit.
   (b) Defining attributes that represent parameters from tested unit.
   (c) Specifying tables that corresponds to methods from tested unit.
   (d) Filling tables with rules that coincide input and result of the tested methods.
4. Receiving complete specification from HQED and storing it in a Eclipse workspace as hml file (for future editing) and hmr file (for sending to HEART).
5. Sending specification in the hmr format to HEART (in server mode).
6. Verifying specification in HEART against in completeness, contradictions, subsumptions and redundancy of rules by using HALVA plugin.
7. Generating test cases using test plugin from HEART.
8. Receiving generated test cases from HEART and storing it in Eclipse.
9. Run prepared tests file in JUnit plugin.

Implementation of the DT-based framework for automatic generation of unit tests is based on the provided architecture. The implementation process can be divided into two main implementation tasks: the first is related to development of the test plugin for HEART while the second is related to development of the HADESCLIPSE plugin for Eclipse.

The test cases generator was implemented in Prolog and works as a plugin for the HEART tool. It consists of three modules:

1. **XTT2 parser**: extracts single rule from XTT2 model.
2. **Test cases generator**: for every extracted rule generates a set of values that are used during testing process.
3. **JUnit generator**: saves test cases into JUnit code based on prepared templates (Listings 1.1 and 1.2).

HADESCLIPSE is the second plugin that was developed. It implements HADES communication protocol in order to provide integration with HEART and HQED

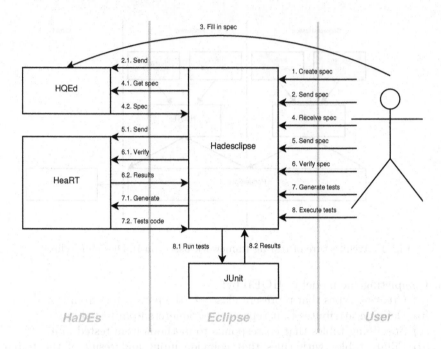

Fig. 2. Communication diagram for testing process

```
1  /* insert package here */
2  import static org.junit.Assert.*;
3  import org.junit.Test;
4
5  class [model]Test{
6      [model] obj[model];
7      /*** here JUnit code for rules goes ***/
8  }
```

Listing 1.1. Header template for JUnit generator

tools. It also extends the Eclipse platform by dedicated creator that facilitates generation of the test cases as well as perspective for rule-based testing (see Figure 3) that provides three dedicated views:

- HQED view for communication with HQED (export/import).
- HEART view for communication with HEART (export/verification/tests generation).
- JUnit view for executing tests.

Nevertheless, the proposed implementation of the framework is just a prototype that has several limitations. Some of them are listed in Section 5.

```
1  @Test
2  void test[tableName][ruleNo]() {
3      //test case
4      obj = new [Model]();
5      /*** line repeated for every condition: ***/
6      obj.set[attName]([value]);
7      obj.[tableName]();
8      /*** line repeated for every action: ***/
9      assertTrue( obj.get[attName]() == [value] );
10     /*** if there is more than one test case for rule, ↵
               above lines are repeated for each ***/
11 }
```

Listing 1.2. Rule template for JUnit generator

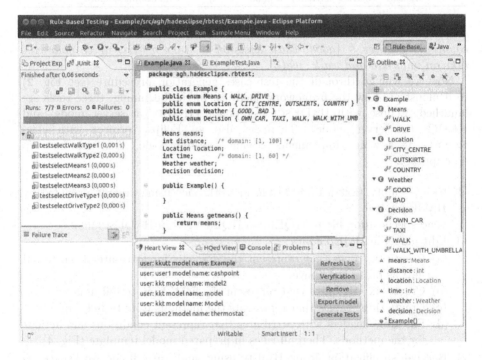

Fig. 3. Rule-based testing perspective in Eclipse

5   Evaluation and Related Work

Let us consider simple system described at the beginning of this paper. Based on
system specification (Tab. 1) and test values selection algorithm (Tab. 2), there is
expectation that generated test cases will look like this presented in Tab. 3. There
is an assumption that attributes have following domains: $distance \in [1,100]$,
$time \in [1,60]$, $means \in \{drive, walk\}$, $location \in \{city\ centre,\ outskirts,$

Table 3. Expected test cases for system presented in Tab. 1

Rule	Test cases	Expected results
1	$distance = 6 \wedge time = 1$	$means = drive$
	$distance = 6 \wedge time = 60$	$means = drive$
2	$distance = 1 \wedge time = 1$	$means = drive$
	$distance = 1 \wedge time = 15$	$means = drive$
	$distance = 5 \wedge time = 1$	$means = drive$
	$distance = 5 \wedge time = 15$	$means = drive$
3	$distance = 1 \wedge time = 16$	$means = walk$
	$distance = 5 \wedge time = 16$	$means = walk$
4	$means = drive \wedge location = city\ centre$	$decision = take\ a\ taxi$
5	$means = drive \wedge location = outskirts$	$decision = drive\ your\ car$
6	$means = walk \wedge weather = bad$	$decision = take\ an\ umbrella\ and\ walk$
7	$means = walk \wedge weather = good$	$decision = walk$

$country\}$, $weather \in \{good,\ bad\}$, $decision \in \{take\ a\ taxi,\ drive\ your\ car,$ $take\ an\ umbrella\ and\ walk,\ walk\}$.

Now we will go through the test cases generation procedure (see Fig. 2) to demonstrate how the framework operates. In the beginning, three tools are launched: Eclipse with HADEsclipse plugin, HQEd (in server mode) and HeaRT (in server mode). There is also an Eclipse project with class `Example.java` which implements assumed system logic. The step by step description is:

1. Create empty (`Example.hml`) file in workspace using creator provided by HADEsclipse.
2. Send specification file to HQEd via HQEd View in HADEsclipse.
3. Edit model in HQEd editor:
   (a) Create six types that represent the domains for attributes from tested unit as presented above.
   (b) Create six attributes that represent the fields from tested unit.
   (c) Create three tables that represents the methods from tested unit.
   (d) Fill table headers with attributes that represent conditions and actions for the methods. Then fill rules in prepared model template (Fig. 4).
4. Receive specification from HQEd using and save it in workspace as `Example.hml` file (for future editing) and `Example.hmr` file (for sending to HeaRT).
5. Send specification file (`Example.hmr`) to HeaRT using HeaRT.
6. Verify specification in HeaRT using HeaRT View.
7. Generate test cases in HeaRT using HeaRT View and save them as `ExampleTest.java` file (Fig. 5). Generated test cases are the same as test cases presented in Tab. 3.
8. Fill in package and enum imports in `ExampleTest.java` and then run prepared tests file in JUnit plugin (right click on file → run as... → JUnit test).

Based on this simple example we can conclude that the tool generates proper
test cases, and valid Java code. After adding package and enum imports, class
compiles without errors. Working with the framework is comfortable, since it
provides very simple GUI with all needed options.

However, the current prototype has some limitations:

- Methods in tested unit are not static.
- Methods in tested unit operate only on unit's fields. They do not receive any
  parameters and don't return anything.
- Each field used as condition in decision table have corresponding set method:
  void set[field](fieldType value).
- Each field used as action in decision table have corresponding get method:
  fieldType get[field](void).
- Only primitive types and enums are supported.
- There is no connections between tables in XTT2 model.

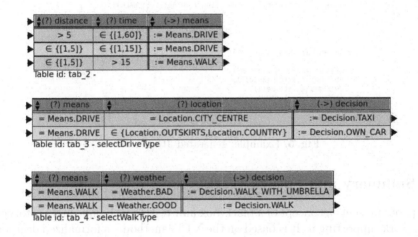

Fig. 4. Example: full specification as XTT2 model

Automated rule-based tests generation was also discussed by M. Sharma and
B.S. Chandra [14]. In their work, system specification is captured as an Excel
spreadsheet. This document is parsed using Java Library (e.g. J-Excel). Test
cases are generated and saved as an XML document. This file is parsed and JUnit
test cases are generated. The authors emphasize the redundancy elimination
achieved by the equivalence classes analysis. Their framework generates minimal
yet complete set of test cases.

```
[J] Example.java    [x] Example.hml    [HMR] Example.plh [HMR]    [J] ExampleTest.java 🔀

 ⓐ   /* insert package here */
 ⊝ import static org.junit.Assert.*;
    import org.junit.Test;

    public class ExampleTest{
        Example objExample;

 ⊝      @Test
        public void testselectWalkType1(){
            //testcase
            objExample = new Example();
 ⓐ          objExample.setmeans(Means.WALK);
 ⓐ          objExample.setweather(Weather.BAD);
            objExample.selectWalkType();
 ⓐ          assertTrue(objExample.getdecision() == Decision.WALK_WITH_UMBRELLA);

        }

 ⊝      @Test
        public void testselectWalkType2(){
            //testcase
            objExample = new Example();
 ⓐ          objExample.setmeans(Means.WALK);
 ⓐ          objExample.setweather(Weather.GOOD);
            objExample.selectWalkType();
 ⓐ          assertTrue(objExample.getdecision() == Decision.WALK);

        }

 ⊝      @Test
        public void testselectMeans1(){
            //testcase
            objExample = new Example();
            objExample.setdistance(6);
            objExample.settime(1);
            objExample.selectMeans();
 ⓐ          assertTrue(objExample.getmeans() == Means.DRIVE);
```

Fig. 5. Example: generated JUnit code

6   Summary and Future Work

The paper presents a concept of a black-box unit testing technique and prototype framework supporting it. It is based on the XTT2 method – a formalized decision table representation method. Decision tables were used to simplify the design of the test cases specification and to provide superior means of ensuring that all important test data is used and all test cases are generated, thanks to the formalized logical model. This work will allow to continue the integration of the XTT2 rule formalism into software engineering process. In fact, the same rule set could be used to generate a design specification ([15,16]) and then for testing.

Future work will include achieving following goals: (a) automatized creation of XTT2 model template, because it is very sensitive to user errors (e.g. typos in names); (b) extended test values selection algorithm that contains validation and covers more cases; (c) consideration of negative test cases scenarios.

References

1. Hunt, A., Thomas, D.: Pragmatic Unit Testing in Java with JUnit. Pragmatic Programmers (2003)

2. Astels, D.R.: Test-Driven Development: A Practical Guide. Prentice Hall (2003)
3. Tahchiev, P., Leme, F., Massol, V., Gregory, G.: JUnit in Action, 2nd edn. Manning Publications (2010)
4. Nalepa, G.J.: Proposal of business process and rules modeling with the XTT method. In: Negru, V., et al. (eds.) SYNASC Ninth International Symposium on Symbolic and Numeric Algorithms for Scientific Computing, Los Alamitos, California, Washington, Tokyo, September 26–29, pp. 500–506. IEEE Computer Society, IEEE, CPS Conference Publishing Service (2007)
5. Nalepa, G.J., Ligęza, A., Kaczor, K.: Formalization and modeling of rules using the XTT2 method. International Journal on Artificial Intelligence Tools 20(6), 1107–1125 (2011)
6. Nalepa, G.J., Kaczor, K.: Proposal of a rule-based testing framework for the automation of the unit testing process. In: Proceedings of the 17th IEEE International Conference on Emerging Technologies and Factory Automation, ETFA 2012, Kraków, Poland (September 28, 2012)
7. Kutt, K.: Proposal of a rule-based testing framework. Master's thesis, AGH University of Science and Technology (July 2013), Supervisor: G. J. Nalepa
8. Anjaneyulu, K.: Expert systems: An introduction. Research Scientist in the Knowledge Based Computer Systems Group at NCST. Resonance article (1998)
9. Ligęza, A., Nalepa, G.J.: A study of methodological issues in design and development of rule-based systems: proposal of a new approach. Wiley Interdisciplinary Reviews: Data Mining and Knowledge Discovery 1(2), 117–137 (2011)
10. Nalepa, G.J.: Architecture of the HeaRT hybrid rule engine. In: Rutkowski, L., Scherer, R., Tadeusiewicz, R., Zadeh, L.A., Zurada, J.M. (eds.) ICAISC 2010, Part II. LNCS (LNAI), vol. 6114, pp. 598–605. Springer, Heidelberg (2010)
11. Nalepa, G., Bobek, S., Ligęza, A., Kaczor, K.: Algorithms for rule inference in modularized rule bases. In: Bassiliades, N., Governatori, G., Paschke, A. (eds.) RuleML 2011 - Europe. LNCS, vol. 6826, pp. 305–312. Springer, Heidelberg (2011)
12. Kaczor, K., Nalepa, G.J., Kutt, K.: Hadesclipse – integrated environment for rules (tool presentation). In: Nalepa, G.J., Baumeister, J. (eds.) Proceedings of 9th Workshop on Knowledge Engineering and Software Engineering (KESE9) Co-ocated with the 36th German Conference on Artificial Intelligence (KI 2013), Koblenz, Germany (September 17, 2013)
13. Nalepa, G.J., Bobek, S., Ligęza, A., Kaczor, K.: HalVA - rule analysis framework for XTT2 rules. In: Bassiliades, N., Governatori, G., Paschke, A. (eds.) RuleML 2011 - Europe. LNCS, vol. 6826, pp. 337–344. Springer, Heidelberg (2011)
14. Sharma, M., Chandra, B.: Automatic generation of test suites from decision table - theory and implementation. In: 2010 Fifth International Conference on Software Engineering Advances (ICSEA), pp. 459–464 (2010)
15. Nalepa, G.J., Ligęza, A.: Designing reliable Web security systems using rule-based systems approach. In: Menasalvas, E., Segovia, J., Szczepaniak, P.S. (eds.) AWIC 2003. LNCS (LNAI), vol. 2663, pp. 124–133. Springer, Heidelberg (2003)
16. Nalepa, G.J., Kluza, K.: UML representation for rule-based application models with XTT2-based business rules. International Journal of Software Engineering and Knowledge Engineering (IJSEKE) 22(4), 485–524 (2012)

Implementing a Supply Chain Management Policy System Based on Rough Set Theory

Henryk Piech[1], Aleksandra Ptak[1], and Ali Jannatpour[2]

[1]Czestochowa University of Technology, Poland,
h.piech@adm.pcz.czest.pl
[2]Department of Computer Science and Software Engineering,
Concordia University, Canada

Abstract. This paper presents a new method for raw material classification based on rough set theory. The classification method is used within the distribution network of a supply chain management system. An expert system is developed based a set of decision rules. The purpose of the expert system is to configure the distribution policies in order to reduce the transportation and storage costs as well as downtime risks.

Keywords: classification, rough set theory, delivery strategy.

1 Introduction

Inventory control is an essential part of supply chain management. Distribution policies involve a wide range of resources and raw materials. They indicate how goods are delivered within the delivery network by maintaining the quantity of resources with respect to the production capacity as well as the market demand. In general, developing a regulated supply policy requires adjusting the quantity of each type of raw material [5,7,9]. A constant supply policy [1,3,4,7] may be implemented using a threshold and a set of variables indicating the intervals between the shipments [2,8]. Consequently, the inventory control is implemented by controlling the quantity level of each raw material with respect to a risk threshold according to the market requirements. In such a model, the quantity levels must be maintained above the risk threshold [6,12,16]. In rare situations, some risks may be taken by keeping some levels below the threshold. Potential costs of downtime may therefore be applied.

The risk analysis is important and yet difficult. In complex environments, using rough sets theory is highly beneficial [11,14]. In such a model, a set of rules is used within an inference engine. In rough sets theory, the decision is made by examining the degree of certainty for each rule within the coverage range . In most cases, the decisions are exclusive. This is achieved by evaluating the amplitudes of the supporting parameters.

2 Constant Supply Policy Using Rough Sets Theory

Very often, real life applications require more advanced extension of the decision support systems. Rough sets theory is one of approachable methods compared

L. Rutkowski et al. (Eds.): ICAISC 2014, Part II, LNAI 8468, pp. 548–557, 2014.

to the evidence theory, fuzzy sets, Bayesian inference, etc. In rough sets theory, the universe consists of a set of basic knowledge formed by any subset of all indiscernible situations, also known as objects. A basic knowledge can either be represented using a crisp set or a rough set. Any union of elementary sets is a crisp set, also referred to as precise. Otherwise the set is rough. Each rough set is also associated with boundary cases. The boundary cases indicate the objects which can not be identified with certainty.

In rough set theory, objects are characterized by a set of parameters. Each parameter represents a criterion, which is used by the inference engine, resulting in indiscernible or difficult situations. The two extremes, representing the boundary cases, are called lower and upper approximation areas [11]. In our model, the lower approximation areas represent certain decisions and therefore are explicitly defined. For instance, suppose the case where all inventory thresholds are maintained: $S = \{s_1, s_2, ..., s_p\}$ The upper approximation areas represent the cases where at least one inventory threshold is exceeded.

$$LA = \bigcup_{i \in U} \{L(i) : L(i) \subseteq S\} = \bigcup_{i \in U} \{L(i) : (l_i < s_i)\}, \qquad (1)$$

where
   LA - the area of the lower approximation,
   i - raw material index,
   $L(i)$- the resource for the selected i^{th} material,
   $l(i)$ - the quantity level of the ith material,
   U - the universe

$$LU = \bigcup_{i \in U} \{L(i) : L(i) \cap S \neq \emptyset\} => \{\exists i : l_i \geq s_i\}. \qquad (2)$$

The uncertainty is obtained by:

$$LB = LU - LA =$$

$$\{(l_1 \leq s_1) \wedge (l_2 \leq s_2) \wedge, ..., \wedge (l_{i-1} \leq s_{i-1}) \wedge (l_{i+1} \leq s_{i+1}) \wedge, ..., \wedge (l_p \leq s_p)\}. \qquad (3)$$

Depending on the inventory control method, each type of raw material may be assigned a different level of risk. Figure 1 illustrates an emergency situation caused by various raw material consumption. Using crisp and rough areas and their associated criteria not only improves the decision making but also allows us to obtain additional parameters such as certainty and coverage. The supply policy allows us to identify the supplementary shipments during over-consumptions, i.e. the quantity level of ith material exceeds the threshold s_i. Although, the supply quantities Q_i are the same, the gaps between the shipping times t_j's are not necessarily equal. In the lower approximation area, all quantity levels are considered to be below threshold. The mathematical distance between the quantity level and the threshold value represent the excess values. Negative values represent under-consumption. The decision strength may be obtained by summing up all the excess values.

$$VN(i) = l(i) - s(i).$$

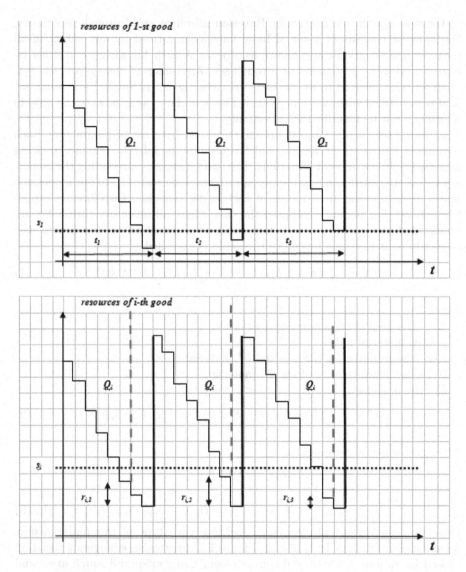

Fig. 1. The effect of shifting the shipments in time, for simultaneous consumption of multiple types of raw materials. The lower figure shows the case when the ith material goes beyond the allowable threshold earlier than the 1st material, $r_{i,j}$ represent the degree of risk for the ith material at the jth stage.

Figure 2 illustrates a sample table of attributes, where the values are normalized. The normalized deterministic value of the risk associated with the ith cluster, represented by $VN(i)$, indicates the strength of the decision whether the raw material i must be included in the shipment or not. The set $\{1, 2, 4\}$ is a lower approximation of the set $\{1, 2, 4, 6\}$; The set $\{5\}$ is the lower approximation of the

Type	ER(i)	VN(i)	Dec(i)
1	H	0,46	yes
2	H	0,25	yes
3	L	0,06	no/yes
4	M	0,12	yes
5	L	0,02	no
6	M	0,09	yes/no

Fig. 2. Sample data for an emergency case where the inventory thresholds are not maintained, $ER(i)$ - risk indicator: L, M, H - representing small, medium, and large risks, $Dec(i)$ - the decision to consider the raw material i in the shipment

set $\{3,5\}$; The set $\{1,2,3,4,6\}$ is the upper approximation of the set $\{1,2,4,6\}$; and the set $\{3,5,6\}$ is the upper approximation of the set $\{3,5\}$. Therefore, the boundary between the upper and lower approximation areas is the set $\{3,6\}$.

Attributes are also divided into two categories: conditions C and decisions D. Conditions address the normalized risks $VN(i)$ whereas decisions use the organizational attribute $dec(i)$. The Formal definition is given in the following:

$$S(i) = supp_i(C, D)/|U| = |C(i) \cap D(i)|/|U| = VN(i), \qquad (4)$$

where
$supp_x(C, D)$ indicates the decision support D by attribute C.

Subsequently, the certainty is estimated by dividing the membership probabilities with regards to the sums of risks in the border area, as formalized in the following:
$DC(i) = supp_x(C, D)/|C(i)| = |C(i) \cap D(i)|/|C(i)| =$
$VN(i : i \in LA))/VN(i) = 1,$
$DC(i) = supp_x(C, D)/|C(i)| = |C(i) \cap D(i)|/|C(i)| =$
$VN(i : i \in LB))/\sum_{k \in LB} VN(k),$
or
$DC(i) = S(i)/\pi(C(i)),$
where
$(C(i)) = |C(i)|/|U|.$

The coverage include all decisions including membership probabilities:
$DCV(i) = supp_x(C, D)/|D(i)| = |C(i) \cap D(i)|/|D(i)| = \frac{VN(i:Dec(i)=Yes)}{\sum_{k:Dec(k)=Yes} VN(k)},$
$DCV(i) = supp_x(C, D)/|D(i)| = |C(i) \cap D(i)|/|D(i)| = \frac{VN(i:Dec(i)=No)}{\sum_{k:Dec(k)=No} VN(k)},$
or
$DC(i) = S(i)/\pi(D(i)),$

where
$$(D(i)) = |D(i)|/|U|$$

Figure 3 presents some sample data. The parameters include the decision strength, the degree of certainty, and the coverage. If $C \rightarrow_i D$ is a decision rule, then

Type	VN(i)	Certainty	Coverage
1	0,46	1	0,5
2	0,25	1	0,27
3	0,06	0,4	0,75
4	0,12	1	0,13
5	0,02	1	0,25
6	0,09	0,6	0,1

Fig. 3. The decision parameters

$$\bigcup_{j \in D(i)} \{C(j) : C(j) \subseteq D(i)\} \tag{5}$$

is the lower approximation of the decision class $D(i)$, for all classes of conditions $C(j)$, where the set

$$\bigcup_{j \in D(i)} \{C(j) : C(j) \cap D(i) \neq \emptyset\} \tag{6}$$

represents the upper approximation.

In order to construct the table of rules, the following significate probabilistic features must be taken into account:

$$\sum_{k \in LB} DC(k) = 1,$$
$$\sum_{k:D(k)=Yes} DCV(k) = 1,$$
$$\sum_{k:D(k)=No} DCV(k) = 1,$$

$$\pi(D(i)) = \sum_{k \in LB} DC(k) * \pi(C(k)) = \sum_{k \in LB} S(k),$$
$$\pi(C'(i)) = \sum_{k:D(k)=Yes} DCV(k) * \pi(D(k)) = \sum_{k \in LB} S(k),$$
$$\pi(C''(i)) = \sum_{k:D(k)=No} DCV(k) * \pi(D(k)) = \sum_{k:D(k)=No} S(k),$$

$$DC'(i) = \frac{DCV(i) * \pi(D(i))}{\sum_{k:D(k)=Yes} DCV(k) * \pi(D(k))} = D(i)/\pi(C'(i)),$$
$$DC''(i) = \frac{DCV(i) * \pi(D(i))}{\sum_{k:D(k)=No} DCV(k) * \pi(D(k))} = D(i)/\pi(C''(i)),$$
$$DCV(i) = \frac{DC(i) * \pi(C(i))}{\sum_{k \in C(i)} DCV(k) * \pi(D(k))} = D(i)/\pi(D(i)),$$

The decision table consists of the rules in the form of "*if* ... *then* ...". The decision algorithm may be implemented by a set of decision rules designating all the possibilities.

An example of such algorithm is given in the following:

	$DC(i)$
$-$	
1)$if\ VN(i) = 0,46\ and\ ER(i) = H\ then\ Dec(i) = Yes$	1
2)$if\ \overline{VN(i)} = 0,25\ and\ ER(i) = H\ then\ Dec(i) = Yes$	1
3)$if\ \overline{VN(i)} = 0,12\ and\ ER(i) = M\ then\ Dec(i) = Yes$	1
4)$if\ \overline{VN(i)} = 0,09\ and\ ER(i) = M\ then\ Dec(i) = Yes$	0,6
5)$if\ \overline{VN(i)} = 0,06\ and\ ER(i) = L\ then\ Dec(i) = No$	0,4
6)$if\ \overline{VN(i)} = 0,02\ and\ ER(i) = L\ then\ Dec(i) = No$	1

As a result, the inverse algorithm will be:

	$DC(i)$
$-$	
1)$if\ Dec(i) = Yes\ then\ ER(i) = H\ and\ VN(i) = 0,46$	0,5
2)$if\ Dec(i) = Yes\ then\ ER(i) = H\ and\ \overline{VN(i)} = 0,25$	0,27
3)$if\ Dec(i) = Yes\ then\ ER(i) = M\ and\ \overline{VN(i)} = 0,12$	0,13
4)$if\ Dec(i) = Yes\ then\ ER(i) = M\ and\ \overline{VN(i)} = 0,09$	0,1
5)$if\ Dec(i) = No\ then\ ER(i) = L\ and\ VN(i) = 0,06$	0,75
6)$if\ Dec(i) = No\ then\ ER(i) = L\ and\ \overline{VN(i)} = 0,02$	0,25.

The "Yes" decisions are interpreted as:

the certainty factor is greater than or equal to $0,12$;
or the certainty factor is greater than or equal to $0,09$.

Similarly, The "No" decisions are interpreted as: the certainty factor is less than or equal to $0,02$;
or the certainty factor is less than or equal to $0,06$.

In the border area, the uncertain "Yes" and "No" decisions are represented by the ratio of probabilities: $0.5 : 0,25$, respectively. Therefore using the inverse algorithm, we conclude that the most probable "Yes" and "No" decisions are satisfied by the degree of coverage equal to 0.5 and 0.25, respectively.

3   Implementing Constant Intervals Using Rough Sets Theory

A regulated supply policy is generally associated with the risk of stock depletion as well as the increase in the cost of storage, in case of early shipments. The recommended shipment time gap for each type of raw material, may be represented by a constant value. The value may be obtained accordingly, i.e. with respect to the storage costs, transport conditions, etc. Figure 4 shows the impact of the changes in the supply levels, where the shipment time gaps are unified. An ideal situation may be represented by using the strategy described in the previous example and some additional data designating an increase in storage cost, in the form of risk parameters. A sample data is given in figure 5. The decision factors are given in figure 6.

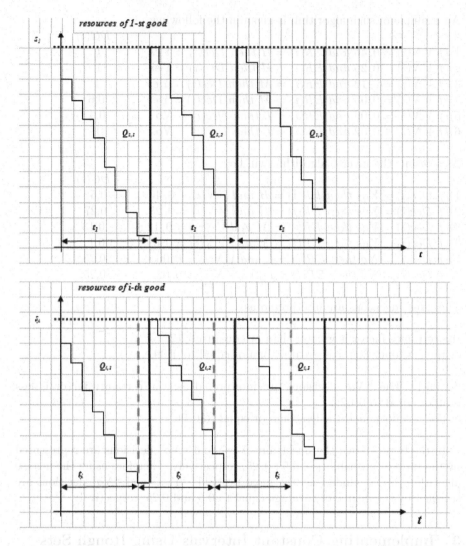

Fig. 4. The impact of changes in the supply levels, as a result of aligning the time gaps between shipments, for various types of raw materials

Suppose the following set of rules:

$DC(i)$

1)$if\ VN(i) = 0,33\ and\ CM(i) = L\ and\ ER(i) = H$
$then\ \overline{Dec(i)} = Yes$ 1

2)$if\ VN(i) = 0,28\ and\ CM(i) = L\ and\ ER(i) = H$
$then\ \overline{Dec(i)} = Yes$ 1

3)$if\ VN(i) = 0,13\ and\ CM(i) = M\ and\ ER(i) = M$
$then\ \overline{Dec(i)} = Yes$ 0,45

Type	CM(i)	ER(i)	VN(i)	Dec(i)
1	L	H	0,33	yes
2	L	H	0,28	yes
3	H	M	0,05	no/yes
4	M	H	0,13	yes/no
5	H	M	0,03	no
6	M	M	0,11	yes/no

Fig. 5. A unified time gap data, $CM(i)$ - the storage cost indicator: L;M;H - indicating small, medium, and large increases

Type	VN(i)	Certainty	Coverage
1	0,33	1	0,39
2	0,28	1	0,33
3	0,05	0,17	0,63
4	0,13	0,45	0,15
5	0,03	1	0,27
6	0,11	0,38	0,13

Fig. 6. Certainty and coverage factors

4)$if\ VN(i) = 0,11\ and\ CM(i) = M\ and\ ER(i) = M$
$then\ \overline{Dec(i)} = Yes$ 0,38
5)$if\ VN(i) = 0,05\ and\ CM(i) = H\ and\ ER(i) = L$
$then\ \overline{Dec(i)} = No$ 0,17
6)$if\ VN(i) = 0,03\ and CM(i) = H\ and\ ER(i) = L$
$then\ \overline{Dec(i)} = No$ 1,0.

Similarly, the inverse decision algorithm is will be:
$-$ $DC(i)$
1)$if\ Dec(i) = Yes$
$then\ CM(i) = L\ and\ ER(i) = H\ and\ \underline{VN(i)} = 0,33$ 0,39
2)$if\ Dec(i) = Yes$
$then\ CM(i) = L\ and\ ER(i) = H\ and\ \underline{VN(i)} = 0,28$ 0,33
3)$if\ Dec(i) = Yes$
$then\ CM(i) = M\ and\ ER(i) = M\ and\ \underline{VN(i)} = 0,15$ 0,15
4)$if\ Dec(i) = Yes$
$then\ CM(i) = M\ and\ ER(i) = M\ and\ \underline{VN(i)} = 0,11$ 0,13
5)$if\ Dec(i) = No$
$then\ CM(i) = H\ and\ ER(i) = L\ and\ \underline{VN(i)} = 0,05$ 0,63
6)$if\ Dec(i) = No$
$then\ CM(i) = H\ and\ ER(i) = L\ and\ \underline{VN(i)} = 0,03$ 0,27.

Thus, a summarized version of the algorithm may be represented by a set of verification rules as in the following:

1)$if\ CM(i) = not\ H\ then\ Dec(i) = Yes$
2)$if\ CM(i) = H\ then\ Dec(i) = No$
or
1)$if\ ER(i) = not\ L\ then\ Dec(i) = Yes$
2)$if\ ER(i) = L\ then\ Dec(i) = No$

4   Conclusions

A rule based system is a simple approach to manage the a supply chain. Supply policies specify the shipment attributes. Implementing an expert system by constructing a set of decision rules using a set of parameters improves the decision making by confirming the correctness of the decision with regards to the supply impact. Such an expert system may be used as a monitoring tool where it can signal upcoming alerts on a selected range of raw materials [15].

References

1. Baumgarten, H.: Logistik-Management. Technische Universitaet Berlin 12 (2004)
2. Blackstock, T.: International Association of Food Industry Suppliers, San Francisco, CA, March 11, 2005 and John Gattorna, Supply Chains Are the Business. Supply Chain Management Review 10(6), 42–49 (2005)
3. Chen, I.J., Paulraj, A., Lado, A.: Strategic purchasing, supply management, and firm performance. Journal of Operations Management 22(5), 505–523 (2004)
4. Cohen, M.A., Huchzermeir, A.: Global supply chain management: A survey of research and applications. In: Tayur, S., Ganeshan, R., Magazine, M. (eds.) Quantitative Models for Supply Chain Management, pp. 669–702. Kluwer, Boston (1999)
5. Lambert, D.M., Cooper, M.C.: Issues in Supply Chain Management. Industrial Marketing Management 29(1), 65–83 (2000)
6. Douglas, M., Lambert, M.C., Cooper, J.D.: Supply Chain Management: Implementation Issues and Research Opportunities. International Journal of Logistics Management 9(2), 1–20 (1998)
7. Douglas, M., Lambert, S.J., Garca-Dastugue, K.L.: Croxton, An evaluation of process-oriented supply chain management frameworks. Journal of Business Logistics 26(1), 25–51 (2005)
8. Lambert, D.M.: Supply Chain Management: Processes, Partnerships, Performance. Supply Chain Management Institute, Sarasota (2008)
9. Gattorna, J.: Supply Chains Are the Business. Supply Chain Management Review 10(6), 42–49 (2006)
10. Croxton, K.L., Garca-Dastugue, S.J., Lambert, D.M., Rogers, D.S.: The Supply Chain Management Processes. The International Journal of Logistics Management 12(2), 13–36 (2001)
11. Pawlak, Z., Sugeno, M.: Decision Rules Bayes, Rule and Rough, New Decisions in Rough Sets. Springer, Berlin (1999)

12. Sawicka, H., Zak, J.: Mathematical and Simulation Based Modeling of the Distribution System of Goods. In: Proceedings of the 23rd European Conference on Operational Research, Bonn, July 5-8, p. 233 (2009)
13. Simchi-Levy, D., Kaminski, P., Simchi-Levy, E.: Designing and Managing the Supply Chain: Concepts, Strategies, and Case Studies. Irwin/McGraw Hill, Boston (2000)
14. Straka, M., Malindzak, D.: Distribution logistics. Express Publicity, Kosice (2008)
15. Tadeusiewicz, R.: Place and role of Intelligence Systems in Computer Science. Computer Methodsin Material Science 10(4), 193–206 (2010)
16. Wisner, J.D., Keong Leong, G., Tan, K.-C.: Supply Chain Management: A Balanced Approach. Thomson South-Western, Mason (2004)

What Is the Primary Language?

Boris Stilman[1,2]

[1] University of Colorado Denver, Denver, CO, USA
Boris.Stilman@UCDenver.edu
[2] STILMAN Advanced Strategies, Denver, CO, USA
boris@stilman-strategies.com

Abstract. This paper includes results of the research on the structure of the Primary Language of the human brain (as introduced by J. von Neumann in 1957). Two components have been investigated, Linguistic Geometry (LG) and the Algorithm of Discovery. I suggest that both components are mental realities "hard-wired" in the human brain. LG is a formal model of human reasoning about armed conflict, an evolutionary product of millions of years of human warfare. It was rediscovered via research on modeling and generalization of the human expert approach to playing chess and applied successfully to modern warfare. Experiences of development of LG have been instructive for discovering the Algorithm of Discovery, the foundation of all the discoveries throughout the history of humanity. This Algorithm is based on multiple thought experiments, which manifest themselves and are controlled by the mental visual streams.

Keywords: Linguistic Geometry, Primary Language, Artificial Intelligence, Algorithm of Discovery, Game Theory, Visual Stream.

1   Linguistic Geometry

Linguistic Geometry (LG) [16]-[26], [34]-[37] is a game-theoretic approach that has demonstrated a significant increase in size of problems solvable in real time (or near real time). After developing the theory and applications of LG for many years, recently, our research branched into investigating role of LG in human culture [38], [39], [27]-[33]. This investigation provided link to the Primary Language and the Algorithm of Discovery.

The word *Linguistic* refers to the model of strategies formalized as a hierarchy of formal languages. These languages and their translations are the constructs that permit us describe strategies leading the game from state to state. These languages utilize a powerful class of generating grammars, the controlled grammars [26], which employ formal semantics of the game to control generation of a string of symbols using mutual influence of the substring generated so far and the grammar's environment.

The word *Geometry* refers to the geometry of the game state space, which is a set of all the states resulting from all legal plays (variants) leading from the start state. Every state could be represented as an abstract board with abstract pieces, i.e., mobile entities, located on this board and acting upon each other. Thus, different states include the

L. Rutkowski et al. (Eds.): ICAISC 2014, Part II, LNAI 8468, pp. 558–569, 2014.

same board with different configurations of pieces resulting from the sequence of moves leading to this state.

In LG, the geometry of the state space is effectively reduced to the geometry of the board. Thus, the state space is reduced to the "projection of the boardxtime" over the "board", by introducing images of planning skirmishes of the pieces reflecting planning physical movements and actions of those pieces over the board. These images are called zones and trajectories. The "elevation" of the board-based analysis of those images back to the space leads to efficient decomposition of the state space, which, in its turn, permits to generate the State Space Chart guiding construction of strategies [26], [29], [31], [32]. This is similar to creating a rough geographical map and drawing routes employing this map. This approach allows us to eliminate search completely. Essentially, LG replaces search by construction or, talking in general terms, analysis by synthesis.

LG is a viable approach for solving board games such as the game of chess as well as practical problems such as mission planning and battle management. Historically, LG was developed from the beginning of the 70s, by generalizing experiences of the most advanced chess players including World Chess Champions and grandmasters [1]-[3], [16], [26]. In the 70s and 80s this generalization resulted in the development of the computer chess program PIONEER utilized successfully for solving chess endgames and complex chess positions with a number of variants considered (tree size) in the order of 10^2, while the state spaces of those problems varied from 10^{10} to 15^{25}. The variants constructed by PIONEER were very close to those considered by the advanced chess experts when analyzing the same problems.

The original version of the theory of LG was developed by generalizing algorithms implemented in the program PIONEER [3], [16], [26]. Simultaneously, some of the similar algorithms were utilized heuristically for economic problems in the former USSR (programs PIONEER 2.0-4.0). Further development of LG, of course, took advantage of these applications. However, the original major framework of LG, the hierarchy of formal languages, constructed in the beginning of the 80s, was based exclusively on the chess domain, the only application of LG available at that time. Remarkably, over the following 30 years, the structure of this framework has never changed.

By the end of the 80s, program PIONEER solved a number of sophisticated endgames and positions but still could not play full games. It was clear for the developers that the main ideas are correct but further development for the chess domain was required. It was also expected that transferring LG to other domains, e.g., defense, should be tried only after the chess model would be completed. Besides incompleteness of this model, a number of other serious limitations based on the awkward nature of the game of chess (in comparison with real life) could have prevented from such transfer. In addition, there was no theoretical evaluation of the accuracy of the LG solutions except for those experiments with program PIONEER approved by the chess experts.

Further generalization led to development of the new type of game theory, LG, changing the paradigm for solving game problems "From Search to Construction" [18]-[26]. The advanced version of LG, presented in [26], had overcome some of the above limitations by further "wild" generalizations and mathematical proofs of correctness of the algorithms and accuracy of the solutions. The new LG of the 90s definitely covered a number of different real life problem domains as many other mathematical theories do. But was it really an adequate model? In Physics, this means predicting results of experiments. In Computer Science, a requirement is similar. Software applications based on the new theory should yield plausible or satisfactory solutions for a new domain. In case of LG, this means consistently generating plans, i.e., military courses of action, comparable or even better than those of military experts.

Beginning from 1999, the LG-based technology was applied to more than 30 real life defense-related projects [12]. On multiple experiments, LG successfully demonstrated the ability to solve extremely complex modern military scenarios in real time. The efficacy and sophistication of the courses of action developed by the LG tools exceeded consistently those developed by the commanders and staff members [36], [37].

Among multiple projects, where the LG-based technology was applied, I will mention RAID (Real-time Adversarial Intelligence and Decision-making) developed for DARPA in 2004-2008 [12], [36]. The LG-RAID software system was intended to advise (in real time) the Blue Commander (American Forces) on the courses of action for both friendly and adversarial forces. The experiments utilized OneSAF battle simulation software so that Blue and Red teams fought via computers installed in different rooms and connected via local network. The simulated battles modeled those in Iraq, Afghanistan, Caucuses, etc. Among voluminous statistical data collected by DARPA in the RAID experiments I will emphasize just one type of data collected in the month-long Experiment 4 conducted in July 2006. After each simulated 2-hour battle (in Bagdad), DARPA requested the Red Commander to answer the question "With whom have you just fought?", i.e., with human Blue Staff or the LG-RAID software. Participation of the Blue human Staff or LG-RAID in each battle was decided right before the battle on a random basis and this decision was unknown to the Red. The Red team was completely isolated from the Blue team to avoid any contacts. In 16 out of 36 2-hour battles (44%), the Red Commander was wrong. One could say that LG-RAID successfully passed an informal *Turing Test* (i.e., true AI or not). It is interesting to notice that even when the Red Commander was guessing correctly, he demonstrated a very high opinion about LG-RAID, albeit indirectly. Indeed, often, when he would correctly guess that he just fought with LG-RAID, his reasoning for thinking that his opponent was LG-RAID was based on the fact that the opposition executed a particularly good strategy such as "very effective defensive posture", "effective shaping fires followed by careful maneuver to establish mid-field position", etc. Amazingly, the observing psychologist noticed that the Red team, the highly qualified military experts (retired colonels) who simulated Iraqi insurgents, have got so scared of the LG-RAID power that close to the end of the experiment during simulated fights they stopped talking to each other and used hand signals instead, being afraid that the almighty LG-RAID is listening through computers …

Forty years of development of LG including numerous successful applications to board games and, most importantly, to a highly diverse set of modern military operation [11], [12], [37] from cruise missiles to military operations in urban terrain to ballistic missile defense to naval engagements, led us to believe that LG is something more fundamental than simply yet another mathematical model of efficient wargaming.

When the LG applications started consistently generate advanced courses of action for a number of defense sub-domains, the developers realized that the game of chess served the role of the eraser of particulars for the real world warfare. From the bird's eye view, military operations are incomparably more complex than this game. Interestingly, this fact was pointed out by many reviewers of our papers with the first generalizations of the original LG in the 90s. All the limitations that could have prevented us from transferring LG to the real world, in a sense, enabled us to see the essence behind numerous particulars. Of course, we still needed an advanced chess player like Dr. Botvinnik who was able to analyze the chess master's approach to solving problems. We could only guess if such a grandmaster-commander capable of doing the same for the military strategies would have ever appeared. With all the ingenuity of such an expert, a task of refining the military strategies down to trajectories and networks of trajectories would have been significantly more complex due to those particulars that mud the picture.

After continuous success in proving the applicability and in taking advantage of the power of LG in applications to the modern warfare over the last 15 years, we decided to investigate if LG would work for the ancient wars. As I have already pointed, LG was developed by generalizing approach utilized by the most advanced experts in playing chess. Theoretically, in several papers [38], [39] we demonstrated that Alexander the Great and Hannibal, in effect, "used" LG-like reasoning for their battles, perhaps even consciously, or, most likely, subconsciously. This means that LG or proto-LG "existed" long before the time when chess was invented, which was about fifteen hundred years ago. Consequently, the game of chess served just as a means for rediscovering LG. We concluded that LG appears to be a part of the human intelligence for probably a million years as the major component essential for survival of the fittest during the constant wars [27].

Moreover, LG could have been a component of the Primary Language (of the human brain) introduced by J. von Neumann in 1957 [42]. Even now nobody knows what this language is about. According to von Neumann's hypothesis, this is the language used by the human brain for thinking, which is different from all the 6,000 live and dead human languages. It must be much older than any of those, which means that it cannot be symbolic, i.e., cannot not utilize strings of symbols, phonetic or written. People thought and made discoveries, such as mastering fire and making bone tools, for at least a million years. At that time human languages did not exist. Moreover, a million years ago, the symbolic part of the human brain, the so-called neo-cortex, could not support symbolic languages because it was yet to be developed [27]. It was developed later as part of the evolution of the Homo sapiens. Consequently, the Primary Language must be analog. However, we could still use modern algorithmic notation to mimic it if we realize what it is. I suggest that the Primary Language is a collection of major algorithms crucial for survival and development of humanity, the underlying "invisible" foundation of all the modern languages and sciences.

A universal applicability of LG in a variety of military domains, especially, in the domain of the ancient warfare [38], [39], its total independence of weaponry, nationality or country, its power in generating human-like strategies suggest that the algorithm of LG utilized by the human brain is "hard-wired" in the Primary Language. Moreover, the age of the Primary Language must be much greater than the age of human natural languages, and so the age of LG [27].

A highly intriguing and difficult issue is an Algorithm of Discovery, i.e., an algorithm of inventing new algorithms and new models. This algorithm should also be a major ancient item "recorded" in the Primary Language. By investigating past discoveries, experiences of construction of various new algorithms, and the heritage of LG, we intended to make a step towards understanding of this puzzle.

2   The Algorithm of Discovery

For several years, I have been developing a hypothesis that there is a universal Algorithm of Discovery driving all the innovations and, certainly, the advances in all sciences [28]-[33]. I suggested that all the discoverers utilized this algorithm. The Algorithm of Discovery should be a major ancient item "recorded" in the Primary Language [42] due to its key role in the development of humanity. This line of research [28]-[33] involved investigating past discoveries and experiences of construction of various new algorithms, especially, those which I was personally involved in [16]-[39]. Another personal trait I utilized in this research is my vast experience in working with advanced experts, especially, chess experts, including renowned World Chess Champion Dr. Botvinnik [1]-[3].

Based on the experiences of great scientists [7]-[9], [14], [40]-[44], research in cognitive science and neuroscience [4]-[6], [10], [13], [15], and from my own experience [16]-[39], I suggested that the essence of the discoveries is in the "visual streams". (By the way, LG is highly visual as well.) These are movie-like visual (for the mind's eye") mental processes. Sometimes, they reflect past reality. More frequently, they reflect artificial mentally constructed reality. This reality is an artificial world with artificial laws of nature including space and time. For example, this could be laws of real or totally different physics or geometry. This world is populated with realistic and/or artificial animated entities. Those entities are mentally constructed, and some of them do not exist in real life. When we run a visual stream we simply observe life events, realistic or artificial, in this world. Of course, those animated events happen according to the laws of this world and we are "lucky" to be present and see what is happening. Usually, scientists have the power to alter this world by reconstructing the laws, the entities, etc. according to the problem statement. Then, the visual stream becomes a movie (or play) showing in the end a solution to the problem staged in this artificial world. Usually, this solution comes without a proof because it was not proved but played in this world. When the solution is known, the proof itself could be broken into small subproblems, staged in the altered mathematical world and eventually discovered. This seemingly shocking reality does not look mysterious to me. These artificial worlds could be modeled employing algorithms, and, consequently, implemented in software. In my opinion, this is the road to the Algorithm of Discovery.

This is how it may work. Within the brain, the visual streams run consciously and subconsciously and may switch places from time to time (in relation to conscious/subconscious use). We may run several visual streams concurrently, morph them, and even use logic for such morphing, although this use is auxiliary. Then we mentally tag some of the objects shown in the movie and create the so-called symbolic shell around the main visual stream. This shell eventually becomes a standard symbolic algorithm that can be communicated to others employing familiar language, logic, mathematics, etc.

By tracing and replaying discoveries in actual development of the theory of LG (Section 1), I made the first steps to revealing the dynamics of visual streams, especially, the means for focusing streams in desired direction [28]-[33]. In this reenactment, I utilized published research papers and introspections of the great scientists as well as other sources [7]-[9], [14], [40]-[44]. From those introspections and research papers, I managed to glean more details about the operations of the Algorithm of Discovery. Replaying various thought experiments permitted to reveal and emphasize various features of this algorithm. Next, I will introduce the reader to a version of this Algorithm as we see it at the current stage of our research. Here, I would like to remark that these results are yet to be implemented in software and their maturity cannot be compared with those in LG.

The Algorithm of Discovery operates as a series of thought experiments, which interface with the rest of the brain and with external environment via imaginary animated movies (plays), which I named visual streams. These streams may or may not reflect the reality. This interface is constructive, i.e., visual streams could be morphed in the desired direction.

The input to the Algorithm is also a visual stream, which includes several visual instances of the object whose structure has to be understood or whose algorithm of construction has to be developed. Sometimes, the object is dynamic, i.e., its structure is changing in time. Then the input visual stream includes this visual dynamics. As a rule, neither the structure of the object nor the details of the dynamics are present in the stream. It simply replicates (mimics) the natural or imaginary phenomenon. The task of the Algorithm of Discovery is to understand its structure including dynamics and/or develop an algorithm for reconstructing this object including its changes in time. This understanding happens in several stages. Importantly, it always ends up with the process of actual reconstruction of the object employing the construction set developed by the Algorithm on the previous stages. If the Algorithm investigates a natural real life object this imaginary reconstruction may be totally unrelated to the construction (replication) utilized by the nature. Usually, this reconstruction process is artificially developed by the Algorithm of Discovery with the only purpose to reveal the structure of the object. However, if the algorithm of natural replication is the goal of discovery than the Algorithm of Discovery will employ a set of different visual streams to reveal the relevant components utilized by the nature.

All the visual streams are divided into classes, Observation, Construction and Validation. They usually follow each other but may be nested hierarchically, with several levels of depth.

The visual streams operate in a very simple fashion similar to a child construction set. The Construction stream utilizes a construction set and a mental visual prototype, a model to be referenced during construction. This is similar to a list of models pictured in a manual (or a visual guide) enclosed to every commercial construction set. It appears that all the thought experiments in LG related to construction investigated so far, [28]-[33], utilized those manuals. Imagine a child playing a construction set. He needs a manual to construct an object by looking constantly at its picture included in this manual. This model comes from the Observation stream as its output. It is not necessarily a real world model. It is not even a model from the problem statement. It is created by the Observation stream out of various multiple instances of the real world objects by abstraction, specifically, by erasing the particulars. A final version of the object constructed by the Construction stream should be validated by the Validation stream.

The Algorithm of Discovery initiates the Observation stream, which must carefully examine the object. It has to morph the input visual stream and run it several times to observe (mentally) various instances of the object from several directions. Often, for understanding the object, it has to observe the whole class of objects considered analogous. If the object is dynamic (a process) it has to be observed in action. For this purpose, the Observation stream runs the process under different conditions to observe it in different situations. The purpose of all those observations is erasing the particulars to reveal the general relations behind them. Once those relations appeared, a construction set and a visual model have to be constructed by the Observation stream. Both are still visual, i.e., specific, – not abstract. However, they should visually represent an abstract concept, usually, a class of objects or processes, whose structure is being investigated. For construction, the Observation stream utilizes the Construction stream with auxiliary purpose (which differs from its prime purpose – see below). Note that the model construction is different from the subsequent reconstruction of the object intended to reveal its structure. This model may differ substantially from the real object or class of objects that are investigated. Its purpose is to serve as a manual to be used for references during reconstruction.

When the model and the construction set are ready, the Algorithm of Discovery initiates the Construction stream with its prime purpose. This purpose is to construct the object (or stage the process) by selecting appropriate construction parts of the set and putting them together. If an object has a sequential nature the construction also takes place sequentially, by repetition of similar steps. At some point of construction, the parts are tagged symbolically and, in the end, visual reasoning with symbolic tagging turns into a conventional symbolic algorithm to be verified by the subsequent Validation stream.

Models and construction sets may vary significantly for different problems. Construction of the model begins from creation of the construction set and the relations between its components. Both items should be visually convenient for construction. The Algorithm of Discovery may utilize a different model for the same object if the purpose of development is different. Such a different model is produced by a different visual stream.

In many cases the Algorithm of Discovery employs "a slave" to visually perform simple tasks for all types of visual streams. This slave may be employed by the Construction stream to "see" construction parts and put them together. More precisely, imagine a child playing a simplistic construction set. To avoid offending children, I had named this personality a Ghost. This Ghost has very limited skills, knowledge and, even, limited visibility. The Observation stream may utilize the Ghost to familiarize itself with the optional construction set, to investigate its properties. Next, the Construction stream may use the Ghost to perform the actual construction employing those properties. Eventually, the Validation stream may use the Ghost to verify visually, if properties of the constructed object match those revealed by the Observation stream. In all cases, the Ghost is guided by the Algorithm of Discovery or, more precisely, by the respective visual streams.

As was already discussed, the initial visual model is usually guided by a very specific prototype, where the Observation stream has actually erased the particulars.

However, this specificity does not reduce generality in any way. This sounds like a paradox. My point is that every component of this model carries an abstract class of components behind it. This way visual reasoning about the model drives reasoning about abstract classes, which is turned eventually into the standard formal reasoning. This happens as follows. A visual model drives construction of the formal symbolic model so that the key items in a visual model have tags representing the respective formal model. At first, the formal model is incomplete. At some stage, a running visual stream is accompanied by a comprehensive formal symbolic shell. Running a shell means doing formal derivation, proof, etc. synchronized with a respective visual stream. While the shell and the stream are synchronized, the visual stream drives execution of the shell, not the other way around. For example, a formal proof is driven by animated events within the respective visual stream. The visual streams, usually, run the creation of the visual model, the construction set and the final construction of the object several times. During those runs as a result of persistent tagging the symbolic shell appears. Multiple runs utilize the same visual components but during initial runs the synchronization of the stream and the shell is not tight. Further on, synchronization is tightened by morphing the visual model and/or adjusting symbolic derivation if they initially mismatch. Eventually, the stream and the shell switch their roles. In the end, it appears that the stream becomes the animated set of illustrations, a movie, driven by the running symbolic shell. For example, during the final runs (and only then), the visual streams, presented in [29]-[33], are driven by the constraints of the abstract board game, the abstract set theory and/or the productions of the controlled grammars. At this point the visual stream and the symbolic shell can be completely separated, and the visual stream can be dropped and even forgotten.

A stream may schedule other streams by creating almost a program with "procedure calls". Essentially, it may schedule a sequence of thought experiments to be executed in the future. These experiments will in their turn initiate new visual streams. In this case, the purpose, the nature, and the general outcome of those experiments should be known to the stream created this sequence. However, this sequence is different from the list of procedure calls in conventional procedural (or imperative) programming. The algorithms of those "procedures", i.e., the algorithms to be produced by the respective thought experiments are generally unknown. The experiments are not programmed – they are staged. The actual algorithm should be developed as a result of execution of such experiment. In a sense, this is similar to the notion of declarative programming when a function is invoked by a problem statement while the function's body does not include an algorithm for solving this problem.

The ability of a visual stream to schedule a sequence of thought experiments permits to create a nested top-down structure of visual streams with several levels of depth. Though, I do not think that the actual depth of nested programmed experiments ever exceeds two or three.

It is likely that all the technological inventions and discoveries of the laws of nature include "optimal construction" or, at least, have optimization components [13]. Thus, various construction steps performed by the Algorithm of Discovery require optimization, which, certainly, makes construction more difficult. As the appearance of this algorithm is lost in millennia it could not certainly utilize any differential calculus even for the problems where it would be most convenient. For the same reason, it could not utilize any approximations based on the notion of a limit of function. In that sense, in order to reveal its optimization components, the most interesting problems to be investigated should lack continuity compelling the Algorithm of Discovery to employ explicitly those components. Based on several case studies [32], I suggested that this optimization is performed by the imaginary movement via approaching a location (or area) in the appropriate imaginary space. Having such space and means, the Algorithm employs an agent to catch sight of this location, pave the way, and approach it. Contrary to the function based approach, which is static by its nature, the Algorithm operates with dynamic processes, the visual streams. Some of those streams approach optimum (in a small number of steps); other streams show dynamically wrong directions that do not lead to the optimum and prevent the Algorithm from pursuing those directions. Both types of visual streams were named "proximity reasoning". I suggested that proximity reasoning plays a special role for the Algorithm of Discovery as the main, if not the only, means for optimization. Important steps of various discoveries include construction of the spaces for proximity reasoning as well as initiating motion within those spaces [32]. Proximity reasoning is a type of visual reasoning [31]. This implies that the Algorithm should reason about the space where distances are "analogous" to the 3D Euclidian distances. Roughly, when we approach something, the distance must be visually reduced, and this should happen gradually. The space for proximity reasoning provides means to evaluate visually if the animated images representing various abstract objects approach each other or specific locations. It is likely that proximity reasoning as the simplest approach to optimization was utilized all the way back through the history of humanity even for the ancient discoveries.

Mosaic reasoning is yet another means to focus the streams of the Algorithm of Discovery [33]. This name was introduced due to the analogy of the Construction stream operation with assembling a mosaic picture of small colorful tiles. Another, maybe, even more transparent analogy is known as a jigsaw puzzle when a picture is drawn on a sheet of paper and then this paper is cut into small pieces, mixed up, to be assembled later into the original picture. As Sir G. Thompson [40] pointed "... the progress of science is a little like making a jig-saw puzzle. One makes collections of pieces which certainly fit together, though at first it is not clear where each group should come in the picture as a whole, and if at first one makes a mistake in placing it, this can be corrected later without dismantling the whole group". Both analogies, the pictorial mosaic and the jigsaw puzzle, represent well the key feature of the Algorithm's construction set. However, I prefer the former because jigsaw puzzle looks more like an assignment in reassembling a construct, a picture, which has already been created and, certainly, well known. In that sense, a tile mosaic is created from scratch, including choosing or even creating necessary tiles. In addition, a jigsaw puzzle is reassembled out of pieces based on random cuts. On the contrary, in pictorial mosaic, in many cases, every tile, or class of tiles, should have unique properties; it should be shaped and colored to match its neighbors precisely. A similar specificity is related to a group of adjacent tiles, the aggregate.

Returning to the Algorithm of Discovery, for many discoveries, the components of the construction set should be developed with absolute precision, in the way that every part should be placed to its unique position matching its neighbors. Let us use the same name, the tiles, for those construction parts of the Algorithm of Discovery. If precision is violated, the final mosaic will be ruined and the discovery will not happen. Though a group of tiles, an aggregate, may be configured properly, its placement in the mosaic may be unclear and may require further investigation. On the other hand, a structure of an aggregate may have to be changed. Moreover, a tile itself may have complex structure which may require tailoring after placement in the mosaic. In some cases, a tile is a network of rigid nodes with soft, stretchable links.

Thus, mosaic reasoning may lead to the observation and construction steps operating with aggregates of the construction tiles. Overall, mosaic reasoning requires tedious analysis of the proper tiles and the matching rules. Investigation of the matching rules is the essential task of the Observation stream. Multiplicity of those rules and their uniqueness with respect to classes of the construction tiles make the actual construction very complex. Selecting a wrong tile, wrong tailoring, choosing a wrong place or incompatible neighbors may ruin the entire mosaic. The matching rules are necessary constraints that control the right placement of the tiles. Missing one of them, usually, leads to the wrong outcome because the Algorithm of Discovery is pointed in the wrong direction.

Some of the matching rules are based on the principle of complementarity. Roughly, a visual protrusion on one tile corresponds to the cavity on the complementary tile. For the Algorithm of Discovery, complementarity expresses itself in the requirement of various kinds of symmetry within the pairs of matching construction tiles. Another set of matching rules is based on the "interchangeability" requirement. In simple terms, if two aggregates that include several tiles are not identical but interchangeabe, their internal structure may be unimportant. This means that we can take one aggregate off the mosaic and replace it with another one, constructed of different tiles. This will certainly change the picture but the whole structure will stand.

As I already mentioned, the Algorithm of Discovery does not search for a solution in the search space. Instead, it constructs the solution out of construction set employing various tools and guides. The right choices of construction tiles and the matching rules developed by the Observation stream permit focusing the Construction stream to produce the desired mosaic, i.e., to make a discovery.

The principles considered in Section 2 resulted from research presented in [28]-[33]. In those papers, I replayed various discoveries via following visual streams, including Observation, Construction and Validation streams in detail, in order to reveal the general rules (constraints) of the thought experiments staged by the Algorithm of Discovery. In our future research, we will continue pursuing the hypothesis that those constraints are the same for all those experiments and reflect the core of the Algorithm of Discovery.

References

1. Botvinnik, M.: Chess, Computers, and Long-Range Planning. Springer, New York (1970)
2. Botvinnik, M.: Blok-skema algorithma igry v shahmaty (in Russian: A Flow-Chart of the Algorithm for Playing Chess). Sovetskoe Radio (1972)
3. Botvinnik, M.: Computers in Chess: Solving Inexact Search Problems. Springer (1984)
4. Brown, J.: The Laboratory of the Mind: Thought Experiments in the Natural Sciences, 2nd edn. Routledge, Taylor &Francis Group, New York (2011)
5. Deheaene, S.: A Few Steps Toward a Science of Mental Life. Mind, Brain and Education 1(1), 28–47 (2007)

6. Deheaene, S.: Edge In Paris. Talk at the Reality Club: Signatures of Consciousness (2009), http://edge.org/3rd_culture/dehaene09/dehaene09_index.html
7. Einstein, A.: Autobiographical Notes. Open Court, La Salle (1991)
8. Gleick, J.: Genius: The Life and Science of Richard Feynman. Pantheon Books, a division of Random House, New York (1992)
9. Hadamard, J.: The Mathematician's Mind: The Psychology of Invention in the Methematical Field. Princeton Univ. Press, Princeton (1996)
10. Kosslyn, S., Thompson, W., Kim, I., Alpert, N.: Representations of mental images in primary visual cortex. Nature 378, 496–498 (1995)
11. Kott, A., McEneaney, W. (eds.): Adversarial Reasoning: Computational Approaches to Reading the Opponent's Mind. Chapman & Hall/CRC (2007)
12. Linguistic Geometry Tools: LG-PACKAGE, with Demo DVD, p. 60, STILMAN Advanced Strategies (2010), This brochure and 8 recorded demonstrations are also available at http://www.stilman-strategies.com
13. Miller, A.: Insights of Genius: Imagery and Creativity in Science and Art. Copernicus, an imprint of Springer-Verlag (1996)
14. Nasar, S.: A Beautiful Mind. Touchstone, New York (2001)
15. Nersessian, N.: Conceptual Change: Creativity, Cognition, and Culture. In: Meheus, J., Nicles, T. (eds.) Models of Discovery and Creativity, pp. 127–166. Springer (2009)
16. Stilman, B.: Formation of the Set of Trajectory Bundles, Appendix 1 to the book. In: Botvinnik, M.M. (ed.) On the Cybernetic Goal of Games, pp. 70–77. Soviet Radio, Moscow (1975) (in Russian)
17. Stilman, B.: Ierarhia formalnikh grammatik dla reshenia prebornikh zadach (Hierachy of Formal Grammars for Solving Search Problems). Tech. Report, 105 p. VNIIE, Moscow (1976) (in Russian)
18. Stilman, B.: A Formal Language for Hierarchical Systems Control. Int. J. Languages of Design 1(4), 333–356 (1993)
19. Stilman, B.: A Linguistic Approach to Geometric Reasoning. Int. J. of Computers & Math. with Appl. 26(7), 29–58 (1993)
20. Stilman, B.: Network Languages for Complex Systems. Int. J. of Computers & Math. with Appl. 26(8), 51–80 (1993)
21. Stilman, B.: Linguistic Geometry for Control Systems Design. Int. J. of Computers and Their Applications 1(2), 89–110 (1994)
22. Stilman, B.: Translations of Network Languages. Int. J. of Computers & Math. with Appl. 27(2), 65–98 (1994)
23. Stilman, B.: Linguistic Geometry Tools Generate Optimal Solutions. In: Eklund, P., Mann, G.A., Ellis, G. (eds.) ICCS 1996. LNCS, vol. 1115, pp. 75–99. Springer, Heidelberg (1996)
24. Stilman, B.: Managing Search Complexity in Linguistic Geometry. IEEE Trans. on Syst., Man, and Cybernetics 27(6), 978–998 (1997)
25. Stilman, B.: Network Languages for Concurrent Multi-agent Systems. Intl. J. of Computers & Math. with Appl. 34(1), 103–136 (1997)
26. Stilman, B.: Linguistic Geometry: From Search to Construction, p. 416. Kluwer Academic Publishers (now Springer) (2000)
27. Stilman, B.: Linguistic Geometry and Evolution of Intelligence. ISAST Trans. on Computers and Intelligent Systems 3(2), 23–37 (2011)
28. Stilman, B.: Discovering the Discovery of Linguistic Geometry. Int. J. of Machine Learning and Cybernetics 4(6), 20 (2012), doi:10.1007/s13042-012-0114-8 (printed in 2013)

29. Stilman, B.: Discovering the Discovery of the No-Search Approach. Int. J. of Machine Learning and Cybernetics, 27 (2012), doi:10.1007/s13042-012-0127-3
30. Stilman, B.: Discovering the Discovery of the Hierarchy of Formal Languages. Int. J. of Machine Learning and Cybernetics, 25 (2012), doi:10.1007/s13042-012-0146-0
31. Stilman, B.: Visual Reasoning for Discoveries. Int. J. of Machine Learning and Cybernetics, 23 (2013), doi:10.1007/s13042-013-0189-x
32. Stilman, B.: Proximity Reasoning for Discoveries. Int. J. of Machine Learning and Cybernetics (under review)
33. Stilman, B.: Mosaic Reasoning for Discoveries. J. of Artificial Intelligence and Soft Computing Research (to be submitted)
34. Stilman, B., Yakhnis, V., Umanskiy, O.: Winning Strategies for Robotic Wars: Defense Applications of Linguistic Geometry. Artificial Life and Robotics 4(3) (2000)
35. Stilman, B., Yakhnis, V., Umanskiy, O.: Knowledge Acquisition and Strategy Generation with LG Wargaming Tools. Int. J. of Comp. Intelligence and Applications 2(4), 385–409 (2002)
36. Stilman, B., Yakhnis, V., Umanskiy, O.: Strategies in Large Scale Problems. In: [11], ch. 3.3, pp. 251–285 (2007)
37. Stilman, B., Yakhnis, V., Umanskiy, O.: Linguistic Geometry: The Age of Maturity. J. of Advanced Computational Intelligence and Intelligent Informatics 14(6), 684–699 (2010)
38. Stilman, B., Yakhnis, V., Umanskiy, O.: Revisiting History with Linguistic Geometry. ISAST Trans. on Computers and Intelligent Systems 2(2), 22–38 (2010)
39. Stilman, B., Yakhnis, V., Umanskiy, O.: The Primary Language of Ancient Battles. Int. J. of Machine Learning and Cybernetics 2(3), 157–176 (2011)
40. Thomson, G.: The Inspiration of Science. Oxford U. Press, London (1961)
41. Ulam, S.: Adventures of a Mathematician. Charles Scribner's Sons, New York (1976)
42. Von Neumann, J.: The Computer and the Brain. Yale U. Press (1958)
43. Watson, J.D.: The Double Helix: A Personal Account of the Discovery of the Structure of DNA, Scribner Classics edn. Atheneum, New York (1968)
44. Watson, J.D., Crick, F.H.C.: A structure for deoxyribose nucleic acid. Nature 171, 737–738 (1953)

Signal Randomness Measure for BSS Ensemble Predictors

Ryszard Szupiluk[1] and Tomasz Ząbkowski[2]

[1] Warsaw School of Economics, Al. Niepodleglosci 162, 02-554 Warsaw, Poland
[2] Warsaw University of Life Sciences, Nowoursynowska 159, 02-776 Warsaw, Poland
rszupi@sgh.waw.pl, tomasz_zabkowski@sggw.pl

Abstract. In this article we present the application of novel noise measure in ensemble method based on blind signal separation methods. In this approach we decompose the set of models' results into basis latent components with destructive or constructive impact on the prediction. The crucial step in such model aggregation is proper identification of destructive components which can be treated as noisy factors. Presented method assesses the randomness of signals using a new measure of variability which helps to compare analyzed signal with some typical noise models. The experiments performed on electric load data using different blind separation algorithms contributed to model improvements.

Keywords: ensemble models, noise detection, measure of randomness.

1 Introduction

In this article we develop a blind signal separation (BSS) methods approach for ensemble predictions [14,15]. Its main idea is based on decomposition of the prediction results into underlying latent basis components. Some of these components may be associated with the prediction and some of them can be treated as noise or interference. Elimination of noises, termed as destructive components, should result in prediction improvement. There are may BSS data decomposition can be effectively used for basis component estimation. In our paper in experiment stage we apply such popular separation method like: SOBI, AMUSE, PCA or ICA algorithms [3,4,6,11]. After basis component estimation, we identify and eliminate the destructive ones, then we perform remixing process including only constructive components to obtain improved prediction results.

In such BSS application the term models ensemble or models aggregation is a consequence of the fact that the final prediction result is a combination of individual results from different models. Unlike the other popular ensemble methods like bagging or boosting [2,5,9], there are no assumptions to the form of aggregated models nor to criteria for model assessment. In other words, we can aggregate models (more specifically, the results of their prediction) regardless to specific criterion. The other important difference in comparison to other ensemble methods is possibility to

L. Rutkowski et al. (Eds.): ICAISC 2014, Part II, LNAI 8468, pp. 570–578, 2014.

aggregate effectively small number of models, even for two aggregated models, in some cases.

The main issue with this method is the correct classification of components into destructive or constructive. Within this study we assume that the random signals or signals with significant degree of random noise, have a negative influence on the prediction and therefore, a priori, they can be considered as destructive [16]. This leads to the issue of assessing signals randomness (noisiness).

The characteristic investigated in this paper is the autocorrelation function and its Fourier transformation called power spectrum [16,17]. Unfortunately, it has some theoretical disadvantages [1,12]. From our point of view, there is practical problem with its functional form which it is difficulty to compare signals which are not pure white noises [14]. The alternative to autocorrelation function analysis is R/S analysis [10,13] but its accuracy strongly depends on individual researcher choices like: regression type or length of data set to perform regression, etc.

From an operational point of view, in BSS aggregation, the goal is to remove the noise or any disruption that has physical nature from the prediction. In this approach, we do not assume, in advance, the specific mathematical characteristics of the interfering signal. Rather, we evaluate its characteristics in terms of volatility, regularity or smoothness, and finally we evaluate whether the analyzed signal is similar to the noise or not. We apply this human perspective within proposed method based on the variability measure which is closely related to the concepts of smoothness and volatility of the signal. We use this measure to assess the similarity between the signal components and some typical noise models.

2   Prediction Results Improvement

We assume that after learning various models we have a set of prediction results. We collect particular prediction results $x_i(k)$, $i = 1,...,m$, in one multivariate variable $\mathbf{x}(k) = [x_1(k),....,x_m(k)]^T$. Now we assume that prediction result is a mixture of the m latent components: constructive $s_j, j \in D_1$ and destructive s_i, $i \in D_2$ where $D_1 \cup D_2 = \{1,2,....,m\}$, $D_1 \cap D_2 = \varnothing$ and $D_1 \neq \varnothing$. Next, we assume that the prediction result are the linear combination of latent components

$$\mathbf{x}(k) = \mathbf{A}s(k) = \mathbf{A}[s_1(k),....,s_m(k)]^T, \tag{1}$$

where $\mathbf{s}(k) \in R^m$, matrix $\mathbf{A} = [a_{ij}] \in R^{m \times m}$ represents the mixing system. The relation (1) stands for decomposition of prediction results $\mathbf{x}$ into latent components vector $\mathbf{s}$ and mixing matrix $\mathbf{A}$. If the destructive part of the signal is removed (the signals are replaced with zero, $s_i(k)$ for $i \in D_2$) and the constructive components are mixed back, the modified prediction results $\hat{\mathbf{x}}(k)$ will be improved (or filtered):

$$\hat{\mathbf{x}}(k) = \mathbf{A}\hat{\mathbf{s}}(k) = \hat{\mathbf{A}}\mathbf{s}(k), \tag{2}$$

where $\hat{s}_j(k) = s_j(k)$ for $j \in D_1$, $\hat{s}_j(k) = 0$ for $j \in D_2$, and $\hat{\mathbf{A}} = [\hat{a}_{ij}]$, where $\hat{a}_{ij} = a_{ij}$ for $j \in D_1$, $\hat{a}_{ij} = 0$ for $j \in D_2$.

The crucial point of the above concept is proper **A** and **S** estimation. It is difficult task because we don't have information which decomposition is most adequate. Therefore, we must test various transformations giving us components of different properties. The most adequate methods to solve the first problem seem to be the blind signal separation (BSS) techniques.

3 Nonlinear and Multistage Remixing System Extension

Proposed concept can be developed by introducing a nonlinear model based on neural network (2) instead of a linear model. We use here the fact that historical values of the target variable are known, therefore the supervised learning is feasible. Adoption of such a non-linear mixing model means that the impact of individual components may be more complex than purely destructive or constructive. The prediction may be also influenced by the interaction between the components or their attenuation. In this approach, the matrix $\hat{\mathbf{A}}$ acts as the matrix with the initial weights for the neural network learning process. The extended nonlinear mixing system can be formulated as MLP neural network [8] where

$$\hat{\mathbf{x}} = \mathbf{g}^{(2)}(\mathbf{B}^{(2)}[\mathbf{g}^{(1)}(\mathbf{B}^{(1)}\mathbf{S} + \mathbf{b}^{(1)})] + \mathbf{b}^{(2)}) . \tag{3}$$

where $\mathbf{g}^{(i)}(.)$ is a vector of nonlinearities, $\mathbf{B}^{(i)}$ is a weight matrix and $\mathbf{b}^{(i)}$ is a bias vector respectively for i-th layer, i=1,2. The first weight layer will produce results related to (2) if we take $\mathbf{B}^{(1)} = \hat{\mathbf{A}}$. If we learn the whole structure starting from system described by $\hat{\mathbf{A}}$ with initial weights of $\mathbf{B}^{(1)}(0) = \hat{\mathbf{A}}$, we can expect the results will be improved.

Next we extend the presented methodology exploring multiple different decompositions. Such approach is motivated by assumption that there may exist different latent components with different statistical properties so different decompositions can be used. For K decompositions with separation $\mathbf{W}_i$ and remixing $\hat{\mathbf{A}}_i$ matrices respectively, and $i = 1...K$ we can employ the transformations one by one we can describe the complete filtration process as

$$\hat{\mathbf{x}} = \mathbf{W}_K \hat{\mathbf{A}}_K ... \mathbf{W}_2 \hat{\mathbf{A}}_2 \mathbf{W}_1 \hat{\mathbf{A}}_1 \mathbf{X} = \mathbf{CX} , \tag{4}$$

where **C** means global filtration matrix. When we apply in each remixing stage the generalised mixing we obtain improved results as

$$\hat{\mathbf{x}} = F_K \left(\hat{\mathbf{A}}_K, \mathbf{W}_K F_{K-1} \left(... F_2 \left(\mathbf{A}_2, \mathbf{W}_2 F_1 (\hat{\mathbf{A}}_1, \mathbf{W}_1 \mathbf{X}) \right) \right) \right), \tag{5}$$

where

$$F_i(\hat{\mathbf{A}}_i, \mathbf{S}_i) = \mathbf{g}_i^{(2)}(\mathbf{B}_i^{(1)}[\mathbf{g}_i^{(2)}(\mathbf{B}_i^{(1)}\mathbf{S}_i + \mathbf{b}_i^{(1)})] + \mathbf{b}_i^{(2)}), \quad \mathbf{B}_i^{(1)}(0) = \hat{\mathbf{A}}_i . \tag{6}$$

The function $F_i(\hat{\mathbf{A}}_i, \mathbf{S}_i)$ might be interpreted as the dual-layer neural network of MLP-type.

4   Destructive Components as Noises

The extraction of primary components using ICA (independent components analysis) leads to the fundamental problem the proposed method which is the classification of the components into constructive or destructive. In this paper, we treat this task as a problem of random noises identification because, by nature, their presence cannot be considered as beneficial for the prediction.

The term *random noise* due to references to such terms as randomness, uncertainty or probability has many definitions, often with deep philosophical interpretations [7,18]. In data analysis practice the random signal or noise is observed when the present values give no precise information about the future values. The most popular example of the noise model is the white noise [7]. It is very convenient case if the analyzed model or data include white noise. In practice, the situation is more complex. There are colored noises with internal dependencies or mixtures of the random noises and deterministic signals.

Generally speaking, we expect that random signal should not include any predictable patterns (internal dependencies, correlations, trends) and shouldn't be smooth. Therefore, for signals with temporal structure we propose a following measure. Let us consider the signal y with temporal structure and observations indexed by $k=1...N$. The variability (and thus unpredictability of the signal) might be measured with the following formula:

$$Q(y) = \frac{\frac{1}{N-1}\sum_{k=2}^{N} |y(k) - y(k-1)|}{\rho(\max(y) - \min(y))}, \tag{7}$$

where ρ symbol means unit indicator and it is introduced to avoid dividing by zero.

The possible values of measure (7) are ranging from 1 to 0. The measure has simple interpretation: it is maximal when the changes in each step are equal to range (maximal change), and is minimal when data are constant. In both cases the signal is totally predictable, but between those marginal states the signal is random. In general case addressed for data $y(t)$ both, with and without temporal structure we can define it as

$$Q_1(y) = \frac{E\{|y(t_1) - y(t_2)|\}}{\rho(E\{\max(y) - \min(y)\})}, \tag{8}$$

or more generally as

$$Q_p(y) = \frac{E\{\|y(t_1) - y(t_2)\|_p\}}{\rho(E\{\max(y) - \min(y)\})}, \tag{9}$$

where $\| . \|_p$ is a given p norm. Measures (7) - (9) allow to evaluate the characteristics of the signal, but the noise detection requires a comparison of the proposed measures with the reference noise models adopted. In our approach, this comparison will be made for several models of noise using the following formula:

$$P = \sum_{p \in K} k_p \big(Q_p(y) - Q_p(y_v) \big)^2 , \tag{10}$$

where k_p is the weight for each square difference to the reference noise; the default value is equal to one.

For the typical noise models generated from Gaussian or normal distributions Q value can be calculated in the following way.

Let us consider random variable $y \sim U[0,1]$. In this case the denominator of formula (8) asymptotically equals 1. The nominator is the expected value of absolute value from difference between two uniform variables $y1, y2 \sim U[0,1]$:

$$E\{| y_1 - y_2 |\} = \int_0^1 \int_{y_2=y_1}^{y_2=1} (y_2 - y_1) dy_2 dy_1 + \int_0^1 \int_{y_2=0}^{y_2=y_1} (y_2 - y_1) dy_2 dy_1 = \frac{1}{3}, \tag{11}$$

Therefore, for $y \sim U[0,1]$ we have $Q(y) = 1/3$.

Let us consider random variable $y \sim N[0,1]$. In this case the nominator of formula (8) might be calculated as expected value of absolute value of variable $z \sim N[0,1]$ (difference of normally distributed variables is normally distributed):

$$E\{| z |\} = \int_{-\infty}^{+\infty} \frac{1}{\sqrt{2\pi}} | z | e^{-\frac{z^2}{2}} dz = \int_0^{+\infty} \frac{2}{\sqrt{2\pi}} z e^{-\frac{z^2}{2}} dz = \sqrt{\frac{2}{\pi}} . \tag{12}$$

The denominator of (8) is more problematic, because normal distribution is unlimited and the extreme values might be both $+\infty$ and $-\infty$. Whereas for N-element representative sample we may take the inverse distribution function of the normal distribution to obtain the minimum value of $\Phi^{-1}(1/N)$ and maximum value of $\Phi^{-1}((N-1)/N)$.

5   Practical Experiment

In the experimental part of our research we focused on electric load prediction problem in the Polish power system. Our task was to forecast the hourly energy consumption for the next 24 hours based on the energy demand observed during last 24 hours and having calendar variables such as: month, day of the month, day of the week, and holiday indicator. The available data covered the time period between years 1988 and 1998, that is 86400 observations on hourly basis.

We trained six MLP neural networks with one hidden layer (with 12, 18, 24, 27, 30, 33 neurons respectively). For the aggregation we used a couple of typical blind separation methods like: AMUSE, SONS, SOBI, ERICA, FPICA, JADE, JADE TD, EASI. The description and implementation details of the separation algorithms can be found in [3,4].

The quality of the results was measured with mean absolute percentage error (MAPE), mean absolute deviation (MAD), mean squared error (MSE), maximal percentage error (MAXPE). For these primary models we performed their decomposition using a broad set of algorithms and calculated the errors' percentage changes observed when using specific decomposition, please refer to Table 1.

For instance, the percentage change for MAPE error was calculated as $\Delta M = ((MAPE_0 - MAPE_1)/MAPE_0) \times 100\%$, where $MAPE_0$ is error for primary model and $MAPE_1$ is error observed after specific aggregation. In similar way, the error percentage change was calculated for MAD, MSE, MAXPE.

Table 1. Percentage change of the best result after the given decomposition and using four quality criteria

Improvement rate in % Decomposition	MAPE	MAD	MSE	MAXP
AMUSE	4.48	4.59	6.96	0.02
SONS	2.30	2.56	3.61	0.34
SOBI	4.49	4.53	7.16	1.27
ERICA	1.33	1.37	2.95	−0.71
FPICA	2.36	2.50	3.74	5.87
JADE	4.42	4.47	6.75	0.35
JADE TD	4.76	4.74	7.47	0.26
EASI	4.73	4.79	7.20	1.39

We can observe that for the analyzed set of models we can benefit significant prediction improvement arte taking into account all errors. Depends on the decomposition algorithm used we can achieve up to 4.76% improvement on MAPE error, up to 4.79% improvement on MAD error, up to 7.47% improvement on MSE error and finally up to 5.87% improvement on MAXP error.

In the following part of the results we will show only to the aggregation using independent component decomposition using the JADE algorithm, but the same procedure applies to other algorithms. Base components for this example are shown in Fig. 1. For this case, the best improvement of prediction on MAPE criterion (reduction of error) was obtained after elimination of the component *s4*. Component *s4* was classified to be the most similar to the noise, since it had the lowest value of P measure, please see Table 2 for details. Finally, Table 3 shows the variance of individual base components.

Table 2. P measure calculated for base components

Signal	s1	s2	s3	s4	s5	s6
Value of P measure	0.0999	0.0937	0.0883	0.0601	0.0803	0.0815

576   R. Szupiluk and T. Ząbkowski

Table 3. Variance observed for base components

Signal	s1	s2	s3	s4	s5	s6
Variance	0.3957	1.5274	1.9478	1.4579	1.1516	1.1592

The other figures show: autocorrelation functions for base components, please see Fig. 2 and the results of R/S analysis, please see Fig. 3.

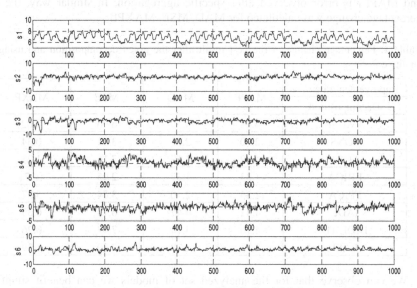

Fig. 1. Base components obtained after JADE algorithm decomposition

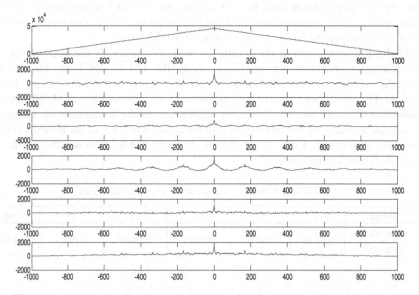

Fig. 2. Autocorrelation functions obtained after JADE algorithm decomposition

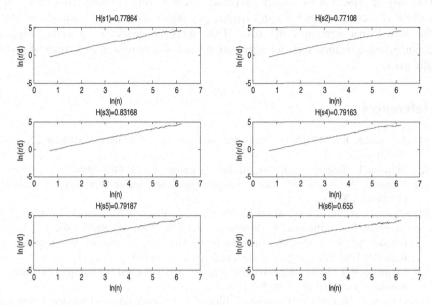

Fig. 3. The results of R/S analysis for base components obtained after JADE algorithm decomposition

The individual graphs of the Fig. 3 show the logarithm values of $E(r/d)$ with respect to the logarithms of interval length, where r is the range, d is standard deviation, and n is the interval length. Above the individual plots there are values of the Hurst exponent included.

Based on the experiments, we can conclude that the results of the correlation analysis as well as R/S analysis did not give good hints for the proper classification of the destructive components. However, the proposed measure is very useful for correct components classification. The other aspect which can influence the prediction quality is neural network recomposition (the inverse operation to the decomposition) which can reduce the errors by additional one to three percentage points.

6   Conclusions

The assessment of signals randomness is complex issue. In practice, we rarely deal with the pure, mathematical models of white or colored noises. The noises can have diverse nature which may be difficult to describe as a one, consistent distribution. The analyzed signal can be a combination of random and deterministic components. Based on the typical autocorrelation characteristics it is difficult to assess clearly the nature of the signal. Limitations and low efficiency of standard applications for signals randomness assessment are motivation to explore new approaches. The one presented in this paper is inspired by the human perception to the noise assessment. The noise is detected based on the particular signal characteristics and its similarity to the volatility of typical noise models. Whereas, the volatility is characterized by a new variability measure, which doesn't require any additional a priori assumptions about the model that generates the data. This approach works in a wide range of decomposition method used for aggregation what was proven in experimental part of this work.

References

[1] Anscombe, F.J.: Graphs in statistical analysis. The American Statistician 27, 17–21 (1973)
[2] Breiman, L.: Bagging predictors. Machine Learning 24, 123–140 (1996)
[3] Cichocki, A., Amari, S.: Adaptive Blind Signal and Image Processing. John Wiley, Chichester (2002)
[4] Cichocki, A., Amari, S., Siwek, K., Tanaka, T., Phan, A.H., Zdunek, R., Cruces, S., Georgiev, P., Washizawa, Y., Leonowicz, Z., Bakardjian, H., Rutkowski, T., Choi, S., Belouchrani, A., Barros, A., Thawonmas, R., Hoya, T., Hashimoto, W., Terazono, Y.: ICALAB Toolboxes, http://www.bsp.brain.riken.jp/ICALAB
[5] Clements, R.T.: Combining forecasts: A review and annotated bibliography. International Journal of Forecasting 5, 559–581 (1989)
[6] Comon, P., Jutten, C.: Handbook of Blind Source Separation: Independent Component Analysis and Applications. Academic Press (2010)
[7] Hamilton, J.D.: Time series analysis. Princeton University Press, Princeton (1994)
[8] Haykin, S.: Neural networks: a comprehensive foundation. Macmillan, New York (1994)
[9] Hoeting, J., Madigan, D., Raftery, A., Volinsky, C.: Bayesian model averaging: a tutorial. Statistical Science 14, 382–417 (1999)
[10] Hurst, H.E.: Long term storage capacity of reservoirs. Transactions of the American Society of Civil Engineers 116, 770–799 (1951)
[11] Hyvarinen, A., Karhunen, J., Oja, E.: Independent Component Analysis. John Wiley, New York (2001)
[12] Rodgers, J.L., Nicewander, W.A.: Thirteen ways to look at the correlation coefficient. The American Statistician 42(1), 59–66 (1988)
[13] Shiryaev, A.N.: Essentials of stochastic finance: facts, models, theory. World Scientific Publishing, Singapore (1999)
[14] Szupiluk, R., Wojewnik, P., Zabkowski, T.: Model Improvement by the Statistical Decomposition. In: Rutkowski, L., Siekmann, J.H., Tadeusiewicz, R., Zadeh, L.A. (eds.) ICAISC 2004. LNCS (LNAI), vol. 3070, pp. 1199–1204. Springer, Heidelberg (2004)
[15] Szupiluk, R., Wojewnik, P., Ząbkowski, T.: Prediction Improvement via Smooth Component Analysis and Neural Network Mixing. In: Kollias, S.D., Stafylopatis, A., Duch, W., Oja, E. (eds.) ICANN 2006. LNCS, vol. 4132, pp. 133–140. Springer, Heidelberg (2006)
[16] Szupiluk, R., Wojewnik, P., Zabkowski, T.: Noise detection for ensemble methods. In: Rutkowski, L., Scherer, R., Tadeusiewicz, R., Zadeh, L.A., Zurada, J.M. (eds.) ICAISC 2010, Part I. LNCS (LNAI), vol. 6113, pp. 471–478. Springer, Heidelberg (2010)
[17] Therrien, C.W.: Discrete Random Signals and Statistical Signal Processing. Prentice Hall, New Jersey (1992)
[18] Vaseghi, S.V.: Advanced signal processing and digital noise reduction. John Wiley and Sons, Chichester (1997)

An Incremental Map-Matching Algorithm Based on Hidden Markov Model

Piotr Szwed and Kamil Pekala

AGH University of Science and Technology
pszwed@agh.edu.pl, kamilkp@gmail.com

Abstract. Map-matching algorithms aim at establishing a vehicle location on a road segment based on positioning data from a variety of sensors: GPS receivers, WiFi or cellular radios. They are integral part of various Intelligent Transportation Systems (ITS) including fleet management, vehicle tracking, navigation services, traffic monitoring and congestion detection. Our work was motivated by an idea of developing an algorithm that can be both utilized for tracking individual vehicles and for monitoring traffic in real-time. We propose a new incremental map-matching algorithm that constructs of a sequence of Hidden-Markov Models (HMMs). Starting from an initial HMM, the next models are developed by alternating operations: expansion and contraction. In the later, the map-matched trace is output. We discuss results of initial experiments conducted for 20 GPS traces, which to test algorithm robustness, were modified by introduction of noise and/or downsampled.

Keywords: GPS, map-matching, Hidden Markov Model, Viterbi.

1 Introduction

Map-matching algorithms aim at establishing a vehicle location on a road segment based on positioning data from a variety of sensors: GPS receivers, WiFi or cellular radios, odometers and others. As all sensors used as input may yield uncertain data, map-matching involves making decision on to which location at several candidate road segments the vehicle should be assigned. The decision can be based on a current sensor reading or on a history comprising a number of past data.

Map-matching is an integral part of various Intelligent Transportation Systems (ITS) including fleet management, vehicle tracking, navigation services, traffic monitoring and congestion detection. Such systems experience growing popularity due to proliferation of smartphone devices capable of receiving positioning data and transferring them over cellular networks. The type of map-matching algorithm that they internally use depends on particular application.

Our work was motivated by an idea of developing an algorithm that can be both utilized for tracking individual vehicles and for monitoring traffic in real-time. Such algorithm must be *incremental*, i.e. should update the information upon arrival of new sensor reading, as opposed to *global*, when a closed

L. Rutkowski et al. (Eds.): ICAISC 2014, Part II, LNAI 8468, pp. 579–590, 2014.

sequence of readings is analyzed. In this paper we propose a new incremental map-matching algorithm, which in order to determine the vehicle trajectory constructs a sequence of Hidden-Markov Models (HMMs). In our approach a HMM state corresponds to a road segment and a sensor reading to an observation in HMM. Starting from an initial HMM, the next models are developed by alternating operations: expansion (new states are added to the model) and contraction (dead ends are deleted, the graph root is moved forward along the detected path and a part of trajectory is output). We report results of initial experiments conducted for 20 GPS traces, which to test algorithm robustness, were modified by introduction of artificial noise and/or downsampled.

The paper is organized as follows: the next Section 2 discusses various types of map-matching algorithms. It is followed by Section 3, in which a model of road network is described. The next Section 4 introduces HMM model and provides the algorithm description. Conducted experiments are reported in Section 5 and finally Section 6 gives concluding remarks.

2   Related Works

More then thirty map-matching algorithms are surveyed by Quddus et. al in [1]. Authors divided them into four groups: geometric, topological, probabilistic and advanced.

Algorithms employing geometric analysis take into account shapes of road segments only, while ignoring, how they are connected. The simplest approach consists in finding the closest map node (a segment endpoint) to the current GPS reading (point-to-point matching). Another option is to find the closest road segment (point-to-curve matching) [2] or to match pairs of points from the vehicle trajectory to the road segments [3]. All those algorithms are very fast, however, they are sensitive to map data (in particular to the density of nodes) and may yield vehicle trajectories, which are not consistent with the connections within the road network [4].

Topological map-matching algorithms utilize information about connections between road segments. This removes leaps between map links that can be observed for algorithms based only on geometrical information. Another features that can be considered are turn angles and also a vehicle state (heading, velocity) [3, 5].

Many positioning devices are capable of delivering a circular or elliptic confidence region associated with each position reading, e.g. the location API for Android devices defines the *accuracy* parameter. The circle radius can be about 10 meters for GPS [6] and 50 m for cellular networks. However, in dense urban area with street canyons and in the presence of trees, the GPS accuracy can degrade substantially. The confidence region can be also estimated using dead reckoning. The idea behind probabilistic algorithms is to select in the match mapping process only those road segments that intersect with the confidence region. If several candidates are found, only one of them with the highest probability is chosen. Such approach was discussed in [7]. An enhanced algorithm that employs such approach at junctions was described in [8].

Advanced algorithms usually combine both topological and probabilistic information, while applying various techniques to assign road links to GPS readings. Kim et al. used Kalman Filter [9] to establish vehicle location along a link after performing point-to-curve matching [10]. Fuzzy Sugeno rules for road segment selection were used in [11, 12]. Gustafsson et al. reported an approach based on particle filter [13], Yang et al. applied Dempster-Shafers evidence theory while determining weights in point-to-curve matching.

Several map-matching algorithms are path-oriented, i.e. they maintain a set of candidate paths. In the algorithm developed by Marchal et al. [14] they ware stored in a collection being sorted according to a path score based on distance to the GPS trace. An idea of using a tree like structure representing a set of candidate paths was proposed by Wu et al. [15]. Both algorithms are *incremantal*, i.e. they update the path representation on arrival of a new GPS reading. On the other hand, if a full GPS trace is initially known a *global* approach based on calculation of Fréchet distance can be applied [16].

Hidden Markov Model (HMM) [17] is a Markov process comprising a number of hidden (unobserved) states. Transitions between states can occur with a certain probabilities. Each state is assigned with a set of observations. One of them is to be output, as the state is reached. For a given state conditional probabilities of observations occurrence (*emission probabilities*) sum up to 1. A problem that can be elegantly formulated with HMM is the *decoding* problem: it consists in finding the most probable sequence of transitions between hidden states that would produce a given sequence of observations. Such sequence can be efficiently determined with the well-known Viterbi algorithm [18].

There are at least four implementations of global map-matching algorithms [19–22] that employ HMM approach. In all of them hidden states correspond to projections of vehicle positions on road segments and observations to location data obtained mainly from GPS sensors. Transition probabilities are established based on links connectivity and/or dead reckoning, whereas emission probabilities assume Gaussian distribution of GPS noise.

In this paper we have taken the similar approach. The main difference that should be emphasized is that our algorithm is incremental, i.e. it does not build a single HMM model for a given GPS trace to be analyzed afterwards with the Vitrebi algorithm, but updates the HMM model on each input and in some situations only applies the Viterbi algorithms. Moreover, the algorithms can be a basis for developing real-time services like vehicle tracking and traffic estimation.

3   Road Network Model

The used road network model is defined as a directed graph $G = (V, E, I)$, where $V \in \mathbb{R}^2$ are graph nodes described by two coordinates: longitude and latitude, $E \in V \times V$ are straight road segments linking two nodes and $I \subset E \times E$ specifies inhibited maneuvers at road junctions. If $((v_1, v_2), (v_2, v_3)) \in I$, then a path containing the sequence (v_1, v_2, v_3) is forbidden according to traffic regulations.

We assume that road links are represented by straight segments. If a road has a curved geometry, e.g. appears on a map as an arc, it can be approximated a sequence of connected segments. This is a typical approach for many map sources, e.g. OSM [23]. Moreover, as performing various geometrical operations we are actually interested in undirected arcs, we define a function $S \colon E \to 2^V$ that maps an edge (v_1, v_2), $v_1 \neq v_2$ onto a a set $\{v_1, v_2\}$ comprising exactly two vertices. We will extend this function to the whole set E, hence $S(E) = \bigcup_{e \in E} S(e)$.

For a given segment $s = \{v_b, v_e\}$ and a point g, we define the projection $p(g, s)$ of g onto s as a point g' belonging to the segment s that minimizes the distance:

$$p(g, s) = \underset{g' = v_b + t(v_e - v_b) \wedge t \in [0,1]}{\arg\min} d(g, g'), \tag{1}$$

where $d(g, g')$ is a distance between g and g' given by the *haversine* formula.

The projection point $p(g, s)$ calculated according to formula (1) can be either an orthogonal projection on a segment or one of its end points (see Fig. 1).

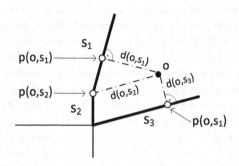

Fig. 1. Projections of a GPS point o and distances to road segments s_1, s_2 and s_3

4   Map Matching Algorithm

The map-matching algorithm comprises three basic operations organized into a pipeline (see Fig. 2). Firstly, an input GPS trace is smoothed with Kalman filter. This allows for compensating noise and removing outliers from the trace. In the next processing step it is checked, whether the distance between two consecutive samples is small enough to match the map scale (or more precisely lengths of typical road links). If the distance is too large, the required number of intermediate samples is generated by applying simple linear interpolation. Finally, the input trace after the two preprocessing steps is interpreted with the proper map-matching algorithm based on Hidden Markov Model (HMM). Due to limited capacity, in this section we will focus on this step only.

Fig. 2. Processing steps of the map-matching algorithm

4.1   Hidden Markov Model

While constructing Hidden Markov Models the approach similar to [21, 22] was taken. A state in HMM describe both a road segment and a projection of a GPS fix on the segment calculated according to formula (1). Thus, each state tuple $(s, p, i) \in Q$ has the following components: e - a road segment, p - a projection point belonging to the segment $S(e)$ and i - a sequence number.

In the assumed model observations O correspond to data obtained from GPS sensor, i.e. they are tuples (x, y, t), whose elements are longitude, latitude and time respectively.

Below we give the definition of Hidden Markov Model reflecting adaptation introduced to support the map matching problem.

Definition 1 (Hidden Markov Model). *Hidden Markov Model is a tuple* $\lambda = (Q, A, O, P_t, P_o, q_0)$, *where*

- *Q is a set of states, $Q \subset E \times \mathbb{R}^2 \times \mathbb{N}$*
- *$A \subset Q \times Q$ is a set of arcs,*
- *O is a set of observations, $O \subset \mathbb{R}^2 \times \mathbb{R}$*
- *$P_t \colon A \to (0, 1]$ is a function that assigns a probability to a transition between states.*
- *$P_o \colon Q \times O \to [0, 1]$ is an emission probability function satisfying $\forall q \in Q \colon \sum_{o \in O} P_o(q, o) = 1$.*
- *q_0 is an initial (root) state.*

Two states $q_1 = (e_1, p_1, i_1)$ and $q_2 = (e_2, p_2, i_2)$, where $e_1 = (v_{11}, v_{12})$ and $e_2 = (v_{21}, v_{22})$, can be connected with an arc $a = (q_1, q_2)$, if $e_1 = e_2$ or there exists a path in a graph $\pi = v_{11}, \dots v_{22}$ linking endpoints of road segments. Currently, in most cases we consider sequences of length 3, i.e. two consecutive segments having common endpoints. Longer sequences can be calculated to handle special situations requiring reinitialization of algorithm. This assumption imposes the requirement that observations (locations obtained form a GPS sensor should be dense enough to be assigned to consecutive segments. If a segment was missed, then the map matching algorithm would probably get lost. The interpolation step (see Fig. 2) was introduced to satisfy this requirement and achieve real-time performance.

In order to calculate a transition probability for an arc a linking states q_1 and q_2 a weight function $\theta(a) \colon A \to [0, 1]$ is used. Basically, it assigns 1 if q_1 and q_2 can be connected by a path, however if the possible path violates traffic rules or physical constraints (e.g. speed greater than 250 km/h) a small value (0.1) is used. Finally, the weights assigned to outgoing arcs for a given state q are normalized applying the formula (2) to give the probabilities.

$$P_t(a) = \tfrac{1}{Z_t}\theta(a),$$
$$\text{where } Z_t = \sum_{\substack{a_i \,:\, a_i=(q,q_i)\in A \\ a=(q,q_a)}} \theta(a_i). \qquad (2)$$

Emission probability P_o is computed for a subset of states in HMM Q_H and an observation o. For a given HMM state $q = (e, p, i)$, where $p = (x_p, y_p)$ is the vehicle position, its GPS observations o can be distributed on XY plane around the point p. Until there is no bias, e.g. related to satellite visibility, the applied distribution should have its mean at the point p and decrease with growing distance between points $d(p, o)$. We have assumed 2-dimensional normal distribution given by (3).

$$P(x, y) = \frac{1}{D} e^{-k\,((x-x_p)^2 + (y-y_p)^2)}. \qquad (3)$$

The D normalizing factor is given as $D = \int_{-\infty}^{\infty} \int_{-\infty}^{\infty} P(x, y)\, dx\, dy$. For k the value 0.01 was taken, what corresponds to a noise giving translations of GPS readings by 10m. In such case $D \approx 314.0$. As the map data used in experiments used longitude and latitude coordinates, we applied, however, a modified version of (3), in which Euclidean distance was replaced by the haversine formula.

4.2 Trace Interpretation Algorithm

The algorithm takes at input a sequence of GPS readings (observations) $\omega = (o_i : i = 1, n)$ and constructs a sequence of Hidden Markov Models $\Lambda = (\lambda_i : 0 = 1, n)$. Basically, it contains two stages: *initialization*, during which the first model λ_1 is built and *processing* that is repeated for successive observations.

Initialization. This stage involves determining a set of possible states (road segments), to which the initial vehicle position might be assigned. The algorithm examines all road segments in a supplied part of the map and chooses only these, whose distances to the measured point are less or equal than a certain threshold r (e.g. 35 meters). At that point the construction a sequence of HMMs, which can be perceived as a trajectory tree, begins. The tree root is set to a fictional state from which the vehicle might have moved to any of the states belonging to initial Hidden Markov Model λ_1. The steps of this stage are listed in Algorithm 1.

Processing. This step is being applied repeatedly for all, but the first GPS observations. Each i-th iteration comprises two phases: *expansion* and *contraction*, during which a new HMM model λ_i is constructed. The expansion phase consists in adding new states and transitions to previous model λ_{i-1}. Its steps are given by Algorithm 2.

Algorithm 1. Initialization

1. For a given observation o_1 calculate a set of road segments, whose distance to o_1 is less or equal r, where r is a certain threshold: $H = \{e \in E: d(o_1, p(o_1, S(e))) \leq r\}$.
2. Assign $Q_1 \leftarrow \{q_0\} \cup \{(e_i, p(o_1, S(e_i)), 1): e_i \in H\}$; q_0 is a fictitious state (a tree root).
3. Connect states with arcs $A_1 \leftarrow \{q_0\} \times Q_H$, where $Q_H = Q_1 \setminus \{q_0\}$.
4. Assign to each arc $a \in A_1$ equal transition probability $P_{t1}(a) = \frac{1}{|Q_H|}$.
5. For each element in Q_H calculate emission probability according to formula (3).

Algorithm 2. Expansion

1. Select the set of states in λ_{i-1} that was added in the previous iteration (heading states) $Q_H = (e, p, k) \in Q: k = i - 1$.
2. Establish a set of edges E_R that are physically reachable from Q_H. As discussed in Section 4.1, currently, only neighbor edges are considered.
3. Calculate a subset $E_{RD} \subset E_R$ comprising those edges, which are placed at a distance less than or equal to a certain threshold r: $E_{RD} = \{e \in E_R: d(o_i, S(e)) \leq r\}$.
4. Insert edges from E_{RD} as new states into the model λ_i. Hence, $Q_i \leftarrow Q_{i-1} \cup \{(e, p(e, S(e)), i): e \in E_{RD}\}$.
5. Link new states with edges: $A_i \leftarrow A_{i-1} \cup Q_H \times (Q_i \setminus Q_{i-1})$
6. Establish transition and emission probabilities according to (2) and (3).

The contraction phase has two goals: firstly orphan nodes without successors are removed, what keeps the detection model compact, secondly the HMM root is moved forward and a next part of the trajectory is output. Operations conducted during this phase are summarized in Algorithm 3.

One of the contraction operation, namely *join handling* requires some comments. A state q_J is a join, if it has two different predecessors:

$$\exists q_a, q_b \in Q_{i-1}: (q_a, q_J), (q_a, q_J) \in A \wedge q_a \neq q_b.$$

Such situation is illustrated in Fig. 3, where states q_2 and q_J are examples of joins. Presence of a join in HMM indicates that during the map matching process vehicle positions were assigned to parallel roads that finally joined at a certain point. Hence, the algorithm faces the problem of selecting the most probable among at least two competing paths. This is achieved with a dedicated procedure that searches the closest parent node q_F, from which (1) *all* paths led to q_J and (2) states belonging to them are reachable only from q_F. If such state exist, the Viterbi algorithm is applied to the subgraph between q_F and q_J and most probable path is kept in the λ_i. States lying beyond the computed path are removed.

Algorithm 3. Contraction

---

1. Remove from Q_i all states with the timestamp less then i, i.e. assign:
   $Q_i \leftarrow Q_i \setminus \{(e, p, k) \colon k < i\}$ and update A_i accordingly.
2. Handle joins.
3. Update the root state q_r:
   a If q_r has exactly one successor q_j in A, output q_r as a next element of the vehicle trajectory. Otherwise, STOP.
   b Assign: $q_r \leftarrow q_j$ and go to a.

The subgraph between q_F and q_2 in Fig. 3 does not satisfy the conditions given above, as there exists a path from q_F to q_3 that is not closed. Similarly, the subgraph between q_1 and q_J cannot be accepted, as q_2 is a join for a path that does not start in q_1. The subgraph between q_F and q_J satisfies the given conditions and, after applying the Viterbi algorithm, can be replaced by a single path between these nodes.

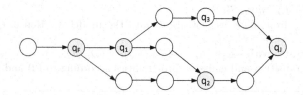

Fig. 3. Example of submodel of HMM, to which Viterbi algorithm is applied to get rid off joins

Handling Special Situations. An exceptional situation in expansion phase occurs if the set E_{RD} established in step 3 of Algorithm 2 is empty. We may conclude then, that the map matching algorithm got lost. There may be several reasons of such situations. It may stem from a noise that was not sufficiently removed by the Kalman filter. The other reason can be that observations are not dense enough to be matched to neighbor map segments. Such effect can be observed at curved roads, e.g. highway links or roundabouts, which are approximated by a number of short straight lines. Basically, we handle this issue by performing reinitialization using Algoritm 1 and obtaining a new model λ_{i0}.

Further processing depends on application of the map matching component within an ITS. If we are particularly interested in reconstructing the trajectory of a tracked vehicle, models λ_{i-1} and λ_{i0} are merged by adding links that are obtained by applying locally A* shortest path algorithm. If the goal of map matching is to calculate traffic parameters based on GPS readings, some tracking errors can be accepted. For such applications λ_{i-1} model is processed with Viterbi algorithm to get the most probable path and the whole matching process restarts from λ_{i0}.

Another specific situation is, when it is known that the sequence of observations ω is finite and ends with o_n. Then for the last model λ_n the most probable trajectory is computed with Viterbi algorithm and the algorithm stops.

5   Experiments

The algorithm was tested on the map of Kraków in Poland. The map originated from OpenStreetMap project [23]. The input dataset was represented by 20 GPS traces, which were recorded during several car trips throughout Kraków with EasyTrials GPS[1] software running on iPhone 5. The total length of traces used in experiments was 148.46km. Both input and map-matched trajectories were stored in GPX format that is supported by JOSM, the OpenStreetMap editor.

The first phase of experiments consisted in determining parameters of a discrete Kalman filter used in the preprocessing phase. It was designed in form of two distinct second order filters processing separately noise for longitude and latitude components. The state variables corresponded, hence, to position and velocity along one of the axes. Initial parameters for both filters were identical. They were determined empirically using the Matlab software for calculations and visualization. The best effects were achieved (and thus those were applied in the final algorithm) with the following set of parameters (see [9] for notation details): process noise covariance matrix $Q = \begin{bmatrix} 1 & 0 \\ 0 & 0.05 \end{bmatrix}$, measurement noise covariance matrix $R = 4.5$ and initial process noise covariance matrix $P = \begin{bmatrix} 0 & 0 \\ 0 & 0 \end{bmatrix}$.

It should be mentioned that the selected parameters reflect features of the used sensor, i.e. this installed in iPhone 5. They may differ for other device. The results of of trace smoothing with the designed filter are shown in Fig. 4. An artificial noise introduced into the original trace yields the zig-zag line, which is smoothed (the black bold line).

Analyzing the traces manually we have observed that invalid paths was obtained (i.e. broken and impossible to repair with A*) in about 30% of the cases, in which the algorithm was forced to perform reinitialization. Moreover, reitialization usually takes more time than the normal algorithm processing step. Thus, to avoid manual annotating of GPS trials, we decided to use the number of reinitialization as a quality metrics.

We have tested the algorithm by feeding the collected data in four forms: original, modified by artificially introduced random noise (magnitude between 0 and 20 meters added to each sample), half sampled (H-S) and half-sampled with the noise. The obtained values are gathered in Table 1. Each table row shows test results for a particular GPS trace. Subcolums marked with RI give number of algorithm reinitializations in the selected mode, RIS denotes average number of reinitalizations per sample.

It is clear and not surprising that the best results were achieved by running the tests with the original input data. However, for applied half-sampling the

---

[1] http://www.easytrailsgps.com/

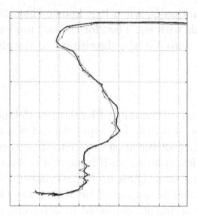

Fig. 4. Example of application of the implemented discrete Kalman filter

Table 1. Test results

No	Length (km)	Samples	Original RI	Original RIS	Noise RI	Noise RIS	H-S RI	H-S RIS	H-S & Noise RI	H-S & Noise RIS
1	9.45	256	0	0	3	0.012	3	0.012	3	0.012
2	8.26	248	3	0.012	10	0.04	2	0.008	1	0.004
3	7.78	261	2	0.008	5	0.019	1	0.004	2	0.008
4	7.67	267	0	0	6	0.022	3	0.011	5	0.019
5	9.67	233	3	0.013	0	0	0	0	0	0
6	6.40	209	0	0	0	0	0	0	0	0
7	5.59	108	0	0	0	0	0	0	1	0.009
8	9.03	259	0	0	10	0.039	0	0	3	0.012
9	7.05	216	1	0.005	1	0.005	1	0.005	0	0
10	7.94	248	2	0.008	4	0.016	1	0.004	0	0
11	7.19	190	0	0	1	0.005	1	0.005	10	0.053
12	11.22	273	1	0.004	7	0.026	1	0.004	2	0.007
13	4.19	118	0	0	0	0	1	0.008	1	0.008
14	5.96	192	2	0.01	2	0.01	0	0	2	0.01
15	9.03	271	0	0	2	0.007	0	0	0	0
16	6.45	242	1	0.004	3	0.012	2	0.008	3	0.012
17	7.95	228	4	0.018	7	0.031	3	0.013	3	0.013
18	7.41	192	1	0.005	3	0.016	2	0.01	2	0.01
19	7.06	283	4	0.014	7	0.025	2	0.007	6	0.021
20	3.16	188	0	0	2	0.011	0	0	1	0.005
Total	148.47	4482	24	0.005	73	0.016	23	0.005	45	0.010

number of reinitializations was practically identical. This effect can be probably attributed to the interpolation. The worse indicator value was obtained for noisy data. Nevertheless, all obtained values are fairly good. In the normal mode the reinitialization occurred once per 6.18km and in about 70% of cases it was possible to recover from errors.

Only initial results of performance tests can now be reported. The algorithm implemented in C# language and published as a RESTfull web service was capable of processing 20 simultaneous feeds with 50 times speed-up, i.e. time intervals between subsequent send operations were 50 times smaller then differences between sample timestamps. This corresponds to 1000 mobile sensors feeding real-time data simultaneously.

6   Conclusions

This paper presents a new map matching algorithm based on Hidden Markov Model. Although the idea of applying HMM to map matching was reported already in a few articles, in works by Krumm et. al [20] and Newson and Krumm [21] only a global algorithm analyzing the whole path was described. The article by Thiagarajan et al. gives yet less details [22]. The paper makes two contributions. Firstly we describe an incremental algorithm that in each iteration updates the HMM model by expanding it with new states corresponding to road segments and contracting to output a certain part of the vehicle trajectory. In most cases the structure of obtained HMM forms a tree similar to that, proposed by Wu et al. [15]. However, our model accepts parallel roads. Our second contribution is the report on performed tests showing that the developed algorithm with applied filtering and interpolation operations is robust enough to handle noisy and downsampled data.

Acknowledgments. This work is supported by the National Centre for Research and Development (NCBiR) under Grant No. O ROB 0021 01/ID 21/2.

References

1. Quddus, M.A., Ochieng, W.Y., Noland, R.B.: Current map-matching algorithms for transport applications: State-of-the art and future research directions. Transportation Research Part C: Emerging Technologies 15(5), 312–328 (2007)
2. White, C.E., Bernstein, D., Kornhauser, A.L.: Some map matching algorithms for personal navigation assistants. Transportation Research Part C: Emerging Technologies 8(1), 91–108 (2000)
3. Greenfeld, J.S.: Matching GPS observations to locations on a digital map. In: National Research Council (US). Transportation Research Board. Meeting (81st: 2002: Washington, DC). Preprint CD-ROM (2002)
4. Quddus, M.A., Ochieng, W.Y., Noland, R.B.: Integrity of map-matching algorithms. Transportation Research Part C: Emerging Technologies 14(4), 283–302 (2006)
5. Quddus, M., Ochieng, W., Zhao, L., Noland, R.: A general map matching algorithm for transport telematics applications. GPS Solutions 7(3), 157–167 (2003)
6. Modsching, M., Kramer, R., ten Hagen, K.: Field trial on GPS accuracy in a medium size city: The influence of built-up. In: 3rd Workshop on Positioning, Navigation and Communication, pp. 209–218 (2006)

7. Zhao, Y.: Vehicle location and navigation systems. Artech House ITS series. Artech House (1997)
8. Ochieng, W.Y., Quddus, M., Noland, R.B.: Map-matching in complex urban road networks. Revista Brasileira de Cartografia 2(55) (2009)
9. Greg Welch, G.B.: An introduction to the Kalman filter, Chapel Hill (2006)
10. Kim, W., Jee, G.I., Lee, J.: Efficient use of digital road map in various positioning for its. In: IEEE Position Location and Navigation Symposium, pp. 170–176 (2000)
11. Syed, S., Cannon, M.: Fuzzy logic-based map matching algorithm for vehicle navigation system in urban canyons. In: Proceedings of the Institute of Navigation (ION) National Technical Meeting, USA (2004)
12. Fu, M., Li, J., Wang, M.: A hybrid map matching algorithm based on fuzzy comprehensive judgment. In: Proceedings of the 7th International IEEE Conference on Intelligent Transportation Systems, pp. 613–617 (2004)
13. Gustafsson, F., Gunnarsson, F., Bergman, N., Forssell, U., Jansson, J., Karlsson, R., Nordlund, P.J.: Particle filters for positioning, navigation, and tracking. IEEE Transactions on Signal Processing 50(2), 425–437 (2002)
14. Marchal, F., Hackney, J., Axhausen, K.: Efficient map-matching of large GPS data sets-tests on a speed monitoring experiment in Zurich. Arbeitsbericht Verkehrs-und Raumplanung 244 (2004)
15. Wu, D., Zhu, T., Lv, W., Gao, X.: A heuristic map-matching algorithm by using vector-based recognition. In: International Multi-Conference on Computing in the Global Information Technology, ICCGI 2007, p. 18 (2007)
16. Brakatsoulas, S., Pfoser, D., Salas, R., Wenk, C.: On map-matching vehicle tracking data. In: Proceedings of the 31st International Conference on Very Large Data Bases, VLDB Endowment, pp. 853–864 (2005)
17. Rabiner, L., Juang, B.: An introduction to hidden Markov models. IEEE ASSP Magazine 3(1), 4–16 (1986)
18. Viterbi, A.: Error bounds for convolutional codes and an asymptotically optimum decoding algorithm. IEEE Transactions on Information Theory 13(2), 260–269 (1967)
19. Hummel, B.: 10. Innovations in GIS. In: Map Matching for Vehicle Guidance. CRC Press (November 2006)
20. Krumm, J., Letchner, J., Horvitz, E.: Map matching with travel time constraints. In: SAE World Congress (2007)
21. Newson, P., Krumm, J.: Hidden Markov map matching through noise and sparseness. In: Proceedings of the 17th ACM SIGSPATIAL International Conference on Advances in Geographic Information Systems, pp. 336–343. ACM (2009)
22. Thiagarajan, A., Ravindranath, L., LaCurts, K., Madden, S., Balakrishnan, H., Toledo, S., Eriksson, J.: Vtrack: accurate, energy-aware road traffic delay estimation using mobile phones. In: Proceedings of the 7th ACM Conference on Embedded Networked Sensor Systems, pp. 85–98. ACM (2009)
23. OpenStreetMap: OpenStreetMap Wiki. (2013), http://wiki.openstreetmap.org/wiki/Main_Page (accessed December 2013)

Machine Learning
for Visual Information Analysis
and Security

Multi-class Classification: A Coding Based Space Partitioning

Sohrab Ferdowsi[1], Sviatoslav Voloshynovskiy[1],
Marcin Gabryel[2], and Marcin Korytkowski[2]

[1] University of Geneva, Centre Universitaire d'Informatique,
Battle Bât. A, 7 route de Drize, 1227 Carouge, Switzerland
[2] Institute of Computational Intelligence, Częstochowa University of Technology
Al. Armii Krajowej 36, 42-200 Częstochowa, Poland

Abstract. In this work we address the problem of multi-class classification in machine learning. In particular, we consider the coding approach which converts a multi-class problem to several binary classification problems by mapping the binary labeled space into several partitioned binary labeled spaces through binary channel codes. By modeling this learning problem as a communication channel, these codes are meant to have error correcting capabilities and thus performance improvement in classification. However, we argue that conventional coding schemes designed for communication systems do not treat the space partitioning problem optimally, because they are heedless of the partitioning behavior of underlying binary classifiers. We discuss an approach which is optimal in terms of space partitioning and advise it as a powerful tool towards multi-class classification. We then review the LDA, a known method for multi-class case and compare its performance with the proposed method. We run the experiments on synthetic data in several scenarios and then on a real database for face identification.

Keywords: Multi-Class Classification, Error Correcting Output Codes, Support Vector Machines, Linear Discriminant Analysis.

1 Introduction

The general multi-class classification is a fundamentally important problem that can find many different applications in different domains. Classification of alphabet letters from a handwritten document, phoneme segmentation in speech processing, face identification and content identification of multimedia segments are among the application examples of this problem. Although studied for many years, it is still considered as an open issue and none of the many proposed methods achieve superior performance under all conditions for different applications.

In binary classification where there are only two classes, many methods exist that are well developed to tackle different classification scenarios. However, they are designed naturally to address the binary case and their extension to multiclass is either not possible or is not straightforward. One way to accommodate

L. Rutkowski et al. (Eds.): ICAISC 2014, Part II, LNAI 8468, pp. 593–604, 2014.

for the multi-class case and still use the existing powerful binary algorithms is to
break a multi-class problem to several binary problems and combine the results
together. This method is done in several ways.

Among the existing methods that convert the multi-class problem to several
binary ones there is the famous one-vs-all approach which considers each of the
classes in each binary classification problem to be classified against the rest. This
requires to run the binary classification algorithm $M - 1$ times. In fact, because
the situation is not symmetric, it might be the case that these binary problems
are very different from each other in nature which might be problematic in
practice. Another method would be to consider each pair of classes together. This
method, known as one-vs-one approach, requires $\frac{M(M-1)}{2}$ binary classifications
to capture all the combinations between the data.

These methods, while could work for small M's, will seriously fail as M grows
because the number of binary classifications to be carried out would be intractable. The fact that in order to identify M objects would naturally require
$\log_2 |\mathcal{M}|$ binary descriptors has motivated an extensive research in the field. A
significant achievement was due to Dietterich [1] who made an analogy between
the problem of classification and communication channel and thus suggested
to consider it as a channel coding problem. This idea was followed by further
research and study, however, no significant results have been reported.

An essential element of Dietterich approach is the selection of coding matrix.
A coding matrix design was proposed in [2] which was shown to be optimal in
terms of space partitioning for the problem of content identification of objects.
In this paper we relax the assumption of identification where in each class there
is only one instance and instead we address the general problem of multi-class
classification where there is an arbitrary number of classes and arbitrary number
of instances in each class as the training examples. We compare it with the Linear
Discriminant Analysis (LDA), an efficient multi-class classification schemes in
different classification scenarios and show that it could be efficiently used also
for the general problem of multi-class classification.

LDA is a powerful technique in statistics that aims at finding a set of
transformed features in a reduced dimension space such that they give best
discrimination among classes. The use of LDA in machine learning, although
not popularized, but has been extensively studied at least for the binary case.
In an experimental study in [3], the use of LDA for multi-class classificaion has
been investigated. It is shown that this method, although with certain limitations regarding its assumption on the distributions of classes, can serve as an
efficient classification method also for the multi-class case.

The paper is organized as follows: In Section 2 we study the problem of multi-
class classification. We review the coding approach for multi-class classification
and introduce a method to optimally solve it. We then consider the LDA method
towards multi-class classification. The experimental results are reported in Section 3. We finally summarize the paper in Section 4.

2   Multi-class Classification

In this section we first consider the binary classification and the SVM approach to solve it. We then define the problem of multi-class classification and explain an important approach towards solving this problem known as Error Correcting Output Codes (ECOC)[1]. Finally, we consider the design method introduced in [2] as the basis for our later discussions.

2.1   Binary Classification Using Support Vector Machines

Here we consider the general formulation of Support Vector Machine (SVM) for binary case. SVM is considered to be one of the most successful machine learning approaches for the binary supervised learning classification. When the two classes are linearly separable, the SVM algorithm tries to find a separating hyperplane such that it has the maximum margin from the closest instances of the two classes. The closest instances from each class are also called support vectors. This criterion, under certain conditions, is proved to guarantee the best generalization performance.

Concretely, given the training instances as $\mathbf{x}(i)$'s with $1 \le i \le s$ and $\mathbf{x}(i) \in \mathbb{R}^N$ and their binary labels as $g(\mathbf{x}(i)) \in \{-1, +1\}$ for each of $\mathbf{x}(i)$'s, we seek to find a hyperplane in $\mathbb{R}^N$ characterized by $\mathbf{w} \in \mathbb{R}^N$ and b such that it correctly classifies all the examples while it has the largest margin. Solving this problem is formulated as the optimization problem of (1). The objective function is maximizing the margin and the constraints try to ensure that the training instances are correctly classified, i.e., their predicted labels are the same as their true labels.

$$\begin{aligned} \underset{\mathbf{w}}{\text{minimize}} \quad & \frac{1}{2}\mathbf{w}^T\mathbf{w} \\ \text{subject to} \quad & g(\mathbf{x}(i))\left(\mathbf{w}^T\mathbf{x}(i) + b\right), \ i = 1, \dots, s. \end{aligned} \tag{1}$$

This optimization problem, or its other variants are treated using quadratic programming techniques and many powerful packages are designed to practically handle it.

For the case where the training instances are not linearly separable, the above formulation can be modified by using the kernels technique. The idea is to use kernels which are pre-designed nonlinear functions that map the input space to a higher dimensional space. It could be the case that the instances in the new space are linearly separable. Therefore, (1) can be modified and used to find the best separating boundary between the instances in the higher dimensional space.

A useful method to gain insight into the spatial geometry of the instances could be derived from Voronoi diagrams. A Voronoi diagram is a way of partitioning the space into convex cells where in each cell there is only one instance from the given examples. The cells are chosen such that all the points in the cell are closest to the corresponding instance than other instances in space. Based on this definition, one could easily confirm that the SVM boundaries, when trained with enough parameters, should in fact follow the Voronoi cells of the set of support vectors. Figure 1 shows this phenomenon.

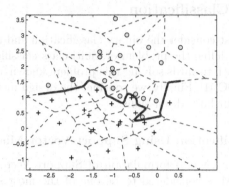

Fig. 1. SVM boundaries (solid lines) following the Voronoi cells (dashed lines) of the support vectors

It is important to mention that in all of these analyses, we are using the l_2-norm as the measure of distance. Other norms could also be studied which could offer advantages for some applications where the distortions have a non-Gaussian character.

2.2   Multi-class Classification: Problem Formulation

A set of training instances are given which contain features, $\mathbf{x}(i) \in \mathbb{R}^N$ and their labels $g(\mathbf{x}(i))$'s belonging to any of the M classes. These labels are assumed to have been generated through an unknown hypothetical mapping function $g : \mathbb{R}^N \longmapsto \{1, 2, ..., M\}$ that we want to approximate based on the given labeled training examples. The labels, unlike the common cases in machine learning, belong to a set of $M \geq 2$ members rather than only two classes. Because most of the existing classification algorithms are naturally designed for $M = 2$ classes, to generalize them for multi-class cases usually requires to consider the problem as several binary classification problems.

2.3   Coding Approach for Multi-class Classification

The main idea behind the Error Correcting Output Codes (ECOC) approach to solve the multi-class problem is to consider it as a communication system where the identity of the correct output class for a given unlabeled example is being transmitted over a hypothetical channel which, due to the imperfections of the training data, the errors in the learning process and non-ideal choice of features is considered to be noisy [1]. Therefore, it would make sense to try to encode the classes using error correcting codes and transmit each of the bits through the channel, i.e., to run the learning algorithm, so that we would be able to cope with the errors in each individual binary classifier. Figure 2 illustrates this idea.

Concretely, we assign randomly to each of the M classes a row of a coding matrix $\mathcal{C}_{(M \times l)}$. Then we run a binary learning algorithm on all the training

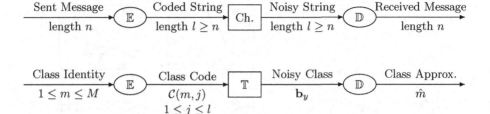

Fig. 2. Communication system and its classification equivalent: $\mathbb{E}$ and $\mathbb{D}$ are the Encoding and Decoding stages in communication, respectively. $\mathbb{T}$ is the training procedure, $\mathcal{C}$ is the coding matrix, $\mathbf{b}_y$ is the derived binary code for the test example.

samples for every column of $\mathcal{C}$ so that we will have l mappings from $\mathbb{R}^N$, the original data space to the one dimensional binary space $\{0, 1\}$, or equivalently, one mapping rule from $\mathbb{R}^N$ to the l-dimensional binary space $\{0, 1\}^l$.

Given a new unlabeled example $\mathbf{y}$, we map it from $\mathbb{R}^N$ to the l-dimensional binary space through the same mapping rule learned as above. We then compare this binary representation $\mathbf{b}_y$ with the items in the database, or equivalently the rows of $\mathcal{C}$ by minimum Hamming distance rule or any other relevant decoding method.

Coding Matrix Design. An important concern in this method is the choice of the coding matrix. Using the techniques from coding theory the main focus of the researchers has been to design elements of $\mathcal{C}$ optimally to be able to combat against noise while keeping the rate of communication as close to 1 as possible, which implies fewer number of binary classifications. Through this end, most design strategies were in essence aiming to maximize the Hamming distance between the rows of $\mathcal{C}$[4].

Another approach in the design of this matrix is to assign the elements randomly. It is shown that this random assignment approach could do as good as the previous coding-oriented designs [5,6].

It is important to mention that in the design of channel codes, e.g., famous codes like BCH or LDPC, it is generally assumed that the channel noise, in our case the bit flippings of $\mathbf{b}_y$ due to the classification process, is *i.i.d.*, or at least is independent of the input codewords. In the case of classification where we have a hypothetical channel representing the behavior of the learning algorithm, however, we can observe that these bit flippings, or equivalently the channel noise samples are highly correlated with the input codewords. Therefore, many of the information theoretic explanations based on notions like typicality could no longer be valid. To address this issue, we consider this problem from a learning theoretic viewpoint.

Optimal Coding. As mentioned earlier in section 1, a coding design was suggested in [2] which was shown to be optimal in terms of space partitioning. An intuitive explanation for this fact is presented below.

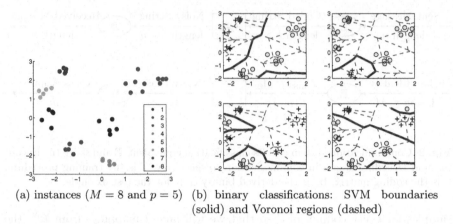

(a) instances ($M = 8$ and $p = 5$)   (b) binary classifications: SVM boundaries
(solid) and Voronoi regions (dashed)

Fig. 3. Instances of the original multi-class problem and the corresponding binary classifications

Figure 3(a) shows the class instances and figure 3(b) shows the the corresponding decision boundaries of a binarized multi-class classification problem with $M = 8$ and $p = 5$ two dimensional instances for every class. As is clear from figure 3(b) and was discussed earlier in 1, the decision boundaries follow the outer Voronoi cells of each class. Notice that the choice of $\mathcal{C}$ dictates that in each of the l classifications, some of the adjacent classes be grouped together and labeled as '0' and some be grouped as '1' and also this labeling and grouping could be changed in each classification.

Therefore, in order to design an optimal coding matrix, we ask the question: Which choice of the elements of $\mathcal{C}$ guaranties learning at least one time these relevant Voronoi regions while avoiding redundant boundary learning? The first requirement links with having good performance via optimal class separability and the latter implies maintaining the number of columns (classifiers) as small as possible, i.e, having maximal rate of communication.

Equivalently, the optimal assignment of codewords should work as a unique and non-redundant encoding of each class with the decision boundaries of SVM classifier following the Voronoi regions between the corresponding classes.

This optimal design, in fact happens when the rows of $\mathcal{C}$ are chosen simply as the modulo-2 equivalent of the the class numbers. Therefore, as an example, in a 20-class problem, the codewords will be of length $l = \lceil \log_2 M \rceil = 5$, the 1st class should be encoded as the binary string '00000', and the 6th class should be encoded as '00101'.

Intuitively, considering each of the two adjacent classes, this approach assigns to each of them a codeword where they differ in at least one position. This satisfies our first objective because it guaranties that each pair of rows of $\mathcal{C}$ that could be assigned to two adjacent classes finds at least one position where the bit values are different. Therefore, they will be mapped into two different classes at least once which implies that the decision boundary will cross between them at least once.

With this approach, the second requirement is also fully satisfied. Since the length of each codeword, i.e, the number of columns of $\mathcal{C}$ equals $l = \lceil \log_2 M \rceil$ which is minimal and the rate of communication is exactly 1.

In essence, the optimality of this approach is based on the fact that we learn the relevant Voronoi regions optimally. In fact learning the Voronoi regions of the support vectors is also equivalent to the maximum likelihood rule under Gaussian assumption for the classes. It is important to mention that we are using SVM classifiers with nonlinear kernels that are properly tuned. Other learning rules do not necessarily learn these Voronoi regions accurately and also the improper choice of kernel parameters does not guarantee learning these regions properly.

While ML decoding rule requires the knowledge of Voronoi regions for all classes, in our approach, these regions are distributed among the l binary classifiers and are learned implicitly. The fusion of the results of all binary classifiers, equivalently produces the entire coverage for all classes defined by their Voronoi regions. Therefore, the results of these fused binary decoding scheme should coincide with the optimal ML decoder.

It is also very important to mention that given a test example to be classified, unlike any other method, the complexity of decoding in this approach comprises only the SVM functional evaluations and does not incur any Hamming distance computation or decoding computations as in LDPC or other coding methods. The reason is due to the fact that a produced codeword is directly referring to a storage point in memory, hence no computation at all. However, the SVM functional evaluations involved could be very high if the nonlinear kernels are too complex.

2.4 Linear Discriminant Analysis

In this part we review the Discriminant Analysis approach which is a collection of techniques in statistical pattern recognition that try to find a set of discriminating features from the data by transforming them into a lower dimensional space. With their small complexity, their powerful behaviour in many classification scenarios and their theoretical importance, they are considered to be a good method of choice for many problems. Here we consider the famous LDA for the multi-class case.

Multi-class LDA Formulation. Given the training dataset as $\mathcal{X} = [\mathbf{x}(1), \mathbf{x}(2),$ $\cdots, \mathbf{x}(s)]^T$ with instance $\mathbf{x}(i) \in \mathbb{R}^N$, labeled as belonging to any of the M classes, c_i's, the objective is to find a transformation $\mathbb{W} \in \mathbb{R}^{N \times (M-1)}$ such that it maps the data into an $M-1$ dimensional space $\tilde{\mathcal{X}} = \mathcal{X}\mathbb{W}$ such that the data could be discriminated more easily. Equivalently, it draws $M-1$ hyperplanes between the M classes.

Given a testing sample $\mathbf{y}$, we transform it to the new space as $\tilde{\mathbf{y}} = \mathbf{y}^T \mathbb{W}$. We then find the transformed class center $\tilde{\mu}_i = \mu_i^T \mathbb{W}$ where $\mu_i = \frac{1}{p_i} \sum_{\mathbf{x} \in c_i} \mathbf{x}$, such that it has the smallest Euclidean distance to $\tilde{\mathbf{y}}$. The sample $\mathbf{y}$ is then classified to c_i.

The transform $\mathbb{W}$ should be found such that in the transformed space, the inter-class distances are the highest while the intra-class distances between the instances are the lowest, which is equivalent to having the maximal distinguishability between the classes.

Concretely, we define the intra-class scatter matrix for class c_i as:

$$\hat{S}_i = \sum_{\mathbf{x} \in c_i} (\mathbf{x} - \mu_i)(\mathbf{x} - \mu_i)^T \tag{2}$$

and the total intra-class scatter matrix as:

$$\hat{S}_{intra} = \sum_{i=1}^{M} \hat{S}_i. \tag{3}$$

The inter-class scatter matrix is defined as:

$$\hat{S}_{inter} = \sum_{i=1}^{M} p_i(\mu_i - \mu)(\mu_i - \mu)^T, \tag{4}$$

where $\mu = \frac{1}{s}\sum_{i=1}^{M} p_i \mu_i$. Jointly maximizing the inter-class scatter of the data in the transformed space and minimizing their intra-class scatters is equivalent to solving the generalized eigenvalue problem in (5),

$$\hat{S}_{inter}\mathbb{W} = \lambda\hat{S}_{intra}\mathbb{W} \tag{5}$$

Based on the $\mathbb{W}$ derived from Eq. 5, the test data $\mathbf{y}$ is classified as:

$$\hat{c} = \underset{i}{\operatorname{argmin}} \|\mathbf{y}\mathbb{W} - \mu_i\mathbb{W}\|_2, \tag{6}$$

which is searching for the closest class center to the test example in the transformed domain.

LDA for Multi-class Classification. LDA, along with its other variants could be considered as reliable methods for multiclass classification. The computational complexity of this approach could be significantly lower than other methods. However, there are certain limitations with this method.

Unlike the SVM classifier discussed above which only considers the boundary instances, LDA assumes an underlying distribution for the data. Therefore, in order for the distribution estimation to be accurate, the number of training instances, compared to the data dimension should not be small. This could be a serious limiting factor, as it could be the case in many applications that the training data are limited. Moreover, the underlying distribution under which the method is successful is assumed to be Gaussian. Therefore, deviations from Gaussianity could seriously affect the performance. We investigate this fact in our experimental results.

It is also important to point out that LDA tries to maximize distinguishability and does not necessarily consider minimizing the training error. For the multiclass case, in the eigenvalue decomposition problem of (5), pairs of classes between which there are large distances, completely dominate the decomposition. Therefore, in the transformed space, the classes with smaller distances will be overlapped [3].

3   Experimental Results

In this section we experimentally study the discussed approaches under different practical scenarios. Since there are many different parameters involved, especially for the multi-class case, to compare different algorithms is not trivial. The data dimension, the size of the training set, the way the instances of different classes are mixed with each other and the underlying distributions of the classes could significantly affect the classification scenario. Especially, when we generalize from binary to the multi-class case, we could see that these parameters and their relative values could radically change the scenario.

Therefore, instead of using only the current available databases which are very limited in terms of being rich in having different combinations of the parameters and therefore capturing a meaningful generality of an arbitrary scenario, we also experimented with synthetic databases. This way we can have the possibility to arbitrarily change these parameters.

We first experiment the case where we generate the data from a Gaussian distribution where we can have control over inter-class and intra-class variances. We then experiment the case where each class is generated as a mixture of Gaussians. We finally report the result of comparison over the *ExtendedYaleB* [7] database for face recognition.

3.1   Synthetic Data

We perform the experiments on the synthetic data in two parts. First we consider Gaussian distribution for the classes. In order to imitate more realistic solutions, we then experiment with the cases where the classes follow mixtures of several Gaussians.

Gaussian Data. We generate centers of classes as $\mathbf{x}_c(i) \in \mathbb{R}^N$ with $\mathbf{X}_c \sim \mathcal{N}(\mathbf{0}, \sigma_{inter}^2 \mathbb{I}_N)$ and $1 \leq i \leq M$. We then generate the jth instance of class c_i as $\mathbf{x}(j) = \mathbf{x}_c(i) + \mathbf{Z}_{intra}$ with $\mathbf{Z}_{intra} \sim \mathcal{N}(\mathbf{0}, \sigma_{intra}^2 \mathbb{I}_N)$. The test data are generated as Additive White Gaussian Noise with covariance matrix $\sigma_z^2 \mathbb{I}_N$ added to the centers of each class. We measure the performance of algorithms with accuracy which is defined as the ratio of all the correctly classified items to the whole test set size.

Figure 4(a) depicts the results of classification when the number of classes were chosen as $M = 16$, the data dimension as $N = 15$ and the inter-class and intra-class scatters were chosen as $\sigma_{inter}^2 = 10$ and $\sigma_{intra}^2 = 1$, respectively. The independent variable was the SNR which is defined as $SNR = 10 \log_{10} \frac{\sigma_{inter}^2}{\sigma_z^2}$. The comparison was made between four methods. The first method is to classify a test item based on its Euclidean distance closeness to the centers of each of the classes, estimated from the training data. This approach, given the Gaussian assumption for each of the classes, is optimal in terms of Maximum-Likelihood rule. The second method is the multi-class LDA. The third method is the discussed ECOC-based space partitioning with optimal coding matrix design. The forth method is ECOC when the matrix was randomly chosen. For the two last methods, the number of classifiers were $l = 4$ and the binary classifiers were SVM with Gaussian kernels. The number of train and test instances per each of the classes were chosen as 100 in all experiments. Figure 4(b) is the result of the same experiment but with a different ratio for inter-class and intra-class scatters. They were chosen as $\sigma^2_{inter} = 1$ and $\sigma^2_{intra} = 1$. As can be seen from figure 4(b), because the instances of each class are very scattered within the instances of the neighboring classes, the underlying binary SVM with Gaussian kernel tends to hugely overtrain on these training data, thus they fail to generalize on the test set. It is important to mention that the good behavior of the first two methods is due to the unrealistic Gaussian setup considered. We will see in the next experiments that this performance could radically decrease as we change the data distribution to more realistic ones.

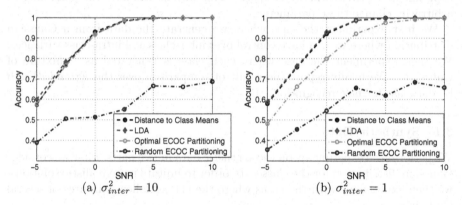

(a) $\sigma^2_{inter} = 10$ (b) $\sigma^2_{inter} = 1$

Fig. 4. Accuracy vs. SNR for Gaussian Data ($M = 16$, $N = 15$)

Gaussian Mixtures. In this part every class is assumed to have 5 Gaussian clouds from which the instances are generated. The class centers are generated as before. The centers of Gaussian clouds for class i, centered on $\mathbf{x}(i)$ are generated from another Gaussian distribution with covariance matrix $\sigma^2_{cloud}\mathbb{I}_N$. The class instances are then generated as Gaussians which are centered on the cloud centers with covariance σ^2_{intra}.

Figure 5(a) is the result of experiment when there were $M = 16$ classes with dimension $N = 15$. The variances were $\sigma^2_{inter} = 1$, $\sigma^2_{cloud} = 1$ and $\sigma^2_{intra} = 1$ and each of the 5 clouds there were 25 training and test examples.

Figure 5(b) is the result of the same experiment with a more scattered clouds than the previous experiment, i.e., $\sigma^2_{cloud} = 10$ was changed.

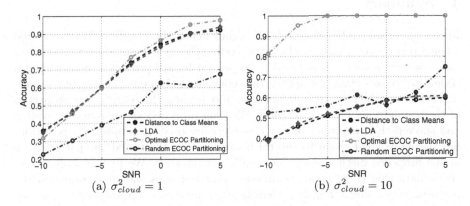

(a) $\sigma^2_{cloud} = 1$ (b) $\sigma^2_{cloud} = 10$

Fig. 5. Accuracy vs. SNR for Mixture of Gaussian Data ($M = 16$, $N = 15$)

As can be seen from 5(b), the first two methods are obviously sub-optimal for this scenario. However, the discussed ECOC-based space partitioning method can successfully cope with it. Also, in all of the experiments, it is clearly seen that random coding, when the number of its binary classifiers is small, cannot provide a good performance. To resolve this, also to avoid the fluctuating results seen in all the figures, one should add more columns to the coding matrix, or equivalently increase the number of binary classifications, while the optimal coding approach achieves the best performance with the least number of binary classifications. This optimality is of course limited and dictated by the choice of underlying classifications.

3.2   Face Identification

To compare the performance of the discussed methods on the real data, we used the *ExtendedYaleB* [7] database for face identification. There were 28 people, from each of them 500 face images were taken under different lighting conditions. We randomly chose 250 images from each for training and 250 for testing. The images were resized to 128×128 pixels and then directly vectorized. Random Projections were used to reduce the dimension of the features from $N = 16384$ to $L = 50$. The instances were then fed to the same four methods. For the last two methods, $l = \lceil log_2 28 \rceil = 5$ binary SVM's with Gaussian kernels were used. Table 1 illustrates the results.

Table 1. Accuracy of different methods on *ExtendedYaleB* Database

Method	Euclidean Distance to Class Means	LDA	Optimal ECOC Partitioning	Random ECOC Partitioning
Accuracy	0.8771	0.8944	**0.9967**	0.7141

4   Summary

In this paper we studied the problem of multi-class classification. We considered a general approach which was based on coding theory in communication systems that converts a multi-class problem to several binary problems by assigning a codeword to each class. We argued that conventional channel codes are not optimal for this problem as they do not take into account the partitioning properties of their underlying binary classifiers. We then proposed an approach for coding and showed that, if proper binary classifiers are used, it is optimally partitioning the multi-label space to several binary spaces. We tested the performance of the proposed methodology under different datasets. We first generated synthetic data that could simulate different real scenarios and then compared the performances under a real face identification database. The method was shown to be superior under more realistic classification scenarios. However, it was seen that because complex binary SVM's were used, one should be careful to avoid over-training of the underlying classifiers.

Acknowledgments. The work presented in this paper was supported by a grant from Switzerland through the Swiss Contribution to the enlarged European Union (PSPB-125/2010).

References

1. Dietterich, T.G., Bakiri, G.: Solving multiclass learning problems via error-correcting output codes. J. Artif. Intell. Res. (JAIR) 2, 263–286 (1995)
2. Ferdowsi, S., Voloshynovskiy, S., Kostadinov, D.: Content identification: binary content fingerprinting versus binary content encoding. In: Proceedings of SPIE Photonics West, Electronic Imaging, Media Forensics and Security V, San Francisco, USA (January 23, 2014)
3. Li, T., Zhu, S., Ogihara, M.: Using discriminant analysis for multi-class classification: an experimental investigation. Knowledge and Information Systems 10(4), 453–472 (2006)
4. Murphy, K.P.: Machine Learning: A Probabilistic Perspective. Adaptive Computation and Machine Learning series. The MIT Press (August 2012)
5. James, G., Hastie, T.: The error coding method and picts. J. Computational and Graphical Statistics 7(3), 377–387 (1998)
6. Voloshynovskiy, S., Koval, O., Beekhof, F., Holotyak, T.: Information-theoretic multiclass classification based on binary classifiers. Signal Processing Systems 65, 413–430 (2011) (accepted)
7. Lee, K., Ho, J., Kriegman, D.: Acquiring linear subspaces for face recognition under variable lighting. IEEE Trans. Pattern Anal. Mach. Intelligence 27(5), 684–698 (2005)

From Single Image to List of Objects Based on Edge and Blob Detection

Rafał Grycuk[1], Marcin Gabryel[1], Marcin Korytkowski[1],
Rafał Scherer[1], and Sviatoslav Voloshynovskiy[2]

[1] Institute of Computational Intelligence, Częstochowa University of Technology
Al. Armii Krajowej 36, 42-200 Częstochowa, Poland
{rafal.grycuk,marcin.gabryel,marcin.korytkowski,
rafal.scherer}@iisi.pcz.pl
http://iisi.pcz.pl
[2] University of Geneva, Computer Science Department,
7 Route de Drize, Geneva, Switzerland
http://sip.unige.ch

Abstract. In this paper we present a new method for obtaining a list of interest objects from a single image. Our object extraction method works on two well known algorithms: the Canny edge detection method and the quadrilaterals detection. Our approach allows to select only the significant elements of the image. In addition, this method allows to filter out unnecessary key points in a simple way (for example obtained by the SIFT algorithm) from the background image. The effectiveness of the method is confirmed by experimental research.

1 Introduction

Content-based image retrieval is one of the greatest challenges of present computer science. Effective browsing and retrieving images is required in many various fields of life e.g. medicine, architecture, forensic, publishing, fashion, archives and many others. In the process of image recognition users search through databases which consist of thousands, even millions of images. The aim can be the retrieval of a similar image or images containing certain objects [4][6]. Retrieving mechanisms use image recognition methods. This is a sophisticated process which requires the use of algorithms from many different areas such as computational intelligence [7][8][12][20][21][22][24][27][29][32], machine learning [23], mathematics [2][13] and image processing [11]. An interesting approach for CBIR, based on nonparametric estimates (see e.g. [14][25][26]) was presented in [10].

One of important aspects of content-based image retrieval is the ability to find specific objects in the image. This is particularly important in the case of large image databases which are searched for specific objects. Many ways to detect objects can be found in the literature and one of them is image segmentation. The goal of the image segmentation is to cluster pixels into salient image regions, i.e. regions corresponding to individual surfaces, objects, or natural parts

L. Rutkowski et al. (Eds.): ICAISC 2014, Part II, LNAI 8468, pp. 605–615, 2014.
© Springer International Publishing Switzerland 2014

of objects. There are many methods for image segmentation: thresholding [3], clustering methods [1], histogram-based methods [30], edge detection [28], stereo vision based methods [16] and many others. We propose a new method for extracting objects from images. This method consists of two parts: the Canny edge detection method [5] and the method for quadrilaterals detection [17]. An important element in our algorithm is the additional step which consists in filtering out the key points from the background. The result is an image with key points only in the most interesting areas of the image.

Our method uses the SIFT (Scale-invariant feature transform) algorithm to detect and describe local features of an image. It was presented for the first time in [18] and is now patented by the University of British Columbia. For each key point which describes the local image feature, we generate a feature vector, that can be used for further processing. SIFT contains four main steps [15][19]: extraction of potential key points, selection of stable key points (resistant to change of scale and rotation), finding key point orientation immune to the image transformation, generating a vector describing the key point. SIFT key points contain 128 values.

The paper consists of several sections. In the next sections we will present methods used in the proposed approach and a method for image segmentation algorithm. The last section presents the experimental results on an original software written in .NET.

2   Canny Edge Detection

The Canny edge detector [5] is one of the most commonly used image processing methods for detecting edges. It takes as input a gray scale image, and produces as output an image showing the positions of tracked intensity discontinuities. The algorithm runs in 5 separate steps:

1. Noise reduction. The image is smoothed by applying an appropriate Gaussian filter.
2. Finding the intensity gradient of the image. During this step the edges should be marked where gradients of the image have large magnitudes.
3. Non-maxima suppression. If the gradient magnitude at a pixel is larger than those at its two neighbors in the gradient direction, mark the pixel as an edge. Otherwise, mark the pixel as the background.
4. Edge tracking by hysteresis. Final edges are determined by suppressing all edges that are not connected to genuine edges.

The effect of the Canny operator is determined by parameters:

- The width of the Gaussian filter used in the first stage directly affects the results of the Canny algorithm,
- The thresholds used during edge tracking by hysteresis. It is difficult to give a generic threshold that works well on all images.

3 Blob Extraction

Blob extraction is one of the basic methods of image processing. It allows to detect and extract a list of blobs (objects) in the image. Unfortunately, obtaining homogeneous objects from an image as a list of pixels is extremely complicated. Especially when we deal with a heterogeneous background, i.e. the objects containing multicolored background. There are many methods for extracting objects (blobs) from images [9]. In this paper we use methods implemented in the AForge.NET library. These algorithms are described by Andrew Kirillov [17]. There are four types of the algorithms: Convex full, Left/Right Edges, Top/Bottom Edges, Quadrilateral. Fig.1 describes these blob detection methods. Figure 6A illustrates Quadrilaterals detection method. As can be seen, round edges of the objects are not detected correctly. Much better results are obtained by the Top/Bottom Edges algorithm (Figure 1C). Edges of objects are detected mostly correctly, with individual exceptions. The Left/Right Edges method behaves similarly (Fig. 1B). The last method has a problem with the detection of vertices inside figures, e.g. star type objects (Fig. 1D). Quadrilateral detection method can be described by the following steps:

1. Locate each separate object in the input image,
2. Find object edge pixels (methods: Top/Bottom, Left/Right),
3. Detect four corners of quadrilateral,

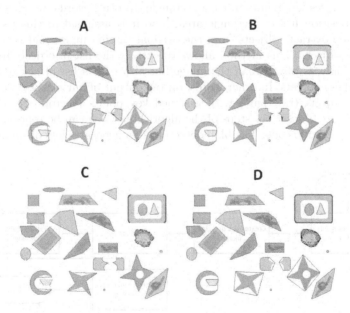

Fig. 1. Comparison of methods for blob detection used in the AForge.NET library [17]

4. Set *distortionLimit*. This value determines how different the object can be. Set 0 to detect perfect quadrilateral,
5. Check how well the analyzed shape fits into the quadrilateral with the assumed parameter (see Fig. 1D).
6. Check each mean distance between given edge pixels and the edge of assumed quadrilateral,
7. If mean distance is not greater then *distortionLimit*, then we can assume that the shape is quadrilateral.

4   Proposed Method for Segmentation Algorithm

In this section we present a new approach to segmentation. When we have a single image described by pixel matrix (e.g. RGB), we can segment it into many objects. This section describes a methodology of this process. The algorithm can be divided into several steps. First of all we need to create mathematical description of the input image. In this step we use the SIFT algorithm. In return we obtain a list of key points (whole image). The next step is to create edge detected image. In this step we use the Canny algorithm described in section 2. Another step detects blobs, with all their properties such as: center of gravity, area, mean color, blob rectangle, position. When we have detected these object contours as blobs, we can extract rectangles for these objects. The next step detects and saves key points in each rectangle. In other words, we check if the key point position lies in rectangle area, if so it is assigned to this rectangle. The last step extracts objects from the original (input) image and saves them as separate objects. This method allows to extract the list of objects from the image, not only as raw part of the image but also with a list of key points assigned to these objects. In other words, on the output of our method we obtain the list of objects (raw part) with assigned key points (vectors) to each object [31]. Figure 2 describes steps of the algorithm, witch can be represented by the following pseudo code: The blob detection step generates lots of small blobs.

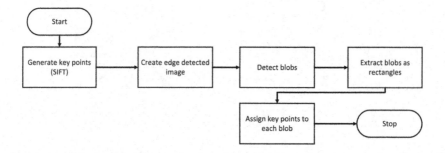

Fig. 2. Block diagram of the proposed method

INPUT: Single image, *singleInputImage*
OUTPUT: Segmented image, list of objects with descriptors assign to each object, *descriptorsList, objectsList*
allDescriptors := Generate_Descriptor(*singleInputImage*);
edgedImage := Canny_Edge_Detector(*singleInputImage*, *thesh*,
threshLinking);
blobs := Detect_Blobs(*edgedImage*);
foreach *blob* ∈ *blobs* **do**
    if *blob.Area* >= *minBlobArea* **then**
        extractedBlob := Extract_Blob(*singleInputImage*, *startPosition*,
        blob.Width, blob.Heigth);
        objectsList.Add_To_List(*extractedBlob*);
        extractedDescriptor := Extract_Descriptor(*allDescriptors*,
        startPosition, blob.Width, blob.Heigth);
        descriptorsList.Add_To_List(*extractedDescriptor*);
    end
end

Algorithm 1. Segmentation steps

The $minBlobArea$ describes min area for extracted objects. All blobs with area equal or greater will be extracted. For blob detection process we use Quadrilaterals detection method (see section 3). The extraction process (blob and descriptor extraction) is realized simply by copying entire blob rectangle into newly created image (pixel by pixel, key point by key point).

Algorithm stages were implemented in .NET C# using AForge and Emgu CV libraries. The first and second step is based on Emgu CV. The third was implemented using AForge. Two last steps were implemented by the authors.

5   Experimental Results

In this section we present the results of the experiments. For this purpose we created simulation application based on described algorithms. On the input we can put a single image and in return we obtain the list of objects with assigned key points. Images in simulations were labelled as follows:

- Input images were labelled by characters (i.e. A,B,C...)
- Extracted objects were labelled by object number and letter of input image (i.e. 1A means first objects from image A.)

Figure 3 presents input images of four simulations. Three of them (A,C,D) are from the same image class (cars), but they were taken from different perspective. In Fig. 4 we present the results of the proposed method. For each input image (A,B,C,D) we obtain a list of objects (1A, 2A,...,1B, 2B...). As we can see the algorithm segmented the image properly. Figure 5 illustrates another type of images i.e. astro images, underwater images, many different objects. These images were given as the algorithm input and were segmented correctly. Object 5G in

Fig. 6 was not entirely extracted. The rest of the objects (image G) were separated properly. Table 1 and tab. 6 represent segmented key points. First column describes object id (i.e. 1A) and the second determine key points count for each object. The third represents input image key point count (before segmentation).

Figure 7A presents the input image after key points detection. As can be seen, the SIFT algorithm detects multiple key points in background of the image. They are located both on objects and background. The next step is Canny edge detection. This part of the algorithm is extremely important. Performing blob detection on the input image is pointless because, the algorithm detects only one blob (the entire image). To eliminate this drawback we use Canny edge detection as preprocessing. Then, on that image type we execute the blob detection algorithm. After that, we extract those blobs simply by copy the entire rectangle represented by this blob. As can be see in Fig. 7B, not significant key points has been reduced. We obtain extracted objects saved as separated images.

Fig. 3. Simulation input images. Experiments A-D.

6   Final Remarks

The presented method is a novel approach for image segmentation. Conducted experiments proved effectiveness of our method. Algorithm takes a single RGB image as input and returns a list of objects as output. Most of extracted objects are detected correctly, but some images contain fragments of other objects. This is caused by intersection of these objects. The next step of our research will be color distinction of obtained objects to remove non homogeneous objects. Our method extracts objects from different types of images, such as: astro images, underwater images and many others.

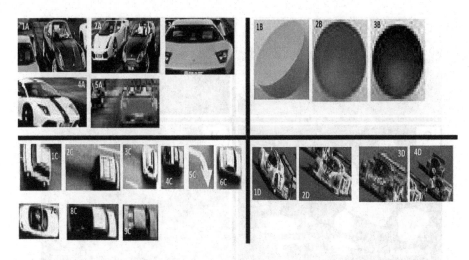

Fig. 4. Objects obtained from images presented in Fig 3. Experiments A-D. Object labels correspond with the input image (eg. 1B, 2B .., are objects belongs to input image B).

Table 1. Key points extraction, experiments A-D. Key points are assigned to each object. The labels correspond with Fig. 4.

Table 2. Key points extraction, experiments E-G. Key points are assigned to each object. The labels correspond with Fig. 6.

Blob number	Object key points count	Input image key points count
1A	138	
2A	65	
3A	248	795
4A	160	
5A	175	
1B	10	
2B	5	47
3B	16	
1C	137	
2C	107	
3C	172	
4C	201	
5C	39	1143
6C	189	
7C	71	
8C	48	
9C	82	
1D	43	
2D	41	247
3D	60	
4D	77	

Blob number	Object key points count	Input image key points count
1E	241	
2E	326	868
3E	281	
1F	63	
2F	53	141
3F	18	
1G	239	
2G	67	
3G	87	
4G	45	
5G	79	
6G	11	835
7G	15	
8G	75	
9G	70	
10G	33	
11G	97	
1H	264	849
2H	301	

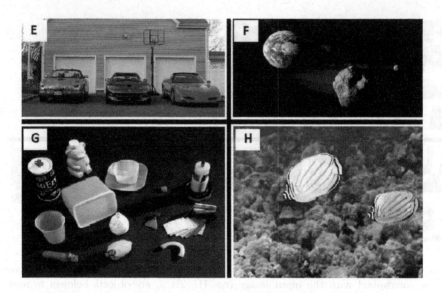

Fig. 5. Simulation input images. Experiments E-H.

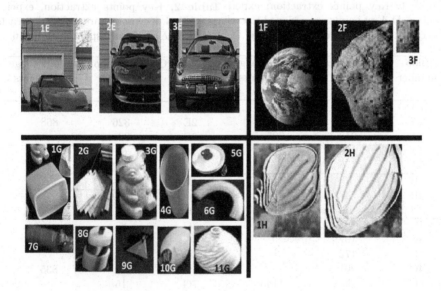

Fig. 6. Objects obtained from images presented in Fig 5. Experiments E-H. Object labels corresponding with input image (e.g. 1G, 2G,..,) are objects that belongs to input image G).

Fig. 7. Background key points removal simulation. Fig. 7A presents the image after key points detection and Fig. 7B after background key points removal.

Acknowledgments. The work presented in this paper was supported by a grant from Switzerland through the Swiss Contribution to the enlarged European Union.

References

[1] Barghout, L., Sheynin, J.: Real-world scene perception and perceptual organization: Lessons from computer vision. Journal of Vision 13(9), 709 (2013)

[2] Bartczuk, L., Przybyl, A., Dziwinski, P.: Hybrid state variables - fuzzy logic modelling of nonlinear objects. In: Rutkowski, L., Korytkowski, M., Scherer, R., Tadeusiewicz, R., Zadeh, L.A., Zurada, J.M. (eds.) ICAISC 2013, Part I. LNCS, vol. 7894, pp. 227–234. Springer, Heidelberg (2013)

[3] Batenburg, K., Sijbers, J.: Optimal threshold selection for tomogram segmentation by projection distance minimization. IEEE Transactions on Medical Imaging 28(5), 676–686 (2009)

[4] Bazarganigilani, M.: Optimized image feature selection using pairwise classifiers. Journal of Artificial Intelligence and Soft Computing Research 1(2), 147–153 (2011)

[5] Canny, J.: A computational approach to edge detection. IEEE Transactions on Pattern Analysis and Machine Intelligence 8(6), 679–698 (1986)

[6] Chang, Y., Wang, Y., Chen, C., Ricanek, K.: Improved image-based automatic gender classification by feature selection. Journal of Artificial Intelligence and Soft Computing Research 1(3), 241–253 (2011)

[7] Cpalka, K.: A new method for design and reduction of neuro-fuzzy classification systems. IEEE Transactions on Neural Networks 20(4), 701–714 (2009)

[8] Cpalka, K., Rutkowski, L.: Flexible takagi sugeno neuro-fuzzy structures for nonlinear approximation. WSEAS Transactions on Systems 4(9), 1450–1458 (2005)

[9] Damiand, G., Resch, P.: Split-and-merge algorithms defined on topological maps for 3d image segmentation. Graphical Models 65(1), 149–167 (2003)

[10] Duda, P., Jaworski, M., Pietruczuk, L., Scherer, R., Korytkowski, M., Gabryel, M.: On the application of fourier series density estimation for image classification based on feature description. In: Proceedings of the 8th International Conference on Knowledge, Information and Creativity Support Systems, Krakow, Poland, November 7-9, pp. 81–91 (2013)

[11] Gabryel, M., Korytkowski, M., Scherer, R., Rutkowski, L.: Object detection by simple fuzzy classifiers generated by boosting. In: Rutkowski, L., Korytkowski, M., Scherer, R., Tadeusiewicz, R., Zadeh, L.A., Zurada, J.M. (eds.) ICAISC 2013, Part I. LNCS, vol. 7894, pp. 540–547. Springer, Heidelberg (2013)

[12] Gabryel, M., Nowicki, R.K., Woźniak, M., Kempa, W.M.: Genetic cost optimization of the $GI/M/1/N$ finite-buffer queue with a single vacation policy. In: Rutkowski, L., Korytkowski, M., Scherer, R., Tadeusiewicz, R., Zadeh, L.A., Zurada, J.M. (eds.) ICAISC 2013, Part II. LNCS, vol. 7895, pp. 12–23. Springer, Heidelberg (2013)

[13] Gabryel, M., Woźniak, M., Nowicki, R.K.: Creating learning sets for control systems using an evolutionary method. In: Rutkowski, L., Korytkowski, M., Scherer, R., Tadeusiewicz, R., Zadeh, L.A., Zurada, J.M. (eds.) SIDE 2012 and EC 2012. LNCS, vol. 7269, pp. 206–213. Springer, Heidelberg (2012)

[14] Greblicki, W., Rutkowska, D., Rutkowski, L.: An orthogonal series estimate of time-varying regression. Annals of the Institute of Statistical Mathematics 35(1), 215–228 (1983)

[15] Grycuk, R., Gabryel, M., Korytkowski, M., Scherer, R.: Content-based image indexing by data clustering and inverse document frequency. In: Mrozek, S.K.D., Kasprowski, P., Małysiak-Mrozek, B., Kostrzewa, D. (eds.) BDAS 2014. CCIS, vol. 424, pp. 374–383. Springer, Heidelberg (2014)

[16] Grycuk, R., Gabryel, M., Korytkowski, M., Scherer, R., Romanowski, J.: Improved digital image segmentation based on stereo vision and mean shift algorithm. In: Parallel Processing and Applied Mathematics 2013. LNCS. Springer, Heidelberg (2014) (manuscript accepted for publication)

[17] Kirillov, A.: Detecting some simple shapes in images (2010), http://www.aforgenet.com

[18] Lowe, D.G.: Object recognition from local scale-invariant features. In: The Proceedings of the Seventh IEEE International Conference on Computer Vision, vol. 2, pp. 1150–1157. IEEE (1999)

[19] Lowe, D.G.: Distinctive image features from scale-invariant keypoints. International Journal of Computer Vision 60(2), 91–110 (2004)

[20] Nowicki, R.: Rough-neuro-fuzzy system with micog defuzzification. In: 2006 IEEE International Conference on Fuzzy Systems, pp. 1958–1965 (2006)

[21] Nowicki, R.: On classification with missing data using rough-neuro-fuzzy systems. International Journal of Applied Mathematics and Computer Science 20(1), 55–67 (2010)

[22] Nowicki, R., Rutkowski, L.: Soft techniques for bayesian classification. In: Neural Networks and Soft Computing, pp. 537–544. Springer (2003)

[23] Peteiro-Barral, D., Guijarro-Bardinas, B., Perez-Sanchez, B.: Learning from heterogeneously distributed data sets using artificial neural networks and genetic algorithms. Journal of Artificial Intelligence and Soft Computing Research 2(1), 5–20 (2012)

[24] Przybył, A., Cpałka, K.: A new method to construct of interpretable models of dynamic systems. In: Rutkowski, L., Korytkowski, M., Scherer, R., Tadeusiewicz, R., Zadeh, L.A., Zurada, J.M. (eds.) ICAISC 2012, Part II. LNCS, vol. 7268, pp. 697–705. Springer, Heidelberg (2012)

[25] Rutkowski, L.: A general approach for nonparametric fitting of functions and their derivatives with applications to linear circuits identification. IEEE Transactions on Circuits and Systems 33(8), 812–818 (1986)

[26] Rutkowski, L.: Non-parametric learning algorithms in time-varying environments. Signal Processing 18(2), 129–137 (1989)

[27] Rutkowski, L., Przybył, A., Cpałka, K., Er, M.J.: Online speed profile generation for industrial machine tool based on neuro-fuzzy approach. In: Rutkowski, L., Scherer, R., Tadeusiewicz, R., Zadeh, L.A., Zurada, J.M. (eds.) ICAISC 2010, Part II. LNCS, vol. 6114, pp. 645–650. Springer, Heidelberg (2010)

[28] Sankaranarayanan, V., Lakshmi, S.: A study of edge detection techniques for segmentation computing approaches. IJCA, Special Issue on CASCT (1), 35–41 (2010)

[29] Starczewski, J.T.: A type-1 approximation of interval type-2 FLS. In: Di Gesù, V., Pal, S.K., Petrosino, A. (eds.) WILF 2009. LNCS, vol. 5571, pp. 287–294. Springer, Heidelberg (2009)

[30] Stockman, G., Shapiro, L.G.: Computer Vision, 1st edn. Prentice Hall PTR, Upper Saddle River (2001)

[31] Tamaki, T., Yamamura, T., Ohnishi, N.: Image segmentation and object extraction based on geometric features of regions. In: Electronic Imaging 1999. International Society for Optics and Photonics, pp. 937–945 (1998)

[32] Zalasiński, M., Cpałka, K.: Novel algorithm for the on-line signature verification. In: Rutkowski, L., Korytkowski, M., Scherer, R., Tadeusiewicz, R., Zadeh, L.A., Zurada, J.M. (eds.) ICAISC 2012, Part II. LNCS, vol. 7268, pp. 362–367. Springer, Heidelberg (2012)

Robust Face Recognition by Group Sparse Representation That Uses Samples from List of Subjects

Dimche Kostadinov[1], Sviatoslav Voloshynovskiy[1], Sohrab Ferdowsi[1], Maurits Diephuis[1], and Rafał Scherer[2]

[1] University of Geneva, Computer Science Department,
7 Route de Drize, Geneva, Switzerland
dimche.kostadinov@unige.ch
http://sip.unige.ch
[2] Institute of Computational Intelligence, Częstochowa University of Technology
Al. Armii Krajowej 36, 42-200 Częstochowa, Poland

Abstract. In this paper we consider group sparsity for robust face recognition. We propose a model for inducing group sparsity with no constraints on the definition of the structure of the group, coupled with locality constrained regularization. We formulate the problem as bounded distance regularized L_2 norm minimization with group sparsity inducing, non-convex constrains. We apply convex relaxation and a branch and bound strategy to find an approximation to the original problem. The empirical results confirm that with this approach of deploying a very simple non-overlapping group structure we outperform several state-of-the-art sparse coding based image classification methods.

Keywords: Face recognition, sparse representation, group sparsity.

1 Introduction

Automatic human face recognition systems are used in a wide range of real world practical applications related to identification, verification, posture/gesture recognition, social network linking and multimodal interaction. In the last ten years, the problem of face recognition was intensively studied in different domains including biometrics, computer vision and machine learning with the main emphasis on recognition accuracy under various acquisition conditions and more recently on security and privacy.

In the past Nearest Neighbor (NN) [3] and Nearest Feature Subspace (NFS) [16] were used for classification. NN classifies the query image by only using its Nearest Neighbor. NN utilizes the local structure of the training data and is therefore easily affected by noise. NFS approximates the query image by using all the images belonging to an identical class, using the linear structure of the data. Class prediction is achieved by selecting that class of images that minimizes the reconstruction error. NFS might fail in the case that classes are highly

L. Rutkowski et al. (Eds.): ICAISC 2014, Part II, LNAI 8468, pp. 616–626, 2014.

correlated to each other. Certain aspects of these problems can be overcome by Sparse Representation based Classification (SRC) [20]. According to SRC, a dictionary is first learned from training images, which can be acquired from the same subject under different viewing conditions or from various subjects. At the recognition stage, a query image is first sparsely encoded using the codewords of the learned dictionary after which the classification is performed by verifying which class yields the smallest coding errors. Other improvement methods over SRC include for example the Gabor feature based SRC (GSRC) method [21] which extracts Gabor features to represent face images and estimates an occlusion dictionary for sparse errors and the metaface learning based SRC method which trains a limited number of metafaces for each class [22]. On the other hand Qinfeng S. at al. [17] argue that the lack of sparsity in the data means that the compressive sensing approach cannot be guaranteed to recover the exact signal and therefore that sparse approximations may not deliver the desired robustness and performance. It has also been shown [2, 1] that in some cases, the locality of the dictionary code words is more essential than the sparsity. Another extension of SRC [14], called Weighted Sparse Representation based Classification (WSRC) integrates the locality structure of the data into a sparse representation in a unified formulation.

While the previous methods can only promote independent sparsity [18], one can partition variables into disjoint groups and promote group sparsity using the so called group Lasso regularization [15]. To induce more sophisticated structured sparsity patterns, it becomes essential to use structured sparsity-inducing norms built on overlapping groups of variables [23, 10]. In a direction related to group sparsity, Elhamifar and Vidal [6] proposed a more robust classification method using a structured sparse representation, while Gao at al. [5] introduced a kernelized version of SRC. The authors in [12] improve SRC by constructing a group structured dictionary by concentrating sub-dictionaries of all classes. Wu at al. [9] introduced a class of structured sparsity inducing norms into the SRC framework to model various corruptions in face images caused by misalignment, shadow (due to illumination change), and occlusion, and develop an automatic face alignment method based on minimizing the structured sparsity norm.

Group Lasso is proven [11] to be robust to Gaussian noise due to the stability associated with the group structure, however this is true and valid when the signal is strongly group sparse or covered by groups with large sizes. Here we present a more general approach with weaker assumptions on the group sparsity structure. That is, we propose a method for inducing group sparsity with an arbitrarily structure coupled with locality constrained regularization, by introducing non-convex constraints on the approximation coefficients. Furthermore we propose an approximate solution using a branch and bound strategy for solving non-convex optimization problems.

The motivation is three fold:

(i) first via this approach we can impose any structure on the sparsity;

(ii) by introducing locality constrained regularization we can control the impact of the locality in the approximation;

(iii) when one adopts the SRC set-up the recognition rate is related to the reconstruction that uses the samples from the correct subject (the one that is related to the probe sample). By defining appropriate simple groups that impose structured sparsity, the approximation might use samples from list of subjects. In this case we have an restricted reconstruction. Letting just a few groups to be (non-zero) active, one might expect an increase in recognition rate due to increase of the total error by the restricted reconstruction.

In this paper we empirically validate our proposed method based on a simple group sparse representation that uses samples from fixed list of subjects (similarly to list decoding) with and without locality constrained regularization, and consider face image variability induced by factors such as noise, lightning, expression or pose.

This paper is organized as follows. In Section 2 we give the basic problem formulation, in Section 3 we present and explain our proposed method. The results of the computer simulations are presented in Section 4. Finally Section 5 concludes the paper.

Notations: We use capital bold letters to denote real valued matrices (e.g, $\mathbf{W} \in \Re^{M \times N}$) and small bold letters to denote real valued vectors (e.g. $\mathbf{x} \in \Re^M$). We use sub and upper indexed vector as sample data (vector) single realization from a given distribution (e.g. $\mathbf{x}_i(m) \in \Re^M$, where m denotes the sample from distribution). We denote an element of a vector as x. The estimate of $\mathbf{x}$ is denoted as $\hat{\mathbf{x}}$. All vectors have finite length, explicitly defined where appropriate. We denote an optimization problem that considers norm approximation without a prior with A, if that problem considers L_1-norm approximation we denote it with A_{L1}, if it considers L_2-norm approximation we denote it with A_{L2}. If the optimization problem that includes a fidelity function (e.g. L_2-norm approximation) and a prior (e.g. L_2-norm prior) we denote the problem with $A_{L2}P_{L2}$. We denote a classifier operating on the L_2-norm by $C2$ and on the L_1-norm by $C1$.

2   Problem Formulation

The face recognition system consists of two stages: *enrolment* and *identification*.

At the enrolment stage, the photos from each subject are acquired and organized in the form of a codebook. We will assume that the recognition system should recognize K subjects. The photo of each subject i, $1 \leq i \leq K$, is acquired under different imaging conditions such as lighting, expression, pose, etc., which will represent the variability of face features and serve as *intra*-class statistics. To investigate the upper limit of performance we will also assume that the frontal face images are aligned to the same scale, rotation and translation (as in [3]). Therefore each subject i is defined by $\mathbf{x}_i(m) \in \Re^N$ vectors representing a concatenation of aligned image columns with $1 \leq m \leq M$. The samples from all subjects are arranged into a codebook represented by a matrix:

$$\mathbf{W} = [\mathbf{x}_1(1), ..., \mathbf{x}_1(m), ..., \mathbf{x}_1(M), ..., \mathbf{x}_i(1),$$
$$..., \mathbf{x}_i(m), ..., \mathbf{x}_i(M), ..., \mathbf{x}_K(1), ..., \mathbf{x}_K(m), ..., \mathbf{x}_K(M)] \quad (1)$$
$$\in \Re^{N \times (K * M)}.$$

At the recognition stage, a probe or query $\mathbf{y} \in \Re^N$ is presented to the system. The system should identify the subject i as accurate as possible based on $\mathbf{y}$ and $\mathbf{W}$. It is also assumed that $\mathbf{y}$ always corresponds to one of the subjects represented in the database.

In the scope of this paper, face recognition is considered as a classification problem where the classifier should produce a decision in favour of some class i whose codebook codewords produce the most accurate approximation of probe $\mathbf{y}$. One important class of approximations is represented by a *sparse linear approximation* [3], when the probe $\mathbf{y}$ is approximated by $\hat{\mathbf{y}}$ in the form of:

$$\hat{\mathbf{y}} = \mathbf{W}\boldsymbol{\alpha}, \quad (2)$$

where $\boldsymbol{\alpha} \in \Re^{M \times K}$ is a sparse coding vector. The coding vector $\boldsymbol{\alpha}$ weights the codebook codewords gathered from all classes to favour the contribution of codewords corresponding to the correct class $\hat{i}$. The model of approximations can be represented as:

$$\mathbf{y} = \hat{\mathbf{y}} + \mathbf{r}, \quad (3)$$

where $\mathbf{r} \in \Re^N$ is the residual error vector of the approximation.

For each class i, let $\boldsymbol{\delta}_i : \Re^{K*M} \to \Re^{K*M}$ be a function that selects the coefficients associated with the ith class. For $\boldsymbol{\alpha} \in R^{K*N}$, $\boldsymbol{\delta}_i(\boldsymbol{\alpha})$ is a new vector whose only nonzero entries are the entries in $\boldsymbol{\alpha}$ that are associated with class i. Using the coefficients that are only associated with the ith class, one can find the class approximation $\hat{\mathbf{y}}_i \in R^M$ to the given test sample $\mathbf{y}$:

$$\hat{\mathbf{y}}_i = \mathbf{W}\boldsymbol{\delta}_i(\boldsymbol{\alpha}), \quad (4)$$

and

$$\mathbf{y} = \hat{\mathbf{y}}_i + \mathbf{r}_i, \quad (5)$$

where $\mathbf{r}_i \in \Re^N$ is the residual error vector of the approximation to class i.

Then the probe $\mathbf{y}$ is classified based on the approximation $\hat{i}$ that minimizes the L_2-norm of the residual error vector between $\mathbf{y}$ and $\hat{\mathbf{y}}_i$. This classifier is denoted as $C2$:

$$C2: \ \hat{i} = \arg \min_{1 \leq i \leq K} (\|\mathbf{r}_i\|_2) = \arg \min_{1 \leq i \leq K} \|\mathbf{W}\boldsymbol{\delta}_i(\boldsymbol{\alpha}) - \mathbf{y}\|_2. \quad (6)$$

Because we use the $\boldsymbol{\delta}_i$ function in this approximation, which is a hard assignment non-linear function, it might change the optimality of the found solution in the L_2 norm, which is known to be unstable. In order to be able to more robustly tackle this problem, we propose a classifier based on the approximation $\hat{i}$ that minimizes the L_1-norm of the residual error vector between $\mathbf{y}$ and $\hat{\mathbf{y}}_i$ and we denote this classifier as $C1$:

$$C1: \quad \hat{i} = \arg\min_{1 \leq i \leq K} (\|\mathbf{r}_i\|_1) = \arg\min_{1 \leq i \leq K} \|\mathbf{W}\boldsymbol{\delta}_i(\boldsymbol{\alpha}) - \mathbf{y}\|_1. \tag{7}$$

In more general case, the equations (6) and (7) correspond to the minimum L_p distance classification, where if $p = 2$ one has the Euclidean distance and if $p = 1$ one has the Manhattan distance. A natural extension to (6) and (7) that might be considered is a bounded distance decoding (BBD) rule when:

$$\hat{i} = \{i \in \{1, \cdots, M\} : \|\mathbf{W}\boldsymbol{\delta}_i(\boldsymbol{\alpha}) - \mathbf{y}\|_p \leq \eta\}, \tag{8}$$

where $\eta \geq 0$. The BDD rule is useful when the classifier should be able to reject probes that are unrelated to the database. In the general case, the BDD will produce a list of candidates that satisfy the above condition. To have only one unique $\hat{i}$ on the list, the parameter η should be chosen accordingly. Geometrically in the L_p space, it means that the L_p spheres with radius η around each approximation for each class should not overlap thus producing a unique classification.

3   Proposed Model for Group Sparsity

Here we propose a model for group sparse approximation with locality constrained regularization. We present a general problem formulation as approximation with priors and non-convex constraints that induce use of data samples from a variable list size of subjects. This is illustrated on Fig. 1.

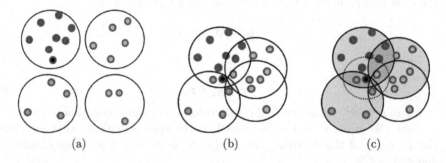

      (a)   (b)   (c)

Fig. 1. a) Ideal case, no noise present, where we have data samples from 4 subjects and the black dot represents the probe sample; b) A case where we have noise and the classes strongly overlap due to small interclass distance; c) Group sparsity constraints form the three active groups represented as circles filed with color, the small circle with dash line represents the boundary of the locality constrained regularization

Let $\mathbf{y}$ be a test sample and $\mathbf{W}$ denote all training samples as in (1), than we define the problem as follows:

$$\min_{\boldsymbol{\alpha}, \boldsymbol{s}, c} \|\mathbf{W}\boldsymbol{\alpha} - \mathbf{y}\|_2 + \lambda * \phi(\boldsymbol{\alpha}, \mathbf{w})$$

subject to

$$\psi(g_k(\boldsymbol{\alpha})) + s(k)/c = 1/c, \forall k \in G,$$

$$\|\boldsymbol{\alpha}\|_1 = 1,$$

$$\sum_{k=1}^{n(G)} s(k) = n(G) - c,$$

$$\mathbf{s} \in \{0, 1\}^{n(G)}, c \in Z, \boldsymbol{\alpha} \in R^{K*M}. \tag{9}$$

In the above equation $\phi(\boldsymbol{\alpha}, \mathbf{w})$ is a proximity prior distribution, describing our prior about the location of the probe sample within all data samples. This prior penalizes distance between $\mathbf{y}$ and each training data $\mathbf{x}_i(m)$:

$$\phi(\boldsymbol{\alpha}, \mathbf{w}) = \sum_{i}^{K*N} |\alpha(i) * w(i)|, \tag{10}$$

where w is a vector defined as:

$$\mathbf{w} = [\|\mathbf{y} - \mathbf{x}_1(1)\|_1, ..., \|\mathbf{y} - \mathbf{x}_i(m)\|_1, ..., \|\mathbf{y} - \mathbf{x}_K(N-1)\|_1, \|\mathbf{y} - \mathbf{x}_K(N)\|_1],$$

In equation (9) G is the set of the defined groups, the group $g_k(\boldsymbol{\alpha})$ is subset of the set that consists of all the approximation coefficients $\boldsymbol{\alpha}$. There are in total $n(G)$ groups, where $n(G)$ is the cardinality of the set G. $\psi(g_k(\boldsymbol{\alpha}))$ is a function that sums the absolute values of all the coefficients $\boldsymbol{\alpha}$ included in the group $g_k(\boldsymbol{\alpha})$:

$$\psi(g_k(\boldsymbol{\alpha})) = \sum_{i \in I_{g_k}} |\alpha(i)|, \tag{11}$$

where I_{g_k} is a set of indexes that denote the coefficients $\boldsymbol{\alpha}$ indexes that belong to the group $g_k(\boldsymbol{\alpha})$.

In general case the structure of the group $g_k(\boldsymbol{\alpha})$, concretely what coefficients $\boldsymbol{\alpha}$ belong to the group $g_k(\boldsymbol{\alpha})$ and the set of groups G can be arbitrary defined. Here we empirically validate the set-up in which we partition the approximation coefficients $\boldsymbol{\alpha}$ into groups that are related to the samples from every subject, this results in a number of non-overlapping groups that is equal to the number of subjects K. Formally we express this as follows:

$$\underbrace{\alpha(1), \alpha(2), ..., \alpha(M)}_{g_1(\boldsymbol{\alpha})}, ..., \underbrace{\alpha(M+1), \alpha(M+2), ..., \alpha(M+M)}_{g_2(\boldsymbol{\alpha})}, ...,$$

$$\underbrace{\alpha((K-1)*M+1), \alpha((K-1)*M+2), ..., \alpha((K-1)*M+M)}_{g_K(\boldsymbol{\alpha})} \tag{12}$$

The integer c is the number of active groups, those groups that have a non-zero sum of absolute values and s is binary slack variable. The first two constraints of the problem ensure to have non-zeros values for the coefficients that are included in the sparsity inducing group and zeros at the remaining coefficients. Note also that these two constraints also enforce to have non-zero values of coefficients for multiple active groups and zero at the all the remaining coefficients. The third constraint ensures the coefficient values to be normalized, the fourth constraint ensures in having exactly c active groups. These last two constraints are important to insure that the first two constants are valid.

This non-convex mixed integer program can be also interpreted as a distance constrained, variable sized list decoder, where the actual list is a list of sparsity inducing groups $g_k(\boldsymbol{\alpha})$. We solve this problem using the branch and bound method [7], (other alternative is the cutting plane method [19]). At each branch we solve a convex relaxation of the problem (9). The number of branches that have to be visited to solve this problem is proportional to the product of the number of groups and the number of active non-zero groups, so the method has bilinear executions of the convexly relaxed problem in these two variables.

Letting the integer c variable be fixed and small, such that it suffices to have data samples from a small list of subjects empirically has proven to be efficient. The problem formulation where c variable is fixed is identical to the problem defined in (9), except that now we have a less complex problem. Applying convex relaxation for the vector of binary variables s, expressing the constrains $\|\boldsymbol{\alpha}\|_1 = 1$ and $\psi_k(\boldsymbol{\alpha}) + s(k)/c = 1/c, \forall k \in G$ in a convexly relaxed form we then have the following convex problem:

$$\min_{\boldsymbol{\alpha},\boldsymbol{s}} \|\mathbf{W}\boldsymbol{\alpha} - \mathbf{y}\|_2 + \lambda * \phi(\boldsymbol{\alpha}, \mathbf{w})$$

$$subject\ to$$

$$\boldsymbol{\alpha} <= \boldsymbol{\alpha}_a,$$

$$\boldsymbol{\alpha} >= -\boldsymbol{\alpha}_a,$$

$$\sum_{i \in I_{g_k}} \alpha_a(i) + s(k)/c = 1/c, \forall k \in G,$$

$$\sum_{i}^{K*N} \alpha_a(i) = 1,$$

$$\sum_{k=1}^{n(G)} s(k) = n(G) - c,$$

$$\boldsymbol{s} >= 0, \boldsymbol{s} <= 1,$$

$$s(i_{CR}) = v_{CR}, \tag{13}$$

where we fix the variable $s(i_{CR})$ to have values $v_{CR} \in \{0, 1\}$ and let the remaining variables of s have values between 0 and 1.

After obtaining the group sparse solution $\hat{\boldsymbol{\alpha}} \in \Re^{M \times K}$, the identification is performed using equation (6) or (7).

4   Computer Simulation

In this section we present the results of the computer simulation, which are organized in two parts. In the first part, we present the results using sparsity priors that promote independent element-wise sparsity and the result using an approximation that induces group sparsity is presented in the second part. In all the parts of the computer simulation, we present the results using two classifiers: $C1$ (equation (6)) and $C2$ (equation (7)).

The computer simulation is carried out on publicly available data. The used database is Extended Yale B for face recognition. This database consists of 2414 frontal face images of 38 subjects captured under various laboratory-controlled lighting conditions [8]. All the images from this database are cropped and normalized to 192x168 pixels.

In our set up, the images from the dataset are rescaled to 10x12 pixels using nearest neighbor interpolation. In all of the computer simulations we use raw, basic, elementary image pixel values (block of image pixel values) as features. To be unbiased in our validation of the results we use 5-fold cross validation, where for a single validation for each subject, half of the images are selected at random for training and the remainder for testing.

All of the optimization problems presented in the previous chapters are solved using CVX [4]. In all of the regularized optimization problems, the regularization parameters were chosen to maximize the classification accuracy.

First we present the results using approximations with sparsity priors that promote independent element-wise sparsity. In this set-up we show the recognition accuracy under several models of approximation:

- $L2$-norm and $L1$-norm approximation as baseline without priors
- $L2$-norm and $L1$-norm approximation with priors that have a Laplacian and Gaussian distribution
- SRC [20]
- LLC [19]
- WSRC [14]

The resulting estimates are tested with the $C1$ and $C2$ classifiers. The details about the set-up of the parameter for all the above models can be found in [13]. The results presented in bold signifies the best achieved results.

Table 1. Identification precision under approximations with sparsity priors that promote independent element-wise sparsity

	A_{L2}		A_{L1}		$G\text{-}A_{LLC}$		$G\text{-}A_{WSRC}$	
	C2	C1	C2	C1	C2	C1	C2	C1
No prior	90.8%	91.0%	87.8%	82.9%	-	-	-	-
P_{L2}	90.6%	91.0%	87.5%	89.3%	**91.6%**	89.8%	-	-
P_{L1}	93.7 %	**94.5%**	91.6%	**94.1%**	-	-	93.2%	**94.0%**

624   D. Kostadinov et al.

In the second series of computer simulations we present the identification accuracy of the proposed approximation that promotes group sparsity (GS) without and with locality constrained regularization (LCR) as defined by equation (10). Here we define a very simple non-overlapping group where the number of groups is equal to the number of subjects and every group covers the data samples from a single subject. We present the results using a fixed number of active groups, where we set the number of active groups (variable c in Equation 12) to 3. In the set-up where we use locality constrained regularization, the Lagrangian multiplier λ is set to 3. Table 2 shows the results for the above method. The results presented in bold signifies the best achieved results.

Table 2. Identification precision under approximations that induces group wise sparsity

A_{GS}		$A_{\text{GS LCR}}$	
C2	C1	C2	C1
93.2%	**95.3%**	93.1%	**94.7%**

As can be seen from Table 1 the $C1$ classifier demonstrates superior performance in comparison to the $C2$ classifier. For the approximations with sparsity priors that promote independent element-wise sparsity the impact of the approximation model is negligible under the P_{L1} prior and $C1$ classifier and the $L2$-norm regularization is non-informative. The best result is achieved for the $G - A_{L2}P_{L1}C1$ setup. Further detailed explanation of the impact of independent element-wise sparsity based on the prior distribution of the approximation coefficients can be found in [13].

As can be seen from Table 2 considering group sparsity again, the $C1$ classifier demonstrates superior performance in comparison to the $C2$ classifier and it's robustness. The best results are achieved using the proposed model without locality constraints regularization and the $C1$ classifier.

5   Conclusion

In this paper we consider group sparsity for robust face recognition. With our proposed model for inducing group sparsity we have empirically shown that using a very simple non-overlapping group structure we outperform several state-of-the-art sparse coding based image classification methods.

One further possible future direction that might bring improvement is to autonomously infer the underling group sparsity structure that is related to the most accurate recognition rate.

Acknowledgements. The research has been partially supported by SNF grant 1200020-146379 and by a grant from Switzerland through the Swiss Contribution to the enlarged European Union PSPB-125/2010.

References

Coates, A.: Demystifying unsupervised feature learning (2012)

Coates, A., Ng, A.Y.: The importance of encoding versus training with sparse coding and vector quantization. In: Proceedings of the 28th International Conference on Machine Learning (ICML 2011), pp. 921–928 (2011)

Cover, T., Hart, P.: Nearest neighbor pattern classification. IEEE Transactions on Information Theory 13(1), 21–27 (1967)

CVX Research, Inc.: CVX: Matlab Software for Disciplined Convex Programming, version 2.0. (August 2012), http://cvxr.com/cvx

Gao, S., Tsang, I.W.-H., Chia, L.-T.: Kernel Sparse Representation for Image Classification and Face Recognition. In: Daniilidis, K., Maragos, P., Paragios, N. (eds.) ECCV 2010, Part IV. LNCS, vol. 6314, pp. 1–14. Springer, Heidelberg (2010)

Elhamifar, E., Vidal, R.: Robust classification using structured sparse representation. In: IEEE CVPR, pp. 1873–1879 (2011)

Friedlander, M.P., Michael, Saunders, A.: A globally convergent linearly constrained lagrangian method for nonlinear optimization. SIAM J. Optim. 15, 863–897 (2002)

Georghiades, A.S., Belhumeur, P.N., Kriegman, D.J.: From few to many: Illumination cone models for face recognition under variable lighting and pose. IEEE Transactions on Pattern Analysis and Machine Intelligence 23, 643–660 (2001)

Huang, J., Huang, X., Metaxas, D.N.: Learning with dynamic group sparsity. In: IEEE ICCV, pp. 64–71 (2009)

Jenatton, R., Audibert, J.Y., Bach, F.: Structured variable selection with sparsity-inducing norms. J. Mach. Learn. Res. 12, 2777–2824 (2011)

Junzhou Huang, T.Z.: The benefit of group sparsity (2009)

Kong, S., Wang, D.: A dictionary learning approach for classification: Separating the particularity and the commonality. In: Fitzgibbon, A., Lazebnik, S., Perona, P., Sato, Y., Schmid, C. (eds.) ECCV 2012, Part I. LNCS, vol. 7572, pp. 186–199. Springer, Heidelberg (2012)

Kostadinov, D., Voloshynovskiy, S., Ferdowsi, S.: Robust human face recognition based on locality preserving sparse over complete block approximation. In: Proceedings of SPIE Photonics West, Electronic Imaging, Media Forensics and Security V, San Francisco, USA, January 23 (2014)

Lu, C.Y., Min, H., Gui, J., Zhu, L., Lei, Y.K.: Face recognition via weighted sparse representation. J. Vis. Comun. Image Represent. 24(2), 111–116 (2013)

Meier, L., Geer, S.V.D., Bühlmann, P., Zürich, E.T.H.: The group lasso for logistic regression. Journal of the Royal Statistical Society, Series B (2008)

Shan, S., Gao, W., Zhao, D.: Face recognition based on face-specific subspace. International Journal of Imaging Systems and Technology 13(1), 23–32 (2003)

Shi, Q., Eriksson, A., van den Hengel, A., Shen, C.: Is face recognition really a compressive sensing problem? In: 2013 IEEE Conference on Computer Vision and Pattern Recognition, pp. 553–560 (2011)

Tibshirani, R.: Regression shrinkage and selection via the lasso. Journal of the Royal Statistical Society, Series B 58, 267–288 (1994)

Wang, J., Yang, J., Yu, K., Lv, F., Huang, T.S., Gong, Y.: Locality-constrained linear coding for image classification. In: IEEE CVPR, pp. 3360–3367 (2010)

Wright, J., Yang, A.Y., Ganesh, A., Sastry, S.S., Ma, Y.: Robust face recognition via sparse representation. IEEE Transactions on Pattern Analysis and Machine Intelligence 31(2), 210–227 (2009)

Yang, M., Zhang, L.: Gabor feature based sparse representation for face recognition with gabor occlusion dictionary. In: Daniilidis, K., Maragos, P., Paragios, N. (eds.) ECCV 2010, Part VI. LNCS, vol. 6316, pp. 448–461. Springer, Heidelberg (2010)

Zhang, L., Yang, M., Feng, Z., Zhang, D.: On the dimensionality reduction for sparse representation based face recognition. In: IEEE ICPR, pp. 1237–1240 (2010)

Zhao, P., Rocha, G., Yu, B.: The composite absolute penalties family for grouped and hierarchical variable selection. Ann. Statist., 2009 (2009)

Using Facial Asymmetry Properties and Hidden Markov Models for Biometric Authentication in Security Systems

Mariusz Kubanek[1], Dorota Smorawa[1], and Mirosław Kurkowski[2]

[1] Czestochowa University of Technology
Institute of Computer and Information Science
Dabrowskiego Street 73, 42-200 Czestochowa, Poland
{mariusz.kubanek,dorota.smorawa}@icis.pcz.pl
[2] University of Luxembourg
Computer Science and Communication Group
6, rue Richard Coudenhove-Kalergi, 1359 Luxembourg, Luxembourg
miroslaw.kurkowski@uni.lu

Abstract. This work concerns the use of biometric features, resulting from the look of a face, for the authentication purposes. For this we propose several different methods of selection and feature analysis during face recognition. The description contains mainly the possibility of the analysis and in later stages also identity verification based on asymmetric facial features. The new authentication method has been introduced on the basis of designated characteristic points of face. The method includes propositions of our own algorithms of face detection, as well as face features extraction methods and their specific coding in the form of observation vectors and recognition using Hidden Markov Models.

Keywords: facial asymmetry, hidden Markov models, face recognition, authentication.

1 Introduction

Authentication is a key point in many computer and electronic security systems. The well-known methods of authentication, such as entering a PIN number, entering login and password or using the ID cards have many difficulties and disadvantages. It is easy to forget the PIN numbers, passwords, as well as lose identification card. In addition, the card can be stolen and protecting passwords broken. Therefore, the traditional methods of people authentication are becoming less popular. On the other hand biometric methods are gaining vast popularity in identification and verification of people. These methods use the digital measurement of certain physical and behavioral characteristics of humans and compare them with the pattern stored in the database. An example of biometric system used in this area can be a system which executes the authentication process on the basis of facial features.

L. Rutkowski et al. (Eds.): ICAISC 2014, Part II, LNAI 8468, pp. 627–638, 2014.
© Springer International Publishing Switzerland 2014

Since the possibility of common and cheap use of computer systems the research concentrates on the construction of fully automatic system of face recognition [1], which combines methods of face localization and extraction of structural characteristics of a face, such as a shape and a size of eyes and a nose, a shape of a face, a colour of a face and other distinguishable features. Using structural features of the face new identification and identity verification methods have been searched, where imperceptible at first dependencies are used as the main recognition factor [2–4]. Such features are e.g. features mentioning asymmetric shape of a face [5–7]. High usefulness of mentioned asymmetric features is described in works [8, 9]. The information about facial asymmetry can be used as an element supporting biometric authentication systems which function on the basis of distinguishable data.

The works about the analysis of facial asymmetry most of the time were based on the construction of feature vectors, received from the image in automatic or semiautomatic way which were compared by one of the known distant method. Such an approach introduces the risk of getting wrong results when characteristic points searched on a face will be determined in an inaccurate way. The introduction of some additional determinants can be useful which coded in appropriate way allow to use hidden Markov models for recognition (HMM). HMM work using vectors with different length so the omission of some features in the process of creation of the observation vector (e.g. by the error because of localization of characteristic points on a face) allows to maintain the stability of the authentication system.

2   Face Detection on the Image

The method based on facial asymmetric features, if it has to work automatically, it must execute automatic face detection in static image or even a frame sequence. It assumes that main data which will be used is static data, so the video sequence should be analysed frame by frame as a static image [10].

In case of face recognition based on whole look, to locate face the method based on specific skin colour is used with regard to a base of photos taken in similar lighting conditions and components of used methods using information about colour.

After appointing the area of face, the detection of facial characteristic points follows, chosen as key elements of determining asymmetry method [10]. There are following characteristic points: corners of both eyes, internal and external, centers of circles describing iris, mouth corners, points describing the width of a nose in its the widest place.

3   Detection of Facial Asymmetry Points

In order to determine correctly the corners of the mouth the method based on specific colour of the mouth is accepted. This method assumes the determination of pixels which fulfil assorted experimentally threshold values. It takes place in a calibration process. The way of the operation on RGB components, which detects colour of the mouth is described in details in work [10]. If you know the shape of the mouth, you can designate the corners of the mouth as utmost in non-zero pixels level. Searching such pixels need to be executed in limited area of the mouth, near horizontal axis.

In case of eyes, the localization takes place by the checked method, based on searching elements on a face which have significant value variation in the level of pixel brightness in small areas (so called gradient method) [11, 12]. Significant value variation can be observed in eye area where white of the eye is similar to maximum white colour and the pupil to maximum black colour, although the iris can contain also white light reflections.

After determining the localization of the eyes next stage requires precise designation of eye corners and center of circle describing the iris, which was described in detail in work [10]. As it will be shown the iris has a very significant importance in this method. A man from the birth till late old age has constant diameter of iris. It amounts 10 mm 0.05 mm. It is essential information because on the basis of constant size of diameter of iris of any man any photo can be scaled to the same real size. A measurement of facial asymmetry in proposed method should be carried out on actual dimensions. The size of iris is determined as a unit "Muld" [8, 13, 14].

The localization of eye corners requires determining the curves which describe lower and upper edges of eyelid. The place of intersection of curves is designated by eye corners. The detection of eyelid edges can be executed on the basis of modified parabolic Hough transform. The eyelid edges can be designated using methods which use information about level luminance of analysed area, the method analysing the depth in image in gray scale [15].

Conducted analyses of luminance levels in the image limited to eye area show that proposed method works quite precisely but only for upper eyelid. The lower eyelid often is not clear enough to determine its edge, maintaining big range of threshold values. Small range of these values causes unfortunately too low versatility of the method and the necessity of constant calibration.

Similar to detection of mouth edges, in case of the eye it is easier to search eyelid edges if you determine approximately the eye corners at the beginning. To narrow the searched area seek only limited subareas.

For the outer eye corner KZ_l the leftmost point of the lowest luminance value is assumed, and for the inner corner KW_l the rightmost point of the least luminance is assumed. In addition the distance from the center of a circle describing the iris is taken into consideration. Similar assumptions are for the right eye. Searching of the edge of upper eyelid takes place by moving from one eye corner to the another along the accepted arc. What is more, the column of the luminance matrix is searched in range $< Y_p - b, Y_p + 2b >$, where Y_p is extreme coordinate gained by searching previous column (for the first column the coordinate of eye corner is assumed). In such a way approximate localization of edges of eye corners is designated. N points is received where n determines assumed number of columns between corners of the eye.

Too low difference of luminance value in case of lower eyelid causes the necessity to use another detection procedure of its edge. One interesting approach can be the use of procedure which uses information about gradient luminance in specified intervals (ILP) in connection with the analysis of components in $(R/G, B/G)$ space. ILP procedure is to divide the eye area into five intervals 30 columns each, and then to execute the project of luminance gradient value within each range according to the following equation:

$$ILP(y) = \sum_{KZ_y-1.5*Iris\_r}^{KZ_y} |I_{lum}(S_i + x)(y) - I_{lum}(S_i + x + 1)(y)| \qquad (1)$$

where: I_{lum} - is an array of luminance values, KZ_y - vertical coordinate of the outer corner, S_i - the initial value of the i-th interval $(i = 1 \dots 5)$. The line containing the point of the edge of lower eyelid in a given interval is determined by the biggest value in ILP table, and the column is determined by half of a given interval. In such a way five points are gained for which the shape of lower eyelid edge can be approximated.

If analysed image contains the information about the colour, the information from the space can be used to determine lower edge of eyelid. An example of such an approach is used in work [16]. The image from RGB space is converted into $(R/G, B/G)$ space according to the following dependence:

$$\begin{cases} I_{RG}(y)(y) = I_R(x)(y)/I_G(x)(y) \\ I_{BG}(y)(y) = I_B(x)(y)/I_G(x)(y) \end{cases} \text{ for } x=0...w, \ y=0...h \qquad (2)$$

where: w, h - width and height of the input image in pixels, I_R, I_G, I_B - R, G and B components in the RGB colour space, I_{RG}, I_{BG} - R/G and B/G components in the representation of the image in $(R/G, B/G)$ space. Depending on accepted threshold values, the analysis of the components in $(R/G, B/G)$ space allows for accurate separation of the area of definite colour. In a presented case searched area is determined according to the following formula:

$$I(x)(y) = \begin{cases} 1 \text{ for } I_{RG}(x)(y) < T_1 \text{ and } I_{BG}(x)(y) > T_2 \\ 0 \text{ otherwise} \end{cases} \qquad (3)$$

for $x = 0...w, y = 0...h$, where: w, h - width and height of the input image in pixels, I_{RG}, I_{BG} - R/G and B/G components in the representation of the image in $(R/G, B/G)$ space, I - search area, T_1, T_2 - threshold values. In addition to Eq. 3 the assumption can be added, that pixel values for green component G should be in the range above the threshold $T3$. All threshold values should be chosen in the experimental way.

The localization of designated five points using ILP procedure is corrected with the edge defined by thresholding in a $(R/G, B/G)$ space.

Some points on the edges of upper and lower eyelid can be determined in a wrong way. Approximation of designated points can be executed using polynomial of third degree in order to level the differences between the real and originally designated localization of eyelid edges. In addition, approximating curves are used to determine final localization of eye corners which the intersection near designated earlier corners determines their proper localization.

Polynomials which approximate the shape of eyelid edges can be designated using the method of smallest squares [7] aiming at minimization of χ^2 size:

$$\chi^2 = \sum_{i=1}^{n} \frac{(y_i - f(x_i))^2}{\sigma_i^2} \tag{4}$$

where: $y_i, f(x_i)$ - the expected value and the value of the function for the i-th point, σ_i^2 - standard deviation for the i-th point, n - number of points.

Because of less accuracy of designating points which describe the eyelid edges near eye corners, the value of standard deviation is assumed individually for each point. In such a way variables of weight values are determined depending on the localization of points between the distance determined by the corners. The presented procedure of detection of the edges of upper and lower eyelid is essential element of functioning the whole method of identity verification on the basis of facial asymmetry. The edges of eyelids are not used directly but they are only one element of procedure of localization eye edges. Correctness of designating the curves which approximate the eyelid edges has large meaning in appointing the eye edges, so in real conditions you have to put a lot of attention to the correct calibration by the selection of the best threshold values.

The last of searched characteristic points are about the width of the nose in its widest place. It is one of the most difficult tasks which in the proposed method of measuring the facial asymmetry should be done. In the case of searching chosen points in eye or mouth area, analysed areas are characterized by large contrast between certain elements in the level of colour or greyscale. In the nose area such big differences in contrast scale are not observed, that is why, the depth of the level of luminance is taken into consideration. The difficulty of analysis results from the fact that the searched nose area changes its position in various people. There is no ideal way to identify clearly which area should be searched. The proposed scheme of determining area assumes that the area will be designated by localized centers of the eyes (the width d) and also by the vertical distance from $0.8k$ to $0.8d$, where d is the distance between the centers of the eyes, and k is the distance between the inner corners of the eyes. Such division results from taken tests on the basis of available pictures. It happens, however, that among some people proposed scheme omits searched points of the nose, so the calibration of system settings is necessary, dedicated to a user.

After correct designation of the area containing the nasal element in its widest place, the further work is about the analysis of the area with additional assumptions about the localization of searched points. It is known that the points will be on both sides in relation to vertical axis of symmetry of the image. To analyse the depth of the image at the level of luminance, searched image is converted into the greyscale (similar to the case of determining the edges of upper eyelid). In the next stage searching the image takes place to find more significant differences in the luminance depth, moving horizontally from the edge of the image to its axis of symmetry. Such differences are probable to find in a good quality picture, without x-rays and unnecessary shadows on the face. After searching all lines among designated points the most extreme point on the left and right of symmetry axis is chosen. The designated points define the limits of the nose in its widest place.

4   Create a Template of the Facial Asymmetry

On the basis of fixed and accepted characteristic points of the face special template of asymmetry is built, and then in later stage the construction of observation vector of facial asymmetry [4]. Facial asymmetry is measurable if everytime for all analysed pictures of the face the same work conditions are fixed and all algorithms and methods of determining characteristic points give correct answers. If the coordinates of the points are in chronological feature vector then the verification or even the identification leads to comparison of the distance between two feature vectors. In real situation working with the fully automated system, various types of obstacles can be seen which more or less influence the correct working of the system. It is necessary to find better solution which allows to level the influence of distracting external factors on efficient operation system.

This paper describes the biometric authentication method on the basis of facial asymmetry using hidden Markov models. Hidden Markov models can generalize in a controlled way which comparing the observation vector amounts to find many similarities between compared vector and the vector which a given model was taught. In practice it means that the models will work correctly despite disturbed correctness of feature vector. This property was used in case of proposed method of identity verification based on vector of asymmetric features. Determining characteristic points every time in simple way is often unattainable. However, if a certain margin of error is taken, the possible functioning of the method will be probable in spite of some discrepancies.

To create the template of facial asymmetry the characteristic points fixed in earlier stages will be used, located in the eye area (internal and external corners, the centers of circles describing the iris), the nose area (extreme points describing the maximum width of the nose) and the mouth area (mouth corners). Creating the template begins with determining the axis of facial symmetry. Proposals to determine perfect axis of symmetry can be found in various scientific studies, however the most reliable axis was determined in the works [13]. A little modified version was accepted in this work. Mainly the symmetry axis of the face is determined on the basis of two points: first A, which is the half of segment determined by inner eye corners, and second B, which is the half of segment determined by mouth corners. On the basis of the symmetry axis of the face the following elements of asymmetry template are determined.

The observation vector of facial asymmetry is built on the basis of determined distances, angles and points of intersection of auxiliary lines. On Fig. 1 a fragment of the template of facial asymmetry is shown with determined distance values.

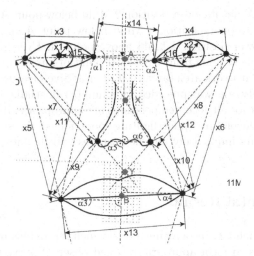

Fig. 1. Fragment of template of facial asymmetry with the designated distance values

In order to code all values describing facial asymmetry using the distance and the angles the rule for computing the ratio between suitable values for the right and left part of the face relative to the axis of symmetry has been assumed: $1 = x1/x2$, $2 = x3/x4$, $3 = x5/x6$, $4 = x7/x8$, $5 = x9/x10$, $6 = x11/x12$, $7 = x13/x14$, $8 = x15/x16$, $9 = \alpha1/\alpha2$, $10 = \alpha3/\alpha4$, $11 = \alpha5/\alpha6$. It has been assumed that the ratio of corresponding values ranges from 0.5 to 2, in extreme cases some dimensions would be twice bigger than the same dimensions for the other parts of the face. Imputing of observation symbols takes place by dividing accepted range (from 0.5 to 2) into sub-bands and accepting one unique observation symbol for each sub-band. In such a way for values from 0.5 to 1 there are number symbols: 1,2,...,20, and for values from 1 to 2 there are number symbols: 21,22,...,40. The first 11 observations in vector of facial asymmetry result directly from value of encoding for 1,2,...,11.

For the sake of greater stability of the work resulting from the accuracy of determining certain characteristic points of the face, obtained observation vector was supplemented by further observations. The observations result from the intersection of the straight lines, determined by:

– the outer corner of the right eye and the right corner of the mouth - and the outer corner of the left eye and the left corner of the mouth, in the point W,
– point X and Y (see Fig. 1)
– the right corner of the mouth and the inner corner of the right eye - and the left corner of the mouth and the inner corner of the left eye, in point Z.

Points W, X, Y and Z are located in the areas which were covered by special network (6 from 10 cells), where one cell for points W and Z has size of 0.5 Muld, whereas for points X and Y one cell has size 0.25 Muld.

All networks are arranged in parallel and symmetric way to the axis of the face. The network for point W has its upper position 11 Muld below point A, the network for point X has its lower position 2 Muld below point A and the network for point Y has its upper position 4 Muld below point A and the network for point Z has its lower position 4 Muld above point A. Every network contains observation symbols ranging from 1 to 60. If point of intersection of the straight lines is beyond the network area (areas 0, 1, 2 or 3) given feature will be omitted. Location of the networks was preceded by a number of studies of different types of faces and almost for all accepted positions are appropriate. It can happen that due to wrong taken picture (poor lighting, poor focus) the system locates the characteristic points imprecisely and next stages will be affected by the initial error.

5   Experimental Results

Depending on a teaching - recognizing model which is provided by hidden Markov models, it requires to form appropriate coded observation vectors. In the proposed method the final observation vector consists of symbols, integers from 1 to 60. The length of feature vector is 15 which is a quite low value. For sure, such an assumption allows to learn the system quickly and add and verify new users. On the other hand there are quite few analysed features in order to make proposed system accessible for big (above 500 people) user base.

When the automatic localization of characteristic points is effective, then tests which verify the identity can be done. First, accept the strategy of creating an observation vector. The first 11 features will be described by the values of observation symbols from 1 to 40. Other 4 features will be in the range from 1 to 60, if the designated point of intersection will be within a code network. When the designated point will be outside the code network, the observation vector will be cut back on the analysed feature. The tests were performed to verify the identity using hidden Markov models for the two variants. The first variant assumed that the length of observation vector is 15 features, with the possibility to reduce to 11. The second variant assumed much greater importance of the features resulting from localized points on code networks, depending on a five times duplication of each properly designated observation. The length of the observation vector for the second variant is contained in the range from 11 to a maximum 31 features. All tests were performed on the users basis containing 500 different faces, taken in certain light conditions and with high resolution (minimum 2.5 mega pixels - 1920 x 1280). For each user two photos are considered, one to learn Markov models, and the other one to test. In addition, the selected pictures are only of those users for whom all designated characteristic points were within the correct location (according to the criteria set out in the initial tests). In Table 1 the results of identity verification are given, obtained for the first and second variant of the tests. There are five different in numbers groups of users registered in the database, in order to analyse the capabilities of the system in multi-user systems.

The results indicate that more data in the observation vector allows to gain better efficiency of verification, thus the second variant is better than the first

Table 1. Results of tests for identity verification based on the asymmetry of the face, for the first and second variant of the test

Num. of Users	Test V1		Test V2	
	FAR [%]	FRR [%]	FAR [%]	FRR [%]
100	2.00	4.00	1.00	4.00
200	2.50	5.50	2.00	5.00
300	3.33	7.66	2.66	6.66
400	6.25	9.75	4.75	8.75
500	7.20	12.80	6.20	11.80

one. It is not a big difference to demonstrate clearly the superiority of any of the proposals. It is clear that with the increase of the number of users in the database, false acceptance and false rejection rate increases significantly. At the 500 users false acceptance rate at the level of more than 30 errors is a dangerous result. However, for a limited number of users (up to 100), it is possible to obtain a highly effective system of identity verification on the basis of the asymmetric features of the face.

About the advantage of the second variant of the tests over the first used hidden Markov models decide. This tool is able to generalize, so even with significant differences in defining observations 12, 13, 14 and 15, and of course with the enlarged vector, it is possible to interpret correctly the asymmetric features. Please note, that for the mentioned studies only photos which automatic localization of the characteristic points of the face was in the accepted criteria were considered. A comparison of test results obtained in accordance with both variants of the tests is presented in Fig. 2.

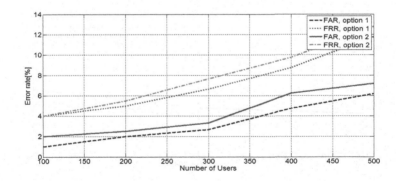

Fig. 2. Comparison of FAR and FRR for the first and second variant of the test

The described cases concerned a pretty selective tests, where only those images were analysed which meet the basic criteria, namely the correct localization of the characteristic points on the face. It is known that in order to identify or verify a person correctly a lot of distinguishable features must be obtained. It concerns especially large databases. In order to illustrate the real possibilities of

636   M. Kubanek, D. Smorawa, and M. Kurkowski

this method, the tests were conducted again, in accordance with the assumptions of the first and second variant but on randomly selected images of the faces from the available database. Also in these tests for each user two different pictures were selected to learn Markov models and to test. In addition, also the photos with a lower resolution and lower quality were used compared to those used in previous tests. The study was conducted in terms of false acceptance and false rejection rates, regardless to the proper functioning of the certain stages of the method. All the results from the first and the second variant tests are given in Table 2. For a better comparison of all tests 500 different people were used in the face database.

Table 2. Results of tests for identity verification based on the asymmetry of the face, for the first and second variant of the test, with no preliminary selection images

Num. of Users	Test V1		Test V2	
	FAR [%]	FRR [%]	FAR [%]	FRR [%]
100	3.00	7.00	7.00	12.00
200	4.50	9.50	7.50	12.50
300	6.00	13.66	8.00	17.66
400	8.25	14.50	9.75	22.00
500	9.20	16.40	11.20	24.80

It can be expected that in conditions close up to the actual error rates reach a worse value. Comparison tests performed for selected images, and the pictures without pre-selection is shown in Fig. 3.

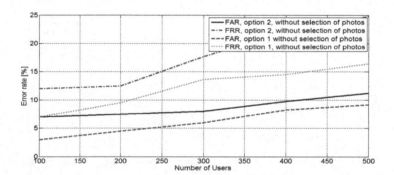

Fig. 3. Comparison of FAR and FRR for the first and second variant of the test, with no preliminary selection

The tests provided one very essential information, namely the creation of observations based on straight lines through characteristic points, intersecting in the face area introduces too big discrepancy during encoding. This leads to worse functioning of the whole method, during the preliminary selection of images.

Finally it is worth mentioning that both the false acceptance rates, as well as the false rejection rates were determined on the basis of the accepted experimentally threshold value, which used hidden Markov models allow.

6   Conclusion and Future Work

The asymmetry of the face is one of the newer trends in research related to biometrics. The described method in this paper relies on pictures of colour faces, taken in a very good quality. It is known that colour pictures depend on lighting conditions rather than the grey-scale pictures. However, at the present stage of research it is hard to reject the information about the colour, due to simpler functioning of certain algorithms in RGB space.

The proposed method of asymmetry uses actually only six characteristic points of the face, on which other elements of algorithms form a template of facial asymmetry. It is clear that this is definitely not enough elements to create a global system for a large number of users. It should be focused on using the information about facial asymmetry from point of supporting identification and verification systems, based on other biometric features. Information about facial asymmetry is often used in medicine as an element indicating the degenerated changes or any disease. In the work [8], the author mentions the use of facial asymmetry to identify physical and mental diseases on the basis of the so-called "ophthalmic geometry". However, as it turned out after the studies in this work, the information about the point of intersection of the two straight lines cannot be used, designated on the basis of points located very close to each other with regard to designated point of the intersection. This approach causes that even an error in determining the base point at the level of one pixel resulting in a large difference in the output (ie, the intersection of two straight lines).

The use of hidden Markov models for the biometric authentication of a person [17] based on facial asymmetry is possible if the right conditions are provided to learn and test the pictures. The models manage better if base points are determined properly, and the template of facial asymmetry has every time a similar shape (within a given user). In other way, the model can give false results, especially when there is a large database of pictures. However, if the errors are corrected, resulting from the faulty determining of the characteristic points of the face, it is worthwhile to use hidden Markov models, which was shown in the second variant of the tests with a preliminary selection of the pictures. First of all, Markov models allow to analyse the data presented in the form of observation vector with different lengths, which increases the flexibility of the system, and in addition it is easy to control the verification process based on the thresholding of a computed response value to the input data by the model.

In summary, the information about facial asymmetry can be used as a further feature in hybrid systems, especially if the number of users in the database of the system is quite significant. In the case of a small number of users (up to several dozen) the correct identity verification is possible at a very safe level.

Acknowledgments. The third author acknowledges the support of the FNR (National Research Fund) Luxembourg under project Galot–Inter/DFG/12/06.

References

1. Wanga J., Youa J., Li Q., Xu Y.: Orthogonal discriminant vector for face recognition across pose, Pattern Recognition, Elsevier, 45, 4069–4079, (2012)
2. Chen W., Flynn P.J, Bowyer K.W.: Fully Automated Facial Symmetry Axis Detection in Frontal Color Images, In Automatic Identi?cation Advanced Technologies, Fourth IEEE Workshop on, 106–111, IEEE, (2005).
3. Choras R.: Automatic Feature Extraction from Ocular Images, Open Journal of Applied Sciences, Vol. 2 No. 4B, 34–38, (2012).
4. Kubanek M., Rydzek S.: A Hybrid Method of User Identification with Use Independent Speech and Facial Asymmetry, Lecture Notes in Artificial Intelligence, 5097, 818–827, (2008).
5. Mitra S., Lazar N.A., Liu Y.: Understanding the Role of Facial Asymmetry in Human Face Identification, Journal Statistics and Computing, 17, 1, 57–70, (2007).
6. Mitra S., Savvides M., Kumar B.V.K.V.: One Bit Facial Asymmetry Code (FAC) Based in the Fourier Domain for Human Recognition, Lecture Notes in Computer Science, 3546, 61–70, (2005).
7. Zhang G.,Wang Y.: Asymmetry Based Quality Assessment of Face Images, Lecture Notes in Computer Science, 5876, 499–508, (2009).
8. Kompanets L.: Biometrics of Asymmetrical Face, Biometric Authentication, Lecture Notes in Computer Science, 3072, 67–73, (2004).
9. Mitra S., Liu Y.: Local facial asymmetry for expression classi?cation, in Proceedings of CVPR, (2004).
10. Kubanek M.: Automatic Methods for Determining the Characteristic Points in Face Image, Lecture Notes in Artificial Intelligence, 6114, Part I, 523–530, (2010).
11. Kubanek M.: Method of Speech recogntion and Speaker Identification with Use Audio-Visual of Polish Speech and Hidden Markov Models, Biometrics, Computer Security Systems and Artificial Intelligence Applications, 45–55, (2006).
12. Kubanek M., Bobulski J., Adrjanowicz L.: Characteristics of the use of coupled hidden Markov models for audio-visual Polish speech recognition, Bulletin of the Polish Academy of Sciences - Technical Sciences, 60, 2, 307–316, (2012).
13. Kompanets L., Kubanek M., Rydzek S.: Czestochowa Precise Model of a Face Based on the Facial Asymmetry, Opthalmogeometry, and Brian Asymmetry Phenomena: the Idea and Algorithm Sketch, Enhanced Methods in Computer Security, Biometric and Artificial Intelligence Systems, 239–251, (2005).
14. Kompanets L., Kubanek M., Rydzek S.: Czestochowa-Faces and Biometrics of Asymmetrical Face, Lecture Notes in Artificial Intelligence, 3070, 742–747, (2004).
15. Hollingsworth K.P., Clark S.: Eye-catching Eyebrows: Training Humans in Periocular Image Verification, IEEE International Conference on Biometrics: Theory, Applications, and Systems, 1–8, (2012).
16. Vezhnevets V.S., Soldatov S., Degtarieva A.: Automatic extraction of frontal facial features, Proc. of the Sixth Asian Conference on Computer Vision (ACCV04), vol 2, 1020–1025, (2004).
17. Bobulski J., Adrjanowicz L.: Two-Dimensional Hidden Markov Models For Pattern Recognition, Lecture Notes in Artificial Intelligence, 7894, Part I, 515–523, (2013).

Spatial Keypoint Representation
for Visual Object Retrieval

Tomasz Nowak[1], Patryk Najgebauer[1], Jakub Romanowski[1], Marcin Gabryel[1],
Marcin Korytkowski[1], Rafał Scherer[1], and Dimce Kostadinov[2]

[1] Institute of Computational Intelligence, Częstochowa University of Technology
Al. Armii Krajowej 36, 42-200 Częstochowa, Poland
{tomasz.nowak,patryk.najgebauer,jakub.romanowski,marcin.gabryel,
rafal.scherer,marcin.korytkowski}@iisi.pcz.pl
http://iisi.pcz.pl
[2] University of Geneva, Computer Science Department,
7 Route de Drize, Geneva, Switzerland
http://sip.unige.ch

Abstract. This paper presents a concept of an object pre-classification method based on image keypoints generated by the SURF algorithm. For this purpose, the method uses keypoints histograms for image serialization and next histograms tree representation to speed-up the comparison process. Presented method generates histograms for each image based on localization of generated keypoints. Each histogram contains 72 values computed from keypoints that correspond to sectors that slice the entire image. Sectors divide image in radial direction form center points of objects that are the subject of classification. Generated histograms allow to store information of the object shape and also allow to compare shapes efficiently by determining the deviation between histograms. Moreover, a tree structure generated from a set of image histograms allows to further speed up process of image comparison. In this approach each histogram is added to a tree as a branch. The sub tree is created in a reverse order. The last element of the lowest level stores the entire histogram. Each next upper element is a simplified version of its child. This approach allows to group histograms by their parent node and reduce the number of node comparisons. In case of not matched element, its entire subtree is omitted. The final result is a set of similar images that could be processed by more complex methods.

Keywords: content-based image retrieval, keypoints, histograms.

1 Introduction

In this paper, we discuss the issue of semantically similar images recognition. Search of semantically similar images consists in finding images with related content such as aircrafts, dogs, cars etc. Phase of image processing is performed at the level of its pixels and there are not considered any other ways of image description (image labels, classes of image and others). Processed image is represented by various local features obtained on the basis of pixels, which may

L. Rutkowski et al. (Eds.): ICAISC 2014, Part II, LNAI 8468, pp. 639–650, 2014.

be colors, shapes or keypoints [30][32][34]. There are many methods of image processing, which are usually intended for specific areas of images processing e.g. face recognition [15], fingerprint [35], various symbols and specific objects. Often these methods are created for a specific purpose and usually they reach the goal much more faster and more accurately than humans can do. However, many contemporary methods ignore a very important feature of images which is spatial distribution of image features [4]. The development of appropriate model of the spatial representation of processed image objects constitutes a major challenge. It is especially difficult in the case for visual classification of any objects belonging to different classes. Images can be also classified by various soft computing techniques [1][3][5][6][7][8][16][17][19][20][21][22][23][24][25][28][29]. Novel approach for image retrieval based on nonparametric estimates (see e.g. [12][26][27]) was presented in [9].

The main problem during image processing is a different perception of the same image by humans and computers. Humans focus on the information carried by the image, remember objects and their names, their relationships and the place in which they are located. Less attention is focused on details in image, trying to simplify and remember generalized information. In many cases humans are unable to reproduce precisely the remembered image, while the computer analyzes the image at a much lower level. Computers do not know what is located in an image, they remember just a group of pixels describing specific image. Pixels are perceived by computers as e.g. three color components pixels. By proper processing this kind of data sets, it is possible to classify processed images.

Most of general purpose algorithms are used to determine automatically interest points also called keypoints. The keypoints are identifiers of image areas which are distinctive from the rest of the image. By applying keypoints it is possible to skip less important parts of the image and focus only on specific areas. However keypoints do not allow search for images which are similar to each other. Important applications of keypoints are finding identical pieces of images, tracking of selected objects in video sequence or to create so-called maps of points that describe local image gradient. Methods based on keypoints often generate a large amount of points that contains only partial information about the image. Their significant and constant amount relative to each image is a problem of searching the common parts of images in their larger group. The disorder is fact that some points from one image does not correspondent to other one which is similar in theory. The search for images related to each other (e.g. two similar objects) with use only keypoints will not work correctly. Not significant change of view point causes that keypoints set will be different than in original image and in result adopting a rigid relationship between points in both images make that will be searched only parts of identical images or relation will be not found. To seek thematically similar objects there is a need to create a specific data structure which will allow to generalize the description of keypoints. In this paper we present a method of generalized keypoints description using histograms. This method of keypoints representation allows to compare similar objects contained in different images, as will be shown in experimental results. In addition, we will present image dictionary built on the basis of histograms, which allows to quick search large image data sets.

The paper is structured as follows. Section 2 shows an overview of popular existing methods of image comparison. Section 3 presents detailed discussion of the problem. Section 4 shows the new method of comparing objects in images. Section 5 shows the results of experiments carried out using the proposed method. Section 6 presents conclusions.

2   Previous Work

Histograms in the processing digital images have a long history. With their help, we can describe many dependencies contained in the image. One of the primary uses of histograms in the process of image processing is to represent the distribution of colors. There are many algorithms based on the analysis of color histograms of the image [11][14][31]. Histograms in the process of image processing are most commonly used to assign the number of pixels in the image to corresponding levels of brightness or color [13]. Histograms are widely considered to be very efficient and concise instrument to provide visual content of a digital image. However, the use of histograms only for the color distribution does not present the image in an unambiguous manner. Many different images may have the same histograms. In this paper we present a method to apply histograms to represent keypoints generated using the SURF algorithm [2]. This approach of keypoints representation will allow to describe their spatial distribution, thus it will be possible to find different objects belonging to the same class. With use of this method we expand the application of the classical approach for comparing images with the keypoints.

To generate keypoints we use the SURF algorithm. The main features of each generated keypoint are: position, orientation, size and descriptor. Algorithms for computing keypoints usually apply a mask defining the local extremes of the image. Such operation is typical for blob detection algorithms (Fig. 1) [33]. The image is processed many times and in each subsequent step the size of the mask is increased, creating a so-called pyramid. This allows to determine the keypoints regardless of their scale. The important advantage of the algorithm is significant acceleration relative to the previous algorithmic solutions. The increase in the efficiency is due to several improvements. In previously used algorithms there were used Gauss masks which required aggregation of all of the pixels repeatedly with a predetermined coefficient. The SURF algorithm is improved by using the so-called Integral Image (1) algorithm which allows rapidly calculating the sum of pixels in a selected area of image. The adopted simplified masks have a negative impact on the accuracy of the calculated descriptors. Integral image is a structure which is represented by the sum of pixels in any rectangular area of the input image I

$$I_{\sum}(x,y) = \sum_{i=0}^{i \leq x} \sum_{j=0}^{j \leq y} I(x,y) \,, \tag{1}$$

where I - processed image, $I_\sum(x, y)$ - the sum of all pixels in the image. Calculation of the sum of the pixels in the selected area of the image (Integral Image) is described by (2)

$$\sum = A - B - C + D, \qquad (2)$$

where A, B, C and D values are the coordinates of the vertices of the selected rectangular area in the image.

Finally, the algorithm generates descriptor and orientation for each of keypoints. Calculated orientation of the keypoint allows generating the same type of descriptors of keypoint regardless of the global orientation of the entire image. The descriptor (3) is a form of description of the local gradient over which keypoint is located

$$V_{sub} = \left[\sum dx, \sum dy, \sum |dx|, \sum |dy| \right]. \qquad (3)$$

Object recognition based on keypoints is usually carried out by matching keypoints from two processed images. Matching is carried out by finding the nearest neighbor in the data base of keypoints. The keypoints are typically used to search for exactly the same objects in another image, e.g. to object tracking in video sequences.

3   Problem Description

Keypoints are very useful in situations when the same objects are present in different images. They are resistant to some degree to change in rotation and scale of image. However, keypoints are not sufficient method in situations where there is a need to find objects of similar shape to each other, but not the exact copy of them (e.g. two different cars). This may be the not the keypoints limitation, but generally this is caused by the way in which they are compared. To find a correlation of a pair of points on the two images, all keypoints are compared point by point and the same rule applies to find similar descriptors of similar keypoints. Such an approach makes it impossible in practice to search for images different than processed one (or its fragments).

As it was mentioned above, often a situation occurs where for two the same objects generate different keypoints. To properly compare objects there should be kept an adequate tolerance between calculated descriptors. Increasing the tolerance results in the ability to create groups of similar descriptors. For example, Table 3 shows a matrix in size 4x4 where we present values of the deviations between two V_{sub} descriptors of two similar keypoints. To illustrate similarity of keypoints which descriptors were compared, we present them in Fig. 1. For humans these points seem to be identical while the standard deviation between these keypoints descriptors is 0.4743. For this reason, descriptors can be assumed to be identical when their standard deviation does not exceed 0.5. The simplest and first adopted method for the representation and indexing of keypoints is to generate stable hash codes based on descriptors. Such a solution would be

Fig. 1. SURF similar keypoints example with 0.47 value of different between descriptor components

Table 1. Deviation $(\Delta V_{sub}(x,y))$ between V_{sub} values of two similar keypoints

(a/b)	1	2	3	5
1	0.0078	0.0042	0.0619	0.0120
2	0.0293	0.0176	0.0282	0.0103
3	0.0210	0.0306	0.0473	0.0027
4	0.0003	0.0298	0.0181	0.0678

advisable due to the potential use of indexing used in data bases. Unfortunately, the nature of constructing descriptors and previously mentioned deviations between descriptors of keypoints cause many problems. To develop efficient and effective method of searching similar objects, there is a need to simplify description of keypoints enough, to be able to correctly classify processed objects. Frequently those encountered problems in finding similar keypoints stemmed from:

- Descriptor presence in the middle of two hash code values,
- Random deviations of the individual values of descriptors,
- Deviations resulting from changes in orientation, position or scale,
- Distortion or image noise in keypoints areas.

During the generation of the keypoints a set of points is created with various number of them. The number of keypoints depends mainly on the size of image and the amount of details contained in image. For example, the number of generated keypoints of the image in size of 1280x800 pixels in most cases exceeds 1000. During comparison process of two images, the large number of calculated keypoints is the reason of significant slow down.

The easiest way to compare keypoints from different images is all-to-all comparison, but with such a large number of points, this may require a significant time complexity of the algorithm. As an example we can consider two sets of keypoints with 1000 points in each of them. In this situation the algorithm needs to calculate one million of keypoint comparisons. To reduce the number of required comparisons of descriptors we can organize them by sorting. Properly sorted points allow for the omission of part of the descriptors during their comparison.

4   Proposed Method

Given a set of keypoints of the test object generated using the SURF algorithm, we set the new point which is the center of this object. The new point will be a center of the coordinate system, based on which we define the distribution of the remaining keypoints in space. Specifying the position of the new points $(\bar{x}, \bar{y})$ we use dependency

$$\bar{x} = \frac{\sum_{i=1}^{n} w_i x_i}{\sum_{i=1}^{n} w_i}, \quad \bar{y} = \frac{\sum_{i=1}^{n} w_i y_i}{\sum_{i=1}^{n} w_i}, \tag{4}$$

where $[x_1, x_2, ..., x_n]$, $[y_1, y_2, ..., y_n]$ are coordinates of the points and $[w_1, w_2, ..., w_n]$ are weights of the points. The next step is calculating angle which was created between the straight line passing through the test keypoints and the X-axis of the coordinate system. It is known that tg angle of inclination graph of a function to the axis X is equal $a = tg\alpha$. Classification of the keypoints we condition from these angles. Assumed intervals from 0° degrees to 360°, with the increment every 5°, for example. $0^o - 5^o$, $5^o - 10^o$ etc. In this way we obtain 72 intervals. In each of the intervals calculated distance between keypoints and the origin (5). Average distance in each of the compartments (6) are moved on a histogram, where the Y axis is normalized average distance, and the X axis the individual invtervals. Storing keypoints in this way causes that similar histograms are generated for similar objects belonging to the same class (Fig.2). Thanks to this solution, we expand the classical approach to search for similar images using keypoints. By generalizing the set of keypoints we created, it is possible to find a similar distribution of points for similar objects. In addition, the transformation of keypoints to histograms allows us to significantly reduce the amount of data that must be processed by a computer.

$$d_i = \sqrt{x_i^2 + y_i^2}, i = 1, ..., n, \tag{5}$$

$$\bar{d}_j = \frac{\sum_{i=1}^{n} d_i}{n}, j = 1, ..., 72, \tag{6}$$

where n is the number of keypoints in tested interval. To compare the histograms we used a method of tree representation of the descriptors. This method originally was used in [18] for comparison of image descriptors generated by the SURF algorithm. This method makes it possible to substantially reduce the amount of required operation during the searching similar strings values, with the possibility to take into account the standard deviation between the values of the compared sequences. The advantage of this method is the ability to add new string value without having to rebuild the entire structure. The method has been adapted to handle the histograms by extending the length of the supported numeric strings from 64 as it was in the case of the SURF algorithm to 72 values, what represents a single histogram. The method works on the principle of generalization of string values. It uses the property resulting from the comparison of numerical sequences with taking into account the threshold of allowable deviation between the strings. It can be assumed that if the deviation of two

Fig. 2. Experimental results for the selected classes. As we can see, each of the subject classes generated different histograms, which however, are relatively similar to each other within every class.

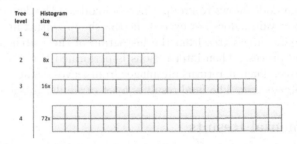

Fig. 3. Type of node descriptor in relations to node tree level

numerical strings is in the allowed range of the deviation between the sums of their values as well.

On the basis of the values of the numeric strings of all histograms, a tree is created which structure is presented in Fig.4. For each histogram is created a sub-tree and placed as the complement in the main tree. Figure 4a presents visualizations of the exemplary completion of a main tree to sub tree of the new histogram. In this process, in the first place searched nodes are shared between the trees, which values the deviation between the string of number is smallest, and does not exceed a given threshold (in the figure they are marked with a bright gray color). Other nodes (indicated in the figure in dark gray) of the sub tree will be copied to the main tree.

Each node of the tree, depending on its level in the hierarchy has a specific subsequence of numbers of histogram as shown in Fig.3, which is a generalization of string values of its child nodes. Free nodes, which are the lowest in the hierarchy tree, keep the original full sequence of 72 values of the image histogram with the name of the image. Then each subsequent node has a string value decreased

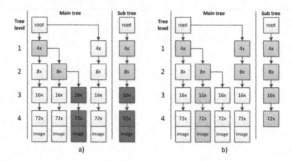

Fig. 4. Visualization of process of single histogram adding to the tree (a) and histogram comparison with the tree (b)

by summing the values of its predecessor. It increases the memory requirements of the method but simultaneously decreasing the number of steps during the image search. In the first step we compare nodes that have histograms that contains sequences of only four values instead of the 72 values of the full image histogram. In addition, each node allows to group other sub nodes if the deviation between their sequences of values does not exceed the threshold. During image searching the method creates a sub tree from the histogram of the searched image as it is in the adding process. Then intersections is performed between the sub tree and the main tree. Then it returns all images from leaves of the main tree that remain from intersection. The final result is a set of similar images.

5   Experimental Results

Experiments were performed on Caltech-101 [10] image database. The Caltech-101 database contains 9.145 images of average resolution of 300x300 pixels. Each image is also assigned to one of 101 image class. Images present various kinds of objects depending on the image category that include animals, plains, everyday objects, etc. For the experiments we limit the number of images per class to 50, because some of class contains much more images in comparison to others. The main task is to find from all the images, images of similar histograms generated from SURF keypoints. Histogram creation process have been discussed in detail in Section 3. After generating histogram the next step is to create from them a tree structure without division into classes. In the case of our experiment, our structure consist 4721 image histograms. The threshold of the maximum allowable deviation between the values of both histograms was set at 5.0. Then each image from the image database is searched in a tree structure. Each time the method finds at least one image that is its duplicate and other similar images. The result of this method is: the number of objects in a given class, the number of retrieved objects and the number of retrieved objects of the same class. The result of the method is also the number of comparison operations performed and number of all combination that would be needed to compare images in the traditional way. The results are presented in Table 2.

Table 2. First column represents class name of image group. Second column presents number of image in each class. Next three column presents dependence between number of matched image form same class to number of all matched images. The last three column presents dependence between number of compared nodes of the tree and number of combination between class image and entire image base.

Class Name	No. of images	No. of matched from same class	No. of matched all images	%	No. of compared node	No. of histgram combination	%
Scissors	39	39	40	97	41764	186069	22
Minaret	50	50	53	94	55418	238550	23
Saxophone	40	44	48	91	47809	190840	25
Faces easy	50	50	56	89	65598	238550	27
Leopards	50	50	56	89	55599	238550	23
Octopus	35	47	53	88	44512	166985	26
Lamp	50	50	58	86	61373	238550	25
Mayfly	40	44	52	84	43585	190840	22
Umbrella	50	50	59	84	59752	238550	25
Metronome	32	32	39	82	36625	152672	23
...							
Brain	50	103	537	19	65693	238550	27
Hedgehog	50	80	404	19	65203	238550	27
Watch	50	84	426	19	72290	238550	30
Cannon	43	48	258	18	55437	205153	27
Crab	50	60	323	18	63903	238550	26
Pizza	50	165	897	18	70091	238550	29
Cougar face	50	62	369	16	73065	238550	30
Gerenuk	34	42	255	16	46552	162214	28
Emu	50	61	404	15	71221	238550	29
Wild cat	34	50	329	15	47016	162214	28
SUM	4721	5561	16468	34	6004834	22523891	27

6   Conclusions and Future Work

On the basis of the experiments it can be concluded that the method can reduce the number of steps during the search in the database. Percent of compared nodes is only 27% of all the nodes which should be compared in a conventional manner. Also, most of the compared nodes are nodes with a smaller histogram than a full 72 values. From experimental results we see that most similar image are in classes like: pizza, brain, dollar_bill. The most unique images in same class and in the entire base are images from classes like: scissors, minaret, saxophone. The proposed method narrows down the number of results and will be useful in a situation when there is a need to quickly select a group of images most similar to the test image, out of a very large group of images.

Acknowledgments. The work presented in this paper was supported by a grant from Switzerland through the Swiss Contribution to the enlarged European Union.

References

1. Bartczuk, Ł., Przybył, A., Dziwiński, P.: Hybrid state variables - fuzzy logic modelling of nonlinear objects. In: Rutkowski, L., Korytkowski, M., Scherer, R., Tadeusiewicz, R., Zadeh, L.A., Zurada, J.M. (eds.) ICAISC 2013, Part I. LNCS, vol. 7894, pp. 227–234. Springer, Heidelberg (2013)
2. Bay, H., Ess, A., Tuytelaars, T., Van Gool, L.: Speeded-up robust features (surf). Comput. Vis. Image Underst. 110(3), 346–359 (2008)
3. Bazarganigilani, M.: Optimized image feature selection using pairwise classifiers. Journal of Artificial Intelligence and Soft Computing Research 1(2), 147–153 (2011)
4. Chang, Y., Wang, Y., Chen, C., Ricanek, K.: Improved image-based automatic gender classification by feature selection. Journal of Artificial Intelligence and Soft Computing Research 1(3), 241–253 (2011)
5. Cpałka, K., Rutkowski, L.: Flexible takagi-sugeno fuzzy systems. In: Proceedings of 2005 IEEE International Joint Conference on Neural Networks, IJCNN 2005, vol. 3, pp. 1764–1769 (July 2005)
6. Cpałka, K., Rutkowski, L.: A new method for designing and reduction of neuro-fuzzy systems. In: 2006 IEEE International Conference on Fuzzy Systems, pp. 1851–1857 (2006)
7. Cpałka, K.: A new method for design and reduction of neuro-fuzzy classification systems. IEEE Transactions on Neural Networks 20(4), 701–714 (2009)
8. Cpałka, K., Rutkowski, L.: Flexible takagi sugeno neuro-fuzzy structures for non-linear approximation. WSEAS Transactions on Systems 4(9), 1450–1458 (2005)
9. Duda, P., Jaworski, M., Pietruczuk, L.: On the application of fourier series density estimation for image classification based on feature description. In: Proceedings of the 8th International Conference on Knowledge, Information and Creativity Support Systems, Krakow, Poland, November 7-9, pp. 81–91 (2013)
10. Fei-Fei, L., Fergus, R., Perona, P.: Learning generative visual models from few training examples: An incremental bayesian approach tested on 101 object categories. Computer Vision and Image Understanding 106(1), 59–70 (2007), Special issue on Generative Model Based Vision
11. Gong, Y., Chuan, C.H., Xiaoyi, G.: Image indexing and retrieval based on color histograms. Multimedia Tools Appl. 2(2), 133–156 (1996)
12. Greblicki, W., Rutkowska, D., Rutkowski, L.: An orthogonal series estimate of time-varying regression. Annals of the Institute of Statistical Mathematics 35(1), 215–228 (1983)
13. Irshad, H., Roux, L., Racoceanu, D.: Multi-channels statistical and morphological features based mitosis detection in breast cancer histopathology. In: 35th Annual International Conference of the IEEE Engineering in Medicine and Biology Society (2013)
14. Hafner, J., Sawhney, H.S., Equitz, W., Flickner, M., Niblack, W.: Efficient color histogram indexing for quadratic form distance functions. IEEE Trans. Pattern Anal. Mach. Intell. 17(7), 729–736 (1995)
15. Kisku, D.R., Rattani, A., Grosso, E., Tistarelli, M.: Face identification by sift-based complete graph topology. CoRR abs/1002.0411 (2010)

16. Laskowski, Ł.: Hybrid-maximum neural network for depth analysis from stereo-image. In: Rutkowski, L., Scherer, R., Tadeusiewicz, R., Zadeh, L.A., Zurada, J.M. (eds.) ICAISC 2010, Part II. LNCS, vol. 6114, pp. 47–55. Springer, Heidelberg (2010)
17. Laskowski, Ł.: A novel continuous dual mode neural network in stereo-matching process. In: Diamantaras, K., Duch, W., Iliadis, L.S. (eds.) ICANN 2010, Part III. LNCS, vol. 6354, pp. 294–297. Springer, Heidelberg (2010)
18. Najgebauer, P., Nowak, T., Romanowski, J., Gabryel, M., Korytkowski, M., Scherer, R.: Content-based image retrieval by dictionary of local feature descriptors. In: Proceedings of the 2014 International Joint Conference on Neural Networks, Beijing, July 6-11 (accepted for publication, 2014)
19. Nowicki, R.: Rough-neuro-fuzzy system with micog defuzzification. In: 2006 IEEE International Conference on Fuzzy Systems, pp. 1958–1965 (2006)
20. Nowicki, R.: On classification with missing data using rough-neuro-fuzzy systems. International Journal of Applied Mathematics and Computer Science 20(1), 55–67 (2010)
21. Nowicki, R., Rutkowski, L.: Soft techniques for bayesian classification. In: Neural Networks and Soft Computing, pp. 537–544. Springer (2003)
22. Peteiro-Barral, D., Guijarro Bardinas, B., Perez-Sanchez, B.: Learning from heterogeneously distributed data sets using artificial neural networks and genetic algorithms. Journal of Artificial Intelligence and Soft Computing Research 2(1), 5–20 (2012)
23. Przybył, A., Cpałka, K.: A new method to construct of interpretable models of dynamic systems. In: Rutkowski, L., Korytkowski, M., Scherer, R., Tadeusiewicz, R., Zadeh, L.A., Zurada, J.M. (eds.) ICAISC 2012, Part II. LNCS, vol. 7268, pp. 697–705. Springer, Heidelberg (2012)
24. Przybył, A., Jelonkiewicz, J.: Genetic algorithm for observer parameters tuning in sensorless induction motor drive, 376–381 (2003)
25. Rutkowski, L., Cpałka, K.: Neuro-fuzzy systems derived from quasi-triangular norms. In: Proceedings of 2004 IEEE International Conference on Fuzzy Systems, vol. 2, pp. 1031–1036 (July 2004)
26. Rutkowski, L.: Sequential estimates of probability densities by orthogonal series and their application in pattern classification. IEEE Transactions on Systems, Man, and Cybernetics SMC-10(12), 918–920 (1980)
27. Rutkowski, L.: Sequential pattern recognition procedures derived from multiple fourier series. Pattern Recognition Letters 8(4), 213–216 (1988)
28. Rutkowski, L., Przybył, A., Cpałka, K., Er, M.: Online speed profile generation for industrial machine tool based on neuro-fuzzy approach. In: Rutkowski, L., Scherer, R., Tadeusiewicz, R., Zadeh, L.A., Zurada, J.M. (eds.) ICAISC 2010, Part II. LNCS, vol. 6114, pp. 645–650. Springer, Heidelberg (2010)
29. Starczewski, J.T.: A type-1 approximation of interval type-2 FLS. In: Di Gesù, V., Pal, S.K., Petrosino, A. (eds.) WILF 2009. LNCS, vol. 5571, pp. 287–294. Springer, Heidelberg (2009)
30. Swain, M.J., Ballard, D.H.: Color indexing. International Journal of Computer Vision 7, 11–32 (1991)
31. Swain, M.J., Ballard, D.H.: Indexing via color histograms. In: Proceedings of the Third International Conference on Computer Vision, pp. 390–393 (December 1990)
32. Wallraven, C., Caputo, B., Graf, A.: Recognition with local features: The kernel recipe. In: Proceedings of the Ninth IEEE International Conference on Computer Vision, ICCV 2003, vol. 2, pp. 257–264. IEEE Computer Society, Washington, DC (2003)

33. Wang, L., Ju, H.: A robust blob detection and delineation method. In: Proceedings of the 2008 International Workshop on Education Technology and Training & 2008 International Workshop on Geoscience and Remote Sensing, ETTANDGRS 2008, pp. 827–830. IEEE Computer Society, Washington, DC (2008)
34. Willamowski, J., Arregui, D., Csurka, G., Dance, C.R., Fan, L.: Categorizing nine visual classes using local appearance descriptors. In: ICPR Workshop on Learning for Adaptable Visual Systems (2004)
35. Zalasiński, M., Cpałka, K.: Novel algorithm for the on-line signature verification. In: Rutkowski, L., Korytkowski, M., Scherer, R., Tadeusiewicz, R., Zadeh, L.A., Zurada, J.M. (eds.) ICAISC 2012, Part II. LNCS, vol. 7268, pp. 362–367. Springer, Heidelberg (2012)

Applications
and Properties of Fuzzy Reasoning
and Calculus

On Orientation Sensitive Defuzzification Functionals

Tomek Bednarek[1], Witold Kosiński[2,3], and Katarzyna Węgrzyn–Wolska[4]

[1] European Commission – Joint Research Centre (JRC)
Institute for Energy and Transport – Cleaner Energy Unit
Westerduinweg 3, NL-1755 LE Petten, The Netherlands
[2] Kazimierz-Wielki University
ul. Chodkiewicza 30, 85-064 Bydgoszcz, Poland
[3] Department of Computer Science
Polish-Japanese Institute of Information Technology
ul. Koszykowa 86, 02-008 Warsaw, Poland
[4] AllianSTIC, ESIGETEL
30, Rue Victor HUGO, Villejuif, France
Tomasz.Bednarek@ec.europa.eu, wkos@pjwstk.edu.pl,
katarzna.wegrzyn@esigetel.fr

Abstract. The aim of the article is to investigate defuzzification functionals in the theory of Ordered Fuzzy Numbers (OFN). The model of OFN was introduced in 2002 to overcome drawbacks of classical (convex) fuzzy numbers. Each OFN is equipped with an additional feature – the orientation. New forms of defuzzification functionals are proposed which are sensitive to the orientation change.

1 Introduction

In our previous two articles [20, 4] the initial and recent versions of Ordered Fuzzy Numbers were presented, that originates from Zadeh's classical model of fuzzy numbers. The Zadeh model is based on the concept of a membership function, like all fuzzy sets, and arithmetic operations defined on them based on the Zadeh extension principle, however with their known drawbacks. In the present article we will confine our interest to recent developments in Ordered Fuzzy Number theory (OFN), especially to defuzzification functionals sensitive to orientation. In Section 2 we give two definitions of Ordered Fuzzy Numbers: classical and extended, together with the main operations defined on them. Possible algebraic and topological structures are introduced there, namely: partially ordered ring, linear space and lattice.

In Section 3 a sensitivity to the orientation change of some functionals on the space of OFN will be defined and then investigated. Those functionals are defuzzification ones and they map results obtained using fuzzy calculus into the non-fuzzy, crisp world. In this way the results can be more easily interpreted in industry, technology (i.e. in control), as well as in the business (i.e. in decision support systems).

2 Main Definition and Structures

The goal of the authors of the previous papers [15–20] was to overcome the known drawbacks of the Zadeh model by constructing a revised concept of a fuzzy number

L. Rutkowski et al. (Eds.): ICAISC 2014, Part II, LNAI 8468, pp. 653–664, 2014.
© Springer International Publishing Switzerland 2014

and at the same time to maintain the algebra of crisp (non-fuzzy) numbers within this concept. In our investigations we wanted, to some extent, to avoid the arithmetic based on both: Zadeh's extension principle and interval calculus on α-sections of membership functions of fuzzy numbers, and to be close to the standard operations used on real numbers. The descriptions of our generalized model of fuzzy numbers given in our first papers can be reformulated in the following definition.

Definition 1. *An Ordered Fuzzy Number A (in Polish: skierowana liczba rozmyta, OFN) is an ordered pair (f, g) of continuous functions $f, g : [0, 1] \to \mathbb{R}$.*

The set of all OFN we denote by $\mathcal{R}$. The functions f and g are called the **branches of fuzzy number** A. Notice that in our definition we do not require that the two continuous functions f and g are inverse functions of some membership function. This means that, referring to classical fuzzy numbers defined by membership functions, corresponding membership function needs not exist for OFN. Notice that a pair of continuous functions (g, f) determine an Ordered Fuzzy Number different than the pair (f, g); graphically the corresponding curves determine two different orientations of 2 Ordered Fuzzy Numbers. In this way to any CFN ([3]) with continuous membership function correspond two OFNs: they will differ by their orientations.

Definition 1 of Ordered Fuzzy Numbers has been recently generalized in [23].

Definition 2. *By an Oriented Fuzzy Number we understand a pair of functions (f, g) defined on the unit interval $[0, 1]$, which are of bounded variation.*

In this way, the space $\mathcal{R}$ is somehow enlarged to the space of functions in $BV(0, 1) \times BV(0, 1)$, elements of which are continuous ([32]), except for a countable number of points. We can call elements of the space of pairs of functions satisfying Def.2 Oriented Fuzzy Numbers (for difference). They form a different space, and we write for it $\mathcal{R}_{BV}$. It is worthwhile to point out that a class of Oriented Fuzzy Numbers represents the whole class of convex fuzzy numbers (CFN).

To be in agreement with further and classical notations of fuzzy sets (numbers), the independent variable of both functions f and g is denoted by y (or s), and the values of them by x. The continuity of both parts implies that their images are bounded intervals, say UP and $DOWN$, respectively (Fig. 1a). We could use the following symbols to mark the boundaries for $UP = [l_A, 1_A^-]$ and for $DOWN = [1_A^+, p_A]$ in Figure 1. In general, these intervals need not be proper.

In Fig. 1 two examples of OFN are given, on each of them to ordered pair of two continuous functions $f(y)$ and $g(y)$ as two quadratic functions and two polynomials of 3-ed order. Corresponding membership functions of convex fuzzy numbers with extra bars, and arrows denoting the orientation of the closed curves are given. In each example on Fig.1:

1)f is increasing, and g is decreasing, moreover 2) $f \le g$ (pointwiese), and the membership function $\mu(x), x \in \mathbf{R}$ is $\mu(x) = f^{-1}(x)$, if $x \in [f(0), f(1)] = [l_A, 1_A^-]$, and $\mu(x) = g^{-1}(x)$, if $x \in [g(1), g(0)] = [1_A^+, p_A]$ and $\mu(x) = 1$ when $x \in [1_A^-, 1_A^+]$. However, whenever functions f and/or g are not invertible or condition 2) is not satisfied, then the membership curve (or relation) in the plane $x - y$ can be defined, only, and composed of the graphs of f and g and the line $y = 1$ over the core

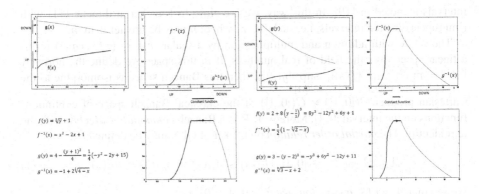

Fig. 1. Graphical representation of OFN and its corresponding membership function

$\{x \in [f(1), g(1)]\}$. If $f(1)$ is less than $g(1)$, we can obtain improper intervals for $[l_A, 1_A^-]$ or $[1_A^+, p_A]$ which have been already discussed in the framework of extended interval arithmetic by Kaucher in [11]. It is worthwhile to point out that a large class of Ordered Fuzzy Numbers (OFN's) satisfying Def. 2 represents the whole class of convex fuzzy numbers ([2, 3, 12, 33, 43]).

If some of the conditions 1) or 2) for f and g formulated above are not satisfied, and the construction of the classical membership function is not possible, Prokopowicz introduced the *corresponding* membership function in [36–38].

Let us define main operations and properties of the space of OFN satisfying Def.1, i.e. on $\mathcal{R}$. Let $A = (f_A, g_A)$, $B = (f_B, g_B)$ and $C = (f_C, g_C)$ be Ordered Fuzzy Numbers. The sum $C = A + B$, product $C = A \cdot B$ and division $C = A \div B$ are defined in $\mathcal{R}$ as follows :

$$f_C(y) = f_A(y) \star f_B(y) \text{ and } g_C(y) = g_A(y) \star g_B(y),$$

where "$\star$" denotes "$+$", "$\cdot$" and "$\div$", respectively, and $A \div B$ is defined when $f_B(y), g_B(y) \neq 0$ for each $y \in [0, 1]$. Many operations can be defined in this way, according to the pairs of functions. Fuzzy Calculator has already been created as a calculation tool, by our co-worker Mr. Roman Koleśnik [14]. It enables easy use of all mathematical objects described as Ordered Fuzzy Numbers.

Let $r \in \mathbb{R}$ and denote by $r^\dagger$ the constant function $r^\dagger(s) = r$ for any $s \in [0, 1]$. Then $r^\ddagger = (r^\dagger, r^\dagger)$ is the Ordered Fuzzy Number representing in $\mathcal{R}$ the number r.

Subtraction in $\mathcal{R}$ is defined as addition of the corresponding negative number, i.e. $-A = (-f_A, -g_A)$. It is obvious that $A + (-A) = 0^\ddagger$. Raising to a power is defined iteratively: $A^n = A^{n-1}A = ((f_A)^n, (g_A)^n)$.

Notice that as long as we are adding Ordered (or Oriented) Fuzzy Numbers which possess their classical membership functions, and moreover, are of the same orientation, the results of addition are in agrement with the α-cut and interval arithmetic known for the classical fuzzy numbers of Zadeh. However, this does not hold, in general, if the numbers have opposite orientations, for the result of addition may lead to improper intervals as noted in [19]. In this way, we are close to Kaucher arithmetic [11] with (improper) directed intervals, i.e. such $[n, m]$ where n may be greater than m.

The set $\mathcal{R}$ with addition and multiplication by a scalar ($rA = (rf_A, rg_A)$) forms a linear space over the field of real numbers. If in this space we define the norm by $||A|| = \max(\sup_{s \in [0,1]} |f(s)|, \sup_{s \in [0,1]} |g(s)|)$, then this Banach space is isomorphic to the Cartesian product $C([0,1]) \times C([0,1])$ of the classical Banach space of continuous functions on the interval $[0,1]$. Moreover, $\mathcal{R}$ is a Banach *commutative algebra* with the unit identity. The *partial order relation* on the set of OFN may be defined by:

$$A \leq B \; \Leftrightarrow \; \forall s \in [0,1] \; [f_A(s) \leq f_B(s) \; \wedge \; g_A(s) \leq g_B(s)] . \tag{1}$$

We say that $A = (f_A, g_A)$ is *non-negative* if $A \geq 0^\ddagger$, i.e.

$$f_A \geq 0 \text{ and } g_A \geq 0. \tag{2}$$

For two numbers A and B we may define their infimum: $\inf(A, B) = C$, where $C = (\inf(f_A, f_B), \inf(g_A, g_B))$, and in an analogous way their supremum, we get the next structure on $\mathcal{R}$, namely a *lattice*. Its sublattice will be a chain of Ordered Fuzzy Numbers related to real numbers. If $A \leq B$, then the set $[A, B] = \{C \in \mathcal{R} \; : \; A \leq C \leq B\}$ will be a sublattice of the lattice $(\mathcal{R}, \leq)$.

It is obvious that in the space $\mathcal{R}_{BV}$ of pairs of functions satisfying Def.2 we may introduced the same operations as in the case of $\mathcal{R}$ with a small correction: division $A \div B$ is defined, if the functions $|f_B|$ and $|g_B|$ are greater than zero. Moreover, the space $\mathcal{R}_{BV}$ can be formed as a Banach space by introducing the norm based on the total variation [1]. What is more interesting: in this space we can distinguish a proper subspace formed of pairs of step functions [26, 27]. If we fix a natural number K and split $[0,1)$ into $K - 1$ subintervals $[a_i, a_{i+1})$, i.e. $\bigcup_{i=1}^{K-1} [a_i, a_{i+1}) = [0, 1)$, where $0 = a_1 < a_2 < ... < a_K = 1$, and define a **step function** f **of resolution** K by putting u_i on each subinterval $[a_i, a_{i+1})$. Thus any such function f is identified with a K-dimensional vector $f \sim u = (u_1, u_2...u_K) \in \mathbf{R}^K$, the K-th value u_K corresponds to $s = 1$, i.e. $f(1) = u_K$. Taking a pair of such functions, we have an Oriented Fuzzy Number from $\mathcal{R}_{BV}$. Now we introduce

Definition 3. *By a Step Oriented Fuzzy Number A of resolution K we mean an ordered pair (f, g) of functions such that $f, g : [0,1] \rightarrow \mathbf{R}$ are K-step functions.*

We use $\mathcal{R}_K$ to denote the set of elements satisfying Def. 3. An example of a Step Oriented Fuzzy Number and its membership function are shown in Fig. 3 (where for the better image the vertical intervals connecting the steps of the functions have been drawn). It is obvious that each element of the space $\mathcal{R}_K$ may be regarded as an approximation of elements from $\mathcal{R}_{BV}$, by increasing the number of steps we obtain the better approximation. The norm of $\mathcal{R}_K$ is assumed to be the Euclidean one for $\mathbf{R}^{2K}$, then we have an inner-product structure at our disposal. The subspace of Step Oriented Fuzzy Numbers (SOFN) is - from a numerical point of view - more suitable in applications [10, 30], and gives the possibility of approximating elements of the whole space $\mathcal{R}_{BV}$.

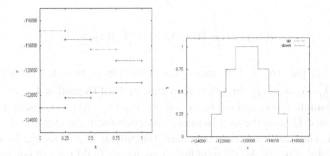

Fig. 2. Step Ordered Fuzzy Number and its corresponding membership relation

3   Defuzzification Functionals

Important role in applications of fuzzy numbers to technological problems are played by fuzzy inference systems. Especially in fuzzy control problems, one uses fuzzy inference systems [5, 35, 41] which are based on fuzzy rules, where a fuzzy conditional part (i.e antecedent part) is linked to a fuzzy conditional part, (i.e. consequent part) by If–Then terms. If a consequent part of a fuzzy rule is fuzzy, i.e. it represents a fuzzy set, then a procedure is needed, in the course of which a fuzzy set or a fuzzy number is associated with a real number. Such procedures are realized by functionals. The classical theory of fuzzy sets and numbers knows a number of such functionals and their properties [2, 3, 5, 12, 31, 34, 35, 40, 42, 45, 46]. Let $c \in \mathbf{R}$ and $A \in \mathcal{R}$ (or $\mathcal{R}_{BV}$).

Definition 4. *A mapping ϕ from the space $\mathcal{R}$ (or $\mathcal{R}_{BV}$) of all OFN's to reals is called a defuzzification functional if it satisfies:*

1. *$\phi(c^{\ddagger}) = c$,*
2. *$\phi(A + c^{\ddagger}) = \phi(A) + c$,*
3. *$\phi(cA) = c\phi(A)$, for any $c \in \mathbf{R}$ and $A \in \mathcal{R}$,*
4. *$\phi(A) \geq 0$, if A is non-negative (cf. (2)),*

where $c^{\ddagger}(s) = (c, c)$, $s \in [0, 1]$ represents the crisp number c.

From Definition 4 it follows that any defuzzification functional must be *homogeneous of order one*, *restrictive additive*, *normalized* and *positive* or *monotonic*. In our previous publication [29] the last condition was not yet presented.

In the case of the space $\mathcal{R}$, thanks to the Banach–Kakutami–Riesz theorem [1] applied to the adjoint space $C([0, 1])^{*}$, each linear and bounded functional on $\mathcal{R} = C([0, 1]) \times C([0, 1])$ satisfying conditions 1) and 4), is represented by

$$\phi(f, g) = \int_{0}^{1} f(s)\nu_1(ds) + \int_{0}^{1} g(s)\nu_2(ds), \tag{3}$$

for arbitrary $f, g \in C([0, 1])$, with two nonnegative Radon measures (ν_1, ν_2) on $[0, 1]$, such that $\nu_1([0, 1]) + \nu_2([0, 1]) = 1$. Since each Radon measure on $[0, 1]$ is represented by a function of bounded variation, we have

$$\phi(f,g) = \int\limits_0^1 f(s)dh_1(s) + \int\limits_0^1 g(s)dh_2(s) \tag{4}$$

for an arbitrary pair (h_1, h_2) of nonnegative functions of bounded variation on $[0,1]$ that satisfy $\int_0^1 dh_1(s) + \int_0^1 dh_2(s) = 1$, in view of 1) of Definition 4.

If we substitute $h_1(s)$ and $h_2(s)$ by $\lambda H(s)$ and $(1 - \lambda)H(s)$, respectively, where $0 \leq \lambda \leq 1$, and $H(s)$ is the step Heaviside function (with the step at $s = 1$), we may obtain all the classical linear defuzzification functionals known for the fuzzy numbers of Zadeh [3, 40], namely: MOM (*middle of maximum*), FOM (*first of maximum*), LOM (*last of maximum*) and RCOM (*random choice of maximum*), depending on the choice of λ; for example if for $h_1(s)$ and $h_2(s)$ we substitute $1/2\ H(s)$, then we get MOM, presented below.

In our new model we can define a number of linear and non-linear defuzzification functionals [25, 44] as the counterparts of defuzzification functionals known for CFN or as the original ones. We will list them below.

3.1   Review of Known Defuzzification Functionals

Middle of Maxima, Φ_{MOM}

$$\Phi_{MOM}(f,g) = \frac{1}{2}(f(1) + g(1)) \tag{5}$$

First Maximum, Φ_{FOM}

$$\Phi_{FOM}(f,g) = f(1) \tag{6}$$

Last Maximum, Φ_{LOM}

$$\Phi_{LOM}(f,g) = g(1) \tag{7}$$

Random Maximum, Φ_{ROM}

$$\Phi_{ROM}(f,g) = \zeta f(1) + (1 - \zeta)g(1), \quad \zeta \in [0,1] \tag{8}$$

where ζ is an arbitrary number from $[0,1]$.

Defuzzification by the Geometrical Mean

$$\phi_{GM}(f,g) = \frac{g(1)g(0) - f(0)f(1)}{g(1) + g(0) - (f(0) + f(1))}, \tag{9}$$

if $f(s) \leq g(s)$ or $g(s) \leq f(s)$ for $s \in [0,1]$ and $f(0) \neq g(0)$, and if $f(0) = g(0)$ and $f(1) = g(1)$, then $\phi_{GM}(f,g) = \dfrac{f(1) + f(0)}{2}$, and

$$\phi_{GM}(f,g) = \frac{f(1) \cdot g(0) - f(0) \cdot g(1)}{f(1) + g(0) - f(0) - g(1)} \tag{10}$$

in all other cases. In this case we can show[39] that ϕ_{GM} possesses all the properties formulated in Def. 4. This nonlinear functional was originally proposed in [44].

Center of Gravity, Φ_{COG}

$$\phi_{COG}(f,g) = \begin{cases} \dfrac{\int_0^1 \frac{f(s)+g(s)}{2}|f(s)-g(s)|ds}{\int_0^1 |f(s)-g(s)|ds}, & \text{when } \int_0^1 |f(s)-g(s)|ds \neq 0 \\ \dfrac{\int_0^1 f(s)ds}{\int_0^1 ds}, & \text{when } \int_0^1 |f(s)-g(s)|ds = 0. \end{cases} \tag{11}$$

This functional is the counterpart of an existing functional ψ_{COG} for convex fuzzy numbers, namely

$$\psi_{COG}(\mu_A) = \frac{\int_{-\infty}^{\infty} x \cdot \mu_A(x)dx}{\int_{-\infty}^{\infty} \mu_A(x)dx}, \tag{12}$$

where μ_A is the membership function of a fuzzy number A from CFN.

Basic Defuzzification Distribution Functional, ϕ_{BADD}

$$\phi_{BADD}(A;\lambda) = \frac{\int_0^1 \frac{f_A(s)+g_A(s)}{2} \cdot |f_A(s)-g_A(s)| \cdot s^{\lambda-1}ds}{\int_0^1 |f_A(s)-g_A(s)| \cdot s^{\lambda-1}ds},$$

where $\lambda \in [0,+\infty)$.

This functional, proposed by [39], is the counterpart of the Yager and Filev's [45] more general defuzzification functional for convex fuzzy numbers called BADD (*BAsic Defuzzification Distribution*) by

$$\psi_{BADD}(\mu_A;\lambda) = \frac{\int_{-\infty}^{\infty} x \cdot [\mu_A(x)]^{\lambda} dx}{\int_{-\infty}^{\infty} [\mu_A(x)]^{\lambda} dx}, \tag{13}$$

where μ_A is the membership function of a fuzzy number A from CFN, and $\lambda \in [0,\infty)$. Notice that this functional is somehow related to the center of gravity of a figure represented in the plane by the power λ to which the function μ_A is raised. However, when calculating the power $\mu^{\lambda}(\cdot)$ one has to remember that in the set of CFN this operation is defined on the α-sections of the membership function μ.

How can one pass from BADD defined for CFN to its counterpart in the space $\mathcal{R}$? First notice that if one takes A as an element of the space of CFN, then it is represented by a membership function μ_A which may possess two representations in the space of OFN, say the pair (f_A, g_A) or the pair (g_A, f_A). Take the first pair and write

$$\mu_A(\sigma) \sim (f_A(\sigma), g_A(\sigma)), \text{ then } [\mu_A(\sigma)]^{\lambda} \sim (f_{\lambda A}(\sigma), g_{\lambda A}(\sigma)),$$

660   T. Bednarek, W. Kosiński, and K. Węgrzyn–Wolska

where $f_{\lambda A}(\sigma) = f_A(\sigma^{\frac{1}{\lambda}})$, $g_{\lambda A}(\sigma) = g_A(\sigma^{\frac{1}{\lambda}})$. Now, using the definition of the center of gravity, we can show cf. [28, 39], that

$$
\psi_{BADD}(\mu_A; \lambda) = \frac{\int_{-\infty}^{\infty} x \cdot [\mu_A(x)]^{\lambda} \, dx}{\int_{-\infty}^{\infty} [\mu_A(x)]^{\lambda} \, dx}
$$
$$
= \frac{\int_0^1 \frac{f_A(s)+g_A(s)}{2} |f_A(s) - g_A(s)| \cdot s^{\lambda-1} ds}{\int_0^1 |f_A(s) - g_A(s)| \cdot s^{\lambda-1} ds} := \phi_{BADD}(A; \lambda).
$$

Notice that the same result can be obtained if we take the opposite orientation, i.e. the representation (g_A, f_A). Hence we have concluded the general for of BADD for OFN from $\mathcal{R}$.

4 Defuzzification Functionals Sensitive to Orientation Change

As we have notice our model of OFN possesses an extra feature: each element of $\mathcal{R}$ has its "orientation reversed" counterpart, i.e. if $A = (f, g) \in \mathcal{R}$ then $\overleftarrow{A} = (g, f) \in \mathcal{R}$. The same we can say about elements of $\mathcal{R}_{BV}$.

In order to help in understanding this new feature, let us consider example [20, 22, 24], and consider a financial company, which has two units A and B. An expert states his opinion about the income of both units. About A he said: "the income is 4 million and this is a downward trend". For B he said: "the income is 3 million and this is an upward trend". He could describe incoming of both units by two (convex) fuzzy numbers. However, how can one describe the trend and the escalation of that trend? Are convex fuzzy numbers or those of $L - R$ type from [8], sufficient? The answer is no or difficult to give, at least. In the model, we have proposed, such a trend and its escalation is possible to describe in the most natural way, by equipping each fuzzy number with an additional feature, called its *orientation*. Concluding, to describe the firm A we will use a fuzzy number "around 4" with the negative orientation, while to the firm B we will use "around 3" with the positive orientation.

Definition 5. *We say that a defuzzification functional ϕ is sensitive to orientation (or in short - orientation sensitive) if there exists a fuzzy number $(f, g) \in \mathcal{R}$ (or $\mathcal{R}_{BV}$) such that*

$$\phi(f, g) \neq \phi(g, f).$$

This class of functionals was recently discussed by Dobrosielski in [7]. Now we give a list of sensitive to orientation functionals which are small modifications of the previously listed functionals.

Orientation Sensitive Maxima, Ψ_{MOM}

$$\Psi_{MOM}(\lambda, f, g) = \lambda f(1) + (1 - \lambda)g(1), \quad \lambda \in [0, 1] \tag{14}$$

First Maximum, Ψ_{FOM}

$$\Psi_{FOM}(f,g) = f(1) = \Phi_{FOM}(\mu) \tag{15}$$

Last Maximum, Ψ_{LOM}

$$\Psi_{LOM}(f,g) = g(1) = \Phi_{LOM}(\mu) \tag{16}$$

Orientation Sensitive Random Maximum, Ψ_{ROM}

$$\Psi_{ROM}(\zeta,f,g) = \zeta f(1) + (1-\zeta)g(1) = \Phi_{ROM}(\mu), \quad \zeta \in [0,1], \tag{17}$$

where ζ is a random number from the interval $[0,1]$, selected on the basis of the probability distribution function, which takes into account the preferred branch of fuzzy numbers appearing there (f,g).

4.1   Orientation Sensitive Center of Gravity, Ψ_{COG}

$$\Psi_{COG}(\zeta,f,g) = \frac{\int_0^1 (\zeta g(s) + (1-\zeta)f(s)) |g(s) - f(s)| ds}{\int_0^1 |g(s) - f(s)| ds} \ , \text{if } f(s) \neq g(s),$$

$$\Psi_{COG}(\zeta,f,g) = \frac{\int_0^1 f(s)ds}{\int_0^1 ds} \ , \text{if } f(s) = g(s). \tag{18}$$

We can see that the modification is related to the new parameter ζ which stands instead of $1/2$; its role is to demonstrate the sensitivity to the change of orientation, since in the numerator of the integrand the middle point of the interval $[f(s), g(s)]$ is substituted by an intermediate point $\zeta g(s) + (1-\zeta)f(s)$.

More examples of orientation sensitive defuzzification functionals, which are under development, will be presented during the Conference, together with some application in control.

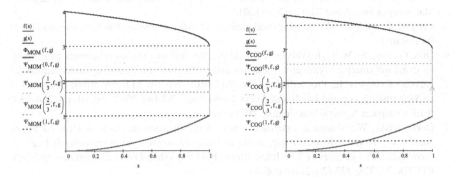

Fig. 3. Sensitive to orientation defuzzification

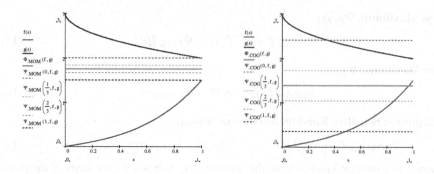

Fig. 4. Middle of maxima and center of gravity with modifications

5 Conclusions

Examples ofefuzzification of OFN with the explicit representations of their branches $f(y) = y^2, g(y) = \sqrt{(-y+1)} + 3$ on Fig.3, and $f(s) = s^3 + 0.5s$, $g(s) = -\sqrt{(s)} + 3$ on Fig.4.

It is rather easy to prove that all new orientation sensitive functionals from Sec. 4 satisfied 4 conditions of Def. 4. The authors of the present paper belief the new functionals will paly an important role in modern controller and fuzzy rule based decision support systems. Especially in the case of Natural Language Processing and in the research on the recognizing entailment in text, when asymmetric information measures defined on pairs of texts are in use [6].

References

1. Alexiewicz, A.: Analiza funkcjonalna. PWN, Warszawa (1969)
2. Buckley, J.J., Eslami, E.: An Introduction to Fuzzy Logic and Fuzzy Sets. Advances in Soft Computing. Physica-Verlag, Springer, Heidelberg (2005)
3. Chen, G., Tat, P.T.: Fuzzy Sets, Fuzzy Logic, and Fuzzy Control Systems. CRS Press, Boca Raton (2001)
4. Chwastyk, A., Kosiński, W.: Fuzzy calculus with applications. Mathematica Applicanda - Matematyka Stosowana 41(1), 47–96 (2013)
5. Czogała, E., Pedrycz, W.: Elements and methods of fuzzy set theory. PWN, Warszawa (1985) (in Polish)
6. Dias, G., Pais, S., Wgrzyn-Wolska, K., Mahl, R.: Recognizing textual entailment by generality using informative asymmetric measures and multiword unit identification to summarize ephemeral clusters. In: Proceedings of the 2011 IEEE/WIC/ACM International Conferences on Web Intelligence and Intelligent Agent Technology, WI-IAT 2011, vol. 01, pp. 284–287. IEEE Computer Society, Washington, DC (2011)
7. Dobrosielski, W.: Trangular extension - new defuzzification methods of Ordered Fuzzy Numbers (Trójktne Rozszerzanie, nowa metoda wyostrzania na skierowanych liczbach rozmytych), Proceedings of XIV International PhD Workshop OWD, Conference Archives, PTETiS, 31, 328–333 (2012) (in Polish)
8. Dubois, D., Prade, H.: Operations on fuzzy numbers, Int. J. System Science 9, 576–578 (1978)

9. Goetschel Jr., R., Voxman, W.: Elementary fuzzy calculus. Fuzzy Sets and Systems 18, 31–43 (1986)

10. Gruszczyńska, A., Krajewska, I.: Fuzzy calculator on step ordered fuzzy numbers. Engineering Thesis, WMFiT, Kazimierz-Wielki University, Bydgoszcz (2008) (in Polish)

11. Kaucher, E.: Interval analysis in the extended interval space IR. Fundamentals of Numerical Computation (Computer-Oriented Numerical Analysis) 2, 33–49 (1980)

12. Kaufman, A., Gupta, M.M.: Introduction to Fuzzy Arithmetic. Van Nostrand Reinhold, New York (1991)

13. Klir, G.J.: Fuzzy arithmetic with requisite constraints. Fuzzy Sets and Systems 91, 165–175 (1997)

14. Koleśnik, R., Kosiński, W., Prokopowicz, P., Frischmuth, K.: On algebra of ordered fuzzy numbers. In: Atanassov, K.T., Hryniewicz, O., Kacprzyk, J. (eds.) Soft Computing – Foundations and Theoretical Aspects. Akad. Oficyna Wydaw, pp. 291–302. EXIT, Warszawa (2004)

15. Kosiński, W., Prokopowicz, P., Ślęzak, D.: Fuzzy numbers with algebraic operations: algorithmic approach. In: Kłopotekk, M., Wierzchoń, S.T., Michalewicz, M. (eds.) Intelligent Information Systems 2002, Sopot, Poland, June 3-6, pp. 311–320. Physica Verlag (2002)

16. Kosiński, W., Prokopowicz, P., Ślęzak, D.: On algebraic operations on fuzzy reals. In: Rutkowski, L., Kacprzyk, J. (eds.) Proc. of the Sixth ICNNSC, Zakopane, Poland, June 11-15. Advances in Soft Computing, pp. 54–61. Physica-Verlag (2002)

17. Kosiński, W.: On algebraic operations on fuzzy numbers. Invited Lecture at ICNNSC 2002, Zakopane, Poland, June 11-15 (2002)

18. Kosiński, W., Prokopowicz, P., Ślęzak, P.: On algebraic operations on fuzzy numbers. In: Kłopotek, M., Wierzchoń, S.T., Trojanowski, K. (eds.) Intelligent Information Processing and Web Mining, Zakopane, Poland, June 2-5, pp. 353–362. Physica (2003)

19. Kosiński, W., Prokopowicz, P., Ślęzak, D.: Ordered fuzzy numbers. Bull. Pol. Acad. Sci., Math. 51(3), 327–338 (2003) Zentralblatt:1102.03310

20. Kosiński, W., Prokopowicz, P.: Algebra liczb rozmytych. Matematyka Stosowana 5/46, 37–63 (2004)

21. Kosiński, W.: On defuzzyfication of ordered fuzzy numbers. In: Rutkowski, L., Siekmann, J.H., Tadeusiewicz, R., Zadeh, L.A. (eds.) ICAISC 2004. LNCS (LNAI), vol. 3070, pp. 326–331. Springer, Heidelberg (2004)

22. Kosiński, W., Prokopowicz, P., Ślęzak, D.: Calculus with Fuzzy Numbers. In: Bolc, L., Michalewicz, Z., Nishida, T. (eds.) IMTCI 2004. LNCS (LNAI), vol. 3490, pp. 21–28. Springer, Heidelberg (2005)

23. Kosiński, W.: On fuzzy number calculus, Int. J. Appl. Math. Comput. Sci. 16(1), 51–57 (2006)

24. Kosiński, W., Prokopowicz, P., Kacprzak, D.: Fuzziness - representation of dynamic changes by ordered fuzzy numbers. In: Seising, R. (ed.) Views on Fuzzy Sets and Systems from Different Perspectives. STUDFUZZ, vol. 243, pp. 485–508. Springer, Heidelberg (2009)

25. Kosiński, W., Piasecki, W., Wilczyńska-Sztyma, D.: On fuzzy rules and defuzzification functionals for ordered fuzzy numbers. In: Burczyński, T., Cholewa, W., Moczulski, W. (eds.) Proc. of AI-Meth 2009 Conference, Gliwice. AI-METH Series, pp. 161–178 (November 2009)

26. Kosiński, W., Wilczyńska-Sztyma, D.: Defuzzification and implication within ordered fuzzy numbers. In: 2010 IEEE International Conference on Fuzzy Systems (FUZZ), pp. 1073–1079 (2010), doi:10.1109/FUZZY.2010.5584226

27. Kosiński, W., Węgrzyn-Wolska, K., Borzymek, P.: Evolutionary algorithm in fuzzy data problem. In: Kita, E. (ed.) Evolutionary Algorithms, pp. 201–218. InTech (April 2011)

28. Kosiński, W., Chwastyk, A.: On defuzzification functionals on the space of Ordered Fuzzy Numbers. Mathematica Applicanda-Matematyka Stosowana 41(1), 47–96 (2013)

29. Kosiński, W., Propopowicz, P., Rosa, A.: Defuzzification functionals of Ordered Fuzzy Numbers. IEEE Trans. Fuzzy Systems 21(6), 1163–1169 (2013)
30. Kościeński, K.: Moduł schodkowych skierowanych liczb rozmytych w sterowaniu ruchem punktu materialnego, Engineering Thesis, PJWSTK, Warszawa (2010)
31. Lęski, J.: Neuro-fuzzy systems. WNT, Warsaw (2008) (in Polish)
32. Lojasiewicz, S.: Wstęp do teorii funkcji rzeczywistych, Biblioteka Matematyczna, Tom 46, PWN, Warszawa (1973)
33. Nguyen, H.T.: A note on the extension principle for fuzzy sets. J. Math. Anal. Appl. 64, 369–380 (1978)
34. Oliveira, J.V.: A set theoretic defuzzification method. Fuzzy Sets and Systems 76(1), 63–71 (1995)
35. Piegat, A.: Modelowanie i sterowanie rozmyte, Akademicka Oficyna Wydawnicza. EXIT, Warszawa (1999)
36. Prokopowcz, P.: Algorytmizacja działań na liczbach rozmytych i jej zastosowania, Ph. D. Thesis, IPPT PAN, Warszawa (2005)
37. Prokopowicz, P.: Methods based on the ordered fuzzy numbers used in fuzzy control. In: Proc. of the Fifth International Workshop on Robot Motion and Control - RoMoCo 2005, Dymaczewo, Poland, pp. 349–354 (June 2005)
38. Prokopowicz, P.: Using ordered fuzzy numbers arithmetic. In: Cader, A., Rutkowski, L., Tadeusiewicz, R., Żurada, J. (eds.) Proc. of the 8th ICAISC, Fuzzy Control in Artificial Intelligence and Soft Computing, Zakopane, Polska, June 25-29, pp. 156–162. Acad. Publ. House EXIT, Warsaw (2006)
39. Rosa, A.: Modelowanie z wykorzystaniem skierownych liczb rozmytych, Engineering Thesis, WMFiT, Kazimierz-Wielki University, Bydgoszcz (2011)
40. Runkler, T.: Selection of appropriate defuzzification methods using application specific properties. IEEE Trans. Fuzzy Systems 5(1), 72–79 (1997)
41. Saade, J.J.: A unifying approach to defuzzification and comparison of the outputs of fuzzy controllers. IEEE Trans. Fuzzy Systems 4(3), 227–237 (1996)
42. Van Leekwijck, W., Kerre, E.E.: Defuzzification: criteria and classification. Fuzzy Sets and Systems 108, 159–178 (1999)
43. Wagenknecht, M.: On the approximate treatment of fuzzy arithmetics by inclusion, linear regression and information content estimation. In: Chojcan, J., Lęski, J. (eds.) Zbiory rozmyte i ich zastosowania, Wydaw. Politechniki Śląskiej, Gliwice, pp. 291–310 (2001)
44. Wilczyńska, D.: On control aspects within ordered fuzzy numbers in the MATLAB environment. Master Thesis, WMFiT, Kazimierz-Wielki University, Bydgoszcz (2007) (in Polish)
45. Yager, R.R., Filev, D.P.: Essentials of Fuzzy Modeling and Control. John Wiley & Sons, New York (1994)
46. Zadeh, L.A.: The concept of a linguistic variable and its application to approximate reasoning, Part I. Information Sciences 8, 199–249 (1975), doi:10.1016/0020-0255(75)90036-5

The Linguistic Modeling
of Fuzzy System as Multicriteria Evaluator
for the Multicast Routing Algorithms

Piotr Prokopowicz, Maciej Piechowiak, and Piotr Kotlarz

Institute of Mechanics and Applied Computer Science
Kazimierz Wielki University, Bydgoszcz, Poland
{piotrekp,mpiech,piotrk}@ukw.edu.pl
http://www.imis.ukw.edu.pl

Abstract. The paper presents the use of fuzzy system in multicriteria evaluation of algorithms that generate multicast trees and optimize realtime data transmission in computer networks. These algorithms take into account a number of factors such as: cost, bandwidth or delay, and their efficiency can be represented by total cost of multicast tree or average path's cost in multicast tree [18]. However, there is a lack of accurate methods for comparing and evaluating these algorithms. In addition, it is difficult to identify with precision the weight of the criteria. The paper describes various proposals models underlying linguistic system that performs two-criteria assessment. These proposals show how to implement linguistic changes and their impact on the results of the fuzzy system.

Keywords: multicriteria fuzzy evaluation, fuzzy system, multicast routing algorithms.

1 Introduction

In many areas of science that are experiencing rapid development there is the problem of mathematical modeling, especially in the evaluation of new technologies. The precise science often does not keep pace with the changes, what is understandable, because the creation of accurate models requires a structured access to multiple data of the same nature. In such situations, the fuzzy set theory seems to be a reasonable choice [25,26]. It allows to create a mathematical model based on linguistic description. The resulting theory using this model may not be optimal, but realizes the basic assumptions and, what is important, is highly intuitive. The knowledge that is the basis of the system, can be obtain from people who understand the matter in the practical literate but not well enough to use the mathematical apparatus to create an accurate model representing their skills. Such an area rapidly developing today is telecommunications. One of the subjects intensively evolving is effective transmission of data in computer networks.

Multicasting is a transmission method used in packet-switched networks for delivering mainly voice and multimedia data at the same time from one to many

L. Rutkowski et al. (Eds.): ICAISC 2014, Part II, LNAI 8468, pp. 665–675, 2014.
© Springer International Publishing Switzerland 2014

receivers. This technique requires efficient routing algorithms defining a tree with a minimum cost between the source node and the particular nodes representing the users. Such a solution prevents from duplication of the same packets in the links of the network. Routing of the sent data occurs only in those nodes of the network that lead directly to destination nodes [16].

The main objective of the publication is to assess the quality of the algorithms that generate multicast tree using fuzzy sets theory. Since there is no specific precise assessment model, it can always be expressed by a linguistic model and on its basis to build a fuzzy system.

The use of fuzzy systems for multi-criteria problems is quite common [6,2]. The same problem is presented in the literature and is called *fuzzy multicriteria analysis*. The paper [5] presents an overview of the developments in this area.

The paper is divided into six sections. Section 2 describes the implemented network model. Section 3 presents the overview of multicast routing algorithms. Section 4 focuses on multicriteria fuzzy evaluators for multicast routing algorithms while Section 5 presents the results of evaluations. Section 6 sums up the paper.

2   Network Model

The network is represented by an undirected, connected graph $G = (V, E)$, where V is a set of nodes, and E is a set of links. With each link $e_{ij} \in E$ between nodes i and j two parameters are coupled: cost c_{ij} and delay d_{ij}. The cost of a connection represents the usage of the link resources; c_{ij} is then a function of the traffic volume in a given link and the capacity of the buffer needed for the traffic. A delay in the link is in turn the sum of the delays introduced by the propagation in a link, queuing and switching in the nodes of the network. The multicast group is a set of nodes that are receivers of the group traffic (identification is carried out according to a unique i address), $M = \{m_1, ..., m_m\} \subseteq V$. The node $s \in V$ is the source for the multicast group M. Multicast tree $T(s, M) \subseteq E$ is a tree rooted in the source node s that includes all members of the group M and is called *Steiner tree*.

The total cost of the Steiner tree $T(s, M)$ can be defined as $\sum_{t \in T(s,M)} c(t)$. The path $p(s, m_i) \subseteq T(s, M)$ is a set of links between s and $m_i \in M$. The cost of path $p(s, m_i)$ can be expressed as: $\sum_{p \in P(s,m_i)} c(p)$, where $P(s, m_i)$ is a set of possible paths between s and $m_i \in M$. The delay is measured between the beginning and the end of the path as: $\sum_{p \in P(s,m_i)} d(p)$. Thus, the maximum delay in the tree can be determined as: $\max_{m \in M}[\sum_{p \in P(s,M)} d(p)]$.

Because of time complexity (the problem is proven to be $\mathcal{NP}$-hard) heuristic algorithms are most preferable for solving this problem.

3   Multicast Routing Algorithms

The implementation of multicasting requires solutions of many combinatorial problems accompanying the building of optimal transmission trees. In the optimization process it can be distinguished: MST – *Minimum Steiner Tree*, and the tree with the shortest paths between the source node and each of the destination nodes – SPT (*Shortest Path Tree*). Finding the MST, which is a $\mathcal{NP}$-complete problem, results in a structure with a minimum total cost [24]. The relevant literature provides a wide range of heuristics solving this (one and multicriterial) problem in polynomial time [12,15,20,21,27]. From the point of view of the application in data transmission, the most commonly used is the KMB algorithm [12] and its modification – KPP algorithm [9] that reflect additional link parameter – delay.

During the first phase of the KPP, a complete graph is constructed whose all vertices are the source node s and the destination nodes $m_x \in M$, while the edges represent the least cost paths connecting any two nodes a and b in the original graph $G = (V, E)$, where $a, b \in \{M \cup s\}$. Then, the minimal spanning tree is determined in this graph taking the delay constraint Δ into consideration, and then the edges of the obtained tree are converted into the paths of the original graph G. Any loops that appeared in this formed structure are removed with the help of the shortest path algorithm, for instance, by Dijkstra algorithm [4]. The computational complexity of the algorithm is $O(\Delta|V|^3)$.

Other methods minimize the cost of each of the paths between the sender and each of the members of the multicast group by forming a tree from the paths having the least costs. In general, at first either the Dijkstra algorithm [4] or the Bellman-Ford algorithm [1] is used, then the branches of the tree that do not have destination nodes are pruned. Several routing algorithms have been proposed in the literature for this problem [3,14,18,23].

In research studies the Constrained Shortest Path Tree (CSPT) is commonly used. It contains constrained shortest paths between the source and each destination node. The CSP problem (*Constrained Shortest Path*) can be stated as the problem of minimizing: $z^* = \min \sum_{e_{ij} \in E} c_{ij} e_{ij}$, subject to: $\sum_{(i,j) \in E} d_{ij} e_{ij} \leq \Delta$, where: $e_{ij} \in \{0, 1\}$ [13].

Lagrange relaxation is a popular technique for calculating lower bounds and finding better solutions than popular CSP heuristics offer [13]. Held and Karp used this first to solve the *traveling salesman problem* [7]. It bases on modified cost function c_λ which is aggregated metric. Problem can be stated as follows:

$$L(\lambda) = \min \sum_{(i,j) \in E} (c_{ij} + \lambda d_{ij}) e_{ij} - \lambda \Delta, \tag{1}$$

for certain λ: $L(\lambda) = z^*$.

The proposed *Path Lagrange Relaxation Algorithm* (PLRA) refers to Jüttner et all idea [8]. Proposed algorithm relay on minimizing aggregated (modified) cost function: $c_\lambda = c + \lambda d$. In each iteration of PLRA, the current value of λ is calculated, in order to increase the dominance of delay in the aggregated cost function, if the optimum solution of c_λ suits the delay requirements (Δ).

The operation performed by the proposed *Multicast Lagrange Relaxation Algorithm* (MLRA) consists in determining the shortest path tree between source node s and each destination node m_i, along which the maximum delay value (Δ)

cannot be exceeded. The paths determined one by one are added to the multicast tree. If there is at least one path that does not meet the requirements multicast tree cannot be constructed. Since the network structure created in that way may contain cycles, in order to avoid them Prim's algorithm has been used.

In the last phase it removes leaves nodes with outdegree 1 that are not multicast nodes. On the basis of links entering the tree and their metrics (cost and delay) the total cost of the constrained tree is calculated.

4   Multicriteria Fuzzy Evaluators for Multicast Routing Algorithms

In order to reliable comparison of multicast algorithms into network topologies with different properties, a flat random graph constructed graphs according to the Waxman method was used [24].

Due to a wide range of solutions presented in the literature of the subject, the following representative algorithms were chosen: KPP [9] and CSPT [3] algorithms and MLRA algorithm proposed in [22]. Such a set of algorithms includes solutions potentially most and least effective in terms of costs of constructed trees. The results were evaluated for three values of maximum delay (Δ: 2000, 2500 and 3000). Fuzzy system which allow to evaluate multicast routing algorithms in the further part of this article will be named Multicriteria Fuzzy Evaluator (MFE). In this section we will look at a number of avaluators taking into account two criteria: total cost of multicast tree (TCMT) and average cost of paths between source and each destination node (ACP). Linguistic model has general assumptions:

- two input variables:
  - total cost of multicast tree (TCMT) – Fig. 1(a),
  - average cost of paths between source and each destination node (ACP) – Fig. 1(a),
- one output variable: quality of multicast tree (QMT) – Fig. 1(b),
- input variables have three values: $SMALL, MEDIUM, HIGH$,
- output variable have five values: $VERYSMALL, SMALL, AVERAGE, HIGH, VERYHIGH$,
- the domain of variables is normalized to interval $[0, 1]$.

Parameters of fuzzy system:
- type of system: Mamdani,
- fuzzyfication method: singleton,
- aggregation operator for premise parts of fuzzy rules: min,
- implication operator in approximate reasoning: min,
- aggregation method for fuzzy conclusions from rules: max,
- defuzzyfication method: center of area. The system was defined in the numerical computing environment MatLab with a Fuzzy Logic Toolbox.

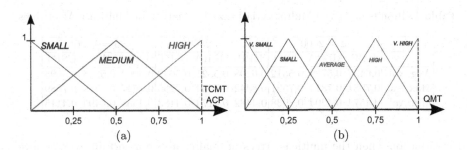

Fig. 1. Linguistic variables: input (a), output (b)

4.1 Trivial Model

This first proposal of linguistic model and fuzzy system discussed in [17] is relatively simple. Its main goal was to design a multi-criteria evaluation system in the proposed implementation. It takes into consideration vital statistics of individual features concerning the assessment of the multicast trees, so its complexity was minimized. It will serve as a reference point for other proposals here.

Basics assumptions used to determine base of linguistic rules:
– total cost of multicast tree – the smaller, the better,
– average cost of paths between source and each destination node – the smaller, the better.

The principles presented earlier lets constitute a set of nine rules used in the fuzzy system:

1. IF $TCMT$ is $SMALL$ AND ACP is $SMALL$ THEN QMT is $VERYHIGH$,
2. IF $TCMT$ is $SMALL$ AND ACP is $MEDIUM$ THEN QMT is $HIGH$,
3. IF $TCMT$ is $SMALL$ AND ACP is $HIGH$ THEN QMT is $AVERAGE$,
4. IF $TCMT$ is $MEDIUM$ AND ACP is $SMALL$ THEN QMT is $HIGH$,
5. IF $TCMT$ is $MEDIUM$ AND ACP is $MEDIUM$ THEN QMT is $AVERAGE$,
6. IF $TCMT$ is $MEDIUM$ AND ACP is $HIGH$ THEN QMT is $SMALL$,
7. IF $TCMT$ is $HIGH$ AND ACP is $SMALL$ THEN QMT is $AVERAGE$,
8. IF $TCMT$ is $HIGH$ AND ACP is $MEDIUM$ THEN QMT is $SMALL$,
9. IF $TCMT$ is $HIGH$ AND ACP is $HIGH$ THEN QMT is $VERYSMALL$,

It is observable that adopted model is very simple. It assumes the uniform distribution of input variables for the fuzzy values. The model assumptions (*the smaller – the better* rules) are trivial. Therefore, the surface of the MFE presented on Fig.3(a) is close to linear.

The results are presented in the form of four values. First three are obvious: average value, maximum value, minimum value.

4.2 Changes in the Linguistic Model

An important advantage of using fuzzy systems is their intuitiveness and ability to model linguistic. Let us now examine the second model, which could reflect

Table 1. Results of Trivial Multicriteria Fuzzy Evaluation for Multicast Algorithms

	$\Delta = 2000$			$\Delta = 2500$			$\Delta = 3000$		
	KPP	MLRA	CSPT	KPP	MLRA	CSPT	KPP	MLRA	CSPT
Avg. val.	0,6137	0,5729	0,5512	0,6208	0,5821	0,5639	0,6004	0,5848	0,5698
Max. val.	0,7981	0,7814	0,7591	0,8342	0,7434	0,7255	0,7647	0,7589	0,7589
Min. val.	0,4574	0,4204	0,3938	0,4482	0,4174	0,4183	0,4558	0,4494	0,4115

the situation when the multicast trees of quality above a certain average level we are interested in a similar way as the best ones. At the same time we want to clearly separate them inferior class of trees. Linguistically, these assumptions can be described as:
– total cost of multicast tree – medium and smaller values are very best,
– average cost of paths between source and each destination node – medium and smaller values are very best.

This can be achieved in different ways:

1. Change the base rules.
2. Change the distribution of fuzzy sets respectively over the output space (QMT).
3. Change the distribution of fuzzy sets respectively over the input space (TCMT and ACP).

Case 1 – Changes in Rules. In the next step, a new base rules were introduced changes are intuitive. For inputs $SMALL$ and $MEDIUM$ proposed quality is $VERYHIGH$. For both $MEDIUM$ inputs estimation is $HIGH$. The possibility of linguistic modeling makes the new assumptions very simple.

1. IF $TCMT$ is $SMALL$ AND ACP is $SMALL$ THEN QMT is $VERYHIGH$,
2. IF $TCMT$ is $SMALL$ AND ACP is $MEDIUM$ THEN QMT is $VERYHIGH$,
3. IF $TCMT$ is $SMALL$ AND ACP is $HIGH$ THEN QMT is $AVERAGE$,
4. IF $TCMT$ is $MEDIUM$ AND ACP is $SMALL$ THEN QMT is $VERYHIGH$,
5. IF $TCMT$ is $MEDIUM$ AND ACP is $MEDIUM$ THEN QMT is $HIGH$,
6. IF $TCMT$ is $MEDIUM$ AND ACP is $HIGH$ THEN QMT is $SMALL$,
7. IF $TCMT$ is $HIGH$ AND ACP is $SMALL$ THEN QMT is $AVERAGE$,
8. IF $TCMT$ is $HIGH$ AND ACP is $MEDIUM$ THEN QMT is $SMALL$,
9. IF $TCMT$ is $HIGH$ AND ACP is $HIGH$ THEN QMT is $VERYSMALL$,

The surface of MFE with the new rules is presented on Fig. 3(b). As can be seen it has non-linear character which clearly reflects assumptions that QMT for input parameters around medium and higher values of interval $[0; 1]$, achieve higher results. A purely linguistic approach is an advantage of such a solution. New assumptions are fulfilled by the right description in words. Unfortunately the advantage is also the flaw, which can be not clear at once. Alteration only of the rule base cause, that we concentrate on linguistic meaning. That in the more complex problem, can lead to the situation when the part of output values isn't used in the rule base. So, it can lead to the discontinuity of the system.

Table 2. Results of modified MFE – changed rules (Case 1)

	$\Delta = 2000$			$\Delta = 2500$			$\Delta = 3000$		
	KPP	MLRA	CSPT	KPP	MLRA	CSPT	KPP	MLRA	CSPT
Avg. val.	0,7957	0,7697	0,7281	0,7921	0,7808	0,7458	0,7947	0,7957	0,7731
Max. val.	0,8854	0,8891	0,8891	0,9040	0,8857	0,8870	0,9144	0,9178	0,9178
Min. val.	0,4970	0,4132	0,3427	0,2802	0,3769	0,3252	0,4848	0,4955	0,2816

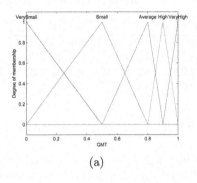 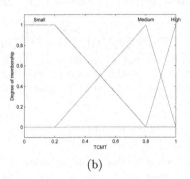

(a)   (b)

Fig. 2. Case 2: changes in output linguistic variable (a) and Case 3: changes in input linguistic variable (b)

Case 2 – Changes in Output Variable. Instead of changing rules, we can change the fuzzy sets in output linguistic variable. The change should take into account the assumption that *small and medium input values are the best.* These changes also are quite intuitive. If we want to emphasize the situation that the results that have so far been secondary interest to us as better results, it should be properly remodel fuzzy set corresponding to the size of *AVERAGE*. Of course, the shift of this size should rearrange also the remaining fuzzy sets. The Fig. 2(a) shows the adopted changes.

It should be emphasized that only the output fuzzy sets has changed. The base of rules remained the same as in the trivial model. MFE surface looks in this case as on Fig. 3(c). It can be observed that the general nature of the graph is similar to Case 1. The decision surface is non-linear and correspond to the expectations.

It should be noticed that such a solution is possible only when linguistic changes relate in a similar way to the all input variables, as in the analyzed example. Affecting only the output values do not have possibilities emphasize the greater importance of one of the inputs.

Case 3 – Changes in Input Variables. Instead of changing the rules and outputs it is possible to make modifications to the input variables. The base of rules is constructed in such a way to produce the best results for smaller inputs. In order to extend a good evaluation on the smaller input values, they must

Table 3. Results of modified MFE – changed output linguistic variable (Case 2)

	$\Delta = 2000$			$\Delta = 2500$			$\Delta = 3000$		
	KPP	MLRA	CSPT	KPP	MLRA	CSPT	KPP	MLRA	CSPT
Avg. val.	0,7920	0,7595	0,7188	0,7886	0,7710	0,7367	0,7911	0,7869	0,7634
Max. val.	0,8816	0,8909	0,8909	0,9202	0,8842	0,8853	0,9333	0,9435	0,9435
Min. val.	0,5108	0,4756	0,4567	0,4426	0,4552	0,4565	0,5035	0,5198	0,4431

Table 4. Results of modified MFE – changed input linguistic variables (Case 3)

	$\Delta = 2000$			$\Delta = 2500$			$\Delta = 3000$		
	KPP	MLRA	CSPT	KPP	MLRA	CSPT	KPP	MLRA	CSPT
Avg. val.	0,8344	0,7908	0,7698	0,8293	0,7960	0,7763	0,8340	0,8129	0,7960
Max. val.	0,9200	0,9200	0,9200	0,9200	0,9200	0,9200	0,9200	0,9200	0,9200
Min. val.	0,6398	0,5351	0,4505	0,3900	0,4955	0,4418	0,6478	0,6427	0,3908

be *covered* with membership function of $SMALL$. Changes proposed here are shown on Fig. 2(b).

For such a revised system surface looks like on Fig. 3(d). The general nature of the surface fulfills requirements – output values grow with decreasing values of the input, but difference between this one and two earlier proposals is observable. This is due to granulation of the input variables. Three values of fuzzy inputs allow fewer opportunities in the field of linguistic expression than five outputs. On the surface of the system a larger part of uniform area can be distinguish. This is due to the extension of the concept of $SMALL$, which covers the input space from 0 to 0.8. Therefore, in accordance with the rules, the values obtained a higher degree of quality assessment QMT. The advantage of this proposal is a greater possibility to differentiate the impact of individual inputs on the result.

5   Research Results

In Tables 2, 3 and 4 authors compared results of the evaluations for linguistic described change. These results come from several cases of modifications for primary proposal.

1. Case 1 – rules modification.
2. Case 2 – output modification.
3. Case 3 – input modification.

It is observable that all alterations, according to assumptions, shifted up quality assessments. Two first cases show particularly high resemblance in the average values of each method. This is understandable because of similar changes in the surfaces of fuzzy system. The third case generates results noticeably higher from two previous, at least not enough in order to change entirely the character of evaluations. Every alteration points the KPP as best method, whereas the CSPT is weakest. Moreover all changes, according to expectations, widen the

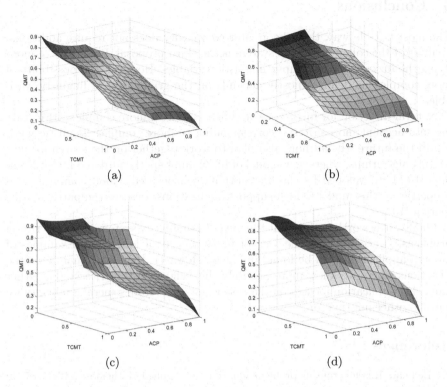

Fig. 3. Output surface plot of Trivial MFE (a), MFE with linguistic modifications of rules (b), MFE with the output fuzzy values modifications (c) and input fuzzy values modifications (d)

scope of the quality, between minimal and with maximal value. It should also be noted that, although space of evaluations is normalized to the range $[0,1]$, the graphs of surfaces presents slightly smaller range. It is directly connected with properties of the defuzzyfication method - center of area.

The problem raised in this publication relates to linguistic modeling of fuzzy system used to multicriterial evaluation of multicast routing algorithms. Analysis of the possibility of using of such methods of evaluation is a purpose.

On the one hand we have specific tools for making the connections in computer networks, on the other lack of clear and strict criteria for assessing the quality of these tools. As shown in the presented examples, a fuzzy system is suitable to solve the problem. Without a detailed mathematical model, we always can use a linguistic model that can be transfered into precise fuzzy system. Discussed examples show that the suggested tool is flexible and allows for the change of characteristics relying on the linguistic description. Each variant has its own advantages and disadvantages.

6   Conclusions

The most flexible way, that the greater complexity does not require additional analysis of the coherence of the system is the third proposal. It consists of modifying the fuzzy sets of the input linguistic variables. However, the possibility of more complex modelling, mostly depends on the granularity of linguistic variable.

Natural direction for further research is to create a more complex MFE, taking into account more criteria, corresponding to more complex linguistic models. In the future, the authors also plan to work together on the search for new routing algorithms, where new model of fuzzy numbers the Ordered Fuzzy Numbers [10,11] (developed by the first author) will be used. Good computational properties of this model (which support applications) deserve the particular attention [19].

Finally, it is worth noting that the idea of using fuzzy system in multi-criteria problems, is accompanies the idea of fuzzy sets for a long time. Examples of modern applications can be found in [2,5,6]. However, they focus mainly on the situations where we know more precisely the weights of the criteria. The other hand this publication focuses on the case when apart from general guidelines we have no other information.

References

1. Bellman, R.: On a routing problem. Quarterly of Applied Mathematics 16(1), 87–90 (1958)
2. Chen, S.-M., Yang, M.-W., Yang, S.-W., Sheu, T.-W., Liau, C.-J.: Multicriteria fuzzy decision making based on interval-valued intuitionistic fuzzy sets. Expert Systems with Applications 39(15), 12085–12091 (2012)
3. Crawford, J.S., Waters, A.G.: Heuristics for ATM Multicast Routing, Proceedings of 6th IFIP Workshop on Performance Modeling and Evaluation of ATM Networks, pp. 5/1–5/18 (July 1998)
4. Dijkstra, E.: A note on two problems in connexion with graphs. Numerische Mathematik 1, 269–271 (1959)
5. Deng, H.: Developments in Fuzzy Multicriteria Analysis. Fuzzy Information and Engineering 1, 109–115 (2009)
6. Dou, Y., Zhu, L., Wang, H.S.: Solving the fuzzy shortest path problem using multi-criteria decision method based on vague similarity measure. Appl. Soft Comput. 12(6), 1621–1631 (2012)
7. Held, M., Karp, R.: The traveling salesman problem and minimum spanning trees. Operation Research 18, 1138–1162 (1970)
8. Juttner, A., Szviatovszki, B., Mecs, I., Rajko, Z.: Lagrange Relaxation Based Method for the QoS Routing Problem. In: IEEE INFOCOM (2001)
9. Kompella V. P., Pasquale J., Polyzos G. C.: Multicasting for Multimedia Applications, In: INFOCOM 1992, pp. 2078–2085 (1992)
10. Kosiński, W., Prokopowicz, P., Kacprzak, D.: Fuzziness – representation of dynamic changes by ordered fuzzy numbers. In: Seising, R. (ed.) Views on Fuzzy Sets and Systems from Different Perspectives, 243th edn. STUD FUZZ, vol. 243, pp. 485–508. Springer, Heidelberg (2009)

11. Kosiński, W., Prokopowicz, P., Ślezak, D.: Ordered fuzzy number. Bulletin of the Polish Academy of Sciences, Ser. Sci. Math. 51(3), 327–338 (2003)
12. Kou, L., Markowsky, G., Berman, L.: A fast algorithm for Steiner trees. Acta Informatica (15), 141-145 (1981)
13. Magnanti, L., Ahuja, K.: Network Flows: Theory. In: Algorithms and Application, Prentice Hall, Upper Saddle River (1993)
14. Mokbel, M.F., El-Haweet, W.A., El-Derini, M.N.: A Delay Constrained Shortest Path Algorithm for Multicast Routing in Multimedia Applications. In: Proceedings of IEEE Middle East Workshop on Networking (1999)
15. Musznicki, B., Tomczak, M., Zwierzykowski, P.: Dijkstra-based Localized Multicast Routing in Wireless Sensor Networks. In: Proceedings of CSNDSP 2012, 8th IEEE, IET International Symposium on Communication Systems, Networks and Digital Signal Processing, Poznań, Poland, July 18-20 (2012)
16. Parniewicz, D., Stasiak, M., Zwierzykowski, P.: Multicast Connections in Mobile Networks with Embedded Threshold Mechanism. In: Kwiecień, A., Gaj, P., Stera, P. (eds.) CN 2011. CCIS, vol. 160, pp. 407–416. Springer, Heidelberg (2011)
17. Piechowiak, M., Prokopowicz, P.: Performance evaluation of multicast routing algorithms with fuzzy sets. In: Choras, R.S. (ed.) Image Processing and Communications Challenges 5. AISC, vol. 233, pp. 357–364. Springer, Heidelberg (2014)
18. Piechowiak, M., Zwierzykowski, P.: Heuristic Algorithm for Multicast Connections in Packet Networks. In: Proceedings of EUROCON 2007 The International Conference on: Computer as a Tool, Warsaw, Poland, pp. 948–955 (September 2007)
19. Prokopowicz, P.: Flexible and Simple Methods of Calculations on Fuzzy Numbers with the Ordered Fuzzy Numbers Model. In: Rutkowski, L., Korytkowski, M., Scherer, R., Tadeusiewicz, R., Zadeh, L.A., Zurada, J.M. (eds.) ICAISC 2013, Part I. LNCS, vol. 7894, pp. 365–375. Springer, Heidelberg (2013)
20. Shaikh, A., Shin, K.G.: Destination-Driven Routing for Low-Cost Multicast. IEEE Journal on Selected Areas in Communications 15(3), 373–381 (1997)
21. Stachowiak, K., Weissenberg, J., Zwierzykowski, P.: Lagrangian Relaxation in the Multicriterial Routing. In: AFRICON 2011, pp. 1–6 (2011)
22. Stasiak, M., Piechowiak, M., Zwierzykowski, P.: Multicast routing algorithm for packet networks with the application of the Lagrange relaxation. In: Proceedings of NETWORKS 2010 – 14th International Telecommunications Network Strategy and Planning Symposium, pp. 197–202 (September 2010)
23. Sun, Q., Langendoerfer, H.: Efficient Multicast Routing for Delay-Sensitive Applications. In: Proceedings of the 2nd Workshop on Protocols for Multimedia Systems (PROMS 1995), pp. 452–458 (1995)
24. Waxmann, B.: Routing of multipoint connections. IEEE Journal on Selected Area in Communications 6, 1617–1622 (1988)
25. Zadeh, L.A.: Fuzzy sets. Information and Control 8, 338–353 (1965)
26. Zadeh, L.A.: The concept of a linguistic variable and its application to approximate reasoning, Part I. Information Sciences 8, 199–249 (1975)
27. Zhu, Q., Parsa, M., Garcia-Luna-Aceves, J.J.: A Source-based Algorithm for Delay-constrained Minimum-cost multicasting. In: INFOCOM 1995: Proceedings of the Fourteenth Annual Joint Conference of the IEEE Computer and Communication Societies, vol. 1, p. 377 (1995)

Optimizing Inventory of a Firm under Fuzzy Data

Irena Sobol[1], Kurt Frischmuth[2], Dariusz Kacprzak[3], and Witold Kosiński[1]

[1] Department of Computer Science
Polish-Japanese Institute of Information Technology
ul. Koszykowa 86, 02-008 Warsaw, Poland
[2] Department of Mathematics, University of Rostock, 18051 Rostock, Germany
[3] Faculty of Computer Science, Bialystok University of Technology
ul. Wiejska 45, 15-351 Białystok
{s8531,wkos}@pjwstk.edu.pl, kurt@math.uni-rostock.de,
d.kacprzak@pb.edu.pl

Abstract. The aim of the article is to propose some tools of inventory management. One is based on the so-called fixed order quantity model which takes into account several elements of inventory cost, such as ordering cost, transportation and storing costs, frozen capital cost, as well as extra discounts. The tool deals with fuzzy concepts represented by Ordered Fuzzy Numbers. The second tool takes into account the dynamics and works on the base of replenishment system. This tool can be regarded as a kind of controller.

1 Introduction

The main objective of a good inventory management system is to keep the inventory costs to the minimum. There are several elements of inventory cost, such as ordering cost, transportation cost, frozen capital cost, cost of loss (i.e. aging), cost of lost sales due to inventory shortages, and others. Several inventory models have been built based on the above. There are two most commonly used inventory models: fixed order quantity system and replenishment system.

In the first system the quantity to be ordered is fixed and re-orders are made once the stock reaches a certain pre-determined level called safety stock. It means that the next order is typically fixed and based on the average consumption during the lead time plus some safety stock. Often in calculation the buffer stock is the one day inventory consumption.

Under the second system the quantity to be ordered is not fixed, the next order is decided based on the lead time of the material, maximum stock level, i.e. the ordered level changes with time.

In the paper we propose two tools of inventory management. One is based on the fixed order quantity model which takes into account several elements of inventory cost, as well as extra discounts. The tool deals with fuzzy concepts represented by Ordered Fuzzy Numbers. The second tool takes into account the dynamics and works on the base of replenishment system. This tool can be regarded as a kind of controller.

Dealing with the first tool the fuzzy optimization problem for the total cost function is formulated within the space, where all variables of the model are fuzzy. After the

L. Rutkowski et al. (Eds.): ICAISC 2014, Part II, LNAI 8468, pp. 676–687, 2014.

choice of a particular defuzzification functional an appropriate theorem is formulated which gives the solution of the fuzzy optimization problem.

Developing the second tool the authors face with situations when material demands are irregular in the production process. This result in nonequal ordered levels as well as in different elapse times between orders.

The organization of the paper is as follows. In Section 2 within the economic order quantity model (EOQ) the problem of management of supply is considered, in which the optimal size of a delivery from outside is determined, which minimizes total costs, when crisp unit costs of purchase, transportation and storage are given. Then a fuzzy optimization problem is formulated together with its solution in Section 3. In Section 4 a problem of management of supply and determining an optimal size of a delivery from outside is considered when the material demand depends on time. Then a solution algorithm is described. The final results of this section is a kind of controller together with a numerical example. In Section 5 some conclusions are formulated. Appendix refers to the model of OFN.

2   Economic Order Quantity Model

Inventory management within an enterprize is an integral part of its operating activities, as it affects its competitive advantage and the liquidity of its financial performance. The purpose of inventory management is to have the stock at a high enough level and operate smoothly, while incurring the lowest possible operating costs,. The present formulation is within the general framework of the model of economic order quantity (EOQ).

We consider an abstract inventory item. To estimate the cost of inventory management we formulate the main assumptions in the EOQ model:

1. the abstract inventory item is split into units,
2. we refer to some time unit, say one year,
3. demands are constant in time,
4. sells are uniform in time and known,
5. the next deliver arrives when just the stock is the one day.

Let us start with deterministic formulation in which the following objects appears:

- D- annual inventory demand, measured in number of units,
- $D/360$- daily demand for supply (assume that a year has 360 days),
- Q- order quantity, measured in number of units,
- Q_0- daily consumption of inventory,
- D/Q- frequency of the deliveries,
- $360/((D/Q)) = t_0$ - time between successive deliveries,
- c_p- unit price of purchase,
- c_T- transportation cost of a single delivery,
- c_S- unit inventory cost per day,
- $r(Q)$- discount function on purchase,
- $S(Q)$- discount function on stored inventory,
- $K(Q)$- total cost,
- K_p- purchase cost,

- K_F- frozen capital cost,
- K_T- transportation (delivery) cost,
- K_S- storage cost,
- R - banking interest rate, used to calculate the cost of frozen capital.

We can write the general expression for the total cost $K(Q)$, as the sum of the purchase cost K_p, the frozen capital cost K_f, the transportation (delivery) cost K_T and the storage cost K_S, i.e.

$$K(Q) = K_p + K_F + K_T + K_S. \tag{1}$$

Suppose that we get the discount $r(Q)$ on purchase and the discount $S(Q)$ on stored inventory depending on the amount of Q, both as step functions:

$$r(Q) = \begin{cases} r_0 = 0 \,, \text{if } 0 < Q < Q_1^r \\ \quad r_1 \quad , \text{if } Q_1^r \le Q \le Q_2^r \\ \quad r_2 \quad , \text{if } Q_2^r \le Q \le D \end{cases} \tag{2}$$

and

$$S(Q) = \begin{cases} S_0 = 0 \,, \text{if } 0 < Q < Q_1^S \\ \quad S_1 \quad , \text{if } Q_1^S \le Q \le Q_2^S \\ \quad S_2 \quad , \text{if } Q_2^S \le Q \le D \end{cases} \tag{3}$$

where Q_1^r, Q_2^r, Q_1^S and Q_2^S are fixed quantities (here 3 steps were assumed, however, more steps can also be considered). The purchase cost K_p depends on the quantity in the single deliver Q, the frequency of deliveries D/Q, the discount $r(Q)$ and the unit price c_p, and is given by

$$K_p = c_p \cdot (1 - r(Q)) \cdot Q \cdot \frac{D}{Q} = c_p \cdot (1 - r(Q)) \cdot D. \tag{4}$$

The cost of frozen capital depends on the number of deliveries D/Q, the money spent on a single delivery, the banking interest rate R, and on the single delivery Q. The form of the purchase cost K_p leads to the following cost K_F of frozen capital:

$$K_F = c_p \cdot (1 - r(Q)) \cdot Q \cdot \frac{D}{Q} \cdot \frac{R}{\frac{D}{Q}} = c_p \cdot (1 - r(Q)) \cdot Q \cdot R. \tag{5}$$

We can see that the expression K_F represents a step function, which is piecewise linear. The cost of the transportation (delivery) K_T depends on the annual frequency of deliveries D/Q and the transportation cost of a single delivery c_T, i.e.

$$K_T = c_T \cdot \frac{D}{Q}. \tag{6}$$

According to the assumptions from 3 to 5, the storage cost K_S depends on the annual frequency of deliveries D/Q, the discount $S(Q)$, the unit inventory cost c_S and the level of inventory between successive deliveries. The level of inventory is given by

$$\int_0^{t_0} \left(-\frac{Q}{t_0} \cdot t + Q + Q_0 \right) = \left(\frac{Q}{2} + Q_0 \right) \cdot t_0, \tag{7}$$

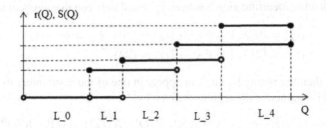

Fig. 1. Graphical representation of discount functions and subintervals L_k, $k = 0, 1, ...4$

and the storage cost by

$$K_S = \frac{D}{Q} \cdot c_S \cdot (1 - S(Q)) \cdot \left(\frac{Q}{2} + Q_0 \right) \cdot t_0 =$$

$$= \frac{D}{Q} \cdot c_S \cdot (1 - S(Q)) \cdot \left(\frac{Q}{2} + Q_0 \right) \cdot \frac{360}{\frac{D}{Q}} = 180 \cdot c_S \cdot (1 - S(Q)) \cdot (Q + 2 \cdot Q_0). \quad (8)$$

Hence the function describing the total cost $K(Q)$ in (1) summed up to

$$K(Q) = c_p \cdot (1 - r(Q)) \cdot (D + Q \cdot R) + c_T \cdot \frac{D}{Q} + 180 \cdot c_S \cdot (1 - S(Q)) \cdot (Q + 2 \cdot Q_0). \quad (9)$$

The optimization problem of inventory management requires us to find the minimum of the cost function $K(Q)$. The argument which gives the minimum is the optimal value of the order quantity. Notice that in $K(Q)$ the first and the last component depend on Q in a piecewise way. Suppose that

$$0 < Q_1^r < Q_1^S < Q_2^r < Q_2^S < D. \quad (10)$$

The search for the optimal value should be performed in a piecewise way, i.e. considering each subinterval $L_0 = (0, Q_1^r), L_1 = [Q_1^r, Q_1^S), L_2 = [Q_1^S, Q_2^r), L_3 = [Q_2^r, Q_2^S), L_4 = [Q_2^S, D]$ (Fig.1). Thus the global optimum is the quantity which gives the minimal cost over these five values calculated from each subinterval. Since

$$\frac{\partial K(Q)}{\partial Q} = c_p \cdot (1 - r(Q)) \cdot R - c_T \cdot \frac{D}{Q^2} + 180 \cdot c_S \cdot (1 - S(Q)) \quad (11)$$

and

$$\frac{\partial K(Q)}{\partial Q} = 0 \Longleftrightarrow Q^* = \sqrt{\frac{c_T \cdot D}{c_p \cdot (1 - r(Q)) \cdot R + 180 \cdot c_S \cdot (1 - s(Q))}} \quad (12)$$

in each of these subintervals L_k, $k = 0, 1, 2, 3, 4$, the local extremum is attained at

$$Q_k^* = \sqrt{\frac{c_T \cdot D}{c_p \cdot (1 - r_i) \cdot R + 180 \cdot c_S \cdot (1 - S_j)}}, \quad (13)$$

where the following idenitification has been assumed between these sets of indexes:

$$0 = k \longleftrightarrow (ij) = (00), 1 = k \longleftrightarrow (ij) = (10), 2 = k \longleftrightarrow (ij) = (11),$$
$$3 = k \longleftrightarrow (ij) = (21), 4 = k \longleftrightarrow (ij) = (22). \tag{14}$$

If $Q_k^* \in L_k,$, then the optimal value can appear in one of these subintervals or at their borders, i.e. it is attained at the argument given by

$$Q_{opt} = \arg \min\{\{K(Q_k^*), k = 0, 1, 2, 3, 4\}, K(Q_1^r), K(Q_1^S), K(Q_2^r), K(Q_2^S), K(D)\}.$$

3   Fuzzy Optimization Problem

The present formulation is within the framework of the model of the Economic Order Quantity (EOQ) and similar to the one proposed in the set of CFN by [9] and repeated by [7]. In the OFN's framework problems in economics and administrative accounting problems were formulated in [1, 3]. Our aim is to give a general solution to the optimization problem with the cost function given by (14) when D, c_p, c_T and c_S are fuzzy and represented by Ordered Fuzzy Numbers (OFN). It will be easy to see that the arithmetic of OFN manifests its superiority over the arithmetic of Convex Fuzzy Numbers (CFN), and the complex calculations performed by authors of [7, 9] can be avoided. The only thing we need to do is choose the defuzzification functional which suits the decision maker the most. For more details on OFN we refer to Appendix.

Let $\Phi(\cdot)$ be the defuzzification functional chosen by the decision maker. Then the problem of minimizing the fuzzy cost $K(Q)$ gives us the economic order quantity. Writting this explicitly

$$\text{find } \arg\{\min \Phi(K(Q)) : Q \in \mathcal{R}\}. \tag{15}$$

The new question arises: how can we find the minimum of this functional? The answer is rather obvious and comes from physics, and is formulated according to the stationary action principle: the minimum of the functional appears at the argument Q where its first variation (the Gâteaux derivative) vanishes. Calculating the first variation of $\Phi(K(Q))$ with respect to Q under given D, c_p, c_T and c_S, we get

$$\delta\Phi(K(Q)) = \partial_K\phi(K)\partial_Q K(Q)\delta Q. \tag{16}$$

The condition $\delta\Phi(K(Q)) = 0$ implies that

$$\partial_K\Phi(K)\partial_Q K(Q)\delta Q = 0, \tag{17}$$

for any variation δQ, where $\partial_K\Phi(K)$ and $\partial_Q K(Q)$ denote functional derivatives, and the argument Q^*, at which the product of these derivatives vanishes, gives us the solution to our optimization problem.

To illustrate this, let us consider a class of linear functionals given by (33). Let us denote the branches of the fuzzy number $K(Q)$ by (f_K, g_K), and for the remaining quantities we adapt the previous notation by using the appropriate subscripts, i.e.

$$D = (f_D, g_D), Q = (f_Q, g_Q), c_p = (f_p, g_p), c_T = (f_T, g_T), c_S = (f_S, g_S). \tag{18}$$

We remain the similar assumption about the discount functions $r(Q)$ and $S(Q)$ as two step functions with the steps represented by relationships (2) and (3), where r_i and S_j are here crisp[1], while the border values $Q_i^r, Q_j^S, i = 1, 2, j = 1, 2$, are Ordered Fuzzy Numbers, which satisfy the inequalities (10). Hence we can define 5 sublattices

$$L_0 = (0, Q_1^r), L_1 = [Q_1^r, Q_1^S), L_2 = [Q_1^S, Q_2^r), L_3 = [Q_2^r, Q_2^S), L_4 = [Q_2^S, D] \,. \quad (19)$$

The linear functional superposed on the fuzzy cost $K(Q)$ has the form

$$\Phi(K(Q))) = \Phi(f_K, g_K) = \int_0^1 f_K(s)dh_1(s) + \int_0^1 g_K(s)dh_2(s) \,, \quad (20)$$

where, due to (9) and the step functions $r(Q)$ and $S(Q)$, the pair of functions f_K, g_K represents 6 pairs, namely

$$f_{K_{ij}}(s) =$$

$$f_p(s)(1 - r_i)(f_D(s) + Rf_Q(s)) + \frac{f_T(s) \cdot f_D(s)}{f_Q(s)} + 180 f_S(s)(1 - S_j)(f_Q(s) + 2Q_0)$$
$$(21)$$

$$g_{K_{ij}}(s) =$$

$$g_p(s)(1 - r_i)(g_D(s) + Rg_Q(s)) + \frac{g_T(s) \cdot g_D(s)}{g_Q(s)} + 180 g_S(s)(1 - S_j)(g_Q(s) + 2Q_0) \,,$$
$$(22)$$

where $i, j, = 0, 1, 2$. As in Sec. 3 we can introduce new index $k = 0, 1, 2, 3, 4$ and use the same identification as in (14) to diminish the number of pairs of functions $(f_{K_{ij}}, g_{K_{ij}})$. Now, we take variation in (16) where the functional is given by (20), to get $\delta\Phi(K(Q)) =$

$$\int_0^1 \left[f_p(s)(1 - r_i)R - \frac{f_T(s) \cdot f_D(s)}{f_Q(s)^2} + 180 f_S(s)(1 - S_j) \right] \delta f_Q(s)dh_1(s)$$

$$+ \int_0^1 \left[g_p(s)(1 - r_i)R - \frac{g_T(s) \cdot g_D(s)}{g_Q(s)^2} + 180 g_S(s)(1 - S_j) \right] \delta g_Q(s)dh_2(s) \quad (23)$$

with $i, j, = 0, 1, 2$. We could consider two cases:

Case A: The functions h_1 are h_2 are absolutely continuous, and
Case B. The functions h_1 and h_2 are singular, i.e. the derivatives $h_1'(s)$ and $h_2'(s)$ are equal to zero almost everywhere.

It is interesting to notice that in the first cases particular forms of h_1 and h_2 in (20) do not effect the optimal value of Q, it does effect, however, the optimal value of the crisp cost $\Phi(K(Q))$. Hence we formulate remark concerning the first case.

---

[1] If there are also fuzzy numbers from $\mathcal{R}$, then final results will be of the same type with 4 extra pairs of functions appearing in a multiplicative way in the expressions for $f_{M_k}(s)$ and $g_{M_k}(s)$ from (25).

Theorem 1. *If the total inventory cost $K(Q)$ arising from fuzzy unit costs of delivery c_T, of inventory c_S, of the annual demand D, of the discount functions $r(Q)$ and $S(Q)$, and of the banking interest rate R, are given by (14) and the decision maker chooses the defuzzification functional Φ in (20), then in **Case A** the economic order quantity is given by two phase optimization procedure:*

– *Phase 1. On each sublattice L_0, L_1, L_2, L_3, L_4 the optimal values are found*

$$q_k^* = \Phi(Q_k^*) \, , \text{with } Q_k^* = (f_{Q_k^*}, g_{Q_k^*}) \, , \tag{24}$$

where

$$f_{Q_k^*}(s) = \left(\frac{f_D(s)f_T(s)}{f_{M_k}(s)}\right)^{1/2}, g_{Q_k^*}(s) = \left(\frac{g_D(s)g_T(s)}{g_{M_k}(s)}\right)^{1/2}, s \in [0,1], \tag{25}$$

with $f_{M_k}(s) = f_P(s)(1-r_i)R + 180 f_S(s)(1-S_j)$, and expression for $g_{M_k}(s)$ is analogous. Here the notation and the identification between the indexes k and (ij) are from (14).

– *Phase 2. From these five values $\Phi(Q_k^*), k = 0,1,2,3,4$ and the values at the boundary numbers: $Q_1^r, Q_1^S, Q_2^r, Q_2^S, D$, the optimal value is calculated according to*

$$Q^{opty} = \tag{26}$$

$$\arg\min\{\{\Phi(K(Q_k^*))\}, \Phi(K(Q_1^r)), \Phi(K(Q_1^s)), \Phi(K(Q_2^r)), \Phi(K(Q_2^s)), \Phi(K(D))\} \, .$$

In [1] we have discussed less complex case. On Fig. 2 the graph of the cost function (9) without discounts and the cost of frozen capital for different values of Q is plotted. The yellow color describes minimal values of K and other colors relate to values of c_S.

4   Optimal Orders under Dynamic Conditions

In the next section we form a solution to the deterministic optimization problem with the help of a controller. In a firm material demands from magazine in production processes are often irregular. It is related to an uneven production or technical problems. Thus the inventory optimization problem becomes more complicated in terms of the order quantity and the frequency of orders, as well as transportation costs. The algorithm described here solves that problem in a relatively easy way by simple algebraic operations. The final result is a controller.

In order to always provide a proper state of the inventory quantity in the magazine, one has to provider appropriate supplies. Each supply requires us to give an optimal order quantity which should be calculated for a given time period t taking into account the actual state of the magazine while minimizing the costs of purchase, transportation and maintaining them in the magazine.

In our solution we keep the previous notations, adding some new variables. Moreover, some new assumptions are also made.

1. Demands are not constant in time and depend on the length of time period for which the order is made.

2. Sells are not uniform and hence actual states of the magazine are different in time.
3. The next deliver arrives after a known period of time that may change by $\pm \delta t$.
4. The safety stock depends on the length of period of time for which the order is made.
5. Cost of transportation depends on the order quantity.
6. There is a discount on purchase.
7. The partitioning of domains of variables does not have to be regular.

For presenting the solution we use the following additional variables (cf. Sec.2):

- M - actual inventory state in the magazine,
- q - possible order quantity used for calculations,
- ΔQ - a value by which Q (or q) might be increased or decreased,
- t - time period for which particular order is made, its value might be changed by some rules of our controller,
- δt - time period by which t may be increased or decreased, or by its multiplicity,
- $D(t)$ - inventory demand for period t, (with safety stock included),
- $\theta(t)$ - safety stock,
- $r(q)$ - discount function on purchase,
- $K_T(q)$ - transportation cost function, in general nonlinear, e.g. a step function,
- P - the set of possible order quantities located on discontinuities of $K(q)$ function, due to the step characteristics of the discount function $r(q)$ and the transportation cost functions $K_T(q)$.

Total Cost Evaluation. If q represents a possible order quantity then the total cost is

$$K(q) = K_p(q) + K_T(q) + K_S(q) \,. \tag{27}$$

Suppose that the discount function on purchase $r(q)$ depending on the amount of q is a step functions, and its form is similar to that $r(Q)$ from Sec.2, with the small change of Q_1^r, Q_2^r into q_1^r, q_2^r, respectively. The cost of transportation (delivery) forms a step function, as well,

$$K_T(q) = \begin{cases} K_0 = 0 \,, if \;\; 0 < q < q_1^T \,, \\ \quad K_1 \quad , if \; q_1^T \le q \le q_2^T \,, \\ \quad K_2 \quad , if \; q_2^T \le q \le D \,, \end{cases} \tag{28}$$

where q_1^r, q_2^r, q_1^T and q_2^T are fixed amounts of item's quantity (here 3 steps were assumed, however, more or less steps can be also considered). The purchase cost $K_p(q)$ depends on the discount $r(q)$ and the unit price c_p by

$$K_p(q) = c_p \cdot (1 - r(q)) \cdot q \,. \tag{29}$$

Due to the discontinuity of both functions $r(q)$ and $k_T(q)$ as well as to the quantized nature of q in deliveries[2] the order quantity Q cannot be an arbitrary number: it should be adjusted even the economic order quantity Q^* has been calculated by solving an

---

[2] If the item to be ordered is coal, it is impossible to buy a fraction of tones; in practice coal is bought in full tons or in full boxcars.

appropriate optimization problem. Hence deliveries can be partitioned by ΔQ and the other relevant functions: $\theta(t)$ and $D(t)$. Notice that arguments at which the function $r(q)$ is discontinuous may be different from those of the function $k_T(q)$. Hence we formulate two rules which form the rule basis of our controller.

1. **IF** t_{old} is the time period for which inventory demand is made **THEN** the new time t_{new} is equal to $t - \delta t$ if the state M is lower than the safety stock $\theta(t)$, or is equal to $t + \delta t$, if the state M is higher than the demand $D(t)$, otherwise $t_{new} = t_{old}$.
2. **IF** P is the set of discontinuity arguments of both functions $r(q)$ and $K_T(q)$ **THEN** the final order quantity Q is the smallest element of P that with the current amount in the magazine would suffice for the next period of time with the minimal cost. **IF** such an element of P does not exist, **THEN** the final order quantity should be equal to the smallest multiple of ΔQ, that with the current amount in the magazine would suffice for the next period of time.

The above rules need explicit relationships to be applied in practice. We assume further that $K_S(q)$ is constant. Hence for the first rule

$$t_{new}(t_{old}, M) = \begin{cases} t_{old} - \delta t \,, \text{if} & M < \theta(t_{old}) \,, \\ t_{old} \,, \text{if } \theta(t_{old}) < M < D(t_{old}) \,, \\ t_{old} + \delta t \,, \text{if} & D(t_{old}) < M \end{cases} \qquad (30)$$

For the second rule we will use the notation $\lfloor \cdot \rfloor$ and $\lceil \cdot \rceil$ in order to keep the quantized nature of q. Hence the optimal order quantity Q^* is the function of M and $D(t_{new})$ and is equal to q^* if such q^* exists which is equal to $\arg \min \{K(q) : \lceil D(t_{new}) - \lfloor M \rfloor \rceil) \leq q \wedge q \in P \wedge K(q) \leq K(\lceil D(t_{new}) - \lfloor M \rfloor \rceil)$, and otherwise $Q^* = \lceil D(t_{new}) - M \rceil$. In the next subsection a numerical example will be presented.

4.1 Particular Example

Let us consider an example of an item measured in number of units, with 8 000 unit as the base quantity, and with the following data: $M = 0, D(t) = t \cdot 8\,000 \cdot 110\%, \delta t = 1$ week, $\theta(t) = D(t) \cdot 10\%/110\% = 800$; $r(q) \in \{0\%$ for $0 \leq q < 5\,000$; 5% for $5\,000 \leq q < 7\,000$; 10% for $7\,000 \leq q < 10\,000$; 15% for $10\,000 \leq q\}$.

In general case the graph $K(q)$ in Fig. 2 does not have to be linear between border values that are not multiples of ΔQ. However, those values are not achievable as an order quantity, hence there is no need to consider them. The circled areas are interesting because of the optimization possibility. Those values of q belong to the set P. In the interval $(4\,000; 4\,999]$ the cost $K(q)$ is in $(19\,500.00; 25\,514.00]$, measured in PLN. But in the next interval with the bigger order, the value $K(q) = 24\,664.00$ PLN appears, which is smaller than the upper limit of the previous interval. It means that ordering bigger amount its cost will be the same or lower. So it is better to buy more, in this case 5 000 units. So the knowledge base can be changed in that particular places.

On Fig.3 partition of q, is presented together with results for q. If t is changed, we have to order our item not for the old value of t but for the new one, according to Eq. (30). This is presented on Fig. 4 together with the final results of the controller for Q.

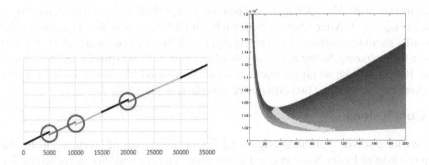

Fig. 2. Left – the graph of $K(q)$ of the controller, right – the graph of $K(Q)$ from (9)

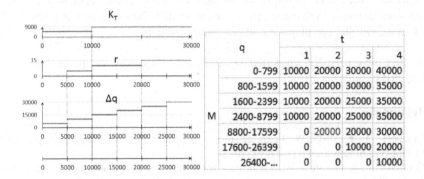

q			t		
		1	2	3	4
	0-799	10000	20000	30000	40000
	800-1599	10000	20000	30000	35000
	1600-2399	10000	20000	25000	35000
M	2400-8799	10000	20000	25000	35000
	8800-17599	0	20000	20000	30000
	17600-26399	0	0	10000	20000
	26400-...	0	0	0	10000

Fig. 3. Partitioning of q based on different factors together with the rules for q

t_{new}	t_{old}			
	1	2	3	4
0-799	t_{old}	$t_{old}-\delta t$	$t_{old}-\delta t$	$t_{old}-\delta t$
800-1599	t_{old}	$t_{old}-\delta t$	$t_{old}-\delta t$	$t_{old}-\delta t$
1600-2399	t_{old}	t_{old}	$t_{old}-\delta t$	$t_{old}-\delta t$
M 2400-8799	t_{old}	t_{old}	t_{old}	$t_{old}-\delta t$
8800-17599	$t_{old}+\delta t$	t_{old}	t_{old}	t_{old}
17600-26399	$t_{old}+\delta t$	$t_{old}+\delta t$	t_{old}	t_{old}
26400-...	$t_{old}+\delta t$	$t_{old}+\delta t$	$t_{old}+\delta t$	t_{old}

Q		t		
	1	2	3	4
0-799	10000	10000	20000	30000
800-1599	10000	10000	20000	30000
1600-2399	10000	20000	20000	25000
M 2400-8799	10000	20000	25000	25000
8800-17599	20000	20000	20000	30000
17600-26399	0	10000	10000	20000
26400-...	0	0	10000	10000

Fig. 4. The knowledge base for changing t together with the final results of the controller

Let us start with $M = 0, t_{old} = 4$. Then we need 30 000 items and decrease t by a week i.e. $t_{new} = 3$. After 3 weeks we are left with 3 600 units in the magazine, so the next order should consist of 30 000 pieces and $t = 3$. This time we were left with 8 100 units in the magazine. So the next order should consist of 25 000 pieces, and $t = 3$, and so on. If there will be no bigger fluctuations in the demand, the controller should give each time the same or just two different results through the whole year.

5 Conclusions

Here we have solved a problem originating from management of inventory, using the setup of Ordered Fuzzy Numbers, and demonstrated its applicability in modelling the influence of imprecise quantities and preferences of decision maker. The final version of the paper will bring a simplifying numerical example.

Thanks to well-defined arithmetic of OFN one can construct an efficient decision support tool when data are imprecise. In the second part of the paper we have introduced some dynamic in management of inventory and show that in a simplest case a rule based controller can play the role of an optimizing tool.

This work was partially supported by Białystok University of Technology grant S/WI/2/2011.

References

1. Chwastyk, A., Kosiński, W.: Fuzzy calculus with applications. Mathematica Applicanda - Matematyka Stosowana 41(1), 47–96 (2013)
2. Goetschel Jr., R., Voxman, W.: Elementary fuzzy calculus. Fuzzy Sets and Systems 18(1), 31–43 (1986)
3. Kosiński, W.K., Kosiński, W., Kościeński, K.: Ordered Fuzzy Numbers approach to an investment project evaluation. Management and Production Engineering Review 4(2), 50–62 (2013)
4. Kosiński, W., Prokopowicz, P., Ślęzak, D.: Fuzzy numbers with algebraic operations: algorithmic approach. In: Klopotek, M., Wierzchoń, S.T., Michalewicz, M. (eds.) Proc.IIS 2002, Sopot, Poland, pp. 311–320. Physica, Heidelberg (2002)
5. Kosiński, W., Prokopowicz, P., Ślęzak, D.: Ordered fuzzy numbers. Bulletin of the Polish Academy of Sciences, Sér. Sci. Math. 51(3), 327–338 (2003)
6. Kosiński, W.: On fuzzy number calculus. Int. J. Appl. Math. Comput. Sci. 16, 51–57 (2006)
7. Kuchta, D.: Miękka matematyka w zarządzaniu. Zastosowanie liczb przedzialowych i rozmytych w rachunkowości zarządczej, Oficyna Wydawnicza Politechniki Wrocławskiej, Wrocław (2001)
8. Nguyen, H.T.: A note on the extension principle for fuzzy sets. J. Math. Anal. Appl. 64, 369–380 (1978)
9. Vuješević, M., Petrović, D., Petrović, R.: EOQ formula when inventory cost is fuzzy. Int. J. Production Economics 45, 499–504 (1996)

Appendix

Proposed recently by the second author and his two coworkers: P.Prokopowicz and D. Ślęzak [4–6] an extended model of convex fuzzy numbers [8] (CFN), called Ordered Fuzzy Numbers (OFN), does not require any existence of membership functions.

In this model we can see an extension of CFN - model, when one takes a parametric representation of fuzzy numbers know since 1986, [2] of convex fuzzy numbers.

Definition 1. *By an Ordered Fuzzy Number we understand a pair of functions* (f, g) *defined on the unit interval* $[0, 1]$, *which are continuous functions (or of bounded variations)* [4–6].

On OFN, denoted by $\mathcal{R}$ (or $\mathcal{R}_{BV}$), four algebraic operations have been proposed between fuzzy numbers and crisp (real) numbers, in which componentwise operations are present. In particular

$$f_C(y) = f_A(y) \star f_B(y), \qquad g_C(y) = g_A(y) \star g_B(y), \qquad (31)$$

where "$\star$" works for "+", "$\cdot$", and "$\div$", respectively, and where $A \div B$ is defined, if the functions $|f_B|$ and $|g_B|$ are bounded from below. Hence any fuzzy algebraic equation $A + X = C$ with A and C as OFN possesses a solution.

A relation of **partial ordering** in the space of all OFN, can be introduced by defining the subset of '**positive**' Ordered Fuzzy Numbers: a number $A = (f, g)$ is not less than zero, and by writing

$$A \geq 0 \quad \text{iff} \quad f \geq 0, \, g \geq 0. \qquad (32)$$

In this way the set $\mathcal{R}$ (or $\mathcal{R}_{BV}$) becomes a partially ordered ring. Notice, that for each two fuzzy numbers $A = (f_A, g_A), B = (f_B, g_B)$ as above, we may define $A \wedge B =: F$ and $A \vee B =: G$, both from $\mathcal{R}$, by the relations: $F = (f_F, g_F)$, if $f_F = \inf\{f_A, f_B\}, g_F = \inf\{g_A, g_B\}$. Similarly, we define $G = A \vee B$ and we get the next structure on $\mathcal{R}$, namely a *lattice*. Its sublattice will be a chain of real numbers. If $A \leq B$, then the set $[A, B] = \{C \in \mathcal{R} : A \leq C \leq B\}$ will be a sublattice of the lattice $(\mathcal{R}, \leq)$.

In dealing with applications of fuzzy numbers we need set of functionals that map each fuzzy number into real, and in a way that is consistent with operations on reals. Those operations are called defuzzifications. To be more strict we introduce.

Definition 2. *A map* Φ *from the space* $\mathcal{R}$ *(or* $\mathcal{R}_{BV}$*) of all OFN's to reals is called a defuzzification functional if is satisfies: 1)* $\Phi(c^{\ddagger}) = c$, *2)* $\Phi(A + c^{\ddagger}) = \phi(A) + c$, *3)* $\Phi(cA) = c\phi(A)$, *for any* $c \in \mathbf{R}$ *and* $A \in \mathcal{R}$. *4)* $\Phi(A) \geq 0$ *if* $A \geq 0$. *where* $c^{\ddagger}(s) = (c, c), s \in [0, 1]$, *represents crisp number (a real)* $c \in \mathbf{R}$.

The linear functionals, as MOM (*middle of maximum*), FOM (*first of maximum*), LOM (*last of maximum*) are given by specification of h_1 and h_2

$$\phi(f_A, g_A) = \int_0^1 f_A(s) dh_1(s) + \int_0^1 g_A(s) dh_2(s), \qquad (33)$$

where h_1, h_2 are nonnegative functions of bounded variation and $\int_0^1 dh_1(s) + \int_0^1 dh_2(s) = 1$. If we substitute $h_1(s)$ and $h_2(s)$ by $\lambda H(s)$ and $(1 - \lambda)H(s)$, respectively, where $0 \leq \lambda \leq 1$, and $H(s)$ is the step Heaviside function (with the step at $s = 1$), we may obtain all the classical linear defuzzification functionals known for the fuzzy numbers of Zadeh, namely: MOM (*middle of maxima*), FOM (*first of maximum*), LOM (*last of maximum*) and RCOM (*random choice of maximum*), depending on the choice of λ; for example if for $h_1(s)$ and $h_2(s)$ we substitute $1/2 \, H(s)$, then we get MOM.

An Approach
to Cardinality of First Order Metasets

Bartłomiej Starosta

Polish-Japanese Institute of Information Technology,
ul. Koszykowa 86,
02-008 Warsaw, Poland
barstar@pjwstk.edu.pl

Abstract. Metaset is a new approach to sets with partial membership relation. Metasets are designed to represent and process vague, imprecise data, similarly to fuzzy sets. They enable expressing fractional certainty of membership, equality, and other relations. Even though the general idea stems from and is firmly suited in the classical set theory, it is directed towards efficient computer implementations and applications.

In this paper we introduce the concept of cardinality for metasets and we investigate its basic properties. For simplicity we focus on the subclass of first order metasets however, the discussed ideas remain valid in general. We also present additional results obtained for finite first order metasets which are relevant for computer applications.

Keywords: metaset, partial membership, set theory, cardinality.

1 Introduction

Metaset is the new concept of set with partial membership relation. It was inspired by the method of forcing [2] in the classical Zermelo-Fraenkel Set Theory (ZFC) [4,3]. Nonetheless it is directed towards artificial intelligence applications and efficient computer implementations. Its scope of practical usage is similar to fuzzy sets [12], intuitionistic fuzzy sets [1] or rough sets [5]. These traditional approaches to partial membership find successful applications in science and industry nowadays. Unfortunately, they are not well suited for computer implementations. They also have other drawbacks like the growth of fuzziness by multiple algebraic operations on fuzzy sets. Therefore, we tried to develop another idea of set with fractional members, which would be closer to ZFC, void of faults of currently used techniques and which would allow for efficient computer implementations.

The results obtained so far indicate success. We defined the basic set-theoretic relations for metasets, which may be satisfied to variety of degrees other than truth or falsity [7]. Algebraic operations for metasets satisfy the axioms of Boolean algebra [9]. The metasets language enables expressing uncertainty [11,10], particularly of membership, in a wider scope than intuitionistic fuzzy sets [8]. Experimental computer application for character recognition based

L. Rutkowski et al. (Eds.): ICAISC 2014, Part II, LNAI 8468, pp. 688–699, 2014.

on metaset approach [6] seems to correctly reflect human perception of simple images.

In this paper we introduce the notion of cardinality for metasets. Instead of analyzing the nature of cardinality and then trying to implement it within the metaset world we just transferred this notion directly from classical crisp sets onto metasets. We use the technique of interpretations for that purpose, as we usually do when defining new relations or operations for metasets (e.g., membership or equality).

For the sake of simplicity we focus in this paper on cardinality of first order metasets. The presented results remain valid in general (see Sec. 7). In computer applications we always deal with finite objects, therefore we also investigate additional results obtained for finite first order metasets. It turns out that objects representing cardinalities of such metasets are quite close to fuzzy numbers.

2 Metasets

A metaset is a classical crisp set with the specific structure which reflects membership degrees of its members.[1] The degrees are expressed as nodes (or rather sets of nodes) of the binary tree $\mathbb{T}$. In fact, they are elements of some Boolean algebra and they can be evaluated as real numbers.

For simplicity, in this paper we deal with first order metasets only.[2] A metaset of this type is a relation between some set and the set of nodes of $\mathbb{T}$. Thus, the mentioned structure which we use to encode the degrees of membership is based on ordered pairs. The first element of each pair is the member and the second element is a node of the binary tree, which contributes to the membership degree of the first element.

Definition 1. *A set which is either the empty set $\emptyset$ or which has the form:*

$$\tau = \{ \langle \sigma, p \rangle : \sigma \text{ is a set, } p \in \mathbb{T} \}$$

is called a first order metaset.

The binary tree $\mathbb{T}$ is the set of all finite binary sequences, i.e., functions whose domains are finite ordinals, valued in 2:[3]

$$\mathbb{T} = \bigcup_{n \in \mathbb{N}} 2^n . \tag{1}$$

The ordering $\leq$ in the tree $\mathbb{T}$ (see Fig. 1) is the reverse inclusion of functions: for $p, q \in \mathbb{T}$ such that, $p: n \mapsto 2$ and $q: m \mapsto 2$, we have $p \leq q$ whenever $p \supseteq q$, i.e., $n \geq m$ and $p_{\restriction m} = q$. The root $\mathbb{1}$ is the largest element of $\mathbb{T}$ in this ordering: it is included in each function and for all $p \in \mathbb{T}$ we have $p \leq \mathbb{1}$.

---

[1] We use the term "degree of membership" rather informally here and throughout the whole paper. For the precise discussion of evaluating degrees of membership and other relations the reader is referred to [11,10].

[2] See [7] for the introduction to metasets in general.

[3] For $n \in \mathbb{N}$, let $2^n = \{ f : n \mapsto 2 \}$ denote the set of all functions with the domain n and the range $2 = \{ 0, 1 \}$ – they are binary sequences of the length n.

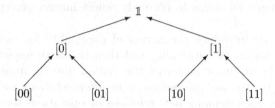

Fig. 1. The levels $\mathbb{T}_0$–$\mathbb{T}_2$ of the binary tree $\mathbb{T}$ and the ordering of nodes. Arrows point at the larger element.

We denote binary sequences which are elements of $\mathbb{T}$ using square brackets, for example: [00], [101]. If $p \in \mathbb{T}$, then we denote its children with $p \cdot 0$ and $p \cdot 1$. A *level* in $\mathbb{T}$ is the set of all finite binary sequences with the same length. The set 2^n consisting of sequences of the length n is the level n, denoted by $\mathbb{T}_n$. The level 0 consists of the empty sequence $\mathbb{1}$ only. A *branch* in $\mathbb{T}$ is an infinite binary sequence, i.e., a function $\mathbb{N} \mapsto 2$. We will write $p \in C$ to mark, that the binary sequence $p \in \mathbb{T}$ is a prefix of the branch C. A branch intersects all levels in $\mathbb{T}$, and each of them only once.

Ordering of nodes in $\mathbb{T}$ is consistent with the ordering of membership degrees they correspond to. The root node $\mathbb{1}$ represents the highest, full membership similar to classical set membership. The first element σ of an ordered pair $\langle \sigma, p \rangle$ contained in a first order metaset τ is called a *potential element* of τ. A potential element may be simultaneously paired with multiple different nodes which contribute to the overall membership degree of the potential element. Nodes on levels with greater numbers contribute less membership information than those which are closer to the root $\mathbb{1}$.

For the given metaset τ, the set of its potential elements:

$$\mathrm{dom}(\tau) = \{ \sigma \colon \exists_{p \in \mathbb{T}} \ \langle \sigma, p \rangle \in \tau \} \tag{2}$$

is called the *domain* of the metaset τ, and the set:

$$\mathrm{ran}(\tau) = \{ p \colon \exists_{\sigma \in \mathrm{dom}(\tau)} \ \langle \sigma, p \rangle \in \tau \} \tag{3}$$

is called the *range* of the metaset τ. The class of first order metasets is denoted by $\mathfrak{M}^1$. Thus,

$$\tau \in \mathfrak{M}^1 \quad \text{iff} \quad \tau \subset \mathrm{dom}(\tau) \times \mathrm{ran}(\tau) \subset X \times \mathbb{T} , \tag{4}$$

where X is some set.

A metaset is *finite* when it is finite as a set of ordered pairs. Consequently, its domain and range are finite. The class of finite first ordered metasets is denoted by $\mathfrak{M}\mathfrak{F}^1$. Thus,

$$\tau \in \mathfrak{M}\mathfrak{F}^1 \quad \text{iff} \quad |\mathrm{dom}(\tau)| < \aleph_0 \wedge |\mathrm{ran}(\tau)| < \aleph_0 . \tag{5}$$

This class is particularly important for computer applications where we deal with finite objects exclusively.

If σ is a first order metaset such, that $\operatorname{ran}(\sigma) = \{\mathbb{1}\}$, then we call it a *canonical metaset*. We denote the class of canonical first order metasets with the symbol $\mathfrak{M}^c$. Such metasets resemble classical crisp sets; they have similar properties. In fact, there is a natural one-to-one correspondence between canonical metasets and crisp sets. Thus,

$$\sigma \in \mathfrak{M}^c \quad \text{iff} \quad \sigma = X \times \{\mathbb{1}\}, \qquad (6)$$

where X is some set (clearly, $X = \operatorname{dom}(\sigma)$).

3 Interpretations of Metasets

An interpretation of a first order metaset is a crisp set. It is produced out of the given metaset with a branch of the binary tree. Different branches determine different interpretations of the given metaset. All of them taken together make up a collection of sets with specific internal dependencies, which represents the source metaset by means of its crisp views.

Properties of crisp sets which are interpretations of the given first order metaset determine the properties of the metaset itself. In particular we use interpretations to define set-theoretic relations for metasets.

Definition 2. *Let τ be a first order metaset and let $\mathcal{C}$ be a branch. The set*

$$\tau_\mathcal{C} = \{\sigma \in \operatorname{dom}(\tau) \colon \langle \sigma, p \rangle \in \tau \wedge p \in \mathcal{C}\}$$

is called the interpretation of the first order metaset τ given by the branch $\mathcal{C}$.

An interpretation of the empty metaset is the empty set, independently of the branch. Generally, interpretations of canonical metasets are independent of the chosen branch.

Proposition 1. *If $\sigma \in \mathfrak{M}^c$, then $\sigma_\mathcal{C} = \operatorname{dom}(\sigma)$, for any branch $\mathcal{C}$.*

The process of producing an interpretation of a first order metaset consists in two stages. In the first stage we remove all the ordered pairs whose second elements are nodes which do not belong to the branch $\mathcal{C}$. The second stage replaces the remaining pairs – whose second elements lie on the branch $\mathcal{C}$ – with their first elements. As the result we obtain a crisp set contained in the domain of the metaset.

Example 1. Let $p \in \mathbb{T}$ and let $\tau = \{\langle \emptyset, p \rangle\}$. If $\mathcal{C}$ is a branch, then

$$p \in \mathcal{C} \to \tau_\mathcal{C} = \{\emptyset\},$$
$$p \notin \mathcal{C} \to \tau_\mathcal{C} = \emptyset.$$

Depending on the branch the metaset τ acquires one of two different interpretations: $\{\emptyset\}$ or $\emptyset$. Note, that $\operatorname{dom}(\tau) = \{\emptyset\}$.

As we see, a first order metaset may have multiple different interpretations – each branch in the tree determines one. Usually, most of them are pairwise equal, so the number of different interpretations is much less than the number of branches. Finite first order metasets always have a finite number of different interpretations. For such metasets we consider the greatest level number of all the levels whose elements may affect interpretations.

Definition 3. *Let* $\tau \in \mathfrak{MF}^1$. *The natural number*

$$\mathfrak{l}_\tau = \begin{cases} \max\{\,|p|: p \in \operatorname{ran}(\tau)\,\} & \text{if } \tau \neq \emptyset, \\ 0 & \text{if } \tau = \emptyset. \end{cases}$$

is called the deciding level for τ.

Since $p \in \mathbb{T}$ is a function, then $|p|$ is its cardinality – the number of ordered pairs which is just the length of the binary sequence p. It is also equal to the level number to which it belongs: $p \in \mathbb{T}_{|p|}$. Thus, $\mathfrak{l}_\tau$ is the length of the longest sequence in $\operatorname{ran}(\tau)$. The following lemma claims that nodes on levels below $\mathfrak{l}_\tau$ (with greater level numbers) do not affect interpretations of τ.

Lemma 1. *Let* τ *be a finite first order metaset and let* $\mathcal{C}'$ *and* $\mathcal{C}''$ *be branches. If initial segments of size* $\mathfrak{l}_\tau$ *of* $\mathcal{C}'$ *and* $\mathcal{C}''$ *are equal, then they produce equal interpretations:*

$$\forall_{n \leq \mathfrak{l}_\tau} \, \mathcal{C}'(n) = \mathcal{C}''(n) \;\to\; \tau_{\mathcal{C}'} = \tau_{\mathcal{C}''}.$$

Proof. Since there are no nodes on levels below $\mathfrak{l}_\tau$ in $\operatorname{ran}(\tau)$, and by the assumption, we obtain $\{\,\langle\sigma,p\rangle \in \tau: p \in \mathcal{C}'\,\} = \{\,\langle\sigma,p\rangle \in \tau: p \in \mathcal{C}''\,\}$. Therefore, $\tau_{\mathcal{C}'} = \{\,\sigma: \langle\sigma,p\rangle \in \tau \wedge p \in \mathcal{C}'\,\} = \{\,\sigma: \langle\sigma,p\rangle \in \tau \wedge p \in \mathcal{C}''\,\} = \tau_{\mathcal{C}''}$.

Note, that for a canonical $\sigma \in \mathfrak{M}^c$ we always have $\mathfrak{l}_\sigma = 0$.

4   Set-Theoretic Relations for Metasets

We briefly sketch the methodology behind the definitions of standard set-theoretic relations for metasets within the scope necessary for the introduction of cardinality. For the detailed discussion of the relations or their evaluation the reader is referred to [9] or [11].

We use interpretations for transferring relations from crisp sets onto metasets.

Definition 4. *We say that the metaset* σ *belongs to the metaset* τ *under the condition* $p \in \mathbb{T}$, *whenever for each branch* $\mathcal{C}$ *containing* p *holds* $\sigma_\mathcal{C} \in \tau_\mathcal{C}$. *We use the notation* $\sigma \,\epsilon_p\, \tau$.

Formally, we define an infinite number of membership relations: each $p \in \mathbb{T}$ specifies another relation ϵ_p. Any two metasets may be simultaneously in multiple membership relations qualified by different nodes: $\sigma \,\epsilon_p\, \tau \wedge \sigma \,\epsilon_q\, \tau$. Membership under the root condition $\mathbb{1}$ resembles the full, unconditional membership of crisp sets, since it is independent of branches. In such case we skip the subscript $\mathbb{1}$ and we just write $\sigma \; \epsilon \; \tau$ instead of $\sigma \; \epsilon_{\mathbb{1}} \; \tau$.

The conditional membership reflects the idea that a metaset μ belongs to a metaset τ whenever some conditions are fulfilled. The conditions are represented by nodes of $\mathbb{T}$. In applications they refer to a modeled reality, e.g.: *the man X is big since X is tall* (i.e., X belongs to a metaset of big people under the condition tall), or *the man X is big since X is tall and fat* (i.e., X belongs to a metaset of big people under two conditions: tall and fat).

There are two substantial properties of this technique exposed by the following two lemmas. Although we show them for the membership relation they also hold for other relations.

Lemma 2. *Let* $\tau, \sigma \in \mathfrak{M}^1$ *and let* $p, q \in \mathbb{T}$. *If* $\sigma \; \epsilon_p \; \tau$ *and* $q \leq p$, *then* $\sigma \; \epsilon_q \; \tau$.

Proof. If $\mathcal{C}$ is a branch containing q then also $p \in \mathcal{C}$. Therefore $\sigma_{\mathcal{C}} \in \tau_{\mathcal{C}}$.

Lemma 3. *Let* $\tau, \sigma \in \mathfrak{M}^1$ *and let* $p \in \mathbb{T}$. *If* $\forall_{q<p} \; \sigma \; \epsilon_q \; \tau$, *then* $\sigma \; \epsilon_p \; \tau$.

Proof. If $\mathcal{C} \ni p$, then it also contains some $q < p$. Therefore, $\sigma_{\mathcal{C}} \in \tau_{\mathcal{C}}$.

In other words: $\sigma \; \epsilon_p \; \tau$ is equivalent to $\sigma \; \epsilon_{p \cdot 0} \; \tau \wedge \sigma \; \epsilon_{p \cdot 1} \; \tau$, i.e., being a member under the condition p is equivalent to being a member under both conditions $p \cdot 0$ and $p \cdot 1$, which are the direct descendants of p. Indeed, by lemma 2 we have $\sigma \; \epsilon_p \; \tau \; \rightarrow \; \sigma \; \epsilon_{p \cdot 0} \; \tau \wedge \sigma \; \epsilon_{p \cdot 1} \; \tau$. And if $\sigma \; \epsilon_{p \cdot 0} \; \tau$, then again, by lemma 2 we have $\forall_{q \leq p \cdot 0} \; \sigma \; \epsilon_q \; \tau$, and similarly for $p \cdot 1$. Consequently, we have $\forall_{q<p} \; \sigma \; \epsilon_q \; \tau$ and by lemma 3 we obtain $\sigma \; \epsilon_{p \cdot 0} \; \tau \wedge \sigma \; \epsilon_{p \cdot 1} \; \tau \; \rightarrow \; \sigma \; \epsilon_p \; \tau$.

Example 2. Recall, that the ordinal number 1 is the set $\{0\}$ and 0 is just the empty set $\emptyset$. Let $\tau = \{\langle 0, [0] \rangle, \langle 1, [1] \rangle\}$ and let $\sigma = \{\langle 0, [1] \rangle\}$. Let $\mathcal{C}^0 \ni [0]$ and $\mathcal{C}^1 \ni [1]$ be arbitrary branches containing $[0]$ and $[1]$, respectively. Interpretations are: $\tau_{\mathcal{C}^0} = \{0\}$, $\tau_{\mathcal{C}^1} = \{1\}$, $\sigma_{\mathcal{C}^0} = 0$ and $\sigma_{\mathcal{C}^1} = \{0\} = 1$. We see that $\sigma \; \epsilon_{[0]} \; \tau$ and $\sigma \; \epsilon_{[1]} \; \tau$. Also, $\sigma \; \epsilon \; \tau$ holds.

Note, that even though interpretations of τ and σ vary depending on the branch, the metaset membership relation is maintained

Similarly to membership we define conditional equality and subset relations for metasets.

Definition 5. *We say that the metaset* σ *is equal to the metaset* τ *under the condition* $p \in \mathbb{T}$, *whenever for each branch* $\mathcal{C}$ *containing* p *holds* $\sigma_{\mathcal{C}} = \tau_{\mathcal{C}}$. *We use the notation* $\mu \approx_p \tau$.

If $p = \mathbb{1}$, then we skip the subscript and we just write $\mu \approx \tau$. Clearly, $\mu = \tau \rightarrow \mu \approx \tau$, but the converse implication fails.

Example 3. Consider $\tau = \{\langle 0, \mathbb{1} \rangle\}$ and $\sigma = \{\langle 0, [0] \rangle, \langle 0, [1] \rangle\}$. Since for any branch $\mathcal{C}$ we have $\tau_{\mathcal{C}} = \{\emptyset\} = \sigma_{\mathcal{C}}$, then $\tau \approx \sigma$ however, $\tau \neq \sigma$.

694   B. Starosta

Definition 6. *We say that the metaset σ is a subset of the metaset τ under the condition $p \in \mathbb{T}$, whenever for each branch $\mathcal{C}$ containing p holds $\sigma_{\mathcal{C}} \subset \tau_{\mathcal{C}}$. We use the notation $\mu \Subset_p \tau$.*

Again, if $p = \mathbb{1}$, then we just write $\mu \Subset \tau$ instead of $\mu \Subset_{\mathbb{1}} \tau$. Note, that if $\sigma, \tau \in \mathfrak{M}^1$ and $p \in \mathbb{T}$, then

$$\sigma \approx_p \tau \quad \leftrightarrow \quad \sigma \Subset_p \tau \wedge \tau \Subset_p \sigma . \tag{7}$$

There are many other properties of set-theoretic relations for metasets which are similar to well known properties for classical sets. We do not discuss them here since they are beyond the scope of this paper. As an example consider the metaset version of extensionality: If $\sigma, \tau \in \mathfrak{M}^1$ and $p \in \mathbb{T}$, then

$$\sigma \approx_p \tau \quad \leftrightarrow \quad \forall_\mu \forall_{q \leq p} \left(\mu \; \epsilon_q \; \sigma \leftrightarrow \mu \; \epsilon_q \; \tau \right) . \tag{8}$$

To prove the above refer to interpretations.

5 Cardinality of First Order Metasets

Cardinality of a crisp set is an ordinal number – the "number of elements" of the set. A metaset may be interpreted as a family of crisp sets (Sec. 3). Therefore, cardinality of a metaset is a family of ordinal numbers. Since each branch in the tree $\mathbb{T}$ determines an interpretation, then this family is indexed with infinite binary sequences, i.e. all the branches in $\mathbb{T}$.

Let **On** denote the class of ordinal numbers and let τ be a first order metaset. We define the cardinality of τ to be a function from the set of all infinite binary sequences into **On**.

Definition 7. *Let $\tau \in \mathfrak{M}^1$. The cardinality of τ, denoted with $\overline{\overline{\tau}}$, is a function $\overline{\overline{\tau}} \colon 2^{\mathbb{N}} \mapsto$ **On** such, that for each branch $\mathcal{C}$ in $\mathbb{T}$ holds:*

$$\overline{\overline{\tau}} \left(\mathcal{C} \right) = \left| \tau_{\mathcal{C}} \right| .$$

The symbol $\left| \tau_{\mathcal{C}} \right|$ denotes the cardinality of the set $\tau_{\mathcal{C}}$.

As we see, the cardinality of τ at the branch $\mathcal{C}$ is the cardinality of the interpretation of τ given by the branch $\mathcal{C}$. The cardinality of the empty metaset is the constant function $2^{\mathbb{N}} \mapsto \{ \emptyset \}$ and generally, the cardinality of a canonical metaset τ is the constant function $2^{\mathbb{N}} \mapsto \{ \left| \mathrm{dom}(\tau) \right| \}$.

To prove that the proposed approach to cardinality is correct we should show that metasets with equal cardinalities are equinumerous, i.e., there exists a one-to-one mapping between them, and vice versa: equinumerosity implies equality of cardinalities. Due to limited scope of this paper we cannot present the proof that indeed such property holds for finite first order metasets.[4] Anyway, we shall try to convince the reader, that metaset cardinality has properties similar to the concept of cardinality for crisp sets. One of the most basic of them says that equal sets have the same cardinality. Translated into metaset language it says, that conditionally equal first order metasets have the same cardinality.

---

[4] It will be published in another paper soon.

Theorem 1. *If $\tau, \sigma \in \mathfrak{M}^1$ and $\tau \approx \sigma$, then $\overline{\overline{\tau}} = \overline{\overline{\sigma}}$.*

Proof. The assumption $\tau \approx \sigma$ implies that for any branch $\mathcal{C} \in \mathbb{T}$ holds $\tau_\mathcal{C} = \sigma_\mathcal{C}$. Therefore, also $|\tau_\mathcal{C}| = |\sigma_\mathcal{C}|$.

Since $\tau = \sigma \to \tau \approx \sigma$, then metasets which are equal sets have identical cardinality. If $\tau \approx_p \sigma$, then cardinalities generally are not equal. However, they are equal as functions restricted to a subset of $2^\mathbb{N}$ consisting of all the sequences containing p.

Example 4. Let $\tau = \{\langle \emptyset, [0] \rangle, \langle \emptyset, [1] \rangle\}$ and $\sigma = \{\langle \emptyset, [0] \rangle\}$. If $\mathcal{C}^0$ is a branch containing $[0]$ and $\mathcal{C}^1 \ni [1]$, then $\tau_{\mathcal{C}^0} = \{\emptyset\} = \sigma_{\mathcal{C}^0}$ and $\tau_{\mathcal{C}^1} = \{\emptyset\}$, whereas $\sigma_{\mathcal{C}^1} = \emptyset$. Therefore, $|\tau_{\mathcal{C}^0}| = |\sigma_{\mathcal{C}^0}|$ and $|\tau_{\mathcal{C}^1}| \neq |\sigma_{\mathcal{C}^1}|$. We also see that $\tau \approx_{[0]} \sigma$ holds, whereas both $\tau \approx_{[1]} \sigma$ and $\tau \approx \sigma$ fail.

Note also, that for $\eta = \{\langle \emptyset, \mathbb{1} \rangle\}$ holds $\overline{\overline{\eta}} = \overline{\overline{\tau}}$, since $\eta \approx \tau$.

We now introduce the partial ordering of metaset cardinalities.

Definition 8. *Let $\tau, \sigma \in \mathfrak{M}^1$. If for each branch $\mathcal{C} \in \mathbb{T}$ holds $|\tau_\mathcal{C}| \leq |\sigma_\mathcal{C}|$, then we say that the cardinality of τ is less than or equal than the cardinality of σ. We use standard notation $\overline{\overline{\tau}} \leq \overline{\overline{\sigma}}$.*

The element $\overline{\overline{\emptyset}}$ is the least one in this ordering. Note, that if τ, η are a first order metasets such, that η is canonical and $\mathrm{dom}(\tau) = \mathrm{dom}(\eta)$, then $\overline{\overline{\tau}} \leq \overline{\overline{\eta}}$ since $\overline{\overline{\tau}}(\mathcal{C}) \leq |\mathrm{dom}(\tau)| = \overline{\overline{\eta}}(\mathcal{C})$, for any branch $\mathcal{C}$.

Proposition 2. *The relation $\leq$ satisfies axioms of partial ordering: it is reflexive, antisymmetric and transitive.*

Proof. Reflexivity means $\overline{\overline{\tau}} \leq \overline{\overline{\tau}}$ for any $\tau \in \mathfrak{M}^1$ and it is satisfied since $|\tau_\mathcal{C}| \leq |\tau_\mathcal{C}|$ holds for any branch $\mathcal{C}$. Antisymmetry ($\overline{\overline{\tau}} \leq \overline{\overline{\sigma}} \wedge \overline{\overline{\sigma}} \leq \overline{\overline{\tau}} \to \overline{\overline{\tau}} = \overline{\overline{\sigma}}$) and transitivity ($\overline{\overline{\tau}} \leq \overline{\overline{\sigma}} \wedge \overline{\overline{\sigma}} \leq \overline{\overline{\eta}} \to \overline{\overline{\tau}} \leq \overline{\overline{\eta}}$) are satisfied similarly by referring to analogous properties for cardinalities of interpretations.

If $\overline{\overline{\tau}} \leq \overline{\overline{\sigma}}$, then – roughly speaking – it means that σ is always, under all conditions, independently of branches, "larger" than or equal to τ. Otherwise, if $\overline{\overline{\tau}} \not\leq \overline{\overline{\sigma}}$, then under some condition there is more of τ (it is "bigger") than σ.

The ordering of metaset cardinalities is consistent with metaset inclusion.

Theorem 2. *If $\tau, \sigma \in \mathfrak{M}^1$ are such, that $\tau \Subset \sigma$, then $\overline{\overline{\tau}} \leq \overline{\overline{\sigma}}$.*

Proof. By the assumption, for any branch $\mathcal{C}$ holds $\tau_\mathcal{C} \subset \sigma_\mathcal{C}$. Therefore, also $|\tau_\mathcal{C}| \leq |\sigma_\mathcal{C}|$, what implies the thesis.

We do not define nor discuss algebraic operations for metasets here (see [9]), however it is worth noting, that the algebraic operations are also consistent with the definition of cardinality. In particular, since (by the definition) the metaset union $\tau \uplus \eta$ of τ and σ coincides with their set-theoretic union $\tau \cup \eta$, i.e., $\tau \uplus \eta = \tau \cup \eta$, then the cardinality of the union makes up an upper bound for the cardinality of operands: $\overline{\overline{\tau}} \leq \overline{\overline{\tau \uplus \eta}}$. Similarly for the intersection $\tau \cap \eta$ (defined in [9]): since $\tau \cap \eta \Subset \tau$, then $\overline{\overline{\tau \cap \eta}} \leq \overline{\overline{\tau}}$.

6 Cardinality in $\mathfrak{MF}^1$

In computer applications we always deal with finite sets. For finite first order metasets the concept of cardinality may be simplified so that it is easily representable as a step function[5] on the unit interval, valued in natural numbers. Such representation facilitates application of metasets to real-life problems.

A branch $\mathcal{C}$ is a binary sequence $\{\mathcal{C}(i)\}_{i \in N}$ which determines a real number $x \in [0 \dots 1]$ by the following formula: $x = 0.\mathcal{C}(0)\mathcal{C}(1)\dots$. There exist pairs of branches which determine equal real numbers. For instance, if $\mathcal{C}^0 = 011\dots$ and $\mathcal{C}^1 = 100\dots$, then $0.011\dots = 0.5 = 0.100\dots$. Generally, different branches $\mathcal{C}' \neq \mathcal{C}''$ determine different interpretations: $\tau_{\mathcal{C}'} \neq \tau_{\mathcal{C}''}$, what may imply different cardinalities $|\tau_{\mathcal{C}'}| \neq |\tau_{\mathcal{C}''}|$ even when $\mathcal{C}'$ and $\mathcal{C}''$ determine the same real value x. For finite first order metasets we may ignore this ambiguity as follows.

The lemma 1 says, that for $\tau \in \mathfrak{MF}^1$ and for branches $\mathcal{C}'$ and $\mathcal{C}''$ that are equal up to the deciding level $\mathfrak{l}_\tau$ the interpretations are equal: $\tau_{\mathcal{C}'} = \tau_{\mathcal{C}''}$. Therefore, also $|\tau_{\mathcal{C}'}| = |\tau_{\mathcal{C}''}|$. Consequently, we may assign to each $p \in \mathbb{T}_{\mathfrak{l}_\tau}$ the unique cardinality $|\tau_{\mathcal{C}}|$ which is given by any branch $\mathcal{C}$ containing p.

Each $p \in \mathbb{T}$ determines an interval $I_p \subset [0 \dots 1)$ of the length $2^{-|p|}$ defined as $I_p = [l_p, \ l_p + 2^{-|p|})$, where $l_p \in [0 \dots 1)$ and

$$
l_p = \begin{cases} \sum_{i=0}^{i=|p|-1} p(i) \cdot 2^{-(i+1)} & \text{for } p \neq \mathbb{1}, \\ 0 & \text{for } p = \mathbb{1}. \end{cases} \tag{9}
$$

For instance, $I_{\mathbb{1}} = [0 \dots 1)$, $I_{[0]} = [0 \dots 1/2)$ and $I_{[1]} = [1/2 \dots 1)$.

Thus, to the given $\tau \in \mathfrak{MF}^1$ and $x \in [0 \dots 1)$ we may assign a unique natural number $|\tau_{\mathcal{C}^x}|$, where $\mathcal{C}^x$ is a branch such, that $x = 0.\mathcal{C}^x(0)\mathcal{C}^x(1)\dots$. We also know that $\mathcal{C}^x$ contains the unique $p \in \mathbb{T}_{\mathfrak{l}_\tau}$ for which $x \in I_p$.

Definition 9. *Let $\tau \in \mathfrak{MF}^1$ and let $\mathfrak{l}_\tau$ be the deciding level for τ. We define the cardinality spectrum for τ as the function $\overline{\overline{\tau}} \colon [0 \dots 1) \mapsto \mathbb{N}$ such, that $\overline{\overline{\tau}}(x) = |\tau_{\mathcal{C}}|$, where $\mathcal{C}$ is an arbitrary branch satisfying the condition:*

$$
\sum_{i=0}^{i=\mathfrak{l}_\tau-1} \mathcal{C}(i) \cdot 2^{-(i+1)} \leq x < 2^{-\mathfrak{l}_\tau} + \sum_{i=0}^{i=\mathfrak{l}_\tau-1} \mathcal{C}(i) \cdot 2^{-(i+1)}
$$

when $\mathfrak{l}_\tau > 0$ or $\mathcal{C}$ is an arbitrary branch when $\mathfrak{l}_\tau = 0$.

In other words, $\overline{\overline{\tau}}(x)$ is the unique cardinality $|\tau_{\mathcal{C}}|$ given by any branch containing $p \in \mathbb{T}_{\mathfrak{l}_\tau}$, where p is a prefix of (is contained in) $\mathcal{C}$ and $x \in I_p$. By the lemma 1 the value of $|\tau_{\mathcal{C}}|$ is constant on I_p, i.e., it is constant for all the branches containing p.

Proposition 3. *If $\tau \in \mathfrak{MF}^1$, then its cardinality spectrum is a step function.*

Thus, for a $\tau \in \mathfrak{MF}^1$ we may split the unit interval $[0 \dots 1)$ into $2^{\mathfrak{l}_\tau}$ disjoint subintervals of equal size $2^{-\mathfrak{l}_\tau}$. The cardinality spectrum for τ is constant and it is equal to some natural number on each of these intervals.

---

[5] A step function is a piecewise constant function having only finitely many pieces.

Example 5. Let $\tau = \{\, \langle \emptyset, [0] \rangle \,\}$. The cardinality spectrum for τ is shown on the Figure 2. As we see, for $x \in [0 \ldots 0.5)$ we have $\overline{\overline{\tau}}(x) = 1$, whereas for $x \in [0.5 \ldots 1)$ we have $\overline{\overline{\tau}}(x) = 0$.

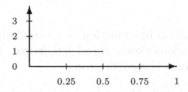

Fig. 2. The cardinality spectrum for $\tau = \{\, \langle \emptyset, [0] \rangle \,\}$ (Ex. 5)

As a real-life application illustrating the examples 5 and 6 let us consider the number of tiny beans or other particles in a large basket. Calculations made by different experts give different results due to errors in calculations or changes in content over time. We represent them all in a single metaset. Its interpretations correspond to different results obtained by the experts.

Example 6. Let $\tau = \{\, \langle \mu, [0] \rangle \,, \langle \eta, [00] \rangle \,, \langle \sigma, [11] \rangle \,\}$, where μ, η, σ are arbitrary different sets. The cardinality spectrum for τ is shown on the Figure 3. The metaset τ contains 0, 1 or 2 elements depending on the interpretation.

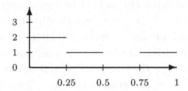

Fig. 3. The cardinality spectrum for $\tau = \{\, \langle \mu, [0] \rangle \,, \langle \eta, [00] \rangle \,, \langle \sigma, [11] \rangle \,\}$ (Ex. 6)

In $\mathfrak{M}\mathfrak{F}^1$ the ordering of cardinalities is consistent with the functional ordering of cardinality spectrums which is imposed by the ordering of natural numbers. Namely, if $\tau, \sigma \in \mathfrak{M}\mathfrak{F}^1$, then

$$\overline{\overline{\tau}} \leq \overline{\overline{\sigma}} \ \leftrightarrow \ \forall_{x \in [0 \ldots 1)} \ \overline{\overline{\tau}}(x) \leq \overline{\overline{\sigma}}(x) \,. \tag{10}$$

This justifies the slight abuse of notation $\overline{\overline{\tau}}$ for cardinality and cardinality spectrum.

7   Generalization and Further Results

We focused on the class of first order metasets in this paper, however the presented results hold for metasets in general. It means, that in the definitions of cardinality (Def. 7) and cardinality spectrum (Def. 9) we may drop the assumption, that the metasets in concern are first order ones.

For completeness, we cite below the general definitions of metaset and interpretation (see [7,11] for a brief discussion of metasets in general).

Definition 10. *A set which is either the empty set $\emptyset$ or which has the form:*

$$\tau = \{ \langle \sigma, p \rangle : \sigma \text{ is a metaset, } p \in \mathbb{T} \}$$

is called a metaset.

Formally, this is a definition by induction on the well founded relation $\in$ (see [4, Ch. VII, §2] for justification of such type of definitions). The general definition of interpretation for metasets is recursive too.

Definition 11. *Let τ be a metaset and let $C \subset \mathbb{T}$ be a branch. The set*

$$\tau_C = \{ \sigma_C \colon \langle \sigma, p \rangle \in \tau \wedge p \in C \}$$

is called the interpretation of the metaset τ given by the branch C.

The discussion of cardinality naturally leads to the idea of cardinal numbers for metasets, i.e., objects representing cardinalities of metasets which are also subject to some arithmetical operations. Such project is undergoing and the results will be published soon. In fact, for first order metasets the algebraic operations on "cardinal metanumbers" are natural consequence of algebraic operations for metasets [9]. The result resembles fuzzy numbers, however the operations are defined differently.

Cardinality is associated with the notion of equinumerosity. In classical set theory for any two sets that have equal cardinality there exists a one-to-one mapping between them and we say in such case that these sets are equinumerous. A notion of equinumerosity similar to the classical one is also defined for metasets. It is worth stressing that two finite first order metasets have equal cardinality if and only if they are equinumerous – just like in the ZFC. The method for establishing equinumerosity in such case is constructible, meaning it is an algorithm which may be easily implemented in a programming language. These results will be published soon.

References

1. Atanassov, K.T.: Intuitionistic Fuzzy Sets. Fuzzy Sets and Systems 20, 87–96 (1986)
2. Cohen, P.: The Independence of the Continuum Hypothesis 1. Proceedings of the National Academy of Sciences of the United States of America 50, 1143–1148 (1963)
3. Jech, T.: Set Theory: The Third Millennium Edition, Revised and Expanded. Springer, Heidelberg (2006)
4. Kunen, K.: Set Theory, An Introduction to Independence Proofs. Studies in Logic and Foundations of Mathematics, vol. 102. North-Holland Publishing Company, Amsterdam (1980)
5. Pawlak, Z.: Rough Sets. International Journal of Computer and Information Sciences 11, 341–356 (1982)
6. Starosta, B.: Application of Meta Sets to Character Recognition. In: Rauch, J., Raś, Z.W., Berka, P., Elomaa, T. (eds.) ISMIS 2009. LNCS (LNAI), vol. 5722, pp. 602–611. Springer, Heidelberg (2009)

7. Starosta, B.: Metasets: A New Approach to Partial Membership. In: Rutkowski, L., Korytkowski, M., Scherer, R., Tadeusiewicz, R., Zadeh, L.A., Zurada, J.M. (eds.) ICAISC 2012, Part I. LNCS (LNAI), vol. 7267, pp. 325–333. Springer, Heidelberg (2012)
8. Starosta, B.: Representing Intuitionistic Fuzzy Sets as Metasets. In: Atanassov, K.T., et al. (eds.) Developments in Fuzzy Sets, Intuitionistic Fuzzy Sets, Generalized Nets and Related Topics. Foundations, vol. I, pp. 185–208. Systems Research Institute, Polish Academy of Sciences, Warsaw (2010)
9. Starosta, B., Kosiński, W.: Meta Sets – Another Approach to Fuzziness. In: Seising, R. (ed.) Views on Fuzzy Sets and Systems. STUDFUZZ, vol. 243, pp. 509–532. Springer, Heidelberg (2009)
10. Starosta, B., Kosiński, W.: Metasets, Intuitionistic Fuzzy Sets and Uncertainty. In: Rutkowski, L., Korytkowski, M., Scherer, R., Tadeusiewicz, R., Zadeh, L.A., Zurada, J.M. (eds.) ICAISC 2013, Part I. LNCS (LNAI), vol. 7894, pp. 388–399. Springer, Heidelberg (2013)
11. Starosta, B., Kosiński, W.: Metasets, Certainty and Uncertainty. In: Atanassov, K.T., et al. (eds.) New Trends in Fuzzy Sets, Intuitionistic Fuzzy Sets, Generalized Nets and Related Topics. Volume I: Foundations, pp. 139–165. Systems Research Institute, Polish Academy of Sciences, Warsaw (2013)
12. Zadeh, L.A.: Fuzzy Sets. Information and Control 8, 338–353 (1965)

Fuzzy System for the Classification of Sounds of Birds Based on the Audio Descriptors

Krzysztof Tyburek, Piotr Prokopowicz, and Piotr Kotlarz

Institute of Mechanics and Applied Computer Science
Kazimierz Wielki University, Bydgoszcz, Poland
{krzysiekkt,piotrekp,piotrk}@ukw.edu.pl
http://www.imis.ukw.edu.pl

Abstract. This paper presents an application of fuzzy systems for the classification of sounds coded by the selected MPEG-7 descriptors. The model of the fuzzy classification system is based on the audio descriptors for a few chosen species of birds: Great Spotted Woodpecker, Greylag, Goldfinch, Chaffinch. The paper proposes two fuzzy models that definitely differ by the description of the input linguistic variables. The results show, that both approaches are effective. However, second one is more flexible in a case of future expanding of the model with next descriptors or species of birds.

Keywords: fuzzy system, fuzzy classification, MPEG-7, audio descriptors, fuzzy classification of audio signals.

1 Introduction

Birds rely on auditory processing for survival. Listening to others enables an bird to classify them as worst enemy, neighbor or stranger, a mate or non-mate, etc. Juvenile songbirds can listen to adult for develop a memory of a normal song that they will use to guide their own life. Our paper presents we would like to present a method for recognize kind of bird by feature of their sounds efficiently. In our study we used definition of MPEG-7 descriptors and fuzzy logic for classification of result. The potential applications for detecting and identifying bird species, particularly automatically, are diverse but can be grouped into the following categories.
1. Species identification.
2. Identification of individuals within a species.
3. Detection of the presence of bird.
4. Approaches to bioacoustic identification.
5. Feature extraction from time domain and frequency domain of bird song.

2 Sound Description With the MPEG-7

The solutions of searching of multimedia data basing on label technique do not always give expecting results. It means that sending queries are not always in

L. Rutkowski et al. (Eds.): ICAISC 2014, Part II, LNAI 8468, pp. 700–709, 2014.
© Springer International Publishing Switzerland 2014

accordance with demanding of person or computer system. Correctly interpretation of sound source is the main issue which occurs during recognition process of sound signals. In this paper researching of sound come from birds: Great Spot–ted Woodpecker, Greylag, Goldfinch, Chaffinch. Researching of sound of bird can be useful for high level of recognizably each other. This problem can be solved by means of MPEG-7 standard which gives a lot of descriptors describing physical features of sound. These descriptors are defined on the base of analysis of digital signals and index of most important their factors. The MPEG-7 Audio standard comprises descriptors and description schemes that can be divided [4–6] into two classes: generic low-level tools and application-specific tools. The generic tools, referred to in the standard as the audio description framework apply to any audio signal and include the scalable series, low-level descriptors (LLDs) and the unform silence segment. The application-specific tools restrict their application domain as a means to afford more descriptive power and include general sound recognition and indexing tools and description tools. The low-level audio descriptors have very general applicability in describing audio. There are seventeen temporal and spectral descriptors [6] that can be divided into six groups. A typical LLD may be instantiated either as a single value for a segment or a sampled series. Then two names for those descriptors are used, as the application requires: AudioLLDScalarType and AudioLLDVectorType, the first type is inherited for scalar values and describing a segment with a single summary, such as power or fundamental frequency, the second one is inherited for vector types describing a series of sampled valued, such spectra. This paper deals with LLDs as well as application-specific tools to recognize audio signal coming from a group of birds. In order to find a feature vector of the group of birds the analysis has been performed in the temporal as well as in frequency domains.

2.1   Time Domain Parameterization

For the purpose of right describing of waveform of sound it is necessary to define descriptor. The descriptor is represented as a fraction of time of separating phases to time of all phases. Log - time of the ending transient (TET) l_{tk}, which is given by:

$$l_{tk} = log(t_{pk} - t_{max}), \tag{1}$$

where:
t_{max} is the time at which the maximal amplitude has been reached,
t_{pk} is the time at which the level of 10 % of maximal value has been reached in the decay stage.

2.2   Frequency Domain Parameterization

Since the frequency domain may contain important information concerning features of the sound it is worthwhile to introduce its parameterization. The base of parameterization of sound spectrum are Fourier transform, wavelet analysis, cepstrum or Wigner–Ville'a transform. The following parameters describing frequency domain of signal were applied:

1. Brightness

$$Br = \frac{\sum\limits_{i=0}^{n} A(i) \cdot i}{\sum\limits_{i=0}^{n} A(i)}, \tag{2}$$

where:
$A(i)$ is amplitude of the i-th partial (harmonic)
i - the frequency of the i-th partial

2. Irregularity of spectrum

$$Ir = log(20 \sum_{i=2}^{N-1} | log \frac{A(i)}{\sqrt[3]{A(i-1) \cdot A(i) \cdot A(i+1)}} |), \tag{3}$$

where:
$A(i)$ is amplitude of the i-th partial (harmonic)
N - number of available harmonics

3   Preparation of Audio Data

The objects of researching was sounds of the birds like Great Spotted Woodpecker, Greylag, Goldfinch, Chaffinch. One of the purposes of the experiments was searching for vector of features which allow to automatic classification of each bird. For parameterization of frequency domain state window length was proposed [8]. It was applied for all samples in experiment. State window length is the fragment of signal (in time domain) which was taken in the same point of time. State window length contains constant amount of samples. The beginning of this window was taken when the level of 10 % of maximal value has been reached. The length of window is determined by resolution of spectrum, according to the formula:

$$f_r = \frac{f_s}{n}, \tag{4}$$

where:
f_r is the spectrum resolution
f_s – sampling frequency (44100 Hz)
n - number of samples.
In the paper f_r equal to $4Hz$ was assumed. It means that number of samples which are assigned to experiment is equal 11025. If testing sound is shorter then

length of window ($n = 11025$) then absent values should be supplemented with zeros to $n = 11025$ [7, 8]. Selecting fragment of signals in time domain were treated DFT and this spectrum was analyzed.

4 Modeling of Fuzzy System

For the realization of classification a fuzzy system was used. The model of this system is based on audio descriptors for the chosen species of birds: Great Spotted Woodpecker, Greylag, Goldfinch, Chaffinch. Each descriptor is represented by a separate linguistic variable. Since the data shall be classified into four categories, we also accept four output variables. Each of them corresponds to a different species.

4.1 Basic Assumptions

All data used in defining the model were normalized to the interval $[0, 1]$. In research two different fuzzy models were proposed. The main difference between them lies in the way of definition of the input linguistic variables. However, common for both are the output variables, defined on the interval $[0, 1]$, where 0 means the lack of recognition of the given species, whereas 1 means the full identification. The output variable out_1 responsible for the recognition of woodpecker, is shown on the Fig.1. Other output variables for classifying the rest of the birds are described in the same way. In addition, both proposals assume that the system will use only four rules. Each rule will select one of the bird species. In this way we obtain the four answer from the fuzzy system, which belong to the numerical interval $[0, 1]$. Thanks to that, the final result of classification

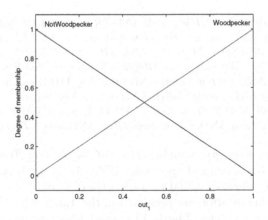

Fig. 1. Linguistic variable out_1

Table 1. Summary of the data used for modeling the fuzzy systems

	Brightness			TET			IR		
	min	max	avg.	min	max	avg.	min	max	avg.
Woodpecker	0	0,21	0,13	0	0,1	0,01	0,48	0,74	0,64
Greylag	0,26	0,43	0,34	0,68	1	0,82	0	0,62	0,37
Goldfinch	0,46	1	0,62	0,03	0,79	0,31	0,3	1	0,66
Chaffinch	0,31	0,55	0,44	0,17	0,7	0,37	0,2	0,73	0,47

can be easily and clear-cut determined with use the *winner takes all* principle. This means that the largest output value indicates an identified species of bird assigned to the given audio signal. Other parameters common for the both propositions:
– method of fuzzyfication - singleton,
– method of aggregation for premise parts of rules - min,
– operator of implication - min,
– defuzzyfication - middle of maximum.

4.2 Fuzzy System - Proposition 1

The input linguistic variables are divided into two values: Small, Big (see Fig.2). To determine the rules mean values for the input data assigned to the species of birds were calculated. On their base fuzzy sets for the premise part of rules were determined. For the average $\leq 0,5$ the *Small* set was taken, for $> 0,5$ fuzzy set *Big*. Tab.1 presents a summary of the minimum, average, and maximum for each of descriptors taking into account the species of birds.

As a result we receive the following rules:

– IF *Brgt* is *Small* AND *TET* is *Small* AND *IR* is *Big* THEN out_1 is *Wdp* AND out_2 is *NotGrlg* AND out_3 is *NotGldfch* AND out_4 is *NotChfnch*
– IF *Brgt* is *Small* AND *TET* is *Big* AND *IR* is *Small* THEN out_1 is *NotWdp* AND out_2 is *Grlg* AND out_3 is *NotGldfch* AND out_4 is *NotChfnch*
– IF *Brgt* is *Big* AND *TET* is *Small* AND *IR* is *Big* THEN out_1 is *NotWdp* AND out_2 is *NotGrlg* AND out_3 is *Gldfch* AND out_4 is *NotChfnch*
– IF *Brgt* is *Small* AND *TET* is *Small* AND *IR* is *Small* THEN out_1 is *NotWdp* AND out_2 is *NotGrlg* AND out_3 is *NotGldfch* AND out_4 is *Chfnch*

where *TET* means linguistic variable *Time of the Ending Transient*, *Brgt* - *Brightness* , *IR* - *Irregularity of Spectrum* , *Wdp* - fuzzy set *Woodpecker*, *Grlg* - *Greylag*, *Gldfch* - *Goldfinch* and *Chfnch* - *Chaffinch*.

The results of classification are presented in the Tab.2. The 40 audio signals was used, ten for every species of birds. First tenth lines represents woodpecker's signals, next ten - greylag, and next for goldfinch, and last - chaffinch. As can be noted, the classification is quite effective. However, the results clearly diverging from the average values are classified incorrectly - see lines numbers

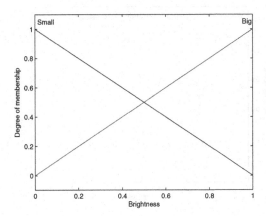

Fig. 2. Input linguistic variable *Brightness*

2,21,22,24,28,32,35,39 . It's a little alarming because the system is based on the fuzzy model, which takes account all available data, including those diverging from the average values.

4.3   Fuzzy System - Proposition 2

To improve the quality of the classification presented in the first proposition, the greater granulation of input variables can be a way. In addition to the terms *Small*, *Big*, could be introduced another fuzzy sets such as: *VerySmall*, *Average*, etc. Note, however, that when increasing the granularity, you need to check the uniqueness of the premise parts of the rules. If in the future we will expand the capabilities of our classification system for another species of birds, there is a rather complex process of updating and matching of linguistic variables and already defined rules.

An alternative solution is split the input variables for the fuzzy sets characteristic for each species. Similar solution to another problem - the classification of flowers (irises) - was presented in [3]. In this way, instead of fuzzy sets defining the size *Small*, *Big*, etc., we introduce sets *Woodpecker*, *Greylag*, *Goldfinch*, *Chaffinch*. Each of them is a triangular fuzzy set (see LR fuzzy sets notation in [1]) and is determined on the the available data. For example lets look at set *Woodpecker* (Fig.3):

$$Woodpecker = \Lambda(x; x_{mean} - 2 \cdot \Delta_L, x_{mean}, x_{mean} + 2\Delta_R), \qquad (5)$$

where $\Delta_L = x_{mean} - x_{min}$, $\Delta_R = x_{max} - x_{mean}$,
$x_{min}/x_{max}/x_{mean}$ – the minimum/maximum/mean value of the descriptor for the given species.

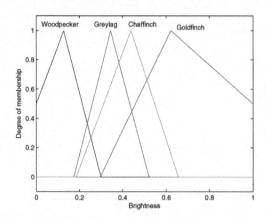

Fig. 3. New fuzzy sets for input linguistic variable *Brightness*

With such definitions of the fuzzy sets we are sure that minimum and maximum have at least $0,5$ membership level in the set assigned to a given species. Same way we deal with the all other input variables (see Fig.3). It is characteristic that we do not take into account properties expected from the fuzzy model such as the completeness or continuity (see [2]). We also do not expect that the values of the fuzzy membership functions sum to unity within a linguistic variable. The rule base looks as follows:

- IF *Brgt* is *Wdp* AND *TET* is *Wdp* AND *IR* is *Wdp* THEN out_1 is *Wdp* AND out_2 is *NotGrlg* AND out_3 is *NotGldfch* AND out_4 is *NotChfnch*
- IF *Brgt* is *Grlg* AND *TET* is *Grlg* AND *IR* is *Grlg* THEN out_1 is *NotWdp* AND out_2 is *Grlg* AND out_3 is *NotGldfch* AND out_4 is *NotChfnch*
- IF *Brgt* is *Gldfch* AND *TET* is *Gldfch* AND *IR* is *Gldfch* THEN out_1 is *NotWdp* AND out_2 is *NotGrlg* AND out_3 is *Gldfch* AND out_4 is *NotChfnch*
- IF *Brgt* is *Chfnch* AND *TET* is *Chfnch* AND *IR* is *Chfnch* THEN out_1 is *NotWdp* AND out_2 is *NotGrlg* AND out_3 is *NotGldfch* AND out_4 is *Chfnch*

We can see that the classification results (Tab.3) do not contain faulty detections. It is primarily the result of increased granulation of input variables comparing to the previous proposal. If we applied a similar granulation there, we would also get a similar effectiveness. However, the second proposition has one basic advantage over the previous one. It is related above all, to the simplicity of expansion defined classifier. Adding the next species of birds does not violate existing structure. You simply add the next fuzzy sets characteristic for the new species. Well, of course you should add a rule that recognizes a new class of data. Similarly, if we want to introduce another descriptor to the model, the changes will be much simpler, more intuitive and easier than with the previous proposition.

Table 2. Results of classification (proposition 1)

	Woodpecker	Greylag	Goldfinch	Chaffinch
1	0,84	0,16	0,16	0,16
2	0,24	0,24	0,24	0,76
3	0,86	0,14	0,14	0,14
4	0,88	0,13	0,13	0,13
5	0,86	0,14	0,14	0,14
6	0,82	0,19	0,19	0,19
7	0,82	0,19	0,19	0,19
8	0,82	0,19	0,19	0,19
9	0,79	0,21	0,21	0,21
10	0,81	0,19	0,19	0,19
11	0,26	0,75	0,26	0,26
12	0,25	0,75	0,25	0,25
13	0,31	0,7	0,31	0,31
14	0,18	0,82	0,18	0,18
15	0,22	0,79	0,22	0,22
16	0,2	0,81	0,2	0,2
17	0,2	0,8	0,2	0,2
18	0,25	0,76	0,25	0,25
19	0,21	0,79	0,21	0,21
20	0,25	0,75	0,25	0,25
21	0,28	0,28	0,28	0,73
22	0,5	0,5	0,5	0,5
23	0,15	0,15	0,85	0,15
24	0,27	0,27	0,27	0,73
25	0,16	0,16	0,84	0,16
26	0,26	0,26	0,74	0,26
27	0,19	0,19	0,81	0,19
28	0,5	0,4	0,5	0,4
29	0,3	0,3	0,71	0,3
30	0,2	0,2	0,81	0,2
31	0,24	0,24	0,24	0,76
32	0,32	0,68	0,32	0,32
33	0,23	0,23	0,23	0,78
34	0,23	0,23	0,23	0,78
35	0,79	0,22	0,22	0,22
36	0,23	0,23	0,23	0,78
37	0,24	0,24	0,24	0,77
38	0,24	0,24	0,24	0,76
39	0,77	0,24	0,24	0,24
40	0,27	0,27	0,27	0,73

Table 3. Results of classification with modified fuzzy system (proposition 2)

	Woodpecker	Greylag	Goldfinch	Chaffinch
1	0,75	0,25	0,25	0,25
2	0,75	0,25	0,25	0,25
3	0,75	0,25	0,25	0,25
4	0,75	0,25	0,25	0,25
5	0,75	0,25	0,25	0,25
6	0,75	0,25	0,25	0,25
7	0,75	0,25	0,25	0,25
8	0,75	0,25	0,25	0,25
9	0,75	0,25	0,25	0,25
10	0,75	0,25	0,25	0,25
11	0,18	0,82	0,18	0,18
12	0,14	0,87	0,14	0,14
13	0,25	0,75	0,25	0,25
14	0,08	0,92	0,08	0,08
15	0,25	0,75	0,25	0,25
16	0,02	0,98	0,02	0,02
17	0,25	0,76	0,25	0,25
18	0,13	0,88	0,13	0,13
19	0,22	0,79	0,22	0,22
20	0,13	0,87	0,13	0,13
21	0,25	0,25	0,75	0,25
22	0,14	0,14	0,86	0,14
23	0,25	0,25	0,75	0,25
24	0,15	0,15	0,86	0,15
25	0,19	0,19	0,81	0,19
26	0,25	0,25	0,76	0,25
27	0,04	0,04	0,97	0,04
28	0,25	0,25	0,76	0,25
29	0,14	0,14	0,86	0,14
30	0,25	0,25	0,76	0,25
31	0,2	0,2	0,2	0,81
32	0,25	0,25	0,25	0,76
33	0,22	0,22	0,22	0,78
34	0,25	0,25	0,25	0,76
35	0,25	0,25	0,25	0,75
36	0,04	0,04	0,04	0,97
37	0,08	0,08	0,08	0,92
38	0,1	0,1	0,1	0,91
39	0,1	0,1	0,1	0,91
40	0,25	0,25	0,25	0,75

5 Summary

Worth to emphasize again that the research presented here are a just preliminary step to further work on the idea of using fuzzy sets in the analysis of audio signals. It should also be noted that the set of data which is the source of the proposed models is too small to build an explicit and definitive conclusions. Nevertheless, the results presented here, clearly shows that the application of fuzzy systems as the classifiers for audio data described by MPEG-7 descriptors is the direction worth of further attention.

In the future, the authors also plan to work together on the search for new effective audio signal descriptors, where new model of fuzzy numbers the Ordered Fuzzy Numbers [9, 10] (developed by the second author) will be used. Good computational properties of this model [11], which support applications, deserve the particular attention.

References

1. Dubois, D., Prade, H.M.: Fuzzy sets and systems: Theory and applications. Academic Press, New York (1980)
2. Driankov, D., Hellendoorn, H., Reinfrank, M.: An Introduction to fuzzy control. Springer, Heidelberg (1996)
3. Siler, W., Buckley, J.J.: Fuzzy Expert Systems and Fuzzy Reasoning. Wiley (2005)
4. Manjunath, B.S., Salembier, P., Sikora, T.: Introduction to MPEG-7, Multimedia Content Description Interface. John Wiley & Sons, Chichester (2002)
5. Martnez, J.M.: MPEG-7 Overview, Klangenfurt (July 2002)
6. Lindsay, A.T., Burnett, I., Quackenbush, S., Jackson, M.: Fundamentals of audio descriptions. In: Manjunath, B.S., Salembier, P., Sikora, T. (eds.) Introduction to MPEG-7: Multimedia Content Description Interface, pp. 283–298. John Wiley and Sons, Ltd. (April 2002)
7. Tyburek, K.: Classification of string instruments in multimedia database especially for pizzicato articulation, Ph. D. thesis. Institute of Fundamental Technological Research Polish Academy of Sciences, Warsaw (November 2006) (in Polish)
8. Tyburek, K., Cudny, W., Kosiski, W.: Pizzicato sound analysis of selected instruments In the freguency domain. Image Processing & Communications 11(1), 53–57 (2006)
9. Kosiński, W., Prokopowicz, P., Ślezak, D.: Ordered fuzzy number, Bulletin of the Polish Academy of Sciences. Ser. Sci. Math. 51(3), 327–338 (2003)
10. Kosiński, W., Prokopowicz, P., Kacprzak, D.: Fuzziness – representation of dynamic changes by ordered fuzzy numbers. In: Seising, R. (ed.) Views of Fuzzy Sets and Systems from Different Perspectives. STUDFUZZ, vol. 243, pp. 485–508. Springer, Heidelberg (2009)
11. Prokopowicz, P.: Flexible and Simple Methods of Calculations on Fuzzy Numbers with the Ordered Fuzzy Numbers Model. In: Rutkowski, L., Korytkowski, M., Scherer, R., Tadeusiewicz, R., Zadeh, L.A., Zurada, J.M. (eds.) ICAISC 2013, Part I. LNCS, vol. 7894, pp. 365–375. Springer, Heidelberg (2013)

Clustering

Clustering

Generalized Tree-Like Self-Organizing Neural Networks with Dynamically Defined Neighborhood for Cluster Analysis

Marian B. Gorzałczany, Jakub Piekoszewski, and Filip Rudziński

Department of Electrical and Computer Engineering
Kielce University of Technology
Al. 1000-lecia P.P. 7, 25-314 Kielce, Poland
{m.b.gorzalczany,j.piekoszewski,f.rudzinski}@tu.kielce.pl

Abstract. The paper presents a generalization of self-organizing neural networks of spanning-tree-like structures and with dynamically defined neighborhood (SONNs with DDN, for short) for complex cluster-analysis problems. Our approach works in a fully-unsupervised way, i.e., it operates on unlabelled data and it does not require to predefine the number of clusters in a given data set. The generalized SONNs with DDN, in the course of learning, are able to disconnect their neuron structures into sub-structures and to reconnect some of them again as well as to adjust the overall number of neurons in the system. These features enable them to detect data clusters of virtually any shape and density including both volumetric ones and thin, shell-like ones. Moreover, the neurons in particular sub-networks create multi-point prototypes of the corresponding clusters. The operation of our approach has been tested using several diversified synthetic data sets and two benchmark data sets yielding very good results.

Keywords: generalized self-organizing neural networks with dynamically defined neighborhood, multi-point prototypes of clusters, cluster analysis, unsupervised learning.

1 Introduction

Data clustering or cluster analysis is an unsupervised process that aims at grouping unlabelled data records from a given data set into an unknown in advance number of cluster or groups. Elements of each cluster should be as "similar" as possible to each other and as "dissimilar" as possible from those of other clusters. Cluster analysis belongs to fundamental issues in data mining and machine learning with wide range of applications, cf., e.g., [15], [1].

This paper presents a technique for cluster analysis based on self-organizing neural networks (SONNs) of spanning-tree-like structures and with dynamically defined neighborhood (henceforward referred to as SONNs with DDN) outlined in Kohonen's work [10]. However, we propose an essential generalization of these networks by introducing original mechanisms that, in the course of learning:

L. Rutkowski et al. (Eds.): ICAISC 2014, Part II, LNAI 8468, pp. 713–725, 2014.

a) automatically adjust the number of neurons in the network, b) allow to disconnect the tree-like structure into sub-trees, and c) allow to reconnect some of the sub-trees preserving the no-loop spanning-tree properties. All these features enable them to detect data clusters of virtually any shape and density including both volumetric clusters and thin, piece-wise linear, shell, polygonal, etc. types of clusters. Similar, to above-listed, mechanisms have been proposed by us in [7], [8], [9] ([5], [6] present their earlier versions) to obtain - for clustering purposes - the so-called dynamic SONNs with one-dimensional neighborhood; they can be treated as a special case of the presently proposed generalized SONNs with DNN. First, their details are presented. Then, an illustration of their operation using several synthetic data sets containing data concentrations of various shapes and densities is given. Finally, their application to the clustering of two benchmark data sets is presented.

An idea of evolving topological structures of self-organizing neural networks has been addressed in the literature. However, some existing solutions do not directly deal with data clustering, e.g. in [11] and [14] evolving neuron trees are used to decrease the computational complexity of Winner-Takes-Most (WTM) learning algorithm. In [16] tree structures are used to visualize the obtained results for the purpose of comparison with conventional decision trees. Among data clustering techniques (to some extent alternative to our approach), evolving topological structures are proposed in [3], [13], and in [4], [2]. However, the approaches of [3], [13] do not enable to detect, in an automatic way, the number of clusters in data sets. In turn, the results of experiments presented in [4], [2] do not provide an information on how effective the proposed approaches are in terms of the automatic detection of the number of clusters in data sets.

2 Generalized SONNs with DDN for Clustering Analysis

First, we consider the conventional SONN with one-dimensional neighborhood. Assume that the network has n inputs $x_1, x_2, \ldots, x_n$ and consists of m neurons arranged in a chain; their outputs are $y_1, y_2, \ldots, y_m$, where $y_j = \sum_{i=1}^{n} w_{ji} x_i$, $j = 1, 2, \ldots, m$ and w_{ji} are weights connecting the i-th input of the network with the output of the j-th neuron. Using vector notation ($\boldsymbol{x} = (x_1, x_2, \ldots, x_n)^T$, $\boldsymbol{w}_j = (w_{j1}, w_{j2}, \ldots, w_{jn})^T$), $y_j = \boldsymbol{w}_j^T \boldsymbol{x}$. The learning data consists of L input vectors $\boldsymbol{x}_l$ ($l = 1, 2, \ldots, L$). The first stage of any Winner-Takes-Most (WTM) learning algorithm that can be applied to the considered network, consists in determining the neuron $j_{\boldsymbol{x}}$ winning in the competition of neurons when learning vector $\boldsymbol{x}_l$ is presented to the network. Assuming the normalization of learning vectors, the winning neuron $j_{\boldsymbol{x}}$ is selected such that

$$d(\boldsymbol{x}_l, \boldsymbol{w}_{j_{\boldsymbol{x}}}) = \min_{j=1,2,\ldots,m} d(\boldsymbol{x}_l, \boldsymbol{w}_j), \tag{1}$$

where $d(\boldsymbol{x}_l, \boldsymbol{w}_j)$ is a distance measure between $\boldsymbol{x}_l$ and $\boldsymbol{w}_j$; throughout this paper, the Euclidian distance measure will be applied

$$d_E(\boldsymbol{x}_l, \boldsymbol{w}_j) = \sqrt{\sum_{i=1}^{n}(x_{li} - w_{ji})^2}. \tag{2}$$

The WTM learning rule can be formulated as follows:

$$\boldsymbol{w}_j(k+1) = \boldsymbol{w}_j(k) + \eta_j(k)N(j, j\boldsymbol{x}, k)[\boldsymbol{x}(k) - \boldsymbol{w}_j(k)], \tag{3}$$

where k is the iteration number, $\eta_j(k)$ is the learning coefficient, and $N(j, j\boldsymbol{x}, k)$ is the neighborhood function. At this point, we have to address the problem of a spanning-tree-like structure of the SONN with DDN. The neighborhood of a given neuron in such a topology is defined along the arcs emanating from that neuron as illustrated in Fig. 1. Therefore, the paths between any two neurons in such a structure are the pieces of SONN with one-dimensional neighborhood. The topological distance $d_{tpl}(j, j\boldsymbol{x})$ between the $j\boldsymbol{x}$-th neuron and some other neurons is equal to 1 if those other neurons are direct neighbors of the $j\boldsymbol{x}$-th one as shown in Fig. 1. The distance $d_{tpl}(j, j\boldsymbol{x}) = 2$ for the neurons that are second along all paths starting at the $j\boldsymbol{x}$-th one (see Fig. 1), etc. The topological distance measure is the basis of the neighborhood function $N(j, j\boldsymbol{x}, k)$. In this paper, the Gaussian-type neighborhood function is used:

$$N(j, j\boldsymbol{x}, k) = e^{-\frac{d_{tpl}^2(j,j\boldsymbol{x})}{2\lambda^2(k)}} \tag{4}$$

where $\lambda(k)$ is the radius of the neighborhood (the width of the Gaussian "bell").

As already mentioned, the generalization of the above-presented SONN with DDN consists in introducing mechanisms that allow the network:

I) to automatically adjust the number of neurons in the network by removing low-active neurons from the network and adding new neurons in the areas of existing high-active neurons,

II) to automatically disconnect the network, as well as to reconnect some of the sub-networks again preserving the no-loop spanning-tree properties.

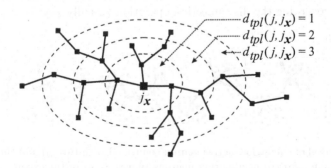

Fig. 1. Examples of neighborhood of the $j\boldsymbol{x}$-th neuron

These two features enable the generalized SONN with DDN to fit in the best way the structures that are "encoded" in data sets to display them to the user. In particular, the number of disconnected sub-networks is equal to the number of clusters detected in a given data set. Moreover, the neurons in a given sub-network create a multi-point prototype of the corresponding cluster. The mechanisms I and II are implemented by activating (under some conditions) - after each learning epoch - five successive operations (cf. [7]):

1) the removal of single, low-active neurons,
2) the disconnection of the network (sub-network) into two sub-networks,
3) the removal of small-size sub-networks,
4) the insertion of additional neurons into the neighborhood of high-active neurons in order to take over some of their activities,
5) the reconnection of two selected sub-networks.

The operations 1, 3 and 4 are the components of the mechanism I, whereas the operations 2 and 5 govern the mechanism II. Based on experimental investigations, the following conditions for activating particular operations have been formulated.

Operation 1: The neuron no. j_r is removed from the network if its activity - measured by the number of its wins win_{jr} - is below an assumed level win_{min}, i.e., $win_{jr} < win_{min}$. win_{min} is experimentally selected parameter (usually, $win_{min} \in \{2, 3, ..., 7\}$). The removal of the j_r-th neuron is followed by reconfiguration of the network topology as shown in Fig. 2. If the j_r-th neuron has only two neighbors (Fig. 2a), they are now topologically connected. In the case of three or more neighbors of the j_r-th unit (Fig. 2b), one of them, say j_1, which is nearest to the j_r-th one in terms of their weight-vector distance, is selected. Then, the remaining neighbors are topologically connected to the j_1-th unit.

Operation 2: The structure of the network is disconnected into two sub-networks by removing the topological connection between two neighboring neurons j_1 and j_2 (see Fig. 3) after fulfilling the following condition: $d_{E,j_1 j_2} > \alpha_{dsc} d_{E,avr}$ where $d_{E,j_1 j_2} = d_E(\boldsymbol{x}_{j_1}, \boldsymbol{x}_{j_2})$ (d_E is defined in (2)), $d_{E,avr} = \frac{1}{P} \sum_{p=1}^{P} d_{E,p}$ is the average distance between two neighboring neurons for all pairs of such neurons in the network ($d_{E,p}$ is the d_E distance for the p-th pair of neighboring neurons, $p = 1, 2, ..., P$), and α_{dsc} is experimentally selected parameter governing the disconnection operation (usually, $\alpha_{dsc} \in [2, 4]$).

a)   b)

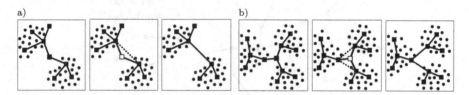

Fig. 2. Removal of single, low-active neuron connected with two (a) and three (in general, more than two) (b) neighboring neurons (illustrations of the exemplary network structure before, during, and after the operation, respectively)

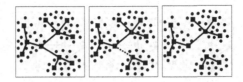

Fig. 3. Disconnection of the network into two sub-networks (illustration of the exemplary network structure before, during, and after the operation, respectively)

Operation 3: A sub-network that contains m_s neurons is removed from the system if $m_s < m_{s,min}$, where $m_{s,min}$ is experimentally selected parameter (usually, $m_{s,min} \in \{3,4\}$).

The operation of the insertion of additional neurons into the neighborhood of high-active neurons in order to take over some of their activities covers 2 cases denoted by 4a and 4b, respectively.

Operation 4a: A new neuron, labelled as (new), is inserted between two neighboring and high-active neurons j_1 and j_2 (see Fig. 4a) if they fulfil the following conditions: $win_{j_1} > win_{max}$ and $win_{j_2} > win_{max}$, where win_{j_1} and win_{j_2} are the numbers of wins of particular neurons and win_{max} is experimentally selected parameter (usually $win_{max} \in \{4, 5, ..., 9\}$). The weight vector $\boldsymbol{w}_{(new)}$ of the new neuron is calculated as follows: $\boldsymbol{w}_{(new)} = \frac{\boldsymbol{w}_{j_1} + \boldsymbol{w}_{j_2}}{2}$.

Operation 4b: A new neuron (new) is inserted in the neighborhood of high-active neuron j_1 surrounded by low-active neighbors (see Fig. 4b) if the following conditions are fulfilled: $win_{j_1} > win_{max}$ and $win_j < win_{max}$ for j such that $d_{tpl}(j, j_1) = 1$, where win_{j_1} and win_{max} are as in Operation 4a and win_j is the number of wins of the j-th neuron. The weight vector $\boldsymbol{w}_{(new)} = [w_{(new)1}, w_{(new)2}, ..., w_{(new)n}]^T$ is calculated as follows: $w_{(new)i} = w_{j_1 i}(1 + \xi_i)$, $i = 1, 2, ..., n$, where ξ_i is a random number from the interval $[-0.01, 0.01]$. Therefore, particular components of high-active neuron j_1, after experimentally selected random modification in the range of $[-1\%, 1\%]$, give the weight vector $\boldsymbol{w}_{(new)}$ of the new neuron. It is a starting point for the new neuron in its further evolution as the learning progresses.

Operation 5: Two sub-networks S_1 and S_2 are reconnected by introducing topological connection between neurons j_1 and j_2 ($j_1 \in S_1$, $j_2 \in S_2$) - see Fig. 5 - after fulfilling condition: $d_{E,j_1 j_2} < \alpha_{con} \frac{d_{E,avr_{S_1}} + d_{E,avr_{S_2}}}{2}$. $d_{E,j_1 j_2}$ is the same

a)   b)

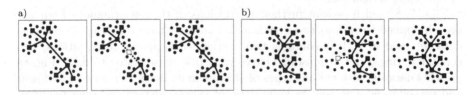

Fig. 4. Insertion of additional neuron between two high-active neighbouring neurons (a) and into the neighborhood of a single high-active neuron (b) (illustrations of the exemplary network structure before, during, and after the operation, respectively)

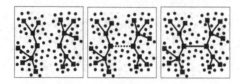

Fig. 5. Reconnection of two sub-networks (illustration of the exemplary network structure before, during, and after the operation, respectively)

as in Operation 2. $d_{E,avr_{S_1}}$ and $d_{E,avr_{S_2}}$ are calculated for sub-networks S_1 and S_2, respectively, in the same way as $d_{E,avr}$ is calculated in Operation 2 for the considered network. α_{con} is experimentally selected parameter that controls the reconnection process (usually, $\alpha_{con} \in [3,5]$).

The conditions that govern Operations 1 through 5 are checked after each learning epoch. The condition that is fulfilled activates the appropriate operation.

In the experiments presented below, the following values of control parameters are selected: $win_{min} = 2$, $win_{max} = 4$, $m_{s,min} = 3$, $\alpha_{dsc} = 3$, and $\alpha_{con} = 4$. Moreover, the learning process is carried out through 10000 epochs, the learning coefficient $\eta_j(k) = \eta(k)$ of (3) linearly decreases over the learning horizon from $7 \cdot 10^{-4}$ to 10^{-6}, the neighborhood radius $\lambda(k) = \lambda$ of (4) is equal to 2, and the initial number of neurons in the network (at the start of the learning process) is equal to 2.

3   Cluster Analysis in Two-Dimensional Synthetic Data Sets

Fig. 6 shows the performance of the generalized SONN with DDN applied to the set of uniformly distributed data (i.e., without any clusters in them). It is a hard-to-pass test for very many clustering techniques, especially those generating a predefined number of clusters - regardless of whether any clusters exist in data or not. Our approach perfectly passes this test. After initial jump to 2, the number of sub-networks (clusters) stabilizes on 1, i.e., the system detects one big cluster in data (see Fig. 6h) and generates a multi-point prototype for it (see neurons of Fig. 6f). Fig. 6g shows the adjustment of the number of neurons in the network in the course of learning.

Figs. 7, 8, and 9 present further illustrations of the performance of our approach applied to various two-dimensional synthetic data sets. Fig. 7a presents data set used in [17]; it contains two overlapped Gaussian distributions, two concentric rings, and a sinusoidal curve with 10% noise added to data. Fig. 8a presents data set with various types of clusters in it. Both, thin piece-wise linear and two-ellipsoidal as well as volumetric of various shapes and densities clusters are considered. Finally, Fig. 9a presents a "classical" two-spiral data set. As the above-listed figures show, in all of these data sets our approach detects the correct numbers of clusters and generates multi-point prototypes for them.

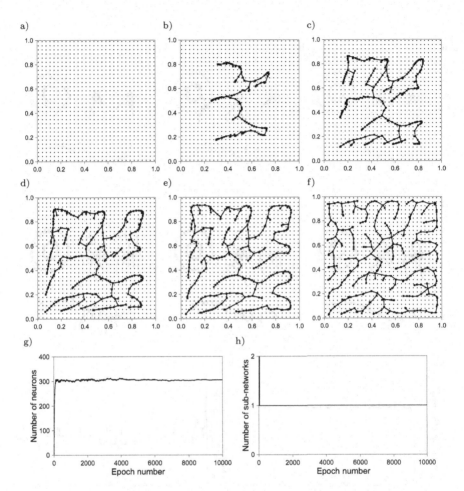

Fig. 6. Synthetic data set (a) and the evolution of the generalized SONN with DDN in it in learning epochs: b) no. 20, c) no. 50, d) no. 100, e) no. 200, and f) no. 10 000 (end of learning), as well as plots of the number of neurons (g) and the number of sub-networks (clusters) (h) vs. epoch number

4   Cluster Analysis in Selected Benchmark Data Sets

Our approach will now be tested using two multidimensional benchmark data sets such as *Breast Cancer Wisconsin (Diagnostic)* and *Congressional Voting Records (BCWD* and *CVR*, for short) [12]. *BCWD* data set has 569 records and 30 numerical attributes, whereas *CVR* data set - 435 records and 16 nominal attributes. It is essential to note that our approach does not utilize the knowledge on class assignments of particular records and on the number of classes (equal to 2

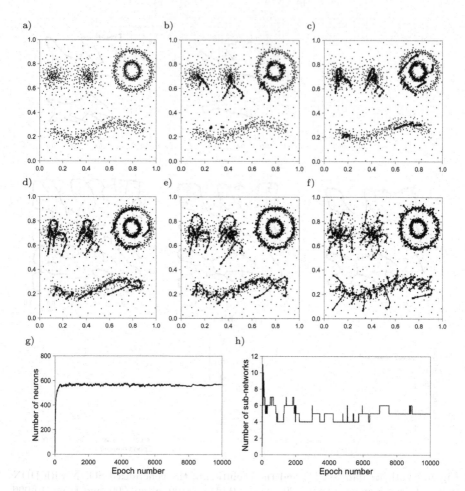

Fig. 7. Synthetic data set (a) and the evolution of the generalized SONN with DDN in it in learning epochs: b) no. 20, c) no. 50, d) no. 100, e) no. 200, and f) no. 10 000 (end of learning), as well as plots of the number of neurons (g) and the number of sub-networks (clusters) (h) vs. epoch number

in both sets). Our approach works in *a fully-unsupervised way*, i.e., it operates on *unlabelled data* and *without any predefinition of the number of clusters (classes)*.

Figs. 10 and 11 as well as Tables 1 and 2 present the performance of our approach applied to both data sets. First, Figs. 10b and 11b show that our approach detects the correct number of clusters in both data sets. Second, since the number of classes and class assignments are known in both original data

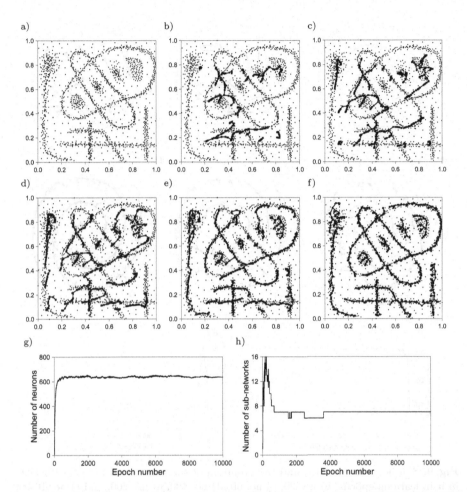

Fig. 8. Synthetic data set (a) and the evolution of the generalized SONN with DDN in it in learning epochs: b) no. 20, c) no. 50, d) no. 100, e) no. 200, and f) no. 10 000 (end of learning), as well as plots of the number of neurons (g) and the number of sub-networks (clusters) (h) vs. epoch number

sets, a direct verification of the obtained results is also possible (see Tables 1 and 2). The percentages of correct decisions, equal to 90.51% (*BCWD* data set) and 94.71% (*CVR* data set), regarding the class assignments are very high (especially, that they have been achieved by the unsupervised-learning systems operating on benchmark data sets).

722   M.B. Gorzałczany, J. Piekoszewski, and F. Rudziński

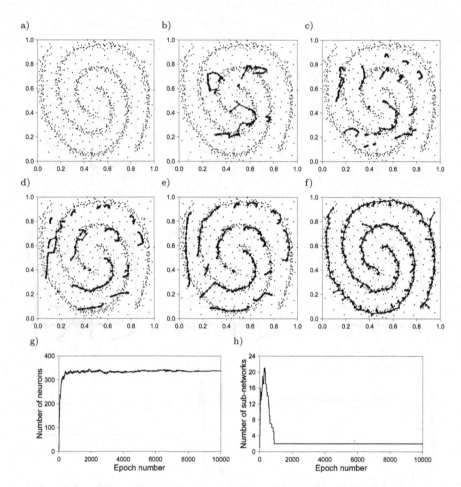

Fig. 9. Synthetic data set (a) and the evolution of the generalized SONN with DDN in it in learning epochs: b) no. 20, c) no. 50, d) no. 100, e) no. 200, and f) no. 10 000 (end of learning), as well as plots of the number of neurons (g) and the number of sub-networks (clusters) (h) vs. epoch number

Table 1. Clustering results for *BCWD* data set

| Class label | Number of records | Number of decisions for sub-network labelled: | | Number of correct decisions | Number of wrong decisions | Percentage of correct decisions |
		Malignant	*Benign*			
Malignant	212	166	46	166	46	78.30%
Benign	357	8	349	349	8	97.76%
ALL	**569**	**174**	**395**	**515**	**54**	**90.51%**

Table 2. Clustering results for *CVR* data set

Class label	Number of records	Number of decisions for sub-network labelled:		Number of correct decisions	Number of wrong decisions	Percentage of correct decisions
		Republican	*Democrat*			
Republican	168	158	10	158	10	94.05%
Democrat	267	13	254	254	13	95.13%
ALL	**435**	**171**	**264**	**412**	**23**	**94.71%**

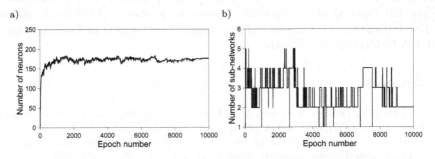

Fig. 10. Plots of the number of neurons (a) and the number of sub-networks (clusters) (b) vs. epoch number (*BCWD* data set)

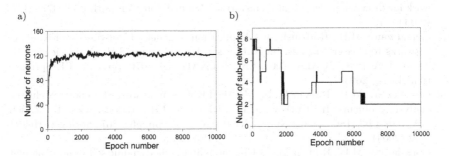

Fig. 11. Plots of the number of neurons (a) and the number of sub-networks (clusters) (b) vs. epoch number (*CVR* data set)

5   Conclusions

The generalized SONNs with DDN that can be effectively applied in complex, multidimensional cluster-analysis problems have been presented in this paper. Our approach works in a fully-unsupervised way, i.e., it operates on unlabelled data and it does not require to predefine the number of clusters in a given data set. The proposed networks, in the course of learning, are able to disconnect their neuron structures into sub-structures and to reconnect some of them again as well as to adjust the overall number of neurons in the system. These features enable them to detect data clusters of virtually any shape and density including both volumetric ones and thin, shell-like ones. Moreover, the neurons in particular sub-networks create multi-point prototypes of the corresponding clusters. The operation of our approach has been illustrated by means of several diversified synthetic data sets and then our approach has been tested using two benchmark data sets (*Breast Cancer Wisconsin* (*Diagnostic*) and *Congressional Voting Records*) yielding very good results.

Acknowledgments. The numerical experiments reported in this paper have been performed using computational equipment purchased in the framework of the EU Operational Programme Innovative Economy (POIG.02.02.00-26-023/09-00) and the EU Operational Programme Development of Eastern Poland (POPW.01.03.00-26-016/09-00).

References

1. Everitt, B.S., Landau, S., Leese, M.: Cluster Analysis, 4th edn. A Hodder Arnold Publication, J. Willey, London (2001)
2. Forti, A., Foresti, G.L.: Growing hierarchical tree SOM: An unsupervised neural network with dynamic topology. Neural Networks 19, 1568–1580 (2006)
3. Fritzke, B.: Growing cell structures - a self-organizing network for unsupervised and supervised learning. Neural Networks 7, 1441–1460 (1994)
4. Ghaseminezhad, M.H., Karami, A.: A novel self-organizing map (SOM) neural network for discrete groups of data clustering. Applied Soft Computing 11, 3771–3778 (2011)
5. Gorzałczany, M.B., Rudziński, F.: Application of genetic algorithms and Kohonen networks to cluster analysis. In: Rutkowski, L., Siekmann, J.H., Tadeusiewicz, R., Zadeh, L.A. (eds.) ICAISC 2004. LNCS (LNAI), vol. 3070, pp. 556–561. Springer, Heidelberg (2004)
6. Gorzałczany, M.B., Rudziński, F.: Modified Kohonen networks for complex cluster-analysis problems. In: Rutkowski, L., Siekmann, J.H., Tadeusiewicz, R., Zadeh, L.A. (eds.) ICAISC 2004. LNCS (LNAI), vol. 3070, pp. 562–567. Springer, Heidelberg (2004)
7. Gorzałczany, M.B., Rudziński, F.: Cluster analysis via dynamic self-organizing neural networks. In: Rutkowski, L., Tadeusiewicz, R., Zadeh, L.A., Żurada, J.M. (eds.) ICAISC 2006. LNCS (LNAI), vol. 4029, pp. 593–602. Springer, Heidelberg (2006)
8. Gorzałczany, M.B., Rudziński, F.: Application of dynamic self-organizing neural networks to WWW-document clustering. ICAISC 2006 1(1), 89–101 (2006); (also presented at 8th Int. Conference on Artificial Intelligence and Soft Computing ICAISC 2006). Zakopane (2006)
9. Gorzałczany, M.B., Rudziński, F.: WWW-newsgroup-document clustering by means of dynamic self-organizing neural networks. In: Rutkowski, L., Tadeusiewicz, R., Zadeh, L.A., Zurada, J.M. (eds.) ICAISC 2008. LNCS (LNAI), vol. 5097, pp. 40–51. Springer, Heidelberg (2008)
10. Kohonen, T.: Self-organizing Maps, 3rd edn. Springer, Heidelberg (2000)
11. Koikkalainen, P., Oja, E.: Self-organizing hierarchical feature maps. In: Proc. of 1990 International Joint Conference on Neural Networks, San Diego, CA, vol. II, pp. 279–284 (1990)
12. Machine Learning Database Repository. University of California at Irvine, http://ftp.ics.uci.edu

13. Martinez, T., Schulten, K.: A "Neural-Gas" network learns topologies. In: Kohonen, T., et al. (eds.) Artificial Neural Networks, pp. 397–402. Elsevier, Amsterdam (1991)
14. Pakkanen, J., Iivarinen, J., Oja, E.: The evolving tree - a novel self-organizing network for data analysis. Neural Processing Letters 20, 199–211 (2004)
15. Pedrycz, W.: Knowledge-Based Clustering: From Data to Information Granules. J. Willey, Hoboken (2005)
16. Samsonova, E.V., Kok, J.N., IJzerman Ad, P.: TreeSOM: Cluster analysis in the self-organizing map. Neural Networks 19, 935–949 (2006)
17. Shen, F., Hasegawa, O.: An incremental network for on-line unsupervised classification and topology learning. Neural Networks 19, 90–106 (2006)

Nonnegative Matrix Factorization for Document Clustering: A Survey

Ehsan Hosseini-Asl[1] and Jacek M. Zurada[1,2]

[1] Electrical and Computer Engineering Department,
University of Louisville, Louisville, KY, USA
[2] Information Technology Institute, Academy of Management, 90-113 Lodz, Poland
{ehsan.hosseiniasl,jacek.zurada}@louisville.edu

Abstract. Nonnegative Matrix Factorization (NMF) is a popular dimension reduction technique of clustering by extracting latent features from high-dimensional data and is widely used for text mining. Several optimization algorithms have been developed for NMF with different cost functions. In this paper we apply several methods of NMF that have been developed for data analysis. These methods vary in using different cost function for matrix factorization and different optimization algorithms for minimizing the cost function. Reuters Document Corpus is used for evaluating the performance of each method. The methods are compared with respect to their accuracy, entropy, purity and computational complexity and residual mean square root error. The most efficient methods in terms of each performance measure are also recognized.

Keywords: Nonnegative Matrix Factorization, Document clustering, optimization algorithm.

1 Introduction

Text mining refers to the detection of trends, patterns, or similarities in natural language text. Given a collection of text documents, often the need arises to classify the documents into groups or clusters based on similarity of content. For a small collections, it is possible to manually perform the partitioning of documents into specific categories. But to partition large volumes of text, the process would be extremely time consuming. Therefore, developing a fast and accurate clustering algorithm is crucial for processing of document data sets.

To classify the documents based on their similarity of content, they should be represented by their features defined as words. In this way, it will generate documents with numerous features attributed. Therefore, a dimension reduction algorithm should be used to define documents with few number of features, which could keep the similarity of content between documents. Several methods exist to reduce the dimensionality of data vectors such as Principal Component Analysis (PCA), Singular Value Decomposition (SVD) and Independent Component Analysis (ICA). Often the data to be analyzed is nonnegative, and the low-rank data are further required to be comprised of nonnegative values

L. Rutkowski et al. (Eds.): ICAISC 2014, Part II, LNAI 8468, pp. 726–737, 2014.

in order to avoid contradicting physical realities. However, these classical tools cannot guarantee to maintain the nonnegativity [1]. Therefore, an approach of finding reduced-rank nonnegative factors to approximate a given nonnegative data matrix becomes a suitable choice. Recently developed Nonnegative Matrix Factorization (NMF) approach allows to create a lower rank data out of original data, while maintaining nonnegativity of matrices entries [1–3].

The NMF technique approximates a data matrix A with the product of low rank matrices W and H, $A \approx WH$ such that the elements of W and H are nonnegative [1, 2]. NMF can be applied to the statistical analysis of multivariate data in the following manner. Given a set of m-dimensional data vectors, the vectors are placed in the columns of an $m \times n$ matrix A where n is the number of examples in the data set. This matrix is then approximately factorized into an $m \times k$ matrix W and an $k \times n$ matrix H. Usually k is chosen to be smaller than n or m, so that W and H are smaller than the original matrix A. This results in a compressed version of the original data matrix [1, 4]. If columns of A are data samples, then the columns of W can be interpreted as basis vectors or parts from which data samples are formed, while the columns of H give the contribution of each basis which when combined form the corresponding data sample. In application of NMF to clustering, it is common to define clusters based on basis vectors, and assigning each data sample to a cluster based on the basis of contribution intensity contained in matrix H.

Several cost functions have been used in the literature to measure the quality of NMF matrix factorization for various types of applications and data type. Euclidean distance is the most common cost function widely used for almost all application including text mining [1]. Kullback-Leibler divergence (KL-divergence) [1, 2], β-divergence [5, 6] are among other methods also used for various applications. However, the main issue is to find the factor matrices (W, H) that achieve the minimum of the chosen cost function. There are several optimization algorithms in the literature to achieve this optimum decomposition [3, 7–11].

Several algorithms have been developed for minimizing cost functions since the advent of NMF. Lee and Seung [1, 2] developed a multiplicative algorithm for solving Euclidean and KL-divergence in 2001. Sparse Coding (SP) and Sparseness Constraint (SC) which impose sparsity on H matrix was proposed by Hoyer in 2002 and 2004 [3, 12]. Alternating Least Square (ALS) [10], ALS using projected gradient descent (ALSPGRAD) [13], Gradient Descent with Constrained Least Square (GD-CLS) [4], Quasi Newton method [9], Alternating Nonnegative Constrained Least Squares using Active Set (ANLS-AS) and Block Principal Pivoting (ANLS-BP) [14, 15], Hierarchical Alternating Least Square (HALS) [16] are various algorithms which were proposed for Euclidean cost function. Fevotte et al. [5, 6] proposed several algorithms for minimizing β-divergence cost function. In 2012, Li et al. [17] convert the general Bregman divergence function to Euclidean distance function using Taylor expansion, and solve the corresponding function using HALS algorithm. Du et al. [18] proposed a half-quadratic optimization algorithm for NMF based on correntropy cost function, where a multiplicative algorithm was developed for calculating W and H.

This paper is organized as follows. Section 2 introduces the algorithms developed for NMF using different cost functions and optimization algorithms. Section 3 discusses the experiment designed for evaluating each NMF algorithms. Results are presented and discussed in Section 4. The discussion and conclusion are presented in Section 5.

2   Algorithms for NMF

To find an approximate factorization, we first need to define cost function $D(A|WH)$ that quantifies the quality of the approximation [1]. Given a data matrix $A \in \mathbb{R}^{m \times n}$ and a positive integer $k \ll (m, n)$, find nonnegative factorization into matrices $W \in \mathbb{R}^{m \times k}$ and $H \in \mathbb{R}^{k \times n}$ as

$$\min_{W,H} D(A|WH) \; subject \; to \; W \geq 0, H \geq 0 \tag{1}$$

where the notation $A \geq 0$ expresses nonnegativity of the entries of A (and not semidefinite positiveness), and where $D(A|WH)$ as the measure for goodness of fit, such that

$$D(A|WH) = \sum_{i=1}^{m} \sum_{j=1}^{n} d([A_{ij}]|[WH_{ij}]) \tag{2}$$

where $d(x|y)$ is a scalar cost function as known in the literature [5]. Several cost function are defined in the literature, where most of them belongs to the Bregman divergence family [19]. Generally, a divergence function is defined as follows

$$D_\alpha(a, b) = \begin{cases} \alpha \frac{a^\alpha - b^\alpha}{\alpha} + b^\alpha (b - a) & : \alpha \in (0, 1] \\ \alpha(\log a - \log b) + (b - a) & : \alpha = 0 \end{cases} \tag{3}$$

where α is chosen to define the type of the divergence function. Obviously, $D_1(a, b) = (a - b)^2$ is the Euclidean distance function, and $D_0(a, b)$ defines KL-divergence [20]. The most common functions found in literature are shown below

$$D_{Euclidean}(A|WH) = \sum_{i=1}^{m} \sum_{j=1}^{n} \frac{1}{2}(A_{ij} - (WH)_{ij})^2 \tag{4}$$

$$D_{KL-divergence}(A|WH) = \sum_{i=1}^{m} \sum_{j=1}^{n} (A_{ij} \log \frac{A_{i,j}}{(WH)_{ij}} - A_{ij} + (WH)_{ij}) \tag{5}$$

A key issue of NMF factorization is to minimize the cost function while keeping elements of W and H matrices to be nonnegative. Another challenge is the existence of local minima due to non-convexity of $D(A|WH)$ in both W and H. Moreover, a unique solution to NMF problem does not exist, since for any invertible matrix B whose inverse is B^{-1}, a term $WBB^{-1}H$ could also be nonnegative and a solution. This is most probably the main reason for non-convexity of $D(A|WH)$ function [20].

2.1   Multiplicative Algorithm

The multiplicative gradient descent approach is equivalent to updating each parameter by multiplying its value at previous iteration by the ratio of the negative and positive parts of the gradient of the cost function with regard to this parameter [2, 9]. The prototypical multiplicative algorithm originated with Lee and Seung for Euclidean and KL-divergence cost functions [1]. Their update algorithms for Euclidean and KL-divergence cost functions are shown at (6) and (7) respectively,

$$H_{ij} \longleftarrow H_{ij} \frac{(W^T A)_{ij}}{(W^T W H)_{ij}}, W_{ij} \longleftarrow W_{ij} \frac{(AH^T)_{ij}}{(WHH^T)_{ij}} \tag{6}$$

$$H_{ij} \longleftarrow H_{ij} \frac{\sum_i W_{ia} A_{il}/(WH)_{il}}{\sum_k W_{ka}}, W_{ia} \longleftarrow W_{ia} \frac{\sum_l H_{al} A_{il}/(WH)_{il}}{\sum_v H_{av}} \tag{7}$$

2.2   Sparse NMF

Sparse Coding (SP) and Sparseness Constraint (SC) which impose sparsity on H matrix were proposed by Hoyer in 2002 and 2004 [3, 12]. Using SP method, Euclidean cost function is penalized by the elements of H matrix,

$$D_{SP}(A|WH) = \sum_{i=1}^{m} \sum_{j=1}^{n} \frac{1}{2}(A_{ij} - (WH)_{ij})^2 + \lambda \sum_{ij} H_{ij} \tag{8}$$

where $\lambda \geq 0$ is the sparseness constant. In SC method, a *Sparseness* measure is computed based on ℓ^1-norm and the ℓ^2-norm for a vector x,

$$Sparseness(x) = \frac{\sqrt{n} - (\sum |x_i|)/\sqrt{\sum x_i^2}}{\sqrt{n} - 1} \tag{9}$$

where n is the dimensionality of x. This function evaluates to unity if and only if x contains only a single non-zero component, and takes a value of zero if and only if all components are equal (up to sign), interpolating smoothly between the two extremes. Using this definition, (4) is minimized under additional constraints,

$$sparseness(w_i) = S_w, \forall i \tag{10}$$

$$sparseness(h_i) = S_h, \forall i \tag{11}$$

where w_i is the i-th column of W and h_i is the i-th row of H. Here, S_w and S_h are the desired sparsenesses of W and H, respectively. These two parameters are set by the user.

2.3 Hybrid Algorithm

In this approach, the multiplicative method is used at each iterative step to approximate only the basis vector matrix W. Then, H is calculated using a Constrained Least Squares (CLS) method to penalize the non-smoothness and non-sparsity of H. The hybrid algorithm is denoted as Gradient Descent with Constrained Least Squares (GD-CLS) [4].

2.4 Alternating Least Square (ALS) Algorithms

In these family of algorithms, a least squares step is followed by another least squares step in an alternating fashion, thus giving rise to the ALS name, as shown in (12) and (13),

$$\min_{W} D(A|WH) \text{ subject to } W \geq 0 \tag{12}$$

$$\min_{H} D(A|WH) \text{ subject to } H \geq 0 \tag{13}$$

ALS algorithms exploit the fact that, while the optimization problem of (4) and (5) is not convex in both W and H, it is convex in either W or H, corresponding to (12) and (13) respectively. Thus, given one matrix, the other matrix can be found with a simple least squares computation. However, the least square problem should result in nonnegative W and H, which means least square algorithm should be of class of nonnegative least square. Several algorithms have been proposed to keep nonegativity constraint in ALS algorithm. The basic ALS algorithm uses nonnegativity threshold on elements of W and H matrices, to remove the nonnegative elements [10]. ALS method based on Projected Gradient Method (ALS-PGD) was proposed in [13], which contains nonnegativity constraint in its gradient based update algorithms.

Kim et al. proposed an Alternating Nonnegative Least Square method (ANLS) based on Active Set (ANLS-AS) and Block Pivoting method (ANLS-BP) to solve nonnegative constrained least squares problem in a fast way [14, 15]. Using ANLS-AS, the following ANLS problem with multiple right hand side,

$$\min_{W>0} \| H^T W^T - A^T \|^2 \tag{14}$$

$$\min_{H>0} \| WH - A \|^2 \tag{15}$$

are converted to the form of (16) alternately,

$$\min_{G>0} \| BG - Y \|^2 \tag{16}$$

where $B \in \mathbb{R}^{p \times q}$ and $Y \in \mathbb{R}^{p \times l}$. Then (16) is decoupled into l independent NNLS problem each with single right-hand side as

$$\min_{G>0} \| BG - Y \|^2 = \min_{g_1>0} \| Bg_1 - Y \|^2, \ldots, \min_{g_l>0} \| Bg_l - Y \|^2 \tag{17}$$

where $G = [g_1, \ldots, g_l] \in \mathbb{R}^{q \times l}$ and $Y = [y_1, \ldots, y_1] \in \mathbb{R}^{p \times l}$. Then each independent NNLS problems is solves using Active Set algorithm proposed in [15].

Using ANLS-BP method, a single right-hand side problem is solved using Block Principle Pivoting (BPP) algorithm proposed, and it was generalized for multiple right-hand side problem [14]. These methods have also been developed to include sparsity and regularity inside the NNLS problem.

2.5   NMF Based on β-divergence

The β-divergence is a family of cost functions parameterized by a single shape parameter β. This cost function could takes the form of Euclidean distance, Kullback-Leibler divergence, and Itakura-Saito divergence as special cases ($\beta = 2, 1, 0$ respectively).

$$d_\beta(x|y) = \begin{cases} \frac{1}{\beta(\beta-1)}(x^\beta + (\beta - 1)y^\beta - \beta x y^{\beta-1}) & : \beta \in \mathbb{R}(0,1) \\ x \log \frac{x}{y} - x + y & : \beta = 1 \\ \frac{x}{y} - \log \frac{x}{y} - 1 & : \beta = 0 \end{cases} \qquad (18)$$

Fevotte et al. [5, 6] proposed algorithms, which are based on a surrogate auxiliary function (a local majorization of the criterion function). They developed a majorization minimization algorithm that leads to multiplicative updates, and a Majorization Equalization (ME) algorithm. We use ME algorithm for NMF based on β-divergence (Beta-ME) in the experiment section.

2.6   NMF Based on Correntropy

The correntropy cost function is defined as

$$D_{Correntropy}(A|WH) = -\sum_{i=1}^{m} \sum_{j=1}^{n} \exp(\frac{-(A_{ij} - (WH)_{ij})^2}{2\sigma^2}) \qquad (19)$$

where σ is a parameter of correntropy measure [21, 22]. The optimization algorithms try to minimize the correntropy, since it is a measure of similarity instead of distance between two elements. Ensari et al. [23, 24] used the general algorithm of Constrained Gradient Descent (CGD) method [25] for solving the correntropy function, and compared the results with the projected gradient descent method of Euclidean cost function. The major disadvantage of CGD is its high sensitivity to σ value of the cost function. Du et al. [18] proposed a half-quadratic optimization algorithm to solve NMF based on correntropy cost function (rCIM), and developed a multiplicative algorithm to solve NMF.

3   Experiment

This section outlines the design procedure of an experiment to evaluate different NMF algorithms. In this procedure, the performance of multiplicative algorithm for Euclidean distance (Euc-Mult) and KL-divergence (KL-Mult), GD-CLS, the basic ALS, ALS-PGD, ANLS-AS, ANLS-BP, Beta-Divergence NMF (Beta-ME), and rCIM methods are evaluated for document clustering. Several experiments have been done for each algorithm, and the results in each experiment were very similar. Therefore, we only show the results of one experiment for each algorithm.

Reuters Documents Corpus has been selected as dataset. It contains 21578 documents and 135 standard topics or document clusters, which are created manually. Each document in the corpus is assigned to one or more topics based on its content. The size of each cluster, which is the number of documents it contains ranges from less than ten to four thousand. For our experiment, documents associated with only one topic are used, and topics which contain less than five documents are discarded [4]. Therefore, 8293 documents with 48 topics were left at the end. In order to evaluate the performance of the NMF algorithms for increasing complexity, i.e., the number of clusters to be created or equal k, clustering results with ten different k values of $[2, 4, 6, 8, 10, 15, 20, 30, 40, 48]$ are computed.

After creating clusters using NMF, each cluster is assigned to a most related document topic. For this purpose, a matrix which shows the distribution of all documents between each created cluster and dataset topics is created. The matrix dimension is $k \times l$, where k is the number of clusters, and l is the number of topics. This matrix is called Document Distribution Matrix (DDM). The maximum value at each column of DDM is found first. Then, the corresponding topic related to this column is assigned to the NMF cluster, corresponding to the row number. At the end of this process, there may be some NMF clusters which are not assigned to any topic. Some of these clusters may contain large number of documents, and omitting them may reduce the accuracy. To assign these NMF clusters to a topic, the maximum value found in a row of DDM, which is related to any of these NMF clusters is used for the topic assignment. It turns out that the related column of the value found indicates the topic to be assigned. This method may results in assigning some NMF clusters to more than one topic.

We evaluate the clustering performance with Accuracy, Root Mean Square Residual (RMSR), Entropy, Purity, and computational time metrics. Accuracy of clustering is assessed with the metric AC used by [7] defined as:

$$AC = \sum_{i=1}^{n} \delta(d_i)/n \qquad (20)$$

where $\delta(d_i)$ is set to 1 if d_i has the same topic label for both NMF cluster and the original topic, and otherwise set to 0, and n is the total number of documents in the collection. The RMSR between A and W and H matrix is defined as:

$$RMSR = \sqrt{\frac{\sum_{ij}(A_{ij} - (WH)_{ij})^2}{m \times n}} \qquad (21)$$

Total entropy for a set of clusters is calculated as the weighted mean of the entropies of each cluster weighted by the size of each cluster [11]. Using DDM, we compute p_{ij} for topic j, the probability that a member of cluster i belongs to topic j as $p_{ij} = n_{ij}/n_i$, where n_i is the number of objects in cluster i and n_{ij} is the number of documents of topic j in cluster i. Entropy of each cluster is defined as:

$$e_i = -\sum_{j=1}^{l} p_{ij} \log_2(p_{ij}) \tag{22}$$

where l is the number of topics. *Entropy* of the full data set is the sum of the entropies of each cluster weighted by its relative size:

$$Entropy = \sum_{i=1}^{k} \frac{n_i}{n} e_i \tag{23}$$

where k is the number of NMF clusters, and n is the total number of documents. *Purity* measures the extent to which each NMF cluster contained documents from primarily one topic [26]. *Purity* of the NMF clustering is obtained as a weighted sum of individual NMF cluster purity values and is given by

$$Purity = \sum_{i=1}^{k} \frac{n_i}{n} P(S_i) \tag{24}$$

where

$$P(S_i) \triangleq \frac{1}{n_i} max_j(n_i^j) \tag{25}$$

where S_i is a particular NMF cluster of size n_i, n_i^j is the number of documents of the i-th topic that were assigned to the j-th NMF cluster, k is the number of clusters, and n is the total number of documents. In general, the larger the *Purity*, the better the clustering solution is. We also compute the computational time (in sec) taken by each NMF algorithms in terms of CPU time.

4   Results

Performance of each NMF algorithm is shown in terms of accuracy AC, RMSR, *Entropy*, and *Purity* in Fig. 1(a), (b), (c), and (d), respectively. The results indicate that KL-Mult yields better performance than any other methods. It shows better AC, the lowest *Entropy*, and the highest *Purity* for different values of k. The results in Fig. 1(b) indicates that Beta-ME is the worst algorithm in terms of RMSR, especially when k is increased. In addition, SC is independent of change of k, while RMSR would decrease by increasing k for other algorithms.

The computational performance of each algorithm is also evaluated in terms of computational time in Fig. 2. Since Beta-ME results in a large values of time (around 7000 sec), it was removed in Fig. 2 to have a better comparison between the other algorithms. The results indicate that KL-Mult is the most

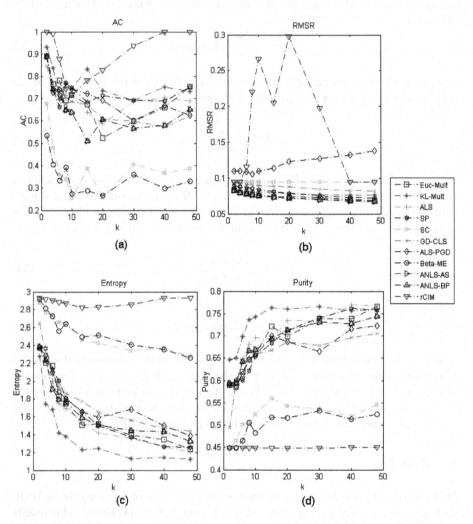

Fig. 1. Comparison of different NMF algorithms using (a) *AC*, (b) RMSR, (c) *Entropy*, (d) *Purity*

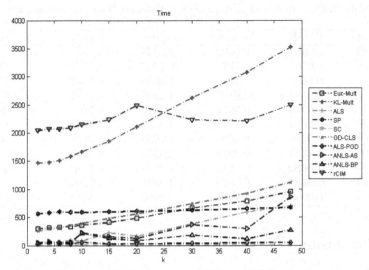

Fig. 2. Comparison between CPU time (sec) of different NMF algorithms using Matlab

time consuming algorithm with increasing computational complexity in terms of k. However, SC and ALS-PGD are the most efficient algorithms. The results of each algorithm for $k = 15$ and $k = 20$ are also tabulated in Table 1 and Table 2, respectively. The most efficient value for each performance measure is shown in bold. The results reveal that KL-Mult has been found to be the most efficient algorithm in terms of accuracy AC, *Entropy* and *Purity*, which are directly related to the clustering performance. However, SC and ALS-PGD are ranked among the fastest algorithms.

Table 1. Comparison of performance of different NMF algorithms, $k = 15$

Algorithm	RMSR	Accuracy	Entropy	Purity	CPU time(sec)
Euc-Mult	0.0736	0.6744	1.5050	0.7217	410
KL-Mult	0.0794	**0.8320**	**1.2338**	**0.7636**	1854
ALS	0.0747	0.6387	1.5380	0.6931	224
SP	0.0813	0.6854	1.6532	0.6835	595
SC	0.0947	0.3867	2.4579	0.5607	**12**
GD-CLS	0.0888	0.6726	1.7785	0.6672	480
ALS-PGD	0.0740	0.7212	1.6549	0.6996	**29**
Beta-ME	0.1135	0.2886	2.4946	0.5172	7547
ANLS-AS	**0.0732**	0.5113	1.5846	0.6929	157
ANLS-BP	**0.0732**	0.5113	1.5846	0.6929	127
rCIM	0.2054	0.7803	2.8225	0.4496	2235

Table 2. Comparison of performance of different NMF algorithms, $k = 20$

Algorithm	RMSR	Accuracy	Entropy	Purity	CPU time(sec)
Euc-Mult	0.0694	0.6602	1.3445	0.7378	788
KL-Mult	0.0767	0.7522	**1.1457**	0.7562	3073
ALS	0.0687	0.7040	1.2639	**0.7699**	590
SP	0.0732	0.6887	1.2635	0.7622	648
SC	0.0946	0.3672	2.3718	0.5197	**14**
GD-CLS	0.0833	0.5745	1.4691	0.6963	924
ALS-PGD	0.0696	0.6690	1.4994	0.7163	**48**
Beta-ME	0.1323	0.2974	2.3553	0.5130	8547
ANLS-AS	**0.0682**	0.5810	1.4348	0.7280	297
ANLS-BP	**0.0682**	0.5810	1.4348	0.7280	117
rCIM	0.0950	**0.9996**	2.9266	0.4499	2214

5   Conclusion

In this paper, we evaluated the performance of the most regular algorithms of NMF for document clustering. NMF based on Euclidean distance, KL-divergence, β-divergence, Correntropy cost function using Multiplicative, Alternating Least Square (ALS), GD-CLS, Alternating Least Square using Active Set (ANLS-AS), and Alternating Least Square using Block Pivoting (ANLS-BP) algorithms were tested. The performance of algorithms were tested on Reuters Document Corpus for document clustering. The most efficient algorithms in terms of accuracy, entropy, purity, computational time and RMSR were identified. The results indicate that KL-divergence cost function with multiplicative update rule yields the most efficient performance in terms of accuracy, entropy and purity. However, this algorithm is time consuming especially for large k. NMF based on Sparseness Constraint (SP) and Alternating Least Square with Projected Gradient Descent (ALS-PGD) method were found to be the fastest algorithms.

References

1. Lee, D.D., Seung, H.S.: Learning the parts of objects by non-negative matrix factorization. Nature 401(6755), 788–791 (1999)
2. Lee, D.D., Seung, H.S.: Algorithms for non-negative matrix factorization. In: Advances in Neural Information Processing Systems, pp. 556–562 (2000)
3. Hoyer, P.O.: Non-negative sparse coding. In: Proceedings of the 12th IEEE Workshop on Neural Networks for Signal Processing, pp. 557–565. IEEE (2002)
4. Shahnaz, F., Berry, M.W., Pauca, V.P., Plemmons, R.J.: Document clustering using nonnegative matrix factorization. Information Processing & Management 42(2), 373–386 (2006)
5. Févotte, C., Bertin, N., Durrieu, J.L.: Nonnegative matrix factorization with the itakura-saito divergence: With application to music analysis. Neural computation 21(3), 793–830 (2009)
6. Févotte, C., Idier, J.: Algorithms for nonnegative matrix factorization with the β-divergence. Neural Computation 23(9), 2421–2456 (2011)

7. Xu, W., Liu, X., Gong, Y.: Document clustering based on non-negative matrix factorization. In: Proceedings of the 26th Annual International ACM SIGIR Conference on Research and Development in Informaion Retrieval, pp. 267–273. ACM (2003)
8. Liu, W., Pokharel, P.P., Principe, J.C.: Correntropy: A localized similarity measure. In: International Joint Conference on Neural Networks, IJCNN 2006, pp. 4919–4924. IEEE (2006)
9. Zdunek, R., Cichocki, A.: Non-negative matrix factorization with quasi-newton optimization. In: Rutkowski, L., Tadeusiewicz, R., Zadeh, L.A., Żurada, J.M. (eds.) ICAISC 2006. LNCS (LNAI), vol. 4029, pp. 870–879. Springer, Heidelberg (2006)
10. Berry, M.W., Browne, M., Langville, A.N., Pauca, V.P., Plemmons, R.J.: Algorithms and applications for approximate nonnegative matrix factorization. Computational Statistics & Data Analysis 52(1), 155–173 (2007)
11. Pang-Ning, T., Steinbach, M., Kumar, V.: Introduction to Data Mining, 1st edn. Addison-Wesley Longman Publishing Co., Inc., Boston (2005)
12. Hoyer, P.O.: Non-negative matrix factorization with sparseness constraints. J. Mach. Learn. Res. 5, 1457–1469 (2004)
13. Lin, C.J.: Projected gradient methods for nonnegative matrix factorization. Neural computation 19(10), 2756–2779 (2007)
14. Kim, H., Park, H.: Nonnegative matrix factorization based on alternating nonnegativity constrained least squares and active set method. SIAM J. Matrix Anal. Appl. 30(2), 713–730 (2008)
15. Kim, J., Park, H.: Fast nonnegative matrix factorization: An active-set-like method and comparisons. SIAM J. Sci. Comput. 33(6), 3261–3281 (2011)
16. Cichocki, A., Anh-Huy, P.: Fast local algorithms for large scale nonnegative matrix and tensor factorizations. IEICE Trans. Fundamentals 92(3), 708–721 (2009)
17. Li, L., Lebanon, G., Park, H.: Fast bregman divergence nmf using taylor expansion and coordinate descent. In: Proceedings of the 18th ACM SIGKDD International Conference on Knowledge Discovery and Data Mining, pp. 307–315. ACM (2012)
18. Du, L., Li, X., Shen, Y.D.: Robust nonnegative matrix factorization via half-quadratic minimization. In: ICDM, pp. 201–210 (2012)
19. Dhillon, I.S., Sra, S.: Generalized nonnegative matrix approximations with bregman divergences. In: NIPS, vol. 18 (2005)
20. Kompass, R.: A generalized divergence measure for nonnegative matrix factorization. Neural computation 19(3), 780–791 (2007)
21. Liu, W., Pokharel, P.P., Principe, J.C.: Correntropy: properties and applications in non-gaussian signal processing. IEEE Trans. Signal Process 55(11), 5286–5298 (2007)
22. Jeong, K.H., Principe, J.C.: Enhancing the correntropy MACE filter with random projections. Neurocomputing 72(1), 102–111 (2008)
23. Ensari, T., Chorowski, J., Zurada, J.M.: Correntropy-based document clustering via nonnegative matrix factorization. In: Villa, A.E.P., Duch, W., Érdi, P., Masulli, F., Palm, G. (eds.) ICANN 2012, Part II. LNCS, vol. 7553, pp. 347–354. Springer, Heidelberg (2012)
24. Ensari, T., Chorowski, J., Zurada, J.M.: Occluded face recognition using correntropy-based nonnegative matrix factorization. In: 11th International Conference on Machine Learning and Applications (ICMLA), vol. 1, pp. 606–609. IEEE (2012)
25. Schmidt, M.: Matlab software (2008), http://www.di.ens.fr/~mschmidt/Software/minConf.html
26. Ding, C., Li, T., Peng, W., Park, H.: Orthogonal nonnegative matrix t-factorizations for clustering. In: Proceedings of the 12th ACM SIGKDD International Conference on Knowledge Discovery and Data Mining, pp. 126–135. ACM (2006)

Fuzzy c-Medoid Graph Clustering

András Király, Ágnes Vathy-Fogarassy, and János Abonyi

University of Pannonia, P.O. Box 158, Veszprém H-8200, Hungary
janos@abonyilab.com

Abstract. We present a modified fuzzy c-medoid algorithm to find central objects in graphs. Initial cluster centres are determined by graph centrality measures. Cluster centres are fine-tuned by minimizing fuzzy-weighted geodesic distances calculated by Dijkstra's algorithm. Cluster validity indices show significant improvement against fuzzy c-medoid clustering.

1   Introduction

Cluster is a group of objects that are more similar to one another than to members of other clusters. The term "similarity" should be understood as mathematical similarity, measured in some well-defined sense. In metric spaces, similarity is often defined by means of a distance norm. In order to develop a special algorithm for graph clustering we developed a novel geodesic distance based fuzzy clustering algorithm where the geodesic distances are defined by the application of Dijskra algorithm on a weighed graph used to represent the high dimensional data. In graph theory, the distance between two vertices in a weighted graph is the sum of weights of edges in a shortest path connecting them. This is an approximation of the geodesic distance that can be measured on the real manifold the (noiseless) data lie on. The proposed approach is able to handle data that lie on a low dimensional manifold of a high dimensional feature space since clustering uses a distance measure which reflects the true embedded manifold.

Classical fuzzy c-means clustering uses some variant of Euclidean measure to compute distances between cluster members and the center. The application of geodesic distances can improve the usability of these methods, since this measure gives a better approximation of real life distances. Recent research validates this distance's applicability like Wu et al. in [1] where large sparse graphs are approximated using geodesic distance based clustering. Nice clustering results are presented by Kim et al. in [2] where a fuzzy-like solution is presented using soft geodesic kernels, while Asgharbeygi and Maleki [3] approximates the geodesic distances from the virtual cluster centers by the law of large numbers. Application for image segmentation can be found in [4,5], Economou et al. use Minimal Spanning Tree algorithm to estimate geodesic distances and the image is presented by an undirected graph. Galluccio et al. in [6] use their algorithm for segmentation of maps, and their main contribution is the initialization of the k-means algorithm, i.e. the proper determination of k, which is done by the

L. Rutkowski et al. (Eds.): ICAISC 2014, Part II, LNAI 8468, pp. 738–748, 2014.

identification os valleys in the 2D projection of total traveling distances in Prim's MST algorithm. Their algorithm is further improved in [5] where large data are handled. Also initialization play the central role in Ren's approach [7], where Kruskal algorithm is used for generating the MST to improve the initial cluster centers.

The main idea and our main contribution of this article is to develop a procedure to reveal hidden, complex structure of high dimensional data, where data is stored using a much simpler graph format, and distances are defined as geodesic distances between vertices. The presented new algorithm is based on the concept of fuzzy c-medoid algorithm, but uses centrality measures to identify highly central cluster centers, operates on a weighted undirected graph and by the usage of geodesic distances it is free of c-medoid's shortcomings, the spherical shape of discovered clusters. Our approach also supports initialization, like identification of most central k points as initial cluster centers.

2 Geodesic Distance Based Fuzzy c-medoid Clustering and Its Initialization Based on Graph Centrality Measures

2.1 A Novel Fuzzy c-medoid Based Clustering Algorithm

The proposed method is built on the fuzzy version of the classical hard k-medoid algorithm (c-medoid method) [8]. However, as a first step, a knn-graph is generated, using k as parameter. Then potential cluster centers are identified using several centrality measures as the most central M points. Distances are measured by the geodesics and calculated by Dijkstra algorithm for each pair of points on the graph. The objective function is almost the same as in fuzzy c-means, but c-medoid accepts measured data points as cluster centers (and not calculated means like in c-means). To find the minimum of the cost function, several methods can be used. The proposed algorithm works well with data sets in different size as we will see in the next section.

1. If data is given by single points, generate knn-graph with parameter k.
2. Calculate centrality values for all data points using one of the centrality measures (degree, betweenness, closeness, eigenvector), and sort the data points according to these centrality values.
3. Select the first M data points as potential cluster centers. This set is denoted by c_M.
4. Calculate the geodesic distances between each potential cluster center and all data points, using Dijkstra algorithm on the knn-graph.
5. Use fuzzy c-medoid algorithm:
   (a) Arbitrarily choose c objects as the initial medoids from the M potential cluster centers.
   (b) Use the calculated geodesic distances (Step 4) to determine how far the data points are from the medoids.

(c) Calculate fuzzy membership degrees as usual by fuzzy partitional clustering methods:

$$\mu_{i,j} = \frac{1}{\sum_{k=1}^{c} \left(\frac{\|\mathbf{x}_i - \mathbf{c}_j\|}{\|\mathbf{x}_i - \mathbf{c}_k\|} \right)^{\frac{2}{(m-1)}}}, \quad 1 \leq i \leq N, 1 \leq j \leq c. \tag{1}$$

(d) Calculate the objective function terms $\sum_{i=1}^{N} (\mu_{i,j})^m \|\mathbf{x}_i - \mathbf{c}_j\|^2, \forall i$ using the determined membership degrees, for all $\mathbf{x}_k$ as potential medoids, and choose the data points as new medoids that minimize the objective function.

$$\mathbf{c}_k = \left\{ \mathbf{x}_j | \mathbf{x}_j \in c_M, j = \arg \min_j \sum_{i=1}^{N} (\mu_{i,j})^m \|\mathbf{x}_i - \mathbf{c}_j\|^2 \right\} \tag{2}$$

(e) If there are any changes, jump to Step 5(b).

This method can handle large data sets because in Step 5(d), only the set of potential cluster centers are used for objective function calculation. In the following, we will present some cluster validity indices which were used for the evaluation of the method.

2.2   Creating a Graph of High Dimensional Data

The suggested method requires a graph structure defined over the data to be analyzed. This network can be given a priori in accordance with the real relationship between the objects (for example cities and the roads connecting them), or it can be defined artificially between them. In the second case there are several possibilities to build up a network among the data. For example we can connect the neighboring objects together, or we can build up the topology representing network [9] of the data as well.

There are two basic approaches to connect neighboring objects together: ϵ-neighboring and k-neighboring. In case of ϵ-neighboring approach two objects x_i and x_j are connected by an edge if they are lying in an ϵ radius environment. The main drawback of this approach is that it does not take the density of the objects into account. If the cloud of the objects contains dense regions and sparse regions too, it is toughish to find a proper value for the parameter ϵ. In the case of the k-neighboring approach, two objects are connected to each other if one of them is in among the k-nearest neighbors of the other, where k is the number of the neighbors to be taken into account. The distance of the objects can be measured in different ways, usually the Euclidean distance is used for this purpose. This method results in the k nearest neighbor graph (knn-graph).

In case of large data sets there is a need to reduce the computational cost. In these cases it is a good choice to apply a vector quantization method on the data, than cluster this reduced data set, and finally project the clustering result to the whole data set (e.g. by applying a k-means algorithm). The Topology Representing Network (TRN) algorithm [9] is one of best known neural network based vector quantization method. It not only quantizes the objects, but also creates the networks of the quantized elements. For this purpose the TRN algorithm distributes representative elements (quantized data points) between the objects by the neural gas algorithm [10], and it creates a network among them by applying the competitive Hebbian rule [11]. As result a graph is given which is a compressed form of the structure of the whole data set.

2.3 Centrality Measures of the Objects

As we have mentioned before, the choice of cluster prototypes significantly influences the clustering result. k-means and k-medoid methods require initial cluster centers as input parameters. The main problem of these methods is that they are sensitive to the selection of the initial centers and may converge to a local minimum of the error function if the initial cluster centers are not properly chosen.

In general clusters are determined based on the distances of the objects or objects and prototypes. To be able to unfold the lower dimensional manifolds embedded nonlinearly in the higher dimensional vector space the utilization of geodesic distance is good choice. To calculate the geodesic distances we have to define a network on the objects (see Section 2.2). When this network is defined central nodes of this graph can be used as initial cluster clusters.

The term centrality expresses the importance of the node in the graph. Importance can be defined in several way so there are several types of measures to express the degree of centrality of a node within a graph. The most widely used centrality measures are: degree centrality, betweenness, closeness and eigenvector centrality. All four measures are based on the structure of the graph and they calculate the measure of the centrality by taking into account the relationships of the objects.

The simplest centrality measure is the *degree centrality*. The degree of a node means the number of the edges connecting to that node. If the graph to be analyzed is a directed graph, we can talk about indegree centrality and outdegree centrality as well. Indegree centrality expresses how many directed edges are incident on a node, and outdegree centrality represents how many directed edges originate at that node. The centrality measure degree is based on that assumption, that significant vertices in the graph have many connections. Formally, the degree of a node v_i can be expressed as follows:

$$C_D(v_i) = deg(v_i) \qquad (3)$$

where $deg(v_i)$ yields the degree of the node v_i. In this from the degree centrality just counts the number of the edges of a vertex. The measure becomes more informative if we normalize it. The normalization of the degree centrality can be made by dividing the value given by the Equation 3 by the maximum number of possible edges, which is $N-1$, where N is the number of the vertices, or we can use the Freeman's general formula as well as follows:

$$C_{D_{norm}}(v_i) = \frac{\sum_{i=1}^{N}[C_D(v^*) - C_D(v_i)]}{[(N-1)(N-2)]} \qquad (4)$$

where $C_D(v^*)$ yields the maximum value of the degree centrality in the network.

The main disadvantage of the degree locality, that it is a purely local measure. The centrality measure *betweenness* [12] takes not only the local environment of the nodes into account, but it considers the whole graph, and it is calculated based on the shortest paths between all possible pairs of vertices. The measure betweenness of a node expresses the number of shortest paths from all vertices to all others that pass through that node. In this approach central nodes establish bridges between the other vertices. Formally, the betweenness can be calculated as:

$$C_B(v_i) = \sum_{j<k} g_{jk}(v_i)/g_{jk} \qquad (5)$$

where g_{jk} is the total number of shortest paths from node v_j to node v_k and $g_{jk}(v_i)$ is the number of those paths that pass through v_i. This measure is usually normalized as well. If the graph is undirected we can calculate the normalized values as follows:

$$C_{B_{norm}}(v_i) = \frac{C_B(v_i)}{[(N-1)(N-2)/2]} \qquad (6)$$

If the graph is directed the division is done by $(N-1)(N-2)$.

The third centrality measure (closeness) is based on the distance of the vertices. *Closeness* [13] expresses how far the nodes are to the other nodes. In this approach the more central the node is, the more close is the node to the other nodes. A node closeness is the the inverse of the sum of its distances to all other nodes. If the graph is weighted the distance is calculated as the sum of the weights along the shortest paths, and if the graph is unweighted it is the number of the hops between the nodes. Therefore the closeness of a node is calculated as follows:

$$C_C(v_i) = \left[\sum_{j}^{N} d(v_i, v_j)\right]^{-1} \qquad (7)$$

where $d(v_i, v_j)$ yields the geodesic distance of objects v_i and v_j. The normalized version of this centrality measure is:

$$C_{C_{norm}}(v_i) = \frac{C_C(v_i)}{N-1} \qquad (8)$$

The *eigenvector centrality* is a more complex centrality measures. It takes not only the structure of the network into account, but the centrality measures of other nodes, too. In this approach the centrality of a node depends on how central its neighbors are. The assumption is that each node's centrality is the weighted sum of the centrality values of the nodes that it is connected to. The weighting factors are arising from the weight of the edges connecting the neighborhood nodes. More precisely, the eigenvector centrality of a node v_i can be determined as:

$$C_E(v_i) = \sum_{j \in M(v_i)} (w_{ji} * C_E(v_j)) \tag{9}$$

where w_{ji} is the weight of the edge connecting nodes v_i and v_j. If the graph is unweighted, w_{ji} is constant (λ) in all cases. Let $G = (E, V)$ to be analyzed, and $A = (a_{i,j})$ the adjacency matrix of the graph G, where $a_{i,j} = 1$ if v_i and v_j are connected, otherwise $a_{i,j} = 0$. In this form the values of the eigenvector centralities ($\mathbf{x}$) can be calculated as follows:

$$x_i = \frac{1}{\lambda} \sum_{j \in G} (a_{ji} * x_j) \tag{10}$$

This formula can be rewritten as eigenvector equation as:

$$\mathbf{Ax} = \lambda \mathbf{x} \tag{11}$$

Multiplying the adjacency matrix by the vector $\mathbf{x}$ again and again each node "pick up" the centrality values of each vertex to which the first vertex is connected and the centrality measures spread across the edges of the graph. This process might eventually reach an equilibrium where the amount coming into a given vertex at each node would remain stable. As result the elements of this vector $\mathbf{x}$ are the eigenvector centralities of the vertices of the graph.

Since the k-nn graph is used to represent the data, the degree centrality measure cannot be used as all nodes have the same degree. According the to the type of the problem the betweenness and the eigenvector centrality measures should be the more informative. This hypothesis will be also tested in the experimental evaluation of the algorithm.

3   Experimental Results

In this section two examples are shown to present the efficiency of the proposed algorithm. A 3 dimensional synthetic data set to illustrate the distribution of the representative elements and the "wine" data set, which defines a well-known clustering problem.

For comparison, the classical fuzzy c-means algorithm is also applied on these data sets. The reason for using fuzzy c-means algorithm is twosome: on the one hand, it will be shown that this algorithm fails if the data lie on a manifold; on the other hand, we have calculated cluster validity indices for this method as well and we have compared these values with cluster validity indices calculated based on the results of geodesic distance and centrality based fuzzy c-medoid clustering.

3.1 Clstering an S-curve

The S-curve data set is a well known and often used data set in manifold exploration. Objects presented by data points lie in the 3 dimensional vector space,
but they form a 2 dimensional nonlinear embedded manifold as can be seen in
Figure 1. In our example the S-curve data set contains 2000 data points.

There were two algorithms applied on this data set: the fuzzy c-means algorithm and our suggested method presented in section 2.1. In both cases we
have tried to find 8 representative data points in the feature space to characterize this data set. Result of the geodesic distance and centrality based fuzzy
c-medoid clustering can be seen in Figure 1. Figure 1 shows the original data
set and the representative elements (cluster centers) marked with diamonds. To
demonstrate how the cluster centers "cover" the whole embedded manifold we
have applied Isomap mapping to visualize our result in a 2 dimensional vector
space (Figure 2). If the classical fuzzy c-means is applied with the same parameters, the algorithm will fail to explore the hidden structure of the data. Results
of the fuzzy c-means algorithm is seen in Figure 3, and it can be determined
that the centers do not lie on the manifold.

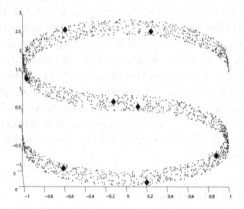

Fig. 1. S-curve data set (dots) and the representative elements (diamonds) determined
by the geodesic distance and centrality based fuzzy c-medoid algorithm

3.2 Wine Data Set

The Wine data, which is available from the University of California, Irvine,
via anonymous ftp *ftp.ics.uci.edu/pub/machine-learning-databases*, contains the
chemical analysis of 178 wines grown in the same region in Italy but derived
from three different cultivars. The problem is to distinguish the three different types based on 13 continuous attributes derived from chemical analysis:

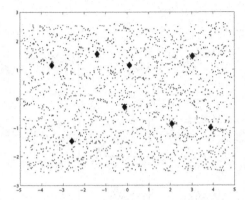

Fig. 2. 2 dimensional Isomap projection of the S-curve data set and the representative elements determined by the geodesic distance and centrality based fuzzy c-medoid algorithm

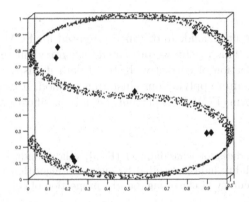

Fig. 3. The S-curve data set and cluster centers of the fuzzy c-means clustering in the feature space

Alcohol, Malic acid, Ash, Alcalinity of ash, Magnesium, Total phenols, Flavanoids, Not-flavanoids phenols, Proanthocyaninsm, Color intensity, Hue, OD280/OD315 of dilluted wines and Proline (Figure 4).

In the following, the number of clusters is three because of the number of the real classes, and the number of neighbors for the neighborhood graph is 8. By this number of neighbors, there is only one component in the neighborhood graph. It is interesting that with 2 neighbors three components were given, but these components do not cover the original classes (the misclassification rate is about 60%). It shows the complexity of this problem as well.

Table 1 shows the values of the validity indices by the wine data set. As above, the recalculated and the original values by FCM show that there may be a certain structure in the data set. However, the validity indices can not show unambiguously which clustering result is the best, since the calculation of

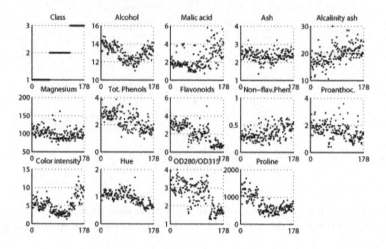

Fig. 4. Wine data set

distances are different, Euclidean distances are used for FCM, while GCM uses geodesic distances. This is why we presented "accuracy" in the last row, which indicates the proportion of correctly clustered data items, i.e. items belonging to the real clusters after applying our clustering method. It can be seen that our algorithm outperforms FCM by 4 percent, i.e. misclassification rate is 4 percent lower.

Table 1. Validity indices for wine data set (FCM: validity indices resulted by classical FCM; GCM: validity indices resulted by our novel algorithm named Geodesic-C-Medoid) and the accuracy of clustering, i.e. the proportion of correctly clustered data points

Validity Index	FCM	GCM
PC	0.33	0.58
CE	1.09	0.28
PI	0.22	0.06
XB	93.24	0.07
Accuracy	69.66%	73.03%

4 Conclusion

We developed an algorithm for mining central objects in graphs and high dimensional data. The modified fuzzy c-medoid clustering algorithm uses geodesic distance measure and selects potential cluster centres among the set of most central objects. Our method doesn't suffer from high computational expenses, since only the set of potential cluster centres are used for objective function calculation. We tested the method using several benchmark problems. The algorithm was capable to explore the hidden structure in the S-Curve Data and the Wine Data sets. We achieved better results applying four different cluster validity indices than the classic Fuzzy C-Means algorithm. The FCM's accuracy was also over-performed by four percent. Our detailed evaluation of the applied initialization using different centrality measures showed unequivocally its necessity. Choosing the centrality measure properly, we proposed a very simple but powerful initial clustering, improving the convergence of the algorithm substantially.

Acknowledgement. This research has been supported by the European Union and the Hungarian Republic through the TÁMOP-4.2.2.C-11/1/KONV-2012-0004 - National Research Center for Development and Market Introduction of Advanced Information and Communication Technologies. The infrasturcure and the publication of the research has been supported by the European Union and the Hungarian Republic through the project TAMOP-4.2.2.A-11/1/KONV-2012-0071. The contribution of Janos Abonyi was supported in the frames of TÁMOP 4.2.4. A/2-11/2012-0001 National Excellence Program- Elaborating and operating an inland student and researcher personal support system.

References

1. Wu, A.Y., Garland, M., Han, J.: Mining scale-free networks using geodesic clustering. In: Proceedings of the 2004 ACM SIGKDD International Conference on Knowledge Discovery and Data Mining, KDD 2004, p. 719 (2004), http://dx.doi.org/10.1145/1014052.1014146, doi:10.1145/1014052.1014146
2. Kim, J., Shim, K.-H., Choi, S.: Soft geodesic kernel k-means. In: IEEE International Conference on Acoustics, Speech and Signal Processing, ICASSP 2007, Honolulu, Hawaii, vol. 2, pp. II–429–II–432 (2007)
3. Asgharbeygi, N., Maleki, A.: Geodesic k-means clustering. In: 19th International Conference on Pattern Recognition, ICPR 2008, Tampa, Florida, pp. 1–4 (2008)
4. Economou, G., Pothos, V., Ifantis, A.: Geodesic distance and mst-based image segmentation. In: XII European Signal Processing Conference (EUSIPCO 2004), pp. 941–944 (2004)
5. Galluccio, L., Michel, O., Comon, P., Hero III, A.O.: Graph based k-means clustering. Signal Processing 92(9), 1970–1984 (2012)
6. Galluccio, L., Michel, O.J.J., Comon, P.: Unsupervised clustering on multi-components datasets: Applications on images and astrophysics data. In: Proceedings of the 16th European Signal Processing Conference, EUSIPCO-2008, Lausanne, Lausanne, pp. 1–6 (2008)
7. Ren, Q., Zhuo, X.: Application of an improved k-means algorithm in gene expression data analysis. In: 2011 IEEE International Conference on Systems Biology (ISB), pp. 87–91 (2011)
8. Feil, B., Abonyi, J.: Geodesic distance based fuzzy clustering. In: Saad, A., Dahal, K., Sarfraz, M., Roy, R. (eds.) Soft Computing in Industrial Applications. Advances in Soft Computing, vol. 39, pp. 50–59. Springer, Heidelberg (2007)

9. Martinetz, T., Schulten, K.: Topology representing networks. Neural Networks 7(3), 522–576 (1994)
10. Martinetz, T., Schulten, K.: Artificial Neural Networks. In: Ch. A "Neural-Gas' Network Learns Topologies, pp. 397–402. Elsevier, Amsterdam (1991)
11. Hebb, D.: The organization of behavior. John Wiley and Son (1949)
12. Freeman, L.: A set of measures of centrality based upon betweenness. Sociometry 40, 35–41 (1977)
13. Sabidussi, G.: The centrality index of a graph. Psychometrika 31, 581–603 (1966)

A Spectral Clustering Algorithm Based on Eigenvector Localization

Małgorzata Lucińska

Kielce University of Technology
Al. 1000-lecia PP. 7, 25-314 Kielce, Poland
lucinska@tu.kielce.pl

Abstract. This paper introduces the SpecLoc algorithm that performs clustering without pre-assigning the number of clusters. This is achieved by the use of a special property of matrix eigenvectors, called weak localization. The signless Laplacian matrix is created on the basis of a mutual neighbor graph. A new measure, introduced in this work, allows for selection of weakly localized eigenvectors. Experiments confirm good performance of the proposed algorithm for weakly separated groups of real datasets, including cancer gene expression matrices.

Keywords: spectral clustering, nearest neighbor graph, signless Laplacian.

1 Introduction

Clustering is a common unsupervised learning technique; its aim is to divide objects into groups, such that members of the same group are more similar each to another (according to some similarity measure) than any two members from two different groups. Being a powerful tool it has been applied in many research areas, like image segmentation [17] and [26], machine learning, data mining, and bioinformatics [23] to name a few. Although many clustering methods have been proposed in the recent decades, see e.g. [12], there is no universal one, that can deal with any clustering problems, since the real world clusters may be of arbitrary complicated shapes, varied densities and unbalanced sizes.

Spectral clustering techniques [14] belong to the most popular and efficient clustering methods. They allow to find clusters even of very irregular shapes. Spectral techniques use eigenvalues and eigenvectors of a suitably chosen matrix to partition the data. The matrix is the affinity matrix (or a matrix derived from it) built on the basis of pairwise similarity of objects to be grouped. Usually one of the key tasks in spectral clustering is the choice of similarity measure, as the structure of the matrix plays a significant role in correct cluster separation. If it is clearly block diagonal, its eigenvalues and eigenvectors will relate back to the structural properties of the set [17]. In such the case the number of clusters is usually given by the value k, that maximizes the eigengap (difference between consecutive eigenvalues). Then the k dominant eigenvalues and the corresponding eigenvectors are used for clustering the original data.

L. Rutkowski et al. (Eds.): ICAISC 2014, Part II, LNAI 8468, pp. 749–759, 2014.

An affinity matrix generated from real-world data is virtually never block-diagonal [33], regardless of a chosen similarity measure. Smaller, or less compact groups may not be identified using just the very top part of the spectrum. More eigenvectors need to be investigated to see these clusters. On the other hand, information included in the top few eigenvectors may also be redundant for clustering, as some of these eigenvectors may represent the same group. An open issue of key importance in spectral clustering is that of choosing the proper number of groups and the right eigenvectors, that reveal the structure of the data. In most spectral algorithms the cluster number is a user defined parameter and the problem of eigenvector selection is overcame by k-means algorithm application to the dominant eigenvectors [21]. Sometimes the number of groups is determined – with varying success rate – in a heuristically motivated way, as for example in [27] and in [16], the algorithm proposed also by the author of this work.

In this paper we present a spectral clustering algorithm SpecLoc, that can simultaneously address both of the above mentioned challenges for a variety of datasets. The number of clusters and the appropriate eigenvectors are determined on the basis of an eigenvector property called localization. Anderson localization [1] refers to the situation, when most of the components of an eigenvector are zero or near-zero, whereas weak localization is characterized by slow decay of the component values away from its main existence subregion [8]. Weak localization of eigenvectors occurs for matrices describing systems with irregular geometry. In the algorithm we find weakly localized eigenvectors, which correspond to different clusters and reveal the structure of the data. To some extent the solution works even in cases of not block-diagonal matrices. In the algorithm we use a mutual k-nearest neighbor affinity matrix and k is the only user defined parameter. We empirically evaluate the proposed approach using real-world test sets, mostly gene expression matrices. The performance of the SpecLoc algorithm is competitive to the other solutions, which likewise do not require the number of clusters to be given.

In section 2 the notation and related definitions are presented, the next section introduces the localization property and its applications. Section 4 explains the main concepts used in the SpecLoc algorithm, which is presented in details in section 5. Then, in section 6, we compare performance of our algorithm with other solutions. Finally, in section 7, the main conclusions are drawn.

2   Notation and Definitions

The set of data points to be clustered will be denoted by $\mathbf{X} = (\mathbf{x}_1, \mathbf{x}_2, ..., \mathbf{x}_n)$. For each pair of points i, j a similarity $s_{ij} \in <0, 1>$ is attached. The value $s_{ij} > 0$ implies the existence of the undirected edge $i \sim j$ in the graph G spanned over the set of vertices $\mathbf{X}$. The matrix $S = [s_{ij}]$ plays a role of an adjacency matrix for G. Let $d_i = \sum s_{ij}$ denote the degree of node i and let D be the diagonal matrix with d_i's on its diagonal. A clustering $\mathcal{C} = (C_1, C_2, ..., C_l)$ is a partition of

X into l nonempty and mutually disjoint subsets. In the graph-theoretic language the clustering represents a multiway cut in G [5].

In the SpecLoc algorithm a signless Laplacian $M = D + S$, introduced by Cvetkovic [4], is used. Cvetkovic proves that the spectrum (i.e. the set of eigenvalues) of M can better distinguish different graphs than spectra of other commonly used graph matrices.

3   Eigenvector Localization

In [8] Filoche *et al.* consider a complex domain with a bottleneck separating the whole domain Ω into two subregions Ω_1 and Ω_2. They prove that whenever λ (an eigenvalue of the Laplacian L in Ω) is far from any eigenvalue of L in Ω_2, the norm of its eigenfunction ϕ in the entire subregion Ω_2 becomes near-zero. Consequently, such an eigenfunction is expelled from Ω_2 and must live in its complement, exhibiting weak localization. Conversely, ϕ can only be substantial in the subregion Ω_2 when λ almost coincides with one of local eigenvalues of the operator L in Ω_2. Thus, they obtain a rigorous scheme elucidating the formation of weak localization. In any partially separated subregion, an eigenfunction of Ω has only two possible choices: (1) either its amplitude is very small throughout this subregion, or (2) this eigenfunction mimics one of the subregions own eigenfunctions. Consequently, an eigenfunction can cross the boundary between two adjacent subregions only if they possess two similar local eigenvalues. More generally, a fully delocalized eigenfunction can only emerge as a collection of local eigenfunctions of all subdomains when they all share a common eigenvalue.

For a few dominant eigenfunctions subregions are disjoint. However, for the next eigenfunctions, initially disjoint subdomains begin to merge to form larger subregions. After reaching the critical point, completely new fully delocalized modes can appear.

Also Delitsyn *et al.* study the behavior of Laplacian eigenfunctions in domains with branches of variable cross-sectional profile [6]. If an eigenvalue is below a threshold which is determined by the shape of the branch, the associate eigenfunction is proved to exponentially decay inside the branch. The numerical simulations have been used to illustrate and extend the theoretical results. It was shown that although the approach was focused on the Dirichlet eigenfunction, these results can be extended to other eigenfunctions.

The above described theory also pertains to the discrete Laplacian eigenproblem. In practice, one can solve Laplacian eigenproblem in a bounded domain by creating a fine mesh (or a spectral graph) that approximates the geometrical structure of the domain, and then using a standard finite element method to compute eigenvalues and eigenfunctions. For each localized eigenfunction in the original domain, one can get an approximated Laplacian eigenvector in the spectral graph which has similar properties of localization [22].

The Anderson localization property was already used in the analysis of gene coexpression network by Jalan *et al.* [13]. To extract these system dependent information they have performed eigenvector analysis of the nearest neighbor adjacency matrix. They have concentrated, however, on highly localized eigenvectors. Similar approach present Slanina *et al.* [29] studying small communities in online social networks. They do not aim at factoring the entire network into some number of modules, or communities, which may or may not be overlapping, but in any case covering, as an ensemble, the whole network. Instead, using Anderson localization, they want to find small parts of the network, which differ structurally from the rest.

Inverse participation ratio (IPR) measures eigenvector localization. It is defined as:

$$I^k = \sum_{l=1}^{N}[u_l^k]^4 \qquad (1)$$

where u_l^k $l = 1, ..., N$ are the components of eigenvector u^k and normalization $\sum_{l=1}^{N}[u_l^k]^2 = 1$ is assumed. The meaning of I^k is illustrated by two limiting cases:

- a vector with identical components $u_l^k = 1/\sqrt{N}$ has $I^k = 1/N$
- a vector with one component $u_l^k = 1$ and the remainders zero has $I^k = 1$.

Thus, the IPR quantifies the reciprocal of the number of eigenvector components that contribute significantly. While IPR says quantitatively to which extent an eigenvector is localized, this information alone is not sufficient, if we want to draw the distinction between Anderson localization, weak localization and extended eigenvectors. For example in [13] it is assumed that Anderson localization occurs if IPR exceeds the threshold of 0.1.

The results of the weak localization in complex domains bring the problem close to the field of spectral theory of graphs. Shi *et al.* in [27] study the spectral properties of an adjacency matrix S and its connection to the data generating distribution P. The authors investigate the case when the distribution P is a mixture of several dense clusters, well separated from each other. In such a case S and L are (close to) block-diagonal matrices. They prove that each of the top eigenvectors of S corresponds exactly to one of the groups. The eigenvectors of each cluster decay to zero at the tail of its distribution if there is a good separation of the groups.

The theory of weak localization sheds new light on spectral clustering methods. It could be useful for identifying not only well separated groups but also close or overlapping clusters.

4   Preliminaries

In the SpecLoc algorithm we apply quite different approach than described in section 4 and use weak localization for determining the eigenvectors, that in the best way reveal a data structure. As the definition of weak localization (given in Introduction) is quite broad, the decision concerning eigenvector localization should be made very carefully. The IPR value seems to be irrelevant since eigenvectors may localize in clusters of variable sizes. We have introduced quite different weak localization measure.

In order to explain in an intuitive manner our policy we analyze eigenvectors of the well known Iris dataset. The set consists of three groups: the first one can be separated very easily whereas the second and third ones are very close to one another. The adjacency matrix is constructed on the basis of the mutual k-nearest neighbor graph, which allows to change the number of edges between the close clusters. The way of constructing the mutual k-nearest neighbor graph is described in section 5. We compare eigenvectors of two different graphs obtained on the basis of quite different numbers of nearest neighbors. Figure 1 shows parts of the second and the third dominant eigenvectors, corresponding to the second and third cluster. Actually they are absolute values of the vector components. We have compared two cases: the picture on the left illustrates the situation, when there are only a few edges between the clusters and the other picture when clusters have many edges in common, so that they are almost inseparable. We can see a difference in the eigenvector shapes. If the clusters share a small number of edges, the difference of the component values between the clusters is significant for both eigenvectors. If the clusters are quite densely connected, the absolute values of eigenvector components show quite even distribution, what indicates their delocalization.

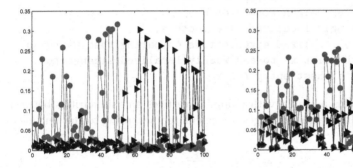

Fig. 1. Weakly localized eigenvectors (left) and delocalized eigenvectors (right)

In order to decide whether the eigenvector A is weakly localized or delocalized it is compared with another eigenvector B. First we calculate the absolute values of the vector components. All the other calculations and comparisons are made on the basis of the absolute values. Then we divide components of A into three subsets: the subset A^+ with component values larger than values of B, the subset A^- with component values smaller than in B, and the subset A^0 with values close to zero and almost equal for A and B. If the vector A is localized in a different cluster than the vector B, the mean value of components from the subset A^+ is much larger than of the subset A^-. We have assumed that for localized eigenvectors, the ratio of the mean values (RMV) should be at least 5. This parameter was chosen experimentally. For the eigenvectors A and B, shown on the left in Figure 1, RMVs equal 12.36 and 8.32 respectively, whereas in the case on the right 4.12 and 2.03.

If eigenvectors A and B are localized in two clusters, which are completely disconnected, the mean value for the set A^- equals zero and it is impossible to calculate the ratio. We assume that in this situation the RMV equals 100. If the vector A is localized in one cluster there must exist at least one vector (localized in another cluster or delocalized), which allows division of the components into two groups: one corresponding to the area of A localization and the other – to the rest of the domain.

5   The SpecLoc Algorithm

Given a set of points $X = x_1, ..., x_n$ in $\Re^D$ that we want to cluster:

The SpecLoc algorithm

```
1. Form the affinity matrix S built on the basis
of mutual k-nearest neighbor graph.
2. Construct the signless Laplacian matrix M=D+S.
3. Find c largest eigenvectors of M.
4. Remove strongly localized eigenvectors.
5. Find weakly localized eigenvectors comparing them pairwise.
6. Assign each point x  to one weakly localized eigenvector,
which has the highest entry for x
```

The algorithm builds a graph, with points as vertices and similarities between points as edges. The weights of edges are calculated according to the Euclidean distance, using:

$$s_{ij} = 1 - \frac{d_{ij}}{d_{max}} \tag{2}$$

where d_{ij} is the Euclidean distance between objects i and j , and d_{max} is the maximum distance between any pair of objects from the dataset. On the basis of the metric we construct the mutual k-nearest neighbor graph, connecting x_i to x_j if x_i is among the k-nearest neighbors of x_j and vice versa. Other metrics could be used, but we decided on this one for simplicity, similarly as in [20].

After constructing the signless Laplacian and finding its top twenty eigenvectors, IPR is calculated for each eigenvector. If IPR is larger than 0.1, the eigenvector is removed as strongly localized. In order to find weakly localized eigenvectors they are compared pairwise, as described in section 4. We have to choose only one eigenvector localized in each cluster. Therefore we must prevent a situation, when two redundant eigenvectors represent the same cluster. In order to avoid the problem the following policy is applied for the eigenvector set V:

```
Output: set W of weakly localized eigenvectors
for each eigenvector A from V
    for each eigenvector B from V, smaller than A
        compare A with B and calculate for them RMVs
        if RMV of A and RMV of B are larger than 5
        and A does not belong to W
            add A and B to W
        if RMV of A is larger than 5 and RMV of B is smaller than 5
        and A  does not belong to W
            add A  to W
        if RMV of A is larger than 5 and RMV of B is smaller than 5
        and A belongs to W
            remove B from the set V
    end
end
remove all repetitions from W
```

If both RMVs calculated on the basis of the vector comparison are smaller than the established threshold, the vectors are delocalized or the areas of their localization are the same. If only the first RMV exceeds the threshold, the second vector is delocalized. There may be cases that a few vector comparisons lead to both RMVs larger than the threshold. We assume that only the vector from the first comparison represents a new cluster, whereas the others are localized in the same cluster.

Weakly localized eigenvectors are used for the final labeling of the data. Each eigenvector represents one cluster and each point is labeled according to the eigenvector with the highest entry for the point.

6   Experimental Results

We have compared the performance of the SpecLoc algorithm (implemented in MATLAB) to three other methods: a spin glass-based algorithm (Spinglass) [25], a fast greedy modularity-based algorithm (FastGreedy) [3], and a MLA-CC algorithm [20]. They are all proposed for graph clustering problems and do not require the definition of the number of clusters. The algorithms use some validation measures adopted by the authors in order to obtain the best partitioning. The comparison of the algorithms is based on the real classification of the datasets with the use of the Adjusted Rand Index (ARI), proposed in [11].

In the experiment thirteen real datasets were used. Ten of them are biological datasets and three are benchmark datasets, often used in cluster analysis. The main aspects of these datasets are explained in Table 1. The biological data were generated from gene expression measurement technologies and employed for clustering cancer tissues (samples). The same benchmark datasets and three algorithms were applied in experiments in [20]. We also use their results for the first three algorithms.

Table 1. Dataset description. n denotes number of samples, l – number of clusters, Dist. Classes – distribution of classes, and D – data dimension

Dataset	Tissue	n	l	Dist. Classes	D
Golub-V1 [10]	Bone marrow	72	2	47, 25	1877
Golub-V2 [10]	Bone marrow	72	3	38, 9, 25	1877
BreastA [31]	Breast	98	3	11, 51, 36	1231
BreastB [32]	Breast	49	2	25, 24	1231
DLBCLC [28]	Blood	58	2	32, 26	3795
Lung [2]	Lung	197	4	139, 21, 20, 17	1000
MultiA [30]	Different	103	4	26, 26, 28, 23	5565
MultiB [24]	Different	32	4	5, 9, 7, 11	5565
Novartis [30]	Different	103	4	26, 26, 28, 23	1000
MiRNA [15]	Blood	218	20	6, 15, 10, 11, 3, 9, 18, 7, 19, 10, 8, 5, 14, 2, 26, 28, 8, 8, 3, 8	217
Yeast [19]	Proteins	1484	10	463, 429, 244, 163, 51, 44, 37, 30, 20, 5	8
Glass [7]	na	214	6	70, 76, 17, 13, 9, 29	9
Iris [9]	na	150	3	50, 50, 50	4
Simulated6 [18]	na	60	6	8, 12, 10, 15, 5, 10	600

The results are shown in Table 2. They are not impressive, but we have to remember that in all the cases the number of clusters is automatically determined by the algorithms. Comparisons with other algorithms, that need the number of clusters to be given as a parameter, would be not fair. Looking at Table 2 we can see the superiority of the SpecLoc algorithm over the other tested solutions. The presented algorithm shows the ability of discovering clusters, that are not visible for the other methods. The number of groups, that it has found, is always the closest to the real data distribution. The SpecLoc algorithm is also competitive to the other cases in terms of the quality of partitioning, measured with the help of the Adjusted Rand Index.

We have compared the performance of the SpecLoc algorithm with our Speclum algorithm, which is also able to determine the number of clusters. In some cases, as for example for the Irys set, the results are the same for both solutions. However, in most of the cases the presented algorithm outperforms the older one either in terms of ARI or on account of the determined number of clusters.

One has to be aware of the fact, that the performance of the presented algorithm, similarly as other spectral algorithms, is quite sensitive to the structure of the graph corresponding to the data. So the use of the mutual k-nearest neighbor graph is an important element of the method. Weak localization will not appear for matrices representing complete graphs. On the other hand eigenvector localization or its lack can constitute an indicator of the quality of partitioning. If all eigenvectors are delocalized, the results, obtained with a help of another spectral algorithm, may be quite poor.

Table 2. Comparison of MLA-CC, Spinglass, FastGreedy, and Specloc algorithms in terms of ARI. l denotes the real number clusters and ls – number of clusters obtained by the appropriate algorithm. The best ARI for each dataset is highlighted in bold.

Dataset	l	MLA-CC		Spinglass		FastGreedy		SpecLoc	
		cl	ARI	cl	ARI	cl	ARI	cl	ARI
Golub-V1	2	3	0.425	3	0.441	2	**0.837**	2	0.600
Golub-V2	3	3	0.395	3	0.428	2	**0.645**	2	0.439
BreastA	3	2	0.654	3	0.721	2	0.741	2	**0.743**
BreastB	4	3	0.202	2	0.269	2	0.269	4	**0.293**
DLBCLC	2	2	-0.017	2	-0.018	2	-0.018	2	**0.335**
Glass	6	6	0.189	3	0.170	2	0.261	5	**0,2654**
Iris	3	4	0.638	3	0.513	2	0.523	3	**0.818**
Lung	4	6	0.303	3	0.151	2	0.117	4	**0.461**
MultiA	4	5	0.702	3	0.664	3	0.633	4	**0.757**
MultiB	4	2	0.027	2	0.027	2	0.027	3	**0.350**
Novartis	4	4	**0.946**	4	**0.946**	3	0.612	4	0.764
Simulated6	6	5	0.871	3	0.326	3	0.326	5	**0.906**
MiRNA	20	8	0.315	2	0.097	2	0.098	9	**0.355**
Yeast	10	3	**0.156**	8	0.084	2	0.082	4	**0.156**

7 Conclusions

In this paper we have described a novel clustering algorithm, that uses weak localization of the Laplacian eigenvectors, to overcome many of the challenges, that traditionally plague clustering algorithms, e.g., finding clusters in the presence of noise and outliers and finding clusters in real data of high dimensionality, where the concepts of distance and density are often ill-defined. The algorithm automatically determines the number of clusters. In particular it can find groups that are relatively weakly distinguished. We have presented an example of this in the context of microarray datasets, where the Specloc algorithm was able to simultaneously find clusters of high dimensional data.

The presented algorithm has only one parameter, the number of neighbors, that is quite easy to establish. First of all, because the degree of eigenvector weak localization (RMV) indicates an appropriate value of the parameter. In the future this local parameter can be determined automatically on the basis of statistic calculation.

Thus, we believe that the Specloc algorithm provides a robust alternative to many other clustering approaches, which are more limited in the types of data and clusters that they can handle.

Acknowledgments. I would like to thank prof. Sławomir T. Wierzchoń for his kind help and constructive comments.

References

1. Anderson, P.W.: Absence of diffusion in certain random lattices. Phys. Rev. 109, 1492–1505 (1958)
2. Bhattacharjee, A., Richards, W.G., Staunton, J., Li, C., Monti, S., Vasa, P., Ladd, C., Beheshti, J., Bueno, R., Gillette, M., Loda, M., Weber, G., Mark, E.J., Lander, E.S., Wong, W., Johnson, B.E., Golub, T.R., Sugarbaker, D.J., Meyerson, M.: Classification of human lung carcinomas by mRNA expression profiling reveals distinct adenocarcinoma subclasses. In: Proc. Natl. Acad. Sci. USA, vol. 98(24), pp. 13790–13795 (2001)
3. Clauset, A., Newman, M.E.J., Moore, C.: Finding community structure in very large networks. Phys. Rev. E 70(6), 66111 (2004)
4. Cvetkovic, D.: Signless Laplacians and line graphs. Bull. Acad. Serbe Sci. Arts, Cl. Sci. Math. Natur., Sci. Math. 131(30), 85–92 (2005)
5. Deepak, V., Meila, M.: Comparison of Spectral Clustering Methods. UW TR CSE-03-05-01 (2003)
6. Delitsyn, A., Nguyen, B.T., Grebenkov, D.S.: Exponential decay of Laplacian eigenfunctions in domains with branches of variable cross-sectional profiles. European Physical Journal B 35, 371 (2012)
7. Evett, I.W., Spiehler, E.J.: Rule induction in forensic science. In: KBS in government, pp. 107–118 (1987) (online Publications)
8. Filoche, M., Mayboroda, S.: Universal mechanism for Anderson and weak localization. Proc. of the National Academy of Sciences 109(37), 14761–14766 (2012)
9. Fisher, R.A.: The use of multiple measurements in taxonomic problems. Ann. Eugen. 7, 179–188 (1936)
10. Golub, T.R., Slonim, D.K., Tamayo, P., Huard, C., Gaasenbeek, M., Mesirov, J.P., Coller, H., Loh, M.L., Downing, J.R., Caligiuri, M.A., Bloomfield, C.D., Lander, E.S.: Molecular classification of cancer: class discovery and class prediction by gene expression monitoring. Science 286(5439), 531–537 (1999)
11. Hubert, L., Arabie, P.: Comparing partitions. J.Classif. 2, 193–218 (1985)
12. Jain, A., Murty, M., Flynn, P.: Data clustering: A review. ACM Computing Surveys 31, 264–323 (1999)
13. Jalan, S., Solymosi, N., Vattay, G., Li, B.: Random matrix analysis of localization properties of gene coexpression network. Phys. Rev. E 81, 46118 (2010)
14. Kannan, R., Vempala, S., Vetta, A.: On clusterings: Good, bad and spectral. In: 41st Symposium on Foundations of Computer Science, FOCS (2000) (2000)
15. Lu, J., Getz, G., Miska, E.A., Alvarez-Saavedra, E., Lamb, J., Peck, D., Sweet-Cordero, A., Ebert, B.L., Mak, R.H., Ferrando, A.A., Downing, J.R., Jacks, T., Horvitz, R.R., Golub, T.R.: Microrna expression profiles classify human cancers. Nature 435(7043), 834–838 (2005)
16. Lucińska, M., Wierzchoń, S.T.: Finding the number of clusters on the basis of eigenvectors. In: Kłopotek, M.A., Koronacki, J., Marciniak, M., Mykowiecka, A., Wierzchoń, S.T. (eds.) IIS 2013. LNCS, vol. 7912, pp. 220–233. Springer, Heidelberg (2013)
17. Meila, M., Shi, J.: A random walks view of spectral segmentation. In: Proc. of 10th International Workshop on Artificial Intelligence and Statistics, AISTATS (2001)

18. Monti, S., Tamayo, P., Mesirov, J., Golub, T.: Consensus clustering: a resampling-based method for class discovery and visualization of gene expression microarray data. Kluwer Academic, Dordrecht. Tech rep, Broad Institute/MIT (2003)
19. Nakai, K., Kanehisa, M.: Expert system for predicting protein localization sites in gram-negative bacteria. Proteins 11, 95–110 (1991)
20. Nascimenro, M.C.V., Carvalho, A.C.P.L.F.: A graph clustering algorithm based on a clustering coefficient for weighted graphs. Journal of the Brazilian Computer Society (Impresso) 17, 19–29 (2011)
21. Ng, A., Jordan, M., Weiss, Y.: On spectral clustering: Analysis and an algorithm. In: Advances in Neural Information Processing Systems, vol. 14 (2001)
22. Nguyen, B.T., Duc, L.T.A., Thuc, N.D., Thach, B.V.: A divide-and-conquer algorithm for a symmetric tri-block-diagonal matrix. In: Proc. of IEEE SoutheastCon 2012 (2012)
23. Pentney, W., Meila, M.: Spectral Clustering of Biological Sequence Data. In: AAAI 2005, pp. 845–850 (2005)
24. Ramaswamy, S., Tamayo, P., Rifkin, R., Mukherjee, S., Yeang, C.H., Angelo, M., Ladd, C., Reich, M., Latulippe, E., Mesirov, J.P., Poggio, T., Gerald, W., Loda, M., Lander, E.S., Golub, T.R.: Multiclass cancer diagnosis using tumor gene expression signatures. In: Proc. Natl. Acad. Sci. USA, vol. 98(26), pp.15,149–15,154 (2001)
25. Reichardt, J., Bornholdt, S.: Statistical mechanics of community detection. Phys. Rev. E 74, 16–110 (2006)
26. Shi, J., Malik, J.: Normalized Cuts and Image Segmentation. IEEE Transactions on Pattern Analysis and Machine Intelligence 22 (1997)
27. Shi, T., Belkin, M., Yu, B.: Data spectroscopy: Eigenspace of convolution operators and clustering. The Annals of Statistics 37(6B), 3960–3984 (2009)
28. Shipp, M.A., Ross, K.N., Tamayo, P., Weng, A.P., Kutok, J.L., Aguiar, R.C.T., Gaasenbeek, M., Angelo, M., Reich, M., Pinkus, G.S., Ray, T.S., Koval, M.A., Last, K.W., Norton, A., Lister, T.A., Mesirov, J.: Diffuse large b-cell lymphoma outcome prediction by gene-expression profiling and supervised machine learning. Nat. Med. 8, 68–74 (2002)
29. Slanina, F., Konopasek, Z.: Eigenvector Localization as a Tool to Study Small Communities in Online Social Networks. Advances in Complex Systems 13(6), 699–723 (2010)
30. Su, A.I., Cooke, M.P., Ching, K.A., Hakak, Y., Walker, J.R., Wiltshire, T., Orth, A.P., Vega, R.G., Sapinoso, L.M., Moqrich, A., Patapoutian, A., Hampton, G.M., Schultz, P.G., Hogenesch, J.B.: Large-scale analysis of the human and mouse transcriptomes. In: Proc. Natl. Acad. Sci., USA, vol. 99, pp. 4465–4470 (2002)
31. van t Veer, L.J., Dai, H., van de Vijver, M.J., He, Y.D., Hart, A.A., Mao, M., Peterse, H.L., van der Kooy, K., Marton, M.J., Witteveen, A.T., Schreiber, G.J., Kerkhoven, R.M., Roberts, C., Linsley, P.S., Bernards, R., Friend, S.H.: Gene expression profiling predicts clinical outcome of breast cancer. Nature 415(6871), 530–536 (2002)
32. West, M., Blanchette, C., Dressman, H., Huang, E., Ishida, S., Spang, R., Zuzan, H., Olson, J.A., Marks, J.R., Nevins, J.R.: Predicting the clinical status of human breast cancer by using gene expression profiles. In: Proc. Natl. Acad. Sci., USA, vol. 98(20), pp. 11462–11467 (2001)
33. Xia, T., Cao, J., Zhang, Y., Li, J.: On defining affinity graph for spectral clustering hrough ranking on manifolds. Neurocomputing 72(1315), 3203–3211 (2008)

HiBi – The Algorithm of Biclustering the Discrete Data

Marcin Michalak, Magdalena Lachor, and Andrzej Polański

Institute of Informatics, Silesian University of Technology
ul. Akademicka 16, 44-100 Gliwice, Poland
{Marcin.Michalak,Magdalena.Lachor,Andrzej.Polanski}@polsl.pl

Abstract. The article presents the new algorithm for hierarchical bi-clustering: *HiBi*. It is dedicated to the analysis of the discrete data. The algorithm uses the set of exact biclusters as the input. In this approach results of exact biclustering algorithm *eBi* are used as the input. As a result of combining biclusters into the more general one, *HiBi* gives the set of inexact biclusters. The algorithm is hierarchical so the final result can be chosen after the algorithm performance. All experiments were performed on artificial datasets.

Keywords: biclustering, hierarchical clustering, binary data, discrete data.

1 Introduction

Clustering is a commonly known branch of data mining which can be described as putting vectors of data into some packages. It is an unsupervised process because the pattern that describes the dependence in the data is unknown. In this paper the problem of grouping cells from matrix is taken into consideration. It may be treated as the special case of clustering when grouping rows and cells due to values of cells is performed at the same time. This problem is described in literature as biclustering. It was suggested in 70's of the last century by Hartigan [4]. Other names of this problem that can be found in the literature are: co-clustering, two-dimensional clustering or two-mode clustering.

In this paper the new algorithm of biclustering binary or discrete value matrix is presented. It is derived from the Ward's idea of hierarchical clustering [16] and previous approach of rough biclustering [8,7]. It is based on the assumption that the set of exact biclusters that cover all of the considered data is given and then its generalisation takes place. This approach is named *HiBi* (from "**Hi**erarchical **Bi**clustering").

This paper is organised as follows: it starts from some basic notions which are very close to the description of the biclustering problem. Then some related and previous works are presented. Afterwards the new idea of biclustering is presented with the backgrounds of Ward's idea. For better understanding of *HiBi* a simple case of biclustering is analysed and then some results of experiments on artificial data are shown. The paper ends with the analysis of the results and the description of several aspects of further works.

L. Rutkowski et al. (Eds.): ICAISC 2014, Part II, LNAI 8468, pp. 760–771, 2014.

2 Basic Notions

Let's start from short description of some useful notions, which will be helpful in the further reading. Also some basics of bicluster evaluation will be presented.

2.1 Features and Co-features

As every matrix is built up of rows and columns it is very important to precise whether an algorithm distinguishes rows from columns or not. In the case when the matrix transposition does not influence final results notions of row and column should be replaced with the new one. In previous research we introduced notions feature and co-feature. If rows are considered as features then columns are considered as co-features. If columns are features then rows are co-features.

A feature is denoted as f and is the element of the set $\mathcal{F}$. A co-feature is denoted as f^*, the element of $\mathcal{F}^*$. The example of this generalisation is presented on the Fig. 1.

	c_1	c_2	c_3
r_1	1	2	3
r_2	4	5	6

Original table

	f_1^*	f_2^*	f_3^*
f_1	1	2	3
f_2	4	5	6

Rows as features

	f_1	f_2	f_3
f_1^*	1	2	3
f_2^*	4	5	6

Rows as co-features

Fig. 1. Illustration of features and co-features

The matrix M is now defined as $M = [\mathcal{F}, \mathcal{F}^*]$ with a set of features and a set of co-features. The bicluster $B = [\mathcal{G}, \mathcal{G}^*]$ will be called the subset of M iff $\mathcal{G} \subseteq \mathcal{F}$ and $\mathcal{G}^* \subseteq \mathcal{F}^*$. This relation is called binclusion (from the "biclustering inclusion").

2.2 Biclusters Evaluation

From this point on, if it is not clearly stated, only the problem of biclustering the binary valued matrices is being considered and only biclusters describing ones are built – zeros are considered as the background. If the discrete valued matrix is mentioned it is assumed that every non-background value is biclustered in such a way that any values different that the considered one are treated as the background (zero) and the considered value is treated as the value one.

In order to give some quality measures to evaluate biclusters, few parameters were introduced in our previous work [14]. Accuracy and coverage are well known measures, used very often in decision rule evaluation, which can also be used to evaluate binary biclustering results. In case of rough biclusters generated with $HRoBi$ another measure called roughness was introduced [8]. This measure will be presented further with the description of this algorithm.

Bicluster $\mathcal{B} \subseteq M$ can be described with two variables:

- area – the number of cells in the bicluster $\overline{\overline{B}}$,
- weight – the number of ones in the bicluster $w(\mathcal{B})$.

Accuracy of a bicluster can be defined as the ratio of a bicluster weight and the area: $acc(\mathcal{B}) = w(\mathcal{B})/\overline{\overline{\mathcal{B}}}$ while coverage is a ratio of $\mathcal{B}$ and M weights: $cov(\mathcal{B}) = w(\mathcal{B})/w(M)$.

3   Related and Previous Works

Biclustering is one of the data mining methods, of unsupervised data analysis. The simplest definition of biclustering can be formulated as finding a similar subset of columns (rows), under a similar subset of rows (columns). It is very widely used in bioinformatics [12,6] and text mining [2,17]. Each detected bicluster is expected to meet some predefined homogeneity criterion [9]. In bioinformatics biclustering is applied to microarray data analysis (continuous data) and to binary data for finding groups of genes regulated by the same factors (microRNA [11], transcription factors [15]) and thus involved in the same biological processes. Up to date several different methods of binary biclustering were proposed in literature [13,5,3]. A part of them is dedicated to find exact biclusters, which consist of all ones and another part of them allows to have some zeros in the bicluster. In the real data analysis it seems to be important to allow for some inaccuracy in bicluster, because bioinformatics data often contain some noise.

In previous works the algorithm of exact biclustering (*eBi* - *exact Biclustering*) was developed. It finds biclusters in binary matrices and in discrete values matrices. It starts from finding two sets of half-biclusters: the first one that is based on rows (or columns) and the second that is based on column (or rows). These steps can be performed in both orders. It is proved that every half-bicluster from the first set has one and only one corresponding half-bicluster from the second set and vice versa. Upon this feature of halfbiclusters, the final bicluster is defined as the pair of corresponding half-biclusters. Results of this algorithm require some postprocessing. The obtained set of biclusters contains very big number of redundant (overlapping) biclusters. The redundancy is eliminated with the "from coverage" strategy. It is very important feature of this algorithm that its results cover all considered data and covers only the considered data – all biclusters have the accuracy equal to 1.

Other algorithm was developed on the basis of *eBi* and is the hierarchical approach to biclustering. *HRoBi* – the algorithm for **H**ierarchical **Ro**ugh **Bi**clustering – is the first approach for rough and hierarchical biclustering. It also represents the idea of the rough definition of the bicluster. This idea comes directly from the Pawlak definition of the rough set [10]. In his representation of the set it is defined with two other sets called upper and lower approximation. The simplest interpretation of rough set and its approximations says that if the element belongs to the lower approximation of the set it surely belongs to the set and if the element does not belong to the upper approximation of the set it surely does not belong to the set. In case when both of approximations are equal we say that the set is exact (is not rough). The border of the rough set is the relative complement of lower approximation in the upper.

HRoBi starts with exact biclusters and joins them to rough biclusters iteratively. In each iteration two different biclusters (or rough biclusters) whose lower approximations have nonempty intersection and give the rough bicluster with the highest inroughness are merged and substituted with the result of merging in the set of biclusters. The algorithm stops when there are no biclusters having nonempty intersection of their lower approximations or the smallest inroughness of biclusters is lower than the level set by the user. This condition helps to assure a compromise between the level of generalisation (smaller number of rough biclusters) and quality of results (smaller inroughness).

Due to the fact that the algorithm is hierarchical the number of rough biclusters in the result set can be set by the user arbitrarily.

The evaluation of the rough bicluster $\mathcal{B}$, defined with its lower $\underline{\mathcal{B}}$ and upper $\overline{\mathcal{B}}$ approximations, is done with the roughness measure (or its complement to one – inroughness). The roughness is defined as the fraction of the number of elements in the border and the upper approximation of the bicluster:

$$\rho(\mathcal{B}) = |b(\mathcal{B})|/|\overline{\mathcal{B}}| = 1 - |\underline{\mathcal{B}}|/|\overline{\mathcal{B}}| = 1 - w(\underline{\mathcal{B}})/|\overline{\mathcal{B}}|$$

where $b(\mathcal{B})$ means the border of the bicluster $\mathcal{B}$.

It is the measure that says how rough is the bicluster and is the fraction of the bicluster border and upper approximation capacities.

4   HiBi - Hierarchical Biclustering

The new presented algorithm belongs to the group of hierarchical methods. In this section also the short description of Ward's algorithm [16] will be presented – the algorithm that was the inspiration for us.

4.1   Hierarchical Clustering - Ward's Approach

Ward's approach starts with the simple assumption that says that each object is a single cluster. Then in each iteration joining of two closest clusters is performed and the new cluster replaces two original ones. The aggregation stops when there is only one cluster containing all objects. It is important to notice that the real result of clustering is not the last cluster but the hierarchical structure describing the order of the clusters joining and the condition of clusters aggregation. The structure is commonly named as the dendrogram.

Results of the Ward's clustering can be also presented as the change of the criterion of joining biclusters in the following iterations. This form does not contain the information about the particular cluster. On the X axis there is the number of the iteration and on the Y axis there is the distance between two merged clusters. This kind of chart is commonly known as the "linkage distance" chart. This kind of chart for the data shown on the Fig. 2a is shown on the Fig. 2b (the X axis is the logarithmic one).

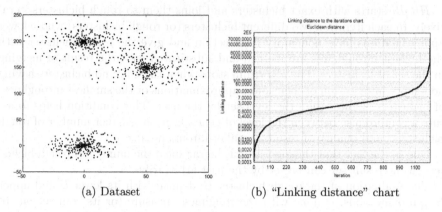

(a) Dataset   (b) "Linking distance" chart

Fig. 2. Grouping of synthetic data in Statistica®

4.2   Hierarchical Biclustering – HiBi

HiBi (**Hi***erarchical* **Bi***clustering*) is the new algorithm of finding biclusters in the binary (or discrete valued) matrix. It partially refers to the approach started with the *HRoBi* algorithm: it also requires an initial set of biclusters and then joins them iteratively. However, in this case the condition for joining is different and obtained results are not rough biclusters but just inexact biclusters.

As it was said, *HiBi* starts with the initial set of exact biclusters (we generated them with *eBi*) and starts joining two of them in each iteration. Joint of two biclusters is defined as the new bicluster which set of rows (columns) is the union of sets of rows (columns) of origin two biclusters. Two biclusters are joined when two conditions are satisfied: a) their joining has the highest accuracy from all possible pairs to be joined, b) their joining accuracy is not smaller than the assumed level.

When the second condition can not be fulfilled by any pair of biclusters the algorithm stops. It means that the end of the algorithm is not equivalent with obtaining the one final bicluster. In every iteration the newly created bicluster has lower accuracy but its coverage is higher than the coverage of each original bicluster. Now we can see how important is the role of the assumed level of accuracy which can be easily interpreted as the minimal accuracy of bicluster. This level is the compromise between the generalisation and the accuracy of results. Assuming the minimal accuracy equal to 0 we can obtain the merging of all biclusters. The performance of the algorithm can be also shown with the "linking distance" chart.

4.3   Interpretation of the *HiBi* "Linking Distance"

The main result of the Ward's clustering is the hierarchical structure describing the order and conditions of joining clusters in each iteration. The results of the *HiBi* can be also shown on the chart called the "linking distance". The minimal bicluster accuracy is presented as the X axis. Then, the number of biclusters is the function of the X. Now from the chart we can read how the minimal assumed bicluster accuracy influences the obtained number of biclusters.

5   HiBi – The Case Study

To understand the idea of *HiBi* let's analyse a small synthetic, binary dataset (Tab.1a). The algorithm starts the generalisation of biclusters from the set of exact biclusters obtained with *eBi* (Tab.1b) and the assumed minimal bicluster accuracy is set to 0 (all biclusters will be joined).

Table 1. Case study matrix M and its biclusters from *eBi*

	f_1^*	f_2^*	f_3^*	f_4^*	f_5^*
f_1	0	0	0	0	0
f_2	0	1	1	1	0
f_3	0	0	1	1	0
f_4	1	1	1	1	0
f_5	0	0	0	0	1

(a) Matrix M

	f	f^*	acc
B_1	f_2, f_4	f_2^*, f_3^*, f_4^*	1
B_2	f_4	$f_1^*, f_2^*, f_3^*, f_4^*$	1
B_3	f_5	f_5^*	1
B_4	f_2, f_3, f_4	f_3^*, f_4^*	1

(b) *eBi* results for M

During each iteration *HiBi* calculates accuracy for each pair of different biclusters in the set. In the next step two biclusters which joining gives the highest value of the considered parameter are joined into one inexact bicluster (Table 2). We use the accuracy of bicluster as the quality measure.

In this case B_1 and B_4 are biclusters joined in the first order. Biclusters B_1 and B_4 are removed from the set of biclusters and they are replaced by the new bicluster B_{14}. The output of previous iteration is an input of the next iteration. In the following iterations the joining of bicluster B_{14} with B_2 and B_{124} with B_4 are done.

The algorithm stops, none pair of remaining biclusters fulfils the assumed criterion: the new bicluster accuracy can not be lower then the assumed level (only one bicluster remained). It is important to note that, if we assume threshold lower than the accuracy of the bicluster that is the projection of "ones" to the rows and columns, then whole dataset will be always generalised into one bicluster.

Table 2. Set of biclusters in the following iterations

iter.		f	f^*	acc
1	B_{14}	f_2, f_3, f_4	f_2^*, f_3^*, f_4^*	0.8889
1	B_2	f_4	$f_1^*, f_2^*, f_3^*, f_4^*$	1
1	B_3	f_5	f_5^*	1
2	B_{124}	f_2, f_3, f_4	$f_1^*, f_2^*, f_3^*, f_4^*$	0.75
2	B_3	f_5	f_5^*	1
3	B_{1234}	f_2, f_3, f_4, f_5	$f_1^*, f_2^*, f_3^*, f_4^*, f_5^*$	0.5

6   Experiments

Experiments were performed on three discrete datasets. Five algorithms were taken into the comparison: *eBi* [14], *HRoBi* [8], *HiBi*, *BicBin* [15] and *BiMax* [12]. Description of *BicBin* and *BiMax* will be presented in the next part of the paper. Each obtained set of biclusters was evaluated with the accuracy and the coverage. The results of comparison are presented in the Table 3a. Each of the mentioned algorithms covers whole dataset (all ones in the binary matrix). Computations for *eBi*, *HiBi*, *HRoBi* and *BicBin* were performed in Matlab® environment. The *BiCat* tool was used to obtain results by the algorithm *BiMax* [1].

The mentioned group of methods generates three types of biclusters – exact, inexact and rough. The exact bicluster is defined as submatrix which only consist of ones (its accuracy is 1), inexact one contains at least one zero while rough bicluster is described by upper and lower approximations.

6.1   Compared Algorithms

Three algorithms – the new one and two previous ones – were compared with two algorithms of binary biclustering. A short description of them is presented below.

The algorithm *BiMax* finds all exact biclusters among binary dataset for the given minimal number of rows and columns. The idea of finding biclusters is to partake dataset into three submatrices. One of them contains only zeros, so it is not considered in the further analysis. In the next steps the algorithm divide remaining submatrices in an recursive way until the current matrix represents a bicluster, it means that it contains only ones [12].

This algorithm works well on sparse binary datasets. It consists of three main components. The score function which evaluates submatrix, the search algorithm to restrict the search space of all possible submatrices and an algorithm to extract all biclusters in an ordered way from a dataset. The algorithm requires two input parameters called α and β in order to emphasise the importance of rows or columns in biclusters. If α and β are not equal than rows or columns are rated higher when score is calculated for a submatrix. The algorithm stops when all ones in dataset are covered by at least one bicluster. Each run of this algorithm gives different results, because its starting point is a random number of rows or columns [15].

6.2   Datasets

To compare our results with other methods three discrete datasets of size 100 x 100 cells were used. The first one (Fig.3a) is similar to the matrix proposed in [12] and consists of several overlapping squares. The second dataset (Fig.3b) was obtained by removing several ones in random places from presented on Fig. 3a. The third dataset (Fig.3c) is the artificial set proposed by authors in [14] and consists of four discrete values. One of them is considered as the background and is not analysed. The matrix contains black cells (#0 – 1415 cells), grey cells (#77 – 1327 cells, three areas) and light grey cells (#237 – 2148 cells, banana shape). Level areas do not have sharp edges and some regions of both grey colours may be considered as overlapping. Numbers correspond to the grey levels on the image.

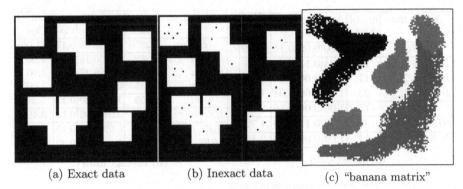

    (a) Exact data   (b) Inexact data   (c) "banana matrix"

Fig. 3. Synthetic datasets

Three algorithms (*eBi*, *BicBin* and *BiMax*) require only the binary matrix as the input. Two other algorithms (*HRoBi* and the new one: *HiBi*) start with the given matrix and the set of exact biclusters. For this purpose the output of *eBi* was used. It also should be mentioned that as in the case of the *eBi* the postprocessed results are considered.

As the *BicBin* requires the setting of α and β parameters (from the range $[0.5; 1.0]$) all values from this range with the step 0.1 were considered. It means that 36 (6×6) experiments were performed for each dataset. In the general comparison only the best results (from the number of biclusters and the maximal average bicluster accuracy) were shown.

The *BiMax* algorithm has two parameters: the minimal number of rows (mnr) and the minimal number of columns (mnc). To assure the coverage of all of the data we assumed each of them equal to 1.

6.3   Results

The results for each dataset are presented separately (every discrete value from the "banana matrix" is considered as the separate dataset). Each table contains calculated value of mean accuracy *AvgAcc*, its standard deviation *StdAcc* and mean coverage *AvgAcc*. *SumCov* is the summary coverage, which is a sum of coverage of all biclusters belonging to the output set. This measure should be analysed in pair with total coverage, which is proportion of ones in dataset covered by at least one bicluster. The total coverage *TotalCov* has been omitted in presented tables, because all of compared algorithms cover whole dataset. If total coverage of output set is complete 1 (what means the 100 %), than *SumCov* should be understood as level of biclusters overlapping.

Table 3. Results for biclustering datasets with different algorithms

Algorithm	no. of bicl.	Avg Acc	Std Acc	Avg Cov	Sum Cov
BiMax	96	1.00	0.00	0.14	13.19
BicBin $\alpha=0.5$ $\beta=0.5$	13	0.94	0.13	0.08	1.06
BicBin $\alpha=0.8$ $\beta=0.5$	17	0.99	0.00	0.06	1.00
BicBin $\alpha=1.0$ $\beta=0.5$	23	1.00	0.00	0.04	1.00
eBi	15	1.00	0.00	0.16	2.38
HRoBi $\rho\geq0.95$	6	0.77	0.14	0.29	1.72
HiBi $acc=0.95$	14	1.00	0.00	0.16	2.18

(a) Exact data

Algorithm	no. of bicl.	Avg Acc	Std Acc	Avg Cov	Sum Cov
BiMax	2850	1.00	0.00	0.17	481.05
BicBin $\alpha=0.5$ $\beta=0.5$	12	0.90	0.15	0.09	1.06
BicBin $\alpha=0.6$ $\beta=0.5$	16	0.90	0.17	0.06	1.00
BicBin $\alpha=1.0$ $\beta=0.5$	45	0.99	0.05	0.02	1.00
eBi	55	1.00	0.00	0.13	7.31
HRoBi $\rho\geq0.8$	17	0.94	0.06	0.18	3.10
HiBi $acc\geq0.95$	26	0.99	0.01	0.15	3.87
HiBi $acc\geq0.8$	11	0,90	0.08	0.23	2.51

(b) Inexact data

Algorithm	no. of bicl.	Avg Acc	Std Acc	Avg Cov	Sum Cov
BiMax	5463	1.00	0.00	0.08	454.81
BicBin $\alpha=0.5$ $\beta=0.5$	11	0.67	0.20	0.10	1.13
BicBin $\alpha=0.9$ $\beta=0.8$	68	0.97	0.10	0.01	1.02
BicBin $\alpha=1.0$ $\beta=0.8$	86	0.99	0.07	0.01	1.01
eBi	103	1.00	0.00	0.10	10.61
HRoBi $\rho\geq0.95$	30	0.92	0.06	0.12	3.64
HiBi $acc\geq0.95$	66	0.99	0.02	0.09	5.77
HiBi $acc\geq0.8$	13	0.85	0.03	0.25	3.21

(c) "banana matrix" v=0

Algorithm	no. of bicl.	Avg Acc	Std Acc	Avg Cov	Sum Cov
BiMax	503	1.00	0.00	0.07	35.80
BicBin $\alpha=0.5$ $\beta=0.5$	13	0.60	0.25	0.08	1.07
BicBin $\alpha=0.6$ $\beta=0.5$	16	0.70	0.26	0.06	1.01
BicBin $\alpha=0.5$ $\beta=1.0$	69	0.97	0.18	0.01	1.01
eBi	75	1.00	0.00	0.08	5.93
HRoBi $\rho\geq0.95$	19	0.90	0.08	0.11	2.05
HiBi $acc\geq0.95$	45	0.99	0.02	0.08	3.55
HiBi $acc\geq0.8$	14	0.86	0.04	0.16	2.23

(d) "banana matrix" v=77

Algorithm	no. of bicl.	Avg Acc	Std Acc	Avg Cov	Sum Cov
BiMax	30194	1.00	0.00	0.11	3247.28
BicBin $\alpha=0.5$ $\beta=0.5$	11	0.67	0.20	0.10	1.13
BicBin $\alpha=0.9$ $\beta=0.8$	68	0.97	0.10	0.01	1.02
BicBin $\alpha=1.0$ $\beta=0.8$	86	0.99	0.07	0.01	1.01
eBi	118	1.00	0.00	0.07	8.66
HRoBi $\rho\geq0.5$	98	1.00	0.01	0.07	7.18
HRoBi $\rho\geq0.3$	108	1.00	0.00	0.07	7.95
HiBi $acc\geq0.95$	71	0.98	0.02	0.09	6.06
HiBi $acc\geq0.8$	15	0.85	0.03	0.21	3.14

(e) "banana matrix" v=237

7   Conclusions

7.1   Brief Analysis

In all cases it can be observed that for the assumed total coverage of the data for the *BiMax* algorithm it generates a vast number of small biclusters (with small coverage). Their only advantage is that they are exact and cover the whole dataset (all considered discrete values). The same effect can be obtained with the *eBi*. Performances of *HiBi* show that it can give comparable and even better results then *BicBin*. More advanced analysis will be performed in the next part of the article on the basis of "linking distance" charts.

7.2   Analysis of the "Linking Distance" Chart

For each dataset we can find the best result of *BicBin* from the both points of view: the minimal number of biclusters and the highest average bicluster accuracy. Figures 4a-4e show the "linking distance" chart generated by *HiBi*.

We can compare average accuracies and minimal accuracies of both algorithms in the following way: for the given result of *BicBin* with the smallest number of biclusters we compare the average accuracies of *BicBin* results and the *HiBi* results (with the same number of biclusters).

We can also compare numbers of biclusters in the analogous way: for the best average of accuracy from the *BicBin* we are looking how many *HiBi* biclusters are needed to assure the same (or better) level of the average bicluster accuracy.

Table 4. "linking distance" charts for all datasets

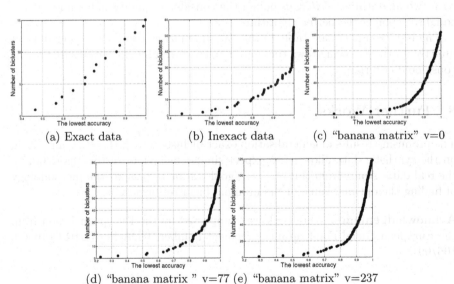

(a) Exact data   (b) Inexact data   (c) "banana matrix" v=0

(d) "banana matrix " v=77 (e) "banana matrix" v=237

Table 5. Direct comparison of *BicBin* and *HiBi* (a-e) and final competition summary (f)

criterion	algorithm	acc	#bicl	winner
accuracy	*BicBin*	1.00	23	
	HiBi	1.00	15	1
no. of bicl.	*BicBin*	0.94	13	
	HiBi	0.95	13	1

(a) Dataset1

criterion	algorithm	acc	#bicl	winner
accuracy	*BicBin*	0.99	45	
	HiBi	0.99	30	1
no. of bicl.	*BicBin*	0.90	12	1
	HiBi	0.83	12	

(b) Dataset2

criterion	algorithm	acc	#bicl	winner
accuracy	*BicBin*	0.99	86	1
	HiBi	0.99	90	
no. of bicl.	*BicBin*	0.67	11	
	HiBi	0.78	11	1

(c) v0

criterion	algorithm	acc	#bicl	winner
accuracy	*BicBin*	0.97	69	
	HiBi	0.97	54	1
no. of bicl.	*BicBin*	0.60	13	
	HiBi	0.78	13	1

(d) v77

criterion	algorithm	acc	#bicl	winner
accuracy	*BicBin*	0.99	86	1
	HiBi	0.99	108	
no. of bicl.	*BicBin*	0.67	11	
	HiBi	0.73	11	1

(e) v237

dataset	criterion	
	accuracy	no. of bicl.
exact	*HiBi*	*HiBi*
inexact	*HiBi*	*BicBin*
#0	*BicBin*	*HiBi*
#77	*HiBi*	*HiBi*
#237	*BicBin*	*HiBi*

(f)

First five tables (5a - 5e) shows the direct comparison of best results generated with two algorithms. *Criterion* points the considered quality index and *winner* equal to 1 points the better algorithm.

The last "competition" table (Table 5f) summarises results for every dataset directly. In the following rows there are names of winning algorithms due to the considered criterion.

8   Further Works

The promising results of generalisation exact biclusters with the *HiBi* algorithm on the synthetic data allow us to expect similar behaviour of the algorithm on the real data. Apart from this our next goal will be to provide the methodology of finding the optimal value of the minimal bicluster accuracy.

Acknowledgements. This work was supported by the European Union from the European Social Fund (grant agreement number: UDA-POKL.04.01.01-00-106/09).

References

1. Barkow, S., Bleuler, S., Prelić, A., Zimmermann, P., Zitzler, E.: BicAT: A Biclustering Analysis Toolbox. Bioinformatics 22(10), 1282–1283 (2006)
2. Chagoyen, M., Carmona-Saez, P., Shatkay, H., Carazo, J., Pascual-Montano, A.: Discovering semantic features in the literature: A foundation for building functional associations. BMC Bioinformatics 7(1), 41 (2006)
3. Gusenleitner, D., Howe, E., Bentink, S., Quackenbush, J., Culhane, A.: iBBiG: Iterative binary bi-clustering of gene sets. Bioinformatics 28(19), 2484–2492 (2012)
4. Hartigan, J.: Direct Clustering of a Data Matrix. Journal of American Statistical Association 67(337), 123–129 (1972)
5. Koyuturk, M., Szpankowski, W., Grama, A.: Biclustering gene-feature matrices for statistically significant dense patterns. In: Proc. of IEEE Computational Systems Bioinformatics Conference, pp. 480–484 (2004)
6. Madeira, S., Oliveira, A.: Biclustering algorithms for biological data analysis: A survey. IEEE/ACM Transactions on Computational Biology and Bioinformatics 1(1), 24–45 (2004)
7. Michalak, M.: Foundations of rough biclustering. In: Rutkowski, L., Korytkowski, M., Scherer, R., Tadeusiewicz, R., Zadeh, L.A., Zurada, J.M. (eds.) ICAISC 2012, Part II. LNCS, vol. 7268, pp. 144–151. Springer, Heidelberg (2012)
8. Michalak, M., Stawarz, M.: HRoBi – The Algorithm for Hierarchical Rough Biclustering. In: Rutkowski, L., Korytkowski, M., Scherer, R., Tadeusiewicz, R., Zadeh, L.A., Zurada, J.M. (eds.) ICAISC 2013, Part II. LNCS, vol. 7895, pp. 194–205. Springer, Heidelberg (2013)
9. Orzechowski, P.: Proximity Measures and Results Validation in Biclustering – A Survey. In: Rutkowski, L., Korytkowski, M., Scherer, R., Tadeusiewicz, R., Zadeh, L.A., Zurada, J.M. (eds.) ICAISC 2013, Part II. LNCS (LNAI), vol. 7895, pp. 206–217. Springer, Heidelberg (2013)
10. Pawlak, Z.: Rough Sets. Journal of Computer and Information Sciences 11(5), 341–356 (1982)
11. Pio, G., Ceci, M., DElia, D., Loglisci, C., Malerba, D.: A Novel Biclustering Algorithm for the Discovery of Meaningful Biological Correlations between microRNAs and their Target Genes. BMC Bioinformatics 14(Suppl. 7) (2013)
12. Prelić, A., Bleuler, S., Zimmermann, P., Wille, A., Bühlmann, P., Gruissem, W., Hennig, L., Thiele, L., Zitzler, E.: A systematic comparison and evaluation of biclustering methods for gene expression data. Bioinformatics 22(9), 1122–1129 (2006)
13. Rodriguez-Baena, D., Perez-Pulido, A., Aguilar, J.: A biclustering algorithm for extracting bit-patterns from binary datasets. Bionformatics 27(19), 2738–2745 (2011)
14. Stawarz, M., Michalak, M.: eBi - The Algorithm for Exact Biclustering. In: Rutkowski, L., Korytkowski, M., Scherer, R., Tadeusiewicz, R., Zadeh, L.A., Zurada, J.M. (eds.) ICAISC 2012, Part II. LNCS, vol. 7268, pp. 327–334. Springer, Heidelberg (2012)
15. Uitert, M., Meuleman, W., Wessels, L.: Biclustering sparse binary genomic data. Journal of Computational Biology 15(10), 1329–1345 (2008)
16. Ward, J.: Hierarchical Grouping to Optimize an Objective Function. Journal of the American Statistical Association 58(301), 236–244 (1963)
17. Wren, J., Garner, H.: Shared relationship analysis: ranking set cohesion and commonalities within a literature-derived relationship network. Bioinformatics 20(2), 191–198 (2004)

Asymmetric k-means Clustering
of the Asymmetric Self-Organizing Map

Dominik Olszewski[1], Janusz Kacprzyk[2], and Sławomir Zadrożny[2]

[1] Faculty of Electrical Engineering,
Warsaw University of Technology, Poland
dominik.olszewski@ee.pw.edu.pl
[2] Systems Research Institute,
Polish Academy of Sciences, Poland
{janusz.kacprzyk,slawomir.zadrozny}@ibspan.waw.pl

Abstract. In this paper, an asymmetric approach to clustering of the asymmetric Self-Organizing Map (SOM) is proposed. The clustering is performed using an improved asymmetric version of the well-known k-means algorithm. The improved asymmetric k-means algorithm is the second proposal of this paper. As a result, we obtain the two-stage fully-asymmetric data analysis technique. In this way, we maintain the structural consistency of the both utilized methods, because they are both formulated in asymmetric version, and consequently, they both properly adjust to asymmetric relationships in analyzed data. The results of our experiments confirm the effectiveness of the proposed approach.

Keywords: Self-Organizing Map, Asymmetric Self-Organizing Map, Clustering, k-means algorithm, Asymmetric k-means algorithm.

1 Introduction

The Self-Organizing Map (SOM) [1] is an example of the artificial neural network architecture. This approach can be also interpreted as a visualization technique, since the algorithm may perform a non-linear projection from a multidimensional space to a 2-dimensional space, this way creating a map structure. The location of points in 2-dimensional grid aims to reflect the similarities between the corresponding objects in multidimensional space. Therefore, the SOM algorithm allows for visualization of relationships between objects in multidimensional space. The asymmetric version of the SOM algorithm was introduced in [2], and the justification of the asymmetric approach was extended in [3].

The visualization provided by SOM may be further analyzed, and consequently, two-stage data processing methods can be developed. An example of such a two-phase technique may be the SOM clustering leading to forming of the clusters on the SOM grid. The approach, proposed in this paper, belongs to such a class of data analysis methods. The SOM clustering, itself, has been extensively studied, and a variety of solutions has been developed [4–7].

L. Rutkowski et al. (Eds.): ICAISC 2014, Part II, LNAI 8468, pp. 772–783, 2014.
© Springer International Publishing Switzerland 2014

The k-means clustering algorithm [8, 9] is a well-known statistical data analysis tool used in order to form arbitrary settled number of clusters in an analyzed dataset. The algorithm aims to separate clusters of possibly most similar objects. Object represented as a vector of d features can be interpreted as a point in d-dimensional space. Hence, the k-means algorithm can be formulated as follows: given n points in d-dimensional space, and the number k of desired clusters, the algorithm seeks a set of k clusters so as to minimize the sum of squared dissimilarities between each point and its cluster centroid. The name "k-means" was introduced in [8], however, the algorithm, itself, was formulated by H. Steinhaus in [9].

The asymmetric version of the k-means clustering algorithm was introduced in [10]. However, the asymmetry in the algorithm in [10] arises caused by use of dissimilarities, which are defined as asymmetric (e.g., the Kullback-Leibler divergence). On the other hand, the paper [11] proposes the asymmetric k-means algorithm using the symmetric similarities, which are asymmetrized by employing the asymmetric coefficients. This kind of approach provides a proper adjustment to the asymmetric relationships in analyzed data. Therefore, in this paper, we utilize the asymmetric version of the k-means algorithm introduced in [11], we improve it, and employ it for cluster analysis on the asymmetric SOM.

1.1 Our Proposal

The improvement of the asymmetric k-means algorithm, introduced in this paper, consists in utilizing the number of objects in clusters in the computation of the asymmetric similarities. In this way, the algorithm more accurately reflects the asymmetric nature of analyzed data. In order to achieve this purpose, we introduce the cluster coefficients, which convey the information about the number of objects in clusters. The novel improved version of the asymmetric k-means algorithm uses both coefficients – the asymmetric coefficients, like it was done in [11], and cluster coefficients, which is the novel proposal of this paper.

Finally, we combine the asymmetric SOM visualization technique and the improved asymmetric k-means algorithm in order to perform the two-stage asymmetric cluster analysis. The SOM visualization method provides only a projection from an input high-dimensional space to an output 2-dimensional space. Any further data analysis should be performed using certain additional appropriate tools. In our research, we continue the data processing using the clustering technique, i.e., the enhanced asymmetric k-means clustering algorithm, and consequently, we obtain clusters of points in 2-dimensional space corresponding to objects in the input high-dimensional space.

The general order of the data analysis in our work is following: First, the asymmetric SOM is generated, and then, the prototypes in the grid of the asymmetric SOM are clustered using the asymmetric k-means algorithm. In other words, the clustering process is carried out on the output data of the asymmetric SOM, i.e., in 2-dimensional space.

In this way, we maintain the structural consistency between the asymmetric SOM and the asymmetric k-means, i.e., both employed methods are asymmetry-

774 D. Olszewski, J. Kacprzyk, and S. Zadrożny

sensitive, and therefore, both can effectively operate on the asymmetric data. As a result, we obtain a fully-asymmetric two-stage data analysis approach.

Recapitulating, this paper proposes:

- the improvement of the asymmetric k-means algorithm,
- the asymmetric k-means clustering of the asymmetric SOM.

2 Asymmetry in Data

The problem of asymmetry in data analysis was relatively rarely studied in the literature. The research of Okada and Imaizumi [12–14] is focused on using the dominance point governing asymmetry in the proximity relationships among objects, represented as points in the multidimensional Euclidean space. They claim that ignoring or neglecting the asymmetry in proximity analysis discards potentially valuable information. On the other hand, Zielman and Heiser in [15] consider the models for asymmetric proximities as a combination of a symmetric similarity component and an asymmetric dominance component. The authors of [2] propose the asymmetric version of the Self-Organizing Map, which is extended in [3]. Finally, the paper [10] introduces the asymmetric version of the k-means clustering algorithm using the dissimilarities, which are defined as asymmetric (e.g., the Kullback-Leibler divergence), and the paper [11] proposes the asymmetric k-means algorithm using the asymmetric coefficients.

When an analyzed dataset appears to have asymmetric properties, the symmetric measures of similarity or dissimilarity (e.g., the most popular Euclidean distance) does not apply properly to this phenomenon, and for most pairs of data points, they produce small values (in case of similarities). Consequently, they do not reflect accurately the relationships between objects. The asymmetry in dataset arises, e.g., in case, when the data associations have a hierarchical nature. The hierarchical connections in data are closely related to the asymmetry. This relation has been noticed in [16]. In case of the dissimilarity, when it is computed in the direction – from a more general entity to a more specific one – it should be greater than in the opposite direction. As stated in [2], asymmetry can be interpreted as a particular type of hierarchy.

An idea to overcome this problem is to employ the asymmetric similarities and dissimilarities. They should be applied in algorithms in such a way, so that they would properly reflect the hierarchical asymmetric relationships between objects in analyzed dataset. Therefore, it should be guaranteed that their application is consistent with the hierarchical associations in data. This can be achieved by use of the asymmetric coefficients and cluster coefficients, inserted in the formulae of symmetric measures. In this way, we can obtain the asymmetric measures on the basis of the symmetric ones. The asymmetric coefficients and cluster coefficients should assure the consistency with the hierarchy. Hence, in case of the similarities, they should assure greater values in the direction – from more specific concept to more general one.

2.1 Asymmetric Coefficients

Asymmetric coefficients convey the information provided by asymmetry. Two coefficients were introduced in [17]. The first one is derived from fuzzy-logic-based index, and the second one is formulated on the basis of the Kullback-Leibler divergence. Both of these quantities are widely used in statistics and probability theory. In our experimental study, we have used the first of these coefficients.

Hence, the fuzzy-logic-based asymmetric coefficient is formulated as follows:

$$a_i = \frac{|x_i|}{\max_j (|x_j|)}, \tag{1}$$

where x_i, $i = 1, \ldots, n$ is the ith object in analyzed dataset, n is the total number of objects, and $|\cdot|$ is the L_1-norm.

This coefficient takes values in the $\langle 0, 1 \rangle$ interval, and it will become large for objects with large L_1-norm.

The asymmetric coefficient is assigned to each object in an analyzed dataset.

2.2 Cluster Coefficients

Cluster coefficients allow to utilize the information about the cluster memberships. In other words, they convey the information about the cardinality of clusters. Cluster centroids are computed on the basis of objects belonging to a given cluster. Consequently, a centroid of a cluster reflects the properties of all objects in that cluster. Therefore, cluster centroids are the entities of a very high level of generality, and consequently, they strongly generate the hierarchy in data analysis. Considering that the hierarchical associations result in asymmetric character of data, the cluster centroids essentially affect the asymmetric relationships between objects in an analyzed dataset, and this fact should be taken into account, when the similarities are computed.

In this paper, we introduce the following cluster coefficient:

$$\eta_j = \begin{cases} \frac{n_j}{\max_i(|x_i|)} & \text{for the direction from object to centroid} \\ \frac{1}{\max_i(|x_i|)} & \text{for the direction from centroid to object} \end{cases}, \tag{2}$$

where n_j, $j = 1, \ldots, k$ is the number of objects in the jth cluster, k is the number of clusters, $i = 1, \ldots, n$, n is the total number of objects, and $|\cdot|$ is the L_1-norm.

This coefficient takes values in the $\langle 0, 1 \rangle$ interval. It becomes larger for clusters with a larger number of objects (when the direction from object to centroid is considered).

The cluster coefficient is assigned to each cluster in an analyzed dataset.

The values of the cluster coefficients need to be updated each time, when the cardinality of a cluster changes. Hence, in case of the k-means clustering algorithm, the values of the cluster coefficients should be updated each time a new object is assigned to a cluster.

3   Asymmetric Self-Organizing Map

The traditional symmetric SOM algorithm provides a non-linear mapping between a high-dimensional original data space and a 2-dimensional map of neurons. The neurons are arranged according to a regular grid, in such a way that the similar vectors in input space are represented by the neurons close in the grid. Therefore, the SOM technique visualize the data associations in the input high-dimensional space.

According to [2], the results obtained by the SOM method are equivalent to the results obtained by minimizing the following error function with respect to the prototypes w_r and w_s:

$$e\left(\mathcal{W}\right) = \sum_r \sum_{x_i \in V_r} \sum_s h_{rs} d^2\left(x_i,\, w_s\right) \tag{3}$$

$$\approx \sum_r \sum_{x_i \in V_r} d^2\left(x_i,\, w_r\right) + K \sum_r \sum_{s \neq r} h_{rs} d^2\left(w_r,\, w_s\right), \tag{4}$$

where x_i, $i = 1, \ldots, n$ is the ith object in high-dimensional space, n is the total number of objects; w_r, $r = 1, \ldots, m$ and w_s, $s = 1, \ldots, m$ are the prototypes of objects in the grid; m is the total number of prototypes/neurons in the grid; h_{rs} is a neighborhood function (e.g., the Gaussian kernel) that transforms nonlinearly the neuron distances (see [1] for other choices of neighborhood functions); $d\left(\cdot,\, \cdot\right)$ is the Euclidean distance; and V_r is the Voronoi region corresponding to prototype w_r. The number of prototypes is assumed to be sufficiently large so that $d^2\left(x_i,\, w_s\right) \approx d^2\left(x_i,\, w_r\right) + d^2\left(w_r,\, w_s\right)$.

In order to formulate the asymmetric version of the SOM algorithm, we will refer to the error function (4).

The asymmetric SOM algorithm is derived in three steps:

Step 1. Transform a symmetric dissimilarity (e.g., the Euclidean distance) into a similarity:

$$s_{is}^{\text{SYM}} = C - d^2\left(x_i, w_s\right), \tag{5}$$

where $d\left(\cdot, \cdot\right)$ is the Euclidean distance, the constant C is the upper boundary of the squared Euclidean distance over the entire dataset, and the rest of notation is described in (4).

Step 2. Transform the symmetric similarity into the asymmetric similarity:

$$s_{is}^{\text{ASYM}} = a_i \left(C - d^2\left(x_i, w_s\right)\right), \tag{6}$$

where a_i is the asymmetric coefficient defined in Subsection 2.1, in (1), and the rest of notation is described in (5). The asymmetric similarity defined in this way using the asymmetric coefficient, guarantees the consistency with the asymmetric hierarchical associations among objects in the dataset.

Step 3. Insert the asymmetric similarity in the error function (4), in order to obtain the energy function, which needs to maximized:

$$E\left(\mathcal{W}\right) = \sum_r \sum_{x_i \in V_r} \sum_s h_{rs} a_i \left(C - d^2\left(x_i, w_s\right)\right), \qquad (7)$$

where the notation is explained in (4), (5), and (6). The energy function (7) can be optimized in the similar way as the error function (4). For detailed information, see [18] or [3].

An important property of the asymmetric SOM algorithm is that it maintains the simplicity of the traditional symmetric approach, and does not increase the computational complexity.

4 Asymmetric Clustering of Asymmetric Self-Organizing Map

In order to obtain a structural consistency in data analysis, the asymmetric SOM, discussed in Section 3, is clustered by means of the asymmetric clustering approach. We have chosen the improved version of the asymmetric k-means algorithm for this purpose. This choice was motivated by the fact that the traditional version of the k-means method is well-known as a very effective and efficient clustering technique, and the asymmetric form of this algorithm assures the consistency with the asymmetric version of the Self-Organizing Map.

The neurons in the grid of the asymmetric SOM are used as input for the asymmetric k-means algorithm. In other words, the clustering process is carried out in the output space of the asymmetric SOM.

The improved asymmetric k-means clustering algorithm consists of two alternating steps:

Step 1. Forming of the clusters: The algorithm iterates over the entire set of neurons (each neuron being represented by the vector of weights determined during the process of the SOM training), and allocates each neuron to the cluster represented by the centroid – nearest to this neuron. The nearest centroid is determined using a chosen similarity measure. Hence, for each neuron ν_r, $r = 1, \ldots, m$ in an analyzed SOM, the following maximal squared similarity has to be found:

$$\max_j\ a_r \eta_j s^2\left(\nu_r, c_j\right), \qquad (8)$$

where $s\left(\cdot, \cdot\right)$ is a chosen similarity measure; a_r, $r = 1, \ldots, m$ is the asymmetric coefficient defined in Subsection 2.1, in (1); η_j, $j = 1, \ldots, k$ is the cluster coefficient defined in Subsection 2.2, in (2); c_j, $j = 1, \ldots, k$ is the centroid of the jth cluster; m is the total number of neurons in the grid; and k is the number of clusters.

Step 2. Finding centroids for the clusters: For each cluster, a centroid is determined on the basis of neurons belonging to this cluster. The algorithm
calculates centroids of the clusters so as to maximize the given energy
function:

$$E\left(\Upsilon_j\right) = \sum_{r=1}^{n_j} a_r \eta_j s^2\left(\nu_r, c_j\right),\qquad(9)$$

where Υ_j, $j = 1, \ldots, k$ is the jth cluster; n_j, $j = 1, \ldots, k$ is the number
of neurons in the jth cluster; and the rest of notation is described in (8).

Both these steps must be carried out with the same dissimilarity measure, in
order to guarantee the monotonicity property of the k-centroids algorithm.

Steps 1 and 2 have to be repeated until the termination condition is met.
The termination condition might be either reaching convergence of the iterative
application of the function (10), or reaching the pre-defined number of cycles.

After each cycle (Step 1 and 2), the value of the energy function (10) needs
to be computed for the entire analyzed set of neurons, in order to track the
convergence of the whole clustering process:

$$E\left(\Upsilon\right) = \sum_{j=1}^{k}\sum_{r=1}^{n_j} a_r \eta_j s^2\left(\nu_r, c_j\right),\qquad(10)$$

where Υ is the whole set of SOM neurons, and the rest of the notation is described
in (8).

The proposed asymmetric version of the k-means clustering algorithm maintains the computational simplicity and efficiency of the classical symmetric
approach, and therefore, the entire proposed asymmetric combination of asymmetric SOM and asymmetric k-means is characterized by the significant advantage of low computational complexity.

Unfortunately, also the well-known drawback of the standard symmetric k-
means algorithm regarding the uncertainty of its convergence process still holds.
Likewise the traditional technique, the proposed method does not assure the
convergence to globally optimal solution. Random initialization of the considered
method is another major issue. The algorithm needs to be multistarted with
random starts in order to return a reasonable solution.

5   Experiments

Our experimental study aims to confirm that clustering of asymmetric SOM by
means of the asymmetric k-means algorithm is superior over clustering of the
traditional symmetric SOM using the traditional symmetric k-means method,
and over clustering of asymmetric SOM using the classical symmetric k-means
algorithm. The experiments have been carried out on real data in the three
different research fields: in the field of words clustering, in the field of sound
signals clustering, and in the field of human heart rhythm signals clustering.

The first part of the experimental study was conducted on the large dataset of high-dimensionality (Subsection 5.3), while the remaining two experimental parts were carried out on smaller datasets, but also of high-dimensionality (Subsection 5.4 and Subsection 5.5). In this way, one can assess the performance of the investigated methods operating on datasets of different size and nature, and consequently, one can better evaluate the effectiveness of the proposed approach.

The words clustering experiment was conducted on the "Bag of Words" dataset from the UCI Machine Learning Repository [19].

The sound signals clustering was carried out on the piano music recordings, and the human heart rhythm signals clustering was conducted using the ECG recordings derived from the MIT-BIH ECG Databases [20].

5.1   Evaluation Criterion

In case of all three parts of our experiments, we have compared the clustering results obtained using the investigated methods. As the basis of the comparisons, i.e., as the clustering evaluation criteria, we have used the accuracy rate [3, 10].

- **Accuracy rate.** This evaluation criterion determines the number of correctly assigned objects divided by the total number of objects.

  Hence, for the ith cluster, the accuracy rate is determined as follows:

$$q_i = \frac{m_i}{n_i}, \tag{11}$$

  where m_i, $i = 1, \ldots, k$ is the number of objects correctly assigned to the ith cluster by the compared algorithms; n_i, $i = 1, \ldots, k$ is the number of objects known to belong to the ith cluster ("gold standard"); and k is the number of clusters.

  And, for the entire dataset, the total accuracy rate is determined as follows:

$$q_{\text{total}} = \frac{m}{n}, \tag{12}$$

  where m is the total number of correctly assigned objects, and n is the total number of objects in the entire dataset.

  The accuracy rates q_i and the total accuracy rate q_{total} assume values in the interval $\langle 0, 1 \rangle$, and naturally, greater values are preferred.

  The total accuracy rate q_{total} was used in our experimental study as the main basis of the clustering accuracy comparison of the three investigated approaches.

Because of the non-deterministic nature of all the examined methods (initializations), each of them was run 50 times, and the average accuracies and uncertainty degrees were calculated in order to obtain reliable results.

5.2 Feature Extraction

Features of the time series considered in Subsection 5.4 and Subsection 5.5 have been extracted using a method based on the discrete Fourier transform (DFT). For the details of the DFT-based feature extraction method the reader is referred to, e.g., [21].

5.3 Words Clustering

In the first part of our experimental study, we have utilized excerpts from the "Bag of Words" dataset from the UCI Machine Learning Repository [19]. It is a high-dimensional dataset of strongly asymmetric nature, especially useful in case of the asymmetric data relationships analysis. It is so, because of the significant differences in frequencies of occurrences of different words in the entire dataset, and because of the natural hierarchical structure of the word, which may be organized along the relation broader/narrower term. Therefore, the experimental investigation on the "Bag of Words" dataset clearly shows the superiority of the proposed asymmetric approach over its traditional symmetric counterpart.

The "Bag of Words" dataset consists of five text collections: Enron e-mail collection, Neural Information Processing Systems (NIPS) full papers, daily KOS blog entries, New York Times news articles, and PubMed abstracts. The total number of analyzed words was approximately 10,868,000.

The investigated methods were forming five clusters representing those five text collections in the "Bag of Words" dataset.

Text Feature Extraction. Feature extraction of the textual data investigated in this part of our experimental study was carried out using the term frequency – inverse document frequency (*tf-idf*) approach. The Vector Space Model (VSM) constructed in this way is particularly useful in our research, because it implicitly captures the terms frequency (both: local – document-dependent and global – collection-dependent), which are the source of the hierarchy-based asymmetric relationships in analyzed data (i.e., in this case, between words).

Experimental Results. The results of this part of our experiments are reported in Table 1, where the total accuracy rates obtained for each investigated approach are presented.

The average (arithmetic average) numbers of words assigned to correct clusters reported in Table 1 (in numerators of the ratio fractions) were rounded to the nearest integer values.

The results of this part of our experimental study show that clustering of the asymmetric SOM using the asymmetric k-means algorithm outperforms clustering of the symmetric SOM using the symmetric k-means, and clustering of the asymmetric SOM using the symmetric k-means. The proposed approach leads to the higher clustering accuracy measured on the basis of the total accuracy rate.

Table 1. Accuracy rates of the words clustering

Investigated approach	q_{total}
Symmetric SOM & symmetric k-means	$8{,}389{,}009/10{,}868{,}000 = 0.7719$
Asymmetric SOM & symmetric k-means	$8{,}945{,}451/10{,}868{,}000 = 0.8231$
Asymmetric SOM & asymmetric k-means	$9{,}817{,}064/10{,}868{,}000 = 0.9033$

5.4   Piano Music Composer Clustering

In this part of our experiments, the investigated methods were forming three clusters representing three piano music composers: Johann Sebastian Bach, Ludwig van Beethoven, and Fryderyk Chopin.

Each music piece was represented by a 30-seconds sound signal sampled with the 44100 Hz frequency. The entire dataset consisted of 32 sound signals.

Experimental Results. The results of this part of our experiments are reported in Table 2, which presents the accuracy rates corresponding to each of the examined approaches.

The average (arithmetic average) numbers of signals assigned to correct clusters reported in Table 2 (in numerators of the ratio fractions) were rounded to the nearest integer values.

The size of the constructed SOM was 11x9 neurons. The number of clusters in the k-means clustering was set to 3.

Table 2. Accuracy rates of the piano music composer clustering

Investigated approach	q_{total}
Symmetric SOM & symmetric k-means	$27/32 = 0.8438$
Asymmetric SOM & symmetric k-means	$30/32 = 0.9375$
Asymmetric SOM & asymmetric k-means	$32/32 = 1.0000$

Also in this part of our experiments, the proposed combination of the asymmetric SOM and the asymmetric k-means clustering appeared to be superior over the other two investigated data analysis approaches.

5.5   Human Heart Rhythms Clustering

The human heart rhythm signals clustering experiment was carried out on the dataset of ECG recordings derived from the MIT-BIH ECG Databases [20].

In this part of our experiments, the investigated methods were forming three clusters representing three types of human heart rhythms: normal sinus rhythm, atrial arrhythmia, and ventricular arrhythmia. This kind of clustering can be interpreted as the cardiac arrhythmia detection and recognition based on the ECG recordings.

We analyzed 20-minutes ECG holter recordings sampled with the 250 Hz frequency. The entire dataset consisted of 63 ECG signals.

Experimental Results. The results of this part of our experiments are presented in Table 3, which is constructed in the same way as in Subsection 5.4.

The size of the constructed SOM was 21x7 neurons. The number of clusters in the k-means clustering was set to 3.

Table 3. Accuracy rates of the human heart rhythms clustering

Investigated approach	q_{total}
Symmetric SOM & symmetric k-means	$45/63 = 0.7143$
Asymmetric SOM & symmetric k-means	$49/63 = 0.7778$
Asymmetric SOM & asymmetric k-means	$56/63 = 0.8889$

Finally, in the last part of our empirical study, the proposed marriage of the asymmetric SOM and the asymmetric k-means clustering produced results superior over the results returned by the two reference methods, confirming the usefulness and effectiveness of the proposed solution.

6   Summary

In this paper, the two-stage data analysis approach was proposed. The first step consisted in data visualization by means of the asymmetric SOM, while in the second step, the asymmetric SOM was clustered using the asymmetric k-means algorithm. This kind of combination assures that in both these steps, the asymmetric relationships in data will be taken into account and properly handled by both methods. In this way, the introduced approach maintains the structural consistency of the entire analysis.

Acknowledgment. This work was supported by the National Science Centre (contract no. UMO-2011/01/B/ST6/06908).

References

1. Kohonen, T.: Self-Organizing Maps, 3rd edn. Springer (2001)
2. Martín-Merino, M., Muñoz, A.: Visualizing Asymmetric Proximities with SOM and MDS Models. Neurocomputing 63, 171–192 (2005)
3. Olszewski, D.: An Experimental Study on Asymmetric Self-Organizing Map. In: Yin, H., Wang, W., Rayward-Smith, V. (eds.) IDEAL 2011. LNCS, vol. 6936, pp. 42–49. Springer, Heidelberg (2011)
4. Shieh, S.L., Liao, I.E.: A New Approach for Data Clustering and Visualization Using Self-Organizing Maps. Expert Systems with Applications 39(15), 11924–11933 (2012)

5. Tasdemir, K., Milenov, P., Tapsall, B.: Topology-Based Hierarchical Clustering of Self-Organizing Maps. IEEE Transactions on Neural Networks 22(3), 474–485 (2011)
6. Wu, S., Chow, T.W.: Clustering of the Self-Organizing Map Using a Clustering Validity Index Based on Inter-cluster and Intra-cluster Density. Pattern Recognition 37(2), 175–188 (2004)
7. Lampinen, J., Oja, E.: Clustering Properties of Hierarchical Self-Organizing Maps. Journal of Mathematical Imaging and Vision 2, 261–272 (1992)
8. MacQueen, J.: Some Methods for Classification and Analysis of Multivariate Observations. In: Proceedings of the Fifth Berkeley Symposium on Mathematical Statistics and Probability, vol. 1, pp. 281–297 (1967)
9. Steinhaus, H.: Sur la Division des Corp Matériels en Parties. Bulletin de l'Académie Polonaise des Sciences, C1. III 4(12), 801–804 (1956)
10. Olszewski, D.: Asymmetric *k*-Means Algorithm. In: Dobnikar, A., Lotrič, U., Šter, B. (eds.) ICANNGA 2011, Part II. LNCS, vol. 6594, pp. 1–10. Springer, Heidelberg (2011)
11. Olszewski, D.: *k*-Means Clustering of Asymmetric Data. In: Corchado, E., Snášel, V., Abraham, A., Woźniak, M., Graña, M., Cho, S.-B. (eds.) HAIS 2012, Part I. LNCS, vol. 7208, pp. 243–254. Springer, Heidelberg (2012)
12. Okada, A., Imaizumi, T.: Multidimensional Scaling of Asymmetric Proximities with a Dominance Point. In: Advances in Data Analysis. Studies in Classification, Data Analysis, and Knowledge Organization, pp. 307–318. Springer, Heidelberg (2007)
13. Okada, A.: An Asymmetric Cluster Analysis Study of Car Switching Data. In: Data Analysis. Studies in Classification, Data Analysis, and Knowledge Organization. Springer, Heidelberg (2000)
14. Okada, A., Imaizumi, T.: Asymmetric Multidimensional Scaling of Two-Mode Three-Way Proximities. Journal of Classification 14(2), 195–224 (1997)
15. Zielman, B., Heiser, W.J.: Models for Asymmetric Proximities. British Journal of Mathematical and Statistical Psychology 49, 127–146 (1996)
16. Muñoz, A., Martin, I., Moguerza, J.M.: Support Vector Machine Classifiers for Asymmetric Proximities. In: Kaynak, O., Alpaydın, E., Oja, E., Xu, L. (eds.) ICANN/ICONIP 2003. LNCS, vol. 2714, pp. 217–224. Springer, Heidelberg (2003)
17. Muñoz, A., Martín-Merino, M.: New Asymmetric Iterative Scaling Models for the Generation of Textual Word Maps. In: Proceedings of the International Conference on Textual Data Statistical Analysis JADT 2002, pp. 593–603 (2002)
18. Heskes, T.: Self-Organizing Maps, Vector Quantization, and Mixture Modeling. IEEE Transactions on Neural Networks 12(6), 1299–1305 (2001)
19. Frank, A., Asuncion, A.: UCI machine learning repository (2010)
20. Goldberger, A.L., Amaral, L.A.N., Glass, L., Hausdorff, J.M., Ivanov, P.C., Mark, R.G., Mietus, J.E., Moody, G.B., Peng, C.K., Stanley, H.E.: PhysioBank, PhysioToolkit, and PhysioNet: Components of a new research resource for complex physiologic signals. Circulation 101(23), e215–e220 (2000), Circulation Electronic Pages
21. Chengalvarayan, R., Deng, L.: HMM-Based Speech Recognition Using State-Dependent, Discriminatively Derived Transforms on Mel-Warped DFT Features. IEEE Transactions on Speech and Audio Processing 2(3), 243–256 (1997)

DenClust: A Density Based Seed Selection Approach for K-Means

Md Anisur Rahman, Md Zahidul Islam*, and Terry Bossomaier

Centre for Research in Complex Systems, School of Computing and Mathematics,
Charles Sturt University, Panorama Avenue, Bathurst, NSW 2795, Australia
{arahman,zislam,tbossomaier}@csu.edu.au
http://csusap.csu.edu.au/~zislam/

Abstract. In this paper we present a clustering technique called Den-Clust that produces high quality initial seeds through a deterministic process without requiring an user input on the number of clusters k and the radius of the clusters r. The high quality seeds are given input to K-Means as the set of initial seeds to produce the final clusters. DenClust uses a density based approach for initial seed selection. It calculates the density of each record, where the density of a record is the number of records that have the minimum distances with the record. This approach is expected to produce high quality initial seeds for K-Means resulting in high quality clusters from a dataset. The performance of DenClust is compared with five (5) existing techniques namely CRUDAW, AGCUK, Simple K-means (SK), Basic Farthest Point Heuristic (BFPH) and New Farthest Point Heuristic (NFPH) in terms of three (3) external cluster evaluation criteria namely F-Measure, Entropy, Purity and two (2) internal cluster evaluation criteria namely Xie-Beni Index (XB) and Sum of Square Error (SSE). We use three (3) natural datasets that we obtain from the UCI machine learning repository. DenClust performs better than all five existing techniques in terms of all five evaluation criteria for all three datasets used in this study.

Keywords: Clustering, Cluster Evaluation, K-Means, Data Mining.

1 Introduction

Clustering groups similar records in a cluster and dissimilar records in different clusters. It extracts hidden patterns, from enormous amount of data, that help in various decision making processes. Therefore, it is crucial to produce good quality clusters from a dataset.

K-Means is a widely used clustering technique, where the number of clusters (k) needs to be provided by a user even before the clustering process starts [1] [2] [3] [4]. Based on a user defined number of clusters, K-Means first randomly selects k number of records as the initial seeds. It then goes through the clustering processes and finally identifies k cluster centers, where each center represents a set of records that belong to the cluster.

---

* Corresponding author.

L. Rutkowski et al. (Eds.): ICAISC 2014, Part II, LNAI 8468, pp. 784–795, 2014.
© Springer International Publishing Switzerland 2014

An drawback of K-Means is its requirement of the user input on k. It can be difficult for a user (data miner) to estimate the correct value for k [5] [6]. Another drawback is the possibility of selecting poor quality initial seeds due to the random seed selection criteria of K-Means. A set of poor quality initial seeds may lead to a poor quality clustering result [1] [7] [8].

An existing clustering technique called CRUDAW [9] obtains the initial seeds and the number of clusters automatically through a deterministic process. The deterministic process of CRUDAW requires a user defined radius r (of a cluster), which is then used for producing the number of clusters and the initial seeds. However, it can be difficult for a user to guess a useful value of r especially when the user does not have good understanding on the dataset.

In this study, we propose a novel clustering technique called DenClust, which produces the number of clusters k and the high quality initial seeds through a deterministic process without requiring a user input on any parameters such as k and r. For the selection of initial seeds from a dataset, DenClust first calculates the density (score) of each record. The score of a record R_i the number of records for which R_i is the nearest neighbor. The record R_j that has the highest score is considered as the first seed S_1. The first seed S_1 and all records for which S_1 is the closest neighbor are then removed from the dataset in order to select the other seeds. For the remaining records of the dataset, DenClust repeats the same process to select the subsequent seeds. The seed selection process continues while the number of the remaining records is greater than a threshold (T) that has a default value. The value of T can be adjusted if necessary.

Since the initial seeds selected by DenClust are the centers of a dense region they are expected to represent the natural clusters. Therefore, the initial seeds are expected to be of high quality. Our empirical analysis to evaluate the quality of initial seeds (presented in Section 4) also supports this expectation. The initial seeds are then given input to K-Means to produce the final clusters of a dataset. High quality initial seeds are expected to produce high quality clusters. Our experimental results also indicate the superiority of DenClust.

To evaluate the performance of DenClust, we implement DenClust and a few other existing clustering techniques namely CRUDAW [9], AGCUK [10], Simple K-Means (SK) [2] [3], Basic Farthest Point Heuristic (BFPH) [11], and New Farthest Point Heuristic (NFPH) [11]. Three external cluster evaluation criteria (F-measure, Entropy and Purity) and two internal cluster evaluation criteria (Xie-Beni Index (XB) and Sum of Square Error (SSE)) [2] [9] [12] are used. We use three natural datasets that we obtain from the UCI Machine learning repository [13]. Our experimental results indicate that the performance of DenClust is better than the existing techniques in terms of all the evaluation criteria. We also compare the computational time of the techniques.

The structure of the paper is as follows. In Section 2, we present some existing clustering techniques. Our proposed clustering technique is presented in Section 3. An analysis of the quality of the initial seeds is presented in Section 4. The experimental results and discussions are presented in Section 5. Finally we give some concluding remarks in Section 6.

2   Background Study

We consider a dataset D having n records $D=\{R_1,R_2,\ldots,R_n\}$, and m attributes $A=\{A_1,A_2,\ldots,A_m\}$. The attributes of a dataset can be categorical and/or numerical. We present a toy dataset in Table 1. The dataset has 10 records and 4 attributes (Age, Marital-Status, Qualification, and Occupation), where Age is a numerical attribute and others are categorical attributes. The domain of Age is [30, 65]. The domain values of Marital-Status, Qualification and Occupation are {Single, Married}, {PhD, Master, Bachelor} and {Academic, Engineer, Physician}, respectively.

Table 1. A toy dataset

Record	Age	Marital-Status	Qualification	Occupation
R_1	65	Married	PhD	Academic
R_2	30	Single	Master	Engineer
R_3	45	Married	Master	Engineer
R_4	30	Single	Bachelor	Physician
R_5	55	Married	PhD	Academic
R_6	35	Single	Bachelor	Physician
R_7	60	Married	PhD	Academic
R_8	45	Single	Bachelor	Physician
R_9	35	Single	Master	Engineer
R_{10}	42	Married	Master	Engineer

Simple K-Means requires a user to input the number of clusters k. It then randomly selects k records as the initial seeds from a data set [2] [3]. All other records are assigned to the nearest seeds to form the initial set of clusters. Based on the records in each cluster, Simple K-Means re-calculates the seed of each cluster [2] [14]. All records of the dataset are assigned again to different clusters in such a way that a record is assigned to the cluster, the seed of which has the minimum distance with the record. The process continues until one of the termination conditions (user defined number of iterations and a minimum difference between the values of the objective function in two consecutive iterations) are satisfied.

Basic Farthest Point Heuristic (BFPH) [11] also requires the number of clusters/seeds as a user input. It then randomly selects a record as the first initial seed. However, unlike Simple K-Means, the other seeds are selected deterministically. The record having the maximum distance with the first seed is selected as the second seed. For the selection of the third seed, the distance between a record and its nearest seed is used. The record having the maximum distance (with its nearest seed) is considered as the third seed. The seed selection process continues until BFPH produces the user defined number of initial seeds or runs out of records. The initial seeds are given to Simple K-means to produce the final clusters.

New Farthest Point Heuristic (NFPH) [11] also requires the number of clusters as an input. However, it selects all seeds (including the first seed) deterministically.

It first calculates the score of each record based on the frequency of each attribute value of the record. The frequencies of the attribute values appearing in a record are added together to obtain the score of the record. The record having the highest score is considered as the first seed. The other seeds are selected by using the same approach of BFPH, where the record having the maximum distance with the first seed is selected as the second seed and so on.

NFPH works on a dataset that has only categorical attributes. In this paper for the experiment of NFPH, if a dataset has a numerical attribute we then categorize values of the numerical attribute to calculate score for each record. The number of categories of a numerical attribute is computed by the square root of the domain size of the numerical attribute.

3 DenClust: A Novel Cluestering Technique

In this study we propose a clustering technique called DenClust, which automatically computes the number of initial seeds without requiring a user input on the parameters such as the number of clusters k and the radius r. It uses a deterministic process to produce the initial seeds that represent the densest regions of a dataset. The initial seeds are then fed into K-Means to produce the final clusters of the dataset. The initial seeds are conceptually similar to the cluster centers since each seed represents a dense region and no duplicate seeds are chosen from the same region. Therefore, the initial seeds selected by Den-Clust are expected to be of high quality and good clustering results are expected when the high quality initial seeds are given input to K-Means. The main steps of DenClust are as follows (see Algorithm 1).

Step 1: Automatic selection of high quality initial seeds.

Step 2: Initial Seeds are fed into K-Means to produce final clusters.

Step 1: Automatic selection of high quality initial seeds.

We consider that out of all attributes $A = \{A_1, A_2, \ldots A_m\}$ of a dataset some can be numerical while the others can be categorical. Let us assume that there are p numerical attributes $A_n = \{A_1, A_2, \ldots A_p\}$ and $(m - p)$ categorical attributes $A_c = \{A_{p+1}, A_{p+2}, \ldots A_m\}$. DenClust first normalizes each numerical attribute in the range between 0 to 1 in order to give equal emphasis to each numerical attribute while calculating the distance between two records. If the ath numerical attribute A_a has the domain $[l, u]$, where l is the lower and u is the upper limit of the domain and $R_{i,a}$ is the ath attribute value of the ith record, then the normalized value of $R_{i,a}$ is $n(R_{i,a}) = \frac{R_{i,a}-l}{u-l}$.

Let, a categorical attribute $A_{p+b} = \{a_{b1}, a_{b2} \ldots a_{bq}\}$ has q domain values. Den-Clust computes the similarity of each pair of values (a_{bi}, a_{bj}), $sim(a_{bi}, a_{bj})$; $\forall i, j$ using an existing technique [15]. However, DenClust is not limited to the technique [15] and any other suitable technique can be used. The similarity of a value pair varies between 0 and 1, where 0 means no similarity and 1 means a complete similarity. The distance between two values of an attribute $\sigma(a_{bi}, a_{bj})$

is calculated as $\sigma(a_{bi}, a_{bj}) = 1 - sim(a_{bi}, a_{bj})$. Therefore, $\sigma(a_{bi}, a_{bj})$ also varies between 0 and 1, where a lower value means a smaller distance. While many existing techniques [3] [16] consider the distance between two categorical values to be either 0 or 1 (and nothing in between), Denclust considers them to be anything between 0 and 1 - based on the similarity between the values. DenClust then calculates distance between all pair of records using Equation 1 as follows.

$$\delta(R_i, R_j) = \sum_{a=1}^{|A_p|} |n(R_{i,a}) - n(R_{j,a})| + \sum_{b=|A_p|+1}^{m} \sigma(R_{i,b}, R_{j,b}) \qquad (1)$$

Algorithm 1. DenClust

Input   : A dataset D, a threshold T (default 0.5%), the number of
             iterations N for K-Means and a threshold ϵ for K-Means
Output: A set of clusters C

Set $S \leftarrow \phi$ /*S is a set of initial seeds. Initially S is set to null*/
/*Step 1: Automatic selection of initial seeds*/
$D' \leftarrow Normalize(D)$ /*Numerical attributes of D are normalized*/
count = 0
while $|D'| \geq T$ **do**
   $Score \leftarrow$ CalculateScore(D')/*Score contains density of each record*/
   $R \leftarrow$ FindMax$(Score)$/*the record R has the maximum density*/
   count = count + 1
   if $Score(R) \geq T$ OR count $\leq$ 2 **then**
      $d \leftarrow$ Neighbor(D', R)/*d is the set of neighbors of R */
      $S \leftarrow S \cup R$/*add R in the set S */
      $D' \leftarrow D' - d$
   else
      break

/*Step 2: Feed the Initial Seeds to K-Means to produce the final clusters*/
Set $O_{cur} \leftarrow 0$, $O_{prev} \leftarrow 0$
for $t \leftarrow 1$ to N **do**
   $C \leftarrow$ PartitionRecord(D', S)/*Partitions the records into clusters */
   $S \leftarrow$ CalculateSeed(C)/*Seed calculation */
   $O_{cur} \leftarrow$ SSE(D', S)/* SSE is the K-Means objective function */
   if ($t > 1$ and $| O_{cur}-O_{prev} | \leq \epsilon$) **then**
      Break;
   $O_{prev} \leftarrow O_{cur}$
$C \leftarrow$ PartitionRecord(D', S) /*Produce the final clusters*/
$C \leftarrow$ Denormalize(C, D) /*The records in C are denormalized*/
return C

Based on the record to record distances, DenClust calculates the density (score) of each record. The score of a record R_i is the number of records that have the minimum distances with R_i. The record R_i having the highest score is selected as the first seed. From the dataset, DenClust next removes the first seed

R_i and all other records for which R_i is the nearest neighbor. From the remaining records of the dataset, the record having the highest score is considered as the second seed. The second seed and all records having their minimum distance with the second seed are removed. DenClust continues the seed selection process while the number of remaining records in the dataset is greater than or equal to T, where we use the default value of T to be 0.5% of the total number of records. Additionally, it only accepts a seed if the seed has at least T records for whom it is the nearest neighbor (See Algorithm 1). However, DenClust choses at least two seeds even if they do not have at least T records associated with them. A justification of the default value of T is provided in Section 4. DenClust also allows a user to input any other value for T if he/she wants to do so.

CRUDAW [9] requires a user defined radius r since it selects the record R_i as a seed, where R_i has the maximum number of records within its r radius. However, DenClust does not require an input on r since it selects a record R_i as a seed, where R_i has the maximum number of records for whom R_i is the nearest neighbor. To identify the nearest neighbor of a record we do not need r.

Step 2: Initial Seeds are fed into K-Means to produce final clusters.

The initial seeds are input to K-Means to produce the final clusters. With high quality initial seeds K-Means is expected to produce high quality clusters [9] [14]. The DenClust algorithm is presented in Algorithm 1.

4   An Analysis of the Quality of the Initial Seeds and the Default T Value

Before we present our experimental results in Section 5, we now perform an empirical analysis for the following two purposes; 1. in order to evaluate the quality of the initial seeds that are chosen by the approach taken by DenClust and 2. in order to explore a suitable value for T. For the first purpose, we compare the DenClust seeds with the seeds that are randomly selected according to the approach of Simple K-Means [2]. Two natural datasets called PID and CMC (avaialble from the UCI machine learning repository [13]) are used in this empirical analysis.

Additionally, for the second purpose we use different T values (2%, 1%, 0.5% and 0.05%) and thereby produce different sets of DenClust seeds from a dataset. The records of the dataset are divided among the seeds (that are selected for a T value) where each record is assigned to its nearest seed. The records assigned to the same seed are considered a cluster. We then evaluate the quality of the clusters by XB index [12] and SSE [2] as presented in Table 2.

For each T value, we also select n seeds randomly where n is the number of seeds that are selected by the DenClust approach for a particular T value. That is, if we get 5 DenClust seeds for $T=2\%$ then we consider $n=5$ and randomly select 5 seeds. The records are assigned in the same way to the seeds and thereby clusters are formed. The quality of the clusters is again evaluated. For each n

Table 2. The quality of the initial seeds

Dataset	T	k	XB(lower the better)		SSE(lower the better)	
			DenClust's Seed	Random Seed	DenClust's Seed	Random Seed
PID	2%	5	0.7687	0.8960	72.7507	73.4431
	1%	5	0.7687	0.8960	72.7507	73.4431
	0.5%	7	0.4899	0.8048	69.8585	70.4048
	0.05%	7	0.4899	0.8048	69.8585	70.4048
CMC	2%	5	0.9066	1.0942	42.4171	45.0816
	1%	5	0.9066	1.0942	42.4171	45.0816
	0.5%	7	0.2590	0.5947	37.3593	39.8319
	0.05%	8	0.4938	1.6867	36.5858	40.5535

value, we select the seeds 10 times to minimize the randomness effect in the results. Table 2 presents the average cluster quality of the 10 runs.

The results shown in Table 2 clearly indicate that DenClust seeds are of higher quality than the seeds that are chosen randomly. Moreover, the results also indicate that $T = 0.5\%$ gives the best result for the PID and CMC datasets. Therefore, in this study we consider 0.5% as the default value of T. In future we will run extensive experiments using a big number of datasets (of different types) in order to get a better understanding on the best default value for T. Since a drawback of DenClust is its sensitivity to a suitable T value, in Fig 1 we show the impact of two different T values ($T=1.5\%$ and $T=1.0\%$) on an example dataset (synthetic) having 200 records and 2 attributes x and y.

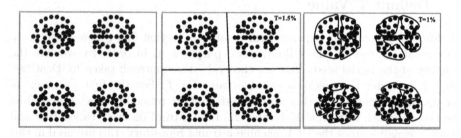

Fig. 1. A two dimensional dataset and its clusters for $T=1.5\%$ and $T=1\%$

5   Experimental Results and Discussion

We evaluate DenClust by comparing it with five (5) existing (high quality) clustering techniques namely CRUDAW [9], AGCUK [10], Simple K-Means (SK) [2] [3], Basic Farthest Point Heuristic (BFPH) [11] and New Farthest Point Heuristic (NFPH) [11]. We compare the performance of the techniques in terms of three external cluster evaluation criteria namely F-measure, Entropy and Purity; and two internal evaluation criteria namely Xie-Beni Index (XB) and Sum of Square Error (SSE) [2] [9]. Note that higher F-measure and Purity values indicate better clustering results, whereas lower Entropy, XB and SSE values indicate the better results.

We use three natural datasets namely Contraceptive Method Choice (CMC), Image Segmentation (IS) and Pima Indian Diabetes (PID) that we obtain from the UCI machine learning repository [13]. We provide a brief introduction to the datasets in Table 3. The CMC dataset has 1473 records and 9 attributes (where 2 of them are numerical and 7 of them are categorical attributes) excluding the class attribute. The class size of the CMC dataset is 3 meaning that the domain size of the class attribute is 3.

Table 3. A brief introduction to the datasets

Dataset	Records	No. of categorical attributes	No. of numerical attributes	Class size
Contraceptive Method Choice (CMC)	1473	7	2	3
Image Segmentation (IS)	2310	0	18	7
Pima Indian Diabetes (PID)	768	0	8	2

Note that we remove the class attribute from a dataset before applying any clustering technique on it, since typically the datasets on which clustering techniques are applied do not have the class attribute i.e. labels for the records. The class attribute values are again used for cluster evaluation purposes using different evaluation criteria such as F-measure, Entropy and Purity [2].

In the experiments, the number of iterations for DenClust, CRUDAW, SK, BFPH and NFPH are considered to be 50 and the threshold T=0.5% and ϵ = 0.005. In the experiments on SK, BFPH, and NFPH we consider the distance between to categorical values of an attribute to be either 0 (if two values are same) or 1(if two values are not same) as suggested by some existing techniques [3] [14]. The original SK, BFPH and NFPH papers only consider numerical values and are unable to handle categorical values.

In the experiments on AGCUK, the number of chromosomes in the initial population and the number of generations are considered 20 and 50, respectively as suggested in the study [10]. The values of r_{max} and r_{min} are considered 1 and 0, respectively based on recommendation of the study [10]. For CRUDAW, the value of T is 1% of all records of a dataset and fuzzy coefficient β=2.2 as recommended in the paper [9].

As mentioned above in the experiments we consider the maximum number of iterations of K-Means (I_{max}) to be 50 as a termination condition. We perform an empirical analysis to justify the selection of I_{max}= 50. We run K-Means on the PID dataset 50 times with just one termination condition ϵ = 0.005. From the 50 runs we aim to find out the number of iterations required by K-Means. We find that typically K-Means terminates in less than 50 iterations when it only uses ϵ as the termination condition. We consider ϵ as the natural termination condition and therefore prefer to choose an I_{max} value that will let the K-Means to terminate based on the value of ϵ, but will take care of unusual situations where ϵ fails to terminate even for a large number of iterations. In Fig 2 we present the number of times (i.e. the frequency) K-Means terminates in a particular number of iterations, out of the 50 runs of K-Means. K-Means terminates 7 times in the 20th iteration. The maximum number of iterations required by K-Means is 45. Therefore, we find that $I_{max} = 50$ is a suitable option.

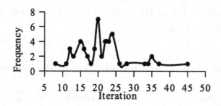

Fig. 2. The frequency versus iteration of K-Means to the PID dataset

We now evaluate DenClust by comparing its clustering results with the results of the five existing techniques as shown in Table 4. For $T= 0.5\%$ of the total number of records, DenClust produces 7 clusters from the PID dataset. The initial number of records associated with the 7 best seeds are 362, 177, 65, 51, 46, 30 and 20, respectively. We also produce 7 clusters by SK, BFPH and NFPH to facilitate a fair comparison of the techniques. Additionally, for CRUDAW and AGCUK we use the results where the techniques also produce 7 clusters from the PID dataset. The clustering result obtained by a technique is then evaluated using the evaluation criteria as shown in Table 4.

Table 4. The evaluation of the clusters on the PID dataset

Evaluation Criteria	Number of Cluster (k)=7; T=0.5%					
	DenClust	CRUDAW	AGCUK	SK	BFPH	NFPH
F-measure(higher the better)	0.7612	0.7059	0.6855	0.7008	0.7143	0.6752
Entropy(lower the better)	0.7612	0.8098	0.8601	0.8203	0.8338	0.7807
Purity (higher the better)	0.7135	0.6953	0.6849	0.6823	0.6698	0.6810
XB(lower the better)	0.3259	1.1486	5.8921	2.0707	2.4154	2.4694
SSE(lower the better)	63.1986	63.3682	73.6601	68.4794	71.6003	70.4184

Due to the random selection of initial seeds, SK and BFPH may produce different clustering results in different runs. Therefore, in this study we run SK and BFPH 10 times. For every run we compute the evaluation criteria values for the set of clusters obtained in the run. Finally, we present the average value of an evaluation criterion over the 10 runs. The results presented in Table 4 indicate that DenClust performs the best on the PID dataset for all evaluation criteria.

We also run similar experiments on the IS and CMC datasets (see Table 5 and Table 6). For both datasets, DenClust produces 7 clusters and therefore we produce 7 clusters by SK, BFPH and NFPH. We run Sk and BFPH 10

Table 5. The evaluation of the clusters on the IS dataset

Number of Cluster (k)=7; T=0.5%						
Evaluation Criteria	DenClust	CRUDAW	AGCUK	SK	BFPH	NFPH
F-measure(higher the better)	0.6006	0.5699	0.3878	0.5743	0.2504	0.2504
Entropy(lower the better)	1.5890	1.7694	2.2157	1.6265	2.7893	2.7900
Purity (higher the better)	0.4879	0.4268	0.2857	0.4602	0.1496	0.1494
XBeni(lower the better)	0.3384	0.3627	0.4242	0.7370	0.9369	0.9871
SSE(lower the better)	173.3157	192.8314	245.5020	180.8747	327.7292	327.8184

times and present the average results of the 10 runs. For the CMC dataset CRDAW also produces 7 clusters, however for the IS dataset CRUDAW and AGCUk produce 4 and 9 clusters, respectively. Since CMC has both numerical and categorical attributes and AGCUK is unable to handle a dataset that has categorical attribute/s AGCUK is not applied on the CMC dataset (see Table 6). It is clear from the tables that DenClust performs better than the five (5) existing techniques in terms of all five evaluation criteria used in this study for all three datasets. That is a very strong result in favor of DenClust in terms of the quality of clusters that it produces.

We now present the execution time required by a technique in Table 7. The configuration of the machine used for the experiments is Intel (R) Core (TM) i5 CPU M430 @ 2.27GHZ and 4 GB of RAM. AGCUK requires the highest execution time, whereas SK requires the least execution time. DenClust requires less execution time than AGCUK, but higher the other techniques. However, DenClust also achieves better clustering results than all techniques in terms of all evaluation criteria for all datasets used in this study. The complexity of Den-Clust and CRUDAW is $O(n^2)$, whereas the complexity of AGCUK, SK, BFPH and NFPH is $O(n)$ [10], [11].

Table 6. The evaluation of the clusters on the CMC dataset

Number of Cluster (k)=7; T=0.5%					
Evaluation Criteria	DenClust	CRUDAW	SK	BFPH	NFPH
F-measure(higher the better)	0.4666	0.4652	0.4637	0.4581	0.4515
Entropy(lower the better)	1.4469	1.451	1.4782	1.4778	1.4755
Purity(higher the better)	0.4691	0.4645	0.4587	0.4549	0.4576
XB(lower the better)	0.2919	0.4156	0.5825	0.4720	0.4358
SSE(lower the better)	33.2266	33.3159	34.505	34.1787	34.0617

Table 7. The execution time (in seconds) of the techniques

Datasets	DenClust	CRUDAW	AGCUK	SK	BFPH	NFPH
PID	38.243	8.464	507.5302	1.613	3.535	4.688
IS	926.977	78.0258	962.768	21.2165	52.625	57.891
CMC	243.632	10.575	NA	1.899	2.9184	4.373

6   Conclusion

In this paper we propose a clustering technique called DenClust that uses a deterministic process for the selection of initial seeds automatically without requiring any user input on the number of clusters and/or the radius of the cluster seeds. DenClust is expected to get high quality initial seeds. An early empirical analysis also indicates the high quality of the seeds selected by DenClust. High quality seeds are then fed into K-Means as the set of initial seeds with an expectation of high quality final clusters. Our experimental results also support the expectation as we find that DenClust performs better than all five existing techniques used in this study in terms of all five evaluation criteria for all three datasets.

In this study we also carry out some early empirical analysis on default values for T and I_{max}. We plan to carry out extensive experiments on them using many datasets in order to find suitable default values for them. The time complexity of DenClust is currently higher than other techniques except AGCUK. Therefore, DenClust is suitable for the applications where a better quality of clustering result is appreciated even if it takes a longer time. For example, a scenario where medical research is carried out on patient datasets in order to discover treatment/prevention strategies and disease pattern. A better clustering result can be appreciated as it is more likely to get better decision/conclusion even if it takes more time.

However, our future research plans include further improvement of the time complexity for DenClust. Out of the three main tasks (1. record to record distance calculation, 2. initial seed selection, and 3. K-Means) of DenClust, Task 2 requires the maximum time. For example, the execution times required by Task 1, Task 2 and Task 3 in the PID dataset are 5.805 sec, 29.894 sec and 2.558 sec, respectively. The trend is similar in the other two datasets as well. We can reduce the time complexity of Task 2 by using some existing techniques. For example, we plan to explore existing techniques [17], [18], [19] for finding the nearest neighbors with the $O(nlogn)$ time complexity. Additionally, we also plan to use the existing techniques [20], [21] for sorting the records in terms of their scores (i.e. densities) where the techniques have the time complexity of $O(nlogn)$. This way we aim to reduce the execution time of the propsed technique. However, the main goal of this paper is to analyse the ability of DenClust to get better quality clustering results. The experimental results clearly support this goal.

References

1. Bai, L., Liang, J., Dang, C.: An initialization method to simultaneously find initial cluster centers and the number of clusters for clustering categorical data. Knowledge-Based Systems 24(6), 785–795 (2011)
2. Tan, P.-N., Steinbach, M., Kumar, V.: Introduction to Data Mining, 1st edn. Pearson Addison Wesley (2005)
3. Huang, Z.: Clustering large data sets with mixed numeric and categorical values. In: The First Pacific-Asia Conference on Knowledge Discovery and Data Mining, Singapore, pp. 21–34 (1997)

4. Khan, F.: An initial seed selection algorithm for k-means clustering of georeferenced data to improve replicability of cluster assignments for mapping application. Applied Soft Computing 12(11), 3698–3700 (2012)
5. Chuan Tan, S., Ming Ting, K., Wei Teng, S.: A general stochastic clustering method for automatic cluster discovery. Pattern Recognition 44(10-11), 2786–2799 (2011)
6. Jain, A.K.: Data clustering: 50 years beyond K-Means. Pattern Recognition Letters 31(8), 651–666 (2010)
7. Bagirov, A.M.: Modified global -means algorithm for minimum sum-of-squares clustering problems. Pattern Recognition 41(10), 3192–3199 (2008)
8. Maitra, R., Peterson, A., Ghosh, A.: A systematic evaluation of different methods for initializing the K-means clustering algorithm. IEEE Transactions on Knowledge and Data Engineering (2010)
9. Rahman, M.A., Islam, M.Z.: CRUDAW: A Novel Fuzzy Technique for Clustering Records Following User Defined Attribute Weights. In: 10th Australasian Data Mining Conference (AusDM 2012), Sydney, Australia. CRPIT Series, vol. 134, pp. 27–42. ACS (2012)
10. Liu, Y., Wu, X., Shen, Y.: Automatic clustering using genetic algorithms. Applied Mathematics and Computation 218(4), 1267–1279 (2011)
11. He, Z.: Farthest-Point Heuristic based Initialization Methods for K-Modes Clustering. CoRR, abs/cs/0610043 (2006)
12. Mukhopadhyay, A., Maulik, U.: Towards improving fuzzy clustering using support vector machine: Application to gene expression data. Pattern Recognition 42(11), 2744–2763 (2009)
13. Bache, K., Lichman, M.: UCI Machine Learning Repository, University of California, Irvine, School of Information and Computer Sciences (2013), http://archive.ics.uci.edu/ml/
14. Rahman, M.A., Islam, M.Z.: Seed-Detective: A Novel Clustering Technique Using High Quality Seed for K-Means on Categorical and Numerical Attributes. In: 9th Australasian Data Mining Conference(AusDM 2011), Ballarat, Australia. CRPIT Series, vol. 121, pp. 211–220. ACS (2011)
15. Giggins, H., Brankovic, L.: VICUS - A Noise Addition Technique for Categorical Data. In: 10th Australasian Data Mining Conference (AusDM 2012), December 4 - 7. CRPIT, vol. 134, pp. 139–148 (2012)
16. Ji, J., Pang, W., Zhou, C., Han, X., Wang, Z.: A fuzzy k-prototype clustering algorithm for mixed numeric and categorical data. Knowledge-Based Systems 30(0), 129–135 (2012)
17. Wang, Y.: Approximating nearest neighbor among triangles in convex position. Information Processing Letters 108(6), 379–385 (2008)
18. Nene, S.A., Nayar, S.K.: A simple algorithm for nearest neighbor search in high dimensions. IEEE Transactions on Pattern Analysis and Machine Intelligence 19(9), 989–1003 (1997)
19. Vaidya, P.M.: An O(n log n) Algorithm for the All-Nearest-Neighbors Problem. Discrete Computational Geometry 4(1), 101–115 (1989)
20. Kocamaz, U.E.: Increasing the efficiency of quicksort using a neural network based algorithm selection model. Information Sciences 229(0), 94–105 (2013)
21. Yang, Y., Yu, P., Gan, Y.: Experimental Study on the Five Sort Algorithms. In: Second International Conference on Mechanic Automation and Control Engineering (MACE), pp. 1314–1317 (2011)

Exploiting Structural Information of Data in Active Learning

Maryam Shadloo, Hamid Beigy, and Siavash Haghiri

Sharif University of Technology
{shadloo,haghiri}@ce.sharif.edu, beygi@sharif.edu

Abstract. In recent years, the active learning algorithms have focused on combining correlation criterion and uncertainty criterion for evaluating instances. Although these criteria might be useful, applying these measures on whole input space globally may lead to inefficient selected instances for active learning. The proposed method takes advantage of clustering to partition input space to subspaces. Then it exploits both labeled and unlabeled data locally for selection of instances by using a graph-based active learning. We define a novel utility score for selecting clusters by combining uncertainty criterion, local entropy of clusters and the factor of contribution of each cluster in queries. Experimental results reveal an elevated performance as compared to several state of the art and widely used active learning strategies.

Keywords: Active Learning, Clustering, Uncertainty Criterion, Correlation Criterion.

1 Introduction

The goal of active learning is to propose the most valuable and informative instances from unlabeled data for labeling, such that active learner achieves high accuracy with minimum cost of labeling. Active learning is well applicable in machine learning problems which there is a huge amount of unlabeled data while labeled data is scare or labeling of the data is expensive and time consuming. Most active learning algorithms use either uncertainty criterion or correlation criterion for evaluating instances, however several active learning algorithms have been proposed which use both criteria[1].

Uncertainty based strategies select instances for which the current statistical model has most uncertainty[2–6]. Another group of query strategies use correlation criterion to select instances with the most density in their neighbourhood. In other words, instances that are most representative of underlying data distribution are selected. Moreover, these strategies favor instances that are far from labeled data[7, 8].

Query strategies that use only uncertainty to assess instances might confront sampling bias problem that adversely affect the performance of active learner. One approach to avoid this problem is exploring the whole input space [9]. Another problem of these strategies is that they tend to select the outliers[10]. Although the model might be uncertain about the outliers, they can't have valuable

L. Rutkowski et al. (Eds.): ICAISC 2014, Part II, LNAI 8468, pp. 796–808, 2014.

information for classification since they are far from other data points. In order to overcome this problem several active learning algorithms have been proposed that combine correlation and uncertainty criteria in evaluating instances.[10–13]. Huang et al., [14] introduced an approach (QUIRE) based on min-max view of margin-based active learning [15] that systematically combines two criteria. This method has long execution time on huge datasets as it uses all data in evaluating instances.

The problem with the most abovementioned approaches is their global view to input space. In this paper, we proposed a two step algorithm for active learning. In brief, we use clustering to partition input space to smaller subspaces and then explore these clusters space based on correlation between clusters, uncertainty of clusters and available label information of clusters. When a cluster is selected an instance will be queried by combining both uncertainty and correlation criterion. Indeed, we have local perspective to exploit both labeled and unlabeled data. Experimental results on several benchmark datasets show that the proposed method achieves better accuracy rather than other algorithms. In addition, in contrast with QUIRE algorithm has an acceptable execution time.

The remainder of this paper is organized as follows: in the next section we review the related work on combining two criteria in active learning. Section 3 describes proposed method. In section 4 we present the experimental results and our observations. It's followed by conclusion and future work in section 5.

2   Related Work

Uncertainty based methods are the most common used active learning strategies. Since they only use labeled data, they usually confront sampling bias and outlier selection problems. In recent years, several active learning algorithms have tried to exploit labeled and unlabeled data in selecting instances. They usually combine uncertainty metric with density or diversity or both of them to evaluate instances[9–13]. To deal with sampling bias problem, Sanjoy Dasgupta and Daniel Hsu present a method that uses hierarchical clustering to explore whole input space [9]. In this approach, quality of hierarchical clustering can heavily affect its performance.The algorithm proposed by Z.Xu et al. [13], uses clustering to select the most representative instances in margin of trained classifier. The main weakness of this strategy is neglecting unlabeled data outside of the margin. Negyun and Slumder [12] suggested another approach in which it is assumed that higher density instances that are close to decision boundary are the most informative instances. Their method reduced error quickly at the first stages of learning, but standard uncertainty sampling outperforms it by additional sampling. With extending this strategy, Donmez et al. [11], proposed a method that dynamically combines it with standard uncertainty sampling.

All mentioned methods are ad-hoc in combining uncertainty and correlation criteria. Therefore, they usually have suboptimal performances[14]. Huang et al. [14], introduced an approach that systematically combined two criteria. It measures utility of instances with exploiting both labeled and unlabeled data in the whole input space. Using whole unlabeled data is the main advantage of this method but it slows down the run time speed so that if there is a huge amount of unlabeled data, the algorithm will perform inefficiently.

In this work, we address this issue with clustering data. The proposed method takes advantage of clustering to explore the whole input space and exploits both labeled and unlabeled data for selecting instances locally in each cluster. Therefore, it addresses sampling bias and other problems related to ignoring correlation criterion and exploring input space.

3   Proposed Method

In this paper, we propose a two step algorithm for selecting valuable instances. In first step, we have a global view to input space and explore whole data space via clustering. In second step we have local view to use both labeled and unlabeled data for querying instances from the selected cluster.

Let $D = \{(x_1, y_1), (x_2, y_2)..., (x_{n_l}, y_{n_l})\} \cup \{x_{l+1}, ..., x_{N=n_l+n_u}\}$ be training data set consists of $n_l \geq 0$ labeled data and $n_u \gg n_l$ unlabeled data, where $y_i = \pm 1$ is the label of x_i. In initial stage of the algorithm, training data is partitioned to n_c clusters. Let $p = \{C_1, C_2, ..., C_{n_c}\}$ be a partition on training data.

Active query strategy selects one cluster C_{sc} from partition p and then selects one instance x_s from the selected cluster.

3.1   Clustering

Rahimi and Recht [16] showed that normalized spectral clustering similar to SVM classifier with RBF kernel lifts dataset to an infinite dimension feature space and separates data with hyper-plan that maximizes gap between data points. Owning to this assumption that separating hyper-plan of data without considering label of them can be closed to separating hyper-plan of SVM classifier, we use spectral clustering. We denote the similarity matrix of training data corresponding to normalized spectral clustering by $W = (w_{i,j})i, j = 1, 2, N$. Using normalized spectral clustering, we partition the whole input space into two parts. We continue clustering larger parts until the size of all parts become less than a fixed value. These parts will be our final clusters.

When a cluster is selected, only data points of that cluster is considered in evaluation process of instances. To incorporate data points of other clusters in assessing instances, we use them in measuring paired affinity of clusters and paired entropy of clusters, which are applied in evaluating clusters. Entropy of each cluster and paired entropy of two clusters are defined as the entropy of labeled data within a cluster, and the entropy of labeled data within union of two clusters respectively. Let $H(.)$ indicates the entropy of a labeled data set[17].

$$H_k = H(D_k{}^L) \tag{1}$$

$$H_{k,l} = H(D_k{}^L \cup D_l{}^L) \tag{2}$$

To calculate paired affinity of clusters, we use overlapping community detection [18]. This algorithm discovers overlapping community in complex networks. It extends disjoint communities with defining and calculating soft partition matrix $\hat{U} = (\hat{u}(i,k))_{i=1,2,,N,k=1,2,...n_c}$ that shows degree of membership of data i to the community k. If this value becomes greater than given threshold, the community k will include node i. Using this algorithm, we find overlapping clusters correspond to disjoint clusters. Let $\tilde{C}_k$, $\tilde{C}_l$ be overlapping clusters correspond to disjoint clusters C_k and C_l. We define data points of cluster C_k which is adjacent to cluster k as $C_{k,l} = C_k \cap \tilde{C}_l$ and compute affinity matrix $A = (a_{k,l})_{k,l=1,2,...n_c}$ as below.

$$a_{k,l} = W(C_{k,l}, C_l) = \sum w_{i,j}{}_{i \in C_{k,l}, j \in C_l} \tag{3}$$

3.2 Selecting Cluster

We define a utility score for evaluating clusters that balances exploration of whole clusters and exploitation of labeled data. The labeled data is used to measure utility of clusters in two ways: Firstly, SVM classifier which is trained by the whole labeled data, is used to measure classification confidence of clusters. Distance from decision boundary can be considered as classification confidence of each instance. Let f^* be decision function of SVM classifier.

$$f^* = arg\ min_{f \in H_\kappa} \frac{\lambda}{2}|f|_{H_\kappa}{}^2 + \sum_{i=1}^{n_l} max(0, 1 - y_i f(x_i)) \tag{4}$$

Where H_κ is the Hilbert space reproduced with kernel function $\kappa(.,.) : \mathbb{R}^h \times \mathbb{R}^h \to \mathbb{R}$. We measure the classification confidence of clusters as following.

$$\Lambda_k = \frac{\sum_{i=n_{l_k}+1}^{N_k} |f^*(x_i)|}{n_{u_k}} \tag{5}$$

Secondly, labeled data of each cluster can be used to measure the utility of it. Non-pure clusters with an entropy greater than zero could be informative. In addition, pure clusters which have non-zero paired entropy with at least one adjacent cluster could have valuable instances for classification. Therefore, we define the local entropy of a cluster by considering the entropy of cluster and paired entropy of it with all its adjacent clusters.

$$\Gamma_k = \frac{(1+\mu)[H_k] + (1-\mu)[\frac{\sum_{l=1}^{n_c} a_{k,l} \times H_{k,l}}{\sum_{l=1}^{n_c} a_{k,l}}]}{2} \tag{6}$$

where $a_{k,l}$ is affinity of cluster k to cluster l and $\mu = \frac{n_l}{n_u}$ shows sampling rate. Equation (6) has two main terms representing the entropy of current cluster and weighted average of all its paired entropy respectively. In Equation (6), μ is used to adjust the importance of two aforementioned terms. As the sampling continues, μ increases the importance of the first term in equation and simultaneously, decreases the importance of the second term. While the sampling rate increases, we should have less attention to pure clusters. Since these clusters are less likely to contain valuable information. The uncertainty metric is measured by aggregating the classification confidence and local entropy of clusters.

$$\Psi_k = \frac{\Gamma_k + \gamma}{\Lambda} \qquad (7)$$

To give a chance of selection to clusters with zero local entropy we add the γ parameter. We empirically fixed this parameter to value 0.25 by cross-validation for all datasets. To explore the whole input space, we use another metric that it is called the indefiniteness of cluster, and measured as following formula.

$$\Phi_k = \frac{n_{u_k}}{n_{l_k}^2 + \epsilon} \qquad (8)$$

If the value of this metric for a cluster would be large it indicates that the cluster has relatively small contribution in queries, so more data must be selected of it. The ϵ is an arbitrarily small quantity. In denominator we squared the number of labeled instances to increase its importance against number of unlabeled data. Finally, we define a utility metric to evaluate clusters by combining the uncertainty and the indefiniteness criteria. The algorithm select a cluster with the highest utility value.

$$f_k = [\Phi_k]^{(1-\mu)} \times [\Psi_k]^{(1+\mu)} \qquad (9)$$

$$sc = argmax_{1 \leq k \leq n_c} f_k \qquad (10)$$

Where $\mu = \frac{n_l}{n_u}$. In equation, the indefiniteness metric conducts active learning to explore the whole input space, while uncertainty metric favors the exploitation of labeled data. We make a balance between these two metrics via the μ parameter. At the early stages of sampling, to discover regions with more information, the exploration is more essential. Gradually, with additional sampling, the trained model and local entropy of clusters become more reliable. Therefore, as the number of queries increases, the power of indefiniteness should be decreased and simultaneously, the power of uncertainty should be increased.

3.3   Selecting Instance

The selected cluster is whether pure or non-pure. In pure clusters we can use correlation criterion such as density and diversity in evaluating instances. Besides correlation criterion, in non pure clusters we can exploit uncertainty criterion. In order to use correlation criterion in pure clusters and both uncertainty and correlation criteria in non-pure clusters, we utilize QUIRE method as graph-based active learning. The selected cluster comprises a labeled data set $D_{l_{sc}} = \{(x_1, y_1), (x_2, y_2)..., (x_{n_{l_{sc}}}, y_{n_{l_{sc}}})\}$ and unlabeled data set $D_{u_{sc}} = \{x_{n_{l_{sc}}+1}, ..., x_{N_{sc}=n_{l_{sc}}+n_{u_{sc}}}\}$.

Let $K = [k(x_i, x_j)]_{|C_{sc}| \times |C_{sc}|}$ be the kernel matrix of the selected cluster and $\Delta = (K + I)^{-1}$. Using QUIRE method we select an instance that minimizes the following evaluation function[14].

$$\hat{El}(D_{l_{sc}}, D_{u_{sc}}, x_i) = max_{y_i=\pm1} \ min \ \hat{Y}^\top \Delta \hat{Y} \tag{11}$$

Where with considering $\hat{Y}_{l_{sc}} = Y_{l_{sc}}$, $\hat{Y}_i = y_i$ and $u_{sc}^i = u_{sc}/i$ the solution to min $\hat{Y}^\top \Delta \hat{Y}$ is given by

$$\hat{Y}_{u_{sc}^i} = -\Delta_{u_{sc}^i, u_{sc}^i}^{-1}(\Delta_{u_{sc}^i, l_{sc}} Y_{l_{sc}} + \Delta_{u_{sc}^i, i} y_i) \tag{12}$$

By approximating Equation(11), representativeness and informativeness terms can be revealed[14]. These two terms are equal respectively by correlation criterion and uncertainty criterion in our literature.

4   Experimental Setup and Results

To evaluate the performance of proposed method we compare it with several widely used active learning algorithms on some benchmark datasets: a1a, australian and letter which are UCI datasets [19] and digit1 and g241n which are semi-supervised learning benchmarks. The letter isn't a binary dataset, therefore we picked two pairs (MvsN,UvsV) from it as binary datasets. In the experiments we compare our approach with the following three baseline active query strategies.

  i Random active learning: It is one strategy to explore the whole input space which samples instances randomly.
 ii Margin-based or SVM active learning: It is the query strategy which exploits labeled data and queries instances closest to decision boundary.
iii QUIRE: It is one of the state of the art active learning algorithms that combine uncertainty and correlation criteria in evaluating instances.

In beginning of active learning that there is no model, we use random method instead of margin-based active learning. To evaluate all approaches, we use repeated holdout and we repeat it 15 times. In each time, we divide the dataset to two parts with equal size as training set and test set. We use two evaluation metrics to assess the performance of all active learning algorithms: trained Classifier accuracy and execution time of algorithm. We use SVM classifier with RBF kernel to evaluate active learning process of each algorithm. In each iteration of individual active learning algorithm, one instance is selected. After querying label of the instance, it is added to labeled data set. Then the SVM classifier is retrained by updated labeled data. We use LIBSVM [20] with default parameters for all datasets except digit1. In the case of digit1 dataset, performances aren't stable owning to default gamma parameter. Thus, we set gamma to 0.5 for digit1. This value is determined via 5-fold-cross validation.

   The introduced method consists of two parameters that must be tuned regarding to the dataset: (1) The standard deviation of RBF kernel matrix used in selection of instances from clusters;(2) The threshold on degree of membership of data used in overlapping community detection algorithm. We apply 5-fold cross validation to evaluate different values of these parameters on diverse datasets.

We empirically conclude that the standard deviation should be set to a value that the mean over paired Gaussian similarity of data becomes approximately 0.0012. The threshold on degree of membership of data affects number of adjacent clusters of each cluster.The results of cross-validation reveals that this parameter should be set to a value such that each cluster have at least one adjacent cluster, but it should not be adjacent to all clusters. The values of these parameters for different datasets are listed in table 1.

Table 1. Values assigned to parameters on various datasets

Data set	a1a	australian	digit1	g241n	MvsN	UvsV
Standard deviation of RBF kernel	0.9	0.23	0.64	5.9	0.14	0.14
Threshold on membership degree	0.25	0.05	0.15	0.3	0.005	0.005

4.1 Results

Figure 1 shows learning curves of all active query strategies on mentioned datasets. The learning curves present number of labeled data on x-axis and classifier accuracy on y-axis. The classifier accuracy is averaged over 15 times. Table 2 lists mean and standard deviation of the AUC (Area Under Curve) values when different percentages of unlabeled data are queried. We also use t-test to evaluate the AUC of our algorithm in comparison to the other algorithms. The results of t-test are represented in table 3. In addition, we compare all algorithms in terms of execution time. The time performance of all algorithms is averaged over 15 runs and shown in table 4. The t-test shows on australian dataset, all algorithms have closed performances. However the learning curves indicate that our algorithm outperforms others, and it finds desired decision boundary with least queries. On g241n dataset, the t-test shows that our method approximately has similar performance to QUIRE and margin-based strategy, but the learning curves show that proposed method and QUIRE algorithm achieve mean of accuracy superior to random and margin-based algorithms. The difference between results of learning curves and t-test indicates the effectiveness of margin-based active learning depends on correctness of trained model. If the initial trained model is not correct, it will affect performance of margin-based active learning adversely. In terms of time performance, proposed method has better performance rather than QUIRE method. So, our method basically outperforms its competitor.

Our observation on digit1 dataset indicates that our method achieves better accuracy than QUIRE and random strategies but its behavior is closed to margin-based strategy. It implies that in this dataset, The uncertainty criterion is more important than the correlation criterion and our algorithm tends to this criterion better than QUIRE method.a1a dataset has opposite trait to digit1 dataset. On this dataset margin-based active learning performs poorly. At the beginning stages of sampling process the margin-based strategy perform well

Table 2. Comparison on AUC values(mean±std)

Data	The Algorithms	percentage of queries					
		5	10	20	30	50	80
a1a	Random	0.748±	0.763±	0.776±	0.786±	0.798±	0.807±
		0.028	0.016	0.014	0.014	0.012	0.01
	Margin	0.757±	0.772±	0.784±	0.791±	0.797±	0.801±
		0.022	0.019	0.022	0.025	0.028	0.031
	QUIRE	0.767±	**0.786±**	**0.802±**	**0.809±**	**0.815±**	**0.819±**
		0.022	0.012	0.009	0.008	0.008	0.008
	Proposed Method	**0.77±**	0.785±	0.799±	0.807±	0.813±	0.818±
		0.018	0.013	0.01	0.008	0.006	0.007
australian	Random	0.677±	0.779±	0.822±	0.834±	0.843±	0.847±
		0.066	0.038	0.017	0.012	0.01	0.01
	Margin	0.689±	0.784±	0.823±	0.834±	0.842±	0.847±
		0.058	0.034	0.015	0.011	0.009	0.009
	QUIRE	0.735±	0.803±	0.831±	0.839±	0.845±	0.849±
		0.046	0.019	0.009	0.008	0.008	0.009
	Proposed Method	**0.75±**	**0.806±**	**0.834±**	**0.842±**	**0.847±**	**0.85±**
		0.102	0.056	0.027	0.02	0.015	0.012
digit1	Random	0.628±	0.763±	0.853±	0.893±	0.925±	0.945±
		0.0840	0.056	0.029	0.019	0.012	0.008
	Margin	**0.776±**	**0.877±**	**0.927±**	**0.947±**	**0.961±**	**0.969±**
		0.024	0.012	0.006	0.005	0.004	0.004
	QUIRE	0.67±	0.824±	0.901±	0.93±	0.951±	0.963±
		0.076	0.04	0.019	0.012	0.007	0.004
	Proposed Method	0.755±	0.865±	0.922±	0.944±	0.96±	0.968±
		0.051	0.03	0.017	0.012	0.008	0.006
g241n	Random	0.508±	0.554±	0.628±	0.688±	0.749±	0.793±
		0.02	0.046	0.054	0.04	0.028	0.021
	Margin	**0.56±**	0.613±	0.67±	0.708±	0.749±	0.78±
		0.033	0.055	0.072	0.087	0.102	0.114
	QUIRE	0.551±	**0.616±**	0.69±	0.738±	0.787±	0.822±
		0.019	0.022	0.015	0.012	0.008	0.005
	Proposed Method	0.547±	0.615±	**0.697±**	**0.745±**	**0.791±**	**0.824±**
		0.012	0.018	0.015	0.012	0.009	0.008
letter(MvsN)	Random	0.622±	0.757±	0.86±	0.895±	0.924±	0.941±
		0.057	0.038	0.022	0.015	0.011	0.009
	Margin	**0.72±**	**0.843±**	**0.912±**	**0.934±**	**0.95±**	0.959±
		0.051	0.028	0.013	0.01	0.008	0.007
	QUIRE	0.664±	0.802±	0.886±	0.916±	0.94±	0.953±
		0.042	0.045	0.023	0.015	0.009	0.006
	Proposed Method	0.714±	0.833±	0.910±	0.931±	0.948±	**0.959±**
		0.058	0.028	0.015	0.01	0.007	0.006
letter(UvsV)	Random	0.55±	0.735±	0.853±	0.889±	0.918±	0.935±
		0.05	0.054	0.025	0.017	0.011	0.009
	Margin	**0.697±**	**0.837±**	**0.908±**	**0.929±**	**0.943±**	**0.952±**
		0.053	0.027	0.014	0.012	0.009	0.008
	QUIRE	0.526±	0.555±	0.703±	0.794±	0.865±	0.903±
		0.029	0.032	0.035	0.024	0.015	0.011
	Proposed Method	0.643±	0.831±	0.899±	0.925±	0.939±	0.95±
		0.041	0.023	0.011	0.008	0.006	0.006

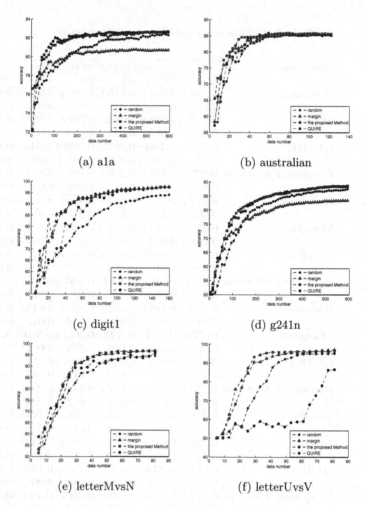

(a) a1a

(b) australian

(c) digit1

(d) g241n

(e) letterMvsN

(f) letterUvsV

Fig. 1. Comparison of classification accuracy on six datasets

but as the queries increases, amazingly it perform weakly. This phenomenon illustrates sampling bias problem of margin-based active learning. Therefore, the correlation criterion in this dataset should be considered. While our strategy and QUIRE strategy have similar performance in terms of accuracy metric, QUIRE strategy has inefficient time performance and can't satisfy the goal of active learning.

On two letter data subsets, the margin-based strategy outperforms others. Over these data subsets variance coefficient of paired similarity of data is small so there is no outlier. Consequently the correlation criterion is not important

Table 3. The Proposed Method versus the other algorithms based on t-test at 0.95 significance level, Win=1, Tie=0, Loss=-1

Data	Competitor Algorithms	percentage Of queries					
		5	10	20	30	50	80
ala	Random	1	1	1	1	1	1
	Margin	1	1	1	1	1	1
	QUIRE	0	0	0	0	0	0
australian	Random	0	0	0	0	0	0
	Margin	1	0	0	0	0	0
	QUIRE	0	0	0	0	0	0
digit1	Random	1	1	1	1	1	1
	Margin	0	0	0	0	0	0
	QUIRE	1	1	1	1	1	1
g241n	Random	0	1	1	1	1	1
	Margin	0	0	0	0	0	0
	QUIRE	0	0	0	0	0	0
letter(MvsN)	Random	1	1	1	1	1	1
	Margin	0	0	0	0	0	0
	QUIRE	0	1	1	1	1	1
letter(UvsV)	Random	1	1	1	1	1	1
	Margin	-1	0	0	0	0	0
	QUIRE	1	1	1	1	1	1
In ALL (Win/tie/loss)	Random	4/2/0	5/1/0	5/1/0	5/1/0	5/1/0	5/1/0
	Margin	2/3/1	1/5/0	1/5/0	1/5/0	1/5/0	1/5/0
	QUIRE	2/4/0	3/3/0	3/3/0	3/3/0	3/3/0	3/3/0

as the uncertainty. The results show the margin based strategy does not confront sampling bias problem, therefore the exploration of whole input space is not required. At the early stages of active query process, the proposed method tends to exploration more, so it is not as effective as margin-based method. But with continuation of sampling, our method yields better performance than margin based active learning. Since the default standard deviation of RBF kernel used in QUIRE strategy is large, on letter UvsV data subset, QUIRE strategy loses its efficiency and falls behind others.

To sum up, our observations demonstrate proposed method can make a balance between two criteria more effectively than QUIRE method and in terms of time performance it is not comparable with QUIRE strategy and outperforms it. It also addresses severe dependency to initial model and sampling bias problems of margin-based strategy.

Table 4. Execution time of the algorithms

Data	The Algorithms	percentage Of queries					
		5	10	20	30	50	80
a1a	Random	0.002	0.004	0.007	0.01	0.015	0.022
	Margin	0.287	1.096	3.853	9.14	25.605	59.458
	QUIRE	422.8	854.83	1478.7	2031.9	2609.1	2872.8
	Proposed Method	1.807	4.826	11.33	19.82	40.08	81.44
australian	Random	0.001	0.002	0.004	0.005	0.007	0.009
	Margin	0.015	0.057	0.196	0.378	0.741	1.48
	QUIRE	11.028	23.59	43.36	56.74	69.06	74.25
	Proposed Method	0.343	0.814	1.589	2.251	3.04	4.185
digit1	Random	0.002	0.003	0.006	0.012	0.017	0.021
	Margin	0.486	1.993	7.125	17.23	49.67	134.4
	QUIRE	330.7	667.4	1135.9	1493.7	1830.8	1998.8
	Proposed Method	1.731	4.886	12.24	24.11	57.56	135.9
g241n	Random	0.003	0.005	0.007	0.013	0.017	0.022
	Margin	0.44	1.76	6.28	15.16	43.79	119.4
	QUIRE	338.6	688.6	1162	1521	1879	2061
	Proposed Method	1.606	4.411	10.87	22.01	56.03	141.6
letter(MvsN)	Random	0.0007	0.001	0.001	0.002	0.003	0.005
	Margin	0.0108	0.022	0.054	0.11	0.251	0.519
	QUIRE	51.31	73.53	116.3	176.7	270.1	388
	Proposed Method	0.378	0.571	0.955	1.539	2.522	3.915
letter(UvsV)	Random	0.0025	0.0042	0.0075	0.010	0.014	0.02
	Margin	0.069	0.2628	0.876	1.675	3.674	7.1
	QUIRE	134	267.6	481.9	664	821.9	889.3
	Proposed Method	0.996	2.366	4.814	6.684	9.578	13.96

5 Conclusion

We introduce a novel active learning algorithm that addresses sampling bias and outlier selection of margin-based strategy by incorporating correlation criterion and exploiting both labeled and unlabeled data in evaluating instances. To solve sampling bias problem of margin-based strategy, the proposed method uses clustering to partition input space into some subspaces. The cluster space is explored based on novel utility metric combining prediction confident of clusters, local entropy of clusters and indefiniteness criteria. We figure out a solution to outlier selection problem by involving correlation criterion and pattern of unlabeled data in active selection of queries. Finally, as result of exploiting both labeled data and unlabeled data locally in each selected cluster, the algorithm performs well in terms of time performance. We aim to extend this method to multi-class learning and also we plan to propose a method that systematically balances between exploration of whole input space and exploitation of labeled data in evaluating clusters. Another future work could be attempting to use other clustering approaches that work well on this task.

References

1. Fu, Y., Zhu, X., Li, B.: A survey on instance selection for active learning. Knowledge and Information Systems 35(2), 249–283 (2013)
2. Balcan, M.-F., Broder, A., Zhang, T.: Margin based active learning. In: Bshouty, N.H., Gentile, C. (eds.) COLT 2007. LNCS (LNAI), vol. 4539, pp. 35–50. Springer, Heidelberg (2007)
3. Lewis, D.D., Catlett, J.: Heterogenous uncertainty sampling for supervised learning. In: Proceedings of the 11th International Conference on Machine Learning (ICML 1994), vol. 94, pp. 148–156 (1994)
4. Tong, S., Koller, D.: Support vector machine active learning with applications to text classification. The Journal of Machine Learning Research 2, 45–66 (2002)
5. Seung, H.S., Opper, M., Sompolinsky, H.: Query by committee. In: Proceedings of the 5th Annual Workshop on Computational Learning Theory, COLT 1992, pp. 287–294. ACM, New York (1992)
6. Freund, Y., Seung, H.S., Shamir, E., Tishby, N.: Selective sampling using the query by committee algorithm. Machine Learning 28(2-3), 133–168 (1997)
7. Sun, S., Hardoon, D.R.: Active learning with extremely sparse labeled examples. Neurocomputing 73(1618), 2980–2988 (2010)
8. Baram, Y., El-Yaniv, R., Luz, K.: Online choice of active learning algorithms. The Journal of Machine Learning Research 5, 255–291 (2004)
9. Dasgupta, S., Hsu, D.: Hierarchical sampling for active learning. In: Proceedings of the 25th International Conference on Machine Learning, ICML 2008, pp. 208–215. ACM, New York (2008)
10. Zhu, J., Wang, H., Yao, T., Tsou, B.K.: Active learning with sampling by uncertainty and density for word sense disambiguation and text classification. In: Proceedings of the 22nd International Conference on Computational Linguistics COLING 2008, vol. 1, pp. 1137–1144 (2008)
11. Donmez, P., Carbonell, J.G., Bennett, P.N.: Dual strategy active learning. In: Kok, J.N., Koronacki, J., Lopez de Mantaras, R., Matwin, S., Mladenič, D., Skowron, A. (eds.) ECML 2007. LNCS (LNAI), vol. 4701, pp. 116–127. Springer, Heidelberg (2007)
12. Nguyen, H.T., Smeulders, A.: Active learning using pre-clustering. In: Proceedings of the 21th International Conference on Machine Learning, ICML 2004, p. 79. ACM, New York (2004)
13. Xu, Z., Yu, K., Tresp, V., Xu, X., Wang, J.: Representative sampling for text classification using support vector machines. In: Sebastiani, F. (ed.) ECIR 2003. LNCS, vol. 2633, pp. 393–407. Springer, Heidelberg (2003)
14. Huang, S.J., Jin, R., Zhou, Z.H.: Active learning by querying informative and representative examples. In: Advances in Neural Information Processing Systems, pp. 892–900 (2010)
15. Hoi, S.C.H., Rong, J., Jianke, Z., Lyu, M.R.: Semi-supervised svm batch mode active learning for image retrieval. In: IEEE Conference on Computer Vision and Pattern Recognition, CVPR 2008, pp. 1–7 (2008)
16. Rahimi, A., Recht, B.: Clustering with normalized cuts is clustering with a hyperplane. Statistical Learning in Computer Vision 56 (2004)

17. Shannon, C.E.: A mathematical theory of communication. SIGMOBILE Mob. Comput. Commun. Rev. 5, 3–55 (2001)
18. Wang, X., Jiao, L., Wu, J.: Adjusting from disjoint to overlapping community detection of complex networks. Physica A: Statistical Mechanics and its Applications 388(24), 5045–5056 (2009)
19. Asuncion, A., Newman, D.J.: UCI machine learning repository (2007)
20. Chang, C.C., Lin, C.J.: LIBSVM: A library for support vector machines (2001)

On Mean Shift Clustering for Directional Data on a Hypersphere

Miin-Shen Yang[1,*], Shou-Jen Chang-Chien[1], and Hsun-Chih Kuo[2]

[1] Department of Applied Mathematics, Chung Yuan Christian University,
Chung-Li 32023, Taiwan
[2] Department of Statistics, National Chengchi University, Wenshan District,
Taipei 11605, Taiwan
msyang@math.cycu.edu.tw

Abstract. The mean shift clustering algorithm is a useful tool for clustering numeric data. Recently, Chang-Chien et al. [1] proposed a mean shift clustering algorithm for circular data that are directional data on a plane. In this paper, we extend the mean shift clustering for directional data on a hypersphere. The three types of mean shift procedures are considered. With the proposed mean shift clustering for the data on a hypersphere it is not necessary to give the number of clusters since it can automatically find a final cluster number with good clustering centers. Several numerical examples are used to demonstrate its effectiveness and superiority of the proposed method.

Keywords: Clustering, Mean shift, Directional data on a hypersphere.

1 Introduction

In 1918, von Mises [13] first introduced a distribution of circular data. Following Watson and Williams [14] investigation of inference problems for the von Mises distribution with the construction of statistical methods on circular data, there has been increasing research on directional data and it has been applied in biology, geology, medicine, meteorology, oceanography [3,6,10,11,12].

Clustering is a useful tool for finding clusters of a data set, grouped with most similarity in the same cluster and most dissimilarity between different clusters [8,16]. Clustering methods can generally be divided into two categories, the probability model-based approach and the nonparametric approach. The nonparametric approach includes partitional and kernel-based methods, while the kernel-based approach includes supervised and unsupervised learning methods. The support vector machine is a well-known supervised kernel-based method [2] and mean shift clustering is a popular unsupervised kernel-based method [5,15]. However, the mean shift clustering is generally used for clustering numeric data.

Recently, Chang-Chien et al. [1] proposed a mean shift clustering algorithm for circular data. In this paper, we extend the mean shift clustering for directional data on a hypersphere. The three types of mean shift procedures are considered. The proposed mean shift clustering for the data on a hypersphere can automatically find a final

---

* Corresponding author.

L. Rutkowski et al. (Eds.): ICAISC 2014, Part II, LNAI 8468, pp. 809–818, 2014.

cluster number with good clustering centers. Several numerical examples are used to demonstrate the effectiveness and superiority of the proposed method.

2   Mean Shift Clustering for the Data on a Hypersphere

In this section, we extend Chang-Chien et al. [1] to the directional data on a hypersphere. Since Chang-Chien et al. [1] used the distance measure for angles to modify the mean shift based clustering algorithm to two dimensional directional data (i.e. circular data), we need to extend the distance measure used in Chang-Chien et al. [1] to high-dimensional directional data. For any two circular (angle) observations θ_1 and θ_2 ($\theta_2 > \theta_1$), Chang-Chien et al. [1] considered the distance between θ_1 and θ_2 with $1 - \cos(\theta_2 - \theta_1)$. For extending two dimensions to high dimensions, we consider high dimensional directional data as points on the unit hypersphere. Thus, the distance measure $1 - x_1^T x_2$ can be used for high dimensional directional data x_1 and x_2. Now, we use this distance measure to define a kernel on high dimension directional data. Let $X = \{x_1, x_2, .., x_n\}$ be a data set on the unit hypersphere and let $H : X \rightarrow [0,1]$ be a kernel function with $H(x) = h(1 - x^T x_j)$. The kernel density estimate using the kernel H is given by

$$\hat{f}_H(x) = \sum_{j=1}^{n} h(x) w(x_j)$$

where $w(x_j)$ is a weight function. By maximizing $\hat{f}_H(x)$ with the constraint $x^T x = 1$, we obtain a general formula for the mode a as follows:

$$a = x = \frac{\sum_{j=1}^{n} h'(1 - x^T x_j) x_j w(x_j)}{\| \sum_{j=1}^{n} h'(1 - x^T x_j) x_j w(x_j) \|} \tag{1}$$

where $w(x_j)$ is a weight function and h' is the derivative of h. Throughout this paper, we have all data points with equal weights. Now, we choose a suitable kernel for equation (1). In general, the performance of the kernel density estimate depends on the bandwidth selection. However, Wu and Yang [15] gave another method to obtain good kernel density estimation where it is different from the bandwidth selection. This technique is to normalize the distance measure and then estimate the stabilization parameters. In the high dimensional directional data case, we define the kernel function $K^p : X \rightarrow [0,1]$ as follows:

$$K^p(x) = \begin{cases} \left(1 - \dfrac{1 - x^T x_j}{\beta} \right)^p = \left(\dfrac{\beta - (1 - x^T x_j)}{\beta} \right)^p & , \text{ if } 1 - x^T x_j \leq \beta \\ 0 & , \text{ if } 1 - x^T x_j > \beta \end{cases} \tag{2}$$

where the parameters β and p are called the normalization and stabilization, respectively. We use the sample standard deviation of the directional data set to estimate β. The parameter β is defined as $\beta=\sqrt{2(1-\overline{R})}$, where $\overline{R}=\left\|\sum_{j=1}^{n}x_j/n\right\|$ is the length of mass vector. The parameter p is used to control the shape of kernel density estimates. Figure 1(a) shows a 3-cluster data set on a unit sphere. In Fig. 1(b)-(d), we show the estimated density shape for the data set as shown in Fig. 1(a) with different values of p. The estimated density shape function using the kernel K^p is given by $\hat{f}_{K^p}(x_i)=\sum_{j=1}^{n}K^p(x_i), i=1,2,..,n$ where $\{\hat{f}_{K^p}(x_j), j=1,2,..,n\}$ denotes the values of the estimated density shape on the data set. Figures 1(b)-(d) shows that the estimated density shape has only one peak, two peaks, and three peaks with $p=1,5$, and 13. Intuitively, the number of peaks and cluster number of data set should be identical. Therefore, p has a great influence on finding the cluster number.

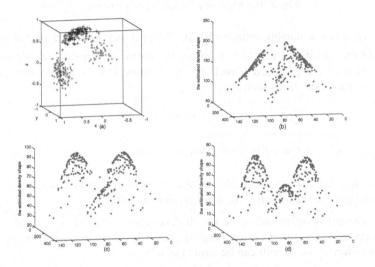

Fig. 1. (a) 3-clusters data set; (b)~(d) Estimated density shapes with $p=1,5$, and 13

The performance of the proposed mean shift clustering (MSC) depends on the stabilization p, and the estimated density shapes are changed with p. Wu and Yang [15] proposed the graphical plot of correlation comparisons in three steps. The first step is to calculate the correlation value of $\{\hat{f}_{K^p}(x_j), j=1,2,..,n\}$ with the pair $(p=2i-1, p=2i+1), i=1,2,..,25$. The suitable operating range for p is between 1 and 50. The reason is that we normalize the kernel function by dividing parameter β. The increasing shift of p depends on the data set. For high-dimensional directional data, we suggest taking 2 for the increasing shift of p. The second step is to plot the points $(i,$ the correlation value with $(p=2i-1, p=2i+1)), i=1,2,..,25$ and connect them with lines. Then, we obtain the graph of correlation comparisons. The final step is to find a suitable estimate for p from the graph. If the correlation value for the jth point is closed to 1, then the value $2j-1$ is a suitable estimate for p. We demonstrate the graphical plot of correlation comparisons on the data set shown in Fig. 1(a) and the result is shown in Fig. 2. From Fig. 2, we can see that $p = 13$ is a suitable estimate since the estimate $p = 13$ provides a good estimated density shape as shown in Fig. 1(d).

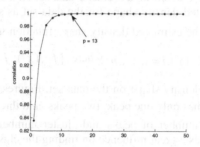

Fig. 2. The graph of correlation comparisons

After we obtain a suitable estimate for p, the next step is to find modes (cluster centers) of the density estimate on X using the mean shift procedure. Substituting the derivative of the proposed kernel K^p in equation (1), we obtain the updated equation for the mode a as follows:

$$a = \frac{\sum_{j=1}^{n}[\max\{\beta - (1 - a^T x_j), 0\} / \beta]^{p-1} x_j w(x_j)}{\|\sum_{j=1}^{n}[\max\{\beta - (1 - a^T x_j), 0\} / \beta]^{p-1} x_j w(x_j)\|} \tag{3}$$

The MSC has three kinds of implementation procedures, which are nonblurring, blurring and general mean shifts. We describe them as follows:

(a) The nonblurring mean shift is to set all data points as initial cluster centers and then update each cluster center using equation (3). Therefore, equation (3) using the nonblurring mean shift can be written as follows:

$$a_i^{(t+1)} = \frac{\sum_{j=1}^{n}[\max\{\beta - (1 - a_i^{(t)T} x_j), 0\} / \beta]^{p-1} x_j w(x_j)}{\|\sum_{j=1}^{n}[\max\{\beta - (1 - a_i^{(t)T} x_j), 0\} / \beta]^{p-1} x_j w(x_j)\|}, \quad i = 1, 2, ..., n$$

(b) The blurring mean shift is to set all data points as initial cluster centers and update each data point x_j with a_j (i.e. $x_j \leftarrow a_j$), $j = 1, 2, .., n$. Therefore, equation (3) using the blurring mean shift can be written as follows:

$$a_i^{(t+1)} = \frac{\sum_{j=1}^{n}[\max\{\beta - (1 - a_i^{(t)T} a_j^{(t)}), 0\} / \beta]^{p-1} a_j^{(t)} w(a_j^{(t)})}{\|\sum_{j=1}^{n}[\max\{\beta - (1 - a_i^{(t)T} a_j^{(t)}), 0\} / \beta]^{p-1} a_j^{(t)} w(a_j^{(t)})\|}, \quad i = 1, 2, ..., n$$

(c) The general mean shift is to choose c initial cluster centers randomly, where c is smaller than n. In general, we take $c = \sqrt{n}$ and c initial cluster centers come from the data set. Therefore, equation (3) using general mean shift can be written as follows:

$$a_i^{(t+1)} = \frac{\sum\limits_{j=1}^{n}[\max\{\beta-(1-a_i^{(t)T}x_j),0\}/\beta]^{p-1}x_j w(x_j)}{\|\sum\limits_{j=1}^{n}[\max\{\beta-(1-a_i^{(t)T}x_j),0\}/\beta]^{p-1}x_j w(x_j)\|}, \quad i=1,2,...,c$$

Note that t denotes the iteration number in (a), (b), and (c).

After the final state of the cluster centers is obtained, we can determine the cluster number and identify clusters by processing the Agglomerative Hierarchical Clustering (AHC) with these cluster centers. There are many linkage methods to process AHC, and in general, we can process AHC simply with the single linkage. According to above illustration, the proposed MSC algorithm for directional data on a hypersphere can be summarized as follows:

MSC for Directional Data on a Hypersphere

Step 1. Choose the kernel function K^p using equation (2).
Step 2. Estimate the stabilization parameter p using the graphical method of
correlation comparisons.
Step 3. Choose one of the three mean shift procedures to find the mean shift $a_i^{(t+1)}$.
Step 4. Use AHC algorithm with merging cluster centers to identify clusters.

For clustering on the unit hypersphere, Kobayashi and Otsu [9] proposed another mean shift-based algorithm, called the von Mises-Fisher (vMF) mean shift. They employed the kernel from the generalized vMF distribution to construct the kernel density estimate and then processed the nonblurring mean shift to find modes of the kernel density estimate. Therefore, the vMF mean shift can be operated without an a priori cluster number. The probability density function of the generalized vMF distribution is given by $F(x;a,\kappa) = C_F(\kappa)f(a^Tx;\kappa)$, where a is the mean direction and κ is the concentration parameter and $C_F(\kappa)$ is the normalization constant. The function f is a monotonically increasing convex function based on inner product a^Tx and the parameter κ. Utilizing the function f as a kernel, the kernel density estimate $p(x)$ is constructed as $p(x) = (C_F(\kappa)/n)\sum_{j=1}^{n}f(x^Tx_j;\kappa)$. To maximize $p(x)$ with the constraint $\|x\|=1$, Kobayashi and Otsu [7] derived the mode estimate a as

$$a = x = \frac{\sum\limits_{j=1}^{n}x_j f'(a^Tx_j;\kappa)}{\|\sum\limits_{j=1}^{n}x_j f'(a^Tx_j;\kappa)\|} \tag{4}$$

where f' is the derivative of f. Equation (4) is similar to equation (1), but with different views. The kernel in equation (1) is based on the distance measure $1-a^Tx_j$ (dissimilarity), but the krenel in equation (4) is based on the inner product (similarity) a^Tx_j and the parameter κ. The vMF mean shift uses the parameter κ to control the concentration of the vMF distribution where the role for the parameter κ is equivalent to a bandwidth. Thus the performance of the vMF mean shift depends on parameter κ. Kobayashi and Otsu [9] emphasized that the parameter value greatly affects the clustering results, so that bad estimates may lead to incorrect results. Our proposed approach is different from Kobayashi and Otsu [9] in that it is independent of the parameter κ. We employ the power parameter stabilization p to control the smoothing of the kernel density estimate. In practice, it is difficult to find a suitable estimate of κ, but it is easy to find the estimate of p by using the graphical plot of the correlation comparisons. Our proposed approach has the advantage of finding better clustering results for high-dimensional directional data.

3   Examples and Numerical Comparisons

Since the vMF mean shift algorithm processes the nonblurring mean shift to find modes of the kernel density estimate, we make comparisons between the MSC with the nonblurring mean shift and the vMF mean shift on numerical and real data sets. The kernel function f and the estimate for κ in Kobayashi and Otsu's method [9] were set as follows:

$$f(x;\kappa) = \begin{cases} 0 & 0 \le x \le \kappa \\ \dfrac{1}{2}(x-\kappa) & \kappa \le x \le 1 \end{cases}$$

and

$$\kappa = \cos\{\underset{i,j}{mean}(\text{the angle between } x_i \text{ and } x_j)/2\}.$$

Here, we also use the same equations in our comparisons.

Example 1. In Fig. 3(a), there is a 10-cluster data set, where each cluster has the same proportion. We implement the vMF mean shift algorithm for the data set in Fig. 3(a). The final states of the cluster centers are shown in Fig. 3(b). We can see that all cluster centers are centralized in 7 locations. This means that the vMF mean shift cannot find the correct cluster number. Based on Fig. 3(b), we obtain incorrect clustering results, as shown in Fig. 3(c). We find that there are five clusters to be identified correctly, but the other five clusters are classified into two clusters along with clusters 4 and 5. If we classify the data set into 10 clusters, then the 10 clusters are obtained as shown in Fig. 3(d). In Fig. 3(d), we can see that the clusters 4 and 5 in Fig. 3(c) still cannot be separated in the correct five clusters. We implement the MSC algorithm for data set in Fig. 3(a). Figure 4(a) is the graphical plot of the correlation comparisons. In Fig. 4(a), the last point is close to 1, that is, $p = 49$ will be a good estimate. The final states of the cluster centers are shown in Fig. 4(b). We observe that all cluster centers can be centralized in 10 distinct locations. The AHC results are shown in Fig. 4(c). The hierarchical tree shows that the suitable cluster number is 10. Fig. 4(d) shows these 10 identified clusters. Compare Fig. 3(a) with Fig. 4(d), we can see that the MSC has good clustering results.

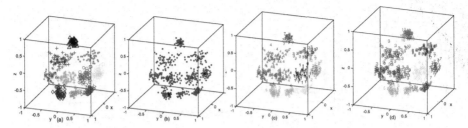

Fig. 3. (a) 10-clusters data set; (b) Final states of cluster centers for the vMF mean shift; (c) Seven identified clusters; (d) Ten identified clusters

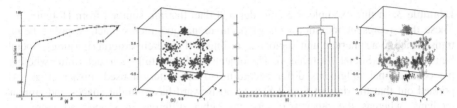

Fig. 4. (a) Graph of correlation with $p = 49$; (b) Final states of cluster centers for the MSC; (c) Hierarchical tree; (d) Ten identified clusters

Example 2. In Fig. 5(a), there is a 6-cluster data set in which we randomly add some noisy points. We implement the vMF mean shift algorithm for the data set. The final states of cluster centers are shown in Fig. 5(b). The results in Fig. 5(b) show that the observed cluster number is 3 for the vMF mean shift. Three identified clusters based on final cluster centers in Fig. 5(b) are shown in Fig. 5(c). In Fig. 5(c), cluster 3 consists of four clusters. If we assign the cluster number of 6 for the vMF mean shift algorithm, then the 6 identified clusters are shown in Fig. 5(d). Figure 5(d) shows that the vMF mean shift algorithm produces bad clustering results. We also implement the MSC algorithm for the data set. The graphical plot of the correlation comparisons is shown in Fig. 6(a). Figure 6(a) shows that $p = 31$ is a suitable estimate. The final states of the cluster centers are shown in Fig. 6(b), which indicates that the cluster centers are centralized to six locations. We process AHC with the final states of cluster centers. The AHC result is shown in Fig. 6(c), which shows that the six clusters match the data structure of the data set. Six identified clusters are shown in Fig. 6(d), which demonstrates that the MSC is not influenced by these noisy points and can produce good clustering results.

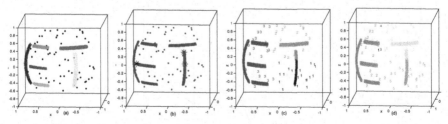

Fig. 5. (a) 6-clusters data set; (b) Final states of cluster centers for the vMF mean shift; (c) Three identified clusters; (d) Six identified clusters

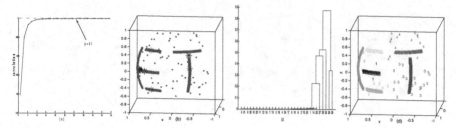

Fig. 6. (a) Graph of correlation with $p = 31$; (b) Final states of cluster centers for the MSBC; (c) Hierarchical tree; (d) Identified clusters

Example 3. In this example, we consider real data that are sourced from Holguin [7]. These data represent measurements of occupational judgments (each response being transformed to a spherical unit vector) according to 4 different criteria (Earnings, Social Status, Reward, Social Usefulness). The objective of this study is to determine whether the occupational judgments differ according to the criterion used. Fisher et al. [4] pointed out that the data of Social Status and Reward have similar shapes and similar medians, whereas the other two sets are rather different in shape and there are significant differences between the median directions. Therefore, we use only the data for Earnings and Social Usefulness, and Fig. 7(a) shows the data set with 48 observations from Earnings and 48 observations from Social Usefulness. We implement the vMF mean shift for this data set. The final states of cluster centers are shown in Fig. 7(b), indicating that cluster centers cannot be centralized in two locations. Therefore, the vMF mean shift algorithm cannot find the correct cluster number for the data set in Fig. 7(a). We classify this data into two clusters as shown in Fig. 7(c). In Fig. 7(c), the first cluster consists of only one point, which is perceived as an outlier. The vMF mean shift algorithm thus produces incorrect clustering results because the estimate for κ is not suitable. We then replace the vMF mean shift algorithm with the proposed MSC algorithm for the data set. The graphical plot of correlation comparisons for the data set is shown in Fig. 8(a) with $p = 9$ being a good estimate. The final states of the cluster centers are shown in Fig. 8(b) with the two different merged locations, and the hierarchical tree is shown in Fig. 8(c). It is clear that the cluster number is 2, as shown in Fig. 8(c). The identified clusters are shown in Fig. 8(d). Comparing the data set in Fig. 7(a) with the identified clusters in Fig. 8(d), we find that only four points are classified into incorrect clusters for the MSC.

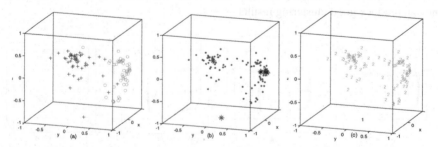

Fig. 7. (a) Data set (Earnings and Social Usefulness); (b) Final states of cluster centers for the vMF mean shift; (c) Two identified clusters

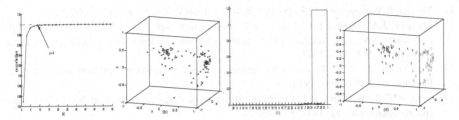

Fig. 8. (a) Graph of correlation with $p = 9$; (b) Final states of cluster centers for the MSC; (c) Hierarchical tree; (d) Two identified clusters

4   Conclusions

In this paper we proposed a mean shift clustering (MSC) algorithm for directional data on a hypersphere where the MSC can automatically find a cluster number with good cluster centers without giving an a priori cluster number. The proposed clustering algorithm presents a new method for the analysis of grouped directional data on a hypersphere. It can also give a good estimated cluster number. For evaluation of the proposed method, we used the numerical and real data to compare the proposed method with the existing method. The results show the accuracy and superiority of the proposed algorithm. Overall, the proposed MSC clustering algorithm gives a new means to analyze grouped directional data on a hypersphere.

References

1. Chang-Chien, S.J., Hung, W.L., Yang, M.S.: On mean shift-based clustering for circular data. Soft Computing 16, 1043–1060 (2012)
2. Cristianini, N., Shawe-Taylor, J.: An Introduction to Support Vector Machines. Cambridge Univ. Press, Cambridge (2000)
3. Fisher, N.I.: Statistical Analysis of Circular Data. Cambridge Univ. Press, Cambridge (1993)
4. Fisher, N.I., Lewis, T., Embleton, B.J.J.: Statistical Analysis of Spherical Data. Cambridge Univ. Press, Cambridge (1987)
5. Fukunaga, K., Hostetler, L.D.: The estimation of the gradient of a density function with applications in pattern recognition. IEEE Trans. Information Theory 21, 32–40 (1975)
6. Gao, K.S., Chia, F., Krantz, I., Nordin, P., Machin, D.: On the application of the von Mises distribution and angular regression methods to investigate the seasonality of disease onset. Stat. in Med. 25, 1593–1618 (2006)
7. Holguin, J.: The Application of Directional Methods in p Dimensions, M.Sc. Thesis, Simon Fraser University, Burnaby, Canada (1980)
8. Kaufman, L., Rousseeuw, P.J.: Finding groups in data: An introduction to cluster analysis. John Wiley, New York (1990)
9. Kobayashi, T., Otsu, N.: Von Mises-Fisher mean shift for clustering on a hypersphere. In: Proc. 20th International Conference on Pattern Recognition, ICPR 2010, pp. 2130–2133 (2010)
10. Lee, A.: Circular data. WIREs Computational Statistics 2, 477–486 (2010)

11. Mardia, K.V., Jupp, P.E.: Directional Statistics. John Wiley, New York (2000)
12. Mooney, J.A., Helms, P.J., Jolliffe, I.T.: Fitting mixtures of von Mises distributions: A case study involving sudden infant death syndrome. Computational Statistics & Data Analysis 41, 505–513 (2003)
13. Von Mises, R.: Uber die die "Ganzzahligkeit" der Atomgewicht und verwandte Fragen. Physikal Z 19, 490–500 (1918)
14. Watson, G.S., Williams, E.J.: On the construction of significance tests on the circle and the sphere. Biometrika 43, 344–352 (1956)
15. Wu, K.L., Yang, M.S.: Mean shift-based clustering. Pattern Recognition 40, 3035–3052 (2007)
16. Yang, M.S.: A survey of fuzzy clustering. Mathematical and Computer Modeling 18, 1–16 (1993)

Author Index

Printed in the United States
By Bookmasters

Printed in the United States
By Bookmasters